Southern Living®
ANNUAL RECIPES
MASTER INDEX
1979 - 1999

Oxmoor House®

Library of Congress Catalog Number: 79-88364
ISBN: 0-8487-1970-0
ISSN: 0272-2003

Printed in the United States of America
First printing 2000

WE'RE HERE FOR YOU!

We at Oxmoor House are dedicated to serving you
with reliable information that expands your imagination
and enriches your life. We welcome your comments and
suggestions. Please write us at:

Oxmoor House, Inc.
Editor, *Southern Living*® *Annual Recipes Master Index*
2100 Lakeshore Drive
Birmingham, AL 35209

To order additional publications, call 1-205-877-6560.

Oxmoor House, Inc.
    Editor-in-Chief: Nancy Fitzpatrick Wyatt
    Senior Foods Editor: Susan Payne Stabler
    Senior Editor, Copy and Homes: Olivia Kindig Wells
    Art Director: James Boone

Southern Living®
    Foods Editor: Susan Hawthorne Nash

Southern Living® *Annual Recipes Master Index 1979-1999*
    Editor: Keri Bradford Anderson
    Director, Production and Distribution: Phillip Lee
    Associate Production Manager: Larry Hunter
    Production Assistant: Faye Porter Bonner

    CONTRIBUTORS
    Indexer: Mary Ann Laurens
    Designer: Carol Middleton
    Copy Assistants: Courtney Hughes, Sally Inzer

INTRODUCTION

*T*hrough the years, many readers have asked us for help finding recipes that have appeared in *Southern Living* magazine. We turn to this *Annual Recipes Master Index* for the answers because it contains every *Southern Living* recipe printed since 1979. This valuable guide—a true cook's companion—lists the exact year and page a recipe appeared in our recipe yearbook, *Southern Living Annual Recipes*.

We've cross-referenced every recipe in the *Southern Living Annual Recipes* collection by the type of dish and by one or more of its main ingredients. The handy step-by-step reference on the following page provides simple instructions on how to find the recipe you want—fast.

It's easy to find your favorite recipes and food columns—and new ones to treasure.

The name of our light section has changed throughout the years, but you can locate light recipes from past columns ("On the Light Side" and "Cooking Light") now under the "Living Light" heading. "From Our Kitchen to Yours" continues to be a reader favorite, and all of this column's tips and secrets are listed for handy reference. The "Quick & Easy," "Dessert of the Month," and "What's for Supper?" columns will also be a big help in the kitchen.

Occasionally, you'll find that the same recipe appears in different volumes of *Southern Living Annual Recipes*. That's because a recipe may appear in the magazine edition for one state before it appears in the edition for another state. This index gives all of the page references to those bonus recipes that have appeared in more than one edition of the magazine and the cookbooks as well as our "Just for Kids" and *Southern Living Cooking School* bonus sections.

We hope you'll be pleased with this index of all our recipes. Use it to find the perfect recipe for any occasion in just seconds.

Susan Hawthorne Nash
Foods Editor

HOW TO FIND A RECIPE–*FAST*

*Look for the main ingredient in the recipe you want or even the basic type of dish
it is (appetizer, cookie, etc.). You can find it either way in this cross-referenced index.
Use the step-by-step guide below to help you find a recipe in record time.*

1. *As you turn through the index, "continued" lines in the upper left corner remind you of the current category.*

2. *Main categories help you cross-reference each recipe by the type of dish and one or more of its main ingredients.*

3. *Boldfaced subcategories help you scan for a recipe through long main categories.*

4. *Frequently, we'll direct you to other categories to help you find similar recipes.*

5. *Each recipe title is alphabetized by its most descriptive word. We've boldfaced the year in which it appeared in* Southern Living® Annual Recipes; *its page number follows.*

6. *An "M" precedes the page numbers of all microwave recipes. It refers to recipes cooked totally or partially in the microwave.*

7. *An alphabetical guide word at the bottom of each page helps you quickly locate main reference categories.*

MASTER INDEX

This index lists all recipes by their complete titles under a specific food category and ingredient. The volume is indicated in bold, followed by the page number. Microwave recipe page numbers are preceded by an "M." For information about how to use this index, see facing page.

ALMONDS

Appetizers

Cheese, Almond, **'88** 173
Cheese Ball, Fruit-and-Nut, **'91** 251
Cheese Ball, Pinecone, **'93** 288
Chicken Almondette Fingers, **'93** 12
Chicken Nut Puffs, **'81** 260
Crostini, Almond-Bacon-Cheese, **'94** 318
Dip, Almond Delight, **'90** 226
Dip with Strawberries, Almond Cream,
   '92 164
Mix, Jalapeño Nut, **'96** 27
Nippy Nuts, **'93** 301
Olives, Almond-Stuffed, **'88** 95
Pastry Cups, Mushroom-Almond, **'88** 210
Pesto-Spiced Nuts, **'95** 173
Rollups, Almond-Ham, **'89** 284
Braid, Almond, **'89** 86
Bread, Cocoa-Nut Swirl, **'80** 257
Bread, Saffron, **'96** 50
Caramelized Almonds, **'92** 303
Coffee Cake, Almond-Blueberry, **'85** 152
Coffee Cake, Apricot-Almond, **'93** 26
Coffee Cake Twist, Almond, **'91** 22
Coffee, Chocolate-Almond, **'84** 54
Coffee Delight, Almond-, **'84** 115
Coleslaw with Grapes and Almonds, **'83** 59
Cream, Peaches 'n' Almond, **'86** 229
Curried Almonds, **'82** 297
Danish, Almond, **'87** 301

Desserts

Apricot-Almond Squares, **'95** 272
Balls, Coconut-Almond, **'84** 256
Balls, Toasted Almond Chip, **'84** 240
Bars, Almond-Chocolate, **'83** 304
Bars, Swedish Almond, **'97** 322
Biscotti, Almond, **'91** 108
Biscotti, Almond-Anise, **'93** 266
Biscotti, Cocoa-Almond, **'96** 280
Biscuits, Raspberry-Almond, **'93** 160
Bread, Mandel, **'97** 220
Brickle Treats, Almond, **'95** 321
Brie, Almond-Raspberry, **'94** M89
Brownies, Date-and-Almond, **'88** 217
Butter-Nut Strips, **'82** 167
Cake, Almond-Butter, **'86** 107
Cake, Almond-Butter Wedding, **'86** 106
Cake, Almond Legend, **'82** 8

Cake, Almond Whipping Cream, **'80** 295
Cake, Apricot-Almond Upside-Down,
   '97 204
Cake, Chocolate-Almond, **'91** 248
Cake, Peach-Almond Pound, **'89** 86
Cake, Peachy Almond-Butter, **'90** 107
Cake Squares, Almond, **'79** 111
Cake, Toasted Almond-Butter, **'99** 315
Cake with Cherry Filling, Chocolate-Almond,
   '84 225
Candied Nuts, **'81** 261
Candy, Almond Brittle, **'80** 255
Cheesecake, Amaretto, **'99** 273
Cheesecake, Black-and-White, **'99** 334
Cheesecake, Chocolate-Almond, **'93** 53
Cheesecake, Coconut-Chocolate-Almond,
   '98 322
Chocolate-Almond Dessert, **'82** 306
Chocolate Almond Velvet, **'81** 148
Cinnamon Stars, Swiss, **'87** 293
Cobbler, Blackberry-Almond, **'81** 132
Combs, Almond, **'84** 136
Confections, Almond Cream, **'87** 198; **'90** 310
Cookies, Almond, **'83** 22, 181; **'91** 51; **'92** 176;
   '97 288; **'99** 49
Cookies, Almond Butter, **'79** 52
Cookies, Almond Lace, **'98** 336
Cookies, Almond Spritz, **'82** 306
Cookies, Chocolate-Almond, **'98** 293
Cookies, Chocolate-Almond Surprise,
   '88 M45
Cookies, Chocolate-Brickle, **'99** 127
Cookies, Cranberry-Almond, **'98** 26
Cookies, Double Chocolate Chunk-Almond,
   '95 178
Cookies, Light Almond, **'83** 151
Cookies, Skillet Almond, **'97** 288
Cookies, Snow, **'99** 167
Cookies, Swedish Almond, **'85** 312
Cookies, Texan-Size Almond Crunch, **'91** 236
Cookies with Ice Cream Balls, Almond
   Brittle, **'96** 202
Cream, Chocolate-Almond, **'91** 108
Cream, Peach Almond, **'82** 108
Cream with Fresh Strawberries, Almond,
   '87 93
Crème Brûlée, Almond, **'95** 323
Crêpes Gelée Amandine, **'83** 126

Crescents, Almond, **'97** 273
Crunch, Almond Butter, **'80** 301
Crunch, Vanilla Almond, **'93** 243
Crust, Vanilla Wafer, **'98** 216
Custard with Raspberries, Almond Crème,
   '88 174
Drops, Cherry-Almond, **'81** 20
Drops, Chocolate-Coconut Almond, **'87** 223
Filling, Almond, **'96** 316
Filling, Almond Cream, **'85** 320; **'91** 248
Filling, Ground Almond, **'87** 14
Filling, Nut, **'91** 35
Float, Nutmeg-Almond, **'84** 106
Frosting, Almond-Butter, **'86** 107
Frosting, Almond Buttercream, **'97** 61;
   '99 155
Frosting, Chocolate-Almond, **'83** 241
Frozen Almond Crunch, **'94** 283
Fudge, Creamy Almond, **'95** 51
Glaze, Honey-Nut, **'87** 15
Ice Cream, Almond, **'98** 221
Ice Cream, Almond-Fudge, **'93** 205
Ice Cream Balls, Almond, **'86** 315
Ice Cream, Peach-Almond, **'89** 156
Leaves, Almond Holly, **'86** 319
Mandelbrot, Rhoda's, **'98** 243
Marzipan Bees, **'98** 100
Meringue Fingers, Chocolate-Almond, **'84** 158
Mocha-Almond Dessert, **'80** 289; **'81** 62
Mousse, Chocolate-Almond, **'93** 316
Pastry, Almond, **'85** 177; **'89** 317; **'92** 30
Pears, Almond-Stuffed, **'83** 207
Petits Fours, Chocolate-Almond, **'93** 255
Pie Amandine, Chocolate, **'83** 300
Pie, Apple-Amandine, **'89** 215
Pie, Cinnamon-Almond-Pecan, **'98** 89
Pie, Creamy Chocolate-Almond, **'85** 102
Pie, Toasted Almond, **'86** 163
Pineapple-Almond Delight, **'85** 96
Praline Sauce, **'93** 214
Pudding, Chocolate-Almond, **'82** 142; **'88** 24
Pudding, Chocolate-Almond Silk, **'96** 266
Pudding, Mandarin-Almond, **'85** M12
Roca, Almond, **'86** 49
Romanoff, Strawberry-Almond, **'98** 99
Sauce, Almond-Vanilla Custard, **'88** M177
Sauce, Angel Food Cake with Amaretto-
   Almond, **'90** 199

ALMONDS, Desserts
(continued)

Shortbread, Apricot-Almond, '99 29
Snaps, Almond, '92 273
Sorbet, Apricot-Almond, '98 126
Sour Cream-Almond Dessert, '92 120
Spread, Almond Cheese, '87 292
Squares, Cream Cheese-Almond, '85 68
Strudel, Pear, '98 253
Tart, Almond, '89 232
Tart, Apricot-Almond, '97 99
Tart, Bakewell, '97 110
Tarts, Almond Tea, '85 120
Tarts, Raspberry-Almond, '99 280
Tart with Brandy Sauce, Peach, '98 119
Tassies, Lucky Almond, '91 13
Toffee Crunch, Almond-, '88 285
Topping, Almond, '86 200
Torte, Chocolate-Almond, '96 M253; '98 273
Tortoni, Coffee-Almond, '81 30
Truffles, Almond, '83 298
Wafers, Almond-Filled, '88 120
Filling, Almond, '87 301
French Toast, Almond, '88 62
French Toast, Amaretto, '98 280
Fruit, Almond-Curried, '83 261
Glazed Almonds, '96 64
Liqueur, Almond-Flavored, '81 287
Main Dishes
Casserole, Chicken-Almond, '94 199
Catfish Amandine, Mandarin, '84 183
Catfish Amandine, Spicy, '89 52
Chicken and Vegetables, Almond, '86 21
Chicken, Creamy Almond, '89 281
Chicken in Orange-Almond Sauce, '79 219;
  '80 13
Chicken, Spicy Almond, '88 150
Fish, Almond Baked, '88 270; '89 203
Fish Amandine, '85 179
Fish Amandine, Fillet of, '80 M54
Flounder Amandine, '89 M196
Orange Lake Amandine, '80 99
Pollo Almendrado, '81 193
Quiche, Almond-Topped Crab, '79 127
Trout Amandine, '99 53
Trout Amandine, Classic, '96 202
Trout Amandine, Gaston's, '96 232
Muffins, Almond, '90 87
Muffins, Banana-Honey-Nut, '88 62
Muffins, Peachy-Almond, '86 301
Phyllo Nests, Nutty, '87 277
Praline Almonds, '97 285
Rice, Almond, '81 195; '85 M112; '89 100; '91 291
Rice, Almond Wild, '86 50
Rice, Indian, '96 202
Rice with Almonds, Curried, '83 M285
Rolls, Almond Crescent, '90 283
Rolls, Cherry-Almond, '84 M198
Salad, Almond-Citrus, '96 274
Salad Amandine, Chicken, '81 37
Salad, Cheesy Fruit-'n'-Nut, '87 56
Salad, Chicken-Almond, '81 133
Salad, Cucumber-Almond, '86 147
Salad Dressing, Almond, '81 37
Salad, Orange-Almond, '99 107
Salad, Sesame-Almond, '89 123
Salad Shanghai, Almond-Chicken, '90 160
Sandwiches, Chicken-Almond Pocket, '81 240;
  '83 69
Sauce, Mandarin-Almond Cream, '84 183
Sauce, Shrimp-and-Almond, '87 282
Slaw, Asian, '99 108

Slaw, Pineapple-Almond, '92 171
Snack Balls, Orange-Almond, '95 214
Soup, Almond, '79 48
Soup, Chicken-Almond Cream, '92 21
Spoons, Dipped Chocolate-Almond, '95 M277
Streusel, Almond-Garlic, '95 159
Sunburst, Almond, '94 245
Sweet-and-Spicy Almonds, '96 274
Syrup, Almond, '82 47
Tea, Almond, '85 43; '86 329; '89 212; '97 226
Tea, Almond-Lemonade, '86 229; '99 207
Tea, Ginger-Almond, '94 131
Toast Amandine, Baked, '82 47
Toasts, Cheddar-Almond, '97 30
Topping, Almond, '85 152; '86 200
Vegetables
Asparagus, Almond, '83 86
Asparagus with Almond Butter, '84 85
Asparagus with Almond Sauce, '91 117
Broccoli Casserole, Almond-, '88 62
Broccoli with Almonds, Glazed, '80 12
Brussels Sprouts Amandine, '79 213
Cabbage with Almonds, Creamed, '79 4
Cauliflower and Peas with Curried Almonds,
  '79 221; '80 82
Cauliflower with Almond Sauce, '82 270
Celery Almondine, '85 116
Celery Amandine, Buttered, '82 98
Eggplant with Almonds, '79 179
Green Beans Amandine, '79 276; '82 M20;
  '97 238
Green Beans with Almonds, '84 253
Green Beans with Almonds, Italian, '81 207
Peas with Almonds, Curried, '88 M294
Potatoes, Almond-Fried, '82 25
Potatoes, Broccoli-and-Almond-Topped, '83 3
Stir-Fry, Almond-Vegetable, '86 222
AMBROSIA
Anytime Ambrosia, '86 182
Baked Ambrosia, '83 303
Bowl, Ambrosia, '80 138; '84 313
Brunch, Ambrosia, '83 57
Cake, Ambrosia, '79 229
Cake Royale, Ambrosia, '89 335
Carrot-Marshmallow Ambrosia, '80 5
Chicken Salad Ambrosia, '85 216
Citrus Ambrosia, '82 287
Cookies, Ambrosia, '81 301; '82 110; '86 313
Cups, Sherbet Ambrosia, '82 159
Custard Sauce Ambrosia, '84 256
Easy Ambrosia, '92 45
Fantastic Ambrosia, '91 277
Fruit Ambrosia, Fresh, '88 184
Fruit Ambrosia, Mixed, '83 10
Ginger Ale Ambrosia, '99 125
Grandma's Ambrosia, '90 254
Honey Bee Ambrosia, '83 267
Layered Ambrosia, '88 304
Mold, Ambrosia, '79 241
Mold, Ambrosia Cream Cheese, '79 249
Old-Fashioned Ambrosia, '80 5
Orange Ambrosia Supreme, '79 37
Pancakes with Orange Syrup, Ambrosia, '89 254
Peach Ambrosia, '83 53
Pie, Ambrosia, '79 284
Pie, Orange Ambrosia, '80 237
Pineapple-Orange Ambrosia, '88 252
Salad, Ambrosia, '83 231; '94 271
Salad, Carrot-Ambrosia, '81 252
Sauce, Hot Ambrosia, '89 335
Sherried Ambrosia, '84 324; '86 317
Spread, Ambrosia, '92 50
Tropical Ambrosia, '79 74

ANCHOVIES
Antipasto, Grandpa's, '98 183
Appetizers, Zesty Anchovy, '83 93
Butter, Lemon-Anchovy, '97 307
Mayonnaise, Anchovy, '86 179
Rémoulade, Criolla, '97 227
Salad, Caesar, '99 265
Salad, Dawn's World-Famous Greek, '98 276
Sauce Niçoise, '96 190
Tapenade, '92 194
APPETIZERS. *See also* **CRACKERS,
    FONDUES, PÂTÉS.**
Almond-Ham Rollups, '89 284
Almonds, Curried, '82 297
Anchovy Appetizers, Zesty, '83 93
Antipasto, Easy, '92 24
Antipasto, Grandpa's, '98 183
Antipasto Relish, '86 327
Apple-Phyllo Rolls, '88 213
Apple Quarters, Honey-Baked, '86 93
Artichoke-and-Shrimp Appetizer, '93 271
Artichoke Appetizer Frittata, '92 58
Artichoke Appetizer, Zesty, '80 146
Artichoke-Caviar Mold, '87 239
Artichoke-Cheese Bottoms, Baked, '94 61
Artichoke Oysters, '96 154
Artichoke-Parmesan Phyllo Bites, '87 54
Artichokes, Marinated, '87 250
Artichokes, Spring, '86 62
Asparagus Croquettes, '85 265
Asparagus, Prosciutto-Wrapped, '91 98
Asparagus Rolls, '79 296; '80 31
Asparagus Rolls, Hot, '93 329
Asparagus Rollups, '79 63
Asparagus Roll-Ups, '84 270
Asparagus with Dill Sauce, '97 59
Asparagus with Garlic Cream, '95 83
Avocado-Crabmeat Cocktail, Sherried, '87 95
Bacon Appetizers, Hot, '80 248
Bacon-Chestnut Wraps, '84 M216
Bacon-Jalapeño-Tomato Quesadillas, '95 240
Bacon-Onion Appetizers, '94 290
Bacon Rolls, '84 270; '93 330
Bacon Rollups, '79 34
Bacon Swirls, '89 214; '98 26
Bacon-Wrapped Crackers, '93 280
Bacon-Wrapped Pineapple Chunks, '84 25
Bacon-Wrapped Water Chestnuts, '79 63
Bagel Chips, '91 138
Bagel Chips, Cinnamon-and-Sugar, '91 139
Bagel Chips, Garlic, '91 139
Bagel Chips, Lemon-and-Herb, '91 139
Bagel Chips, Parmesan Cheese, '91 138
Bagel Crisps, '86 278
Basil-Pepper Appetizers, '98 133
Bean Burrito Appetizers, '94 226
Beef on a Stick, '99 336
Beef on a Stick, Marinated, '85 234
Beef Sticks, '93 331
Beefy Party Snacks, '80 249
Beets, Blue Cheese-Stuffed, '88 211
Biscuits with Ham, Ranch, '97 59
Black Bean Appetizer, '83 50
Black Bean Cakes with Greens and Apple
    Dressing, '92 216
Black-Eyed Pea Pinwheels, '85 300; '86 18
Bread Ring, Braided, '96 322
Breadstick Haystacks, '99 246
Broccoli-Cheese Appetizer, '92 265
Broccoli, Cocktail, '80 192
Broccoli Soup, Mock Cream of, '85 288
Bruschetta, Black Truffle, '99 323
Brussels Sprouts, Marinated, '88 265
Burgers, Saucy Cocktail, '83 217

Burrito Rollups, '90 119
Burritos, Chinese, '87 181
Buzzard's Nests, '93 244
Cakes, Little Bitty, '98 154
Canapés
    Bread, Canapé, '89 292
    Bread, Rye Canapé, '89 293
    Bread, Whole Wheat Canapé, '89 293
    Chicken-Cucumber Canapés, '98 154
    Crab Canapés, '93 130
    Crab Canapés, Cheesy, '86 262
    Crab Canapés, Hot, '86 70; '87 239
    Crabmeat Canapés, '88 150
    Cucumber Canapés, '95 88
    Fruit-Topped Canapés, '85 80
    Green Onion Canapés, '84 M216
    Lemon-Cheese, Canapés, '87 93
    Mushroom Canapés, '80 285; '97 23
    Party Canapés, '86 128
    Roasted Garlic Canapés, '96 95
    Salmon Canapés, Smoked, '99 140
    Shrimp-and-Cucumber Canapés, '93 164
    Shrimp Canapés, '84 116
    Swiss Canapés, Hot, '83 259
    Vegetable Canapés, '91 252
Caponata, '87 166
Caramel Corn, Oven-Made, '91 233
Caramel Good Stuff, Baked, '80 284
Caraway Wafers, '81 261
Carrots, Dilled Baby, '84 80
Carrots, Dill-Spiced, '87 200
Carrots, Pickled, '93 12
Catfish Appetizer, Layered, '92 209
Cauliflower, Crispy Fried, '80 220
Cauliflower, Dilled, '83 93
Cauliflower, French-Fried, '86 211
Cauliflower, Golden Fried, '82 78
Cauliflower, Pickled, '94 183
Cauliflower with Cheese Sauce, Fried, '87 231
Caviar Crown, '83 78
Caviar, Eggplant, '88 262; '99 217
Caviar, Mexican, '98 135
Caviar Pie, '79 154
Caviar Potatoes, '84 80
Caviar Potatoes, Appetizer, '86 223
Caviar, Texas, '86 218; '99 84
Caviar Tomatoes, '91 12
Celery, Creamy Stuffed, '82 102
Celery, Jalapeño Stuffed, '79 70
Celery, Stuffed, '82 98
Celery Trunks, Stuffed, '85 115
Cereal Bites, Buttery, '89 97
Cereal Nibblers, Great, '82 297
Cereal Snack, Toasted, '85 215
Ceviche (Marinated Raw Fish), '80 194
Ceviche, Mexican-Style, '88 115
Cheese. *See also* **APPETIZERS/Dips, Spreads**
    and Fillings.
    Bagel Chips, Parmesan Cheese, '91 138
    Bake, Appetizer Cheese, '92 209
    Ball, Apple Cheese, '98 250
    Ball, Blue Cheese, '80 259; '84 221
    Ball, Blue Cheese-Olive, '82 248
    Ball, Bourbon Cheese, '81 57
    Ball, Brandied Blue Cheese, '85 283
    Ball, Carrot-Cheese, '86 325
    Ball, Cheese, '82 161; '91 200
    Ball, Cheese and Chutney, '87 247
    Ball, Cheese 'n' Beef, '83 230
    Ball, Chicken-Cheese, '93 216
    Ball, Chicken-Curry Cheese, '85 118
    Ball, Cocktail Cheese, '83 174
    Ball, Curried Shrimp Cheese, '86 135
    Ball, Deviled Pecan, '80 258

Ball, Festive Cheese, '79 44; '94 279
Ball, Fruit-and-Nut Cheese, '91 251
Ball, Herbed Cheese, '89 246
Ball, Holiday Cheese, '79 285
Ball, Olive Cheese, '80 258
Ball, Parmesan-Cream Cheese, '89 246
Ball, Party Cheese, '84 258
Ball, Party Pecan Cheese, '81 235
Ball, Peanut Butter-Cheese, '86 136
Ball, Pecan Cheese, '83 127
Ball, Peppered Cheese, '79 100; '94 118
Ball, Pimiento Cheese, '80 258
Ball, Pineapple Cheese, '81 160
Ball, Pineapple-Cheese, '84 26
Ball, Pinecone Cheese, '93 288; '98 265
Balls, Bite-Size Cheese, '92 321
Balls, Cheese and Mushroom, '79 63
Balls, Fried Cheese, '89 181
Ball, Shrimp-Cheese, '85 208
Ball, Smoky Salmon Cheese, '82 247
Balls, Olive-Cheese, '84 206
Balls, Pumpkin Patch Cheese, '99 245
Balls with Sun-Dried Tomatoes, Cheese,
    '94 317
Ball, Tangy Cheese, '81 263, 287
Bar, Savory Cheese, '91 98
Bars, Bacon-Cheese Toast, '79 36
Bars, Camembert, '86 58
Bear Claws, '81 161
Biscuits, Cheese, '79 296; '80 31
Biscuits, Cheesy Sausage, '80 78
Biscuits, Mixer Cheese, '96 22
Biscuits, Petite Ham and Cheese, '79 193
Biscuits, Tiny Cheese, '80 192
Bites, Benne Cheese, '80 121
Bites, Cheese, '93 329
Bites, Cheesy Pecan, '82 248
Bites, Curried Swiss, '85 220
Bites, Lemon-Cheese Party, '95 160
Bites, Parmesan Cheese, '99 221
Bites, Starlight Cheese, '95 329
Bit-of-Brie Appetizer, '88 M8
Bonbons, Cheese, '87 93
Brick, Cheese, '99 170
Brie, Chutney-Bacon, '90 M292
Brie en Croûte, Stuffed, '97 162
Brie, Honey-Mustard, '91 252
Brie in Braided Bread Ring, '96 322
Brie in Rye, Raspberry, '93 252
Brie, Kahlúa-Pecan, '92 289
Brie, Parmesan-Coated, '95 286
Brie, Tropical Breeze, '94 M18
Brie with Fresh Fruit, Caramel, '90 266
Brie, Wrapped, '92 126
Brie Wrapped in Phyllo, '93 173
Caraway Cheese, '89 246
Caraway-Cheese Crisps, '95 284
Cheesecake, Roasted Vegetable, '99 140
Cheesecake, Salsa, '98 33
Cheesecakes, Herbed, '99 182
Cheesecake, Smoked Salmon, '99 92
Cheesecake, Spinach-Herb, '99 139
Cheesecake, Three-Layer, '99 140
Chiles-Rellenos Squares, '91 161
Cracker Nibbles, Cheese, '84 328
Crackers, Cheddar, '84 236
Cream Cheese Appetizer, Baked, '92 58
Cream Cheese Round, Pesto-and-, '90 242
Crème Brûlée, Roquefort-and-Black Pepper,
    '95 324
Crispies, Cheese-Bacon, '84 270
Crispies, Pecan-Cheese, '87 168
Crisps, Blue Cheese, '98 285
Croquettes, Hot Cheese, '89 182

Crostini, Almond-Bacon-Cheese, '94 318
Crostini, Mozzarella, '94 319
Crostini, Roasted Peppers-Feta Cheese, '96 87
Crostini, Swiss-Blue Cheese, '94 318; '96 215
Crostini, Zippy Cheese, '97 90
Cucumber Slices, Cheesy, '84 80
Cups, Cottage Cheese-Spinach, '87 190
Cutouts, Sesame-Cheese, '82 296
Feta Cheesecakes, Little, '86 277
Fiesta Cheesecake, '93 273
Flaming Cheese, '84 187
Fondue, Cheese, '81 40
Fondue, Nacho, '94 332; '95 35
Fondue, Party Cheese, '92 20
Fondue, Pub, '94 332; '95 35
Fondue, Swiss Cheese, '91 48
Fried Cheddar Cheese, '89 182
Fried Cheese Bites, '82 77
Fried Cheese, Italian-Style, '83 250; '89 182
Garnished Cheese, '91 98
Goat Cheese, Dried Tomato Mock, '97 105
Goat Cheese, Mock, '97 105
Goat Cheese, Peppered, '94 128
Goat Cheese Rosemary, '89 270
Goat Cheese with Sun-Dried Tomatoes and
    Rosemary, '93 175
Grapes, Blue Cheese-Pecan, '95 48
Grits, Garlic-Cheese, '97 58
Herb Cheese, Pot-of-, '85 210
Herbed Cheese, '88 152
Herb-Pepper Cheese, '97 90
Kabobs, Peppered Cheese, '91 279
Little Bits, '79 196
Loaf, Four-Layer Cheese, '99 222
Log, Black Pepper-Goat Cheese, '98 285
Log, Cheesy Surprise, '82 247
Log, Garlic Cheese, '85 21
Log, Hawaiian Cheese, '89 246
Log, Roquefort Pecan, '89 247
Logs, Black Pepper Cheese, '90 61
Logs, East Indian Cheese, '88 173
Log, Toasted Pecan Cheese, '86 M288
Marinated Cheese, '90 244; '95 21
Meat-and-Cheese Appetizers, '87 7
Melt, Brie-and-Cranberry Chutney, '98 M318
Mexicali Appetizer, Cheesy, '82 108
Mold, Blue Cheese, '85 210
Mold, Cheese-and-Wine, '84 197
Mold, Cream Cheese-Crabmeat, '90 71
Mold, Garlic-Chive Cheese, '85 210
Mousse, Roquefort, '82 71
Nuggets, Cheesy Ham, '81 290
Olive Appetizers, Cheesy, '85 113
Olive Appetizers, Cheesy-, '87 246
Olive Snack, Open-Faced Cheese-and-, '89 97
Pasta Bites, Pesto-Cheese, '87 251
Pastries, Cream Cheese, '80 250
Pastries, Date-Filled Cheese, '83 259
Pastry, Brie Wrapped in, '80 241
Pastry, Sausage Balls in Cheese, '80 248
Pastry Shells, Miniature Cream Cheese, '87 190
Patty, Lemon-Pepper Cheese, '84 117
Patty Shells, Cream Cheese, '82 249
Peachy Cream Cheese, '92 289
Pepper-Cheese Stacks, '87 80
Peppers, Cheesy Jalapeño, '80 195
Phyllo-Cheese Triangles, '87 246
Phyllo Cheese Triangles, '93 329
Phyllo, Goat Cheese Wrapped in, '99 43
Phyllo Triangles, Cheese-Filled, '83 259
Pie, Cheesy Hors d'Oeuvre, '88 91
Pinwheels, Mexican, '95 21
Pinwheels, Santa's, '91 275
Pita Crisps, Cheesy, '97 45

APPETIZERS, Cheese
(continued)

Potato Skins, Cheesy, '82 78
Puffs, Bavarian Cheese, '80 191
Puffs, Blue Cheese-and-Bacon, '97 98
Puffs, Cheese, '79 110; '97 240
Puffs, Cheese-and-Spinach, '87 246
Puffs, Cream Cheese, '84 151
Puffs, Gouda-Shrimp, '79 234
Puffs, Ham-and-Cheese, '86 277
Puffs, Mexican Cheese, '87 8
Puffs, Oregano Cheese, '95 21
Puffs, Surprise Cheese, '79 295; '80 31
Quesadillas, Green Chile, '90 121
Queso Blanco, '93 322
Queso, Chunky Cheese, '99 279
Quiches, Miniature Bacon-Cheese, '83 93
Quiches, Miniature Cheese, '80 150
Quick Cheese Snack, '89 98
Ring, Cheese, '81 261
Ring, Strawberry-Cheese, '86 14
Roll, Chili-Cheese, '84 114
Roll, Ham-and-Cheese, '79 234
Rollups, Cream Cheese, '98 134
Rollups, Ham-and-Swiss, '85 113
Rollups, Mexican, '98 134
Round, Brie Appetizer, '82 41
Round, Herbed Cheese, '84 300
Rounds, Cheese, '86 262
Rounds, Parmesan, '85 131
Rounds, Parmesan Party, '82 248
Salami-Cheese Snacks, '88 96
Salsa Parmesan, Broiled, '98 33
Sandwiches, Cheese Tea, '92 276
Sandwiches, Cheshire Claret Cheese-and-
Ham Striped Tea, '94 16
Sandwiches, Pimiento Cheese Finger, '99 86
Sesame Cheese Bites, '89 24
Soufflé, Blue Cheese, '91 244
Sour Cream Appetizer, Cheesy, '84 51
Spinach-Cheese Bites, '94 23
Squares, Cream Cheese-Almond, '85 68
Squares, Green Chile-Cottage Cheese, '86 85
Squares, Jalapeño Cheese, '80 195
Squares, Quick Cheese, '84 191
Sticks, Parmesan, '82 297
Sticks, Parmesan-Bacon, '99 65
Sticks, Parmesan Sesame, '81 39
Sticks, Peppery Cheese, '81 M289
Straws, Brie Cheese, '94 216
Straws, Cheese, '80 150; '82 137; '88 77
Straws, Chili-Cheese, '94 216
Straws, Easy-as-Pie Cheese, '94 216
Straws, Italian Cheese, '94 217
Straws, Parmesan Cheese, '94 216
Straws, Sally's Cheese, '97 121
Tartlets, Cheese, '88 211
Tarts, Blue Cheese Appetizer, '85 300; '86 18
Terrine, Basil-Cheese, '96 322
Terrine, Italian Cheese, '93 64
Terrine with Tomato-Basil Vinaigrette, Blue
Cheese, '99 288
Three-Cheese Appetizer, '80 174
Toasts, Cheddar-Almond, '97 30
Toast Treats, Cheese, '83 100
Torte, Showstopping Appetizer, '98 319
Torte, Tomato-Cheese, '97 49
Turnovers, Cheesy Sesame Seed, '91 252
Twists, Double Cheese, '85 131
Twists, Parmesan, '99 323
Vegetable Cheesecake, '96 110
Wafers, Cheese, '80 151; '95 174; '99 279

Wafers, Hope Farm Cheese, '93 282
Wafers, Pam's Cheese, '98 268
Wafers, Pecan-Cheese, '81 119
Wafers, Sage-Pecan Cheese, '93 12
Wedges, Cheesy Party, '84 84
Wonton Chips, Parmesan Cheese, '91 138
Wonton Envelopes, Fried, '95 96
Wontons with Hot Sauce, Cheese, '83 74
Cherries, Stuffed, '85 81
Cherry Pepper Appetizers, Fiery Stuffed, '97 269
Chicken. *See also* **APPETIZERS/Dips,**
Spreads and Fillings.
Balls, Coconut Curried Chicken, '91 165
Balls, Curried Chicken, '91 98
Bites, Curried Chicken, '85 40
Bites, French-Fried Chicken, '85 160
Bites, Savory Chicken, '92 209
B'steeya with Chicken, '98 210
Cakes with Avocado Cream, Southwestern
Chicken-and-Corn, '97 M311
Deep-Fried Walnut Chicken, '87 175
Drummettes, Down-Home Chicken, '93 157
Drummettes, Ginger-Garlic Appetizer, '93 157
Drummettes, Orange-Pecan Chicken, '93 158
Drummettes, Southwestern Chicken, '93 158
Fingers, Chicken Almondette, '93 12
Fingers, Chicken Little, '80 249
Firecrackers, Texas, '95 96; '99 94
Liver and Bacon Roll-Ups, Chicken, '80 200;
'81 57
Livers, Garlic Chicken, '96 105
Livers, Party Chicken, '83 242
Liver Turnovers, Chicken, '79 141
Log, Chicken-Pecan, '81 290
Mushroom Appetizers, Chicken-, '88 210
Nuggets, Baked Chicken, '81 149
Nuggets, Lemon-Chicken, '87 283
Nuggets Supreme, Chicken, '85 160
Nuggets with Pineapple Sauce, Chicken, '84 236
Puffs, Appetizer Chicken, '85 72
Puffs, Chicken Nut, '81 260
Quesadillas, Spicy Chicken, '95 42
Quesadillas with Chipotle Salsa,
Chicken-and-Brie, '99 311
Salad, Old-Fashioned Chicken, '83 79
Sandwiches, Curried Chicken Tea, '97 23
Sesame Chicken, '97 256
Sesame Chicken Appetizers, '89 61
Skewers, Taco-Chicken, '99 119
Sticks, Italian Chicken, '98 25
Sticky Chicken, '97 239
Strips, Sesame Chicken, '98 250
Strips with "Come Back" Dipping Sauce, Miss
Mary's Chicken, '96 213
Tarts, Chicken Salad, '84 257
Tarts, Deviled Chicken, '94 14
Tempura Delight, Chicken, '85 66
Terrine, Vegetable-Chicken, '83 224
Wings, Broiled Chicken, '80 149
Wings, Chinese Chicken, '96 111
Wings, Curried Chicken, '96 110
Wings, Grilled Honey Chicken, '96 111
Wings, Honey-Glazed Chicken, '91 251
Wings, Hot Buffalo, '87 176
Wings, Maple-Glazed Chicken, '99 110
Wings, Satan's, '87 214
Wings, Spicy Buffalo, '95 239
Wings, Spicy Oriental-Style, '96 215
Wings, Sweet-and-Sour Chicken, '90 206;
'96 110
Wings, Tandoori Chicken, '96 110
Wings, Teriyaki Chicken, '85 300; '86 18
Wontons with Hoisin Peanut Dipping Sauce,
Chicken, '99 14

Chile-Sausage Squares, '86 297
Chiles Rellenos, Bite-Size, '87 246
Chiles Rellenos, Roasted, '95 64
Chili in Pastry Cups, '90 68
Chips
Bagel Chips, '91 138
Bagel Chips, Cinnamon-and-Sugar, '91 139
Bagel Chips, Garlic, '91 139
Bagel Chips, Lemon-and-Herb, '91 139
Bagel Chips, Parmesan Cheese, '91 138
Beet Chips, '97 229
Homemade Texas Chips with Guacamole
Spread, '90 119
Pita Chips, '89 19; '91 138
Pita Chips, Baked, '99 138
Plantain Chips, '95 M203
(Plantain Chips), Tostones de Plátano, '92 158
Sweet Potato Chips, '91 138; '93 332; '95 M203
Sweet Potato Chips with Blue Cheese, '93 290
Tortilla Chips, '91 137
Tortilla Chips, Corn, '91 17
Tortilla Chips, Light, '91 257
Wonton Chips, Baked, '91 138; '99 138
Wonton Chips, Cinnamon-and-Sugar, '91 138
Wonton Chips, Garlic, '91 138
Wonton Chips, Lemon-and-Herb, '91 138
Wonton Chips, Parmesan Cheese, '91 138
Chocolate-Almond Cream, '91 108
Chocolate Bites, Snowy, '90 47
Chocolate-Dipped Horns, '93 197
Chocolate-Peanut Butter Snacks, '90 226
Chocolate-Sesame Sticks, '91 316
Chutney, Cranberry, '96 275
Chutney Roll, '83 259
Chutney with Cream Cheese, Cranberry-
Amaretto, '87 244
Cinnamon Sticks, '95 244
Cinnamon Wafers, '84 324
Clam Crisps, '80 151
Clam Puffs, '90 60
Clams Casino, '81 125
Clams Oreganata, '85 104
Clams with Cilantro-Black Walnut Pesto,
Littleneck, '97 164
Cocktail Puffs, '91 106
Confetti Appetizers, '84 191
Corn Salsa, Spicy, '93 322
Crab. *See also* **APPETIZERS/Dips, Spreads**
and Fillings.
Balls, Crabmeat, '88 150
Bites, Crabmeat, '97 98
Bites, Crab-Zucchini, '84 M216
Bites, Spicy Crab, '91 165
Broiled Crab Meltaways, '93 287
Cakes, Crab, '99 267
Cakes, Miniature Crab, '96 306
Cakes with Cress Sauce, Baked Crab, '96 176
Cakes with Maui Sauce, Crab, '99 310
Casserole, Easy Crab, '93 270
Chafing Dish Crabmeat, '89 284
Crisps, Crab, '79 63
Deviled Crab, Devilish, '85 264
Hors d'Oeuvre, Crabmeat, '94 236
Mold, Crab, '85 318
Oysters, Crabmeat Stuffed, '94 328
Pot Stickers, Hoisin Crab, '96 92
Puffs, Crab, '80 20; '84 269
Puffs, Crabmeat, '99 335
Rémoulade, Crabmeat, '93 280
Sandwiches, Miniature Crab Cake, '96 306
Snacks, Crab, '83 93
Topping, Crabmeat, '91 64
Crawfish on Eggplant, Soft-Shell, '88 222
Crème Brûlée, Onion, '95 324

Crème Brûlée, Roasted Garlic, '95 324
Crème Brûlées, Savory, '95 324
Crostini
    Almond-Bacon-Cheese Crostini, '94 318
    Artichoke Crostini, Hot, '94 319
    Artichoke Crostini, Parmesan-, '98 285
    Christmas Crostini, '94 318
    Festive Crostini, '98 183; '99 325
    Green Onion Crostini, '96 93
    Mexican Crostini, '95 142
    Mozzarella Crostini, '94 319
    Peppers-Feta Cheese Crostini, Roasted, '96 87
    Swiss-Blue Cheese Crostini, '94 318; '96 215
    Tomato Crostini, '99 230
    Zippy Cheese Crostini, '97 90
    Zippy Crostini, '97 90
Crunch, Oriental, '96 215
Crunchy Munchies, '94 196
Cucumber Delights, '84 117
Cucumber Fingers, Fried, '86 146
Cucumber Rounds, '88 78
Cucumber Sandwiches, '90 81; '94 14; '97 99
Cucumber Vichyssoise, '94 90
Date-Nut Ball, '92 326
Dates, Apricot-Stuffed, '80 250
Dips. *See also* **APPETIZERS/Caviar.**
    Almond Cream Dip with Strawberries, '92 164
    Almond Delight Dip, '90 226
    Antipasto Dip, '93 313
    Apple Dip, '93 205; '96 M190
    Apricot Dip, '86 178
    Artichoke-Chile Dip, '98 234
    Artichoke Dip, Baked, '95 239
    Artichoke Dip, Deluxe, '80 87
    Artichoke Dip, Florentine, '96 274
    Artichoke Dip, Greek, '97 315
    Artichoke Dip in a Bread Basket, '93 13
    Artichoke Dip, Italian, '97 315
    Artichoke Dip, Mexican, '90 292
    Artichoke Dip, Seasoned Mayonnaise, '80 87
    Artichoke-Seafood Dip, Hot, '80 241
    Artichoke Seafood Dip, Hot, '85 M212
    Avocado Dip, '80 285; '81 57, 306
    Avocado Dip, "Bring-Home-the-Bacon," '92 80
    Avocado Dip, Zippy, '82 9; '83 69
    Bacon-and-Tomato Dip, '90 147
    Bacon Dip, '82 197
    Bacon Dip, Zesty, '92 156
    Bacon-Guacamole Dip, '85 25
    Basket, Dips and Dippers in a, '83 171
    Bean Dip, '89 97
    Bean Dip, Hotshot, '87 195
    Bean Dip, Prairie Fire, '80 195
    Beau Monde Dip in Rye Bread, Party, '83 127
    Beef-and-Spinach Dip, '99 65
    Beef Dip, Chipped, '88 M8
    Beef Dip, Hot Cheesy, '80 85
    Black Bean Dip, '95 93
    Black-Eyed Pea con Queso, '96 274
    Black-Eyed Pea Dip, '81 8
    Black-Eyed Pea Dip, Bill D's, '97 M89
    Blue Cheese Dip, '80 285; '83 169; '93 313
    Braunschweiger-and-Beer Dip, '85 69
    Broccoli Dip, Cheesy, '83 92
    Broccoli-Garlic Dip, '82 59
    Brown Sugar Dip with Fruit, Buttery, '90 243
    Cabbage, Dock Dip in, '86 179
    Cheddar-Bacon Dip, '89 M119
    Cheese-and-Chile Dip, '83 31
    Cheese and Crab Dip, Hot, '81 261
    Cheese-Bean Dip, '85 208
    Cheese-Crab Dip, '91 200
    Cheese Dip, Hot, '91 171
    Cheese Dip, Meaty, '82 59; '92 160

Cheese Dip, Seaside, '85 284
Cheese Dunk, Deviled, '80 265
Cheese-Garlic Dip, '80 192
Cheese-Herb Dip, '89 20
Chicken Dip, Hot, '80 86
Chickpea-and-Red Pepper Dip, '99 138
Chile-Beef Dip, Hot, '83 218
Chile-Cheese Dip, '87 173
Chile con Queso, '80 194; '81 195
Chile con Queso Supreme, '80 265
Chile Dip, Hot, '82 248
Chile Sauce, Hot, '92 156
Chili-and-Black-Eyed Pea Dip, '92 155
Chili-and-Cheese Dip, '89 328
Chili-Cheese Dip, '90 225
Chili con Queso Dip, '86 81
Chili Dip, '82 161; '88 218; '89 47; '91 143
Chili Dip, Cheesy, '90 150
Chive-Cheese Dip, '94 62
Christmas Confetti Dip, '92 279
Clam Dip, '79 151; '80 265
Clam Dip, Hot, '82 59; '89 48
Clam Dip, Zesty, '92 25
Confetti Snack Dip, '79 107
Corn-and-Avocado Dip, Roasted, '91 279
Cottage Cheese Sun-Dried Tomato Dip, '93 13
Crab-and-Cheese Dip, Hot, '94 282
Crab Dip, Creamy, '80 M135
Crab Dip, Festive, '92 285
Crab Dip, Hot, '93 269; '97 89
Crab Dip, Oven-Baked, '82 59
Crab Dip, Tangy, '83 5
Crab Dip, Trawler, '93 238
Crabmeat Dip, Hot, '95 154
Cranberry Fruit Dip, '89 60
Cranberry-Horseradish Dip, '85 65
Cream Cheese Dip, Fruited, '88 261
Cream Cheese-Onion Dip, '79 236
Creamy Texas Dip, '94 161
Crudité Dip, '86 105
Crudité Platter with Dip, '84 139
Cucumber Dipping Sauce, '94 47
Cucumber-Yogurt Dip, '99 93
Curried Dip, '81 262
Curry Dip, '80 84; '81 9; '85 132; '86 184;
    '87 25; '99 138
Curry Dip and Vegetable Platter, '89 327
Curry Dip, Creamy, '84 206
Curry-Onion Dip, '93 313
Delight, Dipper's, '98 93
Deviled Dip, '87 25
Dill Dip, '80 265; '93 330
Dill Dip, Refreshing, '99 324
Dilled Garden Dip, '84 324
Egg Dip, Festive, '79 285
Eggplant Dip, '96 275
Fiesta Dip, '81 206; '92 263; '96 212
Fiesta Dip, Quick, '99 M197
Fish Dip, Smoked, '84 46
Fondue, Cheese, '81 40
Fondue, Fruitcake, '84 258
Fondue, Nacho, '94 332; '95 35
Fondue, Party Cheese, '92 20
Fondue, Peppermint, '94 332; '95 35
Fondue, Pub, '94 332; '95 35
Fondue, Swiss Cheese, '91 48
Fruit Dip, Coconut-Honey, '84 171
Fruit Dip, Creamy, '84 51
Fruit Dip, Fresh, '80 265; '95 94
Fruit Dip, Ginger, '96 190
Fruit Dip, Heavenly, '81 160
Fruit Dip, Marshmallow, '84 171
Fruit Dip, Quick, '90 110
Fruit Dip, Sweet, '89 328

Garbanzo Dip, '93 94
Gazpacho Dip, '95 243
Ginger Dip, '94 12, 19; '99 139
Grand Marnier Dip, '86 142
Green Goddess Dip, '84 159
Guacamole, '79 185; '80 74; '83 179; '91 161;
    '96 170; '99 84
Guacamole, Black Bean, '94 277
Guacamole, Creamy, '79 91; '83 174; '99 119
Guacamole Dip, '86 4; '95 96
Guacamole Dip, Bacon-, '85 25
Guacamole, Easy, '95 94
Guacamole in Shells, '86 74
Guacamole, Margarita, '97 167
Guac, Baine's, '98 88
Ham Dip, Creamy, '93 125
Herbal Dip, '86 14
Holiday Dip, '83 321; '84 289
Honey-Herb Dip, Creamy, '98 135
Horseradish Dip, Creamy, '94 122
Hummas, '92 155
Hummus, '96 158
Hummus, Black-Eyed Pea, '94 123
Hummus, Creamy Dried Tomato, '95 284
Hummus, Low-Fat, '99 137
Hummus, Quick, '95 93
Indonesian Dip, '96 190
Kahlúa Dip, '99 139
Leek Dip, Creamy, '86 77
Lime-Dill Dip, '92 65
Marmalade Dip, '99 324
Mexican Appetizer, Chilled, '87 197
Mexican Fiesta Dip, '98 234
Mint Dip with Fresh Fruit, '87 146
Monster Mash Dip, '93 244
Mushroom Dip, Hot, '89 48
Mustard Dip, Sweet-and-Spicy, '96 M274
Nacho Dip, '83 239; '93 M330
Nacho Dip, Layered, '81 261
Nacho Dip, Quick, '90 168
Niçoise, Sauce, '96 190
Olive-Relish Dip, '84 205
Onion Dip, '94 21
Onion Dip, Cheesy, '83 145
Onion Dip, Chunky, '84 257
Orange Cream, '90 126
Orange Dip, Creamy, '84 117; '87 247
Orange Dip, Spicy, '85 230
Orange Fruit Dip, '96 190
Orange-Lime Dip, '96 248
Orange Sour Cream Dip, '79 208
Oyster Dip, Smoked, '79 233
Parsley-Dill Dip with Fresh Vegetables, '85 79
Peach Dip, Creole, '80 142
Peachy Dip, '92 179
Peanut Butter Dip, '86 135
Peanut Butter-Honey Dip, '85 19
Peanut Butter Lovers' Dip, '93 162
Peas, Passion, '89 17
Pepperoncini-Cream Cheese Dip, '91 252
Pesto Dip, '95 93; '97 226
Pineapple Dip, Cheesy, '80 249
Pineapple-Ginger Dip, '86 104
Pine Nut-Spinach Dip, '99 138
Pizza Dip, '99 65
Plantain Dip, '92 158
Quick Fiesta Dip, '95 M237
Ranch Dip, Skinny, '93 96
Ranch-Style Dip, '90 138; '92 148
Salsa-Bean Dip, '98 285
Salsa, Chunky, '86 130; '90 206
Salsa Cruda, '87 180; '88 148
Salsa, Fresh Summer, '87 89
Salsa, Greek Vegetable, '98 32

APPETIZERS, Dips
(continued)

Salsa Picante, **'84** 108
Sauce, Citrus Dipping, **'97** 208
Sauce, Hoisin Peanut Dipping, **'99** 14
Seafood Dip, **'79** 3
Seafood Dip, Hot Cheesy, **'84** 221
Seafood Dip, Super, **'90** 292
Shrimp Dip, **'86** 84; **'88** M261; **'98** 67
Shrimp Dip, Chunky, **'96** 214
Shrimp Dip, Hot, **'87** 190
Shrimp Dip, Monterey, **'99** M65
Shrimp Dip, Quick, **'79** 153
Shrimp Dip, Zesty, **'80** 150
Six-Layer Dip, **'81** 160
Skinny Dip, Santa Fe, **'94** 137
Sour Cream Dip, **'86** 278
South-of-the-Border Dip, **'81** 235
Spinach-Cheese Dip, Hot, **'89** 48
Spinach con Queso, Easy, **'88** 101
Spinach Dip, **'80** 86; **'86** 159; **'87** 25, 214;
　'93 324
Spinach Dip, Cheesy, **'82** 59
Spinach Dip, Creamy, **'88** 132
Spinach Dip, Hot, **'80** 249
Spinach Dip in Cabbage, **'82** 155
Spinach Dip in Sourdough Round, **'98** 173
Sugar Snap Dip, **'88** 91
Summer Dip, **'94** 157
Swiss-Onion Dip, **'95** 93
Taco Dip, Hot, **'93** 238
Tarragon Dip, **'83** 78
Tennessee Sin, **'95** 218; **'96** 204
Tequila Dip, **'91** 166
Thick-and-Creamy Dip, **'90** 271
Tofu Dip, **'86** 109
Tostada Dip, **'84** 206
Tropical Dip for Fruit, **'91** 252
Tuna-Curry Dip, **'84** 31
Tuna Dip, Low-Cal, **'87** 25
Tuna Dip, Tasty, **'96** 190
Turnip Green Dip, **'91** 13
Turnip Green Dip with Jalapeño-Corn
　Muffins, Hot, **'93** 164
Vegetable Dip, **'79** 52; **'82** 161
Vegetable Dip, Creamy, **'82** 132; **'83** 99, 180
Vegetable Dip, Cucumber-Cheese, **'83** 128
Vegetable Dip, Fresh, **'80** 249
Vegetable Dip, Herb, **'89** 269
Vegetable Dip, Starburst, **'82** 248
Vegetable Dip, Tangy, **'87** 196
Vegetable Dip, Zippy, **'84** 256
Vegetable Garden Dip, **'85** 215
Water Chestnut Dip, **'80** 86; **'86** 183
Yellow Squash-Zucchini Dip, **'89** 48
Yogurt Dip, **'94** 21
Yogurt Dip, Fruited, **'84** 171
Yogurt Herring Dip, **'80** 232
Zesty Party Dip, **'83** 259
Dumplings, Steamed Sesame, **'97** 208
Eggplant Appetizer, **'83** 187
Eggplant Appetizer, Grilled, **'95** 198
Eggplant Caviar, **'88** 262; **'99** 217
Eggplant, Cheesy Fried, **'90** 75
Eggplant, Fried Parmesan, **'87** 166
Eggplant Sticks, Ned's, **'95** 309
Egg Rolls, **'86** 81
Egg Rolls, Chiles Rellenos, **'86** 296
Eggrolls, Shrimp and Pork, **'82** 240; **'83** 18
Egg Rolls, Vegetarian, **'86** 148
Eggs and Ham, Green, **'96** 90
Eggs, Black-and-Blue, **'96** 90

Eggs, Marbleized Garlic-Cheese-Stuffed, **'96** 91
Empanadas, **'92** 156
Endive Boats, **'84** 80
Endive with Arugula Tabbouleh Appetizers, **'98** 67
Endive with Caviar, **'93** 118
Escargots Provençal, **'82** 238; **'83** 156
Eye-of-Round, Burgundy, **'90** 243
Fast Goodies, **'84** 206
Figs with Prosciutto, Walnuts, and Cream, **'96** 194
Filet Mignon, Cajun Blackened, **'95** 85
Flank Steak, Marinated, **'83** 258; **'88** 262
Flank Steak, Red Wine-Marinated, **'95** 283
Frankfurter Appetizers, Bourbon, **'85** 207
Franks, Pickled Party, **'83** 174
Franks, Saucy Appetizer, **'84** M12
Franks, Tipsy, **'85** 52
Frog Legs, Crispy, **'80** 99
Fruit and Cheese Tray, **'83** 171
Fruit Bowl, Sparkling Fresh, **'80** 146
Fruit Cascade, **'86** 104
Fruit Cup, Appetizer, **'86** 131
Fruit Kabobs, **'86** 181
Fruit Kabobs with Coconut Dressing, **'87** 251
Fruit with Curried Rum Sauce, Tropical, **'91** 164
Fruit with Dressing, Chilled, **'85** 222
Fruit with Honey-Sour Cream Dip, Fresh, **'90** 180
Gorp, Elf, **'90** 270
Gorp, Fancy, **'89** 253
Granola, **'93** 197
Granola, Fabulous, **'92** 213
Granola Gorp, **'89** 59
Granola, Nutty, **'90** 95
Green Onion Teasers, **'82** 42
Guacamole. *See also* **APPETIZERS/Dips,**
　Spreads.
　Crisps, Guacamole, **'98** 173
　Mold, Guacamole, **'86** 184
Ham-and-Cheese Balls, Fried, **'84** 221
Ham Appetillas, **'93** 63
Ham-Filled Party Puffs, **'84** 116
Ham-Pineapple Nibbles, **'95** 283
Ham Rolls, **'79** 153
Ham Rolls, Party, **'85** 318
Ham Stack-Ups, **'96** 109
Ham Tapas, Garlic-, **'92** 175
Ham Turnovers, Chile-, **'88** 64
Ham Turnovers, Party, **'82** 39
Ham Twists, Deviled, **'82** 86
Hawaiian Dream Boats, **'86** 151
Hazelnuts, Curried, **'93** 301
Honey-and-Spice Crunch, **'94** 290
Horseradish Squares, Baked, **'92** 24
Hot Munch, Oriental, **'87** 8
Jalapeño Peppers, Fried Stuffed, **'95** 22
Jalapeño Peppers, Stuffed, **'96** 215
Jalapeños, Fiery Fried Stuffed, **'90** 118
Jalapeños, Fried, **'96** 292
Jalapeños, Shrimp-Stuffed, **'88** 115
Jalapeños, Stuffed, **'88** 234
Jezebel Sauce, **'93** 331
June Bugs, **'85** 11
Lettuce Folds, Thai, **'94** 47
Links, Cocktail Smoky, **'90** 168
Mango Chutney Torta, **'96** 322
Meatballs
　Bacon-Wrapped Meatballs, **'79** 81
　Brandied Meatballs, **'83** 78
　Burgundy-Bacon Meatballs, **'80** 283
　Chafing Dish Meatballs, **'81** 260
　Chestnut Meatballs, **'79** 110
　Cocktail Meatballs, **'79** 63, 207
　Flavorful Meatballs, **'84** 206
　German Meatballs, Crisp, **'92** 326
　Ham Balls, **'86** 256

Ham Balls, Appetizer, **'82** 39
Polynesian Meatballs, **'80** 207
Saucy Party Meatballs, **'80** 149
Sauerkraut Meatballs, **'86** 257
Spiced Meatballs, **'79** 284
Sweet-and-Sour Meatballs, **'82** 247; **'99** 325
Sweet-and-Sour Party Meatballs, **'79** 233
Tamale Meatballs, **'80** 194
Venison Sausage Balls, **'80** 42
Zesty Meatballs, **'80** 250
Melon Balls, Minted, **'87** 162
Melon, Berry-Filled, **'86** 93
Mints, Party, **'81** 119
Mirliton Balls, **'90** 217
Mixes, Snack
　Bunny Trail Mix, **'95** 101
　Cereal Snack Mix, **'93** 129
　Creole Snack Mix, **'91** 171
　Crunchy Snack Mix, **'93** 94
　Dried Fruit Mix, **'92** 22
　Granola Snack Mix, **'86** 229
　Jalapeño Nut Mix, **'96** 27
　Mexicali Snack Mix, **'86** 230
　Nutty Snack Mix, **'92** 22
　Party Mix, **'87** 257; **'96** 306; **'97** 108, 322;
　　'98 234
　Quick Party Mix, **'83** 92
　Raisin-Nut Party Mix, **'83** 60
　Rice Mix, Crunchy, **'85** 327
　Sea-and-Ski Cocktail Mix, **'90** 319
　Snack-Attack Party Mix, **'84** 328
　Snack Mix, **'89** 19
　Spicy Party Mix, **'81** M138
Monster Mouths, **'95** 274
Mousses
　Catfish Mousse, **'92** 327
　Caviar Mousse, **'82** 71; **'83** 258; **'85** 86
　Chicken Mousse, Curried, **'95** 328
　Crabmeat Mousse, **'90** 190; **'91** 244
　Crab Mousse, **'79** 117; **'95** 327
　Ham Mousse Pitas, **'95** 328
　Horseradish Mousse, **'84** 126
　Mustard Mousse, **'84** 127; **'86** 184; **'95** 328
　Oyster Mousse, **'81** 245
　Oyster Mousse, Smoked, **'84** 320; **'99** 162
　Salmon Dill Mousse, **'81** 21
　Salmon Mousse, **'83** 79
　Salmon Mousse, Irresistible, **'79** 284
　Shrimp Mousse, **'87** 196, 251
　Tuna Mousse, **'80** 275
Munchies, Reindeer, **'91** 276
Mushrooms. *See also* **APPETIZERS/Canapés.**
　Drunk Mushrooms, **'83** 174
　French-Fried Mushrooms, **'82** 78
　French-Fried Mushrooms with Tartar Sauce,
　　'86 233
　Logs, Mushroom, **'84** 206
　Marinated Herb Mushrooms, **'86** 327
　Marinated Mushroom Caps, **'83** 128
　Marinated Mushrooms, **'80** 82, 270; **'86** 135;
　　'91 306; **'92** 328
　Marinated Mushrooms, Easy, **'86** 217
　Pastry Cups, Mushroom-Almond, **'88** 210
　Rollups, Mushroom, **'85** 318
　Shiitakes Parmigiana, Stuffed, **'98** 25
　Stems, Mushrooms with, **'86** 258
　Stuffed Mushroom Appetizers, **'88** 210
　Stuffed Mushroom Caps, Crab-, **'84** 160
　Stuffed Mushroom Delight, **'87** 281
　Stuffed Mushrooms, **'79** 212; **'81** 239;
　　'83 13, 66, 126, 136; **'93** 172
　Stuffed Mushrooms, Black Olive-, **'86** 258
　Stuffed Mushrooms, Cheese 'n' Bacon-,
　　'86 258

Stuffed Mushrooms, Crab-, '81 190; '97 102
Stuffed Mushrooms, Crawfish-, '86 258
Stuffed Mushrooms, Elegant Cheese-, '81 57
Stuffed Mushrooms, Flavor-, '85 288
Stuffed Mushrooms, Herbed Cheese-, '96 171
Stuffed Mushrooms, Italian Sausage-, '83 127
Stuffed Mushrooms, Parmesan, '83 115
Stuffed Mushrooms, Pâté-, '85 118
Stuffed Mushrooms, Pecan-, '84 261
Stuffed Mushrooms, Pesto-, '86 150
Stuffed Mushrooms, Pistachio-, '86 141
Stuffed Mushrooms, Ricotta-, '85 20
Stuffed Mushrooms, Sausage-, '80 248;
   '91 164
Stuffed Mushrooms, Seasoned, '84 206
Stuffed Mushrooms, Shrimp-, '80 M135;
   '99 324
Stuffed Mushrooms, Spinach-, '86 81;
   '88 131, M261; '89 M133
Stuffed with Crab, Mushrooms, '82 249
Stuffed with Ham, Mushrooms, '97 237
Tapas, Majorcan Mushroom, '95 159
Tarts, Hot Sherried Mushroom, '83 78
Tarts, Mushroom, '88 161
Tipsy Mushrooms, '84 M216
Turnovers, Hot Mushroom, '97 102
Vegetable Mushroom Caps, '81 246
Nachos
Barbecue Nachos, Commissary, '91 171
Best-Ever Nachos, '79 91
Chicken Nachos, '84 244
Easy Nachos, '84 30
Make-Ahead Nachos, '80 M135
South Texas Nachos, '93 321
Southwestern Nachos, '96 170
Supreme, Nachos, '81 306
Texas Oyster Nachos, '87 39
Tex-Mex Nachos, '89 97
Tuna Nachos, '95 127; '96 201
Turkey Nachos, '90 118
Nectarine Cocktail, '85 107
New Potatoes, Ham-Stuffed, '88 211
Nibbles, Party, '90 249
Nuts
Chesapeake Nuts, '93 269
Curried Nuts, Spicy, '82 250
Deviled Nuts, '93 118
Hot Chili Nuts, '81 254
Nippy Nuts, '93 301
Pesto-Spiced Nuts, '95 173
Sherry-Orange Nuts, '86 M289
Soup Nuts, '96 106
Spiced Nuts, '84 257; '91 M316
Spicy Nuts, '82 161
Okra Rellenos, '97 156
Olive Cups, Greek, '99 221
Olive Quiche Appetizers, '86 159
Olives, Caliente Marinated, '95 177
Olives, Herb-Marinated, '92 176
Olives, Lemon-Garlic, '94 118
Onion Blossom, '94 226
Onion Crescent Crunch Sticks, '90 206
Onions, Rosemary Roasted, '98 16
Onion Toasties, '97 225
Orange-Almond Snack Balls, '95 214
Orange-Berry Appetizer, '85 81
Orange Halves, Broiled, '85 288
Oyster Nachos, Texas, '87 39
Oysters à la Casino, '80 296
Oysters Annapolis, '89 195
Oysters, Barbecued, '82 247
Oysters Bienville, Baked, '90 27
Oysters Buccaneer, '87 40
Oysters Chesapeake, '92 254

Oysters, Creamed, '92 254
Oysters in Patty Shells, '85 257
Oysters Italiano, Baked, '89 97
Pasta Bites, Pesto-Cheese, '87 251
Pastry, Processor, '87 67
Peanuts, Sugared, '82 249
Pears, Pineapple-Honey, '86 94
Pecans
Barbecued Pecans, '83 222
Christmas Eve Pecans, '91 276
Coffee 'n' Spice Pecans, '88 256
Curried Pecans, '91 208
Hot-and-Spicy Pecans, '89 161
Hot Pepper Pecans, '85 4
Hot Smoky Pecans, '98 173
Orange-Glazed Pecans, '97 225
Orange Pecans, '87 292
Pear-Pecan Appetizers, '96 262
Pepper Pecans, '87 137; '93 79
Roasted Bacon Pecans, '96 262
Salted Pecans, Southern, '80 285
Savory Southern Pecans, '95 240
Spiced Pecans, '79 296; '80 31
Spicy Pecans, '93 279
Sugar and Spice Pecans, '82 297
Sugar-and-Spice Pecans, '86 121
Sweet-and-Spicy Pecans, '92 321
Toasted Chili Pecans, '85 154
Toasted Pecans, '84 321; '86 229
Toasted Pecans, Buttery, '88 77
Pepper Feet, '93 258
Pepperoni Pie Hors d'Oeuvres, '98 251
Pepperoni Rolls, Ground-, '83 244
Peppers, Marinated Roasted, '92 176
Peppers with Balsamic Vinaigrette,
   Roasted, '94 128
Pesto Rounds, Toasted, '94 289
Pickles, French-Fried, '82 77
Pickles, Fried Dill, '84 206
Pineapple and Strawberries, Skewered, '84 251
Pineapple Delight, Fresh, '79 111
Pineapple Spritz, '86 94
Piroshki, '92 84
Pita Bread Triangles, '88 211
Pita Chips, '89 19; '91 138
Pita Pizza Snack, '94 193
Pita Wedges, Garlic, '93 98
Pizza Bites, '95 244
Pizza-Burger Snacks, '84 30
Pizza, Ham-and-Pineapple, '96 169
Pizza Horns, '89 214
Pizza, Mexican, '99 119
Pizza Party Snacks, '86 262
Pizza Pumpkins, '98 255
Pizzas, Appetizer, '89 M118
Pizzas, Cocktail, '79 110
Pizza Slices, '84 269
Pizza Snacks, Tasty Little, '79 248
Pizzas, Pita, '89 19
Pizza Squares, '87 168
Pizzas, Quick Little, '88 227
Pizza Turnovers, Little, '85 327
Pizzettes, Party, '80 192
Plantain Chips, '95 M203
(Plantain Chips), Tostones de Plátano, '92 158
Pop Graham Munchies, '96 28
Pork Rounds, Sesame, '89 122
Pork Strips, Marinated, '92 219
Potato-Pea Soup, '94 90
Potato Shell Appetizers, '89 M119
Potato Skins, Baked, '86 81
Potato Skin Snack, '91 18
Power Munch, '96 180
Puff Nibbles, '84 191

Puffs, Cajun Hot, '94 277
Quesadilla Torta, '97 325
Quiche, South-of-the-Border, '93 321
Quiche Squares, '84 222
Quiches, Tarragon Cocktail, '84 127
Raisin-Granola Treats, '92 22
Raspberry Party Puffs, '90 170
Ravioli, St. Louis Toasted, '95 117
Ravioli, Sweet, '91 107
Relish Tree, Christmas, '84 257
Reubens, Party, '90 61
Riblets, Sweet-and-Sour, '85 276
Rice Balls, '81 51
Rice with Spring Vegetables, '96 132
Risotto with Greens, '96 132
Risotto with Shellfish and Peas, '96 131
Roasted Red Pepper Rollups, '98 285
Rolls with Thai Dipping Sauce, Summer, '97 236
Rosettes, Savory, '91 107
Rumaki, '80 136
Rumaki, Scallop, '98 M173
Rye Appetizers, Party, '86 262
Salami Rollups, '90 226
Salmon Ball, '80 149; '86 262
Salmon, Drizzled Smoked, '88 91
Salmon Log, '81 22
Salmon Party Log, '98 154
Salmon Party Roll, '83 127
Samosas, '89 266; '96 239
Samurai 'shrooms, '93 258
Sandwiches, Apple Party, '92 234
Sandwiches, Asparagus Spear, '84 165
Sandwiches, Bread Basket of, '86 126
Sandwiches, Calla Lily, '91 106
Sandwiches, Cucumber, '90 81; '94 14; '97 99
Sandwiches, Curried Tea, '91 314
Sandwiches, Dainty Cucumber, '81 119
Sandwiches, Double-Filled Party, '93 159
Sandwiches, Party Ham, '97 240
Sandwiches, Stacking, '86 127
Sandwiches, Tiny Ham-and-Cheese, '99 87
Sandwiches, Turkey Tea, '99 86
Sandwiches, Victoria, '94 16
Sandwiches, Watercress, '90 82
Sandwiches, Watercress-Cucumber, '97 108
Sandwich Wreath, Festive, '86 333
Sausage-Apple Balls, '90 85
Sausage-Bacon Rollups, '88 51
Sausage Balls, '98 93
Sausage-Mushroom-Phyllo Bites, '89 284
Sausage Party Ryes, '89 315
Sausage Pinwheels, '80 209; '93 238
Sausage Quesadillas, '90 118
Sausage, Sweet-and-Sour, '88 296
Sausages with Mustard Sauce, Smoked, '81 56
Scallop Appetizer, '86 155
Scallop Appetizers, Flaky, '86 327
Scallops, Bacon-Wrapped, '87 94
Scallops in Vermouth-Cream Sauce, '96 49
Scallops with Orange-Honey Sauce,
   Bacon-Wrapped, '97 236
Seafood Appetizer, Layered, '88 2
Seafood Mold, Chilled, '86 70
Seafood Tartlets, '87 247
Sea Scallops with Tomato Puree, Seared, '97 201
Sesame Bites, '88 67
Seviche Cocktail, '83 258
Shrimp. *See also* **APPETIZERS/Dips,**
   Canapés, Spreads and Fillings.
Bacon-Shrimp Bites, '98 234; '99 213
Bacon, Shrimp 'n', '98 222
Balls, Curried Shrimp, '94 180
Barbecue Shrimp, '96 210; '97 58
Bayou, Shrimp, '88 261

Boiled Shrimp, Spicy, '84 289
Boiled Shrimp with Cocktail Sauce, '79 151
Braised Shrimp with Garlic Rémoulade,
   '98 133
Cocktail Shrimp, '87 173
Cocktail, Shrimp, '96 174
Coconut-Beer Shrimp, '85 230
Coconut Fried Shrimp, '96 248
Croustades, Shrimp, '97 23
Dilled Shrimp, '88 150
Dippers, Shrimp, '84 324
Double-Dip Shrimp, '99 112
Herbed Jalapeño Cheese, Shrimp with, '87 112
Kabobs, Appetizer Shrimp, '91 251
Kabobs, Shrimp, '80 150
Key West Shrimp, '94 278
Manale, Shrimp, '86 268
Marinated Shrimp and Artichokes, '97 89;
   '98 335
Marinated Shrimp and Cucumber, '91 166
Marinated Shrimp, Icy, '84 215
Marinated Shrimp, Zesty, '87 173
Miniquiches, Shrimp, '87 146
Mold, Shrimp, '87 94
Mold with Asparagus, Shrimp, '93 214
Mushrooms, Shrimp-Stuffed, '80 M135; '99 324
Oven-Fried Shrimp with Marmalade Dip,
   '99 324
Pickled Shrimp, '94 182
Pickle, Shrimp-in-a-, '86 326
Pineapple Appetizer, Shrimp-, '85 80
Pizza Wedges, Shrimp, '89 158
Puffs, Shrimp, '96 211; '98 316
Rémoulade, Shrimp, '83 173
Rock Shrimp Conga, '80 2
Rounds, Shrimp, '98 167
Salsa Picante with Shrimp, '92 210
Sesame Shrimp, '95 92
Sherried Garlic Shrimp, '92 175
Skewers with Vegetable Salsa, Shrimp, '98 32
Smoked Shrimp, Citrus-Marinated, '95 114
Toast, Shrimp, '86 91
Tortilla Bites, '95 42
Tostadas, Shrimp-and-Black Bean, '93 204
Tree, Shrimp, '83 320; '84 288; '85 318
Vegetable Appetizer, Shrimp-and-, '97 161
Snackwiches, '88 172
Snow Peas and Dip, Crunchy, '86 62
Snow Peas, Crab-Stuffed, '85 288
Snow Peas, Stuffed, '84 80
Spanakopita, '96 233
Spinach-and-Cheese Pastries, Greek, '96 76
Spinach-Artichoke-Tomato Puffs, '95 284
Spinach-Filled Phyllo Triangles, '84 52
Spinach Madeleine in Chafing Dish, '85 319
Spinach-Mushroom Cheesecake, '92 326
Spinach Puffs, '95 316
Spinach Quichelets, '87 67
Spinach Quiches, Miniature, '82 38
Spinach-Ricotta Phyllo Triangles, '88 212
Spinach Rollups, '98 251
Spinach Squares, '88 131
Spinach Strudels, '93 249
Spinach Supreme, Layered, '82 38
Spinach Tarts, '82 249
Spinach Triangles, Phyllo-, '87 53
Spreads and Fillings
Aloha Spread, '83 93
Antipasto Spread, '81 25
Apple-Date Spread, '91 231; '92 67

Apricot Brie Spread, '86 275
Apricot-Cream Cheese Spread, '82 161;
   '87 158
Artichoke-Crab Spread, Hot, '85 81
Artichoke Hearts with Caviar, '79 142
Artichoke-Parmesan Spread, '92 95
Artichoke Spread, Chunky, '89 98
Artichoke Spread, Hot, '79 110
Avocado-Cheese Spread, Herbed, '98 335
Beef Spread, Hot, '83 50; '84 M216
Beef Spread in Puff Pastry, Chipped, '98 M335
Beer Cheese, '98 82
Beer Cheese Spread, '81 160; '94 123
Beer-Cheese Spread, '85 69
Black-Eyed Pea Spread, '86 77
Blue Cheese Spread, '90 215; '95 92; '97 240
Boursin Cheese Spread, Buttery, '94 301;
   '96 318
Boursin Cheese Spread, Garlic, '94 301
Braunschweiger-Onion Spread, '79 82
Broccamoli Curry Spread, '88 55
Caraway Spread, '85 276
Carrot-Pecan Spread, '96 108
Carrot Spread, Nutty, '94 123
Catfish Spread, Best-Ever, '98 60
Caviar-Artichoke Mound, '91 244
Caviar-Cream Cheese Spread, '84 256
Caviar Spread, Creamy, '92 58
Cheese-and-Orange Filling, '93 159
Cheese-Horseradish Spread, '84 222
Cheese-Olive Spread, '79 82
Cheese Spread, '86 135
Cheese Spread, Almond, '87 292
Cheese Spread, Confetti, '84 256
Cheese Spread, Creamy Sweet, '79 264
Cheese Spread, Fresh Basil-, '97 108
Cheese Spread, German, '79 82
Cheese Spread, Hawaiian, '87 158
Cheese Spread, Make-Ahead, '93 324
Cheese Spread, Mexican, '90 119
Cheese Spread, Tipsy, '80 150
Cheese Spread, Zippy, '85 4
Cheesy Beer Spread, '87 196
Chicken Salad Party Spread, '88 M8
Chicken Spread, Festive, '87 158
Chicken Spread, Tasty, '84 193
Chili Cheese Spread, '93 242
Chili-Cheese Spread, '99 336
Chive-Mustard Spread, '91 12
Chocolate Chip Cheese Loaves, '91 299
Chutney Spread, Curried, '89 283
Clam Spread, Creamy, '91 274
Coconut-Cranberry Cheese Spread, '92 328
Corn-and-Walnut Spread, '96 26
Corned Beef Spread, '87 196
Crabmeat-Horseradish Spread, '90 292
Crabmeat Spread, '79 81
Crabmeat Spread, Layered, '83 127
Crab Soufflé Spread, '85 4
Crab Spread, '93 167
Crab Spread, Baked, '80 86
Crab Spread, Best-Ever, '98 60
Crab Spread, Superb, '81 235
Cream Cheese Filling, '90 170
Cream Cheese Spread, Deviled, '81 235
Cream Cheese Spread, Fruited, '91 306;
   '93 79
Cream Cheese Spread, Nutty, '89 327
Cream Cheese Spread, Tri-Flavored, '98 134
Cucumber Spread, '79 295; '80 31
Curry Spread, '93 159
Date-Walnut-Cheese Spread, '96 322
Dried Tomato-Cheese Spread, '90 204
Edam-Sherry Spread, '84 257

Egg Mound, Frosted, '79 33
Eggplant-Mushroom Spread, '92 156
Egg, Sour Cream, and Caviar Spread, '85 279
Feta Cheese Spread, '96 265
Fruit and Cheese Spread, '81 245
Fruit-and-Cheese Spread, Nutty, '87 246
Fruit Spread, '85 135
Garbanzo Bean Spread, Herbed, '99 160
Garden Spread, '86 135
Garlic Spread, '85 111
Gouda Cheese Spread, '90 36
Green Onion-Cheese Spread, '92 24
Gruyère-Apple Spread, '81 160
Guacamole Spread, '90 119
Ham and Pimiento Spread, '80 285; '81 56
Ham Spread, Buttery, '95 93; '97 98
Ham Spread, Cold, '82 248
Ham Spread, Country, '87 8
Hearts of Palm Spread, '90 293
Herb-Cheese Spread, '91 124
Herb-Cream Cheese Spread, '83 24
Honey-Nut Spread, '87 157
Horseradish Spread, '90 243
Hummus, '96 158
Italian Spread, '85 135
Jalapeño-Cheese Spread, '82 248
Lentil Spread, '99 288
Liver Spread, '89 161
Liver Spread, Sherried, '80 86
Mullet Spread, '94 159
Mushroom Spread, Hot, '81 190
Olive Spread, Creamy, '81 290
Olive Spread, Tomatoes with, '85 114
Oyster Spread, Smoked, '91 64
Party Bread Spread, '82 161
Party Spread, Spicy, '97 240
Peanut Butter Spread, '92 21
Pear-Cream Cheese Spread, '93 80
Pepper Spread, Roasted, '94 123
Pimiento Cheese, Hot, '87 173
Radish Spread, Fresh, '84 166
Raisin Spread, Creamy, '90 36
Roasted Red Bell Pepper Spread, '97 217
Salmon-and-Horseradish Spread, '87 146
Salmon Spread, '81 149
Salmon Spread, Smoked, '84 324; '98 285
Salmon Spread with Capers, Smoked,
   '98 49
Seafood Spread, '86 M58; '87 146
Seafood Spread, Grandma Reed's, '98 268
Shrimp Spread, '81 306; '85 135; '87 111;
   '93 205
Shrimp Spread, Chunky, '85 300; '86 18
Shrimp Spread, Curried, '87 158
Shrimp Spread, Tempting, '79 57
Shrimp Spread, Zippy, '90 36
Smoked Fish Spread, '92 305
Smoked Whitefish Spread, '92 58
Sombrero Spread, '87 111
Spinach-Bacon Spread, '92 M310
Spinach Spread, '88 132
Spinach Spread, Savory, '82 180
Sweet 'n' Sour Spread, '86 184
Swiss Cheese Spread, '90 60
Tomato-Cheese Spread, '81 157
Tomato-Cheese Spread, Fiery, '87 196
Tomato Spread, '94 123
Tuna Spread, '91 305
Tuna Spread, Chunky, '89 147
Tuna Tapenade, '95 127; '96 201
Turkey Party Spread, '83 282
Turkey Spread, Curried, '92 16
Vegetable Party Spread, '84 166
Vegetable Sandwich Spread, '85 135

Vegetable Spread, '90 144
Vegetable Spread, Garden, '93 184
Watercress Spread, '88 103
White Bean Spread, '95 279
Spring Rolls, '99 238
Squash Nosh, '90 147
Stalks, Splendid, '93 258
Steak-and-Chestnut Appetizers, Marinated,
  '84 323
Strawberries, Spiked, '97 58
Strawberries, Stuffed, '98 155
Strawberries with Chocolate Cream, '85 81
Strawberries with Lemon Cream, '90 170
Strawberries with Walnuts, Stuffed, '85 122
Sugar Peas with Dip, '86 170
Sugar Plums, '92 281
Sugar Snap Pea Appetizers, '86 115
Swamp Sticks, '95 274
Sweet Potato Chips, '91 138; '93 332; '95 M203
Sweet Potato Chips with Blue Cheese, '93 290
Tabbouleh, '88 211
Taco Appetizer, Layered, '84 206
Tamale Balls, Tangy, '89 60
Tamales, Miniature, '85 154
Tapas with Spicy Ranch Dip, Tortellini, '98 318
Tartlets, Country Ham-and-Asparagus, '98 82
Tarts, Party, '95 90
Toasted Appetizers, '94 167
Toast Points, '93 270
Toast Strips, Seasoned, '93 98
Tomato Appetizers, Oven-Baked, '95 172
Tomato Bites, '84 80
Tomatoes, Cucumber-Stuffed Cherry, '88 262
Tomatoes Rockefeller, '97 169
Tomatoes, Stuffed Cherry, '84 160; '88 95, 212;
  '92 25
Tomatoes, Tuna-Stuffed Cherry, '89 214
Tomato Soup, Appetizer, '86 258
Tomato Soup, Savory, '94 91
Tortilla Appetizers, Tex-Mex, '86 297
Tortilla Chips, '91 137
Tortilla Chips, Corn, '91 17
Tortilla Chips, Light, '91 257
Tortilla Dippers, Rolled, '86 4
Tortilla Española, '92 175
Tortilla Snacks, Pesto, '89 19
Tortilla Snack, Two-Cheese, '90 119
Tostadas, Party, '98 M33
Tostados, Hot Chile Salsa with Homemade,
  '88 115
Tuna Mound, '80 276
Tuna Nachos, '95 127; '96 201
Tuna-Pecan Ball, '87 94
Turkey Appetizers, '91 314
Turkey, Country-Fried Wild, '94 306
Turkey Sausage Turnovers, '95 239
Turnovers, Meat, '86 326
Vegetable Appetizer, Tarragon, '83 277
Vegetable Juice Appetizer, Hot, '93 324
Vegetable Nachos, '91 17
Vegetable Party Tray, Fresh, '82 122
Vegetable Platter with Creamy Honey-Herb Dip,
  '98 135
Vegetable Rollups, '98 134
Vegetables Italian, Marinated, '90 242
Vegetables, Marinated, '94 183; '96 213
Vegewiches, '99 86
Veggie Bites, '91 171
Veggies, Fried, '96 19
Venison Tenderloin Appetizers, '88 249
Walnuts, Chinese Fried, '81 254
Watermelon and Prosciutto, '98 164
Wings and Ribs, Thai, '97 M225
Wonton Chips, Baked, '91 138; '99 138

Wonton Chips, Cinnamon-and-Sugar, '91 138
Wonton Chips, Garlic, '91 138
Wonton Chips, Lemon-and-Herb, '91 138
Wonton Nibbles, '85 287
Zucchini Bites, Scalloped, '91 165
Zucchini Caviar, '88 212
Zucchini French Fries, '82 78
Zucchini Fries, '90 147
Zucchini Hors d'Oeuvres, '80 151
Zucchini Pizzas, '88 212
Zucchini-Shrimp Appetizers, '89 311
Zucchini with Cocktail Sauce, French Fried,
  '86 146
APPLES
Acorn Squash, Apple-Stuffed, '83 296; '84 285
Baked. See also APPLES/Desserts.
  à l'Orange, Baked Apples, '90 280
  Apples, Baked, '79 276; '86 40
  Carrot-Apple Bake, '98 232
  Carrot Bake, Apple-, '93 304
  Cheese Bake, Apple-, '92 225
  Easy Baked Apples, '82 22, 238
  Ham and Apples, Baked, '82 M237
  Honey-Baked Apple Quarters, '86 93
  Honey-Baked Apples, '83 234; '84 244
  Honey-Baked Apples and Pear, '97 303
  Imperial Baked Apples, '82 273
  Maple Baked Apples, '85 232
  Mincemeat-Filled Apples, Baked, '80 276
  Orange-Pecan Baked Apples, '85 45
  Orange Sauce, Baked Apples with, '84 314
  Sharpe Baked Apples, '99 83
  Squash and Apple Bake, '79 210
  Stuffed Baked Apples, '89 217
  Sweet Potato-Apple Bake, '83 25; '86 282
Balls, Sausage-Apple, '90 85
Beets and Apples, '80 137; '88 155
Beverages
  Aztec Gold, '99 160
  Berry Sparkler, Apple-, '93 104
  Berry Sparkler, Apple, '94 100
  Cider, Apple, '95 198
  Cider, Apple-Orange, '92 20
  Cider, December, '91 260
  Cider, Holiday, '82 264
  Cider, Hot Apple, '90 21, 225
  Cider, Hot Burgundy, '96 306
  Cider, Hot Mexican, '87 213
  Cider, Hot Molasses, '98 242
  Cider, Hot Mulled, '79 205; '84 323
  Cider, Hot Mulled Apple-Orange, '97 301
  Cider, Hot Spiced, '99 248
  Cider, Hot Spiced Apple, '84 318
  Cider Ice, '83 162
  Cider, Mulled, '91 209; '94 227
  Cider, Mulled Apple, '92 208
  Cider, Mulled Cranberry, '99 278
  Cider Nog, Hot, '98 241
  Cider Nog, Hot Apple, '84 42
  Cider, Red Apple, '80 259
  Cider Sour, Bourbon, '98 242
  Cider, Sparkling Apple, '88 276
  Cider, Spirited Apple, '96 214
  Cider Tea, '98 241; '99 335
  Cooler, Apple, '90 14
  Cooler, Minted Apple, '88 169
  Hot Apple Pie, '99 321
  Juice, Hot Apple, '86 270
  Juice, Perky Cinnamon-Apple, '90 22
  Juice, Sparkling Apple, '95 141
  Julep, Apple, '86 103, 215
  Lemonade, Apple, '89 212
  Limeade, Pink Apple, '89 46
  Mint Juleps, Apple, '97 120

  Punch, Apple Bobbing, '99 246
  Punch, Apple-Tea, '85 82
  Punch, Hot Apple, '84 324
  Punch, Hot Spiced, '80 250
  Shrub, Shenandoah Apple Juice, '79 282
  Tea, Cranberry-Apple, '88 169
  Tea, Hot Apple-Cinnamon, '87 57
  Tea, Iced Apple, '98 84
  Tea, Johnny Appleseed, '85 23
Braised Carrots, Apples, and Celery, '96 107
Breads
  Apple Bread, '79 205; '80 226
  Banana-Apple Bread, '85 250
  Blue Cheese-Apple Sunburst, '94 245
  Butter Bread, Apple, '84 49; '86 69
  Cheddar-Apple Bread, '96 83
  Danish, Deep-Dish Apple, '86 161
  Date-Nut Ring, Apple-, '90 212
  Loaf, Fresh Apple, '82 206
  Loaf, Spiced Apple, '79 215
  Muffins, Apple, '83 96; '84 193; '87 23; '99 234
  Muffins, Apple-Bran, '85 M89
  Muffins, Apple-Carrot, '91 213
  Muffins, Apple-Cinnamon Oat Bran, '89 106
  Muffins, Fresh Apple, '84 264
  Muffins, Pumpkin-Apple, '96 242
  Muffins, Spiced Apple, '79 60
  Muffins, Spicy Apple-Oat, '86 45
  Nut Bread, Apple-, '79 12; '85 281
  Nut Bread, Fresh Apple-, '87 256
  Pinwheel, Quick Apple, '85 42
  Pull-Apart Bread, Apple, '86 330
  Swirl Bread, Apple, '85 4
  Zucchini-Apple Bread, '87 255
Breakfast Delight, '93 195
Burgers, Apple, '86 137
Burgers, Apple-Bacon, '99 202
Butter, Apple, '79 200; '81 217; '92 311
Butter, Half-Hour Apple, '81 203
Butternut Squash, Apple-Stuffed, '81 232
Butter, Slow Cooker Apple, '97 235
Cabbage, Red, '96 272
Cabbage with Apples and Franks, '87 42
Casserole, Apple-Cheese, '84 287
Casserole, Apple-Egg, '85 44
Casserole, Apple Ham, '79 213
Casserole, Cranberry-Apple, '83 311
Casserole, Squash and Apple, '79 209
Casserole, Sweet Potato-and-Apple, '94 280
Casserole, Sweet Potatoes-and-Apple, '90 228
Chard with Onion and Apple, Sautéed, '98 48
Cheese Delight, Apple-and-, '98 97
Chicken, Apple, '85 57
Chicken Breasts, Apple-Bacon Stuffed, '99 313
Chutney, Apple, '92 309
Chutney, Pear-Apple, '89 141
Chutney, Sweet-'n'-Hot Apple, '96 14
Chutney, Sweet Potato, '99 45
Chutney, Tomato-Apple, '84 180
Cider Sauce, '87 224
Cider Sauce, Cheddar-, '98 242
Cinnamon Apples, Rosy, '87 M37
Coffee Cake, Apple, '81 249; '97 326
Coffee Cake, Apple-Pecan, '84 242
Coffee Cake, Fresh Apple, '92 32
Collards with Apples, '98 250
Conserve, Apple-Cranberry, '82 308
Cooked Apples, '93 338
Crêpes, Apple Breakfast, '97 331
Curried Apples, '93 252
Desserts
  Baked Alaska, Apple, '80 226
  Baked Apples with Cookie Crumbs, Orange,
    '95 271

APPLES, Desserts
(continued)

Bars, Apple Butter, **'84** 153
Betty, Apple Brown, **'83** 213
Betty, Pineapple-Apple, **'85** 46
Brandied Apples, **'81** 248
Brandied Apples and Cream, **'82** M237
Brownies, Frosted Apple, **'86** 216
Cake, Apple, **'83** 312; **'84** 262
Cake, Apple Cider Pound, **'84** 10
Cake, Apple Coconut, **'80** 226
Cake, Apple-Ginger Upside-Down, **'94** 180
Cake, Apple-Nut, **'87** 76; **'96** 268
Cake, Apple-Pecan, **'92** 167
Cake, Apple Pie, **'82** 226; **'86** 301
Cake, Apple Slice, **'85** 93
Cake, Apple Spice, **'92** 225
Cake, Apple-Walnut, **'94** 242
Cake, Covered Apple, **'89** 317
Cake, Dried-Apple, **'79** 13
Cake, Dried Apple Stack, **'85** 242
Cake, Fresh Apple-Date, **'83** 300
Cake, Golden Apple-Oatmeal, **'86** 301
Cake, Honey-Apple, **'99** 210
Cake Squares, Apple-Date Dream, **'85** 10
Cake Squares, Apple-Orange, **'84** 150
Candied Red Apples, **'81** 217
Candy Apple Creations, **'94** 256
Candy Apples, **'84** 243
Caramel Apples, **'79** 220; **'89** M231
Caramel Apples, Old English, **'85** 231
Caramel-Peanut Apples, **'93** M244
Charlotte, Apple, **'99** 84
Cheesecake, Dieter's Apple, **'86** 318
Chimichangas, Apple, **'95** 43
Chocolate Apples on a Stick, **'96** 255
Cinnamon Apples with Brandied Date
    Conserve, **'85** 315
Cobbler à la Mode, Apple, **'97** 16
Cobbler, Apple-Pecan, **'84** M198
Cobbler, Apple Walnut, **'79** 154
Cobbler, Apple-Walnut, **'81** 248
Cobbler, Country Apple, **'99** 255
Cobbler, Cranberry-and-Apple, **'84** 306;
    '90 294
Cobbler, Easy Apple, **'83** 174
Cobbler for Two, Apple, **'85** 261
Cobbler, New-Fashioned Apple, **'91** 221
Cobbler with Cinnamon Biscuits,
    Cranberry-Apple, **'99** 256
Compote, Apricot-Apple, **'98** 17
Cookies, Apple Butter Spice, **'79** 291
Cookies, Apple-Filled, **'92** 311
Cookies, Apple-Nut, **'80** 228
Cookies, Apple-Oatmeal, **'85** 215; **'90** 218
Cookies, Fresh Apple, **'84** 36
Cranberry Apple Dessert, **'80** 253
Cranberry Apples, **'99** 246
Crisp, Apple, **'84** 122; **'98** 215
Crisp, Apple-Cheese, **'92** 235
Crisp, Delicious Apple, **'82** 303
Crisp, Granola Apple, **'85** 78
Crisp, Oatmeal Cherry-Apple, **'90** M16
Crisp, Orange-Apple, **'80** 295
Crisp, Tart Apple, **'92** 226
Crumble, Whole Wheat-Apple, **'90** M213
Crunch, Apple-Cranberry, **'86** 300; **'87** 178
Crunch, Apple-Nut, **'82** M238
Cupcakes, Apple-Nut, **'82** 279
Delight, Apple, **'80** 109
Dumplings, Apple, **'82** 273
Dumplings, Cinnamon Apple, **'97** M330

Dumplings, Old-Fashioned Apple, **'84** 226
Dumplings with Maple-Cider Sauce, Apple,
    '95 288
Dumplings with Orange Hard Sauce, Apple,
    '88 224
Dutch Apple Dessert, Creamy, **'91** 19
Enchiladas, Apple, **'99** 63
Filling, Apple-Date, **'83** 301
Filling, Dried Apple, **'85** 242; **'87** 229
Flambé, Hot Apples and Rum, **'92** 88
Flan, Apple, **'81** 309
Foldovers, Apple, **'84** 136
Fritter Rings, Apple, **'88** 44
Fritters, Apple, **'81** 105; **'82** 273; **'85** 14;
    '97 153
Fritters, Apple Holiday, **'86** 314
Goblins, Apple, **'94** 256
Honey-Baked Apple Dessert, **'90** M213
Ice, Cranberry-Apple, **'82** 290
Kuchen, Apple, **'79** 24
Melting Apples, **'88** 19
Mousse, Cran-Apple, **'93** 255
Napoleon, Giant Apple, **'99** 282
Pears, Saucy Apples 'n', **'96** 72
Pecan Apples, Taffy, **'99** 247
Pie, American Apple, **'91** 197
Pie, Apple-Amandine, **'89** 215
Pie, Apple-Bourbon, **'95** 302
Pie, Apple-Cheese, **'85** 284
Pie, Apple Cider, **'84** 227
Pie, Apple-Cranberry, **'97** 276; **'99** M269
Pie, Apple-Cream Cheese, **'81** 247
Pie, Apple Custard, **'88** 236
Pie, Apple-Lemon Chess, **'86** 220
Pie, Apple-Maple, **'97** 276
Pie, Apple-Mincemeat, **'85** 316
Pie, Apple-Pear, **'83** 249
Pie, Apple-Pear Pull-Up, **'98** 259
Pie, Apple-Pineapple, **'97** 276
Pie, Apple-Raisin Brandy, **'89** 58
Pie, Applesauce, **'98** 259; **'99** 26
Pie, Autumn Apple, **'79** 205
Pie, Berry-Apple, **'88** 251
Pie, Blackberry-Apple, **'87** 130
Pie, Brandy-Apple, **'86** 301
Pie, Brandy Raisin-Apple, **'83** 192
Pie, Bumbleberry, **'97** 163
Pie, Caramel-Pecan Apple, **'85** 247
Pie, Cornbread-Sausage-Apple, **'87** 171
Pie, Cran-Apple, **'92** 304
Pie, Cranberry-Apple, **'79** 264
Pie, Cranberry-Apple Holiday, **'81** M269
Pie, Cranberry-Apple-Raisin, **'98** 270
Pie, Dutch Apple, **'81** 105; **'82** 273
Pie, Easy-Crust Apple, **'87** 11
Pie Filling in a Jar, Apple, **'95** 251
Pie, Fresh Apple, **'84** 178
Pie, Grandmother's Apple, **'87** 212
Pie, Grated Apple, **'83** 304
Pie, Holiday Apple, **'87** 260
Pie, Mexican Apple, **'94** 97
Pie, Natural Pear-Apple, **'88** 226
Pie, No-Crust Apple, **'88** 204
Pie, Old-Fashioned Apple, **'82** M299; **'88** 94
Pie, Praline-Apple, **'99** 331
Pie, Red Apple, **'79** 282
Pies, Delicious Fried, **'83** 84
Pies, Fried Apple, **'81** 217; **'86** 302; **'88** 112,
    225; **'94** 61
Pie, Tart Lemon-Apple, **'80** 100
Pie, Upside-Down Southern Apple, **'88** 226
Pie, Warm Apple-Buttermilk Custard, **'99** 98
Pie with Hot Cinnamon Sauce,
    Apple, **'88** 210

Pie with Warm Cinnamon Crème, Apple,
    '99 337
Poached Apples, Spicy, **'90** M141
Pudding, Apple-Raisin Bread, **'88** 175
Pudding, Apple Rice, **'91** 217
Pudding with Hot Rum Sauce, Apple-Nut,
    '79 86
Quesadillas, Apple, **'99** 248
Rings, Apple, **'85** 232
Roll, Apple, **'82** 178
Rolls, Luscious Apple, **'88** 225
Rugelach, Apple, **'97** 220
Sauce, Apple Ambrosia, **'89** 95
Sauce, Apple-Cinnamon, **'93** 42
Sauce, Apple Dessert, **'87** M165
Sauce, Spicy Apple Dessert, **'82** 177
Shortcake, Quick Apple, **'93** 42
Sorbet, Cran-Apple Spice, **'93** 153
Squares, Apple, **'92** 311
Squares, Sour Cream Apple, **'82** 262
Strudel, Apple, **'85** 259; **'89** 267; **'92** 269;
    '97 238
Strudel, Autumn-Apple, **'98** 253
Stuffed Apples, **'99** 247
Sugar-Crusted Apples in Walnut-Phyllo
    Baskets, **'93** 210
Sundae, Hot Apple Spice, **'92** 239
Sundaes, Spicy Apple Ice Cream, **'86** M195
Tart, Apple Cream, **'84** 207
Tart, Apple-Cream Cheese, **'96** 228
Tart, Apricot-Apple Crumb, **'94** 60
Tart, Cranberry-Apple, **'97** M316
Tart, Creamed Apple, **'94** 17
Tart, Deluxe Apple, **'84** 227
Tarte aux Pommes, La, **'80** 125
Tarts, Apple-Pecan, **'80** 282
Tarts, Brandied Apple, **'96** 284; **'99** 28
Tart, Upside-Down Apple, **'98** 35
Tart with Cheese Pastry, Apple, **'88** 225
Topping, Apple-Nut, **'93** 162
Topping, Spicy Apple, **'87** 125
Turnovers, Baked Apple, **'93** 338
Turnovers, Delicious Apple, **'86** 25
Turnovers, Fried Apple, **'81** 161
Turnovers, Orange-Apple, **'99** 294
Turnovers, Puffy Apple, **'87** 276
Waffles with Apples and Caramel,
    Gingerbread, **'98** M237
Dip, Apple, **'93** 205; **'96** M190
Dressing, Apple, **'92** 216
Dressing, Sausage-Apple, **'93** 305; **'94** 296
Dried Apple Side Dish, **'92** 226
Dried Lady Apple Slices, **'95** 263
Fillets, Apple-Carrot Stuffed, **'88** M192
Filling, Apple, **'85** 5; **'96** 53; **'97** 239
French Toast, Apple, **'98** 55
Glazed Apples, **'99** 233
Glazed Apples, Honey-, **'90** 125
Glazed Apples, Orange-, **'82** 51
Golden Apples, **'82** 254
Grilled Ham and Apples, **'96** M303
Honey-Yogurt Apples, **'92** 46
Jelly, Apple, **'82** 149
Jelly, Apple-Mint, **'87** 134
Jelly, Crabapple, **'79** 120; **'81** 217
Jelly, Spiced Apple, **'95** 251
Juice, Nectarines in Apple, **'83** 183
Marmalade, Apple, **'79** 120
Minted Apples, **'99** 231
Monster Mouths, **'95** 274
Muesli, **'89** 208
Omelet Stack, Apple, **'94** 50
Pancake, Apple-Filled, **'86** 96
Pancakes, Apple-Topped, **'93** 339

Pancakes with Cider Sauce, Spicy
    Apple, '87 224
Piggy Apple, '94 194
Poached Lemon Apples, Chilled, '86 182
Pork and Vegetables, Apple Cider, '97 210
Pork Chops and Apples, Baked, '81 10
Pork Chops, Apple, '91 198
Pork Chops, Apple-Crumb Stuffed, '81 234;
    '82 26
Pork Chops, Apple-Glazed, '84 212; '87 35
Pork Chops, Apple-Kraut, '84 50
Pork Chops, Apple-Stuffed, '79 125
Pork Chops, Glazed Apple, '86 300
Pork Chops, Rosemary, '98 329
Pork Chops, Sherry-Apple, '88 40
Pork Chops, Spicy Apple, '87 230
Pork Chops with Apples, Parmesan, '93 338
Pork Chops with Crabapple Peaches, Broiled,
    '81 83
Pork Cutlets, Apple-Glazed, '92 181
Pork Loin with Apples and Mushrooms, Roast,
    '92 218
Pork Tenderloin, Apple-Ginger, '86 75
Pork Tenderloin, Apple-Mushroom, '95 53
Pork Tenderloin with Apples, Celery, and
    Potatoes, Grilled, '95 161
Pot Roast, Spicy Apple, '83 7
Quail, Sage-Smoked Champagne, '97 164
Quiche, Crustless Sausage-Apple, '87 70
Red Cabbage and Apples, '85 32
Red Cabbage, German-Style, '98 279
Relish, Apple, '96 323; '97 27
Relish, Apple-Celery, '89 141
Relish, Cran-Apple, '84 300
Relish, Cranberry, '98 310
Relish, Spicy Apple, '84 M323
Ribs, Apple Barbecued, '80 111
Rice, Apple-Cinnamon, '86 249
Rings, Cinnamon Apple, '82 M237; '90 250
Rings, Cinnamon-Apple, '85 107
Rings, Fried Apple, '81 209
Rings, Honey Apple, '80 243
Rolls, Apple-Phyllo, '88 213
Salads
    Apple Salad, '87 233
    Apricot Salad, Apple-, '88 121
    Aspic, Sunshine Apple, '81 73
    Beet, Apple, and Walnut Salad, '98 269
    Beet Salad, Apple-, '91 237
    Blue Cheese Dressing, Apple Salad with,
        '87 103
    Blue Cheese-Pear-Apple Salad, '81 224
    Carrot Salad, Apple-, '85 22
    Cheesy Apple Salad, '86 301
    Cherry-Apple Salad, '86 31
    Chicken-Apple Salad, '90 216
    Cider Salad, Apple, '83 123
    Coleslaw, Apple, '89 315
    Congealed Apple Salad, '85 252
    Crunch Salad, Apple, '84 232; '86 331
    Crunchy Apple Salad, '80 138
    Curried Apple-Raisin Salad, '80 24
    Double Apple Salad, '84 227
    English Pea-and-Apple Salad, '87 24
    Fresh Apple Salad, '81 207
    Frozen Apple-Cream Salad, '82 80
    Grapefruit-Apple Salad, '89 41
    Greens with Apple and Brie Salad, '93 241
    Ham-and-Apple Salad, '88 139
    Lemony Apple-Bran Salad, '86 223
    Mold, Apple Cider Salad, '85 54
    Mold, Cranberry-Apple, '89 277
    Nut Salad, Apple-, '80 226
    Peanut-Apple Salad, '80 5

Poppyseed Dressing, Apple Wedges with,
    '86 131
Sesame-Apple Toss, '88 21
Slaw, Apple-Carrot, '92 243
Slaw, Apple-Pineapple, '79 241
Slaw, Fresh Apple, '81 63
Slaw, Nutty Apple, '88 216
Slaw, Red Cabbage-and-Apple, '87 31; '91 309
Snow Salad, Apple, '81 224
Spicy Apple Salad, '85 215
Spinach-Apple Salad, '90 89; '92 13; '97 308
Spinach Salad, Apple-, '97 14; '99 222
Stuffed Apple Ring Salad, '91 198
Stuffed Apple Salad, '92 266
Summer Apple Salad, '80 149
Sweet Potato-Apple Salad, '96 240
Swiss-Apple Salad, '84 81
Thai Green Apple Salad, '99 111
Triple Apple Salad, '88 122
Turkey-Apple Salad, '88 123; '90 181
Waldorf, Pineapple, '97 96
Waldorf Salad, '89 278; '97 204
Waldorf Salad, Congealed, '82 80
Waldorf Salad, Creamy, '87 311
Waldorf Salad, Deluxe, '83 81
Waldorf Salad, Frozen, '79 126; '82 145
Waldorf Salad, Jiffy, '88 100
Waldorf Salad, New Wave, '92 36
Waldorf Salad, Old-Fashioned, '81 295
Waldorf Salad, Pineapple, '92 97
Waldorf Salad, Southern Classic, '92 36
Waldorf Salad, Tropical, '89 12
Wild Rice-Green Apple Salad, '92 90
Zucchini Salad, Apple-and-, '97 216
Sandwiches, Apple, '79 164; '80 130
Sandwiches, Apple Breakfast, '92 332
Sandwiches, Apple-Cinnamon Breakfast,
    '85 298
Sandwiches, Apple Party, '92 234
Sandwiches, Sweet Smoky, '97 219
Sauce, Apple Barbecue, '99 173
Sauce, Apple-Bourbon, '99 142
Sauce, Apple-Horseradish, '82 229
Sauce, Apple-Pear, '97 M272
Sauce, Cranberry-Apple, '92 203
Sausage Patties, Apples on, '82 120
Sauté, Chicken-Apple, '97 48
Sautéed Apples, Onions, and Pears over
    Spinach, '94 212
Scalloped Apples, '84 70; '87 156
Scallop, Yam-and-Apple, '91 199
Shells, Sweet Potatoes in Apple, '85 206
Soup, Creamed Butternut-and-Apple, '88 228
Spareribs, Apple-Barbecue, '90 160
Spiced Apples, '93 123
Spiced Apple Slices, '83 289
Spiced Apples, Skillet, '83 234; '84 244
Spread, Apple-Date, '91 231; '92 67
Spread, Feta-and-Apple, '99 106
Spread, Gruyère-Apple, '81 160
Squash, Apple-and-Pecan-Filled, '88 228
Squash, Apple-Stuffed, '85 206
Stir-Fry, Apple-Sesame-Chicken, '92 226
Stuffed Apples, Peanutty, '85 25
Stuffed Apples, Sweet Potato-, '97 216
Stuffing, Apple-Crumb, '81 234; '82 26; '83 39
Stuffing, Apple-Walnut, '95 289
Stuffing, Pork Chops with Cornbread-Apple,
    '99 14
Sweet Potatoes and Apples, '97 249
Sweet Potatoes, Apple-Glazed, '82 303
Sweet Potatoes, Apple-Stuffed, '88 207
Sweet Potatoes, Cinnamon-Apple, '95 M23
Sweet Potatoes Stuffed with Apples, '82 228

Syrup, Spiced Apple, '79 114
Tenderloin with Praline-Mustard Glaze,
    Apple-Stuffed, '97 216
Toast, Apple, '81 278
Topping, Apple, '89 107
Turkey, Apple-Rosemary Roasted, '99 252
Turkey Breast, Apple-Rosemary, '99 253
Veal Chops, Apple, '87 220
Vinaigrette, Apple Cider, '98 284
Vinaigrette, Spinach Salad with Apple-Onion,
    '94 276
APPLESAUCE
Applesauce, '90 255; '97 252
Bread, Applesauce-Honey Nut, '87 300
Bread, Applesauce Nut, '81 305
Bread, Applesauce-Pecan, '90 66
Bread, Bran-Applesauce, '84 229
Butter, Half-Hour Apple, '81 203
Cake, Applesauce, '80 270; '96 67
Cake, Applesauce Carrot, '81 202
Cake, Applesauce-Oatmeal, '92 119
Cake, Applesauce-Spice, '83 42
Cake, Applesauce Spice, '89 296
Cake, My Favorite Applesauce, '87 263
Cakes, Applesauce Snack, '88 215; '89 20
Cake Squares, Applesauce, '86 8
Cake with Bourbon Frosting, Applesauce,
    '88 236
Doughnuts, Applesauce, '81 203
Doughnuts, Applesauce Drop, '90 70
Dressing, Apple, '83 181
Fluff, Applesauce, '91 173
Fruitcake, Applesauce, '83 258
Gingerbread, Applesauce, '94 179
Loaf, Brandy Applesauce, '81 263
Muffins, Applesauce, '84 284; '91 141
Muffins, Applesauce Spice, '88 236
Muffins, Bite-Size Applesauce, '82 104
Oatmeal, Applesauce, '89 108
Pancakes, Applesauce, '79 114
Pie, Applesauce, '98 259; '99 26
Pudding, Applesauce-Graham Cracker, '81 34
Ribs, Apple Barbecued, '80 111
Salad Dressing, Honey-Applesauce, '99 210
Spicy Applesauce, '82 296
Squares, Applesauce-Spice, '86 248
Sweet Potatoes, Applesauce, '91 292; '92 256
APRICOTS
Bake, Sweet Potato-Apricot, '85 206
Beverages
    Bellinis, Apricot, '99 145
    Cooler, Apricot, '81 100
    Cooler, Apricot Mint, '90 165
    Cooler, Apricot-Orange-Carrot, '96 108
    Coolers, Apricot, '99 29
    Fruit Flip, Apricot, '91 18
    Nectar, Hot Apricot, '81 265
    Nectar, Mulled Apricot, '86 229
    Punch, Apricot Spiced, '80 269
    Shake, Apricot, '84 115
    Slush, Apricot, '93 205
    Slush, Apricot Brandy, '91 278
    Slush, Apricot-Citrus, '88 82
    Tea, Hot Spiced Apricot, '88 248
    Wassail, Pineapple-Apricot, '83 275
Bread, Apricot-Nut, '79 24
Bread, Apricot-Orange, '92 285
Bread, Apricot-Pecan, '97 266
Bread, Pineapple-Apricot, '84 7
Bread, Tangy Apricot, '81 249
Butter, Apricot, '82 308; '99 212
Carrots, Apricot, '84 6
Carrots, Apricot Glazed, '80 89
Carrots, Apricot-Glazed, '98 231

APRICOTS

(continued)

Coffee Cake, Apricot-Almond, **'93** 26
Coffee Cake, Apricot Lattice, **'94** 48
Crescents, Apricot-Cheese, **'99** 284
Croissants, Strawberry or Apricot, **'96** 303
Curried Apricots, **'91** 315
Dates, Apricot-Stuffed, **'80** 250
Delight, Apricot, **'81** 42
Desserts
  Almond Squares, Apricot-, **'95** 272
  Baked Apricots, Delicious, **'82** 10
  Balls, Apricot, **'79** 274
  Balls, Crunchy Apricot, **'89** 307
  Bars, Apricot, **'81** 247
  Bars, Apricot-Oatmeal, **'86** 216
  Bars, Apricot-Raisin, **'87** 32
  Cake, Apricot-Almond Upside-Down, **'97** 204
  Cake, Apricot Brandy Pound, **'83** 267
  Cobbler, Peach-Apricot, **'99** 255
  Cobbler with Custard Sauce, Apricot, **'97** 16
  Cobble Up, Apricot, **'82** 138
  Compote, Apricot-Apple, **'98** 17
  Cookie Rolls, Apricot, **'80** 282
  Cookies, Apricot, **'95** 322
  Cookies, Frosted Apricot, **'81** 192
  Cream, Peachy-Apricot, **'86** 163
  Crescents, Apricot, **'90** 181
  Divinity, Apricot, **'83** 297
  Filling, Apricot, **'83** 84; **'86** 107; **'93** 316
  Filling, Lemon-Apricot, **'90** 105
  Flan, Apricot, **'99** 146
  Freeze, Apricot, **'82** 10
  Frosting, Apricot, **'81** 192
  Frozen Apricot Fluff, **'86** 242
  Glaze, Apricot, **'82** 8; **'97** 60; **'98** 260
  Glaze, Apricot-Kirsch, **'87** 14
  Glaze, Sweet Apricot, **'82** 304
  Ice, Apricot Yogurt, **'81** 177
  Ice Cream, Apricot, **'99** 146
  Kolaches, Apricot, **'83** 84; **'94** 291
  Mousse, Apricot, **'82** 72; **'91** 297
  Noodle Kugel, Apricot, **'92** 251
  Pastries, Apricot, **'83** 297
  Pie, Apricot Surprise, **'88** 99
  Pie, Dried Fruit, **'83** 249
  Pies, Apricot Fried, **'86** 269
  Pies, Dried Apricot Hand, **'98** 259
  Pies, Fried Apricot, **'95** 215
  Pies, Special Apricot, **'94** 60
  Pie, Yogurt-Apricot, **'85** 132
  Pinwheels, Apricot, **'87** 276
  Pudding, Apricot Bread, **'85** 24
  Sauce, Apricot, **'82** 212
  Sauce, Apricot Ice Cream, **'91** 57
  Sauce, Apricot-Walnut Hard, **'88** 153
  Sherbet, Apricot, **'81** 177; **'92** 164
  Shortbread, Apricot-Almond, **'99** 29
  Sorbet, Apricot-Almond, **'98** 126
  Soufflé, Baked Apricot, **'88** 267
  Tart, Apricot-Almond, **'97** 99
  Tart, Apricot-Apple Crumb, **'94** 60
  Tart, Apricot-Nut, **'99** 249
  Tarts, Apricot, **'79** 282; **'88** 281
  Tarts, Apricot-Pecan-Brie, **'97** 236
  Tea Cakes, Brandied Apricot, **'91** 241
  Torte, Apricot-Filled Chocolate, **'90** 107
  Torte, Apricot Sponge, **'90** 59
  Torte, Lucy's Apricot Praline, **'95** 243
  Tortoni, Apricot-Yogurt, **'95** 124
  Turnovers, Fried Apricot, **'86** 24
  Wonders, Apricot, **'93** 316

Dip, Apricot, **'86** 178
Dressing, Apricot, **'99** 245
Dressing, Honeydew Salad with Apricot Cream, **'84** 191
Dried Apricot Spiders, **'96** 255
French Toast, Stuffed, **'96** 52
Glaze, Apricot, **'80** 280; **'82** 8; **'86** 197
Glaze for Ham, Apricot, **'85** 256
Glaze, Sweet Potatoes with Apricot, **'89** 331
Granola, **'99** 212
Granola, Superhero, **'98** 206
Jam, Golden Apricot, **'80** 31
Jam, Quick-Cooked Apricot, **'99** 146
Loaf, Apricot-Cranberry, **'79** 235
Loaf, Apricot-Nut, **'81** 8
Loaf, Tasty Apricot-Nut, **'82** 10
Main Dishes
  Chicken, Apricot, **'92** 12
  Chicken Breasts, Apricot, **'88** 301
  Chicken with Apricot Salsa, **'98** 126
  Chicken with Tangy Apricot Glaze, **'98** 275
  Cornish Hens, Apricot-Glazed, **'80** 84; **'87** 306
  Cornish Hens, Apricot-Stuffed, **'84** 6
  Ham and Apricots, **'90** 53
  Ham, Apricot Baked, **'84** 160
  Ham Slice, Apricot-Glazed, **'93** 252
  Lamb Kabobs, Apricot-Grilled, **'98** 102
  Pork Chops, Apricot-Mushroom Stuffed, **'95** 287
  Pork Chops, Apricot-Sauced, **'85** 22
  Pork Chops, Apricot-Stuffed, **'86** 76; **'92** 219
  Pork Chops, Curried Apricot, **'89** 191
  Pork Chops, Mustard-Apricot, **'89** 225
  Pork Chops with Apricot Glaze, Stuffed, **'89** M36
  Pork Loin, Apricot-Pecan Stuffed, **'94** 274
  Sausage-Apricot Breakfast Dish, **'82** 10
Mayonnaise, Apricot, **'97** 320
Rice Pilaf, Apricot, **'99** 146
Rolls, Cheese-Apricot Sweet, **'90** 195
Salad, Apple-Apricot, **'88** 121
Salad, Apricot, **'81** 251; **'83** 123
Salad, Apricot-Chicken, **'99** 163
Salad, Apricot Fruit, **'82** 132
Salad, Apricot Nectar, **'83** 218; **'87** 236
Salad, Creamy Apricot, **'85** 263
Salad, Frosted Apricot, **'80** 248
Salad, Spinach-Apricot, **'94** 63
Salad with Cider Vinaigrette, Harvest, **'99** 322
Salsa, Apricot, **'98** 126
Sauce, Apricot, **'82** 212; **'87** 172
Sauce, Fresh Cranberry-Apricot, **'87** 243
Sauce, Pork Tenderloin with Apricot, **'99** 44
Spread, Apricot Brie, **'86** 275
Spread, Apricot-Cream Cheese, **'82** 161; **'87** 158
Sweet Potatoes, Apricot, **'82** 228
Sweet Potatoes, Apricot-Glazed, **'81** 295
Syrup, Apricot Fruit, **'82** 10
Topping, Apricot Flambé, **'98** 127

ARTICHOKES

Appetizers
  Baked Artichoke-Cheese Bottoms, **'94** 61
  Caviar, Artichoke Hearts with, **'79** 142
  Crostini, Hot Artichoke, **'94** 319
  Crostini, Parmesan-Artichoke, **'98** 285
  Dip, Artichoke-Chile, **'98** 234
  Dip, Baked Artichoke, **'95** 239
  Dip, Deluxe Artichoke, **'80** 87
  Dip, Florentine Artichoke, **'96** 274
  Dip, Greek Artichoke, **'97** 315
  Dip, Hot Artichoke-Seafood, **'80** 241
  Dip, Hot Artichoke Seafood, **'85** M212
  Dip in a Bread Basket, Artichoke, **'93** 13
  Dip, Italian Artichoke, **'97** 315

  Dip, Mexican Artichoke, **'90** 292
  Dip, Seasoned Mayonnaise Artichoke, **'80** 87
  Frittata, Artichoke Appetizer, **'92** 58
  Marinated Artichoke Hearts, **'88** 95
  Marinated Artichokes, **'87** 250
  Marinated Shrimp and Artichokes, **'97** 89; **'98** 335
  Mold, Artichoke-Caviar, **'87** 239
  Mound, Caviar-Artichoke, **'91** 244
  Oysters, Artichoke, **'96** 154
  Phyllo Bites, Artichoke-Parmesan, **'87** 54
  Puffs, Spinach-Artichoke-Tomato, **'95** 284
  Shrimp Appetizer, Artichoke-and-, **'93** 271
  Spread, Antipasto, **'81** 25
  Spread, Artichoke-Parmesan, **'92** 95
  Spread, Chunky Artichoke, **'89** 98
  Spread, Hot Artichoke, **'79** 110
  Spread, Hot Artichoke-Crab, **'85** 81
  Zesty Artichoke Appetizer, **'80** 146
Artichokes, **'92** 107
au Gratin, Crab, Shrimp, and Artichoke, **'90** 240
Bake, Spinach-Artichoke, **'95** 48
Bake, Tomato-and-Artichoke Heart, **'85** 81
Beef with Tomatoes and Artichokes, **'92** 282
Bread, Artichoke, **'93** 140
Casserole, Alii Artichoke, **'93** 294
Casserole, Asparagus-Artichoke, **'86** 279
Casserole, Brussels Sprouts-and-Artichoke, **'94** 279
Casserole, Chicken-and-Artichoke, **'96** 133
Casserole, Italian Green Bean-and-Artichoke, **'85** 81
Casserole, Mushroom-Artichoke, **'87** 241
Casserole, Spinach and Artichoke, **'81** 103
Casserole, Spinach-Artichoke, **'88** 252; **'93** 44
Chicken and Artichoke Hearts, Baked, **'82** 260
Chicken and Artichokes, Italian, **'95** 68
Chicken, Artichoke, **'81** 97
Chicken, Dijon, **'99** 21
Chicken, Sanibel Island, **'97** 66
Chicken with Artichoke Hearts, **'88** 54
Chicken with Artichokes and Mushrooms, **'90** 35
Chicken with Artichokes, Sherried, **'87** 143
Chilled Artichokes with Lemon-Pepper Dressing, **'87** 55
Crabmeat with Artichoke Hearts, Creamed, **'93** 26
Dressing, Artichoke, **'84** 126
Dried Beef with Artichokes, Creamed, **'85** 81
Eggs Sardou, **'92** 93
Flan, Artichoke, **'96** 22
Flatbread, Sicilian Artichoke, **'98** 136
Herb-Mayonnaise Dip, Artichokes with, **'84** 67
Lemon, Artichoke Hearts with, **'90** 98
Linguine, Artichoke and Shrimp, **'95** 210
Marinated Artichoke Hearts, **'95** 66
Marinated Artichokes, **'87** 250; **'88** 41
Marinated Cucumbers and Artichokes, **'82** 111
Pasta with Artichoke Hearts, **'86** 209
Pasta with Catfish and Artichokes, **'90** 123
Pasta with Rosemary, Chicken-Artichoke, **'98** 15
Pie, Artichoke, **'79** 25
Pizza, Grilled, **'97** 190
Pizza with Artichoke and Prosciutto, **'87** 182
Quiche, Artichoke, **'91** 71
Quick 'n' Easy Whole Cooked Artichokes, **'96** M132
Ragoût, Veal-and-Artichoke, **'94** 43
Relish, Jerusalem Artichoke, **'89** 197
Salads
  Artichoke Salad, **'86** 333
  Asparagus-Artichoke Salad, **'85** 162
  Aspic, Tomato-Artichoke, **'84** 320; **'86** 92

Avocado Acapulco, '83 2
Chicken-Rice Salad, Artichoke-, '94 132
Chicken-Rice Salad, Mediterranean
  Artichoke-, '97 321
Chicken Salad with Artichokes, '86 186
Goat Cheese Salad, Artichoke-, '98 118
Italian Salad, '87 145
Marinated Artichoke Salad, '83 241; '95 66
Marinated Cucumbers and Artichokes,
  '82 111
Orzo Salad, Artichokes with, '88 M193
Pasta Salad, Artichoke-, '94 180
Rice Salad, Artichoke-, '80 178; '81 41; '85 81
Rice Salad with Artichoke Hearts, '80 232
Stuffed Tomato Salad, Artichoke-, '82 101
Tomato Salad, Artichoke-, '82 239
Zucchini-Artichoke Salad, '91 229
Salsa, Artichoke-Tomato, '96 182
Sandwich, Beef-and-Artichoke Open-Faced
  Italian, '98 22
Sandwich, Italian Stuffed, '99 15
Sauté, Herbed Artichoke, '96 133
Shrimp Platter with Béarnaise Sauce, Artichoke
  and, '96 132
Soup, Artichoke, '89 269
Soup, Artichoke Cream, '94 62
Soup, Chicken, Artichoke, and Mushroom,
  '92 324
Soup, Cream of Artichoke, '82 232
Soup, Louisiana Oyster-and-Artichoke, '92 81
Soup, Oyster-and-Artichoke, '97 21
Spring Artichokes, '86 62
Steamed Artichokes, '81 59
Strata, Artichoke-Cheese, '90 236
Stuffed Artichokes, '79 76; '82 92; '91 117;
  '99 64
Stuffed Artichokes, Ham-Mushroom-, '95 228
Stuffed Artichokes, Shrimp-, '84 67; '87 55
Stuffed Artichokes, Shrimp, '94 62
Stuffed with Shrimp and Scallops, Artichokes,
  '84 174
Tomatoes with Curry Sauce, Stuffed, '97 170
Veal with Artichoke Hearts, Lemon, '87 219
Vinaigrette, Artichokes, '88 101
Whole Cooked Artichokes, '94 61
ASPARAGUS
Almond Asparagus, '83 86
Almond Butter, Asparagus with, '84 85
Almond Sauce, Asparagus with, '91 117
Basil Butter, Asparagus with, '85 40
Basil Sauce, Asparagus with, '86 33
Bean Sprouts, Asparagus and, '96 95
Beef with Asparagus, '90 100
Caesar, Asparagus, '88 133
Carrots and Asparagus, Sunshine, '99 277
Cashew Butter, Asparagus with, '87 56
Casseroles
  Artichoke Casserole, Asparagus-, '86 279
  Asparagus Casserole, '98 310
  Cheesy Asparagus Casserole, '82 281;
    '83 32
  Chicken-Asparagus Casserole, '83 76; '84 71
  Creamy Asparagus Casserole, '80 76
  Easy Asparagus Casserole, '83 255
  English Pea Casserole, Asparagus-and-,
    '86 324
  Pea Casserole, Asparagus-, '88 M294
  Peas Casserole, Asparagus and, '80 152
  Spaghetti Casserole, Asparagus-, '80 77
  Turkey-Asparagus Casserole, '86 284
Cheesecake, Ham-and-Asparagus, '90 174
Chicken, Asparagus, and Mushrooms with
  Penne Pasta, '98 212
Chicken, Szechuan, '98 155

Chilled Asparagus with Garlic Dipping Sauce,
  '98 136
Company Asparagus, '85 82
Creamed Asparagus on Toast, '95 61
Cream Sauce, Asparagus with, '90 291
Croquettes, Asparagus, '85 265
Curry Sauce, Asparagus with, '90 17
Cutlets, Asparagus, '80 147
Delight, Asparagus, '82 269
Delight, Ham-Asparagus, '86 48
Dill Sauce, Asparagus with, '97 59
Dilly Asparagus, '88 180
Dressing, Asparagus with Warm Citrus, '96 M86
Eggs à la Asparagus, Creamed, '81 201
en Papillote, Shrimp with Asparagus, '86 145
Fettuccine, Ham-and-Asparagus, '94 84
Fish-Asparagus Divan, '87 128
French-Fried Asparagus, '79 66; '83 46
Frittata, Bacon-and-Asparagus, '98 136
Garlic Cream, Asparagus with, '95 83
Goat Cheese Sauce, Asparagus with, '93 116
Goldenrod, Asparagus, '79 66
Guacamole, Mock, '93 36
Ham-Asparagus Dinner, '80 M10
Ham Rolls, Asparagus, '91 117
Holiday Asparagus, '85 260
Jeweled Asparagus, '80 42
Lemon, Asparagus with, '98 103
Lemon Butter, Asparagus in, '80 M123
Lemon Butter, Asparagus with, '87 M151;
  '98 168
Lemon Sauce, Asparagus with, '86 62
Lemon-Sesame Asparagus, '91 31
Loaf, Asparagus-Pimiento, '84 86
Marinated Asparagus, '81 108; '83 46; '84 67, 86;
  '86 92; '87 74
Marinated Asparagus, Easy, '81 148
Marinated Asparagus Spears, '88 130
Marinated Asparagus with Prosciutto, '95 83
Mayonnaise, Asparagus with Hot Wine, '81 83
Meringue, Asparagus, '88 131
Mornay, Asparagus, '99 102
Mushrooms, Asparagus and, '85 108
Orange Butter Sauce, Asparagus with, '85 43
Orange Sauce, Asparagus with, '83 46
Pasta with Asparagus, Tomatoes, and Shrimp,
  Garlicky, '95 82
Pasta with Shrimp and Asparagus, Angel Hair,
  '92 100
Pickled Asparagus, '83 46
Pilaf, Turkey-Asparagus, '88 200
Pimientos, Asparagus with, '98 286
Pork Arlo, '87 229
Prosciutto-Wrapped Asparagus, '91 98
Quiche, Asparagus-Tomato, '88 198
Quiche, Springtime, '83 122
Rarebit, Uptown Welsh, '87 279
Rice and Asparagus, '93 324
Roasted Asparagus with Red Pepper Sauce,
  '98 322
Rolls, Asparagus, '79 296; '80 31
Rolls, Chicken-Asparagus, '86 M211
Rolls, Ham-Asparagus, '79 41
Rolls, Hot Asparagus, '93 329
Rollups, Asparagus, '79 63
Roll-Ups, Asparagus, '84 270
Roulade, Asparagus, '86 102
Salads
  Artichoke Salad, Asparagus-, '85 162
  Asparagus Salad, '88 121; '94 67
  Aspic, Asparagus, '96 65
  Blue Crab Salad with Asian Vinaigrette,
    '98 142
  Chicken Salad, Asparagus-, '89 83

Chicken Salad with Asparagus, Curried,
  '81 36
Congealed Asparagus Salad, '83 260
Crab-and-Asparagus Salad, '92 141
Crabmeat-and-Asparagus, Congealed Salad
  with, '84 86
Cups, Asparagus Salad, '83 47
Easy Asparagus Salad, '88 131
Egg Salad, Asparagus-and-, '86 305
Grilled Asparagus Salad with Orange
  Vinaigrette, '99 102
Horseradish Salad, Asparagus-, '87 80
Lemon-Asparagus Salad, Creamy, '93 116
Marinated Asparagus, '83 46; '84 67, 86;
  '86 92
Marinated Asparagus and Hearts of Palm,
  '90 91
Marinated Asparagus Medley, '91 105
Marinated Asparagus Salad, '79 20
Marinated Asparagus with Prosciutto, '95 83
Mold, Asparagus, '80 104
Mold, Asparagus-Cucumber, '85 252
Mousse Salad, Asparagus, '86 252
Mustard Sauce, Chilled Asparagus in, '88 130
New Potato Salad, Asparagus-and-, '86 69
Papaya Salsa, Asparagus Salad with, '97 144
Peas-and-Asparagus Salad, '83 141
Tarragon Marinade, Asparagus with, '83 47
Tart Asparagus Salad, '81 203
Tomato-Asparagus Salad, '92 79
Tomatoes with Herb Vinaigrette, Asparagus
  and, '99 56
Vinaigrette, Asparagus, '80 77; '90 138
Vinaigrette, Asparagus Salad, '88 56
Vinaigrette, Light Asparagus, '82 50
Yogurt Dressing, Asparagus with, '79 66
Sandwiches, Asparagus-and-Ham Melt, '88 M96
Sandwiches, Asparagus Grill, '79 164; '80 130
Sandwiches, Asparagus Spear, '84 165
Sandwiches, Turkey-Asparagus, '96 74
Sandwich, Warm Asparagus, '99 102
Sauce, Asparagus White, '80 147
Sauté, Asparagus-and-Mushroom, '93 115
Sautéed Asparagus, '79 66
Sesame Asparagus, '96 154
Shrimp Mold with Asparagus, '93 214
Soufflé, Asparagus, '79 66; '83 265; '89 89
Soup, Asparagus, '84 67; '98 290
Soup, Asparagus-Potato, '85 23
Soup, Cream of Asparagus, '84 111
Soup, Creamy Asparagus, '94 225
Soup, Creamy Asparagus-and-Chicken, '95 82
Sour Cream, Asparagus with, '83 46
Spears, Buttered Asparagus, '97 282
Squares, Asparagus, '79 161
Squash Rings, Asparagus in, '87 68
Steamed Asparagus, '92 211
Stir-Fried Asparagus, '87 52
Stir-Fry, Asparagus, '95 83
Stir-Fry Beef and Asparagus, '91 124
Stir-Fry, Sweet Onion-Asparagus, '98 135
Supreme, Asparagus, '80 77; '89 245
Supreme, Cauliflower and Asparagus, '79 287;
  '80 35
Sweet-and-Sour Asparagus, '89 159
Tangy Asparagus, '84 86
Tartlets, Country Ham-and-Asparagus, '98 82
Terrine with Dill Sauce, Asparagus-Seafood,
  '98 157
Tomatoes, Fresh Asparagus and, '94 162
Tomato Sauce, Asparagus with, '83 46
Toss, Asparagus-Carrot-Squash, '91 45
Vinaigrette, Asparagus, '80 77; '90 82, 138;
  '93 174

ASPIC

Apple Aspic, Sunshine, '81 73
Asparagus Aspic, '96 65
Basic Aspic for Garnishing, '84 189
Beet Aspic, '90 123
Blue Cheese Aspic, '96 66
Chicken Salad, Aspic-Topped, '88 88
Coating, White Aspic, '85 151
Cucumber-Curry Dressing, Aspic with, '89 178
Fish Aspic, '84 190
Fish 'n Aspic, '84 190
Gazpacho Aspic, '89 179; '96 65
Grapefruit Aspic, '80 297; '82 112; '83 153
Madeira Aspic, '86 65
Orange-and-Carrot Aspic, '86 199
Rosemary Aspic, Spicy, '99 183
Shrimp-Coleslaw Aspic, '79 88
Shrimp-Cucumber Aspic, '83 108
Sunshine Aspic, '80 103
Three-Layer Aspic, '88 120
Tomato
Artichoke Aspic, Tomato-, '84 320; '86 92
Bloody Mary-Tomato Aspic, '81 77
Chicken in Tomato Aspic, '84 190
Chili Sauce Tomato Aspic, '85 252
Classic Tomato Aspic, '91 229
Crab Aspic, Tomato-, '85 287
Herbed Tomato Aspic, '81 73
Layered Tomato Aspic, '90 99
Light Tomato Aspic, '85 83
Ranch Tomato Aspic, '83 218
Shrimp, Tomato Aspic with, '79 241
Spicy Tomato Aspic, '81 40; '89 288
Tangy Tomato Aspic, '83 124
Two, Aspic for, '83 209
Vegetable Aspic, Cheesy, '81 73
Vegetable Aspic with Horseradish Dressing, Crisp, '87 152

AVOCADOS

Baked Avocado-and-Crabmeat, '84 119
Broiled Crab and Avocado, '79 116
Chicken, Orange-Avocado, '80 38
Cocktail, Sherried Avocado-Crabmeat, '87 95
Crabmeat, Avocado with, '86 119
Cream, Avocado, '92 158
Dagwoods, Chicken-Avocado, '96 200; '99 337
Dip, Avocado, '80 285; '81 57, 306
Dip, "Bring-Home-the-Bacon" Avocado, '92 80
Dip, Gazpacho, '95 243
Dip, Roasted Corn-and-Avocado, '91 279
Dip, Six-Layer, '81 160
Dip, Zippy Avocado, '82 9; '83 69
Dressing, Avocado, '80 15; '92 321; '96 138
Dressing, Avocado Fruit Salad, '82 93
Eggs and Ham, Green, '96 90
Filled Avocados, Shrimp-, '83 2
Gazpacho, Tomato-Avocado-Corn, '97 182
Guacamole
Baine's Guac, '98 88
Coleslaw, Guacamole Mexican, '82 302
Creamy Guacamole, '79 91; '83 174; '99 119
Crisps, Guacamole, '98 173
Dip, Bacon-Guacamole, '85 25
Dip, Guacamole, '86 4; '95 96
Dressing, Guacamole, '92 64
Easy Guacamole, '95 94
Guacamole, '79 185; '80 74; '83 179; '89 226; '90 205; '91 161; '94 116; '96 160, 170; '99 84
Margarita Guacamole, '97 167
Mold, Guacamole, '86 184
Salad, Guacamole, '80 14; '87 181
Salad, Guacamole-Tomato, '81 302
Sandwiches, Guacamole, '82 9; '83 68

Shells, Guacamole in, '86 74
Spicy Guacamole, '93 218
Spread, Guacamole, '90 119
Subs, Guacamole, '84 293
Ice, Avocado, '83 179
Kabobs, Chicken-Avocado, '82 9; '83 68
Mousse with Shrimp Salad, Avocado, '98 333
Omelet, Yogurt-Avocado, '81 33
Pie, Mexican Cheese, '83 69
Potatoes, Avocado-Topped, '83 3
Relish, Avocado, '87 120
Salads
Acapulco, Avocado, '83 2
Avocado Salad, '81 195; '82 9; '83 69; '92 246; '97 250
Chicken-Avocado Salad, '80 139
Chicken-Avocado Salad, Fruited, '82 101
Chicken-Avocado Salad Platter, '83 2
Chicken-Avocado Salad, Tossed, '80 4
Chicken Salad, Avocado-, '87 107
Chicken Salad in Avocados, '85 216
Chicken Salad in Avocados, Fruited, '87 41
Citrus-and-Avocado Salad, '99 26
Citrus-Avocado Salad, '82 265
Congealed Avocado Crunch Salad, '85 26
Congealed Avocado Salad, '84 266
Congealed Avocado Salads, '87 42
Crab-Avocado Salad, '81 114
Dude Ranch Salad, '80 15
Endive Salad, Avocado-, '94 88
Fruit Salad, Avocado, '87 41
Fruit Salad with Honey-Yogurt Dressing, Avocado-, '93 172
Garbanzo Salad, Avocado-, '81 33
Grapefruit-Avocado Salad, '83 316; '84 16; '89 41
Grapefruit Salad, Avocado-, '85 26; '93 282
Melon Salad, Avocado-, '82 164
Mexican Salad Supper, '82 9; '83 68
Orange-Avocado Salad, '99 331
Orange Salad, Avocado-, '91 44
Potato Salad with Avocado, '98 332
Potato Salad with Horseradish Dressing, Avocado-, '96 200
Rice-and-Avocado Salad, '89 146
Romaine Salad, Tangy, '80 155
Shrimp and Avocado Salad, '80 266
Shrimp Salad, Avocado Stuffed with, '82 207
Shrimp Salad on the Half Shell, '86 73
Southwestern Spiral Salad, '98 66
Spanish Avocado Salad, '87 41
Spinach Salad, Green, '79 142
Tomato-Avocado Salad, '86 74
Tomatoes, Avocado-Stuffed, '82 101
Zucchini Salad, Creamy Avocado and, '79 208
Salsa, Avocado, '91 182
Salsa, Avocado-Corn, '94 201; '99 335
Salsa, Avocado-Feta, '96 15
Salsa, Sweet, '98 174
Salsa, Tomato-Avocado, '94 83
Sandwiches, Avocado, Bacon, and Cheese, '87 279
Sandwiches, Avocado-Crabmeat, '83 2
Sandwiches, Avocado Deluxe, '99 72
Sauce, Avocado, '80 198; '83 200
Sauce, Avocado-Tomatillo, '95 206
Sauce, Grilled Swordfish with Avocado-Lime, '97 127
Shells, Ceviche in Avocado, '81 33
Sherbet, Avocado, '83 162
Sherbet, Mexican, '79 155
Sorbet, Avocado, '88 117
Soup, Avocado, '88 160
Soup, Avocado-Banana-Yogurt, '80 78

Soup, Chilled Avocado, '81 34; '87 37; '93 108
Soup, Creamy Avocado, '79 107
Soup, Creamy Avocado-Mushroom, '85 25
Soup, Sherried Avocado, '84 181
Spread, Herbed Avocado-Cheese, '98 335
Stuffed Avocados, Crab-, '86 73
Stuffed Avocados, Salmon-, '86 74
Stuffed Broiled Avocados, '88 246
Tomatoes, Crab-and-Avocado Stuffed, '94 141
Topping, Avocado, '93 309; '94 96
Tostadas, Crispy, '83 2
Whip, Avocado, '79 107

BACON

Appetizers

Bites, Bacon-Shrimp, '98 234; '99 213
Blue Cheese-and-Bacon Puffs, '97 98
Brie, Chutney-Bacon, '90 M292
Cheese-Bacon Crispies, '84 270
Chestnut Wraps, Bacon-, '84 M216
Crackers, Bacon-Wrapped, '93 280
Crostini, Almond-Bacon-Cheese, '94 318
Crostini, Green Onion, '96 93
Dip, Bacon, '82 197
Dip, Bacon-and-Tomato, '90 147
Dip, Bacon-Guacamole, '85 25
Dip, "Bring-Home-the-Bacon" Avocado, '92 80
Dip, Cheddar-Bacon, '89 M119
Dip, Zesty Bacon, '92 156
Eggs, Bacon-Stuffed, '97 52
Hot Bacon Appetizers, '80 248
Meatballs, Burgundy-Bacon, '80 283
Mushrooms, Cheese 'n' Bacon-Stuffed, '86 258
Onion Appetizers, Bacon-, '94 290
Oysters in Bacon, '83 211
Pineapple Chunks, Bacon-Wrapped, '84 25
Popcorn, Bacon-Cheese, '86 74
Quesadillas, Bacon-Jalapeño-Tomato, '95 240
Quiches, Miniature Bacon-Cheese, '83 93
Rolls, Bacon, '84 270; '93 330
Rollups, Bacon, '79 34
Roll-Ups, Chicken Liver and Bacon, '80 200; '81 57
Rollups, Sausage-Bacon, '88 51
Rumaki, '80 M136
Rumaki, Scallop, '98 M173
Scallops, Bacon-Wrapped, '87 94
Scallops with Orange-Honey Sauce, Bacon-Wrapped, '97 236
Shrimp 'n' Bacon, '98 222
Spread, Bacon-Cheese, '83 241
Sticks, Parmesan-Bacon, '99 65
Swirls, Bacon, '89 214; '98 26
Water Chestnuts, Bacon-Wrapped, '79 63
Bagels, Meal-in-One, '88 159
Bake, Bacon, Zucchini, and Cornbread, '99 123
Bake, Lima-Bacon, '86 9
Bars, Bacon-Cheese Toast, '79 36
Beans, Lowcountry Baked, '98 332
Beef-and-Bacon Twirls, '91 163
Biscuit Cups, Bacon, '99 214
Biscuits, Bacon-Cheese, '88 84
Biscuits, Potato-Bacon, '94 214
Bread, Bacon-and-Cheese, '83 255
Bread, Bacon-Cheese French, '92 54
Bread, Bacon Monkey, '94 283; '97 154
Breakfast Bake, '85 45
Breakfast Eye-Openers, '82 231
Breakfast, Farmer's, '81 44
Broccoli Bakers, '99 308
Broccoli with Bacon, '92 302

Bundles, Bean, '80 246
Burgers, Apple-Bacon, '99 202
Burgers, Cheesy Bacon, '81 29
Butterbeans, Bacon, and Tomatoes, '96 36
Butterbeans with Bacon and Green Onions, '96 267
Butternut and Bacon, Skillet, '85 9
Canadian Bacon, Lima Beans with, '83 219; '84 245
Canadian Bacon Squares, Sunrise, '99 103
Canadian-Style Bacon, Glazed, '82 197
Carrots with Bacon and Onion, Glazed, '87 200
Casserole, Bacon and Egg, '81 225
Casserole, Egg-and-Bacon, '85 248
Casseroles, Hot Brown Pasta, '96 290
Casserole with Creole Sauce, Brunch, '98 98
Cauliflower with Parmesan and Bacon, '96 137
Champignons au Vin, '79 47
Chicken Breasts, Apple-Bacon Stuffed, '99 313
Chicken Bundles with Bacon Ribbons, '87 68
Chowder, Fresh Corn and Bacon, '93 203
Chowder, Southern Corn-and-Bacon, '96 166
Coleslaw, Bacon, '83 58
Cookies, Breakfast, '97 52
Cookies, Take-Along Breakfast, '84 59
Cornbread, Cowboy, '81 188
Cornbread, Loaded, '99 214
Corn with Bacon and Caramelized Onion, '99 94
Delight, Bacon-and-Egg, '85 143
Dressing, Green Beans with Bacon, '85 147
Dressing, Hot Bacon, '84 12
Dressing, Jeweled Hot Bacon, '97 196
Dressing, Potatoes with Hot Bacon, '88 M294
Dressing, Sweet Bacon, '93 108
Egg Salad, Bacon-Horseradish, '94 181
Eggs, and Hominy, Bacon, '85 143
Eggs, Bacon Deviled, '86 136
Eggs Benedict, '98 55
Eggs Benedict, Bacon-and-Tomato, '87 195
Eggs, Brunch, '98 93
Eggs Oso Grande, '98 279
Flank Steak, Bacon-Wrapped, '85 59
Franks, Bacon-Wrapped, '81 202
Frittata, Bacon-and-Asparagus, '98 136
Frittata, Potato-Bacon, '95 269; '98 330
Green Beans, Bacon-Topped, '80 M123
Green Beans, Mushroom-Bacon, '91 291; '92 255
Green Beans with Bacon and Mushrooms, '92 13
Greens and Bacon, Shelly, '96 290
Grits, Nassau, '99 214
Hush Puppies, Bacon, '91 201
Kabobs, Scallop-Bacon, '81 111
Linguine Carbonara, '87 108
Meatballs, Bacon-Wrapped, '79 81
Muffins, Bacon-and-Cheese, '89 205
Muffins, Bacon-Cheese, '96 280
Mushrooms with Bacon, Stir-Fried, '80 123
Okra Pilau, '99 184
Oysters, Bacon-Baked, '86 132
Oysters Rockefeller, '98 222
Pancake, Maple-Bacon Oven, '89 255
Pasta, Bacon, '97 52
Peas and Bacon, Sautéed, '89 331
Pecans, Roasted Bacon, '96 262
Pie, Country Breakfast, '93 M328
Pizza, Breakfast, '97 172
Pizza, The King Henry, '95 267
Popcorn, Bacon-Cheese, '86 74
Pork Tenderloin, Spinach-and-Bacon Stuffed, '94 81
Potatoes, Bacon-Stuffed, '86 193
Potatoes, Bacon-Topped Blue Cheese, '79 46
Potatoes, Cheesy Bacon-Stuffed, '81 M61

Quiche, Bacon, '85 60
Quiche Lorraine, '80 M108; '99 M218
Quiche Lorraine, Classic, '81 131
Quiche Lorraine, Mushroom-, '86 242
Quiche Lorraine, Peppery, '81 228
Rice, Bacon-Chive, '83 129
Rice, Bacon Fried, '80 115
Rice, Spicy, '99 214
Rolls, Onion-Bacon, '99 47
Rouladen, '99 242
Rutabaga with Bacon, '83 243
Salad, Bacon-Lettuce-Mozzarella-and-Tomato, '98 209
Salad, Bacon-Topped Potato, '85 59
Salad, BLT Chicken, '87 144
Salad, Eight-Layer, '99 107
Salad, Endive, Bacon, and Pecan, '89 12
Salad, Escarole-and-Bacon, '84 85
Salad, Hot Bacon and Black-Eyed, '85 7
Salad, Spinach and Bacon, '81 143
Salad, Wilted Bacon-and-Lettuce, '85 69
Salad with Bacon, Rice, '79 52
Sandwiches
   Avocado, Bacon, and Cheese Sandwiches, '87 279
   Bagel, Breakfast on a, '94 66
   Beef, Bacon, and Blue Cheese Sandwiches, '96 223
   Breakfast Sandwiches, '82 M123; '89 M230
   Breakfast Sandwiches, Open-Faced, '92 140
   Cheese, and Tomato Sandwiches, Bacon, '84 14
   Cheesy BLT's, '85 92
   Croissants, BLT, '93 158
   Curried BLT Sandwiches, '93 158
   Good-Start Sandwiches, '99 134
   Grilled Bacon, Cheese, and Tomato Sandwiches, '97 170
   Grilled Bacon-Cheese Sandwiches, '83 242
   Hoagies, Bacon, Pimiento, and Cheese, '90 144
   Melts, Tomato-Cheese-Bacon, '99 72
   Open-Faced Cheesy Bacon Sandwiches, '80 78
   Open-Faced Sandwiches, Super, '97 52
   Pita Pockets, BLT in, '93 158
   Poor Boys, Oyster-and-Bacon, '87 40
   Stuffed Sandwich, Italian, '99 15
   Welsh Rarebit with Tomatoes and Bacon, '92 M159
   Wraps, Western, '99 194
Sauté, Orange-Watercress, '98 83
Scallops, Maple, '99 176
Scramble, Bacon-and-Eggs, '80 M267
Soufflés, Parmesan, '97 280
Soup, Bacon-Beer Cheese, '87 M7
Soup, Bacon, Lettuce, and Tomato, '91 207
Soup, Bacon-Topped Cheese, '80 M224
Soup, Bean and Bacon, '83 26
Soup, Potato-Bacon, '84 M38
Spaghetti, Bacon, '86 213; '87 82
Spoonbread, Corn and Bacon, '81 129
Spread, Spinach-Bacon, '92 M310
Squash, Bacon-Flavored, '82 158
Supper Supreme, Sunday, '79 76
Sweet Potatoes, Bacon-Stuffed, '86 224
Tomatoes, Bacon-and-Egg-Stuffed, '80 162
Tomatoes with Bacon, Saucy Fried, '81 210
Tortellini Carbonara, Creamy, '99 171
Trout Stuffed with Crawfish, Bacon-Wrapped, '99 54
Trout, Sweet Onion-Stuffed, '99 52
Vegetable-Bacon Bowl, Marinated, '79 191

BAKING POWDER
Single-Acting Baking Powder, '96 142
BANANAS
Alaskas, Banana Split, '87 10
Baked Bananas, '79 103; '96 163
Baked Bananas, Coffee-Kissed, '98 279
Baked Bananas, Honey-, '81 268
Baked Bananas with Orange Sauce, '79 115
Bars, Banana Breakfast, '79 124
Beverages
   Berry Flip, Banana-, '88 215; '89 20
   "Concrete," All Shook Up, '94 114
   Coolers, Banana, '91 308
   Crush, Banana, '80 88; '83 142
   Flip, Banana, '83 303
   Float, Strawberry-Banana, '87 160
   Frostee, Banana, '91 66
   Funky Monkey, '99 161
   Kabana, Banana, '86 316
   Malt, Banana-Chocolate, '89 170
   Milkshake, Banana, '85 47; '90 179
   Milk Shake, Banana-Pineapple, '84 59
   Milk Shake, Chocolate-Banana, '94 113
   Nog, Banana, '82 290
   Orange-Banana Flip, '82 48
   Orange-Banana Whip, '95 244
   Orange Slush, Banana-, '80 48; '81 155
   Pineapple-Banana Slush, '90 14
   Punch, Banana, '99 161
   Purple Cow, '98 206
   Shake, Banana, '97 172
   Shake, Peanut Butter-Banana, '97 172
   Shake, Pineapple-Banana, '85 215
   Shake, Pineapple-Orange-Banana, '97 172
   Shake, Raspberry-and-Banana, '89 183
   Shake, Strawberry-Banana, '89 35; '97 172
   Slush, Banana, '83 56
   Smoothie, Banana, '87 160; '93 95
   Smoothie, Banana-Blueberry, '90 104
   Smoothie, Honey-Banana, '89 144
   Smoothie, Orange-Banana, '97 173
   Smoothie, Quick Banana-Pineapple, '93 195
   Smoothies, Sunshine, '98 330
   Smoothie, Strawberry-Banana, '81 59
   Smoothie, Tropical, '81 50
   Strawberry Frost, Banana-, '87 199
   Tropical Delight, '89 182
Bisque, Banana-Raspberry, '93 161
Boats, Banana, '82 50
Breads
   Apple Bread, Banana-, '85 250
   Banana Bread, '87 72
   Blueberry Bread, Banana-, '81 163
   Butterscotch Bread, Banana, '79 116
   Chocolate Chip-Banana Bread, '90 267
   Chocolate Chip-Banana Loaf, '85 115
   Cranberry-Banana Bread, '80 281; '90 294
   Date-Banana Loaves, Tropical, '95 143
   Easy Banana Bread, '96 97
   Fruity Banana Bread, '95 78
   Hawaiian Loaf, '80 225
   Honey-Banana Bread, '91 68
   Jam Bread, Banana-, '84 73
   Muffins, Banana, '80 88; '84 75
   Muffins, Banana Bran, '83 48
   Muffins, Banana-Chocolate, '94 197
   Muffins, Banana-Honey-Nut, '88 62
   Muffins, Banana-Nut, '93 140
   Muffins, Banana-Oat, '87 188
   Muffins, Banana Oat Bran, '89 106
   Muffins, Banana-Oatmeal, '84 20
   Muffins, Banana-Orange, '84 148
   Muffins, Banana-Poppyseed, '89 205
   Muffins, Banana-Raisin, '89 218

BANANAS, Breads
(continued)

Muffins, Banana Surprise, **'82** 105
Muffins, Jumbo Banana-Chocolate Chip, **'93** 339
Muffins, Oat Bran-Banana, **'91** 18
Nut Bread, Banana-, **'86** 8, 70
Nut Bread, Hawaiian Banana, **'79** 235
Nut-Raisin Bread, Banana-, **'81** 59
Oat Tea Loaf, Banana-, **'87** 256
Roll, Banana-Nut, **'85** 112
Sour Cream-Banana Bread, **'79** 190
Wheat Bread, Banana, **'81** 14
Whole Wheat Banana Bread, **'80** 88
Whole Wheat-Banana Nut Bread, **'84** 50
Zucchini Bread, Banana-, **'85** 326
Breakfast-in-a-Bowl, **'89** 87
Broiled Bananas with Honey, **'84** 175
Brownies, Chocolate-Banana, **'80** 160
Cake, Banana, **'84** 151
Cake, Banana-Blueberry, **'86** 247
Cake, Banana-Coconut, **'93** 154
Cake, Banana-Nut, **'92** 120
Cake, Banana Pound, **'96** 60; **'98** 195
Cake, Bananas Foster Crunch, **'93** 339
Cake, Banana Split, **'99** 48
Cake, Banana Waldorf, **'85** 118
Cake, Chocolate-Banana, **'86** 138
Cake, Deluxe Light Banana, **'84** 314
Cake, Marvelous Banana, **'79** 115
Cake, Peanut Butter-Banana, **'80** 87
Cake with Coconut Custard, Supreme Banana, **'97** 131
Candied Bananas, **'83** 179
Caramelized Bananas, **'99** 49
Casserole, Sweet Potato-Banana, **'86** 276
Cheesecake, Chocolate-Wrapped Banana, **'99** M48
Chicken with Black Bean Sauce, Banana, **'96** 156
Coffee Cake, Banana, **'81** 288
Coffee Cake, Banana Cream, **'85** 46
Coffee Cake, Banana-Sour Cream, **'80** 186; **'97** 231
Cookies, Banana Oatmeal, **'79** 217
Crêpes Flambé, Banana, **'84** 262
Cupcakes, Banana-Cocoa, **'80** 130
Curried Bananas, Fillets with Horseradish Sauce and, **'85** 230
Delights, Choco-Peanut, **'99** 197
Dessert, Banana Cream, **'81** 180
Dessert in a Nutshell, **'96** 318
Doughnuts, Banana, **'86** 137
Dressing, Banana-Poppy Seed, **'98** 184
Fish, Caribbean Banana, **'95** 202
Flambé, Banana-Peach, **'85** 316
Foster, Bananas, **'79** 18; **'83** M114; **'86** 139; **'96** 99
Foster, Elegant Bananas, **'81** 59
Foster for Two, Bananas, **'80** 115
Foster, Orange-Glazed Bananas, **'91** 91
Foster, Tropical Bananas, **'79** 231
Fritters, Banana, **'79** 213
Frosting, Banana-Nut, **'79** 115
Glacé, Bananas, **'96** 46
Green Bananas Escabeche (Pickled Green Bananas), **'92** 169
Hawaiian, Bananas, **'89** 94
Ice Cream, Banana-Graham, **'91** 56
Ice Cream, Banana Split, **'80** 176
Ice Cream, Straw-Ba-Nut, **'80** 177
Ice Cream, Strawberry-Banana-Nut, **'88** 203

Ice Milk, Banana Yogurt, **'89** 199
Jam, Banana, **'82** 296
Jam, Rosy Peach-Banana, **'80** 142
Nutty Bananas, **'79** 251
Pancakes, Banana-Nut, **'98** 160
Pancakes, Best, **'99** 194
Pancakes, Island, **'87** 225
Pancakes, Wheat Germ-Banana, **'79** 114
Pie, Banana Cream, **'84** 48; **'87** 207
Pie, Blueberry-Banana, **'93** 115
Pie, Caramel-Banana, **'86** M165
Pie, Chocolate-Banana-Pecan Cream, **'94** 210
Pie, Hawaiian Banana Cream, **'90** 105
Pie, Layered Banana Split, **'83** 189
Pie, Luscious Caramel Banana, **'79** 115
Pie, Strawberry-Banana Glazed, **'81** 181
Pie, White Chocolate-Banana Cream, **'94** 314
Pie with Hot Buttered Rum Sauce, Banana, **'88** 204
Pizza, Banana Split-Brownie, **'96** M164
Pops, Banana, **'83** 60; **'84** 44
Pops, Orange-Banana, **'82** 129
Praline Bananas, **'84** 313
Pudding, Almost Banana, **'88** 174
Pudding, Banana, **'82** 53; **'84** 94; **'85** 255; **'88** 16, 32
Pudding, Banana-Mallow, **'86** 139
Pudding, Basic Banana, **'81** 59
Pudding, Creamy Banana, **'89** M130
Pudding, Delicious Banana, **'80** 9
Pudding, Fudge-Banana, **'97** 331
Pudding, No-Bake Banana, **'91** 172; **'99** 197
Pudding, Old-Fashioned Banana, **'92** 94
Pudding Parfait Pops, Banana, **'96** 180
Pudding, Peanut Butter-Banana, **'93** 340
Pudding, Sour Cream Banana, **'98** 90
Pudding, Surprise Banana, **'86** 7
Regal Bananas, **'85** 46
Salad, Banana, **'87** 80
Salad, Banana-Mixed Fruit, **'79** 270
Salad, Banana Split, **'91** 58
Salad, Frozen Banana, **'82** 80, 132
Salad with Celery Seed Dressing, Grapefruit-Banana, **'91** 237
Salsa, Banana, **'96** 85
Salsa, Banana Rum, **'94** 97
Salsa, Caribbean, **'96** 70
Sauce, Banana-Pineapple, **'83** 48
Sauce, Banana Sundae, **'84** 275
Sauce, Strawberry-Banana, **'81** 41
Sherbet, Banana-Orange, **'83** 162
Shortcake, Banana-Pecan, **'93** 43
Slaw, Banana-Nut, **'86** 250
Sorbet, Banana-Orange, **'88** 117
Soufflé, Banana Daiquiri, **'84** 317
Soup, Avocado-Banana-Yogurt, **'80** 78
Soup, Strawberry-Banana, **'86** 181
Spiced Bananas with Rum Sauce, **'99** 247
Splits, Cottage Cheese-Banana, **'87** 56
Splits, French Toast Banana, **'96** M164
Sundae, Breakfast, **'98** 206
Supreme, Banana-Berry, **'81** 205
Supreme, Bananas, **'84** 256
Terrine, Banana Split, **'96** 164
Topping, Pound Cake with Strawberry-Banana, **'89** 200
Topping, Strawberry-Banana, **'87** 125
Trifle, Banana Pudding, **'98** 273
Waffles, Banana-Ginger, **'86** 96
Waffles, Banana-Oatmeal, **'94** 206
Waffles, Banana Split, **'89** 205
BARBECUE. *See also* **GRILLED.**
Beans, Barbecued, **'94** 248
Beans, Barbecued Green, **'86** 252

Beans, Barbecued Lima, **'82** 2
Beans, Barbecued Pork and, **'79** 100
Beans, Commissary Barbecue, **'90** 120
Beans, Skillet Barbecued, **'93** 217
Beef. *See also* **BARBECUE/Ribs.**
Barbecued Beef, **'81** 18
Bourbon Barbecue, **'88** 129
Brisket, Barbecued, **'86** 154; **'88** 218
Brisket, Barbecued Beef, **'83** 11
Brisket, Denton, Texas, Barbecued Beef, **'81** 55
Brisket with Sauce, Barbecued Beef, **'86** 153
Burgers, Barbecued, **'82** 168; **'89** 164
Chuck Roast Barbecue, **'96** 71
Corned Beef Sandwiches, Barbecued, **'83** 130
Cups, Barbecue, **'79** 129
Kabobs, Barbecued Steak, **'79** 89
Liver, Barbecued, **'85** 219
Loaves, Individual Barbecued Beef, **'95** 242
Meatballs, Oven Barbecued, **'82** 233
Meat Loaf, Barbecued, **'80** 60; **'81** 275; **'87** 216
Pot Roast, Barbecued, **'79** 17; **'83** 319
Rib Roast, Barbecued, **'86** 152
Roast, Barbecue, **'98** 245
Roast Barbecue, Beef, **'79** 159
Roast, Barbecued Beef, **'82** 96; **'83** 103
Sandwiches, Barbecue Beef, **'99** 327
Sandwiches, Barbecued Beef, **'81** 25; **'82** 31; **'83** 34
Sandwiches, Debate Barbecue, **'97** 234
Saucy Barbecued Beef, **'82** 156
Steak, Barbecued Flank, **'79** 89
Steak, Marinated Barbecued Chuck, **'80** 156
Steak, Saucy Oven-Barbecued, **'83** 10
Supper, Barbecue Hobo, **'99** 108
Tenderloin, Barbecued Beef, **'94** 26
Bread, Barbecue, **'99** 105
Cabrito, Barbecued, **'86** 153
Chicken
Bake, Barbecued Chicken, **'81** 97
Barbecue Chicken, **'86** 122
Barbecued Chicken, **'82** 97, 106; **'83** 103; **'85** 144; **'86** 153; **'89** 167
Carambola-Glazed Barbecued Chicken, **'92** 246
Chili-Barbecued Chicken, **'98** 170
Cranberry Chicken, Barbecued, **'83** 178
Golden Barbecued Chicken, **'83** 136
Grilled Barbecued Chicken, **'81** 154
Legs and Thighs, Barbecued Chicken, **'94** 94
Lemon Barbecued Chicken, **'93** 215
Marinated Barbecued Chicken, **'79** 90
Old South Barbecued Chicken, **'82** 97; **'83** 103
Orange Barbecued Chicken, **'88** 123
Oven-Barbecued Chicken, Kentucky-Style, **'96** 328
Oven-Barbecued Cranberry Chicken, **'93** 332
Salad, Warm Barbecue Chicken, **'99** 124
Sauce Chicken with White Barbecue, **'97** 322
Saucy Barbecued Chicken, **'83** 11
South-of-the-Border Barbecued Chicken, **'97** 311
Tangy Barbecued Chicken, **'86** 186; **'98** 170
Zesty Barbecued Chicken, **'80** M76
Zippy Barbecued Chicken, **'83** 213
Coleslaw, Barbecue, **'97** 139
Coleslaw, Best Barbecue, **'97** 214
Corn on the Cob, Barbecued, **'81** 128
Dressing, Barbecue, **'99** 124
Dressing, Barbecue Salad, **'80** 74
Fish. *See also* **BARBECUE/Seafood.**
Catfish, Barbecued, **'80** 157
Catfish, Lemon Barbecued, **'89** 202

Fillets, Barbecued Fish, '86 182
Salmon, Barbecued, '81 181
Tacos, Barbecued Fish, '95 339
Tuna, Barbecued, '80 275
Frank Barbecue, Tangy, '79 63
Frankfurters, Barbecued, '83 144
Frankfurters, Oven-Barbecued, '83 11
Franks, Barbecued, '85 192
Lamb, Barbecued, '79 58
Lamb Chops, Barbecued, '79 89
Lamb Shanks, Barbecued, '92 128; '93 113
Muffins, Barbecue, '96 246
Outdoor Cooking, '82 109
Popcorn, Cheesy Barbecue, '95 239
Pork. *See also* **BARBECUE/Ribs.**
Bannister's Barbecue, '92 166
Barbecued Pork, '80 72
Chops, Barbecued Pork, '81 10
Chops, Marinated Barbecued Pork, '79 90
Chops, Oven-Barbecued Pork, '81 234; '82 26; '83 40
Ham Slices, Barbecued, '81 110
Home-Style Barbecue, '88 145
Nachos, Commissary Barbecue, '91 171
Roast, Barbecued Pork Loin, '93 34
Roast Barbecue, Pork, '82 97; '83 104
Roast, Berry Barbecued Pork, '80 288
Shoulder, Barbecued Pork, '81 111; '82 11
Spicy Barbecued Pork, '84 296
Potatoes, Barbecued, '91 311; '92 26
Rabbit, Hickory Barbecued, '82 216
Ribs
Apple Barbecued Ribs, '80 111
Apple-Barbecue Spareribs, '90 160
Baby Back Ribs, Barbecued, '97 234
Barbecued Ribs, '80 111; '85 159; '91 205
Barbecued Spareribs, '81 112; '82 12; '86 232; '95 236
Barbecue Ribs, '99 68
Beef Short Ribs, Barbecued, '83 178
Country-Style Barbecued Ribs, '79 42
Country-Style Ribs, Barbecued, '95 237
Country-Style Spareribs, Barbecued, '80 73
Easy Barbecued Spareribs, '82 97; '83 104
Herbed Barbecued Ribs, '86 185
Oven-Barbecued Pork Ribs, '88 132
Saucy Barbecued Spareribs, '79 14
Short Ribs, Barbecued, '90 148
Smoky Barbecued Ribs, '80 111
Southern Barbecued Spareribs, '79 90
Spicy Barbecued Spareribs, '84 93
Tangy Barbecued Ribs, '83 160
Tangy Barbecued Spareribs, '82 106
Rub, Master Class Barbecue, '98 244
Salad, Barbecue Macaroni, '82 276
Sauces
Apple Barbecue Sauce, '99 173
Bannister's Barbecue Sauce, '92 166
Barbecue Sauce, '84 172; '86 153; '88 218; '91 16, 205; '93 129; '94 27
Barbecue Sauce, Baked Fish with, '84 92
Basting Sauce, '90 120
Beef Marinade, Tangy, '86 113
Beer Barbecue Sauce, '84 173
Blender Barbecue Sauce, Ribs with, '90 12
Bourbon Barbecue Sauce, '85 90
Brisket with Barbecue Sauce, Smoked, '85 144
Crickhollow Barbecue Sauce, '99 200
Dressed-Up Barbecue Sauce, '84 173
Eastern-Style Barbecue Sauce, '88 145
Easy Barbecue Sauce, '79 90; '82 178
Handcrafted Barbecue Sauce, '98 45
John Wills's Barbecue Sauce, '92 255

Lemon Barbecue Sauce, Herbed, '94 154; '98 334
Lemony Barbecue Sauce, '88 M177; '95 31
Maple Syrup Barbecue Sauce, '94 154
Mustard Barbecue Sauce, '84 173
Orange Barbecue Sauce, Spareribs with, '83 11
Oven Barbecue Sauce, '82 233
Paprika Barbecue Sauce, '79 90
Peanut Butter Barbecue Sauce, '81 233
Piquant Barbecue Sauce, '79 159
Savory Barbecue Sauce, '86 153
Special Barbecue Sauce, '82 177
Spicy Southwest Barbecue Sauce, '94 154
Sweet-and-Sour Marinade, '86 113
Sweet Sauce, '90 120
Tangy Barbecue Sauce, '97 323; '99 104
Teriyaki Marinade, '86 114
Texas Barbecue Sauce, '99 210
Texas Barbecue Sauce, LBJ's, '97 42
Thick and Robust Barbecue Sauce, '94 95
Thick and Sweet Barbecue Sauce, '94 95
Thin and Tasty Barbecue Sauce, '94 95
Tomato Barbecue Sauce, Fresh, '84 172
Western-Style Barbecue Sauce, '88 145
White Barbecue Sauce, '94 95
White Barbecue Sauce, Chicken with, '89 M84; '97 322
Zippy Barbecue Sauce, '92 166
Sausage, Barbecued, '86 153
Seafood. *See also* **BARBECUE/Fish.**
Oysters, Barbecued, '82 247
Shrimp and Cornbread-Stuffed Peppers, Barbecued, '97 261
Shrimp, Barbecue, '96 210; '97 58
Shrimp, Barbecued, '82 74; '84 93; '90 28
Shrimp, Cajun Barbecued, '87 95
Turkey Barbecue, '90 158
BARLEY
Baked Barley, '91 133
Casserole, Barley, '84 281
Pilaf, Barley-Vegetable, '91 33
Rolls, Wine-Sauced Beef-and-Barley, '87 269
Salad, Barley, '92 212
Salad, Barley-Broccoli, '90 135
Salad, Black Bean-and-Barley, '94 174
Soup, Hearty Bean-and-Barley, '86 304
Soup, Turkey-Barley, '91 312
Stuffing, Cornish Hens with Barley-Mushroom, '97 242
Vegetables, Barley and, '91 81
BEANS. *See also* **LENTILS.**
Anasazi Beans with Mushrooms, Stewed, '95 226
Bake, Cheesy Beef-and-Bean, '82 89
Baked
Barbecued Beans, '94 248
Barbecued Pork and Beans, '79 100
Beefy Baked Beans, '80 136; '84 149; '85 142
Bourbon Baked Beans, '95 182
Chuckwagon Beans, '81 188
Crowd-Pleasing Baked Beans, '82 127
Easy Baked Beans, '85 141
Favorite Baked Beans, '86 210
Franks, Beans and, '85 142
Franks, Beany Kraut and, '79 64
Franks, Hawaiian Baked Beans and, '80 136
Genuine Baked Beans, '83 26
Ham, Baked Beans with, '80 136
Hamburger-Bean Bake, '95 121
Hawaiian-Style Baked Beans, '86 210
K.C. Baked Beans, '98 244
Lowcountry Baked Beans, '98 332

Maple Heights Baked Beans, '91 223
Meat Baked Beans, Three-, '86 210
Medley, Baked Bean, '80 100
Mixed Baked Beans, '87 92
Molasses Baked Beans, '82 139; '84 327; '86 20; '99 105
More Beans, Baked Beans and, '92 173
Old-Fashioned Baked Beans, '84 25
Picnic Baked Beans, '83 143; '85 142
Polynesian Beans-and-Franks, '84 M11
Pork Chops with Baked Beans, '93 18
Quick Baked Beans, '80 136
Quintet, Baked Beans, '93 105; '94 100
Rum-Laced Bean Bake, '82 283; '83 72
Slow Cooker Bean Bake, '99 88
Smoked Baked Beans, '79 150
Spiced Baked Beans, '85 142
Three-Bean Bake, '81 155; '99 88
White Bean Bake, Turnip Greens and, '94 246
Barbecue Beans, Commissary, '90 120
Barbecued Beans, Skillet, '93 217
Beefy Beans, '82 59
Black. *See also* **BEANS/Salads, Soups.**
Appetizer, Black Bean, '83 50
Black Beans, '93 28
Bow Ties, Black Beans, and Key Limes, '96 291
Broth with Black Beans and Cilantro, Southwestern Scallop, '87 123
Burgers, Black Bean, '98 144
Cakes with Greens and Apple Dressing, Black Bean, '92 216
Cakes with Smoked Salmon Salsa, Corn-and-Black Bean, '96 272
Casserole of Black Beans, '95 27
Chicken with Black Beans and Salsa, Poached, '87 217
Chili Goes Southwest, Basic, '93 326
Chili Marsala, Black Bean, '95 16
Cuban Black Beans, '88 196; '99 56
Cuban Black Beans, Traditional, '98 21
Dip, Black Bean, '95 93
Frijoles con Cerveza (Beans with Beer), '81 66
Garbanzo-Black Bean Medley, '99 236
Guacamole, Black Bean, '94 277
Marinated Black Beans, '93 131
Mexicorn, Black Bean, '96 189
Pancakes with Gazpacho Butter, Black Bean, '92 86
Puree, Spicy Chicken with Black Bean, '97 48
Quesadillas, Chicken-and-Black Bean, '96 288
Relish, Black Bean-Tomatillo, '87 121
Rice, Black Beans and, '80 222; '89 178; '91 82; '95 309
Salsa, Black Bean, '93 155; '94 161; '97 226
Salsa, Black Bean-and-Corn, '94 80
Salsa, Black Bean-Corn, '96 126
Salsa, Corn-Black Bean, '96 15
Salsa, Hill Country, '97 123
Salsa, Orange-Black Bean, '98 231
Salsa with Black Beans and Corn, Southwestern, '96 275
Sandwiches, Caribbean Seafood, '98 105
Sauce, Banana Chicken with Black Bean, '96 156
Sauce, Black Bean, '93 59; '98 46
Sauce, Spicy Beef Fillets with Black Bean, '97 184
Spaghetti, Black Bean, '92 217
Spanish Black Beans, '84 327
Spicy Beef and Black Beans, '99 331
Stew, Baja Pork, '98 283
Strudel, Meatless Mexican, '98 29

BEANS, Black
(continued)

Terrine with Fresh Tomato Coulis and Jalapeño Sauce, Black Bean, **'93** 230
Terrine with Goat Cheese, Black Bean, **'87** 120
Tony's Black Beans, **'96** 289
Tostadas, Rice-and-Black Bean, **'97** 65
Tostadas, Shrimp-and-Black Bean, **'93** 204
Wraps, Western, **'99** 194
Yellow Rice, Black Beans and, **'95** 126
Yellow Rice, Black Beans with, **'82** 2
Yellow Rice, Easy Black Beans and, **'92** 308
Burrito Appetizers, Bean, **'94** 226
Burritos, Meat-and-Bean, **'81** 194
Butterbeans, **'90** 166
Butterbeans, Bacon, and Tomatoes, **'96** 36
Butterbeans with Bacon and Green Onions, **'96** 267
Cabbage Rolls, Southwestern, **'97** 214
Cannellini Beans, Rosemary, **'95** 213
Casserole, Bean-and-Cornbread, **'92** 243
Casserole, Chuck Wagon Bean, **'93** 198
Casserole, Fajita, **'97** 96
Casserole, Spicy Mexican Bean, **'84** 114
Casserole, Three-Bean, **'88** 56
Cassoulet, **'96** 328
Cassoulet, Vegetarian, **'96** 329
Chickpea Stew, Chicken, Kale, and, **'98** 47
Chili, **'98** 95
Chili and Beans, Ranch, **'79** 270; **'80** 11
Chili Bean Roast, **'87** 268; **'88** 102
Chili, Chilly Night, **'99** 317
Chili in a Biscuit Bowl, **'98** 224
Chili, Mom's, **'93** 292
Chili Supper, Hot, **'99** 279
Chili Surprise, **'82** 229
Chili, Turkey-Bean, **'88** M213
Chili, White, **'91** 284
Chili, White Christmas, **'98** 266
Chili with Beans, Easy, **'92** 262
Chili with Beans, Meaty, **'85** 250
Chimichangas, Baked Spicy Beef, **'97** 319
Creole Beans and Rice, **'80** 223
Crostini, Mexican, **'95** 142
Dinner, Quick Mexican, **'98** 224
Dip, Bean, **'89** 97
Dip, Cheese-Bean, **'85** 208
Dip, Chickpea-and-Red Pepper, **'99** 138
Dip, Fiesta, **'96** 212
Dip, Garbanzo, **'93** 94
Dip, Hotshot Bean, **'87** 195
Dip, Layered Nacho, **'81** 261
Dip, Mexican Fiesta, **'98** 234
Dip, Prairie Fire Bean, **'80** 195
Dip, Salsa-Bean, **'98** 285
Dip, South-of-the-Border, **'81** 235
Enchiladas, Three-Bean, **'91** 133
Farmer's Beans and Rice with Rosemary Biscuits, **'99** 16
Franks, Jiffy Beans and, **'91** M172
Franks 'n' Beans, Stove-Top, **'88** 201
Garbanzo Bean Spread, Herbed, **'99** 160
Garbanzo Dinner, Beef-and-, **'84** 31
Green. *See also* **BEANS/Salads, Soups.**
Almonds, Green Beans with, **'84** 253
Amandine, Green Beans, **'79** 276; **'82** M20; **'85** 156; **'97** 238
Appalachian Green Beans, **'81** 215
au Gratin, Green Beans, **'80** 116
Bacon and Mushrooms, Green Beans with, **'92** 13

Bacon Dressing, Green Beans with, **'85** 147
Bacon-Topped Green Beans, **'80** M123
Baked Green Beans, **'91** 159
Bake, Green Bean, **'99** 112
Barbecued Green Beans, **'86** 252
Basil Beans and Tomatoes, **'83** 172
Basil, Green Beans with, **'82** 96
Blue Cheese, Green Beans with, **'88** 57
Bow-Tie Green Beans, **'94** 320
Buffet Green Beans, **'93** 325
Bundles, Bean, **'80** 246; **'83** 67
Bundles, Green Bean, **'83** 180; **'87** 118
Buttered Green Beans, **'92** 54
Caramelized Onions, Green Beans with, **'95** 288
Cashews, Green Beans with, **'89** 202
Casserole, Chicken-Green Bean, **'85** 296
Casserole, Corn-and-Bean, **'90** 208
Casserole, Creamy Chicken-Green Bean, **'97** 158
Casserole, Easy Green Bean, **'87** 284
Casserole, Green Bean, **'79** 106; **'84** 145
Casserole, Green Bean-and-Corn, **'88** 123; **'99** 36
Casserole, Italian Green Bean-and-Artichoke, **'85** 81
Celery, Green Beans and Braised, **'84** 254
Cheese-Topped Green Beans, **'79** 100
Cheesy Green Beans, **'80** 157
Chinese Green Beans, **'96** 330
Creamed Green Beans, French-Style, **'88** 252
Cumin Green Beans, **'82** 90
Dilled Carrots and Green Beans, **'99** 223
Dilled Green Beans, **'82** 106; **'86** 157; **'88** 101; **'89** 203; **'93** 279; **'96** 172; **'99** 170
Dill Green Beans, **'93** 136
Dilly Green Beans, **'80** 116
Excellent, Green Beans, **'94** 321
French Green Beans, **'90** 208
French Quarter Green Beans, **'80** 298; **'81** 26
Fresh Green Beans, **'79** 122
Garlic Green Beans, **'91** 159; **'94** 273
Goldenrod Beans, **'83** 111
Gratin, Gourmet Green Bean, **'99** M334
Greek Green Beans, **'94** 165
Green Beans, **'80** 126; **'87** M151; **'97** 263
Herbed Green Beans, **'83** M147, 177; **'88** M190
Herb Green Beans, **'89** 321
Herbs, Green Beans with, **'82** 90
Indian-Style Green Beans, **'88** 265
Italian Green Beans, **'85** 147; **'90** 164; **'92** 183
Italian, Green Beans, **'87** 10
Italian Green Beans, Sesame, **'82** 174
Italian Green Beans with Almonds, **'81** 207
Italiano, Green Bean, **'94** 248
Italiano, Green Beans, **'86** 144
Lemon-Dill Butter, Green Beans with, **'99** 141
Lemon Green Beans, **'89** 275
Lemon-Walnut Green Beans, **'93** 304
Lemony Green Beans, **'85** 190; **'99** 259
Lorraine's Green Beans, **'99** 319
Marinated Beets, Green Beans, and Carrots, **'88** 162
Marinated Green Beans, **'83** 145
Marinated Italian Beans, **'86** M226
Marinated Vegetables, **'81** 239
Marjoram, Fresh Green Beans with, **'91** 159
Mediterranean-Style Green Beans, **'79** 100
Medley, Green Bean, **'85** 108
Medley, Peppery Green Bean, **'93** 181
Minted Green Beans, **'84** 104
Mushroom-Bacon Green Beans, **'91** 291; **'92** 255

Mushroom Sauce, Green Beans in Sherried, **'93** 206
Mushrooms, Green Beans with, **'82** 21; **'93** 89
Mustard, Green Beans and Tomatoes with, **'87** 83
New Potatoes, Green Beans with, **'87** 164
Nutty Green Beans, **'88** M187
Oregano, Green Beans with, **'97** 218
Oriental Green Beans, **'88** 43
Oriental, Green Beans, **'91** 158
Pecans, Green Beans with Buttered, **'92** 61
Pepper Strips, Green Beans and, **'86** 170
Pickled Beans, Dressed-Up, **'86** 251
Pole Beans, Old-Fashioned, **'80** 100
Potatoes, Down-Home Beans and, **'85** 254
Potatoes, Green Beans and, **'91** 221
Potatoes, Snap Beans and, **'98** 177
Provençal, Green Beans, **'81** 182; **'91** 158
Red Peppers and Pearl Onions, Green Beans with Roasted, **'93** 260
Saucy Green Beans, **'83** 206
Savory Green Beans, **'89** 70, 235
Seasoned Green Beans, **'88** 304
Shallots and Red Bell Pepper, Green Beans with, **'97** 251
Shuck Beans, **'81** 216
Simple Green Beans, **'92** 100
Snap Beans, **'86** 218
Snap Beans, Simple, **'85** 148
Snap, or Wax Beans, Green, **'85** 105
Sour Cream, Green Beans in, **'80** 116
Sour Cream, Green Beans with, **'82** 90
Southern-Style Green Beans, **'79** 283
Spanish Green Beans, **'80** 116
Spanish-Style Green Beans, **'84** 128
Special Green Beans, **'90** 268
Spicy Green Beans with Purple Onion, **'98** 286
Squash, Beans, and Tomatoes, **'83** 148
Stir-Fried Green Beans, **'85** 148; **'86** 305
Surprise, Green Bean, **'86** 9
Sweet-and-Sour Beans, **'87** 197
Sweet-and-Sour Green Beans, **'79** 184; **'81** 158; **'82** 90; **'91** 250
Sweet-and-Sour Green Beans and Carrots, **'83** 6
Sweet-and-Sour Snap Beans, **'89** 173
Tangy Green Beans, **'85** M142; **'89** 314, 332
Tarragon Dressing, Green Beans with Creamy, **'93** 191
Tarragon, Green Beans, **'98** 328
Tomatoes, Bean-Stuffed, **'84** 34
Tomatoes, Green Beans with, **'85** 137
Tomatoes, Green Beans with Cherry, **'86** 177
Tomato-Feta Green Beans, **'99** 59
Tomato Skillet, Bean-and-, **'90** 316
Vegetable-Herb Trio, **'83** 172
Vinaigrette, Green Beans, **'93** 120; **'94** 90; **'96** 177
Vinaigrette, Kentucky Wonder Green Beans, **'94** 158
Walnut Dressing, Green Beans with, **'94** 279
Zucchini, Green Beans with, **'84** 128
Hot Dogs, Beany, **'82** 190
Hummas, **'92** 155
Hummus, **'96** 158
Hummus, Low-Fat, **'99** 137
Hummus, Quick, **'95** 93
Kidney Bean Casserole, **'90** 136
Kidney Beans, Mexican, **'90** 205
Lasagna, Spinach-Bean, **'92** 96
Legumes, Marinated, **'90** 197
Lemon-Mint Beans, **'88** 22

Lima. *See also* BEANS/Salads, Soups.
  Baked Lima Beans, '96 217
  Bake, Lima-Bacon, '86 9
  Barbecued Lima Beans, '82 2
  Beans, Lima, '80 127
  Beef-and-Lima Bean Dinner, '84 292
  Canadian Bacon, Lima Beans with, '83 219;
    '84 245
  Casserole, Ham and Lima, '79 192
  Casserole, Lima Bean, '79 189; '83 313;
    '86 225; '87 284; '95 132
  Casserole, Lima Bean Garden, '83 218;
    '84 246
  Casserole, Spicy Lima Bean, '79 189
  Casserole, Swiss Lima Bean, '80 191
  Cheese and Limas in Onion Shells, '81 86
  Cheese Limas, Spanish, '86 225
  Chilly Lima Beans, '81 206
  Combo, Hot Lima and Tomato, '83 219
  Creole, Lima Beans, '80 191; '85 137
  Deluxe, Lima Beans, '79 289; '80 26
  Fresh Lima Beans and Scallions, '82 133
  Marinated Limas, '86 225
  Medley, Carrot-Lima-Squash, '80 123
  Minted Lima Beans, '98 86
  Rancho Lima Beans, '80 191
  Savory Lima Beans, '83 219; '84 246
  Savory Sauce, Lima Beans and Carrots with,
    '84 196
  Sour Cream, Lima Beans in, '79 189; '88 41
  Spanish-Style Lima Beans, '83 25
  Stew, Brunswick, '97 315
  Succotash, '98 177
  Succotash, Easy, '80 165
  Succotash, Quick, '97 302
  Succotash, Savory, '96 63
  Super Lima Beans, '79 189
  Supper, Sausage-Bean, '86 52
  Mogumbo, '93 32
  Nachos, Best-Ever, '79 91
  Nachos, Easy, '84 30
  Nachos, Make-Ahead, '80 M135
  Nachos, Southwestern, '96 170
  Pasta, Beans and, '99 35
  Pasta with Beans, '99 236
  Pie, Tortilla, '96 135
Pinto. *See also* BEANS/Salads, Soups.
  Beef-and-Bean Supper, '82 2
  Burgers, Pinto, '98 51
  Burritos, Hot Phyllo, '98 312
  Casserole, Beef, Bean, and Cornbread,
    '99 215
  Chalupa, Bean, '80 223
  Chalupas, Bean, '83 313
  Chalupas, Pork, '83 160
  Chili, Tex-Mex, '83 26
  Chili, Vegetable, '97 179
  Cow Camp Pinto Beans, '94 28
  Enchiladas, Spicy Bean, '88 18
  Frijoles Rancheros, '88 148
  Ham, Pinto Beans with, '97 210
  Lasagna, Texas, '98 52
  Mexican Pinto Beans, '93 69; '94 30
  Pie, Pinto Bean, '80 40
  Pinto Beans, '87 303
  Potatoes, Chili-Topped, '98 M289
  Ranch Beans, Laredo, '81 75
  Ranch Beans, Texas, '90 198
  Razorback Beans, '84 328
  Refried Beans, '79 185
  Rice, South Texas Beans and, '85 252
  Sandwiches, Bean Salad, '81 243
  Sausage, Hearty Pintos and, '88 296
  Souper Pintos, Texas, '98 51

  Southwestern Beans, '89 16
  Spicy-Hot Beans, '89 17
  Spicy Hot Pintos, '83 26
  Sweet-Hot Pinto Beans, '86 114
  Texas Beans, '97 139
  Trailride Pinto Beans, '85 154
  Pitas, Fajita, '99 239
  Pizza, Mexican, '99 119
  Pole Beans, Home-Cooked, '96 46
  Pork Chops, Mexican, '99 108
  Quesadillas, Easy, '98 M205
  Quesadilla Torta, '97 325
  Ragoût with Cilantro-Cornmeal Dumplings,
    Bean, '97 209
  Red Bean Salsa, '97 227
  Red Beans and Couscous, '99 22
  Red Beans and Rice, '80 58; '83 89; '84 37;
    '87 45; '90 27; '96 218
  Red Beans and Rice, Cajun, '83 26
  Red Beans and Rice, Delta, '98 146
  Red Beans and Rice, Easy, '90 220; '99 M219
  Red Beans and Rice, New Orleans, '97 235
  Refried Beans, '79 185; '96 160
  Refried Beans, Easy, '99 57
  Rice, Caribbean Beans and, '99 121
Salads
  Black Bean-and-Barley Salad, '94 174
  Black Bean-and-Cheese Salad, '92 217
  Black Bean Salad, '89 217; '97 196; '98 208
  Black Bean Salad, Caribbean Shrimp-and-,
    '93 143
  Cannellini Bean Salad, Tuna-and-, '86 143
  Chicken-Black Bean Salad, '99 124
  Chilled Bean Salad, '80 178
  Corn Salad, Confetti, '96 168
  Cucumber-Bean Salad, '83 81
  Dill-Icious Green Beans, '98 53
  Five-Bean Salad, Hot, '81 149
  Four-Bean Salad, '79 20; '84 82
  Full o' Beans Salad, '81 38
  Garbanzo Salad, '82 2
  Garbanzo Salad, Avocado-, '81 33
  Garden Medley Salad, '80 122
  Green Bean-and-Tomato Salad, '86 180
  Green Bean-Peanut Salad, '86 117
  Green Bean-Potato Salad, '83 80
  Green Bean-Red Potato Salad, '96 175
  Green Bean Salad, '87 90
  Green Bean Salad, Cold, '84 106
  Green Bean Salad, Crispy, '82 239
  Green Bean Salad, German, '92 169
  Green Bean Salad, Hot, '86 298; '87 176
  Green Bean Salad, Lettuce and, '80 79
  Green Bean Salad, Molded, '85 252
  Green Bean Salad, Paprika-, '86 191
  Green Bean Salad, Pickled, '82 239
  Green Bean Salad, Roasted Red Pepper-and-,
    '99 322
  Green Bean Salad, Speedy, '84 283
  Green Bean Salad, Tomato-and-, '97 162
  Green Beans-and-Cheese Salad, '91 159
  Green Bean Slaw, '95 108
  Green Beans Vinaigrette, '83 25
  Green Bean, Walnut, and Feta Salad, '96 273
  Hominy-Bean Salad, '88 266
  Hot German-Style Bean Salad, '91 314
  Kidney Bean-Salami Pasta Toss, '85 165
  Layered Salad, '86 35
  Lima Bean-Tomato Salad, '85 137
  Lima Salad), You Lima My Life (Paprika,
    '96 159
  Marinated Bean-and-Rice Salad, '87 152
  Marinated Bean-Pasta Salad, '94 167;
    '97 328

  Marinated Bean Salad, '85 137, 296; '89 314;
    '93 312; '94 167; '98 331
  Marinated Bean Salad, Crunchy, '84 197
  Marinated Combo Salad, '82 267
  Marinated Corn-Bean Salad, '87 9
  Meal in a Bowl, '96 138
  Mexican Dinner Salad, '98 330
  Mexican Salad, '94 202
  Mexican Tossed Salad, '81 280
  Mexicorn-Bean Salad, '96 184
  Mixed Bean Salad, '83 217
  Niçoise, Salad, '86 35
  Overnight Fiesta Salad, '83 80
  Pinto Salad, '86 169
  Pole Bean-Potato Salad, Hot, '79 74
  Pork-'n'-Bean Salad, '87 83
  Potato-Bean Salad, '82 301
  Quick Bean Salad, '89 128
  Red Bean Slaw, '79 247
  Rice-and-Bean Salad, '85 22
  Rice Salad, Beans-and-, '91 44
  Saucy Bean Salad, '84 18
  Sausage Salad, Bean-and-, '91 313
  Six-Bean Salad, Colorful, '87 82
  Southwest Salad, '81 113
  Spicy Bean Salad, '96 46
  Sprout Salad, Bean, '82 113
  Supreme Bean Salad, '91 202
  Sweet-and-Sour Bean Salad, '85 198; '86 147
  Sweet-and-Sour Beans with Sprouts, '86 32
  Sweet-and-Sour Vegetable Salad, '81 25
  White Bean Salad, Tuna-and-, '98 209
  White Bean-Tuna Salad, '98 208
  Salsa, Pork Chops with Black-and-White,
    '97 200
  Sandwiches, Falafel, '96 23
  Sauce, Picante-Bean, '96 220
  Sauce, Pork-and-Onions with Bean, '85 76
  Sausage-and-Bean Dinner, '95 108
  Sausage, Beans, and Rice, Texas, '84 296
  Sauté, Vegetarian, '95 69
  Shuck Beans, '81 216
Soups
  Bacon Soup, Bean and, '83 26
  Barley Soup, Hearty Bean-and-, '86 304
  Bean-Chicken Soup, '99 283
  "Bean Counter" Soup, '92 80
  Beanolla Soup, '94 248
  Bean Soup, '80 25
  Black Bean Soup, '88 30, 266; '89 28; '93 231;
    '98 291
  Black Bean Soup, Carolina, '92 139
  Black Bean Soup, Marge Clyde's, '96 29
  Cabbage-Bean Soup, '97 301
  Capitol Hill Bean Soup, '80 222
  Chili Bean Soup, '96 71
  Chill-Chaser Soup, '87 282
  Drunken Bean Soup, '87 283
  French Market Soup, '92 49; '94 317
  French Market Soup Mix, '94 317
  Green Bean, Mushroom, and Ham Chowder,
    Creamy '99 M336
  Green Bean Soup, Cream of, '84 111
  Guadalajara Soup, '88 30
  Ham-and-Bean Soup, '84 4
  Ham-and-Bean Soup, Spicy, '94 322
  Hominy Soup, Bean-and-, '95 23
  Italian Soup, Chunky, '99 20
  Leafy Bean Soup, '86 223
  Minestra, '97 246
  Minestrone, Cheesy, '99 17
  Minestrone Soup, '91 258
  Minestrone Soup Mix, '91 258
  Mix, Bean Soup, '99 283

BEANS, Soups
(continued)

Navy Bean Soup, '84 280; '96 19
Navy Bean Soup, Chunky, '83 291
Navy Bean Soup, Savory, '87 282
Pasta Soup, Bean and, '94 220
Polish Sausage Soup, '99 317
Quick Bean Soup, '99 97
Red Bean Soup with Walnuts, '96 243
Refried Bean Soup, '96 136
Sausage-Bean Chowder, '83 20
Sausage-Bean Soup, '85 88
Sausage-Bean Soup, Spicy, '83 229
Sausage, Spinach, and Bean Soup, '99 311
Taco Soup, '99 36
Three-Bean Soup, '89 17
Three-Bean Soup, Spicy, '91 28
Tortellini Soup, '98 68
Turkey Soup, Bean-and-, '93 319
Vegetable-Bean Soup, '83 317
White Bean Chowder with Sage Pesto, '97 22
White Bean Soup, '83 229; '90 201
White Bean Soup, Spicy, '94 225
Stew, Santa Fe Chicken, '97 193
Taco Bake, '97 326
Tacos, Chicken-and-Bean, '93 293
Tomatoes, Stuffed, '96 82
Tostadas, Party, '98 M33
White Bean Pot, '86 194
White Bean Puree, Pork Chops with, '96 226
White Bean Puree, Stuffed Chicken Breasts
   with, '98 270
White Bean Ragoût, '96 232
White Bean Relish, '93 229
White Beans, Caesar Salad with, '93 30
White Bean Spread, '93 30; '95 279; '96 122
BEEF. *See also* **BEEF, GROUND;**
   CASSEROLES/Meat; GRILLED/Beef;
   LIVER; SANDWICHES.
Appetizers, Meat-and-Cheese, '87 7
Asparagus, Beef with, '90 100
Ball, Cheese 'n' Beef, '83 230
Barbecue, Bourbon, '88 129
Barbecued Beef, Saucy, '82 156
Baria, '97 91
Bouilli, '80 58
Bourguignon, Beef, '79 104; '82 288
Bourguignon, Royal Beef, '80 106
Brisket
   Barbecued Beef Brisket, '83 11
   Barbecued Beef Brisket, Denton, Texas,
      '81 55
   Barbecued Beef Brisket with Sauce, '86 153
   Barbecued Brisket, '86 154; '88 218
   Beer, Beef Brisket in, '93 63
   Brisket, '96 228
   GG's Brisket, '97 251
   Home-Style Brisket, '87 303
   Marinated Brisket, '86 129
   Passover Brisket, '95 102
   Pot Roast, Beef Brisket, '93 20
   Roast, Peppery Brisket, '83 319
   Smoke-at-Home Brisket, '93 192
   Smoked Brisket, '89 168
   Smoked Brisket, Heavenly, '95 114
   Smoked Brisket, Texas-, '98 89
   Smoked Brisket with Barbecue Sauce, '85 144
Broccoli, Quick Beef and, '91 123
Broccoli with Chive Gravy, Beef and, '88 214
Burgoo, Five-Meat, '87 3
Burgoo, Kentucky, '88 235; '97 138
Burgoo, Old-Fashioned, '87 3

Burgundy, Beef, '82 259; '83 125, 281; '88 25;
   '95 69
Burgundy, Simple Beef, '90 234
Burgundy with Pearl Onions, Beef, '81 108
Burritos, Carne Guisada, '95 43
Burritos, Cheesy Beef, '85 193
Burritos, Meat-and-Bean, '81 194
Caldo de Rez (Mexican Beef Stew), '89 276
Carne Guisada, '93 68
Chalupa, Bean, '80 223
Chili
   Black Bean Chili Marsala, '95 16
   Bodacious Chili, '95 14
   Chuck Wagon Chili, '81 282; '82 57
   Chunky Chili, '82 M282; '86 3
   con Carne, Chili, '82 310; '83 30; '86 2
   Cowboy Chili, '86 2
   Firestarter Chili, '93 34
   Out West Chili, '95 15
   Red Chili, '93 108
   Red Chili, North Texas, '87 303
   South-of-the-Border Chili, '83 283; '91 283
   Texas Championship Chili, '81 54
   Verde, Chili, '95 14
   Zippy Chili, '87 110
Chimichangas (Fried Burritos), '85 244;
   '86 114
Chimichangas, Oven-Fried Beef, '92 124
Chinese-Style Beef, '87 50
Chipped Beef and Toast, Creamy, '79 180
Chipped Beef Spread in Puff Pastry, '98 M335
Corned Beef
   Birming "Ham," '94 229
   Brunch Bake, Corned Beef, '82 44
   Cabbage au Gratin, Corned Beef and, '83 16
   Cabbage, Corned Beef and, '83 104; '93 64;
      '96 328
   Cabbage, Corned Beef Squares and, '82 86
   Cabbage, Quick Corned Beef and, '79 54
   Dijon Glaze, Corned Beef with, '87 54
   Dinner, Corned Beef, '87 54
   Hash, Corned Beef, '95 262
   Hash, Red Flannel, '79 191
   Reuben Buns, '88 298
   Reuben Casserole, '90 240
   Reuben Cheesecake, '90 175
   Reuben Loaf, '95 338
   Reuben Meat Pie, '80 189
   Reuben Puffs, '98 231
   Reuben Sandwiches, '80 M201
   Reuben Sandwiches, Broiled, '81 240
   Reuben Sandwiches, Crispy, '85 299
   Reuben Sandwiches, Grilled, '81 206
   Reuben Sandwiches, Open-Face, '91 199
   Reuben Sandwich, Rolled, '99 219
   Reuben Soup, Cream of, '97 26
   Reubens, Oven-Grilled, '97 304
   Reubens, Party, '90 61
   Reuben Strudel, '98 28
   Reuben Turnovers, '94 253
   Roll, Corned Beef, '85 66
   Salad, Corned Beef, '80 104
   Salad, Corned Beef-Cauliflower, '83 16
   Salad, Corned Beef-Potato, '85 213
   Salad, Molded Corned Beef, '82 86
   Salad, Potato-Corned Beef, '81 36
   Salad, Vegetable-Corned Beef, '80 148
   Sandwich, Corned Beef and Cheese, '79 214
   Sandwiches, Barbecued Corned Beef, '83 130
   Sandwiches, Corned Beef, '83 291; '85 242;
      '92 23
   Sandwiches, Grilled Corned Beef, '87 54
   Sandwiches, Meal-in-One, '80 218
   Soup, Corned Beef, '83 16

Soup, French Onion-Beef, '87 54
Spread, Corned Beef, '87 196
Creamed Beef and Chicken-Topped Potatoes,
   '83 210
Creamed Chipped Beef, '92 42
Creamed Dried Beef with Artichokes, '85 81
Cubes in Wine Sauce, Beef, '79 264
Curried Beef Dinner, '83 4
Dip, Chipped Beef, '88 M8
Dip, Hot Cheesy Beef, '80 85
Élégante, Beef, '80 125
en Daube, Beef, '79 163
Fajitas, Beef, '88 233
Fajitas, Favorite, '86 114
Filet Mignon, Cajun Blackened, '95 85
Filet of Beef, Marinated Stuffed, '99 165
Fillet of Beef with Blue Cheese Sauce,
   Pan-Roasted, '94 320
Fillet of Beef with Red Pepper Butter, '96 32
Flautas, Rancho Ramillete, '96 M125
Ginger Beef with Bok Choy, '96 99
Goulash, Beef, '83 231
Goulash, Hungarian, '81 227; '92 227
Green Peppers, Beef and, '79 104
Grillades and Grits, '89 47; '93 62
Gumbo, Texas Ranch-Style, '82 226
Gumbo z'Herbes, '94 239
Hash, Beef, '95 24; '99 62
Hash with Cabbage Salad, Austrian, '95 262
Jerky, Beef, '80 269; '81 26
Kabobs
   Barbecued Steak Kabobs, '79 89
   Beef Kabobs, '85 110
   Beef on a Stick, '99 336
   Chile-Beef Kabobs, '94 251
   Deluxe, Beef Kabobs, '82 182
   Hot-and-Spicy Kabobs, '87 193
   Liver Kabobs, '80 185
   Marinated Beef Kabobs, '82 105; '85 159
   Marinated Beef Kabobs with Rice, '84 32
   Marinated Beef Kabobs with Vegetables,
      '99 292
   Marinated Beef on a Stick, '85 234
   Marinated Sirloin Kabobs, '82 162
   Marinated Steak Kabobs, '80 184
   Pineapple-Beef Kabobs, '83 212
   Saucy Beef Kabobs, '83 109
   Shrimp Kabobs, Steak-and-, '80 184
   Spicy Grilled Kabobs, '98 158
   Spirited Beef Kabobs, '87 142
   Steak Kabobs, '82 4; '93 95
   Steak on a Stick, '83 109
   Steak with Vegetables, Skewered, '81 124
   Teriyaki Beef Kabobs, '80 207
   Vegetable Kabobs, Beef-and-, '91 148
   Vegetables, Beef Kabobs with, '90 148
Liver
   Balsamic Vinegar, Beef Liver with, '98 130
   Creamy Liver and Noodle Dinner, '80 11
   Creole Liver, '96 236
   Creole Sauce, Liver in, '87 33
   French-Style Liver, '80 10
   Gravy, Liver and, '80 10
   Herbs, Liver with, '81 277
   Kabobs, Liver, '80 185
   Patties, Beef Liver, '81 277
   Saucy Liver, '81 277
   Sauté, Liver, '81 277
   Spanish-Style Liver, '80 11
   Stroganoff, Liver, '79 54
   Sweet-and-Sour Liver, '81 277
   Tasty Liver, '83 29
Mango-Beef and Rice, '88 138
Meatballs, Quick Processor, '87 111

Medaillons, Italian Beef, '87 305
Medaillons of Beef with Ancho Chile Sauce, '87 122
Medaillons of Beef with Horseradish Cream, '90 96
Mongolian Beef, '85 2, 75
Oriental, Beef and Cauliflower, '80 220
Oriental Beef and Snow Peas, '79 105
Oriental Beef with Pea Pods, '86 M328
Pastichio, '85 194
Pies, Carry-Along Beef, '80 224; '81 56
Pie, Shepherd's, '92 168
Pot Pie, Oriental Beef, '92 253
Pot Pies with Yorkshire Pudding Topping, Beef, '93 45

Ribs
Barbecued Beef Short Ribs, '83 178
Barbecued Short Ribs, '90 148
Braised Short Ribs, '98 44
Grilled Ribs, Sweet-and-Sour, '98 331
Hearty Beef Shortribs, '79 14
Supreme, Beef Shortribs, '79 14
Rice, Beef and Cauliflower over, '93 94

Roasts
à la Beer, Beef, '98 64
à la Mode, Beef, '98 122
Barbecue, Beef Roast, '79 159
Barbecued Beef Roast, '82 96; '83 103
Barbecue Roast, '98 245
Beer-and-Onion Sauce, Roast in, '80 124
Brisket Roast, Peppery, '83 319
Burgundy Gravy, Beef Roast with, '95 263
Burgundy Roast, Beef, '85 291
Chili Bean Roast, '87 268; '88 102; '89 68
Chuck Roast Barbecue, '96 71
Chuck Roast, Fruited, '91 289
Chuck Roast in Sauce, '91 47
Chuck Roast, Marinated, '80 59
Chuck Roast, Orange Marinated, '85 179
Chuck Roast, Slow Cooker, '98 32
Cola Roast, '81 298
Deli-Style Roast Beef, '93 15
Diablo, Beef, '79 17
Easy Banquet Roast, '99 291
Easy Beef Roast, '89 M65
Easy Oven Roast, '93 64
Eye-of-Round, Burgundy, '90 243
Eye of Round, Grilled Beef, '82 91
Eye of Round Roast, '99 60
Eye-of-Round Roast with Fruited Onion Marmalade, '96 323
Eye of Round Roast with Marmalade, '97 27
Eye-of-Round Roast with Rice Gravy, Seasoned, '89 118
Eye of Round, Slow Cooker Spicy Marinated, '99 291
Eye of Round, Spicy Marinated, '99 291
Eye Round Roast, Mexican, '89 190
French-Style Beef Roast, '89 32
Grillades and Grits, '88 126
Grilled Marinated Beef Roast, '93 141
Grilled Pepper Roast, '81 110
Herbed Roast, '91 288
Java Roast, '83 319
Marengo, Beef, '82 284; '83 14
Marinated Roast, '85 3
Marinated Roast Beef, '97 14
Marinated Roast, Dijon Wine-, '91 289
New York Strip Roast, Spicy, '93 131
Patio Steak, '87 141
Pot Pie, Beef Roast, '88 296
Pot Roast, All-Seasons, '86 89
Pot Roast and Gravy, '89 234
Pot Roast and Gravy, Country-Style, '94 308

Pot Roast, Autumn Gold, '83 7
Pot Roast, Barbecued, '79 17; '83 319
Pot Roast, Basic, '81 M208
Pot Roast, Bavarian-Style, '79 17
Pot Roast, Beef Brisket, '93 20
Pot Roast, Bloody Mary, '86 47
Pot Roast, Cardamom, '79 12
Pot Roast, Company, '79 162; '88 M14
Pot Roast, Country, '87 216
Pot Roast, Dillicious, '81 187
Pot Roast, Easy Oven, '86 52
Pot Roast, Favorite, '89 118
Pot Roast, Fruited, '90 211
Pot Roast, Gee's Italian, '96 18
Pot Roast, Hawaiian, '81 298
Pot Roast, Indian, '87 215
Pot Roast in Red Sauce, '87 215
Pot Roast in Sour Cream, '89 117
Pot Roast in White Wine Gravy, '81 299
Pot Roast, Italian, '81 299; '87 95
Pot Roast, Marinated, '85 21
Pot Roast Medley, Vegetable-, '83 319
Pot Roast, Mexican, '98 64
Pot Roast, Mushroom, '79 17; '96 250
Pot Roast of Beef with Vegetables, '98 65
Pot Roast, Old-Fashioned, '98 64
Pot Roast, Peppered, '87 215
Pot Roast, Perfect, '83 7
Pot Roast, Polynesian, '80 59
Pot Roast, Regal, '79 17
Pot Roast, Spicy Apple, '83 7
Pot Roast, Swedish, '80 59
Pot Roast, Sweet-and-Sour, '83 8; '99 291
Pot Roast with Dumplings, '98 245
Pot Roast with Gravy, '80 59
Pot Roast with Herbed Red Sauce, '88 29
Pot Roast with Sour Cream Gravy, '79 17
Pot Roast with Spaghetti, '80 59
Pot Roast with Vegetables, '80 59; '81 M208
Pot Roast with Vegetables, Marinated, '88 M52
Pot Roast, Zesty, '81 206
Pressure-Cooker Roast, '91 289
Prime Rib, Perfect, '96 197
Prime Rib, Smoked, '97 161
Pumpernickel Roast, '97 234
Rib-Eye Beef, Spicy, '84 259
Rib-Eye Roast, Marinated, '90 318
Rib Roast, Barbecued, '86 152
Rib Roast, Standing, '80 246; '84 187; '95 28
Rib Roast with Yorkshire Pudding, Standing, '80 252
Rump Roast, Easy, '93 217
Sandwiches, French Dip, '97 211
Sauerbraten, '98 278
Sauerbraten Beef, Marinated, '93 16
Sauerbraten, Quick, '80 139
Simple Roast, '81 298
Sirloin Roast, Canary, '89 117
Sirloin Tip Roast with Mustard Cream Sauce, Herbed, '88 61
Standing Rib Roast with Yorkshire Pudding, '98 86
Sunday Roast Beef, '99 327
Supreme, Roast Beef, '83 8
Vegetables, Company Beef and, '88 234
Wellington, Beef, '83 319
Rolls, Stuffed Sherried Beef, '79 105
Rolls, Wine-Sauced Beef-and-Barley, '87 269
Roll-Ups, Mexican Beef, '90 176
Roll-Ups, Savory Beef and Cheese, '96 235
Rollups with Rice, Royal Beef, '79 105
Roulades, Beef, '83 47; '85 234
Roulades, Roquefort Beef, '88 215

Salads. See also BEEF/Corned Beef.
Broccoli Salad, Beef-and-, '87 187
Cilantro, Beef Salad with, '97 202
Cucumber-Roast Beef Salad, '89 162
Fajita Salad, Beef, '91 70
Gingered Beef Salad, '88 61
Greek Steak Salad, '92 107
Niçoise, Beef Salad, '99 159
Peking Beef Salad, '88 60
Pepper Steak Salad Cups, '86 206
Roast Beef Salad, '80 223; '81 56; '90 318
Sirloin Salad, Grilled, '94 129
Steak Salad Niçoise, Grilled, '98 148
Steak Salad with Peach Salsa, '97 183
Stir-Fry Beef Salad, '96 129
Tangy Beef Salad, '87 M218
Vinaigrette Salad, Beef, '95 177
Western-Style Beef Salad, '93 321
Zesty Beef Salad, '79 56
Sandwich, Beef-and-Kraut, '91 167
Sandwiches, Beef and Pork Tenderloin, '80 175
Sandwiches, Beef, Bacon, and Blue Cheese, '96 23
Sandwiches, Beef Salad Pocket, '83 267
Sandwiches, Dilly Beef, '98 288
Sandwiches, Dried Beef Pita, '86 160
Sandwiches, Wake-Up, '84 58
Sandwich, Roast Beef Hero, '91 167
Sandwich, Saucy Beef Pocket, '80 92
Seasoning Blend, Meat, '88 29
Shredded Beef over Rice Noodles, '85 74
Sirloin Tips, Braised, '98 45
Soup, Beefy Lentil, '87 282
Soup, Beefy Vidalia Onion, '97 212
Soup, Chunky Italian, '99 20
Soup, Hearty Vegetable-Beef, '84 102
Soup, Steak, '99 260
Soup, Vegetable-Beef, '88 296
Spaghetti, Meaty, '82 19
Spicy Beef and Black Beans, '99 331
Spread, Hot Beef, '83 50; '84 M216

Steaks. See also BEEF/Kabobs, Salads.
American Steakhouse Beef, '93 15
Appetizers, Marinated Steak-and-Chestnut, '84 323
au Poivre, Steak, '88 232
Bacon Twirls, Beef-and-, '91 163
Bake, Asian Noodle Beef, '98 31
Barbecued Beef, '81 18
Barbecued Steak, Saucy Oven-, '83 10
Bean Sprouts, Beef and, '82 281; '83 42
Benedict for Two, Steaks, '85 295
Blackened 'n' Peppered Steak, '95 174
Blue Cheese Steaks, '84 171
Blue Cheese-Walnut Stuffed Fillets, '95 327
Blue, Elegant Beef, '97 97
Bourbon Steak, '90 148
Braised Steaks, Beer-, '87 96
Broiled Oriental Steaks, '83 110
Broiled Steaks, '96 172
Carne Guisada, '94 219
Carpetbagger Steak, '84 87
Chicken-Fried Steak, '92 214; '97 307
Chicken-Fried Steak and Cream Gravy, Threadgill's, '98 62
Chicken-Fried Steak Fingers with Creole Mustard Sauce, '99 142
Chicken-Fried Steak, Matt's, '97 25
Chicken-Fried Steaks, '88 110
Chuck Steak, Marinated Barbecued, '80 156
Coconut-Beef Stir-Fry, '97 18
Continental, Steak, '83 178
Country-Fried Steak and Cream Gravy, '84 8
Country-Fried Steak in Paradise, '98 62

BEEF, Steaks
(continued)

Country-Fried Steak, Mock, **'87** 163
Crêpes, Special Steak, **'91** 24
Curried Beef Steak, **'88** 60
Cutlets, Lemon-Flavored, **'79** 105
de Burgo, Steak, **'84** 117
Diane Flambé, Steak, **'79** 103
Diane, Steak, **'82** 275; **'92** 306
Dianne, Steak, **'83** 47
Fajita Casserole, **'97** 96
Fajita Crêpes, **'94** 116
Fajitas, **'84** 233
Fajitas, Java, **'96** 227
Fajitas, Plum Good, **'94** 115
Fajitas with Pico de Gallo, **'98** 87
Fiery Steak with Pimiento Cheese Salsa,
   '99 331
Filet Mignon, Marinated, **'84** 171
Filet Mignons with Shiitake Madeira Sauce,
   '95 265
Filet Mignon Tarragon, **'94** 46
Filet Mignon with Horseradish Gravy, **'92** 262
Filet Mignon with Mushroom Sauce, **'94** 250
Fillet, Acapulco, **'98** 174
Fillets au Vin, Beef, **'79** 137
Fillets with Black Bean Sauce, Spicy Beef,
   '97 184
Fillets with Horseradish Sauce and Curried
   Bananas, **'85** 230
Fillets with Orange Cream, Beef, **'97** 66
Fingers, Golden Steak, **'85** 110
Flank Steak and Mushrooms, **'87** 61
Flank Steak-and-Spinach Pinwheels, **'95** 56
Flank Steak, Bacon-Wrapped, **'85** 59
Flank Steak, Barbecued, **'79** 89
Flank Steak, Beer-Marinated, **'87** 35
Flank Steak, Cheese-Stuffed, **'98** 182
Flank Steak, Flavorful, **'96** 32
Flank Steak, Ginger-Marinated, **'89** 25
Flank Steak, Grilled, **'80** 152; **'89** 168; **'91** 80;
   '92 166
Flank Steak, Grilled Marinated, **'97** 182
Flank Steak, Herbed, **'92** 127
Flank Steak, Herb-Marinated, **'85** 275
Flank Steak in Mexican Marinade, **'98** 128
Flank Steak, Lemon-Lime, **'95** 55
Flank Steak, Marinated, **'82** 162; **'83** 35, 258;
   '85 86; **'88** 262; **'95** 237
Flank Steak, Oriental, **'83** 178
Flank Steak, Peppery Grilled, **'99** 157
Flank Steak Pinwheels, **'87** 141
Flank Steak, Red Wine-Marinated, **'95** 283
Flank Steak Sandwiches with Apple Barbecue
   Sauce, **'99** 173
Flank Steaks, Delicious Marinated, **'83** 110
Flank Steak Sukiyaki, **'88** 233
Flank Steak, Tangy, **'86** 184
Flank Steak, Tenderized, **'82** 105
Flank Steak Teriyaki, **'81** 110
Flank Steak, Texas, **'86** 185
Flank Steak, Tomato-Stuffed, **'97** 49
Flank Steak with Apple-Bourbon Sauce and
   Roasted Vegetables, Grilled, **'99** 142
Flank Steak with Black Bean-and-Corn Salsa,
   Grilled, **'94** 80
Flank Steak with Noodles, Stuffed, **'90** 101
Flank Steak with Sweet Peppers, Grilled,
   '90 138
French Quarter Steak, **'81** 17
Garlic-Herb Steaks, **'98** 169; **'99** 175
Garlic Steak, **'84** 8

Greek Pocket Steaks, **'81** 262
Grillades and Baked Cheese Grits, **'94** 240
Grilled Black Pepper Steak, **'86** 184
Grilled Steaks, **'96** 172
Grilled Steaks, Mesquite-, **'85** 154
Grilled Steak, Spicy, **'97** 211
Grilled Steaks with Green Chiles, **'85** 144
Grill, Steak Brunch, **'82** 44
Ham-and-Mushroom Sauce, Steak with,
   '83 109
Horseradish Steak, **'88** 39
Kabobs, Spicy Grilled, **'98** 158
Korean Steak, **'89** 190
Lemon-Butter Steak with Brandy Sauce, **'85** 78
lo Mein, Steak, **'90** 100
London Broil, Grilled, **'92** 59
London Broil, Marinated, **'87** 32
London Broil, Peppercorn, **'88** 60
London Broil, Teriyaki, **'92** 282
Marinated Bourbon Steak, **'95** 91
Marinated Steak, **'88** 233
Marinated Steak, Mexican, **'88** 148
Mesquite-Ginger Beef with Fresh Fruit Relish,
   '95 158
Mexican Steak, **'84** 76
Mushroom Sauce, Steak with, **'83** 212
Mush, Steak and Gravy with, **'81** 215
Oriental Beef, **'85** 20
Pan-Grilled Steaks, **'96** 172
Parmesan, Steak, **'93** 41
Parmigiana, Beef, **'84** 8; **'85** 234
Pasta and Sesame-Ginger Butter, Steak with,
   '99 142
Pepper-Beef Steak, **'85** 21
Pepper-Cheese Steaks, Mexican, **'97** 190
Pepper Cream, Steak in, **'94** 117
Pepper Steak, **'81** 273; **'85** 57; **'88** 113
Pepper Steak and Rice, **'81** 17
Pepper Steak, Chinese, **'82** 236
Pepper Steak, Cold, **'91** 208
Pepper Steak, Cracked, **'83** 109
Pepper Stir-Fry Steak, **'81** 240
Pies, Cornish Meat, **'84** 23
Pirate Steak, **'79** 89
Red Wine Marinade, Beef with, **'91** 46
Rib Eyes, Grecian Skillet, **'96** 234
Rib-Eyes, Italian, **'98** 215
Rib-Eye Steaks, Peppered, **'97** 46
Rib-Eye Steaks with Roquefort Glaze, **'89** 310
Ropa Vieja, **'93** 28; **'98** 20
Rouladen, **'99** 242
Round Steak, Braised, **'87** 35
Round Steak over Rice, Burgundy, **'90** M33
Round Steak, Parmesan, **'80** 106
Round Steak, Red Pepper, **'88** 214
Round Steak, Savory Stuffed, **'81** 18
Round Steak, Skillet, **'83** 29
Round Steak, Tangy, **'82** 284; **'83** 14
Round Steak, Tender Grilled, **'85** 3
Saltillo, Beef (Beef with Tomatillos), **'82** 219
Sandwich, Beef-and-Artichoke Open-Faced
   Italian, **'98** 22
Sandwiches, Steak, **'96** 136
Sandwiches, Steak Bagel, **'96** 249
Shrimp, Steak and, **'88** 123
Sirloin, Mustard Marinated, **'94** 41
Sirloin Steak, Secret, **'81** 110
Sirloin Steaks with Thyme Pesto, **'97** 182
Sirloin Supreme, Shrimp and, **'81** 131
Skillet Steak in Red Wine Sauce, **'85** 21
Skillet Steak 'n Potatoes, **'81** 18
Smothered Beef and Onions, **'85** 293
Smothered Steak, **'79** 212
Smothered Steak, Onion-, **'87** M189

Soup, Steak, **'99** 260
Stir-Fried Beef, **'84** 26
Stir-Fried Steak, Fast-and-Easy, **'87** 50
Stir-Fry, Beef-and-Carrot, **'98** 335
Stir-Fry, Beef-and-Vegetable, **'87** 22; **'99** 204
Stir-Fry Beef-and-Vegetables, **'84** 141
Stir-Fry, Italian Beef, **'99** 35
Stir-Fry, Pepper Steak, **'89** 191
Stir-Fry, Steak-and-Vegetable, **'84** 8
Stuffed Steak, Italian-, **'88** 232
Stuffed Steak Rolls, **'82** 135
Stuffed Steaks, Cheese-, **'81** 17
Sweet-and-Sour Marinated Steaks, **'83** 110
Swiss Steak Cheese Skillet, **'80** 106
Swiss Steak, Deviled, **'80** 107
Swiss Steak Monterey, **'99** 23
Swiss Steak, Oven, **'85** 234
Swiss Steak Surprise, **'81** 17
Swiss Steak with Vegetables, **'81** 273
Tabasco Steak, **'95** 207
Tartare, Steak, **'83** 78
Tenderloin Steak, Gingered, **'96** 154
Tenderloin Steaks with Balsamic Sauce, Beef,
   '98 319
Tenderloin Steaks with Peperonata, Beef,
   '97 291
Teriyaki Beef Broil, **'92** 56
Teriyaki, Marinated Steak, **'84** 50
Thai Beef, Spicy Lemon, **'97** 320
Thai Lemon Beef, **'97** 292
Tomatoes and Artichokes, Beef with, **'92** 282
Vegetables, Beef with Chinese, **'81** 211
Vegetables, Beef with Oriental, **'84** 140
Wellingtons, Individual Beef, **'82** 259
Zippy Steak and Gravy, **'90** 35
Stews
Beef Stew, **'86** 51; **'90** 230; **'96** 16
Brown Stew, **'85** 239
Brunswick Stew, Bama, **'87** 4
Brunswick Stew, Easy, **'92** 280
Brunswick Stew, Georgian, **'92** 35
Brunswick Stew, Virginia Ramsey's Favorite,
   '91 16
Burgundy Beef Stew, **'88** 234
Burgundy Stew with Drop Dumplings, **'83** 125
Celery Root Stew, Beef-and-, **'98** 292
Company Beef Stew, **'83** 85; **'97** 198
Dumplings, Beef Stew with, **'84** 3
Dumplings, Beef Stew with Parsley, **'81** 76;
   '82 13; **'85** M246
Emerald Isle Stew, **'95** 71
Hungarian Stew with Noodles, **'80** 263
Irish Stew, **'90** 64
Mexican Stew, **'82** 231
Mexican Stew Olé, **'86** 296
Onion Stew, Beef-and-, **'87** 18
Oven Beef Stew, **'79** 222; **'80** 64
Quick Beef Stew, **'92** 71
Red Chili Stew, **'95** 226
Spicy Beef Stew, **'86** 228
Sweet-and-Sour Beef and Vegetable Stew,
   '85 87
Texas Stew, **'97** 211
Vegetable-Beef Stew, **'94** 323
Vegetable-Beef Stew, Shortcut, **'89** 218
White Wine Stew, **'82** 228
Stir-Fried Beef and Vegetables, **'88** 301
Stir-Fry Beef and Asparagus, **'91** 124
Stir-Fry Beef and Broccoli, **'79** 47
Stir-Fry, Beef-and-Broccoli, **'91** 46
Stir-Fry Beef and Pea Pods, **'80** 19
Stir-Fry, Beef-and-Shrimp, **'93** 32
Stir-Fry, Beef and Snow Pea, **'82** 98
Stir-Fry Beef and Snow Peas, **'83** 22

Stir-Fry, Beef-and-Vegetable, '81 211
Stir-Fry Broccoli and Beef, '83 110
Stir-Fry, Chinese Beef, '83 151
Stir-Fry, Hungarian, '93 64
Stir-Fry, Indian, '92 126
Stir-Fry, Lime-Ginger Beef, '92 65
Stir-Fry, Mongolian Beef, '89 25
Stir-Fry, Peanutty Beef, '95 157
Stir-Fry, Teriyaki, '83 110
Stock, Beef, '95 17
Stock, Brown Meat, '90 31
Stroganoff, Beef, '79 163; '81 179; '91 134;
    '93 18
Stroganoff, Beef Burgundy, '85 31
Stroganoff, Light Beef, '86 36
Stroganoff, Liver, '79 54
Stroganoff, Quick Beef, '92 20; '99 327
Stroganoff Sandwiches, Steak, '85 110
Stroganoff, Sirloin, '81 297
Stroganoff with Parslied Noodles, Steak,
    '85 31
Tacos al Carbón, '86 19
Tacos al Carbón, Tailgate, '79 185
Tamales, '80 195
Tempting Twosome, '81 240
Tenderloin, Barbecued Beef, '94 26
Tenderloin Bundles, Peppered Beef, '89 272
Tenderloin, Chutneyed Beef, '94 270
Tenderloin Deluxe, Beef, '85 109
Tenderloin, Easy Beef, '90 268
Tenderloin, Elegant Beef, '88 244
Tenderloin for Two, Beef, '90 295
Tenderloin, Grilled, '91 166
Tenderloin, Herb Marinated, '83 109
Tenderloin, Lobster-Stuffed Beef, '87 248
Tenderloin, Marinated, '80 146
Tenderloin, Marinated Beef, '81 246; '85 302;
    '93 215
Tenderloin, Mustard Greens-Stuffed, '96 324
Tenderloin Picnic Sandwiches, Beef, '90 91
Tenderloin, Spicy Beef, '88 29
Tenderloin, Spicy Marinated Beef, '83 262
Tenderloin, Spinach-Stuffed, '89 311
Tenderloin, Stuffed, '86 323; '88 50
Tenderloin, Stuffed Tuscany, '99 269
Tenderloin with Five-Onion Sauce, Beef, '98 272
Tenderloin with Mushroom Sauce, Beef, '88 3
Tenderloin with Mushrooms, Beef, '87 115
Tenderloin with Mushroom-Sherry Sauce, Beef,
    '87 306
Tenderloin with Peppercorns, Beef, '91 246
Tips and Noodles, Beef, '86 293
Tips on Rice, Beef, '85 87
Tournedos Diables, '87 60
Tournedos Mouton, '83 262
Turnovers, Roast Beef, '88 273; '89 180
Tzimmes, Sweet Potato-Beef, '92 234
Tzimmes with Brisket, Mixed Fruit, '93 114
Vegetables in a Noodle Ring, Beef and, '85 285
Vegetables, Savory Beef and, '79 163
Wellington, Beef, '93 288
BEEF, GROUND
Acorn Squash, Stuffed, '83 15
Appetizer, Cheesy Mexicali, '82 108
Barbecue Cups, '79 129
Bean Bake, Cheesy Beef-and-, '82 89
Bean Medley, Baked, '80 100
Beans, Beefy, '82 59
Beans, Beefy Baked, '80 136; '84 149; '85 142
Beans, Rancho Lima, '80 191
Beans, Three-Meat Baked, '86 210
Brunswick Stew, Breeden Liles's, '91 14
Burger Boat, '95 70
Burgoo, Harry Young's, '87 3

Burritos, Chinese, '87 181
Burritos, Fiesta, '86 114
Cabbage-and-Beef Rolls, Easy, '88 49
Cabbage, Italian Stuffed, '84 294
Cabbage Rolls, '83 104
Cabbage Rolls, Beef Stuffed, '81 87; '82 7
Cabbage Rolls, Fried, '95 270
Cabbage Rolls, Hungarian, '94 47
Cabbage Rolls, Spicy, '84 2
Cabbage Rolls, Stuffed, '84 217
Cabbage Rollups, Beef-and-, '80 63
Cabbage, Stuffed, '84 282
Calzones, Easy, '99 133
Calzones, Ground Beef, '97 95
Casseroles. *See also* **BEEF,**
    GROUND/Lasagna.
Bean, and Cornbread Casserole, Beef, '99 215
Bean Bake, Hamburger-, '95 121
Biscuit Casserole, Beef-and-, '83 75
Cabbage Beef Bake, Zesty, '80 300
Cavatini, '94 214
Cheese, and Noodle Casserole, Beef, '99 58
Cheeseburger Casserole, '95 255
Cheesy Ground Beef Casserole, '79 44
Cheesy Mexican Casserole, '82 224
Chiles Rellenos Casserole, '98 48
Chili-Rice Casserole, '79 54
Cornbread Casserole, '81 91
Cornbread Skillet Casserole, '83 243; '84 101
County Fair Casserole, '79 130
Creamy Ground Beef Casserole, '81 142
Crusty Beef Casserole, '82 88
Easy Beef Casserole, '86 M58
El Dorado Casserole, '81 140
Enchilada Casserole, '87 287
Enchilada Casserole, Firecracker, '80 260
Enchilada Casserole, Sour Cream, '82 113
Enchiladas, American, '81 170
Enchiladas, Enticing, '99 57
Enchiladas, Quicker, '96 103
Enchiladas, Sour Cream, '87 37
Enchiladas, Weeknight, '93 63
Five-Layer Meal, '81 140
Grits Italiano, '92 43
Hamburger Casserole, '95 210
Hamburger-Corn Bake, '99 58
Italian Cabbage Casserole, '87 42
Italian Casserole, '80 81
Layered Beef Casserole, '82 M203
Layered Grecian Bake, '82 119
Macaroni Bake, Beef-, '94 255
Macaroni-Cheese-Beef Casserole, '95 125
Macaroni Combo, Beef-, '79 194
Matador Mania, '86 19
Mexican Casserole, '92 M22
Mexican Casserole, Cabin, '97 95
Mexican Casserole, Microwave, '90 M231
Mexi Casserole, '83 M87
Moussaka, '97 94
Moussaka Casserole, '79 179
Noodle Bake, Hamburger-, '81 140
Noodles Casserole, Beef-and-, '84 72
Pastitsio, '87 12; '88 11; '99 167
Pizza Bake, Upside-Down, '98 224
Pizza Casserole, '88 273; '89 181
Pizza Casserole, Microwave, '89 M248
Pizza Casserole, Quick, '83 266
Sausage Casserole, Ground Beef and, '80 260
Seashell-Provolone Casserole, '80 189
Shells, Spinach-Stuffed, '99 64
Sour Cream-Noodle Bake, '79 55
Spaghetti and Beef Casserole, '79 129
Spaghetti, Casserole, '95 132
Spinach and Beef Casserole, '79 192

Spinach-Beef-Macaroni Casserole, '83 313
Stroganoff Casserole, '98 48
Taco Bake, '97 326
Taco Beef-Noodle Bake, '81 141
Taco Casserole, '80 33
Taco Squares, Deep-Dish, '91 88
Tamale, Mozzarella, '95 70
Tortilla Bake, Texas, '94 285
Vegetable Casserole, Beefy, '79 248
Vegetable Chow Mein Casserole, Beef-and-,
    '83 313
Zucchini-Beef Bake, '86 146
Chiles Rellenos Egg Rolls, '86 296
Chili
Basic Chili, '82 M11; '93 326
Basic Chili Embellished, '93 327
Basic Chili Goes Southwest, '93 326
Before-and-After Burner, Roy's, '89 316
Biscuit Bowl, Chili in a, '98 224
Cheese-Topped Chili, '82 M11
Cheesy Chili, '82 310
Chili, '87 17; '89 143; '93 89; '98 95
Chilly Night Chili, '99 317
Choo-Choo Chili, '89 316
Cincinnati Chili, '96 18
Company Chili, '82 311; '83 30
con Carne, Beef and Sausage Chili, '83 284
con Carne, Chili, '84 72
con Carne, Favorite Chili, '86 293
con Carne, Quick-and-Easy Chili, '86 2
Dip, Chili, '89 47
Double-Meat Chili, '79 269; '80 12
Easy Chili, '82 310; '83 30
Easy Texas Chili, '90 201
Five-Ingredient Chili, '95 212
Friday Night Chili, '86 228
Greek Chili, '95 16
Hominy Bake, Chili, '81 282; '82 58
Hot Texas Chili, '80 222; '81 77
Hotto Lotto Chili, '89 316
I-Cious, Chili-, '89 315
"In-the-Red" Chili over "Rolling-in-Dough"
    Biscuits, '92 80
Kielbasa Chili, Hearty, '91 28
Lolly's Pop Chili, '89 316
Lunchtime Chili, '81 230
Meaty Chili, '81 282; '82 58
Meaty Chili with Beans, '85 250
Mexican Chili, '89 18
Noodles, Chili with, '81 282; '82 57
Now, Thatsa Chili, '95 16
Pastry Cups, Chili in, '90 68
Potato Chili, Savory, '83 284
Potatoes, Chili-Topped, '83 3; '98 M289
Quick-and-Easy Chili, '92 20
Quick and Simple Chili, '81 282; '82 58
Quick Chili, '83 283
Ranch Chili and Beans, '79 270; '80 11
Rice, Chili with, '82 M11
Roundup Chili, '79 269; '80 12
Sauce, Chili Meat, '83 4
Sausage-Beef Chili, '86 232
Sausage Chili, Beefy, '82 M11
Simple Chili, '79 269; '80 11
Speedy Chili, '92 66
Spiced Chili, Hot, '83 214
Spicy Chili, Old-Fashioned, '79 269; '80 11
Supper, Hot Chili, '99 279
Texas-Style Chili, '82 311; '83 30
Tex-Mex Chili, '83 26
Tree-Hunt Chili, '87 292
Chimichangas, Baked Spicy Beef, '97 319
Chimichangas, Traditional Spicy Beef, '97 319
Cornbread, Beefy Jalapeño, '82 142

BEEF, GROUND
(continued)

Cornbread, Cheesy Beef, **'81** 242
Cornbread Tamale Bake, **'79** 163
Crêpes, Italian, **'90** 157
Crêpes, Sherried Beef, **'85** M29
Crêpes, Southwestern Cornbread, **'98** 42
Curried Beef and Rice, **'88** 164
Dinner, Beef-and-Garbanzo, **'84** 31
Dinner, Beef-and-Lima Bean, **'84** 292
Dinner, Beef-Cabbage, **'81** 179
Dinner, Beefy Sausage, **'80** M9
Dinner, Black-Eyed Pea Skillet, **'86** 6
Dinner, Fiesta, **'85** 110
Dinner, Ground Beef Skillet, **'82** 60
Dinner, Mexican Beef-and-Rice, **'88** 199
Dip, Beef-and-Spinach, **'99** 65
Dip, Hot Chile-Beef, **'83** 218
Dip, Meaty Cheese, **'82** 59; **'92** 160
Dip, Quick Nacho, **'90** 168
Dip, Tostada, **'84** 206
Dumplings, Steamed Sesame, **'97** 208
Eggplant, Baked Stuffed, **'81** 133
Eggplant, Beefy Stuffed, **'81** 204
Eggplant, Cheesy Stuffed, **'79** 188
Empanadas, **'92** 156
Enchiladas. *See also* **BEEF/Casseroles.**
  Hot and Saucy Enchiladas, **'81** 141; **'82** 6
  Skillet Enchiladas, **'82** 89
Fiesta, **'87** 180
Filet Mignon, Mock, **'80** 81
Filet Mignon Patties, Mock, **'82** M68
Fillets, Poor Boy, **'82** 106
Filling, Beef, **'80** 81
Filling, Blue-Corn Crêpes with Beef, **'97** 197
Flips, Pea, **'80** 7
Green Peppers, Beefy Stuffed, **'81** 86
Green Peppers, Mexican, **'80** 65
Gumbo, Carolina, **'95** 70
Gumbo, Ground Beef, **'87** 283
Gumbo Joes, **'88** 158
Hamburgers
  Apple-Bacon Burgers, **'99** 202
  Apple Burgers, **'86** 137
  au Poivre Blanc, Burgers, **'87** 186
  Bacon Burgers, Cheesy, **'81** 29
  Barbecued Burgers, **'82** 168; **'89** 164
  Beefburger on Buns, **'84** 71
  Beerburgers, **'79** 129
  Blue Cheese Burgers, **'89** M66
  Brie-Mushroom Burgers, **'95** 128
  Burgundy Burgers, **'80** 156
  Caramelized Onions, Beef Burgers with, **'98** 143
  Cheeseburger Biscuits, **'79** 194
  Cheeseburger Loaves, **'86** 19
  Cheese Burgers, Beef-and-, **'96** 139
  Cheeseburgers, Fried Green Tomato, **'94** 138
  Cheeseburgers, Inside Out, **'99** 202
  Cheeseburgers, Mini-, **'97** 203
  Cheesy Beef Burgers, **'83** 217
  Chili Burgers, Open-Face, **'81** 24; **'82** 31; **'83** 33
  Cocktail Burgers, Saucy, **'83** 217
  Cracked Pepper Patties, **'89** M131
  Deluxe, Burgers, **'84** 125
  Favorite Burgers, **'89** 165
  Glorified Hamburgers, **'81** 73
  Grilled Hamburgers, **'93** 198
  Grilled Hamburgers, Flavorful, **'81** 110
  Grilled Hamburgers, Spicy, **'98** 158
  Hawaiian, Beefburgers, **'86** 137

Jalapeño-Stuffed Burgers with Roasted Bell Pepper Ketchup, **'97** 318
Mexicali Beef Patties, **'86** 137
Mexicali, Hamburgers, **'93** 217
Mushroom Burgers, **'89** 164
Nutty Burgers, **'87** 185
Old-Fashioned Hamburgers, **'79** 149
Oven Burgers, **'83** 130
Party Burgers, **'83** 164; **'84** 39
Patties, Deviled-Beef, **'87** 22
Patties, Hamburger, **'82** M172
Pineapple Burgers, **'82** 169
Pizza Burger, **'87** 185
Pizza Burgers, **'80** M201; **'81** 73
Pizza Burgers, All-American, **'92** 148
Pizza Burgers, Easy, **'82** 190
Sauce, Hamburgers with Tomato, **'81** 73
Saucy Burgers, **'80** 93
Saucy Hamburgers, Quick, **'82** 60
Sausage Burgers, **'83** 212
Seasoned Burgers, **'85** 158
Seasoned Hamburgers, **'84** 230
Seasoned Stuffed Burgers, **'86** 136
Sour Cream Burgers, Grilled, **'87** 287
Spirals, Burger, **'94** 139
Sprouts, Burgers with, **'89** 164
Steak, Hamburger, **'99** 45
Steak-House Burgers, **'87** 186
Steaks, Company Hamburger, **'82** 169
Steaks with Mustard Sauce, Hamburger, **'84** 230
Stuffed Burgers, **'85** 159
Stuffed Hamburger Steaks, Mushroom-, **'99** 202
Stuffed Southwestern-Style Burgers, **'99** 201
Superburgers, **'79** 89
Super Hamburgers, **'79** 129
Super Supper Burgers, **'82** 110
Surprise Burgers, **'82** 169
Sweet-and-Sour Burgers, **'90** 128
Taco Burgers, **'98** 224
Tahiti Burgers, **'85** 179
Teriyaki Burgers, **'81** 72
Teriyaki, Hamburgers, **'89** 309; **'99** 332
Teriyaki Hamburgers, **'94** 138
Tortilla Burgers, **'94** 138
Triple-Layer Burgers, **'89** 165
Vegetable Burgers, **'89** 164
Vegetable Burgers, Beef-and-, **'84** 125
Vegetable Burgers, Beefy, **'98** 143
Venison Burgers, **'87** 304
Kheema, Indian, **'81** 226
Kielbasa, **'92** 242
Lasagna
  Beefy Lasagna, **'80** 81
  Bun, Lasagna in a, **'90** 176
  Cheesy Lasagna, **'82** 224; **'88** 299
  Easy Lasagna, **'92** M197; **'93** M24
  Lasagna, **'82** 119; **'83** M6; **'98** 95
  Light Lasagna, **'95** 212
  Mexican Lasagna, **'89** 63
  Microwave Lasagna, **'96** M225
  Noodles Lasagna, Lots of, **'91** M127
  Quick Lasagna, **'84** 220
  Quick 'n Easy Lasagna, **'80** M10
  Simple Lasagna, **'81** 188
  South-of-the-Border Lasagna, **'84** 31
  Spinach Lasagna, Cheesy, **'83** 204
  Supreme, Lasagna, **'92** 198; **'93** 24
  Two, Lasagna for, **'81** 91
  Vintage Lasagna, **'79** 194
  White Lasagna, Gourmet, **'96** 225
Log, Stuffed Beef, **'79** 71
Macaroni, Ground Beef and, **'85** 218

Macaroni, Skillet Beef and, **'82** 130
Madras, Beef, **'87** 284
Manicotti, Quick, **'79** 6
Manicotti, Saucy Stuffed, **'83** 288
Manicotti, Special, **'88** 50
Meatballs
  Bacon-Wrapped Meatballs, **'79** 81
  Barbecued Meatballs, Oven, **'82** 233
  Brandied Meatballs, **'83** 78
  Burgundy-Bacon Meatballs, **'80** 283
  Chafing Dish Meatballs, **'81** 260
  Charleston Press Club Meatballs, **'93** 129
  Chestnut Meatballs, **'79** 110
  Chinese Meatballs, **'83** 116; **'87** 194
  Cocktail Meatballs, **'79** 63, 207
  Creole, Meatball-Okra, **'83** 156
  Creole, Meatballs, **'82** 233
  Español, Meatballs, **'82** 110
  Flavorful Meatballs, **'84** 206
  Golden Nugget Meatballs, **'82** 233
  Gravy, Meatballs in, **'79** 136
  Hawaiian Meatballs, **'85** 86
  Hawaiian Meatballs, Tangy, **'79** 129
  Heidelberg, Beef Balls, **'83** 164; **'84** 39
  Horseradish Dressing, Meatballs and Vegetables with, **'91** 32
  Kabobs, Meatball, **'95** 192
  Meatballs, **'89** 237
  Paprikash with Rice, Meatballs, **'85** 31
  Pineapple and Peppers, Meatballs with, **'90** 145
  Pizza Meatballs, **'85** 86
  Polynesian Meatballs, **'80** 207
  Red Delicious Meatballs, **'85** 85
  Royal Meatballs, **'87** 268; **'88** 102; **'89** 67
  Sandwiches, Open-Faced Meatball, **'99** 239
  Sandwich, Giant Meatball, **'92** 196
  Saucy Meatballs, **'85** 68; **'90** 122
  Saucy Party Meatballs, **'80** 149
  Sauerbraten Meatballs, **'85** 85
  Spaghetti-and-Herb Meatballs, **'84** 75
  Spaghetti with Meatballs, **'81** 38
  Spiced Meatballs, **'79** 284
  Spicy Meatballs and Sausage, **'79** 163
  Stew, Meatball, **'79** 198
  Stroganoff, Meatball, **'81** 297
  Stroganoff, Mushroom-Meatball, **'85** 85
  Swedish Meatballs, **'80** 80; **'86** 256
  Sweet-and-Sour Meatballs, **'82** 233; **'86** 240; **'99** 325
  Sweet-and-Sour Party Meatballs, **'79** 233
  Tamale Balls, Tangy, **'89** 60
  Tamale Meatballs, **'80** 194
  Zesty Meatballs, **'80** 250
Meat Loaf
  All-American Meat Loaf, **'92** 341; **'93** 46
  Barbecued Beef Loaves, Individual, **'95** 242
  Barbecued Meat Loaf, **'80** 60; **'81** 275; **'84** 50; **'87** 216
  Basic Meat Loaf, **'88** M14
  Blue Cheese Meat Loaf Roll, **'93** 247
  Cheeseburger Loaf, **'81** 236, 276
  Cheesy Meat Roll, **'82** 136
  Chili Meat Loaf, **'81** 275
  Corny Meat Loaf, **'86** 68
  Crunchy Meat Loaf Oriental, **'79** 212
  Curried Meat Loaf, **'86** 43
  Easy Meat Loaf, **'88** M214; **'95** 125; **'97** 24
  Elegant Meat Loaf, **'89** 243
  Family-Style Meat Loaf, **'93** 18
  Fennel Meat Loaf, **'88** 46
  German Meat Loaf, **'87** 216
  Glazed Beef Loaf, **'86** 19
  Hurry-Up Meat Loaf, **'82** 21

Hurry-Up Meat Loaves, '88 15
Individual Meat Loaves, '81 279; '82 24;
　'83 154; '92 229
Italian Meat Loaf, '79 187
Meat Loaf, '81 170; '89 109
Mexicali Meat Loaf, '81 275
Mexican Meat Loaf, '87 217
Miniature Meat Loaves, '85 24
Mini-Teriyaki Meat Loaf, '90 69
Moist-and-Saucy Meat Loaf, '99 270
Mozzarella-Layered Meat Loaf, '79 71
My-Ami's Meat Loaf, '94 229
Oriental Meat Loaf, '81 M122; '83 M194
Parsleyed Meat Loaf, '83 35
Parsley Meat Loaf, '87 22
Pineapple Loaves, Individual, '81 M121
Pizza Meat Loaf, Cheesy, '81 M121
Roll, Meat Loaf, '79 129
Saucy Meat Loaves, '79 186
Savory Meat Loaf, '87 216
Southwestern Meat Loaf, '93 248
Southwestern Roll with Cilantro Hollandaise
　Sauce, '99 16
Special Meat Loaf, '89 70
Spicy Meat Loaf, '79 71
Spinach Meat Loaf, '96 131
Sprout Meat Loaf, '85 51
Stuffed Beef Log, '79 71
Stuffed Meat Loaf, '79 187
Stuffed Meat Loaf, Rolled, '80 80
Sun-Dried Tomatoes and Herbs, Meat Loaf
　with, '92 192
Supreme, Meat Loaf, '92 33
Swedish Meat Loaf, '81 M121
Tasty Meat Loaf, '83 213
Teriyaki Loaves, Mini, '98 224
Teriyaki Meat Loaf, '98 224
Tex-Mex Meat Loaf for Two, '90 234
Tomato Sauce, Meat Loaf with Chunky,
　'95 264
Triple Meat Loaf, '79 186
Vegetable Loaf, Beef-, '79 164
Vegetable Meat Loaf, '85 M29
Wellington, Meat Loaf, '79 186; '87 284
Wrap, Meat Loaf in a, '89 122
Mexican Dinner, Quick, '98 224
Mexican Stack-Up, '95 69
Mexicorn Main Dish, '96 189
Mix, Ground Beef, '84 71
Mix, Ground Meat, '89 143
Moussaka, '87 166; '90 68
Moussaka, Corn, '87 190
Muffins, Barbecue, '96 246
Mushrooms, Stuffed, '83 13
Noodle Dinner, Beefy, '81 179
Noodles, Easy Beef and, '83 288
Omelet, Beefy Vegetable, '83 188
Omelet con Carne, Tex-Mex, '81 209
Patties, Foo Yong, '80 223
Peppers, Beefed-Up, '82 186
Peppers, Beef-Stuffed, '84 154; '85 146;
　'91 M127
Peppers for Two, Stuffed, '80 84
Peppers, Stuffed, '81 239; '83 66
Peppers Stuffed with Beef, '84 72
Picadillo II, '93 72
Picadillo (Spanish Hash), '91 87
Picadillo (Spicy Beef over Rice), '80 193;
　'84 118; '85 57
Picadillo Tarts, '91 279
Pies
　Broccoli-Beef Pie, '83 196
　Burrito Pie, Mexican, '87 287
　Cheese-Beef Pie, '85 33

Cheeseburger Pie, '89 121
Continental Meat Pie, '95 256; '96 75
Corn Burger Pie, '83 156
Country Pie, '83 155
Enchilada Pie, '83 155
Fried Beef Pies, '96 108
Hamburger Pie, '81 92; '84 13
Mexicali Meat Pie, '81 194
Natchitoches Meat Pies, '84 21; '91 241
Old-Fashioned Meat Pie, '82 110
Potato Pie, Meat-and-, '84 23
Shepherd Pie, '83 116
Sombrero Pie, '81 140
Spaghetti Pie, '81 32
Spaghetti Pie, Weeknight, '95 312
Taco Pie, '88 256
Taco Pie, Crescent, '80 80
Taco Pie, Double-Crust, '88 272; '89 180
Taco Pies, Individual, '82 M282
Vegetable-Beef Pies, '80 286
Pintos, Texas Souper, '98 51
Pitas, Curried Beef, '85 220
Pizza, Best Ever Homemade, '80 233
Pizza-Burger Snacks, '84 30
Pizza, Cheeseburger, '97 318
Pizza Cups, '81 215
Pizza, Double Cheesy Beef-and-Sausage, '86 77
Pizza Horns, '89 214
Pizza, Quick Hamburger, '85 243
Pizzas, Five-Ring, '96 180
Pizza Supreme, '81 214
Pizza, Taco, '98 176
Pizza, Tostada, '81 16; '82 13
Pizza, Upside-Down, '91 185
Potatoes, Taco-Topped, '93 M18
Quiche, Green Chile, '83 31
Ravioli, Homemade, '87 230
Rice, Arabic, '94 200
Rice, Picadillo, '98 237
Rice, Spanish, '81 51
Rice, Spiced Beef and, '84 285
Rice, Spicy Beef and, '83 231
Rolls, Italian Meat, '86 137
Rolls, Spicy Beef, '85 110
Roulades, Beef, '80 80
Salad Cups, Taco, '85 M29
Salad, Dude Ranch, '80 15
Salad in a Shell, Mexican, '86 4
Salad, Mexican, '81 36
Salad, Mexican Chef, '85 84; '92 64
Salad, Mexican Dinner, '98 330
Salad, Mexican Olive, '85 84
Salad, Mexi-Pea, '81 7
Salad, Party Taco, '97 19
Salad, Spicy Chili, '86 71
Salad, Spicy Taco, '87 287
Salad Supper, Mexican, '82 9; '83 68
Salad, Taco, '79 56; '83 145; '84 221; '85 84;
　'90 20
Salisbury Steak Deluxe, '81 170
Sandwiches, Barbecued Beef, '81 25; '82 31;
　'83 34
Sandwiches, Bavarian Pita, '83 31
Sandwiches, Beef-Eater, '86 72
Sandwiches, Hearty Pocket, '80 93
Sandwiches, Hot Pita, '83 217; '87 M6
Sandwiches, Open-Face Pizza, '82 3
Sauce, Italian, '90 67
Sauce, Italian Meat, '83 193
Sauce, Szechuan Noodles with Spicy Beef,
　'97 95
Sausage, Summer, '99 85
Shells, Cheesy Beef-Stuffed, '83 217
Shells, Mexican Stuffed, '91 87

Skillet, Vegetable-Beef, '86 172
Slice, French Beef, '79 125
Sloppy Joe Cups, '98 204
Sloppy Joe Dogs, '85 192
Sloppy Joe Pocket Sandwiches, '81 200
Sloppy Joes, '81 279; '82 24; '83 153; '89 143;
　'91 172
Sloppy Joes, Easy, '82 31, 278; '83 34
Sloppy Joes, Pocket, '85 M328
Sloppy Joe Squares, '97 95
Sloppy Joes, Simple, '82 130
Sloppy Joes, Super, '83 130
Snacks, Beefy Party, '80 249
Soup, Beef-and-Barley Vegetable, '89 31
Soup, Beefy Black-Eyed, '85 6
Soup, Beefy Vegetable, '79 113; '84 M38
Soup, Chunky Italian, '99 20
Soup, Hamburger, '80 263
Soup, Mexican Meatball, '98 315
Soup, Quick Beefy Vegetable, '80 25
Soup, Quick Italian Beef and Vegetable, '96 235
Soup, Spicy Vegetable-Beef, '88 11
Soup, Taco, '94 225; '99 36
Soup, Tamale, '95 213
Soup, Vegetable-Beef, '99 219
Soup, Vegetable-Burger, '82 6
Spaghetti. *See also* **BEEF, GROUND/**
　Casseroles, Meatballs, Pies.
All-in-One Spaghetti, '98 295
Black-Eyed Pea Spaghetti, '81 7
Easy Spaghetti, '83 M317; '84 72; '92 66
Italian Spaghetti, Real, '81 233
Marzetti's Spaghetti, '99 85
Meaty Spaghetti, '82 19
Mushrooms, Spicy Spaghetti with, '85 2
Pepperoni Spaghetti, Quick, '88 40
Pizzazz, Spaghetti with, '80 85
Sauce, Beer Spaghetti, '85 13
Sauce for 4, Easy Spaghetti Meat, '92 244
Sauce for 25, Easy Spaghetti Meat, '92 245
Sauce, Herbed Spaghetti, '85 13
Sauce, Quick Spaghetti and Meat, '94 64
Sauce, Thick Spaghetti, '84 118
Thick-and-Spicy Spaghetti, '83 287
Zucchini Spaghetti, '83 160
Squash, Beef-Stuffed, '83 134
Steak, Matt's Chicken-Fried, '97 25
Steak, Spanish, '80 80
Stew, Campeche Bay Rib-Tickling, '89 317
Stew, Hamburger Oven, '84 4
Stew, Mixed Vegetable, '84 13
Stew, Quick Beef, '86 302
Sticks, Beef, '93 331
Stroganoff, Easy Hamburger, '79 208
Stroganoff, Ground Beef, '84 71
Stroganoff, Hamburger, '82 108, 110
Stroganoff, Quickie, '81 200
Stromboli, '87 283
Supper, Beef-and-Bean, '82 2
Supper, Beef-and-Eggplant, '84 291
Supper, Oriental Beef, '79 192
Supper, Quick Skillet, '84 69
Supreme, Beef, '83 196
Taco Joes, '91 167
Tacoritos, '90 133
Taco Rolls, Chinese, '95 339
Tacos, '80 196
Tacos, Basic, '83 199
Tacos, Corn Chip, '81 67
Tacos, Easy, '96 159
Tacos, Jiffy, '83 M318
Tacos, Microwave, '88 M213
Tacos, Soft Beef, '91 88
Taco Tassies, '95 339

BEEF, GROUND
(continued)

Texas Straw Hat, **'85** 293
Torta Mexican Style, **'89** 122
Tostada Compuestas, **'81** 194
Tostadas, Crispy, **'83** 2
Tostadas, Super, **'83** 199
Turnovers, Meat, **'86** 326
Wontons, Tex-Mex, **'87** 196
Zucchini, Beef-Stuffed, **'86** M139

BEETS
Apples, Beets and, **'80** 137; **'88** 155
Aspic, Beet, **'90** 123
Borscht, Crawfish, **'92** 84
Borscht, Ruby Red, **'83** 176
Cake, Chocolate Beet, **'80** 40
Cake with Almond Topping, Beet, **'86** 200
Chilled Beets and Cauliflower, **'80** 137
Chips, Beet, **'97** 229
Creamy Beets, **'80** 136
Deviled Beets, **'84** 217; **'86** 252
Eggs, Marbleized Garlic-Cheese-Stuffed, **'96** 91
Fritters, Beet, **'96** 36
Fruited Beets, **'97** 28
Glazed Beets, Ginger-Marmalade, **'93** 35
Glazed Beets, Orange-, **'81** 167; **'85** 289; **'86** 187; **'99** 24
Glazed Beets, Strawberry-, **'83** 234
Glazed Fresh Beets, **'81** 167
Greens, Beets 'n', **'95** 179
Harvard Beets, **'83** M195
Ivy League Beets, **'84** 122
Marinated Beets, Green Beans, and Carrots, **'88** 162
Orange Beets, **'91** 219
Orange Beets, Spicy, **'94** 280
Orange-Ginger Beets, **'80** 137
Pickled Beets, **'79** 276; **'81** 216; **'87** 163; **'97** 229
Pickled Beets, Easy, **'80** 137
Pickles, Beet, **'81** 210
Pineapple, Beets with, **'79** 249; **'82** 204
Relish, Beet, **'84** 179
Relish, Colorful Beet, **'85** 136
Rice Ring with Beets, **'79** 225
Salad, Apple-Beet, **'91** 237
Salad, Beet, Apple, and Walnut, **'98** 269
Salad, Beet-Nut, **'79** 74
Salad, Marinated Beet, **'83** 216
Salad Mold, Beet, **'82** 267
Salad, Orange-and-Beet, **'88** 43
Salad, Pickled Beet, **'83** 234
Salad, Red-and-Green, **'90** 55
Salad, Tangy Beet, **'86** 199
Salad with Orange Vinaigrette, Roasted
   Beet-and-Sugared Walnut, **'97** 229
Slaw, "Think Pink," **'94** 247
Soup, Potato-Beet, **'88** 156
Sour Cream Dressing, Beets with, **'88** M295
Spiced Beets, **'79** 22
Spread, Beet-and-Pecan Sandwich, **'99** 274
Stuffed Beets, **'88** 155
Stuffed Beets, Blue Cheese-, **'88** 211
Stuffed Beets, Potato-, **'83** 234
Sweet-and-Sour Beets, **'81** 167; **'82** 22; **'89** 314
Vinaigrette, Beet, **'97** 229
BEVERAGES. *See also* **COFFEE,**
   EGGNOG, TEA.
Alcoholic
Almond-Flavored Liqueur, **'81** 287
Amaretto, **'90** 272
Amaretto Breeze, **'83** 172
Amaretto Slush, **'90** 322; **'95** 90

Apricot Brandy Slush, **'91** 278
Apricot Slush, **'93** 205
Aztec Gold, **'99** 160
Banana Flip, **'83** 303
Banana Kabana, **'86** 316
Bay Bloodies, **'93** 268
Bellinis, **'88** 77
Bellinis, Apricot, **'99** 145
Bellinis, Frosted, **'97** 122
Bloody Mary, **'80** 221
Bloody Mary Bowl, **'99** 268
Bloody Mary, Easy, **'84** 115
Bloody Marys, **'79** 33, 38; **'80** 51
Bloody Marys, Eye-Opener, **'82** 48
Bloody Marys, Overnight, **'81** 270
Bloody Marys, Pitcher, **'81** 198
Bloody Marys, Spicy, **'87** 173; **'90** 207
Blueberry Cordial, **'95** 142
Blue Woo-Woo, **'94** 226
Bole, **'97** 245
Bourbon Blizzard, **'92** 287
Bourbon, Hot Buttered, **'97** 17
Bourbon Slush, **'84** 58
Bourbon Slush, Summertime, **'81** 101
Brandy Alexander, **'92** 283
Brandy Cream, **'84** 312
Brandy Slush, **'89** 110
Brandy Velvet, **'89** 170
Burgundy Bowl, Sparkling, **'83** 276
Champagne Delight, **'83** 304
Champagne Fruit Slush, **'90** 322
Champagne with Orange Juice, **'91** 71
Chocolate, Flaming Brandied, **'80** M290
Chocolate, Hot Laced Marshmallow,
   '93 53
Christmas Blossom, **'99** 321
Cider, Cinnamon Winter, **'95** 337
Cider, December, **'91** 260
Cider, Hot Burgundy, **'96** 306
Cider, Hot Mexican, **'87** 213
Cider, Hot Mulled, **'84** 323
Cider Nog, Hot, **'98** 241
Cider, Red Apple, **'80** 259
Cider Sour, Bourbon, **'98** 242
Cider, Spirited Apple, **'96** 214
Clam Diggers, **'91** 63
Cocktails, Sea Breeze, **'97** 161
Coconut Frost, Pink, **'79** 174; **'80** 128
Coconut-Pineapple Drink, **'83** 172
Cranapple Glogg, Hot, **'90** 22
Cranapple Wine, **'90** 272
Cranberry Cooler, **'86** 229
Cranberry-Rum Slush, **'84** 259
Cranberry-Vodka Refresher, **'91** 210
Cranberry Wine Cup, **'85** 23
Cricket, **'89** 289
Daiquiris, Cranberry, **'81** 245
Daiquiris, Creamy Strawberry, **'91** 66
Daiquiris, Freezer Lime, **'79** 141
Daiquiris, Mint, **'89** 157
Daiquiris, Peach, **'90** 322
Daiquiris, Strawberry, **'90** 125; **'98** 99
Daiquiri, Strawberry, **'81** 156
Daiquiritas, **'82** 160
Daiquiri, Watermelon, **'95** 143; **'98** 165
Dessert, After Dinner-Drink, **'82** 100
Dessert Drink, Creamy, **'86** 131
Dessert Drink, Simply Super, **'83** 303
Frosty Sours, **'81** 156
Fruit 'ritas, **'94** 157
Funky Monkey, **'99** 161
Fuzz Buzz, **'82** 160
Game-Cocktails, **'93** 214
Gin Cooler, Sparkling, **'90** 272

Ginger Beer, **'84** 159
Golden Dream, **'82** 100
Grapefruit Drink, **'95** 238
Hot Apple Pie, **'99** 321
Hot Chocolate Deluxe, **'90** 272
Hot Chocolate, Tennessee, **'96** 214
Kahlúa Beverage Sipper, **'99** 27
Kahlúa Hummer, **'91** 176
Kahlúa Smoothie, **'87** 242
Kahlúa Velvet Frosty, **'82** 244
King Alfonso, **'80** 259
Lemonade, Claret, **'93** 72
Lemonade, Hot Buttered, **'88** 208
Lemon Cooler, **'82** 48
Lime Fizz, **'81** 172
Liqueur Sampler, Miniature, **'95** 332
Magnolia Blossoms, **'87** 72
Magnolias, **'82** 196
Margaritas, **'92** 210; **'93** 273
Margaritas, Frosted, **'84** 115
Margaritas, Frosty, **'83** 172
Margaritas, Lemon-Lime, **'94** 227
Margaritas, Mango, **'96** 126
Margaritas, Orange-Lime, **'97** 140
Margaritas, Pitcher, **'83** 175
Margaritas Supreme, Frozen, **'80** 160
Margaritas, Tart, **'85** 153
Melon Ball Cooler, **'86** 131
Mimosa Hawaiian, **'85** 44
Mimosas, **'86** 91
Minted Delight, **'87** 107
Mint Julep, **'97** 120
Mint Juleps, **'81** 155; **'82** 41; **'85** 40; **'90** 81
Mint Juleps, Apple, **'97** 120
Mix, Bloody Mary, **'89** 110
Mix, Hot Wine, **'81** 287
Mix, Mulled Wine Spice, **'85** 266
Mocha Chocolate Fluff, **'89** 170
Mocha Deluxe Hot Drink, **'82** 289
Mocha Polka, **'89** 171
Mocha, Spirited Hot, **'91** M260
New Orleans, Mr. Funk of, **'95** 57
Oklahoma Sunrise, **'87** 67
Old-Fashioneds, **'86** 270
Old-Fashioned Slush, **'93** 340
Orange Blossom Flips, **'80** 51
Orange Brandy Smash, **'99** 30
Orange-Champagne Cocktail, **'79** 39
Orange Liqueur, **'81** 287
Orange Milk Shake, **'84** 166
Peach Frosty, **'81** 156
Peach Petals, **'90** 104
Peach Smash, **'88** 161
Peppermint Flip, Hot, **'86** 329
Peppermint Patti, The Peabody, **'99** 321
Pimm's Cup, **'96** 214
Piña Coladas, **'95** 203; **'96** 127
Piña Coladas, Frosty, **'83** 176
Piña Coladas, Luscious, **'81** 134
Piña Colada Slush, **'95** 90
Pineapple-Strawberry Slush, **'94** 227
Pink Palace, **'93** 293
Pirate's Painkiller, **'99** 161
Plum Slush, **'84** 139
Punch, Amaretto, **'91** 277
Punch, Anytime Wine, **'79** 232
Punch, Autumn Harvest, **'96** 277
Punch, Berry-Colada, **'96** 277
Punch, Bourbon, **'92** 208
Punch, Bourbon-Citrus, **'94** 227
Punch, Bourbon-Tea, **'87** 57
Punch, Brandy Milk, **'85** 44; **'88** 83
Punch, Brandy Slush, **'87** 72
Punch, Caribbean, **'95** 173

Punch, Champagne, '85 153, 257; '86 101; '96 277; '98 310; '99 30
Punch, Champagne Blossom, '81 50; '99 290
Punch, Chatham Artillery, '80 121
Punch, Citrus-Wine, '98 197
Punch, Cranapple-Vodka, '87 72
Punch, Cranberry, '85 90
Punch, Cranberry Percolator, '88 248
Punch, Extra-Kick, '91 209
Punch, Festive, '94 289
Punch, Frozen Margarita, '95 91
Punch, Fruit, '83 52
Punch, Fruit Juice-and-Vodka, '96 214
Punch, Fruit Juicy Rum, '91 175
Punch, Gin, '80 160
Punch, Golden Gin, '79 233
Punch, Golden Spiked, '79 285
Punch, Health-Kick, '80 174
Punch, Hot Cranberry, '84 41
Punch, Hot Molasses-Milk, '86 329
Punch, Hot Pineapple, '82 264
Punch, Hot Spiced Rum, '96 214
Punch, Hot Wine, '85 265
Punch, Irish Coffee-Eggnog, '95 314
Punch, Jefferson County, '86 267
Punch, Lemonade-Bourbon, '95 287
Punch, Lemon Champagne, '94 176
Punch, Lime, '84 58
Punch, Milk, '79 38
Punch, Mixed Fruit, '95 239
Punch, Mulled Wine, '95 337
Punch, New Orleans Milk, '81 50
Punch, Orange-Lime, '82 160
Punch, Party, '81 265
Punch, Perky Rum, '85 116
Punch, Pimms, '92 167
Punch, Piña Colada, '89 212
Punch, Pineapple, '79 174; '80 128
Punch, Pineapple-Gin, '95 140
Punch, Pink, '96 190
Punch, Raspberry-Rosé, '87 242
Punch, Red Velvet, '89 289
Punch, Refreshing Champagne, '84 259
Punch, Rum, '85 265
Punch, Southern Fruit, '95 238
Punch, Sparkling Champagne, '84 58
Punch, Sparkling Holiday, '81 290
Punch, Spiced Rum, '86 179
Punch, Spiked Tea, '86 101
Punch, Spirited Fruit, '81 100
Punch, Stormy Petrel Rum Thunder, '93 269
Punch, Strawberry Champagne, '90 315
Punch, Streetcar Champagne, '88 82
Punch, Tropical Fruit, '83 176
Punch, Vodka, '85 265
Punch, Wedding, '86 107
Punch, Whiskey, '90 64; '91 175
Punch, Whiskey Sour, '91 209
Punch, Wine, '93 331
Punch, Yacht Club Milk, '89 86
Raspberry Kir, '86 183
Red Roosters, '87 147
Red Ruby, '92 209
Rum, Hot Buttered, '80 259; '82 244; '88 247; '96 213
Rum Slush, Easy, '79 174; '80 129
Sangría, '79 186; '81 67, 196; '82 121; '86 214; '98 178
Sangría, Cranberry, '95 238
Sangría, Easy Citrus, '80 218
Sangría, Easy Frozen, '92 208
Sangría, Grapefruit, '89 92
Sangría, Orange, '81 237
Sangría, Pineapple, '91 176

Sangría, Punchy, '80 160
Sangría, Quick, '81 156
Sangría Slush, White, '90 322
Sangría, Spanish, '83 81
Sangría, Teaberry, '87 147
Sangría, Three-Fruit, '89 212
Sangría, White, '83 180; '94 289
Screwdrivers, '79 33
Sea Mist, '93 167
Sherry Sour, '87 74
Sipper, Sunshine, '86 179
Slush, Mexican, '83 176
Slush with a Punch, '90 322
Spritzer, Cranberry, '91 66; '92 265
Spritzer, Lemon-Mint, '99 175
Spritzers, Bellini, '90 110
Spritzers, Citrus, '91 231; '92 67
Spritzers, Cranberry, '89 213
Spritzers, Grapefruit-White Wine, '96 56
Spritzers, Spiced, '86 229
Spritzers, Wine, '81 94
Strawberry-Banana Smoothie, '81 59
Strawberry Mimosa, Sparkling, '88 169
Strawberry Slush, '98 178
Strawberry Sparkler, '99 49
Sunny Morning, '93 295
Sunrise, St. Pete, '94 227
Syllabub, '81 265; '84 319
Tangerine Sparkler, '98 54
Tart Caribbean Cooler, '81 134
Tea Juleps, '99 90
Tequila Slush, '83 176
Tequila Sunrise, '83 175
Toddy, Molasses Rum, '91 36
Tomato Bouillon, New Year's, '94 24
Tomato-Orange Juice Cocktail, '83 169
Tomato Sipper, Peppy, '94 227
Vanilla Cream, '97 272
Vodka, Frozen Pink, '89 170
Vodka-Orange Slush, '89 92
Vodka Slush, '88 82
Wassail, '83 311
Wassail, Bourbon, '86 270
Wassail, Four-Fruit, '90 22
Whiskey Sours, Frozen, '93 176
Whiskey Sours, Frozen Orange-, '92 67
Whisky Sour Slush, '86 183
Whispers, '86 317
Wine, Christmas Dreams in, '91 260
Wine Cocktail, Citrus, '99 93
Wine Cooler, '82 41
Wine Cooler, Fruited, '86 176
Wine, Hot Mulled, '83 251
Wine, Hot Spiced, '84 41
Wine Tasting, '95 332
Wine Welcomer, '81 100
Yellow Birds, '90 103
Apple-Berry Sparkler, '93 104
Apple Berry Sparkler, '94 100
Apple Cooler, '90 14
Apple Cooler, Minted, '88 169
Apple Juice, Hot, '86 270
Apple Juice, Perky Cinnamon-, '90 22
Apple Juice Shrub, Shenandoah, '79 282
Apple Juice, Sparkling, '95 141
Apple Julep, '86 103, 215
Apricot Bellinis, '99 145
Apricot-Citrus Slush, '88 82
Apricot Cooler, '81 100
Apricot Coolers, '99 29
Apricot Fruit Flip, '91 18
Apricot Mint Cooler, '90 165
Apricot Nectar, Hot, '81 265
Apricot Nectar, Mulled, '86 229

Apricot-Orange-Carrot Cooler, '96 108
Aztec Gold, '99 160
Banana-Berry Flip, '88 215; '89 20
Banana-Chocolate Malt, '89 170
Banana Coolers, '91 308
Banana Crush, '80 88; '83 142
Banana Frostee, '91 66
Banana Nog, '82 290
Banana-Orange Slush, '80 48; '81 155
Banana Slush, '83 56
Banana-Strawberry Frost, '87 199
Berry Shrub, '95 29
Blackberry Breeze, '98 179
Black Russian, Mock, '92 322
Bloodless Mary, '80 146
Breakfast Eye-Opener, '87 199
Brew, Beach, '91 177
Brew, Holiday, '90 272
Brew, Quilter's, '85 43
Brew, Witch's, '93 244
Bullshots, '86 91
Carambola-Yogurt Calypso, '90 169
Caribbean Cooler, '95 203
Carrot Cooler, '89 35
Champagne, Mock Pink, '89 46
Champions' Cooler, '96 M181
Chiller, Royal Cup, '98 218
Chocolate Malt, '86 183
Chocolate, Mexican-Style, '81 187
Chocolate Milk, French, '79 38
Chocolate Sipper, '88 83
Cider, Apple, '95 198
Cider, Apple-Orange, '92 20
Cider, Cherry, '94 288
Cider, Holiday, '82 264
Cider, Hot Apple, '90 21, 225
Cider, Hot Molasses, '98 242
Cider, Hot Mulled, '79 205
Cider, Hot Mulled Apple-Orange, '97 301
Cider, Hot Spiced, '82 290; '99 248
Cider, Hot Spiced Apple, '84 318
Cider, Hot Spicy, '84 265
Cider, Mulled, '91 209; '94 227
Cider, Mulled Apple, '92 208
Cider Nog, Hot, '98 241
Cider Nog, Hot Apple, '84 42
Cider, Sparkling Apple, '88 276
Cider, Spiced Apple, '85 256
Cider, Spiced Cranberry, '84 261; '98 278
Citrus Blush, '98 197
Citrus Cooler, '82 160; '93 105
Citrus Float, '89 171
Citrus Slush, '93 198
Cocoa, Mocha, '83 318
Coco-Berry Calypso, '89 171
Coffee Soda, '97 272
Cooler, Caribbean, '98 333
Cooler, Spring, '86 214
Cranberry Cocktail, Hot, '89 310
Cranberry Drink, Mulled, '92 12
Cranberry Frappé, '82 263
Cranberry Juice, Sparkling, '88 275
Cranberry-Orange Soda, '79 148
Cranberry-Raspberry Drink, '97 154
Cranberry Shimmer, '98 168
Cubes, Berry-Good, '95 201
Cubes, Cranberry, '95 201
Cubes, Florida, '95 201
Cubes, Lemonade, '95 201
Cubes, Lemon-Mint, '95 201
Float, Frosty Fruit, '87 159
Float, Nutmeg-Almond, '84 106
Float, Pineapple Sherbet, '79 148
Floats, Maple-Coffee, '86 195

BEVERAGES
(continued)

Float, Sparkling Cranberry, '86 195
Float, Strawberry-Banana, '87 160
Frappé, Hootenanny, '89 110
Fruit Beverage, Blender, '83 318
Fruit Cooler, Four-, '86 101
Fruit Coolers, '98 197
Fruit Drink, Three-, '79 38; '80 50; '87 199
Fruit Drink, Tropical, '85 43
Fruit Juice Cooler, '92 67
Fruit Juicy, Breakfast, '86 176
Fruit Refresher, '91 203
Fruit Refresher, Four-, '79 174; '80 129
Fruit Slush, '96 157
Fruit Slush, Refreshing, '82 35
Fruit Slushy, '80 146
Fruit Whisper, Tropical, '89 212
Funshine Fizz, '91 66
Ginger-Mint Cooler, '89 92
Grapefruit Cooler, '88 81
Grapefruit Drink, '90 84; '95 238
Grapefruit-Orange Refresher, '82 174
Grapefruit Refresher, '88 85
Grape Juice, Mulled, '90 21
Grape Juice, Spiced White, '92 320
Grape-Lime Cooler, '94 227
Hawaiian Crush, '91 66
Hot Chocolate, '94 290
Hot Chocolate, Creole, '80 M290
Hot Chocolate, Favorite, '83 55
Hot Chocolate, French, '86 328
Hot Chocolate, Mexican, '98 313
Hot Chocolate, Old-Fashioned, '85 23
Hot Chocolate, Special, '82 5
Hot Chocolate, Spiced, '80 50
Hot Chocolate, Spicy, '85 278
Hot Chocolate, Sugar-and-Spice, '95 34
Hot Cocoa, Quick, '82 5
Ice Bowl, '83 152
Ice Cream Ginger Fizz, '83 303
Ice Mold, Strawberry, '91 278
Ice Ring, '95 140
Ice Ring, Strawberry, '94 176
Jogger's Sunrise, '93 213
Kid's Cooler, '90 95
Kona Luscious, '84 54
Lemonade, Apple, '89 212
Lemonade, Berry Delicious, '93 205
Lemonade, Blackberry, '99 130
Lemonade, Blueberry, '98 179
Lemonade by the Glass, '96 161
Lemonade Concentrate, '89 110
Lemonade, Dazzling, '97 99
Lemonade, Fresh Squeezed, '81 172
Lemonade, Fresh-Squeezed, '99 220
Lemonade, Front Porch, '90 156
Lemonade, Hot Buttered, '94 18
Lemonade, Pineapple, '93 194
Lemonade Slush, Pink, '80 151
Lemonade, Strawberry, '80 160
Lemonade, Sweet-Tart, '96 173
Lemonade, Watermelon, '98 165
Lemonade with Frozen Tea Cubes, '85 161
Lemon Frappé, '92 44
Lemon Velvet, '90 15
Limeade, Pink Apple, '89 46
Lime Cooler, '87 160
Lime Fizz, Frosty, '90 104
Malt Special, '85 198
Mango Frappé, '86 216
Margaritas, Mock, '88 209; '99 120

Melon Julep, Rainbow, '80 183
Milk, Santa Claus, '92 281
Milk Shakes. *See* BEVERAGES/Shakes.
Mint Juleps, Apple, '97 120
Mix, Beetle Cider, '82 308
Mix, Bloody Mary, '89 110
Mix, Cappuccino, '90 87
Mix, Deluxe Hot Chocolate, '80 M290
Mix, Hot Cocoa, '81 287
Mix, Hot Mocha-Cocoa, '82 296
Mix, Hot Spiced Cider, '84 42
Mix, Instant Cocoa, '86 332
Mix, Minted Hot Cocoa, '91 316
Mix, Mocha-Flavored Hot Cocoa, '91 316
Mix, Spicy-Hot Chocolate, '85 278
Mocha Espresso, Italian, '82 254
Mocha Frosty, '92 44
Mocha, Hot, '84 60
Mocha, Mexican, '93 M341
Mocha, Quick Viennese, '79 232
Mocha, Swiss-Style, '82 253
Mocha Warmer, '97 272
Orange-Banana Flip, '82 48
Orange-Banana Whip, '95 244
Orange Blush, '80 51
Orange Frosty, '86 101
Orange Juicy, '90 178
Orange-Lemon Mist, '79 288; '80 35
Orange Pick-Me-Up, '80 232
Orange-Pineapple Drink, '89 35
Orange Slush, '82 49
Patio Blush, '92 43; '99 93
Peach Cooler, '85 198
Peaches 'n' Almond Cream, '86 229
Peach Frost, '89 155
Peach Frosty, '83 318
Peach Pick-Me-Up, '89 183
Peach Refresher, '86 103
Peanut Butter Cooler, '84 115
Piña Colada, Mock, '92 322
Piña Colada, Parson's, '89 46
Pineapple-Banana Slush, '90 14
Pineapple Cooler, '90 207
Pineapple Drink, Hot Buttered, '91 260
Pineapple Nectar, Hot, '90 21
Pineapple Slush, '88 82
Pineapple Soda, '90 179
Pineapple Sparkle, Spiced, '92 322
Pineapple-Yogurt Whirl, '91 132
Pink Soda, Blushing, '90 104
Punch. *See also* BEVERAGES/Alcoholic.
Apple Bobbing Punch, '99 246
Apple Punch, Hot, '84 324
Apple-Tea Punch, '85 82
Apricot Spiced Punch, '80 269
Autumn Punch, '88 209
Banana Punch, '99 161
Berry-Colada Punch, '96 277
Berry Punch, '92 67
Brew-Ha-Ha Punch, '98 255
Bubbling Jade Punch, '79 174; '80 129
Bunch, Punch for a, '95 90
Cantaloupe Punch, '81 147
Caribbean Punch, '95 173
Champagne Punch, '99 30
Children's Punch, '85 322
Christmas Eve Punch, '86 314
Christmas Punch, '84 259; '89 330
Cider Punch, Hot, '95 238
Cider Punch, Spiced, '84 258
Citrus Party Punch, '83 141; '92 289
Citrus Punch, '85 319; '93 99
Citrus Punch, Budget, '82 121
Citrus Punch, Fresh, '85 154

Citrus Punch, Party, '84 117
Citrus Punch, Sparkling, '95 337
Cola Punch, '91 144
Cranapple Punch, '83 142
Cranberry-Cherry Punch, '91 176
Cranberry-Cinnamon Punch, '86 270
Cranberry Punch, '83 275; '99 290
Cranberry Punch, Holiday, '85 265
Cranberry Punch, Hot, '80 288; '84 319;
    '85 265
Cranberry Punch, Sparkling, '85 277; '95 101
Cranberry Punch, Spiced, '89 290
Cranberry Punch, Tart, '83 318
Cran-Grape-Tea Punch, '92 209
False-Kick Punch, '82 121
Frozen Punch Ring, '83 152
Fruited Ice-Cube Punch, '98 197
Fruit Juice Punch, '96 214
Fruit Punch, Can-Can, '94 122
Fruit Punch, Florida, '92 247
Fruit Punch, Fresh, '98 155
Fruit Punch, Golden, '80 299; '83 56; '96 278
Fruit Punch, Holiday, '79 232
Fruit Punch, Holiday Hot, '92 286
Fruit Punch, Hot, '83 33
Fruit Punch, Mixed, '90 207; '95 239
Fruit Punch, Party, '82 137
Fruit Punch, Passion, '90 169
Fruit Punch, Slushy, '98 92
Fruit Punch, Southern Fresh, '99 70
Fruit Punch, Spiced, '88 2
Fruit Punch, Summertime, '80 160
Fruit Punch, Tropical, '80 51; '90 169
Fruit Slush Punch, '91 278
Fruit Sparkle, '99 289
Fruity Witches' Brew, '95 273
Ginger Ale-Nectar Punch, '92 171
Goblin Punch, '88 228
Golden Punch, '85 207
Grape Punch, Sparkling, '82 48
Happy New Year Punch, '98 26
Holiday Punch, '87 252
Hot Spiced Punch, '96 214
Irish Coffee-Eggnog Punch, '95 314
Lemonade Punch, Sparkling, '88 276
Lemon Balm Punch, '80 42
Lime-Pineapple Punch, '83 142
Lime Punch, Calypso Presbyterian Church
    Women's, '95 141
Lime Punch, Foamy, '82 264
Lime Slush Punch, '90 273
Margarita Punch, '98 88
Merry Christmas Punch, '79 285
Mocha Punch, '84 58, 166; '86 270; '95 141
Mock Champagne Punch, '93 340
Morning Punch, '88 82
Nectar Punch, '93 283
Orange Blossom Punch, '83 142
Orange-Mint Punch, '82 121
Orange Punch, Refreshing, '81 39
Orange Sherbet Party Punch, '83 142
Orange Soda Punch, '87 214
Parsonage Punch, '79 148
Party Punch, '91 106, 214
Party Punch in a Pail, '94 289
Party Punch, Special, '81 119
Peppermint-Eggnog Punch, '90 273
Percolator Punch, '91 306
Percolator Punch, Hot, '81 288
Pineapple-Citrus Punch, '96 134
Pineapple-Mint Punch, '88 209
Pineapple-Orange Punch, '85 236
Pineapple Punch, '79 174
Pineapple Punch, Frosty, '91 66

Pineapple Punch, Spiced, '83 33; '92 66
Pineapple Sherbet Punch, '95 141
Pink Lady Punch, '81 100
Polka Dot Punch, '95 178
Ponche de Piña, '84 58
Raspberry Sherbet Punch, '95 141
Raspberry Sparkle Punch, '84 57
Sherbet Punch, Double, '79 232
Spiced Punch, Hot, '80 250
Strawberry-Lemonade Punch, '85 116; '91 175
Strawberry Punch, '90 273
Strawberry Punch, Creamy, '86 195
Sunset Punch, '96 278
Tangy Punch, '83 142
Tea Party Punch, '87 147
Tea Punch, '90 143, 207
Tea Punch, Citrus-, '85 116
Traders' Punch, '87 94
Tropical Punch, '90 207
Vegetable Punch, Hot, '93 12
Watermelon Punch, '89 204; '92 190
White Grape Punch, '90 15
White Grape Punch, Spiced, '96 170
Purple Cow, '98 206
Raspberry Cooler, '89 171
Raspberry Fizz, Rosy, '90 179
Raspberry Shrub, Red, '97 132
Sangría, Mock Tea, '99 336
Sangría, Southern, '88 170
Sangría, Virgin, '89 46
Scarlet Sipper, '90 198
Scuppernong Juice, '98 221

Shakes
Apricot Shake, '84 115
Banana Milkshake, '85 47; '90 179
Banana-Pineapple Milk Shake, '84 59
Banana Shake, '97 172
Chocolate-Banana Milk Shake, '94 113
Chocolate Mint Shake, '89 170
"Concrete," Abaco Mocha, '94 114
"Concrete," All Shook Up, '94 114
"Concrete," Cardinal Sin, '94 113
"Concrete," Foxtreat, '94 113
Cranberry Shake, '83 171
Date Shake, '92 44
Fruit Shake, Frosty, '87 23
Fruit Shake, Tangy, '95 129
Mocha Milkshake, '89 35
Orange Milk Shake, '84 166
Orange Shake, Peachy, '81 156
Papaya Shake, '90 169
PBJ Shake, '93 292
Peach Melba Sundae Shake, '93 134
Peanut Butter-Banana Shake, '97 172
Peanut Butter Milkshakes, '85 198
Peanut Butter Shake, '82 48
Pep Shake, '79 38
Pineapple-Banana Shake, '85 215
Pineapple Milkshake, '87 199
Pineapple Milk Shake, '94 113
Pineapple-Orange-Banana Shake, '97 172
Raisin Shake, Amazin', '86 195
Raspberry-and-Banana Shake, '89 183
Raspberry Milk Shakes, '95 238
Strawberry-Banana Shake, '89 35; '97 172
Strawberry-Cheesecake Shake, '92 44
Strawberry Milk Shake, '94 113
Strawberry Milkshake, Fresh, '82 113
Strawberry-Orange Breakfast Shake, '87 186
Strawberry-Pear Shake, '92 139
Strawberry-Pineapple Shake, '84 166
Strawberry Shake, '97 172
Strawberry-Yogurt Shake, '87 199

Summer Shake, '82 161
Sunshine Shake, '79 53
Tropical Shake, '87 200; '93 212
Slush, Santa's, '90 271
Smoothies
Banana-Blueberry Smoothie, '90 104
Banana-Pineapple Smoothie, Quick, '93 195
Banana Smoothie, '87 160; '93 95
Berry Smoothie, Four-, '97 173
Chocoholic Smoothie, '97 173
Chocolate-Mint Smoothie, '84 166
Citrus Smoothie, '98 17; '99 196
Cranberry Smoothie, '86 183; '91 307
Fruit Smoothie, '89 87
Fruit Smoothie, Two-, '89 182
Honey-Banana Smoothie, '89 144
Honey-Yogurt Smoothie, '97 326
Honey-Yogurt Smoothie, Fruited, '88 231; '89 23
Kahlúa Smoothie, '87 242
Mango-Orange Smoothie, '86 216
Orange-Banana Smoothie, '97 173
Peachy-Pineapple Smoothie, '97 173
Pineapple Smoothie, '97 172
Strawberry-Banana Smoothie, '81 59
Strawberry-Peach Smoothie, '89 182
Strawberry Smoothie, '86 183; '97 173
Sunrise Smoothie, '93 139
Sunshine Smoothies, '98 330
Tropical Smoothie, '81 50; '90 169
Spiced Brew, Hot, '91 36
Spices, Barclay House Mulling, '86 289
Spritzers. *See also* **BEVERAGES/Alcoholic.**
Lemon-Mint Spritzer, '99 175
Raspberry Spritzers, '99 207
Strawberry Spritzer, '90 14; '97 272
Strawberry Cooler, '83 56; '84 51
Strawberry Coolers, '92 67
Strawberry-Mint Cooler, '84 57
Strawberry-Orange Slush, '83 172
Strawberry Refresher, Frozen, '93 213
Strawberry Slurp, '81 96
Strawberry Soda, '84 115
Strawberry Soda, Old-Fashioned, '79 49
Strawberry Sparkler, '99 49
Sunshine Fizz, '92 44
Syllabub, Plantation, '79 233
Syrup, Berry, '96 161
Syrup, Ginger, '96 161
Syrup, Mint, '90 89; '96 161; '97 120
Syrup, Orange, '96 161
Syrup, Simple, '99 161
Syrup, Sugar, '96 161
Tahitian Flower, '87 159
Toddy, Jolly, '86 229
Toddy, Tasty, '88 82
Tofruitti Breakfast Drink, '88 26
Tomato Bouillon, '83 8
Tomato-Clam Cocktail, '87 252
Tomato Cocktail, '83 M203
Tomato Juice Cocktail, '79 212; '83 230; '90 12
Tomato Juice Cocktail, Zesty, '83 289
Tomato Juice, Homemade, '81 50
Tomato Juice, Spicy, '85 189
Tomato Refresher, '83 318
Tomato Sipper, Peppy, '94 227
Tomato Sipper, Spicy, '86 229
Tomato Warm-Up, Spicy, '95 328
Tropical Cooler, '84 120
Tropical Delight, '89 182
Tropical Ice, '79 174; '80 129
Tropical Refresher, '85 198; '96 157
Vanilla Cream, '97 272
Vanilla Frosty, French, '79 148

Vegetable Cocktail, Fresh, '82 165
Vegetable Juice Delight, '84 58
Virgin Mary, Spicy, '92 323
Wassail, '84 259, 318; '88 248; '90 273; '97 240; '99 268
Wassail, Christmas, '93 295
Wassail, Cranberry, '88 289
Wassail, Golden, '96 278
Wassail, Holiday, '89 289; '91 260
Wassail, Pineapple-Apricot, '83 275
Watermelon-Berry Slush, '90 137
Watermelon-Strawberry Cooler, '98 178
Zippy Red Eye, '91 209
BISCUITS
Angel Biscuits, '80 49; '90 28; '93 270
Angel Biscuits, Ham-Filled, '80 159
Bacon Biscuit Cups, '99 214
Baking Powder Biscuits, '82 195; '89 144
Basil Biscuits, '93 160
Beaten Biscuits, '86 54
Benne Seed Biscuits, '79 38
Biscuits, '92 31
Blueberry Buttermilk Biscuits, '89 210
Blue Cheese-and-Ham Cornmeal Biscuits, '98 136
Bowl, Chili in a Biscuit, '98 224
Bran Biscuits, '85 228
Bread, Biscuit, '84 284
Buttermilk Biscuits, '83 208; '85 255, 321; '99 32
Buttermilk Biscuits, Basic, '94 214
Buttermilk Biscuits, Deluxe, '82 130
Buttermilk Biscuits, Favorite, '81 191
Buttermilk Biscuits, Fluffy, '84 102
Buttermilk Biscuits, Old-Fashioned, '80 77
Buttermilk Biscuits, Quick, '83 311; '88 15; '92 269
Buttermilk Biscuits with Virginia Ham, '96 142
Buttermilk-Raisin Biscuits, '92 338
Caramel Dessert Biscuits, '95 36
Casserole, Beef-and-Biscuit, '83 75
Casserole, Biscuit-Topped Tuna, '79 113
Cheese
Angel Biscuits, Cheese, '89 211
Bacon-Cheese Biscuits, '88 84
Beer-and-Cheese Biscuits, '94 215
Blue Cheese Biscuits, '88 83
Butter Cheese Dips, '80 46
Cheese Biscuits, '79 296; '80 31; '81 288; '83 253; '85 32; '87 78
Cheeseburger Biscuits, '79 194
Chive Biscuits, Cheese-, '94 324
Easy Cheese Biscuits, '81 99
Ham and Cheese Biscuits, Petite, '79 193
Hot Cheesy Biscuits, '80 186
Lightnin' Cheese Biscuits, '90 283
Mixer Cheese Biscuits, '96 22
Onion Biscuits, Cheesy, '95 98
Pepper-Cheese Biscuit Fingers, '88 283
Refrigerator Biscuits, '96 17
Roquefort Biscuits, Herbed, '84 95
Rosemary Biscuits, '99 17
Sausage Biscuits, Cheesy, '80 78
Tiny Cheese Biscuits, '80 192
Chicken in a Biscuit, '79 263
Cinnamon Biscuits, Cranberry-Apple Cobbler with, '99 256
Cinnamon-Raisin Breakfast Biscuits, '93 159
Cloud Biscuits, '87 15
Coconut Biscuits, Yummy, '95 99
Cornmeal Biscuits, '85 228; '95 98
Cornmeal-Jalapeño Biscuits, '94 214
Country Ham Biscuits, '94 215
Country Ham, Biscuits with, '90 93
Daisy Biscuits, '90 86
Dressing, Cornbread-Biscuit, '79 296

BISCUITS
(continued)

Dumplings and Chicken, Biscuit, '99 326
Easy-Bake Biscuits, '96 157
Elf Biscuits, '99 309
Elgin Biscuits, '93 281
Elsie's Biscuits, '97 129
Feather Biscuits, '80 78
Feather Light Biscuits, '80 246
Flaky Biscuits, '84 228
Grapefruit Juice Biscuits, '83 10
Ham and Biscuits, Southern, '91 12
Ham Biscuits, '99 233
Ham 'n' Angel Biscuits, Kentucky, '90 83
Heart Biscuits, Country Ham in, '86 105
Heart Biscuits with Sausage, Angel, '87 156
Hearty Biscuits, '83 121
Herb Biscuits, Easy, '90 283
Herbed Biscuit Ring, '95 161
Herbed Biscuits, '85 228; '93 67
Honey Angel Biscuits, '95 138
Hot Biscuits, '86 269
Lemon Drop Biscuits, '97 332
Light Biscuits, '89 53
Marmalade Biscuits, Carolina, '85 42
Marmalade Biscuit Squares, '79 193
Mile-High Biscuits, '85 41
Muffins, Biscuit, '98 136
Nannie's Biscuits, '82 156
Nutty Tea Biscuits, '89 210
Oatmeal Biscuits, '89 108
Omelet Biscuits, Deluxe, '98 101
One-Step Biscuits, '82 173
Orange Biscuits, '88 85
Orange Puffs, Upside-Down, '83 57
Pandy's Biscuits, '99 277
Parker House-Style Biscuits, '79 162
Pepperoni Biscuits, '84 95
Potato-Bacon Biscuits, '94 214
Processor Biscuits, Easy, '84 218
Pudding, Biscuit, '79 86; '93 51
Pudding, Chocolate Biscuit Bread, '94 215
Pull-Apart Biscuits, Surprise, '95 46
Quick Biscuits, '89 30
Raised Biscuits, Southern, '82 94
Raisin Biscuits, Glazed, '89 210
Ranch Biscuits with Ham, '97 59
Raspberry-Almond Biscuits, '93 160
Rise-and-Shine Biscuits, '89 211
"Rolling-in-Dough" Biscuits, '92 80
Rosemary Biscuits, '95 91; '99 17
Rye Biscuits, '84 96
Sausage and Biscuits, Southern, '82 43
Sausage, Best Biscuits with, '99 103
Sausage Biscuit Bites, '84 95
Sausage Gravy, Biscuits and, '92 270; '94 20
Scones, Breakfast Drop, '88 83
Scones, Currant, '84 117
Snowflake Biscuits, '90 158
Sour Cream Biscuits, '79 128
Sour Cream Biscuits, Soft-as-a-Cloud, '86 138
Sourdough Biscuits, '82 201
Spoon Biscuits, Mexican Fiesta, '95 161
Sweetened Biscuits, '80 42
Sweet Little Biscuits, '85 305
Sweet Potato Angel Biscuits, '93 312
Sweet Potato Biscuits, '80 287; '84 140; '89 210;
    '98 222
Taco Biscuit Bites, '91 89
Three-Step Biscuits, '98 97
Tomato Biscuits, '86 72
Tomato-Eggplant Biscuit Cakes, '95 170

Tomato-Herb Biscuits, '94 215
Topping, Biscuit, '86 157, 265
Up-and-Down Biscuits, '88 263
Velvet Cream Biscuits, '92 303
Wheat Bran Biscuits, '81 49
Wheat Germ Biscuits, '86 261
Wheat Quick Biscuits, '85 278
Whipping Cream Biscuits, '80 77
Whole Wheat Biscuits, '83 18; '84 60, 268;
    '85 227; '88 83; '91 222
Yeast Biscuits, '87 71, 301
Yeast Biscuits, Refrigerator, '85 48
BISQUE. *See* **SOUPS/Bisques.**
BLACKBERRIES
Bars, Blackberry, '87 130
Bars, Blackberry-Filled, '79 124
Bars, Blackberry Jam, '82 M185
Berry Shrub, '95 29
Breeze, Blackberry, '98 179
Butter, Blackberry, '97 306
Cake, Fresh Blackberry, '81 132
Chantilly, Blackberries, '99 130
Cobbler, Blackberry, '82 139; '83 175; '99 131
Cobbler, Blackberry-Almond, '81 132
Cobbler, Deep-Dish Blackberry, '80 186
Cobbler, Deluxe Blackberry, '81 132
Cobbler, Juicy Blackberry, '89 137
Cobbler, New-Fashioned Blackberry, '87 164
Cobbler, Southern Blackberry, '81 132
Crème Brûlée, Berry, '95 323
Crisp, Lemon-Blackberry, '98 171
Custard, Blackberry, '99 132
Dumplings, Blackberries and, '86 196
Dumplings, Blackberry, '97 253
Flan, Blackberry, '79 182
Gazpacho, Berry, '97 181
Jam, Berry Refrigerator, '89 139
Jam, Blackberry, '82 149; '89 138; '99 M131
Jam, Freezer Blackberry, '84 M181
Jelly, Blackberry, '82 149
Lemonade, Blackberry, '99 130
Napoleons, Berry, '94 120
Parfait, Blackberries-and-Cream, '87 129
Pie, Berry-Apple, '88 251
Pie, Blackberry, '84 141; '86 152
Pie, Blackberry-Apple, '87 130
Pie, Blackberry Cream, '81 132
Pie, Creamy Blackberry, '88 179
Pie, Peach-and-Blackberry, '89 136
Roll, Blackberry, '82 178
Sandwiches, Smoked Turkey, Mozzarella, and
    Blackberry, '99 220
Sauce, Berry, '94 130
Sauce, Blackberry, '86 152; '94 232
Sauce, Ducklings with Blackberry, '82 251
Sauce, Grilled Quail with Red Wine-Blackberry,
    '98 319
Sherbet, 1-2-3 Blackberry, '99 130
Supremes, Blackberry, '99 179
Syrup, Blackberry, '99 131
Tamales, Blackberry Dessert, '94 190
Tart, Cherry and Blackberry, '83 225
Tart, Pick-a-Berry, '91 118
Tarts, Berry Good Lemon, '91 119
Tarts, Blackberry Pudding, '93 200
BLUEBERRIES
à la Frederick, Blueberries, '93 123
Appetizer, Orange-Berry, '85 81
Basket, Summer Berry, '84 158
Berry Tartlets, Fresh, '91 98
Bordeaux, Beauberries, '98 18
Breads
    Banana-Blueberry Bread, '81 163
    Biscuits, Blueberry Buttermilk, '89 210

Buns, Deluxe Blueberry, '81 164
Hot Blueberry Bread, '81 164
Lemon Bread, Blueberry-, '85 190
Muffins, Blueberry, '80 140, 203; '91 140, 203; '99 234
Muffins, Blueberry-Bran, '89 23
Muffins, Blueberry Buttermilk, '80 16
Muffins, Blueberry-Cream Cheese, '86 14
Muffins, Blueberry Ice Cream, '82 143
Muffins, Blueberry-Lemon, '79 7
Muffins, Blueberry-Oat, '92 119
Muffins, Blueberry Oat Bran, '89 106
Muffins, Blueberry-Oatmeal, '87 24
Muffins, Blueberry Streusel, '80 46
Muffins, Blueberry-Streusel, '96 146
Muffins, Easy Blueberry, '81 197
Muffins, Golden Blueberry, '79 235
Muffins, Old-Fashioned Blueberry, '86 161
Muffins, Speedy Blueberry, '95 135
Muffins with Streusel Topping, Blueberry,
    '88 129
Oatmeal Bread, Blueberry-, '83 139
Orange Bread, Blueberry-, '87 140
Orange Nut Bread Blueberry-, '84 141
Pinwheels, Blueberry, '82 205
Tea Bread, Blueberry, '96 146
Buckle, Blueberry, '85 30
Buckle Blueberry, Huckle-, '86 151
Cake, Banana-Blueberry, '86 247
Cake, Blueberry Brunch, '83 183
Cake, Blueberry-Sour Cream, '90 140
Cake, Blueberry Streusel, '92 144
Cheesecake, Blueberries 'n' Cream, '87 140
Cheesecake, Blueberry Chiffon, '87 76
Chutney, Blueberry, '95 190
Cobbler, Blueberry, '83 175
Cobbler, Blueberry Pinwheel, '87 140
Cobbler, Blueberry Upside-Down, '96 146
Cobbler, Easy Blueberry, '83 183
Cobbler, Fresh Blueberry, '80 144
Cobbler, No-Dough Blueberry-Peach, '86 177
Cobbler, Peachy Blueberry, '80 143
Cobbler, Warm Blueberry, '98 153
Coffee Cake, Almond-Blueberry, '85 152
Coffee Cake, Blueberry, '82 206; '85 326; '88 263
Coffee Cake, Blueberry Streusel, '88 154
Coffee Cake, Fresh Blueberry, '81 164
Cointreau, Blueberries and, '82 100
Compote, Berry-Peach, '82 133
Compote, Peach-Berry, '89 112
Conserve, Blueberry, '82 149
Cordial, Blueberry, '95 142
Cream, Lemon-Blueberry, '92 153
Crisp, Blueberry, '84 177
Crumble, Blueberry, '81 84
Crunch, Blueberry, '96 146
Crunch, Fresh Blueberry, '82 143
Delight, Blueberry, '96 17
Dessert, Easy Blueberry, '89 M130
Dessert, Peach-Blueberry, '92 184
Dessert Squares, Chocolate-Blueberry, '87 299
Dream, Blueberry, '88 94
Fritters, Blueberry, '85 152
Gazpacho, Berry, '97 181
Glaze, Blueberry, '83 143
Ice Cream, Blueberry, '88 203
Jam, Blueberry, '79 120; '85 130
Jam, Blueberry Refrigerator, '89 139
Kuchen, Blueberry, '80 143
Lemonade, Blueberry, '98 179
Lemon Curd with Berries, '90 102
Marmalade, Blueberry, '96 145
Napoleons, Blueberry, '96 147
Napoleons, Blueberry-Lemon, '94 122
Pancake, Brunch Popover, '96 28

Pancakes, Blueberry, '85 152; '89 138
Pancakes, Blueberry Buttermilk, '79 114
Pancakes, Blue Cornmeal-Blueberry, '94 115
Pancakes, Sour Cream Blueberry, '81 164
Pie, Blueberry-Banana, '93 115
Pie, Blueberry Cream, '84 142
Pie, Blueberry-Cream Cheese, '88 154
Pie, Blueberry-Peach, '94 158
Pie, Blueberry-Sour Cream, '83 183
Pie, Bumbleberry, '97 163
Pie, Chilled Blueberry, '89 136
Pie, Fresh Blueberry, '83 183; '85 152
Pie, Fresh Blueberry Cream, '80 144
Pie, Fresh Blueberry Streusel, '89 137
Pie, Old-Fashioned Blueberry, '89 136
Pie, Red, White, and Blueberry, '98 162
Pie, Spicy Blueberry, '96 147
Pizza, Blueberry, '96 147
Pudding, Blueberry Bread, '88 154
Pudding, Russian Blueberry-Raspberry, '97 128
Puree, Grapefruit with Pear-Berry, '89 213
Quick Blueberry Slump, '91 20
Raspberry Custard Sauce, Fresh Berries with, '88 163
Salad, Layered Berry, '79 173
Salad, Melon-Berry, '90 180
Salad, Watercress, '97 249
Sauce, Berry, '94 130; '95 103
Sauce, Blueberry, '80 144; '86 248; '88 155; '89 M130; '94 122; '95 135
Sauce, Cinnamon-Blueberry, '86 11
Sauce, Melon Wedges with Berry, '86 178
Sauce, Peach-Berry, '87 M165
Sauce, Peach-Blueberry, '81 170
Sauce, Peach-Blueberry Pancake, '82 177
Shortcake, Warm Blueberry-Nectarine, '97 205
Smoothie, Banana-Blueberry, '90 104
Smoothie, Four-Berry, '97 173
Snow, Berries on, '82 227
Sorbet, Blueberry-Kirsch, '83 120
Squares, Blueberry-Amaretto, '83 220
Tart, Pick-a-Berry, '91 118
Tarts, Berry Good Lemon, '91 119
Topping, Blueberry, '87 125
Trifle, Lemon-Blueberry, '88 210
Yum Yum, Blueberry, '98 91
BOK CHOY
Beef with Bok Choy, Ginger, '96 99
Pork on Mixed Greens, Hot Sesame, '97 19
Salad, Ramen Noodle, '97 18
Stir-Fried Bok Choy, '97 105
Stir-Fry, Bok Choy-Broccoli, '84 2
BOYSENBERRIES
Cobbler, Boysenberry, '82 133
Compote, Berry-Peach, '82 133
Cream Mold, Peachy Berry, '83 130
Cream Supreme, Boysenberries and, '82 133
Crisp, Berry, '83 130
Pie, Boysenberry, '82 133
BRAN
Biscuits, Bran, '85 228
Biscuits, Wheat Bran, '81 49
Bread, Bran-Applesauce, '84 229
Bread, Honey-Oat, '93 232
Bread, Wheat-and-Oat Bran, '92 102
Bread, Whole Wheat Bran, '79 58
Chocolate-Bran Raisin Jumbos, '91 142
Crêpes, Bran, '83 70; '86 44
Cupcakes, Carrot-Bran, '82 16
Eggplant, Ratatouille-Bran Stuffed, '86 44
Muesli, Bran-and-Fruit, '91 134

Muffins
All-Bran Oat Bran Muffins, '91 134
Apple-Bran Muffins, '85 M89
Apple-Cinnamon Oat Bran Muffins, '89 106
Banana Bran Muffins, '83 48
Banana Oat Bran Muffins, '89 106 ·
Big Batch Moist Bran Muffins, '95 214
Blueberry-Bran Muffins, '89 23
Blueberry Oat Bran Muffins, '89 106
Bran Muffins, '84 53
Buttermilk Muffins, Bran-, '85 7
Cranberry Oat Bran Muffins, '89 107
Easy Bran Muffins, '83 55
Ever-Ready Bran Muffins, '81 106
Freezer Bran Muffins, '91 141
High-Fiber Muffins, '85 250
Honey Bran Muffins, '88 171
Honey-Bran Muffins, '89 250
Made of Bran Muffins, '86 103
Maple-Bran Muffins, '90 66
Oat Bran-Banana Muffins, '91 18
Oat Bran Muffins, '89 106
Oatmeal Bran Muffins, '81 236
Oatmeal-Bran Muffins, '91 83
Quick Bran Muffins, '86 85
Raisin Oat Bran Muffins, '89 106
Refrigerator Bran Muffins, '79 6
Sour Cream-Bran Muffins, '87 98
Spiced Bran Muffins, '84 229
Two, Bran Muffins for, '84 211
Whole Wheat Bran Muffins, '88 M274
Pancakes with Cinnamon Syrup, Bran, '91 315
Rolls, Bran, '85 145
Rolls, Bran Yeast, '87 116
Salad, Lemony Apple-Bran, '86 223
Waffles, Oat Bran, '92 139
BREADS. *See also* **APPETIZERS/Crostini;**
BISCUITS; CAKES/Coffee Cakes;
CORNBREADS; CRACKERS; CRÊPES;
CROUTONS; FRENCH TOAST;
MUFFINS; PANCAKES; PIES, PUFFS,
AND PASTRIES/Pastries; ROLLS AND
BUNS; WAFFLES.
Apple Bread, '79 205; '80 226
Apple Butter Bread, '84 49; '86 69
Apple Loaf, Fresh, '82 206
Apple Loaf, Spiced, '79 215
Apple-Nut Bread, '79 12; '85 281
Apple-Nut Bread, Fresh, '87 256
Applesauce-Honey Nut Bread, '87 300
Applesauce Loaf, Brandy, '81 263
Applesauce Nut Bread, '81 305
Applesauce-Pecan Bread, '90 66
Apple Toast, '81 278
Apricot Bread, Tangy, '81 249
Apricot-Cranberry Loaf, '79 235
Apricot-Nut Bread, '79 24
Apricot-Nut Loaf, '81 8
Apricot-Nut Loaf, Tasty, '82 10
Apricot-Orange Bread, '92 285
Apricot-Pecan Bread, '97 266
Artichoke Bread, '93 140
Asparagus Squares, '79 161
Bacon-and-Cheese Bread, '83 255
Bacon-Cheese Toast Bars, '79 36
Banana-Apple Bread, '85 250
Banana-Blueberry Bread, '81 163
Banana Bread, '87 72
Banana Bread, Easy, '96 97
Banana Bread, Fruity, '95 78
Banana Bread, Sour Cream-, '79 190
Banana Bread, Whole Wheat, '80 88
Banana Butterscotch Bread, '79 116
Banana-Jam Bread, '84 73

Banana-Nut Bread, '86 8, 70
Banana Nut Bread, Hawaiian, '79 235
Banana Nut Bread, Whole Wheat-, '84 50
Banana-Nut-Raisin Bread, '81 59
Banana-Nut Roll, '85 112
Banana-Oat Tea Loaf, '87 256
Banana Wheat Bread, '81 14
Banana-Zucchini Bread, '85 326
Barbecue Bread, '99 105
Batter Bread, Soft, '84 253
Batter, Primary, '89 192
Beer Bread, Easy, '79 213; '84 160
Biscuit Bread, '84 284
Blueberry Bread, Hot, '81 164
Blueberry-Lemon Bread, '85 190
Blueberry-Oatmeal Bread, '83 139
Blueberry-Orange Bread, '87 140
Blueberry-Orange Nut Bread, '84 141
Blueberry Tea Bread, '96 146
Blue Cheese-Apple Sunburst, '94 245
Bourbon-Pecan Bread, '93 308; '96 27
Bowls, Toasted Bread, '98 30
Braided Bread Ring, '96 322
Bran-Applesauce Bread, '84 229
Breadstick Haystacks, '99 246
Breakfast Bread, Crunchy, '93 327
Breakfast Bread, Easy, '83 289
Brie Bread, '87 143
Brie Cheese Bake, '87 117
Brown Bread, '84 242; '88 63
Brown Bread, Eighteenth-Century, '79 72
Brown Bread, Steamed Buttermilk, '86 261
Bruschetta, Black Truffle, '99 323
Buttermilk-Cheese Loaf, '91 52
Butternut-Raisin Bread, '79 25
Butternut Spice Loaf, '92 235
Calas, Easy, '92 89
Calas, Quick, '96 64
Carrot Bread, '89 143
Carrot Bread, Tasty, '84 328
Carrot-Nut Loaf, '83 117
Carrot-Pineapple Bread, '82 210
Carrot Puffs, '87 200
Carrot-Walnut Bread, '88 284
Cheddar-Apple Bread, '96 83
Cheddar Cheese-Pepper Bread, '98 25
Cheddar-Nut Bread, '85 41
Cheese Bread, '82 174
Cheese Bread, Dilly, '83 5
Cheese Bread, Easy, '82 74; '86 17
Cheese Bread, Quick, '83 9
Cheese Breadsticks, Italian, '95 126
Cheese Delights, Toasted, '79 37
Cheese-Herb Bread, '85 283
Cheese Loaf, '87 92; '90 93
Cheese Loaves, Little, '86 213
Cheese-Olive Bread, Spicy, '84 150
Cheese Puffs, Bavarian, '80 191
Cheesy Twists, '84 284
Cherry Nut Bread, '81 306; '82 36
Cherry Nut Bread, Maraschino, '79 234
Cherry-Nut Bread, Quick, '85 55
Chocolate Chip-Banana Bread, '90 267
Chocolate Date-Nut Bread, '81 284
Chocolate-Zucchini Bread, '93 308
Cinnamon Loaves, '99 260
Cinnamon Loaves, Miniature, '99 260
Cinnamon Logs, '98 325
Cinnamon Puffs, '81 209
Cinnamon Sticks, '95 244
Cinnamon Toast, Buttery Skillet, '79 36
Citrus-Nut Bread, '83 294
Coconut Bread, '83 140
Cracklin' Cakes, Grannie's, '98 252

BREADS
(continued)

Cranberry-Banana Bread, '80 281; '90 294
Cranberry Bread, '79 242
Cranberry Fruit-Nut Bread, '79 275
Cranberry-Orange Bread, '87 244
Cranberry-Orange Nut Bread, '80 288
Crescent Twists, Pecan, '99 47
Damper, '97 22
Date-Banana Loaves, Tropical, '95 143
Date-Nut Bread, '85 306
Date-Nut Loaf, '85 10
Date-Walnut Loaf, Blue Ribbon, '80 15
Easy Bread, '87 168
Egg Bread, '95 121
Eggnog Bread, '83 294
Feta Cheese-Spinach Roll, '91 22
Flatbread, Mexican, '80 197
Flatbread, Sicilian Artichoke, '98 136
Focaccia, Fast Rosemary-Dried Tomato,
    '98 53
Focaccia, Herb, '97 31
Focaccia, Mustard-and-Onion, '90 321; '92 97
Fou-Fou, '96 325
French Baguettes, Rosemary, '97 165
French Bread, Bacon-Cheese, '92 54
French Bread Bowls, '95 58
French Bread, Cheesy, '88 172; '95 218; '96 205;
    '97 325
French Bread, Chive-Garlic, '89 29
French Bread, Herbed, '82 174; '93 283; '99 47
French Bread, Herb-Seasoned, '83 198
French Bread, Hot Garlic, '81 83
French Bread, Lemony, '97 147
French Bread, Onion-Cheese, '89 29
French Bread, Tangy, '98 166
French Loaf, Herbed, '87 243
Fruit-Nut Bread, Kahlúa, '79 235
Fruit-Nut Twists, '82 253
Fry Bread, '84 140; '85 155
Fry Bread, Indian, '81 56
Garlic Bread, '82 19; '89 282; '91 204; '95 218;
    '96 204
Garlic Bread, Cheesy, '84 150
Garlic Bread, Dilly, '95 218; '96 205
Garlic Bread, Quick, '90 283
Garlic Breadsticks, '79 70
Garlic-Stuffed Bread, Cheesy, '95 176
Gingerbread, Gingery, '96 100
Gingerbread Loaf, '82 14
Gingerbread, Mocha, '81 207; '82 14
Gingerbread, Molasses, '88 203
Gingerbread, Old English, '79 265
Gingerbread, Old-Fashioned, '81 157, 207;
    '82 14; '91 240
Gingerbread, Refrigerator, '80 52
Gingerbread, Spicy, '84 263
Gingerbread Squares, '84 16
Gingerbread, Very Moist, '86 261
Gingerbread with Key Lime Curd, Kahlúa,
    '96 126
Greek Bread, '89 200
Greek Sunburst, '94 245
Ham-and-Cheese Bread, '86 213
Hawaiian Loaf, '80 225
Herb-and-Cheese Pull Aparts, '87 143
Herb Bread, '86 17
Herb Loaf, Toasted, '84 150
Herbs-and-Cheese Bread, '93 56
Herb Sticks, '83 252
Herb-Vegetable-Cheese Bread, '88 172
Hobo Bread, '86 86

Honey-Banana Bread, '91 68
Irish Soda Bread, '90 214; '95 71
Jam-and-Cheese Loaf, '89 246
Koulourakia, '90 193
Lahvosh Cracker Bread Bowls, '95 58
Lemon Bread, '79 275; '87 256
Lemon-Cream Tea Loaf, '84 50
Lemon-Nut Bread, '79 24
Lemon-Pecan Bread, '83 54
Lemon Tea Bread, '92 268; '93 183
Mandel Bread, '97 220
Mango Bread, '96 205
Marbled Loaves with Orange Glaze,
    '99 293
Mayonnaise Bread, '89 29
Mix, Quick Bread, '81 90; '86 8
Molasses-Nut Bread, '84 24
Monkey Bread, Bacon, '94 283; '97 154
Monkey Bread, Cheese-Filled, '91 21
Monkey Bread, Quick, '81 306; '82 36
Mustard-Rye Ovals, '84 149
Nautical Knots, '93 168
Oatmeal Bread, '81 236, 300
Oatmeal Raisin Bread, '81 14
Onion Bread, Easy, '81 162
Onion-Cheese Bread, '79 180; '81 8
Onion-Cheese Supper Bread, '83 112
Onion-Herb Bread, Toasted, '83 266
Onion-Parmesan Bread, '84 284
Orange, Baba au, '86 138
Orange-Cranberry Bread, '85 266
Orange-Cream Cheese Bread, '82 210
Orange-Nut Bread, '82 75
Orange Nut Loaf, '80 226
Orange-Pecan Bread, '79 148
Orange-Pecan Bread, Glazed, '81 250
Orange-Pecan Loaves, '79 215
Orange Praline Toast, '79 36
Orange Puffs, Upside-Down, '83 57
Orange-Pumpkin Bread, '87 300
Orange Tea Bread, '79 234
Pane Cunsado (Fixed Bread), '95 218
Pane Cunsado (Sicilian for "Fixed Bread"),
    '96 205
Papaya Bread, '88 138
Parmesan Cheese Bread, '99 61
Parmesan-Garlic Breadsticks, '99 46
Parmesan Herb Bread, '82 235; '83 41
Parmesan-Pepper Toasts, '98 242
Parmesan Puffs, '98 235
Parmesan Rounds, '79 170
Parmesan Sesame Sticks, '81 39
Parmesan Twists, '83 239; '99 323
Parmesan-Wine Bread, '97 31
Peach Bread, '82 170
Peach Bread, Georgia, '79 161
Peanut Bread, '87 184
Peanut Butter Bread, '88 64; '99 111
Pear Bread, '80 218
Pecan-Cornmeal Rounds, '95 99
Pepper Bread, '85 156
Persimmon Bread, '80 228
Persimmon Date-Nut Bread, '82 218
Pig-in-a-Blanket Bread, '99 134
Pineapple-Apricot Bread, '84 7
Pineapple Bread, '83 139
Pineapple Breakfast Puffs, '98 326
Pineapple-Carrot Bread, '79 106
Pineapple-Nut Bread, '79 215
Pineapple-Pecan Loaf Bread, '87 256
Pita Bread Salad, '95 86
Pita Triangles, Cheesy, '93 70
Pizza Sticks, '98 255
Pizza Sunburst, '94 245

Popovers
Blender Popovers, Perfect, '79 53
Cheddar Cheese Popovers, '85 41
Cheese Popover Puffs, '85 6
Cinnamon Popovers, '90 66
Good Old Southern Popovers, '79 138
Jumbo Popovers, '83 225
Muffin Tin Popovers, '79 138
Parmesan Popovers, '90 66
Pecan Popovers, Giant, '83 208
Pimiento Popovers, '79 138
Popovers, '94 43
Ring, Cheesy Popover, '80 45
Seasoned Popovers, '86 86
Two, Popovers for, '81 304
Whole Wheat Popovers, '90 66
Poppy Seed Bread, '83 140
Poppy Seed Loaf, Quick, '82 75
Poppy Seed-Swiss Cheese Bread, '91 52
Potato Bites, Mashed, '98 249
Prune-Nut Bread, '87 255; '91 55
Puddings
Amish Bread Pudding, '80 8
Apple-Raisin Bread Pudding, '88 175
Apricot Bread Pudding, '85 24
Blueberry Bread Pudding, '88 154
Bread Pudding, '89 M130; '90 219
Buttermilk Bread Pudding with Butter-Rum
    Sauce, '95 134
Cheesy Bread Pudding, '83 68
Chocolate Bread Pudding, '80 8
Chocolate Bread Pudding with Whiskey
    Sauce, '99 277
Cinnamon Toast Pudding with Caramel
    Sauce, '96 284
Custard Sauce, Bread Pudding with,
    '97 313
Durfee's Bread Pudding, '96 48
French Bread Pudding, '85 231
Lemon Bread Pudding, Old-Fashioned,
    '88 95
Mushroom Bread Pudding, '99 58
Old-Fashioned Bread Pudding, '83 213;
    '88 175
Old-Fashioned Bread Pudding with Bourbon
    Custard Sauce, '95 271
Old-Fashioned Bread Pudding with Rum
    Sauce, '88 32
Peachy Bread Pudding, '88 175
Piña Colada Bread Pudding, '98 34
Plum Bread Pudding, Refrigerator, '97 177
Pumpkin Bread Pudding, '98 240
Raisin Bread Pudding, '94 215
Raisin Bread Pudding with Bourbon Sauce,
    '98 336
Soufflé, Creole Bread Pudding, '92 87
Spiced Bread Pudding, '93 52
Sweet Potato Bread Pudding, '94 241
Sweet Roll Pudding, '96 283
Tennessee Bread Pudding with Bourbon
    Sauce, '93 51
Vanilla Sauce, Bread Pudding with, '97 M15
Whiskey Sauce, Bread Pudding with, '80 58;
    '90 230; '92 93
Pull-Away Bread, '98 137
Pull-Away Bread, Cinnamon, '98 137
Pumpkin Bread, '81 8
Pumpkin Bread, Brother Boniface's, '98 26
Pumpkin Bread, Harvest, '90 M215
Pumpkin Bread, Moist, '80 245
Pumpkin Bread, Spiced, '91 233
Pumpkin Bread with Cream Cheese and
    Preserves, '84 264
Pumpkin-Coconut Bread, '87 255

Pumpkin Loaf, Harvest, **'85** 232
Pumpkin-Nut Bread, **'83** 294
Pumpkin-Oatmeal Loaf, **'81** 49
Pumpkin-Pecan Bread, **'87** 221
Raisin-Cranberry Bread, **'81** 305; **'82** 36
Saffron Tea Bread, **'85** 26
Salad, Italian Bread, **'99** 259
Sally Lunn, Quick, **'87** 16
Salt-Rising Bread, **'79** 145
Santa Gertrudis Pan de Campo, **'94** 27
Sausage-Onion Squares, **'83** 112
Scones
    Breakfast Scones, **'88** 231; **'89** 22
    Cheddar Cheese Scones, Golden, **'99** 82
    Cherry-and-Cream Scones, **'99** 49
    Cranberry-Nut Yeast Scones, Merry, **'99** 274
    Cranberry-Orange Scones, **'97** 45
    Cranberry Scones, **'95** 283
    Cream Scones, **'97** 44
    Currant Scones, **'84** 117; **'92** 332
    Hazelnut Scones, **'94** 16
    Lemon-Poppy Seed Scones, **'97** 44
    Lemon-Raisin Scones, **'87** 69
    Mocha-Pecan Scones, **'97** 45
    Orange-Pecan Scones, **'94** 215
    Orange Scones with Orange Butter,
      Double-, **'97** 44
    Scottish Scones, **'97** 44
Seasoned Breadsticks, **'81** 84; **'96** 46
Sesame Bread Twists, **'84** 283
Sesame-Cheddar Sticks, **'81** 150
Sesame-Cheese Breadsticks, **'97** 31
Sesame Sticks, **'83** 9
Sesame Wheat Crisps, **'81** 106
Shortbread, **'85** 266
Shrimp Toast, **'86** 91
Sourdough Dill Bread, **'89** 192
Sourdough Starter, **'89** 192
Sourdough Wedges, **'90** 199
Spinach Bread, **'83** 121; **'87** 144
Spoonbreads
    Barbara Sue's Spoonbread, **'99** 83
    Cheddar Spoonbread, **'82** 196
    Cheese Spoonbread, **'86** 261
    Corn and Bacon Spoonbread, **'81** 129
    Corn-Cheese Spoonbread, **'88** 9
    Corn Spoonbread, **'97** 301
    Dressing, Southwestern-Style Spoonbread,
      '94 273
    Garlic Spoonbread, **'79** 269; **'80** 14
    Golden Spoonbread, **'83** 286; **'84** 17
    Grits Spoonbread, **'79** 38
    Grits with Savory Mushroom Sauce,
      Spoonbread, **'96** 236
    Memmie's Spoonbread, **'95** 27
    Old Virginia Spoonbread, **'84** 102
    Spoonbread, **'80** 43; **'81** 138; **'90** 200; **'95** 156
Squash Bread, **'79** 210
Squash Bread, Spicy, **'83** 121
Stars, Bread, **'93** 286
Starter Food, **'94** 324; **'95** 77
Stollen, **'86** 291
Strawberry Bread, **'81** 250; **'83** 140; **'84** 49
Strawberry Jam Bread, **'79** 216
Strawberry-Nut Bread, **'79** 24
Tacos, Navajo, **'84** 246
Tennessee Sin, **'95** 218; **'96** 204
Three-C Bread, **'81** 284
Toast Points, **'93** 270
Toast Strips, Seasoned, **'93** 98
Tomato-Cheese Bread, **'98** 172; **'99** M157
Tomato-Cheese Bread, Herbed, **'88** 143
Tortillas, Flour, **'81** 303
Tortillas, Never-Fail Flour, **'80** 198

Vegetable Bread, Breakaway, **'82** 74
Wampus Bread, **'81** 305
Wheat Loaf, Nutty, **'90** 65
Whole Wheat Cardamom Bread, **'86** 223
Whole Wheat Coffee Can Bread, Molasses,
    '85 111
Whole Wheat Orange Bread, **'85** 5
Whole Wheat Quick Bread, **'82** 65
Wine-Date Nut Bread, **'82** 253
Yeast
    Almond Braid, **'89** 86
    Almond Danish, **'87** 301
    Anise-Orange Bread, **'83** 295
    Apple Danish, Deep-Dish, **'86** 161
    Apple-Date-Nut Ring, **'90** 212
    Apple Pull-Apart Bread, **'86** 330
    Apple Swirl Bread, **'85** 4
    Armenian Thin Bread, **'94** 108
    Austrian Sweet Bread, **'83** 294
    Austrian Twists, **'80** 45
    Bagels, **'89** 266
    Bagels, Whole Wheat, **'84** 20
    Baguettes, **'85** 70
    Baguettes and Rolls, **'98** 168
    Beer Bread, Best-Ever, **'82** 129
    Beer Bread, Hearty, **'87** 226; **'88** 133
    Beignets, **'84** 56
    Beignets, French Market, **'92** 88; **'93** 219;
      '94 319; **'95** 80
    Binning Bread, **'80** 68
    Bowls, Irish Tater Bread, **'96** 111
    Bowls, Italian Bread, **'98** 292
    Braided Bread, **'88** 76
    Braided Loaf, **'82** 17
    Braids, Festive, **'87** 297
    Braids, Holiday, **'83** 295
    Braid, Sweet Yeast, **'90** 46
    Break-Away Bread, **'86** 56
    Brioche, **'81** 122; **'89** 90
    Brioche Chicken Curry, **'88** 124
    Brioche Loaves, Vienna, **'87** 300
    Brioche, Morrison House, **'96** 53
    Brown Bread, Light-, **'84** 268
    Bubble Bread, **'81** 107
    Bunny Bread, Glazed, **'92** 102
    Butter-Egg Bread, **'85** 269
    Butterhorns, **'84** 267
    Buttermilk-Oatmeal Bread, **'97** 212
    Cake Bread, Golden, **'84** 269
    Canapé Bread, **'89** 292
    Caramel Bread, **'82** 75
    Caramel-Orange Coffee Ring, **'80** 45
    Caraway Breadsticks, **'89** 239
    Caraway Puffs, **'82** 174
    Caraway Seed Bread, Dark, **'80** 256
    Challah, **'92** 62
    Cheddar Cheese Bread, **'84** 268
    Cheese Bread, **'83** 208; **'87** 11
    Cheese Bread, Crusty, **'86** 233
    Cheese-Caraway Batter Bread, **'85** 33
    Cheese Crescents, **'82** 18
    Cheese-Herb Bread, **'84** M144
    Cheese Loaf, Jalapeño-, **'84** 76
    Cheese-Wine Bread, **'87** 254
    Chocolate Loaf Bread, **'88** M188
    Chocolate Pinwheel Loaf, **'80** 256
    Christmas Bread, **'87** 296; **'88** 288
    Christmas Bread, Norwegian, **'79** 234
    Christmas Wreath, **'80** 280
    Cinnamon Loaf, **'82** 18; **'85** 55
    Cinnamon-Nut Bubble Bread, **'80** 22
    Cinnamon-Oat Bread, **'90** 135
    Cinnamon Raisin Bread, **'80** 22
    Cinnamon Swirl Loaf, **'79** 23

Cinnamon Twists, **'83** 53
Cocoa-Nut Swirl Bread, **'80** 257
Coffee Ring, Filled, **'82** 18
Coffee Ring, Sugarplum, **'83** M37
Cornmeal Yeast Bread, **'89** 54
Cottage Cheese-Dill Bread, **'83** 154
Country Ham Bread with Herb Butter, **'99** 18
Cracker Bread, Sesame, **'87** 2
Cream Cheese Braids, **'82** 243; **'97** 287
Cream Cheese Loaves, Processor, **'85** 48
Crescents, Festive, **'80** 281
Croissants, **'83** 54; **'84** 188; **'96** 303
Croissants, Chocolate-Filled, **'96** 303
Croissants, Cinnamon-Sugar, **'96** 303
Croissants, Flaky Butter, **'85** 42
Croissants, Strawberry or Apricot, **'96** 303
Crust Bread, Country, **'80** 225
Dill-Oat Bread, **'91** 95
Dough, Basic Yeast, **'88** 74
Easter Bread, Golden, **'91** 54
Easter Egg Bread, **'84** 94; **'96** 88
Easy Yeast Bread, **'79** 147
Egg Bread, County Fair, **'87** 68
Elephant Ears, **'84** 18
English Muffin Bread, **'95** M79
English Muffin Loaf, **'82** 96
English Muffin Loaves, **'85** 42
Figure-8 Bread, **'79** 171
Flatbread, **'98** 106
Flat Bread, Italian-Style, **'82** 235; **'83** 41
Flatbread, Parmesan-Onion, **'98** 65
Focaccia, Dried Tomato, **'94** 65
Focaccia, Onion, **'93** 77
Focaccia, Roquefort-and-Onion, **'98** 54
Focaccia, Rosemary, **'95** 190
Focaccia with Rosemary, **'96** 84
French Bread, **'79** 158; **'87** 227; **'89** 54;
    '96 191
French Bread, Easy, **'88** 299
French Bread, Glazed, **'88** 75
French Bread, Herbed, **'85** 222; **'86** 166
French Bread, Mom's, **'98** 281
French Bread, New Orleans, **'80** 212
French Bread, Whole Wheat, **'88** 63
French Loaves, Crusty, **'85** 37
French Onion Bread, **'91** 90
French Pistou Bread, Crusty, **'97** 68
Fruit-and-Cheese Braid, **'86** 214
Gingerbread Men, Yeast, **'92** 312
Golden Bread, **'90** 47
Gouda Bread, **'91** 52
Grittibanz (Swiss Bread Figure), **'93** 265
Ham Bread with Herb Butter, Country,
    '86 255
Heartland Loaves, **'89** 287
Herb Bread, **'84** 268
Herb Bread, No-Knead, **'81** 217
Herb-Cheese Bread, **'85** 70
Herbed Bread, **'89** 34
Herb Loaf, Butterflake, **'86** 261
Herb-Sour Cream Bread, **'85** 268
Herman Food, **'82** 200
Holiday Wreath, **'81** 284
Honey-Cinnamon Swirl Bread, **'88** 287
Honey-Curry Bread, **'89** 250
Honey Graham Bread, **'99** 211
Honey-Granola Bread, **'86** 56
Honey Loaves, Hint o', **'81** 104
Honey-Oat Bread, **'89** 107; **'93** 232; **'98** 27
Honey Oatmeal Bread, **'80** 60
Honey Puffs, **'96** 153
Honey Twist, **'79** 80
Honey-Walnut Swirl, **'80** 21
Honey Wheat Bread, **'85** 18, 268

BREADS, Yeast
(continued)

Honey-Wheat Bread, '91 223
Italian Bread, '82 297
Kolecz (Polish Bread), '80 29
Lightbread, Coffee Can, '79 59
Light Yeast Bread, '81 299
Loaf Bread, Hospitality, '86 299
Loaf Bread, Old-Fashioned, '88 75
Loaves, Sweet-Filled Yeast, '90 46
Mandelkrantz, '92 32
Marble Loaf, '80 230
Monkey Bread, '82 243; '95 174
Monkey Bread, Easy, '90 214
Multi-Grain Bread, '86 236
Oat Bread, Caraway-Raisin, '86 44
Oatmeal Bread, '81 300; '92 212; '97 130
Oatmeal Bread, Round, '84 20
Oatmeal-Molasses Bread, '97 194
Oatmeal Pan Bread, Herbed, '97 243
Oatmeal-Raisin Bread, '83 59
Oat-Molasses Bread, '82 139
Old-Fashioned Yeast Bread, '79 284
Olive Bread, '93 78
Olive-Dill Casserole Bread, '92 16
Onion-Dill Bread, Easy, '85 5
Onion-Herb Bread, '90 165
Onion-Poppy Seed Twist, '97 242
Onion-Rye Bread, '99 55
Onion Twist Loaves, '84 300
Pandoro, '93 267
Panettone, '93 266
Parmesan Bread, '92 19; '93 231
Party Bread, '86 218
Peanut Butter Bread, '86 171
Peanut Lover's Bread, '93 211
Pimiento-Cheese Bread, '85 223; '86 166
Pitas, Puffy, '97 69
Pizza Batter Bread, '85 56
Pocket Bread, '79 58
Poppy Seed Loaf, '83 254
Portuguese Round Bread, '83 295
Potato Bread, '85 56
Potato Bread, Old-Fashioned, '86 57
Potato Lightbread, '80 225
Potato Loaves, '86 162
Pull-Apart Yeast Bread, '94 132
Raisin Batter Bread, Salt-Free, '86 33
Raisin Bread, Curried Chicken Salad on, '85 96
Raisin Bread, Homemade, '87 300
Raisin Bread, Round, '89 230
Raisin-Whole Wheat Bread, '93 77
Refrigerator Bread, No-Knead, '83 155
Roasted Red Bell Pepper Bread, '95 241
Rounds, Individual Bread, '83 159
Rye Bread, '84 21
Rye Bread, Swedish Orange-, '85 111
Rye Canapé Bread, '89 293
Rye Loaves, Swedish, '97 68
Rye Sandwich Bread, '82 65
Saffron Bread, '96 50
Sally Lunn, '81 157; '88 163; '94 233
Sandwiches, Stacking, '86 127
Savarin, Holiday, '80 280
Scones, Merry Cranberry-Nut Yeast, '99 274
Sesame-Wheat Breadsticks, '93 114
Soft Breadsticks, '83 115
Sopaipillas, '80 197
Sour Cream Bread, '79 59
Sour Cream-Cheese Bread, '85 33
Sourdough Bread, '82 201

Sourdough Bread Dough, Potato, '94 324; '95 77
Sourdough Bread, Potato, '94 325; '95 77
Sourdough Starter, Herman, '82 200
Sourdough Starter, Potato, '94 324; '95 77
"Sponge," '93 267
Squares, Yeast Bread, '83 155
Starter Food, '94 324
Sugar Plum Bread, '80 256
Sweet Bread Wreath, Glazed, '90 192
Sweet Christmas Loaf, '84 278
Swiss Cheese Bread, '79 60
Swiss Cheese Loaves, Mini, '95 80
Techniques of Breadmaking, '82 17
Trinity Feast Bread, '82 92; '83 83
Walnut Bread, '93 77
Wheat-and-Oat Bran Bread, '92 102
Wheat Bread, Buttermilk, '86 236
Wheat Bread, Pull-Apart Maple, '85 222; '86 166
White Bread, '79 275
White Bread, Cardamom, '82 236; '83 41
White Bread, Old-Fashioned, '81 285
White Bread, Special, '86 57
Whole Wheat Bran Bread, '79 58
Whole Wheat Bread, '83 17
Whole Wheat Bread and Rolls, Hearty, '79 92
Whole Wheat Bread, Anise-, '93 36
Whole Wheat Bread, Quick, '92 25
Whole Wheat Breadsticks, '84 228
Whole Wheat Canapé Bread, '89 293
Whole Wheat Honey Bread, '82 65; '83 106
Whole Wheat-Oatmeal Bread, '87 85
Whole Wheat-Rye Bread, '83 M37
Whole Wheat-White Bread, '82 130
Yogurt Bread, '97 130
Yellow Squash Bread, '84 140
Zucchini-Apple Bread, '87 255
Zucchini Bread, '85 111; '86 93
Zucchini Bread, Spiced, '79 161; '86 162
Zucchini Bread, Spicy, '81 305; '82 36
Zucchini-Carrot Bread, '83 190
Zucchini-Honey Bread, '89 143
Zucchini Loaves, '96 130

BROCCOLI
Appetizer, Broccoli-Cheese, '92 265
au Gratin, Broccoli, '82 M20
Bacon, Broccoli with, '92 302
Bake, Broccoli, '81 246; '89 279
Bakers, Broccoli, '99 308
Beef and Broccoli, Quick, '91 123
Beef and Broccoli with Chive Gravy, '88 214
Burritos, Broccoli, '83 200
Carnival Broccoli, '81 2

Casseroles
Almond-Broccoli Casserole, '88 62
au Gratin, Broccoli-and-Eggs, '85 289
au Gratin, Broccoli-Ham, '90 239
Bake, Broccoli, '89 279
Blue Cheese Casserole, Broccoli-, '85 260
Breakfast Casserole, Broccoli-Cheese, '99 233
Broccoli Casserole, '87 284; '88 M146, 265
Cheese Casserole, Broccoli-, '82 269; '84 9; '94 132
Cheesy Broccoli Bake, '83 255
Cheesy Broccoli Casserole, '84 293; '92 342; '95 M191
Cheesy Italian Broccoli Bake, '83 5
Chicken-Broccoli Casserole, '79 48; '91 315
Chicken Casserole, Broccoli-, '82 33
Company Broccoli Bake, '83 279
Corn Casserole, Broccoli-, '83 313
Crabmeat-Broccoli Casserole, '84 232

Divan Casserole, Chicken, '82 M203
Divan, Chicken, '80 10; '87 M218
Divan, Creamy Turkey, '90 M34
Divan, Curried Chicken, '80 83
Divan, Easy Chicken, '94 310
Divan, Gourmet Chicken, '82 83
Divan, Overnight Chicken, '83 198
Divan Quiche, Chicken, '88 M125
Divan, Quick Turkey, '89 178
Divan, Sherried Chicken, '80 38
Divan, Turkey, '82 268
Egg Casserole, Broccoli-and-, '86 324
English Walnut Broccoli, '89 68
Garden Surprise, '83 112
Ham and Broccoli Casserole, '81 133
Ham and Broccoli Strata, '80 261
Ham-Broccoli Casserole, Quick, '82 40
Italian Broccoli Casserole, '82 6, 280; '83 32
Onion Deluxe, Broccoli-, '81 75
Potato-Broccoli-Cheese Bake, '80 114
Rice Casserole, Broccoli-, '81 101
Sausage and Broccoli Casserole, '80 33
Stuffing, Broccoli with, '95 341
Supreme, Broccoli, '85 68
Swiss Cheese Casserole, Broccoli-, '83 322; '85 M211
Tuna-Broccoli Casserole, Tangy, '83 75
Turkey-and-Broccoli Casserole, '86 332
Winter Broccoli Casserole, '94 280
Cheese Sauce, Broccoli with, '82 107
Chinese Broccoli, '85 M12
Chowder, Broccoli, '79 16
Chowder, Swiss-Broccoli, '80 73
Cocktail Broccoli, '80 192
Crêpes, Royal Brunch, '81 44
Dip, Broccoli-Garlic, '82 59
Dip, Cheesy Broccoli, '83 92
Dip, Santa Fe Skinny, '94 137
Eggs, Broccoli and Creamed, '83 84
Elegant, Broccoli, '81 267
Fettuccine, Broccoli-Parmesan, '93 55
Fettuccine with Broccoli, '90 97
Filling, Broccoli, '81 44
French Sauce, Broccoli with, '81 295
Frittata, Broccoli-Cheese, '81 243
Frittata, Ham-and-Broccoli, '98 101
Fritters, Cheesy Broccoli, '79 53
Garlic Broccoli, '93 35; '95 54; '99 46
Glazed Broccoli with Almonds, '80 12
Herbed Broccoli, '88 101
Hollandaise Sauce, Broccoli with, '79 244, 276
Hollandaise Sauce, Broccoli with Mock, '82 272
Horseradish Sauce, Broccoli with, '81 2; '83 206; '84 33
Horseradish Sauce, Carrots and Broccoli with, '91 246
Italian-Style Broccoli, '88 41
Italienne, Broccoli, '82 300
Jade-Green Broccoli, '80 12
Lemon Broccoli, '88 119; '95 53
Lemon-Broccoli Goldenrod, '84 M89
Lemon Cream, Broccoli with, '89 245
Lemon Dressing, Chilled Broccoli with, '88 270
Lemon Sauce and Pecans, Broccoli with, '86 71
Lemon Sauce, Broccoli with, '91 292; '92 256
Linguine, Broccoli, '98 30
Linguine, Chicken-Broccoli, '98 30
Lo Mein Noodles and Broccoli, '97 18
Marinated Broccoli, '80 79; '81 40; '85 207; '86 157; '88 255
Marinated Fresh Broccoli, '81 M139
Medley, Cauliflower-Broccoli, '81 69
Muffins, Broccoli-Chicken, '96 27
Olive-Butter Sauce, Broccoli with, '83 118

Omelet, Broccoli-Mushroom, '85 45
Onions, Broccoli-Stuffed, '84 154
Orange Broccoli, Easy, '85 267
Orange Sauce, Broccoli with, '80 243
Parmesan, Broccoli, '97 302
Pasta, Broccoli, '84 176
Pasta, Chicken-and-Broccoli, '87 286
Pasta with Broccoli and Sausage, '87 109;
  '97 266
Pasta with Peppers and Broccoli, '91 69
Pickled Broccoli, '81 308
Pie, Broccoli-and-Turkey Pasta, '88 269
Pie, Broccoli-Beef, '83 196
Pie, Broccoli-Cheese, '84 235
Pimiento Broccoli, '86 268
Polonaise, Broccoli, '86 55
Potatoes and Broccoli, Creamy, '92 61
Potatoes, Broccoli-and-Almond-Topped, '83 3
Potatoes, Broccoli-Shrimp Stuffed, '92 M228
Potatoes, Broccoli-Topped Baked, '86 17
Potatoes, Stuffed Mashed, '98 328
Puff, Broccoli, '81 94; '82 95
Quiche, Broccoli-Rice, '81 228
Quiche, Easy Broccoli, '82 34
Quiche, Italian Broccoli, '85 45
Quick-and-Easy Broccoli, '86 55
Rice, Holiday Broccoli with, '87 252
Risotto with Parmesan, Broccoli, '99 120
Rolls, Broccoli-Cheddar, '91 21
Rolls, Ham-and-Broccoli, '86 212; '87 82
Salads
  Barley-Broccoli Salad, '90 135
  Beef-and-Broccoli Salad, '87 187
  Broccoli Salad, '82 24; '85 249; '90 292;
    '95 95; '99 84
  Carrot-Broccoli Salad, '99 26
  Cauliflower-Broccoli Crunch, '88 216
  Cauliflower-Broccoli Salad, '79 20
  Cauliflower-Broccoli Toss, '82 54
  Cauliflower Salad, Broccoli-, '92 97
  Cauliflower Salad, Broccoli and, '81 280
  Cauliflower Salad, Broccoli 'n', '90 32
  Cauliflower Salad, Creamy Broccoli and,
    '81 23
  Cauliflower Toss, Crunchy Broccoli, '83 25
  Chicken Salad, Broccoli-, '90 129
  Congealed Broccoli Salad, '84 124
  Corn Salad, Broccoli-, '87 24
  Creamy Broccoli Salad, '79 143
  Crunchy Broccoli Salad, '83 39
  Curried Broccoli Salad, '86 225
  Fresh Broccoli Salad, '82 34; '87 103
  Mandarin Salad, Broccoli-, '93 325
  Marinated Broccoli, '80 79
  Marinated Broccoli Salad, '83 240
  Marinated Broccoli, Tangy, '80 284
  Medley, Broccoli, '81 206
  Orange Salad, Broccoli-, '94 281
  Pasta Salad, Broccoli-Cauliflower, '88 269
  Pasta Salad, Broccoli-Cheese-, '96 184
  Peanut Salad, Broccoli-, '92 35
  Pepperoni-and-Broccoli Salad, '83 216
  Potato Salad, Hot Broccoli-, '85 23
  Raisin Salad, Creamy Broccoli-, '92 106
  Red Pepper Salad, Broccoli and, '83 224
  Red, White, and Green Salad, '90 18
  Slaw, Sweet Broccoli, '96 20; '98 332
  Slaw, Zesty Broccoli, '93 246
  Supreme, Broccoli Salad, '83 260
  Warm Broccoli Salad, '92 35
Sauce, Broccoli, '91 85
Sauté, Broccoli and Walnut, '95 52
Sautéed Broccoli, '79 246
Savory Broccoli, '79 268; '80 14

Sesame Broccoli, '84 69; '85 8
Sesame, Broccoli with, '80 13
Sesame Seeds, Broccoli with, '82 34
Shrimp Sauce, Broccoli and Cauliflower with,
  '84 248
Soufflé, Broccoli, '81 24
Soufflé, Golden Broccoli, '84 283
Soufflés, Broccoli, '96 218
Soup, Broccoli, '86 161, M194; '87 288
Soup, Broccoli-and-Chicken, '90 202
Soup, Broccoli-Swiss, '86 6
Soup, Cheese-and-Broccoli, '89 276
Soup, Cheesy-Broccoli, '86 258
Soup, Creamed Broccoli, '85 24
Soup, Cream of Broccoli, '79 130; '80 188, M225;
  '82 314; '83 66; '86 259
Soup, Cream-of-Broccoli, '88 56
Soup, Creamy Broccoli, '81 75; '82 13; '83 99;
  '91 307
Soup, Easy Broccoli, '81 307
Soup, Fresh Broccoli, '91 86
Soup, Hot Broccoli, '81 235; '83 44
Soup, Light Cream of Broccoli, '93 17
Soup, Mock Cream of Broccoli, '85 288
Sour Cream Sauce, Broccoli with, '87 127
Spears, Saucy Broccoli, '84 35
Spears, Zesty Broccoli, '79 152
Spread, Broccamoli Curry, '88 55
Stack-Ups, Jiffy Tomato, '80 161
Steamed Broccoli, '80 122
Steamed Broccoli with Tangy Chive Sauce,
  '83 101
Stew, Oyster-Broccoli, '89 242
Stir-Fried Broccoli, '83 227
Stir-Fry Beef and Broccoli, '79 47
Stir-Fry, Beef-and-Broccoli, '91 46
Stir-Fry, Bok Choy-Broccoli, '84 2
Stir-Fry Broccoli, '80 19
Stir-Fry Broccoli and Beef, '83 110
Stir-Fry, Chicken-Broccoli, '82 33
Stir-Fry, Turkey-Broccoli, '91 62
Stroganoff, Chicken-and-Broccoli, '89 M248
Sunshine Sauce, Broccoli with, '84 248
Supreme, Broccoli, '82 34; '85 68
Supreme, Broccoli-Carrot, '89 331
Supreme, Creamy Broccoli, '82 287
Tomatoes, Broccoli-Stuffed, '83 136; '93 216
Toss, Broccoli, '86 294
Toss, Italian Cauliflower-Broccoli, '88 269
Vinaigrette, Potato-Broccoli, '85 84
White Wine, Broccoli with, '80 12
Wine Sauce, Broccoli with, '84 187
Ziti with Sausage and Broccoli, '95 340
BROWNIES. *See also* **COOKIES/Bars and**
  Squares.
  Alaskas, Brownie, '83 299
  Amaretto Brownies, '86 246
  Amaretto-Walnut Brownies, '99 311
  Angel Fluff Brownies, '99 221
  Apple Brownies, Frosted, '86 216
  Basic Brownies, '97 M34
  Biscuit Mix Brownies, '94 M51
  Blonde Brownies, Nutty, '85 249
  Blonde Brownies with Chocolate Chunks, '91 271
  Broadway Brownie Bars, '97 M35
  Buttermilk Brownies, '85 249
  Buttermilk Cake Brownies, '87 198
  Butterscotch Brownies, '85 248
  Cake, Brownie-Carrot, '92 120
  Candy Bar Brownies, '92 204
  Cheesecake Brownies, '85 249
  Chocolate-Banana Brownies, '80 160
  Chocolate Chip Brownies, '81 162
  Chocolate Chip-Peanut Butter Brownies, '84 73

Chocolate-Coconut Brownies, '97 35
Chocolate Ice Cream Brownies, '89 124
Chocolate-Kahlúa Brownies, '93 99
Chocolate-Mint Brownies, '85 M294; '88 80
Chocolate-Mint Brownies, Southern, '93 216
Chocolate-Nut Brownies, '81 129
Chocolate-Peanut Butter Chip Brownies, '91 306
Chocolate-Pecan Brownies, '81 64
Chocolate-Peppermint Brownies, '88 262
Chocolate Tea Brownies, '83 79
Chocolate-Walnut Brownies, '89 325
Choco-Mallow Brownies, '87 198; '90 309
Cinnamon Brownie Bars, '81 230
Cocoa Brownies, Nutty, '81 64
Coconut-Pecan-Frosted Brownies, '97 99
Cookies, Brownie Chip, '90 320
Cookies, Brownie Waffle, '86 245
Cream Cheese Brownies à la Mode, Magnolias,
  '97 M178
Cream Cheese Swirl Brownies, '79 51
Crème de Menthe Brownies, '83 244
Crunch-Crust Brownies, '87 198
Date-and-Almond Brownies, '88 217
Derby Brownies, Special, '90 94
Easy Brownies, '83 245
Favorite Brownies, '86 158
Frosted Brownies, '97 M87
Fudge Brownies, Nutty, '80 M171
German Cream Cheese Brownies, '80 269
Gooey Brownies, '97 133
Heavenly Hash Brownies, '83 245
Honey Brownies, Heavenly, '79 83
Macadamia-Fudge Designer Brownies, '94 51
Marshmallow Brownies, Chewy, '83 306
Mint Dessert, Brownie-, '82 227
Mint Julep Brownies, '93 165
Mississippi Mud Brownies, '89 M25
Mix, Brownie, '82 6
Mocha Brownies, '87 93
Mocha Frosting, Brownies with, '94 292
Mother's Brownies, '93 239
Muffins, Fudge Brownie, '95 M50
No-Bake Brownies, '94 330
Oat Brownies, '89 59
Oatmeal Brownies, '87 199
Oat 'n' Crunch Brownies, '91 233
Passover Brownies, '98 M104
Passover, Brownies for, '99 56
Peanut Butter Brownies, '87 199
Peanut Butter Brownies, Frosted, '92 272
Pistachio-Mint Brownies, '94 50
Pizza, Banana Split-Brownie, '96 M164
Praline Brownies, '93 243
Pretzel Brownies, Saucepan, '85 171
Quick and Easy Brownies, '82 6
Quick Brownies, '87 M302
Raspberry Brownies, '92 274; '97 M35
Rich Brownies, '95 84
Rocky Road Brownies, '86 320
Triple Decker Brownies, '92 319
Walnut-Cream Cheese Brownies, '84 240
White Chocolate Brownies, '89 169; '97 36
BRUSSELS SPROUTS
Amandine, Brussels Sprouts, '79 213
Beer, Brussels Sprouts in, '85 69
Brussels Sprouts, '89 278
Caramelized Onion-and-Pecan Brussels Sprouts,
  '99 254
Carrots and Brussels Sprouts, '82 300
Cashews, Brussels Sprouts with, '81 2
Casserole, Brussels Sprouts-and-Artichoke,
  '94 279
Casserole of Brussels Sprouts, '86 294
Celery, Brussels Sprouts and, '79 21

BRUSSELS SPROUTS

(continued)

Cheese Sauce, Brussels Sprouts with, '79 246
Citrus Brussels Sprouts, Calico, '85 303
Creamed Brussels Sprouts and Celery, '83 322
Creamy Brussels Sprouts, '79 212
Deviled Brussels Sprouts, '84 248
Dijon, Brussels Sprouts, '96 91
Dilled Brussels Sprouts, '88 180
Fried Brussels Sprouts, '81 308
Glazed Brussels Sprouts and Baby Carrots, '97 302
Glorified Brussels Sprouts, '86 282
Lemon Sauce, Brussels Sprouts in, '82 269
Lemon Sprouts, '85 288
Lemony Brussels Sprouts with Celery, '85 25
Marinated Brussels Sprouts, '88 265; '96 252; '97 29
Medley, Brussels Sprouts, '79 212; '85 267
Mustard Sauce, Brussels Sprouts in, '87 253; '90 228
Onion Sauce, Brussels Sprouts in, '81 308
Orange Brussels Sprouts, '84 34
Orange Sauce, Brussels Sprouts in, '86 55
Pierre, Brussels Sprouts, '84 248
Polonaise, Brussels Sprouts, '85 79
Rice, Brussels Sprouts and, '79 288; '80 26
Salad, Brussels Sprouts, '87 233
Salad, Cauliflower-Brussels Sprouts, '83 240
Sautéed Brussels Sprouts with Parmesan
    Soufflés, '97 280
Sesame Brussels Sprouts, '86 55
Shallots and Mustard, Brussels Sprouts
    with, '85 258
Stir-Fry, Brussels Sprouts, '81 308
Tangy Brussels Sprouts, '88 40
Tarragon Brussels Sprouts, '83 291
Wine Butter, Brussels Sprouts in, '86 327

BULGUR

Burgers with Cucumber Sauce, Lamb, '98 102
Lentils, Tex-Mex, '99 288
Salad, Cracked Wheat-Fruit, '96 240
Salad with Citrus and Mint, Wheat, '99 163
Tabbouleh, '93 70; '99 175
Tabbouleh Pitas, '98 105
Tabbouleh Salad, '92 212; '94 174
(Tabbouleh Salad), Boot Scoot Tabbouli, '96 159
Wild Rice Bulgur, '91 83

BUNS. *See* **ROLLS AND BUNS.**

BURRITOS

Bean Burrito Appetizers, '94 226
Beef Burritos, Cheesy, '85 193
Breakfast Burritos, '84 57; '90 192; '97 172; '99 103
Broccoli Burritos, '83 200
Brunch Burritos, '91 77
Burritos, '80 196
Carne Guisada Burritos, '95 43
Chimichangas (Fried Burritos), '81 196; '85 244; '86 114
Chinese Burritos, '87 181
Egg Burritos, Tex-Mex, '95 34
Fiesta Burritos, '86 114
Lentil Burritos, '99 287
Meat-and-Bean Burritos, '81 194
Monterey Burritos, '84 292
Phyllo Burritos, Hot, '98 312
Pie, Mexican Burrito, '87 287
Pork Burritos with Pico de Gallo, '97 140
Rollups, Burrito, '90 119
Vegetable Burritos, '80 197; '90 134; '92 138
Vegetable Burritos with Avocado Sauce, '83 200
Vegetarian Burritos, '93 319
Veggie Burritos, Tony's, '96 289

BUTTER

Acorn Squash-and-Bourbon Butter, '94 266
Ancho Chile Butter, '99 93
Apple Butter, '79 200; '81 217; '92 311
Apple Butter, Half-Hour, '81 203
Apple Butter, Slow Cooker, '97 235
Apricot Butter, '82 308; '99 212
Balls, Butter, '82 189; '89 90
Basil Butter, '87 171; '99 274
Basil Butter, Asparagus with, '85 40
Blackberry Butter, '97 306
Blue Cheese Butter, '97 306
Bourbon Butter, '97 306
Cashew Butter, Asparagus with, '87 56
Cheese Butter, '84 114
Chervil Butter, '83 129
Chervil Butter, Swordfish Steak with, '91 147
Chili Butter, '82 219; '97 306
Chipotle Pepper Butter, '97 307
Chive-Mustard Butter, '98 156
Cilantro Butter, '98 182
Cilantro-Lime Butter, '98 156
Cinnamon Butter, '92 319
Cinnamon-Honey Butter, '89 281
Citrus Butter, '97 307
Clarified Butter, '81 59
Clarifying Butter, '82 189
Cranberry Butter, '97 307
Curls, Butter, '82 51, 189; '89 90
Flavored Butters, '97 306
Frosting, Browned Butter, '97 247
Garlic-Basil Butter, '98 156
Garlic Butter, '83 193; '84 108; '95 89
Gazpacho Butter, '92 86
Ginger Butter, '91 26
Green Peppercorn Butter, '88 60; '90 117
Herb Butter, '86 128, 255, 261, 306; '96 309; '97 306; '99 19
Herb Butter, Cauliflower with, '81 2
Herb Butter, Corn-on-the-Cob with, '84 160
Herbed Caper Butter, '94 62
Herbed Unsalted Butter, '82 67
Herb-Garlic Butter, '96 173
Honey Butter, '93 309; '94 206; '95 139; '97 307
Honey-Orange Butter, '79 36; '85 19
Horseradish-Chive Butter, '86 277
Horseradish-Parsley Butter, '98 156
Jalapeño Butter, '97 306
Jalapeño-Chili Butter, '98 156
Lemon-Anchovy Butter, '97 307
Lemon Butter, '95 32; '96 124
Lemon Butter, Asparagus with, '87 M151; '98 168
Lemon-Dill Butter, Green Beans with, '99 141
Lemon Pepper Butter, '97 307
Lime Butter, Chicken with, '84 68
Maple-Flavored Butter, Whipped, '79 36
Mediterranean Butter, '97 307
Molds, Butter, '89 90
Nectarine Butter, '79 175
Olive Butter, '91 295
Onion Butter, '86 253
Onion Butter, Sweet, '93 124
Orange Butter, '81 8, 42; '90 323; '92 319; '94 115; '97 44
Orange-Pecan Butter, '84 75; '97 15
Peach Butter, '82 308
Peach Butter, Golden, '91 178
Pear Butter, '85 130
Pear Butter, Spiced, '80 218
Pecan Butter, '97 307
Pesto Butter, '97 307
Plum Butter, '88 152
Prune-Orange Butter, '92 49

Raisin Butter, '81 272
Red Pepper Butter, Fillet of Beef with, '96 32
Roasted Garlic Butter, '97 46
Roasted Red Bell Pepper Butter, '95 242
Sage Butter, '96 269
Sauce, Brown Butter, '91 65
Sauce, Butter-Rum, '95 134
Sauce, Garlic Buerre Blanc, '88 222
Sauce, Garlic-Butter, '95 327
Sauce, Garlic-Ginger Butter, '94 89
Sauce, Honey-Butter, '98 45
Sauce, Lemon-Butter, '99 198
Sauce, Pecan-Butter, '91 65
Sauce, Red Wine-Butter, '96 173
Sauce, Strawberry-Butter, '96 87
Sauce, White Butter, '92 107
Seafood Butter, '97 306
Sesame Butter, '97 307
Sesame-Ginger Butter, '99 142
Shrimp Butter, '92 91
Southwestern Butter, '92 320
Spread, Cranberry-Butter, '99 86
Spread, Garlic-Butter, '96 199
Spread, Honey Mustard-Butter, '99 86
Strawberry Butter, '79 36; '81 286; '91 71; '99 44, 234
Sweet Potato Butter, '95 M290
Thyme-Lemon Butter, '96 121
Tomato Butter, '86 128
Tomato-Curry-Orange Butter, '93 159

BUTTERSCOTCH

Bars, Butterscotch, '82 209; '83 297
Bars, Chocolate-Butterscotch, '81 197
Bread, Banana Butterscotch, '79 116
Brownies, Butterscotch, '85 248
Cake, Butterscotch, '91 270
Cake, Butterscotch-Pecan Pound, '92 153
Cheesecake, Butterscotch, '86 188
Cookies, Butterscotch, '87 58
Cookies, Butterscotch-Pecan, '84 36
Fantastic, Butterscotch, '83 76
Filling, Butterscotch, '91 271
Fudge, Butterscotch-Peanut, '98 M282
Fudge, Butterscotch Rum, '88 256
Fudge, Four Chips, '92 318
Fudge Scotch Ring, '79 273
Mousse, Butterscotch, '93 254
Pie, Butterscotch, '97 212
Pie, Butterscotch Cream, '84 48; '87 207
Pie, Butterscotch Meringue, '83 158
Pinwheels, Butterscotch, '90 49
Pralines, Butterscotch, '81 253
Sauce, Butterscotch-Pecan, '82 212
Sticky Buns, Christmas Morning, '97 245
Trail Mix, Bunny, '95 101

C

ABBAGE. *See also* **SAUERKRAUT, SLAWS.**
Apples and Franks, Cabbage with, '87 42
au Gratin, Cabbage, '83 279
Bake, Zesty Cabbage Beef, '80 300
Beef-Cabbage Dinner, '81 179
Bubbling Cabbage, '84 2
Caraway Cabbage, '85 32, 289
Caraway, Cabbage with, '93 181
Casserole, Cabbage, '97 88
Casserole, Cheesy Cabbage, '79 4
Casserole, Creamy Cabbage, '80 63
Casserole, Italian Cabbage, '87 42
Casserole, Savory Cabbage, '82 168
Chop Suey, Cabbage, '81 101
Chow-Chow, '82 196
Chowchow, '87 150

Chowder, Hearty Cabbage, '80 25
Colcannon, '90 64
Corned Beef and Cabbage, '83 104; '93 64; '96 328
Corned Beef and Cabbage au Gratin, '83 16
Corned Beef and Cabbage, Quick, '79 54
Corned Beef Squares and Cabbage, '82 86
Country-Style Cabbage, '81 271
Creamed Cabbage with Almonds, '79 4
Creole Cabbage, '87 189
Duck Breast, Tender, '97 215
Dumplings, Steamed Sesame, '97 208
Egg Rolls, Scrumptious, '96 101
Frankfurter-Cabbage Skillet, '80 166
Hot Cabbage Creole, '87 42
Kielbasa and Cabbage, '85 67; '89 M196
Kielbasa, Cabbage, '87 42
Lemon-Butter Cabbage, '88 156
Medley, Cabbage, '80 64; '83 104
Medley, Cabbage-Onion-Sweet Pepper, '96 252; '97 28
Orange Juice, Cabbage Cooked in, '97 129
Peppers, Carrot-and-Cabbage Stuffed, '99 63
Piccalilli, Kentucky, '81 216
Pork Chops, Chinese, '97 320
Quick Cooked Cabbage, '95 270
Red Cabbage, '96 272
Red Cabbage and Apples, '85 32
Red Cabbage, Braised, '95 343; '99 243
Red Cabbage, Cooked, '97 28
Red Cabbage, German, '94 254
Red Cabbage, German-Style, '84 2; '98 279
Red Cabbage, Pickled, '81 271
Red Cabbage, Sweet-Sour, '79 5
Red Cabbage with Pineapple, '97 215
Relish, Cabbage, '83 260
Relish, Spanish Cabbage, '95 270
Reuben Strudel, '98 28
Rolls, Beef Stuffed Cabbage, '81 87; '82 7
Rolls, Cabbage, '83 104
Rolls, Crunchy Cabbage-Rice, '85 32
Rolls, Easy Cabbage-and-Beef, '88 49
Rolls, Fried Cabbage, '95 270
Rolls, Hot-and-Spicy Cabbage, '84 249
Rolls, Hungarian Cabbage, '94 47
Rolls, Southwestern Cabbage, '97 214
Rolls, Spicy Cabbage, '84 2
Rolls, Stuffed Cabbage, '84 217; '88 18; '92 251
Rolls, Vegetarian Cabbage, '91 86
Rollups, Beef-and-Cabbage, '80 63
Salad, Austrian Hash with Cabbage, '95 262
Salad, Cabbage, '87 120, 233
Salad, Cabbage and Fruit, '79 286
Salad, Chinese Cabbage, '81 271
Salad, Chinese Green, '88 48
Salad, Garden Cabbage, '81 210
Salad, Nutty Cabbage, '87 42
Salad, Overnight Cabbage, '79 83
Salad, Red Cabbage Citrus, '94 72
Salad, Tangy Cabbage, '82 55
Salad, Turkish, '96 137
Salad, Wilted Cabbage, '94 281
Salad, Winter Cabbage, '98 284
Sausage, Cabbage with Polish, '83 104
Sausage-Sauced Cabbage, '81 271
Sausage Surprise, '83 245; '84 42
Scalloped Cabbage, '82 269
Scalloped Cabbage, Cheese, '81 87; '82 7
Skillet Cabbage, '89 314; '90 229
Skillet, Cabbage-and-Tomato, '86 110
Skillet, Rutabaga-Cabbage, '99 285
Soup, Cabbage, '83 291
Soup, Cabbage-Bean, '97 301
Soup, Sweet-and-Sour Cabbage, '89 314

Spinach Dip in Cabbage, '82 155
Stir-Fried Cabbage, '81 75, 271; '85 109
Stuffed Cabbage, '84 282
Stuffed Cabbage, Italian, '84 294
Supper, Cabbage, '89 314
Supreme, Cabbage, '79 4; '83 206
Sweet-and-Sour Cabbage, '86 295; '87 189
Tex-Mex Cabbage, '80 63
Tomatoes, Cabbage and, '83 104
Tomatoes, Tasty Cabbage and, '86 72
Wedges, Saucy Cabbage, '83 86
Wedges, Smothered Cabbage, '81 87; '82 7
Wilted Cabbage, '80 64; '88 229
CAKES. See also **BREADS, CHEESECAKES.**
Acorn Squash Cake, '96 216
Almond-Butter Cake, '86 107
Almond-Butter Cake, Peachy, '90 107
Almond-Butter Cake, Toasted, '99 315
Almond-Butter Wedding Cake, '86 106
Almond Legend Cake, '82 8
Almond Whipping Cream Cake, '80 295
Amaretto Cake, Easy, '85 79
Ambrosia Cake, '79 229
Ambrosia Cake Royale, '89 335
Angel Food
  Amaretto-Almond Sauce, Angel Food Cake with, '90 199
  Cappuccino Mousse Cake, '99 154
  Chocolate Angel Cake, '88 128
  Chocolate Angel Food Cake, '87 21; '90 111; '91 55
  Chocolate Angel Food Cake with Custard Sauce, '88 259
  Coconut Angel Cake, Spiked, '85 279
  Deluxe Angel Food Cake, '86 121
  Ice Cream Angel Cake, '83 23
  Ice-Cream Angel Dessert, Triple Mint, '93 86
  Lemon Angel Cake, '80 147; '97 163
  Orange Angel Food Cake, '96 246
  Orange-Coconut Angel Food Cake, '94 294
  Pineapple-Orange Sauce, Angel Cake with, '84 14
  Surprise, Angel Cake, '93 86
  Trifle, Pineapple Angel Food, '93 86
  White Chocolate Mousse Cake, Strawberry-Studded, '99 154
Apple Cake, '83 312; '84 262
Apple Cake, Dried-, '79 13
Apple-Date Cake, Fresh, '83 300
Apple-Ginger Upside-Down Cake, '94 180
Apple-Nut Cake, '87 76; '96 268
Apple-Oatmeal Cake, Golden, '86 301
Apple-Pecan Cake, '92 167
Apple Pie Cake, '86 301
Applesauce Cake, '80 270; '96 67
Applesauce Cake, My Favorite, '87 263
Applesauce Cake with Bourbon Frosting, '88 236
Applesauce Carrot Cake, '81 202
Applesauce-Oatmeal Cake, '92 119
Applesauce Snack Cakes, '88 215; '89 20
Applesauce-Spice Cake, '83 42
Applesauce Spice Cake, '89 296
Apple Shortcake, Quick, '93 42
Apple Slice Cake, '85 93
Apple Spice Cake, '92 225
Apple Stack Cake, Dried, '85 242
Apple-Walnut Cake, '94 242
Apricot-Almond Upside-Down Cake, '97 204
Banana-Blueberry Cake, '86 247
Banana Cake, '84 151
Banana Cake, Deluxe Light, '84 314
Banana Cake, Marvelous, '79 115

Banana Cake with Coconut Custard, Supreme, '97 131
Banana-Coconut Cake, '93 154
Banana-Nut Cake, '92 120
Banana-Pecan Shortcake, '93 43
Bananas Foster Crunch Cake, '93 339
Banana Split Cake, '99 48
Banana Waldorf Cake, '85 118
Bars and Squares
  Almond Cake Squares, '79 111
  Angel Squares, Mocha, '98 61
  Apple-Date Dream Cake Squares, '85 10
  Apple-Orange Cake Squares, '84 150
  Applesauce Cake Squares, '86 8
  Applesauce-Spice Squares, '86 248
  Buttermilk Fudge Squares, '99 99
  Carrot-Lemon Squares, Golden, '80 40
  Carrot Squares, '79 256
  Cherry Cheesecake Bars, '97 330
  Cinnamon Cake Squares, '87 222
  Cream Cheese Cake Squares, '84 321
  Crumb Cake, Calico, '87 261
  Gingerbread, Gingery, '96 100
  Gingerbread Squares, '84 16
  Ginger Cake, '87 222
  Honey Cake Squares, '89 250
  Honey-Oatmeal Cake, '87 222
  Jam Squares, '81 M289
  Orange Cake Squares, '81 34
  Orange-Pumpkin Cake Squares, '83 242
  Pecan Squares, Easy, '81 230
  Pumpkin Cake Bars, '80 245
  Rhubarb Squares, '92 129
  Strawberry Shortcake Squares, '85 122; '86 124
  Zucchini-Carrot Cake, '93 20
Beerquick Sugar Cake, '96 112
Beet Cake with Almond Topping, '86 200
Birdhouse Cake, '93 284
Birthday Cake, Clowning Around, '94 52
Blackberry Cake, Fresh, '81 132
Blackberry Flan, '79 182
Black Walnut Cake, '80 253; '84 316; '90 308
Blueberry-Sour Cream Cake, '90 140
Blueberry Streusel Cake, '92 144
Boston Cream Pie, '83 220
Bourbon Cake, '98 277
Bourbon-Pecan Cake, '84 25
Brown Mountain Cake, '84 39
Brown Sugar Meringue Cake, '81 70
Brown Sugar Snack Cake, '98 195
Bûche de Noël, '84 304; '87 241
Bûche de Noël Cake, '82 262
Bunny Cake, '94 98
Butter Brickle Cake, '85 118
Butter Brickle Loaf Cakes, '98 137
Butter Cake, Old-Fashioned, '97 60
Butter Pecan Cake, '80 229
Butter Pecan Cake, Caramel-Filled, '88 278
Butterscotch Cake, '91 270
Cajun Cake, '87 138
Candy Bar Cake, '92 204; '98 90
Caramel Cake, '89 55; '90 307
Caramel Layer Cake, Creamy, '81 71
Carolina Dream Cake, '88 278
Carrot
  Applesauce Carrot Cake, '81 202
  Best Carrot Cake, '97 230
  Blue Ribbon Carrot Cake, '81 70
  Brownie Carrot Cake, '92 120
  Carrot Cake, '79 45; '82 137; '84 315; '98 275
  Cheater's Carrot Cake, '96 20
  Coconut-Carrot Cake, Fresh, '80 299
  Coconut-Pecan Carrot Cake, '84 322

CAKES, Carrot
(continued)

Easy Carrot Cake, **'83** 215
Easy Carrot Snack Cake, **'82** 235
Frosted Carrot Cake, **'92** 19
German Carrot-Hazelnut Cake, **'97** 230
Old-Fashioned Carrot Cake, **'83** M232;
  '97 330
Old-Fashioned Carrot Sheet Cake, **'97** 330
Old-South Carrot Cake, **'80** 120
Quick-and-Easy Carrot Cake, **'84** 150
Madeira Syrup and Vanilla Ice Cream, Carrot
  Cakes with, **'98** 247
Miniature Carrot Cakes, **'90** 94
Pecan-Carrot Cake, **'99** 223
Pound Cake, Carrot, **'87** 41
Pudding Cake, Carrot, **'83** 24
Spiced Carrot Cake, **'87** 296
Spicy Fruited Carrot Cake, **'85** 117
Zucchini-Carrot Cake, **'93** 20
Chart, Cake Failure, **'81** 72
Cherry Bourbon Cake, **'82** 287
Cherry Cake, **'79** 165
Cherry Cake, Dried, **'97** 33
Cherry Cake, Quick, **'81** 238
Cherry Upside-Down Cake, **'82** 56
Chocolate. *See also* **CAKES/Angel Food,**
  Pound, Tortes.
Almond Cake, Chocolate-, **'91** 248
Almond Cake with Cherry Filling, Chocolate-,
  '84 225
Banana Cake, Chocolate-, **'86** 138
Banana Loaf, Chocolate Chip-, **'85** 115
Basket Cake, Chocolate-Strawberry, **'98** 100
Beet Cake, Chocolate, **'80** 40
Birthday Cake, Fishin'-for-Fun, **'93** 194
Black Forest Cake, **'81** 126; **'92** 174
Black Forest Cake, Six-Layer, **'85** 125
Black Forest Cherry Cake, **'83** 302
Black Forest Dump Cake, **'85** 13
Brownie Baked Alaska, **'80** 66
Brownie Delight, Chocolate, **'87** 224
Buttercream Cake, Chocolate, **'90** 108
Buttermilk Chocolate Cake, **'79** 13
Buttermilk Fudge Squares, **'99** 99
Cameo Cake, **'94** 58
Candy Cake, Chocolate, **'81** 238
Caramel-Nut Cake, Chocolate-, **'83** 23
Carrot Cake, Brownie, **'92** 120
Cherry Cake, Choco-, **'96** 229
Cherry Cake, Chocolate-, **'84** 200; **'86** 239
Cherry Fudge Cake, **'98** 214
Chiffon Cake with Coffee Buttercream,
  Chocolate, **'95** 277
Chocolate Cake, **'97** 283
Cinnamon Cake, Chocolate-, **'93** 154
Cocoa Crown Cake, **'90** 107
Coconut Cake, Chocolate-, **'83** 23
Coconut-Fudge Cake, **'99** 206
Cola Cake, Quick Chocolate, **'95** 56
Cookies-and-Cream Cake, **'92** 163
Custard Cake, Chocolate, **'88** 175
Decadent Chocolate Cake, **'86** 142
Easy Chocolate Cake, **'80** 140
Easy Perfect Chocolate Cake, **'99** 307
Extra-Rich Chocolate Cake, **'99** 271
Father's Day Cake, **'92** 134
Frosting, Chocolate Cake with Double,
  '86 314
Fudge Cake, **'94** M293; **'98** 110; **'99** 176
Fudge Cake, Best, **'83** 301
Fudge Cake, Brown Sugar, **'86** 316

Fudge Cake, Chocolate, **'80** 279
Fudge Cake, Coconut-, **'99** 206
Fudge Cake for Two, **'81** 205
Fudge Cake, Hot, **'99** 105
Fudge Cake, One-Foot-in-the-Fire, **'90** 252
Fudge Frosting, Chocolate Cake with, **'89** 56
German Chocolate Cake, **'81** 296; **'83** M233
German Chocolate Chip Cake, **'86** 247
Grandma's Chocolate Cake, **'94** 133
Heart, Chocolate-Amaretto, **'98** 56
Kahlúa Cake, Chocolate, **'91** 298
Kahlúa Chocolate Cake, **'81** 303
Layers, Chocolate Cake, **'96** 229
Loaf Cakes, Chocolate Chip, **'98** 137
Marbled Cake, Cocoa, **'82** 265
Marshmallow Cake, No-Egg Chocolate,
  '87 M97
Mayonnaise Cake, Chocolate, **'83** 99
Mocha Cake, Belgian, **'84** 316
Mocha Cake, Double, **'84** 311
Mocha-Chocolate Cake, Dark, **'84** 311
Mousse Cake, Chocolate, **'87** 264; **'98** 270
Nut Cake, Rich Chocolate-, **'86** 8
Pastry Cake, Chocolate, **'91** 196
Peanut Butter Cake, Chocolate-, **'84** 240
Peanut Butter Cake, Fudgy, **'85** 91
Peanut Butter-Fudge Cake, **'96** 254
Peanut Butter Mousse Cake, Chocolate-,
  '98 71
Peanut Cluster Cake, Chocolate-, **'87** 184
Perfect Chocolate Cake, **'82** 244; **'90** 307
Pudding Cake, Hot Fudge, **'88** 255
Pudding, Chocolate Cake, **'81** 99
Pudding, Hot Fudge Sundae Cake, **'88** 167
Pumpkin, Chocolate Cake, **'96** 254
Queen's Chocolate Cake, **'89** 271
Raspberry Cake, Chocolate-, **'92** 173
Raspberry-Fudge Cake, **'97** 34
Rich Chocolate Cake, **'89** 43
Rocky Road Cake, **'81** 178
Roll, Chocolate Cream, **'85** 317
Roll, Chocolate-Frosted Ice Cream, **'84** 200
Roll, Chocolate-Mocha Cream, **'84** 304
Roll, Chocolate Mousse, **'83** 290; **'88** 280
Roll, Chocolate-Orange, **'87** 21
Roll, Make-Ahead Chocolate-Mint Cake,
  '95 220
Rolls, Chocolate Cake, **'94** 312
Roulade, Kahlúa-and-Cream, **'97** 199
Royal, Chocolate Cake, **'86** 239
Rum Cake, Chocolate, **'79** 67
Sachertorte, **'84** 253
Sachertorte, Shortcut, **'99** M243
Shortcake, Chocolate-Raspberry, **'95** 99
Snack Cake, Black Widow, **'93** 245
Snack Cake, Frosted Chocolate, **'90** 194
Sour Cream Cake, Chocolate-, **'87** 222
Sour Cream Cake, Chocolate Chip-, **'85** 115
Sour Cream Chocolate Cake, **'79** 282
Spice Potato Cake, Chocolate-, **'96** 111
Strawberry Shortcake, Chocolate-, **'89** 216
Swiss Chocolate Chip Cake, **'87** 85
Tic-Tac-Toe Cake, **'94** 52
Tiered Cameo Cake, **'94** 125
Toffee Cake, Chocolate-, **'89** 335
Tree Cakes, Miniature Chocolate Truffle,
  '97 M285
Triangle Cake, Chocolate, **'85** 126
Truffle Angel Cake, Chocolate, **'97** 283
Truffle Cake, Chocolate, **'89** 43
Wedding Cake, Cameo, **'94** 124
Wedding Cake, Double Chocolate, **'91** 100
Whipped Cream Cake, Chocolate-Mint,
  '90 265

White Chocolate-Cherry Cake, **'88** 268
White Chocolate Mousse Cake, **'89** 160
White Chocolate Mousse Cake, Strawberry-
  Studded, **'99** 154
White Chocolate-Raspberry Cake, **'98** 323
Yule Log, **'79** 281; **'82** 289
Zucchini Cake, Chocolate, **'85** 156
Cinderella Fantasy Cake, **'98** 70
Cinnamon Crumb Cake, **'85** 290
Cinnamon Streusel Cake, **'84** 151
Coconut
Apple Coconut Cake, **'80** 226
Cake, Coconut, **'92** 120
Carrot Cake, Coconut-Pecan, **'84** 322
Carrot Cake, Fresh Coconut-, **'80** 299
Chocolate-Coconut Cake, **'83** 23
Christmas Coconut Cake, **'82** 262
Cream Cake, Coconut, **'81** 179; **'91** 269
Creamy Coconut Cake, **'84** 43
Fresh Coconut Cake, **'80** 289; **'82** 52; **'85** 281
Fudge Cake, Coconut-, **'99** 206
Hibiscus-Nectar Cake, **'96** 248
Holiday Coconut Cake, **'90** 308
Layer Cake, Coconut-Pineapple, **'80** 140
Layer Cake, Stately Coconut, **'81** 70
Lemon Cake, Coconut-, **'95** 319
Lemon-Coconut Cream Cake, **'81** 179
Lemon-Coconut Sheet Cake, **'85** 117
MaMa's Coconut Cake, **'97** 71
Piña Colada Cake, **'99** 117
Pineapple Cake, Coconut-, **'89** 56
Pineapple Cake, Nanny's Famous Coconut-,
  '97 277
Pineapple Cake Roll, Coconut-, **'84** 304
Regal Coconut Cake, **'83** 299
Rum-Orange Coconut Cake, **'88** 224
Spice Cake, Coconut-, **'84** 255; **'87** 296
Toasted Coconut Cake, **'86** 60
Unforgettable Coconut Cake, **'90** 104
White Chocolate-Coconut Cake, **'87** 263
Coffee Cakes
Almond-Blueberry Coffee Cake, **'85** 152
Almond Coffee Cake Twist, **'91** 22
Almond Sunburst, **'94** 245
Apple Coffee Cake, **'81** 249; **'97** 326
Apple Coffee Cake, Fresh, **'92** 32
Apple Loaf, Spiced, **'79** 215
Apple-Pecan Coffee Cake, **'84** 242
Apricot-Almond Coffee Cake, **'93** 26
Apricot Lattice Coffee Cake, **'94** 48
Banana Coffee Cake, **'81** 288
Banana Cream Coffee Cake, **'85** 46
Banana-Sour Cream Coffee Cake, **'80** 186;
  '97 231
Blueberry Brunch Cake, **'83** 183
Blueberry Coffee Cake, **'82** 206; **'85** 326;
  '88 263
Blueberry Coffee Cake, Fresh, **'81** 164
Blueberry Streusel Coffee Cake, **'88** 154
Braid Coffee Cake, Daisy, **'82** 197
Breakfast Pullapart, **'81** 278
Butterflake Coffee Ring, **'79** 216
Buttermilk Coffee Cake, **'89** 50
Buttermilk Crumb Cake, **'79** 72
Caramel Bread, **'82** 75
Caramel Breakfast Rolls, **'79** 193
Caramel-Orange Coffee Ring, **'80** 45
Caramel Ring, Easy, **'85** M89
Cardamom Coffee Cake, **'83** 246; **'84** 17
Cheesecake Coffee Cake, Deep-Dish, **'90** 50
Cherry Blossom Coffee Cake, **'80** 21
Cherry Coffee Cake, **'94** 49
Chocolate-Chip Coffee Cake, **'79** 249
Chocolate Chip Coffee Cake, **'83** 231; **'97** 232

Christmas-Tree Coffee Cakes, '87 298
Christmas Wreath, '80 280
Cinnamon-Buttermilk Coffee Cake, '80 45
Cinnamon-Cherry Coffee Cake, '98 330
Cinnamon Coffee Cake, '83 M203
Cinnamon Crisps, '81 113
Cinnamon-Nut Bubble Bread, '80 22
Cinnamon-Pecan Coffee Cake, '87 69
Cinnamon-Raisin Coffee Cake, '93 180
Cinnamon Twist Coffee Cake, '84 322
Cinnamon Upside-Down Coffee Cake, '85 256
Coffee Cake, '94 167
Cora's Coffee Cake, '91 186
Cowboy Coffee Cake, '95 84
Cranberry-Coconut Coffee Cake, '93 332
Cranberry Coffee Cake, '81 14; '90 159
Cranberry Crunch Coffee Cake, '97 231
Cranberry-Nut Coffee Cake, '81 250
Cranberry-Orange Coffee Cake, '82 283
Cream Cheese Coffee Cake, '86 290
Crescent Coffee Cake, '81 229
Danish Coffee Ring, '80 20
Fig Coffee Cake, Easy, '80 116
Holiday Coffee Cake, '84 284
Holiday Wreath, '81 284
Honey Twist, '79 80
Lemon Coffee Cake, Lightly, '81 14
Macadamia Ring Coffee Cake, '85 326
Maple-Nut Coffee Twist, '86 290
Marbled Coffee Cake, '86 9
Mix, Quick, '94 167
Muffins, Coffee Cake, '79 7
Oatmeal-Coconut Coffee Cake, '83 312
Orange Breakfast Ring, '81 229
Orange Butter Coffee Cake, '89 229
Orange Coffee Cake, '85 M88
Orange Coffee Cake, Nutty, '95 160
Orange Marmalade Swirl Coffee Cake, '81 107
Orange-Pecan Coffee Cake, '86 86
Overnight Coffee Cake, '80 52; '92 213
Peach Flip, '79 217
Pecan-Topped Coffee Cake, '81 41
Pineapple-Coconut Coffee Cake, '94 49
Raisin Coffee Cake, Spicy, '88 63
Raspberry-Cheese Coffee Cake, '97 231
Raspberry Coffee Cake, '83 112
Raspberry Tea Cake, '91 271
Ring, Coffee Cake, '85 M89
Savarin, Holiday, '80 280
Snack Cake, Coffee, '86 247
Sour Cream Coffee Cake, '81 270; '93 154
Sour Cream-Walnut Coffee Cake, '79 209
Special Coffee Cake, Mama Cle's, '94 287
Strawberry Coffee Cake, '85 46
St. Timothy's Coffee Cake, '91 54
Sugar Cake, Moravian, '87 228
Sugar Cake, Polish, '89 267
Sugarplum Coffee Ring, '79 235; '83 M37
Sweet Roll Dough, '79 80
Tropical Coffee Cake, '80 232; '90 323
Walnut Coffee Cake, '93 124
Whole Wheat Coffee Cake, Crunchy-Topped,
  '79 93
Cola Cake, '81 238
Compromise Cake, The, '90 253
Cranberry Upside-Down Cake, '87 8
Cream Cheese Cake, Regal, '80 140
Cream Cheese Loaf Cake, '84 151
Crème de Menthe Cake, '81 178
Crêpe Cake, Southern Custard, '99 166
Cupcakes
  Apple-Nut Cupcakes, '82 279
  A Tisket, a Tasket, '92 15
  Banana-Cocoa Cupcakes, '80 130

Birthday Balloon Cakes, '92 15
Black Bottom Cups, '82 279
Brownie Cupcakes, '82 280
Carrot-Bran Cupcakes, '82 16
Chocolate Chip Cupcakes, '97 108
Chocolate Chip Cupcakes, Marble, '81 239
Chocolate Cupcakes, '92 14
Chocolate Surprise Cupcakes, '85 91
Cinnamon-Chocolate Cupcakes, '81 M139
Confetti Cupcakes, New Year's, '92 15
Cream Cheese Party Cupcakes, '82 279
Date Cupcakes, '84 7
Graveyard Grumblings, '92 15
Happy Day Cupcakes, '80 129
Ice-Cream Cone Cakes, Fourth-of-July, '92 15
Lemon Moist Cupcakes, '82 112; '83 153
Mocha Cupcakes, '85 250
Orange Cupcakes, '97 32
Piglets, '98 203
Pumpkin Cupcakes, '85 121
Self-Filled Cupcakes, '80 129
Sweetheart Cupcakes, '92 15
Tannenbaum Temptations, '92 14
Turkey Talk, '92 15
Vanilla Cupcakes, '92 14
Vanilla Cupcakes, Golden, '85 121
Yellow Cupcakes, Easy, '83 241
Daffodil Cake, '84 161
Date Nut Cake, '79 176; '80 5
Date-Nut Cake Roll, '89 94
Decorating Techniques, Cake, '83 72, 240;
  '84 224
Easter Egg Cake, '94 98
Easter Rabbit Cake, '94 99
Éclair Cake, '93 42
Fig Cake, '79 32; '99 314
Fig Preserve Cake, '79 140; '84 316
Fig Preserves Cake, '89 335
Friendship Cake, '82 250
Fruit-and-Cereal Brunch Cake, '88 263
Fruit-and-Nut Cake, Stately, '84 226
Fruitcakes
  Applesauce Fruitcake, '83 258
  Aronowitz Fruitcake, '86 285
  Bourbon Fruitcake, '85 315
  Brandy Fruitcake, '82 261
  Burgundy Fruitcake, '85 292
  Cake Mix Fruit Cake, '95 248
  Chocolate Fruitcakes, '95 250
  Classic Fruitcake, '91 258
  Favorite Fruitcake, Family, '88 284
  Fondue, Fruitcake, '84 258
  Grandmother's Fruitcake, '95 248
  Japanese Fruitcake, '83 268; '90 252
  Jeweled Fruitcake, '88 260
  Jill's Fruitcake, '95 249
  Kentucky Fruitcake, '86 266
  Layered Fruitcake, '87 265
  Lemon Fruitcake, '83 258
  Light Fruitcake, '90 309
  Loaf, Fruitcake, '96 286
  Mom's Fruitcake, '85 321
  No-Bake Fruitcake, '95 249
  Old-South Fruitcake, '79 289
  Regal Fruitcake, '83 257
  Sherry-Nut Fruitcake, '84 266
  Spice Cake, Fruit and, '87 M97
  White Fruitcake, '80 280; '85 316
  Zucchini Fruitcake, '88 284
Funnel Cakes, '83 250
Funnel Cakes, Nutty, '91 233
Gift Box Cake, '96 319
Gingerbread, Applesauce, '94 179
Gingerbread Cake Roll, '89 214

Gingerbread Mix, '92 312
Gingerbread, No-Molasses, '92 313
Gingerbread, Old English, '79 265
Gingerbread, Old-Fashioned, '91 240
Gingerbread, Refrigerator, '80 52
Gingerbread, Spicy, '84 263
Gingerbread with Caramel Sauce, Pumpkin,
  '93 235
Gingerbread with Key Lime Curd, Kahlúa,
  '96 126
Ginger-Pear Upside-Down Cake, '97 205
Ginger Shortcakes, '94 179
Graham Cracker Cake, '79 13
Grapefruit Cake, Fresh, '89 308
Holiday Cake, Favorite, '81 264
Honey-Apple Cake, '99 210
Honey Bun Cake, '91 214
Honey Cake, '92 250
Honey Cake, Southern, '89 251
Hummingbird Cake, '82 244; '90 305
Ice Cream Cake, '86 321; '89 71
Ice Cream Cake for Grown-Ups, '88 M192
Ice Cream Cake, Fruity, '87 110
Ice Cream Yule Log, '83 253
Italian Cream Cake, '96 262
Italian Cream Cake, Quick, '99 307
Jam Cake, Spicy, '89 236
Jellyroll, Easy, '82 176
Jellyroll Layer Cake, '85 125
Jellyroll, Spiced, '82 176
Key Lime Cake, '91 214
King Cake, '90 20
Lady Baltimore Cake, '90 45
Lane Cake, '80 121; '83 269; '96 144
Lane Cake, Holiday, '99 306
Lane Cake, Nanny's, '89 55
Lemon Cake, Easy, '83 24
Lemon Cake, Glazed, '86 70
Lemon Cake, Luscious, '93 81
Lemon Cake Pudding, '92 96; '98 35
Lemon Cake Roll, '89 312
Lemon Cake Roll, Elegant, '80 70
Lemon-Cheese Cake, Tart, '88 7
Lemon Gold Cake, '83 301
Lemon Layer Cake, Luscious, '86 61
Lemon Layer Cake, Old-Fashioned, '85 191
Lemon Meringue Cake, '89 296; '99 118
Lemon-Pineapple Cake, '86 60, 239
Lemon-Poppy Seed Cake, '93 154
Lemon Pudding Cake, '83 106
Lemon-Raspberry Cake, '91 247
Lemon Roll, Snow-Capped, '79 68
Lemon Sponge Cups, '83 10
Light Cake, Basic, '90 107
Lime Layer Loaf, '85 96
Little Bitty Cakes, '98 154
Lord Baltimore Cake, '90 45
Mandarin-Rum Cake, '84 150
Mango Cake, '83 150
Maple Nut Cake, '96 17
Maraschino Nut Cake, '83 268
Mincemeat Spice Cake, '79 246
Molasses Snack Cake, '86 20
Moravian Sugar Cake, '95 304
Neapolitan Cake, '88 168
Nutmeg Feather Cake, '81 238
Nutty Cakes, '89 50
Oatmeal Cake, Dutch, '83 95
Orange Blossom Cake, '96 162
Orange Butter Cake, '95 46
Orange Cake, '86 61; '95 320
Orange Cake, Fresh, '83 300
Orange Cake, Mandarin, '83 24
Orange Cake, Williamsburg, '81 120; '82 23

CAKES
(continued)

Orange Chiffon Cake, '91 56
Orange Chiffon Cake, Fresh, '88 179
Orange-Cranberry Cake, '85 314
Orange Cream Cake, '99 118
Orange-Date Cake, '94 60
Orange-Lemon Cake, General Robert E. Lee, '88 92
Orange Liqueur Cake, '87 84
Orange Marmalade Cake, '85 53
Orange Meringue Cake, '86 336; '87 84
Orange-Nut Butter Cake, '80 254
Orange Nut Cake, '80 70
Orange-Pecan Crunch Cake, '83 10
Orange Rum Cake, '79 2
Orange-Slice Cake, '81 264
Orange Streusel Cake, '88 10
Peach Cake, Fresh, '85 178
Peaches and Cream Cake, '80 142
Peaches-and-Cream Cake, '96 118
Peach Shortcakes, Spicy, '89 154
Peach Upside-Down Cake, '87 8
Peachy Picnic Cake, '79 178
Peanut Butter-and-Jelly Cake, '85 34
Peanut Butter-Banana Cake, '80 87
Peanut Butter Cake, '79 51; '83 M233
Peanut Butter Swirl Cake, '86 109
Peanutty Layer Cake, Super, '83 222
Pear Cakes with Praline Sauce, '96 284
Pear Cake with Caramel Drizzle, '86 247
Pear Preserve Cake, '85 52
Pecan Cake, '97 256
Pecan Cake, Kentucky, '84 263
Pecan Cake with Praline Glaze, '82 196
Pecan-Carrot Cake, '99 223
Pecan-Cornmeal Rounds, '95 99
Pecan Pie Cake, '98 254
Pecan Roulade, '87 183
Peppermint Cake, Red Velvet, '98 308
Peppermint Candy Cake, '89 254
Persimmon Cake, '79 205
Petit Fours, Simple, '92 277
Petits Fours, '79 117; '96 282
Petits Fours, Chocolate-Almond, '93 255
Petits Fours, Teatime, '85 119
Pineapple Cake, Heavenly, '83 303
Pineapple-Pecan Upside-Down Cake, '84 25
Pineapple Right-Side-Up Snack Cake, '99 28
Pineapple Upside-Down Cake, '80 102; '88 10
Pineapple Upside-Down Cake, Fresh, '97 204
Pineapple Upside-Down Cake Roll, '96 162
Pineapple Upside-Down Cake, Skillet, '85 242
Pineapple Upside-Down Cake, Stacked, '86 239
Plum Cake, '97 177
Popcorn-Gumdrop Cake, '87 262
Poppy Seed Cake, '92 174; '95 63
Poppy Seed Cake, Lemon-, '93 154
Poppy Seed Cake, Plantation, '79 13
Poppy Seed Loaf Cake, '81 63
Poppy Seed Loaf, Quick, '82 75
Pound
  Apple Cider Pound Cake, '84 10
  Apricot Brandy Pound Cake, '83 267
  Aztec Pound Cake, '96 61
  Banana Pound Cake, '96 60; '98 195
  Black Pepper Pound Cake, '96 61
  Black Walnut Pound Cake, '92 16
  Bourbon-Pecan Pound Cake, '91 270
  Brandied Pound Cake, '89 292
  Brown Sugar Pound Cake, '82 135

Brown Sugar-Rum Pound Cake, '96 60
Buttermilk Pound Cake, '79 285; '85 255; '99 98
Buttermilk Pound Cake, Old-Fashioned, '82 52
Buttermilk Pound Cake, Spiced, '84 73
Butter-Nut Pound Cake, '86 235
Butternut Pound Cake with Caramel Sauce, Betty's, '95 308
Butterscotch-Pecan Pound Cake, '92 153
Caramel Frosting, Pound Cake with, '87 39
Caramel Pound Cake, '98 194
Carrot Pound Cake, '87 41
Cheesy Pound Cake, '96 62
Cherry Pound Cake, Cute-as-a-Button, '95 139
Chocolate Chip Pound Cake, '86 178; '93 105; '94 100
Chocolate Marble Pound Cake, '88 16
Chocolate-Orange Pound Cake, '89 94
Chocolate Pound Cake, '82 88; '84 10; '89 325; '94 288; '98 336
Chocolate Pound Cake with Frosting, '90 284
Chocolate Pound Cake with Fudge Frosting, '87 296
Chocolate-Sour Cream Pound Cake, '83 239; '92 153
Chocolate-Swirled Pound Cake, '97 329
Coconut-Cream Cheese Pound Cake, '85 297; '90 305
Coconut Cream Pound Cake, '84 10
Coconut Pound Cake, '82 87; '91 224
Cream Cheese Pound Cake, '81 290; '86 287; '95 304
Cream Cheese Pound Cake, Crusty, '89 124
Croutons, Cinnamon Pound Cake, '93 161
Daiquiri Pound Cake, '93 83
Eggnog-Pecan Pound Cake, '95 313
Eggnog Pound Cake, '90 253
Favorite Pound Cake, '81 132; '92 171
Five-Flavor Pound Cake, '87 264
Four-Flavor Pound Cake, '91 136
Fruited Pound Cake, '81 265
German Chocolate Pound Cake, '97 M254
Glazed Pound Cake, '89 207
Golden Pound Cake, '90 284
I Remember Pound Cake, '86 180
Irish Cream-and-Coffee Pound Cake, '92 287
Lemon Pound Cake, '82 88
Lemon Pound Cake with Mint Berries and Cream, '99 183
Lemon-Sour Cream Pound Cake, '87 38
Lemony Pound Cake, '96 60
Loaf, Pound Cake, '85 306
Loaf, Pretty and Pink Pound Cake, '96 60
Mahogany Pound Cake, '89 207
Marbled Pecan Pound Cake, '93 313
Marble Pound Cake, '95 29
Milk Chocolate Pound Cake, '90 306
Million Dollar Pound Cake, '90 306
Mini Pound Cakes, '86 148
Mocha Marble Pound Cake, '99 23
Old-Fashioned Buttermilk Pound Cake, '88 16
Old-Fashioned Pound Cake, '80 279; '82 88; '93 120
Orange-Pecan Pound Cake, '93 13
Orange Pound Cake, '87 84, 221; '92 69
Pastel Cake, '97 173
Peach-Almond Pound Cake, '89 86
Pineapple Pound Cake, '79 148
Pound Cake, '92 94
Praline Pound Cake, '82 88
Problems to Avoid Chart, '84 319
Pumpkin Pound Cake, '92 235

Rose-Geranium Pound Cake, Mrs. Willoughby's, '84 318
Rum Pound Cake, Buttered, '83 220
Sandwich, Grilled Pound Cake Dessert, '94 171
S'mores, Grilled Pound Cake, '98 179
Sour Cream-Orange Pecan Pound Cake, '89 207
Sour Cream Pound Cake, '89 56; '92 153
Sour Cream Pound Cake, Cinnamon-Topped, '82 43
Sour Cream Pound Cake, Elegant, '83 79
Sour Cream Pound Cake with Raspberry Sauce, '99 259
Southern Pound Cake, Smoothest, '93 237
Strawberry-Banana Topping, Pound Cake with, '89 200
Sweet Potato Pound Cake, '83 85
Tea Pound Cake, '99 90
Whipping Cream Pound Cake, '90 284
White Chocolate Pound Cake, '91 101
Wine Jelly, Pound Cake with, '98 125
Yogurt Pound Cake, '84 10
Praline Cake, '81 162
Praline Ice Cream Cake, '80 84
Prune Cake, '85 223
Prune Cake and Sauce, '85 118
Prune Cake, Spicy, '79 136
Pudding Cake, Danish, '91 269
Pudding Cake, Saucy, '98 196
Pudding Cake with Blueberry Sauce, Buttermilk-Lemon, '95 135
Pumpkin Cake, '81 272; '93 303; '98 241
Pumpkin Date Cake, '79 251
Pumpkin Kahlúa Cake, '86 292
Pumpkin Layer Cake, '80 245
Pumpkin Roll, '79 206; '91 297
Queen Bee Cake, '81 237
Raisin Layer Cake, Spicy, '79 230
Red Velvet Cake, '93 318; '96 282
Root Beer Float Cake, '99 196
Satin Ribbon Cake, '92 68
Sauerkraut Cake, '94 254
Savarin, '79 171
Shortcakes
  Blueberry-Nectarine Shortcake, Warm, '97 205
  Chicken Shortcakes, Cheesy, '95 98
  Chocolate-Raspberry Shortcake, '95 99
  Orange Shortcake, Fresh, '80 100
  Orange-Strawberry Shortcake, '95 100
  Strawberry Crispy Shortcakes, '93 42
  Strawberry Pinwheel Shortcake, '89 112
  Strawberry Shortcake, '81 96; '83 122; '92 184; '94 162
  Strawberry Shortcake, A Favorite, '88 136
  Strawberry Shortcake, Elegant, '88 37
  Strawberry Shortcake Jubilee, '88 209
  Strawberry Shortcake Shells, '88 196
  Strawberry Shortcakes with Mint Cream, '97 144
Sorghum Cake, '85 239
Sorghum Tea Cakes, '85 239
Spice Cake, '81 162
Spice Cake, Buttermilk, '81 211
Spice Cake, Dark, '82 314; '83 43
Spice Cake, Old South, '84 263
Spice Cake, Sugar 'n, '84 226
Spice Cake with Caramel Frosting, '82 314; '83 42
Spice Cake with Chocolate-Coffee Frosting, '88 268
Spice Cake, Yule Log, '85 314
Spice Layer Cake with Coffee Frosting, '94 86

Sponge

Burnt Sugar Sponge Cake with Berry Sauce, **'95** 103
Chocolaty Sponge Cake, **'86** 60
Coffee Sponge Cake, **'83** 229; **'91** 55
Coffee Sponge Cake, Two-Day, **'86** 75
Daffodil Sponge Cake, **'79** 175; **'80** 6; **'84** 315
Passover Sponge Cake, **'90** 106
Strawberries 'n Cream Sponge Cake Roll, **'81** 95
Yellow Sponge Cake, **'80** 250
Squash Cake, **'86** 200
Stack Cake, Favorite, **'87** 228
Stack Cake, Old-Fashioned, **'81** 216
Strawberry Cake Roll, **'79** 49; **'83** 129; **'84** 305; **'85** 172
Strawberry Cream Cake, **'86** 61
Strawberry Crunch Cake, **'79** 288; **'80** 35
Strawberry Delight Cake, **'85** 30
Strawberry Ice Cream Roll, **'84** 105
Strawberry Meringue Cake, **'86** 240
Strawberry Roll, **'82** 120
Strawberry Roll, Heavenly, **'82** 176
Strawberry Yogurt Layer Cake, **'94** 85
Sweet Potato Cake, **'79** 207; **'89** 295
Sweet Potato Loaf Cake, **'81** 224
Sweet Potato Log Roll, **'82** 227
Sweet Potato Surprise Cake, **'80** 287
Tea Cake, Lemon, **'82** 169
Tea Cakes and Fresh Strawberries, Telia's, **'98** 110
Tea Cakes, Mexican, **'81** 196
Teacakes, Old-Fashioned, **'84** 43
Teddy Bear Cakes, **'92** 278
Tilden Cake with Cherry-Wine Sauce, **'97** 132
Tipsy Squire, **'85** 41

Tortes

Almond Torte, Chocolate-, **'96** M253
Amaretto Torte, **'82** 303
Apricot Praline Torte, Lucy's, **'95** 243
Apricot Sponge Torte, **'90** 59
Black Forest Torte, **'88** 209
Black Forrest Cherry Torte, **'88** 178
Bourbon-Chocolate Torte, **'98** M84
Caramel-Sweet Potato Torte, **'96** 312
Carob-Pecan Torte, **'85** 218
Chocolate-Almond Torte, **'98** 273
Chocolate Mint Torte, **'94** 86
Chocolate-Pecan Torte, **'89** 42
Chocolate Praline Torte, **'84** 165
Chocolate-Strawberry Ice Cream Torte, **'79** 7
Chocolate Torte, Apricot-Filled, **'90** 107
Chocolate Torte, Double-, **'79** 67
Chocolate Torte Royale, **'82** 263
Chocolate Torte, Triple, **'96** 58
Chocolate Velvet Torte, **'86** 316
Graham Cracker-Nut Torte, **'97** 275; **'98** 35
Hazelnut Torte, **'91** 248
Lemon Meringue Torte with Raspberry Sauce, **'93** 82
Mocha Brownie Torte, **'85** 102
Mocha-Pecan Torte, **'86** 26
Mocha Torte, **'99** 66
Mocha Velvet Torte, **'92** 318
Passover Linzer Torte, **'90** 106
Pecan Torte, Heavenly, **'81** 266
Spring Torte, **'91** 57
Strawberry Meringue Torte, **'88** 136
Sugar Cookie Torte, **'79** 68
Toffee Meringue Torte, **'87** 118
White Chocolate Mousse Torte, **'99** 154
Twelfth Night Cake, **'93** 337
Upside Down Cake, Quick, **'90** 219
Upside-Down Sunburst Cake, **'87** 9

Vanilla Chiffon Cake, **'79** 266
Walnut Cream Roll, **'84** 192
Wedding Cake, Rose Garden, **'97** 60
Whipped Cream Cake, **'96** 96
White Cake Batter, Basic, **'99** 117
White Cake, Buttermilk, **'86** 235
White Cake with Strawberries and Chocolate Glaze, **'87** 76
White Cake with Strawberry Frosting, Rich, **'89** 184
Winter Squash-Spice Bundt Cake, **'99** 248
Yogurt-Lemon-Nut Cake, **'89** 169
Zucchini Cake, **'79** 24
Zucchini-Pineapple Cake, **'95** 160
Zuppa Inglese, **'85** 229

CANDIES

Almond Brittle Candy, **'80** 255
Almond Butter Crunch, **'80** 301
Almond Roca, **'86** 49
Almond-Toffee Crunch, **'88** 285
Apples, Candied Red, **'81** 217
Apples, Candy, **'84** 243
Apricot Balls, **'79** 274
Balls, No-Cook Candy, **'85** 14
Bourbon Balls, **'81** 254; **'83** 315; **'90** 83
Bourbon Balls, Chocolate, **'84** 298
Bow, Candy, **'99** M306
Box, White Candy, **'97** M54
Brandy Balls, **'86** 319
Brittle, Microwave Pecan, **'97** M245
Brittle with Crushed Peanuts, **'87** 184
Buckeyes, **'85** 321
Butter Creams, **'80** 302
Buttermilk Candy, **'80** 302
Caramel Corn Candy, **'84** 243
Caramel Good Stuff, Baked, **'80** 284
Caramel O's, **'99** M196
Caramel-Peanut Squares, **'85** 247
Caramels, Coconut-Macadamia, **'98** 305
Chocolate Brittle, **'83** 315
Chocolate Brittle, Quick, **'82** 114
Chocolate Caramels, **'91** 35
Chocolate-Coconut Almond Drops, **'87** 223
Chocolate-Covered Cherries, **'81** 286; **'84** 298; **'97** M55
Chocolate-Covered Pecan Fritters, **'79** 205
Chocolate-Covered Pretzels, **'82** 295
Chocolate Drops, **'84** 111
Chocolate Greeting Card, **'83** 40
Chocolate-Lemon Creams, **'98** M235
Chocolate-Marshmallow Squares, **'92** M50
Chocolate-Nut Log Candy, **'86** 335
Chocolate Nut Teasers, **'91** 35
Chocolate-Peanut Butter Balls, **'80** 87
Chocolate-Peanut Butter Bites, **'92** M317
Chocolate-Peanut Butter Drops, **'92** 322
Chocolate-Peanut Clusters, **'81** 16
Chocolate Peanutty Swirls, **'94** M330
Chocolate Rum Balls, **'80** 302
Chocolate-Rum Balls, **'88** 285
Chocolates, Liqueur Cream-Filled, **'87** 258
Chocolate Spiders, **'85** 236
Chocolates, Spirited, **'86** 278
Chocolate, Tempered, **'91** 35
Chocolate Velvets, **'84** 298
Coconut-Almond Balls, **'84** 256
Coconut-Black Walnut Bonbons, **'82** 307
Coconut Candy, **'79** 272; **'80** 250
Coconut Joys, **'98** 282
Coconut Joys, Chocolate-Covered, **'98** M282
Coffee Buttons, **'99** 66
Corn Brittle, Crunchy, **'85** 208
Crème de Cacao Balls, **'86** 266
Crème de Menthe Chocolates, **'91** 36

Crystal Candy, **'84** 299
Date Candy, **'89** 308
Date Loaf Candy, **'80** 302
Date Logs, **'79** 274
Divinity, Apricot, **'83** 297
Divinity, Cherry, **'97** 316
Divinity, Christmas, **'81** 286
Divinity Ghosts, **'95** 273
Divinity, Lemon, **'97** 316
Divinity, Peanut, **'85** 233; **'87** M278
Divinity, Pink, **'86** 49
Divinity, Strawberry, **'91** 272
Frosting, Chocolate Candy, **'81** 238
Fruit Balls, **'82** 296; **'84** 299

Fudge

Almond Fudge, Creamy, **'95** 51
Buttermilk Fudge, **'95** 52; **'97** 317
Butterscotch-Peanut Fudge, **'98** M282
Butterscotch Rum Fudge, **'88** 256
Caramel Fudge, **'91** 273
Cherry Nut Fudge, **'83** 315
Chocolate Fudge, **'82** 20
Chocolate Fudge, Five Pounds of, **'95** 51
Chocolate-Peanut Butter Fudge, **'87** 257; **'90** 311
Chocolate-Peanut Butter Fudge Squares, **'97** M54
Coffee-Chip Fudge, **'86** 74
Cream Cheese Fudge, **'84** 111
Creamy Dark Fudge, **'82** 295
Creamy Fudge, **'81** 218
Diamond Fudge, **'92** 193
Double-Good Fudge, **'79** M263; **'95** M50
Double Good Fudge, **'87** M278
Fast Fudge, **'79** 274
Four Chips Fudge, **'92** 318
Fudge, **'86** 266
Microwave Chocolate Fudge, **'92** M50
Microwave Fudge, **'91** M92
Mint Fudge, **'95** 50
Mint Fudge, Dinner, **'88** 285
Mocha Fudge, Creamy, **'95** 51
Mocha Fudge, Holiday, **'84** 298
Nut Fudge, Quick, **'83** 316
Nutty White Fudge, **'81** 253
Orange-Walnut Fudge, **'92** 288
Peanut Butter Chewies, Fudge-, **'98** 215
Peanut Butter Fudge, **'80** 302; **'89** 307; **'95** 51
Peanut Butter Fudge, Creamy, **'92** 240
Peanut Butter Fudge, Marbled, **'88** 65
Peanut-Fudge Bites, **'91** M231; **'92** M68
Peanut Fudge, Double, **'85** 91
Pecan Fudge, Creamy, **'84** 321
Penuche, **'79** 272
Pistachio Fudge, **'83** 298
Quick-and-Easy Fudge, **'88** M190
Scotch Ring, Fudge, **'79** 273
Sour Cream Fudge, **'95** 52
Strawberry Fudge Balls, **'93** 80
Tiger Butter, **'86** 48
White Chocolate-Coffee Fudge, **'94** 232
White Chocolate Fudge, **'92** 317; **'95** 51
Kentucky Colonels, **'79** 273
Lollipops, Colorful Molded, **'81** 218
Marzipan, **'83** 306
Millionaires, **'79** M262; **'97** M55
Mints, Cream Cheese, **'93** 79
Mints, Dinner, **'88** 66
Mints, Easy Holiday, **'84** 299
Mints, Party, **'79** 273; **'81** 119
Mints, Special, **'99** 323
Mint Twists, **'86** 106
Molded Candies, **'84** 40
Nut Clusters, **'81** 254

CANDIES
(continued)

Nuts, Candied, '81 261
Orange Balls, '94 331
Orange Peel, Candied, '81 286
Peanut Brittle, '79 M263; '80 87; '84 298; '92 240
Peanut Brittle, Golden, '83 223
Peanut Brittle, Never-Fail, '79 273
Peanut Brittle, Orange, '80 302
Peanut Butter Candy, '93 166
Peanut Butter-Chocolate Balls, '80 269
Peanut Butter-Chocolate Candy Squares, '82 56
Peanut Butter Creams, '79 273
Peanut Butter Easter Eggs, '87 86
Peanut Butter Temptations, '84 29
Peanut Butter Yummies, '83 223
Peanut Clusters, '87 184; '92 288; '98 M282
Peanutty Clusters, '83 143
Pecan Brittle, '91 272
Pecan Clusters, '81 266; '98 305
Pecan Clusters, Roasted, '85 233; '90 310
Pecan-Coconut Clusters, '86 M251
Pecan Rolls, '79 285
Pecans, Brown Sugar, '81 266
Pecans, Glazed, '81 254
Pecans, Honeycomb, '84 300
Pecans, Orange, '84 299
Pecans, Spiced, '79 296; '81 286
Pecans, Spicy, '81 289
Pecans, Sugar-and-Honey, '86 319
Penuche, Coffee, '98 305
Peppermint Patties, '86 278
Potato Candy, '79 273
Pralines
Basic Pralines, '92 313; '93 50
Bourbon Pralines, '92 313; '93 51
Buttermilk Pralines, '99 99
Butterscotch Pralines, '81 253
Café au Lait Pralines, '92 313; '93 51
Chocolate-Mint Pralines, '92 313; '93 51
Chocolate-Peanut Butter Pralines, '92 313; '93 51
Chocolate Pralines, '92 313; '93 51
Cinnamon Pralines, '97 317
Coffee Pralines, Plantation, '86 241
Creamy Pralines, '80 198; '92 289
Dark Praline Clusters, '86 313
Dark Pralines, '83 52
Hot Spicy Pralines, '92 313; '93 51
Maple-Pecan Pralines, '83 222
Mocha Pralines, '92 313; '93 51
New Orleans-Style Pralines, '86 335
Old-Fashioned Pralines, '89 318
Orange Pralines, '92 313; '93 51
Peanut Butter Pralines, '92 313; '93 51
Pecan Pralines, Original, '81 11
Pralines, '79 272; '86 M288; '89 60; '90 48; '99 295
Southern Pralines, '79 M263
Spicy Praline Delights, '84 299
Texas-Size Pralines, '79 186
Vanilla Pralines, '92 313; '93 51
Quemada (Burnt-Sugar Candy), '87 38
Raisin Candy, Mixed, '84 111
Raspberry Cream Chocolates, '91 36
Red Rock Candy, '92 240
Rocky Road, '84 298
Rum Balls, '93 314
Strawberries, Christmas, '94 331
Taffy, Old-Fashioned, '80 302

Toffee, English, '79 273
Toffee, Microwave, '92 M317
Toffee, Nutty, '79 M263
Truffles, Almond, '83 298
Truffles, Amaretto Dessert, '86 319
Truffles, Bittersweet, '94 330
Truffles, Chocolate, '85 114; '89 43; '91 108
Truffles, Chocolate-Cherry Cordial, '99 127
Truffles, Chocolate-Kahlúa, '92 285
Truffles, Chocolate Marble, '97 284
Truffles, Chocolate-Praline, '97 284
Truffles, Hazelnut, '97 M54
Truffles, Orange-Pecan, '95 92
Truffles, White Chocolate, '87 45
Truffles, White Chocolate-Praline, '97 284
Truffles, Yule Street, '90 242
Turtle Candies, '93 M41
White Chocolate Salties, '92 50
White Chocolate Surprises, '91 36
CANNING AND PRESERVING
Apple Rings, Cinnamon, '85 107
Asparagus, Pickled, '83 46
Beets, Pickled, '81 216
Berries (except Strawberries), '80 128
Black-Eyed, Field, and Crowder Peas, '80 126
Cantaloupe, Pickled, '99 171
Carrot Marmalemon, '96 107
Catsup, Homemade, '85 188
Catsup, Spicy Tomato, '83 182
Chili Sauce, '81 175
Chili Sauce, Chunky, '85 188
Chow-Chow, '82 196
Chutney, Pear, '98 243
Confit, Roasted Shallot-Garlic, '94 303
Corn, Cold-Pack, '81 216
Corn, Cream-Style, '80 127; '85 106
Corn, Whole Kernel, '85 106
Cranberry Conserve, '83 279
Fruit Juices, '85 107
Fruit, Unsweetened Mixed, '83 182
Grapes, Spiced, '98 220
Green Beans, '80 126
Green Bean Salad, Pickled, '82 239
Green Beans, Appalachian, '81 215
Green Beans, Dill, '93 136
Green Beans, Dilled, '99 170
Green, Snap, or Wax Beans, '85 105
Green Tomatoes, Pickled, '99 143
Lima Beans, '80 127
Mincemeat, Homemade, '79 245
Nectarines in Apple Juice, '83 183
Okra, '80 127
Okra, Pickled, '98 177
Oranges, Brandied Cranberry, '98 309
Peaches, '80 128
Peaches and Pears, '85 106
Peaches, Honey-Sweet, '85 107
Pear Mincemeat, '79 196
Piccalilli, Kentucky, '81 216
Plums, Brandied, '97 176
Pomegranate Syrup, '96 241
Relish, Green Tomato, '98 124
Sauerkraut, Homemade, '81 216
Squash Pickles, '97 119
Squash, Summer, '80 127; '85 105
Succotash, '85 106
Tomatoes, '80 128; '85 106
Tomatoes, Canned Flavored, '95 217
Tomatoes, Stewed, '83 182
Tomatoes with Okra, '85 106
Tomato Juice, Spicy, '85 189
Tomato Puree, Seasoned, '83 182
Vegetable Soup, '80 128; '85 106

CANTALOUPE. *See* **MELONS.**
CARAMEL
Apples, Caramel, '79 220; '89 M231
Apples, Caramel-Peanut, '93 M244
Apples, Old English Caramel, '85 231
Baked Caramel Good Stuff, '80 284
Bars, Cranberry-Caramel, '98 277
Bars, Gooey Turtle, '96 M189
Bars, Oatmeal-Caramel, '85 247
Bars, Yummy, '92 171
Biscuits, Caramel Dessert, '95 36
Bombe, Caramel-Toffee, '93 214
Bread, Caramel, '82 75
Brie with Fresh Fruit, Caramel, '90 266
Cake, Caramel, '89 55; '90 307
Cake, Caramel-Filled Butter Pecan, '88 278
Cake, Caramel Pound, '98 194
Cake, Chocolate-Caramel-Nut, '83 23
Cake, Creamy Caramel Layer, '81 71
Candy, Caramel Corn, '84 243
Cheesecake, Chocolate-Caramel-Pecan, '91 197
Chocolate Caramels, '91 35
Cobbler, Peach-Caramel, '86 300; '87 178
Coconut-Macadamia Caramels, '98 305
Cookies, Caramel-Filled Chocolate, '92 319
Corn, Baked Caramel, '81 218
Corn, Caramel, '88 64
Corn, Nutty Caramel, '92 317
Corn, Oven-Made Caramel, '91 233
Crème d'Ange, '83 91
Crunch, Caramel, '95 165
Dessert, Coconut-Caramel, '92 44
Dip, Apple, '96 M190
Drizzle, Caramel, '86 247
Filling, Caramel, '88 278
Filling, Caramel Whipped Cream, '96 312
Flans, Caramel-Crowned, '90 227
Flan with Caramel, Baked, '92 231
Fondue, Caramel, '94 331; '95 35
Frosting, Caramel, '81 278, M289; '82 314; '83 43; '84 39, 263; '86 239; '87 265; '89 55, 236; '90 307; '98 195
Frosting, Creamy Caramel, '81 71
Frosting, Easy Caramel, '87 39
Frosting, Favorite Caramel, '83 106
Fudge, Caramel, '91 273
Glaze, Caramel, '98 195
Helado, Caramel-Vanilla (Caramel-Vanilla Ice Cream), '81 67
Ice Cream Dessert, Caramel, '95 36
Millionaires, '79 M262; '97 M55
O's, Caramel, '99 M196
Peaches, Caramel, '93 134
Pecan Triangles, Caramel-, '99 281
Pie, Burnt Caramel, '82 53
Pie, Caramel, '96 72
Pie, Caramel-Banana, '86 M165
Pie, Caramel Ice Cream, '82 181
Pie, Caramel Meringue, '97 109
Pie, Caramel-Nut Crunch, '94 244
Pie, Caramel-Peanut, '86 259
Pie, Caramel-Pecan, '88 282
Pie, Caramel-Pecan Apple, '85 247
Pie, Cracked Caramel-Pumpkin, '99 254
Pie, Luscious Caramel Banana, '79 115
Pie, Maverick Lunar, '98 111
Pies, Coconut-Caramel, '87 260
Popcorn, Caramel, '79 219; '86 M212
Popcorn, Caramel Crunch, '96 255
Popcorn, Crispy Caramel, '85 247
Ring, Caramel-Orange Coffee, '80 45
Ring, Easy Caramel, '85 M89
Rolls, Caramel Breakfast, '79 193
Rolls, Caramel-Nut, '86 312

Rolls, Easy Caramel, '90 195
Sauce, Caramel, '79 79; '91 56, 180; '93 210, 235, 296; '94 234; '95 308; '96 284, 310; '97 178
Sauce, Caramel-Raisin, '88 127
Sauce, Easy Caramel, '87 38
Sauce, Pears with Orange-Caramel, '95 281
Sauce, Toffee-Fudge, '89 95
Sauce, White Caramel, '92 195; '99 28
Squares, Caramel-Peanut, '85 247
Squares, Chocolate-Caramel Layer, '79 83
Sticky Buns, Easy Caramel-Chocolate, '95 36
Surprise, Caramel, '88 202
Syrup, Caramel, '82 43
Syrup, Citrus Compote with Caramel, '98 313
Tart, Caramel Turtle Truffle, '93 M131
Tarts, Caramel, '82 43
Tarts, Tiny Caramel, '99 179
Torte, Caramel-Sweet Potato, '96 312
Waffles with Apples and Caramel, Gingerbread, '98 M237

CARROTS
Aloha Carrots, '85 261
Ambrosia, Carrot-Marshmallow, '80 5
Apricot Carrots, '84 6
Asparagus, Sunshine Carrots and, '99 277
Aspic, Orange-and-Carrot, '86 199
Baby Carrots, Zucchini with, '88 24
Bake, Apple-Carrot, '93 304
Bake, Carrot-Apple, '98 232
Bake, Creamy Carrot, '85 67
Ball, Carrot-Cheese, '86 325
Balls, Carrot, '79 178
Beef à la Mode, '98 122
Bourbonnaise, Baby Carrots, '85 89
Braised Carrots and Celery, '86 327
Braised Carrots, Apples, and Celery, '96 107
Braised Red Cabbage, '99 243
Brandied Carrots, '87 253
Brandy Sauce, Carrots in, '83 86
Breads
  Carrot Bread, '89 143
  Cornbread, Carrot, '80 89; '81 163
  Muffins, Apple-Carrot, '91 213
  Muffins, Carrot-and-Raisin, '87 24
  Muffins, Carrot-Date-Nut, '86 262
  Muffins, Carrot-Pineapple, '81 6
  Muffins, Carrot-Wheat, '88 9
  Muffins, Morning Glory, '93 327
  Pineapple Bread, Carrot-, '82 210
  Pineapple-Carrot Bread, '79 106
  Tasty Carrot Bread, '84 328
  Three-C Bread, '81 284
  Walnut Bread, Carrot-, '88 284
  Zucchini-Carrot Bread, '83 190
Brussels Sprouts, Carrots and, '82 300
Buttered Carrots and Celery, '89 44
Cakes. *See* CARROTS/Desserts.
Caprice, Carrots, '84 6
Cardamom Carrots, '89 271
Casserole, Carrot, '86 279; '87 285
Casserole, Carrot and Zucchini, '83 256
Casserole, Carrot-Pecan, '93 44; '98 231
Casserole, Cauliflower-and-Carrot, '83 280
Casserole, Scrumptious Carrot, '84 328
Casserole, Squash-Carrot, '81 157
Casserole, Zucchini-Carrot, '99 61
Celeriac and Carrots, '91 219
Chicken, Sweet-and-Sour, '97 325
Chowchow, Carrot, '93 218
Classy Carrots, '94 36
Coleslaw, Best Barbecue, '97 214
Coleslaw, Memphis-Style, '98 104
Combo, Carrot, '79 45
Cooler, Apricot-Orange-Carrot, '96 108

Cooler, Carrot, '89 35
Curried Carrots and Pineapple, '90 228
Desserts
  Cake, Applesauce Carrot, '81 202
  Cake, Best Carrot, '97 230
  Cake, Blue Ribbon Carrot, '81 70
  Cake, Brownie Carrot, '92 120
  Cake, Carrot, '79 45; '82 137; '84 315; '98 275
  Cake, Carrot Pound, '87 41
  Cake, Carrot Pudding, '83 24
  Cake, Cheater's Carrot, '96 20
  Cake, Coconut-Pecan Carrot, '84 322
  Cake, Easy Carrot, '83 215
  Cake, Easy Carrot Snack, '82 235
  Cake, Fresh Coconut-Carrot, '80 299
  Cake, Frosted Carrot, '92 19
  Cake, German Carrot-Hazelnut, '97 230
  Cake, Old-Fashioned Carrot, '83 M232; '97 330
  Cake, Old-Fashioned Carrot Sheet, '97 330
  Cake, Old-South Carrot, '80 120
  Cake, Pecan-Carrot, '99 223
  Cake, Quick-and-Easy Carrot, '84 150
  Cakes, Miniature Carrot, '90 94
  Cake, Spiced Carrot, '87 296
  Cake, Spicy Fruited Carrot, '85 117
  Cakes with Madeira Syrup and Vanilla Ice Cream, Carrot, '98 247
  Cake, Zucchini-Carrot, '93 20
  Cookies, Carrot, '82 137
  Cookies, Carrot-Orange, '83 149
  Cookies, Frosted Carrot, '81 7
  Cupcakes, Carrot-Bran, '82 16
  Pie, Carrot Custard, '79 45
  Pie, Carrot Ice Cream, '86 200
Deviled Carrots, '83 322
Dilled Baby Carrots, '84 80; '92 145
Dilled Carrots, '85 24; '90 17
Dilled Carrots and Green Beans, '99 223
Dill-Spiced Carrots, '87 200
Dilly Carrots, '85 85
Fillets, Apple-Carrot Stuffed, '88 M192
Fried Carrot Balls, '82 16
Fried Carrots, Crispy, '94 36
Garden Surprise, '83 112
Ginger Carrots, '83 9; '85 139
Gingered Carrots, '85 95; '92 302
Glazed
  Apricot Glazed Carrots, '80 89
  Apricot-Glazed Carrots, '98 231
  Baby Carrots, Glazed, '91 291; '92 256
  Baby Carrots, Mint-Glazed, '89 102
  Bacon and Onion, Glazed Carrots with, '87 200
  Brown Sugar-Glazed Carrots, '99 24
  Brussels Sprouts and Baby Carrots, Glazed, '97 302
  Candied Carrots, '82 269; '83 225
  Ginger Carrots, '83 9
  Ginger-Cinnamon Carrots, '93 168
  Gingered Carrots, '85 95
  Ginger-Glazed Carrots, '87 68
  Glazed Carrots, '81 304; '83 117; '85 258; '88 304; '89 106, 235
  Golden Carrots, '85 267
  Grapes, Glazed Carrots with, '82 287
  Harvard Carrots, '83 117
  Honey-Glazed Carrots, '80 115; '84 121; '85 18; '92 229; '99 63
  Honey-Kissed Carrots, '84 122
  Horseradish Glaze, Carrots with, '85 66
  Lemon-Glazed Carrots, '84 16
  Light Glazed Carrots, '92 227
  Mint-Glazed Carrots and Peas, '90 291

Onions, Glazed Carrots and, '83 25; '87 128
Orange-Glazed Carrots, '79 12; '81 M165; '90 M98
Orange-Raisin Carrots, '80 24
Peach-Glazed Carrots, '90 13
Pineapple Carrots, '83 198
Rutabaga, Lemon-Glazed Carrots and, '97 46
Spice-Glazed Carrots, '83 M58
Sunshine Carrots, '82 16
Hash Browns, Carrot, '96 107
Herbed Carrots and Onions, '87 31
Horseradish Sauce, Carrots and Broccoli with, '91 246
Julienne Carrots, How to Prepare, '84 120
Julienne Carrots, Sautéed, '82 91
Julienne Carrots with Walnuts, '84 188
Julienne, Tarragon Carrots, '84 329
Julienne, Turnips and Carrots, '86 295
Julienne Zucchini and Carrots, '90 14
Lemon-Carrot Bundles, '91 80
Lemon Carrots, '82 300; '83 111
Loaf, Carrot-Nut, '83 117
Madeira, Carrots, '80 125; '83 281
Marinated Beets, Green Beans, and Carrots, '88 162
Marinated Carrots, '86 108, 111; '91 103
Marinated Carrots, Creamy, '87 200
Marinated Carrots, Crispy, '81 7
Marinated Carrot Strips, '88 176
Marmalade, Carrot-Citrus, '81 148
Marmalemon, Carrot, '96 107
Marsala, Carrots, '83 56
Medley, Carrot-and-Leek, '88 102
Medley, Carrot-Lima-Squash, '80 123
Medley, Parsnip-Carrot, '96 36
Minted Carrots, '81 101
Minted Carrots, Saucy, '82 252
Orange Carrots and Turnips, Sunset, '94 213
Orange-Fennel Carrots, '92 133
Orange Sauce, Carrots in, '82 107
Orange-Spiced Carrots, '88 18
Orangy Carrot Strips, '89 312
Parsleyed Turnips and Carrots, '79 253
Patties, Carrot, '80 89
Pecans, Carrots and Celery with, '84 254
Peppers, Carrot-and-Cabbage Stuffed, '99 63
Pickled Carrots, '93 12
Pie, Carrot, '83 117
Pie, Cauliflower-Carrot, '82 191
Polynesian, Carrots, '79 45
Pudding, Carrot-Potato, '94 279
Puff, Carrot, '84 328; '89 89
Puffs, Carrot, '87 200
Puree, Carrot-and-Sweet Potato, '94 56
Puree, Carrot-Sweet Potato, '92 90
Ring, Festive Carrot, '82 16
Ring, Rice-Carrot, '79 246
Roasted Carrots, '92 340
Roasted Celery Root, Carrots, and Onions, '98 293
Roasted Potatoes, Carrots, and Leeks, '94 276
Rosemary Carrots, '91 219
Salad, Apple-Carrot, '85 22
Salad, Carrot, '82 137
Salad, Carrot-Ambrosia, '81 252
Salad, Carrot-and-Zucchini, '83 240
Salad, Carrot-Broccoli, '99 26
Salad, Carrot-Caraway, '89 105
Salad, Carrot-Pineapple, '91 83
Salad, Carrot-Raisin, '83 117; '84 174; '87 10
Salad, Carrot-Tangerine, '83 316; '84 16
Salad, Creamy Carrot-Nut, '86 331
Salad, Favorite Carrot, '80 33
Salad, Fruity Carrot-and-Seed, '86 223

CARROTS
(continued)

Salad, Harvest Carrot, '89 128
Salad, Honey-Sweet Carrot, '89 161
Salad, Lime-Carrot, '92 65
Salad, Orange-Carrot, '80 89; '84 325
Salad, Shredded Carrot, '80 178
Salad, Simple Carrot, '82 101; '84 152
Salad, Sunny Day, '96 90
Salad, Sunshine Carrot, '82 132
Salad, Sweet-and-Sour Carrot, '98 211
Salad, Turkey-Carrot, '86 283
Salad, Turnip-and-Carrot, '91 212
Salad with Orange-Nutmeg Dressing,
    Carrot-Raisin, '97 305; '98 19
Saucy Carrots, '87 41
Sauté, Carrot-Turnip, '93 241
Sautéed Zucchini and Carrots, '92 62, 99
Savory Sauce, Lima Beans and Carrots with,
    '84 196
Scalloped Carrots, '81 6; '96 107
Scalloped Carrots-and-Celery, '84 M112
Scalloped Carrots, Cheese, '94 36
Slaw, Apple-Carrot, '92 243
Slaw, Shredded Celery Root-and-Carrot, '98 293
Soufflé, Carrot, '79 73; '98 231; '99 25
Soufflé, Carrots, '83 265
Soufflés, Carrot, '96 309
Soup, Carrot, '80 88; '89 146; '98 123
Soup, Carrot Cream, '90 210
Soup, Carrot-Leek, '86 34
Soup, Carrot-Orange, '79 172
Soup, Cheesy Carrot, '81 262
Soup, Chilled Carrot-Mint, '90 M168
Soup, Cream of Carrot, '81 307; '88 46; '91 69
Soup, Cream of Carrot-and-Tomato, '94 176
Soup, Creamy Carrot, '92 218
Soup, Curried Carrot, '82 157
Soup, Potato-Carrot, '88 297
Soup, Savory Carrot, '84 107
Soup with Parslied Croutons, Carrot-and-
    Butternut Squash, '97 217
Special Carrots, '81 108; '84 6
Spiced Carrots Polynesian, '88 85
Spread, Carrot-Pecan, '96 108
Spread, Feta-and-Apple, '99 106
Spread, Nutty Carrot, '94 123
Squares, Carrot, '79 256
Squares, Golden Carrot-Lemon, '80 40
Squash, Stuffed, '98 177
Steamed Carrots, Lemon-Dill, '93 180
Sticks, Carrot, '89 106
Stir-Fry, Beef-and-Carrot, '98 335
Stir-Fry, Turnip-and-Carrot, '96 36
Stuffed Carrots, '86 324; '87 40
Sugar Snaps and Carrots, Creamed, '93 139
Sunshine Carrots, '82 16; '83 25
Supreme, Broccoli-Carrot, '89 331
Swamp Sticks, '95 274
Sweet-and-Sour Carrots, '82 137
Sweet-and-Sour Green Beans and Carrots, '83 6
Tarragon Carrots, '83 173
Tipsy Carrots, '87 40
Toss, Asparagus-Carrot-Squash, '91 45
Toss, Carrot-Fruit, '82 235
Tropical Carrots, '84 34
Veal and Carrots, Company, '85 22
Veal and Carrots in Wine Sauce, '81 31;
    '86 M139
White Wine, Carrots in, '81 109
Wine Sauce, Carrots in, '80 88
Zesty Carrots, '84 5

Zucchini and Carrots, Buttered, '83 252
Zucchini, Carrots and, '84 262
CASSEROLES. *See also* **LASAGNA.**
Apple-Cheese Casserole, '84 287
Barley, Baked, '91 133
Barley Casserole, '84 281
Bean
    Baked Bean Medley, '80 100
    Baked Beans, Hawaiian-Style, '86 210
    Baked Beans, Maple Heights, '91 223
    Baked Beans Quintet, '94 100
    Baked Beans, Three-Meat, '86 210
    Baked Beans with Ham, '80 136
    Beef-and-Bean Bake, Cheesy, '82 89
    Beef, Bean, and Cornbread Casserole, '99 215
    Black Beans, Casserole of, '95 27
    Chuck Wagon Bean Casserole, '93 198
    Cornbread Casserole, Bean-and-, '92 243
    Green Bean and Artichoke Casserole, Italian,
        '85 81
    Green Bean-and-Corn Casserole, '88 123
    Green Bean Casserole, '79 106; '84 145
    Green Bean Casserole, Easy, '87 284
    Green Bean Italiano, '94 145
    Green Bean Salad, Hot, '86 298
    Green Beans au Gratin, '80 116
    Green Beans, French Quarter, '80 298; '81 26
    Green Beans in Sour Cream, '80 116
    Green Beans, Italian, '85 147
    Green Beans Italian, '87 10
    Green Bean Surprise, '86 9
    Green Beans with Sour Cream, '82 90
    Kidney Bean Casserole, '90 136
    Lentils with Cheese, Baked, '84 113
    Lima-Bacon Bake, '86 9
    Lima Bean Casserole, '79 189; '83 313;
        '86 225; '87 284; '95 132
    Lima Bean Casserole, Spicy, '79 189
    Lima Bean Casserole, Swiss, '80 191
    Lima Bean Garden Casserole, '83 218; '84 246
    Lima Beans Deluxe, '79 289; '80 26
    Lima Beans, Savory, '83 219; '84 246
    Lima Beans, Super, '79 189
    Lima Beans with Canadian Bacon, '83 219;
        '84 245
    Lima Casserole, Ham and, '79 192
    Limas, Spanish Cheese, '86 225
    Mexican Bean Casserole, Spicy, '84 114
    Three-Bean Bake, '81 155
    Three-Bean Casserole, '88 56
    White Bean Bake, Turnip Greens and, '94 246
Breakfast and Brunch
    Apple-Egg Casserole, '85 44
    Bacon and Egg Casserole, '81 225
    Bacon-and-Eggs Scramble, '80 M267
    Breakfast Casserole, '91 285; '99 273
    Broccoli-Cheese Breakfast Casserole, '99 233
    Brunch Casserole, '82 124
    Bunch, Brunch for a, '88 57
    Cheese-and-Egg Casserole, '99 268
    Cheese Blintz Casserole, '92 251
    Cheesy Breakfast Casserole, '85 247
    Cheesy Brunch Casserole, Easy, '92 91
    Chile-Hominy Casserole, '88 57
    Chile 'n' Cheese Breakfast Casserole, '88 57
    Corned Beef Brunch Bake, '82 44
    Cornmeal Puff, '82 42
    Cranberry-Apple Casserole, '83 311
    Creole Sauce, Brunch Casserole with, '98 98
    Egg-and-Bacon Casserole, '85 248
    Egg-and-Cheese Casserole, '84 293
    Egg-and-Cheese Puff, '85 45
    Egg Casserole, '83 311; '98 98
    Egg Casserole, Brunch, '86 329

    Egg Casserole, Cheesy, '81 244; '86 15
    Egg Casserole, Scrambled, '80 51; '86 241
    Egg Casserole, Sunday, '95 100
    Egg-Mushroom Casserole, '83 49
    Eggs Bel-Mar, '90 92
    Eggs, Brunch, '98 93
    Eggs, Bruncheon, '83 83
    Eggs, Chile, '88 80
    Eggs, Creole, '82 42
    Eggs, Layered, '96 97
    Egg Soufflé Casserole, '83 55
    Fruit Bake, Hot, '81 270
    Grits, Baked Cheese-and-Garlic, '83 292
    Grits Casserole, Cheesy, '81 270
    Grits Casserole, Garlic, '81 47
    Grits, Garlic-Cheese, '99 270
    Grits, Orange, '81 47
    Grits-Sausage Casserole, '84 75; '86 241
    Grits, Swiss-and-Cheddar Baked, '91 71
    Ham and Egg Casserole, Breakfast, '79 253
    Hash Brown Cheese Bake, '82 50
    Hash Brown Potato Casserole, '81 40
    Hominy, Gold Coast, '83 52
    Huevos Rancheros, '82 197
    Potato Breakfast Casserole, '80 52
    Sausage-and-Egg Casserole, '94 284
    Sausage Breakfast Casserole, '81 270
    Sausage Brunch, Italian, '88 57
    Sausage Casserole, Hawaiian, '85 42
    Sausage Casserole, Swiss, '80 209
    Sausage-Cheese Bake, '88 58
    Sausage, Country Grits and, '83 54
    Sausage Egg Bake, '81 225
    Sausage-Egg Bake, Smoked, '85 248
    Sausage-Mushroom Breakfast Casserole,
        '86 95
    Sausage Strata, '83 243
Broccoli-Ham au Gratin, '90 239
Brown Rice Casserole, '87 118
Cannelloni, '92 17
Cheese Bake, Continental, '81 89
Cheese Casserole, Feather-Light, '79 84
Cheese Casserole, Four, '92 170
Chile-Cheese Casserole, '82 90
Chiles Rellenos Casserole, '79 84; '92 18
Chili Casserole, '90 176
Chili-Rice Casserole, '79 54
Chili-Tamale Pie, '83 68
Egg and Rice Bake, '83 119
Egg Casserole, Saucy Scrambled, '89 213
Eggplant-and-Oyster Louisiane, '95 196
Eggplant-Sausage-Pasta Casserole, Freezer,
    '95 197
Enchilada Casserole, '87 287
Enchilada Casserole, Green, '79 76
Franks, Mexican, '93 78
Fruit Casserole, Sherried, '80 284
Fruit, Gingered Baked, '81 232
Grits, Garlic-Cheese, '86 180
Grits, Garlicky Ham-and-Spinach, '94 177
Grits Italiano, '92 43
Grits with Green Chiles, Cheese, '95 208
Hash Brown-Ham-Cheese Bake, '97 323
Hominy-and-Corn Casserole, '97 291
Hominy Casserole, Cheesy, '83 170
Hominy Casserole), Four-Part Hominy (Cheesy,
    '96 158
Hominy-Chili Casserole, '86 255
Hominy, Hot Cheese, '84 77
Hominy, Jalapeño, '82 51
Hominy with Chiles and Cheese, '86 78
Italian Casserole, '90 238
Kale, Scalloped, '86 224
Lentils-and-Rice Casserole, '93 301

Macaroni and Blue Cheese, '93 248
Macaroni and Cheese, Creamy, '93 249
Macaroni and Cheese, Divine, '99 314
Macaroni and Cheese, Eleanor's, '97 253
Macaroni and Cheese, Old-Fashioned, '92 215
Macaroni and Cheese, Thick-and-Rich, '84 329
Macaroni Bake, Jack-in-the-, '93 249
Macaroni Casserole, '84 220; '87 154
Macaroni, Glorious, '84 76
Macaroni, Gorgonzola, '97 28
Macaroni, Mexican, '96 73
Macaroni Mousse, '96 73
Macaroni-Mushroom Bake, '97 96
Macaroni-Mushroom Bake, Cheesy, '81 243
Manicotti, Make-Ahead, '98 68
Meat. *See also* **CASSEROLES/Pork.**
   Beef-and-Bean Bake, Cheesy, '82 89
   Beef-and-Biscuit Casserole, '83 75
   Beef-and-Noodles Casserole, '84 72
   Beef-and-Vegetable Chow Mein Casserole,
      '83 313
   Beef Bake, Zesty Cabbage, '80 300
   Beef Bake, Zucchini, '86 146
   Beef, Bean, and Cornbread Casserole, '99 215
   Beef Casserole, Crusty, '82 88
   Beef Casserole, Macaroni-Cheese-, '95 125
   Beef Casserole, Spinach and, '79 192
   Beef, Cheese, and Noodle Casserole, '99 58
   Beef-Macaroni Bake, '94 255
   Beef-Macaroni Combo, '79 194
   Beef-Noodle Bake, Taco, '81 141
   Beef Supreme, '83 196
   Beefy Vegetable Casserole, '79 248
   Cavatini, '94 214
   Cheeseburger Casserole, '95 255
   Cheesy Mexican Casserole, '82 224
   Chiles Rellenos Casserole, '79 84; '84 31, 234;
      '92 18; '98 48
   Chili Casserole, Ultimate, '99 239
   Chili Hominy Bake, '81 282; '82 58
   Chili Manicotti, '99 239
   Cornbread Casserole, '81 91
   Cornbread Skillet Casserole, '83 243; '84 101
   Cornbread Tamale Bake, '79 163
   Corned Beef and Cabbage au Gratin, '83 16
   County Fair Casserole, '79 130
   El Dorado Casserole, '81 140
   Enchilada Casserole, Firecracker, '80 260
   Enchilada Casserole, Sour Cream, '82 113
   Fajita Casserole, '97 96
   Five-Layer Meal, '81 140
   Frankaroni Potluck Dish, '88 201
   Franks 'n' Beans, Stove-Top, '88 201
   Ground Beef and Sausage Casserole, '80 260
   Ground Beef Casserole, Cheesy, '79 44
   Ground Beef Casserole, Creamy, '81 142
   Hamburger-Bean Bake, '95 121
   Hamburger Casserole, '95 210
   Hamburger-Corn Bake, '99 58
   Hamburger-Noodle Bake, '81 140
   Hamburger Pie, '81 92
   Hot Doggie Casserole, '88 200
   Italian Casserole, '80 81
   Layered Grecian Bake, '82 119
   Matador Mania, '86 19
   Mexican Casserole, Cabin, '97 95
   Moussaka, '87 166; '90 68; '97 94
   Moussaka Casserole, '79 179
   Moussaka, Corn, '87 190
   Pastichio, '85 194
   Pastitsio, '87 12; '88 11; '99 167
   Pizza Bake, Upside-Down, '98 224
   Pizza Casserole, '88 273; '89 181
   Pizza Casserole, Quick, '83 266

Shells, Spinach-Stuffed, '99 64
Sloppy Joe Squares, '97 95
Sour Cream-Noodle Bake, '79 55
Spaghetti and Beef Casserole, '79 129
Spaghetti Casserole, '84 241
Spinach and Beef Casserole, '79 192
Spinach-Beef-Macaroni Casserole, '83 313
Stroganoff Casserole, '98 48
Taco Bake, '97 326
Taco Beef-Noodle Bake, '81 141
Taco Casserole, '80 33
Taco Squares, Deep-Dish, '91 88
Tamale, Mozzarella, '95 70
Tortilla Bake, Texas, '94 285
Veal and Wild Rice Casserole, '79 180
Veal Cutlet Casserole, '79 109
Venison-Vegetable Bake, '87 304
Ziti, Baked, '94 65
Microwave
   Asparagus-Pea Casserole, '88 M294
   Beans-and-Franks, Polynesian, '84 M11
   Beef Casserole, Easy, '86 M58
   Beef Casserole, Layered, '82 M203
   Beefy Sausage Dinner, '80 M9
   Broccoli Casserole, '88 M146
   Broccoli-Swiss Cheese Casserole, '85 M211
   Carrots-and-Celery, Scalloped, '84 M112
   Chicken Divan, '80 M10
   Chicken Divan Casserole, '82 M203
   Chicken Mexicana, '91 M127
   Chicken Tetrazzini, Cheesy, '83 M87
   Green Beans, Herbed, '83 M147
   Ham-and-Potato Casserole, '83 M87
   Ham-Asparagus Dinner, '80 M10
   Ham Roll Casserole, '91 M127
   Macaroni-Ham Casserole, '81 M177
   Mexican Casserole, '92 M22
   Mexican Casserole, Microwave, '90 M231
   Mexi Casserole, '83 M87
   Okra and Tomatoes, Fresh, '81 M165
   Onion-Potato Bake, '83 M195
   Pineapple, Scalloped, '84 M323
   Pizza Casserole, Microwave, '89 M248
   Pork Casserole, Cheesy, '81 M74
   Potato Casserole, Creamy, '84 M113
   Potatoes, Parmesan, '90 M62
   Sausage and Rice Casserole, Oriental,
      '82 M123
   Sausage Casserole, Easy, '87 M189
   Sausage-Egg Casserole, '86 M12
   Sausage Jambalaya Casserole, '82 M203
   Spinach Delight, '84 M144
   Squash Bake, Cheddar-, '84 M113
   Squash Casserole, Cheesy, '82 M21
   Squash Casserole, Jiffy, '81 M144
   Squash Medley, Fresh, '81 M165
   Tuna Casserole, Easy, '82 M203
   Turkey Casserole, Crunchy, '89 M282
   Zucchini-Egg Casserole, '84 M113
   Zucchini, Italian, '83 M147
Orzo, Mozzarella-and-Olive, '97 249
Paella Casserole, '95 254
Pasta Casseroles, Hot Brown, '96 290
Pineapple Bake, '79 251; '96 84
Pineapple, Baked, '84 287
Pineapple, Scalloped, '79 106
Pork
   Casserole, Pork, '83 116
   Chop Casserole, Peppered Pork, '81 235;
      '82 25; '83 39
   Chop Casserole, Pork, '94 255
   Chops and Potato Scallop, Pork, '82 114
   Chops Italiano, Pork, '80 72
   Chop-Vegetable Casserole, Pork, '90 208

Fiesta Pork Bake, '79 265
Frankfurter Casserole, Layered, '79 64
Franks, Family-Style, '79 54
Ham and Broccoli Casserole, '81 133
Ham and Broccoli Strata, '80 261
Ham-and-Cheese Casserole, '87 78
Ham-and-Cheese Layered Casserole, '98 160
Ham and Lima Casserole, '79 192
Ham and Noodle Casserole, '80 300
Ham-and-Potato Casserole, '96 103
Ham-and-Potato Casserole, Cheesy, '84 326
Ham-and-Rice Casserole, '84 75
Ham and Turkey Bake, Layered, '79 252
Ham Bake, Harvest, '79 210
Ham-Broccoli Casserole, Quick, '82 40
Ham Casserole, '96 302; '98 314
Ham Casserole, Apple, '79 213
Ham Casserole, Golden, '82 119
Ham Casserole, Macaroni-, '83 283
Ham Casserole, Vegetable-and-, '84 91
Ham Medley, Creamy, '84 90
Ham Pie, Golden, '87 78
Ham-Rice-Tomato Bake, '87 78
Ham Strata, '95 308
Ham Strata, Baked, '83 283
Ham Tetrazzini, '84 241
Salami-Corn Casserole, '80 209
Sausage and Broccoli Casserole, '80 33
Sausage and Noodle Casserole, '82 123
Sausage-and-Noodle Casserole, '95 255
Sausage-and-Rice Bake, Creole, '88 58
Sausage and Wild Rice Casserole, '83 196
Sausage Bake, Eggplant, '85 221
Sausage Bake, Hominy-, '88 51
Sausage-Bean Supper, '86 52
Sausage Casserole, '81 112; '82 12
Sausage Casserole, Cheesy, '82 124
Sausage Casserole, Country, '79 192
Sausage Casserole, Crunchy, '81 288
Sausage Casserole, Eggplant-, '84 215
Sausage Casserole, Ground Beef and, '80 260
Sausage Casserole, Skillet, '99 123
Sausage-Chile Rellenos Casserole, '88 52
Sausage Grits, '86 92
Sausage-Lasagna Rollups, '80 236
Sausage-Noodle Bake, '81 92
Sausage-Potato Casserole, '86 217
Sausage-Rice Casserole, '82 50; '83 75
Sausages, Baked Zucchini and, '80 300
Sausage-Stuffed Shells, '96 102
Sausage, Wild Rice and, '86 268
Sausage-Wild Rice Casserole, '84 250
Spaghetti Bake, Pork, '81 11
Spaghetti Casserole, Low-Fat, '99 215
Strata, Christmas Morning, '95 282
Supper Supreme, Sunday, '79 76
Vegetable-Pork Combo, '85 113
Poultry
   Chicken à la Russell, '95 175
   Chicken-Almond Casserole, '94 199
   Chicken-and-Artichoke Casserole, '96 133
   Chicken-and-Chiles Casserole, '93 107
   Chicken-and-Dressing Casserole, '81 263
   Chicken and Green Noodle Casserole, '80 32
   Chicken and Grits, '95 263
   Chicken-and-Pasta Casserole, '97 192
   Chicken and Rice, '95 54
   Chicken and Rice Casserole, '80 260
   Chicken-and-Shrimp Florentine, '89 64
   Chicken-and-Spinach Enchiladas, '91 222
   Chicken and Wild Rice, '79 248
   Chicken-and-Wild Rice Casserole, '97 192
   Chicken-Asparagus Casserole, '83 76; '84 71
   Chicken Bake, Company, '80 301

CASSEROLES, Poultry
(continued)

Chicken Bake, Spicy, **'85** 251
Chicken Bake with Sweet Bacon Dressing, Vegetable-, **'93** 108
Chicken-Broccoli Casserole, **'79** 48; **'91** 315
Chicken-Brown Rice Bake, **'91** 314
Chicken Casserole, **'96** 103, 302
Chicken Casserole, Broccoli-, **'82** 33
Chicken Casserole, Cheesy, **'85** 34
Chicken Casserole, Chow Mein, **'96** 276
Chicken Casserole, Hearty Tex-Mex Squash-, **'99** 312
Chicken Casserole, Macaroni and, **'80** 260
Chicken Casserole, Make-Ahead, **'84** 241
Chicken Casserole, Mexi-, **'93** 69; **'94** 30
Chicken Casserole, Mexican, **'82** 143
Chicken Casserole, Oyster-and-, **'99** 320
Chicken Casserole, Pesto-, **'94** 231
Chicken Casserole, Quick, **'81** 91
Chicken Casserole, Rice-and-, **'87** 154
Chicken Casserole, Simply Good, **'95** 255
Chicken Casserole, Sunday, **'83** 290
Chicken Casserole, Swiss, **'90** 67
Chicken Chili Bake, **'93** 302
Chicken Chimichangas, **'93** 68
Chicken Dinner, Hot-and-Spicy, **'94** M94
Chicken Divan, **'80** M10
Chicken Divan, Curried, **'80** 83
Chicken Divan, Easy, **'94** 310
Chicken Divan, Gourmet, **'82** 83
Chicken Divan, Overnight, **'83** 198
Chicken Divan, Sherried, **'80** 38
Chicken-Eggplant Parmigiana, **'82** 212
Chicken Enchiladas, **'80** 301
Chicken Enchiladas, Creamy, **'97** 250
Chicken Enchiladas, Easy, **'82** 89
Chicken Enchiladas, Three-Cheese, **'99** 330
Chicken Florentine, **'93** 107
Chicken, Fontina-Baked, **'90** 64
Chicken, French Herbed, **'86** 89
Chicken, Garlic-Spinach, **'92** 56
Chicken-Green Bean Casserole, **'85** 296
Chicken-Green Bean Casserole, Creamy, **'97** 158
Chicken, King Ranch, **'95** 193; **'99** 330
Chicken Lasagna Bake, **'95** 55
Chicken, Lemony Pecan, **'96** 82
Chicken-Macaroni Casserole, **'85** 219
Chicken-Noodle Casserole, **'94** 286
Chicken Parmigiana, **'80** 190
Chicken, Poppy Seed, **'99** 195
Chicken-Rice Casserole, **'86** 52; **'99** 215
Chicken-Rice Casserole, Creamy, **'99** 21
Chicken Salad, Baked, **'86** 297
Chicken, Scarborough, **'80** 38
Chicken Skillet Casserole, Spaghetti Squash and, **'94** 134
Chicken-Spaghetti Casserole, **'84** 15
Chicken, Spicy Mexican, **'82** 89
Chicken-Squash Casserole, **'95** 121
Chicken Superb Casserole, **'89** 83
Chicken Supreme Casserole, **'84** 219
Chicken Supreme, Hot, **'81** 76
Chicken, Swiss, **'95** 54
Chicken Tetrazzini, **'79** 268; **'80** M75; **'99** 61
Chicken Thighs, Swiss, **'94** 282
Chicken Tortilla Bake, **'82** 89
Chicken Tortilla Casserole, **'81** 166
Chicken-Wild Rice Casserole, **'84** 241; **'85** 65
Chicken-Wild Rice Supreme, **'79** 77

Chicken with Spinach Fettuccine, Creamy Basil, **'97** 328
Cornish Hens-and-Rice Casserole, **'92** 267
Crêpes Divan, Elegant, **'81** 91
Day-After-the-Holiday Casserole, **'96** 276
Duck and Wild Rice Casserole, **'79** 224
Pollo, Chilaquiles con (Tortillas with Chicken), **'81** 66
Rice Casserole, Mexican, **'83** 31
Shells, Southwestern Stuffed, **'99** 238
Southwestern Casserole, **'99** 216
Turkey-and-Broccoli Casserole, **'86** 332
Turkey-and-Shrimp Florentine Casserole, **'92** 122
Turkey-Asparagus Casserole, **'86** 284
Turkey Bake, Layered Ham and, **'79** 252
Turkey Casserole, **'84** 327; **'96** 302
Turkey Casserole, Golden, **'80** 271
Turkey Casserole, Stuffed, **'88** 246
Turkey Florentine, **'88** 264
Turkey Noodle Bake, **'93** 243
Turkey-Noodle-Poppyseed Casserole, **'90** 239
Turkey-Olive Casserole, **'87** 268
Turkey Parmigiana, **'87** 193
Turkey Salad Bake, **'79** 253
Turkey Salad, Hot, **'86** 297
Turkey-Spinach Casserole, **'84** 71
Turkey-Swiss Casserole, **'86** 283
Turkey Tetrazzini, Herbed, **'86** 47
Wraps, Southwestern, **'99** 238
Provolone Casserole, Seashell-, **'80** 189
Quiche Casserole, **'95** 33
Ravioli, Mediterranean, **'93** 301
Reuben Casserole, **'90** 240
Rice-and-Cheese con Chiles, **'89** 99
Rice and Green Chiles, **'83** 152
Rice au Gratin Supreme, **'86** 78
Rice, Baked, **'94** 270
Rice, Baked Spicy, **'96** 125
Rice Bake, Green, **'79** 43
Rice Casserole, **'87** 45
Rice Casserole, Chili-, **'79** 54
Rice Casserole, Colorful, **'82** 199
Rice Casserole, Green, **'95** 181
Rice Casserole, Jalapeño, **'81** 66
Rice Casserole, Spanish, **'79** 192
Rice Chantilly, **'86** 82
Rice, Easy Mushroom, **'89** 286
Rice, Fiesta, **'84** 76
Rice, Hot Pepper, **'92** 310
Rice Mélange, **'87** 240
Rice, Mexican, **'85** 147
Rice Pilaf, **'86** 82
Rice, Savannah Red, **'95** 27
Rice, Spanish, **'81** 51; **'90** 183
Rice, Spicy, **'85** 256
Rotini Romano, **'87** 193
Seafood
Crab-and-Mushroom Casserole, **'89** 96
Crab-and-Shrimp Casserole, **'84** 71
Crab and Spinach Casserole, Creamy, **'80** 3
Crab Bake, Quick, **'87** 192
Crab Casserole, **'79** 228
Crab Casserole, Deviled, **'91** 238; **'92** 27
Crab Casserole, Easy, **'93** 270
Crab, Dressed, **'82** 276
Crab-Egg Casserole, **'80** 260
Crab Imperial, **'79** 82, 116
Crab Imperial, Elegant, **'83** 245
Crabmeat-Broccoli Casserole, **'84** 232
Crabmeat Imperial, **'82** 311
Crabmeat with Artichoke Hearts, Creamed, **'93** 26
Crab Puff, **'79** 116

Crab, Shrimp, and Artichoke au Gratin, **'90** 240
Crawfish Lasagna, **'91** 89
Crawfish Pasta Casserole, **'97** 106
Fish and Potato Bake, Herbed, **'79** 287; **'80** 34
Fish Casserole, Green Chile-and-, **'84** 32
Miss Hannah's Casserole, **'92** 236
Oyster-and-Chicken Casserole, **'99** 320
Oyster-and-Corn Bake, **'83** 34; **'84** 44
Oyster-and-Spinach Casserole, **'83** 34; **'84** 44
Oyster-and-Wild Rice Casserole, **'83** 34; **'84** 44
Oyster Casserole, **'79** 228
Oyster Casserole, Wild Rice-, **'86** 256
Oysters Johnny Reb, **'82** 42
Oysters, Scalloped, **'79** 225; **'84** 213; **'86** 132; **'95** 318; **'99** 321
Parmesan, Savannah Seafood, **'99** 312
Salmon Casserole, **'81** 22
Salmon Florentine, **'83** 43
Scallop Casserole, **'79** 228
Seafood Casserole, **'87** 109; **'89** 63
Shrimp-and-Chicken Casserole, **'91** 102
Shrimp-and-Noodle Casserole, **'90** 240
Shrimp and Rice Casserole, **'79** 228
Shrimp-and-Rice Casserole, **'94** 328
Shrimp au Gratin, **'85** 79
Shrimp Casserole, **'85** 240
Shrimp Casserole, Chayotes and, **'80** 230
Shrimp Casserole, Spicy, **'96** 62
Shrimp-Crab Puff, **'79** 57
Shrimp Delight, **'79** 192
Shrimp Fettuccine, **'96** 210
Shrimp Florentine Casserole, Turkey-and-, **'92** 122
Shrimp Manicotti, **'97** 96
Tuna and Peas in Wine Sauce, Baked, **'83** 196
Tuna-Broccoli Casserole, Tangy, **'83** 75
Tuna Casserole, **'82** 119; **'96** 103
Tuna Casserole, Biscuit-Topped, **'79** 113
Tuna Casserole, Nippy, **'84** 241
Tuna Casserole with Cheese Swirls, **'88** 256
Tuna Chopsticks, **'94** 255
Tuna-Macaroni Treat, **'82** 131
Tuna Vegetable Casserole, **'81** 135
Shells, Southwestern Stuffed, **'93** 234
Spaghetti, Casserole, **'95** 132
Tamale Casserole, Quick, **'94** 255
Vegetable
Artichoke Casserole, Alii, **'93** 294
Asparagus-and-English Pea Casserole, **'86** 324
Asparagus and Peas Casserole, **'80** 152
Asparagus-Artichoke Casserole, **'86** 279
Asparagus Casserole, **'98** 310
Asparagus Casserole, Cheesy, **'82** 281; **'83** 32
Asparagus Casserole, Creamy, **'80** 76
Asparagus Casserole, Easy, **'83** 255
Asparagus Delight, **'82** 269
Asparagus, Holiday, **'85** 260
Asparagus-Pea Casserole, **'88** M294
Asparagus-Pimiento Loaf, **'84** 86
Asparagus-Spaghetti Casserole, **'80** 77
Asparagus Supreme, **'89** 245
Beets, Fruited, **'97** 28
Black-Eyed Peas with Rice, **'83** 12
Broccoli-and-Egg Casserole, **'86** 324
Broccoli-and-Eggs au Gratin, **'85** 289
Broccoli Bake, **'81** 246; **'89** 279
Broccoli Bake, Cheesy, **'83** 255
Broccoli Bake, Cheesy Italian, **'83** 5
Broccoli Bake, Company, **'83** 279
Broccoli-Blue Cheese Casserole, **'85** 260
Broccoli Casserole, **'87** 284; **'88** M146, 265
Broccoli Casserole, Almond-, **'88** 62

Broccoli Casserole, Cheesy, '84 293; '92 342; '95 M191
Broccoli Casserole, Italian, '82 6, 280; '83 32
Broccoli Casserole, Winter, '94 280
Broccoli-Cheese Casserole, '82 269; '84 9; '94 132
Broccoli-Corn Casserole, '83 313
Broccoli Elegant, '81 267
Broccoli, English Walnut, '89 68
Broccoli-Onion Deluxe, '81 75
Broccoli Puff, '82 95
Broccoli-Rice Casserole, '81 101
Broccoli Supreme, '82 34; '85 68
Broccoli-Swiss Cheese Casserole, '83 322; '85 M211
Broccoli with Lemon Cream, '89 245
Broccoli with Rice, Holiday, '87 252
Broccoli with Stuffing, '95 341
Brussels Sprouts-and-Artichoke Casserole, '94 279
Brussels Sprouts, Casserole of, '86 294
Butternut Casserole, '83 280
Butternut Casserole, Sweet, '83 256
Butternut Squash Casserole, '79 210; '96 216
Butternut Squash Puff, '85 205
Cabbage au Gratin, '83 279
Cabbage, Caraway, '85 32, 289
Cabbage Casserole, '97 88
Cabbage Casserole, Cheesy, '79 4
Cabbage Casserole, Creamy, '80 63
Cabbage Casserole, Italian, '87 42
Cabbage Casserole, Savory, '82 168
Cabbage, Cheese Scalloped, '81 87; '82 7
Cabbage, Scalloped, '82 269
Cabbage Wedges, Smothered, '81 87; '82 7
Cabbage with Apples and Franks, '87 42
Calabaza Mexicano (Mexican Squash), '81 196
Carrot and Zucchini Casserole, '83 256
Carrot-Apple Bake, '98 232
Carrot Bake, Creamy, '85 67
Carrot Casserole, '86 279; '87 285
Carrot Casserole, Scrumptious, '84 328
Carrot-Pecan Casserole, '93 44; '98 231
Carrot Puff, '84 328
Carrots, Scalloped, '81 6; '96 107
Carrots, Zesty, '84 5
Cashew Casserole, '95 166
Cauliflower and Asparagus Supreme, '79 287; '80 35
Cauliflower-and-Carrot Casserole, '83 280
Cauliflower and Peas with Curried Almonds, '80 82
Cauliflower au Gratin, '99 59
Cauliflower Bake, '95 342
Cauliflower Casserole, '86 10, 279
Cauliflower Casserole, Easy, '82 204
Cauliflower Casserole, Festive, '87 232
Cauliflower Casserole, Herbed, '79 221
Cauliflower, Cheddar, '99 318
Cauliflower, Curried, '91 315
Cauliflower Italiano, Cheesy, '82 300
Cauliflower, Main-Dish, '79 221; '80 83
Cauliflower Medley, '80 220
Cauliflower 'n' Chiles Casserole, '87 285
Cauliflower-Pea Casserole, '85 260
Cauliflower Scallop, '88 270
Cauliflower, Spanish-Style, '79 21
Cauliflower Surprise, Crunchy, '99 318
Celery and Cheese Casserole, '79 178
Celery au Gratin, '83 38
Celery, Baked, '82 98
Celery Casserole, '80 246; '96 92
Celery Casserole, Creamy, '82 98; '83 255

Celery, Creamed, '79 247
Celery, Exotic, '83 280
Celery Oriental, '83 206; '85 116
Celery, Saucy, '83 39
Chayote-Cheese Bake, '80 230
Cheesy Vegetable Casserole, '81 103
Chilaquiles, '82 220
Collards Casserole, Parmesan-, '95 233
Corn-and-Bean Casserole, '90 208
Corn and Cheese Casserole, '81 128
Corn-and-Green Chile Casserole, '89 68
Corn and Tomato Casserole, '81 127
Corn-and-Tomato Casserole, '84 145
Corn Bake, Cheesy, '98 244
Corn, Baked Jack, '97 86
Corn, Baked Scalloped, '85 290
Corn Casserole, '79 247; '89 126; '93 141
Corn Casserole, Chili-, '88 266
Corn Casserole, Fresh, '80 165
Corn Casserole, Jalapeño-, '83 256
Corn, Creamy Baked, '90 60
Corn, Elegant Scalloped, '86 268
Corn Pudding, '86 192
Corn, Scalloped, '80 164; '81 128; '86 111; '88 218
Corn with Sour Cream, Baked, '86 170
Corn-Zucchini Bake, '79 178
Creamy Vegetable Casserole, '98 96
Curry Casserole, Vegetable-, '91 286; '92 27
Eggplant and Noodle Casserole, '82 230
Eggplant and Squash, '83 187
Eggplant-and-Tomato Casserole, '83 187
Eggplant and Zucchini, Italian-Style, '79 289; '80 26
Eggplant Bake, '80 82
Eggplant Cakes, '95 196
Eggplant Casserole, '81 205; '84 217; '93 44; '94 214
Eggplant Casserole, Easy, '80 202
Eggplant Casserole, Elegant, '82 168
Eggplant Casserole, Flavorful, '79 92
Eggplant Casserole, Spicy Hot, '93 92
Eggplant Casserole, Super, '80 202
Eggplant Chiles Rellenos, '91 86
Eggplant Creole, '86 110
Eggplant Crêpes with Marinara Sauce, Mini, '99 266
Eggplant, Heavenly, '93 293
Eggplant, Italian, '84 216
Eggplant Italiano, '91 212
Eggplant, Lebanese, '81 24
Eggplant, Mexican, '83 187
Eggplant Parmesan, '83 186; '84 215; '92 18; '95 84
Eggplant Parmigiana, '81 19; '95 197
Eggplant, Rolled Stuffed, '80 63
Eggplant, Scalloped, '91 223
Eggplant-Spinach Casserole, '99 217
Eggplant Supreme, '79 188; '86 170
English Pea Casserole, Cheesy, '83 216
English Pea Casserole, Quick Fresh, '84 145
English Pea-Pimiento Casserole, '83 207
Étouffée, Okra, '98 207
Fresh Vegetable Casserole, '82 225
Garden Casserole, '82 168; '88 122
Garden Medley, '98 236
Garden Surprise, '83 112
Green-and-Gold Scallop, '81 159
Green Bean-and-Corn Casserole, '99 36
Green Bean Bake, '99 112
Green Bean Gratin, Gourmet, '99 M334
Green Beans, Baked, '91 159
Greens Dinner Bake, Grits 'n, '84 281
Green Vegetable Medley, '79 287; '80 34

Hash Brown Cheese Bake, '82 50
Hash Brown-Cheese Bake, '97 323
Hominy, Mexican, '91 133, 162
Hubbard Squash, Tart, '80 214
Lasagna Casserole, Vegetable, '92 198; '93 25
Layered Vegetable Casserole, '91 286; '92 27
Lentils with Cheese, Baked, '84 113
Macaroni Primavera, '96 73
Medley, Baked Vegetable, '81 75
Medley Bake, Vegetable, '81 268
Medley, Vegetable-Cheese, '99 M287
Mexican Vegetarian Casserole, '96 276
Mixed Vegetable Casserole, '83 208, 256; '86 327
Mixed-Vegetable Casserole, '87 154
Mixed Vegetables, Scalloped, '83 5
Mushroom-Artichoke Casserole, '87 241
Mushroom Bake, Windsor, '88 132
Mushroom Casserole, '95 211; '96 47
Mushroom-Cheese Casserole, '83 216
Mushroom Deluxe Casserole, '96 20
Mushroom-Macaroni Casserole, '95 180
Mushrooms Supreme, '84 214
New Potatoes, Cheesy, '85 156
Noodle Casserole, Vegetable, '91 30
Okra Casserole, '79 160
Okra-Tomato Bake, '80 298; '81 26
Onion Bake, Four, '93 304
Onion Casserole, Cheesy, '79 101
Onion Casserole, French, '95 26
Onions, Baked Sweet, '91 79
Pea Casserole, Curry, '87 154
Pea Casserole, Reunion, '87 11
Pea Casserole Supreme, '82 281; '83 32
Peas and Rice, '88 97
Peas, Cajun, '88 3
Peas, Chinese-Style Baked, '86 305
Peas, Mexi-, '88 3
Peas, Party, '79 102
Peas, Sweet-and-Sour, '88 3
Potato-and-Rutabaga Gratin, '96 237
Potato Bake, '83 209
Potato Bake, Creamy, '82 201
Potato Bake, Thyme-, '96 121
Potato-Broccoli-Cheese Bake, '80 114
Potato Casserole, '87 190; '99 274
Potato Casserole, Cheesy, '80 244; '83 53; '92 229
Potato Casserole, Easy, '80 114
Potato Casserole, Fluffy, '80 268
Potato Casserole, Hash Brown, '81 40
Potato Casserole, Holiday, '92 302
Potato Casserole, Irish, '81 263
Potato Casserole, Mashed, '85 296; '99 223
Potato Casserole, Mushroom-, '84 5
Potato Casserole, Peppery, '95 182
Potato Casserole, Processor, '86 159
Potato Casserole, Saucy, '81 276
Potato-Cheese Casserole, '79 101
Potato-Egg Casserole, Cheesy, '84 5
Potato-Eggplant Casserole, '87 166
Potatoes and Eggs au Gratin, '79 107
Potatoes and Turnips, Scalloped, '85 235
Potatoes-and-Zucchini au Gratin, '84 5
Potatoes au Gratin, Shredded, '89 69
Potatoes, Buffet, '98 92
Potatoes, Cheesy Scalloped, '83 82
Potatoes, Christmas, '88 252
Potatoes, Cottage, '89 69
Potatoes, Double-Cheese, '86 6
Potatoes, Easy Oven-Baked, '82 202
Potatoes, Fix-Ahead Mashed, '89 70
Potatoes, Fluffy, '84 296; '85 196
Potatoes for Company, Saucy, '82 202

CASSEROLES, Vegetable
(continued)

Potatoes, Garlic, '84 296; '85 196
Potatoes Gourmet, '80 114
Potatoes, Gruyère, '83 193
Potatoes, Hot Deviled, '84 296; '85 196
Potatoes, Italian-Style, '89 69
Potatoes, Jalapeño, '84 39
Potatoes, Jazzy Mashed, '87 192
Potatoes, Lemon and Nutmeg, '80 36
Potatoes, Light Scalloped, '89 311
Potatoes Lorraine, '87 190
Potatoes, Mexican-Style, '91 78
Potatoes, Missy, '85 259
Potatoes Moussaka, '93 44
Potatoes, Mushroom Scalloped, '87 191
Potatoes, Olive, '80 114
Potatoes, Parmesan, '82 270; '90 M62
Potatoes, Party Scalloped, '87 191
Potatoes, Rosemary's, '98 53
Potatoes, Scalloped, '82 300; '83 211; '92 48
Potatoes, Sour Cream, '84 39
Potatoes, Special Scalloped, '88 162
Potatoes, Two-Cheese, '80 114
Potatoes, Wayside Scalloped, '79 283
Potatoes, Winter Herb Garden Scalloped, '99 289
Potatoes with Feta Cheese, '84 295; '85 196
Potatoes with Ham Bits, Creamy, '87 191
Potatoes with Sweet Marjoram and Parmesan Cheese, Scalloped, '91 246
Potato-Horseradish Gratin with Caramelized Onions, '99 314
Potato-Tomato Bake, '86 17
Potato-Tomato Casserole, Saucy, '79 46
Potato Tuna Bake, Shoestring, '82 211
Pumpkin, Baked, '82 217
Spinach and Artichoke Casserole, '81 103
Spinach-and-Celery Casserole, '84 294
Spinach and Egg Casserole, '82 270
Spinach-Artichoke Bake, '95 48
Spinach-Artichoke Casserole, '88 252; '93 44
Spinach Bake, Creamy, '89 68
Spinach, Baked Macaroni with, '99 244
Spinach Casserole, '79 265; '91 31; '99 271
Spinach Casserole, Cheesy, '81 263
Spinach Casserole, Cottage Cheese-and-, '84 77
Spinach Casserole, Creamy, '86 111
Spinach-Cheese Bake, '88 10
Spinach-Cheese Casserole, '83 216; '89 64
Spinach-Cheese Puff, '84 96
Spinach, Cheesy Topped, '84 85
Spinach, Company, '89 280
Spinach, Creamy Lemon, '82 302
Spinach Fantastic, '93 173
Spinach-Gorgonzola Custards, Savory, '99 313
Spinach, Gourmet Baked, '82 180
Spinach Parmesan, '93 72
Spinach-Parmesan Casserole, '82 281; '83 32
Spinach Rice, '85 146
Spinach Shells, '97 50
Spinach Supreme, '84 77
Spinach Surprise, '82 42
Spinach with Cheese, Scalloped, '79 8
Squares, Checkerboard Vegetable, '96 178
Squash, Amarillo, '99 M218
Squash and Apple Casserole, '79 209
Squash and Egg Casserole, '80 146
Squash and Tomato Bake, '95 180
Squash, Bacon-Flavored, '82 158

Squash Bake, '82 107
Squash Bake, Cheddar-, '84 128
Squash Bake, Cheesy, '80 183
Squash-Carrot Casserole, '81 157
Squash Casserole, '87 163; '89 159; '90 161; '92 342; '96 247, 252; '97 29
Squash Casserole, Baked, '83 149
Squash Casserole, Blender, '81 212
Squash Casserole, Calico, '90 290
Squash Casserole, Cheesy, '79 123
Squash Casserole, Company, '81 183
Squash Casserole, Creamy Rice and, '95 26
Squash Casserole, Crunchy, '84 293
Squash Casserole, Fresh, '82 204
Squash Casserole, Jiffy, '81 M144
Squash Casserole, Summer, '81 102, 184
Squash Casserole, Two-, '79 101
Squash Casserole, Zippy, '80 183
Squash, Country Club, '88 M16
Squash, Greek-Style, '91 285; '92 26
Squash, Mexican, '83 31
Squash Nicholas, '94 236
Squash, Posh, '81 159
Squash, Savory, '99 111
Squash, South-of-the-Border, '89 148; '96 178
Strata, Vegetable-Cheese, '98 98
Sweet Potato-and-Apple Casserole, '94 280
Sweet Potato-Apple Bake, '83 25
Sweet Potato-Apricot Bake, '85 206
Sweet Potato Bake, '80 287
Sweet Potato Bake, Holiday, '90 291
Sweet Potato-Banana Casserole, '86 276
Sweet Potato Casserole, '79 289; '80 26; '85 256; '89 279
Sweet Potato Casserole, Glazed, '90 250
Sweet Potato Casserole, Pear-, '86 280
Sweet Potato Delight, '86 335
Sweet Potato-Eggnog Casserole, '95 291
Sweet Potatoes-and-Apple Casserole, '90 228
Sweet Potatoes-and-Berries Casserole, '84 231
Sweet Potatoes, Bourbon, '86 324; '87 280
Sweet Potatoes, Candied, '86 111; '88 207
Sweet Potatoes, Mashed, '98 269
Sweet Potatoes, Praline-Topped, '98 96
Sweet Potatoes Royale, '91 250
Sweet Potatoes with Sherry and Walnuts, '86 286
Sweet Potato-Rum Casserole, '84 231
Sweet Potato Supreme, '94 196
Sweet Potato Surprise, '81 267
Swiss Vegetable Medley, '95 26
Tomato-and-Artichoke Heart Bake, '85 81
Tomato Casserole, Scalloped, '88 144
Tomatoes, Herbed, '81 102
Tomatoes, Italian-Sauced Green, '85 214
Tomatoes, Scalloped, '84 142
Torta, Mexican, '88 149
Turnip Casserole, '83 242; '84 229
Turnip Casserole, Baked, '82 274
Turnips au Gratin, '84 229
Turnips, Scalloped, '79 254
Vegetarian Casserole, '96 302
Veggies Casserole, '88 123
Vidalia Deep Dish, '89 120
Wine Sauce Casserole, Vegetables in, '95 133
Winter Root Vegetable Casserole, '98 265
Yam-and-Apple Scallop, '91 199
Yams, Brandied, '94 273
Yellow Squash Casserole, '79 179; '85 135; '88 166
Zucchini, and Cornbread Bake, Bacon, '99 123
Zucchini and Tomato Bake, '82 158
Zucchini-and-Tomato Casserole, '88 265

Zucchini, Baked, '83 209
Zucchini-Carrot Casserole, '99 61
Zucchini Casserole, '79 157; '87 154
Zucchini Casserole, Cheese-Egg-, '84 114
Zucchini Casserole, Cheesy, '82 168; '84 145
Zucchini Casserole, Italian, '85 59
Zucchini-Jack Casserole, '85 296
Zucchini-Rice Casserole Italiano, '89 146
Zucchini with Pasta, Stuffed, '97 101
Wild Rice Casserole, '82 199; '95 176

CAULIFLOWER
Almond Sauce, Cauliflower with, '82 270
au Gratin, Cauliflower, '82 204; '99 59
Bake, Cauliflower, '95 342
Baked Swiss Cauliflower, '79 100
Beef and Cauliflower Oriental, '80 220
Beef and Cauliflower over Rice, '93 94
Beets and Cauliflower, Chilled, '80 137
Casserole, Cauliflower, '86 10, 279
Casserole, Cauliflower-and-Carrot, '83 280
Casserole, Cauliflower 'n' Chiles, '87 285
Casserole, Cauliflower-Pea, '85 260
Casserole, Easy Cauliflower, '82 204
Casserole, Festive Cauliflower, '87 232
Casserole, Herbed Cauliflower, '79 221
Cheddar Cauliflower, '99 318
Cheese-Frosted Cauliflower, '85 68
Cheese Sauce, Cauliflower with, '81 101
Cheesy Cauliflower Italiano, '82 300
Crunchy Cauliflower Surprise, '99 318
Curried Cauliflower, '91 315
Dilled Cauliflower, '83 93
Festive Cauliflower, '84 34
French-Fried Cauliflower, '86 211
French-Fried Cauliflower au Gratin, '79 221; '80 82
Fried Cauliflower, '83 5; '84 248; '90 18
Fried Cauliflower, Crispy, '80 220
Fried Cauliflower, Golden, '82 78
Fried Cauliflower with Cheese Sauce, '87 231
Fritters, Cauliflower-Cheddar, '98 25
Frosted Cauliflower, '97 105
Garden Surprise, '83 112
Goldenrod, Cauliflower, '79 21
Gratin, Cauliflower with Chinese Mustard, '94 45
Herb Butter, Cauliflower with, '81 2
Italian-Style Cauliflower, '92 36
Lemon Cauliflower, Easy, '83 322
Main-Dish Cauliflower, '79 221; '80 83
Medley, Cauliflower, '80 220
Medley, Cauliflower-Broccoli, '81 69
Medley, Cauliflower-Snow Pea, '87 305
Oriental Cauliflower, '81 75
Oven-Fried Cauliflower, '99 318
Peas and Cauliflower, '82 288
Peas with Curried Almonds, Cauliflower and, '79 221; '80 82
Pickled Cauliflower, '94 183
Pie, Cauliflower-Carrot, '82 191
Pimiento Sauce, Cauliflower with, '87 232
Quiche, Cauliflower, '83 86
Salads
Broccoli and Cauliflower Salad, '81 280
Broccoli and Cauliflower Salad, Creamy, '81 23
Broccoli and Cauliflower Toss, Crunchy, '83 25
Broccoli-Cauliflower Pasta Salad, '88 269
Broccoli-Cauliflower Salad, '92 97
Broccoli Crunch, Cauliflower-, '88 216
Broccoli 'n' Cauliflower Salad, '90 32
Broccoli Salad, Cauliflower-, '79 20
Broccoli Toss, Cauliflower-, '82 54
Broccoli Toss, Italian Cauliflower-, '88 269
Brussels Sprouts Salad, Cauliflower-, '83 240

Cauliflower Salad, '79 221; '80 83; '81 225;
'84 291; '85 240, 279; '92 36
Celery-and-Cauliflower Salad, '83 39
Corned Beef-Cauliflower Salad, '83 16
Creamy Cauliflower Salad, '82 102
Crunchy Cauliflower Salad, '80 4; '82 75
English Pea Salad, Cauliflower-, '95 66
Green Salad, Crunchy, '89 321
Layered Cauliflower Salad, '83 240
Lemon Salad, Cauliflower-, '81 23
Marinated Cauliflower Salad, '82 303; '84 232
Orange-Cauliflower Salad, '82 266
Parmesan and Bacon, Cauliflower with,
'96 137
Pea Salad, Cauliflower-, '87 231
Pea Salad, Savory Cauliflower and, '81 280
Red, White, and Green Salad, '90 18
Slaw, Cauliflower, '92 167
Sweet-and-Sour Cauliflower Salad, '81 2
Vegetable Salad, Cauliflower-, '85 158
Sauté, Cauliflower, '94 67
Scallop, Cauliflower, '88 270
Shrimp Sauce, Broccoli and Cauliflower with,
'84 248
Soufflé, Cauliflower, '82 76; '89 279; '90 17
Soup, Cauliflower, '90 211; '99 318
Soup, Cauliflower and Caraway, '82 264
Soup, Cream of Cauliflower, '87 M7; '88 12;
'96 277
Soup, Cream of Cauliflower and Watercress,
'83 126
Soup, Creamy Cauliflower, '82 76
Soup, Fresh Cauliflower, '84 279
Spanish-Style Cauliflower, '79 21
Supreme, Cauliflower and Asparagus, '79 287;
'80 35
Toss, Cauliflower, '85 289
Toss, Cauliflower-Olive, '85 198; '86 147

CAVIAR
Artichoke Hearts with Caviar, '79 142
Crown, Caviar, '83 78
Eggplant Caviar, '88 262; '99 217
Eggplant Caviar with Tapenade, '92 194
Eggs, Black-and-Blue, '96 90
Endive with Caviar, '93 118
Homemade Cowboy Caviar, '94 64
Mexican Caviar, '98 135
Mold, Artichoke-Caviar, '87 239
Mound, Caviar-Artichoke, '91 244
Mousse, Caviar, '82 71; '83 258; '85 86; '92 83
Pie, Caviar, '79 154
Potatoes, Appetizer Caviar, '86 223
Potatoes, Caviar, '84 80
Spread, Caviar-Cream Cheese, '84 256
Spread, Creamy Caviar, '92 58
Spread, Egg, Sour Cream, and Caviar, '85 279
Texas Caviar, '86 218; '99 84
Tomatoes, Caviar, '91 12
Zucchini Caviar, '88 212

CELERY
Almondine, Celery, '85 116
Amandine, Buttered Celery, '82 98
Ants on a Float, '91 177
au Gratin, Celery, '83 38
Baked Celery, '82 98
Braised Carrots and Celery, '86 327
Braised Carrots, Apples, and Celery, '96 107
Braised Celery, Green Beans and, '84 254
Brussels Sprouts and Celery, '79 21
Brussels Sprouts with Celery, Lemony, '85 25
Buttered Carrots and Celery, '89 44
Carrots and Celery with Pecans, '84 254
Casserole, Celery, '80 246; '96 92
Casserole, Celery and Cheese, '79 178

Casserole, Creamy Celery, '82 98; '83 255
Casserole, Spinach-and-Celery, '84 294
Chicken-and-Celery Skillet, '88 6
Creamed Brussels Sprouts and Celery, '83 322
Creamed Celery, '79 247
Croutons, Celery, '79 16
Curried Corn and Celery, '86 192
Dressing, Celery-Honey, '80 42
Dressing, Watermelon Salad with Celery-Nut,
'80 182
Exotic Celery, '83 280
Olives Scaciati, '99 266
Orange Sauce, Celery in, '79 70
Oriental, Celery, '83 206; '85 116
Peas and Celery, '93 289
Peas and Celery, Deluxe, '81 267
Pork Tenderloin with Apples, Celery, and
Potatoes, Grilled, '95 161
Potatoes, Whipped Celery, '94 305; '99 45
Potato Puffs, Celeried, '89 279
Relish, Apple-Celery, '89 141
Rice, Holiday, '98 289
Rice, Island, '98 276
Salad, Celery, '79 70
Salad, Celery-and-Cauliflower, '83 39
Salad, Chicken-Celery, '81 187
Salad, Overnight Alfalfa-Celery, '82 97
Salad, Pear-and-Celery, '87 56
Salad, Pineapple-Celery, '85 95
Sauce, Baked Fillets in Lemon-Celery, '84 91
Saucy Celery, '83 39
Scalloped Carrots-and-Celery, '84 M112
Snow Peas with Celery, Skillet, '84 123
Soup, Burnet-Celery, '84 107
Soup, Celery-and-Potato, '84 279
Soup, Cream of Celery, '79 71; '90 210
Soup, Light Cream-of-Celery, '82 279
Soup, Tomato-Celery, '83 M58
Splendid Stalks, '93 258
Stuffed Celery, '82 98; '86 324
Stuffed Celery, Creamy, '82 102
Stuffed Celery, Jalapeño, '79 70
Stuffed Celery Trunks, '85 115
Toss, Celery-Parmesan, '84 34

CELERY ROOT
Carrots, Celeriac and, '91 219
Mashed Potatoes, Celery Root, '98 293
Roasted Celery Root, Carrots, and Onions,
'98 293
Slaw, Shredded Celery Root-and-Carrot, '98 293
Stew, Beef-and-Celery Root, '98 292

CHAYOTES
Bake, Chayote-Cheese, '80 230
Casserole, Chayotes and Shrimp, '80 230
Fried Chayotes, '80 230
Mirlitons, Stuffed, '97 263
Pickles, Chayote Squash, '89 197
Sautéed Chayote Squash with Cilantro,
'95 227
Stuffed Chayote, '92 247

CHEESE. *See also* **APPETIZERS/Cheese;**
CHEESECAKES.
Almond Cheese, '88 173
Apple-Cheese Bake, '92 225
Bake, Brie Cheese, '87 117
Bake, Chicken, Ham, and Cheese, '87 217
Baked Brie, Walnut-, '93 241
Bake, Pineapple-Cheese, '79 106
Bake, Spinach-Ricotta, '88 97
Beef and Black Beans, Spicy, '99 331
Beef Blue, Elegant, '97 97
Beef Parmigiana, '85 234
Beef Roulades, Roquefort, '88 215
Blintzes, Cheese, '82 146; '83 71; '92 84

Blue Cheese, Creamy, '88 173
Bobolis, Easy Cheesy, '92 278
Breads
Apple Bread, Cheddar-, '96 83
Bacon-and-Cheese Bread, '83 255
Bacon-Cheese Toast Bars, '79 36
Batter Bread, Cheese-Caraway, '85 33
Biscuit Cups, Bacon, '99 214
Biscuit Fingers, Pepper-Cheese, '88 283
Biscuits, Bacon-Cheese, '88 84
Biscuits, Beer-and-Cheese, '94 215
Biscuits, Blue Cheese, '88 83
Biscuits, Blue Cheese-and-Ham Cornmeal,
'98 136
Biscuits, Cheese, '81 288; '83 253; '85 32;
'87 78
Biscuits, Cheese Angel, '89 211
Biscuits, Cheeseburger, '79 194
Biscuits, Cheese-Chive, '94 324
Biscuits, Cheesy Onion, '95 98
Biscuits, Deluxe Omelet, '98 101
Biscuits, Easy Cheese, '81 99
Biscuits, Herbed Roquefort, '84 95
Biscuits, Hot Cheesy, '80 186
Biscuits, Lightnin' Cheese, '90 283
Biscuits, Mexican Fiesta Spoon, '95 161
Biscuits, Mixer Cheese, '96 22
Biscuits, Petite Ham and Cheese, '79 193
Biscuits, Refrigerator, '96 17
Biscuits, Rosemary, '99 17
Biscuits, Surprise Pull-Apart, '95 46
Biscuits, Tiny Cheese, '80 192
Blue Cheese-Apple Sunburst, '94 245
Bobolis, Easy Cheesy, '92 278
Bowls, Toasted Bread, '98 30
Breadsticks, Italian Cheese, '95 126
Breadsticks, Parmesan-Garlic, '99 46
Breadsticks, Sesame-Cheese, '97 31
Brie Bread, '87 143
Buns, Cheesy Onion, '85 5
Buns, Hurry-Up Cheese, '81 300
Buns, Onion-Cheese, '88 218
Butter Cheese Dips, '80 46
Buttermilk-Cheese Loaf, '91 52
Cheddar Cheese Bread, '84 268
Cheddar Cheese-Pepper Bread, '98 25
Cheddar-Nut Bread, '85 41
Cheese Bread, '82 174; '83 208; '87 11
Cinnamon Logs, '98 325
Cornbread, Cheddar, '83 285; '84 17
Cornbread, Cheddar-Jalapeño, '85 3
Cornbread, Cheesy Beef, '81 242
Cornbread, Chile-Cheese, '87 171
Cornbread, Cottage Cheese, '80 90
Cornbread, Jalapeño, '98 178
Cornbread, Loaded, '99 214
Cornbread, Sweet Onion, '98 252
Cornbread, Swiss Cheese, '79 60
Cornbread, Vicksburg, '96 35
Cottage Cheese-Dill Bread, '83 154
Cream Cheese Braids, '82 243; '97 287
Cream Cheese Loaves, Processor, '85 48
Cream Cheese Pinches, '87 85
Crescents, Apricot-Cheese, '99 284
Crescents, Cheese, '82 18
Croissants, Cream Cheese, '92 159
Crusty Cheese Bread, '86 233
Danish, Cheese, '97 31
Danish, Cream Cheese, '98 325
Dilly Cheese Bread, '83 5
Easy Cheese Bread, '82 74; '86 17
Flatbread, Parmesan-Onion, '98 65
Flatbread, Sicilian Artichoke, '98 136
Focaccia, Roquefort-and-Onion, '98 54

CHEESE, Breads
(continued)

French Bread, Bacon-Cheese, '92 54
French Bread, Cheesy, '88 172; '95 218;
   '96 205; '97 325
French Bread, Herbed, '99 47
French Bread, Onion-Cheese, '89 29
French Bread, Tangy, '98 166
French Toast au Fromage, '88 288
French Toast, Cottage-Topped, '85 49
French Toast, Stuffed, '96 52; '98 55, 313
French Toast, Three Cheese Stuffed, '93 122
Fruit-and-Cheese Braid, '86 214
Garlic Bread, Cheesy, '84 150
Garlic-Stuffed Bread, Cheesy, '95 176
Gouda Bread, '91 52
Ham-and-Cheese Bread, '86 213
Herb-and-Cheese Pull Aparts, '87 143
Herb Bread, Cheese-, '84 M144; '85 283
Herb-Cheese Bread, '85 70
Herbs-and-Cheese Bread, '93 56
Herb-Vegetable-Cheese Bread, '88 172
Jalapeño-Cheese Loaf, '84 76
Jam-and-Cheese Loaf, '89 246
Lemon-Cream Tea Loaf, '84 50
Little Cheese Loaves, '86 213
Loaf, Cheese, '90 93
Mashed Potato Bites, '98 249
Monkey Bread, Cheese-Filled, '91 21
Muffin Mix, Cheese-and-Pepper, '89 330
Muffins, Bacon-and-Cheese, '89 205
Muffins, Bacon-Cheese, '96 280
Muffins, Blueberry-Cream Cheese, '86 14
Muffins, Caraway-Cheese, '91 213
Muffins, Cheddar, '89 15
Muffins, Cheddar-Raisin, '91 51
Muffins, Cheese, '96 54; '97 287
Muffins, Cheese-and-Pepper, '84 139
Muffins, Cheesy Cornbread, '88 M275
Muffins, Cheesy Sausage, '92 252; '93 144
Muffins, Dilly Cheese, '95 245; '96 55
Muffins, Ham-and-Cheese, '92 252; '93 144
Muffins, Marvelous Cheese, '83 96
Muffins, Pepper-Cheese, '96 280
Muffins, Peppered Cheddar, '99 234
Muffins, Sausage-Cheese, '86 213
Muffins, Sesame-Cheese, '86 16
Olive Bread, Spicy Cheese-, '84 150
Onion-Cheese Bread, '79 180; '81 8
Onion-Cheese Supper Bread, '83 112
Onion-Parmesan Bread, '84 284
Orange-Cream Cheese Bread, '82 210
Pane Cunsado (Fixed Bread), '95 218
Pane Cunsado (Sicilian for "Fixed Bread"),
   '96 205
Parmesan Bread, '92 19; '93 231
Parmesan Cheese Bread, '99 61
Parmesan Herb Bread, '82 235; '83 41
Parmesan Puffs, '98 235
Parmesan Sesame Sticks, '81 39
Parmesan Twists, '83 239; '99 323
Pig-in-a-Blanket Bread, '99 134
Pimiento-Cheese Bread, '85 223; '86 166
Pita Triangles, Cheesy, '93 70
Popover Puffs, Cheese, '85 6
Popover Ring, Cheesy, '80 45
Popovers, Cheddar Cheese, '85 41
Popovers, Parmesan, '90 66
Poppy Seed-Swiss Cheese Bread, '91 52
Pull-Away Bread, '98 137
Quick Cheese Bread, '83 9
Roll, Feta Cheese-Spinach, '91 22

Rolls, Broccoli-Cheddar, '91 21
Rolls, Cheese, '80 286
Rolls, Cheese-Apricot Sweet, '90 195
Rolls, Cottage Cheese, '81 78
Rolls, Crunchy, '97 160
Rolls, Ham-and-Cheese, '82 3
Rolls, Italian Parker House, '99 47
Rolls, Parmesan, '79 181
Rolls, Romano Sesame, '87 144
Rolls, Whole Wheat, '96 50
Scones, Golden Cheddar Cheese, '99 82
Sour Cream-Cheese Bread, '85 33
Spinach Bread, '87 144
Spoonbread, Cheddar, '82 196
Spoonbread, Cheese, '86 261
Spoonbread, Corn-Cheese, '88 9
Sticks, Sesame-Cheddar, '81 150
Swiss Cheese Bread, '79 60
Swiss Cheese Bread, Poppy Seed-, '91 52
Swiss Cheese Loaves, Mini, '95 80
Tennessee Sin, '96 204
Toasted Cheese Delights, '79 37
Toasts, Parmesan-Pepper, '98 242
Tomato-Cheese Bread, '98 172; '99 M157
Tomato-Cheese Bread, Herbed, '88 143
Twists, Cheesy, '84 284
Wine Bread, Cheese-, '87 254
Wine Bread, Parmesan-, '97 31
Bugs in a Rug, '95 178
Burgers, Beef-and-Cheese, '96 139
Burgers, Blue Cheese, '89 M66
Burgers, Brie-Mushroom, '95 128
Burgers, Cheesy Bacon, '81 29
Burgers, Cheesy Beef, '83 217
Burgers, Spinach-Feta, '99 135
Burgers, Stuffed Southwestern-Style, '99 201
Burritos, Breakfast, '90 192; '97 172
Burritos, Cheesy Beef, '85 193
Burritos, Lentil, '99 287
Butter, Cheese, '84 114
Calzones, Spinach-and-Cheese, '95 310
Canadian Bacon Squares, Sunrise, '99 103

Casseroles
Apple-Cheese Casserole, '84 287
Asparagus Casserole, Cheesy, '82 281; '83 32
Beef-and-Bean Bake, Cheesy, '82 89
Beef, Cheese, and Noodle Casserole, '99 58
Blintz Casserole, Cheese, '92 251
Breakfast Casserole, '91 285; '99 273
Breakfast Casserole, Cheesy, '85 247
Broccoli Bake, Cheesy, '83 255
Broccoli-Blue Cheese Casserole, '85 260
Broccoli Casserole, Cheesy, '84 293; '92 342;
   '95 M191
Broccoli-Cheese Breakfast Casserole, '99 233
Broccoli-Cheese Casserole, '82 269; '84 9;
   '94 132
Broccoli-Ham au Gratin, '90 239
Broccoli-Swiss Cheese Casserole, '83 322;
   '85 M211
Brunch Casserole, '82 124
Brunch Casserole, Easy Cheesy, '92 91
Brunch Casserole with Creole Sauce, '98 98
Brunch for a Bunch, '88 57
Cabbage au Gratin, '83 279
Cabbage Casserole, Cheesy, '79 4
Carrots, Cheese Scalloped, '94 36
Cauliflower Surprise, Crunchy, '99 318
Celery and Cheese Casserole, '79 178
Celery au Gratin, '83 38
Chayote-Cheese Bake, '80 230
Cheeseburger Casserole, '95 255
Chicken Casserole, Cheesy, '85 34
Chicken Casserole, Swiss, '90 67

Chicken Enchiladas, Creamy, '97 250
Chicken Enchiladas, Quicker, '97 312
Chicken, Fontina-Baked, '90 64
Chicken, King Ranch, '99 330
Chicken, Poppy Seed, '99 195
Chicken Salad, Hot, '98 290
Chicken, Swiss, '95 54
Chicken Tetrazzini, Cheesy, '83 M87
Chicken Thighs, Swiss, '94 282
Chilaquiles, '82 220
Chile-Cheese Casserole, '82 90
Chile 'n' Cheese Breakfast Casserole, '88 57
Chiles Rellenos Casserole, '79 84; '84 31, 234;
   '92 18; '98 48
Chili Casserole, Ultimate, '99 239
Collards Casserole, Parmesan-, '95 233
Continental Cheese Bake, '81 89
Corn and Cheese Casserole, '81 128
Corn Bake, Cheesy, '98 244
Corn, Baked Jack, '97 86
Corned Beef and Cabbage au Gratin, '83 16
Crab, Shrimp, and Artichoke au Gratin,
   '90 240
Egg-and-Cheese Casserole, '84 293
Egg Casserole, '98 98
Egg Casserole, Cheese-and-, '99 268
Egg Casserole, Cheesy, '81 244; '86 15
Eggplant Crêpes with Marinara Sauce, Mini,
   '99 266
Eggplant Parmesan, '83 186; '84 215; '86 53;
   '95 84
Eggplant Parmigiana, '81 19
Eggplant-Spinach Casserole, '99 217
Eggs, Brunch, '98 93
Enchiladas, Quicker, '96 103
Enchiladas, Three-Cheese Chicken, '99 330
English Pea Casserole, Cheesy, '83 216
Feather-Light Cheese Casserole, '79 84
Florentine Bake, Cheesy, '95 131
Four Cheese Casserole, '92 170
Garden Medley, '98 236
Green Bean Bake, '99 112
Green Bean Gratin, Gourmet, '99 M334
Grits, Baked Cheese, '80 49, 99; '83 311;
   '85 41
Grits, Baked Cheese-and-Garlic, '83 292;
   '84 78
Grits Casserole, Cheesy, '81 270
Grits, Cheese, '86 242
Grits, Garlic-Cheese, '80 47; '81 197; '86 180
Grits, Swiss-and-Cheddar Baked, '91 71
Ground Beef Casserole, Cheesy, '79 44
Ham-and-Cheese Casserole, '87 78
Ham-and-Cheese Layered Casserole, '98 160
Hash Brown-Cheese Bake, '97 323
Hash Brown-Ham-Cheese Bake, '97 323
Hominy Casserole, Cheesy, '83 170
Hominy Casserole), Four-Part Hominy
   (Cheesy, '96 158
Hominy with Chiles and Cheese, '86 78
Lasagna, '98 95
Lasagna, Cheesy, '82 224; '88 299
Lasagna, Cheesy Spinach, '80 32; '83 204
Lasagna, Cheesy Vegetable, '79 84
Lasagna, Crabmeat, '96 290
Lasagna, Gourmet White, '96 225
Lasagna, Italian Sausage, '96 225
Lasagna Maria, '90 191
Lasagna, Mexican, '98 283
Lasagna, Roasted Vegetable-Meat, '99 M332
Lasagna, Texas, '98 52
Lasagna, Vegetable, '99 97
Lentils with Cheese, Baked, '84 113
Lima Bean Casserole, Swiss, '80 191

Limas, Spanish Cheese, '86 225
Macaroni and Blue Cheese, '93 248; '94 44
Macaroni and Cheese, '83 M7; '88 M147, M190; '90 30
Macaroni and Cheese, Baked, '82 199
Macaroni and Cheese, Creamy, '93 249; '94 45
Macaroni-and-Cheese Deluxe, '79 84
Macaroni and Cheese Deluxe, '80 236
Macaroni and Cheese, Divine, '99 314
Macaroni and Cheese, Eleanor's, '97 253
Macaroni and Cheese, Old-Fashioned, '92 215
Macaroni and Cheese, Tasty, '83 288
Macaroni and Cheese, Thick-and-Rich, '84 329
Macaroni-and-Cheese with Wine, '86 78
Macaroni Bake, Jack-in-the-, '93 249; '94 45
Macaroni, Cheese, and Tomatoes, '95 213
Macaroni-Cheese-Beef Casserole, '95 125
Macaroni, Double Cheese, '82 224
Macaroni, Gorgonzola, '97 28
Macaroni, Mexican, '96 73
Macaroni Mousse, '96 73
Macaroni-Mushroom Bake, Cheesy, '81 243
Macaroni Primavera, '96 73
Macaroni with Spinach, Baked, '99 244
Manicotti, Cheesy, '83 216
Manicotti, Make-Ahead, '98 68
Manicotti, Special, '88 50
Manicotti, Stuffed, '83 M6
Mexican Casserole, Cabin, '97 95
Mexican Casserole, Cheesy, '82 224
Mexican Casserole, Microwave, '90 M231
Mushroom-Cheese Casserole, '83 216
Mushroom Deluxe Casserole, '96 20
Mushrooms au Gratin, '81 108
Onion Casserole, Cheesy, '79 101
Orzo, Mozzarella-and-Olive, '97 249
Parmigiana, Eggplant, '95 197
Pineapple Bake, '96 84
Pineapple-Cheese Bake, '79 106
Pizza Bake, Upside-Down, '98 224
Pork Casserole, Cheesy, '81 M74
Pork Parmigiana, Easy, '94 57
Potato Casserole, Cheesy, '80 244; '83 53; '92 229
Potato Casserole, Mashed, '99 223
Potato-Cheese Casserole, '79 101
Potato-Cheese Dream, '91 307
Potato-Egg Casserole, Cheesy, '84 5
Potatoes and Eggs au Gratin, '79 107
Potatoes au Gratin, Shredded, '89 69
Potatoes, Buffet, '98 92
Potatoes, Cheesy Scalloped, '83 82
Potatoes, Cottage, '89 69
Potatoes, Double-Cheese, '86 6
Potatoes Gourmet, '80 114
Potatoes, Gruyère, '83 193
Potatoes, Mushroom Scalloped, '87 191
Potatoes, Rosemary's, '98 53
Potatoes, Scalloped, '83 211
Potatoes, Special Scalloped, '88 162
Potatoes, Winter Herb Garden Scalloped, '99 289
Reuben Casserole, '90 240
Rice-and-Cheese con Chiles, '89 99
Rice au Gratin, '83 129
Rice au Gratin Supreme, '86 78
Rice, Cheese-Parslied, '89 99
Rice Strata, Cheese-, '81 176
Sausage Brunch, Italian, '88 57
Sausage Casserole, Cheesy, '82 124
Sausage Casserole, Swiss, '80 209
Sausage-Cheese Bake, '88 58
Sausage-Chile Rellenos Casserole, '88 52
Seafood Parmesan, Savannah, '99 312

Seashell-Provolone Casserole, '80 189
Spinach Casserole, '99 271
Spinach Casserole, Cheesy, '81 263
Spinach Casserole, Cottage Cheese-and-, '84 77
Spinach-Cheese Bake, '88 10
Spinach-Cheese Casserole, '83 216; '89 64
Spinach-Gorgonzola Custards, Savory, '99 313
Spinach-Parmesan Casserole, '82 281; '83 32
Spinach Ring au Fromage, '79 8
Spinach Shells, '97 50
Squash Bake, Cheddar-, '84 M113, 128
Squash Casserole, Cheesy, '79 123; '82 M21
Squash, Savory, '99 111
Squash, South-of-the-Border, '96 178
Strata, Vegetable-Cheese, '98 98
Stroganoff Casserole, '95 48
Tamale, Mozzarella, '95 70
Tuna Casserole with Cheese Swirls, '88 256
Turkey Parmigiana, '87 193
Turkey-Swiss Casserole, '86 283
Vegetable Casserole, Cheesy, '81 103
Vegetable-Cheese Medley, '99 M287
Vegetable Medley, Swiss, '95 26
Vegetable Squares, Checkerboard, '96 178
Wraps, Southwestern, '99 238
Zucchini Casserole, Cheese-Egg-, '84 114
Zucchini Casserole, Cheesy, '82 168; '84 145
Zucchini-Jack Casserole, '85 296
Catfish Parmesan, '79 184; '86 210; '99 91
Catfish, Parmesan, '92 309
Cheeseburgers, Inside Out, '99 202
Cheeseburgers, Mini-, '97 203
Chicken Alouette, '91 295
Chicken, Baked Parmesan, '83 320
Chicken Breasts, Celebrity, '95 60
Chicken Breasts, Cream Cheese, '90 234
Chicken Breasts Gruyère, '80 189
Chicken Breasts over Angel Hair, Goat Cheese-Stuffed, '97 144
Chicken Breasts Romano, '79 218
Chicken Breasts Saltimbocca, '98 19
Chicken Caprese with Tomato-Basil Cream, '99 240
Chicken Cordon Bleu, '81 304; '82 83; '86 37
Chicken, Crispy Parmesan, '80 M76
Chicken Fiesta, Breast-of-, '88 151
Chicken Monterey, '82 275
Chicken-Mozzarella Melt, Italian, '95 153
Chicken, Oven-Fried, '99 212
Chicken, Oven-Fried Parmesan, '81 97; '82 148
Chicken Packets, '96 104
Chicken Parmesan, '83 184; '95 210
Chicken Parmesan, Baked, '83 137
Chicken Provolone, '93 323
Chicken Rollups, Cheesy, '82 44
Chicken, Roquefort, '89 320
Chicken, Seasoned, '99 316
Chicken Skillet, Cheesy, '80 115
Chiles Rellenos, '88 116; '89 226
Chiles Rellenos, Roasted, '95 64
Chiles Rellenos with Walnut Cream Sauce, Havarti-and-Corn-Stuffed, '93 M275
Chili-Cheese Dogs, '81 M176
Chili, Cheese-Topped, '82 M11
Chili, Cheesy, '82 310
Chimichangas, Baked Spicy Beef, '97 319
Chimichangas, Chicken, '98 95
Chunky Cream Cheese, '85 306
Chutney with Cream Cheese, Cranberry-Amaretto, '87 244
Coffee Cake, Cream Cheese, '86 290
Coffee Cake, Deep-Dish Cheesecake, '90 50

Coffee Cake, Raspberry-Cheese, '97 231
con Queso, Chile, '97 25
Corn on the Cob, Parmesan, '88 M187
Country Ham Puff, Cheesy, '90 88
Crab Bake, Quick, '87 192
Crabmeat au Gratin, '86 154
Crackers, Hot Nut, '90 206
Crackers, Taco-Cheese Animal, '94 197
Cream Puffs with Chicken Salad, Cheesy, '86 260
Cream-Style Cheese, '85 209
Crème Brûlée, Roquefort-and-Black Pepper, '95 324
Crêpe Cups, Florentine, '89 44
Crêpes, Cheese and Mushroom, '81 88
Crêpes, Cheesy Sausage, '82 240; '83 71
Crêpes con Queso, '96 48
Crêpes, Goat Cheese-Filled Cornbread, '98 43
Crêpes, Mushroom-Cheese, '87 289; '88 135
Crêpes, Sausage-Filled, '98 266; '99 25
Crêpes, Spinach-Ricotta, '81 52
Crispies, Pecan-Cheese, '87 168
Crisps, Blue Cheese, '96 106
Crisps, Peppered Cheese, '98 107
Crostini, Feta-Tomato, '92 159
Croutons, Prosciutto, '99 89
Crust, Cheese, '80 286; '86 264
Crust, Cheesy Crumb, '88 86
Crust, Chicken Pot Pie with Cheese, '86 264
Crust, Parmesan, '94 304
Crust, Parmesan Pizza, '93 58
Desserts
Almond-Raspberry Brie, '94 M89
Apple-and-Cheese Delight, '98 97
Bites, Starlight Cheese, '95 329
Blackberry Supremes, '99 179
Blintzes, Cheese, '82 146
Blueberry Yum Yum, '98 91
Brownie Bars, Broadway, '97 M35
Brownies à la Mode, Magnolias Cream Cheese, '97 M178
Brownies, Cream Cheese Swirl, '79 51
Brownies, German Cream Cheese, '80 269
Brownies, Walnut-Cream Cheese, '84 240
Cake, Cheesy Pound, '96 62
Cake, Coconut-Cream Cheese Pound, '85 297; '90 305
Cake, Cream Cheese Loaf, '84 151
Cake, Cream Cheese Pound, '81 290; '86 287; '95 304
Cake, Crusty Cream Cheese Pound, '89 124
Cake, Poppy Seed, '95 63
Cake, Regal Cream Cheese, '80 140
Cake Squares, Cream Cheese, '84 321
Cake, Tart Lemon-Cheese, '88 7
Cake with Wine Jelly, Pound, '98 125
Cannoli, '91 20
Chocolate-Cheese Cups, '91 142
Chocolate Heaven, '98 323
Cobbler, Country Apple, '99 255
Cookies, Breakfast, '97 52
Cookies, Cream Cheese, '80 282
Cottage Cheese Dessert, Creamy, '87 191
Cream Cheese Eggs, '99 118
Cream Cheese Frills, '79 291
Cream, Molded French, '99 72
Crisp, Apple-Cheese, '92 235
Cupcakes, Cream Cheese Party, '82 279
Custard, Goat Cheese, '96 285
Date-Cream Cheese Rollups, '83 298
Date Dessert Cheese, Nutty, '87 299
Frosting, Cherry-Nut Cream Cheese, '96 249
Frosting, Citrus Cream Cheese, '99 223
Frosting, Coconut Cream Cheese, '86 60

CHEESE, Desserts
(continued)

Frosting, Cream Cheese, '79 45; '80 140, 253, 299; '82 135, 244; '83 105, 215, M233; '84 201, 255, 315, 316; '85 118, 121; '86 217, 337; '87 58; '90 305, 308; '92 120; '93 20; '94 254; '95 139; '96 282; '97 230, 277, 330; '98 275; '99 307, 315
Frosting, Deluxe Cream Cheese, '80 120
Frosting, Fluffy Cream Cheese, '80 245
Frosting, Lemon-Cream Cheese, '81 157
Frosting, Nutty Cream Cheese, '85 117; '96 263
Frosting, Orange Cream, '82 14
Frosting, Orange-Cream Cheese, '81 70; '82 16; '92 19
Frosting, Peppermint Cream Cheese, '98 308
Frosting, Pineapple-Cream Cheese, '95 160
Frosting, White Chocolate-Cream Cheese, '94 58; '98 323
Frosting, White Chocolate-Cream Cheese Tiered Cake, '94 125
Fruit, Cheese, and Nuts, '93 324
Fruited Cream Cheese, '85 306
Fruit with Cheese, Luscious Fresh, '79 153
Fudge, Cream Cheese, '84 111
Ginger Cheese, '92 163
Glaze, Cream Cheese, '84 150; '94 242
Kuchen, Cheese, '86 84
Lemon-Cream Cheese Dessert, '84 95
Loaves, Chocolate Chip Cheese, '91 299; '92 264
Mints, Cream Cheese, '93 79
Molds, Heavenly Dessert Cheese, '85 209
Pastries, Cream Cheese, '80 250
Pastries, German, '86 78
Pastry, Apple Tart with Cheese, '88 225
Pastry, Cheddar, '86 206
Pastry, Cheddar Cheese, '80 219; '82 194
Pastry, Cream Cheese, '86 78; '89 136; '96 228, 264
Pastry Mini Shells, Cream Cheese, '99 180
Pastry Shell, Cheese, '85 284
Pastry Shells, Cream Cheese, '86 13
Patty Shells, Cream Cheese, '81 266
Pear-Blue Cheese Gratin, '93 328
Pears Blue, '99 246
Pie, Apple-Cheese, '85 284
Pie, Apple-Cream Cheese, '81 247
Pie, Black-and-White Fudge, '99 249
Pie, Blueberry-Cream Cheese, '88 154
Pie, Chocolate-Cream Cheese, '80 69
Pie, Chocolate Cream Cheese, '92 240
Pie, Cottage Cheese, '82 85
Pie, Fruited Cheese, '92 228
Pie, Lemon Cheese, '81 136; '82 146
Pie, Lemon-Cottage Cheese, '79 44
Pie, Lemon Cottage Cheese, '81 143
Pie, Yogurt-Cheese, '82 121
Quesadillas, Apple, '99 248
Soufflé, Blintz, '88 155
Soufflé, Cream Cheese, '88 11
Spread, Chocolate Cheese, '87 292
Spread, Orange Cheese, '87 292
Squares, Lemony Cream Cheese, '82 159
Strawberry Cheese Delight, '79 50
Strawberry-Cream Cheese Dessert, '83 123
Strudel, Fig, '98 253
Tart, Apple-Cream Cheese, '96 228
Tart, Cream Cheese-Peach, '99 169
Tart, Pine Nut, '97 86
Tarts, Cranberry-Cream Cheese, '80 154

Tarts, Cream Cheese, '84 74; '90 312
Tarts, Lemon-Cheese, '79 2
Tiramisù, '91 21; '94 295; '98 280
Wafers, Hope Farm Cheese, '93 282
Devonshire Cream, Mock, '99 275
Dressing, Blue Cheese, '79 69; '82 166; '86 233; '90 286; '97 98; '98 248; '99 244
Dressing, Blue Cheese Salad, '82 94
Dressing, Cheese Fluff, '91 256
Dressing, Cheesy Barbecue Salad, '92 255
Dressing, Creamy, '95 66
Dressing, Creamy Blue Cheese, '81 150; '91 307
Dressing, Creamy Blue Cheese Salad, '86 123
Dressing, Creamy Roquefort, '84 12
Dressing, Garden Salad with Tomato-Cream Cheese, '79 173
Dressing, Parmesan, '86 192; '97 326
Dressing, Romano, '80 174
Dressing, Roquefort, '79 85; '80 74; '93 128
Dressing, Special Blue Cheese, '80 74
Dressing, Tangy Blue Cheese, '87 81
Dressing, Thick Roquefort Cheese, '97 63
Dressing, Zesty Blue Cheese, '79 104
Dumplings, Chicken Ragoût with Cheddar, '94 44
Dumplings, Goat Cheese, '99 70
Egg Medley, Cheddary, '81 M176
Eggs and Cheese, '95 165
Eggs, Black-and-Blue, '96 90
Eggs, Blue Cheese Stuffed, '93 87
Eggs, Cheddar, '94 M141
Eggs, Cheese-Chive Scrambled, '95 34
Eggs, Chile-Cheese Deviled, '93 87
Eggs, Cottage, '85 44
Eggs, Cottage Cheese Scrambled, '81 142
Eggs, Cottage-Scrambled, '80 49
Eggs, Cream Cheese Scrambled, '81 287
Eggs, Marbleized Garlic-Cheese-Stuffed, '96 91
Empanadas, Easy Turkey, '96 63
Enchiladas, Cheese, '81 194; '85 154; '95 311
Enchiladas, Cheesy Sour Cream, '79 25
Enchiladas, Enticing, '99 57
Enchiladas, Meatless, '93 106
Enchiladas, Saucy Cheese, '84 220
Enchiladas, Vegetable-Cheese, '94 42
Fajitas, Chicken, '99 158
Fettuccine, Broccoli-Parmesan, '93 55
Fettuccine, Crab, '98 142
Fettuccine, Creamy, '96 136
Fig Flowers, '96 195
Fillets, Blue Cheese-Walnut Stuffed, '95 327
Fillets, Parmesan, '86 M112
Fillings
 Blintz Filling, '92 84
 Cheese Filling, '89 91
 Chocolate-Cheese Filling, '90 47
 Cinnamon-Cheese Filling, '90 46
 Cream Cheese Filling, '90 170; '97 287
 Four Cheese Filling, '97 171
 Lemon-Cheese Filling, '79 68; '88 7
 Orange-Cheese Filling, '90 47
 Orange Filling, Cheese-and-, '93 159
 Ricotta Filling, '80 58
 Spinach and Feta Filling, '97 171
 Spinach-Ricotta Filling, '81 53
Firecrackers, Roquefort, '97 19
Flank Steak, Cheese-Stuffed, '98 182
Flautas, Rancho Ramillete, '96 M125
Flounder au Fromage, Baked, '86 234
Flounder, Cheesy Broiled, '84 69
Fondue, Nacho, '94 332
Fondue, Pub, '94 332
Fondue, Warm Goat Cheese, '96 234
Fowl, Fancy, '81 76

French Toast, Ham-and-Cheese Oven, '97 172
Fried Brie, Walnut-, '86 244
Fries, Parmesan Oven, '98 235
Frittata, Bacon-and-Asparagus, '98 136
Frittata, Broccoli-Cheese, '81 243
Frittata, Potato-Bacon, '98 330
Fritters, Cauliflower-Cheddar, '98 25
Fritters, Cheese-Stuffed Potato, '96 153
Fritters, Cheesy Zucchini, '88 44
Frosting. *See* **CHEESE/Desserts.**
Gnocchi à la Narciso, '97 246
Goat Cheese and Greens, '90 54
Grits, Baked Cheese, '94 240
Grits, Cheese, '90 102
Grits, Creamy, '96 24
Grits, Garlic-and-Herb Cheese, '95 122
Grits, Garlic-Cheese, '88 126; '89 47; '97 58; '99 270
Grits, Good Morning, '87 156
Grits, Grillades and Baked Cheese, '94 240
Grits, Gruyère Cheese, '81 47
Grits, Jalapeño Cheese, '85 43
Grits, Margaret's Creamy, '99 18
Grits, Quick Cheese, '83 M203; '96 97
Grits, Saga Blue-Chile, '98 202
Grits, Sausage-Cheese, '90 238
Grits, Sliced Cheese, '84 75
Grits with Green Chiles, Cheese, '95 208
Grouper, Heavenly Broiled, '99 91
Ham-and-Cheese Bundles, '93 63
Ham-and-Cheese Flips, '92 46
Ham and Eggs on Toast with Cheese Sauce, '81 43
Ham-Cheese Chips, '82 34
Ham Dinner, Cheesy, '84 90
Ham, Frosted, '89 71
Ham Towers, Cheesy, '82 M77
Hominy, Hot Cheese, '84 77
Hot Dog Deluxe, '97 140
Hush Puppies, Cheesy Mexican, '91 201
Kabobs, Swiss-Ham, '81 124
Lamb Meat Loaf with Feta Cheese, '97 24
Little Bits, '79 196
Loaf, Cheese, '87 92
Loaf, Cheeseburger, '81 236, 276
Loaf, Pepperoni and Cheese, '82 32
Loaves, Sausage-Cheese, '88 235
Marinated Cheese, '90 244
Mayonnaise, Parmesan, '86 79
Meatballs, Golden Nugget, '82 233
Meatballs, Mock, '81 243
Meat Loaf, Mozzarella-Layered, '79 71
Meat Loaf Roll, Blue Cheese, '93 247
Nachos, Southwestern, '96 170
Nachos, Tuna, '96 201
Noodles and Mushrooms, Cheesy, '79 84
Noodles, Blue Cheese, '98 290
Noodles, Cheesy Parmesan, '83 M7
Noodles, Ham and Swiss on, '87 108
Noodles, Parmesan, '83 118
Omelet, Cheddar-Vegetable, '83 205
Omelet, Cheesy Picante, '86 95
Omelet, Cheesy Vegetable, '85 49
Omelet, Dill-Cheese-Ham, '95 33
Omelet, Golden Cheese-Shiitake, '95 265
Omelet, Ham and Cheese, '79 262; '80 123
Omelet, Herbed Cheese, '93 47
Omelet, Puffed Cheese, '89 227
Omelets, George's, '80 68
Omelet, Shrimp-and-Cheddar, '84 57
Omelet, Shrimp-and-Cheese, '94 31
Omelet, Spinach-Cheese, '83 119
Omelet, Swiss Oven, '80 189
Omelet, Zippy Cheese, '87 287

Orange Cream Cheese, '91 177
Pancakes, Cottage Cheese, '79 115
Pancakes, Cream Cheese, '97 70
Pancakes, Featherweight, '99 43
Pancakes with Goat Cheese, Sweet Potato, '96 271
Parmesan Toasts, '96 66
Pasta and Lentils, Cheesy, '99 287
Pasta, Basil-Cheese, '96 136
Pasta, Mamma Mia, '95 25
Pasta Stuffed with Five Cheeses, '88 197
Pasta with Parmesan, Creamy, '98 233
Pastries, Greek Spinach-and-Cheese, '96 76
Pastry, Cheese, '88 56
Pastry, Cream Cheese, '82 39; '86 78; '89 136
Pastry Shells, Miniature Cream Cheese, '87 190
Pastry Tart Shells, Cheese, '85 216
Pâté, Cream Cheese, '80 154
Pâté, Liver-Cheese, '85 276
Patty Shells, Cream Cheese, '81 266; '82 249
Pears, Cheese-Filled, '81 268
Pears Stuffed with Cheese, '82 290
Peppers, Macaroni-and-Cheese-Stuffed, '80 65
Perch, Parmesan-Crusted, '93 91
Pesto, Ruth's, '96 170
Pie, Breakfast, '86 242
Pie, Broccoli-Cheese, '84 235
Pie, Cheese-Beef, '85 33
Pie, Cheesy Mexican Chicken, '82 142
Pie, Green Chile-Cheese, '84 234
Pie, Ham-and-Cheese, '95 256; '96 75
Pie, Mexican Cheese, '82 9; '83 69
Pie, Mincemeat-Cheese, '80 253
Pie, Onion-Cheese, '88 86
Pie, Quick and Cheesy Corn, '82 191
Pie, Tortilla, '85 M211
Pie, Tumbleweed, '98 205
Pie, Turkey-Cheese, '88 264
Pie, Zucchini-Ham-Cheese, '80 272
Pineapple Gratin, '93 328
Pinwheels, Pepperoni, '96 247
Pizza, Breakfast, '88 288; '97 172
Pizza, Cheese-and-Mushroom, '83 226
Pizza, Cheeseburger, '97 318
Pizza, Double Cheesy Beef-and-Sausage, '86 77
Pizza, Gruyère-Chicken, '87 182
Pizza, Maca-, '99 195
Pizza, Nutty Pesto, '97 267
Pizza, Portobello-Pine Nut, '99 216
Pizzas, Chicken-and-Three-Cheese French Bread, '96 94
Pizzas, Eggplant, '98 183
Pizzas, Five-Ring, '96 180
Polenta Squares, Skillet, '94 22
Polenta Triangles, '98 181
Polenta with Cheese and Okra, Baked, '99 232
Popcorn, Bacon-Cheese, '86 74
Popcorn, Cheese, '98 205
Popcorn, Cheesy Barbecue, '95 239
Popcorn, Sesame-Cheese, '79 220
Pork Chops, Cheese-Stuffed, '84 81
Pork Chops Italian, '98 334
Pork Chops with Apples, Parmesan, '93 338
Pork Chops with Ripieno, '97 245
Pork Tenderloin, Southern-Style Stuffed, '99 45
Pork Tenderloin with Blue Cheese, '86 76
Preserves, Cream Cheese and Peach, '84 264
Pudding, Baked Cheese, '86 78
Pudding, Cheesy Bread, '83 68
Pudding, Corn-Cheese, '80 244
Puff, Egg-and-Cheese, '85 45
Puff, Macaroni and Cheese, '79 5
Puffs, Bavarian Cheese, '80 191
Puffs, Turkey-Cheese, '87 301

Quesadillas, Easy, '98 M205
Quesadillas, Quick, '89 87
Quesadillas, Sausage, '90 118
Quesadillas, Western, '97 65
Quesadillas with Chipotle Salsa, Chicken-and-Brie, '99 311
Quesadillas with Shrimp and Brie, '94 173
Quiches
Bacon-Cheese Quiches, Miniature, '83 93
Benedict Quiche, '80 M107
Blue Cheese Quiche, '84 52
Cheddar-Leek Quiche, '88 198
Cream Cheese Quiche, '96 203
Eggless Quiche, '87 220
Green Onion Quiche, Cheesy, '83 194; '84 42
Ham-and-Cheese Quiches, Individual, '98 24
Ham-Cheese Quiche, '79 26
Ham Quiche, Cheesy, '79 127
Individual Quiches, '98 101
Jalapeño Quiche, Cheesy, '84 31
Lorraine, Perfect Quiche, '79 127
Lorraine, Quiche, '79 40; '80 M108; '99 M218
Miniature Cheese Quiches, '80 150
Sausage-Cheddar Quiche, '79 26
Sausage Quiche, Spicy, '80 M108
South-of-the-Border Quiche, '93 321
Spinach Quiche, Cheesy, '81 228
Squares, Cheesy Hot Quiche, '79 124
Swiss Alpine Quiche, '90 18
Swiss-Zucchini Quiche, '82 49
Tasty Quiche, '82 264
Vegetable Quiche, Cheese-, '81 228
Vegetable Quiche, Light, '97 332
Zucchini Quiche, Cheesy, '83 312
Ramekins, Three-Cheese, '79 26
Rarebit, Cheese, '86 78
Rarebit, Tangy Welsh, '88 159
Rarebit, Uptown Welsh, '87 279
Raspberry Brie in Rye, '93 252
Refried Beans, Easy, '99 57
Rice, Chili-Cheesy, '79 43
Risotto, Crawfish, '99 120
Risotto with Parmesan, Broccoli, '99 120
Risotto with Saffron, Pistachio, '98 272
Roll, Cheesy Meat, '82 136
Rolls, Ham-and-Cheese Lettuce, '89 217
Rollups, Pizza, '99 197
Rounds, Parmesan, '79 170
Rounds, Turkey-Mozzarella, '82 3
Salads
Apple Salad, Cheesy, '86 301
Apple Salad, Swiss-, '84 81
Artichoke-Goat Cheese Salad, '98 118
Aspic, Blue Cheese, '96 66
Aspic, Cheesy Vegetable, '81 73
Baby Lettuces with Vidalia Onion Vinaigrette, Salad of, '99 168
Bacon-Lettuce-Mozzarella-and-Tomato Salad, '98 209
Baked Goat Cheese Salad, '96 26
Banana Splits, Cottage Cheese-, '87 56
Black Bean-and-Cheese Salad, '92 217
Blue Cheese Chicken Salad, '94 81
Blue Cheese Salad, '88 48
Blue Cheese Tossed Salad, '84 195
Broccoli-Cheese-Pasta Salad, '96 184
Cantaloupe-Cheese Salad, '88 184
Cauliflower with Parmesan and Bacon, '96 137
Chicken Salad, Greek, '98 329
Chicken Salad, Parmesan-, '98 234
Chicken Salad with Blue Cheese, '97 97
Citrus-Blue Cheese Salad, '92 220
Coleslaw, Blue Cheese, '89 13; '95 270

Coleslaw, Cottage, '80 64
Cottage Cheese Salad, Different, '85 328; '86 22
Cottage Cheese Salad, Out-of-This-World, '79 44
Cranberry-Cheese Ribbon Salad, '79 241
Crunchy-Creamy Salad, '88 100
Freeze Salad, Party, '82 145
Fruit-'n'-Nut Salad, Cheesy, '87 56
Fruit Salad, Cottage Cheese-and-, '86 16
Garden Salad, Italian, '99 203
Goat Cheese and Black-Eyed Pea Salad, Fearrington House, '95 60
Green Beans-and-Cheese Salad, '91 159
Green Bean, Walnut, and Feta Salad, '96 273
Greens with Parmesan Walnuts, Mixed, '95 301
Ham-and-Cheese Salad, '88 138
Ham-Pecan-Blue Cheese Pasta Salad, '90 62
Harvest Salad with Cider Vinaigrette, '99 322
Layered Salad, Cheesy, '81 37
Lemon-Cheese Salad, '85 240
Lettuce, Cheesy Stuffed, '79 175
Lettuce Salad, Blue Cheese-Stuffed, '94 202
Lime-Cheese Salad, Frosted, '79 286
Macaroni and Cheese Salad, '97 203
Macaroni-Cheese Salad, Dilled, '86 208
Marinated Tomato and Brie Salad, '95 95
Mexican Salad, '81 36
Mold, Ambrosia Cream Cheese, '79 249
Mold, Cheesy Lemon, '79 241
Mold, Creamy Tuna-Cheese, '81 135
Molds, Snowcap Cheese, '79 242
Mushroom Salad, Quick Cheese-, '89 128
Orange-Cottage Cheese Salad, '79 44
Pear-Apple Salad, Blue Cheese-, '81 224
Pear-Swiss Cheese Salad, '91 237
Pea Salad, '98 274
Pea Salad, Cheddar-, '84 82
Pepper Toss, Parmesan, '93 208
"Pig in the Garden" Salad, '92 255
Pine Nut, Rice, and Feta Salad, '96 26; '98 331
Potato Salad, Blue Cheese-, '91 208
Potato Salad, Cottage Cheese-, '79 147, 285
Potato Salad, Hot Parmesan, '79 78
Potato Salad, Warm Goat Cheese and, '96 234
Roquefort Salad, Creamy, '79 73
Spinach-Blue Cheese Salad, '82 166
Spinach Salad with the Blues, '95 66
Suzie or Steven Salad, '98 204
Tomato-Basil-Mozzarella Salad, '95 171
Tomato-Basil Salad, Fresh Mozzarella-, '93 131
Tomatoes, Cottage Cheese Salad in, '86 208
Tomato-Feta Salad, '81 246; '91 168
Tomato-Gruyère-Basil Salad, '99 172
Tomato-Mozzarella Salad, '89 220
Tomato Salad, Cottage-, '85 163
Tuna Salad, Cheese-Sauced, '87 M124
Tuna Salad, Swiss, '86 186
Vegetable Congealed Salad, Cheesy-, '86 199
Vinaigrette with Greens, '98 184
Walnut Salad, Gorgonzola-, '96 170
Warm Cheese Salad, '97 246
Watercress Salad, '97 249
Ziti-Cheddar Salad, '85 165
Salmon Patties, Cheesy, '89 99
Salsa, Avocado-Feta, '96 15
Salsa, Fiery Steak with Pimiento Cheese, '99 331
Sandwiches
Avocado, Bacon, and Cheese Sandwiches, '87 279
Bacon, Cheese, and Tomato Sandwiches, '84 14

CHEESE, Sandwiches
(continued)

Bacon-Cheese Sandwiches, Grilled, '83 242
Bacon, Pimiento, and Cheese Hoagies,
  '90 144
Bacon Sandwiches, Open-Faced Cheesy,
  '80 78
Bagel Sandwiches, Mozzarella-Pepper,
  '98 145
Beef and Cheese Roll-Ups, Savory, '96 235
Beef, Bacon, and Blue Cheese Sandwiches,
  '96 23
BLT's, Cheesy, '85 92
Breakfast Sandwiches, '80 52
Breakfast Sandwiches, Cheesy, '90 140
Brown Bread-Cream Cheese Sandwiches,
  '87 M6
Buns, Snack, '87 279
Calzones, Ground Beef, '97 95
Chicken-and-Cheese Sandwiches, Toasted,
  '85 242
Chicken 'n' Cheese Sandwiches, Grilled,
  '99 240
Chicken Parmigiana Sandwich, '94 65
Chicken Sandwiches, Cheesy, '82 190
Chicken Sandwiches, Gouda Lover's, '99 195
Christmas Tree Sandwiches, '92 279
Corned Beef and Cheese Sandwich, '79 214
Crab-and-Cheese Sandwiches, Hot, '87 279
Eggplant Sandwiches, '99 240
Eggplant, Tomato, and Feta Sandwiches,
  '98 106
Egg Sandwiches, Open-Faced Cheesy, '86 67
Feta Salad Sandwich, Tuscan, '99 289
Focaccia Sandwiches, '98 53
Fruit-and-Cheese Breakfast Sandwiches,
  '89 M21
Gingered Tea Sandwiches, '84 116
Good-Start Sandwiches, '99 134
Grilled Bacon, Cheese, and Tomato
  Sandwiches, '97 170
Grilled Cheese, '97 328
Grilled Cheese Sandwiches, '82 M172; '94 167
Grilled Cheese Sandwich, Mexican, '92 63
Grilled Cheeses, Mexican, '97 170
Grilled Chili con Queso Sandwiches, '96 139
Grilled Sandwiches, Tasty, '84 30
Grilled Spinach Fondue Sandwiches, '99 337
Grills, Double Cheese, '97 170
Grills, Triple Cheese, '97 170
Ham-and-Cheese Pita Pockets, '90 271
Ham-and-Cheese Pita Sandwiches, '87 202;
  '88 44
Ham-and-Cheese Sandwiches, Hot, '85 299
Ham-and-Cheese Sandwiches, Tiny, '99 87
Ham-and-Cheese Sandwich Round, '94 326
Ham-and-Cheese Sandwich, Tex-Mex, '86 4
Ham and Swiss in the Pocket, '83 31
Ham-and-Swiss Sandwiches, '98 287
Ham-and-Swiss Sandwiches, Tangy, '85 164
Ham-and-Turkey Specials, Cheesy, '84 14
Ham 'n' Cheese Chicken Sandwich, '95 153
Ham Sandwiches, Creamy Blue Cheese-,
  '87 279
Herbed Cheese Sandwiches with Artichoke-
  Tomato Salsa, '96 182
Hot Browns, '98 287
Hot Cheddar Cheese Sandwiches, '97 179
Hot French Cheese Sandwiches, '82 3
Lasagna in a Bun, '90 176
Leafy Cheese Sandwiches, '90 56
Monte Cristo Sandwiches, '97 319

Muffin, Stuffin', '99 193
Muffuletta Loaf, '97 86
Muffulettas, '98 184
"Muffy" Sandwich, Fertitta's, '94 34
Open-Faced Mexican Sandwiches, '98 230
Open-Faced Sandwiches, Super, '97 52
Peanut-Cheese-Raisin Sandwiches, '88 140
Pimiento Cheese Finger Sandwiches, '99 86
Pimiento Cheese Sandwiches, '82 278
Pita, Stuffed, '89 87
Sausage-Cheese Muffin Sandwiches, '92 M212
Sebastian, The, '94 184
Shrimp-Cheese Sandwiches, '85 242
Smoked Turkey, Mozzarella, and Blackberry
  Sandwiches, '99 220
Stuffed Sandwich, Deli, '98 287
Sub, Chicken, '98 287
Tea Sandwiches, Cheese, '92 276
Tomato-Cheese-Bacon Melts, '99 72
Tortilla Stack-Ups, '92 196
Tuna Cheesies, '82 191
Tuna Melt, Southwestern, '96 201
Turkey-Cheese Dogs, '97 203
Wraps, Western, '99 194
Yummy Sandwiches, '81 229

Sauces
Blue Cheese Sauce, '90 142; '94 320
Blue Cheese Sauce, Fettuccine with, '98 247
Cheddar Cheese Sauce, '91 286
Cheese Sauce, '79 M156; '81 43, 44, 225;
  '82 M123; '83 49, 138, 188; '84 57; '85 92;
  '86 241; '88 78, 272; '89 181, 229; '90 235;
  '93 48
Cider Sauce, Cheddar-, '98 242
Cottage Cheese Sauce, '87 232
Cream Sauce, Cheesy, '82 79
Devonshire Sauce, Processor, '86 337
Easy Cheese Sauce, '79 22
Garlic-Cheese Sauce, '84 M70
Guilt-Free Cheese Sauce, '93 M95
Lemon-Cheese Sauce, '91 24
Lemony Cheese Sauce, '84 183
Monterey Jack Sauce, '84 293
Mornay Sauce, '80 120; '81 90; '89 195
Mushroom-Cheese Sauce, '83 190; '86 48
Parmesan Cheese Sauce, '79 165; '80 162;
  '85 143
Parmesan Sauce, '92 17
Pesto Sauce, Walnut-Parmesan, '97 104
Rich Cheese Sauce, '81 89
Roquefort Sauce, '89 321
Seafood Cheese Sauce, '89 240
Swiss Cheese Sauce, '79 35; '87 289; '88 135
Swiss Sauce, '83 M195
Swiss Sauce, Creamy, '80 M53
Topper, Vegetable-Cheese Potato, '86 6
Vegetable-Cheese Sauce, '85 M152
Vegetable Sauce, Cheesy, '92 M134
Walnut-Parmesan Pesto Sauce, '96 251
Sausage, Grilled Pork, Cheddar, and Jalapeño,
  '98 311
Scallops, Baked Gruyère, '92 57
Scallops, Chip and Cheese, '80 301
Scallops Mornay, '80 164
Schnitzel, Swiss, '80 189
Shake, Strawberry-Cheesecake, '92 44
Shell, Rice-Cheese, '82 49
Shells, Cheesy Beef-Stuffed, '83 217
Shells, Cream Cheese, '79 2
Shortcakes, Cheesy Chicken, '95 98
Shrimp and Pasta with Two Cheeses,
  '98 49
Shrimp au Gratin, '85 79
Shrimp, Parmesan-Stuffed, '85 103

Soufflés. See also CHEESE/Desserts.
Blue Cheese Soufflé, '91 244
Cheddar Cheese Soufflé, '98 24
Cheese Soufflé, '79 72, 261; '94 116
Chile-Cheese Soufflés, '96 219
Corn-and-Cheese Soufflé, '88 122
Cups, Hot Soufflé, '85 284
Egg Cheese Soufflé, Three-, '87 234
Grits Soufflé, Garlic-Cheese, '99 18
Italian Pizzaola Soufflé, '98 232
Mexican Pizzaola Soufflé, '98 232
Rice-Cheese Soufflé, '79 270
Rolled Cheese Soufflé, '89 13
Individual Frozen Soufflés, '80 52
Individual Soufflés, '80 190
Parmesan Soufflés, '97 280
Spinach Soufflé, Cheese-and-, '98 235
Spinach Soufflé, Cheesy, '81 53
Three-Cheese Soufflés, '96 219
Two, Cheese Soufflé for, '81 226
Soups
Anytime Soup, Cheesy, '81 307; '82 314;
  '83 66
Bacon-Beer Cheese Soup, '87 M7
Bacon-Topped Cheese Soup, '80 M224
Beer-Cheese Soup, '84 246
Bell Pepper-Cheese Chowder, '95 240
Blue Satin Soup, '98 248
Broccoli Soup, Cheese-and-, '89 276
Broccoli Soup, Cheesy-, '86 258
Broccoli-Swiss Soup, '86 6
Carrot Soup, Cheesy, '81 262
Cauliflower Soup, '99 318
Cheddar Cheese Chowder, '97 30
Cheddar Chowder, Hearty, '79 16
Chicken Chowder, Cheesy, '92 21
Chicken-Corn Soup, Cheesy, '97 158
Chicken Noodle Soup, Creamy, '99 20
Chunky Cheese Soup, '98 31
Corn and Cheese Chowder, '80 228
Cream Cheese Soup, Austrian, '98 M85
Cream of Cheese Soup, '83 99
Cream with Greens Soup, '94 277
Favorite Cheese Soup, Uncle Ed's, '94 228
Gazebo Cheese Soup, '90 158
Gazpacho, Shrimp-Cream Cheese, '94 137
Golden Cheese Chowder, '80 73
Ham-and-Cheese Chowder, '89 15
Ham 'n Cheese Chowder, '79 199
Hearty Cheese Soup, '84 4
Herbed Cheese Soup, '96 219
Hot Cheese Chowder, '89 16
Macaroni and Cheese Soup, '95 264
Mexican Cheese Soup, '97 268
Minestrone, Cheesy, '99 17
Monterey Jack Cheese Soup, '81 112;
  '85 M211
Onion-Cheese Soup, '87 81
Onion Soup, Double-Cheese, '85 227
Onion Soup, Double Cheese-Topped, '79 49
Oyster-Cheese Soup, '84 213
Pimiento "Mac and Cheese" Soup, '97 M325
Potato-and-Wild Rice Soup, Cheesy, '89 16
Reuben Soup, Cream of, '97 26
Roquefort Vichyssoise, Velvety, '83 223
Swiss-Broccoli Chowder, '80 73
Tomato Soup with Parmesan Cheese, Cream
  of, '86 161
Tortilla Soup, '99 310
Vegetable-Cheese Soup, '89 15
Vegetable-Cheese Soup, Creamy, '81 244
Vegetable Cheese Soup, Creamy, '83 230
Vegetable Chowder, Cheesy, '80 25; '83 20
Vegetable Soup, Cheesy, '80 73; '97 241

Velvet Soup, Cheese, '80 74; '92 193
Zucchini Soup, Cold, '99 164
Spaghetti, Chicken, '98 329
Spaghetti, Marzetti's, '99 85
Spaghetti, Three-Cheese, '83 105
Spanakopita, '86 58; '96 233
Spiders, Dried Apricot, '96 255
Spreads
Almond Cheese Spread, '87 292
Aloha Spread, '83 93
Apricot Brie Spread, '86 275
Apricot-Cream Cheese Spread, '82 161; '87 158
Artichoke-Parmesan Spread, '92 95
Bacon-Cheese Spread, '83 241
Basil-Cheese Spread, Fresh, '97 108
Beer Cheese Spread, '81 160; '85 69
Beer Spread, Cheesy, '87 196
Blue Cheese Spread, '90 215; '95 79, 92;
   '97 240
Boursin Cheese Spread, Buttery, '94 301;
   '96 318
Boursin Cheese Spread, Garlic, '94 301
Butter, Blue Cheese, '97 306
Caviar-Cream Cheese Spread, '84 256
Cheddar-Swiss Spread, '99 106
Cheese Spread, '96 122; '99 24
Chile-Cheese Spread, '86 297; '99 336
Chili Cheese Spread, '93 242
Chili-Cheese Spread, '99 24
Chocolate Cheese Spread, '87 292
Coconut-Cranberry Cheese Spread, '92 328
Confetti Cheese Spread, '84 256
Cottage Cheese Spread, '87 107
Cottage-Egg Salad Spread, '82 146
Cream Cheese-Olive Spread, '82 35
Cream Cheese Spread, Deviled, '81 235
Cream Cheese Spread, Fruited, '91 306;
   '93 79
Cream Cheese Spread, Peachy, '90 M215
Cream Cheese Spread, Pear-, '93 80
Cucumber and Cream Cheese Spread, '82 140
Date-Walnut-Cheese Spread, '96 322
Edam-Sherry Spread, '84 257
Feta-and-Apple Spread, '99 106
Feta Cheese Spread, '96 265
Four-Cheese Spread, '99 106
Fruit and Cheese Spread, '81 245
Fruit-and-Cheese Spread, Nutty, '87 246
Garlic Pimiento Cheese Spread, '79 58
German Cheese Spread, '79 82
Gouda Cheese Spread, '90 36
Green Onion-Cheese Spread, '92 24
Gruyère-Apple Spread, '81 160
Ham and Pimiento Spread, '80 285
Hawaiian Cheese Spread, '87 158
Herb-Cream Cheese Spread, '83 24
Herbed Avocado-Cheese Spread, '98 335
Herbed Cheese Spread, '87 247
Horseradish Spread, Cheese-, '84 222
Jalapeño-Cheese Spread, '82 248
Make-Ahead Cheese Spread, '93 324
Mexican Cheese Spread, '90 119
Olive Spread, Cheese-, '79 82
Orange Cheese Spread, '87 292
Parmesan-Spinach Spread, '93 55
Party Spread, Spicy, '97 240
Pimiento and Three Cheeses, '86 296
Pimiento Cheese, Chunky, '86 295; '88 91
Pimiento Cheese, Creamy, '86 296
Pimiento Cheese, Fabulous, '98 315
Pimiento Cheese, Incredible, '96 22
Pimiento Cheese, Jalapeño, '98 315
Pimiento Cheese Spread, '82 35; '83 93;
   '86 127; '99 106, 276

Pimiento Cheese Spread, Creamy, '92 159
Pimiento Cheese Spread, Low-Calorie,
   '85 215
Pimiento Cheese, West Texas, '84 9
Pimiento Cheese, White Cheddar, '99 106
Pineapple-Cheese Spread, '86 126; '91 167
Pineapple-Cream Cheese Spread, '82 35
Sandwich Spread, Benedictine, '80 299
Swiss Cheese Spread, '90 60
Tomato-Cheese Spread, '81 157
Tomato-Cheese Spread, Fiery, '87 196
Tropical Cheese Spread, '95 46
Vegetable Sandwich Spread, '83 174
Waldorf Cheese Spread, '88 173
Zesty Cheese Spread, '82 140
Zippy Cheese Spread, '85 4
Steak Cheese Skillet, Swiss, '80 106
Steak Parmesan, '93 41
Steak, Parmesan Round, '80 106
Steaks, Blue Cheese, '84 171
Steaks, Cheese-Stuffed, '81 17
Steaks, Mexican Pepper-Cheese, '97 190
Strata, Artichoke-Cheese, '90 236
Strata, Tomato-Cheese, '81 209
Stromboli, '88 272; '89 181
Strudel, Chicken-Goat Cheese, '98 28
Strudel, Meatless Mexican, '98 29
Strudel, Reuben, '98 28
Stuffing, Catfish with Cream Cheese, '89 52
Supper Supreme, Sunday, '79 76
Sweet Potato Chips with Blue Cheese, '93 290
Tart, Dried Tomato-Cheese, '90 203
Tart, Ham-and-Cheese, '92 332
Tart, Herb-Cheese, '87 98
Tart Milan, '87 70
Tart Shells, Cheese, '88 88
Tarts, Sausage 'n' Cheese, '88 51
Tart, Tomato-Basil, '98 132
Tenderloin, Stuffed Tuscany, '99 269
Terrine, Italian Cheese, '93 64
Terrine with Goat Cheese, Black Bean, '87 120
Terrine with Tomato-Basil Vinaigrette, Blue
   Cheese, '99 288
Tomato, Basil, and Cheese, '95 165
Topping, Blue Cheese Burger, '93 218
Topping, Cheese, '86 233
Topping, Yogurt-Cheese, '88 55
Tortellini, Creamy, '99 171
Tortellini with Rosemary-Parmesan Sauce,
   '92 284
Tortillas, Cheesy, '81 62
Tortilla Snack, Two-Cheese, '90 119
Tortilla Stack, Cheesy Chicken-, '86 3
Toss, Ham and Cheese, '79 55
Tostadas, Quick Chicken, '99 159
Trout Florentine, Cheesy, '85 53
Turkey Parmesan, '82 268
Turnovers, Sausage-Cheese, '88 231; '89 22
Twists, Cheese, '92 125
Veal Parmigiana, '81 227
Vegetables. *See also* **CHEESE/Casseroles.**
Artichoke-Cheese Bottoms, Baked, '94 61
Artichokes, Stuffed, '99 64
Asparagus Mornay, '99 102
Asparagus on Toast, Creamed, '95 61
Asparagus with Goat Cheese Sauce, '93 116
Broccoli-and-Eggs au Gratin, '85 289
Broccoli au Gratin, '82 M20
Broccoli Bakers, '99 308
Broccoli Fritters, Cheesy, '79 53
Broccoli Parmesan, '97 302
Broccoli with Cheese Sauce, '82 107
Brussels Sprouts with Cheese Sauce, '79 246
Cabbage, Cheese Scalloped, '81 87; '82 7

Cabbage Rolls, Southwestern, '97 214
Cauliflower au Gratin, '82 204; '99 59
Cauliflower au Gratin, French-Fried, '79 221;
   '80 82
Cauliflower, Baked Swiss, '79 100
Cauliflower, Cheddar, '99 318
Cauliflower, Cheese-Frosted, '85 68
Cauliflower, Frosted, '97 105
Cauliflower Italiano, Cheesy, '82 300
Cauliflower with Cheese Sauce, '81 101
Cherry Tomatoes, Cheesy, '83 135
Chiles Rellenos, Cheese, '96 24
Chiles Rellenos (Stuffed Chiles), '82 220;
   '83 150
Corn-and-Swiss Cheese Bake, '92 133
Corn, Grilled Parmesan, '82 127
Eggplant, Cheesy Fried, '90 75
Eggplant, Cheesy Stuffed, '79 188; '82 208
Eggplant, Fried Parmesan, '87 166
Eggplant Parmesan, '82 230; '92 18
Eggplant, Parmesan Fried, '79 189
Eggplant Parmesan, No-Fry, '92 172
Eggplant, Scalloped, '91 223
Fries, Cheesy Oven, '91 187
Green Beans au Gratin, '80 116
Green Beans, Cheese-Topped, '79 100
Green Beans, Cheesy, '80 157
Green Beans, Tomato-Feta, '99 59
Green Beans with Blue Cheese, '88 57
Hash Brown Cheese Bake, '82 50
Jalapeño Cheese Pie, '96 292
Jalapeños, Hot Stuffed, '99 123
Lentils with Cheese, Baked, '84 113
Limas in Onion Shells, Cheese and, '81 86
Loaf, Pureed Vegetable-Cheese, '85 297
Mushrooms, Herbed Cheese-Stuffed, '96 171
Mushrooms, Parmesan Stuffed, '83 115
Mushrooms, Ricotta-Stuffed, '85 20
New Potatoes, Cheesy, '85 156
New Potatoes, Crispy Roasted, '98 166
Okra with Cheese, '80 185
Onion Bake, Cheese, '82 32
Onion Bake, Romano, '90 98
Onions, Cheese-Stuffed, '90 34
Onions, Parmesan, '93 170
Onions, Sherried Cheese, '82 32
Parmesan Vegetables, '97 147
Pie, Savory Summer, '99 159
Potato Boats, Southwestern, '96 33
Potato Bowls, Mashed, '97 199
Potato-Broccoli-Cheese Bake, '80 114
Potato-Cheese Puff, '95 269
Potato Croquettes, Baked, '97 30
Potato Croquettes, Parmesan, '84 210
Potatoes, Accordion, '98 69
Potatoes Alfredo, '89 204
Potatoes-and-Zucchini au Gratin, '84 5
Potatoes au Gratin, '93 90, 217
Potatoes, Bacon-Topped Blue Cheese, '79 46
Potatoes, Basil-Cheese, '90 M316
Potatoes, Blue Cheese, '98 247
Potatoes, Blue Cheese Mashed, '92 330
Potatoes, Blue Cheese Stuffed, '81 276;
   '92 M228
Potatoes, Blue Cheese-Stuffed, '89 69
Potatoes, Cheesy, '82 211
Potatoes, Cheesy Bacon-Stuffed, '81 61
Potatoes, Cheesy Caraway, '86 17
Potatoes, Cheesy Chive, '90 M316
Potatoes, Cheesy Chive-Stuffed, '91 128
Potatoes, Cheesy Crab-Stuffed, '86 17
Potatoes, Cheesy Frank-Topped, '83 3
Potatoes, Cheesy Scalloped, '96 33
Potatoes, Chicken-Cheese Stuffed, '86 55

CHEESE, Vegetables
(continued)

Potatoes, Chili-Cheese, '90 M62
Potatoes, Chive-Cream Cheese Mashed, '92 330
Potatoes, Crab-Stuffed, '99 307
Potatoes, Cream Cheese Mashed, '97 14
Potatoes, Creamy Cheese, '88 M146
Potatoes, Creamy Cheese-and-Chive, '99 308
Potatoes, Creamy Chive-and-Gorgonzola Stuffed, '99 308
Potatoes, Feta Mashed, '92 330
Potatoes, Garlic-Gruyère Mashed, '98 322
Potatoes, Golden, '96 139
Potatoes, Harvest Mashed, '98 248
Potatoes, Horseradish Mashed, '98 69
Potatoes, Parmesan, '82 270; '90 M62; '92 M341; '93 M46
Potatoes, Parmesan-Cream, '97 54
Potatoes, Parmesan-Paprika, '99 169
Potatoes, Roasted Garlic-Parmesan Mashed, '97 263
Potatoes Roquefort, '79 211
Potatoes, Stuffed Mashed, '98 328
Potatoes, Two-Cheese, '80 114
Potatoes with Cheese Sauce, Baked, '83 239
Potatoes with Cheese Sauce, Stuffed, '87 192
Potatoes with Feta Cheese, '84 295; '85 196
Potatoes with Sweet Marjoram and Parmesan Cheese, Scalloped, '91 246
Potato Fans, Parmesan-, '88 M190
Potato Gratin, Dual, '93 328
Potato Skins, Cheese, '84 M239
Potato Soufflé, Cheesy, '89 332
Potato Wedges, Parmesan, '95 181
Rice au Gratin, '83 129
Rutabaga au Gratin, '79 254
Spinach-Cheese Puff, '84 96
Spinach, Cheesy Topped, '84 85
Spinach, Creamed, '96 252
Spinach Parmesan, '93 72
Spinach Pie Parma, '96 203
Spinach Pie with Muenster Crust, '95 48
Spinach, Savory Parmesan, '85 68
Spinach with Cheese, Scalloped, '79 8
Spinach with Feta, Lemon, '85 190
Spuds, Mushroom-Swiss, '96 M238
Squash and Tomato Bake, '95 180
Squash Bake, Cheesy, '80 183
Squash Boats, Parmesan-Stuffed, '79 156
Squash, Cheesy Stuffed, '82 134
Squash, Greek-Style, '92 26
Squash Soufflé, Cheesy, '82 146
Stalks, Splendid, '93 258
Summer Vegetables, Cheesy, '94 119
Sweet Potato Blues, Stacked, '95 290
Swiss Chard Bundles, '94 48
Tomato Cheese Puffs, '81 48
Tomatoes, Baked Cheddar, '85 43
Tomatoes, Cheese Herbed-Topped, '86 108
Tomatoes, Cheese-Stuffed, '91 69
Tomatoes, Cheese-Topped, '81 160
Tomatoes, Cheesy Grilled, '79 150
Tomatoes, Cheesy Puff-Top, '86 187
Tomatoes, Cheesy Stuffed, '80 161
Tomatoes, Chile-Cheese Stuffed, '94 141
Tomatoes, Greek, '98 173
Tomatoes, Parmesan, '80 161
Tomatoes, Parmesan-Stuffed, '92 182
Tomatoes, Provençal, '98 267
Tomatoes, Romano Broiled, '80 42

Tomatoes with Cheese Sauce over Toast, '88 159
Tomato-Feta Green Beans, '99 59
Tomato Tart, Herbed, '96 94
Turnip au Gratin, '79 289
Turnips au Gratin, '88 229; '89 244
Turnips in Cheese Sauce, '84 229
Yellow Squash with Cheese Sauce, Stuffed, '80 162
Zucchini and Tomato au Gratin, '82 208
Zucchini Fries, Parmesan-, '95 129
Zucchini, Ham and Cheese Stuffed, '79 157
Zucchini Parmesan, '81 108; '82 103
Zucchini, Parmesan, '81 234
Zucchini Pie, Cheesy, '82 103
Zucchini with Feta, Greek Grilled, '95 190
Vermicelli, Shrimp and Feta Cheese on, '87 108
Vinaigrette, Blue Cheese, '90 55, 280
Vinaigrette, Garlic-Blue Cheese, '92 57
Wafers, Cheese, '95 174
Wafers, Hope Farm Cheese, '93 282
Wafers, Italian, '87 36
Wafers, Sage-Pecan Cheese, '93 12
Walnut-Baked Brie, '93 241

CHEESECAKES
Amaretto Cheesecake, '81 150; '99 273
Amaretto-Irish Cream Cheesecake, '90 266
Apple Cheesecake, Dieter's, '86 318
Banana Cheesecake, Chocolate-Wrapped, '99 M48
Bars, Cherry Cheesecake, '97 330
Bavarian Cheesecake, '97 55
Black-and-White Cheesecake, '99 334
Black Forest Cheesecake, '84 74; '89 93; '94 21; '97 330
Blueberries 'n' Cream Cheesecake, '87 140
Blueberry Chiffon Cheesecake, '87 76
Brownies, Cheesecake, '85 249
Brown Sugar-and-Spice Cheesecake, '89 93
Butter Pecan Cheesecake, '86 61
Butterscotch Cheesecake, '86 188
Candy Bar Cheesecake, '85 298; '86 120
Cherry Cheesecake, '79 50
Cherry-Topped Cheesecake, '80 23
Chocolate-Almond Cheesecake, '93 53
Chocolate-Amaretto Cheesecake, '85 M294; '93 97
Chocolate-Caramel-Pecan Cheesecake, '91 197
Chocolate Cheesecake, '81 16; '82 305
Chocolate Cheesecake, Rich, '84 74; '85 38
Chocolate Cheesecakes, Tiny, '92 288
Chocolate Cheesecake with Whipped Cream Frosting, '89 42
Chocolate Chip Cheesecake, '85 114
Chocolate Cookie Cheesecake, '91 298
Chocolate-Glazed Triple-Layer Cheesecake, '86 315; '90 310
Chocolate Marble Cheesecake, '89 93
Chocolate-Mint Baked Alaska Cheesecake, '94 142
Chocolate-Mint Cheesecake, '91 104
Chocolate-Raspberry Truffle Cheesecake, '91 270
Chocolate Swirl Cheesecake, '84 295; '85 26
Coconut-Chocolate-Almond Cheesecake, '98 322
Coffee Cake, Deep-Dish Cheesecake, '90 50
Cottage Cheese Cheesecake, '80 24
Cream Cheesecake, Rich, '83 270
Crème de Menthe Cheesecake, '82 263; '89 93
Daiquiri Chiffon Cheesecake, '88 66
Deluxe Cheesecake, '80 23
Frozen Cheesecake with Raspberry Sauce, '84 73
Fruit-Glazed Cheesecake, '80 24; '90 162
Fudge Cheesecake, '98 M213
Fudge-Filled Cheesecake, Warm, '98 34

German Chocolate Cheesecake, '87 265
Glazed Cheesecake, '83 142
Grasshopper Cheesecake, '80 191
Individual Cheesecakes, So Easy, '85 30
Kahlúa Cheesecake, Heavenly, '84 152
Key Lime Cheesecake with Strawberry-Butter Sauce, '96 87
Lemon Cheesecake, '86 194; '91 308; '92 24
Lemon Cheesecake, Luscious, '90 M196
Lemon Cheesecake with Orange-Pineapple Glaze, '81 60
Lemon Delight Cheesecake, '95 219
Light-and-Easy Cheesecake, '88 55
Make-Ahead Cheesecake Pie, '81 233
Marbled Cheesecake, '87 261
Marble Mint Cheesecake, '84 152
Margarita Cheesecake, '92 211
Mile-High Cheesecake, '86 334
Miniature Cheesecakes, '82 305; '90 170
Mint Cheesecake Bites, '99 282
Mocha Cheesecake, '98 278
Mocha-Chocolate Cheesecake, '88 258
Mocha Swirl Cheesecake, '87 262
Orange Cheesecake, '81 84; '85 38
Passover Cheesecake, '91 53
Peaches 'n' Cream Cheesecake, '88 137
Peanut Butter Cheesecake, '94 142
Pear-Berry Cheesecake, '82 M141
Pear-Glazed Cheesecake, '79 67
Pecan Cheesecake, '85 38
Peppermint Cheesecake, Frozen, '94 143
Petite Cheesecakes, Holiday, '86 321
Phyllo Cheesecakes, Little, '87 275
Piña Colada Cheesecake, '92 70
Pineapple Cheesecake, '81 32
Pineapple Cheesecake, Ultimate, '85 38
Praline Cheesecake, '83 270; '89 93
Praline-Crusted Cheesecake, '99 295
Pumpkin Cheesecake, '80 254; '85 280; '96 268
Raspberry-Lemon Sauce, Cheesecake with, '96 30
Raspberry Sauce, Cheesecake with, '87 116
Ricotta Cheesecake, Italian, '95 303
Savory
Chicken Cheesecake, Curried, '90 174
Chicken-Chile Cheesecake, '92 42
Feta Cheesecakes, Little, '86 277
Fiesta Cheesecake, '93 273
Ham-and-Asparagus Cheesecake, '90 174
Herbed Cheesecakes, '99 182
Margarita Cheesecake, '94 142
Reuben Cheesecake, '90 175
Salsa Cheesecake, '98 33
Shrimp-and-Gruyère Cheesecake, '92 57
Smoked Salmon Cheesecake, '99 92
Spinach-Herb Cheesecake, '99 139
Spinach-Mushroom Cheesecake, '92 326
Spinach Pesto Cheesecake, '90 175
Vegetable Cheesecake, '96 110
Vegetable Cheesecake, Layered, '91 62; '92 51
Vegetable Cheesecake, Roasted, '99 140
Shake, Strawberry-Cheesecake, '92 44
Sour Cream Cheesecake, '86 320
Squares, Cheesecake, '84 151
Strawberry Cheesecake, Almost, '86 32
Sweet Potato Cheesecake, '80 287; '96 312
Tarts, Cream Cheese, '84 74
Three-Layer Cheesecake, '99 140
Ultimate Cheesecake, '98 260
Vanilla Cheesecake, Creamy, '89 93
White Chocolate Cheesecake, '87 44; '88 267; '94 180
Yam Cheesecake, '81 224

CHERRIES

à la Mode, Cherries, '88 202
Bars, Cherry Cheesecake, '97 330
Bars, Delightful Cherry, '86 217
Bread, Cherry Nut, '81 306; '82 36
Bread, Maraschino Cherry Nut, '79 234
Bread, Quick Cherry-Nut, '85 55
Cake, Black Forest Cherry, '83 302
Cake, Cherry, '79 165
Cake, Cherry Bourbon, '82 287
Cake, Cherry Fudge, '98 214
Cake, Cherry Upside-Down, '82 56
Cake, Choco-Cherry, '96 229
Cake, Chocolate-Cherry, '84 200; '86 239
Cake, Cute-as-a-Button Cherry Pound, '95 139
Cake, Dried Cherry, '97 33
Cake, Maraschino Nut, '83 268
Cake, Quick Cherry, '81 238
Cake, Upside-Down Sunburst, '87 9
Cake, White Chocolate-Cherry, '88 268
Cheesecake, Black Forest, '89 93; '94 21; '97 330
Cheesecake, Cherry, '79 50
Cheesecake, Cherry-Topped, '80 23
Chocolate-Covered Cherries, '81 286; '84 298; '97 M55
Chocolates, Cherry, '95 321
Chutney, Glazed Ham with Cherry-Peach, '97 315
Cider, Cherry, '94 288
Cloud, Cherry-Berry on a, '79 94
Cobbler, Berry-Cherry, '83 270
Cobbler, Cherry, '82 91, 139; '99 156
Cobbler, Colossal Cherry, '89 137
Cobbler, Fresh Cherry, '84 178
Cobbler, Raspberry-Cherry, '93 230
Coffee Cake, Cherry, '94 49
Coffee Cake, Cherry Blossom, '80 21
Coffee Cake, Cinnamon-Cherry, '98 330
Compote, Cherry, '83 139
Compote, Watermelon-Cherry, '90 180
"Concrete," Cardinal Sin, '94 113
Cookies, Cherry Bonbon, '93 52
Cookies, Cherry Pecan, '82 136
Cookies, Chocolate-Cherry, '85 324
Cookies, Chocolate-Covered Cherry, '99 280
Cookies, Christmas Cherry, '88 282
Cookies, Coconut-Cherry, '79 292
Cookies, Frosted Chocolate-Cherry, '89 294
Cream, Maraschino Russian, '79 231
Crêpes, Cherry, '91 67
Crêpes Flambé, Cherry, '79 18
Crisp, Cherry, '91 20
Crisp, Oatmeal Cherry-Apple, '90 M16
Crowns, Cherry, '92 275
Dessert, Cherry Cordial, '84 312
Dessert, Holiday Cherry, '80 255
Divinity, Cherry, '97 316
Drops, Cherry-Almond, '81 20
Filling, Cherry, '83 302; '84 225; '88 178
Frosting, Cherry, '86 217
Frosting, Cherry-Nut Cream Cheese, '96 249
Frosting, Chocolate-Cherry, '89 294
Fudge, Cherry Nut, '83 315
Glaze, Cherry, '83 143; '93 52; '98 260
Ice Cream, Black Forest, '88 203
Ice Cream, Cherry, '84 184; '99 156
Ice Cream, Cherry-Nut, '86 129
Ice Cream, Cherry-Pecan, '88 203
Jubilee, Cherries, '79 18; '83 139
Jubilee, Quick Cherries, '82 M100
Jubilite, Cherries, '86 317
Kirsch, Melon Balls and Cherries in, '91 91
Muffins, Cherry, '82 105

Muffins, Cherry-Nut, '90 87
Muffins, Dried Cherry, '94 59
Nuggets, Cherry Nut, '81 286
Pies
Berry Pie, Cherry-, '92 316
Coconut Crumb Cherry Pie, '92 30
Cranberry-Cherry Pie, Tart, '87 299
Cream Pie with Almond Pastry, Cherry, '92 30
Easy Cherry Pie, '82 M299
Filling, Dried Cherry Fried Pie, '96 109
Fresh Cherry Pie, '88 178
Lemony Cherry Pie, '92 30
No-Bake Cherry Confetti Pie, '93 114
Pecan Pie, Cherry-, '92 30
Prize-Winning Cherry Pie, '82 57
Red Cherry Pie, '83 192
Scrumptious Cherry Pie, '83 250
Pork Roast, Cherry-Glazed, '91 84
Punch, Cranberry-Cherry, '91 176
Relish, Cherry-Honey, '97 32
Rolls, Cherry-Almond, '84 M198
Sabayon, Cherries, '88 178
Salads
Apple Salad, Cherry-, '86 31
Best Cherry Salad, '82 302
Cola Salad, Cherry, '80 104
Cola Salad, Cherry-, '91 224; '95 94
Congealed Cherry Salad, '89 278
Festive Cherry Salad, '84 265
Fresh Cherry Salad, '83 120
Frozen Black Cherry Salad, '89 163
Frozen Cherry Salad, '79 126
Frozen Cherry Salad, Delicious, '81 252
Fruit Salad, Cherry, '87 236
Honey-Lime Dressing, Cherry Salad with, '83 139
Orange Salad, Cherry-, '79 74; '82 56
Port Wine-Cherry Salad, '86 11
Sherry Dressing, Cherry Salad with, '79 165
Sweet Cherry Salad, '89 326
Wine Salad, Elegant Cherry-, '82 56
Salsa, Cherry, '99 156
Sauce, Cherry, '79 91; '83 276; '84 91; '91 67
Sauce, Cherry-Wine, '95 285; '97 132
Sauce, Chocolate-Cherry, '85 189
Sauce, Chocolate Cherry, '87 M165
Sauce, Elegant Cherry, '79 M156
Sauce, Ham Balls with Spiced Cherry, '81 112; '82 12
Sauce, Maraschino-Orange, '96 164
Sauce, Roast Ducklings with Cherry, '86 312
Sauce, Roast Pork with Spiced Cherry, '89 324
Sauce, Royal Cherry, '85 224; '86 83
Sauce, Spicy Cherry, '83 244
Scones, Cherry-and-Cream, '99 49
Sherried Cherries, '93 289
Slump, Cherry, '83 139
Snow, Berries on, '82 227
Spread, Cherry, '93 309
Squares, Cherry, '97 273
Squares, Surprise Cherry, '82 57
Stuffed Cherries, '85 81
Syrup, Cherry-Lemonade, '86 214
Tart, Cherry and Blackberry, '83 225
Tart, Chocolate-Cherry, '97 33
Tarts, Cheery Cherry, '80 238
Topping, Cherry-Pineapple, '87 126
Torte, Black Forest Cherry, '88 178
Truffles, Chocolate-Cherry Cordial, '99 127
CHICKEN
Acapulco, Chicken, '84 32
à la King, Chicken, '79 218; '83 137; '87 197; '94 41
à la King, Easy Chicken, '93 14

Almond Chicken and Vegetables, '86 21
Almond Chicken, Creamy, '89 281
Almond Chicken, Spicy, '88 150
à l'Orange, Chicken, '84 277
Alouette, Chicken, '91 295
Andalusia, Chicken, '87 103
Appetizers, Chicken-Mushroom, '88 210
Appetizers, Sesame Chicken, '89 61
Apple Chicken, '85 57
Apricot Chicken, '92 12
Apricot Chicken Breasts, '88 301
Apricot Glaze, Chicken with Tangy, '98 275
Ariosto, Shrimp and Chicken, '79 31
Artichoke Chicken, '81 97
Artichoke Hearts, Chicken with, '88 54
Artichokes and Mushrooms, Chicken with, '90 35
Artichokes, Italian Chicken and, '95 68
Bag, Chicken in a, '86 M57; '87 23
Bake, Chicken, Ham, and Cheese, '87 217
Bake, Chicken-Italian Dressing, '91 199
Bake, Chicken-Tomato, '83 35
Bake, Crispy Chicken, '83 115
Baked Breast of Chicken with Marinated Bermuda Onions, '92 194
Baked Chicken and Artichoke Hearts, '82 260
Baked Chicken and Dressing, '79 296
Baked Chicken, Breaded, '81 76
Baked Chicken Breasts, Sherried, '79 83
Baked Chicken Breasts, Wine-, '83 177
Baked Chicken, Citrus Herb, '85 303
Baked Chicken, Fancy, '79 85
Baked Chicken, Herb-, '82 229
Baked Chicken in Wine, '81 109
Baked Chicken, Italian, '82 84
Baked Chicken, Marmalade, '99 286
Baked Chicken Parmesan, '83 137
Baked Chicken, Tomato-, '81 281; '82 30
Baked Chicken with Tarragon Sauce, '94 126
Baked Chicken with Wine-Soaked Vegetables, '84 277
Baked Hen with Cranberry Pan Gravy, '94 308
Baked Honey Chicken, '99 110
Baked in Wine, Chicken, '97 128
Baked Italian Chicken, '83 184
Baked Lemon Chicken, '85 190
Baked Mustard Chicken, '87 10
Baked Parmesan Chicken, '83 320
Bake, Herb Chicken, '82 186
Bake, Individual Chicken, '90 279
Bake, Mushroom-Chicken, '89 147
Bake, Parslied Chicken, '90 65
Bake, Pineapple Chicken, '82 120
Bake, Saucy Chicken, '84 220
Bake, Savory Chicken, '98 31
Bake, Seasoned Chicken, '94 278
Ball, Chicken-Cheese, '93 216
Ball, Chicken-Curry Cheese, '85 118
Balls, Coconut Curried Chicken, '91 165
Balls, Curried Chicken, '91 98
Banana Chicken with Black Bean Sauce, '96 156
Barbecued
Bake, Barbecued Chicken, '81 97
Bundles, Chicken-Mushroom, '80 157
Chicken, Barbecue, '86 122
Chicken, Barbecued, '82 97, 106; '83 103; '85 144; '86 153; '89 167
Chili-Barbecued Chicken, '98 170
Cranberry Chicken, Barbecued, '83 178
Glazed Barbecue Chicken, Carambola-, '92 246
Golden Barbecued Chicken, '83 136
Grilled Barbecued Chicken, '81 154
Legs and Thighs, Barbecued Chicken, '94 94

CHICKEN, Barbecued
(continued)

Lemon Barbecued Chicken, **'93** 215
Marinated Barbecued Chicken, **'79** 90
Old South Barbecued Chicken, **'82** 97; **'83** 103
Orange Barbecued Chicken, **'88** 123
Oven-Barbecued Chicken, Kentucky-Style, **'96** 328
Oven-Barbecued Cranberry Chicken, **'93** 332
Saucy Barbecued Chicken, **'83** 11
South-of-the-Border Barbecued Chicken, **'97** 311
Tangy Barbecued Chicken, **'86** 186; **'98** 170
White Barbecue Sauce, Chicken with, **'89** M84; **'97** 322
Zesty Barbecued Chicken, **'80** M76
Zippy Barbecued Chicken, **'83** 213
Basil Chicken, **'87** 171
Bengalese Chicken, **'79** 12
Bird's-Nest Chicken, **'88** 152
Birds of Paradise, **'82** 224
Biscuit, Chicken in a, **'79** 263; **'80** 30
Bites, Curried Chicken, **'85** 40
Bites, Savory Chicken, **'92** 209
Black Bean Puree, Spicy Chicken with, **'97** 48
Bourbon Chicken with Gravy, **'94** 252
Bourbon-Laced Tipsy Chicken with Peaches, **'97** 136
Bourbon-Purple Onion Relish, Chicken with, **'95** 253
Braised Bourbon Chicken, **'86** 51
Braised Chicken Breast in Lemon Cream Sauce, **'94** 184
Brandado, Chicken, **'84** 195
Breaded Chicken Breasts, **'89** M196
Breast of Chicken, Herbed, **'79** 100
Breasts, Celebrity Chicken, **'95** 60
Breasts Diane, Chicken, **'99** 213
Breasts, Greek Chicken, **'95** 170; **'98** 19
Breasts, Island Chicken, **'84** 68
Breasts Lombardy, Chicken, **'82** 242
Breasts, Salsa-Topped Chicken, **'94** 144
Breasts Saltimbocca, Chicken, **'98** 19
Breasts, Saucy Chicken, **'83** 184; **'87** 167
Breasts with Herb Butter, Chicken, **'89** 120
Breasts with Orange-Ginger Sauce, Chicken, **'97** 47
Breasts with Sage Orzo, Chicken, **'98** 169
Brioche Chicken Curry, **'88** 124
Broiled Chicken Breast Tarragon, **'89** 310
Broiled Chicken, Island, **'84** 288
Broth, Easy Microwave Chicken, **'90** M167
B'steeya with Chicken, **'98** 210
Bundles, Cheesy Chicken-and-Ham, **'84** 261
Bundles, San Antonio-Style Chicken, **'85** 251
Bundles with Bacon Ribbons, Chicken, **'87** 68
Burgers, Open-Faced Chicken-Onion, **'94** 139
Burgoo, Five-Meat, **'87** 3
Burgoo, Harry Young's, **'87** 3
Burgoo, Kentucky, **'97** 138
Burgoo, Old-Fashioned, **'87** 3
Buttermilk-Pecan Chicken, **'89** 166; **'97** 252
Cacciatore, Chicken, **'99** 213
Cajun Chicken over Rice, **'87** 268; **'88** 102; **'89** 67
Cakes with Avocado Cream, Southwestern Chicken-and-Corn, **'97** M311
Canapés, Chicken-Cucumber, **'98** 154
Caprese with Tomato-Basil Cream, Chicken, **'99** 240
Caramelized Chicken with Cranberry Conserve, **'98** 320

Cashew Chicken, **'79** 255; **'80** 8; **'83** 21
Cashew, Chicken, **'88** 38
Cashews, Chicken with, **'79** 207
Casseroles
à la Russell, Chicken, **'95** 175
Almond Casserole, Chicken-, **'94** 199
Artichoke Casserole, Chicken-and-, **'96** 133
Asparagus Casserole, Chicken-, **'83** 76; **'84** 71
Basil Chicken with Spinach Fettuccine, Creamy, **'97** 328
Breast-of-Chicken Fiesta, **'88** 151
Breasts, Creamy Baked Chicken, **'83** 24
Broccoli Casserole, Chicken-, **'79** 48; **'91** 315
Broccoli-Chicken Casserole, **'82** 33
Brown Rice Bake, Chicken-, **'91** 314
Cacciatore, Chicken, **'80** 39; **'83** 118; **'84** 9; **'86** 42
Cacciatore, Quick Chicken-and-Rice, **'88** 38
Cheesy Chicken Casserole, **'85** 34
Chicken Casserole, **'96** 103, 302
Chilaquiles con Pollo (Tortillas with Chicken), **'81** 66
Chile Chicken with Salsa, Baked, **'88** 147
Chiles Casserole, Chicken-and-, **'93** 107
Chili Bake, Chicken, **'93** 302
Chimichangas, Chicken, **'93** 68; **'94** 30
Chow Mein Chicken Casserole, **'96** 276
Company Chicken Bake, **'80** 301
Countryside Chicken Bake, **'88** 39
Dilly Chicken, **'90** 65
Divan Casserole, Chicken, **'82** M203
Divan, Chicken, **'80** M10; **'87** M218
Divan, Curried Chicken, **'80** 83
Divan, Easy Chicken, **'94** 310
Divan, Elegant Crêpes, **'81** 91
Divan, Gourmet Chicken, **'82** 83
Divan, Overnight Chicken, **'83** 198
Divan, Sherried Chicken, **'80** 38
Dressing Casserole, Chicken-and-, **'81** 263
Enchiladas, Chicken, **'80** 301; **'86** 296; **'90** 121
Enchiladas, Chicken-and-Spinach, **'91** 222
Enchiladas, Creamy Chicken, **'97** 250
Enchiladas, Easy Chicken, **'82** 89; **'86** 231
Enchiladas, Quicker Chicken, **'97** 312
Enchiladas, Three-Cheese Chicken, **'99** 330
Enchiladas with Tomatillo Sauce, Chicken, **'95** 206
Florentine, Chicken, **'93** 107
Florentine, Chicken-and-Shrimp, **'89** 64
Fontina-Baked Chicken, **'90** 64
Garlic-Spinach Chicken, **'92** 56
Good Chicken Casserole, Simply, **'95** 255
Green Bean Casserole, Chicken-, **'85** 296
Green Bean Casserole, Creamy Chicken-, **'97** 158
Grits, Chicken and, **'95** 263
Herbed Chicken, French, **'86** 89
Hot-and-Spicy Chicken Dinner, **'94** M94
King Ranch Chicken, **'95** 193; **'99** 330
Lasagna Bake, Chicken, **'95** 55
Lasagna, Chicken, **'87** M302; **'88** 90; **'92** 197; **'93** 25; **'96** 16
Lasagna, Creamy Ham-and-Chicken, **'95** 88
Lasagna Florentine, Chicken, **'95** 158
Macaroni and Chicken Casserole, **'80** 260
Macaroni Casserole, Chicken-, **'85** 219
Make-Ahead Chicken Casserole, **'84** 241
Manicotti, Creamy Chicken, **'85** 60
Mexicana, Chicken, **'91** M127
Mexican Chicken Casserole, **'82** 143
Mexican Chicken, Spicy, **'82** 89
Mexi-Chicken Casserole, **'93** 69; **'94** 30
Noodle Casserole, Chicken-, **'94** 286
Noodle Casserole, Chicken and Green, **'80** 32

Oyster-and-Chicken Casserole, **'99** 320
Paella Casserole, **'95** 254
Parmigiana, Chicken, **'80** 190
Parmigiana, Chicken-Eggplant, **'82** 212
Pasta Casserole, Chicken-and-, **'97** 192
Pecan Chicken, Lemony, **'96** 82
Pesto-Chicken Casserole, **'94** 231
Poppy Seed Chicken, **'99** 195
Quick Chicken Casserole, **'81** 91
Rice-and-Chicken Casserole, **'87** 154
Rice Casserole, Chicken-, **'86** 52; **'99** 215
Rice Casserole, Chicken and, **'80** 260
Rice Casserole, Creamy Chicken-, **'99** 21
Rice, Chicken and, **'95** 54
Salad, Baked Chicken, **'86** 297; **'87** 176
Scarborough Chicken, **'80** 38
Shrimp-and-Chicken Casserole, **'91** 102
Southwestern Casserole, **'99** 216
Spaghetti Casserole, Chicken-, **'84** 15
Spaghetti Squash and Chicken Skillet Casserole, **'94** 134
Spicy Chicken Bake, **'85** 251
Squash Casserole, Chicken-, **'95** 121
Squash-Chicken Casserole, Hearty Tex-Mex, **'99** 312
Sunday Chicken Casserole, **'83** 290
Superb Casserole, Chicken, **'89** 83
Supreme Casserole, Chicken, **'84** 219
Supreme, Hot Chicken, **'81** 76
Swiss Chicken, **'95** 54
Swiss Chicken Casserole, **'90** 67
Swiss Chicken Thighs, **'94** 282
Tangy Chicken, **'85** 251
Tetrazzini, Cheesy Chicken, **'83** M87
Tetrazzini, Chicken, **'79** 268; **'80** M75; **'83** 288; **'99** 61
Tortilla Bake, Chicken, **'82** 89
Tortilla Casserole, Chicken, **'81** 166
Vegetable-Chicken Bake with Sweet Bacon Dressing, **'93** 108
Wild Rice Casserole, Chicken-, **'84** 241; **'85** 65
Wild Rice Casserole, Chicken-and-, **'97** 192
Wild Rice, Chicken and, **'79** 248
Wild Rice Supreme, Chicken-, **'79** 77
Cassoulet, **'96** 328
Celery Skillet, Chicken-and-, **'88** 6
Chafing Dish Chicken, **'82** 284
Chalupas, Chicken, **'79** 185
Chalupas, Chicken-Olive, **'81** 227
Champagne Chicken, **'85** 251
Champagne Sauce, Chicken Breasts with, **'86** 49
Charcoal Broiled Chicken, **'79** 90
Charlemagne, Chicken, **'86** 293
Cheesecake, Chicken-Chile, **'92** 42
Cheesecake, Curried Chicken, **'90** 174
Chili, White, **'91** 284
Chili, White Christmas, **'98** 266
Chili, White Lightning Texas, **'92** 321
Chimichangas, Chicken, **'98** 95
Chimichangas, Oven-Fried Chicken, **'90** 175
Chinese, Chicken, **'94** 33
Chinese Chicken and Vegetables, **'81** 212
Chinese Chicken, Lazy Day, **'81** 3
Chinese-Style Chicken Dinner, **'89** 247
Chinese-Style Dinner, **'84** 26
Chop Suey, Chicken, **'81** 227
Chowder, Cheesy Chicken, **'92** 21
Chowder, Chicken, **'83** 20
Chowder, Creamy Chicken-Vegetable, **'92** 20
Chowder, Curried Chicken-and-Corn, **'92** 21
Chow Mein, Chicken, **'90** 68; **'98** 283
Chutney Chicken, **'86** 249
Coconut Chicken, **'98** 20
Coconut Chicken with Fresh Fruit, **'93** 294

Coconut Milk, Chicken in, '97 202
Company Chicken, '80 39; '83 125
Continental, Chicken, '82 274
Cordon Bleu, Chicken, '81 304; '82 83; '86 37; '93 126
Cordon Bleu, Company Chicken, '82 274
Cordon Bleu in Mushroom Sauce, Chicken, '86 198
Cordon Bleu, Pasta, '97 327
Corn Flake Chicken, '91 172
Country Captain Chicken, '94 252
Country Poulet, '86 292
Couscous, Chicken with, '97 325
Crabmeat Stuffing, Chicken Breasts with, '85 302
Cracked Wheat, "Fried," '89 31
Cream Cheese Chicken Breasts, '90 234
Creamed Chicken, '82 49, 284; '83 14
Creamed Chicken and Vegetables, '91 90
Creamed Chicken, Company, '82 84
Creamed Chicken in a Shell, '79 138
Creamed Chicken in Patty Shells, '86 123
Creamed Chicken over Confetti Rice Squares, '81 282; '82 31
Creamed Chicken over Cornbread, '86 231
Creamed Chicken Toppers, '99 240
Creamed Ham and Chicken, '81 M74
Creole, Chicken, '86 231; '89 33; '90 146
Creole Chicken, '94 93; '95 261
Creole Chicken and Rice, '92 262
Crêpes, Chicken, '80 39
Crêpes, Chicken-Vegetable, '83 70
Crêpes, Creamy Chicken, '81 200
Crêpes Divan, Elegant, '81 91
Crispy Chicken, '84 152
Croissants, Chutney-Chicken, '92 22
Croquettes and Mushroom Sauce, Chicken, '91 220
Croquettes, Chicken, '81 133
Croquettes, Crispy Chicken, '88 206
Crunchy Chicken, Janet's, '96 22
Curried Chicken, '86 43
Curried Chicken, Quick, '89 219; '99 92
Curried Chicken, Regal, '84 110
Curry, Chicken, '84 110; '85 220; '86 21; '89 219
Curry, Indian-Style Chicken, '97 119
Curry, Turban Chicken, '94 266
Cutlets with Lemon, Chicken, '85 8
Dagwoods, Chicken-Avocado, '96 200; '99 337
Dante's Chicken, '88 25
Delicacy, Chicken, '99 M23
Deviled Chicken, Zesty, '90 232
Dijon Chicken, '81 156; '99 21
Dijon Chicken with Pasta, '90 318
Dijon-Herb Chicken, '89 120
Dilled Chicken Paprika, '86 41
Dinner, Chicken-Mushroom, '81 3
Dinner, Chicken Peach, '79 77
Dinner, Curried Chicken Skillet, '95 47
Dinner, Healthful Chicken, '83 232
Dip, Hot Chicken, '80 86
Dixie Manor, Chicken à la, '85 3
Dressing, Chicken and, '99 42
Dressing, Chicken and Rice, '79 288
Dressing, Chicken Cornbread, '90 159
Dressing, Tipsy Chicken and, '88 151
Drummettes, Down-Home Chicken, '93 157
Drummettes, Ginger-Garlic Appetizer, '93 157
Drummettes, Orange-Pecan Chicken, '93 158
Drummettes, Southwestern Chicken, '93 158
Drumsticks, Breaded Chicken, '99 110
Drumsticks, Cajun-Style, '87 159
Drumsticks, Tangy, '97 120
Dumplings and Chicken, Biscuit, '99 326

Dumplings, Chicken and, '97 208
Dumplings, Chicken and Potato, '99 326
Dumplings, Chicken and Tortilla, '99 327
Dumplings, Country Chicken and, '85 254
Dumplings, Easy Chicken and, '86 21
Dumplings, Old-Fashioned Chicken and, '79 55; '83 228; '93 302
Dumplings, Quick Chicken and, '95 125
Dumplings with Herbed Broth, Chicken and, '95 338
Dumplings with Vegetables, Chicken and, '85 M56
Easy Chicken, '89 M129
Egg Bread, Chicken on, '95 120
Eggs, Chicken-Stuffed, '98 102
Empanadas, '92 156
Enchiladas, Chicken-Chile, '97 313
Enchiladas, Creamy, '93 174
Enchiladas Terrificas, '84 32
Enchiladas Verde, Chicken, '93 274
Enchiladas with Spicy Sauce, Chicken, '84 76
Enchiladas with Tomatillo Sauce, Chicken, '94 231
English Muffin Delight, '82 45
en Papillote, Chicken and Vegetables, '86 145
Fajita Fettuccine, '94 84
Fajita in a Pita, '90 177
Fajitas, Chicken, '88 231; '89 100; '90 204; '99 158
Fajita Spuds, Chicken, '96 238
Fancy Fowl, '81 76; '82 13
Fennel and Mushrooms, Chicken with, '97 93
Fettuccine, Cajun Chicken, '96 198
Fettuccine, Chicken and Dried Tomatoes over, '98 233
Fettuccine, Chicken-and-Tomatoes over, '90 204
Fettuccine, Chicken-Pecan, '86 52
Fiesta Chicken, Spicy, '84 234
Filling, Chicken, '81 200
Filling, Chicken Divan, '81 91
Filling, Chicken-Olive, '81 227
Filling, Crêpe, '96 48
Filling, Curried Chicken, '88 125
Filling Luau, Chicken, '79 81
Fingers, Buttermilk-Pecan Chicken, '93 165
Fingers, Chicken Little, '80 249
Fingers, Herb-Baked Chicken, '86 249
Fingers, No-Fry-Pan Chicken, '91 120
Fingers, Spicy Chicken, '91 162
Firecrackers, Texas, '95 96; '99 94
Flautas, '83 199
Flautas with Guacamole, Chicken, '89 226
Florentine with Mushroom Sauce, Chicken, '87 250
Foil, Chicken in, '91 134; '94 93
Foil-Wrapped Chicken, '99 108
Fricassee, White Chicken, '98 122
Fried
  Beaumont Fried Chicken, '88 92
  Best Ever Sunday Chicken, '89 234
  Best Fried Chicken, Our, '97 311
  Bites, French-Fried Chicken, '85 160
  Buttermilk Fried Chicken, Company, '86 177
  Cheese-Stuffed Chicken Thighs, Fried, '88 206
  Cream Gravy, Fried Chicken with, '85 241
  Crispy Fried Chicken Breasts, '80 155
  Curried Fried Chicken, '85 160
  Delicious Fried Chicken, '86 156
  Dixie Fried Chicken, '88 14
  Drummettes with Horseradish Sauce, Fried Chicken, '88 207
  Drumsticks, Buttermilk, '87 175
  Edna's Fried Chicken, '99 126

Finger Chicken, '96 89
Fingers, Chicken Almondette, '93 12
Garlic-Flavored Fried Chicken, '79 147
Garlic Fried Chicken, '82 148
Gravy, Fried Chicken, '95 235
Herbed Fried Chicken, '87 91
Herb-Seasoned Fried Chicken, '80 8
Kudzu Fried Chicken, '95 198
Lemon-Fried Chicken, '79 77
Lemon Fried Chicken, '82 275
Mandarin Chicken, Crispy, '86 119
Mexican Fried Chicken, '81 166; '87 176
Nuggets, Golden Chicken, '80 159
Nuggets, Lemon-Chicken, '87 283
Oven-Fried Chicken, '84 118; '93 90; '95 236; '99 212
Oven-Fried Chicken, Crisp, '94 220
Oven-Fried Chicken, Crunchy, '87 163
Oven-Fried Chicken, Crusty, '79 77
Oven-Fried Chicken, Golden-Brown, '86 21
Oven-Fried Chicken Legs, Jalapeño, '94 94
Oven-Fried Chicken, Nutty, '85 160
Oven-Fried Chicken, Southern, '86 37
Oven-Fried Chicken, Spicy, '97 307
Oven-Fried Chicken with Honey-Butter Sauce, '85 18
Oven-Fried Parmesan Chicken, '81 97; '82 148
Oven-Fried Pecan Chicken, '84 288
Oven-Fried Sesame Chicken, '79 77
Pan-Fried Chicken, Virginia, '96 142
Sesame Chicken, '82 148
Southern Fried Chicken Breasts, '98 20
Southern Fried Chicken, Our Best, '95 235
Special Fried Chicken, '88 220
Spicy Country-Fried Chicken, '82 148
Spicy Fried Chicken, '83 5; '88 129; '94 162
Spinach-Stuffed Chicken Breasts, Fried, '88 206
Sunday Dinner Fried Chicken, '88 110
Super Fried Chicken, '82 148
Timely Fried Chicken, '98 274
Traditional Fried Chicken, '82 148
Walnut Chicken, Deep-Fried, '87 175
Wings, Hot Buffalo, '87 176
Fried Rice, Chicken-Cashew, '99 171
Fruited Chicken en Crème, '83 264
Garden, Chicken-in-a-, '80 18
Garlic Chicken, Forty-Cloves-of-, '95 261
Garlic Chicken, Moroccan, '99 15
Ginger Chicken and Cashews, '85 M11
Ginger-Nut Chicken, '90 M33
Glazed Chicken and Pears, '99 21
Glazed Chicken, Fruit-, '80 211
Gold Nugget Chicken, '95 120
Gravy, Chicken, '99 34
Gravy, Chicken Smothered in, '99 41
Greek Lemon Chicken, '90 65
Grilled Bahamian Chicken with Cha-Cha Salsa, '97 160
Grilled Basil Chicken, '93 201
Grilled Chicken, '89 200; '92 170; '94 167
Grilled Chicken and Onions, Grits with, '99 17
Grilled Chicken and Vegetables, '99 200
Grilled Chicken Breasts, '84 172
Grilled Chicken Breasts with Lemon-Yogurt Coleslaw, '98 148
Grilled Chicken, Garlic-, '87 180
Grilled Chicken, Honey-Glazed, '99 213
Grilled Chicken, Honey-Lime, '96 189; '98 332
Grilled Chicken, Lemon-Herb, '95 87
Grilled Chicken, Smoky, '85 160
Grilled Chicken with Cha-Cha Salsa, '98 333
Grilled Chicken with Dill Sauce, '88 162

CHICKEN
(continued)

Grilled Chicken with Tabbouleh Salad, **'91** 70
Grilled Chicken with Vegetables Vinaigrette, **'91** 26
Grilled Cumin Chicken, **'87** 142
Grilled Ginger-Glazed Chicken, **'98** 166
Grilled Ginger-Orange Chicken, **'91** 26
Grilled Herbed Chicken Quarters, **'96** 171
Grilled Jalapeño Chicken, **'93** 213
Grilled Lime-Jalapeño Chicken, **'91** 87
Grilled Margarita-Marinated Chicken, **'97** 167
Grilled Tarragon-Dijon Thighs, **'97** 120
Grilled Teriyaki Chicken, **'92** 59
Grilled Yogurt-Lemon Chicken, **'81** 111
Gruyère, Chicken Breasts, **'80** 189
Gumbo, Chicken, **'79** 199; **'90** 26
Gumbo, Chicken-Andouille, **'98** 14
Gumbo, Chicken and Oyster, **'81** 198
Gumbo, Chicken-and-Sausage, **'89** 275; **'90** 256; **'94** 20
Gumbo, Chicken-Ham-Seafood, **'81** 6
Gumbo, Combo, **'81** 198
Gumbo, Easy Chicken, **'83** 156
Gumbo, Old-Style Shrimp, **'98** 97
Gumbo, The Gullah House, **'92** 237
Gumbo, Wild Game, **'91** 290
Gumbo with Smoked Sausage, Chicken, **'81** 199
Gumbo Ya Ya, **'87** 210
Hawaiian Chicken, **'82** 274
Hawaiian, Chicken, **'84** 88
Herb Chicken, Smoky, **'95** 116
Herbed Chicken, Sunny, **'86** 156
Herbed Chicken, Tangy, **'87** M302
Herb-Seasoned Chicken Breasts, **'93** M325
Honey Chicken, **'82** 55; **'88** 67
Honey-Curry Chicken, **'87** 36
Honey Sauce, Chicken in, **'89** 82
Honolulu Chicken, **'85** 52
Imperial Chicken, **'81** 238; **'98** 91
Italian Chicken, **'86** 122; **'91** 206
Italian Chicken Cutlets, **'89** 82
Italian Chicken-Mozzarella Melt, **'95** 153
Jalapeño, Easy Chicken, **'92** 310
Jambalaya, **'90** 26
Jambalaya, Chicken-and-Sausage, **'88** 200; **'91** 216
Jambalaya, 1-2-3, **'97** 301
Jambalaya, Red Rice, **'91** 18
Jambalaya, Smoky Cajun, **'96** 62
Jerk Chicken, Jamaican, **'96** 120; **'99** 121
Kabobs, Chicken, **'87** 141
Kabobs, Chicken-Avocado, **'82** 9; **'83** 68
Kabobs, Good-and-Easy Chicken, **'85** 87
Kabobs, Hawaiian, **'85** 157
Kabobs, Marinated Chicken, **'84** M144
Kabobs, Oriental Chicken, **'95** 193
Kabobs, Pineapple-Chicken, **'86** M328
Kabobs, Sesame Chicken, **'82** 165
Kabobs, Soy-Chicken, **'86** 156
Kabobs Supreme, Chicken, **'81** 124
Kiev, Chicken, **'80** 39
Kiev, Cranberry Chicken, **'87** 250
Kiev, Oven-Baked Chicken, **'86** 37
Kiev, Oven Chicken, **'82** 83
King Ranch Chicken, **'94** 26
la France, Chicken, **'86** 248
Lemonade Chicken, **'82** 163
Lemon and Wine, Chicken in, **'83** 281
Lemon Chicken, **'81** M138; **'86** 173; **'96** 49
Lemon Chicken and Vegetables, **'88** 118
Lemon Chicken Breasts, **'89** 18

Lemon Chicken, Sweet, **'79** 218
Lemon-Chicken, Sweet, **'84** 69
Lemon-Dill Chicken, **'93** 19
Lemon-Dill Chicken Sauté, **'91** 186
Lemon-Frosted Chicken, **'88** 170
Lemon-Garlic Chicken, **'89** M132; **'90** 35
Lemon-Herb Chicken, **'85** 127
Lemon Marinade, Chicken in, **'98** 128
Lemon-Pepper Chicken, **'89** 104
Lemon-Rosemary Chicken, **'94** 201
Lemon-Spinach Chicken, **'97** 104
Lime Butter, Chicken with, **'84** 68
Lime-Roasted Chicken Breasts, **'97** 100
Linguine, Chicken-Broccoli, **'98** 30
Livers
  Bits and Livers, Chicken, **'84** 222
  Chopped Chicken Livers, Grandma Rose's, **'96** 105
  en Brochette, Chicken Livers, **'84** 222
  Fried Chicken Livers, **'96** 105
  Garlic Chicken Livers, **'96** 105
  Italian Sauce, Chicken Livers in, **'83** 117
  Kabobs, Rumaki, **'82** 182
  Mushrooms, Chicken Livers with, **'81** 133
  Omelet, Chicken Liver, **'82** 44
  Orange Sauce, Chicken Livers in, **'82** 218
  Party Chicken Livers, **'83** 242
  Pâté, Chicken Liver, **'79** 153; **'81** 235; **'83** 108; **'84** 205; **'88** M132
  Pâté Maison, **'84** 222
  Potatoes, Chicken Livers and, **'82** 218
  Rice, Chicken Livers with, **'80** 200; **'81** 58; **'84** 292
  Rice Dish, Chicken Livers and, **'82** 218
  Risotto, Chicken Livers, **'82** 218
  Roll-Ups, Chicken Liver and Bacon, **'80** 200; **'81** 57
  Rumaki, **'80** M136
  Sautéed Chicken Livers, **'80** 200; **'81** 57
  Scrumptious Chicken Livers, **'84** 230
  Spread, Sherried Liver, **'80** 86
  Stroganoff, Chicken Livers, **'80** 200; **'81** 57
  Supreme, Chicken Livers, **'81** 298
  Turnovers, Chicken Liver, **'79** 141
  Wine Sauce, Chicken Livers in, **'81** 104
  Wine Sauce, Chicken Livers with Marsala, **'81** 76
Log, Chicken-Pecan, **'81** 290
Luzianne, Poulet, **'86** 197
Madrid, Chicken, **'97** 326
Marengo, Chicken, **'92** 70
Marinara, Chicken, **'86** 77
Marinated Breast of Chicken, **'87** 123
Marinated Chicken, **'87** 61
Marinated Chicken, Balsamic, **'98** 130
Marinated Chicken Breasts, **'90** 54
Marinated Chicken Strips and Vegetables, **'90** 110
Marsala, Chicken, **'83** 137; **'89** 237
Medaillons in Pepper Pesto, Chicken-Rice, **'90** 97
Mediterranean Chicken, **'91** 27; **'94** 72
Medley, Creamy Ham-and-Chicken, **'92** 272
Mexican Chicken, **'80** 124
Milano, Chicken, **'84** 220
Minted Chicken, **'81** 102
Mole, Chicken, **'81** 193
Mole Sauce, Chicken with, **'93** 34
Monterey, Chicken, **'82** 275
Mornay Sauce, Chicken Breasts in, **'81** 273
Mousse, Curried Chicken, **'95** 328
Muffins, Broccoli-Chicken, **'96** 27
Murphy, Chicken, **'89** 82
Mushroom Sauce, Chicken with, **'99** 22

Mushrooms, Chicken-Stuffed, **'80** 162
Mustard Chicken, **'80** 222; **'86** 293; **'93** 239
Mustard Cream Sauce, Chicken in, **'92** 181
Nachos, Chicken, **'84** 244
Nuggets, Baked Chicken, **'81** 149; **'89** 18
Nuggets, Golden Chicken, **'80** 159; **'81** 237
Nuggets, Lemon-Chicken, **'86** 337
Nuggets Supreme, Chicken, **'85** 160
Nuggets with Pineapple Sauce, Chicken, **'84** 236
Omelet, Indian, **'99** 92
Onion-Crusted Chicken, **'88** 40
Orange-Almond Sauce, Chicken in, **'79** 219; **'80** 13
Orange-Avocado Chicken, **'80** 38
Orange Chicken, **'83** 278; **'86** M140
Orange Chicken Breasts with Parslied Rice, **'87** 242
Orange Chicken, Skillet-Seared, **'96** 68
Orange, Lime, and Ginger Sauce, Chicken with, **'92** 123
Orange Sauce, Chicken Breasts with, **'79** 77
Orange Sauce, Chicken in, **'83** 8
Orange Sauce, Skillet Chicken in, **'94** 252
Oregano Chicken, **'95** 84
Oriental Chicken, **'80** 40, 208; **'82** 131
Oriental Chicken with Peanuts, **'82** 236
Oriental Chicken with Pineapple, **'86** 42
Oriental Stuffed Pockets, **'79** 14
Packets, Chicken, **'96** 104
Paella, **'97** 328
Paella, Chicken-Pork-Shrimp, **'82** 245
Paella, Chicken-Seafood, **'88** 68
Paella, Shrimp-and-Chicken, **'94** 168
Paella, Spanish, **'85** 26
Paella Valenciana, **'82** 246
Paprika Chicken, **'95** 125
Parchment, Chicken and Leeks in, **'97** 290
Parmesan, Chicken, **'83** 184; **'95** 210
Parmesan Chicken, Crispy, **'80** M76
Pasquale, Chicken, **'83** 67
Pasta and Chicken, Taste-of-Texas, **'92** 78
Pasta and Garden Vegetables, **'87** 192
Pasta, Chicken-and-Broccoli, **'87** 286
Pasta, Chicken Caesar, **'97** 87
Pasta Platter, Cold, **'88** 42
Pasta Primavera, Chicken-, **'91** 72
Pasta, Quick Chicken and, **'93** 14
Pasta with Rosemary, Chicken-Artichoke, **'98** 15
Pastry, Chicken in, **'86** 122
Pâté, Vegetable-Chicken, **'86** 66
Peach Sauce, Chicken with, **'98** 334
Peachy Chicken, **'90** 212
Peanut Butter-Marmalade Chicken, **'81** 282; **'82** 30
Pecan Chicken, **'90** 54; **'99** 332
Pecan-Rice Dressing, Chicken with, **'85** M57
Pecan-Sausage Stuffing, Chicken Breasts with, **'94** 212
Penne Pasta, Chicken, Asparagus, and Mushrooms with, **'98** 212
Pepper-Sage Chicken, **'96** 237
Peppers, Chicken Breasts with Curried, **'90** 227
Peppers, Curried Chicken-Stuffed, **'87** 19
Peppers, Devilish Chicken, **'80** 65
Pesto Chicken and Pasta, **'89** M132
Pesto Chicken with Basil Cream, **'89** 158
Phyllo, Chicken in, **'87** 286
Phyllo Pastry, Chicken Breasts in, **'91** 105
Piccata, Chicken, **'83** 35; **'84** 230
Piccata, Herbed Chicken, **'88** 28
Pie, Biscuit-Topped Chicken, **'86** 157, 264
Pie, Cheesy Mexican Chicken, **'82** 142
Pie, Chicken, **'81** 281; **'82** 31
Pie, Chicken Dumpling, **'95** 245; **'96** 55

Pie, Chicken Pot, **'81** 210; **'82** 114; **'84** 21; **'94** 21; **'95** 54, 256; **'96** 75
Pie, Chicken-Vegetable Pot, **'81** 281; **'82** 30
Pie, Deluxe Chicken, **'88** 298
Pie, Double-Crust Chicken, **'87** 111
Pie, Double-Crust Chicken Pot, **'90** 220
Pie, Easy Chicken Pot, **'83** 156; **'89** 218
Pie, Egg-Stra Special Chicken, **'86** 264
Pie, Greek Chicken Phyllo, **'92** 328
Pie, Montezuma Tortilla, **'83** 199
Pie, Nana's Chicken, **'90** 25
Pie, Old-Fashioned Chicken Pot, **'92** 271
Pie, Savory Southern Chicken, **'90** 24
Pie, Thick 'n' Crusty Chicken Pot, **'87** 267; **'88** 102; **'89** 67
Pie with Cheese Crust, Chicken Pot, **'86** 264
Pilaf, Chicken, **'82** 246
Pilaf, Chicken-Vegetable, **'97** 51
Pilau, Chicken, **'99** 184
Piña Colada Chicken, **'86** 21
Pineapple Chicken, **'83** M194; **'85** 3
Pineapple, Chicken and, **'81** 281; **'82** 30
Pineapple Chicken, Oriental, **'84** 288
Piquant Chicken, **'86** 76
Piquant, Chicken, **'94** 19
Pita, Oriental Chicken, **'89** 216
Pita, Peppery Chicken in, **'93** 62
Pitas, Acadian Stuffed, **'90** 177
Pitas, Fajita, **'99** 239
Pizza, Chicken, **'94** 218
Pizza, Chicken-and-Purple Onion, **'97** 47
Pizza, Gruyère-Chicken, **'87** 182
Pizza, Mexican Chicken, **'97** 321
Pizzas, Chicken-and-Three-Cheese French Bread, **'96** 94
Pizza, Southwest Deluxe, **'95** 268
Plum Sauce, Chicken with, **'82** 236
Poached Chicken and Vegetables, Ginger-, **'98** 229
Poached Chicken Breast in Wine, **'91** 184
Poached Chicken Breasts, Wine-, **'85** 58
Poached Chicken Breast with Turned Vegetables and Chive Sauce, **'94** 309
Poached Chicken, Whole, **'98** 229
Poached Chicken with Black Beans and Salsa, **'87** 217
Poached Chicken with Creamy Mustard Sauce, Champagne-, **'94** 24
Poblano Chicken, Creamy, **'98** 42
Pollo Almendrado (Chicken in Almond Sauce), **'81** 193
Pollo con Calabacita (Mexican Chicken with Zucchini), **'82** 219
Pollo en Mole de Cacahuate (Chicken with Peanut Mole Sauce), **'80** 194
Pollo en Pipián, Mexican, **'88** 31
Poppy Seed Chicken, **'94** 108
Potatoes, Chicken-Cheese Stuffed, **'86** 55
Potatoes, Creamed Beef and Chicken-Topped, **'83** 210
Potatoes, Gumbo, **'95** 22
Potatoes, Sweet-and-Sour-Topped, **'83** 4
Pot, Chicken in a, **'81** 3
Pretzel-Crusted Chicken, **'94** 252
Princess Chicken, **'86** 122
Provolone, Chicken, **'93** 323
Puffs, Appetizer Chicken, **'85** 72
Puffs, Chicken Nut, **'81** 260
Quesadillas, Chicken-and-Black Bean, **'96** 288
Quesadillas, Spicy Chicken, **'95** 42
Quesadillas with Chipotle Salsa, Chicken-and-Brie, **'99** 311
Quiche, Chicken Divan, **'88** M125
Quiche, Chicken-Pecan, **'91** 206

Quiche Noël, **'82** 310
Quick, Chicken, **'90** 117
Ragoût with Cheddar Dumplings, Chicken, **'94** 44
Raspberry Chicken, **'97** 66
Rice and Chicken, Salsa, **'99** 109
Rice, Chicken Caruso and, **'89** 177
Rice, Chicken with Curried, **'98** 127
Rice, Moorish Chicken with, **'98** 127
Rice Pilaf, Chicken Breasts with Fruited, **'92** 307
Rice, Shortcut Chicken and, **'90** 220
Rice, Spicy Chicken and, **'88** 200
Roast Chicken, **'93** 14
Roast Chicken and Brown Rice, **'83** 268
Roast Chicken and Vegetables, **'81** 3
Roast Chicken with Pineapple-Mustard Glaze, **'89** 83
Roast Chicken with Rice, **'95** 261
Roasted Chicken and Potatoes, **'98** 289
Roasted Chicken, Herb-, **'87** 155
Roasted Chicken, Hot Oven-, **'98** 108
Roasted Chicken, Lemon-, **'95** 24
Roasted Chicken, Lemon-Garlic, **'98** 108
Roasted Chicken, Rice-Stuffed, **'88** 38
Roasted Chicken, Savory, **'98** 21
Roasted Chicken, Slow-, **'98** 108
Roasted Chicken with Lemon, Garlic, and Rosemary, **'97** 61
Roasted Chicken with Poblano Vinaigrette and Corn Pudding, **'99** 71
Roasted Chicken with Vegetables, **'98** 108
Roasted Citrus Chicken, Clay Oven-, **'98** 108
Roasted Stuffed Chicken, **'98** 109
Rockefeller Chicken, **'79** 219
Rolls à la Swiss, Chicken-and-Ham, **'92** 42
Rolls, Chicken-Asparagus, **'86** M211
Rolls, Crispy Chicken, **'84** 288
Rolls Élégante, Chicken, **'80** 210
Rolls, Hearts of Palm Chicken, **'89** 201
Rolls, Hearty Salad, **'81** 206
Rolls Jubilee, Chicken, **'87** 118
Rolls, Mexican Chicken, **'93** 242
Rolls, Pesto-Stuffed Chicken, **'93** 82
Rolls, Southwestern Cabbage, **'97** 214
Rollups, Cheesy Chicken, **'82** 44
Rollups, Chicken, **'85** 179; **'88** 38
Rollups, Chicken and Spinach, **'80** 90; **'82** M68
Rollups, Imperial Chicken, **'80** 217
Rollups in Gravy, Chicken, **'83** 184
Rollups, Sunshine Chicken, **'85** 251
Romano, Chicken alla, **'83** M58
Romano, Chicken Breasts, **'79** 218
Romanoff, Chicken, **'84** 292
Roquefort Chicken, **'89** 320
Rosemary Chicken, Pinot Noir Risotto with, **'97** 214
Rotelle, Chicken and Tomato with, **'87** 108
Saffron Chicken with Prunes, **'97** 264
Salads
Almond-Chicken Salad Shanghai, **'90** 160
Almond Salad, Chicken-, **'81** 133
Aloha Chicken Salad, **'80** 297
Amandine, Chicken Salad, **'81** 37
Ambrosia, Chicken Salad, **'85** 216
Apple Salad, Chicken-, **'90** 216
Apricot-Chicken Salad, **'99** 163
Apricot Salsa, Chicken with, **'98** 126
Artichoke-Chicken-Rice Salad, **'94** 132
Artichoke-Chicken-Rice Salad, Mediterranean, **'97** 321
Artichokes, Chicken Salad with, **'86** 186
Asian Chicken Salad, **'99** 124
Asparagus-Chicken Salad, **'89** 83
Aspic-Topped Chicken Salad, **'88** 88

Avocado-Chicken Salad, **'87** 107
Avocado Salad, Chicken-, **'80** 139
Avocado Salad, Fruited Chicken-, **'82** 101
Avocado Salad Platter, Chicken-, **'83** 2
Avocado Salad, Tossed Chicken-, **'80** 4
Avocados, Chicken Salad in, **'85** 216
Baked Chicken Salad, **'86** 297; **'87** 176
Barbecue Chicken Salad, Warm, **'99** 124
Basil-Chicken-Vegetable Salad, **'92** 162
Black Bean Salad, Chicken-, **'99** 124
Black-Eyed Pea Salad, Chicken-and-, **'97** 305
BLT Chicken Salad, **'87** 144
Blue Cheese Chicken Salad, **'94** 81
Blue Cheese, Chicken Salad with, **'97** 97
Broccoli-Chicken Salad, **'90** 129
Caesar Salad, Chicken, **'96** 26
Celery Salad, Chicken-, **'81** 187
Chef's Salad, **'98** 209
Chicken Salad, **'86** 232, 261; **'96** 67
Chop Suey Salad, **'81** 37
Chutney-Chicken Salad, **'87** 74
Chutney Salad, Chicken, **'82** 108
Coconut-Chicken Salad, Curried Poached Pears with, **'97** 93
Coleslaw, Chicken, **'84** 2
Cream Puff Bowl, Chicken Salad in, **'86** 232
Crisp Salad, Crunchy, **'95** 28
Crunchy Chicken Salad, **'86** 157, 207
Curried Chicken-and-Orange Salad, **'87** 144
Curried Chicken-Rice Salad, **'92** 190
Curried Chicken Salad, **'79** 219; **'84** 66; **'85** 96; **'86** 131; **'89** 176
Curried Chicken Salad, Royal, **'96** 200
Curried Chicken Salad with Asparagus, **'81** 36
Dilled Chicken Salad, **'91** 212
Exotic Luncheon Salad, **'83** 210
Fancy Chicken Salad, **'79** 55
Filling, Chicken Salad, **'87** 106
Fried Chicken Ginger Salad, **'93** 290
Fruit, Chicken Salad with, **'82** 171
Fruited Chicken Salad, **'84** 25, 290; **'88** 88; **'90** 318
Fruited Chicken Salad in Avocados, **'87** 41
Fruit Salad, Chicken-, **'82** 79; **'90** 234
Fruity Chicken Salad, **'83** 157
Grapes, Chicken Salad with, **'86** 117
Greek Chicken Salad, **'97** 92; **'98** 329
Green Salad with Chicken, Mixed, **'80** 54
Grilled Asian Chicken Salad, **'96** 158
Grilled Chicken-and-Fruit Salad, **'96** 155
Grilled Chicken on Greens, **'99** 201
Grilled Chicken-Rice Salad, **'98** 148
Grilled Chicken Salad, Moroccan, **'95** 231
Grilled Chicken Salad with Raspberry Dressing, **'95** 202
Hoisin Chicken-and-Pasta Salad, **'99** 125
Hot Chicken Salad, **'81** 201; **'83** 196; **'98** 290
Hot Chicken Salad, Country Club-Style, **'86** 10
Hot Chicken Salad, Crunchy, **'80** 138
Hot Chicken Salad Pinwheel, **'80** 139
Italian, Chicken Salad, **'89** 18
Layered Chicken Salad, **'89** 162
Macadamia Chicken Salad, **'80** 138
Macaroni-Chicken Salad, **'85** 296; **'86** 302
Macaroni-Chicken Salad, Dilled, **'92** 142
Mama Hudson's Chicken Salad, **'93** 238
Mandarin Chicken, Carousel, **'79** 88
Mango, Chicken Salad with, **'86** 215
Marinated Chicken-Grape Salad, **'85** 74
Marinated Chicken-Raspberry Salad, **'93** 190
Mexican Chicken Salad, **'85** 84; **'88** 272
Minted Chicken Salad, **'92** 104
Mold, Chicken-Cucumber, **'80** 175
Mold, Chicken Salad, **'83** 80; **'84** 163

Nectarine Chicken Salad, '79 175
Noodle Salad, Chicken, '95 25
Old-Fashioned Chicken Salad, '83 79
Oriental Chicken Salad, '85 216; '88 271;
  '91 43; '96 92
Oriental, Chicken Salad, '90 146
Overnight Salad, '97 305; '98 18
Parmesan-Chicken Salad, '98 234
Pasta-Chicken Salad, Tarragon, '87 155
Pasta Salad, Chicken, '88 89
Pasta Salad, Grilled Chicken-, '94 64
Peachy Chicken Salad, '97 193
Pea Salad, Chicken-, '83 218
Persian Chicken Salad, '81 12
Pineapple-Chicken Salad Pie, '80 138
Pineapple-Nut Chicken Salad, '83 80
Pocket, Chicken Salad in a, '88 139
Polynesian Chicken Salad, '88 272
Poulet Rémoulade, '87 144
Rice Salad, Chicken-, '81 203; '97 93
Rice Salad, Chicken-and-, '97 92
Rice Salad, Hot Chicken-and-, '83 22
Rice Salad, Nutty Chicken-, '83 157
Ring, Chicken Salad, '90 123
Ring Salad, Chicken Jewel, '83 282
Roasted Chicken Salad, '93 14
Rolls, Hearty Salad, '81 206
Sandwiches, Asian Chicken Salad, '98 223
Sandwiches, Chicken-Salad Finger, '85 119
Sandwiches, Hot Chicken Salad, '96 74
South Sea Island Chicken Salad, '97 88
Southwestern Chicken Salad, '88 88
Spaghetti Salad, Chicken-, '90 146
Special Chicken Salad, '85 82; '87 183;
  '88 M193
Spinach-Strawberry Salad, Chicken-, '97 92
Spinach Tossed Salad, Chicken-and-, '83 157
Spread, Chicken Salad Party, '88 M8
Stack-Up Salad, Chicken, '83 80
Summer Chicken Salad, '83 145
Summery Chicken Salad, '95 138
Super Chicken Salad, '82 174
Supreme, Chicken Salad, '79 107, 152; '89 176
Taco Chicken Salad, Ranch, '97 315
Taco Salad, Chicken, '94 M136
Tahitian Chicken Salad, '84 120
Tarragon Chicken Salad, '90 199
Tarts, Chicken Salad, '84 257
Thai Chicken Salad, '95 177
Tortellini Salad, Chicken, '87 288
Tortilla Salads, Mexican Chicken, '95 129
Tropical Chicken Boats for Two, '82 186
Tropical Chicken Salad, '85 216; '96 127
Twist, Chicken Salad with a, '84 221
Vegetable-Chicken Salad, '91 287
Vegetable-Chicken Vinaigrette Salad, '86 135
Walnut-Chicken Salad, '89 14; '96 243
Walnut Salad, Sunburst Chicken-and-, '93 91
Wild Rice-Chicken Salad, '83 146; '99 55
Saltimbocca alla Romana, Chicken, '80 212
San Antonio-Style Chicken, '81 166
Sandwich, Chicken Parmigiana, '94 65
Sandwich, Crispy Chicken, '81 114
Sandwiches, Baked Chicken, '79 164; '80 130;
  '84 165
Sandwiches, Cheesy Chicken, '82 190
Sandwiches, Chicken-Almond Pocket, '81 240;
  '83 69
Sandwiches, Chicken-Benedict Bagel, '96 250
Sandwiches, Chicken Club, '86 160

Sandwiches, Curried Chicken Tea, '97 23
Sandwiches, Gouda Lover's Chicken, '99 195
Sandwiches, Grilled Chicken 'n' Cheese, '99 240
Sandwiches, Hot Brown, '80 202
Sandwiches, Hot Chicken, '83 291
Sandwiches, Marinated Chicken, '86 M45
Sandwiches, Puffed Chicken, '82 35
Sandwiches, Southwestern Chicken, '96 23
Sandwiches, Summer Open-Faced, '99 201
Sandwiches, Toasted Chicken-and-Cheese,
  '85 242
Sandwich, Ham 'n' Cheese Chicken, '95 153
Sandwich, Jamaican Chicken, '95 153
Sandwich, Jerk Chicken, '98 333
Sandwich, Marinated Chicken in a, '86 185
Sanibel Island Chicken, '97 66
Saté, Chicken, '99 134
Sauce, Chicken Curry, '90 117
Sauce, Creamy Chicken, '81 91
Sauce, Curry, '95 18
Saucy Chick-Wiches, '81 25; '82 31; '83 34
Sausage with Fennel, Chicken, '98 312
Sauté, Chicken-Apple, '97 48
Sautéed Chicken Breasts, '87 36
Sauté, Savory Chicken, '88 254; '89 120
Sauté, Sherry-Chicken, '87 218
Sauté, Sweet Pepper-Chicken, '89 104
Scallopini with Lemon Sauce, Chicken, '86 156
Scallopini with Peppers, Chicken, '85 78
Scotch Cream, Chicken in, '88 42
Seasoned Browned Chicken, '85 25
Seasoned Chicken, '99 316
Seasoned Chicken, Crunchy, '87 217
Seasoning Blend, Poultry, '88 28
Sesame Chicken, '85 252; '86 122; '97 256;
  '98 20
Sesame Chicken, Hawaiian, '81 106
Sesame Chicken Strips, '98 250
Sesame Chicken with Noodles, '88 M125
Sesame-Crusted Chicken with Pineapple Salsa,
  '96 226
Sesame-Dijon Chicken, '98 96
Shells, Southwestern Stuffed, '99 238
Sherried Chicken, '79 214
Sherried Chicken with Artichokes, '87 143
Sherry Chicken with Rice, '81 97
Shortcakes, Cheesy Chicken, '95 98
Sicilian Chicken, '97 142
Skewers, Taco-Chicken, '99 119
Skillet, Cheesy Chicken, '80 115
Skillet Chicken, '81 180
Skillet Chicken Dinner, '86 249; '89 247
Skillet Chicken, Spicy, '94 220
Skillet Company Chicken, '82 60
Skillet, Confetti Chicken, '97 327
Skillet Dinner, Antipasto, '97 327
Skillet Dinner, Chicken-and-Rice, '98 127
Snow Peas, Chicken with, '83 187
Soufflé, Chicken-Chestnut, '79 107
Soups
  Artichoke, and Mushroom Soup, Chicken,
    '92 324
  Asparagus-and-Chicken Soup, Creamy, '95 82
  Bean-Chicken Soup, '99 283
  Broccoli-and-Chicken Soup, '90 202
  Chicken Soup, '81 98
  Chowder, Chicken-and-Roasted Vegetable,
    '97 21
  Chowder Sauterne, Chicken, '84 235
  Chunky Chicken-Noodle Soup, '88 12
  Corn Soup, Cheesy Chicken-, '97 158
  Cream of Chicken Soup, '85 243
  Cream Soup, Chicken-Almond, '92 21
  Curried Chicken Soup, '86 34

  Enchilada Soup, Chicken, '86 22
  French Soup Maigre, '98 125
  Ham, and Oyster Soup, Chicken, '79 198
  Homemade Chicken Soup, '82 34
  Lime Soup, '88 31
  Mexican Chicken Soup, '84 234
  Noodle Soup, Chicken, '80 264; '95 45; '98 30
  Noodle Soup, Creamy Chicken, '99 20
  Pepper-and-Chicken Soup, Roasted, '90 58
  Quick Chicken Soup, '86 M72
  Rice Soup, Chicken-and-, '88 236
  Sopa de Lima, '79 211
  Spicy Chicken Soup, '97 268
  Stock, Chicken, '95 18
  Tortilla Soup, '98 291; '99 310
  Vegetable Soup, Chicken-, '88 18; '99 60
  Wild Rice Soup, Creamy Chicken-and-,
    '98 M334
Soy and Wine, Chicken in, '84 26
Soy-Garlic Chicken, '98 128
Spaghetti, Chicken, '83 105; '87 221; '98 329
Spaghetti, Chicken-Vegetable, '92 281; '98 296
Spanish Chicken, '98 183
Special Occasion Chicken, '91 206
Spiced Chicken, Crunchy, '85 M57
Spiced Fruited Chicken with Almond Rice,
  '81 195
Spicy Chicken Dish, '87 267; '88 103; '89 66
Spinach Fettuccine, Easy Chicken with, '88 89
Spinach Noodles, Chicken and, '82 19
Spread, Festive Chicken, '87 158
Spread, Low-Fat Chicken, '82 290
Spread, Tasty Chicken, '84 193
Spring Rolls, '99 238
Steamed Dinner, Easy, '83 M314
Stews
  Brunswick Chicken Stew, '87 4
  Brunswick Stew, '80 264; '97 138, 315
  Brunswick Stew, Bama, '87 4
  Brunswick Stew, Breeden Liles's, '91 14
  Brunswick Stew, Chicken, '97 234
  Brunswick Stew, Dan Dickerson's, '91 16
  Brunswick Stew, Gay Neale's, '91 17
  Brunswick Stew, Georgian, '92 35
  Brunswick Stew, Jeff Daniel's, '91 16
  Brunswick Stew, Sonny Frye's, '87 4
  Brunswick Stew, Van Doyle's Family-Size,
    '91 14
  Brunswick Stew, Virginian, '92 34
  Brunswick Stew, Virginia Ramsey's Favorite,
    '91 16
  Chicken Stew, '97 26
  Chili-Chicken Stew, '90 319
  Dumplings, Chicken Stew and, '84 4
  Kale, and Chickpea Stew, Chicken, '98 47
  Santa Fe Chicken Stew, '97 193
  Strader Stew, '89 28
Sticks, Italian Chicken, '98 25
Sticky Chicken, '97 239
Stir-Fried Chicken Curry, '87 51
Stir-Fried Chicken, Zesty, '83 82
Stir-Fry, Apple-Sesame-Chicken, '92 226
Stir-Fry Chicken à l'Orange, '83 82
Stir-Fry, Chicken and Snow Pea, '95 157
Stir-Fry, Chicken and Vegetable, '82 237
Stir-Fry, Chicken-and-Vegetable, '96 19
Stir-Fry Chicken and Vegetables, '86 249
Stir-Fry Chicken-and-Vegetables, '86 68
Stir-Fry, Chicken-Broccoli, '82 33
Stir-Fry, Chicken-Vegetable, '83 151; '84 13, 141
Stir-Fry Chicken with Vegetables, '96 128
Stir-Fry, Chicken-Zucchini, '84 50
Stir-Fry, Chinese Chicken, '90 100
Stir-Fry, Easy Chicken, '91 124

Stir-Fry, Herb-Chicken, '89 177
Stir-Fry, Hurry-Up Chicken, '91 124
Stir-Fry, Kyoto Orange-Chicken, '87 96
Stir-Fry, Mexican, '92 126
Stir-Fry, Orange-Chicken, '84 68
Stir-Fry, Pineapple-Chicken, '89 176
Stir-Fry, Shiitake-Chicken, '89 61
Stir-Fry, Sweet-and-Sour Chicken, '98 204
Stir-Fry Vegetables with Chicken, '84 195
Stock, Light Poultry, '90 31
Strips, Nutty Chicken, '99 111
Strips with "Come Back" Dipping Sauce, Miss
    Mary's Chicken, '96 213
Strips, Zippy Chicken, '84 205
Stroganoff, Chicken, '99 41
Stroganoff, Chicken-and-Broccoli, '89 M248
Strudel, Chicken-Goat Cheese, '98 28
Stuffed Chicken Breasts, '82 36; '85 291; '88 50;
    '89 274
Stuffed Chicken Breasts, Apple-Bacon, '99 313
Stuffed Chicken Breasts, Hawaiian, '99 64
Stuffed Chicken Breasts over Angel Hair, Goat
    Cheese-, '97 144
Stuffed Chicken Breasts, Peach-, '79 177
Stuffed Chicken Breasts Sardou, '87 269
Stuffed Chicken Breasts, Walnut-, '85 293
Stuffed Chicken Breasts with White Bean Puree,
    '98 270
Stuffed Chicken Breasts with White Grape
    Sauce, '80 38
Stuffed Chicken, Crab-, '84 101
Stuffed Chicken in Puff Pastry, Spinach-, '92 125
Stuffed Chicken, Rice-, '81 4
Stuffed Chicken Rolls, Spinach-, '86 248
Stuffed Chicken Thighs, '82 84
Stuffed Chicken, Vegetable-, '89 M65
Stuffed Chicken, Wild Rice-, '79 219
Stuffed Chicken with Sautéed Peppers and
    Mushrooms, Herb-, '91 26
Stuffed Chicken with Tomato-Basil Pasta, Basil-,
    '94 M204
Sub, Chicken, '98 287
Sunday Chicken, '95 228
Sunshiny Chicken, '81 309
Supremes de Volaille à Blanc (Chicken Breasts
    in Cream Sauce), '82 83
Sweet-and-Sour Chicken, '79 106; '83 184;
    '84 218; '86 217, 240; '90 161; '91 202;
    '97 325
Sweet-and-Sour Chicken Nuggets, '90 168
Sweet-and-Sour Chicken Wings, '90 206
Sweet-and-Sour Lemon Chicken, '84 93
Sweet-and-Sour Shrimp and Chicken, '87 267;
    '88 103; '89 66
Szechuan Chicken, '98 155
Szechuan Chicken with Angel Hair Pasta, '97 91
Szechwan Chicken, '83 85
Szechwan Chicken with Cashews, '81 212
Tacos, Chicken-and-Bean, '93 293
Tacos, Pizza-Flavored Chicken, '95 340
Tahitian Chicken, '84 68
Tamales, Chicken, '88 151
Tangy Chicken, '85 251; '86 292; '87 35
Tarragon Chicken, '86 231
Tarts, Deviled Chicken, '94 14
Tempura Delight, Chicken, '85 66
Teriyaki, Chicken, '80 M76
Teriyaki Chicken, '91 163
Teriyaki Chicken Wings, '85 300; '86 18
Terrine, Chicken-Vegetable, '84 131
Terrine, Cold Chicken-Leek, '92 145
Terrine Ring, Chicken, '84 132
Terrine, Vegetable-Chicken, '83 224
Tomato Aspic, Chicken in, '84 190

Tomatoes and Sausage, Chicken with, '97 266
Tortilla Stack, Cheesy Chicken-, '86 3
Toss, Quick Chicken, '87 M124
Tostadas, Chicken, '93 204; '95 122
Tostadas, Quick Chicken, '99 159
Undercover Chicken, '97 64
Valencia, Chicken-and-Rice, '85 113
Vegetable Platter, Chicken-and-, '88 M52
Vegetables, Chicken and, '88 165
Vegetables, Jim's Chicken and, '99 237
Vegetables with Ginger-Soy Sauce, Chicken and,
    '91 32
Vermouth, Chicken and Vegetables, '87 M37
Véronique, Chicken, '84 260; '85 302
Waffles, Southern Chicken-Pecan, '82 231
Walnut Chicken, '85 126
Walnut Chicken and Vegetables, '85 194
Walnut Chicken, Crispy, '90 89
Wellington, Chicken Breasts, '84 22
White Wine, Chicken in, '81 97
Wild Rice, Chicken-Fried, '89 24; '91 132
Wild Rice, Elegant Chicken with, '80 M76
Wine Sauce, Chicken and Mushrooms in, '81 109
Wine Sauce, Chicken in, '80 8
Wings, Broiled Chicken, '80 149
Wings, Chinese Chicken, '96 111
Wings, Curried Chicken, '96 110
Wings, Grilled Honey Chicken, '96 111
Wings, Honey-Glazed Chicken, '91 251
Wings, Maple-Glazed Chicken, '99 110
Wings, Satan's, '87 214
Wings, Spicy Buffalo, '95 239
Wings, Spicy Oriental-Style, '96 215
Wings, Sweet-and-Sour Chicken, '96 110
Wings, Tandoori Chicken, '96 110
Wontons, Chicken, '92 284
Wontons with Hoisin Peanut Dipping Sauce,
    Chicken, '99 14
Wraps, Southwestern, '99 238
Yogurt Chicken, Savory, '91 238; '92 28
Yogurt-Sesame Chicken, '90 216

CHILI
Bake, Chili Hominy, '81 282; '82 58
Basic Chili, '82 M11; '93 326
Basic Chili Embellished, '93 327
Basic Chili Goes Southwest, '93 326
Before-and-After Burner, Roy's, '89 316
Biscuit Bowl, Chili in a, '98 224
Black Bean Chili Marsala, '95 16
Bodacious Chili, '95 14
Burgers, Open-Face Chili, '82 31; '83 33
Casserole, Chili, '90 176
Casserole, Chili-Rice, '79 54
Casserole, Hominy-Chili, '86 255
Casserole, Ultimate Chili, '99 239
Cheese-Topped Chili, '82 M11
Cheesy Chili, '82 310
Chili, '87 17; '93 89; '98 95
Chilly Night Chili, '99 317
Choo-Choo Chili, '89 316
Chuck Wagon Chili, '81 282; '82 57
Chunky Chili, '82 M282; '86 3
Cincinnati Chili, '96 18
Company Chili, '82 311; '83 30
con Carne, Beef and Sausage Chili, '83 284
con Carne, Chili, '82 310; '83 30; '84 72; '86 2
con Carne, Favorite Chili, '86 293
con Carne, Quick-and-Easy Chili, '86 2
Cowboy Chili, '86 2
Dip, Cheesy Chili, '80 150
Dip, Chili, '82 161; '88 218; '89 47; '91 143
Dip, Chili-and-Cheese, '89 328
Dog, Dinglewood Pharmacy's Scrambled, '95 118
Dogs, Chili-Cheese, '81 M176

Double-Meat Chili, '79 269; '80 12
Easy Chili, '82 310; '83 30
Easy Chili with Beans, '92 262
Easy Texas Chili, '90 201
Eggplant Chili, '85 88
Firestarter Chili, '93 34
Five-Ingredient Chili, '95 212
Friday Night Chili, '86 228
Greek Chili, '95 16
Hot Spiced Chili, '83 214
Hotto Lotto Chili, '89 316
I-Cious, Chili-, '89 315
"In-the-Red" Chili over "Rolling-in-Dough"
    Biscuits, '92 80
Kielbasa Chili, Hearty, '91 28
Lolly's Pop Chili, '89 316
Lunchtime Chili, '81 230
Manicotti, Chili, '89 247; '99 239
Meat Loaf, Chili, '81 275
Meaty Chili, '81 282; '82 58
Meaty Chili with Beans, '85 250
Mexican Chili, '89 18
Microwave Chili, '91 M232
Mom's Chili, '93 292
Noodles, Chili with, '81 282; '82 57
Now, Thatsa Chili, '95 16
Out West Chili, '95 15
Pastry Cups, Chili in, '90 68
Pie, Chili-Tamale, '82 9; '83 68
Potato Chili, Savory, '83 284
Potatoes, Chili-Topped, '83 3; '98 M289
Potatoes, South-of-the-Border Stuffed, '86 54
Quick-and-Easy Chili, '92 20
Quick and Simple Chili, '81 282; '82 58
Quick Chili, '83 283
Ranch Chili and Beans, '79 270; '80 11
Red Chili, '93 108
Red Chili, North Texas, '87 303
Rice, Chili with, '82 M11
Roundup Chili, '79 269; '80 12
Salad, Spicy Chili, '86 71
Sauce, Chili, '81 175; '94 287
Sauce, Chili Meat, '83 4
Sauce, Chunky Chili, '85 188
Sauce, Spicy Chili, '87 127
Sausage-Beef Chili, '86 232
Sausage Chili, Beefy, '82 M11
Simple Chili, '79 269; '80 11
Soup, Chili Bean, '96 71
Soup, Chili Vegetable, '94 120
South-of-the-Border Chili, '83 283; '91 283
Southwestern Chili, '91 284
Spaghetti, Herbed Chili-, '84 222
Speedy Chili, '92 66
Spicy Chili, Old-Fashioned, '79 269; '80 11
Stew, Red Chili, '95 226
Supper, Hot Chili, '99 279
Surprise, Chili, '82 229
Texas Championship Chili, '81 54
Texas Chili, Hot, '80 222; '81 77
Texas-Style Chili, '82 311; '83 30
Tex-Mex Chili, '83 26
Topping, Chili, '84 246; '94 22
Tree-Hunt Chili, '87 292
Turkey-Bean Chili, '88 M213
Vegetable Chili, '91 28; '97 179
Vegetarian Chili, '84 280, 327; '91 284
Venison Chili, '82 216; '86 3; '87 304
Venison Chili, Hot, '91 283
Verde, Chili, '95 14
White Chili, '91 284
White Christmas Chili, '98 266
White Lightning Texas Chili, '92 321
Zippy Chili, '87 110

CHOCOLATE. *See also* **BROWNIES;**
CANDIES/Fudge.
Apples on a Stick, Chocolate, '96 255
Bags, Chocolate-Raspberry, '95 97
Banana Pops, '84 44
Bars and Cookies
    Almond Chip Balls, Toasted, '84 240
    Almond-Chocolate Bars, '83 304
    Almond Cookies, Chocolate-, '98 293
    Almond Cream Confections, '87 198;
      '90 310
    Almond Surprise Cookies, Chocolate-,
      '88 M45
    Biscotti, Chocolate Chip-Cinnamon, '96 281
    Biscotti, Chocolate-Hazelnut, '95 80
    Biscotti Cioccolata, '93 268
    Biscotti, Cocoa-Almond, '96 280
    Blond Nut Squares, '82 156
    Bonbons, Chocolate-Filled, '89 162
    Bran Raisin Jumbos, Chocolate-, '91 142
    Brazil Squares, '82 306
    Brickle Cookies, Chocolate-, '99 127
    Butter Cookies, Chocolate-Tipped, '84 258;
      '90 312
    Butter Pecan Turtle Bars, '90 70
    Butterscotch Bars, Chocolate-, '81 197
    By-Cracky Bars, '84 212
    Cake Mix Cookies, '97 133
    Caramel-Filled Chocolate Cookies, '92 319
    Caramel Layer Squares, Chocolate-, '79 83
    Cereal Bars, Chewy Chocolate, '97 317
    Cherry Chocolates, '95 321
    Cherry Cookies, Chocolate-, '85 324
    Cherry Cookies, Chocolate-Covered, '99 280
    Chess Squares, Chocolate, '92 45
    Chewies, Chocolate, '93 216
    Chewies, Easy Chocolate, '93 296; '94 234
    Chewy Chocolate Chip Squares, '91 175
    Chewy Chocolate Cookies, '80 208; '97 166
    Chip Bars, Chocolate, '81 130
    Chip Cookies, '84 120
    Chip Cookies, Chocolate, '86 245; '90 193
    Chip Cookies, Chocolate-Chocolate, '82 35
    Chip Cookies, Mom Ford's Chocolate, '94 287
    Chippers, Chocolate, '92 206
    Chips Cookies, Loaded-with-, '87 223
    Chip Squares, Chocolate-, '83 170; '89 143
    Cinnamon Bars, Chocolate, '82 209
    Cocoa Drop Cookies, '80 217
    Cocoa Kiss Cookies, '85 171
    Coconut Robin's Nests, '98 M111
    Coconut Squares, Chocolate-, '90 70
    Coconut Swirls, '97 274
    Coffee Kisses, Chocolate-Dipped, '96 313
    Congo Squares, '96 94
    Crème de Menthe Bars, Chocolate-, '86 245
    Crème de Menthe Bites, Chocolate, '88 285
    Crème de Menthe Squares, '93 256
    Crispies, Chocolate-Peanut, '93 80
    Crispy Cookies, Chocolate, '85 115
    Crumble Bars, Choco-, '79 292
    Crunch Cookies, Chocolate, '91 316
    Crunchies, Chocolate, '92 50
    Date-Nut Chocolate Chip Cookies, Rich,
      '92 207
    Deluxe Chocolate Chip Cookies, '79 216
    Devil Doggies, '84 37
    Different Chocolate Chip Cookies, '83 114
    Double Chip Cookies, '81 301
    Double Chocolate Chip Cookies, '79 217
    Double Chocolate Chunk-Almond Cookies,
      '95 178
    Double-Chocolate Cookies, '95 272
    Doubly-Good Chocolate Cookies, '82 M185

Dream Bars, Chocolate, '79 256; '82 298
Drop Cookies, Chocolate, '84 36
Fibber McGee Cookies, '95 72
Flying Brooms, '98 255
Forget 'em Cookies, '83 256
Frosted Chocolate-Cherry Cookies, '89 294
Fudge Bars, '86 93
Fudge Bars, Yummy, '87 158
Fudge-Pecan Chewies, Alabama, '95 143
Fudge Puddles, '94 292
German Chocolate Chess Squares, '94 51
Giant Chocolate Chip Cookies, '84 119
Gingerbread Cookies, Chocolate-, '94 293
Graham Cracker Layered Cookies, Chocolate,
  '98 94
Jumbo Chocolate Chip Cookies, '82 110
Keyboard Cookies, '94 M330
Kissy Cookies, '93 331
Light Chocolate Chip Cookies, '86 46
Log Cookies, Chocolate-Tipped, '87 294
Lollapalooza, '94 194
Macaroon Cookies, Chocolate, '88 217
Macaroons, Chocolate, '83 300; '87 57
Meltaways, Chocolate, '81 302
Melt-Aways, Chocolate Chip, '84 118
Meringue-Chocolate Chip Bars, '84 118
Meringue Kiss Cookies, '86 121
Mint Chip Cookies, Chocolate-, '86 245
Mint Cookies, Chocolate-, '92 206
Mint Snaps, Chocolate-, '83 103; '84 96
Monster Cookies, '84 36
Nugget Cookies, '79 291
Nut Chews, Chocolate-, '81 92
Nut Freezer Cookies, Chocolate-, '88 217
Nutty Choco Snacks, '83 305
Nutty Oatmeal-Chocolate Chip Cookies,
  '82 M185
Oatmeal Bars, Chocolate-Topped, '86 110
Oatmeal-Chocolate Chippers, '90 218
Oatmeal-Chocolate Morsel Cookies, '95 46
Oatmeal Cookies, Chocolate-, '80 105
Oatmeal Cookies, Chocolate Chip-, '84 119
Oatmeal-Peanut Butter Chocolate Chip
  Cookies, '92 207
Oatmeal-Toffee Lizzies, Crispy, '95 136
Olympic Medal Cookies, '96 180
Orange-Chocolate Cookies, '83 113
Orange Delights, Chocolate-, '93 52
Peanut Blossom Cookies, '95 245; '96 55;
  '97 324
Peanut Butter and Chocolate Chunk Cookies,
  '94 169
Peanut Butter-and-Fudge Bars, '80 M172
Peanut Butter Bars, '84 243
Peanut Butter-Chocolate Chip Cookies,
  Freezer, '86 230
Peanut Butter-Chocolate Kiss Cookies, '86 49
Peanut Butter Cones, Chocolate-, '85 14
Peanut Butter Cookies, Chocolate-, '85 90
Peanut Butter Cookies, Chocolate Chip-,
  '99 68
Peanut Butter Cups, Chocolate-, '85 14;
  '97 134
Peanut Butter Fingers, '79 256
Peanut Butter Squares, Chocolate Chip-,
  '84 118
Peanut Chip Cookies, Choco-, '92 318
Peanut Cookies, Chocolate-, '83 223
Peppermint Cookies, Chocolate-Chocolate
  Chip-, '97 289
Peppermint Squares, Chocolate-, '81 119
Pinwheel Cookies, '93 316
Pinwheel Cookies, Chocolate, '86 245
Pinwheels, '95 321

Polka Dots, '95 272
Pudding Cookies, Chocolate Chip-, '93 21
Pumpkin-Chocolate Chip Cookies, '93 235
Raisin Oatmeal Cookies, Chocolate-, '95 136
Rudolph Cookies, '99 M309
Sandwich Cookies, Chocolate, '81 192
Sandwich Cookies, Choco-Nut, '84 200
Sandwiches, Chocolate Cookie Ice Cream,
  '87 147
Scotch Bars, Chewy, '98 M291
Seashells, Chocolate, '91 178
Shortbread Cookies, Chocolate, '99 147
Shortbread, Marble-Topped Hazelnut,
  '99 M29
Shortbread Wafers, Cocoa, '88 243
Snappers, Jumbo Chocolate, '81 218
Snowball Cookies, Chocolate, '82 295
Snowflake Cookies, Chocolate, '89 329
Spice Cookies, Lemon-Iced Chocolate,
  '97 123
Sugar-Coated Chocolate Cookies, '92 274
Sugar Cookies, Double-Chocolate, '92 206
Super Chocolate Chunk Cookies, '88 217
Surprise Bonbon Cookies, '88 119
Surprise Cookies, Choco, '80 60
Teasers, Chocolate, '87 44
Toffee Treats, '89 330
Turtle Bars, Gooey, '96 M189
White Chocolate Chip-Oatmeal Cookies,
  '99 127
White Chocolate Cookies, Chunky
  Macadamia Nut, '92 207
White Chocolate-Macadamia Nut Cookies,
  '94 315
White Chocolate-Orange Dream Cookies,
  '98 294
Whoopie Pies, '86 246
Witches' Hats, '98 256
Yummy Bars, '92 171
Zucchini Cookies, Spicy, '97 273
Baskets with Berry Cream, Chocolate, '92 118
Beverages
    Brandied Chocolate, Flaming, '80 M290
    Café au Lait, German Chocolate, '92 264
    Café Colombian Royal, '80 M290
    Café Mexicano, '92 208
    Cappuccino, Chocolate Castle, '84 53
    Cocoa Mix, Instant, '86 332
    Coffee, Chocolate, '82 43; '97 17
    Coffee, Chocolate-Almond, '84 54
    Coffee, Cocoa-, '83 55
    Coffee, Mexican, '83 175, 275; '88 247; '91 78;
      '93 310; '94 97
    "Concrete," Abaco Mocha, '94 114
    "Concrete," Cardinal Sin, '94 113
    "Concrete," Foxtreat, '94 113
    Hot Chocolate, '94 290
    Hot Chocolate, Creole, '80 M290
    Hot Chocolate Deluxe, '90 272
    Hot Chocolate, Favorite, '83 55
    Hot Chocolate, French, '86 328
    Hot Chocolate, Mexican, '98 313
    Hot Chocolate Mix, Deluxe, '80 M290
    Hot Chocolate Mix, Spicy, '85 278
    Hot Chocolate, Old-Fashioned, '85 23
    Hot Chocolate, Special, '82 5
    Hot Chocolate, Spiced, '80 50
    Hot Chocolate, Spicy, '85 278
    Hot Chocolate, Sugar-and-Spice, '95 34
    Hot Chocolate, Tennessee, '96 214
    Hot Cocoa Mix, '81 287
    Hot Cocoa Mix, Minted, '91 316
    Hot Cocoa Mix, Mocha-Flavored, '91 316
    Hot Cocoa, Quick, '82 5

King Alfonso, '80 259
Malt, Banana-Chocolate, '89 170
Malt, Chocolate, '86 183
Marshmallow Chocolate, Hot Laced, '93 53
Mexican-Style Chocolate, '81 187
Milk, French Chocolate, '79 38
Milk Shake, Chocolate-Banana, '94 113
Mocha Blend, '95 276
Mocha Chocolate Fluff, '89 170
Mocha Cocoa, '83 318
Mocha-Cocoa Mix, Hot, '82 296
Mocha Coffee, '85 M329
Mocha Cream, Café, '84 54
Mocha Deluxe Hot Drink, '82 289
Mocha Espresso, Italian, '82 254
Mocha Frosty, '92 44
Mocha, Hot, '84 60
Mocha, Mexican, '93 M341
Mocha Polka, '89 171
Mocha Punch, '84 58, 166; '95 141
Mocha, Quick Viennese, '79 232
Mocha, Spirited Hot, '91 M260
Mocha Warmer, '97 272
Peppermint Patti, The Peabody, '99 321
Shake, Chocolate Mint, '89 170
Sipper, Chocolate, '88 83
Smoothie, Chocoholic, '97 173
Smoothie, Chocolate-Mint, '84 166
Bites, Snowy Chocolate, '90 47
Black-Bottom Goodies, '89 251
Bombe, Double-Chocolate, '97 282
Bread, Chocolate Chip-Banana, '90 267
Bread, Chocolate Date-Nut, '81 284
Bread, Chocolate Loaf, '88 M188
Bread, Chocolate-Zucchini, '93 308
Bread, Cocoa-Nut Swirl, '80 257
Brickle Squares, Chocolate, '94 290
Buns, Chocolate-Cinnamon, '85 5
Buns, Chocolate Sticky, '81 300; '82 124
Cakes and Tortes
Almond Cake, Chocolate-, '91 248
Almond Cake with Cherry Filling, Chocolate-, '84 225
Almond Torte, Chocolate-, '96 M253; '98 273
Amaretto Heart, Chocolate-, '98 56
Angel Cake, Chocolate, '88 128
Angel Cake, Chocolate Truffle, '97 283
Angel Food Cake, Chocolate, '87 21; '90 111; '91 55
Angel Food Cake with Custard Sauce, Chocolate, '88 259
Angel Squares, Mocha, '98 61
Apricot-Filled Chocolate Torte, '90 107
Banana Cake, Chocolate, '86 138
Banana Loaf, Chocolate Chip-, '85 115
Basket Cake, Chocolate-Strawberry, '98 100
Beet Cake, Chocolate, '80 40
Birthday Balloon Cakes, '92 15
Birthday Cake, Fishin'-for-Fun, '93 194
Black Forest Cake, '81 126; '92 174
Black Forest Torte, '88 209
Bourbon-Chocolate Torte, '98 M84
Brownie Delight, Chocolate, '87 224
Brown Mountain Cake, '84 39
Bûche de Noël, '84 304; '87 241
Bûche de Noël Cake, '82 262
Buttercream Cake, Chocolate, '90 108
Buttermilk Chocolate Cake, '79 13
Buttermilk Fudge Squares, '99 99
Candy Cake, Chocolate, '81 238
Caramel-Nut Cake, Chocolate-, '83 23
Carrot Cake, Brownie, '92 120
Cheesecake Bites, Mint, '99 282
Cheesecake, Black-and-White, '99 334

Cheesecake, Black Forest, '84 74; '89 93; '94 21; '97 330
Cheesecake, Candy Bar, '86 120
Cheesecake, Chocolate, '81 16; '82 305
Cheesecake, Chocolate-Almond, '93 53
Cheesecake, Chocolate-Amaretto, '85 M294; '93 97
Cheesecake, Chocolate-Caramel-Pecan, '91 197
Cheesecake, Chocolate Chip, '85 114
Cheesecake, Chocolate Cookie, '91 298
Cheesecake, Chocolate-Glazed Triple-Layer, '86 315; '90 310
Cheesecake, Chocolate Marble, '89 93
Cheesecake, Chocolate-Mint, '91 104
Cheesecake, Chocolate-Mint Baked Alaska, '94 142
Cheesecake, Chocolate-Raspberry Truffle, '91 270
Cheesecake, Chocolate Swirl, '84 295; '85 26
Cheesecake, Chocolate-Wrapped Banana, '99 M48
Cheesecake, Coconut-Chocolate-Almond, '98 322
Cheesecake, Fudge, '98 M213
Cheesecake, German Chocolate, '87 265
Cheesecake, Marbled, '87 261
Cheesecake, Marble Mint, '84 152
Cheesecake, Mocha, '98 278
Cheesecake, Mocha-Chocolate, '88 258
Cheesecake, Mocha Swirl, '87 262
Cheesecake, Rich Chocolate, '84 74; '85 38
Cheesecakes, Tiny Chocolate, '92 288
Cheesecake, Warm Fudge-Filled, '98 34
Cheesecake, White Chocolate, '87 44; '88 267; '94 180
Cheesecake with Whipped Cream Frosting, Chocolate, '89 42
Cherry Cake, Choco-, '96 229
Cherry Cake, Chocolate-, '84 200; '86 239
Cherry Fudge Cake, '98 214
Chiffon Cake with Coffee Buttercream, Chocolate, '95 277
Chocolate Cake, '97 283
Cinnamon Cake, Chocolate-, '93 154
Cocoa Crown Cake, '90 107
Coconut Cake, Chocolate-, '83 23
Coconut Cake, White Chocolate-, '87 263
Coconut-Fudge Cake, '99 206
Coffee Cake, Chocolate-Chip, '79 249
Coffee Cake, Chocolate Chip, '83 231; '97 232
Cola Cake, Quick Chocolate, '95 56
Crumb Cakes, Calico, '87 261
Cupcakes, Banana-Cocoa, '80 130
Cupcakes, Brownie, '82 280
Cupcakes, Chocolate, '92 14
Cupcakes, Chocolate Chip, '97 108
Cupcakes, Chocolate Surprise, '85 91
Cupcakes, Cinnamon-Chocolate, '81 M139
Cupcakes, Marble Chocolate Chip, '81 239
Cupcakes, Mocha, '85 250
Cupcakes, Self-Filled, '80 129
Cups, Black Bottom, '82 279
Custard Cake, Chocolate, '88 175
Decadent Chocolate Cake, '86 142
Double-Chocolate Torte, '79 67
Easy Chocolate Cake, '80 140
Easy Perfect Chocolate Cake, '99 307
Extra-Rich Chocolate Cake, '99 271
Father's Day Cake, '92 134
Frosting, Chocolate Cake with Double, '86 314
Fruitcakes, Chocolate, '95 250
Fudge Cake, '94 M293; '98 110; '99 176

Fudge Cake, Best, '83 301
Fudge Cake, Brown Sugar, '86 316
Fudge Cake, Chocolate, '80 279
Fudge Cake, Coconut-, '99 206
Fudge Cake for Two, '81 205
Fudge Cake, Hot, '99 105
Fudge Cake, One-Foot-in-the-Fire, '90 252
Fudge Frosting, Chocolate Cake with, '89 56
German Chocolate Cake, '81 296; '83 M233
German Chocolate Chip Cake, '86 247
Grandma's Chocolate Cake, '94 133
Graveyard Grumblings, '92 15
Kahlúa Cake, Chocolate, '91 298
Kahlúa Chocolate Cake, '81 303
Layers, Chocolate Cake, '96 229
Loaf Cakes, Chocolate Chip, '98 137
Marbled Cake, Cocoa, '82 265
Marshmallow Cake, No-Egg Chocolate, '87 M97
Mayonnaise Cake, Chocolate, '83 99
Mint Torte, Chocolate, '94 86
Mocha Brownie Torte, '85 102
Mocha Cake, Belgian, '84 316
Mocha Cake, Double, '84 311
Mocha-Chocolate Cake, Dark, '84 311
Mocha Cream Roll, Chocolate-, '84 304
Mocha-Pecan Torte, '86 26
Mocha Torte, '99 66
Mocha Velvet Torte, '92 318
Mousse Cake, Chocolate, '87 264; '98 270
Mousse Cake, Chocolate-Peanut Butter, '98 71
Mousse Cake, Strawberry-Studded White Chocolate, '99 154
Mousse Cake, White Chocolate, '89 160
Mousse Roll, Chocolate, '88 280
Mousse Torte, White Chocolate, '99 154
Nut Cake, Rich Chocolate-, '86 8
Pastry Cake, Chocolate, '91 196
Peanut Butter Cake, Chocolate-, '84 240
Peanut Butter Cake, Fudgy, '85 91
Peanut Butter-Fudge Cake, '96 254
Peanut Cluster Cake, Chocolate-, '87 184
Pecan Torte, Chocolate-, '89 42
Perfect Chocolate Cake, '82 244; '90 307
Petits Fours, Chocolate-Almond, '93 255
Piglets, '98 203
Pound Cake, Chocolate, '82 88; '84 10; '89 325; '94 288; '98 336
Pound Cake, Chocolate Chip, '86 178; '93 105; '94 100
Pound Cake, Chocolate Marble, '88 16
Pound Cake, Chocolate-Orange, '89 94
Pound Cake, Chocolate-Sour Cream, '83 239; '92 153
Pound Cake, Chocolate-Swirled, '97 329
Pound Cake, German Chocolate, '97 M254
Pound Cake, Mahogany, '89 207
Pound Cake, Marble, '95 29
Pound Cake, Marbled Pecan, '93 313
Pound Cake, Milk Chocolate, '90 306
Pound Cake, White Chocolate, '91 101
Pound Cake with Frosting, Chocolate, '90 284
Pound Cake with Fudge Frosting, Chocolate, '87 296
Praline Torte, Chocolate, '84 165
Pudding Cake, Hot Fudge, '88 255
Pudding Cake, Warm Chocolate, '92 324
Pudding, Chocolate Cake, '81 99
Pumpkin, Chocolate, '96 254
Queen's Chocolate Cake, '89 271
Raspberry Cake, Chocolate-, '92 173
Raspberry-Fudge Cake, '97 34
Rich Chocolate Cake, '89 43

CHOCOLATE, Cakes and Tortes
(continued)

Rocky Road Cake, '81 178
Roll, Chocolate Cream, '85 317
Roll, Chocolate-Frosted Ice Cream, '84 200
Roll, Chocolate Mousse, '83 290
Roll, Chocolate-Orange, '87 21
Roll, Make-Ahead Chocolate-Mint Cake, '95 220
Rolls, Chocolate Cake, '94 312
Roulade, Kahlúa-and-Cream, '97 199
Roulage, Chocolate-Cranberry, '94 313
Roulage, Chocolate-Orange, '94 314
Roulage, Mint-Chocolate, '94 314
Royal, Chocolate Cake, '86 239
Royale, Chocolate Torte, '82 263
Rum Cake, Chocolate, '79 67
Sachertorte, '84 253
Sachertorte, Shortcut, '99 M243
Shortcake, Chocolate-Raspberry, '95 99
Shortcake, Chocolate-Strawberry, '89 216
Snack Cake, Black Widow, '93 245
Snack Cake, Frosted Chocolate, '90 194
Sour Cream Cake, Chocolate-, '87 222
Sour Cream Cake, Chocolate Chip-, '85 115
Sour Cream Chocolate Cake, '79 282
Spice Potato Cake, Chocolate-, '96 111
Sponge Cake, Chocolaty, '86 60
Strawberry Ice Cream Torte, Chocolate-, '79 7
Sugar Cookie Torte, '79 68
Swiss Chocolate Chip Cake, '87 85
Tannenbaum Temptations, '92 14
Toffee Cake, Chocolate-, '89 335
Tree Cakes, Miniature Chocolate Truffle, '97 M285
Triangle Cake, Chocolate, '85 126
Triple Chocolate Torte, '96 58
Truffle Cake, Chocolate, '89 43
Turkey Talk, '92 15
Velvet Torte, Chocolate, '86 316
Wedding Cake, Double Chocolate, '91 100
Whipped Cream Cake, Chocolate-Mint, '90 265
White Chocolate-Cherry Cake, '88 268
White Chocolate Mousse Cake, '89 160
White Chocolate Mousse Cake, Strawberry-Studded, '99 154
White Chocolate Mousse Torte, '99 154
White Chocolate-Raspberry Cake, '98 323
Yule Log, '79 281; '82 289
Zucchini Cake, Chocolate-, '85 156
Candies
Almond Roca, '86 49
Bourbon Balls, '83 315; '90 83
Bourbon Balls, Chocolate, '84 298
Brittle, Chocolate, '83 315
Brittle, Quick Chocolate, '82 114
Butter Creams, '80 302
Caramels, Chocolate, '91 35
Cherries, Chocolate-Covered, '81 286; '84 298; '97 M55
Coconut Almond Drops, Chocolate-, '87 223
Coconut Joys, '98 282
Coconut Joys, Chocolate-Covered, '98 M282
Coffee Buttons, '99 66
Cream-Filled Chocolates, Liqueur, '87 258
Creams, Chocolate-Lemon, '98 M235
Crème de Cacao Balls, '86 266
Crème de Menthe Chocolates, '91 36
Drops, Chocolate, '84 111
Fudge, '86 266
Fudge Balls, Strawberry, '93 80

Fudge Bites, Peanut-, '91 M231; '92 M68
Fudge, Cherry Nut, '83 315
Fudge, Chocolate, '82 20
Fudge, Chocolate-Peanut Butter, '87 257; '90 311
Fudge, Coffee-Chip, '86 74
Fudge, Cream Cheese, '84 111
Fudge, Creamy, '81 218
Fudge, Creamy Almond, '95 51
Fudge, Creamy Dark, '82 295
Fudge, Creamy Mocha, '95 51
Fudge, Creamy Pecan, '84 321
Fudge, Diamond, '92 193
Fudge, Dinner Mint, '88 285
Fudge, Double-Good, '79 M263; '95 M50
Fudge, Double Good, '87 M278
Fudge, Double Peanut, '85 91
Fudge, Fast, '79 274
Fudge, Five Pounds of Chocolate, '95 51
Fudge, Four Chips, '92 318
Fudge, Holiday Mocha, '84 298
Fudge, Marbled Peanut Butter, '88 65
Fudge, Microwave Chocolate, '92 M50
Fudge, Mint, '95 50
Fudge, Orange-Walnut, '92 288
Fudge, Peanut Butter, '89 307
Fudge-Peanut Butter Chewies, '98 215
Fudge, Pistachio, '83 298
Fudge, Quick-and-Easy, '88 M190
Fudge, Quick Nut, '83 315
Fudge Scotch Ring, '79 273
Fudge Squares, Chocolate-Peanut Butter, '97 M54
Fudge, White Chocolate, '92 317; '95 51
Fudge, White Chocolate-Coffee, '94 232
Greeting Card, Chocolate, '83 40
Kentucky Colonels, '79 273
Marshmallow Squares, Chocolate-, '92 M50
Millionaires, '79 M262; '97 M55
Mints, Dinner, '88 66
Molded Candies, '84 40
Nut Clusters, '81 254
Nut Log Candy, Chocolate-, '86 335
Nut Teasers, Chocolate, '91 35
Peanut Butter Balls, Chocolate-, '80 87
Peanut Butter Bites, Chocolate-, '92 M317
Peanut Butter-Chocolate Balls, '80 269
Peanut Butter-Chocolate Candy Squares, '82 56
Peanut Butter Creams, '79 273
Peanut Butter Drops, Chocolate-, '92 322
Peanut Clusters, '92 288; '98 M282
Peanut Clusters, Chocolate-, '81 16
Peanutty Clusters, '83 143
Peanutty Swirls, Chocolate-, '94 M330
Pecan Clusters, '98 305
Pecan Clusters, Roasted, '90 310
Pecan Fritters, Chocolate-Covered, '79 205
Pralines, Chocolate, '92 313; '93 51
Pralines, Chocolate-Mint, '92 313; '93 51
Pralines, Chocolate-Peanut Butter, '92 313; '93 51
Pralines, Mocha, '92 313; '93 51
Pretzels, Chocolate-Covered, '82 295
Raspberry Cream Chocolates, '91 36
Rocky Road, '84 298
Rum Balls, Chocolate, '80 302
Rum Balls, Chocolate-, '88 285
Spiders, Chocolate, '85 236
Spirited Chocolates, '86 278
Tempered Chocolate, '91 35
Tiger Butter, '86 48
Toffee, English, '79 273
Toffee, Microwave, '92 M317

Toffee, Nutty, '79 M263
Truffles, Almond, '83 298
Truffles, Amaretto Dessert, '86 319
Truffles, Bittersweet, '94 330
Truffles, Chocolate, '85 114; '89 43; '91 108
Truffles, Chocolate-Cherry Cordial, '99 127
Truffles, Chocolate-Kahlúa, '92 285
Truffles, Chocolate Marble, '97 284
Truffles, Chocolate-Praline, '97 284
Truffles, Hazelnut, '97 M54
Truffles, Orange-Pecan, '95 92
Truffles, White Chocolate, '87 45
Truffles, White Chocolate-Praline, '97 284
Truffles, Yule Street, '90 242
Turtle Candies, '93 M41
Velvets, Chocolate, '84 298
White Chocolate Salties, '92 50
White Chocolate Surprises, '91 36
Cannoli, '80 58
Charlotte Russe, Chocolate, '87 74
Cheese Cups, Chocolate-, '91 142
Cinnamon-Chocolate Cream, '94 199
Cocoa to Chocolate Equivalents, '84 200
Combo, Strawberry-Chocolate, '85 96
Cones, Chocolate-Coffee, '96 M316
Cream, Chocolate-Almond, '91 108
Cream, Heavenly Chocolate, '88 128
Cream, Strawberries with Chocolate, '85 81
Crème Brûlée, Black-and-White, '98 267
Crème Brûlée, Chocolate, '95 323
Crème Brûlée, White Chocolate-Macadamia Nut, '95 323
Crêpes, Chocolate, '86 164
Crêpes, Chocolate Chantilly, '82 183
Crêpes, Chocolate Dessert, '84 84; '85 262
Crêpes, Chocolate Dream, '86 164
Crêpes, Chocolate-Orange, '85 263
Crêpes, Fruit-Filled Chocolate, '89 325
Croissants, Chocolate-Filled, '96 303
Crust, Chocolate, '87 264; '90 M15
Crust, Chocolate-Coconut, '87 261
Crust, Chocolate Crumb, '87 261
Crust, Chocolate-Macadamia Crumb, '96 254
Crust, Chocolate Wafer, '89 42, 93
Cups, Chocolate, '80 207
Cups, Chocolate Crinkle, '93 270
Cups, Chocolate Lace, '87 133
Cups, Chocolate-Mint, '80 71
Cups, Chocolate-Walnut, '85 213
Cups, Miniature Chocolate, '87 132
Custard, Chocolate, '88 258
Custard, Chocolate-Topped Amaretto, '87 M37
Date-Nut Delight, Chocolate, '88 168
Decadence, Chocolate, '89 183
Delights, Choco-Peanut, '99 197
Dessert, Chilled Chocolate, '83 177
Dessert, Chocolate-Almond, '82 306
Dessert, Chocolate-Coffee Frozen, '85 172
Dessert, Chocolate Dream, '83 198
Dessert, Chocolate Ladyfinger, '86 162
Dessert, Chocolate-Mint, '82 100
Dessert, Chocolate-Rum, '81 247
Dessert, Chocolate Truffle, '88 281
Dessert, Choco-Maple Frozen, '86 300; '87 178
Dessert, Cool Chocolate-Mint, '80 109
Dessert, Easy Chocolate, '79 75
Dessert, Frozen Chocolate, '83 76
Dessert, Fudge-Peanut Ice Cream, '88 167
Dessert, Hello Dolly, '95 168
Dessert, Layered Ice Cream, '83 189
Dessert, Nutty Fudgy Frozen, '94 28
Dessert, Peanut-Chocolate, '80 86
Dessert Squares, Chocolate-Blueberry, '87 299
Dessert, Triple Cream, '94 244

Dessert with Kahlúa Cream, Fudge, '91 197
Dip, Chocolate, '92 50
Doughnuts, Chocolate, '83 95
Doughnuts, Chocolate-Covered, '84 55
Doughnuts, Chocolate-Glazed Potato, '85 6
Dream Drops, '99 328
Éclairs, Chocolate, '96 191
Flan, Layered, '89 45
Fondue, Brandied Chocolate, '93 162
Fondue, Chocolate, '91 142
Fondue, Dessert, '89 281
Fondue, White Chocolate, '92 287
Frostings, Fillings, and Toppings
  Almond Frosting, Chocolate-, '83 241
  Buttercream, Chocolate, '84 156
  Buttercream Frosting, Chocolate, '96 229;
    '98 M100
  Butter Frosting, Chocolate, '89 271
  Buttermilk Frosting, Chocolate-, '99 99
  Candy Frosting, Chocolate, '81 238
  Cheese Filling, Chocolate-, '90 47
  Cherry Frosting, Chocolate-, '89 294
  Chocolate Filling, '96 316
  Chocolate Frosting, '80 M171; '81 265;
    '82 262; '83 79, 99, M233, 253; '84 200;
    '85 323; '86 8, 93, 138, 239, 314; '87 M97,
    198, 199, 293; '89 M25; '90 194, 252, 265,
    284, 309; '91 248; '92 319; '93 239; '94 133;
    '96 253, 254; '97 M87, 254; '99 271
  Cocoa Frosting, '86 60; '96 253, 254
  Coconut Chocolate Frosting, '79 13
  Coffee Frosting, Chocolate-, '84 36; '88 269
  Cola Frosting, Chocolate-, '95 56
  Cream, Chocolate, '94 57
  Creamy Chocolate Frosting, '85 314; '86 316;
    '87 241; '99 307
  Creamy Chocolate Glaze, '82 88
  Fluffy Chocolate Frosting, '86 336; '87 58
  Fudge Filling, '94 292
  Fudge Frosting, '81 303; '87 296; '89 56;
    '94 51
  Fudge Frosting, Chocolate, '83 105
  Fudge Frosting, Quick, '81 278
  Ganache, Chocolate, '93 255; '97 282
  Ganache Cream, '92 318
  Glaze, Chocolate, '81 119; '83 220; '84 10, 55,
    253; '85 6; '86 315, 316; '89 325; '90 310;
    '91 M296; '93 52; '97 M35, 231; '99 206
  Glaze, Creamy Chocolate, '98 90
  Glaze, French Chocolate, '98 M57
  Glaze, White Cake with Strawberries and
    Chocolate, '87 76
  Gravy, Chocolate, '99 35, 88
  Honey Chocolate Frosting, '79 83
  Honey Glaze, Chocolate-, '82 306
  Hot Fudge Ice Cream Topping, '98 317
  Kahlúa Frosting, Chocolate, '91 298
  Marshmallow Frosting, Chocolate-, '83 245
  Marzipan Bees, '98 100
  Midnight Filling, Chocolate, '96 120
  Mint Chocolate Frosting, '99 M176
  Mocha Butter Cream Frosting, '79 281
  Mocha-Buttercream Frosting, '86 26
  Mocha Cream, '94 47
  Mocha Cream Filling, '84 305
  Mocha Frosting, '83 301; '84 316; '87 224;
    '94 292; '97 35
  Mocha Frosting, Creamy, '82 289; '84 311;
    '91 248
  Nut Frosting, Chocolate, '80 140
  Peanut Butter Frosting, Chocolate-, '84 240;
    '87 222
  Peanut Butter-Fudge Frosting, '87 184
  Peanut Topping, Chocolate-, '79 222

Perfect Chocolate Frosting, '90 307
Rich Chocolate Filling, '79 68
Rich Chocolate Frosting, '84 304
Rum Frosting, Chocolate, '79 67
Satiny Chocolate Frosting, '85 126; '89 43
Truffle Filling, Chocolate, '87 69
Whipped Cream Frosting, '89 43
White Chocolate Buttercream Frosting,
  '97 M284
White Chocolate-Cream Cheese Frosting,
  '94 58; '98 323
White Chocolate-Cream Cheese Tiered Cake
  Frosting, '94 125
White Chocolate Filling, '89 160
White Chocolate Frosting, '88 280; '91 101;
  '97 M111
Garnishes, Chocolate, '85 16
Garnishes, Lacy Chocolate, '89 43
Gâteau Panache, '83 269
Granola with Chocolate Morsels, '86 69
Grapefruit, Chocolate-Topped, '89 88
Horns, Chocolate-Dipped, '93 197
Ice Cream, Almond-Fudge, '93 205
Ice Cream Balls, Easy, '84 106
Ice Cream Balls, Nutty, '89 72
Ice Cream, Chocolate, '80 176; '86 129
Ice Cream, Chocolate Chunk-Peanut Butter,
  '85 297; '86 120
Ice Cream, Chocolate Cookie, '95 245
Ice Cream, Chocolate-Covered Peanut, '88 203
Ice Cream, Double-Chocolate, '88 203
Ice Cream, Mexican Chocolate, '91 162
Ice Cream, Mint-Chocolate Chip, '88 202
Ice Cream, Mocha, '88 202; '97 M145
Ice Cream, Orange Pekoe-Chocolate, '99 90
Ice Cream Party Squares, '91 214
Ice Cream Sandwiches, Chocolate, '89 72
Ice Cream Squares, Mint-Chocolate Chip,
  '94 245
Kahlúa Delight, '83 67
Leaves, Chocolate, '88 281; '89 42; '98 270
Loaf, Chocolate Pinwheel, '80 256
Loaves, Chocolate Chip Cheese, '91 299; '92 264
Log, Chocolate Cream, '94 220
Meringue Acorns, '93 284
Meringue Fingers, Chocolate-Almond, '84 158
Mexican Fiesta Confection, '82 223
Mint Freeze, Chocolate, '88 167
Mississippi Mud, '96 253
Mocha Alaska Dessert, '84 191
Mocha Chiffon, '86 75
Mocha Delight, Frozen, '96 179
Mocha Dessert, Frozen, '84 311
Mocha Freeze, Royal, '84 53
Mocha Squares, Frozen, '81 187
Mousse. *See also* **CHOCOLATE/Cakes and
  Tortes, Pies and Tarts.**
  Almond Mousse, Chocolate-, '93 316
  Amaretto-Chocolate Mousse, '86 50
  Amaretto-Chocolate Mousse, Elegant, '86 337
  au Grand Marnier, Chocolate Mousse,
    '91 296
  Baked Alaska, Chocolate Mousse, '85 195
  Blender Chocolate Mousse, '82 71
  Blender-Quick Chocolate Mousse, '80 269
  Brandy-Chocolate Mousse, '85 102
  Chocolate Mousse, '88 280; '97 282
  Creamy Chocolate Mousse, '87 133
  Honeyed Chocolate Mousse, '87 223
  Kid-Pleasin' Chocolate Mousse, '90 271
  Loaf with Raspberry Puree, Chocolate
    Mousse, '97 34
  Orange Mousse, Chocolate-, '81 16, 205
  Parfait, Chocolate Mousse, '94 90

Parfaits, Chocolate-Peanut Butter Mousse,
  '98 71
Present, Chocolate Mousse, '99 281
Quick Chocolate Mousse, '85 87
Quick White Chocolate Mousse, '99 155
Rum Mousse, Chocolate, '86 189
Truffle Mousse with Raspberry Sauce,
  Chocolate, '95 327
White Chocolate Mousse, '91 247; '93 315;
  '97 282; '98 M57, M111; '99 155
Muffins, Banana-Chocolate, '94 197
Muffins, Chocolate Chip, '90 87
Muffins, Fudge Brownie, '95 M50
Muffins, Jumbo Banana-Chocolate Chip, '93 339
Muffins, Peanut Butter-Chocolate Chip, '94 167
Napoleons, Coffee, '95 276
Napoleons, Peanut Butter-and-Chocolate,
  '94 121
Parfait, Bodacious Peanut, '95 167
Parfait, Chocolate Mousse, '94 90
Parfaits, Chocolate-Crème de Menthe, '85 161
Parfaits, Chocolate-Mint, '90 M15
Parfaits, Chocolate-Peanut Butter Mousse,
  '98 71
Parfaits, Chocolate-Peppermint, '88 65
Parfaits, Hooray, '96 229
Parfaits, Mocha-Mallow, '80 219
Parfaits, Speedy, '83 76
Parfait, White Chocolate-Raspberry Swirl,
  '93 315
Pies and Tarts
  Almond Pie, Creamy Chocolate-, '85 102
  Amandine, Chocolate Pie, '83 300
  Amaretto Heavenly Tarts, Chocolate-, '88 4
  Amaretto Mousse Pie, Chocolate-, '80 180;
    '81 30
  Banana-Pecan Cream Pie, Chocolate-, '94 210
  Bavarian Pie, Chocolate, '89 326
  Berry Pie, Heavenly Chocolate-, '85 102
  Best-Ever Chocolate Pie, '88 M45
  Black Bottom Mocha-Cream Tart, '92 304
  Black Bottom Pie, '82 53
  Black-Bottom Pie, '98 161
  Bluegrass Chocolate Tarts, '90 84
  Bourbon-Chocolate-Pecan Tarts, '96 264
  Bourbon Pie, Chocolate, '88 99
  Brownie-Mint Pie, '97 303
  Brownie Pie, Crustless, '82 33
  Brownie Pie, Frozen Chocolate, '96 57
  Caramel Turtle Truffle Tart, '93 M131
  Cherry Tart, Chocolate-, '97 33
  Chess Pie, Chocolate, '81 161; '86 220; '92 13
  Chess Tarts, Chocolate, '92 214
  Chilled Chocolate Pie, '88 99
  Chip Pie, Chocolate, '85 114
  Coffee Tart, '99 67
  Cream Cheese Pie, Chocolate-, '80 69
  Cream Cheese Pie, Chocolate, '92 240
  Cream Pie, Chocolate, '83 192; '84 49;
    '87 208; '94 208
  Creamy Chocolate Pie, '85 298; '86 119
  Custard Tart, Chocolate, '99 27
  Double Chocolate Pie, '82 M282
  Easy Chocolate Pie, '83 158
  Fox Hunter's Pie, '97 109
  French Silk Pie, '80 247
  French Silk Tarts, '79 236
  Frozen Chocolate-Macadamia Nut Pie,
    '96 254
  Frozen Chocolate Pie, '80 154
  Frozen Chocolate Pie with Pecan Crust,
    '89 291; '98 180
  Fudge Pie, '87 168; '89 252
  Fudge Pie, Black-and-White, '99 249

CHOCOLATE, Pies and Tarts
(continued)

Fudge Pie, Chocolate, '98 336
Fudge Pie, Sweetheart, '86 316; '90 313
Fudge Truffle-Pecan Tart, '99 315
German Chocolate Pie, '93 129
Heaven, Chocolate, '98 323
Heavenly Chocolate Pie, '87 260
Ice Cream Pie, Chocolate-, '87 224
Ice Cream Pie, Chocolate, '91 56
Ice Cream Pie, Chocolate-Mint, '81 144
Ice Cream Pie, Chocolate-Peanut Butter, '98 244
Ice Cream Sundae Pie, '94 244
Kahlúa Pie, '83 191
Kentucky Derby Tarts, '79 102
Meringue Pie, Chocolate, '80 238; '82 206; '83 158; '92 216
Meringue Pie, Chocolate-Filled, '86 121
Microwave Chocolate Pie, '90 M15
Midnight Delights, '95 278
Mocha Crunch Pie, Chocolate-, '81 136
Mocha Meringue Pie, '80 242
Mocha Pie, '94 168
Mousse Pie, Chocolate, '81 136
Mousse Pie, Chocolate-Amaretto, '80 180; '81 30
Mud Pie, Decadent, '89 252
Mud Pie, Mississippi, '89 26
Mud Pie, Tipsy, '80 255; '97 251
Party Tarts, '95 90
Peanut Butter Pie, Chocolate-, '85 91
Peanut Butter Swirl Pie, Chocolate-, '87 262
Peanut Butter Tarts, Chocolate-, '92 277
Pecan Chess Pie, Chocolate-, '93 251
Pecan Pie, Bourbon-Chocolate, '98 258
Pecan Pie, Choco-, '82 86
Pecan Pie, Chocolate, '80 237; '83 12; '90 184
Pecan Pie, Chocolate-, '91 272
Pecan Tart with Caramel Sauce, Chocolate-, '93 296; '94 234
Praline Pie, Chocolate-, '86 259
Silk Pie, Chocolate, '88 67
Strawberry-Chocolate Truffle Pie, '89 112
Tin Roof Pie, '85 91
Turtle Pecan Pie, '93 250
Whipped Cream Pie, Chocolate, '79 124
White Chocolate-Banana Cream Pie, '94 314
White Chocolate Chess Tart, '95 303
Pineapple with Raspberry Sauce, Chocolate-Drizzled, '90 57
Pizza, Chocolate, '91 298
Plunge, Chocolate, '94 332; '95 35
Pots de Chocolat, Petits, '82 272
Pots de Crème, '81 15; '84 M145
Pots de Crème au Chocolate, '93 53
Pots de Crème, Chocolate, '93 296; '94 234
Pots de Crème for Two, '89 275
Pots de Crème, Mocha, '88 M45
Pots de Crème, Rum-Flavored, '85 102
Pots de Crème with Orange Meringues, Chocolate, '95 318
Pudding, Brownie, '79 265; '80 295
Pudding, Chocolate-Almond, '82 142; '88 24
Pudding, Chocolate-Almond Silk, '96 266
Pudding, Chocolate Biscuit Bread, '94 215
Pudding, Chocolate Bread, '80 8
Pudding, Creamy Chocolate, '83 106
Pudding, Fudge-Banana, '97 331
Pudding, Fudgy Chocolate, '96 285
Pudding, Hot Fudge, '81 208
Pudding, Hot Fudge Sundae Cake, '88 167

Pudding with Lemon Meringue, Chocolate, '88 258
Pudding with Whiskey Sauce, Chocolate Bread, '99 277
Reindeer Food, Magic, '99 M309
Roulage, '90 266
Roulage, Chocolate-Mocha, '80 216
Roulage, Frozen Chocolate, '90 56
Roulage, White Chocolate, '92 230
Sack, Large Chocolate, '93 314
Sack, Small Chocolate, '93 314
Sauces
Amaretto-Chocolate Sauce, '92 154
Bittersweet Chocolate Sauce, '92 319
Cherry Sauce, Chocolate-, '85 189
Cherry Sauce, Chocolate-, '87 M165
Chocolate Sauce, '83 189; '84 208, 313; '86 322; '90 57; '91 56, 57; '93 276; '94 121; '97 178, 331
Cinnamon-Fudge Sauce, '85 141
Classic Chocolate Sauce, '85 207
Creamy Chocolate Sauce, '88 M177
Dark Chocolate Sauce, '93 296; '94 234, 283; '96 310; '98 336
Dark Chocolate Sauce, Poached Pears with, '90 M141
Double Chocolate Sauce, '83 79
Easy Chocolate Sauce, '92 148
Fudge Sauce, '91 174
Heavenly Chocolate Sauce, '79 79; '82 167
Honey-Chocolate Sauce, '89 251
Hot Fudge Sauce, '82 181, 295; '84 143; '97 255
Hot Fudge Sauce, Easy, '84 69; '94 194
Hot Fudge Sauce, Quick, '82 212
Kahlúa Chocolate Sauce, '85 155
Mint Sauce, Chocolate-, '93 86; '94 314; '98 217
Mint Sauce, Quick Chocolate, '86 M58
Mocha Sauce, '98 57
Orange Sauce, Chocolate-, '86 165; '94 314
Peanut Butter Sauce, Chocolate-, '79 91, M156
Peppermint Sauce, Chocolate-, '94 205
Praline Sauce, Chocolate-, '85 M295
Supreme, Chocolate Sauce, '85 189
Toffee-Fudge Sauce, '89 95
White Chocolate Sauce, '92 164; '96 310
Scones, Mocha-Pecan, '97 45
Shavings, Chocolate Hearts and, '86 26
Shell, Chocolate-Coconut Pie, '82 210; '83 100
Shell, Chocolate Pastry, '87 262
Shell, Chocolate Tart, '99 315
Shells with Kahlúa Cream, Chocolate, '88 195
S'mores, Grilled Pound Cake, '98 179
Snacks, Chocolate-Peanut Butter, '90 226
Sorbet, Chocolate, '97 111
Soufflé au Chocolat Cointreau, '94 56
Soufflé, Chocolate, '84 317; '94 46
Soufflé, Chocolate Mint, '81 16
Soufflé, Light Chocolate, '83 278
Soufflé with White Chocolate Mousse, Chocolate, '98 57
Soup, Mexican Chocolate, '96 277
Spoons, Dipped Chocolate-Almond, '95 M277
Spread, Chocolate Cheese, '87 292
Sticks, Chocolate-Sesame, '91 316
Sticky Buns, Easy Caramel-Chocolate, '95 36
Strawberries, Chocolate-Dipped, '98 M100
Strawberries Dipped in White Chocolate, '90 83
Sundae Dessert, Hot Fudge, '84 313; '86 322
Sundaes, Cocoa-Kahlúa, '83 M58
Supreme, Chocolate, '84 94
Tacos, Dessert, '97 141

Torte, Frozen Viennese, '93 171
Trifle, Chocolate, '88 258; '93 326
Velvet, Chocolate Almond, '81 148
Waffles, Fudge, '94 205
Waffles with Strawberry Cream, Chocolate, '88 153
Whip, Chocolate, '89 326
Yogurt, Mocha Sauce with Chocolate, '92 243
Zuppa Inglese, '99 M267
CHOP SUEY
Cabbage Chop Suey, '81 101
Chicken Chop Suey, '81 227
Salad, Chop Suey, '81 37
CHOWDERS. *See also* **GUMBOS, SOUPS.**
Bell Pepper-Cheese Chowder, '95 240
Bluefish Chowder, '84 282
Broccoli Chowder, '79 16
Cabbage Chowder, Hearty, '80 25
Cheddar Cheese Chowder, '97 30
Cheddar Chowder, Hearty, '79 16
Cheese Chowder, Golden, '80 73
Cheese Chowder, Hot, '89 16
Chicken-and-Corn Chowder, Curried, '92 21
Chicken-and-Roasted Vegetable Chowder, '97 21
Chicken Chowder, '83 20
Chicken Chowder, Cheesy, '92 21
Chicken Chowder Sauterne, '84 235
Chicken-Vegetable Chowder, Creamy, '92 20
Clam-and-Sausage Chowder, '94 104
Clam Chowder, '79 182; '81 32; '85 9; '86 36; '89 95; '90 202
Clam Chowder, New England, '86 M72; '98 289
Clam Chowder, Ocracoke, '79 31
Clam Chowder, Tomato-, '84 251
Corn and Bacon Chowder, Fresh, '93 203
Corn-and-Bacon Chowder, Southern, '96 166
Corn and Cheese Chowder, '80 228
Corn Chowder, '81 128; '83 20; '84 M38; '85 10; '90 202; '91 132; '97 241; '98 31
Corn Chowder, Delicious, '82 279
Fish Chowder, '79 152; '84 M38
Fish Chowder, Basque, '86 36
Fish Chowder, Chunky, '92 331
Fish Chowder, Creamy, '79 16
Fish Chowder, Tasty, '80 188
Green Bean, Mushroom, and Ham Chowder, Creamy, '99 M336
Greens Chowder, Mixed, '97 262
Ham-and-Cheese Chowder, '89 15
Ham and Corn Chowder, '79 16
Ham-and-Corn Chowder, '82 40
Ham Chowder, Creamy, '88 M53
Ham 'n Cheese Chowder, '79 199
Harvest Chowder, '83 317
Mushroom Chowder, '79 16
Mushroom-Potato Chowder, '92 331
Okra Chowder, Quick, '80 185
Oyster Chowder, '83 229
Oyster-Corn Chowder, '83 211
Potato Chowder with Ham, '99 141
Potato-Corn Chowder, '94 66
Potato-Vegetable Chowder, '98 335
Pumpkin-Corn Chowder, '97 219
Red Snapper Chowder, '85 217
Salmon Chowder, '97 125
Sausage-Bean Chowder, '83 20
Seafood Chowder, '85 9; '92 122
Seafood Chowder, Curried, '94 103
Seafood Chowder, Southern, '83 20
Shrimp and Corn Chowder, '79 199
Shrimp Chowder, '89 218
Sweet Potato Chowder, Asian, '97 213
Swiss-Broccoli Chowder, '80 73
Turkey Chowder, '85 10; '91 312

Turkey-Corn Chowder, '81 98; '96 279
Vegetable Chowder, Cheesy, '80 25; '83 20
Vegetable Chowder, Easy, '97 304
Vegetable Chowder, Hearty, '88 56
Vegetable Chowder, Oven-Roasted, '95 229
White Bean Chowder with Sage Pesto, '97 22

CHOW MEIN
Beef-and-Vegetable Chow Mein Casserole, '83 313
Chicken Casserole, Chow Mein, '96 276
Chicken Chow Mein, '90 68
Noodles, Chow Mein over Crispy, '85 286
Pork Chow Mein, '80 208; '90 101
Shrimp Chow Mein, '82 30

CHRISTMAS
  Beverages
    Blossom, Christmas, '99 321
    Milk, Santa Claus, '92 281
    Punch, Christmas, '84 259; '89 330
    Punch, Christmas Eve, '86 314
    Punch, Merry Christmas, '79 285
    Tea, Christmas Fruit, '83 275
    Wassail, Christmas, '93 295
  Bread, Christmas, '87 296; '88 288
  Bread, Norwegian Christmas, '79 234
  Bread Stars, '93 286
  Buns, Christmas Morning Sticky, '97 245
  Cake, Christmas Coconut, '82 262
  Candy Canes and Wreaths, Braided, '92 276
  Chili, White Christmas, '98 266
  Cinnamon Ornaments, '85 284
  Coeur à la Crème, Christmas, '86 278
  Coffee Cakes, Christmas-Tree, '87 298
  Cookies
    Calendar, Cookie Advent, '85 325
    Candy Canes and Wreaths, Braided, '92 276
    Cards, Christmas Cookie, '84 302
    Cherry Cookies, Christmas, '88 282
    Date Cookies, Christmas, '88 287
    Eggnog Christmas Cookies, '79 255
    Elf Biscuits, '99 309
    Elf Cookie, '80 279, 303
    Fruit Squares, Christmas, '88 282
    Gingerbread Bowl, Christmas, '93 266
    Gingerbread Cookies, '80 278
    Gingerbread Men, '99 294
    Gingerbread Snowflake Cookies, '98 324
    Gingerbread Votives, '98 309
    Jammies, Christmas, '95 322
    Lizzies, Christmas, '87 257
    Moravian Christmas Cookies, '91 282
    Mrs. Claus Cookie, '80 279, 303
    Nutcracker Cookies, '97 286
    Painted Cookies, '86 322
    Reindeer Cookies, Jolly, '91 273
    Rudolph Cookie, '80 279, 303
    Rudolph Cookies, '99 M309
    Santa Claus Cookie, '80 278, 303
    Santa Cookies, Easy, '95 321
    Santa's Whiskers, '85 323
    Sleigh Cookie, '80 279, 303
    Spiced Christmas Cookies, '87 294
    Spritz Cookies, Christmas, '96 314
    Strawberries, Christmas, '87 293
    Sugarplum Fairy Wands, '97 M286
    Sugarplum Sticks, '95 321
    Swedish Christmas Cookies, '79 290
    Tree Cookies, Christmas, '93 286
    Trees, Christmas, '89 294
    Votives, Edible, '98 309
    Wreaths, Christmas, '97 288
  Corn, Christmas, '93 325
  Cottage, Quick-Fix Christmas, '91 280
  Cottage, Sugarplum, '88 309

Cranberry Hearts, '93 286
Crostini, Christmas, '94 318
Custard, Boiled Christmas, '95 329
Dessert, White Christmas, '82 261
Dip, Christmas Confetti, '92 279
Divinity, Christmas, '81 286
Doughnuts, Snowy, '93 286
Grittibanz (Swiss Bread Figure), '93 265
Icing, Royal, '98 324
Jam, Christmas, '88 288
Jam, Christmas Brunch, '81 286
Jelly, Christmas Freezer, '86 M288
Ketchup, Christmas, '97 254
Loaf, Sweet Christmas, '84 278
Munchies, Reindeer, '91 276
Nuggets, Golden North Pole, '99 M309
Orange Baskets, '93 286
Ornaments, Edible, '94 316
Paints, Powdered Sugar, '97 286
Pandoro, '93 267
Panettone, '93 266
Peanut Butter Elf Bites, '91 275
Pecans, Christmas Eve, '91 276
Pie, White Christmas, '88 281; '93 289
Pinecones, Peanut Butter-Suet, '93 286
Pinwheels, Santa's, '91 275
Potatoes, Christmas, '88 252
Potpourri, Christmas, '94 317
Pretzel Garlands, '93 286
Pudding with Brandy Sauce, Baked Christmas, '88 279
Reindeer Food, Magic, '99 M309
Reindeer Nibbles, '92 280
Relish Tree, Christmas, '84 257
Salad, Christmas, '88 249
Salad, Christmas Snow, '82 266
Salad, Cranberry Christmas, '79 243
Salad, Eggnog Christmas, '86 281
Sandwiches, Christmas Tree, '92 279
Sandwich Wreath, Festive, '86 333
Santa's Hat, '92 279
Santa's Whiskers, '85 323
Scent, Christmas, '84 325
Snowman, Marshmallow, '96 311
Spices, Barclay House Mulling, '86 289
Strata, Christmas Morning, '95 282
Strawberries, Christmas, '87 293; '94 331
Sugarplum Fairy Wands, '97 M286
Sugar Plums, '92 281
Tannenbaum Temptations, '92 14
Wine, Christmas Dreams in, '91 260
Wreath, Christmas, '80 280
Wreath, Della Robbia Fruit, '87 294
Wreaths, Braided Candy Canes and, '92 276

CHUTNEYS. *See also* **PESTOS, RELISHES, SALSAS, SAUCES, TOPPINGS.**
Apple Chutney, '92 309
Apple Chutney, Sweet-'n'-Hot, '96 14
Blueberry Chutney, '95 190
Cantaloupe Chutney, Fresh, '97 148
Cherry-Peach Chutney, Glazed Ham with, '97 315
Commander's Chutney, '87 245
Cranberry-Amaretto Chutney with Cream Cheese, '87 244
Cranberry Chutney, '80 243; '83 260; '84 265; '96 275; '98 276, 318
Cranberry-Orange Chutney, '79 292
Fruit Chutney, Autumn, '88 M230
Fruit Chutney, Fall, '97 218
Kiwifruit-Onion Chutney, '93 125
Mango Chutney, '89 141; '96 182
Mango Chutney, Blue-Ribbon, '96 206
Orange-Cranberry Chutney, '86 266
Pâté, Chutney-Cheese, '84 152

Peach Chutney, '84 179; '96 207
Pear-Apple Chutney, '89 141
Pear Chutney, '95 251; '98 243
Pepper Chutney, Jeweled, '94 316
Plum Chutney, '84 179
Rhubarb Chutney, '87 245
Roll, Chutney, '83 259
Rosy Chutney, '80 120
Sauce, Chutney-Mustard, '89 242
Sweet Potato Chutney, '99 45
Tomato-Apple Chutney, '84 180
Tomato Chutney, '99 143

CLAMS
Backyard Clambake, '81 92
Bisque, Clam, '86 228
Casino, Clams, '81 125
Casino, Maryland Clams, '89 196
Chase, Clams, '79 85
Chowder, Clam, '79 182; '81 32; '85 9; '86 36; '89 95; '90 202
Chowder, Clam-and-Sausage, '94 104
Chowder, New England Clam, '86 M72; '98 289
Chowder, Ocracoke Clam, '79 31
Chowder, Tomato-Clam, '84 251
Cocktail, Tomato-Clam, '87 252
Crisps, Clam, '80 151
Dip, Clam, '79 151; '80 265
Dip, Hot Clam, '82 59; '89 48
Dip, Zesty Clam, '92 25
Fritters, Clam, '79 151; '86 71
Linguine, Clam, '95 212
Linguine, Quick Clam, '90 233
Littleneck Clams with Cilantro-Black Walnut Pesto, '97 164
Oreganata, Clams, '85 104
Pizza, Baby Clam, '87 182
Puffs, Clam, '90 60
Quiche, Clam, '83 215
Sauce, Linguine in Clam, '81 83
Sauce, Linguine with Clam, '84 124; '88 90; '89 178
Sauce, Pasta with Clam, '84 291
Sauce, Pasta with Pesto-Clam, '98 17
Sauce, Tricolor Pasta with Clam, '93 272
Sauce, Vermicelli and Sprouts with Red Clam, '86 143
Sauce, Vermicelli with Clam, '85 295
Sauce with Linguine, Clam, '84 9
Shells, Baked Clam, '87 94
Soup, Clam Florentine, '85 23
Spread, Creamy Clam, '91 274
Steamed Clams Chesapeake, '89 196

COBBLERS. *See* **PIES, PUFFS, AND PASTRIES/Cobblers, Crisps, and Crumbles.**
COCONUT. *See also* **AMBROSIA.**
Balls, Coconut-Almond, '84 256
  Bars and Cookies
    Brownies, Chocolate-Coconut, '97 35
    Brownies, Coconut-Pecan-Frosted, '97 99
    Cherry Cookies, Coconut-, '79 292
    Chocolate Macaroon Cookies, '88 217
    Clear-the-Cupboard Cookies, '99 278
    Crinkle Sunflower Cookies, '83 149
    Crisp Coconut Cookies, '89 162
    English Cherubs, '83 257
    Golden Bars, '84 255
    Graham Cracker Layered Cookies, '98 94
    Graham Cracker Layered Cookies, Chocolate, '98 94
    Granola Bars, Coconut, '85 202
    Hawaiian Bars, '84 153
    Kisses, Coconut, '90 106
    Macadamia Cookies, Coconut-, '98 294

COCONUT, Bars and Cookies
(continued)

    Macaroons, Chewy Peanut Butter, **'95** 214
    Macaroons, Chocolate, **'83** 300
    Macaroons, Coconut, **'79** 52
    No-Bake Bars, Creamy, **'97** 166
    Oatmeal-Coconut Cookies, **'80** 218
    Oatmeal Cookies, Crispy Coconut-, **'93** 80
    Peanut Butter-Coconut Cookies, **'83** 113
    Robin's Nests, Coconut, **'98** M111
    Shortbread Cookies, Coconut, **'93** 316
    Squares, Chocolate-Coconut, **'90** 70
    Swirls, Coconut, **'97** 274
Biscuits, Yummy Coconut, **'95** 99
Bonbons, Coconut-Black Walnut, **'82** 307
Bread, Coconut, **'83** 140
Bread, Pumpkin-Coconut, **'87** 255
Broth with Noodles, Thai Coconut, **'98** 295
Cakes
    Angel Cake, Spiked Coconut, **'85** 279
    Apple Coconut Cake, **'80** 226
    Banana-Coconut Cake, **'93** 154
    Banana Split Cake, **'99** 48
    Brown Sugar Snack Cake, **'98** 195
    Carrot Cake, Fresh Coconut-, **'80** 299
    Cheesecake, Coconut-Chocolate-Almond, **'98** 322
    Chocolate-Coconut Cake, **'83** 23
    Christmas Coconut Cake, **'82** 262
    Coconut Cake, **'92** 120
    Coffee Cake, Cranberry-Coconut, **'93** 332
    Coffee Cake, Oatmeal-Coconut, **'83** 312
    Coffee Cake, Pineapple-Coconut, **'94** 49
    Cream Cake, Coconut, **'81** 179; **'91** 269
    Creamy Coconut Cake, **'84** 43
    Fresh Coconut Cake, **'80** 289; **'82** 52; **'85** 281
    Fudge Cake, Coconut-, **'99** 206
    Hibiscus-Nectar Cake, **'96** 248
    Holiday Coconut Cake, **'90** 308
    Italian Cream Cake, **'96** 262
    Italian Cream Cake, Quick, **'99** 307
    Layer Cake, Stately Coconut, **'81** 70
    Lemon Cake, Coconut-, **'95** 319
    Lemon-Coconut Cream Cake, **'81** 179
    Lemon-Coconut Sheet Cake, **'85** 117
    MaMa's Coconut Cake, **'97** 71
    Orange-Coconut Angel Food Cake, **'94** 294
    Piña Colada Cake, **'99** 117
    Pineapple Cake, Coconut-, **'89** 56
    Pineapple Cake, Nanny's Famous Coconut-, **'97** 277
    Pineapple Layer Cake, Coconut-, **'80** 140
    Pound Cake, Coconut, **'82** 87; **'91** 224
    Pound Cake, Coconut Cream, **'84** 10
    Pound Cake, Coconut-Cream Cheese, **'85** 297; **'90** 305
    Regal Coconut Cake, **'83** 299
    Roll, Coconut-Pineapple Cake, **'84** 304
    Rum-Orange Coconut Cake, **'88** 224
    Spice Cake, Coconut-, **'84** 255; **'87** 296
    Toasted Coconut Cake, **'86** 60
    Unforgettable Coconut Cake, **'90** 104
    White Chocolate-Coconut Cake, **'87** 263
Calypso, Coco-Berry, **'89** 171
Candy, Coconut, **'79** 272; **'80** 250
Caramels, Coconut-Macadamia, **'98** 305
Chicken Balls, Coconut Curried, **'91** 165
Chicken, Coconut, **'98** 20
Chicken with Fresh Fruit, Coconut, **'93** 294
Cloud, Coconut, **'80** 70
Clusters, Pecan-Coconut, **'86** M251
Coffee, Coconut, **'97** 17

Cookies. *See* **COCONUT/Bars and Cookies.**
Cream, Orange-Coconut, **'84** 24
Crust, Chocolate-Coconut, **'87** 261
Crust, Coconut, **'89** 160
Custard, Coconut, **'86** 109; **'97** 131
Dessert, Chilled Coconut, **'83** 116
Dessert, Coconut-Caramel, **'92** 44
Dessert in a Nutshell, **'96** 318
Dessert, Macaroon-Sherbet Frozen, **'79** 212
Dip, Coconut-Honey Fruit, **'84** 171
Dressing, Coconut, **'87** 251
Dressing, Coconut-Orange, **'97** 93
Dressing, Orange-Coconut, **'80** 158
Dressing, Tangy Coconut-Fruit, **'84** 171
Drink, Coconut-Pineapple, **'83** 172
Drops, Chocolate-Coconut Almond, **'87** 223
Filling, Coconut, **'81** 265
Filling, Coconut Cream, **'84** 200
Filling, Piña Colada, **'99** 117
Filling, Sour Cream-Coconut, **'92** 120
Frosting, Coconut, **'82** 262; **'91** 269
Frosting, Coconut Chocolate, **'79** 13
Frosting, Coconut Cream Cheese, **'86** 60
Frosting, Coconut-Pecan, **'81** 296; **'83** M233; **'84** 43, 322; **'97** 99
Frosting, Creamy Coconut, **'80** 287
Frosting, Lemon-Coconut, **'90** 253
Frosting, Nutty Coconut, **'86** 8
Frost, Pink Coconut, **'79** 174; **'80** 128
Fruit Bowl, Coconut, **'83** 111
Granola, **'99** 212
Ice Cream, Coconut, **'98** 180
Ice Cream, Coconut Fried, **'85** 141
Ice Cream, Fresh Coconut, **'79** 166
Joys, Chocolate-Covered Coconut, **'98** M282
Joys, Coconut, **'98** 282
Macaroon Charlotte, **'81** 296
Macaroon-Stuffed Peaches, **'79** 178
Milk, Chicken in Coconut, **'97** 202
Mousse, Coconut-Pineapple, **'94** 198
Muffins, Coconut, **'95** 214
Muffins, Coconut-Molasses, **'82** 210
Nests, Strawberry Coconut, **'88** 136
Nog, Coconut, **'83** 275
Pears, Spicy Coconut, **'83** 207
Pecan Coils, Coconut-, **'90** 196
Pies
    Blender Coconut Pie, **'84** 236
    Buttermilk-Coconut Pie, **'94** 246
    Caramel Pies, Coconut-, **'87** 260
    Cherry Pie, Coconut Crumb, **'92** 30
    Chess Pie, Coconut, **'86** 220
    Coconut Pie, **'93** 115
    Cream Pie, Coconut, **'80** 238; **'81** 136; **'82** 85; **'84** 49; **'87** 207; **'89** 236; **'90** 312; **'98** 161
    Cream Pie, Fresh Coconut, **'80** 289
    Cream Pie, Surprise Coconut, **'92** 43
    Crunch Pie, Coconut, **'90** 105
    Custard Pie, Coconut, **'82** 33
    French Coconut Pie, **'90** 162
    Macadamia Nut Pie, Coconut-, **'97** 110
    Macaroon Pie, Coconut, **'88** 204
    Magic Coconut Pie, **'79** 53
    Mock Coconut Pie, **'86** 200
    Orange Chess Pie, Coconut-, **'89** 169
    Orange-Coconut Cream Pie, **'94** 208
    Orange-Coconut Pie, **'90** 90
    Pecan Chess Pie, Coconut-, **'81** 248
    Pecan Pie, Coconut, **'81** 161
    Pineapple-Coconut Chess Pie, **'92** 214
    Pineapple Pie, Coconut-, **'84** 256
    Quick Coconut Pie, **'83** 115
    Shell, Chocolate-Coconut Pie, **'82** 210; **'83** 100
    Toasted Coconut Pie, **'90** 105

Pirate's Painkiller, **'99** 161
Pudding, Piña Colada Bread, **'98** 34
Puffs, Coconut, **'87** 277
Relish, Pineapple-Coconut, **'96** 323; **'97** 27
Salad, Cantaloupe Colada, **'97** 148
Salad, Chunky Fruit-and-Coconut, **'84** 24
Salad, Curried Poached Pears with Coconut-Chicken, **'97** 93
Sauce, Coconut, **'98** 34
Sauce, Coconut-Orange, **'85** 189
Sauce, Creamy Light Coconut, **'82** 177
Shrimp, Coconut-Beer, **'85** 230; **'89** 23
Shrimp, Coconut Fried, **'96** 248
Soufflé, Coconut, **'79** 73; **'85** 212
Spread, Coconut-Cranberry Cheese, **'92** 328
Spread, Coconut-Pineapple, **'93** 309
Stir-Fry, Coconut-Beef, **'97** 18
Sweet Potatoes, Coconut-Broiled, **'84** 231
Sweet Potatoes, Coconut-Orange, **'84** 252
Sweet Potatoes, Coconut-Stuffed, **'82** 204
Tarts with Macadamia Nut Crusts, Coconut Cream, **'97** 62
Tropical Snow, **'86** 34
COFFEE
Beverages
    After-Dinner Coffee, **'81** 262
    Almond-Coffee Delight, **'84** 115
    Blends, Coffee, **'95** 276
    Brandied Coffee, **'81** 244
    Brandy Coffee, **'97** 17
    Cappuccino, Café, **'82** 253
    Cappuccino, Chocolate Castle, **'84** 53
    Cappuccino Coffee Dessert, **'92** 264
    Cappuccino, Flaming, **'79** 293
    Cappuccino, Iced, **'99** 333
    Cappuccino Sipper, **'99** 29
    Chiller, Royal Cup, **'98** 218
    Chocolate-Almond Coffee, **'84** 54
    Chocolate Coffee, **'82** 43; **'97** 17
    Cocoa-Coffee, **'83** 55
    Coconut Coffee, **'97** 17
    Colombian Royal, Café, **'80** M290
    Colonial Coffee, **'89** 290
    "Concrete," Abaco Mocha, **'94** 114
    Cream, Café, **'82** 312
    Cream, Icy Rum Coffee, **'83** 172
    Creamy Coffee, **'81** 244
    Dessert Drink, Simply Super, **'83** 303
    Dessert, Light Coffee, **'88** 260
    Diablo, Café, **'80** 259
    Espresso, Amaretto, **'92** 263
    Floats, Maple-Coffee, **'86** 195
    Freeze, Amaretto-Coffee, **'99** 161
    Frosted Coffee, **'81** 244
    German Chocolate Café au Lait, **'92** 264
    Hazelnut-Coffee Ice, **'94** 233
    Holiday Coffee, **'90** 273
    Hot Buttered Bourbon, **'97** 17
    Irish Coffee, Creamy, **'79** 232
    Irish Coffee, Flaming, **'79** 293
    Irish Coffee Nog, **'84** 258; **'93** 340
    Irish Cream Nog, **'82** 312
    Kahlúa Beverage Sipper, **'99** 27
    Kahlúa Delight, Make-Ahead, **'84** M89
    Kona Luscious, **'84** 54
    Liqueur, Coffee-Flavored, **'86** 266
    Maple Coffee, **'97** 17
    Mexican Coffee, **'83** 175, 275; **'88** 247; **'91** 78; **'93** 310; **'94** 97
    Mexicano, Café, **'92** 208
    Mix, Cappucino, **'90** 87
    Mix, Fireside Coffee, **'87** 241
    Mix, Hot Mocha-Cocoa, **'82** 296
    Mix, Mocha-Flavored Hot Cocoa, **'91** 316

Mocha Blend, '95 276
Mocha Chocolate Fluff, '89 170
Mocha Cocoa, '83 318
Mocha Coffee, '85 M329
Mocha Cream, Café, '84 54
Mocha Deluxe Hot Drink, '82 289
Mocha Espresso, Italian, '82 254
Mocha Frosty, '92 44
Mocha, Hot, '84 60
Mocha, Mexican, '93 M341
Mocha Milkshake, '89 35
Mocha Polka, '89 171
Mocha, Quick Viennese, '79 232
Mocha, Spirited Hot, '91 M260
Mocha, Swiss-Style, '82 253
Mocha Warmer, '97 272
Nog, Brandied Coffee, '86 329
Orange Blend, '95 276
Orange Coffee, '96 313
Orange Coffee, Viennese, '84 54
Pontalba, Cafe, '92 83
Praline Coffee, '97 17
Praline-Flavored Coffee, '87 69
Punch, Coffee, '80 50; '83 275; '88 83
Punch, Coffee-and-Cream, '85 116
Punch, Coffee-Eggnog, '86 281
Punch, Coffee Eggnog, '92 264
Punch, Creamy Coffee, '81 50
Punch, "Eye-Opener" Coffee, '92 80
Punch, Irish Coffee-Eggnog, '95 314
Punch, Mocha, '84 58, 166; '86 270; '95 141
Punch, Rich-and-Creamy Coffee, '82 121
Refresher, Velvet Coffee, '79 149
Royal, Café, '80 259
Shake, Peach-Coffee Milk, '84 284
Soda, Coffee, '97 272
Spiced Brew, Hot, '91 36
Spiced Coffee, Special, '84 284
Spiced-Up Coffee, '89 92
Vienna Blend, '95 276
Viennese, Café, '82 254
Buttercream, Coffee, '95 277
Buttons, Coffee, '99 66
Cake, Cappuccino Mousse, '99 154
Cake, Coffee Sponge, '83 229; '91 55
Cake, Extra-Rich Chocolate, '99 271
Cake, Two-Day Coffee Sponge, '86 75
Chill, Coffee-and-Cream, '99 126
Cones, Chocolate-Coffee, '96 M316
Cookies, Java Shortbread, '94 233
Cream Puffs, Java, '81 187
Crème Brûlée, Coffee, '95 323
Crêpes, Coffee Ice Cream, '84 85
Dessert, Chocolate-Coffee Frozen, '85 172
Dip, Kahlúa, '99 139
Fajitas, Java, '96 227
Filling, Chocolate Midnight, '96 120
Filling, Coffee, '96 316
Frosting, Chocolate-Coffee, '84 36; '88 269
Frosting, Coffee, '94 86
Frosting, Coffee Buttercream, '99 155
Fudge, Coffee-Chip, '86 74
Fudge, White Chocolate-Coffee, '94 232
Granita, Coffee-Kahlúa, '88 118
Ice Cream, Coffee, '88 202
Ice Cream Crunch, Coffee, '82 182
Kisses, Chocolate-Dipped Coffee, '96 313
Mallow, Coffee, '80 109
Meringues with Butterscotch Mousse, Coffee,
   '93 254
Mocha. *See also* **COFFEE/Beverages.**
   Angel Squares, Mocha, '98 61
   Blend, Mocha, '95 276
   Brownies, Mocha, '87 93

Buttercream, Mocha, '89 42
Cake, Belgian Mocha, '84 316
Cake, Dark Mocha-Chocolate, '84 311
Cake, Double Mocha, '84 311
Cake, Mocha Marble Pound, '99 23
Cheesecake, Mocha, '98 278
Cheesecake, Mocha-Chocolate, '88 258
Cheesecake, Mocha Swirl, '87 262
Chiffon, Mocha, '86 75
"Concrete," Abaco Mocha, '94 114
Cupcakes, Mocha, '85 250
Dessert, Frozen Mocha, '84 311
Dessert, Mocha Alaska, '84 191
Dessert, Mocha-Almond, '80 289; '81 62
Filling, Mocha, '80 55; '82 262
Filling, Mocha Cream, '81 187; '84 305
Freeze, Royal Mocha, '84 53
Frosting, Creamy Mocha, '82 289; '84 311;
   '91 248
Frosting, Mocha, '83 301; '84 316; '87 224;
   '94 292; '97 35; '99 66
Frosting, Mocha Butter Cream, '79 281
Frosting, Mocha-Buttercream, '86 26
Frozen Mocha Delight, '96 179
Frozen Mocha Squares, '81 187
Fudge, Creamy Mocha, '95 51
Gingerbread, Mocha, '81 207; '82 14
Ice Cream, Mocha, '88 202; '97 M145
Parfaits, Mocha-Mallow, '80 219
Pie, Chocolate-Mocha Crunch, '81 136
Pie, Mocha, '94 168
Pie, Mocha Meringue, '80 242; '88 163
Pots de Crème, Mocha, '88 M45
Pralines, Mocha, '92 313; '93 51
Pudding, Pecan-Mocha, '89 M130
Roll, Chocolate Mocha Cream, '84 304
Roulage, Chocolate-Mocha, '80 216
Sauce, Mocha, '98 57
Sauce with Chocolate Yogurt Mocha, '92 243
Scones, Mocha-Pecan, '97 45
Tart, Black Bottom Mocha-Cream, '92 304
Torte, Mocha, '99 66
Torte, Mocha Brownie, '85 102
Torte, Mocha Velvet, '92 318
Mousse, Coffee, '84 126
Mousse, Coffee-Nut, '86 319
Mousse Present, Chocolate, '99 281
Mousse, Quick-as-a-Wink, '84 311
Napoleons, Coffee, '95 276
Nuggets, Coffee, '95 278
Parfaits, Coffee Crunch, '82 159
Pecans, Coffee 'n' Spice, '88 256
Penuche, Coffee, '98 305
Pie, Coffee, '96 148
Pie, Coffee Cream, '94 209
Pie, Coffee Ice Cream, '79 231
Pie, Coffee Pecan, '82 74
Pie, Decadent Mud, '89 252
Pie, Tipsy Mud, '97 251
Pralines, Café au Lait, '92 313; '93 51
Pralines, Plantation Coffee, '86 241
Tart, Coffee, '99 67
Tiramisù, '98 280
Tortoni, Coffee-Almond, '81 30
Tortoni, Creamy Coffee, '88 268
Wafers, Kahlúa, '99 147
COFFEE CAKES. *See* **CAKES/Coffee Cakes.**
COLESLAW. *See* **SLAWS.**
COLLARD GREENS. *See* **GREENS.**
COOKIES. *See also* **BROWNIES.**
   Almond-Anise Biscotti, '93 266
   Almond Biscotti, '91 108
   Almond Brittle Cookies with Ice Cream Balls,
      '96 202

Almond Butter Cookies, '79 52
Almond Chip Balls, Toasted, '84 240
Almond Cookies, '83 22, 181; '91 51; '92 176
Almond Cookies, Light, '83 151
Almond Cookies, Skillet, '97 288
Almond Cookies, Swedish, '85 312
Almond Snaps, '92 273
Almond Spritz Cookies, '82 306
Apple-Filled Cookies, '92 311
Apricot Cookies, '95 322
Bars and Squares
   Almond Bars, Swedish, '97 322
   Almond Brickle Treats, '95 321
   Almond Cake Squares, '79 111
   Almond-Chocolate Bars, '83 304
   Almond Cream Confections, '87 198; '90 310
   Apple Butter Bars, '84 153
   Apple Kuchen, '79 24
   Apricot-Almond Squares, '95 272
   Apricot Bars, '81 247
   Apricot-Oatmeal Bars, '86 216
   Apricot-Raisin Bars, '87 32
   Banana Breakfast Bars, '79 124
   Blackberry Bars, '87 130
   Blackberry-Filled Bars, '79 124
   Blackberry Jam Bars, '82 M185
   Blondie Swirls, '85 248
   Blond Nut Squares, '82 156
   Brazil Squares, '82 306
   Butter Pecan Pie Squares, '81 262
   Butter Pecan Turtle Bars, '90 70
   Butterscotch Bars, '82 209; '83 297
   By-Cracky Bars, '84 212
   Caramel-Pecan Triangles, '99 281
   Carrot-Lemon Squares, Golden, '80 40
   Carrot Squares, '79 256
   Cherry Bars, Delightful, '86 217
   Cherry Squares, '97 273
   Cherry Squares, Surprise, '82 57
   Choco-Crumble Bars, '79 292
   Chocolate-Butterscotch Bars, '81 197
   Chocolate-Caramel Layer Squares, '79 83
   Chocolate Cereal Bars, Chewy, '97 317
   Chocolate Chess Squares, '92 45
   Chocolate Chip Bars, '81 130
   Chocolate Chip-Peanut Butter Squares,
      '84 118
   Chocolate Chip Squares, '83 170; '89 143
   Chocolate Chip Squares, Chewy, '91 175
   Chocolate Cinnamon Bars, '82 209
   Chocolate-Coconut Squares, '90 70
   Chocolate-Crème de Menthe Bars, '86 245
   Chocolate Crème de Menthe Bites, '88 285
   Chocolate Dream Bars, '79 256; '82 298
   Chocolate-Peanut Crispies, '93 80
   Chocolate-Peppermint Squares, '81 119
   Cinnamon Chews, '84 110
   Cinnamon Sand Bars, '91 178
   Coconut Granola Bars, '85 202
   Coffee Bars, Frosted, '79 256
   Congo Squares, '96 94
   Cranberry-Caramel Bars, '98 277
   Crème de Menthe Squares, '93 256
   Date Bars, '84 313; '95 322
   Date Bars, No-Bake, '79 256
   Date Bars, Nutty, '84 153
   Date-Nut Bars, '80 166
   Date-Oat Bars, '80 M172
   English Cherubs, '83 257
   Fudge Bars, '86 93
   Fudge Bars, Yummy, '87 158
   German Chocolate Chess Squares, '94 51
   Golden Bars, '84 255
   Graham Cracker Layered Cookies, '98 94

COOKIES, Bars and Squares
(continued)

Graham Cracker Layered Cookies, Chocolate, '98 94
Granola Bars, '83 305; '95 214
Granola Bars, Fruit and Nut, '81 49
Granola Bars, No-Bake, '97 220
Hawaiian Bars, '84 153
Honey Cake Squares, '89 250
Jam-It Bars, '87 159
Jam Squares, '81 M289
Janhagel Cookies, '86 195
Key Lime Bars with Macadamia Crust, '99 282
Layer Squares, Novelty, '90 70
Lemon Bars Deluxe, '79 35
Lemon Bars, Tangy, '86 217
Lemon-Pecan Squares, '89 124
Lemon Squares, '81 197; '97 329
Lemon Yogurt Wheat Bars, '79 93
Lime Squares, '79 2
Marmalade Biscuit Squares, '79 193
Meringue-Chocolate Chip Bars, '84 118
Mincemeat-Spice Bars, '88 231; '89 22
Mystery Bars, '93 239
Nutmeg Logs, Frosted, '85 324
Nutty Choco Snacks, '83 305
Oatmeal Bars, Chocolate-Topped, '86 110
Oatmeal-Caramel Bars, '85 247
Oatmeal-Date Bars, Layered, '85 10
Peanut Bars, '89 307
Peanut Bars, Chewy, '80 M172
Peanut Butter-and-Fudge Bars, '80 M172
Peanut Butter Bars, '84 243; '93 166
Peanut Butter Fingers, '79 256
Peanut Butter Frosts, '84 153
Peanut Butter-Jam Bars, '94 291
Peanut Butter Logs, No-Bake, '84 211
Peanut Butter 'n' Jelly Bars, '83 305
Peanut Butter Squares, '83 116
Pecan Bars, '82 209
Pecan Bars, Gooey, '94 133
Pecan Squares, '79 205; '90 69; '98 336
Pecan Squares, Easy, '81 230
Pecan Squares, Twice-Baked, '79 291
Pumpkin Bars, '80 40
Pumpkin Nut Bars, '82 217
Raisin Bars, '94 228
Raspberry Bars, '82 209; '84 212
Rhubarb Squares, '91 146
Rhubarb Squares, Rosy, '79 111
Scotch Bars, Chewy, '98 M291
Shortbread, Butter-Mint, '99 28
Shortbread, Orange, '91 272
Strawberry Bars, '81 301
Toffee Treats, '89 330
Tropical Bars, '80 284
Turtle Bars, Gooey, '96 189
Wheat Germ Squares, Spicy, '80 44
Yummy Bars, '92 171
Zucchini Bars, '85 77
Benne Seed Wafers, '96 315
Bird's Nest Cookies, '93 284
Biscotti, Anise, '96 282
Biscotti, Chocolate Chip-Cinnamon, '96 281
Biscotti Cioccolata, '93 268
Biscotti, Cocoa-Almond, '96 280
Biscotti, Fruitcake, '96 281
Bonbon Cookies, Surprise, '88 119
Bourbon Balls, '81 254
Bourbon Dunkers, Crunchy, '85 90
Brutti Ma Buoni (Ugly but Good), '93 267
Butter Cookies, '85 322
Butter Cookies, Chocolate-Tipped, '84 258; '90 312
Butter Cookies, Holiday, '92 317
Butter Cookies, Melt-Away, '81 20
Butter-Nut Strips, '82 167
Butter Pecan Cookies, '82 139
Cake Mix Cookies, '97 133
Cats' Tongues, '96 145
Cheesecake Cookies, Chewy, '82 109
Cherry Bonbon Cookies, '93 52
Cherry Crowns, '92 275
Cherry Nut Nuggets, '81 286
Chocolate-Almond Cookies, '98 293
Chocolate-Cherry Cookies, Frosted, '89 294
Chocolate Chewies, Easy, '93 296; '94 234
Chocolate Chip Cookies, Giant, '84 119
Chocolate Chip Melt-Aways, '84 118
Chocolate Cookies, Caramel-Filled, '92 319
Chocolate Cookies, Chewy, '97 166
Chocolate Cookies, Sugar-Coated, '92 274
Chocolate-Covered Cherry Cookies, '99 280
Chocolate Crunch Cookies, '91 316
Chocolate-Filled Bonbons, '89 162
Chocolate-Mint Snaps, '83 103; '84 96
Chocolate-Peanut Butter Cones, '85 14
Chocolate-Peanut Butter Cookies, '85 90
Chocolate-Peanut Butter Cups, '85 14
Chocolate Seashells, '91 178
Chocolate Snappers, Jumbo, '81 218
Chocolate Snowflake Cookies, '89 329
Chocolate Spice Cookies, Lemon-Iced, '97 123
Chocolate-Tipped Log Cookies, '87 294
Choco-Nut Sandwich Cookies, '84 200
Christmas
Calendar, Cookie Advent, '85 325
Candy Canes and Wreaths, Braided, '92 276
Cards, Christmas Cookie, '84 302
Cherry Cookies, Christmas, '88 282
Date Cookies, Christmas, '88 287
Eggnog Christmas Cookies, '79 255
Elf Biscuits, '99 309
Elf Cookie, '80 279, 303
Fruit Squares, Christmas, '88 282
Gingerbread Bowl, Christmas, '93 266
Gingerbread Cookies, '80 278
Gingerbread Men, '99 294
Gingerbread Snowflake Cookies, '98 324
Gingerbread Votives, '98 309
Jammies, Christmas, '95 322
Lizzies, Christmas, '87 257
Moravian Christmas Cookies, '91 282
Mrs. Claus Cookie, '80 279, 303
Nutcracker Cookies, '97 286
Painted Cookies, '86 322
Reindeer Cookies, Jolly, '91 273
Rudolph Cookie, '80 279, 303
Rudolph Cookies, '99 M309
Santa Claus Cookie, '80 278, 303
Santa Cookies, Easy, '95 321
Santa's Whiskers, '85 323
Sleigh Cookie, '80 279, 303
Spiced Christmas Cookies, '87 294
Spritz Cookies, Christmas, '96 314
Strawberries, Christmas, '87 293
Sugarplum Fairy Wands, '97 M286
Sugarplum Sticks, '95 321
Swedish Christmas Cookies, '79 290
Tree Cookies, Christmas, '93 286
Trees, Christmas, '89 294
Votives, Edible, '98 309
Wreaths, Christmas, '97 288
Cinnamon Balls, '79 23
Cinnamon Sticks, Italian, '93 204
Cinnamon Wafers, '81 192
Cocoa Kiss Cookies, '85 171
Coconut Cookies, Crisp, '89 162
Coconut-Oatmeal Cookies, Crispy, '93 80
Coconut Swirls, '97 274
Coffee Kisses, Chocolate-Dipped, '96 313
Cream, Cookies and, '96 179
Curled Cookies, French, '87 16
Drop
Almond Cookies, '97 288; '99 49
Almond Lace Cookies, '98 336
Ambrosia Cookies, '81 301; '82 110; '86 313
Apple Butter Spice Cookies, '79 291
Apple Cookies, Fresh, '84 36
Apple-Nut Cookies, '80 228
Apple Oatmeal Cookies, '85 215
Apple-Oatmeal Cookies, '90 218
Apricot Cookies, Frosted, '81 192
Banana Oatmeal Cookies, '79 217
Benne Seed Cookies, '84 318
Breakfast Cookies, '97 52
Breakfast Cookies, Take-Along, '84 59
Brownie Chip Cookies, '90 320
Butterscotch Cookies, '87 58
Butterscotch-Pecan Cookies, '84 36
Candy Bit Cookies, '81 192
Carrot Cookies, '82 137
Carrot Cookies, Frosted, '81 7
Carrot-Orange Cookies, '83 149
Cashew Crunch Cookies, '92 17
Cherry-Almond Drops, '81 20
Chip Cookies, Double, '81 301
Chips Cookies, Loaded-with-, '87 223
Chocolate-Bran Raisin Jumbos, '91 142
Chocolate-Brickle Cookies, '99 127
Chocolate Chewies, '93 216
Chocolate Chip Cookies, '84 120; '86 245; '90 193
Chocolate Chip Cookies, Deluxe, '79 216
Chocolate Chip Cookies, Different, '83 114
Chocolate Chip Cookies, Double, '79 217
Chocolate Chip Cookies, Jumbo, '82 110
Chocolate Chip Cookies, Light, '86 46
Chocolate Chip Cookies, Mom Ford's, '94 287
Chocolate Chip Cookies, Nutty Oatmeal-, '82 M185
Chocolate Chip-Oatmeal Cookies, '84 119
Chocolate Chip-Peanut Butter Cookies, '99 68
Chocolate Chippers, '92 206
Chocolate Chip-Pudding Cookies, '93 21
Chocolate-Chocolate Chip Cookies, '82 35
Chocolate-Chocolate Chip-Peppermint Cookies, '97 289
Chocolate Chunk-Almond Cookies, Double, '95 178
Chocolate Chunk Cookies, Super, '88 217
Chocolate Cookies, Double-, '95 272
Chocolate Cookies, Doubly-Good, '82 M185
Chocolate Crispy Cookies, '85 115
Chocolate Drop Cookies, '84 36
Chocolate Macaroon Cookies, '88 217
Chocolate Macaroons, '83 300; '87 57
Chocolate-Mint Chip Cookies, '86 245
Chocolate-Mint Cookies, '92 206
Chocolate-Nut Chews, '81 92
Chocolate-Oatmeal Cookies, '80 105
Chocolate-Orange Delights, '93 52
Chocolate-Peanut Butter Cups, '97 134
Chocolate-Peanut Cookies, '83 223
Chocolate-Raisin Oatmeal Cookies, '95 136
Chocolate Sandwich Cookies, '81 192
Choco-Peanut Chip Cookies, '92 318
Clear-the-Cupboard Cookies, '99 278
Cocoa Drop Cookies, '80 217
Coconut-Cherry Cookies, '79 292

Coconut Kisses, '90 106
Coconut-Macadamia Cookies, '98 294
Coconut Macaroons, '79 52
Coconut Robin's Nests, '98 M111
Cranberry-Almond Cookies, '98 26
Cream Cheese Cookies, '80 282
Date-Nut Chocolate Chip Cookies, Rich, '92 207
Devil Doggies, '84 37
Fibber McGee Cookies, '95 72
Forget 'em Cookies, '83 256
Fruitcake Cookies, '79 291; '86 320; '88 286;
   '96 314; '98 294
Fruitcake Cookies, Holiday, '81 301
Fruitcake Drop Cookies, '92 275
Fruit Cookies, Bourbon, '86 334
Fruit Cookies, Spicy Holiday, '83 298
Fruit Drops, Candied, '89 329
Fudge-Pecan Chewies, Alabama, '95 143
Gumdrop Cookies, '79 292
Jack-o'-Lantern Cookies, '87 214
Lace Cookies, '86 8
Lemonade Cookies, '79 51
Lemon Yummies, '81 301
Macadamia Nut White Chocolate Cookies,
   Chunky, '92 207
Melting Moments, '85 191
Meringue Kiss Cookies, '86 121
Meringue Surprise Cookies, '86 320
Mincemeat Drop Cookies, '79 246
Molasses Cookies, Chewy, '87 257
Molasses Cookies, Crispy-Chewy, '90 218
Monster Cookies, '84 36
Nugget Cookies, '79 291
Oatmeal-Chocolate Chippers, '90 218
Oatmeal-Chocolate Morsel Cookies, '95 46
Oatmeal Cookies, '92 82; '99 280
Oatmeal Cookies, Cake Mix, '96 247
Oatmeal Cookies, Cinnamon, '84 72
Oatmeal Cookies, Crunchy, '85 202
Oatmeal Cookies, Easy, '80 105
Oatmeal Cookies, Nutty, '81 130
Oatmeal Cookies, Old-Fashioned, '80 106;
   '85 250
Oatmeal Cookies, Orange-Glazed, '80 60
Oatmeal Cookies, Peanutty, '80 106; '83 95
Oatmeal Cookies, Pudding-, '98 215
Oatmeal Cookies, Spicy, '81 197
Oatmeal Cookies, Toasted, '92 273; '95 136
Oatmeal-Date Cookies, '82 109
Oatmeal Krispies, '85 115
Oatmeal-Peanut Butter Chocolate Chip
   Cookies, '92 207
Oatmeal-Peanut Butter Cookies, '85 171
Oatmeal-Raisin Cookies, '87 221; '93 127
Oatmeal-Raisin Cookies, Frosted, '79 290
Oatmeal-Spice Cookies, Giant, '80 105
Oatmeal Sunshine Cookies, '89 59
Oats-and-Peanut Cookies, '89 60
Olympic Medal Cookies, '96 180
Orange-Chocolate Cookies, '83 113
Orange Cookies, Frosted, '83 114
Orange Crinkles, '95 272
Orange Slice Cookies, '98 324
Peanut Butter Cookies, No-Bake, '94 197
Peanut Butter Macaroons, Chewy, '95 214
Peanut Butter-Oatmeal Cookies, '81 218
Peanut Cookies, Salted, '87 92
Pecan Crispies, '99 337
Pecan Lace Shells, '97 167
Pecan Sandies, Basil-, '97 166
Persimmon Cookies, '96 242
Persimmon-Raisin Cookies, '85 232
Pineapple Cookies, '79 216
Polka Dots, '95 272

Potato Chip Cookies, '86 93
Praline Cookies, '91 271
Pumpkin-Chocolate Chip Cookies, '93 235
Pumpkin Drop Cookies, '79 206
Pumpkin-Walnut Cookies, Frosted, '82 217
Rainy Day Cookies, '94 168
Raisin Cookies, Alltime Favorite, '80 24
Raisin-Granola Treats, '92 22
Sour Cream Cookies, Southern, '83 113
Sour Cream-Nutmeg Cookies, '85 171
Sugar Cookies, Nutmeg, '79 136
Sugar Cookies, Stir-and-Drop, '92 174
Sunflower Cookies, Crinkle, '83 149
Tea Cakes, Dropped, '90 156
Toffee Crunch Cookies, '93 80
Walnut Spice Kisses, '89 295
White Chocolate Chip-Oatmeal Cookies,
   '99 127
White Chocolate-Macadamia Nut Cookies,
   '94 315
White Chocolate-Orange Dream Cookies,
   '98 294
Zucchini Cookies, Spicy, '97 273
Easter Basket and Eggs, '95 101
Eggnog Logs, '92 274
Finikia, '96 21
Flying Brooms, '98 255
Ginger Cookies, '85 306; '96 314
Ginger Crinkles, '83 149
Gingersnaps, '79 146; '91 299; '92 264
Gingersnaps, Best-Ever, '79 208
Hazelnut Bonbons, Crisp, '97 274
Hazelnut Cookies, '84 111
Hazelnut Crinkle Cookies, '98 294
Hazelnut-Lemon Logs, '84 117
Heavenly Delights, '85 324
Jumbles, Mrs. Jemison's, '97 133
Keyboard Cookies, '94 M330
Kissy Cookies, '93 331
Lace Cookies, Florentine, '88 120
Lemon Cookies, Sunshine, '86 69
Lemon Crinkle Cookies, '81 287
Lemon Crisps, '95 272
Lemon Zephers, '81 172
Lollipop Cookies, '94 196
Macadamia-Oat Snowballs, '92 274
Madeleines, Snow-Capped, '85 120
Mailing Cookies, Tips on, '83 305
Mandel Bread, '97 220; '99 57
Mandelbrot, Rhoda's, '98 243
Meringue Cookies, '98 71
Miracle Cookies, '83 149
Mix, Quick, '94 167
Molasses Crinkles, '92 276
Oat Cookies, Crispy, '88 203; '90 311
Oatmeal Cookies, Special, '81 236
Orange Fingers, '86 57
Peanut Blossom Cookies, '95 245; '96 55; '97 324
Peanut Butter and Chocolate Chunk Cookies,
   '94 169
Peanut Butter-Chocolate Kiss Cookies, '86 49
Peanut Butter-Cinnamon Cookies, '84 30
Peanut Butter Cookies, '82 56
Peanut Butter Cookies, Double-Chip, '89 169
Peanut Butter Cookies, Easy, '92 272
Peanut Butter Cookies, Quick, '86 109
Peanut Butter-Oatmeal Cookies, '84 72
Peanut Butter Temptations, '84 29
Peanut-Date Balls, '81 92
Peanut Truffle Cookies, '93 212
Pecan-Butter Cookies, '83 113
Pecan Crescent Cookies, '85 324
Pecan Pie Cookies, '92 289
Peppermint Candy Cookies, '88 286

Peppermint Sandwich Cookies, '92 277
Peppermint Wreaths, Melt-Away, '85 324
Pizzelles, '83 298
Pumpkin Cookies, Peppy, '89 253
Refrigerator
   Almond Crescents, '97 273
   Almond Crunch Cookies, Texan-Size, '91 236
   Apple Rugelach, '97 220
   Apricot Kolaches, '83 84
   Berliner Kranse, '96 311
   Biscotti, Chocolate-Hazelnut, '95 80
   Biscotti, Light, '91 310
   Brown Sugar-Pecan Cookies, '91 236
   Brown Sugar Wafers, '96 213
   Buckin' Bronco Cookies, '90 95
   Butter Cookie Dough, Basic, '95 320
   Butter Cookies, Valentine, '81 20
   Cardamom Cookies, '79 12
   Cheese Wafers, Hope Farm, '93 282
   Cherry Chocolates, '95 321
   Cherry Pecan Cookies, '82 136
   Chocolate-Almond Surprise Cookies, '88 M45
   Chocolate-Cherry Cookies, '85 324
   Chocolate-Gingerbread Cookies, '94 293
   Chocolate Meltaways, '81 302
   Chocolate-Nut Freezer Cookies, '88 217
   Chocolate Pinwheel Cookies, '86 245
   Chocolate Snowball Cookies, '82 295
   Chocolate Teasers, '87 44
   Choco Surprise Cookies, '80 60
   Coffee Nuggets, '95 278
   Crème de Menthe Cookies, '86 230
   Crescents, '85 321
   Date-Cream Cheese Rollups, '83 298
   Date Nut Roll, '79 249
   Fruit Rugelach, '97 220
   Fudge Puddles, '94 292
   Gingerbirds, '93 283
   Gingerbread Men, '84 299
   Gingerbread Men, Miniature, '84 318
   Ginger Icebox Cookies, '93 205
   Gingersnaps, Raisin, '85 324
   Holiday Garland Cookies, '83 299
   Holiday Riches, '83 257
   Jack-o'-Lantern Cookies, '95 273
   Lemon Thyme Cookies, '96 124
   Lollipop Cookies, '95 322
   Memory Book Cookies, '92 45
   Molasses Cookies, '86 20
   Oatmeal Cookies, Crispy, '89 328
   Oatmeal-Date Sandwich Cookies, '83 257
   Oatmeal-Toffee Lizzies, Crispy, '95 136
   Orange Crispies, '84 205
   Orange Refrigerator Cookies, '86 230
   Orange-Slice Cookies, '89 294
   Peanut Butter-Chocolate Chip Cookies,
      Freezer, '86 230
   Peanut Butter-Coconut Cookies, '83 113
   Peanut Butter Cookie Ice Cream Sandwiches,
      '93 199
   Peanut Butter Cookies, '87 58
   Peanut Butter Crisps, '79 50
   Peanut Butter Slice-and-Bakes, '82 M185
   Peanut Butter Snaps, '81 237
   Pecan-Cheese Wafers, '81 119
   Pecan Crescent Cookies, '97 274
   Pecan Crisps, Sugar, '86 230
   Peppermint Rounds, '94 19
   Pfeffernusse, German, '98 293
   Pinwheel Cookies, '93 316
   Raspberry Sandwich Cookies, '82 306
   Ravioli, Sweet, '91 107
   Ribbon Cookies, '87 293
   Sandwich Cookies, Grandmother's, '82 306

COOKIES, Refrigerator
(continued)

Sesame-Cheese Cutouts, '82 296
Shortbread, Brown Sugar, '98 278
Shortbread, Cinnamon, '98 202
Shortbread Cookie Crumbs, '83 298
Shortbread Cookies, '87 58
Shortbread Cookies, Angel, '97 M285
Shortbread Cookies, Crispy, '83 113
Shortbread, Rum-Currant, '98 277
Snowball Surprises, '93 315
Sour Cream Cookies, Dutch, '83 149
Spice Cookies, Slice-of-, '79 290
Spice-Molasses Cookies, '89 289
Spooky Eyes, '95 273
Spring Bonnet Cookies, '97 111
Springerle, '81 251
Sugar Cookies, Crisp, '84 243
Sugar Cookies, Golden, '88 286
Sugar Cookies, Molasses, '80 270
Sugar Cookies, Pastel, '99 179
Sugar Cookies, Red-, '81 21
Sugar Cookies, Symbol, '91 282
Sugar Cookies, Valentine, '82 20
Sugar 'n Spice Cookies, '81 21
Swedish Cookies, '82 306
Taco-Cheese Animal Crackers, '94 197
Tea Cakes, Old-Fashioned, '91 72; '99 319
Tea Cookies, '83 170
Vanilla Crescents, '82 307
Vanilla Slice-and-Bake Cookies, '85 171
Wafers, Italian, '87 36
Walnut Cookies, '81 301; '97 275; '98 35
Watermelon Cookies, '92 179
Rolled
Almond-Filled Wafers, '88 120
Almond Holly Leaves, '86 319
A-Pees, '97 133
Apricot Cookie Rolls, '80 282
Apricot Kolaches, '94 291
Apricot Wonders, '93 316
Bears, Red-Bellied, '92 277
Biscochitos, '92 230
Chocolate Cookies, Chewy, '80 208
Cinnamon Stars, Swiss, '87 293
Cream Cheese Frills, '79 291
Crème de Menthe Cookies, '80 282
Cutout Cookies, Frosted, '85 236
Cutout Cookies, Old-Fashioned, '92 273
Date-Filled Cookies, '91 95
Fruit Cookies, Rolled, '80 15
Fruit-Nut Twists, '82 253
Gingerbread Animal Cookies, '86 70
Gingerbread Cookies, '80 278; '92 343
Gingerbread Man Cookies, '88 227
Gingerbread Men, '85 259; '99 294
Gingerbread Men Cookies, '85 319
Gingerbread People, '92 312
Gingerbread Snowflake Cookies, '98 324
Ginger Cookies, Swedish, '85 323
Grandmother's Cookies, '85 319
Ice Box Filled Cookies, '79 112
Lemon Pecan Dainties, '80 208
Lemony Cutout Cookies, '85 323
Maple Sandwich Cookies, '85 322
Mincemeat Cookies, '79 51
Mincemeat Sweetheart Cookies, '87 293
Oat Crispies, '83 96
Oatmeal-Coconut Cookies, '80 218
Oatmeal Cookies, Date-Filled, '86 314
Oatmeal Cookies, Slice-and-Bake, '80 105
Oatmeal Nut Crispies, '80 208

Orange-Pecan Cookies, '88 119
Ornaments, Edible, '94 316
Peanut Butter Cookies, Double, '80 209
Peanuttiest Cookies, Crisp, '88 65
Pear Mincemeat Cookies, '84 264
Pecan Cookies, Easy, '80 208
Peppermint Cookies, '95 322
Pinwheels, '95 321
Pueblo Indian Cookies, '95 228
Pumpkin Cookies, Great, '91 234
Raspberry Swirl Cookies, '90 111
Rugelach, '92 252
Scones, Currant, '84 117
Sherry Snaps, '87 94
Shortbread, Apricot-Almond, '99 29
Shortbread Cookies, '99 147
Shortbread Cookies, Butter Pecan, '80 282
Shortbread Cookies, Chocolate, '99 147
Shortbread Cookies, Coconut, '93 316
Shortbread, Easy Roll-Out, '81 21
Shortbread, Raspberry, '99 29
Shortbread Sugarplums, Pecan-, '83 298
Snowflake Cookies, '92 278
Snow Flurries, '92 275
Strawberry Cookie Tarts, '89 112
Sugar Cookies, '94 271
Sugar Cookies, Crescent, '87 294
Sugar Cookies, Molasses, '80 270
Sugar Cookies, Moravian, '85 321
Sugar Cookies, Old-Fashioned, '86 313
Sugar Cookies, Orange, '89 329
Sugar Cookies, Rolled, '79 291
Sweetheart Cookies, '93 53
Tea Cakes, Back-Home, '90 156
Teacakes, Currant, '80 88
Tea Cakes, Decorative, '90 156
Tea Cakes, Grandma's, '90 156
Teacakes, Old-Fashioned, '84 43
Tea Cakes, Sorghum, '85 239
Wafers, Kahlúa, '99 147
Sandwich Cookies, Viennese, '87 293
Sesame Cookies, Italian, '85 311
Shortbread, Brown Sugar, '93 331
Shortbread Cookie, Old-Fashioned, '88 242
Shortbread Cookies, Java, '94 233
Shortbread Cookies, Praline, '88 242
Shortbread Cookies, Spiced, '88 242
Shortbread Madeleines, Orange, '88 242
Shortbread, Marble-Topped Hazelnut, '99 M29
Shortbread, Peanut Butter, '95 321
Shortbread, Scottish, '94 242; '95 34
Shortbread Wafers, Cocoa, '88 243
Snow Cookies, '99 167
Spice Cookies, '87 M278
Spice Thins, '95 322
Spider Cookies, '93 M166
Spooky Ghosts, '98 M256
Spritz Cookies, Butter, '91 175
Spritz Hearts, '91 107
Sugar Cookies, '97 288
Sugar Cookies, Cinnamon, '84 73
Sugar Cookies, Double-Chocolate, '92 206
Sugar Cookies, Molasses, '82 140
Sugar Cookies, Sour Cream, '79 51
Sugar Cookies, Winning, '97 108
Swedish Heirloom Cookies, '81 129; '90 311
Tea Cakes, Brandied Apricot, '91 241
Tea Cakes, Mexican, '81 196
Thumbprint Cookies, Childhood, '85 323
Thumbprint Cookies, Praline, '89 328
Turkey Treats, '93 256
Turtle Cookies, Snappin', '85 323
Waffle Cookies, Brownie, '86 245
Walnut Cookies, Simply, '91 236

Wedding Cookies, '82 M185
Whoopie Pies, '86 246
Witches' Hats, '98 256
COOKING LIGHT. *See* **LIVING LIGHT.**
CORN
Bacon and Caramelized Onion, Corn with, '99 94
Bake, Corn-and-Swiss Cheese, '92 133
Baked Corn, Creamy, '90 60
Balls, Zesty Corn Dressing, '82 307
Boil, Monroe County Corn, '96 167
Cabbage Rolls, Southwestern, '97 214
Cakes with Avocado Cream, Southwestern
    Chicken-and-Corn, '97 M311
Cakes with Smoked Salmon Salsa, Corn-and-
    Black Bean, '96 272
Casseroles
Baked Jack Corn, '97 86
Bean Casserole, Corn-and-, '90 208
Broccoli-Corn Casserole, '83 313
Cheese Casserole, Corn and, '81 128
Cheesy Corn Bake, '98 244
Chili-Corn Casserole, '88 266
Corn Casserole, '79 247; '89 126; '93 141
Creamy Corn, '79 213; '90 207
Escalloped Corn, '79 251
Fresh Corn Casserole, '80 165
Green Bean-and-Corn Casserole, '88 123; '99 36
Green Chile Casserole, Corn-and-, '89 68
Hamburger-Corn Bake, '99 58
Hominy-and-Corn Casserole, '97 291
Jalapeño-Corn Casserole, '83 256
Moussaka, Corn, '87 190
Oyster-and-Corn Bake, '83 34; '84 44
Salami-Corn Casserole, '80 209
Scalloped Corn, '80 164; '81 128; '86 111;
    '88 218
Scalloped Corn, Baked, '85 290
Scalloped Corn, Elegant, '86 268
Scalloped Corn for Two, '82 208
Sour Cream, Baked Corn with, '86 170
Tomato Casserole, Corn and, '81 127
Tomato Casserole, Corn-and-, '84 145
Zucchini Bake, Corn-, '79 178
Chiles Rellenos with Walnut Cream Sauce,
    Havarti-and-Corn-Stuffed, '93 M275
Christmas Corn, '93 325
Cob
Baked Corn on the Cob, Seasoned, '82 134
Barbecued Corn on the Cob, '81 128
Corn on the Cob, '79 122
Foil-Baked Corn on the Cob, '81 128
Foiled Corn on the Cob, '80 165
Grill, Corn on the, '94 161; '97 191
Grilled Corn-on-the-Cob, '90 166
Grilled Corn with Maple Vinaigrette, '98 171
Grilled Parmesan Corn, '82 127
Herb Butter, Corn-on-the-Cob with, '84 160
Herb Butter Sauce, Corn with, '79 150
Hickory-Smoked Corn, '85 145
Lemony Corn on the Cob, '89 200
Mexican Corn on the Cob, '96 167
Microwaved Corn on the Cob, '80 M122
Parmesan Corn on the Cob, '88 M187
Parslied Corn, '90 155
Roasted Red Pepper Corn, '91 122
Spicy Corn-on-the-Cob, '84 149
Spicy Corn on the Cob, '87 M151
Cold-Pack Corn, '81 216
Combo, Zucchini-Corn, '86 218
Cornbread, Sour Cream, '96 17
Creamed Corn, '97 136
Creamed Corn, Freezer-Fresh, '96 46
Creamed Corn, Southern-Style, '81 M165;
    '92 201

Creamed Fresh Corn, '82 158
Cream-Style Corn, '80 127; '85 106
Creamy Corn, '79 213; '90 207
Creole Corn, '81 128
Creole, Corn-and-Okra, '89 127
Creole, Okra-Corn, '83 157
Crêpes, Blue-Corn, '97 197
Crêpes with Beef Filling, Blue-Corn, '97 197
Curried Corn and Celery, '86 192
Curried Corn and Sweet Red Peppers, '95 47
Custard, Fresh Corn, '89 127
Deviled Corn, '86 192
Dinner, Corn-and-Ham Skillet, '83 190
Dip, Quick Fiesta, '99 M197
Dip, Roasted Corn-and-Avocado, '91 279
Dressing, Corny Cornbread, '99 258
Flan, Corn, '98 246; '99 25
Flan, Corn-Chive, '94 172
Fresh Corn, Seasoned, '83 M147
Fried Corn, '89 127; '94 158
Fried Corn, Buttermilk, '96 167
Fried Corn, Skillet, '83 190
Frittata, Corn-and-Squash, '89 144
Frittata, Skillet Corn, '87 90
Fritters, Corn, '86 192; '94 22; '98 207
Fritters, Corn-and-Crab, '97 227
Fritters, Corn-Jalapeño, '96 153
Fritters, Golden Corn, '80 165; '81 128
Fritters, Skillet-Fried Corn, '85 14
Hush Puppies, Corn Soufflé, '98 M328
Hush Puppies with Corn, '83 286; '84 17
Indian Corn, '96 287
Limping Susan, '90 155
Macque Choux (Smothered Corn), '94 236
Meat Loaf, Corny, '86 68
Medley, Corn-and-Okra, '99 203
Medley, Okra-Corn-Tomato, '81 159
Medley, Peas-and-Corn, '85 138
Medley, Skillet Corn, '86 192
Medley, Summer Garden, '84 158
Medley, Zucchini-and-Corn, '80 298; '81 25
Mexican Corn, '80 157, 165
Mexican Corn, Spicy, '93 90
Mexi-Corn, '82 M21
Mexicorn, '96 189
Mexicorn, Black Bean, '96 189
Mexicorn Main Dish, '96 189
Muffins, Corn, '98 313
Muffins, Corn-Oat, '89 108
Muffins, Sunny Corn, '96 166
Muffins, Tex-Mex Corn, '92 253; '93 144
Okra and Corn in Cream, '79 160
Okra, Corn, and Peppers, '87 M151
Okra, Corn, and Tomatoes, '95 203
Pancakes, Corn, '93 43
Peppers, Corn-Stuffed, '84 104
Peppers, Ham-and-Corn Stuffed, '81 87
Pie, Quick and Cheesy Corn, '82 191
Pie with Fresh Tomato Salsa, Buttercrust Corn, '95 181
Poblanos, Corn-Stuffed, '97 269
Pork Chops, Mexican, '99 108
Pork Chops, Southwestern, '98 131
Posole, '95 226
Pudding, Baked Corn, '83 314
Pudding, Corn, '79 276; '81 128; '86 192; '90 219; '98 124; '99 71, 270
Pudding, Corn-Cheese, '80 244
Pudding, Creamy Corn, '81 267
Pudding, Dashiell Corn, '98 274
Pudding, Easy Corn, '83 280
Pudding, Fresh Corn, '80 157, 165; '89 172
Pudding, Tee's Corn, '95 318
Puppies, Corn, '97 140

Quesadilla Torta, '97 325
Quiche, Jalapeño-Corn, '85 122
Quick Corn Fix-Up, '81 M4
Relish, Corn, '81 129, 175; '83 189; '84 107; '85 136; '87 120, 245; '92 241
Relish Dogs, Corn, '85 192
Relish, Easy Corn, '83 260
Relish, Quick Corn, '90 13
Relish, Summer Corn, '89 127
Relish, Sweet Corn, '93 119
Relish, Virginia Corn, '79 283
Salads
    Bean Salad, Mexicorn-, '96 184
    Broccoli-Corn Salad, '87 24
    Chilled Corn Salad, '79 20
    Confetti Corn Salad, '96 168
    Corn Salad, '80 247; '81 139; '85 236; '91 27; '95 214
    Festive Corn Salad, '92 263
    Fresh Corn Salad, '91 126; '94 162
    Garden Medley Salad, '80 122
    Marinated Corn-Bean Salad, '87 9
    Marinated Corn Salad, '89 126
    Pea Salad, Corn-and-, '90 181
    Roasted Corn Salad, '97 196
    Shoepeg Corn Salad, '81 23
    Shuck Salad, Corn-in-the-, '93 236
    Slaw, Corn and Cabbage, '79 135
    Tangy Corn Salad, '88 176
    Tasty Corn Salad, '84 289
    Wheat Berry-and-Roasted Corn Salad, '94 175
    Wild Rice-and-Corn Salad, '98 288
    Zucchini-Corn Marinated Salad, '98 236
Salsa, Avocado-Corn, '94 201; '99 335
Salsa, Black Bean-and-Corn, '94 80
Salsa, Black Bean-Corn, '96 126
Salsa, Corn-Black Bean, '96 15
Salsa, Grilled Corn, '99 162
Salsa, Mexi-Corn, '91 279
Salsa, Spicy Corn, '93 322
Salsa, Sweet Corn, '95 156
Salsa with Black Beans and Corn, Southwestern, '96 275
Salsa, Yellowfin Tuna with Corn, Pepper, and Tomato, '94 164
Sauce, Fresh Corn, '98 43
Sauté, Corn, '80 165
Sautéed Corn and Okra, '84 158
Soufflé, Corn-and-Cheese, '88 122
Soufflés, Zucchini-Corn, '97 203
Soufflé, Zucchini-and-Corn, '83 265
Soups
    Bisque, Crab-and-Corn, '87 137
    Bourbon Soup, Corn-and-, '92 194
    Chicken-Corn Soup, Cheesy, '97 158
    Chowder, Corn, '81 128; '83 20; '84 M38; '85 10; '90 202; '91 132; '97 241; '98 31
    Chowder, Corn and Cheese, '80 228
    Chowder, Curried Chicken-and-Corn, '92 21
    Chowder, Delicious Corn, '82 279
    Chowder, Fresh Corn and Bacon, '93 203
    Chowder, Ham, '79 16
    Chowder, Ham-and-Corn, '82 40
    Chowder, Oyster-Corn, '83 211
    Chowder, Potato-Corn, '94 66
    Chowder, Pumpkin-Corn, '97 219
    Chowder, Shrimp and Corn, '79 199
    Chowder, Southern Corn-and-Bacon, '96 166
    Chowder, Turkey-Corn, '81 98; '96 279
    Corn Soup, '80 56; '85 243; '87 156
    Crab Soup, Fresh Corn-and-, '92 183
    Cream of Corn Soup, '90 210
    Favorite Corn Soup, '85 155
    Gazpacho, Tomato-Avocado-Corn, '97 182

Grilled Corn Soup, '87 121
Pimiento-Corn Soup, '89 126
Pumpkin-Corn Soup with Ginger-Lime Cream, '95 227
Shrimp-and-Corn Soup, '84 88
Sweet Corn Soup with Shiitakes and Shrimp, '99 168
Tortilla Soup, '98 291
Spoonbread, Corn, '97 301
Spoonbread, Corn and Bacon, '81 129
Spoonbread, Corn-Cheese, '88 9
Spread, Corn-and-Walnut, '96 26
Succotash, Easy, '80 165
Succotash, Savory, '96 63
Timbales, Corn-and-Zucchini, '92 100
Tomatoes-and-Corn, Creole-Style, '84 142
Tomatoes, Corn-Stuffed, '82 270
Tomatoes, Stuffed, '96 82
Tomatoes with Corn, Baked, '80 161
Vinaigrette, Okra-Corn-and-Tomato, '90 173
Waffles, Corn-Chile, '94 206
Whole Kernel Corn, '85 106
Zucchini and Corn, '86 177
Zucchini and Corn, Dilled, '83 173
Zucchini, Corn and, '83 190
CORNBREADS. *See also* **HUSH PUPPIES.**
    Bake, Bacon, Zucchini, and Cornbread, '99 123
    Bake, Cornbread Tamale, '79 163
    Basic Cornbread, '99 257
    Beef Cornbread, Cheesy, '81 242
    Biscuits, Cornmeal-Jalapeño, '94 214
    Bites, Corn Dog, '85 245
    Black-Eyed Pea Cornbread, '98 44
    Bowls, Cornbread, '95 58
    Buttermilk Cornbread, '79 34; '82 70; '99 235
    Carrot Cornbread, '80 89; '81 163
    Casserole, Bean-and-Cornbread, '92 243
    Casserole, Beef, Bean, and Cornbread, '99 215
    Casserole, Cornbread, '81 91
    Casserole, Cornbread Skillet, '83 243; '84 101
    Cheddar Cornbread, '83 285; '84 17
    Cheddar-Jalapeño Cornbread, '85 3
    Chicken over Cornbread, Creamed, '86 231
    Chile-Cheese Cornbread, '87 171
    Chile Cornbread, '86 254
    Confetti Cornbread, '94 170
    Cornbread, '80 272; '86 231; '87 197; '92 324; '93 122
    Cornish Hens, Cranberry-Cornbread Stuffed, '95 325
    Cottage Cheese Cornbread, '80 90
    Cowboy Cornbread, '81 188
    Cracklin' Cornbread, '92 216
    Cracklin' Cornbread, Grannie's, '98 252
    Cracklin' Cornbread, Southern, '80 119
    Crackling Cornbread, '85 200
    Crackling Cowboy Cornbread, '82 114
    Crêpes, Cornbread, '98 42
    Crêpes, Goat Cheese-Filled Cornbread, '98 43
    Crêpes, Southwestern Cornbread, '98 42
    Crispy Cornbread, '92 340
    Croutons, Cornbread, '93 192
    Croutons, Honeyed Cornbread, '94 106
    Crust, Turkey and Peppers in Cornbread, '95 312
    Crusty Cornbread, '85 255
    Dieter's Cornbread, '87 164
Dressings
    Biscuit Dressing, Cornbread-, '79 296
    Chicken and Dressing, '99 42
    Chicken Cornbread Dressing, '90 159
    Cornbread Dressing, '86 286; '88 254; '92 267; '98 269
    Corny Cornbread Dressing, '99 258
    Crawfish-Cornbread Dressing, '99 257

CORNBREADS, Dressings
(continued)

Fruited Cornbread Dressing, **'80** 262
Green Chile-Cornbread Dressing, **'93** 306;
  '94 296
Herb-Seasoned Cornbread Dressing,
  '83 315
Kentucky Cornbread Dressing, **'86** 281
Light Cornbread Dressing, **'92** 324
Nannie's Cornbread Dressing, **'95** 306
Old-Fashioned Cornbread Dressing, **'84** 321
Oyster-Cornbread Dressing, Ma E's
  Traditional, **'96** 35
Quail and Dressing, **'99** 42
Quail Stuffed with Cornbread Dressing,
  '93 280
Roast Turkey and Cornbread Dressing,
  '89 324
Sage-Cornbread Dressing, **'84** 283
Sage Dressing, Cornbread-, **'80** 262
Sausage, and Pecan Dressing, Cornbread,
  '99 257
Sausage-Cornbread Dressing, **'95** 289
Sausage-Cornbread Dressing, Turkey with,
  '83 287
Sausage Dressing, Cornbread-, **'82** 307;
  '85 280
Sausage Dressing, Cornbread-and-, **'83** 213
Savory Cornbread Dressing, **'88** 303
Spoonbread Dressing, Southwestern-Style,
  '94 273
Sweet Cornbread Dressing, **'97** 303
Texas Cornbread Dressing, **'82** 243
Easy Cornbread, **'94** 158
Fresh Cornbread, **'80** 165
Green Chile Cornbread, **'82** 134
Herbed Cornbread, **'90** 214
Hoecake, Hot Water, **'81** 56
Hoecakes, Green Onion, **'88** 112
Honey Cornbread, **'83** 286; **'84** 17
Hot Water Cornbread, **'88** 92
Jalapeño Cornbread, **'85** 200; **'94** 78; **'98** 178
Jalapeño Cornbread, Beefy, **'82** 142
Jalapeño Pepper Bread, **'83** 121
Lacy Corncakes, **'81** 242
Lightbread, Corn, **'81** 137
Light Cornbread, Old Southern, **'81** 242
Loaded Cornbread, **'99** 214
Loaf, Cornbread, **'85** 200
Menfolks' Cornbread, **'82** 156
Mexican Cornbread, **'80** 198; **'81** 137;
  '84 140, 242; **'93** 182
Mexican Cornbread, Hot, **'83** 286; **'84** 17
Mexican Cornbread, Quick, **'81** 242
Mexican Flatbread, **'80** 197

Muffins
Angel Cornbread Muffins, Heavenly, **'98** 43
Blue Corn Muffins, **'89** 145; **'92** 52; **'94** 114
Cheesy Cornbread Muffins, **'88** M275
Cornmeal Muffins, **'80** 90; **'88** 92; **'96** 248
Corn Muffins, **'82** M282; **'84** 16
Four-Grain Muffins, **'80** 46
Jalapeño-Corn Muffins, **'93** 164
Miniature Cornmeal Muffins, **'93** 119
Quick Corn Muffins, **'88** 15
Sage-Corn Muffins, **'83** 207
Sour Cream Corn Muffins, **'95** 176
Southern Cornbread Muffins, **'85** 201
Spicy Cornbread Muffins, **'90** 59
Tex-Mex Corn Muffins, **'93** 144
Tomato Corn Muffins, **'81** 137
Yeast Muffins, Cornmeal, **'92** 49

Mush, **'81** 215
Old-Fashioned Cornbread, **'81** 242
Onion Cornbread, **'88** 283
Onion-Topped Cornbread, **'84** 153
Oysters Casino on Cornbread, **'79** 34
Paprika Cornbread, **'90** 213
Pastry, Cornmeal, **'81** 140
Pecan Cornbread, **'94** 169; **'98** 252
Picante Cornbread, **'94** 169
Pie, Cornbread-Sausage-Apple, **'87** 171
Pie, Cornbread-Tamale, **'92** 123
Pie, Sausage-and-Cornbread, **'90** 25
Puff, Cornmeal, **'82** 42
Quick-and-Easy Cornbread, **'83** 9
Quick Cornsticks, **'81** 192
Salad, Cornbread, **'87** 172
Salad, Mexican Cornbread, **'95** 210
Seasoned Cornbread, **'90** 320
Serrano Chile Blue Cornbread, **'94** 114
Skillet Cornbread, **'81** 31; **'84** 102; **'85** 200;
  '90 13; **'97** 137
Soufflé Cornbread, **'96** 34
Sour Cream Cornbread, **'81** 137; **'96** 17
Southern Cornbread, **'79** 123; **'81** 56; **'83** 12
Southern Corncakes, **'88** 166
Spinach Cornbread, **'95** 49
Spoonbread, **'81** 138
Spoonbread, Cheddar, **'82** 196
Spoonbread, Golden, **'83** 286; **'84** 17
Spoonbread, Old Virginia, **'84** 102
Spoonbread, Ozark, **'85** 202
Spoon Cornbread, **'98** 252
Sticks, Angel Corn, **'84** 20
Sticks, Blue Ribbon Corn, **'84** 102
Sticks, Buttermilk Corn, **'80** 120
Sticks, Corn, **'79** 275; **'89** 54; **'90** 214
Sticks, Cornbread, **'87** 15
Sticks, Favorite Corn, **'85** 202
Sticks, Firecracker Corn, **'85** 241
Sticks, Garlic-Thyme Corn, **'93** 242
Sticks, Golden Cornbread, **'94** 213
Sticks, Old-Fashioned Corn, **'90** 232
Sticks, Quick Corn, **'88** 15
Sticks, Savory Corn, **'93** 33
Sticks, Southern Corn, **'81** 242
Stuffed Peppers, Barbecued Shrimp and
  Cornbread-, **'97** 261
Stuffing, Cornbread, **'94** 305
Stuffing, Pork Chops with Cornbread-Apple,
  '99 14
Supper, Cornbread-Vegetable, **'97** 319
Supreme, Cornbread, **'93** 67
Sweet Onion Cornbread, **'98** 252
Swiss Cheese Cornbread, **'79** 60
Toasted Cornbread, **'82** 174
Tomatoes, Cornbread-Stuffed, **'97** 169
Ultimate Cornbread, **'80** 90
Vicksburg Cornbread, **'96** 35
Waffles, Cornbread, **'79** 265; **'91** 90; **'98** 42
Waffles, Cornmeal, **'85** 201
Wampus Bread, **'81** 305; **'82** 36

CORNISH HENS
à l'Orange, Cornish Hens, **'95** 325
Barley-Mushroom Stuffing, Cornish Hens with,
  '97 242
Brandied Cornish Hens, **'81** 259
Brown Rice, Cornish Hens with, **'82** 275
Buttered Cornish Hens, Brandy-, **'79** 292;
  '80 32
Cajun-Fried Cornish Hens, **'95** 326
Casserole, Cornish Hens-and-Rice, **'92** 267
Chutney-Mustard Glaze, Game Hens with, **'93** 66
Company Cornish Hens, **'83** 263
Cranberry Cornish Hens, **'86** 303

Cranberry-Orange Sauce, Cornish Hens with,
  '86 119
Cranberry Sauce, Cornish Hens with, **'79** 180
Elegant Cornish Hens, **'80** 227; **'81** 52
Flambé, Cornish Hens, **'80** 227; **'81** 52
Fruited Stuffing, Cornish Hens with, **'90** 191
Glazed Cornish Hens, Apricot-, **'80** 84; **'87** 306
Glazed Cornish Hens, Jelly-, **'89** 193; **'93** 251
Glazed Cornish Hens, Orange-, **'83** 267; **'99** 293
Glazed Stuffed Cornish Hens, Orange-, **'84** M89
Grilled Cornish Hens, **'88** 243; **'92** 59
Grilled Cornish Hens, Asian, **'99** 41
Grilled Cornish Hens, Orange-Glazed, **'86** 250
Grilled Cornish Hens with Tropical Fruit,
  '97 310
Herbed Cornish Hens, **'82** 271
Marinated Cornish Hens, Sherry-, **'91** 148
Mesquite-Smoked Cornish Hens, **'92** 144
Orange-Ginger Hens with Cranberry Salsa,
  '98 321
Orange Glaze, Cornish Hens with, **'79** 244
Port and Sour Cream, Cornish Hens in, **'86** 323
Roast Cornish Hens, **'86** 89
Roasted Cornish Hens, Herb-, **'88** 29
Roasted Cornish Hens, Lemon, **'82** 260
Roasted Cornish Hens with Vegetables,
  Tarragon, **'94** 79
Roasted Rock Cornish Hens, **'82** 66
Smoked Cornish Hens, **'86** 142, 154; **'88** 168
Stuffed Cornish Hens, **'85** 261
Stuffed Cornish Hens, Apricot-, **'84** 6
Stuffed Cornish Hens, Cranberry-Cornbread,
  '95 325
Stuffed Cornish Hens, Rice-, **'82** 302
Tarragon, Cornish Hens, **'95** 326
Tarragon, Cornish Hens with, **'83** 143
Teriyaki Cornish Hens, **'86** 198
Texas-Style Game Hens, **'87** 61
Vermouth, Cornish Hens in, **'86** 33
Wild Rice Stuffing, Cornish Hens with, **'79** 222;
  '80 64; **'82** 136

COUSCOUS
Chicken, Moroccan Garlic, **'99** 15
Chicken with Couscous, **'97** 325
Fruit, Couscous with Mixed, **'95** 232
Lemon Couscous, **'96** 154
Red Beans and Couscous, **'99** 22
Salad, Basil-and-Tomato Couscous, **'94** 175
Salad, Curried Couscous, **'91** 44
Salad, Shrimp-and-Couscous, **'96** 157
Salad with Dried Tomato Vinaigrette, Couscous,
  '96 244
Spinach-and-Onion Couscous, **'98** 23
Tabbouleh Couscous, **'96** 251; **'97** 103
Tabbouleh Salad, **'91** 70
Vegetables and Couscous, **'96** 136

CRAB
Appetizers
Balls, Crabmeat, **'88** 150
Bites, Crabmeat, **'97** 98
Bites, Crab-Zucchini, **'84** M216
Bites, Spicy Crab, **'91** 165
Broiled Crab Meltaways, **'93** 287
Cakes, Miniature Crab, **'96** 306
Cakes with Cress Sauce, Baked Crab,
  '96 176
Cakes with Jalapeño Tartar Sauce,
  Chesapeake Bay Crab, **'96** 69
Cakes with Maui Sauce, Crab, **'99** 310
Canapés, Cheesy Crab, **'86** 262
Canapés, Crab, **'93** 130
Canapés, Crabmeat, **'88** 150
Canapés, Hot Crab, **'86** 70; **'87** 239
Chafing Dish Crabmeat, **'89** 284

Cherry Tomatoes, Crab-Stuffed, '82 289;
  '88 78
Cocktail Puffs, '91 106
Cocktail, Sherried Avocado-Crabmeat, '87 95
Deviled Crab, Devilish, '85 264
Dip, Cheese-Crab, '91 200
Dip, Creamy Crab, '80 M135
Dip, Festive Crab, '92 285
Dip, Hot Cheese and Crab, '81 261
Dip, Hot Crab, '93 269; '97 89
Dip, Hot Crab-and-Cheese, '94 282
Dip, Hot Crabmeat, '95 154
Dip, Oven-Baked Crab, '82 59
Dip, Tangy Crab, '83 5
Dip, Trawler Crab, '93 238
Hors d'Oeuvre, Crabmeat, '94 236
Mold, Crab, '85 318
Mousse, Crab, '79 117; '95 327
Mousse, Crabmeat, '90 190; '91 244; '94 159
Mushroom Caps, Crab-Stuffed, '84 160
Mushrooms, Crab-Stuffed, '81 190; '97 102
Mushrooms Stuffed with Crab, '82 249
Oysters, Crabmeat Stuffed, '94 328
Pâté, Crab, '79 233
Pot Stickers, Hoisin Crab, '96 92
Puffs, Crab, '80 20; '84 269
Puffs, Crabmeat, '99 335
Sandwiches, Miniature Crab Cake, '96 306
Snacks, Crab, '83 93
Snow Peas, Crab-Stuffed, '85 288
Spread, Baked Crab, '80 86
Spread, Best-Ever Crab, '98 60
Spread, Crab, '93 167
Spread, Crabmeat-Horseradish, '90 292
Spread, Crab Soufflé, '85 4
Spread, Hot Artichoke-Crab, '85 81
Spread, Layered Crabmeat, '83 127
Spread, Superb Crab, '81 235
Topping, Crabmeat, '91 64
au Gratin, Crabmeat, '86 154
au Gratin, Crab, Shrimp, and Artichoke, '90 240
Baked Avocado-and-Crabmeat, '84 119
Bake, Easy Crab, '95 209
Bake, Quick Crab, '87 192
Benedict, Crab, '92 63
Benedict, Lion, '93 121
Blue Crabs, Festive, '85 103
Blue Crabs, Spicy Steamed, '84 162
Blue Crabs, Steamed, '89 195
Bow Ties with Crab and Vegetables, '98 233
Broiled Crab and Avocado, '79 116
Brunch Scramble, Crabmeat, '95 32
Burgers, Potato-Crusted Crab, '94 139
Cakes, Baltimore Crab, '92 117
Cakes, Chesapeake Bay Crab, '89 194; '95 155
Cakes, Country Crab, '95 20
Cakes, Crab, '81 125; '90 71; '91 122;
  '98 140, 222; '99 267
Cakes, Crispy Fried Crab, '80 119
Cakes, Down-East Crab, '79 151
Cakes, Gulf Coast Crab, '94 71
Cakes, Mock Crab, '95 159
Cakes, Victoria Crab, '92 195
Cakes, Virginia Jumbo Lump Crab, '97 180
Cakes with Tomato Cream, Crab, '94 70
Casserole, Crab, '79 228
Casserole, Crab-and-Mushroom, '89 96
Casserole, Crab-and-Shrimp, '84 71
Casserole, Crab-Egg, '80 260
Casserole, Crabmeat-Broccoli, '84 232
Casserole, Creamy Crab and Spinach, '80 3
Casserole, Deviled Crab, '91 238; '92 27
Casserole, Easy Crab, '93 270
Chicken, Crab-Stuffed, '84 101

Cornbread, Crab with Chile, '86 254
Creamed Crabmeat with Artichoke Hearts,
  '93 26
Crêpes, Crab, '79 165
Crêpes, Sautéed Crab, '84 84
Crisps, Crab, '79 63
Delight, Crab-and-Egg, '84 261
Deviled Crab, '85 104; '92 117
Dressed Crab, '82 276
Eggs New Orleans, Crabmeat and, '82 45
Eggs, Shrimp and Crab Scrambled, '79 261
Étouffée, Crab-and-Shrimp, '89 96
Fettuccine, Crab, '98 142
Filling, Crab, '89 13
Flounder, Crab-Stuffed, '80 120
Fresh Crab, Preparing, '82 127
Fried Soft-Shell Crabs, '95 154
Fritters, Corn-and-Crab, '97 227
Fritters, Crab, '98 142
Hash with Three-Pepper Hollandaise, Lump
  Crab, '96 52
Imperial, Crab, '79 82, 116; '89 194; '95 155;
  '96 148
Imperial, Crabmeat, '82 311; '83 72
Imperial, Easy Crab, '93 128
Imperial, Elegant Crab, '83 245
Imperial, Pineapple-Crab, '84 M286
Imperial, Speedy Crabmeat, '90 M112
Karen, Crabmeat, '93 49
Lasagna, Crabmeat, '96 290
Lobster Tails, Crab-Stuffed, '95 326
Marinière, Mashed Potatoes with Crab,
  '99 165
Meunière, Soft-Shell Crab, '80 57
Mold, Cream Cheese-Crabmeat, '90 71
Mushrooms on Toast Points, Crabmeat and,
  '82 M91
Oysters and Crabmeat, Creamy, '83 211
Potatoes, Cheesy Crab-Stuffed, '86 17
Potatoes, Crabmeat-Topped, '83 3; '95 22
Potatoes, Crab-Stuffed, '91 311; '92 26; '99 307
Puff, Crab, '79 116
Puff, Shrimp-Crab, '79 57
Quiche, Almond-Topped Crab, '79 127
Quiche, Crab, '82 M122, 243
Quiche, Quick Crab, '84 96
Quiche, Sherried Crab, '83 180
Quiche, Simple Crab, '85 207
Ravigote, Crabmeat, '82 250; '92 329
Relish, Crabmeat, '99 198
Salads
  Asparagus Salad, Crab-and-, '92 141
  Avocado Salad, Crab-, '81 114
  Avocados, Crab-Stuffed, '86 73
  Avocado with Crabmeat, '86 119
  Blue Crab Salad with Asian Vinaigrette,
    '98 142
  Cakes with Greens and Dijon Dressing, Crab,
    '96 176
  Caribbean Crabmeat Salad with Creamy
    Gingered Dressing, '97 263
  Chesapeake Crab Salad, '89 195
  Congealed Salad with Crabmeat-and-
    Asparagus, '84 86
  Crabmeat Salad, '91 169
  Cucumber-and-Crab Salad, '98 208
  Delightful Crab Salad, '87 145
  Louis, Crab, '95 94
  Luncheon Salad, Crabmeat, '82 207
  Macaroni-Crabmeat Salad, '81 153
  Marinated Crab-and-Endive Salad, '93 22
  Rémoulade, Crabmeat, '93 280
  Shrimp Pasta Salad, Crabmeat-, '86 208
  Tomato Salad, Crab-Stuffed, '80 148

Wild Rice Salad, Crab-, '86 207
Wild Rice Salad, Crab and, '79 116
Sandwiches, Avocado-Crabmeat, '83 2
Sandwiches, Crabmeat, '84 285
Sandwiches, Deluxe Crabmeat, '81 M74
Sandwiches, Hot Crab-and-Cheese, '87 279
Sandwiches, Mango-Crab Salad, '99 72
Sandwiches, Open-Face Crab Tomato, '81 29
Sandwiches, Open-Faced Crab, '87 106
Sandwiches, Puffy Crab, '83 291
Sauce Piquante, Crab and Shrimp, '83 92
Sauce, Quick Crab Marinara, '85 M151
Sauce, Stone Crab Mustard, '80 3
Sauce, Tangy Stone Crab, '80 3
Sautéed Crabmeat, Roussos, '84 88
Shrimp Bundles, Crab-Stuffed, '81 176
Shrimp, Crab-Stuffed, '84 259
Soft-Shell Crabs, Chesapeake, '89 194
Soft-Shell Crabs, Fried Stuffed, '98 140
Soups
  Beaufort Crab Soup, '92 238
  Bisque, Crab, '88 251
  Bisque, Crab-and-Corn, '87 137
  Bisque, Crab-and-Leek, '94 104
  Bisque, Crab-and-Spinach, '97 241
  Bisque, Stone Crab, '96 86
  Chowder, Maryland Crab, '97 23
  Corn-and-Crab Soup, Fresh, '92 183
  Crabmeat Soup, '84 123
  Cream of Crab Soup, '88 302
  Cream of Crab Soup, Steamboat's, '81 127
  Creamy Crab Soup, '80 M224
  Elegant Crab Soup, '80 188
  Gazpacho, Crab, '97 181
  Gumbo, Crab and Shrimp, '81 200
  Gumbo, Shrimp-Crab, '98 15
  Gumbo with Whole Crabs, Seafood, '85 2
  Old-Fashioned Crab Soup, '90 71
  Plantation Crab Soup, '92 237
  Quick Crab Soup, '84 279
  She-Crab Soup with Marigold, '79 32
Spread, Crabmeat, '79 81
Stroganoff, Crab, '79 116
Strudel, Crab-and-Mushroom, '98 28
Stuffed Soft-Shell Crabs, '83 91
Stuffed Soft-Shell Crabs, Steamboat's, '81 127
Stuffing, Chicken Breasts with Crabmeat, '85 302
Stuffing, Crabmeat, '94 68
Stuffing, Tropical Orange Roughy with Crab,
  '99 122
Supreme, Crab, '79 181
Tomatoes, Crab-and-Avocado Stuffed, '94 141
Tostadas, Crab, '93 203
Veal with Crabmeat, New Orleans, '86 94
CRACKERS
Bacon-Wrapped Crackers, '93 280
Bisque Crackers, Easy, '83 252
Blue Cheese Crisps, '96 106
Bread, Sesame Cracker, '87 2
Cheddar Crackers, '84 236
Cheese Cracker Nibbles, '84 328
Cheese Crisps, Peppered, '98 107
Cranberry Crackers, '99 258
Critter Crackers, '93 193
Dessert Crackers, '87 3
Fennel-Rye Crackers, '87 2
Florida Crackers, '86 179
Hot Nut Crackers, '90 206
Hush Puppies, Cracker, '80 99
Oatmeal-Wheat Germ Crackers, '84 236
Olive-Rye Snack Crackers, '84 191
Pie, Cracker, '79 113
Snackers, Cracker, '86 229; '93 197
Soup Nuts, '96 106

CRACKERS
(continued)

Tortilla-Lime Crackers, **'99** 17
Vegetable Crackers, **'96** 105
CRANBERRIES
Acorn Squash, Cranberry-Filled, **'81** M231
  Beverages
    Apple-Berry Sparkler, **'93** 104
    Apple Berry Sparkler, **'94** 100
    Beach Brew, **'91** 177
    Cider, Mulled Cranberry, **'99** 278
    Cider, Spiced Cranberry, **'84** 261; **'98** 278
    Cocktails, Sea Breeze, **'97** 161
    Cooler, Cranberry, **'86** 229
    Cubes, Cranberry, **'95** 201
    Daiquiris, Cranberry, **'81** 245
    Fizz, Cranberry-Ginger, **'99** 93
    Float, Sparkling Cranberry, **'86** 195
    Frappé, Cranberry, **'82** 263
    Juice, Sparkling Cranberry, **'88** 275
    Lemonade, Spiced Cranberry, **'87** 292
    Mulled Cranberry Drink, **'92** 12
    New Orleans, Mr. Funk of, **'95** 57
    Punch, Cranberry, **'83** 275; **'85** 90; **'99** 290
    Punch, Cranberry-Cherry, **'91** 176
    Punch, Cranberry-Cinnamon, **'86** 270
    Punch, Cranberry Percolator, **'88** 248
    Punch, Cran-Grape-Tea, **'92** 209
    Punch, Holiday Cranberry, **'85** 265
    Punch, Hot Cranberry, **'80** 288; **'84** 41, 319; **'85** 265
    Punch, Hot Spiced, **'80** 250
    Punch, Pink Lady, **'81** 100
    Punch, Sparkling Cranberry, **'85** 277; **'95** 101
    Punch, Spiced Cranberry, **'89** 290
    Punch, Tart Cranberry, **'83** 171
    Raspberry Drink, Cranberry-, **'97** 154
    Red Roosters, **'87** 147
    Refresher, Cranberry-Vodka, **'91** 210
    Sangría, Cranberry, **'95** 238
    Shake, Cranberry, **'83** 171
    Shimmer, Cranberry, **'98** 168
    Slush, Cranberry-Rum, **'84** 259
    Smoothie, Cranberry, **'86** 183; **'91** 307
    Soda, Cranberry-Orange, **'79** 148
    Spritzer, Cranberry, **'91** 66; **'92** 265
    Spritzers, Cranberry, **'89** 213
    Tea, Cranberry, **'94** 131; **'97** 121, 160
    Tea, Cranberry-Apple, **'88** 169
    Tea, Pink Sangría, **'95** 200
    Wassail, Cranberry, **'88** 289
    Wine Cup, Cranberry, **'85** 23
Brandied Cranberries, **'86** 269; **'95** 306
Bread, Cranberry, **'79** 242
Bread, Cranberry-Banana, **'80** 281; **'90** 294
Bread, Cranberry Fruit-Nut, **'79** 275
Bread, Cranberry-Orange, **'87** 244
Bread, Cranberry-Orange Nut, **'80** 288
Bread, Orange-Cranberry, **'85** 266
Bread, Raisin-Cranberry, **'81** 305; **'82** 36
Butter, Cranberry, **'97** 307
Casserole, Cranberry-Apple, **'83** 311
Casserole, Sweet Potatoes-and-Berries, **'84** 231
Chicken, Barbecued Cranberry, **'83** 178
Chicken Kiev, Cranberry, **'87** 250
Chicken, Oven-Barbecued Cranberry, **'93** 332
Chutney, Cranberry, **'80** 243; **'83** 260; **'84** 265; **'96** 275; **'98** 276, 318
Chutney, Cranberry-Orange, **'79** 292
Chutney Melt, Brie-and-Cranberry, **'98** M318
Chutney, Orange-Cranberry, **'86** 266

Chutney with Cream Cheese, Cranberry-Amaretto, **'87** 244
Cocktail, Hot Cranberry, **'89** 310
Coffee Cake, Cranberry, **'81** 14; **'90** 159
Coffee Cake, Cranberry-Coconut, **'93** 332
Coffee Cake, Cranberry Crunch, **'97** 231
Coffee Cake, Cranberry-Nut, **'81** 250
Coffee Cake, Cranberry-Orange, **'82** 283
Conserve, Apple-Cranberry, **'82** 308
Conserve, Caramelized Chicken with Cranberry, **'98** 320
Conserve, Cranberry, **'79** 243; **'83** 279; **'85** 266
Cornish Hens, Cranberry, **'86** 303
Cornish Hens, Cranberry-Cornbread Stuffed, **'95** 325
Crackers, Cranberry, **'99** 258
Cream, Cranberry, **'90** 66
Croissant, Turkey-Cranberry, **'96** 320
Desserts
    Apple Dessert, Cranberry, **'80** 253
    Apples, Cranberry, **'99** 246
    Bake, Hot Cranberry, **'91** 250
    Bars, Cranberry-Caramel, **'98** 277
    Cake, Cranberry Upside-Down, **'87** 8
    Cake, Orange-Cranberry, **'85** 314
    Cloud, Cranberry, **'90** 287
    Cobbler, Cranberry, **'81** 275
    Cobbler, Cranberry-and-Apple, **'84** 306; **'90** 294
    Cobbler, Cranberry-Peach, **'92** 322
    Cobbler, Easy Cranberry, **'86** 260
    Cobbler Roll, Cranberry, **'80** 288; **'81** 248
    Cobbler with Cinnamon Biscuits, Cranberry-Apple, **'99** 256
    Compote, Berry, **'81** 275
    Compote, Cranberry, **'97** 264
    Cookies, Cranberry-Almond, **'98** 26
    Crêpes, Cranberry, **'85** 262
    Crisp, Cranberry-Pear, **'83** 207; **'97** 16
    Crunch, Apple-Cranberry, **'86** 300; **'87** 178
    Glaze, Cranberry, **'84** 306
    Ice, Cranberry-Apple, **'82** 290
    Ice, Tangy Cranberry, **'87** 305
    Ice, Tart Cranberry-Orange, **'86** 317
    Jubilee, Cranberries, **'85** 312; **'90** 293
    Jubilee, Tasty Cranberry, **'84** 305; **'85** 189
    Mousse, Cran-Apple, **'93** 255
    Orange Surprise, Cran-, **'94** 143
    Pie, Apple-Cranberry, **'97** 276; **'99** M269
    Pie, Autumn Apple, **'79** 205
    Pie, Berry-Apple, **'88** 251
    Pie, Cran-Apple, **'92** 304
    Pie, Cranberry-Apple, **'79** 264
    Pie, Cranberry-Apple Holiday, **'81** M269
    Pie, Cranberry-Apple-Raisin, **'98** 270
    Pie, Cranberry-Pecan, **'92** 316
    Pie, Cranberry-Raisin, **'80** 283; **'85** 316
    Pie, Cranberry Streusel, **'98** 258
    Pie, Cran-Raspberry, **'87** 244
    Pie, Festive Cranberry Freezer, **'84** 306
    Pie, Frosty Cranberry, **'79** 259
    Pie, Nutty Cranberry, **'82** M298
    Pie, Peach-Cranberry, **'83** 249
    Pie, Tart Cranberry-Cherry, **'87** 299
    Pie, Walnut-Cranberry, **'87** 259
    Pizzas, Cranberry Dessert, **'96** 320
    Pockets, Cranberry, **'96** 320
    Pudding, Cranberry, **'84** 306
    Roulage, Chocolate-Cranberry, **'94** 313
    Sherbet, Cranberry, **'88** 280
    Sorbet, Cranberry, **'82** 251
    Sorbet, Cranberry Juice, **'85** 259
    Soufflé, Cranberry-Topped Holiday, **'84** 306
    Supreme, Cranberry, **'85** 280

    Surprise Dessert, Cranberry, **'79** 242
Tart, Cranberry-Apple, **'97** M316
Tart, Cranberry-Nut, **'84** 305
Tartlets, Fresh Cranberry, **'87** 244
Tarts, Cranberry-Cream Cheese, **'80** 154
Tarts, Cranberry Holiday, **'83** 279
Tarts, Cran-Raspberry Meringue, **'92** 286
Dip, Cranberry Fruit, **'89** 60
Dip, Cranberry-Horseradish, **'85** 65
Dipper's Delight, **'98** 93
Dressing, Cranberry-Orange, **'91** 287
Dressing, Orange Salad with Honey-Berry, **'89** 250
Frosted Cranberries, **'82** 280
Fruit Bake, Cranberry-Mustard, **'90** 287
Glaze, Chili-Cranberry, **'98** 320
Glaze, Cranberry, **'84** 306; **'86** 171; **'88** 244
Glaze, Cranberry-Honey, **'89** 273
Gravy, Baked Hen with Cranberry Pan, **'94** 308
Ham, Cranberry Broiled, **'88** 301
Ham, Cranberry Glazed, **'81** 274
Ham, Cranberry-Orange Glazed, **'81** 295
Hearts, Cranberry, **'93** 286
Jam, Christmas, **'88** 288
Jam, Christmas Brunch, **'81** 286
Jelly, Cranberry-Wine, **'81** 290
Ketchup, Christmas, **'97** 254
Lamb, Cranberry Leg of, **'90** 52
Loaf, Apricot-Cranberry, **'79** 235
Loaf, Cranberry-Ham, **'82** M77
Mexican Cranberries, **'94** 273
Muffins, Cranberry, **'81** 249
Muffins, Cranberry Oat Bran, **'89** 107
Muffins, Cranberry-Pecan, **'84** 269
Muffins, Cranberry Streusel Cake, **'88** M274
Muffins, Miniature Cranberry, **'90** 294
Orange Delight, Cranberry-, **'90** 168
Oranges, Brandied Cranberry, **'98** 309
Pork Chops, Cranberry, **'80** 288; **'90** 53
Pork Chops, Orange-Cranberry, **'86** 335; **'87** 84
Pork, Cranberry, **'90** 293
Pork Roast, Berry Barbecued, **'80** 288
Relish, Cran-Apple, **'84** 300
Relish, Cranberry, **'81** 275; **'83** 144; **'85** 258, 264; **'86** 283; **'87** 245; **'91** 257; **'92** 341; **'95** 318; **'98** 310
Relish, Cranberry-Nut, **'86** 275
Relish, Cranberry-Orange, **'81** M289; **'88** 254; **'99** 15
Relish, Cranberry-Pear, **'85** 232
Relish, Frozen Cranberry, **'95** 302
Relish, Holiday Cranberry, **'88** 304
Relish, Lemony Cranberry, **'79** 243
Relish, Old-Fashioned Cranberry, **'82** 297
Relish, Tipsy Cranberry, **'92** M310
Ring, Cranberry, **'90** 291
Rolls, Cranberry-Pineapple, **'86** 275
Salads
    Cheese Ribbon Salad, Cranberry-, **'79** 241
    Christmas Salad, Cranberry, **'79** 243
    Congealed Cranberry Salad, **'90** 124
    Congealed Salad, Cranberry, **'91** 296
    Congealed Salad, Lemon-Cranberry, **'87** 311
    Cranberry Salad, **'88** 250; **'99** 290
    Cup, Berry Grapefruit, **'79** 242
    Festive Cranberry Salad, **'81** 264, 296
    Frosted Cranberry Salad, **'90** 288
    Frozen Cranberry-Pineapple Salad, **'91** 237
    Green Salad, Cranberry-Topped, **'87** 311
    Holiday Cranberry Salad, **'82** 266, 288; **'95** 301
    Holiday Jewel Salad, **'81** 252
    Holiday Salad, Cranberry, **'89** 277
    Jellied Cranberry Salad, **'83** 279; **'85** 281
    Layered Cranberry Salad, **'84** 322; **'86** 325

Mold, Cranberry, **'79** 250
Mold, Cranberry-Apple, **'89** 277
Mold, Cranberry Gelatin, **'92** 271
Oriental, Cranberry, **'79** 126
Ring, Cranberry Salad, **'80** 247
Ring, Spicy Peach-Cranberry, **'85** 264
Tart Cranberry Salad, **'79** 286
Whipped Cream Salad, Cranberry-, **'83** 261
Wild Rice-and-Cranberry Salad, **'99** 272
Sauces
Apple Sauce, Cranberry-, **'92** 203
Apricot Sauce, Fresh Cranberry-, **'87** 243
Baked Cranberry Sauce, **'88** 257
Cranberry Sauce, **'86** 278; **'88** 280; **'92** 269
Dried Cranberry Sauce, Pork Medaillons with Port Wine and, **'95** 330
Fresh Cranberry Sauce, **'79** 283; **'84** 275
Jalapeño-Cranberry Sauce, **'92** 310
Juice Sauce, Cranberry, **'85** 224; **'86** 83
Orange Sauce, Cornish Hens with Cranberry-, **'86** 119
Raisin Sauce, Baked Ham with Cranberry-, **'88** 244
Salsa, Cranberry, **'98** 321; **'99** 316
Salsa, Cranberry-Citrus, **'97** 290
Salsa, Grilled Turkey Breast with Cranberry, **'95** 252
Salsa with Sweet Potato Chips, Cranberry, **'93** 332
Spiced Cranberry Sauce, **'96** 267
Tart Cranberry Sauce, **'83** 261
Wine Sauce, Cranberry, **'83** 276
Scones, Cranberry, **'95** 283
Scones, Cranberry-Orange, **'97** 45
Scones, Merry Cranberry-Nut Yeast, **'99** 274
Spiced Cranberries, **'82** 254, 287
Spread, Coconut-Cranberry Cheese, **'92** 328
Spread, Cranberry-Butter, **'99** 86
Stuffing, Cranberry-Pecan, **'96** 309
Stuffing, Crown Roast of Pork with Cranberry-Sausage, **'88** 49
Turkey Loaf, Cranberry-Glazed, **'86** 171
Vinaigrette, Cranberry, **'98** 321
Vinegar, Cranberry, **'91** 288
Wild Rice, Cranberry-Pear, **'83** 279
CRAWFISH
Borscht, Crawfish, **'92** 84
Cakes with Cilantro-Lime Cream, Crawfish, **'98** 129
Casserole, Crawfish Pasta, **'97** 106
Delicacy, Crawfish, **'99** M23
Dressing, Crawfish-Cornbread, **'99** 257
Dressing, Louisiana Crawfish, **'90** 103
Étouffée, Crawfish, **'83** 91; **'86** 156; **'90** 103; **'94** 239
Fettuccine, Crawfish, **'96** 98
Fettuccine, Crawfish and Tasso, **'96** 290
Lasagna, Crawfish, **'91** 89
Mushrooms, Crawfish-Stuffed, **'86** 258
Risotto, Crawfish, **'99** 120
Salad, Dilled Crawfish, **'83** 126
Soft-Shell Crawfish on Eggplant, **'88** 222
Spaghetti, Crawfish, **'85** 104
Stroganoff, Crawfish, **'91** 89
Trout Stuffed with Crawfish, Bacon-Wrapped, **'99** 54
CRÈME BRULÉE. *See* **CUSTARDS.**
CRÈME FRAÎCHE
Fraîche, Crème, **'85** 39; **'91** 99
Sauce, Crème Fraîche, **'79** 281; **'93** 135
CRÊPES
Apple Breakfast Crêpes, **'97** 331
Basic Crêpes, **'84** 83; **'86** 38
Beef Crêpes, Sherried, **'85** M29

Beef Roulades, **'80** 80
Blintzes, Cheese, **'92** 84
Blue-Corn Crêpes, **'97** 197
Blue-Corn Crêpes with Beef Filling, **'97** 197
Bran Crêpes, **'83** 70; **'86** 44
Breakfast Crêpes, Country-Style, **'79** 22
Brunch Crêpes, Nutritious, **'80** 44
Brunch Crêpes, Royal, **'81** 44
Cannelloni Crêpes, **'86** 143
Cheese and Mushroom Crêpes, **'81** 88
Cheese Blintzes, **'82** 146; **'83** 71
Cheesy Party Wedges, **'84** 84
Cherry Crêpes, **'91** 67
Chicken Crêpes, **'80** 39
Chicken Crêpes, Creamy, **'81** 200
Chicken-Vegetable Crêpes, **'83** 70
con Queso, Crêpes, **'96** 48
Coquilles St. Jacques Crêpes, **'83** 13
Cornbread Crêpes, **'98** 42
Cornbread Crêpes, Goat Cheese-Filled, **'98** 43
Cornbread Crêpes, Southwestern, **'98** 42
Cornmeal Sombreros, **'93** 277
Crab Crêpes, **'79** 165
Crab Crêpes, Sautéed, **'84** 84
Crêpes, **'82** 38, 46, 146, 240; **'83** 13, 71, 122, 127, 205, 282; **'84** 186; **'86** 216; **'87** 126; **'88** 295; **'89** 44; **'90** 157; **'91** 24; **'92** 41, 88; **'93** 123; **'94** 116; **'96** 191; **'97** 332; **'98** 266; **'99** 25, 166
Cups, Florentine Crêpe, **'89** 44
Desserts
Amandine, Crêpes Gelée, **'83** 126
Amaretto-and-Orange Crêpes, **'86** 260
Banana Crêpes Flambé, **'84** 262
Basic Dessert Crêpes, **'82** 183; **'85** 262; **'86** 275
Cheese Blintzes, **'82** 146
Cherry Crêpes Flambé, **'79** 18
Chocolate Chantilly Crêpes, **'82** 183
Chocolate Crêpes, **'86** 164
Chocolate Crêpes, Fruit-Filled, **'89** 325
Chocolate Dessert Crêpes, **'84** 84; **'85** 262
Chocolate Dream Crêpes, **'86** 164
Chocolate-Orange Crêpes, **'85** 263
Coffee Ice Cream Crêpes, **'84** 85
Cranberry Crêpes, **'85** 262
Dessert Crêpes, **'84** 84; **'86** 260; **'87** 290; **'88** 134
Dixie Dessert Crêpes, **'79** 222
Fruit Crêpes, Tropical, **'87** 77
Fruit Filling, Crêpes with, **'81** 96
Low-Calorie Crêpes, **'87** 77
Mango-Pineapple Crêpes, **'86** 216
Orange Dream Crêpes, **'82** 183
Peach Crêpes, **'82** 184
Peach Crêpes, Fresh, **'84** 186
Plain Crêpes, **'83** 70
Processor Crêpes, Basic, **'87** 289; **'88** 135
Raspberry Crêpes, **'87** 126
Spicy Dessert Crêpes, **'84** 262
Strawberry Dessert Crêpes, **'83** 122
Strawberry Ice Cream Crêpes, **'87** 290; **'88** 135
Suzette, Raspberry Crêpes, **'84** 84
Suzettes, Light Crêpes, **'83** 71
Tropical Crêpes, **'86** 275
Whole Wheat Crêpes, **'83** 70
Divan, Elegant Crêpes, **'81** 91
Eggplant Crêpes with Marinara Sauce, Mini, **'99** 266
Entrée Crêpes, **'79** 264
Fajita Crêpes, **'94** 116
Filling, Crêpe, **'96** 48
Florentine Crêpe Pie, **'79** 34

Florentine, Crêpes, **'80** 190
Ham-and-Egg Crêpes, **'83** 204
Ham-and-Egg Crêpes with Mushroom Sauce, **'82** 46
Italian Crêpes, **'90** 157
Lemon Crêpes with Fruit Filling, **'82** 46
Light Crêpes, **'86** 143
Mushroom-Cheese Crêpes, **'87** 289; **'88** 135
Plain Crêpes, **'83** 70
Processor Crêpes, Basic, **'87** 289; **'88** 135
Raspberry Crêpes with Yogurt Filling, Fresh, **'93** 123
Sausage Crêpes, **'88** 295
Sausage Crêpes, Cheesy, **'82** 240; **'83** 71
Sausage-Filled Crêpes, **'79** 39; **'98** 266; **'99** 25
Spinach-Ricotta Crêpes, **'81** 52
Steak Crêpes, Special, **'91** 24
Turkey Crêpes, **'92** 41
Turkey Crêpes, Elegant, **'83** 282
Virginia Crêpes, **'79** 264
Whole Wheat Crêpes, **'80** 44; **'83** 70
Zucchini Crêpes, **'79** 157
CRISPS. *See* **PIES, PUFFS, AND PASTRIES/Cobblers, Crisps, and Crumbles.**
CROUTONS
Bagel Croutons, **'93** 192
Bourbon Croutons, **'93** 234
Bread Croutons, Hawaiian, **'94** 107
Bread, Quick Crouton, **'90** 138
Celery Croutons, **'79** 16
Cinnamon Pound Cake Croutons, **'93** 161
Cornbread Croutons, **'93** 192
Cornbread Croutons, Honeyed, **'94** 106
Crispy Italian Croutons, **'84** 126
Crostini, **'92** 56
Croûtes, Croutons and, **'93** 30
Croutons, **'86** M288
Dilled Croutons, **'93** 161
Egg Roll Fan, Sesame, **'94** 107
Fried Okra Croutons, Salad Greens and Veggies with, **'96** 178
Garlic Croutons, **'92** 71
Garlic-Flavored Croutons, **'86** 47
Herb Croutons, **'81** 150
Microwave Croutons, **'86** M227
Parslied Croutons, Carrot-and-Butternut Squash Soup with, **'97** 217
Pita Croutons, **'93** 192; **'96** 64; **'98** 329
Prosciutto Croutons, **'99** 89
Pumpernickel Croutons, **'94** 62
Seasoned Croutons, **'96** 326
Tortilla Triangles, **'94** 107
Vegetable-Flavored Croutons, **'84** 148
CRUMBLES. *See* **PIES, PUFFS, AND PASTRIES/Cobblers, Crisps, and Crumbles.**
CUCUMBERS
Bisque, Shrimp-Cucumber, **'79** 172
Canapés, Chicken-Cucumber, **'98** 154
Canapés, Cucumber, **'95** 88
Canapés, Shrimp-and-Cucumber, **'93** 164
Chips, Cucumber, **'85** 176
Cool Cucumbers, **'84** 152
Creamy Cucumbers, **'92** 62
Delights, Cucumber, **'84** 117
Dills, Lazy Wife, **'87** 149
Dip, Cucumber-Cheese Vegetable, **'83** 128
Dip, Cucumber-Yogurt, **'99** 93
Dip, Refreshing Dill, **'99** 324
Dressing, Benedictine, **'98** 83
Dressing, Creamy Cucumber Salad, **'82** 79
Dressing, Cucumber, **'80** 74; **'90** 144
Dressing, Cucumber-Curry, **'89** 179

CUCUMBERS
(continued)

Dressing, Cucumber-Mint, **'87** 153
Dressing, Tomato, Onion, and Cucumber in Italian, **'81** 83
Fried Cucumber Fingers, **'86** 146
Gazpacho-Stuffed Endive, **'95** 287
Gazpacho, White, **'97** 181
Lemony Cucumbers, **'89** 102
Marinated Cucumbers and Artichokes, **'82** 111
Marinated Cucumbers and Squash, **'86** 146
Marinated Shrimp and Cucumber, **'91** 166
Mold, Chicken-Cucumber, **'86** 175
Mold, Lemon-Cucumber, **'87** 90
Pasta, Asian Cucumbers and, **'96** 177
Pepper Combo, Cucumber-and-, **'88** 176
Pickled Cucumber Rounds, Easy, **'90** 143
Pickles, Cucumber Sandwich, **'81** 174
Pickles, Dill, **'81** 174
Pickles, Freezer Cucumber, **'99** 87
Pickles, Lime, **'96** 206
Pickles, Mixed, **'81** 174
Pickles, Quick Sweet, **'87** 149
Pickles, Sour Cucumber, **'85** 176
Pickles, Sweet Icicle, **'85** 176
Pico de Gallo, **'98** 174
Red Snapper Rolls, Cucumber-Stuffed, **'83** 176
Relish, Cucumber, **'85** 176; **'96** 23
Rounds, Cucumber, **'88** 78
Salads
  Almond Salad, Cucumber-, **'86** 147
  Asian Greens, Cucumber, **'98** 66
  Aspic, Shrimp-Cucumber, **'83** 108
  Bean Salad, Cucumber-, **'83** 81
  Congealed Salad, Pineapple-Cucumber, **'83** 118
  Cooler, Simple Cucumber, **'86** 147
  Crab Salad, Cucumber-and-, **'98** 208
  Creamy Cucumber Salad, **'86** 147; **'92** 97
  Dilled Cucumber and Tomato Salad, **'81** 153
  Dilled Cucumber on Tomatoes, **'84** 142
  Dilled Cucumber Salad, **'82** 229; **'92** 72; **'93** 65
  Grapefruit-Cucumber Salad, **'80** 100
  Marinated Cucumber Salad, **'82** 111
  Marinated Tomato-and-Cucumber Salad, **'92** 216
  Mold, Asparagus-Cucumber, **'85** 252
  Mold, Creamy Cucumber, **'84** 164
  Mold, Cucumber Salad, **'82** 111; **'83** 81, 253
  Mousse, Cucumber, **'79** 11; **'88** 121
  Mousse with Dill Sauce, Cucumber, **'95** 216
  Pineapple Salad, Cucumber-, **'84** 124
  Roast Beef Salad, Cucumber-, **'89** 162
  Scallions, Cukes and, **'91** 168
  Slaw, Creamy Cucumber, **'89** 49
  Sour Cream, Cucumbers in, **'79** 52; **'80** 178
  Tomato-and-Cucumber Summer Salad, **'93** 141
  Tomato-Cucumber-Onion Salad, **'81** 239
  Tomato-Cucumber Salad, **'86** 218; **'92** 199
  Tomato-Cucumber Salad with Yogurt-Herb Dressing, **'92** 96
  Tomato Salad, Cucumber-, **'90** 144
  Tuna Boats, Cucumber, **'83** 136
  Vinaigrette Oriental, Cucumber-, **'85** 198; **'86** 147
  Yogurt-Cucumber Salad, **'82** 122
  Yogurt Salad, Cucumber-, **'87** 33
Salsa, Cucumber, **'95** 131
Salsa, Cucumber-Dill, **'95** 107
Sandwiches, Cucumber, **'88** 159; **'90** 81; **'94** 14; **'97** 99

Sandwiches, Cucumber Pinwheel, **'85** 120
Sandwiches, Dainty Cucumber, **'81** 119
Sandwiches, Watercress-Cucumber, **'97** 108
Sauce, Cucumber, **'82** 111; **'84** M286; **'92** 41
Sauce, Cucumber Cream, **'92** 33
Sauce, Cucumber-Dill, **'86** 5; **'91** 62; **'92** 51
Sauce, Cucumber Dipping, **'94** 47
Sauce, Lamb Burgers with Cucumber, **'98** 102
Sauce, Lemony Cucumber, **'89** 245
Sauce, Tomato-Cucumber, **'98** 45
Sauce, Tuna Steaks with Cucumber, **'97** 180
Sesame Cucumbers, **'85** 85
Sherbet, Jalapeño-Mint, **'98** 202
Slices, Cheesy Cucumber, **'84** 80
Slices, Fresh Cucumber, **'86** 177
Soup, Chilled Cucumber, **'79** 144
Soup, Chilled Cucumber-Buttermilk, **'95** 134
Soup, Cold Cucumber, **'79** 130; **'81** 130
Soup, Cold Minted Cucumber, **'86** 34
Soup, Cold Potato-Cucumber, **'88** 160
Soup, Cream of Cucumber, **'81** 98
Soup, Creamy Cucumber, **'80** 171
Soup, Cucumber-Yogurt, **'82** 157; **'83** 205
Soup, Dilled Cucumber, **'90** M167
Sour Cream, Cucumber and Onion in, **'81** 69
Sour Cream, Cucumbers and, **'93** 203
Sour Cream, Cucumbers in, **'99** 243
Spread, Cucumber, **'79** 295; **'80** 31; **'93** 158
Spread, Cucumber and Cream Cheese, **'82** 140
Spread, Shrimp-Cucumber, **'79** 81
Stuffed Cucumbers, **'81** 237
Tartlets, Smoked Salmon and Cucumber, **'95** 216
Tomatoes, Cucumber-Stuffed Cherry, **'88** 262
Topping, Lamb Pockets with Dilled Cucumber, **'87** 104
Vichyssoise, Cucumber, **'94** 90
Vichyssoise with Mint Cream, Cucumber, **'94** 246
CUPCAKES. *See* CAKES/Cupcakes.
CURRANTS. *See* RAISINS.
CURRY
Almonds, Cauliflower and Peas with Curried, **'79** 221
Almonds, Curried, **'82** 297
Appetizers
  Bites, Curried Swiss, **'85** 220
  Cheese Ball, Chicken-Curry, **'85** 118
  Cheese Ball, Curried Shrimp, **'86** 135
  Chicken Balls, Coconut Curried, **'91** 165
  Chicken Balls, Curried, **'91** 98
  Chicken Bites, Curried, **'85** 40
  Chicken Tea Sandwiches, Curried, **'97** 23
  Dip and Vegetable Platter, Curry, **'89** 327
  Dip, Curried, **'81** 262
  Dip, Curry, **'80** 84; **'81** 9; **'85** 132; **'86** 184; **'87** 25; **'99** 138
  Dip, Curry-Onion, **'93** 313
  Dip, Tuna-Curry, **'84** 31
  Hazelnuts, Curried, **'93** 301
  Pecans, Curried, **'91** 208
  Popcorn Mix, Curried, **'86** 326
  Sandwiches, Curried Tea, **'91** 314
  Sauce, Curry, **'94** 54
  Shrimp Balls, Curried, **'94** 180
  Spread, Broccamoli Curry, **'88** 55
  Spread, Curried Chutney, **'89** 283
  Spread, Curried Shrimp, **'87** 158
Apples, Curried, **'93** 252
Apricots, Curried, **'91** 315
Bananas, Fillets with Horseradish Sauce and Curried, **'85** 230
Beef and Rice, Curried, **'88** 164
Beef Dinner, Curried, **'83** 4
Beef Pitas, Curried, **'85** 220

Beef Steak, Curried, **'88** 60
Bread, Honey-Curry, **'89** 250
Butter, Tomato-Curry-Orange, **'93** 159
Carrots and Pineapple, Curried, **'90** 228
Casserole, Curry Pea, **'87** 154
Casserole, Vegetable-Curry, **'91** 286; **'92** 27
Cauliflower, Curried, **'91** 315
Chicken. *See also* CURRY/Appetizers.
  Brioche, Chicken Curry, **'88** 124
  Cheesecake, Curried Chicken, **'90** 174
  Country Captain Chicken, **'94** 252
  Curried Chicken, **'86** 43
  Curry, Chicken, **'84** 110; **'85** 220; **'86** 21; **'89** 219
  Divan, Curried Chicken, **'80** 83
  Filling, Curried Chicken, **'88** 125
  Fried Chicken, Curried, **'85** 160
  Honey-Curry Chicken, **'87** 36
  Indian-Style Chicken Curry, **'97** 119
  Mousse, Curried Chicken, **'95** 328
  Peppers, Chicken Breasts with Curried, **'90** 227
  Peppers, Curried Chicken-Stuffed, **'87** 19
  Quick Curried Chicken, **'89** 219; **'99** 92
  Regal Curried Chicken, **'84** 110
  Sauce, Chicken Curry, **'90** 117
  Skillet Dinner, Curried Chicken, **'95** 47
  Soup, Curried Chicken, **'86** 34
  Stir-Fried Chicken Curry, **'87** 51
  Turban Chicken Curry, **'94** 266
  Wings, Curried Chicken, **'96** 110
Chops, Pineapple-Curry Glazed, **'82** 106
Chowder, Curried Chicken-and-Corn, **'92** 21
Chowder, Curried Seafood, **'94** 103
Corn and Celery, Curried, **'86** 192
Corn and Sweet Red Peppers, Curried, **'95** 47
Dressing, Cucumber-Curry, **'89** 179
Dressing, Curried, **'84** 115
Dressing, Curry, **'80** 242; **'82** 78; **'97** 63
Eggs, Curried Deviled, **'93** 87
Eggs, Saucy Shrimp-Curried, **'84** 143
Fish, Curried Baked, **'87** 5
Fish, Curry-Baked, **'91** 196
Fruit, Almond-Curried, **'83** 261
Fruit Bake, Curried, **'87** 241
Fruit, Hot Curried, **'79** 225; **'81** 264; **'84** 287; **'95** 72
Fruit Medley, Curried, **'95** 329
Ham and Peaches, Curried, **'82** 60
Ham Steak, Curried, **'82** 120
Ham with Rice, Curried, **'80** 111
Hurry Curry, **'79** 103
Kheema, Indian, **'81** 226
Lamb Curry with Rice, **'80** 83; **'81** 10
Lamb with Rice Mold, Curried, **'85** 36
Mayonnaise, Curry, **'95** 66
Meat Loaf, Curried, **'86** 43
Mushrooms, Curried, **'84** 214
Nuts, Spicy Curried, **'82** 250
Onions, Curried, **'90** 34
Peas with Almonds, Curried, **'88** M294
Pecans, Curried, **'91** 208
Pork Chops, Curried Apricot, **'89** 191
Pork Tenderloin, Curried, **'86** 76
Rice and Shrimp, Curried, **'83** 231
Rice, Chicken with Curried, **'98** 127
Rice, Curried, **'90** 183; **'97** 51; **'98** 237
Rice, Curry-Spiced, **'86** M226
Rice Mix, Fruited Curry-, **'86** 326
Rice Mold, Curried, **'85** 36
Rice, Quick Curried, **'86** 81
Rice with Almonds, Curried, **'83** M285
Rice with Curry, Raisin, **'85** 83

Rice with Pineapple, Curried, '79 142
Salad Dressing, Curry, '96 326
Salads
  Apple-Raisin Salad, Curried, '80 24
  Broccoli Salad, Curried, '86 225
  Chicken-and-Orange Salad, Curried, '87 144
  Chicken-Rice Salad, Curried, '92 190
  Chicken Salad, Curried, '79 219; '84 66;
    '85 96; '86 131; '89 176
  Chicken Salad, Royal Curried, '96 200
  Chicken Salad with Asparagus, Curried,
    '81 36
  Coleslaw, Curried, '85 139
  Coleslaw, Curried Pineapple, '88 172
  Couscous Salad, Curried, '91 44
  Gift, Curried Salad, '96 326
  Indian Curry Salad, Hot, '83 23
  Melon and Shrimp Curry Salad, '97 129
  Pears with Coconut-Chicken Salad, Curried
    Poached, '97 93
  Potato Salad, Curried, '99 137
  Rice Salad, Curried, '80 84; '85 147, 220;
    '96 240
  Rice Salad, Curry, '89 146
  Shrimp Salad, Aloha, '95 46
  Spinach Salad, Curry, '80 242
  Tuna Salad, Curried, '86 208
  Tuna Salad with Grapes, Curried, '87 201
  Turkey Salad, Chutney Curried, '98 314
  Turkey Salad, Curried, '88 140
Sandwiches, Curried BLT, '93 158
Sauce, Asparagus with Curry, '90 17
Sauce, Curried Rum, '91 164
Sauce, Curried Sour Cream, '90 174
Sauce, Curry, '79 156; '83 138; '84 M71; '95 18;
  '97 170; '99 92
Sauce, Curry-Mustard, '96 249
Sauce, Halibut with Orange-Curry, '87 91
Sauce, Pineapple-Curry, '79 252
Sauce, Turkey Slices with Curried Cream, '91 60
Seasoning Salt, Gourmet, '97 254
Shrimp, Curried, '84 110
Shrimp Curry, '99 91
Shrimp Curry, Creamy, '90 145
Shrimp Curry, Polynesian, '89 23
Shrimp Curry, Sour Cream, '80 83
Shrimp Curry, Sour Cream and, '81 10
Shrimp Malai Curry, '84 110
Shrimp, Quick Curried, '84 M198
Snapper, Honey-Curried, '85 181
Soup, Cold Curried Pea, '91 120
Soup, Curried, '81 130
Soup, Curried Carrot, '82 157
Soup, Curried Chicken, '86 34
Soup, Curried Mushroom, '84 M89
Soup, Curried Pumpkin, '96 242
Soup, Curried Turkey, '86 332
Spread, Curried Shrimp, '87 158
Spread, Curried Turkey, '92 16
Spread, Curry, '93 159
Stir-Fry, Indian, '92 126
Tomatoes, Curried Green, '93 138
Topping, Curry Salad, '96 326
Tuna Melts, Curried, '95 46
Turkey Pie, Crumb-Crust Curried, '86 265
Vegetable Curry, '99 91
Vegetables, Curried, '89 219
Vegetables with Curry, Stir-Fried, '87 51
Vinaigrette, Ginger-Curry, '97 146
Vinaigrette, Warm Curry, '93 107
CUSTARDS. *See also* **MOUSSES, PUDDINGS.**
  Acorn Squash, Custard-Filled, '86 334
  Almond Crème Custard with Raspberries,
    '88 174

Amaretto Custard, Chocolate-Topped, '87 M37
Amaretto Custard, Range-Top, '87 77
Amaretto Custard with Raspberries, '86 152
Ambrosia, Custard Sauce, '84 256
Baked Custard, '80 219
Baked Custard, Creamy, '86 7
Baked Custard, Easy, '85 52
Baked Vanilla Custard, '82 129
Blackberry Custard, '99 132
Boiled Christmas Custard, '95 329
Boiled Custard, Favorite, '81 181
Boiled Custard, Perfect, '81 34
Cake, Chocolate Custard, '88 175
Cake, Southern Custard Crêpe, '99 166
Chocolate Custard, '88 258
Citrus Custard with Fresh Fruit, '93 70
Coconut Custard, '86 109; '97 131
Corn Custard, Fresh, '89 127
Crema, '80 175
Crème Brûlée, Almond, '95 323
Crème Brûlée, Basic, '95 323
Crème Brûlée, Berry, '95 323
Crème Brûlée, Black-and-White, '98 267
Crème Brûlée, Chocolate, '95 323
Crème Brûlée, Coffee, '95 323
Crème Brûlée, Double Raspberry, '95 323
Crème Brûlée, Ginger, '95 323
Crème Brûlée, Onion, '95 324
Crème Brûlée, Orange, '95 323
Crème Brûlée, Peppermint, '95 323
Crème Brûlée, Roasted Garlic, '95 324
Crème Brûlée, Roquefort-and-Black Pepper,
  '95 324
Crème Brûlées, Savory, '95 324
Crème Brûlée, White Chocolate-Macadamia Nut,
  '95 323
Crème Patissière, '84 207
Easy Custard with Nutmeg, '90 316
Filling, Creamy Custard, '81 180
Filling, Custard, '82 52, 298; '85 281
Filling, Egg Custard, '87 14
Flans
  Almendra, Flan, '80 199
  Apricot Flan, '99 146
  Baked Flan with Caramel, '92 231
  Blackberry Flan, '79 182
  Caramel-Crowned Flans, '90 227
  Corn-Chive Flan, '94 172
  Corn Flan, '98 246; '99 25
  de Leche (Flan with Milk), Flan, '92 169
  de Queso, Flan, '95 303
  Flaming Flan, '85 313
  Flan, '88 247
  Individual Flans, '85 52
  Layered Flan, '89 45
  Luscious Flan, '90 56
  Orange Flan, '84 95
  Pumpkin Flan, '82 217
  Spanish Flan, '85 51, 311
  Sweet Potato Flan, '95 291
Goat Cheese Custard, '96 285
Ice Cream, Vanilla Custard, '96 145
Lemon-Buttermilk Custards, '89 49
Lemon Custard in Meringue Cups, '80 295;
  '81 172
Mexican Custard, Light, '88 149
Napoleon Cream, '84 138
Orange Custard Pudding, '88 174
Peach Custard Dessert, Fresh, '86 162
Pears in Custard, Poached, '88 20
Pie, Apple Custard, '88 236
Pie, Carrot Custard, '79 45
Pie, Coconut Custard, '82 33
Pie, Custard Pecan, '87 184

Pie, Old-Fashioned Egg Custard, '82 261
Pie, Perfect Custard, '82 92
Pie, Quick 'n' Easy Custard, '96 28
Preserves, Custard, '98 126
Pumpkin Custard, '88 279
Rice Custard, Baked, '92 308
Sauce, Bourbon Custard, '95 271
Sauce, Buttermilk Custard, '96 183
Sauce, Custard, '85 41; '88 154, 251, 259;
  '89 291; '97 16, 313
Sauce, Fresh Berries with Raspberry Custard,
  '88 163
Sauce, Vanilla Custard, '99 27
Spinach-Gorgonzola Custards, Savory, '99 313
Stirred Custard, '92 45; '99 126
Stirred Custard, Old-Fashioned, '85 52
Stirred Custard over Fruit, '84 83
Tart, Chocolate Custard, '99 27
Tocino del Cielo, '93 29
Vanilla Cream, '83 M115
Vanilla Custard, '99 27

Dates
Ball, Date-Nut, '92 326
Bars and Cookies
  Balls, Date-Nut, '85 10
  Balls, Peanut-Date, '81 92
  Brownies, Date-and-Almond, '88 217
  Chocolate Chip Cookies, Rich Date-Nut,
    '92 207
  Christmas Date Cookies, '88 287
  Cranberry-Caramel Bars, '98 277
  Date Bars, '84 313; '95 322
  Filled Cookies, Date-, '91 95
  Fruit Cookies, Rolled, '80 15
  No-Bake Date Bars, '79 256
  Nut Bars, Date-, '80 166
  Nutty Date Bars, '84 153
  Oat Bars, Date-, '80 M172
  Oatmeal-Date Bars, Layered, '85 10
  Oatmeal-Date Cookies, '82 109
  Oatmeal-Date Sandwich Cookies, '83 257
Breads
  Apple-Date-Nut Ring, '90 212
  Banana Loaves, Tropical Date-, '95 143
  Chocolate Date-Nut Bread, '81 284
  Muffins, Carrot-Date-Nut, '86 262
  Muffins, Date, '79 142
  Muffins, Date-Nut, '84 75; '99 234
  Muffins, Orange-Date, '92 119; '97 243
  Muffins, Surprise Date, '79 216
  Nut Bread, Date-, '85 306
  Nut Loaf, Date-, '85 10
  Persimmon Date-Nut Bread, '82 218
  Walnut Loaf, Blue Ribbon Date-, '80 15
  Wine-Date Nut Bread, '82 253
Cake, Bourbon, '98 277
Cake, Date Nut, '79 176; '80 5
Cake, Fresh Apple-Date, '83 300
Cake, Orange-Date, '94 60
Cake, Pumpkin Date, '79 251
Cake, Queen Bee, '81 237
Cake Roll, Date-Nut, '89 94
Cake Squares, Apple-Date Dream, '85 10
Candy, Date, '89 308
Candy, Date Loaf, '80 302
Cheese, Nutty Date Dessert, '87 299
Chocolate Date-Nut Delight, '88 168
Conserve, Brandied Date, '85 315
Cupcakes, Date, '84 7
Dessert Squares, Date, '89 255
Dressing, Date, '87 57

DATES

(continued)

Filling, Apple-Date, '**83** 301
Filling, Date, '**80** 15; '**83** 257; '**86** 314
Filling, Date Cream, '**81** 303
June Bugs, '**85** 11
Logs, Date, '**79** 274
Pastries, Date-Filled Cheese, '**83** 259
Pie, Date-Pecan, '**80** 15
Pie, Dried Fruit, '**83** 249
Pudding, Steamed Date, '**79** 86
Relish, Lemon-Date, '**96** 271
Rice), Basted Dates and Basted Rice (Date-Nut, '**96** 158
Roll, Date Nut, '**79** 249
Rollups, Date-Cream Cheese, '**83** 298
Salad, Festive Fruit, '**80** 16
Sandwich, Date-Nut Lettuce, '**94** 202
Sauce, Date-Nut Sundae, '**82** 167
Spread, Apple-Date, '**91** 231; '**92** 67
Spread, Breakfast Date, '**84** 7
Spread, Date-Walnut, '**87** 292
Spread, Date-Walnut-Cheese, '**96** 322
Squares, Date, '**90** 49
Stuffed Date Drops, '**97** 247
Stuffed Dates, Apricot-, '**80** 250

DESSERT OF THE MONTH

Bananas, Caramelized, '**99** 49
Beverage Sipper, Kahlúa, '**99** 27
Bombe, Double-Chocolate, '**97** 282
Brownies à la Mode, Magnolias Cream Cheese, '**97** M178
Cake, Banana Split, '**99** 48
Cake, Best Carrot, '**97** 230
Cake, Buttermilk Pound, '**99** 98
Cake, Chocolate-Peanut Butter Mousse, '**98** 71
Cake, German Carrot-Hazelnut, '**97** 230
Cake, Mama's Coconut, '**97** 71
Cake, Nanny's Famous Coconut-Pineapple, '**97** 277
Cake, Pastel, '**97** 173
Cake, Pecan-Carrot, '**99** 223
Cake with Coconut Custard, Supreme Banana, '**97** 131
Cake with Wine Jelly, Pound, '**98** 125
Candied Rose Petals, '**98** 57
Caramels, Coconut-Macadamia, '**98** 305
Cheesecake, Bavarian, '**97** 55
Cheesecake, Chocolate-Wrapped Banana, '**99** M48
Cheesecake, Praline-Crusted, '**99** 295
Cheesecake, Warm Fudge-Filled, '**98** 34
Cobbler à la Mode, Apple, '**97** 16
Cobbler with Custard Sauce, Apricot, '**97** 16
Coffee Buttons, '**99** 66
Cookies, Chocolate-Brickle, '**99** 127
Cookies, Chocolate Shortbread, '**99** 147
Cookies, Gingerbread Snowflake, '**98** 324
Cookies, Orange Slice, '**98** 324
Cookies, Shortbread, '**99** 147
Cookies, White Chocolate Chip-Oatmeal, '**99** 127
Cream, Spanish, '**99** 27
Crisp, Cranberry-Pear, '**97** 16
Crust, Gingersnap, '**98** 161
Crust, Peanut-Graham, '**99** 49
Crust, Vanilla Wafer, '**98** 216
Custard, Coconut, '**97** 131
Custard, Vanilla, '**99** 27
Filling, Pineapple, '**97** 277
Frosting, Amaretto Buttercream, '**98** 57

Frosting, Chocolate-Buttermilk, '**99** 99
Frosting, Citrus Cream Cheese, '**99** 223
Frosting, Cream Cheese, '**97** 230, 277
Frosting, Mocha, '**99** 66
Frosting, Seven-Minute, '**97** 71
Ganache, Chocolate, '**97** 282
Glaze, Buttermilk, '**97** 230; '**99** 98
Glaze, Chocolate, '**97** 231
Glaze, Pineapple, '**97** 55
Heart, Chocolate-Amaretto, '**98** 56
Ice Cream, Mocha, '**97** M145
Ice Cream, Rum-Raisin, '**97** 145
Ice Cream Sandwiches, '**99** 147
Icing, Royal, '**98** 324
Jelly, Wine, '**98** 125
Meringue, '**97** 109
Mousse, Chocolate, '**97** 282
Mousse Parfaits, Chocolate-Peanut Butter, '**98** 71
Mousse, White Chocolate, '**97** 282; '**98** M57, M111
Pecan Clusters, '**98** 305
Penuche, Coffee, '**98** 305
Pie, Black-and-White Fudge, '**99** 249
Pie, Black-Bottom, '**98** 161
Pie, Caramel Meringue, '**97** 109
Pie, Coconut Cream, '**98** 161
Pie, Coconut-Macadamia Nut, '**97** 110
Pie, Fox Hunter's, '**97** 109
Pie, Georgia Peach-and-Praline, '**98** 196
Pie, Lemony Ice Cream, '**99** 207
Pie, Maverick Lunar, '**98** 111
Pie, Peach Melba, '**98** 216
Pie, Pear Streusel, '**97** 109
Pie, Raspberry Baked Alaska, '**98** 216
Pie, Red, White, and Blueberry, '**98** 162
Pie, Triple Mint Ice Cream, '**98** 217
Pie, Warm Apple-Buttermilk Custard, '**99** 98
Pralines, '**99** 295
Pralines, Buttermilk, '**99** 99
Preserves, Custard, '**98** 126
Pudding, Lemon Cake, '**98** 35
Pudding, Piña Colada Bread, '**98** 34
Sauce, Caramel, '**97** 178
Sauce, Chocolate, '**97** 178
Sauce, Chocolate-Mint, '**98** 217
Sauce, Coconut, '**98** 34
Sauce, Custard, '**97** 16
Sauce, Mocha, '**98** 57
Sauce, Raspberry, '**98** 216
Sauce, Vanilla Custard, '**99** 27
Sherbet, Buttermilk, '**99** 99
Shortcake, Warm Blueberry-Nectarine, '**97** 205
Soufflé with White Chocolate Mousse, Chocolate, '**98** 57
Soup, Fresh Fruit, '**98** 196
Spritzers, Raspberry, '**99** 207
Squares, Buttermilk Fudge, '**99** 99
Strudel, Autumn-Apple, '**98** 253
Strudel, Fig, '**98** 253
Strudel, Pear, '**98** 253
Tart, Apricot-Nut, '**99** 249
Tart, Bakewell, '**97** 110
Tart, Chocolate Custard, '**99** 27
Tart, Coffee, '**99** 67
Tart, Golden Peach Meringue, '**98** 197
Tart, Upside-Down Apple, '**98** 35
Tea, Almond-Lemonade, '**99** 207
Torte, Mocha, '**99** 66
Truffles, Chocolate-Cherry Cordial, '**99** 127
Wafers, Kahlúa, '**99** 147
Waffles with Apples and Caramel, Gingerbread, '**98** M237

DESSERTS. *See also* **AMBROSIA; BROWNIES; CAKES; CHEESECAKES; COOKIES; CUSTARDS; ICE CREAMS; MERINGUES; MOUSSES; PIES, PUFFS, AND PASTRIES; PUDDINGS; SHERBETS; SOUFFLÉS/Dessert.**

Alaska, Peachy Melba, '**88** 266
Alaskas, Brownie, '**83** 299
Almond Dessert, Sour Cream-, '**92** 120
Amaretto Cream Tortoni, '**85** 161

Apple

Baked Alaska, Apple, '**80** 226
Baked Apples and Pear, Honey-, '**97** 303
Baked Apples, Imperial, '**82** 273
Baked Apples, Orange-Pecan, '**85** 45
Baked Apples with Orange Sauce, '**84** 314
Baked Mincemeat-Filled Apples, '**80** 276
Brandied Apples, '**81** 248
Brandied Apples and Cream, '**82** M237
Brown Betty, Apple, '**83** 213
Caramel Apples, Old English, '**85** 231
Charlotte, Apple, '**99** 84
Cheese Crisp, Apple-, '**92** 235
Cinnamon Apples with Brandied Date Conserve, '**85** 315
Compote, Apricot-Apple, '**98** 17
Cooked Apples, '**93** 338
Cranberry Apple Dessert, '**80** 253
Cranberry Apples, '**99** 246
Cranberry Crunch, Apple-, '**86** 300; '**87** 178
Crisp, Delicious Apple, '**82** 303
Crisp, Granola Apple, '**85** 78
Crumble, Whole Wheat-Apple, '**90** M213
Delight, Apple, '**80** 109
Dumplings, Apple, '**82** 273
Dumplings with Orange Hard Sauce, Apple, '**88** 224
Dutch Apple Dessert, Creamy, '**91** 19
Enchiladas, Apple, '**99** 63
Flambé, Hot Apples and Rum, '**92** 88
Flan, Apple, '**81** 309
Fritters, Apple, '**82** 273
Golden Apples, '**82** 254
Honey-Baked Apple Dessert, '**90** M213
Kuchen, Apple, '**79** 24
Melting Apples, '**88** 19
Nut Crunch, Apple-, '**82** M238
Oatmeal Cherry-Apple Crisp, '**90** M16
Orange-Apple Crisp, '**80** 295
Pecan Apples, Taffy, '**99** 247
Poached Lemon Apples, Chilled, '**86** 182
Rings, Apple, '**85** 232
Rings, Cinnamon Apple, '**82** M237
Saucy Apples 'n' Pears, '**96** 72
Sour Cream Apple Squares, '**82** 262
Sundae, Hot Apple Spice, '**92** 239
Apricot-Apple Compote, '**98** 17
Apricot Cream, Peachy-, '**86** 163
Avocado Whip, '**79** 107
Baklava, '**96** 20

Banana

Alaska, Banana Split, '**87** 10
Baked Bananas, '**96** 163
Baked Bananas, Coffee-Kissed, '**98** 279
Baked Bananas with Orange Sauce, '**79** 115
Berry Supreme, Banana-, '**81** 205
Candied Bananas, '**83** 179
Caramelized Bananas, '**99** 49
Cream Dessert, Banana, '**81** 180
Flambé, Banana-Peach, '**85** 316
Flip, Banana, '**83** 303
Foster, Bananas, '**79** 18; '**83** M114; '**86** 139; '**88** 20; '**96** 99
Foster, Elegant Bananas, '**81** 59

Foster for Two, Bananas, '80 115
Foster, Tropical Bananas, '79 231
Glacé, Bananas, '96 46
Pie, Layered Banana Split, '83 189
Pops, Banana, '83 60; '84 44
Pops, Orange-Banana, '82 129
Praline Bananas, '84 313
Regal Bananas, '85 46
Soufflé, Banana Daiquiri, '84 317
Spiced Bananas with Rum Sauce, '99 247
Splits, French Toast Banana, '96 M164
Supreme, Bananas, '84 256
Bavarian Cream with Fresh Fruit, '88 137
Bavarian Cream with Raspberry Sauce, '91 180
Bavarian Dessert, Light, '86 6
Berried Treasure, '89 124
Berries on Snow, '82 227
Berries with Raspberry Custard Sauce, Fresh,
    '88 163
Berry Basket, Summer, '84 158
Berry Compote, '81 275
Berry Grapefruit Cup, '79 242
Beverages. See also BEVERAGES.
    Berry Smoothie, Four-, '97 173
    Brandy Alexander, '92 283
    Brandy Float, Blazing, '85 314
    Cappuccino Coffee Dessert, '92 264
    Champagne Delight, '83 304
    Chocoholic Smoothie, '97 173
    Creamy Dessert Drink, '86 131
    Golden Dream, '82 100
    Grape Juice-Fruit Refresher, '86 182
    Ice Cream Ginger Fizz, '83 303
    Orange-Banana Smoothie, '97 173
    Pineapple Smoothie, '97 172
    Pineapple Smoothie, Peachy-, '97 173
    Strawberry Smoothie, '97 173
    Super Dessert Drink, Simply, '83 303
Biscotti, Light, '91 310
Biscuits, Elf, '99 309
Biscuits, Sweet Little, '85 305
Blackberries and Dumplings, '86 196
Blackberries Chantilly, '99 130
Blackberry Dessert Tamales, '94 190
Blackberry Flan, '79 182
Blueberries and Cointreau, '82 100
Blueberry-Amaretto Squares, '83 220
Blueberry Crumble, '81 84
Blueberry Crunch, '96 146
Blueberry Crunch, Fresh, '82 143
Blueberry Delight, '96 17
Blueberry Dessert, Easy, '89 M130
Blueberry Dream, '88 94
Blueberry Pizza, '96 147
Blueberry Yum Yum, '98 91
Boysenberries and Cream Supreme, '82 133
Bread, Fry, '85 155
Brie, Almond-Raspberry, '94 M89
Brownie Ice Cream Sandwich Shells, '88 195
Brûlé, Petit, '93 219
Buñuelos, '80 199
Buñuelos, King-Size, '86 5
Butter-Nut Strips, '82 167
Butterscotch Fantastic, '83 76
Cakes, Funnel, '83 250
Cakes, Spanish Wind, '84 157
Cannoli, '80 58; '91 20
Cantaloupe Compote, '81 147
Cantaloupe Cream Delight, '82 179
Cantaloupe Delight, '89 204
Caramel Dessert Biscuits, '95 36
Caramel Fondue, '94 331; '95 35
Caramel Surprise, '88 202
Charlotte, Macaroon, '81 296

Charlotte, Peach, '79 68
Charlotte, Pineapple, '90 288
Charlotte Russe, '80 71; '82 M142; '90 288
Charlotte Russe, Chocolate, '87 74
Charlotte Russe, Fresh Lemon, '80 13
Charlotte Russe, Lemon, '84 192
Charlotte Russe, Wine Jelly and, '82 305
Charlotte Russe with Strawberry Sauce, '92 85
Cheese Blintzes, '82 146; '83 71
Cheese Kuchen, '86 84
Cheese Molds, Heavenly Dessert, '85 209
Cheese, Nutty Date Dessert, '87 299
Cheese Squares, Lemony Cream, '82 159
Cherries à la Mode, '88 202
Cherries Jubilee, '79 18; '83 139
Cherries Jubilee, Quick, '82 M100
Cherries Jubilite, '86 317
Cherries Sabayon, '88 178
Cherries, Sherried, '93 289
Cherry-Berry on a Cloud, '79 94
Cherry Compote, '83 139
Cherry Dessert, Holiday, '80 255
Chocolate. See also DESSERTS/Frozen,
    Sauces.
    Almond Dessert, Chocolate-, '82 306
    Almond Meringue Fingers, Chocolate-,
        '84 158
    Bags, Chocolate-Raspberry, '95 97
    Baskets with Berry Cream, Chocolate, '92 118
    Black-Bottom Goodies, '89 251
    Bombe, Double-Chocolate, '97 282
    Brickle Squares, Chocolate, '94 290
    Brownie-Mint Dessert, '82 227
    Buttercream, Chocolate, '84 156
    Charlotte Russe, Chocolate, '87 74
    Chilled Chocolate Dessert, '83 177
    Cinnamon-Chocolate Cream, '94 199
    Coffee Mallow, '80 109
    Cones, Chocolate-Coffee, '96 M316
    Cream, Heavenly Chocolate, '88 128
    Crêpes, Chocolate Dream, '86 164
    Crêpes, Fruit-Filled Chocolate, '89 325
    Cups, Chocolate, '80 207
    Cups, Chocolate Crinkle, '93 270
    Cups, Chocolate Lace, '87 133
    Cups, Chocolate-Mint, '80 71
    Cups, Miniature Chocolate, '87 132
    Date-Nut Delight, Chocolate, '88 168
    Decadence, Chocolate, '89 183
    Dip, Chocolate, '92 50
    Dream Dessert, Chocolate, '83 198
    Easy Chocolate Dessert, '79 75
    Fondue, Dessert, '89 281
    Fondue, White Chocolate, '92 287
    Fudge Dessert with Kahlúa Cream, '91 197
    Hello Dolly Dessert, '95 168
    Ladyfinger Dessert, Chocolate, '86 162
    Loaves, Chocolate Chip Cheese, '91 299;
        '92 264
    Log, Chocolate Cream, '94 220
    Midnight Delights, '95 278
    Mint Dessert, Chocolate-, '82 100
    Mint Dessert, Cool Chocolate-, '80 109
    Mississippi Mud, '96 253
    Peanut-Chocolate Dessert, '80 86
    Pizza, Chocolate, '91 298
    Plunge, Chocolate, '94 332; '95 35
    Pots de Chocolat, Petits, '82 272
    Pots de Crème, '81 15; '84 M145
    Pots de Crème au Chocolate, '93 53
    Pots de Crème, Chocolate, '93 296; '94 234
    Pots de Crème for Two, '89 275
    Pots de Crème, Mocha, '88 M45
    Pots de Crème, Rum-Flavored, '85 102

Pots de Crème with Orange Meringues,
    Chocolate, '95 318
Roll, Chocolate Cream, '85 317
Roll, Chocolate Mousse, '83 290
Roulage, '90 266
Roulage, Chocolate-Cranberry, '94 313
Roulage, Chocolate-Mocha, '80 216
Roulage, Chocolate-Orange, '94 314
Roulage, Mint-Chocolate, '94 314
Roulage, White Chocolate, '92 230
Rum Dessert, Chocolate-, '81 247
Sack, Large Chocolate, '93 314
Sack, Small Chocolate, '93 314
Shells with Kahlúa Cream, Chocolate, '88 195
Squares, Chocolate-Blueberry Dessert,
    '87 299
Strawberry-Chocolate Combo, '85 96
Sundae Dessert, Hot Fudge, '84 313
Supreme, Chocolate, '84 94
Trifle, Chocolate, '88 258; '93 326
Truffle Dessert, Chocolate, '88 281
Turtle Bars, Gooey, '96 M189
Waffles with Strawberry Cream, Chocolate,
    '88 153
Cinnamon Crisps, '93 106
Coconut Cloud, '80 70
Coconut Dessert, Chilled, '83 116
Coeur à la Crème, Christmas, '86 278
Coffee-Almond Tortoni, '81 30
Coffee-and-Cream Chill, '99 126
Cookies and Cream, '96 179
Corn, Indian, '96 287
Cottage Cheese Dessert, Creamy, '87 191
Crackers, Dessert, '87 3
Cranberries, Brandied, '86 269
Cranberries Jubilee, '85 312; '90 293
Cranberry Apple Dessert, '80 253
Cranberry Bake, Hot, '91 250
Cranberry Compote, '97 264
Cranberry Dessert Pizzas, '96 320
Cranberry Jubilee, Tasty, '84 305
Cranberry-Pear Crisp, '97 16
Cranberry Pockets, '96 320
Cranberry Supreme, '85 280
Cranberry Surprise Dessert, '79 242
Cream, Bavarian, '86 M165
Cream Cheese, Chunky, '85 306
Cream Cheese Eggs, '99 118
Cream Cheese, Fruited, '85 306
Cream Cheese Squares, Lemony, '82 159
Cream, Molded French, '85 311; '99 72
Cream Puffs, Captivating, '81 180
Cream Puffs, Java, '81 187
Cream Puffs, Strawberry, '81 95
Cream Puffs, Tutti-Frutti, '79 231
Cream Puff Tree, '96 310
Cream, Spanish, '99 27
Crème Celeste, '88 94
Crème d'Ange, '83 91
Crème Pâtissière, '84 207
Crêpes, Basic Dessert, '82 157; '86 275
Crêpes, Dessert, '86 260; '87 290; '88 134
Crêpes, Dixie Dessert, '79 222
Crêpes Flambé, Cherry, '79 18
Crêpes, Strawberry Dessert, '83 122
Crêpes Suzettes, Light, '83 71
Date Dessert Squares, '89 255
Date-Nut Balls, '85 10
De-Light-Ful Dessert, '95 220
Doughnuts, Orange Spiced, '79 136
Éclair Cake, '93 42
Éclairs, Miniature Orange, '95 92
Éclairs, Minted Miniature, '88 66
Éclairs, Pistachio-Cream, '91 296

DESSERTS
(continued)

Éclairs with Pecan Sauce, '83 219
Eggnog Dessert, '95 314
Figs, Sugar-Crusted, '96 195
Flan. *See* CUSTARDS.
Frozen
    After Dinner-Drink Dessert, '82 100
    Almond Crunch, Frozen, '94 283
    Amaretto Chantilly, '89 14
    Amaretto Freeze, '82 182
    Amber Bombe, '80 255
    Applesauce Fluff, '91 173
    Apricot Fluff, Frozen, '86 242
    Apricot Freeze, '82 10
    Baked Alaska, '84 105; '85 295
    Baked Alaska, Apple, '80 226
    Baked Alaska, Brownie, '80 66
    Baked Alaska, Chocolate Mousse, '85 195
    Banana Pudding Parfait Pops, '96 180
    Banana Split Alaskas, '87 10
    Banana Split Pie, Layered, '83 189
    Banana Split Terrine, '96 164
    Bars, Creamy No-Bake, '97 166
    Bombe, Ice Cream, '90 269
    Bombe with Raspberry Sauce, Creamy,
      '89 322
    Cantaloupe Cream, Frozen, '82 159
    Cantaloupe Whip, '89 198
    Caramel-Toffee Bombe, '93 214
    Charlotte, Spumoni, '90 193
    Cherry Cordial Dessert, '84 312
    Chocolate Almond Velvet, '81 148
    Chocolate-Coffee Frozen Dessert, '85 172
    Chocolate Dessert, Frozen, '83 76
    Chocolate Mint Freeze, '88 167
    Chocolate Roulage, Frozen, '90 56
    Chocolate-Walnut Cups, '85 213
    Chocolate Whip, '89 326
    Choco-Maple Frozen Dessert, '86 300; '87 178
    Cinnamon Ice Cream Sombreros, '93 276
    Citrus Cup, Snowball, '79 2
    Coconut-Caramel Dessert, '92 44
    Coffee Dessert, Light, '88 260
    Coffee Ice Cream Crunch, '82 182
    Coffee Tortoni, Creamy, '88 268
    Cookies 'n' Cream Dessert, Gold-Dusted,
      '94 271
    Cream, Betty's Holiday, '95 303
    Cream Dessert, Triple, '94 244
    Elegant Ending, '86 145
    Frappé, Hawaiian, '81 178
    Fruit Cream Freeze, '82 144
    Fruit Cups, Frozen, '93 197
    Fruit Freeze, Holiday, '88 283
    Fruit Ice, Mixed, '88 85
    Fudge-Peanut Ice Cream Dessert, '88 167
    Fudgy Frozen Dessert, Nutty, '94 28
    Grand Marnier Cream, '84 312
    Grapefruit Freeze, '93 242
    Grasshopper Freeze, Creamy, '81 180
    Ice-Cream Angel Dessert, Triple Mint, '93 86
    Ice Cream Bombe, '82 305
    Ice Cream Delight, '80 69
    Ice Cream Dessert, Caramel, '95 36
    Ice Cream Dessert, Decadent, '91 56
    Ice Cream Dessert, Layered, '83 189;
      '84 94, 105; '86 163
    Ice Cream Dessert, Mint, '88 66
    Ice Cream Dessert, Toffee, '87 110
    Ice Cream Party Squares, '91 214
    Ice Cream Pumpkin, '96 255

Ice Cream Sandwiches, Chocolate Cookie,
    '87 147
Ice Cream Treats, Crunchy, '86 300; '87 178
Ice, Hazelnut-Coffee, '94 233
Ice, Mimosa, '94 24
Lemon-Chiffon Frozen Yogurt, '85 54
Lemon Cream, Frozen, '83 118
Lime-Mint Refresher, '82 144
Lime Whip, '89 199
Little Bits, '79 196
Macaroon-Sherbet Frozen Dessert, '79 212
Mint Patty Alaska, '80 219
Mocha Alaska Dessert, '84 191
Mocha Delight, Frozen, '96 179
Mocha Dessert, Frozen, '84 311
Mocha Freeze, Royal, '84 53
Mocha Squares, Frozen, '81 187
Orange Alaska, '83 177
Orange Dessert, Frozen, '92 44
Oranges Grand Marnier, '92 82
Ozark Pudding, Frozen, '88 127
Peach Freeze, Creamy, '82 144
Peach Torte, Frozen, '93 135
Peanut Butter Delight, Frozen, '88 137
Pineapple Delight, Fresh, '79 111
Pineapple-Orange Bars, '82 129
Pops, Banana, '83 60; '84 44
Pops, Berry, '99 133
Pops, Deep Blue Sea, '94 143
Pops, Fruit, '87 168
Pops, Hawaiian Orange-Pineapple, '94 143
Pops, Kiwi Margarita, '99 133
Pops, Orange-Banana, '82 129
Pops, Orange Float, '99 132
Pops, Pineapple-Yogurt, '91 173
Pops, Purple People Eater, '99 132
Pops, Sangría, '99 133
Pops, Strawberry-Cinnamon, '99 132
Popsicles, Smoothie Strawberry, '82 112
Praline Freeze, '89 60
Pumpkin Dessert, Frozen, '88 167
Rainbow Delight, Frozen, '84 105
Raspberry Dessert, Frozen, '84 192
Raspberry Fluff, '89 198
Sherbet Ambrosia Cups, '82 159
Sherbet Dessert, Layered, '87 109
Strawberry Cups, Frozen, '91 173
Strawberry Delight, Frozen, '82 112, 174
Strawberry Frost, '82 24; '83 154
Strawberry Puff, '82 5
Strawberry Whip, '89 198
Texas Tornadoes for Grown-Ups, '94 143
Torte, Frozen Viennese, '93 171
Tortoni, Apricot-Yogurt, '95 124
Vanilla Almond Crunch, '93 243
Vanilla Frozen Yogurt, '87 125
Vanilla Soufflé, Frozen, '79 230; '82 173
Watermelon Frost, '86 196
Fruit
    Amaretto Crème on Fresh Fruit, '93 176
    Bake, Nutty Fruit, '83 127
    Beauberries Bordeaux, '98 18
    Bowl, Fresh Fruit, '89 137
    Caribbean Fruit Dessert, '84 314
    Cheese, and Nuts, Fruit, '93 324
    Cheese, Luscious Fresh Fruit with, '79 153
    Chilled Fruit with Dressing, '85 222
    Combo, Fresh Fruit, '86 178
    Compote, Baked Fruit, '80 276; '84 314
    Compote, Baked Mustard Fruit, '85 47
    Compote, Champagne Fruit, '81 309; '82 124
    Compote, Chilled Fruit, '83 123
    Compote, Citrus, '98 17
    Compote, Dried Fruit, '98 18

Compote, Fresh Fruit, '79 162; '82 197, 272;
    '84 82; '94 190
Compote, Fruit, '86 330
Compote, Gingered Fruit, '88 184
Compote, Hot Fruit, '81 203; '83 53
Compote, Jicama-Fruit, '92 49
Compote, Mixed Fruit, '93 123
Compote, Warm Praline Fruit, '85 260
Compote, Wine Fruit, '81 272
Compote with Caramel Syrup, Fruit, '98 313
Crisp, Fruit, '94 168
Cup, Fruit, '81 141; '91 202
Cup with Rum, Fruit, '83 55
Curried Fruit, Hot, '95 72
Dumplings, Delicious Fruit, '97 210
Flame, Sherried Fruit, '85 313
Flaming Fruit Dessert, '83 302
Fondue, Fruitcake, '84 258
Gazpacho, Tropical, '95 204
Gingered Fruit, '83 151
Glazed Fruit, '85 83
Hot Fruit Delight, '83 281
Island Fruit Chill, '98 180
Kabobs with Mint Marinade, '82 157
Lemon Curd, Fresh Fruit with, '88 21
Medley, Chinese Fruit, '83 22
Medley, Fancy Fruit, '84 82
Medley, Fresh Fruit, '81 141
Medley, Frosty Fruit, '82 226
Medley of Fruit, Tropical, '86 53
Meringue Shells, Fruited, '87 32
Mint-Balsamic Tea, Fresh Fruit with, '95 232
Orange, Fruit Dessert, '84 314
Planter's Punch Dessert, '95 175
Rainbow Fruit Dessert, '85 108
Soup Dessert, Fruit, '79 172
Soup, Fresh Fruit, '98 196
Spiced Fruit Delight, '82 229
Spiced Fruit Dessert, '82 50
Tequila, Fruit in, '82 223
Trifle, Tropical, '95 204
Turnovers, Fruit, '79 150
Gâteau Panache, '83 269
Gel with Stirred Custard, Sherried, '99 126
Glacé, Sabayon, '89 306
Grahams, Praline, '92 239
Honeydew-Berry Dessert, '83 120
Honeydew Melon with Grapes, '91 91
Ice-Cream Dessert, Toffee, '97 134
Jelly, Wine, '98 125
Kahlúa Cream, '87 134
Kahlúa Delight, '83 67
Kahlúa Delight, Make-Ahead, '84 M89
Kahlúa Velvet Dessert, '85 M294
Kiwi and Cream in Meringue Cups, '81 279
Kiwi-and-Orange Dessert, '93 295
Kiwi-Berry Pizza, '86 198
Kiwifruit Pizza, '89 306
Kiwi Jubilee, '83 120
Kugel, Apricot Noodle, '92 251
Kugel, Sweet, '90 254
Lemon Angel Rolls with Raspberry Sauce,
    '94 294
Lemon-Cream Cheese Dessert, '84 95
Lemon Cups, Baked, '87 128
Lemon Curd, '89 334
Lemon Curd with Berries, '90 102
Lemon Delight, '82 227
Lemon Dessert, Layered, '88 134
Lemon Solid, '93 279
Little Nothings, '79 135
Lollapalooza, '94 194
Madeleines, '88 79
Mango Dessert Tamales, '94 190

Mango Pan Dowdy, '83 150
Maple Nut Dessert, '81 84
Maraschino Russian Cream, '79 231
Margarita Tacos, '97 167
Maverick Lunar Pie, '98 111
Melon Ball Compote, '85 157
Melon Balls and Cherries in Kirsch, '91 91
Melon Balls in Watermelon Sauce, '79 177
Melon-Mint Julep, '86 196
Melons in Mint Sauce, '85 164
Melon Wedges with Berry Sauce, '86 178
Meringue Baskets with Fresh Fruit and Ice Cream, '98 179
Meringue Cream Cups, Lemon, '84 23
Meringue Flowers, '84 156
Meringue, Piping, '84 156
Meringues, Baked Pear, '85 232
Meringues, Strawberry, '84 188
Mocha-Almond Dessert, '80 289; '81 62
Mocha Chiffon, '86 75
Nectarines Royale, '85 132
Nuggets, Golden North Pole, '99 M309
Oatmeal Cherry-Apple Crisp, '90 M16
Orange. See also **DESSERTS/Frozen.**
　Baked Apples, Orange-Pecan, '85 45
　Baked Orange Elegance, '80 13
　Baskets, Orange, '81 308
　Champagne Oranges, '93 83
　Chiffon Dessert, Orange, '93 295
　Cream Dessert, Orange, '80 254; '84 165
　Cream, Orange, '81 12
　Cream, Orange Chantilly, '84 156
　Cream, Orange-Coconut, '84 24
　Crisp, Orange-Apple, '80 295
　Delight, Pumpkin-Orange, '86 321
　Dip, Creamy Orange, '84 117
　Doughnuts, Orange Spiced, '79 136
　Éclairs, Miniature Orange, '95 92
　Flambé, Dessert Orange, '85 313
　Frosted Oranges, '83 270
　Fruit Dessert Orange, '84 314
　Grand Marnier, Oranges, '92 82
　Kiwi-and-Orange Dessert, '93 295
　Molded Dessert, Orange, '83 302
　Parfaits, Chilled Orange, '80 219
　Parfaits, Orange Cream, '94 198
　Pears Flambé, Orange-Poached, '85 313
　Poached Oranges, Wine-, '84 M323
　Rice Cream with Mandarin Oranges, '85 317
　Sections with Chocolate and Raspberry Sauce, Orange, '97 33
　Slices, Burgundy-Spiced Orange, '93 294
　Soufflé, Chilled Orange, '84 317; '86 189
　Soufflé, Frozen Orange, '79 211
　Soufflé, Orange Dessert, '83 206
　Strawberries with Brandied Orange Juice, '82 160
　Tapioca Crème, Orange-, '82 M283
　Tapioca Fluff, Orange, '87 31
Pancakes, Dessert Ginger, '88 153
Pancakes, Luau Dessert, '88 154
Parfaits
　Blackberries-and-Cream Parfait, '87 129
　Chocolate-Crème de Menthe Parfaits, '85 161
　Chocolate-Mint Parfaits, '90 M15
　Chocolate Mousse Parfait, '94 90
　Chocolate-Peanut Butter Mousse Parfaits, '98 71
　Chocolate-Peppermint Parfaits, '88 65
　Coffee Crunch Parfaits, '82 159
　Eggnog Bavarian Parfait, '79 255
　Family, Parfait, '94 130
　Hooray Parfaits, '96 229
　Kiwi Parfait, '86 199; '87 55

Lime Parfaits, '80 153
Mocha-Mallow Parfaits, '80 219
Orange Cream Parfaits, '94 198
Orange Parfaits, Chilled, '80 219
Peach Parfait, '82 166
Peanut Butter Parfaits, Crunchy, '79 176; '80 6
Peppermint Parfait, '93 315
Pineapple Parfait, '84 83
Speedy Parfaits, '83 76
Strawberry-Lemon Parfaits, '84 198
Strawberry Parfait, '79 99
Strawberry Parfaits, Frosty, '85 213
Strawberry Parfait, Surprise, '86 151
Strawberry-Yogurt Parfait, Crunchy, '79 124
Surf-and-Sand Parfaits, '93 169
Tropical Trilogy Parfait, '92 247
White Chocolate-Raspberry Swirl Parfait, '93 315
Pavlova, '92 101
Peach. See also **DESSERTS/Frozen, Sauces.**
　Baked Peaches, '92 179
　Blueberry Dessert, Peach-, '92 184
　Brandy Peaches, '85 275
　Caramel Peaches, '93 134
　Cardinale, Peach, '89 155
　Champagne, Peaches, '79 146
　Charlotte, Peach, '79 68
　Compote, Berry-Peach, '82 133
　Compote, Peach-Berry, '89 112
　Cream, Bavarian Peach, '82 171
　Cream, Peach Almond, '82 108
　Cream, Peaches and, '95 196
　Cream, Peachy-Apricot, '86 163
　Crisp, Gingered Peach, '97 303
　Crisp, Peach, '92 13
　Custard Dessert, Fresh Peach, '86 162
　Dumplings, Peach, '85 177
　Foster, Peaches, '86 240
　Ginger Peaches with Rum, '84 M323
　Gingersnap Peaches, '85 M329
　Honeyed Peaches 'n' Cream, '93 134
　Layered Peach Dessert, '95 196
　Marinated Peaches, '91 91
　Melba, Peach, '81 83; '83 M114
　Melt-Away Dessert, Peachy, '87 298
　Oven-Baked Peaches with Ginger, '82 170
　Parfait, Peach, '82 166
　Quick Peach Dessert, '85 178
　Sherbet Cooler, Peachy, '91 187
　Spiced Peach Dessert, '83 9
　Spiced Peaches with Nutty Dumplings, '87 164
　Split, Peach, '85 277
　Strawberry Sauce, Peaches with, '85 8
　Stuffed Peaches, Macaroon-, '79 178
　Stuffed Peach Halves, '86 196
　Sundaes Flambé, Peach, '81 88
　Trifle, Peach, '92 179
　Wine Sauce, Peaches in, '79 184
Peanut Butter Dessert, '92 164
Peanut-Buttery Dessert, Crunchy, '92 204
Pear. See also **DESSERTS/Sauces.**
　Amaretto Pears with Meringue, '90 M58
　Baked Apples and Pear, Honey-, '97 303
　Baked in Molasses-Port Sauce, Pears, '97 195
　Baked Pears à la Mode, '95 129
　Baked Pears Elegant, '91 48
　Belle Helene, Pears, '86 164
　Blue, Pears, '99 246
　Coconut Pears, Spicy, '83 207
　Crème Chantilly, Holiday Pears with, '91 297
　Crème de Menthe Pears, '94 50
　Crisp, Cranberry-Pear, '97 16

Crisp, Raspberry-Pear, '89 109
Dumplings, Pear, '97 210
Flaming Pears, '84 313
Gratin, Pear-Blue Cheese, '93 328
Maple-Sugared Pears, '81 232
Meringues, Baked Pear, '85 232
Orange-Caramel Sauce, Pears with, '95 281
Poached in Red Wine, Pears, '83 302
Poached Pear Fans with Raspberry-Orange Sauce, '88 22
Poached Pears Flambé, Orange-, '85 313
Poached Pears in Custard, '88 20
Poached Pears in Wine, '82 194
Poached Pears, Lemon, '82 74
Poached Pears, Vanilla, '90 57
Poached Pears with Berry Sauce, Wine-, '86 144
Poached Pears with Dark Chocolate Sauce, '90 M141
Poached Pears with Honey-Yogurt Sauce, '92 306
Poached Pears with Raspberry Sauce, '84 213; '87 69; '88 223
Poached Pears with White Caramel Sauce, '99 28
Red Wine, Pears in, '82 254
Stewed Pears, '98 280
Stuffed Pears, Almond-, '83 207
Sundaes, Quick Pear, '86 71
Pecans, Sugared, '82 167
Peppermint Bavarian, '80 153
Peppermint Fondue, '94 332
Peppermint Wafer Dessert, '79 176; '80 7
Pineapple-Almond Delight, '85 96
Pineapple Boats with Rum Sauce, '97 192
Pineapple Dessert Chimichangas, '86 4
Pineapple Filling, '97 277
Pineapple, Meringue-Topped, '84 178
Pineapple 'n' Cream, '88 202
Pineapple, Scalloped, '79 106; '82 254
Pineapple with Natillas Sauce, Baked, '83 179
Pineapple with Raspberry Sauce, Chocolate-Drizzled, '90 57
Pizza Dessert, Rocky Road, '99 196
Pizzelles, '83 298
Plum Crunch, Layered, '86 174
Plums in Port Wine, '97 176
Port Wine Jelly with Whipped Cream, '84 254
Pots de Crème, Easy, '93 281
Praline Horns, '96 316
Profiteroles, '84 208
Prune Bavarian, '86 223
Prunes in Merlot, '98 18
Pumpkin Chiffon, '82 216; '86 283; '88 260
Pumpkin Chiffon Dessert, '88 128
Pumpkin Flan, '97 219
Pumpkin Mold, '82 311
Pumpkin-Orange Delight, '86 321
Pumpkin Swirl, Easy, '93 234
Raspberry Dream, '83 108
Raspberry-Jellyroll Dessert, '85 95
Raspberry Jellyrolls, '93 M255
Raspberry-Pear Crisp, '89 109
Raspberry Prunes, '82 124
Raspberry-Strawberry Bavarian, '89 15
Reindeer Food, Magic, '99 M309
Rhubarb Crisp, '91 146; '92 130
Rhubarb-Strawberry Bavarian, '86 140
Rhubarb Whip, '79 112
Rice Cream with Mandarin Oranges, '85 317
Roulage, Toffee-Pecan, '94 312
Rum Balls, '93 314
Sabayon, '93 272
Santa's Hat, '92 279

DESSERTS
(continued)

Sauces
Almond-Vanilla Custard Sauce, '88 M177
Amaretto-Chocolate Sauce, '92 154
Amaretto-Cinnamon Sauce, '93 171
Amaretto-Strawberry Sauce, '87 M165
Ambrosia Sauce, Hot, '89 335
Apple Ambrosia Sauce, '89 95
Apple-Cinnamon Sauce, '93 42
Apple Dessert Sauce, '87 M165
Apple Dessert Sauce, Spicy, '82 177
Apple Topping, Spicy, '87 125
Apricot Ice Cream Sauce, '91 57
Apricot Sauce, '82 212
Apricot-Walnut Hard Sauce, '88 153
Banana-Pineapple Sauce, '83 48
Banana Sundae Sauce, '84 275
Berry Mimosa Sauce, '90 315
Berry Sauce, '87 290; '88 135; '94 130; '95 103
Bittersweet Chocolate Sauce, '92 319
Blackberry Sauce, '86 152; '94 232
Blueberry Sauce, '88 155; '89 M130; '94 122;
   '95 135
Blueberry Topping, '87 125
Bourbon Cream Sauce, '98 84
Bourbon Praline Sauce, '81 170
Bourbon Sauce, '93 51; '98 336
Brandied Hard Sauce, '80 264; '83 250;
   '85 313
Brandy-Butter Sauce, '79 230
Brandy-Macadamia Sauce, '82 311
Brandy Sauce, '88 279; '98 119
Brown Sugar Sauce, '90 314
Buttered Rum Sauce, '83 249
Buttered Rum Sauce, Hot, '88 204
Buttermilk Custard Sauce, '96 183
Buttermilk Sauce, '95 183
Butter Pecan Sauce, '91 174
Butter-Rum Sauce, '95 134
Butterscotch-Pecan Sauce, '82 212
Caramel-Raisin Sauce, '88 127
Caramel Sauce, '79 79; '91 56, 180;
   '93 210, 235, 296; '94 234; '95 308;
   '96 284, 310; '97 178
Caramel Sauce, Easy, '87 38
Caramel Sauce, White, '92 195
Cherry-Pineapple Topping, '87 126
Cherry Sauce, '79 91
Cherry Sauce, Elegant, '79 M156
Cherry-Wine Sauce, '97 132
Chocolate and Raspberry Sauce, Orange
   Sections with, '97 33
Chocolate-Cherry Sauce, '85 189
Chocolate Cherry Sauce, '87 M165
Chocolate-Mint Sauce, '93 86; '94 314;
   '98 217
Chocolate Mint Sauce, Quick, '86 M58
Chocolate-Orange Sauce, '86 165; '94 314
Chocolate-Peanut Butter Sauce, '79 91, M156
Chocolate-Peppermint Sauce, '94 205
Chocolate-Praline Sauce, '85 M295
Chocolate Sauce, '83 189; '84 208, 313;
   '86 322; '90 57; '91 56, 57; '93 276; '94 121;
   '97 178, 331
Chocolate Sauce, Classic, '85 207
Chocolate Sauce, Creamy, '88 M177
Chocolate Sauce, Dark, '93 296; '94 234, 283;
   '96 310; '98 336
Chocolate Sauce, Double, '83 79
Chocolate Sauce, Easy, '92 148
Chocolate Sauce, Heavenly, '79 79; '82 167

Chocolate Sauce Supreme, '85 189
Cinnamon-Blueberry Sauce, '86 11
Cinnamon-Fudge Sauce, '85 141
Cinnamon Sauce, Apple Pie with Hot, '88 210
Coconut-Orange Sauce, '85 189
Coconut Sauce, '98 34
Coconut Sauce, Creamy Light, '82 177
Cranberry Jubilee, Tasty, '85 189
Cranberry Sauce, '86 278; '88 280
Crème Anglaise, '92 164
Crème Fraîche Sauce, '79 281; '93 135
Custard Sauce, '85 41; '88 154, 251, 259;
   '89 291; '97 16, 313
Date-Nut Sundae Sauce, '82 167
Fig Sauce, '79 140
Fruit Dessert Sauce, Hot, '87 299
Fruit Puree, '94 190
Fruit Sauce, Golden, '89 281
Fruit Sauce, Quick, '82 212
Fudge Sauce, '91 174
Fudge Sauce, Easy Hot, '84 69; '94 194
Fudge Sauce, Hot, '82 181, 295; '84 143;
   '97 255
Fudge Sauce, Quick Hot, '82 212
Golden Sauce, '88 267
Hard Sauce, '80 265; '82 14
Hard Sauce, Special, '86 318
Honey-Chocolate Sauce, '89 251
Honey-Orange Sauce, '85 108
Honeyscotch Sundae Sauce, '82 167
Honey-Yogurt Sauce, '92 307
Kahlúa Chocolate Sauce, '85 155
Lemon Cream Sauce, '93 200
Lemon Dessert Sauce, '87 M165
Lemon Sauce, '84 258, 306; '85 77, 190;
   '91 240; '96 283
Lemon Sauce, Tart, '85 191
Lemon Sauce, Zesty, '97 318
Mandarin Dressing, '89 137
Mandarin Orange Sauce, '89 204
Mango Sauce, '83 120
Marshmallow Sauce, '91 91
Melba Sauce, '87 77
Mint Sauce, '96 127
Mint Sauce, Party, '82 212
Mocha Sauce, '98 57
Orange Dessert Sauce, '86 337; '87 58
Orange Hard Sauce, '88 225
Orange Sauce, Fresh, '85 209
Peach-Berry Sauce, '87 M165
Peach-Blueberry Pancake Sauce, '82 177
Peach Blueberry Sauce, '81 170
Peach-Praline Sauce, '85 161
Peach Sauce, '84 144
Peach Sauce, Creamy, '85 189
Peach Sauce, Fresh, '87 167
Peanut Butter Ice Cream Sauce, '84 30
Peanut Dessert Sauce, '86 M251
Pear Sauce, '92 164
Pecan Sauce, '83 219
Piña Colada Topping, Chunky, '87 125
Pineapple Ice Cream Sauce, '81 M289
Pineapple-Rhubarb Sauce, '88 94
Pineapple-Rum Sauce, '84 275
Plum Sauce, Fresh, '94 129
Praline Ice Cream Sauce, '85 189
Praline Ice Cream Sauce, Southern, '86 M227
Praline Sauce, '83 25; '84 143; '89 95; '92 282;
   '93 214; '94 206, 312; '96 285
Raspberry-Amaretto Sauce, '88 130
Raspberry-Lemon Sauce, Cheesecake with,
   '96 30
Raspberry-Orange Sauce, '88 22; '92 154
Raspberry-Peach Topping, '87 126

Raspberry Sauce, '82 289; '83 108;
   '84 73, 213; '87 69, 117, 183; '88 267;
   '89 183, 322; '91 96, 180, 270; '92 130;
   '93 82, 99, 315; '94 295; '95 327;
   '96 183, 310; '98 157, 216; '99 167, 259
Raspberry Sauce, Crimson, '79 91; '85 30
Raspberry Sauce Dessert, '80 147
Raspberry Sauce Flambé '84 142
Raspberry Sauce, Fresh, '93 120
Rhubarb Sauce, Chilled, '88 94
Rum-Butter Sauce, '86 301
Rum-Fruit Sauce, '84 312
Rum-Raisin Sauce, '84 7; '94 295
Rum Sauce, '88 32; '94 241
Rum Sauce, Brown Sugar-, '85 231
Rum Sauce, Hot, '79 86
Rum Sundae Sauce, '93 162
Sherry Sauce, '84 109
Spicy Sauce, '93 52
Strawberries Arnaud Sauce, '93 50
Strawberry-Banana Topping, '87 125
Strawberry-Butter Sauce, '96 87
Strawberry-Orange Sauce, '96 95
Strawberry-Peach Sauce, '92 154
Strawberry Sauce, '84 144; '87 93, 198; '92 85;
   '94 121
Strawberry Sauce, Brandied, '88 196
Strawberry Sauce, Fresh, '82 177
Strawberry Sauce, Old-Fashioned,
   '94 130
Strawberry Sauce, Peaches with, '85 8
Strawberry Sauce with Crunchy Topping,
   '81 170
Strawberry Sauce with Dumplings, '84 314
Taffy Dessert Sauce, '86 20
Tea-Berry Sauce, '94 130; '99 334
Toffee-Fudge Sauce, '89 95
Toffee Sauce, '94 72
Vanilla Crème Sauce, '94 243; '96 155
Vanilla Custard Sauce, '99 27
Vanilla Sauce, '97 M15
Watermelon Sauce, Melon Balls in, '79 177
Whiskey Sauce, '90 230; '92 87, 93; '99 277
White Caramel Sauce, '99 28
White Chocolate Sauce, '92 164; '96 310
Savarin, '79 171
Sherbet-Cantaloupe Surprise, '91 105
Sopaipillas, '80 197; '88 112; '91 78
Sopaipillas, Pineapple, '83 179
Soufflés
Banana Daiquiri Soufflé, '84 317
Brandy Alexander Soufflé, '82 173; '83 M114
Chocolate-Mint Soufflé, '81 16
Chocolate Soufflé, Light, '83 278
Chocolate Soufflé with White Chocolate
   Mousse, '98 57
Coconut Soufflé, '85 212
Daiquiri Soufflé, Elegant, '80 69
Devonshire Soufflé, Chilled, '88 279
Grand Marnier Soufflé, '79 281
Grasshopper Soufflé, '81 248; '86 188
Kahlúa Soufflé, '82 173
Lemon-Lime Soufflé, Cold, '84 24
Lemon Soufflé, '82 170
Lemon Soufflé, Tart, '85 82
Orange Dessert Soufflé, '83 206
Orange Soufflé, Chilled, '84 317; '86 189
Orange Soufflé, Frozen, '79 211
Pineapple Dessert Soufflé, '80 153
Raspberry Soufflé, '86 188
Raspberry-Topped Soufflé, '85 317
Vanilla Soufflé, Frozen, '79 230; '82 173
Vanilla Soufflés with Vanilla Crème Sauce,
   '96 155

Soup, Sherry-Berry Dessert, '91 180
Spumoni and Berries, '91 204
Strawberry. *See also* **DESSERTS/Frozen,
    Parfaits, Sauces.**
  Almond Cream with Fresh Strawberries,
    '87 93
  Arnaud, Strawberries, '93 50
  Banana-Berry Supreme, '81 205
  Bavarian, Raspberry-Strawberry, '89 15
  Bavarian, Rhubarb-Strawberry, '86 140
  Best-Dressed Berries, '96 317
  Brandied Orange Juice, Strawberries with,
    '82 160
  Carousel, Strawberry, '91 247
  Cheese Delight, Strawberry, '79 50
  Cherry-Berry on a Cloud, '79 94
  Chilled Strawberry Dessert, '84 164
  Chocolate Combo, Strawberry-, '85 96
  Coconut Nests, Strawberry, '88 136
  Compote, Peach-Berry, '89 112
  Cream Cheese Dessert, Strawberry-, '83 123
  Cream in Vanilla Lace Cups, Strawberry,
    '98 93
  Cream Puffs, Strawberry, '81 95
  Cream, Strawberries and, '82 100
  Cream, Strawberries 'n', '90 30
  Cream, Strawberries with Strawberry, '84 108
  Crêpes, Strawberry Dessert, '83 122
  Deep-Fried Strawberries, '84 109
  Delight, Strawberry, '81 95
  Dipped Strawberries, '94 17
  French Cream, Strawberries with, '83 191
  Frost, Strawberry, '81 279; '82 24; '83 154
  Glazed Strawberry Dessert, '84 33
  Honeydew-Berry Delight, '83 120
  Jamaica, Strawberries, '85 161; '93 239
  Juliet, Strawberries, '84 82
  Lemon Dessert, Strawberry-, '86 162
  Marsala, Strawberries, '88 171
  Meringues, Strawberry, '84 188
  Napoleons, Strawberry, '81 126
  Pizza, Kiwi-Berry, '86 198
  Pizza, Strawberry, '79 94
  Raspberry Custard Sauce, Fresh Berries with,
    '88 163
  Rock Cream with Strawberries, Old-
    Fashioned, '90 125
  Romanoff, Strawberries, '84 108; '88 95;
    '91 126
  Romanoff, Strawberry-Almond, '98 99
  Ruby Strawberries, '82 100
  Sabayon, Strawberries, '79 94
  Shortcake Squares, Strawberry, '85 122
  Soup, Sherry-Berry Dessert, '91 180
  Spumoni and Berries, '91 204
  Strawberry Dessert, '83 123
  Stuffed Strawberries with Walnuts, '85 122;
    '86 124
  Summer Strawberry Dessert, '92 143
  Sweet-and-Sour Strawberry Dessert, '92 54
  Swirl, Strawberry, '84 108
  Trifle, Easy Strawberry, '88 201
  Yogurt Delight, Strawberry, '85 77
  Yogurt Dessert, Strawberry-, '90 295
  Zabaglione, Strawberries, '81 95
Sundaes
  Apple Spice Sundae, Hot, '92 239
  Cantaloupe Sundae, '89 166
  Cocoa-Kahlúa Sundaes, '83 M58
  Hot Fudge Sundae Dessert, '86 322
  Mauna Loa Sundaes, '80 126
  Peach Sundaes Flambé, '81 88
  Pear Sundaes, Quick, '86 71
  Strawberry Sundaes, Hot, '81 M5

Syrup, Madeira, '98 247
Tacos, Dessert, '97 141
Tea Cakes and Fresh Strawberries, Telia's,
    '98 110
Tiramisù, '91 21; '94 295; '98 280
Toffee Dessert, English, '88 136
Tortilla Baskets, '94 97
Trifles
  Angel Food Trifle, '91 184
  Banana Pudding Trifle, '98 273
  English Trifle, '93 289
  Individual Trifles, Easy, '92 239
  Island Trifle, '92 238
  Lemon-Blueberry Trifle, '88 210
  Lemon Trifle, All Seasons, '95 219
  Olde English Trifle, '95 331
  Pineapple Angel Food Trifle, '93 86
  Raspberry Trifle, '88 259
  Raspberry Trifles, Individual, '99 112
  Rum Trifle, '86 322
  Savannah Trifle, '80 121
  Strawberry Trifle, Easy, '88 201
  Toffee Trifle, '94 168
Tropical Snow, '86 34
Vacherin Moka, '80 55
Vanilla Cream, '83 M115
Vanilla Lace Cups, '98 M93
Vanilla Sherry Dessert, Glorified, '81 85
Waffles, Banana Split, '89 205
Waffles with Apples and Caramel, Gingerbread,
    '98 M237
Waffles with Mandarin Orange Sauce, Dessert
    Pumpkin, '89 204
Waffle, Whole Wheat Dessert, '79 92
White Christmas Dessert, '82 261
Wine Jelly, Rosy, '85 306
Yule Log, '79 281; '82 289
Zuppa Inglese, '99 M267
DOUGHNUTS
  Applesauce Doughnuts, '81 203
  Applesauce Drop Doughnuts, '90 70
  Banana Doughnuts, '86 137
  Beignets, '84 56
  Cake Doughnuts, Quick, '82 226
  Chocolate-Covered Doughnuts, '84 55
  Chocolate Doughnuts, '83 95
  Cinnamon Puffs, '81 209
  Dutch Doughnuts, '81 50
  Fry Bread, '84 140
  Glazed Doughnuts, '83 94
  Jelly-Filled Doughnuts, '84 55
  Orange Spiced Doughnuts, '79 136
  Pineapple Drop Doughnuts, '83 95
  Potato Doughnuts, Chocolate-Glazed, '85 6
  Potato Doughnuts, Old-Fashioned, '84 56
  Puffs, Doughnut, '86 85
  Puffs, Wheat Quick Doughnut, '85 278
  Pumpkin Doughnut Drops, '90 323
  Snowy Doughnuts, '93 286
  Spice Doughnuts, '84 56
  Sufganiyot (Jelly-Filled Doughnuts), '90 255
  Whole Wheat Doughnuts, '84 56
DOVE. *See* **GAME.**
DRESSINGS. *See also* **SALAD DRESSINGS,
    STUFFINGS.**
  Cajun Dressing, '82 307
  Chicken and Dressing, Baked, '79 296
  Cornbread
    Biscuit Dressing, Cornbread-, '79 296
    Chicken and Dressing, '99 42
    Chicken Cornbread Dressing, '90 159
    Cornbread Dressing, '86 286; '88 254; '92 267;
      '98 269
    Corny Cornbread Dressing, '99 258

    Crawfish-Cornbread Dressing, '99 257
    Fruited Cornbread Dressing, '80 262
    Green Chile-Cornbread Dressing, '93 306;
      '94 296
    Herb-Seasoned Cornbread Dressing, '83 315
    Kentucky Cornbread Dressing, '86 281
    Light Cornbread Dressing, '92 324
    Nannie's Cornbread Dressing, '95 306
    Old-Fashioned Cornbread Dressing, '84 321
    Oyster-Cornbread Dressing, Ma E's
      Traditional, '96 35
    Quail and Dressing, '99 42
    Quail Stuffed with Cornbread Dressing,
      '93 280
    Sage-Cornbread Dressing, '84 283
    Sage Dressing, Cornbread-, '80 262
    Sausage, and Pecan Dressing, Cornbread,
      '99 257
    Sausage-Cornbread Dressing, '95 289
    Sausage-Cornbread Dressing, Turkey with,
      '83 287
    Sausage Dressing, Cornbread-, '82 307;
      '85 280
    Sausage Dressing, Cornbread-and-, '83 213
    Savory Cornbread Dressing, '88 303
    Sweet Cornbread Dressing, '97 303
    Texas Cornbread Dressing, '82 243
    Turkey and Cornbread Dressing, Roast,
      '89 324
  Corn Dressing Balls, Zesty, '82 307
  Crawfish Dressing, Louisiana, '90 103
  Creole Dressing, '95 289
  Eggplant Dressing, '90 236
  Fruit-and-Pecan Dressing, '84 252
  Fruit Dressing, Baked, '87 253
  Giblet Dressing, '91 255
  Grandmother's-Dressing, '91 254
  Green Onion Dressing, '96 17
  Grits Dressing, '93 306; '94 296
  Oyster Bread Dressing, '82 251
  Oyster Dressing, '79 250
  Peanut Dressing, Roast Turkey with, '79 283
  Pecan-Rice Dressing, Chicken with, '85 M57
  Pecan-Sage Dressing, '80 262
  Pretzel Dressing, '86 280
  Rice Dressing, '91 217
  Rice Dressing, Chicken and, '79 288
  Rice Dressing, Mexican, '87 253
  Rice Dressing, Roast Turkey with, '82 286
  Rice Dressing, Southern, '99 256
  Roasted Garlic Dressing, '99 269
  Sausage-Apple Dressing, '93 305; '94 296
  Sausage Dressing, '86 280
  Sausage Dressing, Harvest, '88 254
  Seasoned Dressing, Stuffed Turkey Breast with,
    '83 320; '84 128
  Spoonbread Dressing, Southwestern-Style,
    '94 273
  Squash Dressing, '83 315; '86 280; '95 290
  Squash Dressing, Turkey with, '87 248
  Turkey and Dressing, Easy, '79 296
  Turkey-and-Dressing Pie, '84 326
  Turkey Dressing, '85 298
  Turkey Dressing, Fruited, '99 257
  Whole Wheat-Mushroom Dressing,
    '84 283
  Zucchini Dressing, '86 282
DUCK. *See* **GAME.**
DUMPLINGS
  Apple Dumplings, '82 273
  Apple Dumplings, Cinnamon, '97 M330
  Apple Dumplings, Old-Fashioned, '84 226
  Apple Dumplings with Maple-Cider Sauce,
    '95 288

DUMPLINGS
(continued)

Apple Dumplings with Orange Hard Sauce, '88 224
Beef Stew with Dumplings, '84 3
Biscuit Dumplings and Chicken, '99 326
Blackberries and Dumplings, '86 196
Blackberry Dumplings, '97 253
Cheddar Dumplings, Chicken Ragoût with, '94 44
Chicken and Dumplings, '97 208
Chicken and Dumplings, Country, '85 254
Chicken and Dumplings, Easy, '86 21
Chicken and Dumplings, Old-Fashioned, '79 55; '83 228; '93 302
Chicken and Dumplings, Quick, '95 125
Chicken and Dumplings with Herbed Broth, '95 338
Chicken and Dumplings with Vegetables, '85 M56
Chicken Dumpling Pie, '96 55
Chicken Stew and Dumplings, '84 4
Cilantro-Cornmeal Dumplings, Bean Ragoût with, '97 209
Cornmeal Dumplings, Turnip Greens with, '82 211
Drop Dumplings, Burgundy Stew with, '83 125
Fruit Dumplings, Delicious, '97 210
Gnocchi à la Narciso, '97 246
Goat Cheese Dumplings, '99 70
Green Peas and Dumplings, '80 102
Old-Fashioned Dumplings, '81 191
Parsley Dumplings, Beef Stew with, '81 76; '82 13; '85 M246
Peach Dumplings, '80 143; '85 177; '96 172
Pear Dumplings, '97 210
Potato Dumplings, Chicken and, '99 326
Potato Dumplings, Venison Stew with, '87 304
Pot Roast with Dumplings, '98 245
Sesame Dumplings, Steamed, '97 208
Shrimp with Dumplings, Stewed, '79 31
Strawberry Sauce with Dumplings, '84 314
Tomato Dumplings, '88 144; '97 209
Tortilla Dumplings, Chicken and, '99 327

EGGNOG
Beverages
Blender Eggnog, '93 341
Breakfast Nog, Speedy, '82 47
Christmas Eggnog, '87 242
Cider Nog, Hot, '98 241
Cider Nog, Hot Apple, '84 42
Coconut Nog, '83 275
Coffee Nog, Brandied, '86 329
Cooked Custard Eggnog, '91 305
Creamy Eggnog, '80 259; '83 303; '85 300
Easy Eggnog, '91 305
Edenton Eggnog, '84 251
Eggnog, '83 318
Holiday Brew, '81 265
Holiday Eggnog Deluxe, '79 232
Irish Coffee Nog, '84 258; '93 340
Irish Cream Nog, '82 312
Mock Eggnog with Orange and Nutmeg, '92 323
Orange Spiced Nog, '82 48
Punch, Coffee-Eggnog, '86 281
Punch, Coffee Eggnog, '92 264
Punch, Holiday Eggnog, '86 281

Punch, Irish Coffee-Eggnog, '95 314
Punch, Peppermint-Eggnog, '90 273
Sparkling Eggnog, '79 232
Thick and Creamy Eggnog, '80 261
Bread, Eggnog, '83 294
Cake, Eggnog-Pecan Pound, '95 313
Cake, Eggnog Pound, '90 253
Casserole, Sweet Potato-Eggnog, '95 291
Cookies, Eggnog Christmas, '79 255
Dessert, Eggnog, '95 314
French Toast, Eggnog, '95 313
Parfait, Eggnog Bavarian, '79 255
Pie, Eggnog, '80 254; '83 205; '86 317; '87 295
Pie, Eggnog Chiffon, '86 281
Pie, Fluffy Eggnog, '81 M269
Salad, Eggnog Christmas, '86 281
Tarts, Creamy Eggnog, '79 255

EGGPLANT
Almonds, Eggplant with, '79 179
Appetizer, Eggplant, '83 187
Appetizer, Grilled Eggplant, '95 198
Balsamic-Flavored Eggplant, '95 342
Biscuit Cakes, Tomato-Eggplant, '95 170
Cakes, Eggplant, '95 196
Caponata, '87 166; '98 50
Casseroles
Bake, Eggplant, '80 82
Cakes, Eggplant, '95 196
Chiles Rellenos, Eggplant, '91 86
Creole Eggplant, '86 110
Crêpes with Marinara Sauce, Mini Eggplant, '99 266
Easy Eggplant Casserole, '80 202
Eggplant Casserole, '81 205; '84 217; '93 44; '94 214
Elegant Eggplant Casserole, '82 168
Flavorful Eggplant Casserole, '79 92
Frittata, Fresh Vegetable, '93 140
Heavenly Eggplant, '93 293
Italian Eggplant, '84 216
Italian-Style Eggplant and Zucchini, '79 289; '80 26
Lebanese Eggplant, '81 24
Mexican Eggplant, '83 187
Moussaka, '87 166; '90 68; '97 94
Moussaka Casserole, '79 179
Moussaka, Potatoes, '93 44
Noodle Casserole, Eggplant and, '82 230
Oyster Louisiane, Eggplant-and-, '95 196
Parmesan, Eggplant, '82 230; '83 186; '84 215; '86 53; '92 18; '95 84
Parmesan, No-Fry Eggplant, '92 172
Parmigiana, Chicken-Eggplant, '82 212
Parmigiana, Eggplant, '81 19; '82 186; '95 197
Potato-Eggplant Casserole, '87 166
Sausage Bake, Eggplant-, '85 221
Sausage Casserole, Eggplant-, '84 215
Sausage-Pasta Casserole, Freezer Eggplant-, '95 197
Scalloped Eggplant, '91 223
Spanish Eggplant, '79 21
Spicy Hot Eggplant Casserole, '93 92
Spinach Casserole, Eggplant-, '99 217
Super Eggplant Casserole, '80 202
Supreme, Eggplant, '79 188; '86 170
Tomato Casserole, Eggplant-and-, '83 187
Caviar, Eggplant, '88 262; '99 217
Caviar, Homemade Cowboy, '94 64
Caviar with Tapenade, Eggplant, '92 194
Crawfish on Eggplant, Soft-Shell, '88 222
Creole, Eggplant, '82 107; '83 86; '86 110
Dip, Eggplant, '96 275
Dressing, Eggplant, '90 236
Easy Eggplant, '87 M151

French-Fried Eggplant, '81 204
Fried Eggplant, '79 178; '83 187; '88 111
Fried Eggplant, Cheesy, '90 75
Fried Eggplant, Parmesan, '79 189
Fried Parmesan Eggplant, '87 166
Fritters, Eggplant, '91 211
Gravy, Roast Duck with Sweet Potato-Eggplant, '83 90
Grilled Eggplant, '80 202; '89 174
Grilled Eggplant, Sage-, '96 269
Italiano, Eggplant, '91 212
Jackstraw Eggplant, '82 230
Julienne, Eggplant, '85 221
Main Dish, Sausage-Eggplant, '80 211
Medley, Eggplant-Shrimp, '79 188
Mexicano, Eggplant à la, '82 229
Oven-Fried Eggplant, '91 187
Patties, Eggplant, '83 186
Pizza, Eggplant, '85 221
Pizzas, Eggplant, '98 183
Provençal, Eggplant, '92 82
Ratatouille, Eggplant-Zucchini, '81 205
Relish, Eggplant, '95 342
Salad, Eggplant, '90 99
Sandwiches, Baked Eggplant, '82 230
Sandwiches, Eggplant, '99 240
Sandwiches, Eggplant, Tomato, and Feta, '98 106
Sandwiches, Open-Face Eggplant, '95 124
Sautéed Eggplant and Zucchini, '82 96
Sauté, Eggplant, '96 135
Slices, Quick Eggplant, '90 75
Soup, Eggplant Supper, '85 221
Soup, Herbed Eggplant, '90 173
Spaghetti Squash with Sesame Eggplant, '92 252
Spicy Eggplant, '99 217
Spicy Oriental Eggplant, '96 130
Spread, Eggplant, '86 278
Spread, Eggplant-Mushroom, '92 156
Squash, Eggplant and, '83 187
Stacks, Eggplant, '91 211
Sticks, Ned's Eggplant, '95 309
Stuffed
à la Creole, Eggplant, '96 177
Baked Stuffed Eggplant, '81 133
Beefy Stuffed Eggplant, '81 204
Cheesy Stuffed Eggplant, '79 188; '82 208
Creole Stuffed Eggplant, '82 230
Eggplant, Stuffed, '80 158
Ham-Stuffed Eggplant, '80 162
Italian-Stuffed Eggplant, '90 74
Mushroom-Stuffed Eggplant, '83 136
Ratatouille-Bran Stuffed Eggplant, '86 44
Ratatouille-Stuffed Eggplant, '83 187
Rolled Stuffed Eggplant, '80 63
Sausage Stuffed Eggplant, '81 204
Sausage-Stuffed Eggplant, '91 211
Seafood Stuffed Eggplant, '79 187
Shrimp-Stuffed Eggplant, '92 99
Supper, Beef-and-Eggplant, '84 291
Tophats, Eggplant, '79 188
Zaalouk, Eggplant, '98 210
EGGS. *See also* **QUICHES, SOUFFLÉS.**
Armadillo Eggs, '97 270
Baked Egg Crisps, '83 57
Baked Eggs Florentine, '86 M12
Baked Eggs in Spinach Nests, '82 70
Baked in Mushroom Sauce, Eggs, '93 47
Bake, Egg and Rice, '83 119
Bedeviled Eggs, '86 67
Benedict, Bacon-and-Tomato Eggs, '87 195
Benedict, Easy Eggs, '80 M268
Benedict, Eggs, '79 40, 254; '85 49; '98 55
Benedict, Light Eggs, '93 M68
Benedict, Lion, '93 121

Benedict with Cheese Sauce, Eggs, '81 225
Brandied Cream Sauce, Eggs in, '82 70
Bread, Butter-Egg, '85 269
Bread, County Fair Egg, '87 68
Bread, Easter Egg, '84 94; '96 88
Breakfast Eye-Openers, '82 231
Breakfast, Farmer's, '81 44
Brunch Eggs, '85 44
Brunch, Texas, '82 70
Bunwiches, '80 92
Burritos, Brunch, '91 77
Burritos, Tex-Mex Egg, '95 34
Casseroles
   Apple-Egg Casserole, '85 44
   Bacon and Egg Casserole, '81 225
   Bacon Casserole, Egg-and-, '85 248
   Bel-Mar, Eggs, '90 92
   Breakfast Bake, '85 45
   Broccoli-and-Egg Casserole, '86 324
   Broccoli-and-Eggs au Gratin, '85 289
   Brunch Casserole with Creole Sauce, '98 98
   Brunch Egg Casserole, '86 329
   Brunch Eggs, '98 93
   Bruncheon Eggs, '83 83
   Cheese-and-Egg Casserole, '99 268
   Cheese Casserole, Egg-and-, '84 293
   Cheese-Egg-Zucchini Casserole, '84 114
   Cheesy Egg Casserole, '81 244; '86 15
   Chile Eggs, '88 80
   Crab-Egg Casserole, '80 260
   Creole Eggs, '82 42
   Egg Casserole, '83 311; '98 98
   Frittata, Fresh Vegetable, '93 140
   Ham and Egg Casserole, Breakfast, '79 253
   Layered Eggs, '96 97
   Mushroom Casserole, Egg-, '83 49
   Potato-Egg Casserole, Cheesy, '84 5
   Potatoes and Eggs au Gratin, '79 107
   Sausage-and-Egg Casserole, '94 284
   Sausage Breakfast Casserole, '81 270
   Sausage Egg Bake, '81 225
   Sausage-Egg Bake, Smoked, '85 248
   Sausage-Egg Casserole, '86 M12
   Scrambled Egg Casserole, Saucy, '89 213
   Soufflé Casserole, Egg, '83 55
   Spinach and Egg Casserole, '82 270
   Squash and Egg Casserole, '80 146
   Strata, Cheese-Rice, '81 176
   Strata, Sausage, '84 101
   Strata, Tomato-Cheese, '81 209
   Sunday Egg Casserole, '95 100
   Zucchini-Egg Casserole, '84 M113
Cheddar Eggs, '94 M141
Cheese, Eggs and, '95 165
Cottage Eggs, '85 44
Crabmeat and Eggs New Orleans, '82 45
Creamed Eggs à la Asparagus, '81 201
Creamed Eggs, Broccoli and, '83 84
Creamed Eggs in Patty Shells, '80 M267
Creamed Eggs in Toast Cups, '83 83
Creole, Eggs, '92 86
Creole, Skillet Eggs, '85 143
Crêpes, Ham-and-Egg, '83 204
Crêpes with Mushroom Sauce, Ham-and-Egg,
   '82 46
Croissant Eggwiches, '91 160
Croquettes, Tuna-Egg, '80 275
Delight, Bacon-and-Egg, '85 143
Delight, Crab-and-Egg, '84 261
Delight, Mushroom-Egg, '83 14
Deviled Eggs. *See* **EGGS/Stuffed.**
Dip, Festive Egg, '79 285
Dressing, Egg, '86 79
Eagle Nest Egg, '99 194

Featherbed Eggs, '93 122
Florentine, Eggs, '79 39; '83 56
Florentine-Style Eggs, '82 38
Foo Yong, Egg, '80 19; '86 232
Foo Yong Patties, '80 223
Foo Yong, Shrimp Egg, '83 22
Frittata, Bacon-and-Asparagus, '98 136
Frittata, Bell Pepper, '96 204
Frittata, Broccoli-Cheese, '81 243
Frittata, Corn-and-Squash, '89 144
Frittata, Firecracker Pasta, '94 230
Frittata, Ham-and-Broccoli, '98 101
Frittata, Potato, '89 145
Frittata, Potato-Bacon, '95 269; '98 330
Frittata, Spinach, '81 53
Frittata, Vegetable, '92 48; '93 183
Ham and Eggs à la Swiss, '88 158
Ham and Eggs, Creamed, '82 40
Ham and Eggs, Creamy, '87 286
Ham and Eggs on Toast with Cheese Sauce,
   '81 43
Ham and Eggs, Savory, '82 231
Hard-Cooked Eggs (garnish), '82 280
Hash Brown Skillet Breakfast, '82 5
Herb Sauce, Eggs in, '88 80
Hominy, Bacon, Eggs, and, '85 143
Huevos Rancheros, '82 197; '91 77
Medley, Cheddary Egg, '81 M176
Mexicana, Eggs, '82 146
Mound, Frosted Egg, '79 33
Muffin, Stuffin', '99 193
Mushroom Eggs, Sherried, '83 49
Mushrooms and Eggs in Patty Shells, '85 143;
   '88 197
Mushrooms and Eggs, Saucy, '79 138
Nests, Fluffy Egg, '79 128
Noodles, Egg Foo Yong, '98 233
Omelets
   Apple Omelet Stack, '94 50
   Baked Omelets, '94 50
   Biscuits, Deluxe Omelet, '98 101
   Broccoli-Mushroom Omelet, '85 45
   Cheese Omelet, Herbed, '93 47
   Cheese Omelet, Puffed, '89 227
   Cheese Omelet, Zippy, '87 287
   Cheese-Shiitake Omelet, Golden, '95 265
   Cheesy Picante Omelet, '86 95
   Chicken Liver Omelet, '82 44
   Country Omelets, '91 128
   Creole Sauce, Omelets with, '89 228
   Dill-Cheese-Ham Omelet, '95 33
   Fines Herbes, Omelette aux, '92 82
   Fluffy Omelet, '84 56
   George's Omelets, '80 68
   Ham and Cheese Omelet, '79 262; '80 123
   Indian Omelet, '99 92
   Italian Omelet, '92 47
   Mexican Omelet, '79 128; '81 225
   Mexican Omelet, Easy, '88 114
   Mushroom Omelet, Rolled, '82 70
   Mushroom Sauce, Puffy Omelets with, '85 40
   Olé Omelet, '87 M124
   Olé, Omelet, '94 31
   Oyster Omelets, Smoked, '84 96
   Potato Omelet, Family-Size, '94 31
   Potato-Sprout Omelet, '79 128
   Primavera, Omelet, '87 71
   Rising Sun Omelet, '82 281; '83 42
   Rolled Omelet, '89 228
   Sandwich, Omelet, '86 95
   Sausage Filling, Omelet with, '81 43
   Sausage Omelet, Puffy, '80 M268
   Shrimp-and-Cheddar Omelet, '84 57
   Shrimp-and-Cheese Omelet, '94 31

Shrimp-and-Vegetable Oven Omelet, '99 286
Sour Cream-Ham Omelet, '79 261
Spanish Omelet, '81 201; '83 243; '84 101
Spanish-Style Omelets, '83 188
Spinach-Cheese Omelet, '83 119
Strawberry-Sour Cream Omelet, '89 229
Sunrise Omelet, '83 289
Swiss Oven Omelet, '80 189
Tarragon Omelet, '89 144
Tex-Mex Omelet con Carne, '81 209
Vegetable Omelet, Beefy, '83 188
Vegetable Omelet, Cheddar-, '83 205
Vegetable Omelet, Cheesy, '85 49
Vegetable Omelet, Fresh, '84 211
Vegetable Omelet, Golden, '82 M123
Vegetable Omelet, Puffy, '83 188
Vegetable-Pasta Oven Omelet, '99 286
Vegetarian Omelet, '84 114
White Wine Omelet, '79 103
Yogurt-Avocado Omelet, '81 33
Zucchini Omelet, '81 99
Oso Grande, Eggs, '98 279
Paint, Egg Yolk, '86 322
Peanut Butter Easter Eggs, '87 86
Pickled Eggs, Beet, '84 287
Pickled Eggs, Rosy, '86 68
Pickled Eggs, Spiced, '84 288
Pie, Country Breakfast, '93 M328
Pie, Egg Custard, '99 82
Pie, Egg-Stra Special Chicken, '86 264
Pie, Old-Fashioned Egg Custard, '82 261
Pillows, Egg, '92 332
Pizza, Breakfast, '85 44
Pizza, Ham-and-Eggs Crescent, '93 47
Poached Eggs, '92 87, 93; '93 121
Poached Eggs, Basic, '82 58
Poached Eggs, French-Style, '82 58
Potatoes with Eggs and Meat, '91 311; '92 25
Potato Nests, Mashed, '94 141
Puff, Egg-and-Cheese, '85 45
Rancheros, Easy Eggs, '88 81
Rice, Egg Fried, '79 252; '80 19
Roll-Ups, Spicy Egg, '90 140
Roulade with Mushroom Filling, Egg, '88 84
Salads
   Asparagus-and-Egg Salad, '86 305
   Bacon-Horseradish Egg Salad, '94 181
   Deviled Egg Salad, '83 124
   Ham-and-Egg Potato Salad, '86 84
   Ham 'n Egg Salad, '81 36
   Rice Salad, Egg-, '84 18; '86 169
   Shrimp-and-Egg Salad Sandwiches, '94 182
   Shrimp-Egg Salad, Tossed, '80 4
   Spread, Cottage-Egg Salad, '82 146
   Spread, Egg Salad, '86 127
   Tacos, Mexican Egg Salad, '94 181
   Tuna-Egg Salad, '81 135
   Vegetable and Egg Salad, Green, '79 191
   Yolkless Egg Salad, '94 181
Sandwiches, Breakfast, '82 M123; '89 M230
Sandwiches, Confetti, '79 236
Sandwiches, Eggsclusive, '79 164; '80 130
Sandwiches, Eggs-Tra Special, '81 240;
   '83 69
Sandwiches, Open-Faced Cheesy Egg,
   '86 67
Sandwiches, Open-Face Egg, '83 292; '84 78;
   '86 160
Sandwiches, Saucy Egg, '91 160
Sardou, Eggs, '92 93
Saucy Eggs, '83 84
Saucy Eggs on Toast, '81 209
Sauté, Vegetable-Egg, '96 204
Scotch Eggs, '79 261; '83 289; '98 101

EGGS
(continued)

Scrambled
Bacon-and-Eggs Scramble, '80 M267
Buttermilk Scrambled Eggs, '79 72
Casserole, Scrambled Egg, '80 51; '86 241
Cheese-Chive Scrambled Eggs, '95 34
Cottage Cheese Scrambled Eggs, '81 142
Cottage-Scrambled Eggs, '80 49
Country Eggs, '86 330
Country-Style Scrambled Eggs, '79 22
Crabmeat Brunch Scramble, '95 32
Cream Cheese Scrambled Eggs, '81 287
Creamy Scrambled Eggs, '90 82
Enchiladas, Scrambled Egg, '97 153
Home-Style Scrambled Eggs, '84 66
Mexican-Style Scrambled Eggs, '85 50
Migas, '87 180; '94 26; '98 312
Onion Scrambled Eggs, Creamy, '83 M203
Shrimp and Crab Scrambled Eggs, '79 261
Sonora, Eggs, '80 196
Spanish Scrambled Eggs, '83 49; '84 60
Special Scrambled Eggs, '81 103
Supreme, Scrambled Eggs, '79 39
Tostadas, Scrambled Egg, '86 95
Wild Rice, Scrambled Eggs with, '80 42
Soufflés, Little Egg, '83 57
Soufflé, Three-Egg Cheese, '87 234
Soup, Egg Drop, '83 21; '86 16
Soup, Egg-Drop, '85 M12
Soup, Egg Flower, '81 307; '82 313; '83 65
Soup, Egg-Lemon, '96 88
Soup, Lemon-Egg Drop, '93 81
Spread, Cottage-Egg Salad, '82 146
Spread, Egg Salad, '86 127
Spread, Egg, Sour Cream, and Caviar, '85 279
Spread, Ham-and-Egg, '79 59
Spread, Vegetable-Egg, '87 106
Stuffed
Bacon-Stuffed Eggs, '97 52
Black-and-Blue Eggs, '96 90
Blue Cheese Stuffed Eggs, '93 87
Chicken-Stuffed Eggs, '98 102
Creamed Eggs, '86 67
Creamy Stuffed Eggs, '84 143
Crunchy Stuffed Eggs, '86 67
Deluxe, Eggs, '82 79
Deviled Eggs, '86 176; '94 161
Deviled Eggs, Bacon, '86 136
Deviled Eggs, Best, '80 159
Deviled Eggs, Chile-Cheese, '93 87
Deviled Eggs, Creamed, '82 79
Deviled Eggs, Curried, '93 87
Deviled Eggs, Easy, '82 127
Deviled Eggs, Nippy, '80 217
Deviled Eggs, Pimiento-, '84 143
Deviled Eggs, Saucy, '82 80
Deviled Eggs Surprise, '79 83
Deviled Eggs, Sweet, '93 88
Deviled Eggs, Tex-Mex, '97 247
Deviled Eggs with Smoked Oysters, '84 161
Deviled Eggs, Zesty, '84 205
Devil's Island Eggs, '82 79
Eggs, Stuffed, '80 155; '88 95
Garlic-Cheese-Stuffed Eggs, Marbleized, '96 91
Green Eggs and Ham, '96 90
Ham Devils, '93 88
Herb-Sour Cream Stuffed Eggs, '93 87
Mustard Eggs, Spicy, '84 143
Pecan-Stuffed Eggs, '80 78
Shrimp-Curried Eggs, Saucy, '84 143
Stuffed Eggs, Easy, '93 87

Tomato Slices, Stuffed Eggs-and-, '84 152
Tuna-Stuffed Eggs, '83 83
Substitute, Homemade Egg, '92 47
Sunny-Side-Up Eggs, '79 38
Tacos, Breakfast, '80 43
Tomatoes, Bacon-and-Egg-Stuffed, '80 162
Tortillas, Chorizo and Egg, '81 193
Tortillas, Egg-and-Sausage, '83 246; '84 42
Tulsa Eggs, '87 95
ENCHILADAS
American Enchiladas, '81 170
Apple Enchiladas, '99 63
Bean Enchiladas, Spicy, '88 18
Bean Enchiladas, Three-, '91 133
Casserole, Enchilada, '87 287
Casserole, Firecracker Enchilada, '80 260
Casserole, Green Enchilada, '79 76
Casserole, Sour Cream Enchilada, '82 113
Cheese Enchiladas, '81 194; '85 154; '95 311
Cheese Enchiladas, Saucy, '84 220
Chicken-and-Spinach Enchiladas, '91 222
Chicken-Chile Enchiladas, '97 313
Chicken Enchiladas, '80 301; '86 296; '90 121
Chicken Enchiladas, Creamy, '97 250
Chicken Enchiladas, Easy, '82 89; '86 231
Chicken Enchiladas, Quicker, '97 312
Chicken Enchiladas, Three-Cheese, '99 330
Chicken Enchiladas Verde, '93 274
Chicken Enchiladas with Spicy Sauce, '84 76
Chicken Enchiladas with Tomatillo Sauce,
   '94 231; '95 206
Creamy Enchiladas, '93 174
Dove Enchiladas, '85 270
Duck Enchiladas with Red Pepper-Sour Cream,
   Smoked, '87 121
Egg Enchiladas, Scrambled, '97 153
Enticing Enchiladas, '99 57
Green Chile-Sour Cream Enchiladas, '84 234
Hot and Saucy Enchiladas, '81 141; '82 6
Meatless Enchiladas, '93 106
New Mexican Flat Enchiladas, '85 244
Pie, Enchilada, '83 155
Pork Enchiladas, '97 M94
Quicker Enchiladas, '96 103
Sauce, Enchilada, '81 194
Sauce, Red Chile Enchilada, '85 245
Shrimp Enchiladas in Tomatillo Sauce, '95 310
Skillet Enchiladas, '82 89
Soup, Chicken Enchilada, '86 22
Soup, Shrimp Enchilada, '94 103
Sour Cream Enchiladas, '83 200; '87 37
Sour Cream Enchiladas, Cheesy, '79 25
Spinach Enchiladas, '83 60; '84 14
Terrificas, Enchiladas, '84 32
Weeknight Enchiladas, '93 63
ESCARGOTS
Provençal, Escargots, '82 238; '83 156
ESCAROLE. *See* **GREENS.**

FAJITAS
Beef Fajitas, '88 233
Beef Fajita Salad, '91 70
Casserole, Fajita, '97 96
Chicken Fajitas, '88 231; '89 100; '90 204; '99 158
Chicken Fajita Spuds, '96 238
Crêpes, Fajita, '94 116
Fajitas, '84 233
Favorite Fajitas, '86 114
Fettuccine, Fajita, '94 84
Java Fajitas, '96 227
Pico de Gallo, Fajitas with, '98 87
Pita, Fajita in a, '90 177

Pitas, Fajita, '99 239
Plum Good Fajitas, '94 115
FETTUCCINE
Alfredo, Fettuccine, '80 236; '86 158
Blue Cheese Noodles, '98 290
Blue Cheese Sauce, Fettuccine with, '98 247
Broccoli and Sausage, Pasta with, '97 266
Broccoli, Fettuccine with, '90 97
Broccoli-Parmesan Fettuccine, '93 55
Chicken and Dried Tomatoes over Fettuccine,
   '98 233
Chicken and Pasta, Pesto, '89 M132
Chicken-and-Tomatoes over Fettuccine, '90 204
Chicken-Artichoke Pasta with Rosemary, '98 15
Chicken Fettuccine, Cajun, '96 198
Chicken-Pecan Fettuccine, '86 52
Chicken with Pasta, Dijon, '90 318
Cordon Bleu, Pasta, '97 327
Crab Fettuccine, '98 142
Crawfish and Tasso Fettuccine, '96 290
Crawfish Fettuccine, '96 98
Creamy Fettuccine, '92 283; '96 136
Eggplant Sauté, '96 135
Fajita Fettuccine, '94 84
Greens, Pasta with, '95 211
Ham-and-Asparagus Fettuccine, '94 84
Parsley, Fettuccine with, '83 115
Peas and Pasta, '93 139
Pepper Pasta, '89 321
Poppy Seeds, Fettuccine with, '91 48
Primavera, Fettuccine, '89 238; '94 85
Prosciutto, Party Pasta with, '94 176
Salmon Fettuccine, '90 123
Scallop-Mushroom Fettuccine, '96 198
Shrimp and Tomatoes, Fettuccine with, '96 198
Shrimp Élégante, '83 48
Shrimp Fettuccine, '94 84; '96 210
Shrimp-Tomato Pasta, '98 172
Shrimp with Dried Tomato Pesto, Fettuccine
   and, '94 249
Shrimp with Fettuccine, Dilled, '99 141
Spinach Fettuccine, '82 179
Spinach, Fettuccine and, '88 90
Spinach Fettuccine, Creamy Basil Chicken with,
   '97 328
Spinach Fettuccine, Easy Chicken with, '88 89
Spinach Fettuccine, Fresh, '83 60
Spinach Fettuccine with Mustard Greens, '94 247
Spinach Sauce, Fettuccine with, '84 329
Supreme, Fettuccine, '83 288; '86 333
Thai-Style Noodles with Peanut Basil Sauce,
   '98 133
Tomato-Olive Pasta Toss, '86 209
Vegetable Fettuccine, '83 312
Vegetables, Fettuccine and, '97 178
FIGS
Cake, Fig, '79 32; '99 314
Cake, Fig Preserve, '79 140; '84 316
Cake, Fig Preserves, '89 335
Cobbler, Cajun Fig, '94 196
Cobbler, Fig, '79 140
Cobbler, Super Fig, '86 206
Coffee Cake, Easy Fig, '80 116
Flowers, Fig, '96 195
Ice Cream, Fig, '87 139
Jam, Fig, '86 206
Marinated Grilled Figs, '96 194
Muffins, Fig, '86 206
Pickled Figs, '79 140
Pies with Fruit Salsa, Lone Star Fried, '97 124
Preserves, Fig, '79 140; '82 150; '89 140; '96 195
Preserves, Quick Strawberry-Fig, '96 194
Prosciutto, Walnuts, and Cream, Figs with,
   '96 194

Sauce, Fig, '79 140
Snacks, Sliced Fig, '86 206
Strudel, Fig, '98 253
Sugar-Crusted Figs, '96 195

FILLINGS

Savory

Apple Filling, '96 53
Baria, '97 91
Beef Filling, '80 81
Blintz Filling, '92 84
Broccoli Filling, '81 44
Cheese-and-Orange Filling, '93 159
Chicken Divan Filling, '81 91
Chicken Filling, '81 200
Chicken Filling, Curried, '88 125
Chicken Filling Luau, '79 81
Chicken-Olive Filling, '81 227
Chicken Salad Filling, '87 106
Crab Filling, '89 13
Cream Cheese Filling, '97 287
Crêpe Filling, '96 48
Four Cheese Filling, '97 171
Fruit Filling, '94 245
Mushroom Filling, '81 89; '88 84
Omelet Filling, Greek, '80 68
Omelet Filling, Spanish, '80 68
Peanut Filling, '93 211
Pesto, '89 158
Shrimp and Dill Filling, '97 171
Shrimp Filling, '89 320
Shrimp Salad Filling, '87 106
Spinach and Feta Filling, '97 171
Spinach Filling, '95 316
Spinach-Mushroom Filling, '80 215
Spinach-Ricotta Filling, '81 53

Sweet

Almond Cream Filling, '85 320; '91 248
Almond Filling, '87 301; '96 316
Almond Filling, Ground, '87 14
Amaretto Filling, '87 241
Apple-Date Filling, '83 301
Apple Filling, '85 5; '97 239
Apple Filling, Dried, '85 242; '87 229
Apricot Filling, '83 84; '86 107; '93 316
Butterscotch Filling, '91 271
Caramel Filling, '88 278
Caramel Whipped Cream Filling, '96 312
Chantilly Crème, '80 280
Cheese Filling, '89 91
Cherry Filling, '83 302; '84 225; '88 178
Cherry Fried Pie Filling, Dried, '96 109
Chocolate Buttercream, '84 156
Chocolate-Cheese Filling, '90 47
Chocolate Filling, '96 316
Chocolate Filling, Rich, '79 68
Chocolate Midnight Filling, '96 120
Chocolate Truffle Filling, '87 69
Cinnamon-Cheese Filling, '90 46
Coconut Cream Filling, '84 200
Coconut Filling, '81 265
Coffee Filling, '96 316
Cran-Apple Mousse, '93 255
Cream Cheese Filling, '90 170
Cream Filling, '83 220; '84 37; '87 198; '90 311
Crème Fraîche, '91 99
Custard Filling, '82 52, 298; '85 281
Custard Filling, Creamy, '81 180
Custard Filling, Egg, '87 14
Date Cream Filling, '81 303
Date Filling, '80 15; '83 257; '86 314
Fluffy Filling, '81 192; '86 246
Fluffy White Filling, '90 252
Fruit Filling, Nutty, '99 306
Fruit Fried Pie Filling, Mixed, '96 109

Fruit-Nut Filling, '80 289
Fudge Filling, '94 292
Honey Filling, '88 287
Honey-Walnut Filling, '80 21
Lane Cake Filling, '89 55; '96 144
Lemon-Apricot Filling, '90 105
Lemon-Cheese Filling, '79 68; '88 7
Lemon Cream, '91 119
Lemon Cream Filling, '84 23; '87 14
Lemon Filling, '81 172; '84 137; '85 191;
   '86 235; '87 293; '89 312; '90 308; '94 122;
   '95 319; '97 255; '99 118
Lemon Filling, Creamy, '80 70
Lemon-Orange Filling, '81 71
Mint-Cream Filling, '96 229
Mocha Cream Filling, '81 187; '84 305
Mocha Filling, '80 55; '82 262
Napoleon Cream, '84 138
Nut-and-Fruit Filling, '84 263
Nut Filling, '91 35
Orange-Cheese Filling, '90 47
Orange Cream Filling, '99 118
Orange Curd Filling, '96 120
Orange Filling, '79 229; '86 336; '87 84;
   '88 224; '89 287; '96 316
Orange-Pineapple Fried Pie Filling, '96 109
Pastry Cream, Luscious, '82 304
Peach Filling, '89 154; '90 107; '96 119
Peach Pie Filling, Fresh, '95 195
Peanut Butter Filling, '96 229
Pecan Pie Filling, '98 254
Peppermint Filling, '81 119; '89 254
Piña Colada Filling, '99 117
Pineapple Filling, '80 140; '83 179; '84 153;
   '89 57; '97 277
Praline Buttercream, '95 243
Praline Filling, '89 328
Raisin Filling, '90 86
Raspberry Filling, '90 111
Ricotta Filling, '80 58
Sour Cream-Coconut Filling, '92 120
Whipped Cream Filling, '90 265, 307; '99 307
White Chocolate Cream Filling, '92 230
White Chocolate Filling, '89 160

FISH. *See also* **CLAMS, CRAB, CRAWFISH,**
   LOBSTER, OYSTERS, SALMON,
   SCALLOPS, SEAFOOD, SHRIMP,
   TUNA.

Amandine, Fillet of Fish, '80 M54
Amberjack Sandwiches, Grilled, '91 195
Asparagus Divan, Fish-, '87 128

Baked

Almond Baked Fish, '88 270; '89 203
Barbecue Sauce, Baked Fish with, '84 92
Creamy Baked Fillets, '84 91
Crunchy Baked Fish Fillets, '85 217
Fast Fish Bake, '85 218
Herbed Fish and Potato Bake, '79 287; '80 34
Lemon-Celery Sauce, Baked Fillets in, '84 91
Saucy Fish Bake, '79 75
Southern Baked Fish, '82 73

Beer-Batter Fish, '85 68
Bluefish Chowder, '84 282
Broiled Fish Fillets Piquante, '84 91
Broiled Herb Fish Fillets, '79 99
Cakes, Fish, '85 54

Catfish

Amandine, Mandarin Catfish, '84 183
Amandine, Spicy Catfish, '89 52
Appetizer, Layered Catfish, '92 209
Baked Catfish, '94 67
Barbecued Catfish, '80 157
Barbecued Catfish, Lemon, '88 271; '89 202
Blackened Catfish, '97 82

Breaded Catfish with Creole Sauce, '90 28
Breaded Herbed Fish Fillets, '91 121
Broiled Manchac, Catfish, Middendorf's,
   '84 183
Cakes, Catfish, '94 70
Cakes, Creole Catfish, '97 82
Cream Cheese Stuffing, Catfish with, '89 52
Eldorado de Colorado, Catfish, '84 183
Fingers, Crackermeal Catfish, '89 53
Fried Catfish, '82 135; '83 169
Fried Catfish, Classic, '97 82
Fried Catfish, Crisp, '82 242
Fried Catfish, Crisp-, '88 110
Fried Catfish, Front Porch, '96 233
Fried Catfish, Golden, '80 99
Fry, Burk's Farm-Raised Catfish, '95 158
Fry, Catfish, '84 184
Grilled Catfish Cajun-Style, '90 129
Grilled Catfish with Red Salsa, '90 172
Grilled Catfish with Relish, '92 54
Grilled Fish with Heather Sauce, Catfish Inn's,
   '84 182
Gumbo, Catfish, '90 278; '91 216
Jack's Catfish, '99 32
Kiev-Style, Catfish, '84 184
Lafitte, Catfish, '97 83
Louisiana, Catfish, '93 291
Meunière, Catfish, '80 57
Microwave Catfish, '89 M52
Mousse, Catfish, '92 327
Oven-Fried Catfish, '95 106; '99 174
Oven-Fried Catfish, Southern, '87 163
Parmesan, Catfish, '79 184; '86 210; '99 91
Parmesan Catfish, '92 309
Pasta with Catfish and Artichokes, '90 123
Pecan, Catfish, '85 53
Pecan Catfish, '98 329
Pilaf, Catfish, '94 171
Sesame, Catfish, '81 106
Smoked Catfish, '84 47
Spicy-Seasoned Catfish, '89 M66
Spread, Best-Ever Catfish, '98 60
Stew, Cajun-Style Catfish, '88 12
Stir, Catfish, '84 184
Stuffed Catfish, Crown Room's Shrimp-,
   '84 182
Stuffed Catfish, Soufflé-, '84 183

Ceviche in Avocado Shells, '81 33
Ceviche (Marinated Raw Fish), '80 194; '82 220
Ceviche, Mexican-Style, '88 115
Chart, Fat and Lean Fish, '85 180
Chowder, Chunky Fish, '92 331
Chowder, Creamy Fish, '79 16
Chowder, Fish, '79 152; '84 M38
Chowder, Tasty Fish, '80 188
Corned Fish, '79 32
Dinner, Jollof Rice, '91 230; '92 325
Dip, Smoked Fish, '84 46
en Papillote, Fish with Snow Peas, '86 144
Fillet of Fish à l'Orange, '89 180
Fillets, Lemon-Coated, '80 M53
Florentine, Fish, '86 35

Flounder

Amandine, Flounder, '89 M196
Ambassador, Flounder, '86 234
Aspic, Fish 'n, '84 190
Baked Flounder, '79 31; '90 316
Baked Flounder au Fromage, '86 234
Baked Flounder Supreme, '79 75
Broiled Flounder, '88 28; '89 310
Broiled Flounder, Cheesy, '84 69
Broiled Flounder, Pesto, '86 150
Broil, Flounder-Grapefruit, '85 53
Caesar's Fish, '90 76

FISH, Flounder
(continued)

Casserole, Green Chile-and-Fish, '84 32
Chowder, Basque Fish, '86 36
Creole-Style Flounder, '85 180
Crunchy Flounder, Quick, '90 76
Crust, Fish in a, '84 294
Delight, Fish, '86 M212
Dijon, Flounder, '85 95
Fried Fish, '79 151
Fried Fish, Crispy, '84 92
Fried Flounder, Crispy, '84 93
Fried Flounder, Seasoned, '79 214
Grilled Flounder Fillets, '83 213
Hollandaise-Shrimp Sauce, Flounder with,
 '86 234
Italian Fish, '88 270; '89 203
Monterey, Fish, '84 293
Nicole, Flounder, '85 217
Oven-Fried Fish Fillets, '79 75
Papillote, Ocean, '84 M287
Poached Fish with Greek Sauce, '91 M183
Rolls, Vegetable-Filled Fish, '86 M251
Rollups, Shrimp-Stuffed, '82 234
Royal Flounder Fillets, '91 128
Sesame Flounder, '89 33
Shrimp Sauce, Flounder Fillets in, '83 227
Stuffed Flounder, Crab-, '80 120; '81 176
Stuffed Flounder Fillets, '86 234
Stuffed Flounder, Grand Lagoon, '94 68
Stuffed Flounder Rolls, Vegetable-, '87 6
Stuffed Flounder Rolls with Citrus Sauce,
 '85 180
Stuffed with Shrimp, Flounder, '88 51
Thermidor, Flounder, '85 190
Vegetable Medley, Flounder-, '85 217
Wine Sauce, Fillet of Flounder in, '80 179;
 '81 30
Wrap, Fish in a, '97 64
Fresh Fish, Preparing, '82 127
Fried Fish, Golden, '82 134
Fried Fish, Southern, '92 168
Grecian Seafood, '97 314
Greek Fish with Vegetable Sauce, '82 72
Grilled Fish and Vegetables, '89 179
Grilled Fish, Easy, '91 194
Grilled Fish with Caribbean Salsa, Montego Bay,
 '96 70
Grill Fish, How to Charcoal-, '84 48
Grouper
Baked Fish, '98 122
Baked Grouper, Creamy, '85 292
Batter-Fried Grouper Sandwiches, '96 197
Breaded Grouper Fillets, '89 M36
Broiled Grouper, Heavenly, '99 91
Creole Fish, '87 M79
Gourmet Fish, '86 71
Grilled Grouper, '86 185
Grilled Herbed Grouper, '99 178
Grilled Marinated Grouper, '90 166
Guadalajara Grouper, '98 17
Herb-Coated Fish, '86 M112
Hot Spicy Grouper, '94 78
Macadamia, Grouper, '85 127
Marinated Grouper, Garlic-Basil, '94 160
Pan-Fried Fish Fillets, '91 196
Pan-Fried Grouper with Vanilla Wine Sauce,
 '94 241
Parmesan Fillets, '86 M112
Pesto Grouper with Orzo, '97 321
Sausage, Shrimp, '97 164
Sauté, Shrimp-and-Grouper, '87 91

Spectacular, Grouper, '84 163
Steamed Fish and Vegetables, '91 32
Stuffed Fillets, Apple-Carrot, '88 M192
Vegetables, Grouper with Confetti, '88 M189
Vegetables, Grouper with Sautéed, '90 M233
Gumbo, Easy Fish, '81 6
Haddock, Baked, '80 179; '81 30
Haddock Fillets in White Wine, '90 76
Haddock Fillets with Zucchini Stuffing,
 '88 M191
Haddock Italiano, '81 M4
Halibut, Chinese-Style Fried, '80 179; '81 30
Halibut Steaks Italiano, '88 M191
Halibut Steak, Wine-Herb, '94 171
Halibut with Champagne Sauce, Baked, '90 29
Halibut with Cider, '79 182
Halibut with Orange-Curry Sauce, '87 91
Halibut with Swiss Sauce, '83 M195
Hash, Smoked Fish, '92 306
Heroes, Neptune, '84 281
Herring Dip, Yogurt, '80 232
Italian Fish, Easy, '86 M112
Kabobs, Fish, '98 223
Mackerel Creole, '80 126
Mackerel, Lemon-Baked, '79 182
Mackerel, Rosemary-Garlic, '92 200
Mackerel, Smoked Salmon or, '84 46
Mahimahi in Grape Sauce, '91 218
Mahi Mahi, Macadamia, '88 164
Mahimahi, Middle Eastern, '96 92
Mahi-Mahi with Lemon Mayonnaise, '99 178
Marinated Beer-Battered Fish, '86 180
Mix, Fish Herb, '98 51
Monkfish, Greek-Style, '87 M79
Mullet, Festive, '79 75
Mullet, Smoked, '84 47
Mullet Spread, '94 159
Orange Roughy
Asian-Inspired Orange Roughy, '99 122
Baked Fish, Curried, '87 5
Baked Fish, Curry-, '91 196
Baked Fillets, Crispy, '99 90
Basil-Orange Roughy with Vegetables, '92 98
Caper Sauce, Fish in, '95 209
Caribbean Fish, '99 109
Dijon, Orange Roughy, '99 122
Fillets, Quick Fish, '96 196
Fillets Tomatillo, '94 135
Fillets with Herb Sauce, Orange Roughy,
 '91 29
Florentine in Parchment, Fish, '87 22
Kiwi Orange Roughy, '87 193
Mustard Fish, Spicy, '99 90
Pan-Fried Roughy with Tomato-Basil Salsa,
 '99 123
Pecan Roughy with Brown Butter Sauce,
 '91 64
Pesto-Crusted Orange Roughy, '96 156
Sour Cream, Fish with, '89 180
Spinach Pesto, Orange Roughy with,
 '88 M192
Steamed Orange Roughy with Herbs, '95 189
Stew, Fish-and-Vegetable, '87 220
Stir-Fry, Orange Roughy, '98 50
Stir-Fry, Orange Roughy-and-Vegetable, '91 50
Tropical Orange Roughy with Crab Stuffing,
 '99 122
Vegetable Dinner, Fish-and-, '91 196
Vegetable-Topped Orange Roughy, '93 67
Oven-Fried Fish, '91 172; '94 172
Oven-Fried Fish, Mexi-Style, '90 76
Perch Fillets, Buttery Baked, '81 134
Perch, Parmesan-Crusted, '93 91
Poached Fish in Creamy Swiss Sauce, '80 M53

Pollock with Summer Squash Relish, '92 200
Potatoes, Fish-Stuffed, '92 306
Potato Platter, Fish-and-, '89 M248
Redfish Court Bouillon, '83 290; '84 93
Salad, Smoked Fish-Potato, '84 233
Salad, Smoky Seafood, '84 46
Sautéed Seafood Platter, '83 89
Scamp, Tangy Broiled, '87 5
Sea Bass, Hong Kong-Style, '96 196
Seasoning Blend, Fish-and-Seafood, '88 28
Seviche Cocktail, '83 258
Shad Roe with Lemon-Butter Sauce, Baked,
 '84 252
Shark, Marinated, '79 151
Skillet Fish Dinner, '88 199
Smoked Fish, '92 305
Smoked Fish Log, '85 144
Snapper
Baked Snapper à l'Orange, '85 181
Baked Snapper and Stuffing, '82 72
Baked Snapper with Tarragon Stuffing,
 '82 136
Blackened Red Snapper, '90 27
Captain's Spicy One, '81 125
Caribbean Banana Fish, '95 202
Caribbean Snapper, '87 5
Chowder, Red Snapper, '85 217
Company Red Snapper, '82 72
Destin, Snapper, '88 222
Dill, Snapper with, '84 190
Fingers with Banana Salsa, Snapper, '96 85
Glazed Snapper with Rosemary, '98 51
Gumbo, Savannah Snapper, '94 105
Honey-Curried Snapper, '85 181
Horseradish-Crusted Red Snapper, '96 227
Huachinango à la Veracruzana (Veracruz-
 Style Red Snapper), '80 193
Louisiane, Red Snapper, '85 217
Orangy Snapper, '88 23
Oven-Fried Snapper, '90 75
Pecan-Crusted Snapper with Crabmeat
 Relish, Lemony, '99 198
Peppered Snapper with Creamy Dill Sauce,
 '94 42
Poached Fish with Vegetables, '89 332; '90 18
Poached Red Snapper, '85 127
Poached Snapper, '83 101
Provençal, Snapper, '91 M170
Rome, Fillet of Snapper, '80 57
Southwestern Snapper, '91 195
Spanish-Style Fillets, '86 M112
Spicy Snapper, '89 179
Stuffed Red Snapper Rolls, Cucumber-,
 '83 176
Stuffed Red Snapper with Lime, '83 246
Stuffed Snapper, '87 138
Vegetables, Yellowtail Snapper with Julienne,
 '93 31
Veracruz, Red Snapper, '88 149; '92 142
Wine Sauce, Red Snapper in, '85 138
Sole Divan, '87 21
Sole Fillets, Herbed, '82 21
Sole Fillets in Wine Sauce, '81 109
Sole in Papillote, '82 22
Sole Provençal, Fillet of, '85 78
Sole Royale, '89 104
Sole, Saucy, '82 M68
Sole Véronique, '85 181
Sole with Cucumber Sauce, '84 M286
Soup with Garlic Mayonnaise, Rich Fish, '92 56
Spread, Smoked Fish, '92 305
Steaks, Soy Fish, '86 M112
Stock, Fish, '95 19
Stock, Homemade Fish, '92 237

Surprise, Fish, '84 231
Sweet-and-Sour Fish, '80 M54
Swordfish, Foil-Baked, '87 5
Swordfish-Shiitake Skewers, '97 168
Swordfish, Skewered, '86 256
Swordfish Steaks, Orange-Ginger Marinated,
    '93 271
Swordfish Steak with Chervil Butter, '91 147
Swordfish Stir-Fry, '96 128
Swordfish with Caper Sauce, Grilled, '95 230
Swordfish with Cashew-and-Cracked Pepper
    Crust, '96 196
Tacos, Barbecued Fish, '95 339
Trout
    Amandine, Classic Trout, '96 202
    Amandine, Fish, '85 179
    Amandine, Gaston's Trout, '96 232
    Amandine, Orange Lake, '80 99
    Amandine, Trout, '99 53
    Baked Fish Fillets, Creamy, '85 217
    Baked Trout, '95 106
    Cakes with Lemon-Butter Sauce, Mountain
        Trout, '92 337
    Cornmeal-Crusted Trout, '99 52
    Delmonico, Trout, '80 57
    Fillets with Capers, Trout, '95 252
    Florentine, Cheesy Trout, '95 53
    Grilled Rainbow Trout with Mushroom
        Stuffing, '97 162
    Grilled Trout, '95 106
    Grilled Trout with Ginger and Soy Sauce, '85 228
    Laurie, Trout, '88 270; '89 202
    Pecan-Crusted Trout with Orange Sauce,
        '98 M82
    Poached Trout, '95 106
    Salad with Black Pepper Vinaigrette,
        Trout-and-Tomato, '98 284
    Smoked Trout, '84 47
    Spread, Smoked Trout, '84 47
    Stuffed Rainbow Trout, '93 121
    Stuffed Trout, Sweet Onion-, '99 52
    Stuffed with Crawfish, Bacon-Wrapped Trout,
        '99 54
    Sunshine Trout, '84 M286
    Tomato Sauce, Fish in, '85 75
    Wine Sauce, Trout in, '80 180; '81 31
Two, Fish for, '92 60
Vegetables, Cheesy Fish and, '94 254
Veracruz Fish with Shrimp, '86 130
Whitefish Spread, Smoked, '92 58
FLAN. *See* **CUSTARDS/Flan.**
FOKTY. *See* **FROM OUR KITCHEN TO YOURS.**
FONDUE
Caramel Fondue, '94 332; '95 35
Cheese Fondue, '81 40
Cheese Fondue, Party, '92 20
Chocolate Fondue, '91 142
Chocolate Fondue, Brandied, '93 162
Chocolate Plunge, '94 332; '95 35
Dessert Fondue, '89 281
Fruitcake Fondue, '84 258
Goat Cheese Fondue, Warm, '96 234
Nacho Fondue, '94 332; '95 35
Peppermint Fondue, '94 332; '95 35
Pub Fondue, '94 332; '95 35
Spinach Fondue Sandwiches, Grilled, '99 337
Swiss Cheese Fondue, '91 48
White Chocolate Fondue, '92 287
FRANKFURTERS
Appetizer Franks, Saucy, '84 M12
Appetizers, Bourbon Frankfurter, '85 207
Bacon-Wrapped Franks, '81 202
Barbecued Frankfurters, '83 144; '84 M12
Barbecued Frankfurters, Oven-, '83 11

Barbecued Franks, '85 192
Barbecue, Tangy Frank, '79 63
Beans and Franks, '85 142
Beans and Franks, Hawaiian Baked, '80 136
Beans and Franks, Jiffy, '91 M172
Beans-and-Franks, Polynesian, '84 M11
Beans, Stove-Top Franks 'n', '88 201
Beany Hot Dogs, '82 190
Cabbage with Apples and Franks, '87 42
Casserole, Hot Doggie, '88 200
Casserole, Layered Frankfurter, '79 64
Chafing Dish Franks, '83 143
Chili-Cheese Dogs, '81 M176
Corn Dog Bites, '85 245; '93 79
Corn Dogs, Favorite, '83 144
Corn Puppies, '97 140
Corn Relish Dogs, '85 192
Crusty Franks, '80 166
Delicious, Hot Dogs, '81 202
Deluxe, Hot Dog, '97 140
Family-Style Franks, '79 54
Grilled Stuffed Franks, '82 163
Hash Browns, Franks and, '80 166
Hawaiian Franks, '81 202
Jubilee, Hot Dog, '81 113
Kraut and Franks, Beany, '79 64
Mexicali Hot Dogs, '82 131
Mexican Franks, '93 78
Pickled Party Franks, '83 174
Pigs in a Blanket, '95 178
Pigs on a Roll, Three Little, '98 203
Pizza Dogs, Grilled, '97 139
Pizzas, Hot Dog, '93 78
Potatoes, Cheesy Frank-Topped, '83 3
Potatoes, Frank-Filled, '84 M11
Potluck Dish, Frankaroni, '88 201
Sandwiches, Frankfurter, '84 M11
Sauce, Hot Diggity Dog, '93 198
Saucy Franks, '88 201
Scrambled Dog, Dinglewood Pharmacy's,
    '95 118
Skillet Dinner, Frankfurter, '80 166
Skillet, Frankfurter-Cabbage, '80 166
Skillet, Hot Dog and Spaghetti, '83 144
Sloppy Joe Dogs, '85 192
Soup, Split Pea and Frankfurter, '79 64
Spanish Frankfurters, '80 166
Spicy Frankfurters, '81 202
Stuffed Franks and Potatoes, '81 202
Supper, Hot Dog, '93 78
Tipsy Franks, '85 52
FRENCH TOAST
Almond French Toast, '88 62
Amandine, Baked Toast, '82 47
Amaretto French Toast, '98 280
Apple French Toast, '98 55
au Fromage, French Toast, '88 288
Banana Splits, French Toast, '96 M164
Caribbean French Toast, '92 46
Cinnamon French Toast, '84 211
Cottage-Topped French Toast, '85 49
Easy French Toast, '82 M172
Eggnog French Toast, '95 313
Grand Marnier Fruit Sauce, French Toast with,
    '90 93
Ham-and-Cheese Oven French Toast, '97 172
Macadamia French Toast, '86 96
Macadamia Nut French Toast, '95 282
Orange Butter, French Toast with, '81 42
Orange French Toast, '83 292; '84 78; '86 329
Orange Sauce, French Toast with, '82 47
Oven-Baked French Toast, '82 47; '90 192
Oven-Baked French Toast, Easy, '93 195
Overnight French Toast, '89 227

Overnight French Toast Deluxe, '79 216
Pain-Perdu Po-Boy, '93 291
Painted French Toast, '98 206
Peach-Filled French Toast, '98 160
Peachy French Toast, '98 56
Peanut Butter French Toast, '93 166
Potato-Crusted Texas Toast, '94 142
Praline French Toast, '98 55
Sandwiches, Strawberry-French Toast, '91 160
Slender French Toast, '86 103
Stuffed French Toast, '96 52; '98 55, 313
Stuffed French Toast, Orange-, '98 54
Stuffed French Toast, Three Cheese, '93 122
Waffled French Toast, '82 47
FRITTERS
Apple Fritter Rings, '88 44
Apple Fritters, '81 105; '82 273; '85 14; '97 153
Apple Holiday Fritters, '86 314
Banana Fritters, '79 213
Beet Fritters, '96 36
Blueberry Fritters, '85 152
Broccoli Fritters, Cheesy, '79 53
Buñuelos, '93 29
Cauliflower-Cheddar Fritters, '98 25
Clam Fritters, '79 151; '86 71
Corn-and-Crab Fritters, '97 227
Corn Fritters, '86 192; '94 22; '98 207
Corn Fritters, Golden, '80 165; '81 128
Corn Fritters, Skillet-Fried, '85 14
Corn-Jalapeño Fritters, '96 153
Crab Fritters, '98 142
Eggplant Fritters, '91 211
Ham Fritters, '82 39
Ham Fritters with Creamy Sauce, '81 105
Honey Puffs, '96 153
Okra, Fritter-Fried, '86 218
Okra Fritters, '79 160; '98 159
Orange Fritters, Puffy, '81 169
Oyster Fritters, '79 31; '97 20
Pear Fritters, Ol' Timey, '86 51
Pecan Fritters, Chocolate-Covered, '79 205
Pineapple Fritters, '88 112
Potato Fritters, Cheese-Stuffed, '96 153
Potato-Ham Fritters, '98 249
Squash Fritters, '89 68
Squash-Jalapeño Fritters, '98 249
Sweet Potato Fritters, '88 44
Sweet Potato Fritters, Golden, '79 9
Zucchini Fritters, '81 163
Zucchini Fritters, Cheesy, '88 44
FROG LEGS
Crispy Frog Legs, '80 99
Fried Frog Legs, '88 110
FROM OUR KITCHEN TO YOURS (FOKTY)
Alcohol, substituting in recipes, '92 314; '99 148
Apples, '84 227, 228
    adding to meat loaf, '98 138
    amounts to buy, '84 228
    preventing browning after cutting, '84 228
    selecting for cooking, '84 227, 228
    selecting for eating, '84 227, 228
    storing, '84 228
Appliances, kitchen. *See* **FOKTY/Kitchen,
    Dishwasher, Food processor, Freezer,
    Microwave oven, Ovens, Refrigerator.**
Arrowroot, as a thickening agent, '83 147
Avocados, softening, '96 76
Baking soda, as ice melter, '98 36
Barbecue, '94 155. *See also* **FOKTY/Grilling.**
    chicken, '94 155
    recipe, Barbecue Ribs, '99 68
    tongs, using to reach things, '97 206
Bay leaves, removing from soups, '95 314;
    '96 51

Beans, dried, '88 4; **'99** 250
amount of folate in, **'99** 250
buying, **'88** 4
cooking, **'88** 4; **'99** 100
soaking, **'88** 4
storing, **'88** 4
Beef, '83 38; **'92** 65, 66; **'94** 140
browning, **'83** 38
buying, **'83** 38; **'90** 276; **'92** 65
cooking methods, **'83** 38
fat content of, **'92** 65, 66; **'94** 140
handling properly, **'87** 208; **'94** 140; **'96** 76
making gravy from pan drippings, **'83** 38
storing, **'94** 140
tenderizing, **'83** 38
Beers
selecting, **'99** 250
tasting, **'99** 250
types of, **'99** 250
Berries. *See also* **FOKTY/Blueberries.**
selecting, **'99** 148
storing, **'99** 148
Beverages, '83 191; **'90** 276, 277; **'97** 174;
'98 218. *See also* **FOKTY/Beers,**
Buttermilk, Coffee, Eggnog, Ice,
Tea, Water, Wines.
chilling quickly, **'96** 21
determining amounts to buy for entertaining,
'90 276, 277
freezing, **'92** 314
garnishing, **'97** 56
glasses, **'97** 184
ice molds, **'86** 331
placement of in basic table setting, **'90** 182
placement of when entertaining, **'90** 277
recipe, Royal Cup Chiller, **'98** 218
substituting for alcohol in recipes, **'92** 314;
'99 148
Biscuits, '89 211, 212; **'92** 52. *See also*
FOKTY/Breads, Rolls, Yeast.
baking, **'89** 211, 212
cutting dough, **'89** 211; **'95** 30; **'97** 36
freezing, **'89** 212
kneading, **'92** 52
making dough for, **'89** 211; **'92** 52
reheating, **'89** 212
removing burned bottoms from, **'96** 51
storing leftovers, **'89** 212
using food processor to make, **'89** 211, 212;
'96 256
Blueberries, freezing before adding to batter,
'98 138
Breads, '82 198; **'84** 92; **'89** 268; **'92** 52, 102,
314; **'93** 183. *See also* **FOKTY/Biscuits,**
Muffins, Rolls, Yeast.
cutting, **'91** 144, 145
doubling recipes, **'91** 22
freezing, **'89** 268; **'90** 315; **'91** 95; **'92** 102
as gifts, **'91** 95
metal dough scraper, **'90** 126; **'92** 52
microwave oven, **'89** 268
quick breads, **'84** 92; **'89** 268
rising procedures, **'87** 12; **'89** 268; **'98** 72
testing for doneness, **'84** 92; **'92** 314
yeast breads, **'84** 92; **'87** 12; **'89** 268; **'92** 314
yeast rolls, **'83** 323
Broccoli, '84 249
cutting, **'93** 132
preparing, **'84** 249
selecting, **'84** 249

Broths. *See* **FOKTY/Soups.**
Brussels sprouts, '84 249
preparing, **'84** 249
selecting, **'84** 249
Butter, '82 189; **'95** 314; **'99** 296
availability of, **'82** 189
balls, how to make, **'82** 189
clarifying, **'82** 189; **'97** 232
curls, how to make, **'82** 189
fat content of, **'82** 189
storing, **'82** 189
substituting for in baked goods, **'90** 314;
'97 134
Buttermilk, freezing, **'92** 314; **'97** 72
Butterscotch, **'98** 238
Cactus (Nopales), '94 29
cooking, **'94** 29
selecting, **'94** 29
storing, **'94** 29
Cakes, '89 57, 58; **'91** 144, 200, 201;
'92 154, 155, 314; **'94** 59. *See also*
FOKTY/Fruitcakes.
baking techniques, **'89** 57; **'98** 218
cheesecakes, cutting, **'96** 140
cheesecakes, disguising cracks in, **'96** 112
cheesecakes, eliminating cracks in, **'91** 300
cooling, **'92** 155; **'96** 208; **'99** 128, 328
cutting, **'91** 144; **'92** 314; **'95** 30
decorating, **'94** 59; **'99** 328
dry ingredients, **'87** 12; **'92** 155
freezing, **'89** 58; **'90** 314, 315; **'99** 328
frosting, **'89** 57, 58
greasing pans, **'92** 314
jellyroll cakes, **'92** 314
mixing procedures, **'89** 57; **'92** 154, 155;
'99 328
pan sizes, **'92** 154, 314; **'96** 332
pound cakes, **'84** 92, 319 (baking tips chart);
'92 154, 155
repairing disasters, **'96** 21
as snacks, **'91** 200, 201
storing, **'89** 57, 58; **'92** 155; **'99** 328
substituting flours, **'92** 155
testing for doneness, **'84** 92; **'92** 155;
'96 112, 332
Campsite cooking, '86 172
cleaning up, **'86** 172
making lists, **'86** 172
packing, **'86** 172
planning, **'86** 172
Candy, crushing hard, **'96** 21, 76
Canning fruits and vegetables, '84 180;
'89 141, 142; **'93** 136, 137; **'99** 180. *See also*
FOKTY/Paraffin.
boiling water bath, **'84** 180; **'89** 141, 142;
'91 300; **'93** 136, 137
equipment, **'93** 137; **'97** 278; **'99** 180
packing, **'84** 180; **'89** 141, 142
safety, **'84** 180; **'89** 141, 142; **'91** 300; **'93** 137
steam pressure method of, **'84** 180;
'89 141, 142
Caramel, **'98** 238
Casseroles
doubling recipes, **'91** 22, 23, 96
freezing, **'90** 314; **'91** 96; **'96** 112
preventing spoilage of, **'87** 208
Cast-iron cookware, '93 33; **'99** 50
caring for, **'93** 33; **'99** 50
cleaning, **'99** 50
seasoning, **'93** 33; **'99** 50
Cauliflower, '84 249
cutting, **'93** 132
preparing, **'84** 249; **'99** 100
selecting, **'84** 249

Centerpieces, **'90** 205; **'97** 232
Champagne. *See* **FOKTY/Wines.**
Cheese, '82 109
buying, **'85** 210; **'90** 276
cooking with, **'85** 210; **'87** 12
freezing, **'82** 109; **'85** 211
handling properly, **'87** 208
serving, **'85** 210, 211
shredding, **'95** 31 (illustration)
as snacks, **'91** 200, 201
storing, **'85** 210
Cheesecakes. *See* **FOKTY/Cakes.**
Chicken, '87 12; **'88** 39; **'94** 155, 253
barbecuing, **'94** 155
boning, **'88** 39
cooking, **'87** 12; **'88** 39; **'95** 246; **'97** 112
cutting up, **'94** 253
handling properly, **'87** 208; **'99** 128
microwaving, **'88** 39
packaging of, **'88** 39
preparing for stir-frying, **'91** 160
Children in the kitchen, **'91** 92; **'92** 102, 207
China, '88 301
removing marks from, **'88** 301
storing, **'88** 301
washing, **'88** 301
Chinese cooking, '85 76
equipment, **'85** 76
garnishing, **'85** 76
preparing food for, **'85** 76
Chocolate, '86 246, 247; **'92** 314; **'93** 317
dipping, **'86** 330, 331
garnishing with, **'86** 247; **'93** 317; **'94** 59;
'96 230, 256
illustrations for chocolate sacks,
'93 317
kinds of, **'86** 246, 247
melting, **'92** 314; **'93** 317; **'96** 21, 332
substitutions, **'86** 246, 247
using to line pie shells, **'97** 36
white chocolate, **'86** 246, 247; **'94** 59
Cholesterol, '90 72
and food labels, **'90** 72
Cleaning up. *See* **FOKTY/Recipe**
preparation.
Clothing for "chefs," **'97** 278
Club soda, using to remove stains, **'96** 304
Coconut, **'98** 238
Coffee
beverages, **'98** 218
freezing excess, **'98** 306
Cookbooks, making notations in, **'96** 160
Cookies, '91 234; **'92** 207, 208; **'95** 30
baking, **'92** 208; **'98** 326
cooling, **'92** 208; **'96** 208; **'98** 326
crushing, **'95** 30
equipment, **'92** 208
freezing, **'90** 314; **'92** 207, 208
freezing dough, **'97** 112
as gifts, **'91** 95
mixing procedures, **'92** 207
recipe, Chocolate Chip-Peanut Butter
Cookies, **'99** 68
shaped cookie cutters, **'97** 56
slicing dough, **'96** 140, 230; **'97** 112
storing, **'92** 208
testing for doneness, **'84** 92
Cooking directions, basic, '87 12, 208.
See also **FOKTY/Handling food properly,**
Recipe preparation.
chicken, **'87** 12
shrimp, **'87** 12
Cooking oils, '98 112
varieties of, **'98** 112

Cooking spray. *See* **FOKTY/Vegetable cooking spray.**
Cookware, **'85** 329; **'86** 227; **'90** 50; **'93** 33, 183, 220. *See also* **FOKTY/ Cast-iron cookware, Kitchen.**
  caring for, **'85** 329; **'93** 33, 183
  keeping metal handles cool, **'97** 184
  for microwave, **'86** 227
  selecting, **'85** 329; **'86** 227; **'93** 220
Corn
  cutting from the cob, **'96** 192
  removing silks, **'98** 198
Cornbread, **'87** 16
  cornmeal, **'87** 16
  ingredients in, **'87** 16
  making cornbread, **'87** 16
Cornmeal, **'87** 16
  making cornbread, **'87** 16
  understanding the label, **'87** 16
Cornstarch, **'83** 146, 147
  as a thickening agent, **'83** 146, 147
Crab, cracking, **'95** 156
Cranberries
  buying, **'92** 314
  enhancing canned sauce, **'99** 296
  freezing, **'92** 314
  frosted cranberries (garnish), **'82** 280
Crystal, **'88** 300, 301
  removing discolorations and stains, **'88** 300, 301
  repairing chips, **'88** 300
  storing, **'88** 300
  washing, **'88** 300, 301
Custards
  preparing and storing properly, **'87** 208 (chart)
  testing for doneness, **'84** 92
  thickening, **'83** 147
Cutting boards, **'87** 208; **'98** 138, 198
  acrylic, **'87** 208
  cleaning, **'87** 208; **'99** 224
  food safety, **'87** 208
  wooden, **'87** 208
Desserts. *See also* **FOKTY/Butterscotch, Cakes, Candy, Caramel, Cookies, Custards, Fruits, Garnishes, Meringue, Piecrust, Puddings, Soufflés, Tarts.**
  gelatin molds, **'99** 100
  using ready-made products, **'97** 174
Dishwasher, **'87** 130
Drying foods, **'93** 23
  cherry tomatoes, **'93** 23
  equipment, **'93** 23
  safety, **'93** 23
  uses for, **'93** 23
Eggnog, freezing, **'92** 314
Eggs, **'83** 147, 214; **'89** 26. *See also* **FOKTY/Meringue.**
  cooking methods, **'83** 214; **'98** 112
  handling properly, **'87** 208 (chart)
  pasteurized egg substitute, **'89** 26
  preventing curdling, **'82** 198; **'83** 147
  using raw egg whites, **'91** 300
  using raw egg yolks, **'89** 26
  yolks, thick and lemon colored, **'83** 214
Entertaining, **'84** 122, 123; **'88** 276; **'90** 182, 276, 277; **'91** 300; **'94** 17, 18
  beverage glasses, **'97** 184
  determining amounts of food to buy, **'90** 276 (chart)
  determining traffic flow, **'84** 122, 123; **'86** 191; **'90** 276, 277
  making preparations for, **'84** 122; **'86** 191; **'94** 17, 18; **'96** 21; **'97** 154

  outdoors, **'86** 191; **'96** 230
  presenting food, **'84** 122; **'88** 276; **'97** 56, 174; **'98** 112
  "referral coffee," **'97** 154
  selecting menus for, **'84** 122; **'86** 191; **'88** 276; **'90** 276; **'97** 308
  serving food safely, **'91** 300; **'96** 230
  setting up a bar for, **'90** 277
  sharing recipes, **'97** 72
  table setting, **'90** 182 (illustration), 276; **'96** 192; **'97** 184
  tailgating, **'96** 230
Equivalents of ingredients, **'91** 22, 23
Etiquette, **'90** 225
  basic manners at the table, **'90** 225; **'96** 208
  tipping in restaurants, **'96** 140
Fat, dietary, **'82** 189; **'90** 72; **'91** 200, 201; **'92** 65, 66; **'93** 207
  in beef, **'92** 65, 66
  in butter, **'82** 189; **'90** 314
  eliminating in snacks, **'91** 200, 201
  and food labels, **'90** 72; **'92** 65; **'93** 207
  in margarine, **'82** 189; **'90** 314
  storing, **'82** 189
Fish, **'84** 48; **'87** 79, 80; **'90** 130; **'94** 105, 106. *See also* **FOKTY/Seafood, Shrimp, Surimi.**
  boning, **'96** 256
  buying, **'84** 48; **'87** 79, 80; **'90** 130; **'94** 106; **'97** 112; **'99** 68
  cooking, **'87** 80
  deep frying, **'98** 238
  eliminating odors on hands, **'82** 109
  fat fish, **'87** 79
  freezing, **'87** 80
  grilling, **'84** 48; **'92** 52
  handling properly, **'87** 208
  lean fish, **'87** 79
  market forms of, **'87** 79
  selecting fish for grilling, **'84** 48; **'90** 130
  storing, **'87** 80; **'90** 130; **'94** 105, 106; **'97** 112
  substituting, **'90** 130
  thawing, **'87** 80; **'90** 130
  transporting fresh, **'94** 105, 106
Flour, **'82** 197, 198
  all purpose, **'82** 197, 198; **'87** 12; **'99** 224
  bread, **'99** 224
  cake flour, **'82** 197, 198; **'87** 12
  cracked wheat, **'82** 197, 198
  self rising, **'82** 197, 198
  sifting, **'82** 197, 198; **'87** 12
  storing, **'82** 197, 198
  types of, **'82** 197, 198; **'96** 256; **'99** 224
  whole wheat, **'99** 224
Flowers
  crystallizing edible, **'94** 59; **'99** 100
  edible, **'96** 304
  keeping fresh, **'99** 100
  toxic, **'96** 304
Food processor, **'82** 109; **'86** 13
  chopping nuts, **'92** 314; **'95** 208
Food safety. *See* **FOKTY/Handling food properly.**
Freezer, **'83** 14, 15; **'86** 50, 51; **'87** 112, 208; **'93** 83, 84
  amount of food to store in, **'87** 112
  casseroles in, **'87** 112
  cleaning, **'84** 11; **'87** 112
  constant freezer temperature, **'86** 50; **'99** 50
  defrosting, **'87** 112; **'99** 50
  foods that freeze well, **'86** 50; **'87** 112; **'90** 314, 315
  fruits in, **'87** 112
  labeling foods in, **'84** 11; **'86** 51; **'87** 112

  leftovers, freezing safely, **'87** 112; **'96** 140, 160; **'99** 50
  organizing foods in, **'87** 112
  and power loss, **'83** 14, 15; **'93** 83, 84
  preventing sogginess of particular foods to be frozen, **'87** 112
  refreezing foods, **'83** 15; **'93** 83, 84; **'99** 50
  reheating frozen foods, **'87** 112
  sausage, **'87** 238
  vegetables in, **'87** 112
  wraps and containers for freezing foods, **'86** 50, 51; **'87** 112
Fruitcakes, **'83** 285; **'86** 331; **'95** 343
  purchasing candied fruit for, **'92** 314
  shortcut for, **'99** 224
  storing, **'83** 285; **'86** 331
Fruits, **'83** 94; **'85** 233; **'89** 141, 142; **'92** 248, 249, 250. *See also* **FOKTY/Apples, Avocados, Berries, Blueberries, Cranberries, Coconut, Garnishes, Kiwifruit, Lemons, Mangoes, Melons, Oranges, Peaches, Pears, Persimmons, Raspberries, Strawberries, Tomatillos.**
  canning, **'84** 180; **'89** 141, 142
  in centerpieces, **'90** 205
  as "containers" for food, **'97** 174
  cooking with, **'97** 36
  dressing for fruit salad, **'97** 134
  exotic fruits, **'92** 248, 249, 250
  fall fruits, **'85** 233
  freezing, **'87** 112
  grating citrus peel, **'95** 314; **'96** 140; **'98** 138
  nutritive values of, **'92** 248, 249, 250
  preparing, **'92** 248, 249, 250; **'97** 134
  selecting, **'84** 186, 187; **'92** 248, 249, 250
  as snacks, **'91** 200, 201
  storing, **'83** 94; **'92** 248, 249, 250
  using yogurt instead of puree, **'97** 206
Frying foods, **'84** 211; **'88** 112, 113. *See also* **FOKTY/Lard.**
  cooking fat to use, **'88** 113
  equipment, **'88** 113
  safety, **'90** 22
  techniques, **'88** 113
Gardening, **'98** 112
Garlic, **'93** 182
  baker, **'94** 332
  conversions of bottled for fresh, **'99** 50
  press, **'94** 332; **'97** 134
  tool for peeling easily, **'97** 154
Garnishes, **'82** 138, 280; **'89** 100; **'90** 108; **'93** 317; **'94** 59; **'96** 230, 256. *See also* **FOKTY/Flowers.**
  butter curls, **'82** 189
  candy holly leaves, **'99** 328
  chocolate, **'86** 247; **'94** 59; **'96** 230, 256
  chocolate leaves, **'96** 230
  chocolate sacks, **'93** 317
  containers as garnishes, **'97** 174
  curling garnishes, **'89** 100
  eggs, hard-cooked, **'82** 280
  fruit garnishes, **'82** 280; **'96** 230; **'97** 36
  illustrations, **'89** 100; **'90** 108; **'93** 317
  making ahead, **'89** 100
  pastry garnishes, **'96** 230
  piped garnishes, **'82** 280; **'86** 330; **'90** 108
  soup garnish, **'96** 160
  sugar, lemon, **'97** 56
  sugar, powdered, **'96** 51
  utensils for creating, **'89** 100; **'90** 108
  vegetable garnishes, **'82** 280; **'89** 100, 243; **'95** 343
  whipped cream, **'86** 330

FROM OUR KITCHEN TO YOURS (FOKTY)
(continued)

Gelatin, **'83** 124, 125; **'91** 300
  chilling, **'83** 124; **'86** 13
  molds, determining size of, **'82** 313
  molds, substituting, **'99** 100
  softening, **'91** 300
  unmolding, **'83** 124, 125; **'86** 330
  using fresh fruits and vegetables in, **'91** 300
Gifts, nonfood, **'97** 134; **'98** 326
  gift certificates, **'97** 308
Gifts of food, **'86** 289; **'91** 95, 96; **'95** 343;
  '96 112
  containers for, **'86** 289; **'91** 95, 96; **'98** 36
  freezing, **'91** 95, 96; **'95** 343
  mailing, **'86** 289; **'95** 343
  mail orders from favorite restaurants, **'97** 308
  storing, **'91** 95, 96
  wrapping, **'86** 289; **'95** 343
Gingerroot, **'94** 29
  cooking with, **'92** 314; **'94** 29
  freezing, **'98** 138
  grating, **'98** 138
  selecting, **'94** 29
  in stir-frying, **'92** 314
  storing, **'92** 314; **'98** 138
Gloves, disposable, **'96** 76
Grating citrus rind, **'95** 314; **'96** 140; **'98** 138
Gravies, **'83** 38; **'86** 330
  serving and storing properly, **'87** 208 (chart)
Greens
  cleaning, **'96** 304; **'97** 206
  radicchio, **'97** 232
Grilling, **'82** 109; **'83** 191; **'84** 48; **'86** 172;
  '88 145, 146; **'92** 202; **'93** 103, 104. *See also*
  FOKTY/Smoking (cooking method).
  avoiding flare-ups, **'88** 145; **'92** 202;
    '99 148, 180
  basting, **'82** 109; **'88** 146; **'93** 103
  charcoal, **'82** 109; **'93** 103, 104
  cleanup, **'93** 104
  cooking times, **'95** 194 (chart)
  direct/indirect cooking methods, **'88** 145;
    '93 103, 104; **'95** 194; **'97** 206; **'99** 148
  equipment, **'82** 109; **'88** 146; **'92** 52; **'93** 103;
    '95 274; **'99** 148
  flavoring with wood chips, **'88** 145; **'93** 103
  kabobs, **'88** 146; **'93** 103; **'99** 180
  safety, **'99** 148
  temperature of fire, **'82** 109; **'88** 145, 146;
    '95 195
  thermometer, **'93** 103, 104; **'95** 195;
    '99 148
Grits, eliminating lumps in, **'97** 154
Grocery shopping, **'84** 11; **'91** 187, 188
  best time for, **'84** 11
  comparative shopping, **'91** 188
  determining best values, **'91** 188 (chart)
  making lists for, **'82** 312; **'83** 284; **'84** 11
  planning menus, **'82** 312; **'83** 284; **'84** 11
  saving time and money, **'91** 187, 188
  stocking up, **'91** 188
  using coupons, **'91** 188
Ham, **'89** 333, 334; **'90** 276
  cooking in microwave oven, **'89** 333, 334
  determining amount to buy for entertaining,
    '90 276
  freezing, **'89** 334
  preparing, **'89** 333, 334
  reducing saltiness during cooking, **'97** 134
  selecting, **'89** 333
  storing, **'89** 334

Handling food properly, **'87** 208; **'89** 26;
  '91 300; **'92** 202; **'93** 23, 83, 84; **'96** 76, 230;
  '99 224. *See also* **FOKTY/Beef, Canning,**
  Chicken, Eggs, Fish, Turkey.
  chart, **'87** 208
  egg whites, raw, **'91** 300
  egg yolks, raw, **'89** 26
  holiday hot lines, **'97** 278; **'98** 306
  when entertaining, **'91** 300; **'96** 230
  when grilling, **'99** 148
Herbs, **'85** 58; **'89** 121; **'99** 208. *See also*
  FOKTY/Seasonings, Spices.
  amounts to use, **'89** 121; **'95** 30
  chart, **'89** 121
  cooking with, **'85** 58
  drying, **'85** 58; **'98** 198
  freezing, **'85** 58
  gathering fresh, **'85** 58; **'89** 121
  storing, **'85** 58; **'89** 121; **'98** 198
  substituting fresh for salt, **'99** 208
  types of, **'99** 208
Holiday
  baking, **'98** 326
  hot lines, **'97** 278; **'98** 306
Ice
  dry ice, **'83** 14, 15
  molds, **'86** 331
Ice cream, **'82** 171; **'86** 215
  adding fresh fruit to homemade,
    '82 171
  homemade, **'82** 171
  varieties of, **'86** 215
Ingredients, uncommon, **'97** 232
Kitchen, **'83** 191; **'84** 10, 11, 148, 149; **'90** 22, 50;
  '93 220; **'94** 332
  aluminum foil cooking bags, **'99** 68
  appliances, **'87** 130
  baking pans, **'98** 138; **'99** 128
  baking stone, **'99** 68
  basic equipment, **'90** 50; **'93** 220; **'94** 332;
    '97 56, 308; **'98** 138
  cookware, **'85** 329; **'90** 50; **'93** 220; **'96** 160;
    '98 326
  countertops, **'84** 148, 149
  fire extinguisher for, **'99** 50
  gadgets, **'86** 13; **'90** 126; **'94** 332; **'95** 343;
    '97 154; **'98** 36, 218
  keeping cool in summer, **'83** 191
  knives, **'91** 144, 145
  organizing, **'84** 10, 11
  safety in, **'84** 37; **'90** 22; **'96** 256
  shears, **'91** 160; **'92** 52
  toolbox, **'96** 21
Kiwifruit, peeling, **'95** 31 (illustration)
Knives, **'84** 11; **'91** 144, 145
  buying, **'91** 144, 145
  sharpening, **'91** 144, 145
  storing, **'84** 11
  using properly, **'86** 13; **'91** 144, 145
  varieties of, **'91** 144, 145 (illustration)
Labels, food, **'90** 72; **'92** 65; **'93** 207; **'94** 140
  chart, **'90** 72
  margarine or "spread" labels,
    '97 134
  sample label, **'93** 207
  "sell by" date, **'99** 128
  understanding, **'90** 72; **'93** 207
Lamb, **'88** 59
  buying, **'88** 59
  cooking, **'88** 59; **'95** 105 (chart)
  seasoning, **'95** 105
  selecting, **'88** 59
  storing, **'88** 59; **'95** 105 (chart)
Lard, **'96** 160

Leftovers, **'82** 313; **'87** 112, 208; **'92** 314;
  '95 30, 274; **'96** 230
  bread slices, **'82** 313
  buns, **'82** 313
  freezing, **'87** 112, 208; **'92** 314
  of jams and jellies, **'97** 232
Lemons, using for routine kitchen cleanup, **'96** 51
Lettuce, **'86** 80; **'95** 67
  coring, **'86** 80
  selecting, **'86** 80
  storing, **'86** 80
  types of, **'86** 80 (illustration)
  yields, **'86** 80
List making, **'82** 312; **'83** 284; **'84** 11, 122; **'86** 172
  and grocery shopping, **'88** 165; **'91** 188
  and meal planning, **'82** 312; **'83** 284; **'84** 11;
    '91 188
  telephone numbers for emergencies, **'84** 37
Low-fat, low-calorie foods
  substituting fresh herbs for salt, **'99** 208
  using frozen juice concentrate as a sweetener,
    '99 208
  using lemon or lime juice, **'99** 208
Mailing food, **'86** 289
Mangoes, **'94** 192
Manners. *See* **FOKTY/Etiquette.**
Margarine, **'82** 189
  availability of, **'82** 189
  diet margarine, **'82** 189
  fat content of, **'82** 189; **'90** 314
  storing, **'82** 189
  substituting in baked goods, **'90** 314; **'97** 134
Marinating, **'88** 165; **'95** 30
  containers to use, **'87** 208
Masa harina, **'94** 192
Mayonnaise
  recipe, Homemade Mayonnaise, **'99** 180
Meal planning, **'82** 312, 313; **'83** 191, 284;
  '84 122, 123; **'86** 13; **'88** 165, 276; **'99** 30. *See*
  also **FOKTY/Campsite cooking, Snacks.**
  advance planning, **'82** 312, 313; **'86** 172
  for a crowd, **'82** 313; **'86** 191
  for holidays, **'83** 284
  making lists, **'82** 312; **'83** 284; **'84** 11, 122;
    '86 172
  party menus, **'82** 313; **'84** 122, 123; **'86** 191;
    '88 276
Measuring, **'85** 192, 193; **'86** 13; **'98** 36
  butter, **'85** 192, 193
  determining cup measurement of dish,
    '85 193; **'96** 332
  dry measuring utensils, **'85** 192, 193
  how to measure accurately, **'85** 192, 193
  liquid measuring utensils, **'85** 192, 193
  sifting ingredients for, **'82** 197, 198;
    '85 192, 193; **'87** 12
  solid shortening, **'85** 192, 193
Meat loaf, additives, **'98** 138
Meats, **'89** 191, 192; **'91** 300; **'92** 202; **'99** 224.
  See also **FOKTY/Beef.**
  garnishing, **'97** 56
  handling properly, **'87** 208; **'99** 224
  meat-cure mix, **'91** 300
  serving safely, **'87** 208; **'91** 300
  standing time, **'89** 192
  suggested cooking temperatures, **'89** 191, 192;
    '92 202
  using a meat thermometer, **'89** 191, 192; **'92** 202
Melons, **'88** 183
  cantaloupe, **'88** 183
  honeydew, **'88** 183
  selecting, **'88** 183
  storing, **'88** 183
  watermelon, **'88** 183; **'96** 192; **'98** 198

Meringue, '83 214
  baking, **'83** 214
  equipment, **'83** 214
  humidity, effects of, **'83** 214
  making, **'83** 214
  powder, **'92** 314
  preventing weeping, **'83** 214; **'95** 246
  recipe, Dream Drops, **'99** 328
Microwave oven, '83 191; **'84** 211; **'86** 113, 227;
  '87 130; **'92** 176; **'99** 296
  cleaning, **'87** 130; **'99** 128
  cookware for, **'86** 227
  drying herbs in, **'98** 198
  features, **'86** 113
  recipe, Microwave Fudge, **'91** 92
  removing odors from, **'99** 30
  roasting peppers in, **'92** 176
  safety when using, **'91** 92
  sizes, **'86** 113
  steaming vegetables in, **'99** 296
  using to clean microwave cookware, **'98** 256
  variations of, **'86** 113
  wattage, **'86** 113
Muffins, preparing ahead, **'97** 174
Mushrooms
  as garnish, **'82** 280
  shiitake, **'97** 232
  slicing, **'98** 198
  storing, **'92** 314
Nopales. See **FOKTY/Cactus.**
Nutrition, '90 72; **'91** 200, 201; **'92** 65
  food labels, **'90** 72; **'92** 65
  snacks, **'91** 200, 201
Oils. See **FOKTY/Cooking oils, Olive oils,**
  Vegetable oil.
Olive oils, '89 175; **'98** 112
  flavored, **'89** 175
  selecting, **'89** 175
  storing, **'89** 175
  varieties of, **'89** 175; **'98** 112
Onions, '88 87; **'95** 30; **'98** 36
  caramelizing, **'98** 72
  chopping, **'92** 314; **'95** 246; **'97** 134
  cooking with, **'88** 87
  eliminating odor on hands, **'82** 109; **'94** 332;
  '96 51
  extracting onion juice, **'88** 87
  grating, **'92** 314; **'95** 30; **'97** 134
  paste, **'98** 218
  selecting, **'88** 87
  using in salads, **'96** 192
  varieties of, **'88** 87 (illustrations)
Oranges
  types of, **'99** 250
  using in recipes, **'99** 250
Outdoor cooking. See **FOKTY/Campsite**
  cooking, Grilling, Smoking (cooking
  method).
Ovens, '83 191; **'84** 211; **'86** 113; **'87** 130
  checking oven temperature, **'96** 230
  cleaning, **'87** 130
  convection, **'86** 113
  conventional, **'86** 113
  microwave, **'83** 191; **'84** 211; **'86** 113, 227;
  '87 130; **'92** 176
  preheating, **'86** 13
Pan sizes, **'96** 332; **'97** 112 (chart)
Paraffin, '89 244
  as a seal in canning, **'84** 180; **'89** 142; **'91** 300
Parchment paper, **'99** 250
Parsley, keeping fresh, **'98** 72
Pastas, '87 177; **'96** 208
  basic categories, **'87** 177
  cooking, **'87** 177; **'95** 30

  measuring, **'87** 177
  reheating, **'87** 177; **'95** 31
  storing, **'87** 177
  substituting, **'87** 177
Pastry. See **FOKTY/Piecrust.**
Peaches, uses for overripe fruit, **'97** 174
Peanut butter, **'96** 256
Peanuts, '83 228, 229
  boiling, **'83** 228
  chopping, **'83** 229
  roasting, **'83** 228
Pears, '85 233
  cooking, **'85** 233
  peeling, **'85** 233
  ripening, **'85** 233
  selecting, **'85** 233
Peas, dried, '88 4
  buying, **'88** 4
  cooking, **'88** 4
  soaking, **'88** 4
  storing, **'88** 4
Pecans, '83 228, 229; **'94** 59
  chopping, **'83** 229; **'95** 208
  as garnish, **'94** 59
  toasting, **'83** 228
Pepper, ground, cayenne, or red, **'98** 58
Peppers, '85 4; **'92** 176; **'94** 29; **'95** 30, 208
  as garnish, **'82** 280; **'89** 100
  freezing, **'85** 4
  removing skins of, **'85** 4
  roasting, **'92** 176
  selecting, **'94** 29
  storing, **'94** 29
  substituting, **'85** 4
  types of, **'85** 4; **'98** 218
  working with hot peppers, **'85** 4; **'94** 29;
  '95 208
Persimmons, '85 233
  freezing, **'85** 233
  preparing, **'85** 233
  selecting, **'85** 233
Pesto, paste, **'98** 218
Pickles, '87 150
  pickling vegetables, **'87** 150
  spoilage, **'87** 150
Piecrust, '82 234, 235; **'92** 52, 314; **'94** 210;
  '95 246; **'96** 76
  crumb crust, **'99** 250
  equipment, **'82** 234; **'94** 332; **'95** 208
  finishing, **'82** 234; **'98** 36
  flavor variations of, **'97** 72
  glazing, **'82** 235
  lining with melted chocolate, **'97** 36
  mixing, **'82** 234; **'92** 52; **'95** 246
  preventing overbrowning, **'92** 314; **'95** 30
  preventing sogginess, **'86** 330; **'91** 300;
  '92 314
  puff pastry, **'97** 56
  recipe, Water-Whipped Baked Pastry Shell,
  '95 246
  rolling, **'82** 234; **'92** 314
  variations of, **'82** 234, 235
Planning meals. See **FOKTY/Meal planning.**
Plastic containers, storing, **'99** 250
Poaching, '85 127
  eggs, **'85** 127
  equipment, **'85** 127
  fish, **'85** 127
  fruits, **'85** 127
  liquid to use, **'85** 127
Pork
  cooking, **'95** 246
  nutritional value, **'98** 198
  recipe, Barbecue Ribs, **'99** 68

Potatoes, '84 210, 211. See also **FOKTY/Sweet**
  potatoes.
  methods of mashing, **'97** 278
  preparing, **'84** 210, 211; **'97** 206; **'99** 100
  selecting, **'84** 210, 211; **'98** 256
  storing, **'84** 211; **'98** 256
  using to absorb too much pepper or salt in
  cooking, **'96** 76
Poultry. See **FOKTY/Chicken, Turkey.**
Pound cakes. See **FOKTY/Cakes.**
Puddings, '86 330; **'96** 256. See also
  FOKTY/Custards.
  preventing "skin" from forming, **'86** 330
Pumpkins, '85 233
  as jack-o'-lanterns, **'97** 232
  preparing for cooking, **'85** 233
  selecting, **'85** 233
  storing, **'85** 233
  substituting canned for fresh, **'98** 256
  using pumpkin shell as serving container,
  '98 256
Raspberries, making sauce, **'92** 314
Recipe preparation, '86 13; **'91** 22, 23; **'93** 235;
  '96 76; **'99** 30. See also **FOKTY/Cooking**
  directions, Handling food properly,
  Substitutions.
  baking techniques, **'89** 57; **'98** 218
  cleaning up, **'86** 13; **'95** 31 (illustration);
  '98 198, 256; **'99** 100, 128, 224
  cutting recipes for smaller yields, **'97** 184
  determining solutions to problems, **'93** 235;
  '96 21, 76
  doubling recipes, **'91** 22, 23; **'92** 66;
  '95 30
  equipment, **'86** 13; **'96** 160, 208; **'98** 218
  freezing berries, **'98** 138
  greasing bakeware, **'98** 238
  measuring, **'86** 13; **'95** 274
  parchment paper, **'99** 250
  planning menus, **'86** 13
  preparing ingredients, **'86** 13;
  '95 30, 31 (illustration), 208
  presentation, **'99** 128, 148
  shortcuts in, **'96** 256
  tasting along the way, **'98** 138
  tubes of paste: onion, pesto, tomato,
  '98 218
  utensils, **'86** 13
Recipes, organizing, **'98** 198
Recycling, '92 28
  items to be recycled, **'92** 28
  packaging of products, **'92** 28
  setting up home recycling center,
  '92 28
  the three Rs, **'92** 28
Refrigerator, '83 94; **'87** 130
  canned foods (opened), **'83** 94
  cleaning, **'84** 11; **'87** 130
  dairy products, **'83** 94
  food storage chart, **'83** 94
  meats, **'83** 94
Rice, '87 46
  cooking, **'95** 30; **'98** 238
  flavoring, **'87** 46
  preparing, **'87** 46
  reheating, **'87** 46
  storing, **'87** 46
  types of, **'87** 46; **'99** 208
Rolls, '83 323. See also **FOKTY/Biscuits,**
  Breads, Yeast.
  glazing, **'83** 323
  removing burned bottoms from, **'96** 51
  variations of, **'83** 323
  yeast, **'83** 323

FROM OUR KITCHEN TO YOURS (FOKTY)
(continued)

Roux, '87 211, 212
  color of, '87 211, 212
  cooking temperature, '87 211
  cooking times, '87 211
  ingredient amounts, '87 211
  microwave roux, '87 211, 212
  oven roux, '87 211
  reducing fat in roux, '87 212
  utensils to use, '87 212
Safety, '84 37, 180; '90 22; '91 92, 300. *See also*
    FOKTY/Handling food properly.
  canning fruits and vegetables, '84 180;
    '91 300
  extinguishing a range-top fire, '99 50
  first aid for burns, '90 22; '99 50
  in the kitchen, '84 37; '90 22; '96 256;
    '99 50
  preventing burns in the kitchen, '84 37; '90 22
  when serving food, '91 300
  when using the microwave, '91 92
Salad dressings, '97 184
Salads, '82 313; '91 300
  congealed, '82 313; '91 300
  equipment, '94 332
  washing salad greens, '97 36
Sauces, '83 146, 147; '92 314; '94 274; '95 30
  chilling quickly, '86 13
  reduction sauces, '94 274; '96 332
  thickening, '83 146, 147
Sausage, '87 238
  classifications of, '87 238
  freezing, '87 238
  meat-cure mix, '91 300
Scallops, '99 180
  amounts to buy, '99 180
  cooking, '99 180
  selecting, '99 180
  types of, '99 180
Seafood, '90 130. *See also* **FOKTY/Crab, Fish,**
    Scallops, Shellfish, Shrimp, Surimi.
Seasonings, '92 121, 344; '93 182; '96 304. *See*
    also **FOKTY/Herbs, Spices.**
  in recipes, '91 22
  recipes for seasoning blends, '92 121
  storing, '82 198; '84 11; '92 121; '98 36
  substitutions, '92 344
Shelf life, '83 65
  of canned foods, '83 65
  chart, '83 65
  of packaged mixes, '83 65
  of staples, '83 65
Shellfish, '94 105, 106
  buying, '94 106
  transporting fresh, '94 105, 106
Shopping. *See* **FOKTY/Grocery shopping.**
Shrimp, '87 12; '94 105, 106
  cooking, '87 12
  deveining, '92 52
  grilling, '92 52
  selecting, '94 106
  transporting fresh, '94 105
Sifting, '82 197, 198; '85 192, 193; '87 12
  flour, '82 197, 198; '87 12
  powdered sugar, '85 192; '87 12
Silver, '88 300
  avoiding spotting and pitting, '88 300
  cleaning, '88 300
  removing tarnish from, '88 300
  serving spoons, '99 296
  storing, '88 300

Smoking (cooking method), '95 116
  adding the food, '95 116
  cleaning the smoker, '95 117
  filling the water pan, '95 116
  maintaining the temperature, '95 116
  soaking the wood, '95 116
  starting the fire, '95 116
Snacks, '91 200, 201
  nutritious, '91 200, 201
  planning, '91 200, 201
  recipes for, '91 200, 201
Sodium, '90 72
  content of in surimi, '90 130
  and food labels, '90 72
Soufflés, '84 92
  testing for doneness, '84 92
Soups, '89 30; '95 274; '96 160. *See also*
    FOKTY/Stews.
  as appetizers, '98 112
  broths, '89 30; '98 138
  freezing, '89 30
  as gifts, '91 95
  presentation, '98 112
  pureeing, '99 250
  reheating, '89 30
  removing bay leaf, '95 314
  stocks, '89 30; '95 30
  storing, '89 30
Spaghetti sauce, substituting vegetable juice for
    tomato sauce, '98 256
Spices, '87 297; '99 180. *See also* **FOKTY/**
    Herbs, Seasonings.
  amounts to use, '87 297; '99 208
  buying, '87 297; '98 58
  checking for freshness, '84 11; '87 297;
    '98 58
  grinding your own, '87 297; '98 58
  sprinkle opening, '99 180
  storing, '82 198; '84 11; '87 297; '98 58
  substituting, '87 297
  toasting, '98 58
  whole spices, '87 297; '98 58
Squash, winter, '88 229, 230
  cooking, '88 229, 230
  determining amount to buy, '88 229
  selecting, '88 229, 230
  storing, '88 229, 230
  types of, '88 229, 230
Stains, removing, '96 304; '99 100
Stews, baking in oven, '98 256
Stir frying, '95 30
Stocks. *See* **FOKTY/Soups.**
Strawberries, '82 109
  buying, '82 109
  as garnish, '82 138
  preparing, '99 100
Substitutions, '92 344; '96 208; '98 256
  alcohol, '92 314; '99 148
  emergency substitutions, '92 344 (chart)
  flour, '99 224
  lemon juice, '99 100
  using tofu as a substitution, '99 128
  vinegar, '99 100
Sugar, '85 19
  making colored sugar, '86 331
  making lemon sugar, '97 56
  measuring, '85 19; '87 12
  powdered sugar, '87 12; '96 51
  preventing brown sugar from drying out, '85 19
  sifting powdered sugar, '85 192; '87 12
  softening brown, '98 198
  substitutions, '85 19
  types of, '85 19
Surimi, '90 130

Sweet potatoes, '88 208. *See also*
    FOKTY/Potatoes.
  cooking, '88 208
  handling, '88 208
  selecting, '88 208
  storing, '88 208
  substituting canned for fresh, '88 208
  yams, '88 208
Table setting, '90 182, 225
  centerpieces, '90 205; '98 72
  for formal entertaining, '90 182
  illustration, '90 182
Tahini, '96 304
Tamales, '94 192. *See also* **FOKTY/Masa harina.**
  making tamale dough, '94 192
Tapioca, as a thickening agent, '83 147
Tarts, '95 274
Tea, '85 120, 121
  brewing, '85 120, 121
  storing, '85 121
  types of, '85 120, 121
Thawing food, '83 14, 15; '86 330; '87 208;
    '88 165
  turkey, '83 284; '86 330
Thermometers, '89 191, 192; '92 202; '98 306
  deep-fat frying, '84 37
  instant-read, '89 191, 192; '92 202, 314;
    '93 104
  meat, '89 191, 192; '92 202
  storing, '89 192; '92 202
  testing for accuracy, '89 192; '92 202; '96 230
Thickening agents, '83 146, 147. *See also*
    FOKTY/Arrowroot, Cornstarch, Eggs,
    Tapioca.
Tofu, '99 128
Tomatillos, about, '97 232
Tomatoes, '85 181, 182; '93 23; '95 30
  drying cherry tomatoes, '93 23
  freezing leftover paste, '96 160
  as garnish, '82 280; '89 100
  paste, '98 218
  peeling large amount of, '82 138; '85 181, 182
  recipe, Marinated Dried Cherry Tomatoes,
    '93 23
  ripening, '85 181
  seeding, '85 182
  selecting, '85 181
  slicing, '85 181, 182
  storing, '85 181
  stuffing, '85 182
Tortillas, '95 44
  equipment, '95 44
  how to cook, '95 44
  how to shape, '95 44
  recipe, Flour Tortillas, '95 44
  reheating, '95 44
  storing, '95 44
Turkey, '83 284, 285; '93 306, 307
  carving, '93 306, 307
  chart, '83 285
  cooking, '83 284, 285; '86 330; '98 306
  determining amounts to buy for entertaining,
    '90 276; '99 296
  handling properly, '87 208
  leftovers, storing, '83 285; '98 306
  recipe, Benny Sauce Marinated Turkey, '98 306
  selecting fresh or frozen, '99 296
  stuffing, '83 284; '98 306
  thawing, '83 284; '86 330; '98 306; '99 296
U.S. Department of Agriculture (USDA), '89 142;
    '90 72; '92 65, 202; '93 83
Vegetable cooking spray, '92 208; '98 138
  cleanup, easy, '82 198, 314; '84 48; '92 314;
    '93 104; '95 31

Vegetable oil, '82 189; **'84** 211; **'88** 112, 113; **'98** 112
  deep-fat frying thermometer, **'84** 37; **'88** 113
  preventing fire, **'84** 37; **'88** 112, 113
Vegetables, '82 138; **'83** 94; **'84** 180, 211, 249; **'86** 140, 141; **'89** 243, 244; **'92** 344; **'93** 132; **'94** 29, 92; **'95** 30. *See also* **FOKTY/ Broccoli, Brussels sprouts, Canning, Cauliflower, Corn, Garnishes, Greens, Lettuce, Mushrooms, Onions, Peas, Peppers, Potatoes, Pumpkins, Squash, Sweet potatoes, Tomatoes.**
  basic cooking methods, **'82** 138; **'84** 249; **'94** 29, 92 (chart)
  canning, **'84** 180; **'93** 136, 137
  as "containers" for food, **'97** 174
  cutting, **'86** 13; **'92** 52; **'93** 132; **'94** 29; **'96** 21; **'98** 72
  determining amounts to buy for entertaining, **'90** 276
  freezing, **'87** 112
  grilling, **'83** 191; **'92** 52; **'95** 274; **'97** 56
  growing your own, **'98** 112
  microwaving, **'82** 138; **'83** 191; **'99** 296
  preparing, **'86** 140, 141; **'89** 243, 244; **'98** 238; **'99** 100
  seasoning, **'94** 92 (chart)
  selecting, **'84** 249; **'86** 140, 141; **'89** 243, 244; **'94** 29
  steaming, **'99** 296
  stir-frying, **'82** 138; **'83** 191
  storing, **'83** 94; **'84** 211; **'86** 140, 141; **'89** 243, 244; **'94** 29; **'96** 208
  substitutions, **'92** 344
  winter vegetables, **'84** 249; **'88** 229
Vinegar
  as a stain remover, **'99** 100
  as a substitute in recipes, **'99** 100
  using to enhance flavors, **'99** 100
Water, adding flavor to bottled or tap water, **'96** 21
Web sites, watermelon, **'98** 198
Whipping cream, **'97** 72
White chocolate. *See* **FOKTY/Chocolate.**
Wines, '85 292, 293; **'98** 162; **'99** 30, 328
  amounts to buy for entertaining, **'99** 328
  champagne, **'85** 293; **'96** 21; **'98** 306; **'99** 328
  chilling, **'99** 328
  removing the cork, **'99** 328
  selecting, **'85** 292; **'99** 30, 68, 100, 128, 224, 328
  selecting in restaurants, **'96** 140
  serving, **'85** 292, 293; **'99** 328
  storing, **'85** 292
  sugar content of, **'99** 328
Wok cooking, '85 76
  equipment, **'85** 76
  preparing food for, **'85** 76
Yams. *See* **FOKTY/Sweet potatoes.**
Yeast, '89 268. *See also* **FOKTY/Biscuits, Breads, Rolls.**
  kinds of, **'89** 268
  using leftover, **'99** 50
Yogurt, instead of fruit puree, **'97** 206
FROSTINGS. *See also* **FILLINGS, GLAZES, TOPPINGS.**
Almond Buttercream Frosting, **'97** 61; **'99** 155
Almond-Butter Frosting, **'86** 107
Amaretto Buttercream Frosting, **'98** 57
Amaretto Frosting, **'86** 246
Apricot Frosting, **'81** 192
Banana-Nut Frosting, **'79** 115
Boiled Frosting, **'90** 45; **'92** 14; **'93** 318
Bourbon Frosting, **'88** 236
Brandy Cream Frosting, **'86** 239
Browned Butter Frosting, **'97** 247

Brown Sugar Frosting, **'79** 13; **'87** 296; **'91** 236
Brown Sugar Meringue Frosting, **'81** 70
Buttercream Frosting, **'85** 322; **'92** 230; **'93** 53, 285; **'96** 96; **'98** 155
Butter Cream Frosting, **'88** 279
Buttercream Frosting, White, **'93** 337
Buttercream Icing, **'83** 73
Buttercream, Spiced, **'84** 226
Butter Frosting, **'80** 129
Butter Frosting, Browned, **'86** 248
Butter Frosting, Williamsburg, **'81** 120; **'82** 23
Buttermilk Frosting, **'85** 249
Butter Pecan Frosting, **'80** 229
Butter Whip Frosting, **'96** 119
Caramel Frosting, **'81** 278, M289; **'82** 314; **'83** 43; **'84** 39, 263; **'86** 239; **'87** 265; **'89** 55, 236; **'90** 307; **'98** 195
Caramel Frosting, Creamy, **'81** 71
Caramel Frosting, Easy, **'87** 39
Caramel Frosting, Favorite, **'83** 106
Carob Frosting, **'85** 218
Carolina Dream Frosting, **'88** 278
Cheese Spread, Tropical, **'95** 46
Cherry Frosting, **'86** 217
Cherry-Nut Cream Cheese Frosting, **'96** 249
Chocolate
  Almond Frosting, Chocolate-, **'83** 241
  Buttercream Frosting, Chocolate, **'96** 229; **'98** M100
  Butter Frosting, Chocolate, **'89** 271
  Buttermilk Frosting, Chocolate-, **'99** 99
  Candy Frosting, Chocolate, **'81** 238
  Cherry Frosting, Chocolate-, **'89** 294
  Chocolate Frosting, **'80** M171; **'81** 265; **'82** 262; **'83** 79, 99, M233, 253; **'84** 200; **'85** 323; **'86** 8, 93, 138, 239, 314; **'87** M97, 198, 199, 293; **'89** M25; **'90** 194, 252, 265, 284, 309; **'91** 248; **'92** 319; **'93** 239; **'94** 133; **'96** 253, 254; **'97** M87, 254; **'99** 271
  Cocoa Frosting, **'86** 60
  Coconut Chocolate Frosting, **'79** 13
  Coffee Frosting, Chocolate-, **'84** 36; **'88** 269
  Cola Frosting, Chocolate-, **'95** 56
  Creamy Chocolate Frosting, **'85** 314; **'86** 316; **'87** 241; **'99** 307
  Fluffy Chocolate Frosting, **'86** 336; **'87** 58
  Fudge Frosting, **'81** 303; **'87** 296; **'89** 56; **'94** 51
  Fudge Frosting, Chocolate, **'83** 105
  Fudge Frosting, Quick, **'81** 278
  Ganache, Chocolate, **'93** 255
  Honey Chocolate Frosting, **'79** 83
  Kahlúa Frosting, Chocolate, **'91** 298
  Marshmallow Frosting, Chocolate-, **'83** 245
  Mint Chocolate Frosting, **'99** M176
  Mocha Buttercream, **'89** 42
  Mocha Butter Cream Frosting, **'79** 281
  Mocha-Buttercream Frosting, **'86** 26
  Mocha Frosting, **'83** 301; **'84** 316; **'87** 224; **'94** 292; **'97** 35; **'99** 66
  Mocha Frosting, Creamy, **'82** 289; **'84** 311; **'91** 248
  Nut Frosting, Chocolate, **'80** 140
  Peanut Butter Frosting, Chocolate-, **'84** 240; **'87** 222
  Peanut Butter-Fudge Frosting, **'87** 184
  Perfect Chocolate Frosting, **'90** 307
  Rich Chocolate Frosting, **'84** 304
  Rum Frosting, Chocolate, **'79** 67
  Satiny Chocolate Frosting, **'85** 126; **'89** 43
  White Chocolate Buttercream Frosting, **'97** M284
  White Chocolate-Cream Cheese Frosting, **'94** 58; **'98** 323

  White Chocolate-Cream Cheese Tiered Cake Frosting, **'94** 125
  White Chocolate Frosting, **'88** 280; **'91** 101; **'97** 111
Cinnamon-Cream Frosting, **'84** 311
Cinnamon Frosting, Buttery, **'81** M139
Coconut Cream Cheese Frosting, **'86** 60
Coconut Frosting, **'82** 262; **'91** 269
Coconut Frosting, Creamy, **'80** 287
Coconut Frosting, Nutty, **'86** 8
Coconut-Pecan Frosting, **'81** 296; **'83** M233; **'84** 43, 322; **'97** 99
Coffee Buttercream, **'95** 277
Coffee Buttercream Frosting, **'99** 155
Coffee Frosting, **'94** 86
Cola Frosting, **'81** 238
Colored Frostings, **'90** 21
Cream Cheese Frosting, **'79** 45; **'80** 140, 253, 299; **'82** 135, 244; **'83** 105, 215, M233; **'84** 201, 255, 315, 316; **'85** 118, 121; **'86** 217, 337; **'87** 58; **'90** 305, 308; **'92** 120; **'93** 20; **'94** 254; **'95** 139; **'96** 282; **'97** 230, 277, 330; **'98** 275; **'99** 307, 315
Cream Cheese Frosting, Deluxe, **'80** 120
Cream Cheese Frosting, Fluffy, **'80** 245
Cream Cheese Frosting, Nutty, **'85** 117; **'96** 263
Crème Chantilly, **'87** 9; **'91** 297
Crème de Menthe Frosting, **'86** 245; **'93** 256; **'97** 35
Decorating Techniques, Cake, **'83** 72, 240
Decorator Frosting, **'82** 20, 307; **'83** 106; **'87** 86; **'91** 282; **'93** 285
Decorator Frosting, Creamy, **'79** 117
Decorator Frosting, Green, **'93** 286
Decorator Frosting, Yellow, **'93** 283
Divinity Frosting, **'79** 229
Fluffy Frosting, **'79** 246; **'86** 235; **'88** 268; **'89** 254; **'90** 308
Fluffy White Frosting, **'90** 105; **'95** 319
Fondant, Faux, **'98** M154
Fondant, Rolled, **'92** 69
Ganache Cream, **'92** 318
Grapefruit Frosting, **'89** 308
Heavenly Frosting, **'80** 140
Lemon
  Buttercream Frosting, Lemon, **'83** 301; **'86** 61; **'91** 247
  Butter Cream Frosting, Lemon-, **'85** 117
  Coconut Frosting, Lemon-, **'90** 253
  Cream Cheese Frosting, Lemon-, **'81** 157
  Creamy Lemon Frosting, **'79** 93
  Lemon Frosting, **'85** 191; **'86** 217; **'93** 81
  Orange-Lemon Frosting, **'88** 92
  White Frosting, Lemony, **'88** 7
Maple Frosting, **'82** 217; **'85** 322; **'96** 17
Meringue Frosting, **'86** 336; **'87** 84; **'99** 118
Meringue Frosting, Italian, **'98** 70
Mint Cream Frosting, **'93** 216
Mint Frosting, **'88** 80
Never Fail Frosting, **'86** 314
Orange
  Buttercream Frosting, Orange, **'80** 70; **'99** 117
  Butter Frosting, Orange, **'83** 300
  Cream Cheese Frosting, Citrus, **'99** 223
  Cream Cheese Frosting, Orange, **'81** 70; **'82** 16; **'92** 19
  Cream Frosting, Orange, **'81** 207; **'82** 14
  Creamy Orange Frosting, **'83** 24, 241
  Lemon Frosting, Orange-, **'88** 92
  Orange Frosting, **'81** 7; **'86** 61; **'88** 119
Panocha Frosting, **'89** 296
Peanut Butter Frosting, **'83** 223; **'84** 153; **'85** 34
Peanut Butter Swirl Frosting, **'86** 109
Peanut Frosting, Creamy, **'80** 87

FROSTINGS
(continued)

Pecan Frosting, '86 86
Peppermint Birthday Cake Frosting, Pink,
   '92 269
Peppermint Cream Cheese Frosting, '98 308
Peppermint Frosting, Quick, '98 308
Pineapple-Cream Cheese Frosting, '95 160
Piping Icing, '92 69
Piping Icing, Tips for, '84 302
Powdered Sugar Frosting, '96 319
Quick Pour Frosting, '85 119
Royal Icing, '80 278; '81 21; '83 73; '84 303;
   '85 323; '87 295; '88 309; '91 281; '98 324
Rum Buttercream Frosting, '99 117
Rum Cream, '88 154, 224
Sea Foam Frosting, '81 211; '91 271
Seven-Minute Double Boiler Frosting, '81 278
Seven-Minute Frosting, '80 289; '83 299, 301;
   '87 296; '89 55, 57; '94 98, 99; '97 71
Snow Peak Frosting, '82 53; '85 281
Spiced Cream, '89 215
Strawberry Frosting, '89 184
Toffee Frosting, English, '85 125
Vanilla Buttercream Frosting, '92 239; '94 99;
   '96 229; '97 111; '99 117
Vanilla Frosting, '84 36; '85 236; '92 14, 274
Vanilla-Rum Frosting, '85 324
Whipped Cream Frosting, '83 229; '85 125;
   '87 263; '89 43; '93 86; '96 229
White Chocolate-Cream Cheese Frosting, '94 58
White Frosting, '83 268
White Frosting, Fluffy, '81 278
White Frosting, Luscious, '81 71
FRUIT. *See also* **specific types.**
Acorn Squash, Fruited, '85 235
Acorn Squash, Fruit-Stuffed, '81 295
Appetizers
   Bowl, Sparkling Fresh Fruit, '80 146
   Brie, Tropical Breeze, '94 M18
   Brown Sugar Dip with Fruit, Buttery, '90 243
   Canapés, Fruit-Topped, '85 80
   Cascade, Fruit, '86 104
   Cheese Ball, Fruit-and-Nut, '91 251
   Cup, Appetizer Fruit, '86 131
   Curried Rum Sauce, Tropical Fruit with,
      '91 164
   Dip, Ginger Fruit, '96 110
   Dip, Orange Fruit, '96 190
   Fresh Fruit, Mint Dip with, '87 146
   Fresh Fruit with Lemon Sauce, '82 290
   Kabobs with Coconut Dressing, Fruit, '87 251
   Soup, Cold Fresh Fruit, '87 157
   Soup, Swedish Fruit, '82 313; '83 65
   Spread, Fruit and Cheese, '81 245
   Spread, Fruited Cream Cheese, '91 306
   Spread, Nutty Fruit-and-Cheese, '87 246
Bake, Cranberry-Mustard Fruit, '90 287
Baked Fruit, Gingered, '81 232
Baked Fruit, Ginger-Orange, '93 313
Baked Spiced Fruit, '89 305
Bake, Hot Fruit, '81 270
Bake, Mustard Fruit, '90 291
Bake, Nutty Fruit, '83 127
Bars, Fruit and Nut Granola, '81 49
Beets, Fruited, '97 28
Beverages
   Apricot Fruit Flip, '91 18
   Blender Fruit Beverage, '83 318
   Breakfast Fruit Juicy, '86 176
   Brew, Fruity Witches', '95 273
   Champagne Fruit Slush, '90 322

Champions' Cooler, '96 M181
Citrus Blush, '98 197
Cocktails, Sea Breeze, '97 161
Cooler, Four-Fruit, '86 101
Cooler, Fruited Wine, '86 176
Cooler, Fruit Juice, '92 67
Coolers, Fruit, '98 197
Float, Frosty Fruit, '87 159
Four-Fruit Refresher, '79 174
Frappé, Hootenanny, '89 110
Honey-Yogurt Smoothie, Fruited, '88 231;
   '89 23
Ice Tropical, '79 174
Patio Blush, '99 93
Punch, Autumn Harvest, '96 277
Punch, Can-Can Fruit, '94 122
Punch, Caribbean, '95 173
Punch, Citrus-Wine, '98 197
Punch, Florida Fruit, '92 247
Punch for a Bunch, '95 90
Punch, Fresh Fruit, '98 155
Punch, Fruit, '83 52
Punch, Fruited Ice-Cube, '98 197
Punch, Fruit Juice, '96 214
Punch, Fruit Juice-and-Vodka, '96 214
Punch, Fruit Juicy Rum, '91 175
Punch, Fruit Slush, '91 278
Punch, Golden Fruit, '80 299; '83 56; '96 278
Punch, Happy New Year, '98 26
Punch, Holiday Fruit, '79 232
Punch, Holiday Hot Fruit, '92 286
Punch, Hot Fruit, '83 33
Punch, Hot Spiced, '96 214
Punch, Hot Spiced Rum, '96 214
Punch, Margarita, '98 88
Punch, Mixed Fruit, '90 207; '95 239
Punch, Party Fruit, '82 137
Punch, Passion Fruit, '90 169
Punch, Polka Dot, '95 178
Punch, Slushy Fruit, '98 92
Punch, Southern Fresh Fruit, '99 70
Punch, Southern Fruit, '95 238
Punch, Spiced Fruit, '88 2
Punch, Spirited Fruit, '81 100
Punch, Summertime Fruit, '80 160
Punch, Sunset, '96 278
Punch, Tropical Fruit, '81 51; '83 176; '90 169
Refresher, Fruit, '91 203
'ritas, Fruit, '94 157
Sangría, Mock Tea, '99 336
Sangría, Three-Fruit, '89 212
Shake, Frosty Fruit, '87 23
Shake, Tangy Fruit, '95 129
Shake, Tropical, '93 212
Slush, Fruit, '96 157
Slushy, Fruit, '80 146
Smoothie, Citrus, '98 17
Smoothie, Fruit, '89 87
Smoothie, Two-Fruit, '89 182
Sparkle, Fruit, '99 289
Sparkler, Tangerine, '98 54
Tea, Christmas Orange, '83 275
Tea Cooler, Fruited, '94 131
Tea, Fruit-and-Mint Iced, '98 84
Tea, Fruited Mint, '88 79; '91 81
Tea, Hot Russian, '97 274
Tea, Hot Spiced Fruit, '87 242
Tea, Refreshing Fruit, '97 122
Tea-Ser, Tropical, '95 200
Tea, Spiced Iced, '97 121
Three-Fruit Drink, '79 38; '80 50; '87 199
Tropical Fruit Drink, '85 43
Tropical Fruit Whisper, '89 212
Tropical Refresher, '96 157

Wassail, '97 240; '99 268
Wassail, Golden, '96 278
Boats, Honeydew Fruit, '81 147
Braid, Fruit-and-Cheese, '86 214
Brandied Fruit, Hot, '80 48
Bread, Cranberry Fruit-Nut, '79 275
Bread, Fruity Banana, '95 78
Bread, Kahlúa Fruit-Nut, '79 235
Canning and Preserving
   Apple Rings, Cinnamon, '85 107
   Berries (except Strawberries), '80 128
   Conserve, Dried Fruit, '82 308
   Dehydration Chart, Fruit and Vegetable, '84 147
   Freezing Chart, Fruit, '85 187
   Jam, Tri-Berry Lemon, '98 214
   Juices, Fruit, '85 107
   Mixed Fruit, Unsweetened, '83 182
   Peaches, '80 128
   Peaches and Pears, '85 106
   Peaches, Honey-Sweet, '85 107
   Preserves, Fruity, '98 214
   Syrup, Fruit, '86 176
Chafing Dish Fruit, '89 305
Chilled Fruit with Dressing, '85 222
Chutney, Autumn Fruit, '88 M230
Chutney, Fall Fruit, '97 218
Compotes
   Amaretto-Hot Fruit Compote, '90 250
   Baked Fruit Compote, '80 276; '84 314; '87 228
   Baked Mustard Fruit Compote, '85 47
   Beauberries Bordeaux, '98 18
   Brandied Fruit Compote, '96 286
   Champagne Fruit Compote, '81 309; '82 124
   Chilled Fruit Compote, '83 123
   Citrus Compote, '98 17
   Citrus Compote with Caramel Syrup, '98 313
   Dried Fruit Compote, '98 18
   Festive Fruit Compote, '94 279
   Fresh Fruit Compote, '79 162; '82 197, 272;
      '84 82; '94 190
   Fruit Compote, '86 330
   Gingered Fruit Compote, '88 184
   Hot Fruit Compote, '81 203; '83 53; '86 324;
      '90 124
   Jícama-Fruit Compote, '92 49
   Mixed Fruit Compote, '93 123
   Praline Fruit Compote, Warm, '85 260
   Pudding Compote, Fresh Fruit, '86 151
   Raspberry Puree, Fruit Compote with, '88 81
   Wine Fruit Compote, '81 272
Cornish Hens with Tropical Fruit, Grilled, '97 310
Couscous with Mixed Fruit, '95 232
Cup, Fruit, '81 141; '91 202
Cup, Mixed Fruit, '94 60
Cups, Honeydew Fruit, '82 179
Cup, Tipsy Fruit, '81 268
Curried Fruit, Almond-, '83 261
Curried Fruit Bake, '87 241
Curried Fruit, Hot, '79 225; '81 264; '84 287;
   '95 72
Delight, Fruit, '86 131
Delight, Winter Fruit, '80 243
Desserts. *See also* **FRUIT/Fruitcakes.**
   Amaretto Crème on Fresh Fruit, '93 176
   Balls, Fruit, '82 296; '84 299
   Bavarian Cream with Fresh Fruit, '88 137
   Biscotti, Fruitcake, '96 281
   Brandied Fruit Starter, '82 249
   Brie with Fresh Fruit, Caramel, '90 266
   Briwatts with Fruit, '98 211
   Cake, Fruit-and-Cereal Brunch, '88 263
   Cake, Fruit and Spice, '87 M97
   Cake, Fruited Pound, '81 265
   Cake, Fruity Ice Cream, '87 110

Cake, Holiday Lane, '99 306
Cake, Southern Custard Crêpe, '99 166
Cake, Spicy Fruited Carrot, '85 117
Cake, Stately Fruit-and-Nut, '84 226
Caribbean Fruit Dessert, '84 314
Cheese, and Nuts, Fruit, '93 324
Cheesecake, Fruit-Glazed, '80 24; '90 162
Cobbler, Fruit, '99 33
Cobbler, Quick Fruit, '91 20
Cookies, Bourbon Fruit, '86 334
Cookies, Fruitcake, '79 291; '86 320; '88 286; '96 314; '98 294
Cookies, Fruitcake Drop, '92 275
Cookies, Holiday Fruitcake, '81 301
Cookies, Rolled Fruit, '80 15
Cookies, Spicy Holiday Fruit, '83 298
Cream Cheese, Fruited, '85 306
Cream Freeze, Fruit, '82 144
Cream Puffs, Tutti-Frutti, '79 231
Crêpes, Fruit-Filled Chocolate, '89 325
Crêpes, Tropical, '86 275
Crêpes, Tropical Fruit, '87 77
Crisp, Fruit, '94 168
Cup, Fruit, '81 141
Cup, Snowball Citrus, '79 2
Cup, Vanilla Fruit, '80 183
Curried Fruit, Hot, '95 72
Custard over Fruit, Stirred, '84 83
Custard with Fresh Fruit, Citrus, '93 70
Drops, Candied Fruit, '89 329
Dumplings, Delicious Fruit, '97 210
Elegant Fruit, '91 91
Filling, Crêpes with Fruit, '81 96
Filling, Fruit-Nut, '80 289
Filling, Mixed Fruit Fried Pie, '96 109
Filling, Nutty Fruit, '99 306
Filling, Tutti-Frutti, '79 231
Flaming Fruit Dessert, '83 302
Freeze, Holiday Fruit, '88 283
Fresh Fruit with Cheese, Luscious, '79 153
Frozen Fruit Cream, '94 129
Frozen Fruit Cups, '93 197
Glazed Fruit, '85 83
Ice Cream, Tutti-Frutti, '86 129
Ice, Fruit, '86 176
Ice, Mixed Fruit, '81 178; '88 85
Ice, Tropical, '99 105
Island Fruit Chill, '98 180
Kabobs, Fruit, '86 181
Kabobs with Mint Marinade, Fruit, '82 157
Lemon Curd, Fresh Fruit with, '88 21
Marinated Fruit Bowl, '80 297
Meringue Baskets with Fresh Fruit and Ice Cream, '98 179
Meringue Shells, Fruit-Filled, '86 151
Meringues, Tropical, '98 71
Parfait, Tropical Trilogy, '92 247
Pie, Bumbleberry, '97 163
Pie, Crispy-Crust Fruit, '88 68
Pie, Fruitcake, '80 237
Pie, Fruited Cheese, '92 228
Pie, Fruit-Topped Vanilla Cream, '84 49
Pie, Japanese Fruit, '80 238
Pies, Baked Fruit, '84 7
Pizza, Peanut Butter-Fruit, '94 60
Planter's Punch Dessert, '95 175
Pops, Fruit, '87 168
Pudding, Fruited Rice, '86 95
Pudding, Summer, '98 217
Puff, Giant Fruit, '85 72
Puff Pastry Baskets, Tropical, '93 177
Puree, Fruit, '94 190
Rainbow Fruit Dessert, '85 108
Refresher, Grape Juice-Fruit, '86 182

Rugelach, Fruit, '97 220
Rumtopf, '95 142
Sauce, Fruit, '81 177
Sauce, Golden Fruit, '89 281
Sauce, Hot Fruit Dessert, '87 299
Sauce, Quick Fruit, '82 212
Sauce, Rum-Fruit, '84 312
Shells, Fruited Meringue, '87 32
Sherbet, Freezer Fruit, '86 334
Sherbet, Frozen Fruit, '79 155
Sherbet, Fruit Punch, '86 129
Sherbet, Instant Fruit, '85 158
Sherried Fruit Flame, '85 313
Slush, Refreshing Fruit, '82 35
Sorbet, Tropical, '97 110
Soup Dessert, Fruit, '79 172
Soup, Fresh Fruit, '98 196
Spiced Fruit Dessert, '82 50
Squares, Christmas Fruit, '88 282
Sugarplum Sticks, '95 321
Tart, Fancy Fruit, '82 128; '91 119
Tart, Fresh Fruit, '84 178; '90 58
Tart, King Cake Fruit, '96 57
Tartlets, Fresh Fruit, '93 96
Tart, Open-Face Fruit, '84 207
Tart, Rainbow Fruit, '82 304
Tarts, Bowl-Me-Over Fresh Fruit, '93 200
Tequila, Fruit in, '82 223
Topping, Fruity Dessert, '82 167
Trifle, Olde English, '95 331
Turnovers, Fruit, '79 150
Winter Fruit with Custard Sauce, '88 251
Dips
Coconut-Honey Fruit Dip, '84 171
Cranberry Fruit Dip, '89 60
Cream Cheese Dip, Fruited, '88 261
Fresh Fruit Dip, '80 265; '95 94
Heavenly Fruit Dip, '81 160
Marshmallow Fruit Dip, '84 171
Quick Fruit Dip, '90 110
Sweet Fruit Dip, '89 328
Tropical Dip for Fruit, '91 252
Yogurt Dip, Fruited, '84 171
Dressings. *See also* **FRUIT/Stuffings.**
Avocado Fruit Salad Dressing, '82 93
Baked Fruit Dressing, '87 253
Coconut-Fruit Dressing, Tangy, '84 171
Cornbread Dressing, Fruited, '80 262
Fluffy Fruit Dressing, '79 69
Fresh Fruit Dressing, '87 134
Lime-Honey Fruit Salad Dressing, '87 81
Marmalade-Fruit Dressing, '84 171
Nutty Fruit Dressing, '88 68
Pecan Dressing, Fruit-and-, '84 252
Salad Dressing for Fruit, '86 40
Salad, Dressing for Fruit, '87 81
Salad Dressing for Fruit, '79 69; '93 184
Turkey Dressing, Fruited, '99 257
Whipped Cream Fruit Dressing, '79 270
Filling, Fruit, '94 245
Filling, Lemon Crêpes with Fruit, '82 46
Fresh Fruit Combo, '86 178
Fresh Fruit with Lemon-Yogurt Dressing, '93 17
Fruitcakes
Applesauce Fruitcake, '83 258
Aronowitz Fruitcake, '86 285
Bourbon Fruitcake, '85 315
Brandy Fruitcake, '82 261
Burgundy Fruitcake, '85 292
Cake Mix Fruit Cake, '95 248
Chocolate Fruitcakes, '95 250
Classic Fruitcake, '91 258
Favorite Fruitcake, Family, '88 284
Fondue, Fruitcake, '84 258

Grandmother's Fruitcake, '95 248
Japanese Fruitcake, '83 268; '90 252
Jeweled Fruitcake, '88 260
Jill's Fruitcake, '95 249
Kentucky Fruitcake, '86 266
Layered Fruitcake, '87 265
Lemon Fruitcake, '83 258
Light Fruitcake, '90 309
Loaf, Fruitcake, '96 286
Mom's Fruitcake, '85 321
No-Bake Fruitcake, '95 249
Old-South Fruitcake, '79 289
Regal Fruitcake, '83 257
Sherry-Nut Fruitcake, '84 266
White Fruitcake, '80 280; '85 316
Zucchini Fruitcake, '88 284
Garnishes, '82 280; '85 339
Gazpacho, Berry, '97 181
Gazpacho, Citrus, '96 70
Gingered Fruit, '83 151
Granola, Fruity, '84 148
Grilled Fruit with Honey Yogurt, '95 87
Hawaiian Fruit Dish, '82 112
Honey-Sour Cream Dip, Fresh Fruit with, '90 180
Hot Fruit Delight, '83 281
Kabobs, Fruit, '86 181; '89 85
Kabobs, Fruity Mermaid, '91 177
Kabobs, Grilled Fruit, '97 147
Kabobs, Winter Fruit, '89 34
Main Dishes
Brisket, Mixed Fruit Tzimmes with, '93 114
Chicken Breasts with Fruited Rice Pilaf, '92 307
Chicken en Crème, Fruited, '83 264
Chicken, Fruit-Glazed, '80 211
Chicken with Almond Rice, Spiced Fruited, '81 195
Chicken with Fresh Fruit, Coconut, '93 294
Chuck Roast, Fruited, '91 289
Cornish Hens with Fruited Stuffing, '90 191
Goose, Fruit- and Pecan-Stuffed, '83 268
Goose, Fruited Stuffed Wild, '88 248
Goose, Fruit Stuffed, '83 320
Ham Slice, Fruited, '83 M317
Pork Chops, Fruited, '87 194
Pork Chops, Fruited Stuffed, '86 197
Pork Chops, Fruit-Stuffed, '82 136
Pork Chops, Fruit-Topped, '94 41
Pork Chops with Rice, Fruit-Glazed, '82 73
Pork Loin, Fruitcake-Stuffed, '95 250
Pork Medaillons with Fresh Fruit, '97 104
Pork Pilaf, Fruited, '82 246
Pork Tenderloins, Fruit-Stuffed, '87 270
Pot Roast, Fruited, '90 211
Salad, Main Dish Fruit, '83 119
Spareribs, Fruit-Stuffed, '79 14
Turkey-and-Fruit Kabobs, '88 140
Marinade, Fruit with Lime, '98 92
Marinated Fruit, '91 67
Marinated Fruit, Minted, '92 138
Marmalade, Citrus, '97 32
Marmalade, Delicious Fruit, '81 285
Marmalade, Fruited Onion, '96 323; '97 27
Medleys
Baked Fruit Medley, '81 297
Chilled Fruit Medley, '84 60
Chinese Fruit Medley, '83 22
Cup Medley, Fruit, '85 47
Curried Fruit Medley, '95 329
Fancy Fruit Medley, '84 82
Fresh Fruit Medley, '81 141
Frosty Fruit Medley, '82 226
Fruit Medley, '89 235
Midsummer Fruit Medley, '88 182

Fruit 105

FRUIT, Medleys
(continued)

Minted Fruit Medley, '80 182
Tropical Medley of Fruit, '86 53
Mélange, Fruit, '88 M295
Mélange, Melon, '84 139
Mint-Balsamic Tea, Fresh Fruit with, '95 232
Mix, Dried Fruit, '92 22; '96 286
Muesli, Bran-and-Fruit, '91 134
Muesli, Homestyle, '91 315
Muffins, Fruited Wheat, '79 93
Nuggets, Dried Fruit, '86 326
Oatmeal, Fruited, '88 19
Pick, Fruit-on-a-, '90 179
Poblanos Stuffed with Pork and Fruit, '97 269
Preserving. *See* **FRUIT/Canning and Preserving.**
Relish, Fresh Fruit, '95 158
Rhapsody, Fruit, '80 158
Rice, Far East Fruited, '81 175
Rice Mix, Fruited, '90 267; '97 317
Rice Mix, Fruited Curry-, '86 326
Rice Pilaf, Fruit-and-Vegetable, '84 196
Rice, Sweet Jamaican, '96 71
Salads
Almond-Citrus Salad, '96 274
Apricot Fruit Salad, '82 132
Avocado Fruit Salad, '87 41
Avocado-Fruit Salad with Honey-Yogurt Dressing, '93 172
Banana-Mixed Fruit Salad, '79 270
Berry-Citrus Twist, '95 100
Bowl, Fresh Fruit, '89 137
Cabbage and Fruit Salad, '79 286
Cantaloupe, Fruit-Filled, '83 120
Carrot-and-Seed Salad, Fruity, '86 223
Carrot-Fruit Toss, '82 235
Chef Salad, Fruited, '85 222
Chef's Fruit Salad, '86 35
Cherry Fruit Salad, '87 236
Chicken-and-Fruit Salad, Grilled, '96 155
Chicken-Avocado Salad, Fruited, '82 101
Chicken-Fruit Salad, '82 79
Chicken Fruit Salad, '90 234
Chicken Salad, Fruited, '84 25, 290; '88 88; '90 318
Chicken Salad, Fruity, '83 157
Chicken Salad in Avocados, Fruited, '87 41
Chicken Salad, Summery, '95 138
Chicken Salad, Tropical, '96 127
Chicken Salad with Fruit, '82 171
Citrus-and-Avocado Salad, '99 26
Citrus and Greens with Orange-Ginger Dressing, '96 240
Citrus-Cilantro Dressing, Fruit Salad with, '93 310; '94 97
Citrus Dressing, Fruit Salad with, '88 6
Coconut Fruit Bowl, '83 111
Coconut Salad, Chunky Fruit-and-, '84 24
Coleslaw, Fruited, '83 209; '85 139
Coleslaw, Three-Fruit, '86 250
Colorful Fruit Bowl, '91 58
Colorful Fruit Salad, '82 113
Congealed Fresh Fruit, Jeweled, '95 89
Cottage Cheese-and-Fruit Salad, '86 16
Cottage-Fruit Split, '86 169
Cracked Wheat-Fruit Salad, '96 240
Cream Dressing, Fruit Salad with, '89 277
Creamy Fruit Salad, '84 265
Creamy Holiday Fruit Salad, '90 251
Cup, Mixed Fruit, '87 233
Cups, Royal Fruit, '81 146

Curried Fruit Salad, '85 107
Date Dressing, Fruit Salad with, '87 57
Dressed-Up Fruit, '82 5
Easy Fruit Salad, '80 221
Easy Patio Fruit Salad, '88 184
Fall Salad with Ginger Dressing, '82 194
Favorite Fruit Salad, '99 220
Festive Fruit Salad, '80 16
Freeze, Fruity Lemon, '82 145
Fresh Fruit Cup with Mint Dressing, '80 183
Fresh Fruit Salad, '82 165; '97 122
Fresh Fruit Salad with Celery-Honey Dressing, '80 42
Fresh Fruit Salad with Poppy Seed Dressing, '91 168
Frisky Fruit Salad, '85 46
Frozen Fruit Salad, '83 110; '97 158
Frozen Fruit Salad, Dreamy, '79 126
Frozen Fruit Salad, Luscious, '81 204
Frozen Fruit Salad, Summertime, '89 111
Frozen Salad Christmas Wreath, '79 241
Fruit Salad, '83 209; '89 277
Gingered Fruit Salad, '95 95
Glazed Fruit Salad, '83 48; '84 290
Green Fruit Salad with Honey-Lime Dressing, '93 71
Ham Salad, Fruited, '81 36, 146
Harvest Salad with Cider Vinaigrette, '99 322
Heavenly Salad, '81 252
Holiday Fruit Salad, '87 236
Honeydew Fruit Bowl, '84 186
Honey Dressing, Fruit Salad with, '87 129
Honey Fruit Salad, '80 276
Honey-Lemon Dressing, Fruit Salad with, '93 21
Hurry-Up Fruit Salad, '87 236
Jícama-Fruit Salad, '86 83
Layered Fruit Salad, '84 290; '89 277; '91 58
Lemonade Fruit Salad, '84 24
Lettuce and Fruit Salad with Poppy Seed Dressing, '80 152
Main Dish Fruit Salad, '83 119
Marinated Fruit Deluxe, '81 146
Mélange Delight, Fruit, '81 302
Melon-Citrus Mingle, '79 177
Minted Fruit Toss, '99 160
Mint-Gin Fruit Salad, '92 92
Mint Sauce, Fruit Salad with, '88 M96
Mold, Sherried Fruit, '90 124
Multi-Fruit Salad, '93 184
Nut Salad, Cheesy Fruit-'n'-, '87 56
Old-Fashioned Fruit Salad, '82 80
Orange Cream, Fresh Fruit Salad with, '90 126
Orange Fruit Cup, '91 277
Oriental Dressing, Fruit Salad with, '91 277
Pasta Salad, Fruited, '92 108
Peachy Fruit Salad, '89 206
Persimmon Fruit Salad, '79 206
Picks, Fruit on, '80 159
Pineapple Cream Dressing, Fruit Cups with, '83 81
Pineapple Dressing, Fruit Salad with, '85 207
Pineapple-Fruit Salad, Icy, '87 9
Platter, Fresh-Fruit Salad, '92 213
Platter, Fruit Salad, '83 261
Poppy Seed Dressing, Fruit Salad with, '88 78
Potato Salad, Fruity, '85 214
Quick-and-Easy Fruit Salad, '81 99
Raspberry Fruit Mounds, '79 35
Refreshing Fruit Salad, '85 92
Rum, Fruit Cup with, '83 55
Sangría Fruit Cups, '89 34
Shrimp Salad, Fruited, '86 156
Sour Cream Fruit Salad, '80 138
Sparkling Fruit Salad, '82 266

Spiced Autumn Fruit Salad, '87 228
Spiced Fruit Salad, '98 54
Springtime Fruit Salad, '81 96
Summer Fruit Salad, '82 164; '92 171
Summer Salad, Favorite, '80 158
Sunny Fruit Salad, '91 58
Sweet-and-Sour Fruit Salad, '80 13; '84 125
Tossed Fruit Salad, '92 106
Tropical Fruit Salad, '89 306
Tropical Fruit Salad with Fresh Mint Dressing, '84 126
Turkey-Fruit Salad, '79 56
Turkey Fruit Salad, '83 233; '84 244
Turkey Salad, Fruit-and-, '89 176
Turkey Salad, Fruit-and-Spice, '94 325
Turkey Salad, Fruitful, '84 197
Twenty-Four-Hour Fruit Salad, '96 279
Watermelon Fruit Basket, '84 161
Wheat Salad with Citrus and Mint, '99 163
Winter Fruit Salad, '80 248; '82 23
Winter Fruit with Poppy Seed Dressing, '95 317
Wreath, Della Robbia Fruit, '87 294
Yogurt Fruit Salad, '81 114; '96 247
Yogurt-Granola Fruit Medley, '91 58
Salsa, Cranberry-Citrus, '97 290
Salsa, Fruit, '97 124
Salsa, Grilled Shrimp with Citrus, '97 141
Salsa, Key Lime Pie with Minted Tropical, '99 333
Sandwiches, Fruit-and-Cheese Breakfast, '89 M21
Sandwiches, Glazed Breakfast Fruit, '93 178
Sauce, Citrus Dipping, '97 208
Sauce for Fruit, Tangy, '90 161
Sauce, Grand Marnier Fruit, '90 93
Sherried Fruit Casserole, '80 284
Sherried Fruit Mélange, '80 158
Soup, Chilled Fresh Fruit, '88 160
Soup, Dried Fruit, '79 23
Soup, Fruit, '87 98
Soup, Yogurt Fruit, '86 176
Spiced Fruit, '79 23
Spiced Fruit, Cold, '90 269
Spiced Fruit Delight, '82 229
Spiced Fruit, Warm, '86 39
Spiced Winter Fruit, '83 262
Spread, Fruit, '85 135
Spread, Fruited Cream Cheese, '91 306; '93 79
Spread, Sugarless Fruit, '84 60
Strudel, Fruit Basket, '87 276
Stuffing and Shiitake Sauce, Pork Tenderloin with Fruit, '97 218
Stuffing Mix, Fruited, '89 331
Summer Fruit Fantasy, '91 178
Sundae, Breakfast, '98 206
Syrup, Apricot Fruit, '82 10
Terrine with Raspberry Sauce, Fruit, '98 157
Topping, Fruit, '81 42; '87 225; '89 50
Tropical Fruit Fluff, '88 68
Tropical Fruit Tray, '93 72
Twists, Fruit-Nut, '82 253
White Wine, Fruit in, '81 48
Wontons, Fruit-Filled, '85 287
Wreath, Tex-Mex, '96 241
FUDGE. *See* **CANDIES/Fudge.**

Game

Birds in Wine Marinade, Game, '94 306
Chili, Double-Meat, '79 269; '80 12
Dove and Sausage Gumbo, '81 199
Dove au Vin, '95 309
Dove Enchiladas, '85 270
Doves, Pan-Roasted, '87 240
Doves, Sherried, '91 290

Duck and Duckling
Baked Duck, Sherried, '79 224
Blackberry Sauce, Ducklings with, '82 251
Breasts, Blackened Duck, '93 259
Breasts, Charcoaled Marinated Duck, '79 226
Breasts, Smoked Duck, '87 121
Breasts with Raspberry Sauce, Duck, '87 240
Breast, Tender Duck, '97 215
Casserole, Duck and Wild Rice, '79 224
Enchiladas with Red Pepper-Sour Cream,
Smoked Duck, '87 121
Foxfire Duck, '89 241
Grilled Duck with Orange Sauce, '94 305
Gumbo, Duck, Oyster, and Sausage, '79 226
Holiday Duckling, '80 251
Kabobs with Almond Rice, Grilled Duck,
'91 291
Muscovy Duck with Parsnip Mash,
Honey-Orange-Glazed, '97 262
Orange Duck, Chafing Dish, '79 226
Orange Gravy, Duck with, '81 259
Pâté, Duck, '79 226
Pâté, Duck Liver, '79 227
Roast Ducklings with Cherry Sauce, '86 312
Roast Duckling with Orange Sauce, '81 125
Roast Duckling with Tangerine Stuffing, '90 16
Roast Duckling with Wine Jelly, '88 243
Roast Duck with Sweet Potato-Eggplant
Gravy, '83 90
Roast Long Island Duckling, '84 87
Wild Duck, Buffet, '86 268
Wild Duck with Orange Gravy, Roast, '89 323
Wild Duck with Pecan Stuffing, '85 269
Goose, Fruit- and Pecan-Stuffed, '83 268
Goose, Fruited Stuffed Wild, '88 248
Goose, Fruit-Stuffed, '83 320
Goose with Currant Sauce, Wild, '87 240
Gumbo, Wild Game, '91 290
Gumbo Ya Ya, '87 210
Mallard, Prairie Wings, '83 252
Pepper Feet, '93 258
Pheasant Muscatel, '85 269
Pheasants with Port Wine Sauce, '84 252
Pot Pie with Parmesan Crust, Game, '94 304
Quail
Baked Quail with Cornbread Stuffing, '94 305
Baked Quail with Mushroom Gravy, '89 273
Baked Quail with Mushrooms, '81 259
Breasts, Southern Quail, '85 270
Currant Jelly Sauce, Quail with, '86 94
Dressing, Quail and, '99 42
Étouffée, Roasted Quail, '96 34
Foxfire Quail, '89 240
Fried Quail, '82 45
Fried Quail, Seasoned, '88 220
Fried Quail with Onion Gravy, '82 214
Glazed Quail with White Bean Ragoût,
Maple-, '96 232
Gravy, Georgia Quail with, '87 240
Gravy, Quail Smothered in, '99 41
Grilled Breakfast Quail, '88 220
Grilled Quail, '92 90
Grilled Quail, Asian, '99 41
Grilled Quail with Red Wine-Blackberry
Sauce, '98 319
Hatcreek Quail, '89 270
J.W. Quail, '89 240
Magnificent Quail, '82 214
Marinated Quail, '80 221
Mushrooms, Quail with, '85 138
Orange Sauce in Potato Baskets, Quail with,
'86 193
Pan-Roasted Chipotle-Marinated Quail, '98 201
Red Plum Sauce, Quail with, '80 48

Smoked Champagne Quail, Sage-, '97 164
Smoked Quail, '93 236
Stroganoff, Quail, '99 41
Stuffed Quail, Hawkeye-, '89 241
Stuffed with Cornbread Dressing, Quail,
'93 280
Superb, Quail, '81 303
Rabbit, Hickory Barbecued, '82 216
Rabbit, Santa Fe Spanish, '94 307
Squab, Baked Stuffed, '82 260
Stew, Hunter's, '85 270
Turkey, Country-Fried Wild, '94 306
Venison
Bake, Venison-Vegetable, '87 304
Burgers, Venison, '87 304
Chili, Hot Venison, '91 283
Chili, Venison, '82 216; '86 3; '87 304
Chutney-Mustard Sauce, Bostick Venison
with, '89 242
Country-Fried Venison, '81 233
Kabobs, Venison, '82 215; '88 249
Loin, Mushroom-Crusted Venison, '94 302
Roast, Grilled Venison, '93 278
Roast, Lillie Bell's Venison, '89 242
Roast, Venison, '82 226
Roast with Red Wine Gravy, Venison, '85 270
Sauce, Venison Reduction, '94 303
Sausage Balls, Venison, '80 42
Soup, Venison, '82 216
Steak, Country-Fried Venison, '83 262
Steaks, Country-Style Venison, '82 215
Steaks, Grilled Venison, '82 215
Stew, Venison, '86 294
Stew, Venison Sausage, '87 238
Stew with Potato Dumplings, Venison, '87 304
Stock, Venison, '94 302
Tenderloin Appetizers, Venison, '88 249
Tomatoes, Venison and, '85 270
GARLIC
Beans, Molasses Baked, '99 105
Black Beans, Cuban, '99 56
Bread, Barbecue, '99 105
Broccoli, Garlic, '99 46
Bruschetta, Black Truffle, '99 323
Burgers, Spinach-Feta, '99 135
Butter, Garlic, '83 193; '84 108; '95 89
Butter, Garlic-Basil, '98 156
Butter, Roasted Garlic, '97 46
Canapés, Roasted Garlic, '96 95
Chicken and Potatoes, Roasted, '98 289
Chicken Breasts, Greek, '98 19
Chicken, Forty-Cloves-of-Garlic, '95 261
Chicken, Garlic-Spinach, '92 56
Chicken, Lemon-Garlic, '90 35
Chicken, Soy-Garlic, '98 128
Confit, Roasted Shallot-Garlic, '94 303
Crème Brûlée, Roasted Garlic, '95 324
Crisps, Garlic, '99 60
Croutons, Garlic, '92 71
Dressing, Basil-and-Garlic, '94 55
Dressing, Garlic-Ginger Vinaigrette, '92 195
Dressing, Southern Rice, '99 256
Garbanzo-Black Bean Medley, '99 236
Gazpacho, Classic Tomato, '99 172
Green Beans, Garlic, '91 159
Grits, Baked Cheese-and-Garlic, '83 292; '84 78
Grits Casserole, Garlic, '81 47
Grits, Garlic-and-Herb Cheese, '95 122
Grits, Garlic Cheese, '80 47; '81 197
Grits, Garlic-Cheese, '86 180; '88 126; '89 47; '97
58; '99 270
Grits, Garlicky Ham-and-Spinach, '94 177
Grits Soufflé, Garlic-Cheese, '99 18
Hamburgers Teriyaki, '99 332

Jelly, Garlic, '99 283
Jelly, Garlic Pepper, '99 221
Kale with Tomatoes, Spicy, '99 243
Lamb Chops with Minted Apples, '99 230
Lamb Extraordinaire, '99 242
Leg of Lamb, Garlic-and-Herb Stuffed, '99 241
Leg of Lamb, Roast, '99 242
Marinade, Garlic-Basil, '94 160
Mayonnaise, Garlic, '92 56
Mayonnaise, Roasted Garlic, '97 47
Mushrooms, Garlic and, '95 165
Oil, Roasted Garlic, '96 122
Olives Scaciati, '99 266
Pasta, Tomato-Garlic, '94 177
Pasta with Marinara Sauce, Garlic, '92 78
Pesto, Garlic, '84 108
Pesto, Roasted Garlic-Basil, '98 145
Pesto, Roasted Garlic-Rosemary, '97 46
Pork Loin, Garlic-Honey Marinated, '99 334
Pork, Smoked, '99 81
Potatoes, Garlic Mashed, '92 330; '97 308
Potatoes, Garlic-Parsley, '90 290
Potatoes, Garlic-Roasted, '95 87
Potatoes, Roasted Garlic Mashed, '95 288
Potatoes, Roasted Garlic-Parmesan Mashed,
'97 263
Puree, Roasted Garlic, '92 55
Rack of Lamb, Mint-Crusted, '98 118
Rémoulade, Braised Shrimp with Garlic, '98 133
Risotto, Crawfish, '99 120
Roasted Garlic, '94 177; '96 304
Roasted Garlic Bulbs, '97 46
Roasted Garlic Dressing, '99 269
Roasted Garlic, Herbed, '94 177
Sauce, Chilled Asparagus with Garlic Dipping,
'98 136
Sauce, Garlic, '92 56
Sauce, Garlic Beurre Blanc, '88 222
Sauce, Lemon-Butter, '99 198
Sauce, Parsley-Garlic, '83 138; '84 M76
Sauce, Red Pepper-Garlic, '98 140
Sauce, Red Wine Garlic, '94 250
Sauce, Roasted Garlic, '95 268; '98 176
Sauce, Roasted Garlic-Tomato, '97 46
Shrimp di Santo, '99 265
Shrimp, Grilled Garlic, '99 178
Shrimp with Fettuccine, Dilled, '99 141
Soup, Tortilla, '99 310
Spread, Tri-Flavored Cream Cheese, '98 134
Steak, Garlic, '84 8
Steaks, Garlic-Herb, '98 169; '99 175
Turkey, Rosemary Roasted, '99 312
Vegetable Medley, Herbed, '99 46
Vinaigrette, Garlic, '95 65
Vinaigrette, Garlic-Blue Cheese, '92 57
Vinaigrette, Roasted Garlic, '97 47
Vinegar, Shallot-Tarragon-Garlic, '93 191
GARNISHES
Butter
Balls, Butter, '82 189; '89 90
Curls, Butter, '82 51, 189; '89 90
Molds, Butter, '89 90
Flowers, edible
Candied Flowers and Raspberries, '98 155
Pansies, Candied, '96 118
Rose Petals and Mint Leaves, Candied, '99 155
Rose Petals, Candied, '98 57
Roses and Leaves, Crystallized, '97 61
Candy Bow, '99 M306
Candy Box, White, '97 M54
Chocolate
Cups, Chocolate, '80 207
Cups, Chocolate Crinkle, '93 270
Cups, Miniature Chocolate, '87 132

GARNISHES, Chocolate
(continued)

　　Curls, Chocolate, **'85** 338
　　Hearts and Shavings, Chocolate, **'86** 26
　　Lacy Chocolate Garnishes, **'89** 43
　　Leaves, Chocolate, **'88** 281; **'89** 42; **'98** 270
　　Sack, Large Chocolate, **'93** 314
　　Sack, Small Chocolate, **'93** 314
　Eggs, Hard-Cooked, **'82** 280
　Fruit
　　Citrus Cups, **'85** 339
　　Citrus Cups, Notched, **'82** 280
　　Cranberries, Frosted, **'82** 280; **'85** 339
　　Grapes, Frosted, **'82** 51; **'85** 339
　　Lemon Peel, Candied, **'94** 199
　　Lemon Roses, **'82** 280; **'85** 338
　　Lemon Slices, Fluted, **'82** 51
　　Orange Rind, Candied, **'96** 162; **'97** 32
　　Orange Rose, **'85** 338
　　Orange Zest, Candied, **'95** 320
　　Vegetable and Fruit Garnishes, **'82** 280
　Guide, Garnishing, **'82** 138
　Holiday Trees, **'98** 308
　Holly Leaves, **'99** M306
　Marinade, Dill, **'87** 115
　Marinade, Garlic-and-Oregano, **'87** 115
　Marinade, Sweet-and-Sour, **'87** 115
　Marzipan Bees, **'98** 100
　Pastry Garnish, **'98** 254
　Piped Garnishes, **'82** 280
　Vegetable
　　Broccoli Bouquet, **'87** 115
　　Carrot Curls, **'85** 338
　　Carrot Flowers, **'85** 338
　　Celery Fans, **'85** 339
　　Fruit Garnishes, Vegetable and, **'82** 280
　　Green Onion Fans, **'85** 339
　　Green Pepper Cups, **'85** 339
　　Mushrooms, Aztec, **'82** 51
　　Mushrooms, Fluted, **'82** 280; **'85** 338
　　Onion Mum, **'85** 339
　　Onion Mums, **'96** 318
　　Onion Rose, **'87** 114
　　Radish Rose, **'85** 339
　　Squash Buttercup, **'87** 114
　　Tomato Cups, **'85** 339
　　Tomato Flower, Marinated Pasta in, **'87** 115
　　Tomato Rose, **'82** 51; **'85** 338
　　Zucchini Fan, **'87** 114
GIFTS
　Bars, Chewy Chocolate Cereal, **'97** 317
　Cake, Gift Box, **'96** 319
　Cookies, Skillet Almond, **'97** 288
　Cream Cheese Braids, **'97** 287
　Divinity, Cherry, **'97** 316
　Divinity, Lemon, **'97** 316
　Extract, Vanilla, **'97** 288
　Filling, Cream Cheese, **'97** 287
　Fudge, Buttermilk, **'97** 317
　Gadgets, Off-the-Wall, **'95** 332
　Gifts That Measure Up, **'95** 332
　Glaze, **'99** 284
　Glaze, Powdered Sugar, **'97** 287
　Hot Handlers, **'95** 332
　Jambalaya Mix, **'98** 317
　Jelly, Garlic, **'99** 283
　Miniature Liqueur Sampler, **'95** 332
　Muffins, Cheese, **'97** 287
　Pralines, Cinnamon, **'97** 317
　Rice Mix, Fruited, **'97** 317
　Rolls, Cinnamon, **'99** M284
　Salad Gift, Asian, **'96** 327

Salad Gift, Caesar, **'96** 326
Salad Gift, Curried, **'96** 326
Sauce, Zesty Lemon, **'97** 318
Soup Mix, Bean, **'99** 283
Topping, Hot Fudge Ice Cream, **'98** 317
Topping, Maple-Pecan Ice Cream, **'98** 317
Wine Tasting, **'95** 332
Wreaths, Christmas, **'97** 288
GLAZES. *See also* **FILLINGS, FROSTINGS,**
　　TOPPINGS.
　Apricot Glaze, **'80** 280; **'82** 8; **'86** 197; **'97** 60;
　　'98 260
　Apricot Glaze for Ham, **'85** 256
　Apricot Glaze, Sweet, **'82** 304
　Apricot-Kirsch Glaze, **'87** 14
　Berry Glaze, **'83** 225
　Blueberry Glaze, **'83** 143
　Brandy Glaze, Powdered Sugar-, **'86** 291
　Brown Sugar Glaze, **'83** 312; **'96** 268
　Buttermilk Glaze, **'79** 140; **'81** 70; **'84** 316;
　　'97 230; **'99** 98
　Caramel Glaze, **'85** 320; **'98** 195
　Cherry Glaze, **'83** 143; **'93** 52; **'98** 260
　Chili-Cranberry Glaze, **'98** 320
　Chocolate Glaze, **'81** 119; **'83** 220; **'84** 10, 55,
　　253; **'85** 6; **'86** 315, 316; **'89** 325; **'90** 310;
　　'91 M296; **'93** 52; **'97** M35, 231; **'99** 206
　Chocolate Glaze, Creamy, **'82** 88; **'98** 90
　Chocolate Glaze, French, **'98** M57
　Chocolate-Honey Glaze, **'82** 306
　Cinnamon Glaze, **'88** 83
　Citrus Glaze, **'82** 128; **'89** 205
　Cranberry Glaze, **'84** 306; **'86** 171; **'88** 244
　Cranberry-Honey Glaze, **'89** 273
　Cream Cheese Glaze, **'84** 150; **'94** 242
　Daiquiri Glaze, **'93** 83
　Dijon Glaze, **'87** 54
　Drizzle Glaze, **'87** 94
　Drizzling Icing, **'91** 35
　Glaze, **'99** 284
　Honey Glaze, **'88** 287
　Honey-Nut Glaze, **'87** 15
　Irish Cream Glaze, **'92** 287
　Kahlúa Glaze, **'86** 292
　Lemon Glaze, **'79** 285; **'86** 194; **'87** 41; **'92** 269;
　　'93 154, 183; **'97** 123, 332
　Orange Butter Glaze, **'90** 194
　Orange Glaze, **'79** 2; **'80** 257; **'81** 34, 107;
　　'82 75, 206; **'83** 33, 114, 140, 267; **'84** 161;
　　'86 298; **'92** 263; **'95** 320; **'99** 293
　Orange Glaze, Nutty, **'80** 45
　Orange-Pineapple Glaze, **'81** 60
　Paint, Egg Yolk, **'86** 322
　Pineapple Glaze, **'83** 143; **'85** 38; **'97** 55
　Powdered Sugar Glaze, **'79** 24; **'82** 92, 283;
　　'83 83, 295; **'85** 55; **'90** 95; **'97** 287
　Praline Glaze, **'82** 196
　Root Beer Glaze, **'99** 196
　Rum Glaze, Buttered, **'83** 220
　Scuppernong-Orange Glaze, **'98** 220
　Snowy Glaze, **'82** 295
　Strawberry Glaze, **'80** 35; **'83** 142
　Sugar Glaze, **'86** 161; **'90** 47
　Teriyaki Glaze, **'94** 82
　Topping Glaze, **'87** 69
　Vanilla Glaze, **'85** M89; **'89** 211
GOOSE. *See* **GAME.**
GRANOLA
　Apple Crisp, Granola, **'85** 78
　Bars, Coconut Granola, **'85** 202
　Bars, Fruit and Nut Granola, **'81** 49
　Bars, Granola, **'83** 305; **'95** 214
　Bars, No-Bake Granola, **'97** 220
　Bread, Honey-Granola, **'86** 56

Chocolate Morsels, Granola with, **'86** 69
Crunchy Granola, **'81** 218; **'84** 144
Easy Granola, **'81** 49
Fabulous Granola, **'92** 213
Fruit Medley, Yogurt-Granola, **'91** 58
Fruity Granola, **'84** 148
Gorp, Granola, **'89** 59
Granola, **'79** 190; **'93** 197; **'99** 212
Healthful Granola, **'97** 204
Homemade Granola, **'84** 58
Mix, Bunny Trail, **'95** 101
Mix, Granola, **'94** 168
Mix, Granola Snack, **'86** 229
Muffins, Granola, **'95** 78
Nutty Granola, **'90** 95
Orange Granola, Sunny, **'84** 212
Pancakes, Granola-Squash, **'94** 267
Peanut Butter Granola, **'82** 296
Peanut Granola, Crunchy, **'90** 48
Raisin-Granola Treats, **'92** 22
Reindeer Nibbles, **'92** 280
Sunshine Granola, **'79** 37
Superhero Granola, **'98** M206
Toasty Granola, **'79** 37
Whole Wheat Granola, **'82** 167
GRAPEFRUIT
　Beverages
　　Cocktails, Sea Breeze, **'97** 161
　　Cooler, Grapefruit, **'88** 81
　　Drink, Grapefruit, **'90** 84; **'95** 238
　　Freeze, Grapefruit, **'93** 242
　　Refresher, Grapefruit, **'88** 85
　　Refresher, Grapefruit-Orange, **'82** 174
　　Sangría, Grapefruit, **'89** 92
　　Spritzers, Grapefruit-White Wine, **'96** 56
　　Tea, Grapefruit, **'92** 67
　　Three-Fruit Drink, **'80** 50
　Biscuits, Grapefruit Juice, **'83** 10
　Broiled Grapefruit, **'85** 7; **'96** 55
　Broiled Grapefruit, Holiday, **'88** 251
　Broiled Grapefruit, Sherried, **'80** 50
　Broil, Flounder-Grapefruit, **'85** 53
　Cake, Fresh Grapefruit, **'89** 308
　Chocolate-Topped Grapefruit, **'89** 88
　Compote, Spicy Grapefruit-Berry, **'91** 19
　Cup, Berry Grapefruit, **'79** 242
　Delight, Winter Fruit, **'80** 243
　Dressing, Grapefruit French, **'80** 101
　Dressing, Grapefruit Salad, **'84** 262
　Frosting, Grapefruit, **'89** 308
　Ice, Grapefruit, **'91** 122
　Ice, Pink Grapefruit, **'85** 304
　Marmalade, Combination Citrus, **'80** 50
　Marmalade, Grapefruit, **'82** 308
　Minted Grapefruit, **'88** 81
　Pear-Berry Puree, Grapefruit with, **'89** 213
　Pie, Grapefruit Meringue, **'96** 56
　Salads
　　Apple Salad, Grapefruit-, **'89** 41
　　Aspic, Grapefruit, **'80** 297; **'82** 112; **'83** 153
　　Avocado-Grapefruit Salad, **'85** 26;
　　　'93 282
　　Avocado Salad, Grapefruit-, **'83** 316; **'84** 16;
　　　'89 41
　　Banana Salad with Celery Seed Dressing,
　　　Grapefruit-, **'91** 237
　　Combo Salad, Grapefruit, **'80** 50
　　Congealed Grapefruit Salad, **'84** 325; **'85** 279
　　Congealed Salad, Grapefruit, **'83** 190
　　Cucumber Salad, Grapefruit-, **'80** 100
　　Grapefruit Salad, **'83** 124; **'84** 325; **'88** 122
　　Greens and Grapefruit Salad, **'95** 301
　　Orange-Grapefruit Salad, **'93** 294
　　Orange Salad, Grapefruit-, **'91** 276

Shrimp Salad, Grapefruit-and-, '88 5
Winter Salad, Grapefruit, '84 24
Sorbet, Grapefruit-Mint, '93 153
Sorbet, Pink Grapefruit and Tarragon, '95 163
Spiced Pink Grapefruit, '96 55
Supreme, Grapefruit, '80 50

GRAPES

Beverages
Cooler, Grape-Lime, '94 227
Juice, Scuppernong, '98 221
Mulled Grape Juice, '90 21
Punch, Sparkling Grape, '82 48
Punch, Spiced White Grape, '96 170
Punch, White Grape, '90 15
Tea, White Grape Iced, '98 84
Tea, White Grape Juice, '87 57
Blue Cheese-Pecan Grapes, '95 48
Caribbean Grapes, '95 48
Carrots with Grapes, Glazed, '82 287
Chicken Véronique, '84 260; '85 302

Desserts
Beauberries Bordeaux, '98 18
Cobbler, Muscadine, '98 221
Granita, Grape, '88 118
Ice Cream, Scuppernong, '88 216
Ice, Grape, '83 162
Ice, Muscadine, '82 202
Pie, Grape, '85 212
Pie, Grape Juice, '79 123
Pie, Muscadine, '82 202
Pie, Scuppernong, '88 216
Pops, Purple People Eater, '99 132
Refresher, Grape Juice-Fruit, '86 182
Tart, Green Grape, '87 77
Tarts, Scuppernong Pudding, '98 221
Frosted Grapes, '82 51; '85 339
Glaze, Scuppernong-Orange, '98 220
Green Grapes Supreme, '88 81
Ham Véronique, '85 90
Honeydew Melon with Grapes, '91 91
Honeyed Grapes, '95 47
Jelly, Grape, '89 140
Jelly, Grape-Burgundy Freezer, '85 130
Jelly, Quick Grape, '89 M156
Jelly, Scuppernong, '98 220
Jelly, Thyme-Grape, '89 193
Jelly, Wild Muscadine, '79 32
Marmalade, Muscadine, '98 220
Mold, Double Grape-Cantaloupe, '79 173
Pork Loin, Scuppernong-Orange Glazed, '98 220
Salad, Chicken, '96 67
Salad, Marinated Chicken-Grape, '85 74
Salad Mold, Grape, '83 120
Salad Véronique, Macaroni, '85 164
Salad with Grapes, Chicken, '86 117
Salad with Grapes, Curried Tuna, '87 201
Sauce, Pears in Muscadine, '88 216
Sauce, White Grape, '80 38
Scallops Véronique, '83 144
Slaw, Grape-Poppy Seed, '86 225
Sole Véronique, '85 181
Spiced Grapes, '98 220
Wild Rice with Grapes, '95 48

GRAVIES. *See also* **SAUCES.**
Black-Eyed Pea Gravy, '87 12
Burgundy Gravy, Beef Roast with, '95 263
Chicken Gravy, '99 34
Chive Gravy, Beef and Broccoli with, '88 214
Chocolate Gravy, '99 35, 88
Cranberry Pan Gravy, Baked Hen with, '94 308
Cream Gravy, '88 15; '97 25
Cream Gravy, Country-Fried Steak with, '84 8
Cream Gravy, Fried Chicken with, '85 241
Currant Gravy, '83 276

Dill-Cream Gravy, Pork Chops with, '84 81
Fried Chicken Gravy, '95 235
Fried Ripe Tomatoes with Gravy, '82 180
Giblet Gravy, '79 283; '88 253
Giblet Gravy, Roast Turkey and, '94 308
Gravy, '88 303
Ham with Gravy, Virginia, '86 15
Horseradish Gravy, Filet Mignon with, '92 262
Milk Gravy, Buttermilk-Marinade Turkey with Peppery, '98 311
Mushroom Gravy, '99 34
Mushroom Gravy, Baked Quail with, '89 273
Onion Gravy, Fried Quail with, '82 214
Onion Gravy, Pork Chops in, '99 222
Orange Gravy, '81 259; '89 323
Pork Chops and Gravy, '96 71
Red-Eye Gravy, Country Ham with, '79 37; '99 34
Redeye Gravy, Country Ham with, '86 254; '98 271
Red-Eye Gravy, Ham and, '88 221
Red Wine Gravy, Venison Roast with, '85 270
Sage Gravy, '96 269
Sausage Gravy, '92 271; '94 20; '97 243
Sour Cream Gravy, '92 301
Sour Cream Gravy, Pot Roast with, '79 17
Southwestern Gravy, '99 34
Sweet Potato-Eggplant Gravy, Roast Duck with, '83 90
Tasso Gravy, '92 236; '96 270
Tomato Gravy, '93 18; '99 35
Tomato Gravy, Spicy, '95 172
Turkey Gravy, '91 255; '94 306
White Wine Gravy, '89 322
White Wine Gravy, Pot Roast in, '81 299

GREENS. *See also* **SWISS CHARD.**
Bacon, Shelly Greens and, '96 290
Bake, Grits 'n Greens Dinner, '84 281
Beets 'n' Greens, '95 179
Chowder, Mixed Greens, '97 262
Collard Greens, '95 233; '96 272
Collard Greens, Seasoned, '82 211
Collards, '79 32
Collards and Sausage, Pasta with, '94 230
Collards Casserole, Parmesan-, '95 233
Collards, Risotto with, '96 203
Collards, Southern-Style, '82 107
Collards, Uptown, '92 23
Collards with Apples, '98 250
Edna's Greens, '96 144
Escarole-and-Bacon Salad, '84 85
Escarole, Easy Cooked, '84 85
Grits and Greens, '95 233
Gumbo z'Herbes, '94 239
Kale, Scalloped, '86 224
Kale Soup, Creamy, '96 203
Kale, Sweet-and-Sour, '80 298
Kale with Salsa, Southwest, '94 246
Kale with Tomato and Onion, '92 244
Kale with Tomatoes, Spicy, '99 243
Mustard Greens and Potatoes, '86 224
Mustard Green Soup, Cream of, '93 280
Mustard Greens, Spinach Fettuccine with, '94 247
Mustard Greens-Stuffed Tenderloin, '96 324
Pasta with Greens, '95 211; '96 47
Pork Tenderloin, Southern-Style Stuffed, '99 45
Risotto with Greens, '96 132
Salad with Warm Pecan Dressing, Mess o' Greens, '98 250
Sauce, Cress, '96 176
Stewed Tomatoes and Greens, '95 234
Stir-Fried Greens, '94 33; '97 270

Turnip-and-Carrot Salad, '91 212
Turnip-and-Collard Greens, '92 215
Turnip Green Dip, '91 13
Turnip Green Dip with Jalapeño-Corn Muffins, Hot, '93 164
Turnip Greens, '90 13, 232; '95 306
Turnip Greens and Ham Hock, Southern, '80 119
Turnip Greens and White Bean Bake, '94 246
Turnip Greens, Fresh, '92 339
Turnip Greens, Old-Fashioned, '85 255
Turnip Greens, Saucy, '83 12
Turnip Greens with Cornmeal Dumplings, '82 211
Turnip Greens with Turnips, '84 230
Watercress-and-Mushroom Salad, '88 104
Watercress Mousse, '88 104
Watercress Soup, '88 104
Watercress Soup, Cream of, '96 66
Watercress Spread, '88 103

GRILLED. *See also* **BARBECUE.**

Beef
Burgers, All-American Pizza, '92 148
Burgers, Beefy Vegetable, '98 143
Burgers, Burgundy, '80 156
Burgers, Favorite, '89 165
Burgers, Grilled Sour Cream, '87 287
Burgers, Mushroom, '89 164
Burgers, Nutty, '87 185
Burgers, Party, '83 164; '84 39
Burger Spirals, '94 139
Burgers, Sausage, '83 212
Burgers, Seasoned, '85 158
Burgers, Steak-House, '87 186
Burgers, Stuffed, '85 159
Burgers, Sweet-and-Sour, '90 128
Burgers, Tortilla, '94 138
Burgers, Triple-Layer, '89 165
Burgers with Caramelized Onions, Beef, '98 143
Burgers with Roasted Bell Pepper Ketchup, Jalapeño-Stuffed, '97 318
Burgers with Sprouts, '89 164
Cheeseburgers, Fried Green Tomato, '94 138
Eye of Round, Grilled Beef, '82 91
Fajita Salad, Beef, '91 70
Fajitas, Favorite, '86 114
Fajitas, Java, '96 227
Fajitas, Plum Good, '94 115
Fajitas with Pico de Gallo, '98 87
Filet Mignon, Marinated, '84 171
Fillet, Acapulco, '98 114
Fillets with Orange Cream, Beef, '97 66
Flank Steak and Mushrooms, '87 61
Flank Steak, Cheese-Stuffed, '98 182
Flank Steak, Flavorful, '96 32
Flank Steak, Ginger-Marinated, '89 25
Flank Steak, Grilled, '80 152; '89 168; '91 80; '92 166
Flank Steak, Grilled Marinated, '97 182
Flank Steak in Mexican Marinade, '98 128
Flank Steak, Lemon-Lime, '95 55
Flank Steak, Marinated, '82 162; '83 35; '85 86; '95 237
Flank Steak, Oriental, '83 178
Flank Steak, Peppery Grilled, '99 157
Flank Steak Pinwheels, '87 141
Flank Steak Sandwiches with Apple Barbecue Sauce, '99 173
Flank Steaks, Delicious Marinated, '83 110
Flank Steak, Tangy, '86 184
Flank Steak, Tenderized, '82 105
Flank Steak Teriyaki, '81 110
Flank Steak, Texas, '86 185
Flank Steak with Apple-Bourbon Sauce and Roasted Vegetables, Grilled, '99 142

GRILLED, Beef
(continued)

Flank Steak with Black Bean-and-Corn Salsa, Grilled, '94 80
Flank Steak with Sweet Peppers, Grilled, '90 138
Grilled Steaks, '96 172
Hamburgers, Flavorful Grilled, '81 110
Hamburgers, Grilled, '93 198
Hamburgers, Old-Fashioned, '79 149
Hamburgers, Spicy Grilled, '98 158
Hamburgers, Teriyaki, '94 138
Hamburgers Teriyaki, '99 332
Kabobs, Beef, '85 110
Kabobs, Beef-and-Vegetable, '91 148
Kabobs Deluxe, Beef, '82 182
Kabobs, Marinated Beef, '82 105; '85 159
Kabobs, Meatball, '95 192
Kabobs, Pineapple-Beef, '83 212
Kabobs, Saucy Beef, '83 109
Kabobs, Spicy Grilled, '98 158
Kabobs, Spirited Beef, '87 142
Kabobs, Teriyaki Beef, '80 207
Kabobs with Rice, Marinated Beef, '84 32
Kabobs with Vegetables, Beef, '90 148
Kabobs with Vegetables, Marinated Beef, '99 292
London Broil, Teriyaki, '92 282
Marinated Beef on a Stick, '85 234
Medaillons of Beef with Horseradish Cream, '90 96
Pigs on a Roll, Three Little, '98 203
Pizza, Taco, '98 176
Poor Boy Fillets, '82 106
Prime Rib, Smoked, '97 161
Red Wine Marinade, Beef with, '91 46
Rib-Eyes, Italian, '98 215
Rib-Eye Steaks, Peppered, '97 46
Ribs, Sweet-and-Sour Grilled, '98 331
Roast, Grilled Marinated Beef, '93 141
Roast, Grilled Pepper, '81 110
Round Steak, Tender Grilled, '85 3
Salad, Beef Vinaigrette, '95 177
Sirloin Kabobs, Marinated, '82 162
Sirloin Salad, Grilled, '94 129
Sirloin Steak, Secret, '81 110
Sirloin Steaks with Thyme Pesto, '97 182
Steak-and-Shrimp Kabobs, '80 184
Steak, Bourbon, '90 148
Steak Continental, '83 178
Steak, Curried Beef, '88 60
Steak, Grilled Black Pepper, '86 184
Steakhouse Beef, American, '93 15
Steak Kabobs, '93 95
Steak Kabobs, Marinated, '80 184
Steak, Marinated Bourbon, '95 91
Steak, Mesquite-Grilled, '85 154
Steak on a Stick, '83 109
Steak, Patio, '87 141
Steak, Pirate, '79 89
Steak Salad Niçoise, Grilled, '98 148
Steaks, Blue Cheese, '84 171
Steaks, Garlic-Herb, '99 175
Steaks, Mexican Pepper-Cheese, '97 190
Steak, Spicy Grilled, '97 211
Steaks, Sweet-and-Sour Marinated, '83 110
Steaks with Green Chiles, Grilled, '85 144
Steak, Tabasco, '95 207
Steak with Ham-and-Mushroom Sauce, '83 109
Steak with Mushroom Sauce, '83 212
Steak with Pimiento Cheese Salsa, Fiery, '99 331
Steak with Vegetables, Skewered, '81 124
Superburgers, '79 89

Tacos al Carbón, '86 19
Tacos al Carbón, Tailgate, '79 185
Tenderloin, Grilled, '91 166
Tenderloin, Herb Marinated, '83 109
Tenderloin, Marinated Beef, '83 215
Tenderloin with Mushrooms, Beef, '87 115
Tomatoes and Artichokes, Beef with, '92 282
Tournedos Diables, '87 60
Bratwurst, Grilled, '94 253
Bread, Barbecue, '99 105
Bread, Greek, '89 200
Bread, Lemony French, '97 147
Burgers, Pizza, '89 165
Cantaloupe Wedges, Grilled, '87 162
Chicken
Bahamian Chicken with Cha-Cha Salsa, Grilled, '97 160
Barbecued Chicken, Grilled, '81 154
Basil Chicken, Grilled, '93 201
Basil-Stuffed Chicken with Tomato-Basil Pasta, '94 204
Breast of Chicken, Marinated, '87 123
Breasts, Grilled Chicken, '84 172
Breasts with Lemon-Yogurt Coleslaw, Grilled Chicken, '98 148
Bundles with Bacon Ribbons, Chicken, '87 168
Burgers, Open-Faced Chicken-Onion, '94 139
Charcoal Broiled Chicken, '79 90
Cumin Chicken, Grilled, '87 142
Dill Sauce, Grilled Chicken with, '88 162
Fajitas, Chicken, '99 158
Foil-Wrapped Chicken, '99 108
Garlic-Grilled Chicken, '87 180
Ginger-Glazed Chicken, Grilled, '98 166
Ginger-Orange Chicken, Grilled, '91 26
Greens, Grilled Chicken on, '99 201
Grilled Chicken, '89 200; '92 170
Grits with Grilled Chicken and Onions, '99 17
Herbed Chicken Quarters, Grilled, '96 171
Honey-Glazed Grilled Chicken, '99 213
Honey-Lime Grilled Chicken, '96 189; '98 332
Jalapeño Chicken, Grilled, '93 213
Jamaican Jerk Chicken, '99 121
Jerk Chicken, Jamaican, '96 120
Kabobs, Chicken, '87 141
Kabobs, Hawaiian, '85 157
Kabobs, Oriental Chicken, '95 193
Kabobs, Sesame Chicken, '92 165
Kabobs, Soy-Chicken, '86 156
Kabobs Supreme, Chicken, '81 124
Lemonade Chicken, '82 163
Lemon-Herb Grilled Chicken, '95 87
Lemon-Mustard Chicken, '99 109
Lime-Jalapeño Chicken, Grilled, '91 87
Margarita-Marinated Chicken, Grilled, '97 167
Marinated Chicken, '87 61
Marinated Chicken Breasts, '90 54
Marinated Chicken in a Sandwich, '86 185
Mushroom Bundles, Chicken-, '80 157
Orange, Lime, and Ginger Sauce, Chicken with, '92 123
Pesto Chicken with Basil Cream, '89 158
Provolone, Chicken, '93 323
Rumaki Kabobs, '82 182
Salad, Grilled Asian Chicken, '96 158
Salad, Grilled Chicken-and-Fruit, '96 155
Salad, Grilled Chicken-Pasta, '94 64
Salad, Grilled Chicken-Rice, '98 148
Salad, Moroccan Grilled Chicken, '95 231
Salad, Thai Chicken, '95 177
Salad with Mango Chutney, Grilled Chicken, '96 182
Salad with Raspberry Dressing, Grilled Chicken, '95 202

Salsa, Grilled Chicken with Cha-Cha, '98 333
Sandwiches, Chicken-Benedict Bagel, '96 250
Sandwiches, Open-Faced Mexican, '98 230
Sandwiches, Summer Open-Faced, '99 201
Sandwich, Ham 'n' Cheese Chicken, '95 153
Sandwich Jamaican Chicken, '95 153
Sandwich, Jerk Chicken, '98 333
Saté, Chicken, '99 134
Sausage with Fennel, Chicken, '98 312
Smoky Grilled Chicken, '85 160
South-of-the-Border Barbecued Chicken, '97 311
Soy-Garlic Chicken, '98 128
Tabbouleh Salad, Grilled Chicken with, '91 70
Tarragon-Dijon Thighs, Grilled, '97 120
Teriyaki Chicken, '91 163
Teriyaki Chicken, Grilled, '92 59
Vegetables, Grilled Chicken and, '99 200
Vegetables Vinaigrette, Grilled Chicken and, '91 26
White Barbecue Sauce, Chicken with, '97 322
Wings, Grilled Honey Chicken, '96 111
Wings, Maple-Glazed Chicken, '99 110
Yogurt-Lemon Chicken, Grilled, '81 111
Cornish Hens, Asian Grilled, '99 41
Cornish Hens, Grilled, '88 243; '92 59
Cornish Hens, Jelly-Glazed, '93 251
Cornish Hens, Orange-Glazed Grilled, '86 250
Cornish Hens, Sherry-Marinated, '91 148
Cornish Hens with Tropical Fruit, Grilled, '97 310
Dogs, Grilled Pizza, '97 139
Duck Breasts, Charcoal Marinated, '79 226
Duck Kabobs with Almond Rice, Grilled, '91 291
Duck with Orange Sauce, Grilled, '94 305
Duck with Parsnip Mash, Honey-Orange-Glazed Muscovy, '97 262
Fennel and Radicchio with Orange Vinaigrette, Grilled, '95 253
Figs, Marinated Grilled, '96 194
Fish. *See also* GRILLED/Seafood.
Amberjack Sandwiches, Grilled, '91 195
Caribbean Fish, '99 109
Catfish Cajun-Style, Grilled, '90 129
Catfish with Red Salsa, Grilled, '90 172
Catfish with Relish, Grilled, '92 54
Easy Grilled Fish, '91 194
Fillets Tomatillo, '94 135
Flounder Fillets, Grilled, '83 213
Grouper, Garlic-Basil Marinated, '94 160
Grouper, Grilled, '86 185
Grouper, Grilled Herbed, '99 178
Grouper, Grilled Marinated, '90 166
Grouper, Hot Spicy, '94 78
Heather Sauce, Catfish Inn's Grilled Fish with, '84 182
Kabobs, Fish, '98 223
Mahi-Mahi with Lemon Mayonnaise, '99 178
Montego Bay Grilled Fish with Caribbean Salsa, '96 70
Rainbow Trout with Mushroom Stuffing, Grilled, '97 162
Salmon Fillets with Sweet Corn Relish, '93 119
Salmon, Orange-Basil, '97 165
Salmon Quesadilla with Cucumber Salsa, Grilled, '95 131
Salmon Steaks, Grilled, '94 278
Salmon Steaks, Grilled Herbed, '93 176
Salmon Steaks, Mint-Marinated, '96 175
Salmon Steaks with Lemon-Mustard Sauce, '97 124
Salmon Steaks with Tarragon Butter, '87 155
Salmon Steaks with Tarragon Sauce, Grilled, '97 42
Swordfish-Shiitake Skewers, '97 168

Swordfish, Skewered, '86 256
Swordfish Steaks, Orange-Ginger Marinated, '93 271
Swordfish Steak with Chervil Butter, '91 147
Swordfish with Avocado-Lime Sauce, Grilled, '97 127
Swordfish with Caper Sauce, Grilled, '95 230
Trout, Grilled, '95 106
Tuna, Grilled Florida, '93 128
Tuna, Inland Grilled, '96 197
Tuna Steaks, Grilled, '90 129
Tuna Steaks on Mixed Greens with Lemon-Basil Vinaigrette, Seared, '94 205
Tuna Steaks with Cucumber Sauce, '97 180
Tuna with Poblano Salsa, Grilled, '91 135
Tuna with Sautéed Vegetables, '98 222
Yellowfin Tuna with Corn, Pepper, and Tomato Salsa, '94 164
Franks, Grilled Stuffed, '82 163
Fruit Kabobs, Grilled, '97 147
Fruit with Honey Yogurt, Grilled, '95 87
Game Hens, Texas-Style, '87 61
Grits, Hot Grilled, '97 191
Ham. *See* **GRILLED/Pork.**
Lamb
Burgers, Mesquite-Grilled Lamb, '88 59
Chops, Grilled Lamb, '91 163
Chops, Joan's Rosemary Lamb, '97 42
Chops, Peppercorn-Crusted Lamb, '92 142
Chops, Teriyaki Lamb, '87 60
Chops with Rosemary Sauce and Wild Rice-Fennel Pilaf, Grilled Lamb, '97 127
Chops with Shrimp, Lamb, '88 58
Kabobs, Apricot-Grilled Lamb, '98 102
Kabobs, Lamb, '85 159; '95 192
Kabobs, Lamb Shish, '93 70
Kabobs, Overnight Shish, '81 124
Kabobs, Rosemary Marinated Lamb, '93 203
Kabobs, Saucy Lamb, '89 167
Kabobs, Savory Lamb, '80 184
Kabobs, Shish, '82 182
Kabobs Teriyaki, Shish, '85 37
Leg of Lamb, Greek-Style, '93 170
Leg of Lamb, Grilled, '96 88; '98 103
Mango Salsa, Grilled Lamb with, '95 104
Rosemary-Skewered Lamb, '97 190
Sandwiches, Lamb, '97 107
Steaks with Béarnaise Sauce, Lamb, '85 37
Sweet Pepper Relish, Grilled Lamb with, '95 104
Liver Kabobs, '80 185
Melon Salad with Orange-Raspberry Vinaigrette, Grilled, '95 144
Pie, Pear-Praline, '97 192
Pineapple Boats with Rum Sauce, '97 192
Pizza, Grilled, '97 190
Pizzas, Grilled, '93 178; '98 176
Polenta with Black Bean Salsa, Grilled, '93 155
Pork
Burgers, Hearty Sauced Pork, '84 125
Burgers, Sausage, '83 212
Chops, Apricot-Stuffed Pork, '92 219
Chops, Country Pride Pork, '79 159
Chops, Glazed Pork, '86 185
Chops, Grilled Pork, '88 113; '98 246
Chops, Hawaiian Grilled Pork, '85 159
Chops, Herbed Pork, '97 147
Chops, Honey-Glazed, '97 200
Chops, Lemon-Herb Pork, '84 81
Chops, Marinated Grilled Pork, '81 110
Chops, Mexican Pork, '99 108
Chops, Pineapple-Curry Glazed, '82 106
Chops, Rosemary Pork, '98 329
Chops with Ancho Cream Sauce, Boneless Pork, '95 205

Chops with Black-and-White Salsa, Pork, '97 200
Chops with Tangy Barbecue Sauce, Pork, '99 104
Ham and Apples, Grilled, '96 M303
Ham, Easy Grilled, '92 134
Ham, Golden Grilled, '79 90
Ham, Hickory-Grilled, '92 81
Ham Kabobs, Honey, '80 156
Ham Kabobs, Swiss-, '81 124
Ham 'n' Cheese Chicken Sandwich, '95 153
Ham Slice, Apricot-Glazed, '93 252
Honey-and-Herb Grilled Pork, '90 148
Jalapeño Grilled Pork, '99 160
Kabobs, Margarita Pork, '98 M223
Kabobs, Pineapple-Pork, '99 144
Kabobs, Spicy Pork, '82 182
Loin, Grandma Ruth's Grilled Pork, '96 250
Loin, Honey-Grilled Pork, '92 219
Loin, Minted Pork, '99 96
Medaillons, Grilled Pork, '93 229
Ribs, Adams', '95 236
Ribs, Lemon Grilled, '81 154
Ribs, Smoky, '84 172
Ribs with Plum Sauce, Crispy, '98 182
Roast, Company Pork, '99 276
Roast, Grilled Pork, '97 323
Salsa, Grilled Pork with, '90 128
Sausage, Grilled Pork, Cheddar, and Jalapeño, '98 311
Spareribs, Baked and Grilled, '97 211
Spareribs, Grilled Maple, '99 136
Spareribs, Honey-Glazed, '82 163
Spareribs in Plum Sauce, '99 136
Spareribs, Peach-Glazed, '86 14
Spareribs, Spicy, '89 168
Steaks, Glazed Pork, '83 178
Superburgers, '79 89
Tenderloin, Coriander-Pepper Pork, '99 145
Tenderloin, Garlic Grilled Pork, '90 172
Tenderloin, Grilled Marinated Pork, '91 199
Tenderloin, Grilled Pork, '91 163; '94 88
Tenderloin, Marinated Pork, '84 175
Tenderloin, Molasses-Grilled Pork, '96 265
Tenderloins, Grilled Pork, '88 98; '94 158
Tenderloins, Honey-Grilled, '92 199
Tenderloin Towers, Pork, '86 75
Tenderloin with Apples, Celery, and Potatoes, Grilled Pork, '95 161
Tenderloin with Brown Sauce, Grilled Pork, '89 32
Tenderloin with Molasses Sauce, Grilled Pork, '97 193
Tenderloin with Mustard Sauce, Pork, '99 145
Tenderloin with Onion-Balsamic Sauce, Pork, '99 44
Tenderloin with Parmesan-Pepper Toasts, Herbed Pork, '98 242
Quail, Asian Grilled, '99 41
Quail, Grilled, '92 90
Quail, Grilled Breakfast, '88 220
Quail, Marinated, '80 221
Quail, Sage-Smoked Champagne, '97 164
Quail with Red Wine-Blackberry Sauce, Grilled, '98 319
Sandwiches, Grilled Garden, '98 315
Seafood. *See also* **GRILLED/Fish.**
Brochette, Seafood, '87 96
Oriental Marinade, Seafood in, '98 128
Oysters Mornay, Grilled, '89 195
Oysters Supreme, Smoky, '87 60
Po'Boy, Grilled Seafood, '96 244
Scallop-Bacon Kabobs, '81 111
Scallop Kabobs, Grilled, '83 101

Scallop Kabobs, Sea, '82 162
Scallops, Marinated Grilled, '84 171
Scallops Tostada, Grilled, '87 120
Scallops with Cilantro-Lime Vinaigrette, Grilled Orange, '94 77
Shrimp and Cornbread-Stuffed Peppers, Barbecued, '97 261
Shrimp-and-Scallop Kabobs, Grilled, '92 210
Shrimp, Grilled, '85 103
Shrimp, Grilled Garlic, '99 178
Shrimp, Grilled Margarita-Marinated, '97 167
Shrimp, Grilled Marinated, '87 173
Shrimp, Grilled Sweet-and-Sour, '97 100
Shrimp, Grilled Zucchini-Wrapped, '98 200
Shrimp Kabobs, Marinated, '85 158
Shrimp Kabobs, Steak-and-, '80 184
Shrimp, Marinated and Grilled, '87 141
Shrimp Skewers with Vegetable Salsa, '98 32, 223
Shrimp with Citrus Salsa, Grilled, '97 141
S'mores, Grilled Pound Cake, '98 179
Tortilla Bites, '95 42
Turkey-and-Fruit Kabobs, '88 140
Turkey Breast, Citrus-Marinated, '94 272
Turkey Breast, Smoky, '89 323
Turkey Breast with Cranberry Salsa, Grilled, '95 252
Turkey Burgers, Grilled, '91 61
Turkey Drumsticks, Grilled, '89 168
Turkey, Seasoned Smoked, '97 85
Turkey Steaks, Grilled Marinated, '93 170
Turkey Tenderloins, Lime-Buttered, '92 127
Vegetables
Acorn Squash with Rosemary, Grilled, '96 266
à la Grill, Vegetables, '88 130
Asparagus Salad with Orange Vinaigrette, Grilled, '99 102
Barbecue Hobo Supper, '99 108
Burgers, Vegetable, '89 164
Cilantro Butter, Grilled Vegetables with, '98 182
Corn, Grilled Parmesan, '82 127
Corn-on-the-Cob, Grilled, '90 166
Corn on the Cob, Lemony, '89 200
Corn on the Cob, Mexican, '96 167
Corn on the Grill, '94 161; '97 191
Corn Salsa, Grilled, '99 162
Corn Soup, Grilled, '87 121
Corn with Herb Butter Sauce, '79 150
Corn with Maple Vinaigrette, Grilled, '98 171
Eggplant Appetizer, Grilled, '95 198
Eggplant, Balsamic-Flavored, '95 342
Eggplant, Grilled, '80 202
Eggplant, Sage-Grilled, '96 269
Gazpacho, Grilled Vegetable, '97 181
Grilled Vegetables, '84 172; '92 124; '96 123, 173
Italian-Style Grilled Vegetables, '92 143
Kabobs, Beef-and-Vegetable, '91 148
Kabobs, Fresh Vegetable, '92 101
Kabobs, Grilled Vegetable, '93 170
Kabobs, Tangy Marinated Vegetable, '88 142
Kabobs, Vegetable, '87 116
Marinated Grilled Vegetables, '95 162
Medley, Grilled Vegetable, '98 158
Mushroom Burgers, '97 101; '99 135
Okra and Tomatoes, Grilled, '98 124
Onion Flowers with Pecans, Grilled, '96 217
Onion Salad, Grilled, '99 96
Onions, Grilled Stuffed, '95 180
Onions, Smoky Sweet, '97 191
Parmesan Vegetables, '97 147
Pasta, Grilled Vegetable, '97 142
Pepper Kabobs, Pretty, '90 166

GRILLED, Vegetables
(continued)

Peppers, Marinated Roasted, '97 123
Pepper Tacos, Grilled, '95 340
Pizza, Grilled Vegetable, '98 176
Pizzas, Grilled Vegetable, '97 323
Portabello Mushrooms, Grilled, '95 123
Portobello Burger, Grilled, '98 331
Potatoes, Grilled Herb, '84 172
Potatoes, Grilled Irish, '97 53
Potatoes, Italian Grilled, '98 171
Potatoes, Smoked Baked, '97 25
Salad, Grilled Vegetable, '94 203
Shiitakes, Grilled, '95 265
Skewers, Grilled Vegetable, '94 160
Squash and Onion, Grilled, '79 150
Squash-and-Pepper Kabobs, Summery,
'95 193
Squash and Tomatoes, Grilled Summer, '99 144
Squash Fans, Grilled, '97 118
Sweet Potatoes, Grilled, '93 213
Tomato, Bell Pepper, and Portobello Salad,
Grilled, '98 211
Tomatoes, Cheesy Grilled, '79 150
Tomatoes, Grilled, '85 158; '99 173
Tomatoes with Basil Vinaigrette, Grilled,
'97 168
Zucchini Fans, Grilled, '89 200
Zucchini with Feta, Greek Grilled, '95 190
Venison Kabobs, '82 215; '88 249
Venison Roast, Grilled, '93 278
Venison Steaks, Grilled, '82 215
GRITS
Bake, Grits 'n Greens Dinner, '84 281
Cakes, Southwestern Grits, '93 61
Casserole, Garlic Grits, '81 47
Casserole, Grits-Sausage, '84 75; '86 241
Cheese
Baked Cheese-and-Garlic Grits, '83 292;
'84 78
Baked Cheese Grits, '80 49, 99; '83 311;
'85 41; '94 240
Baked Cheese Grits, Grillades and, '94 240
Baked Grits, Swiss-and-Cheddar, '91 71
Casserole, Cheesy Grits, '81 270
Cheese Grits, '86 242; '90 102
Creamy Grits, '96 24
Creamy Grits, Margaret's, '99 18
Garlic-and-Herb Cheese Grits, '95 122
Garlic Cheese Grits, '80 47; '81 197
Garlic-Cheese Grits, '86 180; '88 126; '89 47;
'97 58; '99 270
Green Chiles, Cheese Grits with, '95 208
Grilled Grits, Hot, '97 191
Gruyère Cheese Grits, '81 47
Jalapeño Cheese Grits, '85 43
Quick Cheese Grits, '83 M203; '96 97
Saga Blue-Chile Grits, '98 202
Sausage-Cheese Grits, '90 238
Sliced Cheese Grits, '84 75
Soufflé, Garlic-Cheese Grits, '99 18
Chicken and Grits, '95 263
Chicken and Onions, Grits with Grilled, '99 17
Chiles Rellenos, Southern-Style, '96 24
Country Grits and Sausage, '83 54
Creamy Grits, '92 237, 238; '93 60
Dressing, Grits, '93 306; '94 296
Eggs Creole, '92 86
Fried Grits, '83 292; '84 78
Good Morning Grits, '87 156
Greens, Grits and, '95 233
Grillades and Grits, '88 126; '89 47; '93 62

Ham-and-Spinach Grits, Garlicky, '94 177
Italiano, Grits, '92 43
Nassau Grits, '81 47; '99 214
Orange Grits, '81 47
Pan-Fried Grits, '93 62
Patties, Grits, '83 52
Pie, Crustless Grits-and-Ham, '86 103
Pie, Grits Fiesta, '92 43
Pie, Pineapple-Grits, '96 236
Pudding, Grits, '96 28
Quiche, Ham-and-Grits Crustless, '94 89
Risotto, Redneck, '98 107
Salad, Stacked Grits-Spinach, '98 66
Sausage Grits, '86 92
Sausage, Grits with, '99 233
Scrambled Grits, '80 48
Shrimp-Manchego-Chorizo Grits with Red Bean
Salsa, '97 227
Shrimp Stew and Grits, '80 118
Shrimp Stew over Grits, '89 47
Soufflé, Grits, '80 30
Soufflé, Mexican Grits, '79 55
Spoonbread, Grits, '79 38
Spoonbread Grits with Savory Mushroom Sauce,
'96 236
Stew over Grits, Shrimp, '88 126
Stuffing, Grits, '96 270
Timbales, Chives-Grits, '90 172
Timbales, Grits, '88 223
Tomato Grits, Hot, '95 171
GUMBOS. See also CHOWDERS,
JAMBALAYAS, SOUPS, STEWS.
Carolina Gumbo, '95 70
Chicken
Andouille Gumbo, Chicken-, '98 14
Chicken Gumbo, '79 199; '90 26
Easy Chicken Gumbo, '83 156
Gullah House Gumbo, The, '92 237
Ham-Seafood Gumbo, Chicken-, '81 6
Oyster Gumbo, Chicken and, '81 198
Sausage Gumbo, Chicken-and-, '89 275;
'90 256; '94 20
Smoked Sausage, Chicken Gumbo with,
'81 199
Ya Ya, Gumbo, '87 210
Dove and Sausage Gumbo, '81 199
Duck, Oyster, and Sausage Gumbo, '79 226
Fish
Catfish Gumbo, '90 278; '91 216
Easy Fish Gumbo, '81 6
Snapper Gumbo, Savannah, '94 105
Ground Beef Gumbo, '87 283
Mogumbo, '93 32
Okra Gumbo, '86 210; '91 206
Okra Gumbo, Deep South, '79 48
Okra Gumbo Freezer Mix, '86 210
Seafood
Cajun Seafood Gumbo, '94 238
Champion Seafood Gumbo, '86 293
Chicken-Ham-Seafood Gumbo, '81 6
Combo Gumbo, '81 198
Crab and Shrimp Gumbo, '81 200
Crabs, Seafood Gumbo with Whole, '85 2
Creole Gumbo, '86 228
Creole Gumbo, Quick, '82 87
Creole Seafood Gumbo, '82 278
Ham and Seafood Gumbo, '81 199
Okra Gumbo, Light Seafood-, '86 155
Oyster Gumbo, Chicken and, '81 198
Seafood Gumbo, '79 198, 286; '80 34; '81 5;
'83 90; '84 87, 92; '87 210; '90 154; '96 98
Shrimp-Crab Gumbo, '98 15
Shrimp Gumbo, '81 199
Shrimp Gumbo, Old-Style, '98 97

Shrimp Gumbo, Quick, '86 71
Southern Gumbo, '82 242
Spicy Seafood Gumbo, '91 207
Texas Ranch-Style Gumbo, '82 226
Turkey Gumbo, '82 268; '85 258
Wild Game Gumbo, '91 290
z'Herbes, Gumbo, '94 239

HAM. See also PORK.
Acorn Squash, Ham-Stuffed, '81 239; '83 66
Appetizers
Appetillas, Ham, '93 63
Balls, Appetizer Ham, '82 39
Balls, Fried Ham-and-Cheese, '84 221
Balls, Ham, '86 256
Balls with Spiced Cherry Sauce, Ham, '81 112;
'82 12
Biscuits, Country Ham in Heart, '86 105
Biscuits, Cured Ham and, '85 320
Biscuits, Kentucky Ham 'n' Angel, '90 83
Biscuits, Petite Ham and Cheese, '79 193
Biscuits, Southern Ham and, '91 12
Biscuits with Country Ham, '90 93
Biscuits with Ham, Ranch, '97 59
Chips, Ham-Cheese, '82 34
Deviled Ham Twists, '82 86
Dip, Creamy Ham, '93 125
Eggs and Ham, Green, '96 90
Meat-and-Cheese Appetizers, '87 7
Mousse Pitas, Ham, '95 328
Mushrooms Stuffed with Ham, '97 237
New Potatoes, Ham-Stuffed, '88 211
Nuggets, Cheesy Ham, '81 290
Pâté, Ham, '85 279
Pineapple Nibbles, Ham-, '95 283
Prosciutto, Walnuts, and Cream, Figs with,
'96 194
Prosciutto, Watermelon and, '98 164
Prosciutto-Wrapped Asparagus, '91 98
Puffs, Ham-and-Cheese, '86 277
Puffs, Ham-Filled Party, '84 116
Roll, Ham-and-Cheese, '79 234
Rolls, Ham, '79 153
Rollups, Almond-Ham, '89 284
Rollups, Ham-and-Swiss, '85 113
Sandwiches, Party Ham, '97 240
Sandwiches, Tiny Ham-and-Cheese, '99 87
Spread, Buttery Ham, '95 93; '97 98
Spread, Cold Ham, '82 248
Spread, Country Ham, '87 8
Spread, Ham, '86 126
Spread, Ham and Pimiento, '80 285; '81 56
Stack-Ups, Ham, '96 109
Tapas, Garlic-Ham, '92 175
Tennessee Ham, '95 263
Tennessee Sin, '95 218; '96 204
Turnovers, Chile-Ham, '88 64
Turnovers, Party Ham, '82 39
Apricots, Ham and, '90 53
Artichokes, Ham-Mushroom-Stuffed, '95 228
Baked
Apricot Baked Ham, '84 160
Bourbon Glaze, Baked Ham with, '98 M271
Burgundy Ham, Baked, '94 326
Cranberry-Raisin Sauce, Baked Ham with,
'88 244
Festive Baked Ham, '83 263
Maple-Raisin Sauce, Baked Ham with, '83 215
Marinated Baked Ham, '86 94; '88 133
Orange-Honey Glaze, Baked Ham with, '90 53
Orange Sauce, Baked Ham with, '86 294
Pineapple-Baked Ham, '86 48

Plum Ham, '80 110
  Royale, Ham, '84 260
  Slice, Baked Ham, '83 12
Balls, Ham, '84 91; '86 256
Barbecued Ham Slices, '81 110
Birming "Ham," '94 229
Biscuits, Blue Cheese-and-Ham Cornmeal, '98 136
Biscuits, Ham, '99 233
Biscuits, Ham-Filled Angel, '80 159
Biscuits, Surprise Pull-Apart, '95 46
Black-Eyed Peas, Cajun, '96 218
Black-Eyed Peas with Ham Hocks, '79 122
Bread, Ham-and-Cheese, '86 213
Broiled Ham, Cranberry, '88 301
Bundles, Ham-and-Cheese, '93 63
Burritos, Breakfast, '97 172
Cakes, Hawaiian Ham, '79 252
Casseroles
  Apple Ham Casserole, '79 213
  Apples, Baked Ham and, '82 M237
  Asparagus Dinner, Ham-, '80 M10
  Asparagus Ham Rolls, '91 117
  au Gratin, Broccoli-Ham, '90 239
  Beans with Ham, Baked, '80 136
  Breakfast Casserole, '91 285
  Broccoli Casserole, Ham and, '81 133
  Broccoli Casserole, Quick Ham-, '82 40
  Cheese Casserole, Ham-and-, '87 78
  Cheese Layered Casserole, Ham-and-, '98 160
  Chicken, Ham, and Cheese Bake, '87 217
  Creamy Ham Medley, '84 90
  Egg Casserole, '98 98
  Egg Casserole, Breakfast Ham and, '79 253
  Golden Ham Casserole, '82 119
  Ham Casserole, '96 302; '98 314
  Harvest Ham Bake, '79 210
  Hash Brown-Ham-Cheese Bake, '97 323
  Lasagna, Creamy Ham-and-Chicken, '95 88
  Lima Casserole, Ham and, '79 192
  Macaroni-Ham Casserole, '81 M177; '83 283
  Noodle Casserole, Ham and, '80 300
  Pasta Casseroles, Hot Brown, '96 290
  Potato Casserole, Cheesy Ham-and-, '84 326
  Potato Casserole, Ham-and-, '83 M87; '96 103
  Potatoes with Ham Bits, Creamy, '87 191
  Potato-Pineapple Bake, Ham-, '93 302
  Quiche Casserole, '95 32
  Rice Casserole, Ham-and-, '84 75
  Rice-Stuffed Ham Rolls, '83 190
  Rice-Tomato Bake, Ham-, '87 78
  Roll Casserole, Ham, '91 M127
  Spaghetti, Ham-and-Turkey, '95 19
  Spinach-and-Ham Rollups, '86 84
  Spinach-Ham Rolls, '88 78
  Spinach Roll-Ups, Ham and, '81 143
  Strata, Baked Ham, '83 283
  Strata, Ham, '95 308
  Strata, Ham and Broccoli, '80 261
  Tetrazzini, Ham, '82 M77; '84 241
  Turkey Bake, Layered Ham and, '79 252
  Vegetable-and-Ham Casserole, '84 91
Cheesecake, Ham-and-Asparagus, '90 174
Cheesy Ham Dinner, '84 90
Cheesy Ham Towers, '82 M77
Chicken-and-Ham Bundles, Cheesy, '84 261
Chicken Breasts Saltimbocca, '98 19
Chicken Medley, Creamy Ham-and-, '92 272
Chowder, Creamy Green Bean, Mushroom, and
  Ham, '99 M336
Chowder, Creamy Ham, '88 M53
Chowder, Ham-and-Cheese, '89 15
Chowder, Ham and Corn, '79 16
Chowder, Ham-and-Corn, '82 40
Chowder, Ham 'n Cheese, '79 199

Chowder with Ham, Potato, '99 141
Citrus-and-Spice Ham, '88 40
Cordon Bleu, Chicken, '81 304; '82 83; '93 126
Cordon Bleu, Company Chicken, '82 274
Cordon Bleu, Veal, '87 219
Country Ham
  Biscuits, Country Ham, '94 215
  Biscuits, Country Ham in Heart, '86 105
  Biscuits with Country Ham, '90 93
  Bread with Herb Butter, Country Ham,
    '86 255; '99 18
  Brown Sugar Coating, Country Ham with,
    '90 88
  Chips, Country Ham, '92 338
  Cider-Baked Country Ham, '82 195
  Cider, Country Ham in Apple, '80 251
  Cornbread, Crab with Chile, '86 254
  Country Ham, '99 19
  Grits Stuffing, Country Ham with, '96 270
  Kentucky Hot Brown, '86 254
  Kentucky Jack, '86 254
  Oven-Braised Country Ham, '90 87
  Oysters and Ham, Edwards', '86 253
  Puff, Cheesy Country Ham, '90 88
  Quiche, Country Ham, '87 287
  Raisin Sauce, Country Ham with, '99 19
  Red-Eye Gravy, Country Ham with, '79 37;
    '99 34
  Redeye Gravy, Country Ham with, '86 254;
    '98 271
  Roasted Country Ham, Edwards', '86 253
  Sauce, Country Ham, '90 117; '96 24
  Sotterley Plantation Country Ham, '93 270
  Stuffed Country Ham, '90 317
  Stuffed Country Ham, Maryland, '88 49
  Swirls, Veal-and-Smithfield Ham, '86 253
  Tartlets, Country Ham-and-Asparagus, '98 82
  Virginia Ham, Buttermilk Biscuits with,
    '96 142
  Virginia Ham with Gravy, '86 15
  Wine, Country Ham in, '81 260
Creamed Ham and Chicken, '81 M74
Creamed Ham and Eggs, '82 40
Creamy Ham Towers, '79 138
Crêpes, Ham-and-Egg, '83 204
Crêpes with Mushroom Sauce, Ham-and-Egg,
  '82 46
Croquettes, Ham, '82 119
Curried Ham and Peaches, '82 60
Curried Ham Steak, '82 120
Curried Ham with Rice, '80 111
Deviled Delight, '83 130
Devils, Ham, '93 88
Eggplant, Ham-Stuffed, '80 162
Egg Rolls, Chinese, '96 101
Eggs, Creamy Ham and, '87 286
Eggs on Toast with Cheese Sauce, Ham and,
  '81 43
Eggs, Savory Ham and, '82 231
Enchiladas, Scrambled Egg, '97 153
Fettuccine, Ham-and-Asparagus, '94 84
Flips, Ham-and-Cheese, '92 46
French Toast, Ham-and-Cheese Oven, '97 172
Frittata, Ham-and-Broccoli, '98 101
Fritters, Ham, '82 39
Fritters, Potato-Ham, '98 249
Fritters with Creamy Sauce, Ham, '81 105
Frosted Ham, '89 71
Glazed
  Apricot-Glazed Ham Slice, '93 252
  Brown Sugar Glaze, Smithfield Ham with,
    '86 253
  Cherry-Peach Chutney, Glazed Ham with,
    '97 315

Cranberry Glazed Ham, '81 274
Cranberry-Honey Glaze, Baked Ham with,
  '89 273
Cranberry-Orange Glazed Ham, '81 295
Currant-Glazed Ham, '91 249
Fruited Ham Slice, '83 M317
Honey-Glazed Ham Slice, '81 104
Honey-Orange Glazed Ham, '83 320
Marmalade-Glazed Ham, '89 M196
Molasses-Glazed Ham, '84 24
Orange-Glazed Ham, '89 324
Peachy Glazed Ham, '96 189
Steak, Glazed Ham, '91 13
Strawberry-Glazed Ham, '91 84
Stuffed Ham, Glazed, '84 321
Sunshine-Glazed Ham, '84 252
Sweet-and-Sour Glazed Ham, '88 M15
Sweet-Sour Glazed Ham, '83 311
Green Peppers, Ham-Stuffed, '80 65
Griddle Cakes, Ham, '89 255
Grilled Ham and Apples, '96 M303
Grilled Ham, Easy, '92 134
Grilled Ham, Golden, '79 90
Grilled Ham, Hickory-, '92 81
Grits, Garlicky Ham-and-Spinach, '94 177
Gumbo, Chicken-Ham-Seafood, '81 6
Gumbo, Combo, '81 198
Gumbo, Ham and Seafood, '81 199
Hash Brown Bake, '95 281
Hopping John with Ham, '81 7
Jambalaya, Creole, '87 210
Jambalaya de Covington, '87 211
Kabobs, Honey Ham, '80 156
Kabobs, Swiss-Ham, '81 124
Loaves
  Chili-Sauced Ham Ring, '81 M122
  Country Ham Loaves, '86 255
  Cranberry-Ham Loaf, '82 M77
  Glazed Ham Loaf, '79 187; '90 212
  Ham Loaf, '79 180; '80 272
  Ham Loaves, '90 235
  Hawaiian Ham Loaf, '79 71
  Pineapple Upside-Down Ham Loaf, '79 253
  Ring, Ham, '84 91
  Saucy Ham Loaf, '86 M328
  Spicy Ham Loaf, '80 110
  Supreme Ham Loaf, '79 242
  Upside-Down Ham Loaf, '82 40
Muffins, Ham-and-Cheese, '92 252; '93 144
Noodles, Ham and Swiss on, '87 108
Omelet, Dill-Cheese-Ham, '95 33
Omelet, Ham and Cheese, '79 262; '80 123
Omelet, Rolled, '89 228
Omelet, Sour Cream-Ham, '79 261
Omelets with Creole Sauce, '89 228
Pancakes, Potato-Ham, '96 138
Patties, Ham, '81 99
Patties, Ham-Sprout, '85 51
Patties, Pineapple-Ham, '80 110
Patties, Spicy Ham, '90 235
Peas and Ham, Southern, '85 138
Peas and Pasta, '99 68
Peppers, Ham-and-Corn Stuffed, '81 87
Peppers with Rice and Ham, Stuffed, '82 131
Pie, Crustless Grits-and-Ham, '86 103
Pie, Golden Ham, '87 78
Pie, Ham-and-Cheese, '95 256; '96 75
Pie, Ham Pot, '90 25
Pie, Spaghetti-Ham, '93 19
Pie with Cheese Crust, Ham, '80 286
Pie, Zucchini-Ham-Cheese, '80 272
Pineapple-Flavored Ham, '87 160
Pinto Beans with Ham, '97 210
Pinwheels, Ham, '90 235

HAM

(continued)

Pizza, Ham-and-Eggs Crescent, '93 47
Pizza, Ham-and-Pineapple, '96 169
Pizza, Southern Classic, '95 268
Po-Boy, Pain-Perdu, '93 291
Potatoes, Ham Stuffed, '79 210
Potatoes, Jalapeño-Ham Stuffed, '81 M61
Potatoes, Stuffed Mashed, '98 328
Praline Ham, '85 302; '96 303
Prosciutto Croutons, '99 89
Prosciutto, Party Pasta with, '94 176
Prosciutto, Pizza with Artichoke and,
  '87 182
Quiches
  Cheese Quiche, Ham-, '79 26
  Cheese Quiches, Individual Ham-and-, '98 24
  Cheesy Ham Quiche, '79 127
  Crustless Ham Quiche, '84 235
  Grits Crustless Quiche, Ham-and-, '94 89
  Ham Quiche, '80 110
  Jalapeño Quiche, Cheesy, '84 31
  Mushroom Quiche, Ham-and-, '81 11
  Vegetable Quiche, Ham-and-, '84 326
Raisin Ham, '80 124
Raisin Sauce, Ham with, '82 M76
Red-Eye Gravy, Ham and, '88 221
Rice, Charleston, '97 310
Rice, Savannah Red, '80 119
Roast of Ham, Brandied, '98 320
Roast, Peachy Ham, '86 118
Rolls à la Swiss, Chicken-and-Ham, '92 42
Rolls, Ham-and-Broccoli, '86 212; '87 82
Rolls, Ham-and-Cheese, '82 3
Rolls, Ham-and-Cheese Lettuce, '89 217
Rolls, Ham-Asparagus, '79 41
Salads
  Apple Salad, Ham-and-, '88 139
  Asparagus with Prosciutto, Marinated, '95 83
  Baked Ham Salad, Crunchy, '83 23
  Boats, Salad, '80 93
  Cheese Salad, Ham-and-, '88 138
  Cheese Toss, Ham and, '79 55
  Coleslaw, Ham, '84 195
  Congealed Ham Salad, '81 36
  Egg Salad, Ham 'n, '81 36
  Fruited Ham Salad, '81 36, 146
  Hearty Ham Salad, '82 40
  Italian Ham Salad, Spicy, '85 74
  Macaroni-Ham Salad, '85 218
  Macaroni Salad, Ham and, '79 220
  Mandarin Ham-and-Rice Salad, '87 145
  Noodle Salad, Ham-, '85 249
  Pasta Salad, Ham-and-, '90 128
  Pasta Salad, Ham-Dijon, '92 191
  Pasta Salad, Ham-Pecan-Blue Cheese, '90 62
  Pasta Salad with Ham, '92 108
  Pilaf Mold, Ham, '86 222
  Potato Salad, Ham and, '80 272
  Potato Salad, Ham-and-, '95 94
  Potato Salad, Ham-and-Egg, '86 84
  Prosciutto Salad, Melon-and-, '92 191
  Rice Salad, Colorful Ham-and-, '90 319
  Rice Toss, Ham-, '82 40
  Rolls, Hearty Salad, '81 206
  Spread, Ham Salad, '87 92
  Sweet Potato Salad, Hawaiian Ham-, '82 232
  Tropical Ham Salad, '89 175
Sandwiches. *See also* **HAM/Appetizers.**
  Asparagus-and-Ham Melt Sandwiches,
    '88 M96
  Asparagus Delight, Ham-, '86 48

Baked Ham Sandwiches, '81 29
Blue Cheese-Ham Sandwiches, Creamy,
  '87 279
Cheese-and-Ham Striped Tea Sandwiches,
  Cheshire Claret, '94 16
Cheese Chicken Sandwich, Ham 'n',
  '95 153
Cheese Sandwiches, Hot Ham-and-,
  '85 299
Cheese Sandwich Round, Ham-and-, '94 326
Cheese Sandwich, Tex-Mex Ham-and-, '86 4
Club Sandwiches, Double-Decker, '91 231;
  '92 68
Croissant Sandwiches, '89 161
Eggs à la Swiss, Ham and, '88 158
Focaccia Sandwiches, '98 53
French Market Sandwiches, '98 230
Giant Ham-and-Pepper Sandwich, '96 74
Hamwiches, '96 246
Hideaways, Ham, '81 29
Hot Browns, '98 287
Hot Ham Sandwiches, '79 214
Hot Rods, Ham, '86 136
Meal-in-One Sandwiches, '80 218
Monte Cristo Sandwiches, '83 134; '97 319
Muffin, Stuffin', '99 193
Muffuletta, Doodles, '94 35
Muffulettas, '98 184
Open-Faced Sandwiches, '79 214
Open-Face Ham Sandwiches, '82 40; '85 8
Pineapple-Ham Sandwich Loaf, '91 167
Pineapple Slaw Sandwiches, Ham-and-,
  '96 199
Pita Pockets, Ham-and-Cheese, '90 271
Pita Sandwiches, Denver, '86 M12
Pita Sandwiches, Ham-and-Cheese, '87 202;
  '88 44
Pita, Stuffed, '89 87
Pocket, Ham and Swiss in the, '83 31
Rollups, Pizza, '99 197
Salad Sandwich, Tangy Ham, '80 272
Sebastian, The, '94 184
Stroganoff on Cheesy Onion Biscuits, Ham,
  '95 98
Stuffed Sandwich, Deli, '98 287
Swiss Sandwiches, Ham-and-, '98 287
Swiss Sandwiches, Tangy Ham-and-, '85 164
Torta, Mediterranean, '98 23
Turkey Specials, Cheesy Ham-and-, '84 14
Virginia Ham Sandwiches, '80 155
Yummy Sandwiches, '81 229
Sauce, Steak with Ham-and-Mushroom,
  '83 109
Skillet Dinner, Corn-and-Ham, '83 190
Skillet Dinner, Ham, '85 179
Skillet Ham-and-Vegetables, '84 90
Skillet, Ham-Noodle, '87 78
Skillet, Ham Spaghetti, '83 283
Slice with Cinnamon Apple Rings, Holiday Ham,
  '90 250
Smoked Ham, '86 92
Soufflé, Virginia Ham Breakfast, '93 121
Soufflé with Cucumber Sauce, Ham, '92 41
Soup, Chicken, Ham, and Oyster, '79 198
Soup, Creamy Kale, '96 203
Soup, Ham-and-Bean, '84 4
Soup, Hearty Ham, '82 4
Soup, Pot Liquor, '98 273
Soup, Spicy Ham-and-Bean, '94 322
Spread, Deviled Ham, '79 81
Spread, Ham-and-Egg, '79 59
Spread, Ham Salad, '87 92
Spread, Hawaiian Ham, '87 106
Spread, Horseradish-Ham, '91 167

Stew, Blakely Brunswick, '87 4
Stew, Ham-and-Black-Eyed Pea, '93 20
Stew, Quick Okra, '97 88
Stir-Fry, Easy Ham, '86 332
Stir-Fry, Ham and Zucchini, '79 47
Stroganoff, Ham, '82 40
Stromboli, '88 272; '89 181
Stuffed Ham, '86 323
Succotash, Savory, '96 63
Superburgers, '79 89
Supper, Top-of-Stove, '86 332
Tart, Ham-and-Cheese, '92 332
Tart Milan, '87 70
Tart, Supreme Ham, '84 22
Tennessee Ham, '95 263
Turnip Greens and Ham Hock, Southern,
  '80 119
Véronique, Ham, '85 90
Waffles, Ham, '80 44
Zucchini, Ham and Cheese Stuffed, '79 157
HEARTS OF PALM
Chicken Rolls, Hearts of Palm, '89 201
Marinated Asparagus and Hearts of Palm, '90 91
Salad, Different Vegetable, '82 143
Salad, Hearts of Palm, '81 252; '89 276; '96 86
Salad, Hearts-of-Palm, '87 138
Salad with Basil-and-Garlic Dressing, Hearts of
  Palm, '94 55
Salad with Lemon-Dill Vinaigrette, Green, '99 27
Sandwich, Hearts of Palm, '92 191
Spread, Hearts of Palm, '90 293
HOMINY
Bacon, Eggs, and Hominy, '85 143
Bake, Chili Hominy, '81 282; '82 58
Bake, Hominy-Sausage, '88 51
Casserole, Cheesy Hominy, '83 170
Casserole, Chile-Hominy, '81 29
Casserole), Four-Part Hominy (Cheesy Hominy,
  '96 158
Casserole, Hominy-and-Corn, '97 291
Casserole, Hominy-Chili, '86 255
Caviar, Texas, '86 218
Cheese Hominy, Hot, '84 77
Chiles and Cheese, Hominy with, '86 78
Gold Coast Hominy, '83 52
Jalapeño Hominy, '82 51
Mexican Hominy, '86 255; '91 133, 162
Mexihominy, '96 189
Salad, Hominy-Bean, '88 266
Skillet, Hominy-Sausage, '81 29
Soup, Bean-and-Hominy, '95 23
Soup, Black, White, and Red All Over, '95 126
Soup, Southwest, '86 255
HONEY
Ambrosia, Honey Bee, '83 267
Apple Quarters, Honey-Baked, '86 93
Apples and Pear, Honey-Baked, '97 303
Apples, Honey-Baked, '83 234; '84 244
Apples, Honey-Yogurt, '92 46
Apples, Stuffed, '99 247
Bananas, Honey-Baked, '81 268
Breads
  Applesauce-Honey Nut Bread, '87 300
  Banana Bread, Honey-, '91 68
  Biscuits, Honey Angel, '95 138
  Buns, Honey-Oat, '98 27
  Cinnamon Swirl Bread, Honey-, '88 287
  Curry Bread, Honey-, '89 250
  Graham Bread, Honey, '99 211
  Granola Bread, Honey-, '86 56
  Muffins, Banana-Honey-Nut, '88 62
  Muffins, Honey Bran, '88 171
  Muffins, Honey-Bran, '89 250
  Muffins, Honey-Oatmeal, '84 229

Muffins, Honey-Wheat, '83 96; '88 263
Muffins, Oatmeal-Honey, '83 95
Muffins, Orange-Honey, '88 284
Muffins, Peanut Butter-Honey, '82 56
Oat Bread, Honey-, '89 107; '93 232; '98 27
Oatmeal Bread, Honey, '80 60
Rolls, Dilled Honey-Wheat, '83 254
Rolls, Honey Wheat, '83 278
Rolls, Super Honey, '80 115
Wheat Bread, Honey, '85 18, 268
Wheat Bread, Honey-, '91 223
Whole Wheat Honey Bread, '82 65; '83 106
Zucchini-Honey Bread, '89 143
Brie, Honey-Mustard, '91 252
Brownies, Heavenly Honey, '79 83
Buns, Honey Oatmeal, '83 154
Butter, Cinnamon-Honey, '89 281
Butter, Honey, '93 309; '94 206; '95 139; '97 307
Butter, Honey-Orange, '79 36; '85 19
Cake, Honey, '92 250
Cake, Honey-Apple, '99 210
Cake, Honey-Oatmeal, '87 222
Cake, Southern Honey, '89 251
Cake Squares, Honey, '89 250
Carrots, Honey-Glazed, '80 115; '84 121; '85 18; '99 63
Carrots, Honey-Kissed, '84 122
Chicken, Baked Honey, '99 110
Chicken, Honey, '82 55; '88 67
Chicken, Honey-Curry, '87 36
Chicken, Honey-Glazed Grilled, '99 213
Chicken, Honey-Lime Grilled, '96 189; '98 332
Chicken Wings, Grilled Honey, '96 111
Chicken Wings, Honey-Glazed, '91 251
Chops, Honey-Glazed, '97 200
Cornbread, Honey, '83 286; '84 17
Crunch, Honey-and-Spice, '94 290
Dip, Coconut-Honey Fruit, '84 171
Dip, Creamy Honey-Herb, '98 135
Dip, Peanut Butter-Honey, '85 19
Dressings
Applesauce Salad Dressing, Honey-, '99 210
Basil-Honey Dressing, '97 30
Berry Dressing, Orange Salad with Honey-, '89 250
Buttermilk-Honey Dressing, '96 243
Celery-Honey Dressing, '80 42
Dijon-Honey Dressing, '89 45; '99 333
Dijon Salad Dressing, Creamy Honey-, '99 245
French Dressing, Honey, '87 81
Honey Dressing, '79 242; '83 146; '87 129
Lemon Dressing, Fruit Salad with Honey-, '93 21
Lemon Dressing, Honey-, '95 133
Lime Dressing, Honey-, '83 139; '93 71
Lime-Honey Dressing, '92 213
Lime-Honey Fruit Salad Dressing, '87 81
Mustard Dressing, Honey-, '90 55, 111, 146
Orange Salad with Honey Dressing, '89 14
Spinach Salad with Honey Dressing, '90 16
Tomato-Honey French Dressing, '81 105
Vinaigrette, Honey-Mustard, '94 249
Vinaigrette, Honey-Orange, '91 255
Vinaigrette, Lemon-Honey, '96 65
Walnut Dressing, Honey-, '93 107
Yogurt Dressing, Honey-, '93 172
Duck with Parsnip Mash, Honey-Orange-Glazed Muscovy, '97 262
Filling, Honey, '88 287
Filling, Honey-Walnut, '80 21
Flavored Honey, '97 30
Frosting, Honey Chocolate, '79 83
Glaze, Chocolate-Honey, '82 306
Glaze, Cranberry-Honey, '89 273

Glaze, Honey, '88 287
Glaze, Honey-Nut, '87 15
Grapes, Honeyed, '95 47
Ham, Honey-Orange Glazed, '83 320
Ham Slice, Honey-Glazed, '81 104
Ice Cream, Honey, '99 212
Ice Cream, Honey-Vanilla, '95 178
Jelly, Honey-Lemon, '97 29
Kabobs, Honey Ham, '80 156
Leeks, Honey-Glazed, '86 62
Lemon Honey, '94 16; '96 124
Loaves, Hint o' Honey, '81 104
Marinade, Garlic-Honey, '93 102
Marinade, Honey-Mustard, '93 103
Mousse, Honeyed Chocolate, '87 223
Mustard, Hot Honey, '93 240
Mustard, Peppered Honey, '95 312
Onions, Honey, '81 86
Onions, Honey-Paprika Sweet, '92 52
Pancakes, Honey, '91 139
Peaches, Honey-Sweet, '85 107
Peaches 'n' Cream, Honeyed, '93 134
Pear Honey, '90 159
Pear Honey, Gingered, '97 62
Pears, Honey-Baked, '93 47
Pears, Pineapple-Honey, '86 94
Pecans, Honeycomb, '84 300
Pecans, Sugar-and-Honey, '86 319
Pork Chops, Honey-Lime, '85 14
Pork Loin, Garlic-Honey Marinated, '99 334
Pork Tenderloin, Honey-Mustard, '95 52
Pork Tenderloins, Pepper-Honey, '98 33
Preserves, Honeyed Peach, '85 130
Puffs, Honey, '96 153
Relish, Cherry-Honey, '97 32
Rice, Honey, '85 83
Rings, Honey Apple, '80 243
Rutabaga, Honey, '91 220
Salad, Honey Fruit, '80 276
Sauces
Butter Sauce, Honey-, '85 18; '98 45
Chicken in Honey Sauce, '89 82
Chocolate Sauce, Honey-, '89 251
Cinnamon-Pecan-Honey Pancake Sauce, '88 46
Honey Sauce, '99 210
Lemon Mustard Sauce, Honey-, '84 275
Lime Sauce, Honey-, '82 85
Mustard Sauce, Honey-, '85 13
Mustard Sauce, Smoked Ribs with Honey-, '92 168
Orange-Honey Sauce, '97 236
Orange Sauce, Honey-, '85 108
Poppy Seed Sauce, Honey-, '93 13
Sundae Sauce, Honeyscotch, '82 167
Yogurt Sauce, Honey-, '92 307
Shrimp, Tangy Honeyed, '94 32
Smoothie, Fruited Honey-Yogurt, '88 231; '89 23
Smoothie, Honey-Banana, '89 144
Smoothie, Honey-Yogurt, '97 326
Snapper, Honey-Curried, '85 181
Spareribs, Honey-Glazed, '82 163
Spread, Honey, '81 229
Spread, Honey Mustard-Butter, '99 86
Spread, Honey-Nut, '87 157
Stir-Fry, Honey-Butternut, '93 184
Swirl, Honey-Walnut, '80 21
Syrup, Honey, '96 21
Syrup, Maple-Honey-Cinnamon, '85 19
Tart, Honey-Pecan, '99 212
Tea, Honey, '81 105
Topping, Honey, '83 154
Turkey Salad, Honey-Mustard, '92 309
Twist, Honey, '79 80

Vegetables, Honey-Dijon, '98 311
Vegetables, Honey-Glazed Roasted Fall, '99 244
Vegetables, Honey-Mustard Marinated, '93 236
Vegetables, Honey-Roasted, '97 29
Vinaigrette, Sweet Potato Salad with Rosemary-Honey, '98 243
Whip, Peaches with Honey-Lime, '85 108
Yogurt, Orange Slices with Honey, '91 68
HONEYDEW. *See* **MELONS.**
HORS D'OEUVRES. *See* **APPETIZERS.**
HOT DOGS. *See* **FRANKFURTERS.**
HUSH PUPPIES
Acorn Squash Puppies, '94 268
Aunt Jenny's Hush Puppies, '84 88
Bacon Hush Puppies, '91 201
Baked Hush Puppies, '89 53; '95 108
Beer Hush Puppies, Fiery, '86 233
Corn, Hush Puppies with, '83 286; '84 17
Corn Soufflé Hush Puppies, '98 M328
Cracker Hush Puppies, '80 99
Creole Hush Puppies, '98 43
Easy Hush Puppies, '81 191; '85 14
Golden Hush Puppies, '82 135
Green Onion-Tomato Hush Puppies, '97 84
Hush Puppies, '84 102; '87 15; '92 168; '99 32
Mexican Hush Puppies, '90 214
Mexican Hush Puppies, Cheesy, '91 201
Mississippi Hush Puppies, '97 84
Onion Hush Puppies, '85 14
Peppery Hush Puppies, '80 221; '88 111
Shrimp Puppies, Hot-to-Trot, '97 84
Tomato-Onion Hush Puppies, '91 201
Topsail Island Hush Puppies, '79 152

ICE CREAMS. *See also* SHERBETS.
Alaska, Apple Baked, '80 226
Alaska, Baked, '84 105; '85 295
Alaska, Brownie Baked, '80 66
Alaska, Mint Patty, '80 219
Alaskas, Banana Split, '87 10
Almond-Fudge Ice Cream, '93 205
Almond Ice Cream, '98 221
Amaretto Freeze, '82 182
Apricot Ice Cream, '99 146
Balls, Almond Ice Cream, '86 315
Balls, Easy Ice Cream, '84 106
Balls, Nutty Ice Cream, '89 72
Banana-Graham Ice Cream, '91 56
Bananas Foster, Elegant, '81 59
Banana Split Ice Cream, '80 176
Banana Split Pie, Layered, '83 189
Beverages
Almond Float, Nutmeg-, '84 106
Amaretto Breeze, '83 172
Apple Juice Shrub, Shenandoah, '79 282
Banana Flip, '83 303
Banana-Pineapple Milk Shake, '84 59
Banana Smoothie, '87 160
Berry Smoothie, Four-, '97 173
Brandy Cream, '84 312
Champagne Delight, '83 304
Chocoholic Smoothie, '97 173
Chocolate-Mint Smoothie, '84 166
Coffee Floats, Maple-, '86 195
Coffee Punch, Creamy, '81 50
Coffee Refresher, Velvet, '79 149
Coffee Soda, '97 272
Cranberry Float, Sparkling, '86 195
Cranberry-Orange Soda, '79 148
Cranberry Shake, '83 171
Fruit Float, Frosty, '87 159
Ginger Fizz, Ice Cream, '83 303

ICE CREAMS, Beverages
(continued)

Golden Dream, '82 100
Kahlúa Velvet Frosty, '82 244
Lime Cooler, '87 160
Lime Fizz, '81 172
Lime-Pineapple Punch, '83 142
Mocha Punch, '84 166
Orange Milk Shake, '84 166
Orange Shake, Peachy, '81 156
Peach Frosty, '81 156
Peanut Butter Milkshakes, '85 198
Peanut Butter Shake, '82 48
Pineapple Smoothie, Peachy-, '97 173
Pineapple Soda, '90 179
Pink Soda, Blushing, '90 104
Punch, Parsonage, '79 148
Raisin Shake, Amazin', '86 195
Raspberry Fizz, Rosy, '90 179
Rum Coffee Cream, Icy, '83 172
Shake, Pep, '79 38
Strawberry-Banana Float, '87 160
Strawberry Milkshake, Fresh, '82 113
Strawberry-Pineapple Shake, '84 166
Strawberry Punch, Creamy, '86 195
Strawberry Smoothie, '86 183
Strawberry Soda, Old-Fashioned, '79 149
Tahitian Flower, '87 159
Vanilla Cream, '97 272
Vanilla Frosty, French, '79 148
Whispers, '86 317
Black Forest Ice Cream, '88 203
Blueberry Ice Cream, '88 203
Bombe, Amber, '80 255
Bombe, Ice Cream, '82 305; '90 269
Bombe with Raspberry Sauce, Creamy, '89 322
Bourbon Ice Cream, '87 139
Brownie Dessert, Special-Occasion, '87 139
Brownies, Chocolate Ice Cream, '89 124
Butter Crisp Ice Cream, '92 132
Butter Pecan Ice Cream, '80 176; '86 129;
'88 202
Butter-Pecan Ice Cream, '96 134
Cake for Grown-Ups, Ice Cream, '88 M192
Cake, Fruity Ice Cream, '87 110
Cake, Ice Cream, '86 321; '89 71
Cake, Ice Cream Angel, '83 23
Cake, Praline Ice Cream, '80 84
Candy Crunch Ice Cream, '79 166
Cantaloupe Ice Cream, '79 177
Caramel Ice Cream Dessert, '95 36
Caramel-Vanilla Helado (Caramel-Vanilla Ice
Cream), '81 67
Cherry Ice Cream, '84 184; '99 156
Cherry-Nut Ice Cream, '86 129
Cherry-Pecan Ice Cream, '88 203
Chocolate Chunk-Peanut Butter Ice Cream,
'85 297; '86 120
Chocolate Cookie Ice Cream, '95 245
Chocolate-Covered Peanut Ice Cream, '88 203
Chocolate Ice Cream, '80 176; '86 129
Chocolate Ice Cream, Double-, '88 203
Chocolate Ice Cream, Mexican, '91 162
Cinnamon Ice Cream, '95 126
Cinnamon Ice Cream Sombreros, '93 276
Coconut Ice Cream, '98 180
Coconut Ice Cream, Fresh, '79 166
Coffee Ice Cream, '88 202
Coffee Ice Cream Crunch, '82 182
Cookies and Cream Ice Cream, '88 203
Crêpes, Coffee Ice Cream, '84 85
Crêpes, Strawberry Ice Cream, '87 290

Delight, Ice Cream, '80 69
Dessert, Decadent Ice Cream, '91 56
Dessert, Layered Ice Cream, '83 189; '84 94, 105;
'86 163
Fennel Ice Cream, '95 281
Fig Ice Cream, '87 139
Frangelica Cream, '89 291
French-Fried Ice Cream, '85 141
Fried Ice Cream, Coconut, '85 141
Fried Ice Cream Puffs, '85 141
Fruit Cream, Frozen, '94 129
Fudge-Peanut Ice Cream Dessert, '88 167
Galore and More, Ice Cream, '91 144
Granitas
Coffee-Kahlúa Granita, '88 118
Ginger Tea Granita, '98 334
Grape Granita, '88 118
Honeydew Granita, '87 162
Mint Tea Granita, '88 117
Orange Granita, '88 118
Raspberry Liqueur Granita, '88 117
Watermelon Granita, '96 179; '98 165
Wild Raspberry Tea Granita, '99 89
Hawaiian Frappé, '81 178
Honey Ice Cream, '99 212
Honey-Vanilla Ice Cream, '95 178
Ice Milks
Banana Yogurt Ice Milk, '89 199
Strawberry Ice Milk, Fresh, '92 94
Ices
Apricot Yogurt Ice, '81 177
Avocado Ice, '83 179
Champagne Ice, '90 315
Cider Ice, '83 162
Cranberry-Apple Ice, '82 290
Cranberry Ice, Tangy, '87 305
Cranberry-Orange Ice, Tart, '86 317
Fruit Ice, '86 176
Fruit Ice, Mixed, '81 178
Grapefruit Ice, '91 122
Grape Ice, '83 162
Kiwi Ice, '84 315
Merlot Ice, '93 323
Muscadine Ice, '82 202
Peach Ice, '81 178
Peach-Yogurt Ice, '84 83
Pink Grapefruit Ice, '85 304
Raspberry Ice, '92 268
Strawberry Ice, '84 175; '85 108
Strawberry-Orange Ice, '86 196
Tropical Ice, '99 105
Watermelon Ice, '91 173
Wine Ice, '83 163
Irish Cream Ice Cream, '98 221
Italian-Style Ice Cream, '79 245
Lemonade Ice Cream, '88 202
Lemon Ice Cream, '79 142; '83 170; '91 65;
'97 160
Lemon Ice Cream Tarts, '80 152
Lime Ice Cream, Fresh, '97 160
Loaf, Pink Lemonade Ice Cream, '88 202
Log, Ice Cream Yule, '83 253
Making Ice Cream, About, '82 171
Mango Ice Cream, '86 216
Mint-Chocolate Chip Ice Cream, '88 202
Mint-Chocolate Chip Ice Cream Squares, '94 245
Mint Ice-Cream Angel Dessert, Triple, '93 86
Mint Ice Cream Dessert, '88 66
Mocha Ice Cream, '88 202; '97 M145
Oatmeal in a Slow Cooker with Ice Cream,
'99 193
Orange Ice Cream, '97 160
Orange Pekoe-Chocolate Ice Cream, '99 90
Orange-Pineapple Ice Cream, '86 117

Parfaits, Chocolate-Crème de Menthe, '85 161
Parfaits, Coffee Crunch, '82 159
Parfait, Strawberry, '79 99
Parfait, Surprise Strawberry, '86 151
Peach-Almond Ice Cream, '89 156
Peach Ice Cream, '81 184; '82 171; '83 159;
'86 15; '93 135; '98 221
Peach Ice Cream, Creamy, '85 177
Peach Ice Cream, Deluxe, '80 176; '90 314
Peach Ice Cream, Fresh, '95 195
Peanut Butter Ice Cream, '81 103; '88 64, 203
Peanut Ice Cream, '92 132
Peppermint Ice Cream, '80 176; '86 129
Pies
Banana Split Pie, Layered, '83 189
Caramel Ice Cream Pie, '82 181
Carrot Ice Cream Pie, '86 200
Chocolate-Ice Cream Pie, '87 224
Chocolate Ice Cream Pie, '91 56
Chocolate-Mint Ice Cream Pie, '81 144
Chocolate-Peanut Butter Ice Cream Pie,
'98 244
Coffee Ice Cream Pie, '79 231
Divine Ice Cream Pie, Absolutely, '82 181
Double-Delight Ice Cream Pie, '89 72
Heavenly Ice Cream Pie, '82 181
Kona Ice Cream Pie, '83 189
Lemon Ice Cream Pie, '80 70
Lemony Ice Cream Pie, '99 207
Meringue-Pecan Crust, Ice Cream Pie with,
'88 127
Mincemeat Ice Cream Pie, '99 285
Mint Ice Cream Pie, Triple, '98 217
Nutty Ice Cream Pie, '91 180
Peanutty Ice Cream Pie, '82 56
Peppermint Candy-Ice Cream Pie, '87 260
Pumpkin Ice Cream Pie, '81 272
Pumpkin-Ice Cream Pie, '87 243
Rum-Fruit Sauce, Ice Cream Pie with, '84 312
Spectacular, Ice-Cream Pie, '90 314
Sundae Pie, Ice Cream, '94 244
Piña Colada Ice Cream, '91 181
Pineapple-Mint Ice Cream, '84 186
Praline Freeze, '90 48
Praline Ice Cream, '89 318
Pralines and Cream Ice Cream, '82 184; '83 159
Pumpkin, Ice Cream, '96 255
Rainbow Candy Ice Cream, '88 202
Raspberry Ice Cream, '80 176
Raspberry Ice Cream, Fresh, '86 152
Roll, Chocolate-Frosted Ice Cream, '84 200
Roll, Strawberry Ice Cream, '84 105
Rum-Raisin Ice Cream, '97 145
Salad, Ice Cream, '79 126
Sandwiches, Chocolate Cookie Ice Cream,
'87 147
Sandwiches, Chocolate Ice Cream, '89 72
Sandwiches, Ice Cream, '99 147
Sandwiches, Oatmeal Crispy Ice Cream, '93 199
Sandwiches, Peanut Butter Cookie Ice Cream,
'93 199
Sandwich Shells, Brownie Ice Cream, '88 195
Scuppernong Ice Cream, '88 216
Snow Ice Cream, '88 10
Sorbets
Apricot-Almond Sorbet, '98 126
Avocado Sorbet, '88 117
Banana-Orange Sorbet, '88 117
Berry Sorbet, Very, '90 85
Blueberry-Kirsch Sorbet, '83 120
Chocolate Sorbet, '97 111
Cran-Apple Spice Sorbet, '93 153
Cranberry Juice Sorbet, '85 259
Cranberry Sorbet, '82 251

Grapefruit-Mint Sorbet, '93 153
Lemon Sorbet, '93 153
Mango Sorbet, '86 196
Merlot Sorbet, '97 111
Orange Sorbet, Fresh, '92 143
Peach Sorbet, '93 153; '97 110
Pear-Lemon Sorbet, '88 116
Pink Grapefruit and Tarragon Sorbet, '95 163
Strawberry-Champagne Sorbet, '83 162;
    '95 20
Strawberry Margarita Sorbet, '89 111
Strawberry-Passion Fruit Sorbet, '98 180
Strawberry Sorbet, '88 117; '93 153
Tropical Sorbet, '97 110
Watermelon Sorbet, '92 190; '99 166
Spiced Ice Cream, '98 259; '99 26
Squares, Ice Cream Party, '91 214
Straw-Ba-Nut Ice Cream, '80 177
Strawberries and Cream, '92 132
Strawberry-Banana-Nut Ice Cream, '88 203
Strawberry Ice Cream, '80 177; '98 221
Strawberry Ice Cream Crêpes, '88 135
Strawberry Ice Cream, Fresh, '89 111
Strawberry Ice Cream, Homemade, '84 184
Strawberry Ice Cream, Old-Fashioned, '79 94
Strawberry Ice Cream, Very, '81 155
Sundaes
  Apple Ice Cream Sundaes, Spicy, '86 M195
  Cocoa-Kahlúa Sundaes, '83 M58
  Hot Fudge Sundae Dessert, '84 313
  Mauna Loa Sundaes, '80 126
  Peach Sundaes Flambé, '81 88
  Pear Sundaes, Quick, '86 71
  Strawberry Sundaes, Hot, '81 M5
Toffee Ice Cream, '88 202
Toffee Ice Cream Dessert, '87 110
Toffee Ice-Cream Dessert, '97 134
Treats, Crunchy Ice Cream, '86 300; '87 178
Tropical Paradise, Frozen, '89 206
Tutti-Frutti Ice Cream, '86 129
Vanilla Custard Ice Cream, '92 148; '96 145;
    '98 221
Vanilla Ice Cream, '80 176; '86 129; '91 174
Vanilla Ice Cream, Basic, '88 202
Vanilla Ice Cream, Country, '82 143
Vanilla Ice Cream, Old-Fashioned, '97 166
Vanilla Ice Cream Spectacular, '82 166
ICE CUBES. *See* BEVERAGES.
ICINGS. *See* FROSTINGS.

JAMBALAYAS
Black-Eyed Pea Jambalaya, '92 70
Cajun Jambalaya, Smoky, '96 62
Chicken-and-Sausage Jambalaya, '88 200;
    '91 216
Creole Jambalaya, '81 51; '87 210
de Covington, Jambalaya, '87 211
Good Luck Jambalaya, '87 11
Jambalaya, '84 282; '98 317
Mix, Jambalaya, '98 317
1-2-3 Jambalaya, '97 301
Oven Jambalaya, '84 44
Red Rice Jambalaya, '91 18
Sausage Jambalaya, '80 210; '84 249
Seafood Jambalaya, Three-, '82 126
Shrimp Jambalaya, Creole, '92 99
Smoked Sausage Jambalaya, '79 42
Trail Jambalaya, '93 179
Tuna Jambalaya, '83 44
JAMS AND JELLIES
Apple Jelly, '82 149
Apple Jelly, Spiced, '95 251

Apple-Mint Jelly, '87 134
Apricot Jam, Golden, '80 31
Apricot Jam, Quick-Cooked, '99 146
Banana Jam, '82 296
Basil Jelly, '82 301
Blackberry Jam, '82 149; '89 138; '99 M131
Blackberry Jelly, '82 149
Blueberry Jam, '79 120; '85 130
Cantaloupe-Peach Jam, '95 143
Champagne Jelly, '90 248
Chile Piquín Jelly, '94 28
Christmas Brunch Jam, '81 286
Christmas Jam, '88 288
Conserves
  Apple-Cranberry Conserve, '82 308
  Blueberry Conserve, '82 149
  Cranberry Conserve, '79 243; '85 266
  Cranberry Conserve, Caramelized Chicken
    with, '98 320
  Fruit Conserve, Dried, '82 308
  Peach Conserve, '79 120
Crabapple Jelly, '79 120; '81 217; '89 139
Cranberry-Wine Jelly, '81 290
Di-Calcium Phosphate Solution, '89 138
Fig Jam, '86 206
Freezer
  Blackberry Jam, Freezer, '84 M181
  Christmas Freezer Jelly, '86 M288
  Garlic Pepper Jelly, '99 221
  Grape-Burgundy Freezer Jelly, '85 130
  Peach Jam, Freezer, '83 182; '84 M182
  Peach-Plum Freezer Jam, '85 130
  Plum Jam, Freezer, '89 M156
  Raspberry Freezer Jam, '84 M181
  Strawberry Freezer Jam, '84 M182
  Strawberry Preserves, Freezer, '82 112
Garlic Jelly, '99 283
Grape Jelly, '89 140
Grape Jelly, Quick, '89 M156
Grape Jelly, Thyme-, '89 193
Green Pepper Jelly, Unusual, '82 132
Green Tomato Jam, '79 121
Honey-Lemon Jelly, '97 29
Jalapeño Jelly, '92 230; '96 292
Jalapeño Pepper Jelly, Quick, '96 275
Kudzu Blossom Jelly, '95 198
Lemon Jam, Tri-Berry, '98 214
Lime Jelly, '94 23
Marmalades
  Apple Marmalade, '79 120
  Blueberry Marmalade, '96 145
  Carrot-Citrus Marmalade, '81 148
  Citrus Marmalade, '80 101; '97 32
  Citrus Marmalade, Combination, '80 50
  Citrus Marmalade, Mixed, '81 43
  Fruit Marmalade, Delicious, '81 285
  Grapefruit Marmalade, '82 308
  Kumquat Marmalade, '90 48
  Muscadine Marmalade, '98 220
  Onion Marmalade, Fruited, '97 27
  Orange Marmalade, '81 42
  Orange-Pineapple Marmalade, '82 150;
    '89 M156
  Peach-Orange Marmalade, '82 150
  Pear Marmalade, '79 196
  Strawberry-Pineapple Marmalade, '85 130
  Watermelon-and-Ginger Marmalade, '98 164
Mint Jelly, '79 121; '82 301
Muscadine Jelly, Wild, '79 32
Onion Jelly, '93 135
Peach-Banana Jam, Rosy, '80 142
Peach Jam, '93 135
Pear Jam, Paradise, '84 300
Pear Jam, Spiced, '98 214

Pepper Jelly, '79 121
Pineapple Jam, '81 147
Pineapple-Orange Mint Jelly, '92 105
Plum Jelly, '82 150
Port Wine Jelly with Whipped Cream, '84 254
Preserves
  Custard Preserves, '98 126
  Fig Preserves, '79 140; '82 150; '89 140;
    '96 195
  Fruity Preserves, '98 214
  Mango-Pineapple Preserves, '79 137
  Peach Preserves, '81 147; '89 140
  Peach Preserves, Honeyed, '85 130
  Peach Preserves, Old-Fashioned, '82 150
  Pear Preserves, '82 195
  Strawberry-Fig Preserves, Quick, '96 194
  Strawberry Preserves, '79 120; '81 96
  Strawberry Preserves Deluxe, '82 150
  Tomato Preserves, '98 214
  Watermelon Preserves, '79 120
Raspberry Jam, Mock, '96 168
Red Bell Pepper Jam, '95 242
Red Pepper Jelly, '89 M156
Red Zinger Jelly, '99 89
Refrigerator
  Berry Refrigerator Jam, '89 139
  Blueberry Refrigerator Jam, '89 139
  Plum Refrigerator Jam, '89 139
Rose Geranium Jelly, '82 301
Rosemary Jelly, '82 301
Sage Jelly, '82 301
Sangría Jelly, '93 341
Scuppernong Jelly, '98 220
Strawberry Jam, '89 138
Strawberry Jelly, '81 147
Thyme Jelly, '82 301
Wine Jelly, '88 243; '98 125
Wine Jelly, Rosy, '85 306
JÍCAMA
Compote, Jícama-Fruit, '92 49
French-Fried Jícama, '81 88
Parsleyed Jícama, '81 88
Pico de Gallo, '98 174
Salad, Jícama, '87 123
Salad, Jícama-and-Orange, '88 246
Salad, Jícama-Fruit, '86 83
Salad, Jícama-Orange, '86 83; '90 122
Soup with Crunchy Jícama, Tomatillo, '97 143
Tomatillo Soup with Crunchy Jícama, '92 245
Wreath, Tex-Mex, '96 241

KABOBS
Antipasto Kabobs, '94 144
Beef
  Beef Kabobs, '85 110
  Chile-Beef Kabobs, '94 251
  Deluxe Beef Kabobs, '82 182
  Grilled Kabobs, Spicy, '98 158
  Hot-and-Spicy Kabobs, '87 193
  Marinated Beef Kabobs, '82 105; '85 159
  Marinated Beef Kabobs with Rice, '84 32
  Marinated Beef Kabobs with Vegetables,
    '99 292
  Meatball Kabobs, '95 192
  Pineapple-Beef Kabobs, '83 212
  Saucy Beef Kabobs, '83 109
  Sirloin Kabobs, Marinated, '82 162
  Spirited Beef Kabobs, '87 142
  Steak-and-Shrimp Kabobs, '80 184
  Steak Kabobs, '82 4; '93 95
  Steak Kabobs, Barbecued, '79 89
  Steak Kabobs, Marinated, '80 184

KABOBS, Beef
(continued)

Steak on a Stick, '83 109
Steak with Vegetables, Skewered, '81 124
Stick, Beef on a, '99 336
Teriyaki Beef Kabobs, '80 207
Vegetable Kabobs, Beef-and-, '91 148
Vegetables, Beef Kabobs with, '90 148
Cantaloupe Wedges, Grilled, '87 162
Cheese Kabobs, Peppered, '91 279
Fish Kabobs, '98 223
Fruit Kabobs, '86 181; '89 85
Fruit Kabobs, Grilled, '97 147
Fruit Kabobs, Winter, '89 34
Fruit Kabobs with Coconut Dressing, '87 251
Fruit Kabobs with Mint Marinade, '82 157
Fruity Mermaid Kabobs, '91 177
Ham Kabobs, Honey, '80 156
Ham Kabobs, Swiss-, '81 124
Lamb Kabobs, '85 159; '86 90; '92 129; '95 192
Lamb Kabobs, Apricot-Grilled, '98 102
Lamb Kabobs, Rosemary Marinated, '93 203
Lamb Kabobs, Saucy, '89 167
Lamb Kabobs, Savory, '80 184
Lamb, Rosemary-Skewered, '97 190
Lamb Shish Kabobs, '79 142; '93 70
Liver Kabobs, '80 185
Oysters Brochette, '80 56
Pepper Kabobs, Pretty, '90 166
Pork Kabobs, Margarita, '98 M223
Pork Kabobs, Pineapple-, '99 144
Pork Kabobs, Spicy, '82 182
Poultry
Chicken-Avocado Kabobs, '82 9; '83 68
Chicken, Garlic-Grilled, '87 180
Chicken Kabobs, '87 141
Chicken Kabobs, Good-and-Easy, '85 87
Chicken Kabobs, Marinated, '84 M144
Chicken Kabobs, Oriental, '95 193
Chicken Kabobs, Pineapple-, '86 M328
Chicken Kabobs, Sesame, '82 165
Chicken Kabobs, Soy-, '86 156
Chicken Kabobs Supreme, '81 124
Chicken Livers en Brochette, '84 222
Chicken Saté, '99 134
Chicken, Sesame, '97 256
Chicken Skewers, Taco-, '99 119
Chicken with Cha-Cha Salsa, Grilled Bahamian, '97 160
Duck Kabobs with Almond Rice, Grilled, '91 291
Hawaiian Kabobs, '85 157
Turkey-and-Fruit Kabobs, '88 140
Rumaki Kabobs, '82 182
Salmon Kabobs, '81 182
Scallop-Bacon Kabobs, '81 111
Scallop Kabobs, Grilled, '83 101
Scallop Kabobs, Sea, '82 162
Scallops en Brochette with Vegetables, '80 163
Seafood Brochette, '87 96
Shish Kabobs, '82 182; '85 M112
Shish Kabobs, Overnight, '81 124
Shish Kabobs Teriyaki, '85 37
Shrimp
Appetizer Shrimp Kabobs, '91 251
Barbecued Shrimp, '90 28
Marinated and Grilled Shrimp, '87 141
Marinated Shrimp, Grilled, '87 173
Marinated Shrimp Kabobs, '84 276; '85 158
Scallop Kabobs, Grilled Shrimp-and-, '92 210
Shrimp Kabobs, '80 150, 184

Steak-and-Shrimp Kabobs, '80 184
Vegetable Salsa, Shrimp Skewers with, '98 32, 223
Squash-and-Pepper Kabobs, Summery, '95 193
Swordfish-Shiitake Skewers, '97 168
Tomatoes with Basil Vinaigrette, Grilled, '97 168
Vegetable Kabobs, Fresh, '81 158; '92 101
Vegetable Kabobs, Grilled, '93 170
Vegetable Kabobs, Marinated, '83 M195
Vegetable Kabobs, Tangy Marinated, '88 142
Vegetable Skewers, Grilled, '94 160
Venison Kabobs, '82 215; '88 249
Watermelon, Sherried, '92 117
KIWIFRUIT
Chutney, Kiwifruit-Onion, '93 125
Dessert, Kiwi-and-Orange, '93 295
Glacé, Sabayon, '89 306
Ice, Kiwi, '84 315
Jubilee, Kiwi, '83 120
Meringue Cups, Kiwi and Cream in, '81 279
Muffins, Kiwifruit, '87 255
Orange Roughy, Kiwi, '87 193
Parfait, Kiwi, '86 199; '87 55
Pizza, Kiwi-Berry, '86 198; '87 55
Pizza, Kiwifruit, '89 306
Pops, Kiwi Margarita, '99 133
Salad, Peach-and-Kiwi, '90 180
Salad, Spinach-Kiwifruit, '87 305
Salsa, Hot Kiwifruit, '94 82
Tart, Kiwifruit, '89 232
Tart, Kiwifruit-Peach, '88 20
KUGEL
Apricot Noodle Kugel, '92 251
Nu Awlins Kugel, '94 229
Sweet Kugel, '90 254
Vegetable-Noodle Kugel, '96 228

L

LAMB
Barbecued Lamb, '79 58
Burgers, Mesquite-Grilled Lamb, '88 59
Burgers with Cucumber Sauce, Lamb, '98 102
Burgoo, Five-Meat, '87 3
Casserole, Moussaka, '79 179
Chops
Barbecued Lamb Chops, '79 89
Broiled Lamb Chops, '85 22
Dijonaise, Gourmet Lamb Chops, '82 93
Dijon Lamb Chops, '84 277
Dijon-Rosemary Lamb Chops, '95 285; '99 333
Grilled Lamb Chops, '91 163
Grilled Lamb Chops with Rosemary Sauce and Wild Rice-Fennel Pilaf, '97 127
Herbs, Lamb Chops with, '90 164
Minted Apples, Lamb Chops with, '99 230
Orange Lamb Chops, '83 35
Peppercorn-Crusted Lamb Chops, '92 142
Rosemary Lamb Chops, Joan's, '97 42
Sage Lamb Chops, '96 M328
Shrimp, Lamb Chops with, '88 58
Teriyaki, Lamb Chops, '85 109
Teriyaki Lamb Chops, '87 60
Curried Lamb with Rice, '82 93
Curried Lamb with Rice Mold, '85 36
Curry with Rice, Lamb, '80 83; '81 10
Fillets of Lamb with Vegetables, '85 36
Grape Leaves, Stuffed, '94 48
Grilled Lamb with Sweet Pepper Relish, '95 104
Kabobs
Grilled Lamb Kabobs, Apricot-, '98 102
Lamb Kabobs, '85 159; '86 90; '92 129; '95 192

Marinated Lamb Kabobs, Rosemary, '93 203
Rosemary-Skewered Lamb, '97 190
Saucy Lamb Kabobs, '89 167
Savory Lamb Kabobs, '80 184
Shish Kabobs, '82 182; '85 M112
Shish Kabobs, Lamb, '79 142; '93 70
Shish Kabobs, Overnight, '81 124
Shish Kabobs Teriyaki, '85 37
Leg of Lamb
Cranberry Leg of Lamb, '90 52
Extraordinaire, Lamb, '99 242
Glazed Lamb, Honey-Mustard, '90 52
Glazed Leg of Lamb, '86 90
Greek-Style Leg of Lamb, '93 170
Grilled Lamb with Mango Salsa, '95 104
Grilled Leg of Lamb, '96 88; '98 103
Half of Leg of Lamb, '86 90
Hawaii, Lamb, '81 58
Hunter Sauce, Leg of Lamb with, '95 317
Leg of Lamb, '86 90; '95 285
Mustard Sauce, Leg of Lamb with, '89 71
Roasted Lamb Rosemary, '88 244
Roasted Rosemary Lamb, '86 89
Roast, Garlic-Rolled Lamb, '92 128; '93 113
Roast Leg of Lamb, '87 96; '99 242
Sandwiches, Lamb, '97 107
Smoked Leg of Lamb, '98 102
Stuffed Leg of Lamb, '82 93; '87 248
Stuffed Leg of Lamb, Garlic-and-Herb, '99 241
Meatballs with Yogurt Sauce, Lamb, '85 132
Meat Loaf, Greek, '96 251; '97 103
Meat Loaf, Minted Lamb, '93 248
Meat Loaf with Feta Cheese, Lamb, '97 24
Mint-Crusted Lamb, '99 163
Moussaka, '87 166
Pie, Lamb, '90 26
Pilaf, Hearty Lamb, '83 101
Pockets with Dilled Cucumber Topping, Lamb, '87 104
Quenelles, Veal-Vermicelli Soup with, '94 14
Rack, Greek Lemon Lamb, '97 247
Rack of Lamb, '89 270
Rack of Lamb, Marinated, '94 55
Rack of Lamb, Mint-Crusted, '98 118
Rack of Lamb with Cherry-Wine Sauce, Hazelnut-Crusted, '95 284
Rack of Lamb with Herb Mustard Glaze, '81 260
Roasted Lamb with Vegetables, '98 266
Roast of Lamb, Crown, '81 58
Roast, Rolled Lamb, '95 285
Salad, Spinach-Lamb, '85 58
Shanks, Barbecued Lamb, '92 128; '93 113
Shanks Milanaise, Lamb, '82 93
Steak, Destin Lamb, '92 129; '93 113
Steaks with Béarnaise Sauce, Lamb, '85 37
Stewed Lamb with Five Spices, '92 72
Stew, Emerald Isle, '95 71
Stew-in-a-Loaf, Lamb, '85 37
Stew, Lamb, '79 293; '88 58
Stew, Lamb-and-Okra, '97 156
Stew with Popovers, Lamb, '94 43
Stir-Fry, Indian, '92 126
LASAGNA
Beefy Lasagna, '80 81
Bun, Lasagna in a, '90 176
Cheesy Lasagna, '82 224; '88 299
Chicken Lasagna, '87 M302; '88 90; '92 197; '93 25; '96 16
Chicken Lasagna Bake, '95 55
Chicken Lasagna Florentine, '95 158
Crabmeat Lasagna, '96 290
Crawfish Lasagna, '91 89
Easy Lasagna, '92 M197; '93 M24
Gourmet White Lasagna, '96 225

Ham-and-Chicken Lasagna, Creamy, '95 88
Italian Sausage Lasagna, '96 225
Lasagna, '82 119; '83 M6; '98 95
Lean Lasagna, '86 37
Light Lasagna, '95 212
Maria, Lasagna, '90 191
Mexican Lasagna, '89 63; '98 283
Microwave Lasagna, '96 M225
Noodles Lasagna, Lots of, '91 M127
One-Step Lasagna, '89 M129
Pizza, Lasagna, '85 285
Quick Lasagna, '84 220
Quick 'n Easy Lasagna, '80 M10
Roasted Vegetable-Meat Lasagna, '99 M332
Rolls, Pepper-Topped Lasagna, '89 M36
Sausage Lasagna, '83 288
Sausage-Lasagna Rollups, '80 236
Sausage Pinwheels, Lasagna, '79 6
Simple Lasagna, '81 188
South-of-the-Border Lasagna, '84 31
Supreme, Lasagna, '92 198; '93 24
Texas Lasagna, '98 52
Tofu Lasagna, '83 312
Tuna Lasagna, '83 44; '84 123
Turkey Lasagna, '83 239; '91 130
Turkey-Picante Lasagna, '97 93
Two, Lasagna for, '81 91
Vegetable
  Casserole, Vegetable Lasagna, '92 198; '93 25
  Cheesy Vegetable Lasagna, '79 84
  Colorful Vegetable Lasagna, '87 19
  Florentine, Creamy Lasagna, '91 94
  Florentine, Lasagna, '88 196
  Garden Lasagna, '83 119
  Spaghetti Squash Lasagna, '84 127
  Spinach-Bean Lasagna, '92 96
  Spinach Lasagna, '79 25; '81 243
  Spinach Lasagna, Cheesy, '80 32; '83 204
  Vegetable Lasagna, '84 201; '93 320; '95 211; '96 47; '99 97
  Zucchini Lasagna, '85 194
Vintage Lasagna, '79 194
Zesty Lasagna, '87 M188
LEEKS
Bisque, Crab-and-Leek, '94 104
Chicken and Leeks in Parchment, '97 290
Dilled Lemon-Butter, Leeks in, '90 M98
Dilly Leek Combo, '82 26
Dip, Creamy Leek, '86 77
Glazed Leeks, '82 26
Glazed Leeks, Honey-, '86 62
Linguine, Leeks and Peppers with, '98 68
Medley, Carrot-and-Leek, '88 102
Orange Sauce, Leeks in, '88 86
Quiche, Cheddar-Leek, '88 198
Roasted Potatoes, Carrots, and Leeks, '94 276
Soup, Carrot-Leek, '86 34
Soup, Cream of Leek, '99 276
Soup, Leek-and-Potato, '84 112
Soup, Leek-Vegetable, '86 304
Soup, Watercress-and-Leek, '86 161
Tarragon Leeks, '84 66
Terrine, Cold Chicken-Leek, '92 145
Veal Cutlets with Leeks and Zinfandel Cream, '96 237
Vinaigrette, Warm Leeks, '98 47
LEMON
Apples, Chilled Poached Lemon, '86 182
Artichoke Hearts with Lemon, '90 98
Asparagus, Lemon-Sesame, '91 31
Asparagus with Lemon, '98 103
Bagel Chips, Lemon-and-Herb, '91 139

Basil, Cream of Tomato Soup with Lemon, '96 124
Beans, Lemon-Mint, '88 22
Beverages
  Apple Lemonade, '89 212
  Berry Delicious Lemonade, '93 205
  Blackberry Lemonade, '99 130
  Blueberry Lemonade, '98 179
  Caribbean Cooler, '95 203
  Claret Lemonade, '93 72
  Concentrate, Lemonade, '89 110
  Cooler, Lemon, '82 48
  Cranberry Lemonade, Spiced, '87 292
  Cubes, Lemonade, '95 201
  Cubes, Lemon-Mint, '95 201
  Dazzling Lemonade, '97 99
  Frappé, Lemon, '92 44
  Fresh Squeezed Lemonade, '81 172
  Fresh-Squeezed Lemonade, '99 220
  Front Porch Lemonade, '90 156
  Glass, Lemonade by the, '96 161
  Hot Buttered Lemonade, '88 208; '94 18
  Margaritas, Lemon-Lime, '94 227
  Margaritas, Mock, '99 120
  Mist, Orange-Lemon, '79 288; '80 35
  Orange-Mint Lemonade, '88 82
  Piña Coladas, '95 203
  Pineapple Lemonade, '93 194
  Punch, Lemonade-Bourbon, '95 287
  Punch, Lemon Balm, '80 42
  Punch, Lemon Champagne, '94 176
  Punch, Pink, '96 190
  Punch, Sparkling Lemonade, '88 276
  Punch, Strawberry-Lemonade, '85 116; '91 175
  Sipper, Sunshine, '86 179
  Slush, Pink Lemonade, '80 151
  Spritzer, Lemon-Mint, '99 175
  Strawberry Lemonade, '80 160
  Sweetened Preserved Lemons, '95 141
  Sweet-Tart Lemonade, '96 161
  Syrup, Cherry-Lemonade, '86 214
  Tea, Almond-Lemonade, '86 229; '99 207
  Tea Cubes, Lemonade with Frozen, '85 161
  Tea, Lemon, '82 156
  Tea, Lemon-Mint, '85 162
  Tea, Sparkling Summer, '96 172
  Tea Tingler, Lemon, '95 200
  Velvet, Lemon, '90 15
  Watermelon Lemonade, '98 165
Breads
  Biscuits, Lemon Drop, '97 332
  Blueberry-Lemon Bread, '85 190
  French Bread, Lemony, '97 147
  Lemon Bread, '79 275; '87 256
  Muffins, Blueberry-Lemon, '79 7
  Muffins, Fresh Lemon, '79 161
  Muffins, Lemon, '88 119, M275
  Muffins, Lemon-Raspberry, '92 119
  Muffins, Poppy Seed-Lemon, '96 280
  Nut Bread, Lemon-, '79 24
  Pecan Bread, Lemon-, '83 54
  Scones, Lemon-Poppy Seed, '97 44
  Scones, Lemon-Raisin, '87 69
  Spirals, French Lemon, '81 94
  Tea Bread, Lemon, '92 268; '93 183
  Tea Loaf, Lemon-Cream, '84 50
Broccoli Goldenrod, Lemon-, '84 M89
Broccoli, Lemon, '88 119; '95 53
Brussels Sprouts with Celery, Lemony, '85 25
Butter, Asparagus in Lemon, '80 M123
Butter, Asparagus with Lemon, '87 M151; '98 168
Butter, Citrus, '97 307

Butter, Green Beans with Lemon-Dill, '99 141
Butter, Lemon, '95 32; '96 124
Butter, Lemon-Anchovy, '97 307
Butter, Lemon Pepper, '97 307
Butter, Thyme-Lemon, '96 121
Cabbage, Lemon-Butter, '88 156
Canapés, Lemon-Cheese, '87 93
Carrot Bundles, Lemon-, '91 80
Carrot Marmalemon, '96 107
Carrots and Rutabaga, Lemon-Glazed, '97 46
Carrots, Lemon, '82 300; '83 111
Carrots, Lemon-Dill Steamed, '93 180
Carrots, Lemon-Glazed, '84 16
Cauliflower, Easy Lemon, '83 322
Cheese Party Bites, Lemon-, '95 160
Cheese Patty, Lemon-Pepper, '84 117
Corn on the Cob, Lemony, '89 200
Couscous, Lemon, '96 154
Cream, Broccoli with Lemon, '89 245
Cream, Strawberries 'n Lemon, '85 120
Crêpes with Fruit Filling, Lemon, '82 46
Cucumbers, Lemony, '89 102
Curd, Lemon, '94 315
Desserts
  Apples, Chilled Poached Lemon, '86 182
  Bars Deluxe, Lemon, '79 35
  Bars, Lemon Yogurt Wheat, '79 93
  Bars, Tangy Lemon, '86 217
  Cake, Coconut-Lemon, '95 319
  Cake, Easy Lemon, '83 24
  Cake, General Robert E. Lee Orange-Lemon, '88 92
  Cake, Glazed Lemon, '86 70
  Cake, Lemon Angel, '80 147; '97 163
  Cake, Lemon-Coconut Cream, '81 179
  Cake, Lemon-Coconut Sheet, '85 117
  Cake, Lemon Gold, '83 301
  Cake, Lemon Meringue, '89 296; '99 118
  Cake, Lemon-Pineapple, '86 60, 239
  Cake, Lemon-Poppy Seed, '93 154
  Cake, Lemon Pound, '82 88
  Cake, Lemon Pudding, '83 106
  Cake, Lemon-Raspberry, '91 247
  Cake, Lemon-Sour Cream Pound, '87 38
  Cake, Lemon Tea, '82 169
  Cake, Lemony Pound, '96 60
  Cake, Lightly Lemon Coffee, '81 14
  Cake, Luscious Lemon, '93 81
  Cake, Luscious Lemon Layer, '86 61
  Cake, Old-Fashioned Lemon Layer, '85 191
  Cake Roll, Elegant Lemon, '80 70
  Cake Roll, Lemon, '89 312
  Cake, Tart Lemon-Cheese, '88 7
  Cake with Blueberry Sauce, Buttermilk-Lemon Pudding, '95 135
  Cake with Mint Berries and Cream, Lemon Pound, '99 183
  Cake, Yogurt-Lemon-Nut, '89 169
  Candied Lemon Peel, '94 199
  Charlotte Russe, Fresh Lemon, '80 13
  Charlotte Russe, Lemon, '84 192
  Cheesecake, Lemon, '86 194; '91 308; '92 24
  Cheesecake, Lemon Delight, '95 219
  Cheesecake, Luscious Lemon, '90 M196
  Cheesecake with Orange-Pineapple Glaze, Lemon, '81 60
  Chocolate-Lemon Creams, '98 M235
  Cookies, Lemonade, '79 51
  Cookies, Lemon Crinkle, '81 287
  Cookies, Lemon-Iced Chocolate Spice, '97 123
  Cookies, Lemon Thyme, '96 124
  Cookies, Lemony Cutout, '85 323
  Cookies, Sunshine Lemon, '86 69

LEMON, Desserts
(continued)

Cream Cheese Dessert, Lemon-, '84 95
Cream, Frozen Lemon, '83 118
Cream, Lemon, '82 237; '91 119
Cream, Lemon-Blueberry, '92 153
Cream Puffs, Lemon, '93 254
Cream Puffs, Strawberry-Lemon, '87 75
Cream, Strawberries with Lemon, '90 170
Crisp, Lemon-Blackberry, '98 171
Crisps, Lemon, '95 272
Cupcakes, Lemon Moist, '82 112; '83 153
Cups, Baked Lemon, '87 128
Curd, Fresh Fruit with Lemon, '88 21
Curd, Lemon, '87 139; '89 334
Curd with Berries, Lemon, '90 102
Custard in Meringue Cups, Lemon, '80 295;
     '81 172
Custards, Lemon-Buttermilk, '89 49
Dainties, Lemon Pecan, '80 208
Delight, Lemon, '82 227
Divinity, Lemon, '97 316
Filling, Creamy Lemon, '80 70
Filling, Lemon, '81 172; '84 137; '85 191;
     '86 235; '87 293; '89 312; '90 308; '94 122;
     '95 319; '97 255; '99 118
Filling, Lemon-Apricot, '90 105
Filling, Lemon-Cheese, '79 68; '88 7
Filling, Lemon Cream, '84 23; '87 14
Filling, Lemon-Orange, '81 71
Frosting, Creamy Lemon, '79 93
Frosting, Lemon, '85 191; '86 217; '93 81
Frosting, Lemon Buttercream, '83 301; '86 61;
     '91 247
Frosting, Lemon-Butter Cream, '85 117
Frosting, Lemon-Coconut, '90 253
Frosting, Lemon-Cream Cheese, '81 157
Frosting, Lemony White, '88 7
Frosting, Orange-Lemon, '88 92
Fruitcake, Lemon, '83 258
Glaze, Lemon, '79 285; '86 194; '87 41;
     '92 269; '93 154, 183; '97 123
Ice Cream, Lemon, '79 142; '83 170; '91 65;
     '97 160
Ice Cream, Lemonade, '88 202
Layered Lemon Dessert, '88 134
Logs, Hazelnut-Lemon, '84 117
Mandel Bread, '99 57
Melting Moments, '85 191
Meringue, Chocolate Pudding with Lemon,
     '88 258
Meringue Cream Cups, Lemon, '84 23
Mousse, Lemon Cloud, '90 90
Mousse, Strawberry-Lemon, '82 128
Mousse with Raspberry Sauce, Lemon, '91 96;
     '92 130
Napoleons, Blueberry-Lemon, '94 122
Parfaits, Strawberry-Lemon, '84 198
Pastry Shell, Lemon in, '84 137
Pears, Lemon Poached, '82 74
Pie, Angel, '79 123
Pie, Apple-Lemon Chess, '86 220
Pie, Aunt Kitty's Lemon, '98 275
Pie, Best-Ever Lemon Meringue, '94 208
Pie, Buttermilk Lemon, '81 120; '82 23
Pie, Buttermilk-Lemon, '88 297
Pie, Buttermilk-Lemon Cream, '88 99
Pie, Deluxe Lemon Meringue, '81 172; '90 313
Pie, Frozen Lemonade, '92 101
Pie, Frozen Lemon Cream, '82 86
Pie, Lemonade, '91 42
Pie, Lemon-Buttermilk, '91 272

Pie, Lemon Cheese, '81 136; '82 146
Pie, Lemon Chess, '79 32; '82 196
Pie, Lemon-Cottage Cheese, '79 44
Pie, Lemon Cottage Cheese, '81 143
Pie, Lemon Fluff, '92 342; '93 46
Pie, Lemon Ice Cream, '80 70
Pie, Lemon Meringue, '85 M112; '86 130
Pie, Lemon-Orange, '85 172
Pie, Lemon Parfait, '94 310
Pie, Lemon-Pecan, '93 251
Pie, Lemon-Sour Cream, '82 169
Pie, Lemon Sponge, '83 192
Pie, Lemon-Strawberry, '88 127
Pie, Lemon Twirl, '84 94
Pie, Lemony Cherry, '92 30
Pie, Lemony Ice Cream, '99 207
Pie, Slice of Lemon, '84 23
Pie, Tart Lemon, '91 275
Pie, Tart Lemon-Apple, '80 100
Pie, Whipped Lemon, '79 124
Pops, Deep Blue Sea, '94 143
Pops, Sangría, '99 133
Pudding, Layered Lemon, '82 128
Pudding, Lemon, '79 86; '81 99
Pudding, Lemon Cake, '92 96; '98 35
Pudding, Lemon Fluff, '85 304
Pudding, Lemon-Pear, '96 283
Pudding, Old-Fashioned Lemon Bread, '88 95
Roll, Snow-Capped Lemon, '79 68
Rolls with Raspberry Sauce, Lemon Angel,
     '94 294
Sauce, Cheesecake with Raspberry-Lemon,
     '96 30
Sauce, Lemon, '84 258, 306; '85 77, 190;
     '91 240; '96 283
Sauce, Lemon Cream, '93 200
Sauce, Lemon Dessert, '87 M165
Sauce, Tart Lemon, '85 191
Sherbet, Lemon, '91 309
Sherbet, Lemon Cream, '79 114
Sherbet, Lemon-Pineapple, '96 330
Solid, Lemon, '93 279
Sorbet, Lemon, '93 153
Sorbet, Pear-Lemon, '88 116
Soufflé, Cold Lemon-Lime, '84 24
Soufflé, Lemon, '82 170, 252; '94 199
Soufflés, Quick Lemon Sauce, '88 43
Soufflé, Tart Lemon, '85 82
Soufflé with Raspberry-Amaretto Sauce,
     Frozen Lemon, '88 130
Sponge Cups, Lemon, '83 10
Squares, Golden Carrot-Lemon, '80 40
Squares, Lemon, '81 197; '97 329
Squares, Lemon-Pecan, '89 124
Squares, Lemony Cream Cheese, '82 159
Strawberry-Lemon Dessert, '86 162
Tart), Caky Flaky Tart (Tart Lemon, '96 159
Tarts, Berry Good Lemon, '91 119
Tarts, Dainty Lemon, '82 304
Tarts, Golden Lemon, '85 191
Tart Shells, Lemon, '88 195
Tarts, Lemon, '82 156; '83 79
Tarts, Lemon-Cheese, '79 2
Tarts, Lemon Ice Cream, '80 152
Tarts, Lemon-Sour Cream, '81 304
Tart, Strawberry-Lemon, '89 111
Topping, Lemon-Pineapple, '86 60
Torte with Raspberry Sauce, Lemon
     Meringue, '93 82
Trifle, All Seasons Lemon, '95 219
Trifle, Lemon-Blueberry, '88 210
Yogurt, Lemon-Chiffon Frozen, '85 54
Yummies, Lemon, '81 301
Zephers, Lemon, '81 172

Dressing, Chilled Broccoli with Lemon, '88 270
Dressing, Creamy Lemon, '88 M193
Dressing, Fruit Salad with Honey-Lemon, '93 21
Dressing, Green Salad with Lemony French,
     '85 67
Dressing, Honey-Lemon, '95 133
Dressing, Lemon-and-Herb, '92 108
Dressing, Lemon-Caper, '96 69
Dressing, Lemon Cream, '82 170
Dressing, Lemon-Herb, '97 92
Dressing, Lemon-Herb Salad, '82 67
Dressing, Lemon-Molasses, '97 195
Dressing, Lemon-Pepper, '87 55
Dressing, Lemon Salad, '79 8
Dressing, Lemon-Yogurt, '93 17
Dressing, Lemon-Yogurt Slaw or Salad, '88 54
Dressing, Tomato Slices with Lemon, '87 167
Glaze, Lemon, '97 332
Green Beans, Lemon, '89 275
Green Beans, Lemon-Walnut, '93 304
Green Beans, Lemony, '85 190; '99 259
Honey, Lemon, '94 16; '96 124
Jam, Tri-Berry Lemon, '98 214
Jelly, Honey-Lemon, '97 29
Knots, Glazed Lemon, '86 290
Linguine, Lemon, '97 228
Main Dishes
Beef, Spicy Lemon Thai, '97 320
Beef, Thai Lemon, '97 292
Catfish, Lemon Barbecued, '88 271; '89 202
Chicken and Vegetables, Lemon, '88 118
Chicken, Baked Lemon, '85 190
Chicken Breasts, Lemon, '89 18
Chicken, Clay Oven-Roasted Citrus, '98 108
Chicken Cutlets with Lemon, '85 8
Chicken, Greek Lemon, '90 65
Chicken, Grilled Yogurt-Lemon, '81 111
Chicken in Lemon and Wine, '83 281
Chicken in Lemon Marinade, '98 128
Chicken, Lemon, '81 M138; '86 173; '96 49
Chicken, Lemonade, '82 163
Chicken, Lemon Barbecued, '93 215
Chicken, Lemon-Dill, '93 19
Chicken, Lemon-Fried, '79 77
Chicken, Lemon Fried, '82 275
Chicken, Lemon-Frosted, '88 170
Chicken, Lemon-Garlic, '89 M132; '90 35
Chicken, Lemon-Garlic Roasted, '98 108
Chicken, Lemon-Herb, '85 127
Chicken, Lemon-Herb Grilled, '95 87
Chicken, Lemon-Mustard, '99 109
Chicken, Lemon-Pepper, '89 104
Chicken, Lemon-Roasted, '95 24
Chicken, Lemon-Rosemary, '94 201
Chicken, Lemon-Spinach, '97 104
Chicken, Lemony Pecan, '96 82
Chicken Nuggets, Lemon-, '86 337; '87 283
Chicken Piccata, Herbed, '88 28
Chicken Sauté, Lemon-Dill, '91 186
Chicken, Sweet-and-Sour Lemon, '84 93
Chicken, Sweet Lemon, '79 218
Chicken, Sweet Lemon-, '84 69
Chicken with Lemon, Garlic, and Rosemary,
     Roasted, '97 61
Cornish Hens, Lemon Roasted, '82 260
Cutlets, Lemon-Flavored, '79 105
Fillets, Lemon-Coated, '80 M53
Flank Steak, Lemon-Lime, '95 55
Flounder Thermidor, '85 190
Lamb Rack, Greek Lemon, '97 247
Linguine with Garlic and Lemon, '88 91
Mackerel, Lemon-Baked, '79 182
Pork Chops, Lemon-Herb, '84 81; '89 M132
Pork Chops, Lemony, '88 118

Pork Piccata, **'94** 57; **'99** 332
Ribs, Lemon Baked, **'81** 166
Ribs, Lemon Grilled, **'81** 154
Shrimp and Pasta, Lemon, **'96** 124
Shrimp in Lemon Butter, **'84** 163
Shrimp, Lemon-Garlic Broiled, **'82** 29; **'86** 182
Shrimp, Luscious Lemon, **'88** 150
Snapper with Crabmeat Relish, Lemony
  Pecan-Crusted, **'99** 198
Spareribs, Lemony Sweet, **'80** 73
Steak with Brandy Sauce, Lemon-Butter,
  '85 78
Tuna with Lemon and Capers, **'97** 180
Turkey-Basil Piccata, **'96** 49
Turkey Piccata, **'91** 137
Turkey Piccata with Caper Sauce, **'98** 49
Veal, Lemon, **'93** 35
Veal Piccata, **'92** 181
Veal Piccata, Lemon, **'86** 118
Veal with Artichoke Hearts, Lemon, **'87** 219
Marinade, Lemon-Soy, **'91** 194
Marmalade, Citrus, **'80** 101
Mayonnaise, Lemon, **'95** 32; **'98** 144; **'99** 178
Mayonnaise, Lemon-Cream, **'85** 264
Mayonnaise, Lemon-Dill, **'99** 267
Mold, Cheesy Lemon, **'79** 241
Mold, Lemon-Cucumber, **'87** 90
New Potatoes, Lemon-Buttered, **'84** 149;
  '90 268; **'98** 159
New Potatoes, Lemony, **'82** 158
Olive Oil, Lemon-Infused, **'95** 231
Olives, Lemon-Garlic, **'94** 118
Pancakes with Strawberry Butter, Lemon, **'99** 44
Pasta, Lemon-Garlic, **'95** 181
Pilaf, Lemon, **'97** 322
Pilaf, Lemon-and-Pine Nut, **'97** 51
Potatoes, Herbed Lemon Mashed, **'93** 208
Potatoes, Lemon and Nutmeg, **'80** 36
Potatoes, Lemon-Herb Stuffed, **'83** 173
Potatoes, Lemon-Steamed, **'86** 177
Potatoes, Oregano-and-Lemon Skillet, **'93** 54
Potato Wedges, Lemon, **'88** 21
Potato Wedges, Lemony, **'90** M61
Relish, Lemon-Date, **'96** 271
Relish, Lemony Cranberry, **'79** 243
Rice, Lemon, **'89** 166
Rice, Lemony, **'99** 46
Risotto, Lemon-Lime, **'97** 213
Roses, Lemon, **'82** 280
Salads
  Apple-Bran Salad, Lemony, **'86** 223
  Asparagus Salad, Creamy Lemon-, **'93** 116
  Cauliflower-Lemon Salad, **'81** 23
  Cheese Salad, Lemon-, **'85** 240
  Congealed Lemon-Tomato Salad, **'89** 178
  Congealed Salad, Lemon-Cranberry, **'87** 311
  Congealed Salad, Lemon-Vegetable, **'85** 22
  Cream Salad, Lemon-, **'88** 250
  Freeze, Fruity Lemon, **'82** 145
  Fruit Salad, Lemonade, **'84** 24
  Onion Salad, Lemon-, **'85** 252
  Potato Salad, Lemon-Basil, **'97** 63
Sauces
  Asparagus with Lemon Sauce, **'86** 62
  Barbecue Sauce, Herbed Lemon, **'94** 154;
    '98 334
  Barbecue Sauce, Lemony, **'88** M177; **'95** 31
  Basting Sauce, Lemon, **'95** 32
  Broccoli with Lemon Sauce, **'91** 292; **'92** 256
  Broccoli with Lemon Sauce and Pecans,
    '86 71
  Brussels Sprouts in Lemon Sauce, **'82** 269
  Butter Sauce, Lemon-, **'84** 252; **'92** 337;
    '99 198

Celery Sauce, Baked Fillets in Lemon-, **'84** 91
Cheese Sauce, Lemon-, **'91** 24
Cheese Sauce, Lemony, **'84** 183
Cream Sauce, Braised Chicken Breast in
  Lemon, **'94** 184
Cream Sauce, Lemon, **'99** 53
Cucumber Sauce, Lemony, **'89** 245
Garlic Sauce, Shrimp in Lemon, **'83** 67
Honey-Lemon Mustard Sauce, **'84** 275
Hot Lemon-Herb Sauce, **'91** 286
Lemon Sauce, **'82** 290
Meunière Sauce, Lemon, **'88** 222
Mustard Sauce, Salmon Steaks with Lemon-,
  '97 124
New Potatoes with Lemon Sauce, **'86** 130
Parsley Sauce, Lemon, **'81** 106
Parsley Sauce, Lemon-, **'93** 48
Tartar Sauce, Lemony, **'95** 32
Zesty Lemon Sauce, **'97** 318
Slices, Fluted Lemon, **'82** 51
Soup, Egg-Lemon, **'96** 88
Soup, Lemon-Egg Drop, **'93** 81
Spinach, Creamy Lemon, **'82** 302
Spinach with Feta, Lemon, **'85** 190
Spinach with Lemon and Pepper, **'97** 105
Sprouts, Lemon, **'85** 288
Squeezers, Lemon, **'95** 32
Sugar, Lemon-Mint, **'95** 32
Sugar Snap Peas with Basil and Lemon, **'93** 66
Sweetened Preserved Lemons, **'95** 141
Vegetables, Honey-Glazed Roasted Fall, **'99** 244
Vegetables, Lemon, **'93** 83
Vermicelli, Lemon, **'84** 329
Vinaigrette, Lemon, **'95** 31
Vinaigrette, Lemon-Basil, **'94** 205
Vinaigrette, Lemon-Dill, **'99** 27
Vinaigrette, Lemon-Honey, **'96** 65
Vinegar, Lemon, **'95** 31; **'96** 124
Vinegar, Lemon-Mint, **'85** 124
Vinegar, Raspberry-Lemon, **'87** 134
Vinegar, Spicy Oregano-Lemon, **'85** 124
Wild Rice, Pecan-Lemon, **'92** 211
Wonton Chips, Lemon-and-Herb, **'91** 138
Yogurt Coleslaw, Grilled Chicken Breasts with
  Lemon-, **'98** 148
Zucchini, Lemon-Garlic, **'89** 226
LENTILS
  Baked Lentils with Cheese, **'84** 113
  Burgers, Lentil, **'95** 123
  Burritos, Lentil, **'99** 287
  Casserole, Lentils-and-Rice, **'93** 301
  Pasta and Lentils, Cheesy, **'99** 287
  Pilaf, Rice-and-Lentil, **'88** 17
  Rice, Lentils and, **'99** 236
  Salad, Lentils-and-Rice, **'90** 197
  Salad, Mediterranean Lentil, **'96** 239
  Salad, Winter, **'97** 304; **'98** 19
  Samosas, **'96** 239
  Sauce, Lentil Spaghetti, **'90** 198
  Soup, Beefy Lentil, **'87** 282
  Soup, Lentil, **'83** 292; **'86** 304; **'91** 28; **'97** 304;
    '98 19
  Soup, Spanish-Style Lentil, **'96** 239
  Spread, Lentil, **'99** 288
  Stew, Lentil-Rice, **'82** 232
  Supper, Lentil-and-Rice, **'84** 202
  Tacos, Lentil, **'88** 197
  Tex-Mex Lentils, **'99** 288
  Vegetables, Savory Lentils and, **'98** 29
LIGHT & EASY. *See* **LIVING LIGHT.**
LIME
  Beverages
    Apple Limeade, Pink, **'89** 46
    Cooler, Grape-Lime, **'94** 227

Cooler, Lime, **'87** 160
Daiquiris, Freezer Lime, **'79** 141
Fizz, Frosty Lime, **'90** 104
Fizz, Lime, **'81** 172
Fuzz Buzz, **'82** 160
Margaritas, Frosted, **'84** 115
Margaritas, Frosty, **'83** 172
Margaritas, Lemon-Lime, **'94** 227
Margaritas, Mock, **'99** 120
Margaritas, Orange-Lime, **'97** 140
Margaritas, Pitcher, **'83** 175
Punch, Brew-Ha-Ha, **'98** 255
Punch, Calypso Presbyterian Church
  Women's Lime, **'95** 141
Punch, Foamy Lime, **'82** 264
Punch, Lime, **'84** 58
Punch, Lime-Pineapple, **'83** 142
Punch, Lime Slush, **'90** 273
Punch, Orange-Lime, **'82** 160
Tea, Lime, **'98** 198
Tea, Lime-Mint, **'97** 122
Butter, Cilantro-Lime, **'98** 156
Candied Lime Strips, **'94** 137
Crackers, Tortilla-Lime, **'99** 17
Cream, Cilantro-Lime, **'98** 129
Cream, Ginger-Lime, **'95** 227
Desserts
  Cake, Key Lime, **'91** 214
  Cheesecake with Strawberry-Butter Sauce,
    Key Lime, **'96** 87
  Cream, Lime-Rum, **'93** 169
  Curd, Key Lime, **'96** 126
  Ice Cream, Fresh Lime, **'97** 160
  Key Lime Bars with Macadamia Crust, **'99** 282
  Loaf, Lime Layer, **'85** 96
  Mousse Freeze, Luscious Lime, **'81** 173
  Parfaits, Lime, **'80** 153
  Parfaits, Surf-and-Sand, **'93** 169
  Pie, Key Lime, **'91** 42; **'96** 171
  Pie, Lime Chiffon, **'86** 130
  Pie, Lime Fluff, **'84** 43
  Pie, Manny and Isa's Key Lime, **'95** 118
  Pies, Key Lime, **'95** 86; **'97** 162
  Pies, Lime Party, **'92** 65
  Pie with Minted Tropical Salsa, Key Lime,
    '99 333
  Refresher, Lime-Mint, **'82** 144
  Sherbet, Creamy Lime, **'84** 165
  Sherbet, Lime, **'82** 159; **'89** 202
  Soufflé, Cold Lemon-Lime, **'84** 24
  Squares, Lime, **'79** 2
  Tart in Coconut Crust, Key Lime, **'89** 160
  Tart, Lime, **'98** 272
  Tart, Lime-Pineapple, **'88** 6
  Tornadoes for Grown-Ups, Texas, **'94** 143
  Whip, Lime, **'89** 199
Dip, Lime-Dill, **'92** 65
Dip, Orange-Lime, **'96** 248
Dressing, Asparagus with Warm Citrus, **'96** M86
Dressing, Honey-Lime, **'83** 139; **'93** 71
Dressing, Lime, **'79** 2; **'83** 120
Dressing, Lime-Honey, **'92** 213
Dressing, Lime-Honey Fruit Salad, **'87** 81
Dressing, Lime-Parsley, **'85** 131
Dressing, Lime Sherbet, **'80** 221
Dressing, Spinach Salad with Chili-Lime, **'94** 63
Jelly, Lime, **'94** 23
Main Dishes
  Beef Stir-Fry, Lime-Ginger, **'92** 65
  Bow Ties, Black Beans, and Key Limes,
    '96 291
  Chicken Breasts, Lime-Roasted, **'97** 100
  Chicken, Grilled Lime-Jalapeño, **'91** 87
  Chicken, Honey-Lime Grilled, **'96** 189; **'98** 332

LIME, Main Dishes
(continued)

Chicken with Lime Butter, '84 68
Chicken with Orange, Lime, and Ginger
Sauce, '92 123
Flank Steak, Lemon-Lime, '95 55
Pork Chops, Honey-Lime, '91 33
Red Snapper with Lime, Stuffed, '83 246
Turkey Tenderloins, Lime-Buttered, '92 127
Veal, Amaretto-Lime, '93 54
Marinade, Fruit with Lime, '98 92
Marinade, Southwestern, '99 141
Marmalade, Citrus, '80 101
Mayonnaise, Flavored, '97 328
Muffins, Key Lime, '95 50
Mustard, Key Lime, '94 278
Pesto, Cilantro, '98 145
Pickles, Lime, '96 206
Rice, Lime-Flavored, '84 175
Risotto, Lemon-Lime, '97 213
Salad, Emerald, '81 143
Salad, Frosted Lime-Cheese, '79 286
Salad, Lime-Carrot, '92 65
Salad, Pear-Lime, '84 152
Salad, Pineapple-Lime, '84 320
Salad, Snowy Emerald, '87 311
Sauce, Grilled Swordfish with Avocado-Lime,
'97 127
Sauce, Honey-Lime, '82 85
Sauce, Lime Hollandaise, '93 121
Sauce, Lime-Saffron, '94 71
Sauce, Sour Cream-Lime, '91 286
Sopa de Lima, '79 211
Soup, Lime, '88 31
Vinaigrette, Cilantro-Lime, '94 77
Vinaigrette, Pistachio-Lime, '97 148
Whip, Peaches with Honey-Lime, '85 108

LINGUINE
Alfredo, Bourbon-Pecan, '96 291
Artichoke and Shrimp Linguine, '95 210
Artichoke Hearts, Pasta with, '86 209
Basil Pasta, Fresh Tomato Sauce over, '93 176
Bay Scallops, Linguine with, '97 201
Beef Stir-Fry, Italian, '99 35
Broccoli Linguine, '98 30
Carbonara, Linguine, '87 108
Chicken-Broccoli Linguine, '98 30
Chicken, Sicilian, '97 142
Chicken, Taste-of-Texas Pasta and, '92 78
Clam Linguine, '95 212
Clam Linguine, Quick, '90 233
Clam Sauce, Linguine in, '81 83
Clam Sauce, Linguine with, '84 124; '88 90;
'89 178
Clam Sauce with Linguine, '84 9
Cracked Pepper Linguine, '97 228
Favorite Pasta, My, '95 213
Garlic and Lemon, Linguine with, '88 91
Leeks and Peppers with Linguine, '98 68
Lemon Linguine, '97 228
Mussels Linguine, '90 M112
Parmesan, Creamy Pasta with, '98 233
Pasta Verde, '84 201
Peas and Pasta, '99 68
Pesto and Pasta, '92 98
Pesto Pasta, Asian, '95 189
Pesto Primavera, '96 170
Red Pepper Sauce, Linguine with, '93 127
Salad, Pasta, '84 139
Salad Pasta, Caesar, '95 230
Seafood Delight, '86 208
Seafood Linguine, '79 227

Seafood Sauce, Linguine with, '83 232
Shrimp and Linguine, Spicy, '92 34
Shrimp and Pasta, Mediterranean, '95 286
Shrimp and Pasta, Sautéed, '96 288
Shrimp Marinara, '84 233
Shrimp, Spicy Pasta and, '97 67
Spinach, Linguine with, '91 30
Tomato-Cream Sauce, Linguine with, '86 158
Vegetables, Traveling Linguine with Roasted,
'93 178
Verde, Pasta, '84 201
Whole Wheat Linguine, '84 177
Zucchini with Pasta, Stuffed, '97 101

LIVER
Appetizers
Chicken Liver and Bacon Roll-Ups, '80 200;
'81 57
Chicken Livers, Party, '83 242
Chicken Liver Turnovers, '79 141
Pâté, Chicken Liver, '79 153; '81 235; '83 108;
'84 205
Pâté, Country, '86 66
Pâté, Duck Liver, '79 227
Pâté, Liver-Cheese, '85 276
Pâté with Cognac, '86 159
Pâté with Madeira Sauce, Liver, '93 323
Rumaki, '80 M136
Spread, Liver, '89 161
Spread, Sherried Liver, '80 86
Barbecued Liver, '85 219
Beef Liver Patties, '81 277
Beef Liver with Balsamic Vinegar, '98 130
Calf's Liver with Vegetables, '85 219
Chicken
Chopped Chicken Livers, Grandma Rose's,
'96 105
en Brochette, Chicken Livers, '84 222
Fried Chicken Livers, '96 105
Garlic Chicken Livers, '96 105
Italian Sauce, Chicken Livers in, '83 117
Marsala Wine Sauce, Chicken Livers with,
'81 76
Mushrooms, Chicken Livers with, '81 133
Omelet, Chicken Liver, '82 44
Orange Sauce, Chicken Livers in, '82 218
Party Chicken Livers, '83 242
Pâté, Chicken Liver, '79 153; '81 235; '83 108;
'84 205
Potatoes, Chicken Livers and, '82 218
Rice, Chicken Livers with, '80 200; '81 58;
'84 292
Rice Dish, Chicken Livers and, '82 218
Risotto, Chicken Livers, '82 218
Roll-Ups, Chicken Liver and Bacon, '80 200;
'81 57
Rumaki Kabobs, '82 182
Sautéed Chicken Livers, '80 200; '81 57
Scrumptious Chicken Livers, '84 230
Stroganoff, Chicken Livers, '80 200; '81 57
Supreme, Chicken Livers, '81 298
Turnovers, Chicken Liver, '79 141
Wine Sauce, Chicken Livers in, '81 104
Creole Liver, '85 219; '86 108; '96 236
Creole Sauce, Liver in, '87 33
French-Style Liver, '80 10
Gravy, Liver and, '80 10
Herbs, Liver with, '81 277
Italiano, Liver, '85 219
Kabobs, Liver, '80 185
Loaf, Skillet Liver, '80 11
Noodle Dinner, Creamy Liver and, '80 11
Saucy Liver, '81 277
Sauté, Liver, '81 277
Spanish-Style Liver, '80 11

Stroganoff, Liver, '79 54
Sweet-and-Sour Liver, '81 277
LIVING LIGHT
Andouille, '92 242
Appetizers
Ambrosia, Sherried, '84 324
Apple-Phyllo Rolls, '88 213
Artichokes, Marinated, '87 250
Artichokes with Herb-Mayonnaise Dip, '84 67
Beets, Blue Cheese-Stuffed, '88 211
Buzzard's Nests, '93 244
Carrot-Cheese Ball, '86 325
Cheese Tartlets, '88 211
Cherry Tomatoes, Crab-Stuffed, '82 289
Cherry Tomatoes, Stuffed, '88 212
Chicken-Mushroom Appetizers, '88 210
Chicken Wontons, '92 284
Chips, Bagel, '91 138
Chips, Baked Pita, '99 138
Chips, Baked Wonton, '91 138; '99 138
Chips, Cinnamon-and-Sugar Bagel, '91 139
Chips, Cinnamon-and-Sugar Wonton, '91 138
Chips, Corn Tortilla, '91 17
Chips, Garlic Bagel, '91 139
Chips, Garlic Wonton, '91 138
Chips, Lemon-and-Herb Bagel, '91 139
Chips, Lemon-and-Herb Wonton, '91 138
Chips, Light Tortilla, '90 278; '91 257
Chips, Parmesan Cheese Bagel, '91 138
Chips, Parmesan Cheese Wonton, '91 138
Chips, Pita, '89 19; '91 138
Chips, Plantain, '95 M203
Chips, Sweet Potato, '91 138; '95 M203
Chips, Tortilla, '91 137
Crab Cakes with Jalapeño Tartar Sauce,
Chesapeake Bay, '96 69
Crackers, Cranberry, '99 258
Crostini, Festive, '99 324
Crudité Platter with Dip, '84 139
Dip, Cheese-Herb, '89 20
Dip, Chickpea-and-Red Pepper, '99 138
Dip, Creamy Ham, '93 125
Dip, Curry, '87 25; '99 138
Dip, Deviled, '87 25
Dip, Dilled Garden, '84 324
Dip, Festive Crab, '92 285
Dip, Garbanzo, '93 94
Dip, Ginger, '99 139
Dip, Kahlúa, '99 139
Dip, Low-Cal Tuna, '87 25
Dip, Marmalade, '99 324
Dip, Monster Mash, '93 244
Dip, Pine Nut-Spinach, '99 138
Dip, Quick Fruit, '90 110
Dip, Ranch-Style, '90 138
Dip, Refreshing Dill, '99 324
Dip, Santa Fe Skinny, '94 137
Dip, Skinny Ranch, '93 96
Dip, Spinach, '87 25
Dip, Tofu, '86 109
Dip, Vegetable Garden, '85 215
Eggplant Appetizer, Grilled, '95 198
Fruit Kabobs with Coconut Dressing, '87 251
Fruit with Lemon Sauce, Fresh, '82 290
Goat Cheese Wrapped in Phyllo, '99 43
Hummus, '96 158
Hummus, Low-Fat, '99 137
Meatballs, Sweet-and-Sour, '99 325
Mix, Crunchy Snack, '93 94
Mix, Snack, '89 19
Mousse, Shrimp, '87 251
Mushroom-Almond Pastry Cups, '88 210
Mushroom Appetizers, Stuffed, '88 210
Mushrooms, Shrimp-Stuffed, '99 324

Mushrooms, Spinach-Stuffed, '89 M133
Nectarine Cocktail, '85 107
New Potatoes, Ham-Stuffed, '88 211
Orange Halves, Broiled, '85 288
Oysters Bienville, Baked, '90 27
Oysters Italiano, Baked, '89 97
Pasta Bites, Pesto-Cheese, '87 251
Pâté, Black-Eyed Pea, '93 97
Pâté, Lentil, '92 285
Pâté, Mock, '87 251
Pears Stuffed with Cheese, '82 290
Pita Bread Triangles, '88 211
Pita Wedges, Garlic, '93 98
Pizzas, Pita, '89 19
Popcorn, Chili, '91 17
Popcorn Mix, Curried, '86 326
Popcorn with Pizzazz, '93 245
Potato Skin Snack, '91 18
Pretzels, Whole Wheat, '89 20
Quesadillas, Green Chile, '90 121
Scallop Appetizer, '86 155
Shrimp Dippers, '84 324
Shrimp with Marmalade Dip, Oven-Fried,
    '99 324
Snow Peas, Crab-Stuffed, '85 288
Spinach-Ricotta Phyllo Triangles, '88 212
Spread, Artichoke-Parmesan, '92 95
Spread, Broccamoli Curry, '88 55
Spread, Feta Cheese, '96 265
Spread, Low-Fat Chicken, '82 290
Spread, Roasted Red Bell Pepper, '97 217
Spread, Smoked Salmon, '84 324
Steak-and-Chestnut Appetizers, Marinated,
    '84 323
Tabbouleh, '88 211
Tortilla Snacks, Pesto, '89 19
Vegetable Appetizer, Tarragon, '83 277
Vegetable Nachos, '91 17
Zucchini Caviar, '88 212
Zucchini Pizzas, '88 212
Zucchini-Shrimp Appetizers, '89 311
Apple-Cheese Bake, '92 225
Apples, Baked, '86 40
Apple Side Dish, Dried, '92 226
Apples, Stuffed Baked, '89 217
Apples with Orange Sauce, Baked, '84 314
Barley, Baked, '91 133
Beans, Molasses Baked, '99 105
Beverages
Apple Cooler, '90 14
Apple Julep, '86 103
Apricot Fruit Flip, '91 18
Apricot Mint Cooler, '90 165
Banana Coolers, '91 308
Banana Nog, '82 290
Banana Smoothie, '93 95
Bellini Spritzers, '90 110
Black Russian, Mock, '92 322
Bourbon Blizzard, '92 287
Brew, Witch's, '93 244
Caribbean Cooler, '95 203
Carrot Cooler, '89 35
Cider, Hot Spiced, '82 290; '99 248
Cocoa, Mocha, '83 318
Cranberry Cocktail, Hot, '89 310
Cranberry Smoothie, '91 307
Eggnog, '83 318
Eggnog with Orange and Nutmeg, Mock,
    '92 323
Fruit Beverage, Blender, '83 318
Fruit Refresher, '91 203
Fruit Slush, '96 157
Fruit Smoothie, '89 87
Grapefruit Refresher, '88 85

Hot Chocolate, Mexican, '98 313
Lemon Velvet, '90 15
Milkshake, Mocha, '89 35
Mocha, Hot, '84 60
Orange Juicy, '90 178
Orange-Pineapple Drink, '89 35
Orange Slush, '82 49
Peach Cooler, '86 6
Peach Frosty, '83 318
Peach Refresher, '86 103
Piña Colada, Mock, '92 322
Piña Coladas, '95 203
Pineapple-Banana Slush, '90 14
Pineapple Sparkle, Spiced, '92 322
Pineapple-Yogurt Whirl, '91 132
Punch, Apple-Tea, '85 82
Punch, Citrus, '93 99
Punch, Holiday, '87 252
Punch, Holiday Hot Fruit, '92 286
Punch, Hot Apple, '84 324
Punch, Tart Cranberry, '83 318
Punch, White Grape, '90 15
Scarlet Sipper, '90 198
Shake, Frosty Fruit, '87 23
Shake, Strawberry-Banana, '89 35
Shake, Strawberry-Orange Breakfast, '87 186
Shake, Strawberry-Pear, '92 139
Strawberry Cooler, '83 56
Strawberry Spritzer, '90 14
Tea Mix, Spiced, '86 32
Tea Mix, Sugar-Free Spiced, '91 258
Tofruitti Breakfast Drink, '88 26
Tomato-Clam Cocktail, '87 252
Tomato Refresher, '83 318
Tropical Refresher, '96 157
Vegetable Cocktail, Fresh, '82 165
Virgin Mary, Spicy, '92 323
Watermelon-Berry Slush, '90 137
Breads
Apricot-Orange Bread, '92 285
Apricot-Pecan Bread, '97 266
Banana Bread, '87 72
Banana Bread, Fruity, '95 78
Barbecue Bread, '99 105
Biscuits and Sausage Gravy, '94 20
Biscuits, Angel, '90 28
Biscuits, Cheese-Chive, '94 324
Biscuits, Easy-Bake, '96 157
Biscuits, Herbed, '93 67
Biscuits, Light, '89 53
Biscuits, Oatmeal, '89 108
Biscuits, Orange, '88 85
Biscuits, Whole Wheat, '84 60; '91 222
Biscuits, Yeast, '87 71
Bowls, Italian Bread, '98 292
Caraway Breadsticks, '89 239
Cinnamon-Oat Bread, '90 135
Cornbread, '92 324
Cornbread, Dieter's, '87 164
Cornbread, Jalapeño, '94 78
Cornbread, Mexican, '93 182
Cornbread Supreme, '93 67
Cornmeal Yeast Bread, '89 54
Corn Sticks, '89 54
Cranberry-Banana Bread, '90 294
Crouton Bread, Quick, '90 138
English Muffin Bread, '95 M79
Flatbread, '98 106
Focaccia, Rosemary, '95 190
French Bread, '89 54
French Pistou Bread, Crusty, '97 68
French Toast, Cottage-Topped, '85 49
French Toast, Slender, '86 103
Garlic Bread, '82 19; '91 204

Herbed Bread, '89 34
Honey-Oat Bread, '89 107
Hush Puppies, Baked, '89 53; '95 108
Muffins, All-Bran Oat Bran, '91 134
Muffins, Apple, '84 193
Muffins, Applesauce, '91 141
Muffins, Banana-Oat, '87 188
Muffins, Banana-Raisin, '89 218
Muffins, Blueberry, '91 140, 203
Muffins, Bran-Buttermilk, '85 7
Muffins, Corn, '98 313
Muffins, Cornmeal, '91 19
Muffins, Cornmeal Yeast, '92 49
Muffins, Corn-Oat, '89 108
Muffins, Freezer Bran, '91 141
Muffins, Granola, '95 78
Muffins, Honey Bran, '88 171
Muffins Made of Bran, '86 103
Muffins, Miniature Cranberry, '90 294
Muffins, Oat Bran, '89 106
Muffins, Oat Bran-Banana, '91 18
Muffins, Oatmeal-Bran, '91 83
Muffins, Spicy Apple-Oat, '86 45
Muffins, Spicy Cornmeal, '90 59
Muffins, Yogurt, '88 55
Oat Bread, Caraway-Raisin, '86 44
Oatmeal-Molasses Bread, '97 194
Onion-Herb Bread, '90 165
Pitas, Puffy, '97 69
Pumpkin-Pecan Bread, '87 221
Rolls, Dinner, '89 312
Rolls, Honey Wheat, '83 278
Rolls, Old-Fashioned Cinnamon, '92 226
Rolls, Parsley-Garlic, '93 319
Rolls, Vegetable Salad, '82 278
Rolls, Whole Wheat, '90 111
Rolls, Yogurt Crescent, '91 123
Rye Loaves, Swedish, '97 68
Sourdough Wedges, '90 199
Spoonbread, '90 200
Swiss Cheese Loaves, Mini, '95 80
Toasts, Parmesan-Pepper, '98 242
Toast Strips, Seasoned, '93 98
Whole Wheat Cardamom Bread, '86 223
Breakfast-in-a-Bowl, '89 87
Burritos, Hot Phyllo, '98 312
Chorizo, '92 241
Chutney, Blueberry, '95 190
Chutney, Fall Fruit, '97 218
Chutney, Mango, '96 182
Chutney, Peach, '96 207
Chutney, Pear, '98 243
Couscous with Mixed Fruit, '95 232
Crab Cakes, Country, '95 20
Crêpes, Basic, '86 38
Crêpes, Bran, '83 70; '86 44
Crêpes, Ham-and-Egg, '83 204
Crêpes, Light, '86 143
Crêpes, Low-Calorie, '87 77
Crêpes, Plain, '83 70
Crêpes Suzettes, Light, '83 71
Crêpes, Whole Wheat, '83 70
Croutons, Bagel, '93 192
Croutons, Cornbread, '93 192
Croutons, Garlic, '92 71
Croutons, Pita, '93 192
Crust, Whole Wheat, '94 78
Desserts
Alaska, Orange, '83 177
Alaska, Peachy Melba, '88 266
Ambrosia, Baked, '83 303
Ambrosia, Layered, '88 304
Apple Crisp, Tart, '92 226
Apples à l'Orange, Baked, '90 280

LIVING LIGHT, Desserts
(continued)

Applesauce Fluff, '91 173
Apples, Caramel-Peanut, '93 M244
Apples, Melting, '88 19
Bananas Foster, '88 20; '96 99
Bananas with Honey, Broiled, '84 175
Bananas with Rum Sauce, Spiced, '99 247
Bars, Apricot-Raisin, '87 32
Bars, Pineapple-Orange, '82 129
Bavarian Dessert, Light, '86 6
Berries, Best-Dressed, '96 317
Biscotti, Chocolate-Hazelnut, '95 80
Biscotti, Light, '91 310
Blackberries and Dumplings, '86 196
Blintzes, Cheese, '83 71
Blueberry Crisp, '84 177
Brownies, Chocolate-Kahlúa, '93 99
Brownies, Chocolate-Walnut, '89 325
Cake, Apple-Nut, '87 76
Cake, Apple Spice, '92 225
Cake, Banana-Coconut, '93 154
Cake, Black Widow Snack, '93 245
Cake, Blueberry Streusel, '92 144
Cake, Chocolate Angel Food, '87 21; '90 111
Cake, Chocolate-Cinnamon, '93 154
Cake, Chocolate Custard, '88 175
Cake, Chocolate Pound, '89 325
Cake, Cinderella Fantasy, '98 70
Cake, Deluxe Light Banana, '84 314
Cake, Four-Flavor Pound, '91 136
Cake, Frosted Carrot, '92 19
Cake, Heavenly Pineapple, '83 303
Cake, Lemon-Poppy Seed, '93 154
Cake, Mocha Marble Pound, '99 23
Cake, Orange Angel Food, '96 246
Cake, Orange-Coconut Angel Food, '94 294
Cake, Orange Pound, '87 221
Cake, Pound, '92 94
Cake, Pumpkin, '93 303
Cake, Red Velvet, '93 318
Cake Roll, Lemon, '89 312
Cake Roll, Make-Ahead Chocolate-Mint,
  '95 220
Cake, Strawberry Yogurt Layer, '94 85
Cake, Warm Chocolate Pudding, '92 324
Cake, Winter Squash-Spice Bundt, '99 248
Cake with Amaretto-Almond Sauce, Angel
  Food, '90 199
Cake with Coffee Frosting, Spice Layer,
  '94 86
Cake with Custard Sauce, Chocolate Angel
  Food, '88 259
Cake with Pineapple-Orange Sauce, Angel,
  '84 14
Cake with Raspberry Sauce, Sour Cream
  Pound, '99 259
Cake with Strawberries and Chocolate Glaze,
  White, '87 76
Cantaloupe Whip, '89 198
Cheesecake, Almost Strawberry, '86 32
Cheesecake, Black Forest, '94 21
Cheesecake, Blueberry Chiffon, '87 76
Cheesecake, Chocolate-Amaretto, '93 97
Cheesecake, Dieter's Apple, '86 318
Cheesecake, Fudge, '98 M213
Cheesecake, Lemon, '91 308
Cheesecake, Lemon Delight, '95 219
Cheesecake, Light-and-Easy, '88 55
Cheesecake with Raspberry-Lemon Sauce,
  '96 30
Cherries Jubilite, '86 317

Chocolate-Bran Raisin Jumbos, '91 142
Chocolate-Cheese Cups, '91 142
Chocolate-Coffee Cones, '96 M316
Chocolate Cream Log, '94 220
Chocolate Cream Roll, '85 317
Chocolate Fondue, '91 142
Chocolate Glaze, '89 325
Chocolate-Orange Roll, '87 21
Chocolate Whip, '89 326
Chocolat, Petits Pots de, '82 272
Cobbler, Cranberry-and-Apple, '90 294
Cobbler, Fresh Cherry, '84 178
Cobbler, New-Fashioned Apple, '91 221
Cobbler, New-Fashioned Blackberry, '87 164
Cobbler, Peach, '84 178
Cobbler, Raspberry-Cherry, '93 230
Coffee Cake, Sour Cream, '93 154
Coffee Dessert, Light, '88 260
Compote, Baked Fruit, '84 314
Compote, Fresh Fruit, '82 272; '84 82
Compote, Jícama-Fruit, '92 49
Compote, Melon Ball, '85 157
Compote, Spicy Grapefruit-Berry, '91 19
Compote with Caramel Syrup, Citrus, '98 313
Cookies, Almond, '91 51
Cookies, Apple-Oatmeal, '85 215
Cookies, Light Almond, '83 151
Cookies, Light Chocolate Chip, '86 46
Cookies, Meringue, '98 71
Cookies, Oatmeal-Raisin, '87 221; '93 127
Cranberries Jubilee, '90 293
Cream Puffs, Strawberry-Lemon, '87 75
Crêpes, Fruit-Filled Chocolate, '89 325
Crêpes, Tropical Fruit, '87 77
Crust, Gingersnap, '90 296
Crust, Graham Cracker, '86 32; '88 55; '91 308
Crust, Lattice, '90 294
Custard, Baked Rice, '92 308
Custard, Baked Vanilla, '82 129
Custard, Coconut, '86 109
Custard, Light Mexican, '88 149
Custard over Fruit, Stirred, '84 83
Custard, Range-Top Amaretto, '87 77
Custard with Raspberries, Almond Crème,
  '88 174
De-Light-Ful Dessert, '95 220
Filling, Almond, '96 316
Filling, Chocolate, '96 316
Filling, Coffee, '96 316
Filling, Lemon, '89 312
Filling, Orange, '96 316
Flambé, Banana-Peach, '85 316
Flan, Luscious, '90 56
Flan, Pumpkin, '97 219
Frosting, Boiled, '93 318
Frosting, Coffee, '94 86
Frosting, Italian Meringue, '98 70
Frosting, Orange-Cream Cheese, '92 19
Fruitcake, Classic, '91 258
Fruitcake, Jeweled, '88 260
Fruit Cup, '91 202
Fruit Dessert, Caribbean, '84 314
Fruit Dessert, Flaming, '83 302
Fruit Dessert Orange, '84 314
Fruit Dessert, Rainbow, '85 108
Fruit Dessert, Spiced, '82 50
Fruit, Gingered, '83 151
Fruit, Glazed, '85 83
Fruit Medley, Fancy, '84 82
Fruit with Lemon Curd, Fresh, '88 21
Fruit with Mint-Balsamic Tea, Fresh, '95 232
Glaze, Lemon, '93 154
Honeydew-Berry Dessert, '83 120
Ice, Cranberry-Apple, '82 290

Ice, Grapefruit, '91 122
Ice, Kiwi, '84 315
Ice Milk, Banana Yogurt, '89 199
Ice Milk, Fresh Strawberry, '92 94
Ice, Mixed Fruit, '88 85
Ice, Peach-Yogurt, '84 83
Ice, Strawberry, '84 175; '85 108
Ice, Strawberry-Orange, '86 196
Ice, Tangy Cranberry, '87 305
Ice, Tart Cranberry-Orange, '86 317
Ice, Tropical, '99 105
Ice, Watermelon, '91 173
Kiwi Jubilee, '83 120
Lemon Angel Rolls with Raspberry Sauce,
  '94 294
Lemon Curd with Berries, '90 102
Lime Strips, Candied, '94 137
Lime Whip, '89 199
Mandelbrot, Rhoda's, '98 243
Melon Mélange, '84 139
Melon-Mint Julep, '86 196
Meringue Mixture, Basic, '98 70
Meringue Mushrooms, '96 317
Meringue Shells, Fruited, '87 32
Meringues, Peach Melba, '87 76
Meringues, Tropical, '98 71
Meringues with Buttermilk Custard Sauce,
  Peach Melba, '96 183
Mocha Sauce with Chocolate Yogurt, '92 243
Mousse, Coffee-Nut, '86 319
Mousse, Peach, '85 54
Mousse, Strawberry-Lemon, '82 128
Orange-Mallow Cream, '94 295
Orange Molded Dessert, '83 302
Oranges and Pineapple, Glazed, '86 318
Parfait, Peach, '82 166
Parfait, Pineapple, '84 83
Pastry, Light, '92 95
Peach-Blueberry Dessert, '92 184
Peach Dessert, Spiced, '83 9
Peaches with Honey-Lime Whip, '85 108
Peaches with Nutty Dumplings, Spiced,
  '87 164
Peaches with Strawberry Sauce, '85 8
Peach Halves, Stuffed, '86 196
Pear Fans with Raspberry-Orange Sauce,
  Poached, '88 22
Pears Baked in Molasses-Port Sauce, '97 195
Pears in Custard, Poached, '88 20
Pears in Orange Sauce, Poached, '82 19
Pears Poached in Red Wine, '83 302
Pears, Vanilla Poached, '90 57
Pears with Berry Sauce, Wine-Poached,
  '86 144
Pears with Honey-Yogurt Sauce, Poached,
  '92 306
Pears with Meringue, Amaretto, '90 M58
Pie, Buttermilk, '92 95
Pie, Chocolate Bavarian, '89 326
Pie, Eggnog, '83 205
Pie, Fresh Apple, '84 178
Pie, Frozen Chocolate Brownie, '96 57
Pie, Fruited Cheese, '92 228
Pie, New-Fashioned Pumpkin, '90 296
Pineapple, Meringue-Topped, '84 178
Pineapple with Raspberry Sauce, Chocolate-
  Drizzled, '90 57
Plum Slush, '84 139
Pops, Orange-Banana, '82 129
Pops, Pineapple-Yogurt, '91 173
Praline Horns, '96 316
Prune Bavarian, '86 223
Pudding, Almost Banana, '88 174
Pudding, Apple-Raisin Bread, '88 175

Pudding, Chocolate-Almond Silk, '96 266
Pudding, Layered Lemon, '82 128
Pudding, Lemon Cake, '92 96
Pudding, Light Plum, '86 318
Pudding, Old-Fashioned Banana, '92 94
Pudding, Old-Fashioned Bread, '88 175
Pudding, Orange Custard, '88 174
Pudding, Peachy Bread, '88 175
Pudding, Raisin-Pumpkin, '84 315
Pudding, Russian Blueberry-Raspberry, '97 128
Pudding with Whiskey Sauce, Bread, '90 230
Pumpkin Chiffon, '86 283; '88 260
Quesadillas, Apple, '99 248
Raspberry Fluff, '89 198
Raspberry-Pear Crisp, '89 109
Rice Cream with Mandarin Oranges, '85 317
Roulage, Frozen Chocolate, '90 56
Sauce, Buttermilk Custard, '96 183
Sauce, Chocolate, '90 57
Sauce, Creamy Light Coconut, '82 177
Sauce, Custard, '88 259
Sauce, Golden, '88 267
Sauce, Honey-Orange, '85 108
Sauce, Honey-Yogurt, '92 307
Sauce, Mango, '83 120
Sauce, Melba, '87 77
Sauce, Pineapple-Orange, '84 14
Sauce, Raspberry, '88 267; '93 99; '94 295; '96 183; '99 259
Sauce, Raspberry-Orange, '88 22
Sauce, Rum-Raisin, '94 295
Sauce, Special Hard, '83 318
Sauce, Spicy Apple Dessert, '82 177
Sauce, Whiskey, '90 230
Sherbet, Easy Pineapple, '92 199
Sherbet, Fresh Mint, '88 23
Sherbet, Instant Fruit, '85 158
Sherbet, Lemon, '91 309
Sherbet, Nectarine, '89 199
Sherbet, Peach, '90 179
Sherbet, Pineapple, '84 83; '89 199
Sherbet, Watermelon, '92 124
Shortcake, Strawberry, '92 184
Sorbet, Blueberry-Kirsch, '83 120
Sorbet, Fresh Orange, '92 143
Sorbet, Mango, '86 196
Sorbet, Pink Grapefruit and Tarragon, '95 163
Sorbet, Strawberry-Champagne, '95 20
Soufflé, Baked Apricot, '88 59
Soufflé, Light Chocolate, '83 278
Soufflé, Orange Dessert, '83 206
Soufflé, Raspberry-Topped, '85 317
Soufflé, Tart Lemon, '85 82
Spumoni and Berries, '91 204
Strawberries Juliet, '84 82
Strawberries Marsala, '88 171
Strawberries 'n' Cream, '90 30
Strawberry Cups, Frozen, '91 173
Strawberry Dessert, Glazed, '84 33
Strawberry Dessert, Summer, '92 143
Strawberry Puff, '82 5
Strawberry Whip, '89 198
Strawberry-Yogurt Dessert, '90 295
Tapioca Fluff, Orange, '87 31
Tart, Fancy Fruit, '82 128
Tart, Fresh Fruit, '84 178; '90 58
Tart, Green Grape, '87 77
Tart, Kiwifruit-Peach, '88 20
Tartlets, Fresh Fruit, '93 96
Tart, Pear, '92 72
Tarts, Cran-Raspberry Meringue, '92 286
Tart Shell, '87 77; '88 20
Tarts, Orange, '96 317

Tiramisù, '94 295
Topping, Blueberry, '87 125
Topping, Cherry-Pineapple, '87 126
Topping, Chunky Piña Colada, '87 125
Topping, Raspberry, '85 317
Topping, Raspberry-Peach, '87 126
Topping, Reduced-Calorie Whipped, '85 55
Topping, Spicy Apple, '87 125
Topping, Strawberry, '86 32
Topping, Strawberry-Banana, '87 125
Torte, Apricot Sponge, '90 59
Torte, Chocolate Mint, '94 86
Torte, Triple Chocolate, '96 58
Tortoni, Apricot-Yogurt, '95 124
Trifle, All Seasons Lemon, '95 219
Trifle, Angel Food, '91 184
Trifle, Olde English, '95 331
Trifle, Raspberry, '88 259
Trifle, Tropical, '95 204
Truffles, Chocolate-Kahlúa, '92 285
Wafers, Cinnamon, '84 324
Watermelon Frost, '86 196
Yogurt, Frozen Fresh Peach, '90 139
Yogurt, Lemon-Chiffon Frozen, '85 54
Yogurt, Vanilla Frozen, '87 125
Di-Calcium Phosphate Solution, '89 138
Dressing, Light Cornbread, '92 324
Dressing, Savory Cornbread, '88 303
Eggs and Omelets
  Benedict, Eggs, '85 49
  Benedict, Light Eggs, '93 M68
  Cheddar-Vegetable Omelet, '83 205
  Florentine, Eggs, '83 56
  Garden Omelet, '99 174
  Italian Omelet, '92 47
  Primavera, Omelet, '87 71
  Roulade with Mushroom Filling, Egg, '88 84
  Scrambled Eggs, Mexican-Style, '85 50
  Scrambled Eggs, Spanish, '84 60
  Substitute, Homemade Egg, '92 47
  Vegetable Omelet, Cheesy, '85 49
Enchiladas, Three-Bean, '91 133
Fettuccine and Spinach, '88 90
Fettuccine Primavera, '92 238
Filling, Chicken Salad, '87 106
Filling, Mushroom, '88 84
Filling, Shrimp Salad, '87 106
Fruit Kabobs, Winter, '89 34
Fruit Medley, Chilled, '84 60
Fruit, Minted Marinated, '92 138
Fruit Nuggets, Dried, '86 326
Fruit-on-a-Pick, '90 179
Fruit, Warm Spiced, '86 39
Fruit with Lemon-Yogurt Dressing, Fresh, '93 17
Glaze, Cranberry-Honey, '89 273
Glaze, Teriyaki, '94 52
Grapefruit, Broiled, '85 7
Grits, Cheese, '90 102
Grits, Garlic-and-Herb Cheese, '95 122
Guacamole, Mock, '93 36
Ham-and-Cheese Lettuce Rolls, '89 217
Jam, Berry Refrigerator, '89 139
Jam, Blackberry, '89 138
Jam, Blueberry Refrigerator, '89 139
Jam, Plum Refrigerator, '89 139
Jam, Strawberry, '89 138
Jelly, Crabapple, '89 139
Jelly, Grape, '89 140
Kielbasa, '92 242
Linguine with Garlic and Lemon, '88 91
Linguine with Red Pepper Sauce, '93 127
Low Sodium
  Applesauce, Spicy, '82 296
  Asparagus with Basil Sauce, '86 33

Beef and Rice, Spicy, '83 231
Beef Burgundy, '83 281
Beef Goulash, '83 231
Beef Roast, French-Style, '89 32
Biscuits, Flaky, '84 228
Bread, Bran-Applesauce, '84 229
Bread, Salt-Free Raisin Batter, '86 33
Breadsticks, Whole Wheat, '84 228
Brussels Sprouts, Calico Citrus, '85 303
Butter, Herbed Unsalted, '82 67
Carrots Madeira, '83 231
Catsup, Spicy Tomato, '83 182
Cereal Snack, Toasted, '85 215
Chicken à l'Orange, '84 277
Chicken-and-Vegetables, Stir-Fry, '86 68
Chicken, Citrus-Herb Baked, '85 303
Chicken, Creole, '89 33
Chicken Dinner, Healthful, '83 232
Chicken, Herb-Baked, '82 229
Chicken in Lemon and Wine, '83 281
Chicken Piccata, '83 35
Chicken-Tomato Bake, '83 35
Chicken with Wine-Soaked Vegetables, Baked, '84 277
Chili Surprise, '82 229
Cookies, Sunshine Lemon, '86 69
Cornish Hens in Vermouth, '86 33
Cornish Hens, Roasted Rock, '82 66
Dressing, Basil, '88 24
Dressing, Lemon-Herb Salad, '82 67
Dressing, Orange-Yogurt, '85 304
Fish, Curried Baked, '87 5
Flank Steak, Marinated, '83 35
Flounder Rolls, Vegetable-Stuffed, '87 6
Flounder, Sesame, '89 33
Fruit Delight, Hot, '83 281
Fruit Delight, Spiced, '82 229
Fruit, Unsweetened Mixed, '83 182
Green Beans, Minted, '84 104
Ice, Pink Grapefruit, '85 304
Jam, Banana, '82 296
Jam, Freezer Peach, '83 182
Lamb Chops, Dijon, '84 277
Lamb Chops, Orange, '83 35
Linguine with Seafood Sauce, '83 232
Meat Loaf, Corny, '86 68
Meat Loaf, Parsleyed, '83 35
Mocha-Cocoa Mix, Hot, '82 296
Mousse, Orange, '86 69
Muffins, Honey-Oatmeal, '84 229
Muffins, Spiced Bran, '84 229
Mustard, Lower Sodium Horseradish, '86 325
Nectarines in Apple Juice, '83 183
Onions, Glazed, '84 104
Orange Scampi, '85 303
Pastry Shell, Sesame, '82 67
Peppers, Corn Stuffed, '84 104
Pie, Nutty Pumpkin, '82 67
Pork, Roast Loin of, '84 276
Pork Tenderloin with Brown Sauce, Grilled, '89 32
Potato Bake, Chive-, '82 229
Potatoes, Yogurt-Stuffed, '88 24
Pretzels with Lower Sodium Horseradish Mustard, Herb, '86 325
Pudding, Chocolate-Almond, '88 24
Pudding, Lemon Fluff, '85 304
Ratatouille, '84 105
Rice and Shrimp, Curried, '83 231
Rice, Calico Brown, '86 33
Rolls, Low-Sodium Refrigerator, '82 67
Rolls, Low-Sodium Yeast, '84 228
Salad, Asparagus-and-New Potato, '86 69
Salad, Citrus Green, '85 304

LIVING LIGHT, Low Sodium
(continued)

Salad, Dilled Cucumber, '82 229
Salad Mold, Golden Citrus, '85 303
Salad, Mushroom-and-Pepper, '86 68
Salad, Sesame-Citrus Green, '86 33
Salmon, Poached, '83 35
Salmon Steaks, Marinated, '87 6
Sauce, Apple-Horseradish, '82 229
Sauce, Brown, '89 32
Sauce, Green Herb, '83 36
Sauce, Seafood, '83 36
Scallops, Sherried, '83 281
Scamp, Tangy Broiled, '87 5
Seasoning Blend, '82 296
Shake, Pineapple-Banana, '85 215
Shrimp Kabobs, Marinated, '84 276
Shrimp, Special Boiled, '83 36
Snapper, Caribbean, '87 5
Snapper, Orangy, '88 23
Soup, Chunky Chicken-Noodle, '88 12
Soup, Chunky Mushroom, '88 12
Soup, Cream of Cauliflower, '88 12
Soup, Spicy Vegetable-Beef, '88 11
Squash Sauté, '82 67
Squash, Vegetable-Stuffed, '84 104
Stew, Cajun-Style Catfish, '88 12
Stew, White Wine, '82 228
Stuffing, Low-Sodium, '82 66
Swordfish, Foil-Baked, '87 5
Tomatoes, Stewed, '83 182
Tomato Puree, Seasoned, '83 182
Tropical Snow, '86 34
Veal, Savory, '83 281
Veal Spaghetti, '84 276
Vegetable Stir-Fry, '84 104
Waffles, Whole Wheat, '84 228
Zucchini, Herbed, '84 104
Zucchini with Baby Carrots, '88 24
Macaroni and Cheese, Baked, '82 199
Macaroni with Pesto, Whole Wheat, '89 238
Main Dishes
Asparagus Roulade, '86 102
Beans and Rice, Red, '90 27
Beef, American Steakhouse, '93 15
Beef-and-Barley Rolls, Wine-Sauced, '87 269
Beef and Cauliflower over Rice, '93 94
Beef-and-Rice Dinner, Mexican, '88 199
Beef and Vegetables, Company, '88 234
Beef-and-Vegetable Stir-Fry, '87 22; '99 204
Beef, Bean, and Cornbread Casserole, '99 215
Beef Burgundy, '88 25
Beef Chimichangas, Oven-Fried, '92 124
Beef, Chinese-Style, '87 50
Beef Fajitas, '88 233
Beef Fillets with Black Bean Sauce, Spicy, '97 184
Beef Hash, '95 24
Beef Kabobs, Chile-, '94 251
Beef Kabobs, Spirited, '87 142
Beef Kabobs with Rice, Marinated, '84 32
Beef, Marinated Sauerbraten, '93 16
Beef Medaillons, Italian, '87 305
Beef Patties, Deviled-, '87 22
Beef Stir-Fry, Chinese, '83 151
Beef Stroganoff, '91 134
Beef Stroganoff, Light, '86 36
Beef Tenderloin Bundles, Peppered, '89 272
Beef Tenderloin for Two, '90 295
Beef Tenderloin Steaks with Peperonata, '97 291
Beef with Asparagus, '90 100

Black Beans and Rice, '91 82
Black Beans and Yellow Rice, Easy, '92 308
Burgers, Barbecued, '89 164
Burgers, Beefy Vegetable, '98 143
Burgers, Black Bean, '98 144
Burgers, Favorite, '89 165
Burgers, Lentil, '95 123
Burgers, Mushroom, '89 164; '97 101
Burgers, Pizza, '89 165
Burgers, Salmon, '98 144
Burgers, Seasoned, '85 158
Burgers, Triple-Layer, '89 165
Burgers, Vegetable, '89 164
Burgers, Walnut, '89 163
Burgers with Caramelized Onions, Beef, '98 143
Burgers with Sprouts, '89 164
Burritos, Cheesy Beef, '85 193
Cabbage Rolls, Stuffed, '88 18
Cannelloni, '92 17
Carne Guisada, '94 219
Casserole, Bean-and-Cornbread, '92 243
Casserole, Breakfast, '91 285
Casserole, Chiles Rellenos, '92 18
Casserole, Crab-and-Mushroom, '89 96
Casserole, Freezer Eggplant-Sausage-Pasta, '95 197
Casserole, Low-Fat Spaghetti, '99 215
Casserole, Southwestern, '99 216
Casserole, Turkey-and-Shrimp Florentine, '92 122
Catfish, Baked, '94 67
Catfish, Oven-Fried, '95 106; '99 174
Catfish, Parmesan, '92 309
Catfish, Southern Oven-Fried, '87 163
Catfish with Creole Sauce, Breaded, '90 28
Chicken à la King, '94 41
Chicken and Dumplings, Old-Fashioned, '93 302
Chicken and Leeks in Parchment, '97 290
Chicken and Rice, Spicy, '88 200
Chicken-and-Sausage Jambalaya, '88 200
Chicken and Spinach Noodles, '82 19
Chicken and Vegetables, Ginger-Poached, '98 229
Chicken and Vegetables, Stir-Fry, '86 249
Chicken and Vegetables, Walnut, '85 194
Chicken and Vegetables with Ginger-Soy Sauce, '91 32
Chicken-Apple Sauté, '97 48
Chicken, Asparagus, and Mushrooms with Penne Pasta, '98 212
Chicken, Baked Honey, '99 110
Chicken Bake, Individual, '90 279
Chicken Breast in Wine, Poached, '91 184
Chicken Breasts, Hawaiian Stuffed, '99 64
Chicken Breasts, Lime-Roasted, '97 100
Chicken Breasts Sardou, Stuffed, '87 269
Chicken Breasts, Wine-Baked, '83 177
Chicken Breasts with Fruited Rice Pilaf, '92 307
Chicken Breasts with Orange-Ginger Sauce, '97 47
Chicken Cacciatore, '86 42
Chicken Chili Bake, '93 302
Chicken, Chutney, '86 249
Chicken Cordon Bleu, '86 37; '93 126
Chicken, Creamed, '82 49
Chicken Croquettes and Mushroom Sauce, '91 220
Chicken, Crunchy Oven-Fried, '87 163
Chicken, Curried, '86 43
Chicken Curry, Stir-Fried, '87 51
Chicken Cutlets with Lemon, '85 8

Chicken, Dante's, '88 25
Chicken Dinner, Skillet, '86 249
Chicken Drumsticks, Breaded, '99 110
Chicken Enchiladas, '90 121
Chicken Fingers, Herb-Baked, '86 249
Chicken Fingers, No-Fry-Pan, '91 120
Chicken-Fried Wild Rice, '91 132
Chicken Gumbo, '90 26
Chicken in a Bag, '87 23
Chicken in Foil, '91 134
Chicken in Orange Sauce, '83 8
Chicken Kabobs, Sesame, '82 165
Chicken Kiev, Oven-Baked, '86 37
Chicken la France, '86 248
Chicken Lasagna, '88 90
Chicken-Leek Terrine, Cold, '92 145
Chicken, Lemon-Frosted, '88 170
Chicken, Lemon-Mustard, '99 109
Chicken, Lemon-Roasted, '95 24
Chicken Marengo, '92 70
Chicken Marsala, '89 237
Chicken, Orange, '83 278
Chicken, Oven-Fried, '93 90
Chicken Paprika, Dilled, '86 41
Chicken, Pineapple, '83 M194
Chicken Pot Pie, '94 21
Chicken-Rice Casserole, '99 215
Chicken Rolls, Spinach-Stuffed, '86 248
Chicken, Salsa Rice and, '99 109
Chicken, Savory Roasted, '98 21
Chicken, Sicilian, '97 142
Chicken, Southern Oven-Fried, '86 37
Chicken Spaghetti, '87 221
Chicken Stir-Fry, Apple-Sesame-, '92 226
Chicken Stir-Fry, Chinese, '90 100
Chicken Strips and Vegetables, Marinated, '90 110
Chicken, Sweet-and-Sour, '91 202
Chicken Tostadas, '95 122
Chicken-Vegetable Stir-Fry, '83 151; '84 13
Chicken, Whole Poached, '98 229
Chicken Wings, Maple-Glazed, '99 110
Chicken with Artichoke Hearts, '88 54
Chicken with Artichokes, Sherried, '87 143
Chicken with Black Bean Puree, Spicy, '97 48
Chicken with Mole Sauce, '93 34
Chicken with Mushroom Sauce, '99 22
Chicken with Orange, Lime, and Ginger Sauce, '92 123
Chicken with Pineapple, Oriental, '86 42
Chicken with Pineapple Salsa, Sesame-Crusted, '96 226
Chicken with Prunes, Saffron, '97 264
Chicken with Salsa, Baked Chile, '88 147
Chicken with Spinach Fettuccine, Easy, '88 89
Chicken with Tabbouleh Salad, Grilled, '91 70
Chicken with Tomato-Basil Pasta, Basil-Stuffed, '94 M204
Chicken with Vegetables, Stir-Fry, '96 128
Chiles Rellenos, Light, '93 156
Chiles Rellenos with Tomatillo Sauce, Roasted, '94 203
Chile Verde, Light, '88 148
Chili, '93 89
Chili, Firestarter, '93 34
Chili, Hot Venison, '91 283
Chili, South-of-the-Border, '91 283
Chili, Southwestern, '91 284
Chili, Vegetarian, '91 284
Chili, White, '91 284
Cornbread-Tamale Pie, '92 123
Cornish Hens, Herbed, '82 271
Cornish Hens, Mesquite-Smoked, '92 144

Cornish Hens, Orange-Glazed Grilled, '86 250
Cornish Hens with Vegetables, Tarragon Roasted, '94 79
Crab-and-Shrimp Étouffée, '89 96
Crab Cakes, '91 122
Crabmeat au Gratin, '86 154
Cracked Wheat, "Fried," '89 31
Crawfish Étouffée, '86 156
Crawfish Fettuccine, '96 98
Crêpes, Cannelloni, '86 143
Crêpes, Chicken-Vegetable, '83 70
Eggplant Parmesan, '92 18
Enchiladas, Spicy Bean, '88 18
Fajita Fettuccine, '94 84
Fajita in a Pita, '90 177
Fajitas, Java, '96 227
Fettuccine and Shrimp with Dried Tomato Pesto, '94 249
Fettuccine, Ham-and-Asparagus, '94 84
Fettuccine Primavera, '94 85
Fettuccine, Shrimp, '94 84
Filet Mignon with Mushroom Sauce, '94 250
Fillets, Apple-Carrot Stuffed, '88 M192
Fillets Tomatillo, '94 135
Fish and Vegetables, Steamed, '91 32
Fish, Caribbean Banana, '95 202
Fish Dinner, Skillet, '88 199
Fish Fillets, Breaded Herbed, '91 121
Fish Florentine, '86 35
Fish Florentine in Parchment, '87 22
Fish with Greek Sauce, Poached, '91 M183
Flank Steak, Grilled Marinated, '97 182
Flank Steak Sukiyaki, '88 233
Flank Steak with Black Bean-and-Corn Salsa, Grilled, '94 80
Flank Steak with Noodles, Stuffed, '90 101
Flank Steak with Sweet Peppers, Grilled, '90 138
Flounder, Creole-Style, '85 180
Flounder Rolls with Citrus Sauce, Stuffed, '85 180
Frijoles Rancheros, '88 148
Frittata, Vegetable, '92 48
Game Hens with Chutney-Mustard Glaze, '93 66
Goulash, Hungarian, '92 227
Grits-and-Ham Pie, Crustless, '86 103
Grouper, Grilled Marinated, '90 166
Grouper, Hot Spicy, '94 78
Haddock Fillets with Zucchini Stuffing, '88 M191
Halibut Steaks Italiano, '88 M191
Halibut with Champagne Sauce, Baked, '90 29
Halibut with Swiss Sauce, '83 M195
Hamburger Pie, '84 13
Ham-Potato-Pineapple Bake, '93 302
Ham with Cranberry-Honey Glaze, Baked, '89 273
Hopping John with Grilled Pork Medaillons, '93 229
Jambalaya, '90 26
Jambalaya, Black-Eyed Pea, '92 70
Jambalaya, Red Rice, '91 18
Kabobs, Hawaiian, '85 157
Lamb Chops, Broiled, '85 22
Lamb Chops, Joan's Rosemary, '97 42
Lamb Chops, Peppercorn-Crusted, '92 142
Lamb Chops with Herbs, '90 164
Lamb Chops with Rosemary Sauce and Wild Rice-Fennel Pilaf, Grilled, '97 127
Lamb with Five Spices, Stewed, '92 72
Lasagna, Cheesy Spinach, '83 204
Lasagna, Creamy Ham-and-Chicken, '95 88

Lasagna in a Bun, '90 176
Lasagna, Lean, '86 37
Lasagna, Light, '95 212
Lasagna, Spinach-Bean, '92 96
Lasagna, Vegetable, '84 201; '99 97
Lasagna, Zucchini, '85 194
Lentil-and-Rice Supper, '84 202
Lentils-and-Rice Casserole, '93 301
Linguine with Clam Sauce, '88 90
Liver, Creole, '86 108
Liver in Creole Sauce, '87 33
Lobster Tails with Spiced Orange Sauce, '86 155
London Broil, Marinated, '87 32
Mackerel, Rosemary-Garlic, '92 200
Manicotti, Spinach, '82 199
Meatballs and Vegetables with Horseradish Dressing, '91 32
Meat Loaf, '89 109
Meat Loaf, Curried, '86 43
Meat Loaf, Oriental, '83 M194
Meat Loaf, Parsley, '87 22
Migas, '98 312
Orange Roughy-and-Vegetable Stir-Fry, '91 50
Orange Roughy, Pesto-Crusted, '96 156
Orange Roughy, Vegetable-Topped, '93 67
Orange Roughy with Herbs, Steamed, '95 189
Orange Roughy with Spinach Pesto, '88 M192
Pasta, Creamy Turkey-Basil, '89 216
Pasta, Mamma Mia, '95 25
Pasta Primavera, Almost, '86 38
Pasta Salad, Main-Dish, '82 199
Pasta, Vegetable Stir-Fry, '96 29
Pasta Verde, '84 201
Pasta with Fennel, '98 46
Pasta with Peanut Sauce, '95 252
Pastichio, '85 194
Pear Breakfast Treat, '87 72
Peppers Stuffed with Shrimp-and-Orzo Salad, '91 203
Perch, Parmesan-Crusted, '93 91
Pie, Italian Meat, '89 109
Pizza, Breakfast, '90 178
Pizza, Chicken-and-Purple Onion, '97 47
Pizza, Garden, '89 108
Pizzas, Veggie, '99 97
Pizza, Turkey-Vegetable, '90 139
Pizza, Vegetable, '94 218
Pizza, Veggie, '94 78
Pizza, Whole Wheat, '84 33
Polenta with Black Bean Salsa, Grilled, '93 155
Pollock with Summer Squash Relish, '92 200
Pork-and-Noodles Skillet Dinner, '88 199
Pork, Chinese Roast, '91 308
Pork Chop Dinner, '88 25
Pork Chops, Apricot-Sauced, '85 22
Pork Chops, Creole-Style, '91 49
Pork Chops, Fruit-Topped, '94 41
Pork Chops, Honey-Lime, '91 33
Pork Chops in Gravy, '91 137
Pork Chops with Tangy Barbecue Sauce, '99 104
Pork Chops with White Bean Puree, '96 226
Pork Chow Mein, '90 101
Pork, Cranberry, '90 293
Pork Loin Roast, Barbecued, '93 34
Pork Medaillons, Grilled, '93 229
Pork Medaillons with Port Wine and Dried Cranberry Sauce, '95 330
Pork, Oven-Roasted Vegetables and, '99 259
Pork Roast, Oven-Barbecued, '91 50
Pork Roast, Stuffed Crown, '89 272
Pork, Stir-Fried, '87 51

Pork, Sweet-and-Sour, '85 34, 194
Pork Tenderloin, Apple-Mushroom, '95 53
Pork Tenderloin, Honey-Mustard, '95 52
Pork Tenderloin, Marinated, '84 175
Pork Tenderloin, Molasses-Grilled, '96 265
Pork Tenderloin, Sesame, '95 53
Pork Tenderloins, Fruit-Stuffed, '87 270
Pork Tenderloin, Spinach-and-Bacon Stuffed, '94 81
Pork Tenderloin with Apples, Celery, and Potatoes, Grilled, '95 161
Pork Tenderloin with Fruit Stuffing and Shiitake Sauce, '97 218
Pork Tenderloin with Molasses Sauce, Grilled, '97 193
Pork Tenderloin with Orange Marmalade, '91 49
Pork Tenderloin with Parmesan-Pepper Toasts, Herbed, '98 242
Pot Roast, Marinated, '85 21
Quail with Mushroom Gravy, Baked, '89 273
Quesadillas, Chicken-and-Black Bean, '96 288
Quesadillas, Quick, '89 87
Quiche, Eggless, '87 220
Quiche, Fiesta, '92 47
Quiches, Individual Spinach, '86 38
Quiche, Spinach, '85 49; '91 204
Quiche, Swiss-Zucchini, '82 49
Ravioli, Mediterranean, '93 301
Red Beans and Couscous, '99 22
Red Snapper, Blackened, '90 27
Red Snapper Rolls, Cucumber-Stuffed, '83 176
Red Snapper Veracruz, '88 149; '92 142
Rice-and-Lentil Pilaf, '88 17
Risotto with Vegetables, '98 193
Roast Beef, Deli-Style, '93 15
Salmon Burgers, '95 24
Salmon Fillets with Red Wine Garlic Sauce, '94 250
Salmon in Parchment, '95 311
Salmon Loaf with Cucumber-Dill Sauce, '86 5
Salmon-Pesto Vermicelli, '92 200
Salmon Steaks with Tarragon Sauce, Grilled, '97 42
Salmon with Ginger Vinaigrette, Sesame-Crusted, '95 162
Salmon with Horseradish Sauce, Poached, '91 183
Salmon with Yellow Pepper Sauce, Poached, '98 230
Sausage, Dieters' Spicy, '85 49
Scallop Kabobs, Grilled, '83 101
Scallops in Vegetable Nests, '91 70
Scallops with Cilantro-Lime Vinaigrette, Grilled Orange, '94 77
Scallops with Orange-Ginger Sauce, Sesame-Crusted, '97 125
Scallops with Tomato-Mango Salsa, Seared, '95 122
Shells, Spinach-Stuffed, '99 64
Shrimp and Pasta, Sautéed, '96 288
Shrimp-and-Vegetable Medley Stir-Fry, '99 205
Shrimp, Barbecued, '90 28
Shrimp, Beer-Broiled, '87 142
Shrimp Cancun en Papillote, '91 136
Shrimp Enchiladas in Tomatillo Sauce, '95 310
Shrimp Étouffée, '90 229
Shrimp, Grilled Sweet-and-Sour, '97 100
Shrimp Skillet, Quick, '87 50
Shrimp, Stir-Fry, '96 129
Shrimp, Sweet-and-Sour, '83 278

Shrimp with Citrus Salsa, Grilled, **'97** 141
Shrimp with Cranberry-Citrus Salsa, Sautéed, **'97** 290
Shrimp with Orzo, Fire-Roasted, **'99** 42
Shrimp with Peanut Sauce, **'93** 303
Sirloin, Mustard Marinated, **'94** 41
Sirloin Steaks with Thyme Pesto, **'97** 182
Snapper à l'Orange, Baked, **'85** 181
Snapper, Honey-Curried, **'85** 181
Snapper, Poached, **'83** 101
Snapper with Creamy Dill Sauce, Peppered, **'94** 42
Snow Peas and Red Pepper, Sesame, **'84** 175
Sole Divan, **'87** 21
Sole Véronique, **'85** 181
Spaghetti, Meaty, **'82** 19
Spinach-and-Cheese Calzones, **'95** 310
Steak au Poivre, **'88** 232
Steak Diane, **'92** 306
Steak, Fast-and-Easy Stir-Fried, **'87** 50
Steak in Red Wine Sauce, Skillet, **'85** 21
Steak, Italian-Stuffed, **'88** 232
Steak Kabobs, **'82** 4; **'93** 95
Steak lo Mein, **'90** 100
Steak, Marinated, **'88** 233
Steak, Mexican Marinated, **'88** 148
Steak, Mock Country-Fried, **'87** 163
Steak, Pepper-Beef, **'85** 21
Stew, Burgundy Beef, **'88** 234
Swordfish-Shiitake Skewers, **'97** 168
Swordfish Stir-Fry, **'96** 128
Swordfish with Avocado-Lime Sauce, Grilled, **'97** 127
Swordfish with Caper Sauce, Grilled, **'95** 230
Tacoritos, **'90** 133
Tagine, Vegetable, **'96** 289
Tenderloins, Honey-Grilled, **'92** 199
Tenderloin, Spinach-Stuffed, **'89** 311
Tofu, Stroganoff, **'84** 202
Tomato with Tuna Pasta, Stuffed, **'88** 54
Trout, Baked, **'95** 106
Trout Fillets with Capers, **'95** 252
Trout, Grilled, **'95** 106
Trout, Poached, **'95** 106
Tuna Croquettes with Parsley Sauce, **'86** 108
Tuna Steaks on Mixed Greens with Lemon-Basil Vinaigrette, Seared, **'94** 205
Tuna with Poblano Salsa, Grilled, **'91** 135
Tuna with Rosemary, Broiled, **'93** 127
Tuna with Tangy Mustard Sauce, **'92** 201
Turkey-Asparagus Pilaf, **'88** 200
Turkey Breast and Gravy, Roast, **'88** 303
Turkey Breast, Stuffed, **'87** 270
Turkey Breast with Cranberry Salsa, Grilled, **'95** 252
Turkey Breast with Special Gravy, Roast, **'86** 282
Turkey Burgers, **'98** 22
Turkey Cutlets, Oven-Fried, **'91** 121
Turkey Cutlets with Pepper Salsa, Spicy, **'88** 26
Turkey Lasagna, **'91** 130
Turkey, Lazy Day, **'93** 93
Turkey Piccata, **'91** 137
Turkey Tenderloins with Lingonberry Sauce, **'97** 289
Veal and Carrots, Company, **'85** 22
Veal, Lemon, **'93** 35
Veal Marsala, **'91** 310
Veal Picante, **'87** 31

Veal Piccata with Capers, **'87** 142
Veal Scallopini, **'83** 8
Vegetables and Chicken, Glazed Stir-Fry, **'99** 205
Vegetarian Supper, **'86** 222
Veggie-and-Pork Stir-Fry, Mixed, **'99** 206
Vermicelli and Sprouts with Red Clam Sauce, **'86** 143
Vermicelli, Scallop-Vegetable, **'87** 143
Zucchini Frittata, **'86** 103
Zucchini with Pasta, Stuffed, **'97** 101
Marinade, Soy-and-Ginger, **'96** 129
Mayonnaise, Basil, **'98** 144
Mayonnaise, Dried Tomato, **'98** 144
Mayonnaise, Lemon, **'98** 144
Mayonnaise, Mediterranean, **'98** 144
Mayonnaise, Onion, **'98** 144
Mayonnaise, Roasted Red Pepper, **'98** 144
Meatballs, **'89** 237
Meatballs, Turkey, **'89** 237
Meat Mixture, Basic, **'92** 241
Muesli, Bran-and-Fruit, **'91** 134
Oatmeal, Applesauce, **'89** 108
Oatmeal, Fruited, **'88** 19
Olive Oil, Basil-Infused, **'95** 231
Olive Oil, Lemon-Infused, **'95** 231
Pancakes, Honey, **'91** 139
Pancakes, Oatmeal, **'89** 107
Pancakes, Shredded Wheat, **'84** 59
Pancakes, Whole Wheat-Oat, **'93** 16
Pasta, Asian Pesto, **'95** 189
Pasta-Basil Toss, **'87** 33
Pasta, Caesar Salad, **'95** 230
Pasta, Garden, **'82** 199
Pasta, Grilled Vegetable, **'97** 142
Pasta Provençale, **'88** 90
Pasta, Tomato-Basil, **'94** 204
Peaches, Spicy Baked, **'86** 39
Pears, Wine-Poached, **'98** 230
Pickles, Lime, **'96** 206
Pico de Gallo, **'96** 227
Pizza Crust, Special, **'90** 139
Pizza Crusts, Skillet, **'94** 218
Pizza on a Bagel, **'93** M94
Pizza, Plum-and-Sweet Onion, **'98** 193
Preserves, Fig, **'89** 140
Preserves, Peach, **'89** 140
Relish, Cranberry, **'86** 283; **'91** 257
Relish, Green Tomato, **'98** 124
Relish, Holiday Cranberry, **'88** 304
Relish, Papaya-Basil, **'82** 82
Relish, Sweet Onion, **'96** 206
Relish, White Bean, **'93** 229

Rice
Apple-Cinnamon Rice, **'86** 249
Black-Eyed Peas, Rice with, **'93** 66
Blended Rice, **'96** 68
Casserole, Colorful Rice, **'82** 199
Herb Rice, **'91** 257
Lime-Flavored Rice, **'84** 175
Mexican Rice, Spicy, **'88** 149
Mix, Fruited Curry-Rice, **'86** 326
Onion Rice, Seasoned, **'82** 166
Orange Rice, **'82** 200
Peppered Rice, **'82** 4
Pilaf, Browned Rice, **'87** 305
Pilaf, Brown Rice, **'90** 136; **'91** 82
Shell, Rice-Cheese, **'82** 49
Southwestern Rice, **'90** 121
Spanish Rice with Tofu, **'88** 26
Tomatoes and Basil, Rice with, **'95** 232
Wild Rice and Mushrooms, **'83** 278
Wild Rice Bulgur, **'91** 83
Yellow Rice, **'91** 136

Salad Dressings
Balsamic Dressing, **'99** 259
Blue Cheese Dressing, **'82** 166
Blue Cheese Dressing, Creamy, **'91** 307
Blue Cheese Vinaigrette, **'90** 280
Caper Vinaigrette, **'91** 310
Cilantro-Lime Vinaigrette, **'94** 77
Cilantro Vinaigrette, **'97** 126
Coconut Dressing, **'87** 251
Creamy Dressing, **'93** 318
Cucumber-Mint Dressing, **'87** 153
Cucumber Salad Dressing, Creamy, **'82** 79
Curry Dressing, **'82** 78
French Dressing, Miracle, **'82** 79
Fruit, Salad Dressing for, **'86** 40
Herb Salad Dressing, **'86** 40
Honey-Mustard Dressing, **'90** 111
Horseradish Dressing, **'87** 152; **'91** 32
Lemon-Basil Vinaigrette, **'94** 205
Lemon-Caper Dressing, **'96** 69
Lemon-Molasses Dressing, **'97** 195
Lemon-Yogurt Dressing, **'93** 17
Lemon-Yogurt Slaw or Salad Dressing, **'88** 54
Lime Dressing, **'83** 120
Orange-Poppy Seed Dressing, **'87** 187
Papaya Seed Dressing, **'95** 204
Pineapple-Poppy Seed Dressing, **'85** 55
Raspberry Dressing, **'87** 153; **'95** 202
Soy-Sesame Dressing, **'87** 153
Spicy Southwestern Dressing, **'94** 136
Spring Garden Dressing, **'85** 157
Stay Trim Dressing, **'86** 40
Sweet-and-Sour Dressing, **'87** 305
Tangy Dressing, **'83** 9
Thousand Island Dressing, Special, **'82** 79
Vinaigrette Dressing, **'95** 231
Wine Vinegar Dressing, **'93** 126
Yogurt Dressing, **'85** 59, 215; **'88** 27
Yogurt Dressing, Sweet-Hot, **'86** 40
Yogurt-Herb Dressing, **'92** 96
Yogurt-Honey Poppy Seed Dressing, **'83** 177

Salads
Ambrosia, Brunch, **'83** 57
Apple-Apricot Salad, **'88** 121
Apple-Bran Salad, Lemony, **'86** 223
Apple Cider Salad Mold, **'85** 54
Apple Salad, Spicy, **'85** 215
Apple Salad, Triple, **'88** 122
Apple Toss, Sesame-, **'88** 21
Asparagus, Marinated, **'84** 67
Asparagus Salad, **'88** 121; **'94** 67
Asparagus Vinaigrette, Light, **'82** 50
Aspic, Light Tomato, **'85** 83
Aspic, Three-Layer, **'88** 120
Aspic, Tomato-Crab, **'85** 287
Aspic with Horseradish Dressing, Crisp Vegetable, **'87** 152
Barley-Broccoli Salad, **'90** 135
Bean-and-Rice Salad, Marinated, **'87** 152
Bean Salad, Marinated, **'85** 137, 296
Bean Salad, Supreme, **'91** 202
Beans with Sprouts, Sweet-and-Sour, **'86** 32
Beef-and-Broccoli Salad, **'87** 187
Beef Fajita Salad, **'91** 70
Beef Salad, Stir-Fry, **'96** 129
Black Bean-and-Barley Salad, **'94** 174
Black Bean Salad, **'89** 217
Black-Eyed Pea Salad, **'95** 203; **'99** 174
Black-Eyed Pea Salad, Marinated, **'93** 190
Broccoli-Corn Salad, **'87** 24
Brown Rice-and-Vegetable Salad, **'84** 202
Brown Rice Confetti Salad, **'94** 174
Caesar Salad, **'92** 71
Caesar Salad, Baby Romaine, **'97** 128

Cantaloupe, Fruit-Filled, '83 120
Carrot-and-Seed Salad, Fruity, '86 223
Carrot-Pineapple Salad, '91 83
Carrot-Raisin Salad, '84 174
Cauliflower-Vegetable Salad, '85 158
Cherry-Apple Salad, '86 31
Cherry Salad, Fresh, '83 120
Chicken-and-Walnut Salad, Sunburst, '93 91
Chicken-Fruit Salad, '82 79
Chicken Noodle Salad, '95 25
Chicken Pasta Salad, '88 89
Chicken-Raspberry Salad, Marinated, '93 190
Chicken Salad, Blue Cheese, '94 81
Chicken Salad, Crunchy, '86 207
Chicken Salad, Grilled Asian, '96 158
Chicken Salad, Moroccan Grilled, '95 231
Chicken Salad, Special, '85 82
Chicken Salad, Tarragon, '90 199
Chicken Salad with Mango Chutney, Grilled,
   '96 182
Chicken Salad with Raspberry Dressing,
   Grilled, '95 202
Chicken Taco Salad, '94 M136
Chile-Tomato Salad, Spicy, '88 121
Citrus Salad, Tangy, '89 34
Coleslaw, Crunchy, '86 295
Coleslaw, Light and Creamy, '93 318
Composé, Salad, '93 126
Corn Salad, '85 236
Cottage Cheese Salad in Tomatoes, '86 208
Couscous Salad, Basil-and-Tomato, '94 175
Couscous Salad with Dried Tomato
   Vinaigrette, '96 244
Crab-and-Asparagus Salad, '92 141
Crab-Wild Rice Salad, '86 243
Cucumber Mousse, '88 121
Cucumber Salad, Dilled, '92 72
Cucumber-Yogurt Salad, '87 33
English Pea-and-Apple Salad, '87 24
Fennel and Radicchio with Orange
   Vinaigrette, Grilled, '95 253
Freezer Salad, '94 118
Fruit Cups, Sangría, '89 34
Fruit, Dressed-Up, '82 5
Fruit Salad, Chef's, '86 35
Fruit Salad, Curried, '85 107
Fruit with Mint-Balsamic Tea, Fresh, '95 232
Garden-Patch Salad Molds, '86 283
Garden Salad, Summer, '87 153
Gazpacho Molded Salad, '92 323
Grapefruit Salad, '88 122
Grape Salad Mold, '83 120
Green Beans with Creamy Tarragon Dressing,
   '93 191
Green Salad, Mixed, '90 230
Greens, Crimson, '87 153
Greens with Blue Cheese Vinaigrette, Mixed,
   '90 280
Greens with Raspberry Dressing, Peppery,
   '95 254
Hominy-Bean Salad, '88 266
Italian Bread Salad, '99 259
Italian Salad, Cheesy, '84 33
Jicama-Orange Salad, '90 122
Layered Salad, '86 35
Legumes, Marinated, '90 197
Lentils-and-Rice Salad, '90 197
Lettuce, Confetti-Stuffed, '87 24
Lettuces with Mustard Vinaigrette, Baby,
   '93 67
Lima Bean-Tomato Salad, '85 137
Macaroni-Cheese Salad, Dilled, '86 208
Macaroni-Chicken Salad, Dilled, '92 142
Macaroni-Tuna Salad, Whole Wheat, '84 193

Mandarin Salad Molds, '85 54
Meal-in-One Salad, '86 43
Melon Ball Bowl with Cucumber-Mint
   Dressing, '87 153
Mixed Greens with Raspberries and Walnuts,
   '98 194
Mushroom-Zucchini Salad, '85 8
New Potato Salad, '84 139
Niçoise, Salad, '86 35
Oriental Salad Bowl, '87 153
Paella Salad, '86 207
Pasta-and-Tomato Salad, Herbed, '92 144
Pasta Salad, '84 139; '89 217
Pasta Salad, Garden, '86 188
Peaches in a Garden Nest, '87 154
Pork Salad, Oriental, '92 140
Potato Salad, '90 122
Potato Salad, Dill, '99 104
Potato Salad, Hot-and-Light, '93 90
Potato Salad, Pesto, '90 164
Potato Slices, Marinated, '93 98
Rice-and-Vegetable Salad, '86 42
Rice-Shrimp Salad, '92 142
Roasted Vegetable Salad with Dried Peach
   Vinaigrette, '97 265
Romaine with Caper Vinaigrette, Hearts of,
   '91 310
Salmon-and-Wild Rice Salad, Oriental, '94 173
Salmon Salad, Chilled Poached, '96 68
Seafood Salad Sussex Shores, '93 98
Shrimp-and-Couscous Salad, '96 157
Shrimp-and-Rice Salad, '92 307
Shrimp Salad, Fruited, '86 156
Shrimp Salad, Marinated, '85 82
Slaw, Apple-Carrot, '92 243
Slaw, Cabbage-Pineapple, '92 182
Slaw, Chinese Cabbage, '89 312
Slaw, Green Bean, '95 108
Slaw, Healthy, '92 183
Slaw, Red Cabbage-and-Apple, '87 31
Spinach-Blue Cheese Salad, '82 166
Spinach-Kiwifruit Salad, '87 305
Spinach Salad, Citrus, '90 59
Spinach Salad, Wilted, '93 125
Spinach Salad with Orange Dressing, '87 187
Sprout Salad, '90 137
Steak Salad Cups, Pepper, '86 206
Steak Salad with Peach Salsa, '97 183
Strawberry Salad, Frozen, '94 119
Sweet Potato Salad with Rosemary-Honey
   Vinaigrette, '98 243
Tabbouleh Salad, '91 70; '94 174
Tofu Salad, '88 27
Tomato-Cucumber Salad, '92 199
Tomato-Cucumber Salad with Yogurt-Herb
   Dressing, '92 96
Tomatoes Stuffed with Sea Slaw, '89 96
Tortellini Salad, '89 237
Tuna-and-Cannellini Bean Salad, '86 143
Tuna Chef Salad, '82 78
Tuna-Mac in Tomatoes, '87 188
Tuna-Pasta Salad, '92 141
Tuna Salad, Curried, '86 208
Turkey Waldorf Salad with Yogurt Dressing,
   '88 53
Turnip Salad, '85 235
Vegetable Salad, Crispy Marinated, '84 193
Vegetable Salad, Grilled, '94 203
Vegetable Salad, Italian, '82 19
Vegetable Salad, Marinated, '84 13
Vegetable Salad, Minted, '88 23
Vegetable Salad, Tarragon-, '85 288
Vegetable Salad, Winter, '86 42
Vegetables, Zesty Marinated, '82 272

Wheat Berry-and-Roasted Corn Salad, '94 175
Wild Rice Salad, '93 191
Sandwiches
Bagel, Breakfast on a, '94 66
Breakfast Sandwiches, Open-Faced, '92 140
Cheese Sandwiches with Artichoke-Tomato
   Salsa, Herbed, '96 182
Chicken Pita, Oriental, '89 216
Chicken Sandwiches, Marinated, '86 M45
Crab Sandwiches, Open-Faced, '87 106
Eggplant Sandwiches, Open-Face, '95 124
Eggplant, Tomato, and Feta Sandwiches,
   '98 106
Flank Steak Sandwiches with Apple Barbecue
   Sauce, '99 173
Garden Sandwiches, Open-Faced, '87 105
Ham Sandwiches, Open-Face, '85 8
Heroes, Healthy, '90 177
Lamb Pockets with Dilled Cucumber Topping,
   '87 104
Open-Face Sandwiches, '84 13
Picnic Loaf, Mediterranean, '96 156
Pimiento Cheese Sandwiches, '82 278
Pitas, Acadian Stuffed, '90 177
Pita Sandwiches, '84 139
Pita, Stuffed, '89 87
Pizza Sandwiches, Open-Face, '85 22
Seafood Po'Boy, Grilled, '96 244
Seafood Sandwiches, Caribbean, '98 105
Shrimp Salad Sandwiches, '90 178
Sloppy Toms, '91 51
Tabbouleh Pitas, '98 105
Tofu-Veggie Sandwiches, Open-Face, '86 5
Turkey-in-the-Slaw Sandwich, '90 177
Turkey-Roasted Pepper Sandwiches, Smoked,
   '94 66
Vegetable Pockets, '85 215
Vegetarian Melt, Open-Faced, '87 106
Vegetarian Pita Sandwiches, '84 193
Sauces and Gravies
Alfredo Sauce, '94 84
Barbecue Sauce, Apple, '99 173
Barbecue Sauce, Easy, '82 178
Barbecue Sauce, LBJ's Texas, '97 42
Barbecue Sauce, Special, '82 177
Barbecue Sauce, Tangy, '99 104
Basil-Brown Butter Sauce, '93 92
Champagne Sauce, '90 29
Cheese Sauce, Guilt-Free, '93 M95
Creole Sauce, '90 28
Cucumber-Dill Sauce, '86 5
Dill Sauce, Creamy, '94 42
Ginger-Soy Sauce, '91 33
Ginger Vinaigrette, '95 162
Gravy, '88 303
Gravy, Sausage, '94 20
Greek Sauce, '91 183
Hollandaise Sauce, Mock, '85 49; '93 68
Horseradish Sauce, '91 183
Jalapeño Sauce, '93 230
Jalapeño Tartar Sauce, '96 69
Lemon-Chive Sauce, '86 249
Lemon-Molasses Dressing, '97 195
Lemon Sauce, '82 290
Mandarin Sauce, '84 60
Mandarin-Teriyaki Sauce, '96 68
Marinade, Tangy Light, '82 178
Marinara Sauce, '82 178; '89 239; '92 18
Mediterranean Sauce, '94 83
Mushroom Sauce, '83 205; '91 221
Mushroom Sauce, Spicy Sherried, '89 239
Mustard-Hollandaise Sauce, Mock, '87 269
Mustard Sauce, '87 22
Mustard Sauce, Easy, '94 83

LIVING LIGHT, Sauces and Gravies
(continued)

Mustard Sauce, Light, **'82** 178
Mustard Sauce, Tangy, **'92** 201
Parmesan Sauce, **'92** 17
Parsley Sauce, **'86** 108
Pesto, Dried Tomato, **'94** 249
Pesto, Sage, **'97** 22
Picante Sauce, Processed, **'91** 257
Pizza Sauce, **'84** 33
Rancheros Sauce, **'88** 148
Red Chile Sauce, **'94** 251
Reduction Sauce, Cider-Port Wine, **'96** 245
Red Wine Garlic Sauce, **'94** 250
Rosemary Sauce, **'97** 127
Salsa, **'88** 147
Salsa, Artichoke-Tomato, **'96** 182
Salsa, Black Bean, **'93** 155
Salsa, Black Bean-and-Corn, **'94** 80
Salsa, Cranberry-Citrus, **'97** 290
Salsa Cruda, **'88** 148
Salsa, Cucumber-Dill, **'95** 107
Salsa, Dried Chile, **'97** 265
Salsa, Fiesta Onion, **'94** 82
Salsa, Fresh Vegetable, **'98** 194
Salsa, Hot Kiwifruit, **'94** 82
Salsa, Peach, **'97** 183
Salsa, Pepper, **'88** 26
Salsa, Pineapple, **'96** 226
Salsa, Poblano, **'91** 135
Salsa, Tomato-Avocado, **'94** 83
Salsa, Vegetable, **'96** 208
Salsa Verde, Roasted, **'96** 182
Sauerbraten Sauce, **'93** 16
Seafood Sauce, **'89** 239
Seafood Sauce, Red, **'95** 107
Spaghetti Sauce, Lentil, **'90** 198
Swiss Sauce, **'83** M195
Tarragon Sauce, **'83** 56; **'97** 42
Tartar Sauce, **'95** 107; **'99** 174
Tomato Sauce, **'85** 193, 244
Tomato Sauce, Spicy, **'88** 19
Vegetable-Cheese Potato Topper, **'86** 6
White Sauce, Low-Calorie Medium, **'87** 26
Zesty Sauce, **'94** 82
Zippy Sauce, **'86** 44
Sausage, Country, **'92** 242
Sausage, Italian, **'92** 242
Seasoning, Herb, **'99** 63
Sorbet, Pink Grapefruit and Tarragon, **'95** 163
Soups and Stews
Asparagus Soup, **'84** 67
Bean-and-Hominy Soup, **'95** 23
Bean and Pasta Soup, **'94** 220
Bean-and-Turkey Soup, **'93** 319
Bean Soup, Leafy, **'86** 223
Bean Soup, Quick, **'99** 97
Beef-and-Barley Vegetable Soup, **'89** 31
Beef Stew, **'90** 230
Beef Stew, Quick, **'92** 71
Bisque, Squash, **'84** 280
Black Bean Soup, **'88** 266; **'98** 291
Black Bean Soup, Carolina, **'92** 139
Black Bean Soup, Marge Clyde's, **'96** 29
Borscht, Ruby Red, **'83** 176
Bouillon, Court-, **'98** 229
Bouillon, Tomato, **'83** 8
Broccoli Soup, Creamy, **'91** 307
Broccoli Soup, Light Cream of, **'93** 17
Broccoli Soup, Mock Cream of, **'85** 288
Broccoli-Swiss Soup, **'86** 6
Cantaloupe Soup, **'83** 120

Carrot-and-Butternut Squash Soup with
    Parslied Croutons, **'97** 217
Carrot-Leek Soup, **'86** 34
Carrot Soup, **'98** 123
Chicken, Artichoke, and Mushroom Soup,
    '92 324
Chicken, Kale, and Chickpea Stew, **'98** 47
Chicken Soup, Curried, **'86** 34
Chicken-Vegetable Soup, **'88** 18
Chili Vegetable Soup, **'94** 120
Chili, Vegetarian, **'84** 280
Chowder, Basque Fish, **'86** 36
Chowder, Chicken-and-Roasted Vegetable,
    '97 21
Chowder, Clam, **'86** 36; **'89** 95
Chowder, Corn, **'91** 132
Chowder, Maryland Crab, **'97** 23
Chowder, Potato-Corn, **'94** 66
Chowder, Seafood, **'92** 122
Chowder with Sage Pesto, White Bean, **'97** 22
Corn-and-Crab Soup, Fresh, **'92** 183
Crab Soup, Cream of, **'88** 302
Cucumber Soup, Cold Minted, **'86** 34
Cucumber-Yogurt Soup, **'83** 205
Fish-and-Vegetable Stew, **'87** 220
French Market Soup, **'92** 49
Gazpacho, Chilled, **'84** 138
Gazpacho, Citrus, **'96** 70
Gazpacho, Tropical, **'95** 204
Gumbo, Catfish, **'90** 278
Gumbo, Chicken-and-Sausage, **'94** 20
Gumbo, Light Seafood-Okra, **'86** 155
Gumbo, Seafood, **'96** 98
Ham-and-Bean Soup, Spicy, **'94** 322
Hot-and-Sour Soup, **'91** 50
Mex-Tex Soup, **'90** 278
Minestrone Soup, **'86** 144; **'91** 258
Minestrone Soup Mix, **'91** 258
Navy Bean Soup, **'84** 280
Okra-and-Shrimp Soup, **'94** 323
Peach Soup, **'93** 120
Pepper Soup, Spicy, **'93** 98
Plum Soup, **'85** 107
Potato Soup, Hearty, **'98** 292
Roasted Pepper-and-Chicken Soup, **'90** 58
Roasted Red Pepper Soup, **'96** 245
Seafood Stew, **'84** 280
Spinach Soup, Oriental, **'83** 151
Split Pea Soup, **'90** 198; **'94** 322
Sweet Potato-and-Sausage Soup, **'95** 23
Tomato Soup, **'89** 217
Tomato Soup, Easy, **'84** 14
Tomato Soup Plus, **'88** 170
Tortilla Soup, **'94** 136; **'98** 291
Turkey-Tomato Stew, **'90** 279
Vegetable-Beef Stew, **'94** 323
Vegetable Soup, **'86** 187; **'88** 266; **'98** 291
Vegetable Soup, Light, **'84** 280
Vegetable Stew, Mixed, **'84** 13
Zucchini Soup with Fresh Vegetable Salsa,
    Chilled, **'98** 194
Sour Cream, Mock, **'83** 71, 205
Spice Mix, Tex-Mex, **'94** 135
Spice Rub, Moroccan, **'95** 231
Spread, Blue Cheese, **'95** 79
Spread, Cottage Cheese, **'87** 107
Spread, Hawaiian Ham, **'87** 106
Spread, Light Strawberry, **'85** 55
Spread, Low-Calorie Pimiento Cheese, **'85** 215
Spread, Peachy-Raisin, **'86** 326
Spread, Raisin-Nut, **'95** 79
Spread, Strawberry, **'95** 79
Spread, Sugarless Fruit, **'84** 60
Spread, Tasty Chicken, **'84** 193

Spread, Vegetable-Egg, **'87** 106
Syrup, Maple, **'93** 16
Topping, Apple, **'89** 107
Topping, Oat Crunch, **'89** 108
Topping, Yogurt-Cheese, **'88** 55
Tortellini with Rosemary-Parmesan Sauce,
    '92 284
Tortilla Rollups, **'89** 87
Vegetables
Acorn Squash, Fruited, **'85** 235; **'90** 228
Acorn Squash with Nutmeg, **'85** 267
Acorn Squash with Rosemary, Grilled, **'96** 266
Artichokes, Shrimp-Stuffed, **'84** 67
Artichokes, Stuffed, **'99** 64
Artichokes Stuffed with Shrimp and Scallops,
    '84 174
Asparagus, Company, **'85** 82
Asparagus, Stir-Fried, **'87** 52
Asparagus Vinaigrette, **'90** 138
Barley and Vegetables, **'91** 81
Beans, Lemon-Mint, **'88** 22
Beans, Texas Ranch, **'90** 198
Beets, Ginger-Marmalade Glazed, **'93** 35
Beets, Harvard, **'83** M195
Beets, Orange, **'91** 219
Beets, Orange-Glazed, **'86** 187
Beets, Pickled, **'87** 163
Black Bean Terrine with Fresh Tomato Coulis
    and Jalapeño Sauce, **'93** 230
Black-Eyed Peas, **'93** 180
Black-Eyed Peas, Creole, **'98** 22
Black-Eyed Peas, Seasoned, **'85** 138
Black-Eyed Peas, Spicy Hot, **'90** 135
Broccoli and Walnut Sauté, **'95** 52
Broccoli Casserole, **'88** 265
Broccoli, Easy Orange, **'85** 267
Broccoli, Garlic, **'93** 35; **'95** 54
Broccoli, Lemon, **'95** 53
Broccoli, Sesame, **'85** 8
Broccoli Toss, **'86** 294
Broccoli with Horseradish Sauce, **'84** 33
Broccoli with Tangy Chive Sauce, Steamed,
    '83 101
Brussels Sprouts, Casserole of, **'86** 294
Brussels Sprouts, Glorified, **'86** 282
Brussels Sprouts in Mustard Sauce, **'90** 228
Brussels Sprouts, Marinated, **'88** 265
Brussels Sprouts Medley, **'85** 267
Bundles, Vegetable, **'93** 181
Burritos, Tony's Veggie, **'96** 289
Burritos, Vegetable, **'90** 134; **'92** 138
Butterbeans, **'90** 166
Butternut-Orange Bake, **'86** 295
Cabbage, Skillet, **'90** 229
Cabbage, Sweet-and-Sour, **'86** 295
Cabbage with Caraway, **'93** 181
Carrots and Onions, Herbed, **'87** 31
Carrots and Pineapple, Curried, **'90** 228
Carrots, Dilled Baby, **'92** 145
Carrots, Ginger, **'83** 9
Carrots, Glazed, **'88** 304
Carrots, Golden, **'85** 267
Carrots, Lemon-Dill Steamed, **'93** 180
Carrots, Light Glazed, **'92** 227
Carrots, Marinated, **'86** 108
Carrots Marsala, **'83** 56
Carrots, Orange-Spiced, **'88** 18
Carrots Polynesian, Spiced, **'88** 85
Carrots, Rosemary, **'91** 219
Carrot Strips, Orangy, **'89** 312
Carrots, Tropical, **'84** 34
Cauliflower Sauté, **'94** 67
Cauliflower-Snow Pea Medley, **'87** 305
Celeriac and Carrots, **'91** 219

Celery-Parmesan Toss, '84 34
Chard with Onion and Apple, Sautéed, '98 48
Corn Casserole, Chili-, '88 266
Corn, Creamy Baked, '90 60
Corn-on-the-Cob, Grilled, '90 166
Corn Pudding, Fresh, '89 172
Corn, Roasted Red Pepper, '91 122
Corn, Southern-Style Creamed, '92 201
Corn, Spicy Mexican, '93 90
Crêpes, Vegetable-Filled Bran, '86 44
Crunchy Vegetables, '99 43
Eggplant Casserole, Spicy Hot, '93 92
Eggplant, Ratatouille-Bran Stuffed, '86 44
Eggplant, Spicy Oriental, '96 130
English Pea Medley, '85 236
English Peas, Deluxe, '84 68
French Fries, Oven, '91 122
French Fries, Seasoned, '96 245
Green Bean Medley, Peppery, '93 181
Green Beans and Potatoes, '91 221
Green Beans, Herbed, '83 177
Green Beans, Indian-Style, '88 265
Green Beans, Italian, '90 164; '92 183
Green Beans Italiano, '86 144
Green Beans, Lemony, '99 259
Green Beans, Seasoned, '88 304
Green Beans with Mushrooms, '93 89
Green Beans with New Potatoes, '87 164
Green Beans with Oregano, '97 218
Green Beans with Tomatoes, '85 137
Green Tomatoes, '89 174
Green Tomatoes, Oven-Fried, '91 122
Grilled Vegetables, '92 124
Grilled Vegetables, Italian-Style, '92 143
Grilled Vegetables, Marinated, '95 162
Hominy, Mexican, '91 133
Kabobs, Marinated Vegetable, '83 M195
Kale with Tomato and Onion, '92 244
Kidney Bean Casserole, '90 136
Leeks Vinaigrette, Warm, '98 47
Lima Beans Creole, '85 137
Marinated Vegetables, '88 170; '99 105
Medley, Chinese Vegetable, '84 33
Mixed Vegetables, '83 M195
Mushrooms, Flavor-Stuffed, '85 288
Mushrooms, Grilled Portabello, '95 123
Mushrooms, Microwave Portabello, '95 M123
Mushrooms, Sautéed Portabello, '95 123
Mushrooms, Savory Fresh, '85 268
New Potatoes, Herbed, '83 9
New Potatoes, Roasted, '90 138
New Potato Medley, '90 279
Okra-and-Tomato Bake, '89 173
Okra and Tomatoes, Grilled, '98 124
Okra, Corn, and Tomatoes, '95 203
Okra, Oven-Fried, '91 121
Onion-Potato Bake, '83 M195
Onion Rings, Crispy Baked, '95 247
Onions and Wine, Stuffed, '85 268
Onions, Stuffed Vidalia, '89 172
Onions Stuffed with Peas, '84 68
Parsnips, Glazed, '91 220
Peas-and-Corn Medley, '85 138
Peas and Ham, Southern, '85 138
Peas and Peppers, Stir-Fried, '87 51
Peperonata, '97 291
Pepper Kabobs, Pretty, '90 166
Peppers, Carrot-and-Cabbage Stuffed, '99 63
Peppers, Stuffed, '84 202
Pilaf, Barley-Vegetable, '91 33
Potato-Cheese Dream, '91 307
Potatoes and Turnips, Scalloped, '85 235
Potatoes au Gratin, '93 90
Potatoes, Buttermilk-Basil Mashed, '95 330

Potatoes, Cottage, '93 M92
Potatoes, Double-Cheese, '86 6
Potatoes, Herbed, '91 220
Potatoes, Light Scalloped, '89 311
Potatoes, Mexican-Stuffed, '91 131
Potatoes, Mushroom-Dill-Topped, '86 41
Potatoes, Rosemary-Roasted, '95 20
Potatoes, Scalloped, '92 48
Potatoes, Stuffed, '89 173
Potatoes, Twice Baked Cottage-Style, '91 135
Potatoes, Vegetable-Topped Stuffed, '85 235
Potato, Twice-Baked, '90 M295
Potato Wedges, '94 M119
Potato Wedges, Lemon, '88 21
Ragoût, Vegetable, '89 172
Ratatouille, Microwave, '95 M232
Red Cabbage-and-Apple Slaw, '91 309
Rice Toss, Vegetable-, '96 309
Rice, Vegetables and, '93 91
Risotto Primavera, '95 163
Roasted Summer Vegetables, '98 213
Rutabaga, Honey, '91 220
Rutabagas, Mashed, '86 295
Sautéed Vegetable Medley, '83 101
Sauté, Tossed Vegetable, '92 138
Snap Beans, Sweet-and-Sour, '89 173
Snow Peas with Red Pepper, '90 102
Spaghetti Squash Sauté, '98 212
Spinach Quiche, '85 49; '91 204
Spinach Soufflé, '86 108
Squash Casserole, '87 163
Squash Stuffed with Spinach Pesto, '89 M133
Steamed Garden Vegetables, '93 155
Steamed Herbed Vegetables, '93 M303
Steamed Vegetable Medley, '90 29
Stir-Fried Vegetables, '90 136
Stir-Fried Vegetables with Curry, '87 51
Stir-Fry, Almond-Vegetable, '86 222
Stir-Fry, Mixed Veggie, '99 206
Stir-Fry, Vegetable, '99 204
Stir-Fry, Vegetable Medley, '99 205
Stir-Fry Vegetables, Glazed, '99 205
Sugar Snap Peas with Basil and Lemon, '93 66
Summer Vegetables, '91 136
Summer Vegetables, Cheesy, '94 119
Sweet Potato-Apple Bake, '86 282
Sweet Potatoes-and-Apple Casserole, '90 228
Sweet Potato Puff, '85 235
Sweet Potato Puree, '92 306
Tomato Coulis, Fresh, '93 230
Tomatoes and Okra, '87 164
Tomatoes, Bean-Stuffed, '84 34
Tomatoes, Cheese Herbed-Topped, '86 108
Tomatoes, Cheesy Puff-Top, '86 187
Tomatoes, Grilled, '85 158
Tomatoes, Parmesan-Stuffed, '92 182
Tomatoes, Spinach-Topped, '88 265
Tomatoes, Stuffed Scalloped, '90 29
Tomatoes with Basil Vinaigrette, Grilled, '97 168
Tomato Slices, Herbed, '89 173
Torta, Mexican, '88 149
Turnips and Carrots Julienne, '86 295
Turnips, Braised, '91 219
Zucchini-and-Tomato Casserole, '88 265
Zucchini and Tomato with Herbs, '92 182
Zucchini-Basil Delight, '85 267
Zucchini-Basil Scramble, '87 34
Zucchini Dressing, '86 282
Zucchini Fans, '91 33
Zucchini Spears, Oven-Fried, '91 121
Zucchini, Stuffed, '86 187; '89 M133
Zucchini with Feta, Greek Grilled, '95 190
Zucchini with Pecans, '87 31

Vinegar, Raspberry Wine, '93 191
Vinegar, Shallot-Tarragon-Garlic, '93 191
Waffles, Light, '91 139
Waffles, Oat Bran, '92 139
Waffles, Oatmeal, '89 107
Wild Rice-Fennel Pilaf, '97 127
Yogurt Snack, '88 55

LOBSTER
Beef Tenderloin, Lobster-Stuffed, '87 248
Clambake, Backyard, '81 92
Crab-Stuffed Lobster Tails, '95 326
Creamy Lobster, '79 181
How to Cook Lobster, '81 169
Medaillons in Garlic-Chive Butter Sauce, Lobster, '90 96
Orange Sauce, Lobster Tails with Spiced, '86 155
Salad, Lobster, '89 249; '90 69
Salad, Lobster and Orange, '82 207
Salad with Tarragon Vinaigrette, Lobster, '97 163
Soup, Spicy Thai Lobster, '94 102
Taco with Yellow Tomato Salsa and Jícama Salad, Warm Lobster, '87 122
Thermidor, Lobster, '85 103

Macadamia
Beans, Hawaiian-Style Baked, '86 210
Brownies, Macadamia-Fudge Designer, '94 51
Caramels, Coconut-Macadamia, '98 305
Coffee Cake, Macadamia Ring, '85 326
Cookies, Chunky Macadamia Nut White Chocolate, '92 207
Cookies, Coconut-Macadamia, '98 294
Cookies, White Chocolate-Macadamia Nut, '94 315
Crème Brûlée, White Chocolate-Macadamia Nut, '95 323
Crust, Chocolate-Macadamia Crumb, '96 254
Crust, Key Lime Bars with Macadamia, '99 282
Crusts, Coconut Cream Tarts with Macadamia Nut, '97 62
French Toast, Macadamia, '86 96
French Toast, Macadamia Nut, '95 282
Grouper Macadamia, '85 127
Mahi Mahi, Macadamia, '88 164
Oat Snowball, Macadamia, '92 274
Pie, Coconut-Macadamia Nut, '97 110
Pie, Frozen Chocolate-Macadamia Nut, '96 254
Pie, Hawaiian Banana Cream, '90 105
Pie, Macadamia, '80 238
Pie, Pear-Macadamia, '93 260
Salad, Macadamia Chicken, '80 138
Sauce, Brandy-Macadamia, '82 311
MACARONI. *See also* **PASTAS.**
Beans, Pasta with, '99 236
Beef and Macaroni, Skillet, '82 130
Beef-Macaroni Bake, '94 255
Beef-Macaroni Combo, '79 194
Casserole, Chicken-Macaroni, '85 219
Casserole, Macaroni, '84 220; '87 154
Casserole, Macaroni and Chicken, '80 260
Casserole, Macaroni-Ham, '81 M177; '83 283
Casserole, Mushroom-Macaroni, '95 180
Casserole, Spinach-Beef-Macaroni, '83 313
Cheese
    Baked Macaroni and Cheese, '82 199
    Baked Macaroni with Spinach, '99 244
    Blue Cheese, Macaroni and, '93 248; '94 44
    Casserole, Macaroni-Cheese-Beef, '95 125
    Creamy Macaroni and Cheese, '93 249; '94 45
    Deluxe, Macaroni-and-Cheese, '79 84
    Deluxe, Macaroni and Cheese, '80 236

MACARONI, Cheese
(continued)

Divine Macaroni and Cheese, '99 314
Double Cheese Macaroni, '82 224
Eleanor's Macaroni and Cheese, '97 253
Gorgonzola Macaroni, '97 28
Jack-in-the-Macaroni Bake, '93 249; '94 45
Macaroni and Cheese, '83 M7; '88 M147, M90;
    '90 30
Mexican Macaroni, '96 73
Mousse, Macaroni, '96 73
Mushroom Bake, Cheesy Macaroni-, '81 243
Mushroom Bake, Macaroni-, '97 96
Old-Fashioned Macaroni and Cheese, '92 215
Peppers, Macaroni-and-Cheese-Stuffed,
    '80 65
Pizza, Maca-, '99 195
Primavera, Macaroni, '96 73
Puff, Macaroni and Cheese, '79 5
Tasty Macaroni and Cheese, '83 288
Thick-and-Rich Macaroni and Cheese, '84 329
Tomatoes, Macaroni, Cheese, and, '95 213
Wine, Macaroni-and-Cheese with, '86 78
Dinner, Sausage Skillet, '83 29
Glorious Macaroni, '84 76
Ground Beef and Macaroni, '85 218
Mexican Luncheon, '87 192
Oysters with Macaroni, Scalloped, '80 297
Salads
Acini di Pepe Salad, '83 163
Barbecue Macaroni Salad, '82 276
Cheese Salad, Macaroni and, '97 203
Chicken Salad, Dilled Macaroni-, '92 142
Chicken Salad, Macaroni-, '85 296; '86 302
Confetti Macaroni Salad, '82 132; '85 297
Crabmeat Salad, Macaroni-, '81 153
Crunchy Macaroni Salad, '82 24
Dilled Macaroni-Cheese Salad, '86 208
Dilled Macaroni Salad, '89 161
Garden Macaroni Salad, '84 290; '92 64
Gourmet Macaroni Salad, '81 253
Ham and Macaroni Salad, '79 220
Ham Salad, Macaroni-, '85 218
Hearty Macaroni Salad, '84 90
Kidney Bean-Salami Pasta Toss, '85 165
Macaroni Salad, '87 92
Olive Clubhouse Salad, '81 114
Overnight Pasta Salad, '82 276
Pineapple Macaroni Salad, '79 220
Refreshing Macaroni Salad, '80 177
Salmon-and-Macaroni Salad, '81 114
Salmon Salad, Macaroni-, '82 232
Shell Macaroni Salad, '92 163
Shell Salad, Macaroni, '87 38
Shrimp Macaroni Salad, '79 220
Shrimp-Macaroni Salad, '85 219
Shrimp Salad, Festive Macaroni-, '85 165
Shrimp Salad, Macaroni-, '85 121
Spiral Macaroni Salad, '82 276
Sweet-and-Sour Macaroni Salad, '85 166
Taco Macaroni Salad, '85 165
Tuna Macaroni Salad, '83 44, 145
Tuna-Macaroni Salad, '84 66
Tuna Salad, Whole Wheat Macaroni-, '84 193
Turkey Macaroni Salad, '83 282
Two, Macaroni Salad for, '81 31
Vegetable Salad, Macaroni-, '86 209
Véronique, Macaroni Salad, '85 164
Soup, Macaroni and Cheese, '95 264
Soup, Pimiento "Mac and Cheese," '97 M325
Supper Supreme, Sunday, '79 76
Tomatoes, Tuna-Mac in, '87 188
Toss, Corkscrew Macaroni, '83 163
Treat, Tuna-Macaroni, '82 131
Whole Wheat Macaroni with Pesto, '89 238
MANGOES
Beef and Rice, Mango-, '88 138
Bread, Mango, '96 205
Cake, Mango, '83 150
Chutney, Blue-Ribbon Mango, '96 206
Chutney, Mango, '89 141; '96 182
Cooler, Caribbean, '98 333
Crêpes, Mango-Pineapple, '86 216
Dessert Tamales, Mango, '94 190
Frappé, Mango, '86 216
Ice Cream, Mango, '86 216
Margaritas, Mango, '96 126
Orange Smoothie, Mango-, '86 216
Pan Dowdy, Mango, '83 150
Pie, Green Mango, '79 137
Pie, Mango-Ginger, '88 138
Pork Loin, Tropical, '96 86
Preserves, Mango-Pineapple, '79 137
Relish, Mango, '89 198
Salad, Fresh Mango, '84 126
Salad, Mango, '79 137
Salad Sandwiches, Mango-Crab, '99 72
Salad with Mango, Chicken, '86 215
Salsa, Mango, '91 182; '95 104; '98 232
Salsa, Minted Mango, '96 206
Salsa, Seared Scallops with Tomato-Mango,
    '95 122
Salsa, Tropical, '96 14
Sauce, Mango, '83 120
Sauce, Mango-Spiced Rum, '86 215
Slaw, Mango, '93 31; '94 71
Sorbet, Mango, '86 196
Soup, Chilled Mango-Cantaloupe, '96 205
Torta, Mango Chutney, '96 322
Vinegar, Mango-Cilantro, '95 190
MANICOTTI
Cannelloni, '85 60; '92 17
Cheesy Manicotti, '83 216
Chicken Manicotti, Creamy, '85 60
Chili Manicotti, '89 247; '99 239
Make-Ahead Manicotti, '98 68
Quick Manicotti, '79 6
Seafood Manicotti, '94 195
Shrimp Manicotti, '97 96
Special Manicotti, '88 50
Spinach Manicotti, '82 199
Stuffed Manicotti, '83 M6
Stuffed Manicotti, Saucy, '83 288
Stuffed Manicotti, Spinach-, '88 255
Zucchini Manicotti, '84 194
MARINADES
Asian Marinade, '99 141
Basic Marinade, '99 141
Beef Marinade, Tangy, '86 113
Cinnamon-Soy Marinade, '93 103
Citrus Marinade, '93 103
Garlic-Basil Marinade, '94 160
Garlic-Honey Marinade, '93 102
Honey-Mustard Marinade, '93 103
Lemon Marinade, Chicken in, '98 128
Lemon-Molasses Dressing, '97 195
Lemon-Soy Marinade, '91 194
Light Marinade, Tangy, '82 178
Lime Marinade, Fruit with, '98 92
Marinade, '86 153; '92 283
Mexican Marinade, Flank Steak in, '98 128
Minty Marinade, '92 105
Oriental Marinade, '93 102
Oriental Marinade, Seafood in, '98 128
Raspberry Vinaigrette, '96 275
Southwestern Marinade, '93 102; '99 141
Soy-and-Ginger Marinade, '96 129
Sweet-and-Sour Marinade, '86 113
Teriyaki Marinade, '86 114; '93 102
Vegetable Marinade, '92 231
MARMALADES. *See* **JAMS AND JELLIES/
    Marmalades.**
MARSHMALLOWS
Ambrosia, Carrot-Marshmallow, '80 5
Bars, Broadway Brownie, '97 M35
Bars, Chewy Chocolate Cereal, '97 317
Bird's Nests, '95 102
Brownies, Chewy Marshmallow, '83 306
Brownies, Choco-Mallow, '87 198; '90 309
Brownies, No-Bake, '94 330
Cake, No-Egg Chocolate Marshmallow, '87 97
Chocolate, Hot Laced Marshmallow, '93 53
Coffee Mallow, '80 109
Cream, Orange-Mallow, '94 295
Dip, Marshmallow Fruit, '84 171
Frosting, Chocolate-Marshmallow, '83 245
Fudge, Butterscotch-Peanut, '98 M282
Monster Mouths, '95 274
Munchies, Pop Graham, '96 28
Parfaits, Mocha-Mallow, '80 219
Pie, Coffee, '96 148
Piglets, '98 203
Pizza Dessert, Rocky Road, '99 196
Popcorn Balls, Marshmallow, '90 226
Pudding, Banana-Mallow, '86 139
Salad, Waldorf, '97 204
Sauce, Marshmallow, '91 91
S'mores, Grilled Pound Cake, '98 179
Squares, Chocolate-Marshmallow, '92 M50
Sugarplum Fairy Wands, '97 M286
MAYONNAISE
Aioli (Garlic Mayonnaise), '88 221
Aïoli, Picante, '99 53
Anchovy Mayonnaise, '86 179
Apricot Mayonnaise, '97 320
Basil Mayonnaise, '98 144
Cilantro Mayonnaise, '98 51
Citrus Mayonnaise, Creamy, '92 107
Curry Mayonnaise, '95 66
Dill-Garlic Mayonnaise, '92 320
Dill Mayonnaise, '96 197
Dip, Artichokes with Herb-Mayonnaise, '84 67
Dip, Seasoned Mayonnaise Artichoke, '80 87
Dressing, Mayonnaise, '86 11
Dressing, Southwestern Mayonnaise, '99 245
Dried Tomato Mayonnaise, '98 144
Flavored Mayonnaise, '94 167; '96 123; '97 328
Garlic Mayonnaise, '92 56
Herbed Mayonnaise, '82 85, 192
Homemade Mayonnaise, '80 155; '90 81; '99 180
Homemade Mayonnaise, Easy, '84 12
Italian Herbed Mayonnaise, '92 320
Lemon-Cream Mayonnaise, '85 264
Lemon-Dill Mayonnaise, '99 267
Lemon Mayonnaise, '95 32; '98 144;
    '99 178
Mediterranean Mayonnaise, '98 144
Onion Mayonnaise, '98 144
Parmesan Mayonnaise, '86 79
Raspberry Mayonnaise, '97 107
Roasted Garlic Mayonnaise, '97 47
Roasted Red Pepper Mayonnaise, '98 144
Russian Mayonnaise, '80 137
Sauce, Herb-Mayonnaise, '85 73
Sauce, Zesty, '97 312
Spread, Dijon-Mayo, '96 199
Tasty Mayonnaise, '82 192
Thyme Mayonnaise, '96 121
Watercress Mayonnaise, '93 119
Wine Mayonnaise, Hot, '81 83

MEATBALLS

Appetizers

Brandied Meatballs, '83 78
Chafing Dish Meatballs, '81 260
Chestnut Meatballs, '79 110
Flavorful Meatballs, '84 206
German Meatballs, Crisp, '92 326
Ham Balls, '86 256
Ham Balls, Appetizer, '82 39
Hawaiian Meatballs, Tangy, '79 129
Polynesian Meatballs, '80 207
Red Delicious Meatballs, '85 85
Saucy Party Meatballs, '80 149
Sauerkraut Meatballs, '86 257
Spiced Meatballs, '79 284
Sweet-and-Sour Meatballs, '82 247; '99 325
Sweet-and-Sour Party Meatballs, '79 233
Tamale Balls, Tangy, '89 60
Tamale Meatballs, '80 194
Zesty Meatballs, '80 250
Bacon Meatballs, Burgundy-, '80 283
Bacon-Wrapped Meatballs, '79 81
Beef Balls Heidelberg, '83 164; '84 39
Charleston Press Club Meatballs, '93 129
Chinese Meatballs, '83 116; '87 194
Cocktail Meatballs, '79 63, 207
Creole, Meatball-Okra, '83 156
Creole, Meatballs, '82 233
Español, Meatballs, '82 110
Golden Nugget Meatballs, '82 233
Gravy, Meatballs in, '79 136
Ham Balls, '84 91; '86 256
Hawaiian Meatballs, '85 86
Kabobs, Meatball, '95 192
Lamb Meatballs with Yogurt Sauce, '85 132
Meatballs, '89 237
Mock Meatballs, '81 243
Oven Barbecued Meatballs, '82 233
Pineapple and Peppers, Meatballs with, '90 145
Pizza Meatballs, '85 86
Processor Meatballs, Quick, '87 111
Royal Meatballs, '87 268; '88 102; '89 67
Sandwiches, Open-Faced Meatball, '99 239
Sandwich, Giant Meatball, '92 196
Saucy Meatballs, '85 68; '90 122
Sauerbraten Meatballs, '85 85
Soup, Mexican Meatball, '98 315
Spaghetti-and-Herb Meatballs, '84 75
Spaghetti with Meatballs, '81 38
Spicy Meatballs and Sausage, '79 163
Stew, Meatball, '79 198; '98 30
Stroganoff, Meatball, '81 297
Stroganoff, Mushroom-Meatball, '85 85
Swedish Meatballs, '80 80; '86 256
Sweet-and-Sour Meatballs, '82 233, 247; '86 240
Turkey Meatballs, '89 237
Veal Meatballs, European, '85 30
Venison Sausage Balls, '80 42

MEAT LOAF

All-American Meat Loaf, '92 341; '93 46
Barbecued Meat Loaf, '80 60; '81 275; '84 50;
   '87 216
Basic Meat Loaf, '88 M14
Beef Loaf, Glazed, '86 19
Beef Loaves, Individual Barbecued, '95 242
Beef-Vegetable Loaf, '79 164
Blue Cheese Meat Loaf Roll, '93 247
Cheeseburger Loaf, '81 236, 276
Cheesy Meat Roll, '82 136
Chili Meat Loaf, '81 275
Corny Meat Loaf, '86 68
Crunchy Meat Loaf Oriental, '79 212
Curried Meat Loaf, '86 43
Easy Meat Loaf, '88 M214; '95 125; '97 24

Elegant Meat Loaf, '89 243
Family-Style Meat Loaf, '93 18
Fennel Meat Loaf, '88 46
German Meat Loaf, '87 216
Greek Meat Loaf, '96 251; '97 103
Ham Loaf, '79 180; '80 272
Ham Loaf, Cranberry-, '82 M77
Ham Loaf, Glazed, '79 187; '90 212
Ham Loaf, Hawaiian, '79 71
Ham Loaf, Pineapple Upside-Down, '79 253
Ham Loaf, Saucy, '86 M328
Ham Loaf, Spicy, '80 110
Ham Loaf, Supreme, '79 242
Ham Loaf, Upside-Down, '82 40
Ham Loaves, '90 235
Ham Loaves, Country, '86 255
Ham Ring, '84 91
Ham Ring, Chili-Sauced, '81 M122
Hurry-Up Meat Loaf, '82 21
Hurry-Up Meat Loaves, '88 15
Individual Meat Loaves, '81 279; '82 24; '83 154;
   '92 229
Italian Meat Loaf, '79 187
Lamb Meat Loaf with Feta Cheese, '97 24
Liver Loaf, Skillet, '80 111
Meat Loaf, '81 170; '89 109
Mexicali Meat Loaf, '81 275
Mexican Meat Loaf, '87 217
Miniature Meat Loaves, '85 24
Mini-Teriyaki Meat Loaf, '90 69
Mozzarella-Layered Meat Loaf, '79 71
My-Ami's Meat Loaf, '94 229
Oriental Meat Loaf, '81 M122; '83 M194
Parsleyed Meat Loaf, '83 35
Parsley Meat Loaf, '87 22
Pineapple Loaves, Individual, '81 M121
Pizza Meat Loaf, Cheesy, '81 M121
Reuben Loaf, '95 338
Roll, Meat Loaf, '79 129
Saucy Meat Loaves, '79 186
Savory Meat Loaf, '87 216
Southwestern Meat Loaf, '93 248
Special Meat Loaf, '89 70
Spicy Meat Loaf, '79 71
Sprout Meat Loaf, '85 51
Stuffed Beef Log, '79 71
Stuffed Meat Loaf, '79 187
Stuffed Meat Loaf, Rolled, '80 80
Sun-Dried Tomatoes and Herbs, Meat Loaf with,
   '92 192
Supreme, Meat Loaf, '92 33
Swedish Meat Loaf, '81 M121
Tasty Meat Loaf, '83 213
Tex-Mex Meat Loaf for Two, '90 234
Triple Meat Loaf, '79 186
Turkey Loaf, '92 33
Turkey Loaf, Cranberry-Glazed, '86 171
Turkey Loaf, Ground, '86 171
Turkey Meat Loaf, Spinach-Stuffed, '97 24
Veal Meat Loaf, '93 292
Vegetable Meat Loaf, '85 M29
Wellington, Meat Loaf, '79 186; '87 284
Wrap, Meat Loaf in a, '89 122

MELONS

Balls and Cherries in Kirsch, Melon, '91 91
Balls, Fiery Sweet Melon, '92 311
Balls, Mellowed-Out Melon, '88 182
Bowl with Cucumber-Mint Dressing, Melon Ball,
   '87 153

Cantaloupe

Berry-Filled Melon, '86 93
Chutney, Fresh Cantaloupe, '97 148
Compote, Cantaloupe, '81 147
Compote, Melon Ball, '85 157

Cream Delight, Cantaloupe, '82 179
Delight, Cantaloupe, '89 204
Frozen Cantaloupe Cream, '82 159
Fruit-Filled Cantaloupe, '83 120
Fruit Medley, Minted, '80 182
Grilled Cantaloupe Wedges, '87 162
Ice Cream, Cantaloupe, '79 177
Jam, Cantaloupe-Peach, '95 143
Mold, Double-Grape Cantaloupe, '79 173
Pickled Cantaloupe, '99 171
Pickled Cantaloupe, Sweet, '89 197
Pie, Cantaloupe, '86 163
Pie, Cantaloupe Cream, '79 177
Pie, Cantaloupe Meringue, '88 182
Punch, Cantaloupe, '81 147
Salad, Avocado-Melon, '82 164
Salad, Cantaloupe, '86 182
Salad, Cantaloupe-Cheese, '88 184
Salad, Cantaloupe Colada, '97 148
Salad, Cantaloupe Cooler, '79 176
Salad, Cantaloupe Green, '91 126
Salad, Cantaloupe-Pecan, '86 178
Salad, Melon-Berry, '90 180
Salad with Dill Dressing, Melon, '88 182
Salad with Pistachio-Lime Vinaigrette,
   Cantaloupe-Spinach, '97 148
Sherbet, Cantaloupe, '88 183
Sherbet-Cantaloupe Surprise, '91 105
Sherbet, Frosty Cantaloupe, '82 144
Soup, Cantaloupe, '83 120; '88 160
Soup, Chilled Cantaloupe, '81 156; '97 148
Soup, Chilled Mango-Cantaloupe, '96 205
Soup, Fresh Cantaloupe, '84 190
Soup, Melon, '80 182
Southern Plantation Cantaloupe, '82 179
Sundae, Cantaloupe, '89 166
Sweet-and-Hot Melon, '92 163
Wedges with Berry Sauce, Melon, '86 178
Whip, Cantaloupe, '89 198
Citrus Mingle, Melon-, '79 177
Cooler, Melon, '81 146
Fruit Bowl, Sparkling Fresh, '80 146
Fruit Cup with Mint Dressing, Fresh, '80 183
Fruit Deluxe, Marinated, '81 146

Honeydew

Boats, Honeydew Fruit, '81 147
Bowl, Honeydew Fruit, '84 186
Cooler, Melon Ball, '86 131
Cups, Honeydew Fruit, '82 179
Dessert, Honeydew-Berry, '83 120
Granita, Honeydew, '87 162
Grapes, Honeydew Melon with, '91 91
Salad, Fruited Ham, '81 146
Salad, Melon and Shrimp Curry, '97 129
Salad, Melon-Berry, '90 180
Salad with Apricot Cream Dressing,
   Honeydew, '84 191
Salad with Dill Dressing, Melon, '88 182
Soup, Melon, '80 182
Wedges with Berry Sauce, Melon, '86 178
Julep, Melon-Mint, '86 196
Julep, Rainbow Melon, '80 183
Mélange, Melon, '84 139
Minted Melon, '96 123
Minted Melon Cocktail, '81 146
Mint Sauce, Melons in, '85 164
Salad, Congealed Melon Ball, '84 125
Salad, Georgia Summer, '92 179
Salad, Melon-and-Prosciutto, '92 191
Salad, Summertime Melon, '82 101
Salad with Orange-Raspberry Vinaigrette,
   Grilled Melon, '95 144
Salsa, Hot Melon, '95 144
Soup, Swirled Melon, '87 162

MELONS
(continued)

Watermelon
Balls, Minted Melon, '87 162
Basket, Watermelon Fruit, '84 161
Compote, Watermelon-Cherry, '90 180
Cookies, Watermelon, '92 179
Cooler, Melon Ball, '86 131
Cooler, Watermelon-Strawberry, '98 178
Daiquiri, Watermelon, '95 143; '98 165
Frost, Watermelon, '86 196
Granita, Watermelon, '96 179; '98 165
Ice, Watermelon, '91 173
Lemonade, Watermelon, '98 165
Marmalade, Watermelon-and-Ginger, '98 164
Mousse, Frozen Watermelon, '91 96; '92 130
Pickles, Watermelon Rind, '81 174; '98 164
Pie, Watermelon, '95 144
Preserves, Watermelon, '79 120
Prosciutto, Watermelon and, '98 164
Punch, Watermelon, '89 204; '92 190
Salad with Celery-Nut Dressing, Watermelon, '80 182
Salsa, Watermelon, '98 164
Sauce, Melon Balls in Watermelon, '79 177
Sherbet, Light Watermelon, '81 147
Sherbet, Watermelon, '79 155; '92 124
Sherried Watermelon, '92 117
Slush, Watermelon-Berry, '90 137
Sorbet, Watermelon, '92 190; '99 166
Sparkle, Watermelon, '84 191

MERINGUES
Acorns, Meringue, '93 284
Asparagus Meringue, '88 131
Baked Pear Meringues, '85 232
Bars, Meringue-Chocolate Chip, '84 118
Basket, Summer Berry, '84 158
Baskets with Fresh Fruit and Ice Cream, Meringue, '98 179
Cake, Brown Sugar Meringue, '81 70
Cake, Cinderella Fantasy, '98 70
Cake, Orange Meringue, '86 336; '87 84
Cakes, Spanish Wind, '84 157
Coconut Kisses, '90 106
Coffee Kisses, Chocolate-Dipped, '96 313
Coffee Meringues with Butterscotch Mousse, '93 254
Cooked Meringue, '86 130
Cooked Meringue, Easy, '82 207; '83 158
Cookies, Forget 'em, '83 256
Cookies, Meringue, '98 71
Cookies, Meringue Kiss, '86 121
Cookies, Meringue Surprise, '86 320
Cran-Apple Mousse Filling, Meringues with, '93 254
Cups, Kiwi and Cream in Meringue, '81 279
Cups, Lemon Custard in Meringue, '80 295; '81 172
Cups, Lemon Meringue Cream, '84 23
Dream Drops, '99 328
Fingers, Chocolate-Almond Meringue, '84 158
Flowers, Meringue, '84 156
Frosting, Brown Sugar Meringue, '81 70
Frosting, Italian Meringue, '98 70
Frosting, Meringue, '86 336; '87 84; '99 118
Ghosts, White Meringue, '99 246
Holiday Meringues, '88 280
Meringue, '87 207; '94 208; '97 109
Mixture, Basic Meringue, '98 70
Mushrooms, Meringue, '96 317
Orange Meringues, '95 318
Pavlova, '92 101

Peach Melba Meringues, '87 76
Peach Melba Meringues with Buttermilk Custard Sauce, '96 183
Pears with Meringue, Amaretto, '90 58
Pineapple, Meringue-Topped, '84 178
Piping Meringue, '84 156
Shell, Cinnamon Meringue, '82 263
Shells, Fruited Meringue, '87 32
Shells, Fruit-Filled Meringue, '86 151
Strawberry Meringues, '84 188
Strawberry Meringue Torte, '88 136
Toffee Meringue Torte, '87 118
Tropical Meringues, '98 71
Vacherin Moka, '80 55

MICROWAVE. *Includes microwave conversions.*
See also **CASSEROLES/Microwave.**
Appetizers
Bacon-Chestnut Wraps, '84 M216
Brie-and-Cranberry Chutney Melt, '98 M318
Brie Appetizer, Bit-of-, '88 M18
Brie, Chutney-Bacon, '90 M292
Brie, Tropical Breeze, '94 M18
Canapés, Green Onion, '84 M216
Cheese Log, Toasted Pecan, '86 M288
Cheese Sticks, Peppery, '81 M289
Crab-Zucchini Bites, '84 M216
Dip, Apple, '96 M190
Dip, Bill D's Black-Eyed Pea, '97 M89
Dip, Cheddar-Bacon, '89 M119
Dip, Chili-and-Cheese, '89 M328
Dip, Chipped Beef, '88 M8
Dip, Creamy Crab, '80 M135
Dip, Hot Artichoke Seafood, '85 M212
Dip, Mexican Artichoke, '90 M292
Dip, Monterey Shrimp, '99 M65
Dip, Nacho, '93 M330
Dip, Quick Fiesta, '95 M237; '99 M197
Dip, Shrimp, '88 M261
Dip, Sweet-and-Spicy Mustard, '96 M274
Franks, Saucy Appetizer, '84 M12
Mix, Spicy Party, '81 M138
Mushrooms, Shrimp-Stuffed, '80 M135
Mushrooms, Spinach-Stuffed, '88 M261; '89 M133
Mushrooms, Tipsy, '84 M216
Nachos, Make-Ahead, '80 M135
Nuts, Sherry-Orange, '86 M289
Nuts, Spiced, '91 M316
Pâté, Chicken Liver, '88 M132
Pecans, Spicy, '81 M289
Pizzas, Appetizer, '89 M118
Plantain Chips, '95 M203
Popcorn, Caramel, '86 M212
Popcorn, Garlic, '83 M315
Potato Shell Appetizers, '89 M119
Potato Skins, Cheese, '84 M239
Rumaki, '80 M136
Rumaki, Scallop, '98 M173
Spread, Artichoke-Parmesan, '92 M95
Spread, Chicken Salad Party, '88 M8
Spread, Hearts of Palm, '90 M293
Spread, Hot Beef, '84 M216
Spread, Seafood, '86 M58
Spread, Spinach-Bacon, '92 M310
Sweet Potato Chips, '95 M203
Tostadas, Party, '98 M33
Wings and Ribs, Thai, '97 M225
Apples, Honey-Glazed, '90 M125
Apples, Rosy Cinnamon, '87 M37
Apples, Spicy Poached, '90 M141
Beverages
Café Colombian Royal, '80 M290
Champions' Cooler, '96 M181
Chocolate, Flaming Brandied, '80 M290

Coffee, Mocha, '85 M329
Hot Chocolate, Creole, '80 M290
Hot Chocolate Mix, Deluxe, '80 M290
Mocha, Mexican, '93 M341
Mocha, Spirited Hot, '91 M260
Spoons, Dipped Chocolate-Almond, '95 M277
Tomato Cocktail, '83 M203
Blanching Chart, Microwave, '80 M181
Breads
Caramel Ring, Easy, '85 M89
Cheese-Herb Bread, '84 M144
Chocolate Loaf Bread, '88 M188
Coffee Cake, Cinnamon, '83 M203
Coffee Cake, Orange, '85 M88
Coffee Cake Ring, '85 M89
Coffee Ring, Sugarplum, '83 M37
English Muffin Bread, '95 M79
French Toast, Easy, '82 M172
Muffins, Apple-Bran, '85 M89
Muffins, Cheesy Cornbread, '88 M275
Muffins, Cinnamon-Nut, '85 M88
Muffins, Corn, '82 M282
Muffins, Cranberry Streusel Cake, '88 M274
Muffins, Fudge Brownie, '95 M50
Muffins, Lemon, '88 M275
Muffins, Whole Wheat Bran, '88 M274
Pumpkin Bread, Harvest, '90 M215
Rolls, Cherry-Almond, '84 M198
Rolls, Cinnamon, '99 M284
Rolls, Dinner, '93 M326
Rolls, Easy Orange, '89 M131
Tomato-Cheese Bread, '99 M157
Whole Wheat-Rye Bread, '83 M37
Butter, Sweet Potato, '95 M290
Chart, Shortcuts, '89 M134
Chutney, Autumn Fruit, '88 M230
Croutons, '86 M288
Croutons, Microwave, '86 M227
Desserts. *See also* **MICROWAVE/Sauces.**
Apple Crumble, Whole Wheat-, '90 M213
Apple Dessert, Honey-Baked, '90 M213
Apple-Nut Crunch, '82 M238
Apple Rings, Cinnamon, '82 M237
Apples and Cream, Brandied, '82 M237
Apples, Caramel, '89 M231
Apples, Caramel-Peanut, '93 M244
Apples, Easy Baked, '82 M238
Bananas Foster, '83 M114
Banana Splits, French Toast, '96 M164
Bars, Blackberry Jam, '82 M185
Bars, Chewy Peanut, '80 M172
Bars, Chewy Scotch, '98 M291
Bars, Date-Oat, '80 M172
Bars, Gooey Turtle, '96 M189
Bars, Peanut Butter-and-Fudge, '80 M172
Blueberry Dessert, Easy, '89 M130
Brie, Almond-Raspberry, '94 M89
Brownie Bars, Broadway, '97 M35
Brownies à la Mode, Magnolias Cream Cheese, '97 M178
Brownies, Basic, '97 M34
Brownies, Biscuit Mix, '94 M51
Brownies, Chocolate-Mint, '85 M294
Brownies, Frosted, '97 M87
Brownies, Mississippi Mud, '89 M25
Brownies, Nutty Fudge, '80 M171
Brownies, Passover, '98 M104
Brownies, Quick, '87 M302
Cake for Grown-Ups, Ice Cream, '88 M192
Cake, Fruit and Spice, '87 M97
Cake, Fudge, '94 M293
Cake, German Chocolate, '83 M233
Cake, German Chocolate Pound, '97 M254

Cake, No-Egg Chocolate Marshmallow, '87 M97
Cake, Old-Fashioned Carrot, '83 M232
Cake, Peanut Butter, '83 M233
Cakes, Miniature Chocolate Truffle Tree, '97 M285
Candies, Turtle, '93 M41
Candy Bow, '99 M306
Candy Box, White, '97 M54
Caramel O's, '99 M196
Charlotte Russe, '82 M142
Cheesecake, Chocolate-Amaretto, '85 M294
Cheesecake, Chocolate-Wrapped Banana, '99 M48
Cheesecake, Fudge, '98 M213
Cheesecake, Luscious Lemon, '90 M196
Cheesecake, Pear-Berry, '82 M141
Cherries, Chocolate-Covered, '97 M55
Cherries Jubilee, Quick, '82 M100
Chocolate-Coffee Cones, '96 M316
Chocolate-Lemon Creams, '98 M235
Chocolate-Marshmallow Squares, '92 M50
Chocolate-Mint Parfaits, '90 M15
Chocolate-Peanut Butter Bites, '92 M317
Chocolate Peanutty Swirls, '94 M330
Cobbler, Apple-Pecan, '84 M198
Cobbler, Sweet Potato, '99 M255
Coconut Joys, Chocolate-Covered, '98 M282
Coconut Robin's Nests, '98 M111
Cookies, Angel Shortbread, '97 M285
Cookies, Chocolate-Almond Surprise, '88 M45
Cookies, Doubly-Good Chocolate, '82 M185
Cookies, Keyboard, '94 M330
Cookies, Nutty Oatmeal-Chocolate Chip, '82 M185
Cookies, Rudolph, '99 M309
Cookies, Spice, '87 M278
Cookies, Spider, '93 M166
Cookies, Wedding, '82 M185
Cream, Bavarian, '86 M165
Cream, Vanilla, '83 M115
Crème, Orange-Tapioca, '82 M283
Crust, Chocolate, '90 M15
Crust, Graham Cracker, '88 M45; '91 M234
Crust, Microwaved Graham Cracker, '82 M141
Cupcakes, Cinnamon-Chocolate, '81 M139
Cups, Vanilla Lace, '98 M93
Custard, Chocolate-Topped Amaretto, '87 M37
Divinity, Peanut, '87 M278
Dumplings, Cinnamon Apple, '97 M330
Fondant, Faux, '98 M154
Frosting, Buttery Cinnamon, '81 M139
Frosting, Caramel, '81 M289
Frosting, Chocolate, '80 M171; '83 M233; '87 M97; '89 M25; '97 M87
Frosting, Chocolate Buttercream, '98 M100
Frosting, Coconut-Pecan, '83 M233
Frosting, Cream Cheese, '83 M233
Frosting, Mint Chocolate, '99 M176
Frosting, White Chocolate Buttercream, '97 M284
Fudge, Butterscotch-Peanut, '98 M282
Fudge, Double-Good, '79 M263; '95 M50
Fudge, Double Good, '87 M278
Fudge, Microwave, '91 M92
Fudge, Microwave Chocolate, '92 M50
Fudge, Quick-and-Easy, '88 M190
Fudge Squares, Chocolate-Peanut Butter, '97 M54
Glaze, Chocolate, '91 M296; '97 M35
Glaze, French Chocolate, '98 M57

Holly Leaves, '99 M306
Ice Cream, Mocha, '97 M145
Jam Squares, '81 M289
Jellyrolls, Raspberry, '93 M255
Kahlúa Delight, Make-Ahead, '84 M89
Kahlúa Velvet Dessert, '85 M294
Millionaires, '79 M262; '97 M55
Mousse, White Chocolate, '98 M57, M111
Nuggets, Golden North Pole, '99 M309
Oatmeal Cherry-Apple Crisp, '90 M16
Oranges, Wine-Poached, '84 M323
Pastry, Basic, '81 M268
Pastry, Basic Microwave, '82 M142; '85 M113
Pastry, Double-Crust, '82 M298
Peaches, Gingersnap, '85 M329
Peach Melba, '83 M114
Peanut Brittle, '79 M263
Peanut Butter Slice-and-Bakes, '82 M185
Peanut Clusters, '98 M282
Peanut-Fudge Bites, '91 M231; '92 M68
Pears with Dark Chocolate Sauce, Poached, '90 M141
Pecan Brittle, '91 M272
Pecan Brittle, Microwave, '97 M245
Pecan-Coconut Clusters, '86 M251
Pie, Apple-Cranberry, '99 M269
Pie, Best-Ever Chocolate, '88 M45
Pie, Caramel-Banana, '86 M165
Pie, Cranberry-Apple Holiday, '81 M269
Pie, Double Chocolate, '82 M282
Pie, Easy Cherry, '82 M299
Pie, Festive Pumpkin, '81 M269
Pie, Fluffy Eggnog, '81 M269
Pie, Frosty Pumpkin-Praline, '91 M234
Pie, Glazed Strawberry, '82 M142
Pie, Lemon Meringue, '85 M112
Pie, Microwave Chocolate, '90 M15
Pie, Nutty Cranberry, '82 M298
Pie, Old-Fashioned Apple, '82 M299
Pie, Old-Fashioned Pecan, '81 M269
Pie, Quick Pumpkin, '88 M230
Pizza, Banana Split-Brownie, '96 M164
Plums, Poached, '90 M141
Pots de Crème, '84 M145
Pots de Crème, Mocha, '88 M45
Pralines, '86 M288
Pralines, Old-Fashioned, '89 M318
Pralines, Southern, '79 M263
Pudding, Bread, '89 M130
Pudding, Brown Sugar-Pecan, '86 M165
Pudding, Butternut Squash, '89 M313; '90 M19
Pudding, Chocolate-Almond, '82 M142
Pudding, Creamy Banana, '89 M130
Pudding, Mandarin-Almond, '85 M12
Pudding, Pecan-Mocha, '89 M130
Pudding, Pumpkin, '89 M313; '90 M20
Reindeer Food, Magic, '99 M309
Sachertorte, Shortcut, '99 M243
Shortbread, Marble-Topped Hazelnut, '99 M29
Soufflé, Brandy Alexander, '83 M114
Spooky Ghosts, '98 M256
Strawberries, Chocolate-Dipped, '98 M100
Sugarplum Fairy Wands, '97 M286
Sundaes, Cocoa-Kahlúa, '83 M58
Sundaes, Hot Strawberry, '81 M5
Sundaes, Spicy Apple Ice Cream, '86 M195
Tart, Caramel Turtle Truffle, '93 M131
Tart, Cranberry-Apple, '97 M316
Toffee, Microwave, '92 M317
Toffee, Nutty, '79 M263
Torte, Bourbon-Chocolate, '98 M84
Torte, Chocolate-Almond, '96 M253

Truffles, Hazelnut, '97 M54
Truffles, Yule Street, '90 M242
Waffles with Apples and Caramel, Gingerbread, '98 M237
Zuppa Inglese, '99 M267

Eggs and Omelets
Baked Eggs Florentine, '86 M12
Benedict, Easy Eggs, '80 M268
Benedict, Light Eggs, '93 M68
Casserole, Saucy Scrambled Egg, '89 M213
Cheddar Eggs, '94 M141
Creamed Eggs in Patty Shells, '80 M267
Medley, Cheddar Egg, '81 M176
Olé Omelet, '87 M124
Sausage Omelet, Puffy, '80 M268
Scramble, Bacon-and-Eggs, '80 M267
Scrambled Eggs, Creamy Onion, '83 M203
Vegetable Omelet, Golden, '82 M123
Frosting. See MICROWAVE/Desserts.
Fruit Bake, Cranberry-Mustard, '90 M287
Fruit Compote, Hot, '90 M124
Fruit Mélange, '88 M295
Granola, Superhero, '98 M206
Grits, Quick Cheese, '83 M203
Jam, Blackberry, '99 M131
Jam, Freezer Blackberry, '84 M181
Jam, Freezer Peach, '84 M182
Jam, Freezer Plum, '89 M156
Jam, Raspberry Freezer, '84 M181
Jam, Strawberry Freezer, '84 M182
Jelly, Christmas Freezer, '86 M288
Jelly, Quick Grape, '89 M156
Jelly, Red Pepper, '89 M156
Macaroni and Cheese, '83 M7; '88 M147, M190
Main Dishes
Beans and Franks, Jiffy, '91 M172
Beans-and-Franks, Polynesian, '84 M11
Beef Casserole, Easy, '86 M58
Beef Casserole, Layered, '82 M203
Beef Roast, Easy, '89 M65
Beef with Pea Pods, Oriental, '86 M328
Broccoli-Ham au Gratin, '90 M239
Burgers, Blue Cheese, '89 M66
Casserole, Mexi, '83 M87
Casserole, Mexican, '92 M22
Casserole, Microwave Mexican, '90 M231
Catfish, Microwave, '89 M52
Catfish, Spicy-Seasoned, '89 M66
Chicken alla Romano, '83 M58
Chicken-and-Broccoli Stroganoff, '89 M248
Chicken and Cashews, Ginger, '85 M11
Chicken-and-Corn Cakes with Avocado Cream, Southwestern, '97 M311
Chicken and Dumplings with Vegetables, '85 M56
Chicken and Pasta, Pesto, '89 M132
Chicken and Spinach Rollups, '82 M68
Chicken-and-Vegetable Platter, '88 M52
Chicken and Vegetables Vermouth, '87 M37
Chicken-Asparagus Rolls, '86 M211
Chicken, Barbecued, '89 M167
Chicken Breasts, Breaded, '89 M196
Chicken Breasts, Herb-Seasoned, '93 M325
Chicken, Crispy Parmesan, '80 M76
Chicken, Crunchy Spiced, '85 M57
Chicken Delicacy, '99 M23
Chicken Dinner, Hot-and-Spicy, '94 M94
Chicken Divan, '80 M10; '87 M218
Chicken Divan Casserole, '82 M203
Chicken Divan Quiche, '88 M125
Chicken, Easy, '89 M129
Chicken, Ginger-Nut, '90 M33
Chicken in a Bag, '86 M57
Chicken Kabobs, Marinated, '84 M144

Chicken Kabobs, Pineapple-, **'86** M328
Chicken Lasagna, **'87** M302
Chicken, Lemon, **'81** M138
Chicken, Lemon-Garlic, **'89** M132
Chicken Mexicana, **'91** M127
Chicken, Orange, **'86** M140
Chicken, Pineapple, **'83** M194
Chicken, Tangy Herbed, **'87** M302
Chicken Teriyaki, **'80** M76
Chicken Tetrazzini, **'80** M75
Chicken Tetrazzini, Cheesy, **'83** M87
Chicken Toss, Quick, **'87** M124
Chicken, Vegetable-Stuffed, **'89** M65
Chicken with Noodles, Sesame, **'88** M125
Chicken with Pecan-Rice Dressing, **'85** M57
Chicken with Tomato-Basil Pasta, Basil-
   Stuffed, **'94** M204
Chicken with White Barbecue Sauce, **'89** M84
Chicken with Wild Rice, Elegant, **'80** M76
Chicken, Zesty Barbecued, **'80** M76
Chiles Rellenos with Walnut Cream Sauce,
   Havarti-and-Corn-Stuffed, **'93** M275
Chili-Cheese Dogs, **'81** M176
Chili, Microwave, **'91** M232
Chili, Turkey-Bean, **'88** M213
Cornish Hens, Orange-Glazed Stuffed,
   '84 M89
Crab Imperial, Pineapple-, **'84** M286
Crabmeat and Mushrooms on Toast Points,
   '82 M91
Crabmeat Imperial, Speedy, **'90** M112
Crab, Shrimp, and Artichoke au Gratin,
   '90 M240
Crawfish Delicacy, **'99** M23
Crêpes, Sherried Beef, **'85** M29
Dinner, Easy Steamed, **'83** M314
Filet Mignon Patties, Mock, **'82** M68
Fillets, Apple-Carrot Stuffed, **'88** M192
Fillets, Lemon-Coated, **'80** M53
Fillets, Parmesan, **'86** M112
Fillets, Spanish-Style, **'86** M112
Fish Amandine, Fillet of, **'80** M54
Fish-and-Potato Platter, **'89** M248
Fish-and-Vegetable Dinner, **'91** M196
Fish, Creole, **'87** M79
Fish Delight, **'86** M212
Fish, Easy Italian, **'86** M112
Fish, Herb-Coated, **'86** M112
Fish in Creamy Swiss Sauce, Poached,
   '80 M53
Fish Rolls, Vegetable-Filled, **'86** M251
Fish Steaks, Soy, **'86** M112
Fish, Sweet-and-Sour, **'80** M54
Fish with Greek Sauce, Poached, **'91** M183
Flautas, Rancho Ramillete, **'96** M125
Flounder Amandine, **'89** M196
Flounder, Baked, **'90** M316
Frankfurters, Barbecued, **'84** M12
Grits, Sausage-Cheese, **'90** M238
Grouper Fillets, Breaded, **'89** M36
Grouper with Confetti Vegetables, **'88** M189
Grouper with Sautéed Vegetables, **'90** M233
Haddock Fillets with Zucchini Stuffing,
   '88 M191
Haddock Italiano, **'81** M4
Halibut Steaks Italiano, **'88** M191
Halibut with Swiss Sauce, **'83** M195
Ham and Apples, Baked, **'82** M237
Ham and Apples, Grilled, **'96** M303
Ham and Chicken, Creamed, **'81** M74

Ham-Asparagus Dinner, **'80** M10
Hamburger Patties, **'82** M172
Ham Casserole, Macaroni-, **'81** M177
Ham Loaf, Cranberry-, **'82** M77
Ham Loaf, Saucy, **'86** M328
Ham, Marmalade-Glazed, **'89** M196
Ham Ring, Chili-Sauced, **'81** M122
Ham Roll Casserole, **'91** M127
Ham Slice, Fruited, **'83** M317
Ham Steak, Glazed, **'91** M13
Ham, Sweet-and-Sour Glazed, **'88** M15
Ham Tetrazzini, **'82** M77
Ham Towers, Cheesy, **'82** M77
Ham with Bourbon Glaze, Baked, **'98** M271
Ham with Raisin Sauce, **'82** M76
Kabobs, Shish, **'85** M112
Kielbasa and Cabbage, **'89** M196
Lamb Chops, Sage, **'96** M328
Lasagna, **'83** M6
Lasagna, Easy, **'92** M197; **'93** M24
Lasagna, Lots of Noodles, **'91** M127
Lasagna, Microwave, **'96** M225
Lasagna, One-Step, **'89** M129
Lasagna, Quick 'n Easy, **'80** M10
Lasagna, Roasted Vegetable-Meat, **'99** M332
Lasagna Rolls, Pepper-Topped, **'89** M36
Lasagna, Zesty, **'87** M188
Manicotti, Stuffed, **'83** M6
Meat Loaf, Basic, **'88** M14
Meat Loaf, Cheesy Pizza, **'81** M121
Meat Loaf, Easy, **'88** M214
Meat Loaf, Oriental, **'81** M122; **'83** M194
Meat Loaf, Swedish, **'81** M121
Meat Loaf, Vegetable, **'85** M29
Monkfish, Greek-Style, **'87** M79
Mussels Linguine, **'90** M112
Orange Roughy with Spinach Pesto, **'88** M192
Oysters on the Half Shell, Dressed, **'87** M79
Paella, Party, **'88** M189
Papillote, Ocean, **'84** M287
Patties, Cracked Pepper, **'89** M131
Peppers, Beef-Stuffed, **'91** M127
Peppers, Hearty Stuffed, **'88** M214
Pie, Country Breakfast, **'93** M328
Pineapple Loaves, Individual, **'81** M121
Pizza Casserole, Microwave, **'89** M248
Pizza, Jiffy Jazzed-Up, **'83** M314
Pizza, Taco, **'89** M177
Pork Casserole, Cheesy, **'81** M74
Pork Chop, Saucy, **'86** M140
Pork Chops, Lemon-Herb, **'89** M132
Pork Chops, Pineapple, **'87** M124
Pork Chops with Apricot Glaze, Stuffed,
   '89 M36
Pork Enchiladas, **'97** M94
Pork Kabobs, Margarita, **'98** M223
Pork Loin Roast with Red Currant Sauce,
   '89 M84
Potatoes, Chili-Topped, **'98** M289
Potatoes, Frank-Filled, **'90** M11
Pot Roast, Basic, **'81** M208
Pot Roast, Company, **'88** M14
Pot Roast with Vegetables, **'81** M208
Pot Roast with Vegetables, Marinated,
   '88 M52
Quesadillas, Easy, **'98** M205
Quiche, Benedict, **'80** M107
Quiche, Crab, **'82** M122
Quiche Lorraine, **'80** M108; **'99** M218
Quiche, Spicy Sausage, **'80** M108
Quiche, Spinach-Mushroom, **'81** M74
Quiche, Vegetable, **'87** M219
Red Beans and Rice, Easy, **'99** M219
Ribs, Sweet-and-Sour, **'89** M84

Round Steak over Rice, Burgundy, **'90** M33
Salmon Patties, Open-Faced, **'87** M218
Sausage and Rice Casserole, Oriental,
   '82 M123
Sausage Casserole, Easy, **'87** M189
Sausage Dinner, Beefy, **'80** M9
Sausage-Egg Casserole, **'86** M12
Sausage Jambalaya Casserole, **'82** M203
Shrimp Creole, **'90** M220
Shrimp, Garlic-Buttered, **'86** M226
Shrimp in Cream Sauce, **'84** M286
Shrimp, Quick Curried, **'84** M198
Shrimp, Sweet-and-Sour, **'90** M112
Sloppy Joes, Pocket, **'85** M328
Snapper Provençal, **'91** M170
Sole, Saucy, **'82** M68
Sole with Cucumber Sauce, **'84** M286
Spaghetti, Easy, **'83** M317
Spaghetti Pie, **'81** M32
Spinach-Tenderloin Pinwheels, **'89** M118
Steak, Onion-Smothered, **'87** M189
Taco Pies, Individual, **'82** M282
Tacos, Jiffy, **'83** M318
Tacos, Microwave, **'88** M213
Tortilla Pie, **'85** M211
Trout, Sunshine, **'84** M286
Trout with Orange Sauce, Pecan-Crusted,
   '98 M82
Tuna Casserole, Easy, **'82** M203
Turkey Breast and Gravy, Savory Seasoned,
   '89 M309
Turkey Casserole, Crunchy, **'89** M282
Turkey Divan, Creamy, **'90** M34
Turkey-Noodle-Poppyseed Casserole,
   '90 M239
Turkey Scaloppine, Easy, **'95** M192
Veal and Carrots in Wine Sauce, **'86** M139
Veal, Italian Style, **'82** M68
Welsh Rarebit with Tomatoes and Bacon,
   '92 M159
Zucchini, Beef-Stuffed, **'86** M139
Marmalade, Orange-Pineapple, **'89** M156
Mustard, Coarse-and-Sweet, **'86** M288
Noodles, Cheesy Parmesan, **'83** M7
Pancakes with Apple-Pear Sauce, Oatmeal Mini-,
   '97 M272
Pastry, Microwaved Quiche, **'81** M74; **'82** M122
Pastry, Quiche, **'80** M107
Peaches, Bay Laurel, **'90** M124
Peaches with Rum, Ginger, **'84** M323
Pears, Gingered, **'89** M231
Pears, Marmalade Breakfast, **'83** M203
Pears, Spiced Fall, **'89** M231
Pineapple, Scalloped, **'84** M323
Pizza on a Bagel, **'93** M94
Pumpkin, Cooked Fresh, **'88** M230
Pumpkin Seeds, Seasoned, **'91** M234
Pumpkin Seeds, Toasted, **'88** M230
Relish, Cranberry-Orange, **'81** M289
Relish, Quick Corn, **'90** M13
Relish, Spicy Apple, **'84** M323
Relish, Tipsy Cranberry, **'92** M310
Rice, Almond, **'85** M112
Rice, Basic Long-Grain, **'83** M285
Rice, Basic Quick-Cooking, **'83** M285
Rice, Chicken-Flavored, **'84** M144
Rice, Curry-Spiced, **'86** M226
Rice, Herb, **'91** M257
Rice, Herbed, **'83** M285
Rice, Jiffy Spanish, **'90** M176
Rice, Oriental, **'85** M12, 146
Rice, Parsleyed, **'85** M58
Rice with Almonds, Curried, **'83** M285
Risotto, Microwave, **'97** M213

Salads

Artichokes with Orzo Salad, '88 M193
Beef Salad, Tangy, '87 M218
Chef Salad, Microwave, '90 M146
Chicken Salad, Special, '88 M193
Chicken Taco Salad, '94 M136
Fast-and-Easy Salad, '85 M328
Fried Okra Salad, '97 M157
Fruit Salad with Mint Sauce, '88 M96
Green Beans-and-Cheese Salad, '91 M159
Pork-and-Spinach Salad, Mandarin, '88 M126
Potato Salad, Chunky, '81 M138
Potato Salad, German-Style, '88 M194
Spaghetti Squash Salad, '99 M322
Spinach Salad, Sweet-Sour, '85 M112
Spinach Salad, Wilted, '81 M4
Taco Salad Cups, '85 M29
Tomato-Pasta Salad, '97 M160
Tuna Salad, Cheese-Sauced, '87 M124

Sandwiches

Asparagus-and-Ham Melt Sandwiches,
'88 M96
Breakfast Pita Pockets, '89 M21
Breakfast Sandwiches, '82 M123; '89 M230
Brown Bread-Cream Cheese Sandwiches,
'87 M6
Burgers, Pizza, '80 M201
Crabmeat Sandwiches, Deluxe, '81 M74
Frankfurter Sandwiches, '84 M11
Fruit-and-Cheese Breakfast Sandwiches,
'89 M21
Grilled Cheese Sandwiches, '82 M172
Hot Brown Sandwiches, '80 M202
Pita Sandwiches, Denver, '86 M12
Pita Sandwiches, Hot, '87 M6
Pizza Sandwiches, Open-Face, '84 M198
Pork Sandwiches, Party, '88 M273
Reuben Sandwiches, '80 M201
Sausage-Cheese Muffin Sandwiches, '92 M212
Tuna Sandwiches, Hot, '86 M194

Sauces and Gravies

Almond-Vanilla Custard Sauce, '88 M177
Amaretto-Strawberry Sauce, '87 M165
Apple Dessert Sauce, '87 M165
Apple-Pear Sauce, '97 M272
Barbecue Sauce, Lemony, '88 M177
Béchamel Sauce, '84 M239
Blueberry Sauce, '89 M130
Cheese Sauce, '79 M156; '82 M123
Cheese Sauce, Guilt-Free, '93 M95
Cheesy Vegetable Sauce, '92 M134
Cherry Sauce, Elegant, '79 M156
Chocolate Cherry Sauce, '87 M165
Chocolate Mint Sauce, Quick, '86 M58
Chocolate-Peanut Butter Sauce, '79 M156
Chocolate-Praline Sauce, '85 M295
Chocolate Sauce, Creamy, '88 M177
Crab Marinara Sauce, Quick, '85 M151
Cream Sauce, Sherried, '85 M152
Curry Sauce, '79 M156; '84 M71
Dill Sauce, '84 M70
Dill Sauce, Creamy, '79 M156
Garlic-Cheese Sauce, '84 M70
Hollandaise Sauce, '80 M107, M268; '88 M177
Horseradish-Mustard Sauce, Creamy,
'88 M177
Horseradish Sauce, '88 M273
Lemon Dessert Sauce, '87 M165
Mint Sauce, '88 M96
Mushroom Sauce, '84 M70
Mustard Sauce, '84 M70
Orange Sauce, '84 M286
Orange Sauce, Sweet, '93 M325
Parsley-Garlic Sauce, '84 M70

Peach-Berry Sauce, '87 M165
Peanut Dessert Sauce, '86 M251
Pineapple Ice Cream Sauce, '81 M289
Praline Ice Cream Sauce, Southern, '86 M227
Sour Cream Sauce, '82 M68
Swiss Sauce, '83 M195
Taco Sauce, '82 M283
Tomato Sauce, Herbed Fresh, '85 M151
Tomato Sauce, Italian, '82 M68
Vanilla Sauce, '97 M15
Vegetable-Cheese Sauce, '85 M152
White Sauce, Basic, '79 M156
Sausage in a Bun, '89 M22
Shortcuts, '89 M134

Soups and Stews

Bacon-Beer Cheese Soup, '87 M7
Beef Stew with Parsley Dumplings, '85 M246
Broccoli Soup, '86 M194
Broccoli Soup, Cream of, '80 M225
Carrot-Mint Soup, Chilled, '90 M168
Carrot Soup, Creamy, '92 M218
Cauliflower Soup, Cream of, '87 M7
Cheese Soup, Bacon-Topped, '80 M224
Cheese Soup, Monterey Jack, '85 M211
Chicken-and-Wild Rice Soup, Creamy,
'98 M334
Chicken Broth, Easy Microwave, '90 M167
Chicken Soup, Quick, '86 M72
Chili, Basic, '82 M11
Chili, Beefy Sausage, '82 M11
Chili, Cheese-Topped, '82 M11
Chili, Chunky, '82 M11
Chili with Rice, '82 M11
Chowder, Corn, '84 M38
Chowder, Creamy Green Bean, Mushroom,
and Ham, '99 M336
Chowder, Creamy Ham, '88 M53
Chowder, Fish, '84 M38
Chowder, New England Clam, '86 M72
Crab Soup, Creamy, '80 M224
Cream Cheese Soup, Austrian, '98 M85
Cucumber Soup, Dilled, '90 M167
Egg-Drop Soup, '85 M12
Garden Harvest Soup, Italian, '90 M167
Mushroom Soup, '86 M73
Mushroom Soup, Curried, '84 M89
Onion Soup, French, '86 M212
Onion Soup, Shortcut French, '85 M328
Oyster-and-Artichoke Soup, Louisiana,
'92 M81
Pea Soup, Spring, '88 M96
Potato-Bacon Soup, '84 M38
Potato Soup, Cream of, '80 M224
Potato-Yogurt Soup, '92 M217
Strawberry Soup Supreme, '81 M144
Tomato-Celery Soup, '83 M58
Tomato-Vegetable Soup, '81 M177
Vegetable Soup, Beefy, '84 M38
Vegetable Soup, Chunky, '89 M283
Spoons, Dipped Chocolate-Almond, '95 M277
Spread, Peachy Cream Cheese, '90 M215
Topper, Sticky Bun Toast, '99 M72
Topping, Streusel, '88 M275

Vegetables

Acorn Rings, Easy Glazed, '81 M231
Acorn Squash, Cranberry-Filled, '81 M231
Acorn Squash, Sausage-Stuffed, '81 M231
Artichokes, '92 M107
Artichokes, Quick 'n' Easy Whole Cooked,
'96 M132
Artichokes, Stuffed, '91 M117
Asparagus-Carrot-Squash Toss, '91 M45
Asparagus in Lemon Butter, '80 M123
Asparagus, Lemon-Sesame, '91 M31

Asparagus-Pea Casserole, '88 M294
Asparagus with Almond Sauce, '91 M117
Asparagus with Lemon Butter, '87 M151
Asparagus with Warm Citrus Dressing,
'96 M86
Beans, Marinated Italian, '86 M226
Beets, Harvard, '83 M195
Beets with Sour Cream Dressing, '88 M295
Black-Eyed Peas, Fresh, '81 M165
Broccoli au Gratin, '82 M20
Broccoli Casserole, Cheesy, '95 M191
Broccoli, Chinese, '85 M12
Broccoli Goldenrod, Lemon-, '84 M89
Broccoli, Marinated Fresh, '81 M139
Broccoli-Swiss Cheese Casserole, '85 M211
Butternut Squash, Apple-Stuffed, '81 M232
Butternut Squash Ring, '81 M232
Carrots-and-Celery, Scalloped, '84 M112
Carrots, Orange-Fennel, '92 M133
Carrots, Orange-Glazed, '81 M165; '90 M98
Carrots, Peach-Glazed, '90 M13
Carrots, Spice-Glazed, '83 M58
Corn-and-Bean Casserole, '90 M208
Corn Fix-Up, Quick, '81 M4
Corn, Mexi-, '82 M21
Corn on the Cob, Microwaved, '80 M122
Corn on the Cob, Parmesan, '88 M187
Corn on the Cob, Spicy, '87 M151
Corn, Parslied, '90 M155
Corn, Seasoned Fresh, '83 M147
Corn, Southern-Style Creamed, '81 M165
Eggplant, Easy, '87 M151
Fresh Vegetables, Microwaving, '82 M138
Garden Harvest, '85 M142
Green Bean Gratin, Gourmet, '99 M334
Green Beans, '87 M151
Green Beans Amandine, '82 M20
Green Beans, Bacon-Topped, '80 M123
Green Beans, Baked, '91 M159
Green Beans, French, '90 M208
Green Beans, Garlic, '91 M159
Green Beans, Herbed, '83 M147; '88 M190
Green Beans, Nutty, '88 M187
Green Beans Oriental, '91 M158
Green Beans, Tangy, '85 M151
Green Beans with Marjoram, Fresh, '91 M159
Green Peas, Company, '91 M31
Julienne Vegetables with Walnuts, '86 M251
Kabobs, Marinated Vegetable, '83 M195
Leeks in Dilled Lemon-Butter, '90 M98
Medley, Garden Vegetable, '91 M45
Medley, Vegetable, '89 M129
Medley, Vegetable-Cheese, '99 M287
Mixed Vegetables, '83 M195
Mushrooms, Microwave Portabello, '95 M123
New Potatoes, Herbed, '83 M148
New Potatoes, Seasoned, '87 M151
Okra and Tomatoes, Fresh, '81 M165
Okra, Corn, and Peppers, '87 M151
Okra Medley, '88 M185
Onion-Potato Bake, '83 M195
Onions and Peppers, Sautéed, '83 M148
Onions, Micro-Baked, '82 M32
"Pasta," Garden-Fresh, '94 M134
Peas and Peppers, Minted, '90 M99
Peas in a Potato Nest, '84 M239
Peas with Almonds, Curried, '88 M294
Pepper Cups, Hot Vegetable, '88 M188
Platter, Vegetable, '88 M187
Potato Casserole, Creamy, '84 M113
Potatoes, Basil-Cheese, '90 M316
Potatoes, Blue Cheese Stuffed, '92 M228
Potatoes, Broccoli-Shrimp Stuffed, '92 M228
Potatoes, Cheesy Bacon-Stuffed, '81 M61

Potatoes, Chili-Cheese, '90 M62
Potatoes, Chili-Topped, '98 M289
Potatoes, Cottage, '93 M92
Potatoes, Creamy Cheese, '88 M146
Potatoes, Hearty Stuffed, '89 M282
Potatoes, Jalapeño-Ham Stuffed, '81 M61
Potatoes, Micro-Baked, '81 M61
Potatoes, Parmesan, '90 M62; '92 M341; '93 M46
Potatoes, Quick Baked, '92 M134
Potatoes, Quick Browned, '82 M172
Potatoes, Seafood-Stuffed, '95 M192
Potatoes, Shrimp-Sauced, '81 M61
Potatoes, Soufflé, '90 M14
Potatoes, Summertime, '86 M195
Potatoes, Taco-Topped, '93 M18
Potatoes, Twice-Baked, '91 M185
Potatoes with Béchamel Sauce, Stuffed, '84 M239
Potatoes with Chives, '81 M61
Potatoes with Hot Bacon Dressing, '88 M294
Potatoes, Zesty Stuffed, '94 M46
Potato Fans, Parmesan, '84 M240
Potato Fans, Parmesan-, '88 M190
Potato, Twice-Baked, '90 M295
Potato Wedges, '94 M119
Potato Wedges, Lemony, '90 M61
Ratatouille, Microwave, '95 M232
Snow Peas and Tomatoes, Basil, '88 M185
Spaghetti Squash with Meat Sauce, '88 M180
Spinach Casserole, '91 M31
Spinach Delight, '84 M144
Spuds, Mushroom-Swiss, '96 M238
Squash, Amarillo, '99 M218
Squash-and-Pepper Toss, Crisp, '87 M152
Squash Bake, Cheddar-, '84 M113
Squash Casserole, Jiffy, '81 M144
Squash, Country Club, '88 M16
Squash Medley, Fresh, '81 M165
Squash Mexican, Stuffed, '90 M200
Squash Stuffed with Spinach Pesto, '89 M133
Squash Toss, Simple, '85 M142
Steamed Herbed Vegetables, '93 M303
Stir-Fry, Vegetable, '82 M172
Sweet Potatoes, Applesauce, '91 M292; '92 M256
Sweet Potatoes, Cinnamon-Apple, '95 M23
Sweet Potatoes, Orange-Baked, '88 M294
Tomatoes with Walnut-Rice Stuffing, '91 M102
Tomatoes, Zippy Mustard, '86 M226
White Squash, Stuffed, '90 M201
Zucchini and Carrots, Julienne, '90 M14
Zucchini Boats, '85 M143
Zucchini-Egg Casserole, '84 M113
Zucchini, Italian, '83 M147
Zucchini, Stuffed, '89 M133
Vinaigrette Dressing and Croutons, '86 M288
Waffles, Honey-Buttered Peanut Butter, '94 M206

MINCEMEAT
Apples, Baked Mincemeat-Filled, '80 276
Apples, Stuffed, '99 247
Bars, Mincemeat-Spice, '88 231; '89 22
Cake, Mincemeat Spice, '79 246
Cakes, Mini-Mincemeat Nut, '88 257
Cookies, Mincemeat, '79 51
Cookies, Mincemeat Drop, '79 246
Cookies, Mincemeat Sweetheart, '87 293
Cookies, Pear Mincemeat, '84 264
Homemade Mincemeat, '79 245
Peaches, Mincemeat, '85 178

Peaches with Mincemeat, Brandied, '81 47
Pear Mincemeat, '79 196; '84 264; '88 226
Pies
Apple-Mincemeat Pie, '85 316
Cheese Pie, Mincemeat-, '80 253
Chiffon Pie, Mincemeat, '79 245
Holiday Mincemeat Pie, '80 282; '87 213
Ice Cream Pie, Mincemeat, '99 285
Kentucky Mincemeat Pie, '95 302
Peach Pie, Mincemeat-, '80 295; '81 188
Pear Mincemeat Pie, '84 264; '88 226
Pear-Mincemeat Pie, '98 258
Pear-Mince Pie, '81 271
Spirited Mince Pie, '92 316
Pudding, Steamed Mincemeat, '80 264
Salad, Holiday Mincemeat, '85 263
Salad, Mincemeat, '94 282
MOUSSES. *See also* **CUSTARDS, PUDDINGS.**
Amaretto Mousse, '86 188
Apricot Mousse, '82 72; '91 297
Asparagus Mousse Salad, '86 252
Avocado Mousse with Shrimp Salad, '98 333
Butter Pecan Mousse, '95 286
Butterscotch Mousse, '93 254
Catfish Mousse, '92 327
Caviar Mousse, '82 71; '85 86; '92 83
Chicken Mousse, Curried, '95 328
Chocolate
Almond Mousse, Chocolate-, '93 316
Amaretto-Chocolate Mousse, '86 50
Amaretto-Chocolate Mousse, Elegant, '86 337
au Grand Marnier, Chocolate Mousse, '91 296
Baked Alaska Chocolate Mousse, '85 195
Blender Chocolate Mousse, '82 71
Blender-Quick Chocolate Mousse, '80 269
Brandy-Chocolate Mousse, '85 102
Cake, Cappuccino Mousse, '99 154
Cake, Chocolate Mousse, '87 264; '98 270
Cake, Chocolate-Peanut Butter Mousse, '98 71
Cake, Strawberry-Studded White Chocolate Mousse, '99 154
Chocolate Mousse, '88 280; '97 282
Creamy Chocolate Mousse, '87 133
Honeyed Chocolate Mousse, '87 223
Kid-Pleasin' Chocolate Mousse, '90 271
Loaf with Raspberry Puree, Chocolate Mousse, '97 34
Orange Mousse, Chocolate-, '81 16, 205
Parfait, Chocolate Mousse, '94 90
Peanut Butter Mousse Parfaits, Chocolate-, '98 71
Pie, Chocolate-Amaretto Mousse, '80 180; '81 30
Pie, Chocolate Mousse, '81 136
Present, Chocolate Mousse, '99 281
Quick-as-a-Wink Mousse, '84 311
Quick Chocolate Mousse, '85 87
Roll, Chocolate Mousse, '88 280
Rum Mousse, Chocolate, '86 189
Truffle Mousse with Raspberry Sauce, Chocolate, '95 327
White Chocolate Mousse, '91 247; '93 315; '97 282; '98 57, M111; '99 155
White Chocolate Mousse, Quick, '99 155
White Chocolate Mousse Torte, '99 154
Coconut-Pineapple Mousse, '94 198
Coffee Mousse, '84 126
Coffee-Nut Mousse, '86 319
Crabmeat Mousse, '90 190; '91 244; '94 159
Crab Mousse, '79 117; '95 327
Cran-Apple Mousse, '93 255
Crème de Menthe Mousse, '80 109
Cucumber Mousse, '79 11; '88 121

Cucumber Mousse with Dill Sauce, '95 216
Ham Mousse Pitas, '95 328
Horseradish Mousse, '84 126
Lemon Cloud Mousse, '90 90
Lemon Mousse with Raspberry Sauce, '91 96; '92 130
Lime Mousse Freeze, Luscious, '81 173
Macaroni Mousse, '96 73
Margarita Tacos, '97 167
Mustard Mousse, '84 127; '86 184; '95 328
Orange Mousse, '86 69; '94 198
Oyster Mousse, '81 245
Oyster Mousse, Smoked, '84 320; '99 162
Peach Macaroon Mousse, '80 153
Peach Mousse, '85 54
Peppermint Candy Mousse, '82 71; '94 198
Peppermint Mousse, '93 315
Pineapple Mousse, Elegant, '79 230
Pumpkin Mousse, '91 96; '92 130
Raspberry Mousse, '81 34
Raspberry Mousse in Chocolate Crinkle Cups, '93 270
Rhubarb Mousse, '88 93
Roquefort Mousse, '82 71
Salmon Dill Mousse, '81 21
Salmon Mousse, Irresistible, '79 284
Sherried Mousse, '81 247
Shrimp Mousse, '79 57; '87 196, 251
Strawberry-Lemon Mousse, '82 128
Strawberry Mousse, '81 95
Strawberry Mousse, Fresh, '82 72
Tuna Mousse, '80 275
Watercress Mousse, '88 104
Watermelon Mousse, Frozen, '91 96; '92 130
MUFFINS
Almond Muffins, '90 87
Almond Muffins, Peachy-, '86 301
Apple
Apple Muffins, '83 96; '84 193; '87 23; '99 234
Applesauce Muffins, '84 284; '91 141
Bite-Size Applesauce Muffins, '82 104
Bran Muffins, Apple-, '85 M89
Carrot Muffins, Apple-, '91 213
Cinnamon Oat Bran Muffins, Apple-, '89 106
Fresh Apple Muffins, '84 264
Oat Muffins, Spicy Apple-, '86 45
Pumpkin-Apple Muffins, '96 242
Spiced Apple Muffins, '79 60
Spice Muffins, Applesauce, '88 236
Banana
Banana Muffins, '80 88; '84 75
Bran Muffins, Banana, '83 48
Chocolate Chip Muffins, Jumbo Banana-, '93 339
Chocolate Muffins, Banana-, '94 197
Honey-Nut Muffins, Banana-, '88 62
Nut Muffins, Banana-, '93 140
Oat Bran-Banana Muffins, '91 18
Oat Bran Muffins, Banana, '89 106
Oatmeal Muffins, Banana-, '84 20
Oat Muffins, Banana-, '87 188
Orange Muffins, Banana-, '84 148
Poppyseed Muffins, Banana-, '89 205
Raisin Muffins, Banana-, '89 218
Surprise Muffins, Banana, '82 105
Barbecue Muffins, '96 246
Basic Cupcake Muffins, '90 87
Basic Sweet Muffins, '99 234
Biscuit Muffins, '98 136
Blueberry
Blueberry Muffins, '80 143; '91 140, 203; '99 234
Bran Muffins, Blueberry-, '89 23
Buttermilk Muffins, Blueberry, '80 16

Cream Cheese Muffins, Blueberry-, '86 14
Easy Blueberry Muffins, '81 197
Golden Blueberry Muffins, '79 235
Ice Cream Muffins, Blueberry, '82 143
Lemon Muffins, Blueberry-, '79 7
Oat Bran Muffins, Blueberry, '89 106
Oatmeal Muffins, Blueberry-, '87 24
Oat Muffins, Blueberry-, '92 119
Old-Fashioned Blueberry Muffins, '86 161
Speedy Blueberry Muffins, '95 135
Streusel Muffins, Blueberry, '80 46
Streusel Muffins, Blueberry-, '96 146
Streusel Topping, Blueberry Muffins with,
    '88 129

Bran
All-Bran Oat Bran Muffins, '91 134
Apple-Bran Muffins, '85 M89
Apple-Cinnamon Oat Bran Muffins, '89 106
Banana Bran Muffins, '83 48
Banana Oat Bran Muffins, '89 106
Big Batch Moist Bran Muffins, '95 214
Blueberry-Bran Muffins, '89 23
Blueberry Oat Bran Muffins, '89 106
Bran Muffins, '84 53
Buttermilk Muffins, Bran-, '85 7
Cranberry Oat Bran Muffins, '89 107
Easy Bran Muffins, '83 55
Ever-Ready Bran Muffins, '81 106
Fiber Muffins, High-, '85 250
Freezer Bran Muffins, '91 141
Honey Bran Muffins, '88 171
Honey-Bran Muffins, '89 250
Made of Bran, Muffins, '86 103
Maple-Bran Muffins, '90 66
Quick Bran Muffins, '86 85
Raisin Oat Bran Muffins, '89 106
Refrigerator Bran Muffins, '79 6
Sour Cream-Bran Muffins, '87 98
Spiced Bran Muffins, '84 229
Two, Bran Muffins for, '84 211
Whole Wheat Bran Muffins, '88 M274
Breakfast Bites, '86 15
Broccoli-Chicken Muffins, '96 27
Carrot-and-Raisin Muffins, '87 24
Carrot-Date-Nut Muffins, '86 262
Carrot-Pineapple Muffins, '81 6
Carrot-Wheat Muffins, '88 9

Cheese
Bacon-and-Cheese Muffins, '89 205
Bacon-Cheese Muffins, '96 280
Caraway-Cheese Muffins, '91 213
Cheddar Muffins, '89 15
Cheddar Muffins, Peppered, '99 234
Cheddar-Raisin Muffins, '91 51
Cheese Muffins, '96 54; '97 287
Cornbread Muffins, Cheesy, '88 M275
Cream Cheese Muffins, Blueberry-, '86 14
Dilly Cheese Muffins, '95 245; '96 55
Ham-and-Cheese Muffins, '92 252; '93 144
Marvelous Cheese Muffins, '83 96
Pepper-Cheese Muffins, '96 280
Pepper Muffin Mix, Cheese-and-, '89 330
Pepper Muffins, Cheese-and-, '84 139
Sandwiches, Sausage-Cheese Muffin, '92 M212
Sausage-Cheese Muffins, '86 213
Sausage Muffins, Cheesy, '92 252; '93 144
Sesame-Cheese Muffins, '86 16
Cherry Muffins, '82 105
Cherry Muffins, Dried, '94 59
Cherry-Nut Muffins, '90 87
Chive Muffins, '91 34
Chocolate Chip Muffins, '90 87
Cinnamon-Nut Muffins, '85 M88
Cinnamon-Pecan Muffins, '84 219

Coconut-Molasses Muffins, '82 210
Coconut Muffins, '95 214
Coffee Cake Muffins, '79 7; '98 160
Corn
Angel Cornbread Muffins, Heavenly, '98 43
Blue Corn Muffins, '89 145; '92 52
Cheesy Cornbread Muffins, '88 M275
Cornmeal Muffins, '80 90; '88 92; '91 19;
    '96 248
Corn Muffins, '82 M282; '84 16; '98 313
Jalapeño-Corn Muffins, '93 164
Miniature Cornmeal Muffins, '93 119
Oat Muffins, Corn-, '89 108
Quick Corn Muffins, '88 15
Sage-Corn Muffins, '83 207
Sour Cream Corn Muffins, '95 176
Southern Cornbread Muffins, '85 201
Southwestern Muffins, '91 34
Spicy Cornbread Muffins, '90 59
Sunny Corn Muffins, '96 166
Tex-Mex Corn Muffins, '92 253; '93 144
Tomato Corn Muffins, '81 137
Yeast Muffins, Cornmeal, '92 49
Cranberry Muffins, '81 249
Cranberry Muffins, Miniature, '90 294
Cranberry Oat Bran Muffins, '89 107
Cranberry-Pecan Muffins, '84 269
Cranberry Streusel Cake Muffins, '88 M274
Date Muffins, '79 142
Date Muffins, Surprise, '79 216
Date-Nut Muffins, '84 75; '99 234
Dino-Mite Muffins, '94 197
Egg Muffins, One-, '83 9
English Muffins, '87 49; '88 76
English Muffins, Raisin, '80 75
Fig Muffins, '86 206
French Breakfast Puffs, '96 67
Fudge Brownie Muffins, '95 M50
Gingerbread Muffins, '81 285
Gingerbread Muffins, Last-Minute, '82 105
Grain Muffins, Four-, '80 46
Granola Muffins, '95 78
Ham-and-Cheese Muffins, '92 252; '93 144
Herb Muffins, '96 280
Honey Bran Muffins, '88 171
Honey-Bran Muffins, '89 250
Honey-Oatmeal Muffins, '84 229
Honey-Wheat Muffins, '83 96; '88 263
Jam Muffins, '79 7
Jelly-Filled Muffins, '80 16
Key Lime Muffins, '95 50
Kiwifruit Muffins, '87 255
Lemon Muffins, '88 119, M275
Lemon Muffins, Fresh, '79 161
Lemon-Raspberry Muffins, '92 119
Magic Muffins, '79 244
Mayonnaise Muffins, '83 57; '86 16
Merry Muffins, '82 253
Mix, Quick, '94 167
Mix, Quick Bread, '81 90
Monster Muffins, '94 256
Morning Glory Muffins, '93 327
Muffins, '81 90
Nut Crunch Muffins, Best Ever, '82 65; '83 106
Nut Muffins, Tasty, '79 208
Nutty Muffins, '86 141
Oat
All-Bran Oat Bran Muffins, '91 134
Apple-Cinnamon Oat Bran Muffins, '89 106
Apple-Oat Muffins, Spicy, '86 45
Banana Muffins, Oat Bran-, '91 18
Banana Oat Bran Muffins, '89 106
Banana-Oatmeal Muffins, '84 20
Banana-Oat Muffins, '87 188

Best-Ever Oatmeal Muffins, '84 242
Blueberry Oat Bran Muffins, '89 106
Blueberry-Oatmeal Muffins, '87 24
Blueberry-Oat Muffins, '92 119
Bran Muffins, Oatmeal, '81 236
Bran Muffins, Oatmeal-, '91 83
Corn-Oat Muffins, '89 108
Cranberry Oat Bran Muffins, '89 107
Honey Muffins, Oatmeal-, '83 95
Honey-Oatmeal Muffins, '84 229
Oat Bran Muffins, '89 106
Oatmeal Muffins, '82 129, 210; '84 72, 140;
    '92 163
Orange-Oatmeal Muffins, '85 202
Raisin Oat Bran Muffins, '89 106
Okra Muffins, Fresh, '93 161
Onion-Dill Muffins, '92 253; '93 144
Orange
Banana-Orange Muffins, '84 148
Blossom Muffins, Orange, '96 54
Date Muffins, Orange-, '92 119; '97 243
Ginger Muffins, Orange-, '89 41
Honey Muffins, Orange-, '88 284
Honey Spread, Orange Juice Muffins with,
    '81 229
Oatmeal Muffins, Orange-, '85 202
Orange Muffins, '79 236; '81 107; '83 54;
    '89 205; '97 271
Pecan Muffins, Orange-, '83 96; '99 56
Pecan-Orange Muffins, '97 163
Raisin Muffins, Orange-, '97 153
Streusel-Topped Orange Muffins, '84 74
Peach Muffins, Special, '84 74
Peanut Butter-Chocolate Chip Muffins, '94 167
Peanut Butter-Honey Muffins, '82 56
Peanut Butter Muffins, '80 86; '87 158; '99 111
Peanut Butter Muffins, Jelly-Topped, '96 279
Peanut Muffins, '91 223
Pear-Ginger Muffins, '91 240
Pecan Muffins, '80 16
Pecan Muffins, Chunky, '88 9
Pecan Muffins, Country, '83 222
Pineapple Muffins, '81 14, 250
Plum Good Muffins, '83 96
Poppy Seed-Lemon Muffins, '96 280
Poppy Seed Muffins, '81 63; '91 34
Prune Muffins, Miniature, '85 223
Prune Muffins, Spicy, '97 271
Pumpkin Muffins, '79 206, 275; '81 272
Pumpkin Muffins, Nutty, '86 291
Raisin Muffins, Breakfast, '84 59
Raisin-Nut Muffins, '92 46
Raisin Oat Bran Muffins, '89 106
Raisin-Pecan Ginger Muffins, '88 9
Raspberry-Streusel Muffins, '96 54
Rum Muffins, Hot Buttered, '96 280
Rum-Nut Muffins, '90 87
Sandwiches, Sausage-Cheese Muffin,
    '92 M212
Sausage-Cheese Muffins, '86 213
Sausage Muffins, '88 52; '95 49
Sausage Muffins, Cheesy, '92 252; '93 144
Sour Cream Muffins, '90 283
Sour Cream Muffins, Mini, '88 283
Squash Muffins, '91 69
Strawberry Muffins, '99 234
Sunshine Muffins, '86 9
Sweet Potato Muffins, '81 224; '85 6; '87 280;
    '92 31
Taylor House Muffins, '96 48
Tea Muffins, '82 105
Tropical Muffins, '84 299
Twin Mountain Muffins, '96 280
Wheat Germ-Prune Muffins, '81 106

MUFFINS
(continued)

Wheat Muffins, Fruited, **'79** 93
Whole Wheat Bran Muffins, **'88** M274
Whole Wheat Raisin Muffins, **'85** 207
Yam Muffins, **'79** 7
Yeast Muffins, Quick, **'84** 69
Yellow Squash Muffins, **'81** 163
Yogurt-Muesli Muffins, **'90** 215
Yogurt Muffins, **'88** 55
Zucchini Muffins, **'83** 121; **'86** 146

MUSHROOMS
Appetizers, Chicken-Mushroom, **'88** 210
Artichokes, Ham-Mushroom-Stuffed, **'95** 228
Aztec Mushrooms, **'82** 51
Balls, Cheese and Mushroom, **'79** 63
Burger, Grilled Portobello, **'98** 331
Canapés, Mushroom, **'97** 23
Casserole, Mushroom-Macaroni, **'95** 180
Champignons au Vin, **'79** 47
Cheesecake, Spinach-Mushroom, **'92** 326
Coquilles St. Jacques, **'97** 201
Creamed Mushrooms on Toast, **'81** 190
Curried Mushrooms, **'84** 214
Dip, Hot Mushroom, **'89** 48
Drunk Mushrooms, **'83** 174
Egg Rolls, Chinese, **'96** 101
Egg Rolls, Scrumptious, **'96** 101
English Peas with Mushrooms, **'98** 286
Filling in a Peel, Mushroom, **'84** 214
Filling, Mushroom, **'81** 89; **'82** 259; **'83** 51; **'88** 84
Filling, Spinach-Mushroom, **'80** 215
Fluted Mushrooms, **'82** 280
French-Fried Mushrooms, **'82** 78
French-Fried Mushrooms with Tartar Sauce, **'86** 233
Garlic and Mushrooms, **'95** 165
Gravy, Mushroom, **'99** 34
Hot Browns, **'98** 287
Logs, Mushroom, **'84** 206
Main Dishes
Beef, Marinated Stuffed Filet of, **'99** 165
Beef Tenderloin with Mushrooms, **'87** 115
Bouchées aux Fruits de Mer, **'98** 267
Burgers, Brie-Mushroom, **'95** 128
Burgers, Mushroom, **'89** 164; **'97** 101; **'99** 135
Casserole, Crab-and-Mushroom, **'89** 96
Casserole, Egg-Mushroom, **'83** 49
Casserole, Sausage-Mushroom Breakfast, **'86** 95
Chicken and Mushrooms in Wine Sauce, **'81** 109
Chicken, Asparagus, and Mushrooms with Penne Pasta, **'98** 212
Chicken Bake, Mushroom-, **'89** 147
Chicken Livers with Mushrooms, **'81** 133
Chicken Madrid, **'97** 326
Chicken-Mushroom Bundles, **'80** 157
Chicken-Mushroom Dinner, **'81** 3
Chicken Stroganoff, **'99** 41
Chicken with Artichokes and Mushrooms, **'90** 35
Chicken with Fennel and Mushrooms, **'97** 93
Chicken with Sautéed Peppers and Mushrooms, Herb-Stuffed, **'91** 26
Crabmeat and Mushrooms on Toast Points, **'82** M91
Creamed Mushrooms in Wild Rice Ring, **'80** 270
Crêpes, Cheese and Mushroom, **'81** 88
Crêpes, Coquilles St. Jacques, **'83** 13
Crêpes, Mushroom-Cheese, **'87** 289; **'88** 135
Egg Delight, Mushroom-, **'83** 14

Eggs, Saucy Mushrooms and, **'79** 138
Eggs, Sherried Mushroom, **'83** 49
Flank Steak and Mushrooms, **'87** 61
Fricassee, White Chicken, **'98** 122
Hamburger Steaks, Mushroom-Stuffed, **'99** 202
Macaroni-Mushroom Bake, Cheesy, **'81** 243
Muffin Stacks, Mushroom-Topped, **'80** 271
Omelet, Broccoli-Mushroom, **'85** 45
Omelet, Rolled Mushroom, **'82** 70
Patty Shells, Mushrooms and Eggs in, **'85** 143
Pizza, Cheese-and-Mushroom, **'83** 226
Pizza, Portobello-Pine Nut, **'99** 216
Pork Chops, Apricot-Mushroom Stuffed, **'95** 287
Pork Chops, Weeknight, **'97** 200
Pork Loin with Apples and Mushrooms, Roast, **'92** 218
Pork Loin with Mushrooms and Garlic, Roasted, **'92** 301
Pork, Moo Shu, **'99** 237
Pork Tenderloin, Apple-Mushroom, **'95** 53
Potatoes, Shrimp-and-Mushroom Stuffed, **'99** 308
Pot Roast, Mushroom, **'79** 17; **'96** 250
Quail Stroganoff, **'99** 41
Quail with Mushroom Gravy, Baked, **'89** 273
Quail with Mushrooms, **'85** 138
Quail with Mushrooms, Baked, **'81** 259
Quiche, Ham-and-Mushroom, **'81** 11
Quiche Lorraine, Mushroom-, **'86** 242
Quiche, Mushroom, **'81** 244
Quiche, Spinach-Mushroom, **'81** M74
Quiche, Zucchini-Mushroom, **'79** 127
Ragoût of Wild Mushrooms with Creamy Grits, **'92** 238
Rib-Eyes, Italian, **'98** 215
Rice, Baked Mushroom, **'92** 170
Risotto, Redneck, **'98** 107
Salmon with Mushrooms and Green Onions, Fresh, **'93** 180
Scallop-Mushroom Fettuccine, **'96** 198
Scallops and Mushrooms, Creamy, **'83** 144
Shrimp and Mushrooms with Angel Hair Pasta, **'92** 34
Shrimp-Mushroom Italienne, Green Pasta with, **'79** 170
Spaghetti with Mushrooms, Spicy, **'85** 2
Spinach and Mushrooms with Bow Tie Pasta, **'95** 341
Stir-Fry, Shiitake-Chicken, **'89** 61
Stroganoff, Chicken, **'99** 41
Stroganoff, Mushroom, **'81** 298
Stroganoff, Mushroom-Meatball, **'85** 85
Stroganoff, Quail, **'99** 41
Swordfish-Shiitake Skewers, **'97** 168
Tart, Smoked Portabello Mushroom, **'94** 163
Veal-and-Mushrooms Marsala, **'89** 44
Veal-Cepe Sauté, **'89** 62
Veal Scallopini with Shiitakes, **'99** 232
Venison Loin, Mushroom-Crusted, **'94** 302
Vermicelli with Mushrooms, **'79** 195
Marinated
Caps, Marinated Mushroom, **'83** 128
Easy Marinated Mushrooms, **'86** 217
Herb Mushrooms, Marinated, **'86** 327
Marinated Mushrooms, **'80** 82, 270; **'81** 69; **'86** 135; **'91** 306; **'92** 328
Mexican Marinated Mushrooms, **'81** 66
Special Marinated Mushrooms, **'83** 13
Meringue Mushrooms, **'96** 317
Omelet, Golden Cheese-Shiitake, **'95** 265
Pastry Cups, Mushroom-Almond, **'88** 210
Pâté de Champignon, **'93** 171
Pâté in Pastry, Turkey-Mushroom, **'92** 327

Pâté, Mushroom, **'89** 157
Patty Shells, Mushrooms and Eggs in, **'85** 143; **'88** 197
Patty Shells, Mushrooms in, **'80** 283
Phyllo Bites, Sausage-Mushroom-, **'89** 284
Piroshki, **'92** 84
Portabello Mushrooms, Grilled, **'95** 123
Portabello Mushrooms, Microwave, **'95** M123
Portabello Mushrooms, Sautéed, **'95** 123
Rice, Holiday, **'98** 289
Rollups, Mushroom, **'85** 318
Salads
Cheesy-Mushroom Salad, Quick, **'89** 128
Chicken Salad, Asian, **'99** 124
Fabulous Mushroom Salad, **'81** 190
Fresh Mushroom Salad, **'93** 65
Greens, Cucumber Asian, **'98** 66
Greens with Walnuts, Mixed, **'99** 107
Marinated Mushroom Salad, **'88** 215; **'90** 181
Marinated Mushrooms in Rosemary-Red Wine Vinaigrette, **'97** 63
Pepper Salad, Mushroom-and-, **'86** 68
Portobello Salad, Grilled, **'99** 216
Portobello Salad, Grilled Tomato, Bell Pepper, and, **'98** 211
Rice Salad with Fresh Mushrooms, **'80** 231
Spinach and Mushroom Salad, **'80** 112
Spinach-Enoki Salad, **'89** 62
Watercress-and-Mushroom Salad, **'88** 104
Zucchini Salad, Mushroom-, **'85** 8
Sandwiches, Toasted Mushroom, **'87** 281
Sandwiches with Curry-Mustard Sauce, Mushroom Bagel, **'96** 249
Sauces. *See also* **MUSHROOMS/Gravy.**
Beef Tenderloin with Mushroom Sauce, **'88** 3
Chanterelle Brown Sauce, **'89** 62
Cheese Sauce, Mushroom-, **'83** 190; **'86** 48
Chicken Florentine with Mushroom Sauce, **'87** 250
Chicken with Mushroom Sauce, **'99** 22
Creole Sauce, **'98** 98
Dill Sauce, Mushroom-, **'80** 271
Eggs Baked in Mushroom Sauce, **'93** 47
Filet Mignon with Mushroom Sauce, **'94** 250
Ham-and-Mushroom Sauce, Steak with, **'83** 109
Madeira Sauce, Filet Mignons with Shiitake, **'95** 265
Mole Sauce, Burgundy, **'98** 174
Mushroom Sauce, **'81** 90, 200; **'82** 46; **'83** 71, 205, 212; **'84** M70; **'85** 40; **'86** 198; **'87** 36, 186, 284; **'91** 221
Onion-Mushroom Sauce, **'85** 224; **'86** 84
Savory Mushroom Sauce, **'96** 236
Sherried Mushroom Sauce, Green Beans in, **'93** 206
Sherried Mushroom Sauce, Spicy, **'89** 239
Sherry Sauce, Beef Tenderloin with Mushroom-, **'87** 306
Shiitake Sauce, Pork Tenderloin with Fruit Stuffing and, **'97** 218
Steak with Mushroom Sauce, **'83** 212
Tomatoes with Mushroom Sauce, Broiled, **'81** 103
Vermicelli, Mushroom Sauce Supreme on, **'86** 158
Wine Sauce, Mushroom-, **'84** 84; **'86** 24
Zucchini-Mushroom Sauce, **'93** 71
Shiitakes, Grilled, **'95** 265
Side Dishes
Acorn Squash-Mushroom Puree, **'93** 305
à la King, Mushrooms, **'89** 285
Asparagus and Mushrooms, **'85** 108
Asparagus-and-Mushroom Sauté, **'93** 115

au Gratin, Mushrooms, **'81** 108
Baked Mushroom Rice, **'95** 84
Baked Mushrooms, Creamy, **'87** 127
Bake, Windsor Mushroom, **'88** 132
Bread Pudding, Mushroom, **'99** 58
Casserole, Mushroom, **'95** 211; **'96** 47
Casserole, Mushroom-Artichoke, **'87** 241
Casserole, Mushroom-Cheese, **'83** 216
Casserole, Mushroom Deluxe, **'96** 20
Casserole, Mushroom-Potato, **'84** 5
Creamed Oyster Mushrooms, **'89** 61
Dressing, Whole Wheat-Mushroom, **'84** 283
Eggplant, Mushroom-Stuffed, **'83** 136
Fresh Mushrooms, Savory, **'85** 268
Green Beans, Mushroom-Bacon, **'91** 291;
    '92 255
Green Beans with Bacon and Mushrooms,
    '92 13
Green Beans with Mushrooms, **'82** 21; **'93** 89
Green Peas with Mushrooms, **'80** 101
Heavenly Mushrooms, **'87** 281
Herbed Mushrooms, **'84** 214; **'88** 176
Macaroni-Mushroom Bake, **'97** 96
Newburg, Mushroom, **'88** 252
Noodles and Mushrooms, Cheesy, **'79** 84
Panuchos, Mushroom, **'83** 51
Pasta 1-2-3, Mushroom, **'97** 102
Peas and Mushrooms, **'83** 141
Peas and Mushrooms, Buttered, **'82** 204
Peas with Mushrooms, Creamy, **'84** 196
Pepper-Mushroom Medley, **'90** 98
Portobello Mushrooms, Sautéed, **'96** 273
Potatoes, Buffet, **'98** 92
Potatoes, Mushroom-Dill-Topped, **'86** 41
Potatoes, Mushroom Scalloped, **'87** 191
Quiche, Mushroom, **'80** 222; **'89** 285
Quiches, Wild Rice-and-Mushroom, **'93** 237
Rice, Easy Mushroom, **'89** 286
Sautéed Mushrooms, **'84** 35
Sautéed Mushrooms, Easy, **'81** 131
Sautéed Mushroom Spectacular, **'83** 206
Sauté, Mixed Mushroom, **'89** 62
Seasoned Mushrooms, **'83** 291
Sherried Mushrooms, **'83** 13
Soufflés, Mushroom, **'87** 282
Sour Cream-Dill Sauce, Mushrooms in, **'84** 215
Sparkling Mushrooms, **'94** 24
Spinach and Mushrooms with Bow Tie Pasta,
    '95 341
Spinach with Mushrooms, **'80** 19
Stir-Fried Mushrooms with Bacon, **'80** 123
Supreme, Mushrooms, **'84** 214
Tarts, Mushroom, **'88** 161
Tomatoes, Mushroom-Stuffed, **'86** 218; **'96** 106
Turnovers, Tiny Mushroom, **'86** 24
Vermouth, Mushrooms in, **'89** 203
Wild Mushroom-and-Onion Pot Pies, **'98** 296
Wild Rice and Mushrooms, **'83** 278
Wild Rice with Morels, **'89** 62
Wine Sauce, Mushrooms with, **'85** 292
Yellow Squash, Mushroom-Stuffed, **'84** 154
Zesty Mushrooms, **'93** 218
Zucchini with Mushrooms, Sautéed, **'94** 135
Soups
Avocado-Mushroom Soup, Creamy, **'85** 25
Bisque, Brisk Mushroom, **'81** 190
Chicken, Artichoke, and Mushroom Soup,
    '92 324
Chowder, Creamy Green Bean, Mushroom,
    and Ham, **'99** M336
Chowder, Mushroom, **'79** 16
Chowder, Mushroom-Potato, **'92** 331
Chunky Mushroom Soup, **'88** 12
Consommé aux Champignons, **'79** 48

Consommé, Brown Rice, **'98** 288
Corn Soup with Shiitakes and Shrimp, Sweet,
    '99 168
Cream of Mushroom Soup, **'84** 5; **'85** 93, 261
Creamy Mushroom Soup, **'79** 243; **'81** 307
Curried Mushroom Soup, **'84** M89
Elegant Mushroom Soup, **'83** 99
Fresh Mushroom Soup, **'81** 109; **'90** 190
Mushroom Soup, **'82** 286; **'86** M73; **'94** 54
Onion Soup, Mushroom-, **'80** 25
Oyster-and-Mushroom Soup, **'87** 39
Rice Soup, Mushroom-, **'90** 32
Sherried Mushroom Soup, **'96** 104
Shiitake Soup, Cream of, **'95** 265
Wild Mushroom Soup, **'98** 281
Spread, Eggplant-Mushroom, **'92** 156
Spread, Hot Mushroom, **'81** 190
Spuds, Mushroom-Swiss, **'96** M238
Stewed Anasazi Beans with Mushrooms, **'95** 226
Strudel, Crab-and-Mushroom, **'98** 28
Stuffed
Appetizers, Stuffed Mushroom, **'88** 210
Black Olive-Stuffed Mushrooms, **'86** 258
Canapés, Mushroom, **'80** 285
Cheese 'n' Bacon-Stuffed Mushrooms, **'86** 258
Cheese-Stuffed Mushrooms, Elegant, **'81** 57
Chicken-Stuffed Mushrooms, **'80** 162
Crab, Mushrooms Stuffed with, **'82** 249
Crab-Stuffed Mushroom Caps, **'84** 160
Crab-Stuffed Mushrooms, **'81** 190; **'97** 102
Crawfish-Stuffed Mushrooms, **'86** 258
Delight, Stuffed Mushroom, **'87** 281
Flavor-Stuffed Mushrooms, **'85** 288
Florentine, Stuffed Mushrooms, **'82** 270
Ham, Mushrooms Stuffed with, **'97** 237
Italian Sausage-Stuffed Mushrooms, **'83** 127
Parmesan Stuffed Mushrooms, **'83** 115
Pâté-Stuffed Mushrooms, **'85** 118
Pecan-Stuffed Mushrooms, **'84** 261
Pesto-Stuffed Mushrooms, **'86** 150
Pistachio-Stuffed Mushrooms, **'86** 141
Ricotta-Stuffed Mushrooms, **'85** 20
Samurai 'shrooms, **'93** 258
Sausage-Stuffed Mushrooms, **'80** 248; **'91** 164
Seasoned Stuffed Mushrooms, **'84** 206
Shiitakes Parmigiana, Stuffed, **'98** 25
Shrimp-Stuffed Mushrooms, **'80** M135;
    '99 324
Spinach-Stuffed Mushrooms, **'86** 81;
    '88 131, M261; **'89** M133
Stems, Mushrooms with, **'86** 258
Stuffed Mushrooms, **'79** 212; **'81** 239;
    '83 13, 66, 126, 136; **'93** 172
Vegetable Mushroom Caps, **'81** 246
Stuffing, Cornish Hens with Barley-Mushroom,
    '97 242
Stuffing, Grilled Rainbow Trout with Mushroom,
    '97 162
Stuffing, Sausage-and-Wild Mushroom, **'96** 267
Tapas, Majorcan Mushroom, **'95** 159
Tarts, Hot Sherried Mushroom, **'83** 78
Tipsy Mushrooms, **'84** M216
Tomatoes, Veracruz, **'97** 169
Tomatoes with Curry Sauce, Stuffed, **'97** 170
Turnovers, Hot Mushroom, **'89** 285; **'97** 102
MUSSELS. *See* **SEAFOOD.**
MUSTARD
Bourbon Mustard, **'93** 240
Brie, Honey-Mustard, **'91** 252
Brussels Sprouts Dijon, **'96** 91
Brussels Sprouts with Shallots and Mustard,
    '85 258
Butter, Chive-Mustard, **'98** 156
Chicken, Dijon, **'99** 21

Chicken, Lemon-Mustard, **'99** 109
Chicken, Mustard, **'93** 239
Coarse-and-Sweet Mustard, **'86** M288
Compote, Baked Mustard Fruit, **'85** 47
Dip, Sweet-and-Spicy Mustard, **'96** M274
Dressing, Dijon-Honey, **'89** 45; **'99** 333
Dressing, Honey-Mustard, **'90** 55, 111, 146
Dressing, Mustard, **'80** 112
Dressing, Tangy Mustard, **'93** 323
Fish, Spicy Mustard, **'99** 90
Flounder Dijon, **'85** 95
Fruit Bake, Mustard, **'90** 291
Glaze, Apple-Stuffed Tenderloin with
    Praline-Mustard, **'97** 216
Glaze, Game Hens with Chutney-Mustard, **'93** 66
Glaze, Roast Chicken with Pineapple-Mustard,
    '89 83
Herbed Mustard, **'87** 134
Homemade Mustard, **'81** 77
Homemade Mustard, Zesty, **'82** 55
Honey Mustard, Hot, **'93** 240
Honey Mustard, Peppered, **'95** 312
Horseradish Mustard, **'93** 240
Horseradish Mustard, Lower Sodium, **'86** 325
Hot German Mustard, **'82** 298
Hot Mustard, Chinese, **'85** 12
Hot Mustard, Really, **'95** 312
Hot Sweet Mustard, **'85** 12
Jalapeño Mustard, **'93** 240; **'95** 312
Key Lime Mustard, **'94** 278
Lamb Chops, Dijon-Rosemary, **'99** 333
Marinade, Honey-Mustard, **'93** 103
Mousse, Mustard, **'84** 127; **'86** 184; **'95** 328
Orange Roughy Dijon, **'99** 122
Pork Tenderloin, Honey-Mustard, **'95** 52
Raspberry Mustard, **'95** 313
Sauces
Asparagus in Mustard Sauce, Chilled, **'88** 130
Barbecue Sauce, Mustard, **'84** 173
Chutney-Mustard Sauce, **'89** 242
Cream Sauce, Chicken in Mustard, **'92** 181
Cream Sauce, Mustard, **'88** 61
Creamy Mustard Sauce, **'80** 272; **'86** 257;
    '87 232; **'93** 240
Creamy Mustard Sauce, Champagne-Poached
    Chicken with, **'94** 24
Creole Mustard Sauce, **'99** 142
Curry-Mustard Sauce, **'96** 249
Dijon-Caper Cream Sauce, Broiled Salmon
    with, **'98** 329
Easy Mustard Sauce, **'94** 83
Extra-Special Mustard Sauce, **'79** 82
Hamburger Steaks with Mustard Sauce, **'84** 230
Hollandaise Sauce, Mock Mustard-, **'87** 269
Honey-Lemon Mustard Sauce, **'84** 275
Honey-Mustard Sauce, **'85** 13
Honey-Mustard Sauce, Smoked Ribs with,
    '92 168
Horseradish-Mustard Sauce, Creamy,
    '88 M177
Hot Mustard Sauce, **'93** 240
Leg of Lamb with Mustard Sauce, **'89** 71
Lemon-Mustard Sauce, Salmon Steaks with,
    '97 124
Light Mustard Sauce, **'82** 178
Mild Mustard Sauce, **'85** 224; **'86** 84
Mustard Sauce, **'80** 222, 283; **'83** 21, 321;
    '84 M70, 289; **'85** 148; **'86** 185; **'87** 22;
    '89 122, 333; **'90** 19, 97; **'92** 302; **'93** 118;
    '99 270
Pork Tenderloin with Mustard Sauce, **'99** 145
Sausage Sandwiches with Mustard Sauce,
    '84 250
Scallops with Mustard Sauce, **'84** 163

MUSTARD, Sauces
(continued)

Smoked Sausages with Mustard Sauce, '81 56
Sour Cream Sauce, Mustard-, '81 68
Stone Crab Mustard Sauce, '80 3
Sweet Mustard Sauce, '85 12
Tangy Mustard Sauce, '92 201
Tarragon-Mustard Sauce, Turkey Cutlets with, '93 239
Vinaigrette Sauce, Mustard-, '84 174
Vinegar Sauce, Shrimp with Mustard-, '93 240
Spread, Chive-Mustard, '91 12
Spread, Honey Mustard-Butter, '99 86
Spread, Mustard, '86 105
Sweet Cider Mustard, '95 312
Vegetables, Honey-Dijon, '98 311
Vegetables, Honey-Mustard Marinated, '93 236
Vinaigrette, Baby Lettuces with Mustard, '93 67
Vinaigrette, Greens with Dijon, '98 332
Vinaigrette, Honey-Mustard, '94 249
Vinaigrette, Mustard, '96 184

NECTARINES
Apple Juice, Nectarines in, '83 183
Butter, Nectarine, '79 175
Cocktail, Nectarine, '85 107
Royale, Nectarines, '85 132
Salad, Nectarine Chicken, '79 175
Sherbet, Nectarine, '89 199
Shortcake, Warm Blueberry-Nectarine, '97 205

NOODLES
Broccoli and Sausage, Pasta with, '87 109
Cakes with Coconut-Beef Stir-Fry, Noodle, '97 18
Caraway Buttered Noodles, '87 230
Casserole, Eggplant and Noodle, '82 230
Casserole, Vegetable Noodle, '91 30
Egg Foo Yong Noodles, '98 233
Green Noodles, '80 211
Hoisin Noodles with Shrimp, '98 233
Kugel, Apricot Noodle, '92 251
Kugel, Nu Awlins, '94 229
Kugel, Sweet, '90 254
Kugel, Vegetable-Noodle, '96 228
Lo Mein Noodles and Broccoli, '97 18
Main Dishes
Beef and Noodles, Easy, '83 288
Beef Bake, Asian Noodle, '98 31
Beef over Rice Noodles, Shredded, '85 74
Beefy Noodle Dinner, '81 179
Casserole, Beef-and-Noodles, '84 72
Casserole, Beef, Cheese, and Noodle, '99 58
Casserole, Chicken and Green Noodle, '80 32
Casserole, Chicken-Noodle, '94 286
Casserole, Ham, '96 302
Casserole, Ham and Noodle, '80 300
Casserole, Sausage and Noodle, '82 123
Casserole, Sausage-and-Noodle, '95 255
Casserole, Shrimp-and-Noodle, '90 240
Casserole, Stroganoff, '98 48
Casserole, Turkey-Noodle-Poppyseed, '90 239
Cheesy Noodles and Mushrooms, '79 84
Chicken and Spinach Noodles, '82 19
Chicken with Noodles, Sesame, '88 M125
Chili with Noodles, '81 282; '82 57
Chow Mein over Crispy Noodles, '85 286
Ham and Swiss on Noodles, '87 108
Hamburger-Noodle Bake, '81 140
Ham-Noodle Skillet, '87 78
Italian Sauce with Noodles, '84 250
Lasagna, Lots of Noodles, '91 M127

Liver and Noodle Dinner, Creamy, '80 11
Pork-and-Noodle Bake, '88 98
Pork-and-Noodles Skillet Dinner, '88 199
Ring, Noodle, '85 285
Sausage and Mixed Vegetables, Pasta with, '87 249
Sausage-Noodle Bake, '81 92
Scallops and Pasta, Fresh, '83 164
Shrimp and Noodles, Creamy, '92 100
Sour Cream-Noodle Bake, '79 55
Stew with Noodles, Hungarian, '80 263
Szechuan Noodles with Spicy Beef Sauce, '97 95
Taco Beef-Noodle Bake, '81 141
Turkey Noodle Bake, '93 243
Veal Sauce, Noodles with, '80 236
Orange Noodles, '84 177
Pad Thai, '97 202
Pancake, Szechuan Ginger Stir-Fry with Noodle, '97 292
Parmesan Noodles, '83 118
Parmesan Noodles, Cheesy, '83 M7
Parslied Noodles, '85 31
Ramen Noodle Satay, '98 233
Salad, Chicken Noodle, '95 25
Salad, Ham-Noodle, '85 249
Salad, Ramen Noodle, '88 41; '97 18
Soup, Chicken Noodle, '80 264; '95 45; '98 30
Soup Mix, Turkey-Noodle, '89 330
Soup, Turkey-Noodle, '91 312
Spinach with Noodles, Creamed, '84 29
Thai Coconut Broth with Noodles, '98 295
White Noodles, '80 211
NUTS. *See* **ALMONDS; APPETIZERS/Nuts; MACADAMIA; PEANUTS; PECANS; WALNUTS.**

OATMEAL. *See also* **GRANOLA.**
Applesauce Oatmeal, '89 108
Bake, Pear-Oatmeal, '89 208
Breads
Biscuits, Oatmeal, '89 108
Blueberry-Oatmeal Bread, '83 139
Buns, Honey-Oat, '98 27
Buns, Honey Oatmeal, '83 154
Buttermilk-Oatmeal Bread, '97 212
Caraway-Raisin Oat Bread, '86 44
Dill-Oat Bread, '91 95
Herbed Oatmeal Pan Bread, '97 243
Honey-Oat Bread, '89 107; '98 27
Honey Oatmeal Bread, '80 60
Loaf, Banana-Oat Tea, '87 256
Loaf, Pumpkin-Oatmeal, '81 49
Molasses Bread, Oatmeal-, '97 194
Muffins, Banana-Oat, '87 188
Muffins, Banana-Oatmeal, '84 20
Muffins, Best-Ever Oatmeal, '84 242
Muffins, Blueberry-Oat, '92 119
Muffins, Blueberry-Oatmeal, '87 24
Muffins, Corn-Oat, '89 108
Muffins, Honey-Oatmeal, '84 229
Muffins, Oat Bran, '89 106
Muffins, Oat Bran-Banana, '91 18
Muffins, Oatmeal, '82 129, 210; '84 72, 140; '92 163
Muffins, Oatmeal Bran, '81 236
Muffins, Oatmeal-Bran, '91 83
Muffins, Oatmeal-Honey, '83 95
Muffins, Orange-Oatmeal, '85 202
Muffins, Spicy Apple-Oat, '86 45
Oatmeal Bread, '81 236, 300; '92 212; '97 130
Oatmeal Raisin Bread, '81 14

Oatmeal-Raisin Bread, '83 59
Oat-Molasses Bread, '82 139
Rolls, Oatmeal-Cinnamon-Pecan, '96 50
Round Oatmeal Bread, '84 20
Whole Wheat-Oatmeal Bread, '87 85
Breakfast Oatmeal Surprise, '93 178
Breakfast Oatmeal, Swiss Style, '81 49
Brownies, Oat, '89 59
Brownies, Oatmeal, '87 199
Brownies, Oat 'n' Crunch, '91 233
Burgers, Black Bean, '98 144
Burgers, Pinto, '98 51
Cake, Applesauce-Oatmeal, '92 119
Cake, Dutch Oatmeal, '83 95
Cake, Golden Apple-Oatmeal, '86 301
Cake, Honey-Oatmeal, '87 222
Cake, Saucy Pudding, '98 196
Cereal, Full-of-Fiber Hot, '89 208
Coffee Cake, Oatmeal-Coconut, '83 312
Cookies
Apple-Nut Cookies, '80 228
Apple-Oatmeal Cookies, '85 215; '90 218
Banana Oatmeal Cookies, '79 217
Bars, Apricot-Oatmeal, '86 216
Bars, Chocolate-Topped Oatmeal, '86 110
Bars, Date-Oat, '80 M172
Bars, Layered Oatmeal-Date, '85 10
Bars, Oatmeal-Caramel, '85 247
Bars, Yummy Fudge, '87 158
Breakfast Cookies, '97 52
Breakfast Cookies, Take-Along, '84 59
Cake Mix Oatmeal Cookies, '96 247
Carrot Cookies, Oatmeal-, '94 292
Chocolate Chip Cookies, Nutty Oatmeal-, '82 M185
Chocolate Chip-Oatmeal Cookies, '84 119
Chocolate Chippers, Oatmeal-, '90 218
Chocolate Morsel Cookies, Oatmeal-, '95 46
Chocolate-Oatmeal Cookies, '80 105
Chocolate-Raisin Oatmeal Cookies, '95 136
Cinnamon Oatmeal Cookies, '84 72
Clear-the-Cupboard Cookies, '99 278
Coconut Cookies, Oatmeal-, '80 218
Coconut-Macadamia Cookies, '98 294
Coconut-Oatmeal Cookies, Crispy, '93 80
Crackers, Oatmeal-Wheat Germ, '84 236
Cranberry-Caramel Bars, '98 277
Crispies, Oat, '83 96
Crispy Oat Cookies, '88 203; '90 311
Crispy Oatmeal Cookies, '89 328
Crunchy Oatmeal Cookies, '85 202
Date Cookies, Oatmeal-, '82 109
Date-Filled Oatmeal Cookies, '86 314
Date Sandwich Cookies, Oatmeal-, '83 257
Easy Oatmeal Cookies, '80 105
Fibber McGee Cookies, '95 72
Granola Bars, No-Bake, '97 220
Krispies, Oatmeal, '85 115
Lace Cookies, '86 8
Macadamia-Oat Snowballs, '92 274
Nut Crispies, Oatmeal, '80 208
Nutty Oatmeal Cookies, '81 130
Oatmeal Cookies, '92 82; '99 280
Old-Fashioned Oatmeal Cookies, '80 106; '85 250
Olympic Medal Cookies, '96 180
Orange-Glazed Oatmeal Cookies, '80 60
Orange Slice Cookies, '98 324
Peanut Butter Chocolate Chip Cookies, Oatmeal-, '92 207
Peanut Butter Cookies, Oatmeal-, '85 171
Peanut Butter-Oatmeal Cookies, '81 218; '84 72
Peanut Cookies, Oats-and-, '89 60
Peanutty Oatmeal Cookies, '80 106; '83 95

Pudding-Oatmeal Cookies, '98 215
Raisin Cookies, Frosted Oatmeal-, '79 290
Raisin Cookies, Oatmeal-, '87 221; '93 127
Slice-and-Bake Oatmeal Cookies, '80 105
Special Oatmeal Cookies, '81 236
Spice Cookies, Giant Oatmeal-, '80 105
Spicy Oatmeal Cookies, '81 197
Sunshine Cookies, Oatmeal, '89 59
Toasted Oatmeal Cookies, '92 273; '95 136
Toffee Lizzies, Crispy Oatmeal-, '95 136
White Chocolate Chip-Oatmeal Cookies,
  '99 127
Crisp, Oatmeal Cherry-Apple, '90 M16
Crust, Nutty Oat, '89 251
Fruited Oatmeal, '88 19
Granola, '99 212
Granola Bars, '83 305
Granola, Crunchy, '81 218; '84 144
Granola, Easy, '81 49
Granola, Fruity, '84 148
Granola, Healthful, '97 204
Granola, Homemade, '84 58
Granola, Sunny Orange, '84 212
Granola, Superhero, '98 M206
Hamburgers, Meatless Walnut, '96 243
Ice Cream Sandwiches, Oatmeal Crispy, '93 199
Mix, Rolled Oats, '84 72
Muesli, '89 208
Muesli, Homestyle, '91 315
Pancakes, Oat, '89 227
Pancakes, Oatmeal, '80 44; '89 107
Pancakes, Oatmeal-Brown Sugar, '88 203
Pancakes, Whole Wheat-Oat, '93 16
Pancakes with Apple-Pear Sauce, Oatmeal Mini-,
  '97 M272
Piecrust, Crisp Cereal, '83 100
Piecrust, Oatmeal, '79 79
Slow Cooker with Ice Cream, Oatmeal in a,
  '99 193
Topping, Oat Crunch, '89 108
Topping, Oatmeal Cookie, '95 291
Waffles, Banana-Oatmeal, '94 206
Waffles, Oatmeal, '89 107
Waffles, Oatmeal-Nut, '83 96

OILS. See also SEASONINGS.
Basic Recipe, '96 122
Basil Oil, '96 122
Black Pepper Oil, '96 122
Chile Pepper Oil, '96 122
Chili Oil, '96 234
Chive Oil, '96 122
Dill Oil, '96 122
Ginger Oil, '96 122
Mint Oil, '96 122
Olive Oil, Basil-Infused, '95 231
Olive Oil, Lemon-Infused, '95 231
Oregano Oil, '96 122
Parsley Oil, '96 234
Roasted Garlic Oil, '96 122
Rosemary Oil, '96 122
Sage Oil, '96 122
Thyme Oil, '96 122
Vanilla Oil, '94 243

OKRA
Bake, Okra-and-Tomato, '89 173
Bake, Okra-Tomato, '80 298; '81 26
Bisque, Okra-and-Shrimp, '97 156
Caponata, Okra, '97 157
Casserole, Okra, '79 160
Chowder, Quick Okra, '80 185
Corn, and Peppers, Okra, '87 M151
Corn, and Tomatoes, Okra, '95 203
Cream, Okra and Corn in, '79 160
Creole, Corn-and-Okra, '89 127

Creole, Meatball-Okra, '83 156
Creole Okra, '81 182
Creole, Okra-Corn, '83 157
Dills, Okra, '97 157
Étouffée, Okra, '98 207
Fresh Okra and Tomatoes, '87 89
Fried
  Cheese, Okra with, '80 185
  Crispy Fried Okra, '86 169
  Croutons, Salad Greens and Veggies with
    Fried Okra, '96 178
  Deep-Fried Okra, '90 154
  Fingers, Okra, '85 196
  French-Fried Okra, '82 126
  Fried Okra, '79 122; '86 211; '87 89; '88 111
  Fritter-Fried Okra, '86 218
  Fritters, Okra, '79 160; '92 133; '98 159
  Green Tomatoes, Fried Okra and, '93 160
  Green Tomatoes, Okra and, '79 160
  Old-Time Fried Okra, '80 185
  Oven-Fried Okra, '91 121
  Potatoes, Fried Okra and, '97 136
  Potato Fry, Okra-, '81 159
  Puffs, Okra, '83 157
  Rellenos, Okra, '97 156
  Salad, Fried Okra, '97 M157
Goulash, Okra, '93 160
Grilled Okra and Tomatoes, '98 124
Gumbo, Deep South Okra, '79 48
Gumbo Freezer Mix, Okra, '86 210
Gumbo, Light Seafood-Okra, '86 155
Gumbo, Okra, '86 210; '91 206
Gumbo, Old-Style Shrimp, '98 97
How to Can Okra, '80 127
Medley, Corn-and-Okra, '99 203
Medley, Okra, '88 M185
Medley, Okra-Corn-Tomato, '81 159
Muffins, Fresh Okra, '93 161
Pickled Okra, '98 177
Pickles, Okra, '81 173
Pilaf, Okra, '80 185; '82 126; '93 160
Pilau, Okra, '99 184
Plantation Okra, '82 126
Polenta with Cheese and Okra, Baked, '99 232
Salad, Okra, '90 155
Sautéed Corn and Okra, '84 158
Skillet Okra, '95 179
Soup, Charleston Okra, '87 156
Soup, Okra-and-Shrimp, '94 323
Soup, Sausage and Okra, '80 209
Soup with Fou-Fou, Okra, '96 325
Stewed Okra, Southern, '82 134
Stew, Lamb-and-Okra, '97 156
Stew, Old-Fashioned Okra, '84 158
Stew, Quick Okra, '97 88
Stir-Fried Okra, '96 177
Surprise, Okra, '79 160; '84 158
Tomato Combo, Okra-, '83 157
Tomatoes and Okra, '86 170; '87 164
Tomatoes, Fresh Okra and, '81 M165
Tomatoes, Okra and, '80 185; '81 139; '92 215;
  '98 286
Tomatoes with Okra, '85 106
Vinaigrette, Okra-Corn-and-Tomato, '90 173

OLIVES
Antipasto, Easy, '85 114
Antipasto, Grandpa's, '98 183
Appetizers, Cheesy Olive, '85 113
Appetizers, Cheesy-Olive, '87 246
Ball, Blue Cheese-Olive, '82 248
Ball, Olive Cheese, '80 258
Balls, Pumpkin Patch Cheese, '99 245
Black Olives, Shrimp Spaghetti with, '85 13
Black Olive-Stuffed Mushrooms, '86 258

Bread, Olive, '93 78
Bread, Olive-Dill Casserole, '92 16
Butter, Mediterranean, '97 307
Butter, Olive, '91 295
Casserole, Turkey-Olive, '87 268
Caviar, Mexican, '98 135
Chalupas, Chicken-Olive, '81 227
Cheesecake, Three-Layer, '99 140
Chicken-and-Rice Valencia, '85 113
Chicken Breasts, Greek, '98 19
Chicken, Spanish, '98 183
Crostini, Festive, '98 183
Dip, Monterey Shrimp, '99 M65
Filling, Chicken-Olive, '81 227
Greek Olive Cups, '99 221
Lemon-Garlic Olives, '94 118
Marinated Olives, Caliente, '95 177
Marinated Olives, Herb-, '92 176
Muffuletta Loaf, '97 86
Muffulettas, '98 184
Orzo, Mozzarella-and-Olive, '97 249
Pizzas, Eggplant, '98 183
Potatoes, Olive, '80 114
Relish with Coriander, Green Olive, '96 323;
  '97 27
Salad, Doodles Olive, '94 35
Salad, Greek Chicken, '97 92; '98 329
Salad, Italian Olive, '94 35
Salad, Mexican Olive, '85 84
Salad Mix, Muffy, '94 34
Salad, Olive, '98 184
Salad, Olive Clubhouse, '81 114
Salad, Olive-Potato, '85 114
Salad with Sherry Vinaigrette, Shrimp, Orange,
  and Olive, '93 177
Sandwich, Deli Stuffed, '98 287
Sauce, Roasted Red Pepper, '98 16
Scaciati, Olives, '99 266
Snack, Open-Faced Cheese-and-Olive, '89 97
Spread, Antipasto, '81 25
Spread, Cheese-Olive, '79 82
Spread, Cream Cheese-Olive, '82 35
Spread, Creamy Olive, '81 290
Spread, Feta-and-Apple, '99 106
Spread, Tomatoes with Olive, '85 114
Stuffed Olives, Almond-, '88 95
Tapenade, '92 194
Toss, Cauliflower-Olive, '85 198; '86 147
Toss, Tomato-Olive Pasta, '86 209

OMELETS
Apple Omelet Stack, '94 50
Baked Omelets, '94 50
Broccoli-Mushroom Omelet, '85 45
Cheese Omelet, Herbed, '93 47
Cheese Omelet, Puffed, '89 227
Cheese Omelet, Zippy, '87 287
Cheese-Shiitake Omelet, Golden, '95 265
Cheesy Picante Omelet, '86 95
Chicken Liver Omelet, '82 44
Country Omelets, '91 128
Creole Sauce, Omelets with, '89 228
Dill-Cheese-Ham Omelet, '95 33
Filling, Greek Omelet, '80 68
Filling, Spanish Omelet, '80 68
Fluffy Omelet, '84 56
Garden Omelet, '99 174
George's Omelets, '80 68
Ham and Cheese Omelet, '79 262; '80 123
Indian Omelet, '99 92
Mexican Omelet, '79 128; '81 225
Mushroom Omelet, Rolled, '82 70
Mushroom Sauce, Puffy Omelets with, '85 40
Olé Omelet, '87 M124
Olé, Omelet, '94 31

OMELETS
(continued)

Oyster Omelets, Smoked, '84 96
Potato Omelet, Family-Size, '94 31
Potato-Sprout Omelet, '79 128
Primavera, Omelet, '87 71
Rising Sun Omelet, '82 281; '83 42
Rolled Omelet, '89 228
Sandwich, Omelet, '86 95
Sausage Filling, Omelet with, '81 43
Sausage Omelet, Puffy, '80 M268
Shrimp-and-Cheddar Omelet, '84 57
Shrimp-and-Cheese Omelet, '94 31
Shrimp-and-Vegetable Oven Omelet, '99 286
Sour Cream-Ham Omelet, '79 261
Spanish Omelet, '81 201; '83 243; '84 101
Spanish-Style Omelets, '83 188
Spinach-Cheese Omelet, '83 119
Strawberry-Sour Cream Omelet, '89 229
Sunrise Omelet, '83 289
Swiss Oven Omelet, '80 189
Tarragon Omelet, '89 144
Tex-Mex Omelet con Carne, '81 209
Vegetable Omelet, Beefy, '83 188
Vegetable Omelet, Cheddar-, '83 205
Vegetable Omelet, Cheesy, '85 49
Vegetable Omelet, Fresh, '84 211
Vegetable Omelet, Golden, '82 M123
Vegetable Omelet, Puffy, '83 188
Vegetable-Pasta Oven Omelet, '99 286
Vegetarian Omelet, '84 114
White Wine Omelet, '79 103
Yogurt-Avocado Omelet, '81 33
Zucchini Omelet, '81 99
ONIONS
Appetizers, Bacon-Onion, '94 290
Bake, Cheese Onion, '82 32
Baked Onions, Micro-, '82 M32
Baked Onions, Spicy, '84 65
Baked Onions, Sweet-and-Sour, '90 34
Bake, Four Onion, '93 304
Bake, Onion-Potato, '83 M195
Bake, Romano Onion, '90 98
Barbecued Onions, '88 86
Beans, K.C. Baked, '98 244
Beef à la Beer, '98 64
Beef à la Mode, '98 122
Beef and Onions, Smothered, '85 293
Black Beans, Cuban, '99 56
Breads
Biscuits, Cheesy Onion, '95 98
Buns, Cheesy Onion, '85 5
Buns, Onion-Cheese, '88 218
Cheese Bread, Onion-, '79 180; '81 8
Cheese Supper Bread, Onion-, '83 112
Cornbread, Onion, '88 283
Cornbread, Onion-Topped, '84 153
Cornbread, Sweet Onion, '98 252
Dill Bread, Easy Onion-, '85 5
Easy Onion Bread, '81 162
Flatbread, Parmesan-Onion, '98 65
Focaccia, Mustard-and-Onion, '90 321; '92 97
Focaccia, Onion, '93 77
Focaccia, Roquefort-and-Onion, '98 54
French Bread, Onion-Cheese, '89 29
French Onion Bread, '91 90
Herb Bread, Onion-, '90 165
Herb Bread, Toasted Onion-, '83 266
Hush Puppies, Onion, '85 14
Hush Puppies, Tomato-Onion, '91 201
Loaves, Onion Twist, '84 300
Muffins, Onion-Dill, '92 253; '93 144

Parmesan Bread, Onion-, '84 284
Poppy Seed Twist, Onion-, '97 242
Rolls, Onion-Bacon, '99 47
Rolls, Onion Twist, '89 288
Rolls, Poppy Seed Onion, '81 63
Rye Bread, Onion-, '99 55
Sesame Rolls, Onion-and-, '95 292
Burgers, Open-Faced Chicken-Onion, '94 139
Butter, Onion, '86 253
Caramelized Onion-and-Pecan Brussels Sprouts,
'99 254
Caramelized Onions, Beef Burgers with, '98 143
Caramelized Onions, Green Beans with, '95 288
Caramelized Onions, Mediterranean, '96 273
Caramelized Onions, Potato-Horseradish Gratin
with, '99 314
Carrots with Bacon and Onion, Glazed, '87 200
Casserole, Cheesy Onion, '79 101
Chard with Onion and Apple, Sautéed, '98 48
Cheese Onions, Sherried, '82 32
Chicken in Coconut Milk, '97 202
Chicken, Onion-Crusted, '88 40
Chicken Sandwich, Jerk, '98 333
Chicken, Slow-Roasted, '98 108
Chicken with Rice, Moorish, '98 127
Chili, White Christmas, '98 266
Chutney, Cranberry, '98 276
Confit, Roasted Shallot-Garlic, '94 303
Couscous, Spinach-and-Onion, '98 23
Crème Brûlée, Onion, '95 324
Crunch Sticks, Onion Crescent, '90 206
Curried Onions, '90 34
Deluxe, Broccoli-Onion, '81 75
Dip, Cheesy Onion, '83 145
Dip, Chunky Onion, '84 257
Dip, Cream Cheese-Onion, '79 236
Dip, Curry-Onion, '93 313
Dip, Swiss-Onion, '95 93
Dressing, Cornbread, '98 269
Dressing, Green Pepper-Onion Salad, '84 12
Dressing, Onion-French, '84 283
Fried
Beer-Battered Onion Rings, '92 52
Crisp Fried Onion Rings, '84 65
Crispy Fried Onion Rings, '80 108
Crispy Onion Rings, '86 110
Deluxe Fried Onion Rings, '80 108
Easy Onion Rings, '80 108
Favorite Fried Onion Rings, '81 86
French-Fried Onion Rings, '88 111
French-Fried Onion Rings Supreme, '80 109
Green Onions, Fried, '81 106
Leonard's-Style Onion Rings, '90 120
Rings, Fried Onion, '83 85; '85 69
Rings, South-of-the-Border Onion, '96 217
Glazed Carrots and Onions, '83 25; '87 128
Glazed Onions, '84 104; '97 306; '99 24
Gourmet Onions, '81 86
Gravy, Fried Quail with Onion, '82 214
Gravy, Pork Chops in Onion, '99 222
Gravy, Southwestern, '99 34
Green Beans, Lorraine's, '99 319
Green Beans with Purple Onion, Spicy, '98 286
Green Onions. *See also* **ONIONS/Fried,**
Soups.
Butterbeans with Bacon and Green Onions,
'96 267
Canapés, Green Onion, '84 M216
Cheese Ball, Pinecone, '98 265
Crostini, Green Onion, '96 93
Cukes and Scallions, '91 168
Dip, Onion, '94 21
Dressing, Green Onion, '96 17
Eggs, Creamy Onion Scrambled, '83 M203

Hoecakes, Green Onion, '88 112
Hush Puppies, Green Onion-Tomato, '97 84
Lima Beans and Scallions, Fresh, '82 133
Mayonnaise, Mediterranean, '98 144
Pie, Green Onion, '98 159
Pie, Tumbleweed, '98 205
Pork-and-Onions with Bean Sauce, '85 76
Quiche, Cheesy Green Onion, '83 194; '84 42
Relish, Green Onion, '84 65
Salmon with Mushrooms and Green Onions,
Fresh, '93 180
Sauce, Onion-Mushroom, '85 224; '86 84
Sautéed Onions and Peppers, '83 M148
Spread, Green Onion-Cheese, '92 24
Teasers, Green Onion, '82 42
Tempura-Battered Green Onions, '96 93
Grilled Onion Flowers with Pecans, '96 217
Grilled Squash and Onion, '79 150
Grits with Grilled Chicken and Onions, '99 17
Herbed Carrots and Onions, '87 31
Herbed Onions, '84 149
Honey Onions, '81 86
Hush Puppies, Corn Soufflé, '98 M328
Italian Dressing, Tomato, Onion, and Cucumber
in, '81 83
Kale with Tomato and Onion, '92 244
Kuchen, Onion, '90 34
Marinade, Basic, '99 141
Marmalade, Fruited Onion, '96 323; '97 27
Mayonnaise, Onion, '98 144
Meat Loaf, Moist-and-Saucy, '99 270
Medley, Cabbage-Onion-Sweet Pepper, '96 252;
'97 28
Mums, Onion, '96 318
Patties, Potato-Onion, '95 269
Pearl Onions, Beef Burgundy with, '81 108
Pearl Onions, Glazed, '85 258
Pearl Onions, Green Beans with Roasted Red
Peppers and, '93 260
Pearl Onions, Snap Peas and, '89 280
Pearl Onions, Sweet-and-Sour, '96 216
Peas with Onions, Buttered, '80 242
Pickled Cocktail Onions, '89 197
Pickled Refrigerator Onion Rings, '84 265
Pie, Onion, '82 191
Pilau, Sausage, '99 184
Polenta Triangles, '98 181
Pot Roast, Sweet-and-Sour, '99 291
Pudding, Kathy's Onion, '95 318
Quiche, Onion, '83 121
Relish, Pepper-Onion, '84 180
Rice, Braised, '98 45
Rice, Red, '97 138
Rice, Seasoned Onion, '82 166
Risotto, Easy Baked, '99 120
Risotto with Saffron, Pistachio, '98 272
Roasted Celery Root, Carrots, and Onions,
'98 293
Roasted Onions, Rosemary, '98 16
Roast, Pumpernickel, '97 234
Ropa Vieja, '98 20
Salad, Lemon-Onion, '85 252
Salad, Roasted Onion, '95 65
Salad, Tomato-Cucumber-Onion, '81 239
Salad with Peppered Cheese Crisps, Roasted
Onion Pasta, '98 107
Salsa Verde, '96 160
Sauce, Beef Tenderloin with Five-Onion, '98 272
Sauce, Brussels Sprouts in Onion, '81 308
Sauce, Onion, '82 72; '87 248
Sauce, Onion-Balsamic, '99 44
Sauce, Onion Cream, '87 232
Sauce, Onion-Parsley, '85 148
Sauce, Pepper-Onion, '84 125

Sauerbraten, '98 278
Sautéed Apples, Onions, and Pears over
Spinach, '94 212
Selecting and Storing Onions, '84 65
Shallot Salad, Caramelized, '96 308
Shells, Cheese and Limas in Onion, '81 86
Shrimp, Marinated, '98 317
Soufflé, Onion, '79 247
Soups
Cheese Onion Soup, Double-, '85 227
Cheese Soup, Onion-, '87 81
Classic Onion Soup, '84 65
Creamy Onion Soup, '90 211
Double Cheese-Topped Onion Soup, '79 49
Easy Onion Soup, '85 226
French Onion-Beef Soup, '87 54
French Onion Soup, '79 49; '80 188; '83 126;
'85 226; '86 M212; '90 31; '93 246
French Onion Soup, Shortcut, '85 M328
French Onion Soup, Toasty, '81 306
Green Onion Soup, '84 112
Green Onion Soup, Creamed, '83 82
Mushroom-Onion Soup, '80 25
Onion Soup, '99 96
Oven-Browned Onion Soup, '79 49
Potato Soup, Creamy Onion-and-, '92 51;
'97 304
Rich Onion Soup, '85 226
Superb Onion Soup, '81 86
Three-Onion Soup, '96 217
Vichyssoise, '86 181
Vidalia Onion Soup, Beefy, '97 212
Sour Cream, Cucumber and Onion in, '81 69
Spaghetti with Smothered Onions, '97 229
Spread, Braunschweiger-Onion, '79 82
Squares, Creamy Onion, '79 48
Squares, Sausage-Onion, '83 112
Steak, Onion-Smothered, '87 M189
Stew, Beef-and-Onion, '87 18
Stuffed
Baked Onions, Stuffed, '82 32
Baked Stuffed Onions, '83 135
Baked Sweet Onions, '98 130
Broccoli-Stuffed Onions, '84 154
Cheese-Stuffed Onions, '90 34
Peas, Onions Stuffed with, '84 68
Ratatouille-Stuffed Onions, '96 91
Sweet Onions, Stuffed, '91 79
Vidalia Onions, Stuffed, '89 172
Wine, Stuffed Onions and, '85 268
Stuffing, Rice-and-Onion, '88 246
Sweet
Baked Sweet Onions, '91 79
Blossom, Onion, '94 226
Butter, Sweet Onion, '93 124
Caramelized Florida Sweet Onions, Balsamic,
'94 163
Caramelized Onion, Corn with Bacon and,
'99 94
Casserole, French Onion, '95 26
Chutney, Kiwifruit-Onion, '93 125
Creole Onions, '82 32
Eye of Round, Slow Cooker Spicy Marinated,
'99 291
Eye of Round, Spicy Marinated, '99 291
Grilled Stuffed Onions, '95 180
Honey-Paprika Sweet Onions, '92 52
Hot Onions, Sweet-, '85 139
Jelly, Onion, '93 135
Marinated Bermuda Onions, '92 194
Parmesan Onions, '93 170
Pie, Onion-Cheese, '88 86
Pizza, Chicken-and-Purple Onion, '97 47
Pizza, Plum-and-Sweet Onion, '98 193

Pot Pies, Wild Mushroom-and-Onion, '98 296
Relish, Onion, '91 79
Relish, Purple Onion, '95 253
Relish, Sweet Onion, '93 124; '96 206; '99 204
Ribs and Onions, Tangy, '99 136
Rings, Crispy Baked Onion, '93 247
Risotto, Onion, '99 94
Salad Bowl, Spinach-and-Onion, '81 157
Salad, Grilled Onion, '99 96
Salad, Marinated Orange-Onion, '91 231; '92 68
Salad, Orange-Onion, '89 41
Salsa, Fiesta Onion, '94 82
Sauce, Spicy, '99 291
Sauce, Vidalia Onion, '99 52
Shortcake, Onion, '92 51
Slaw, Sweet Onion, '98 171
Smoky Sweet Onions, '97 191
Stir-Fry, Sweet Onion-Asparagus, '98 135
Tart, Caramelized Onion, '99 96
Tarts, Sweet Onion, '95 229
Trout, Sweet Onion-Stuffed, '99 52
Vidalia Deep Dish, '89 120
Vidalia Onion Sauté, '89 119
Vidalia Onions with Pecans and Roasted
Carrots, Roasted, '92 340
Vidalia Sandwiches on Salt-Rising Bread,
'79 145
Vidalias, Marinated, '89 119
Vidalia-Tomato Salad, '84 65
Vinaigrette, Spinach Salad with Apple-Onion,
'94 276
Vinaigrette, Vidalia Onion, '99 168
Sweet Potatoes with Cumin, Mashed, '99 244
Taters, Buck's, '95 72
Toasties, Onion, '97 225
Turkey, New Year's, '97 255
Turnips and Onions, '83 242
Veal and Onions, Herbed, '79 108
Vinaigrette, Asian, '97 146
Vinegar Sauce, Whole Onions with Warm,
'94 172
ON THE LIGHT SIDE. *See* **LIVING LIGHT.**
ORANGES. *See also* **AMBROSIA.**
Appetizer, Orange-Berry, '85 81
Apples, Orange-Glazed, '82 51
Baked Fruit, Ginger-Orange, '93 313
Baked Oranges, '79 247; '89 41
Baked Orange Slices, '89 88
Baskets, Orange, '93 286
Beverages
Blend, Orange, '95 276
Blush, Orange, '80 51
Brandy Smash, Orange, '99 30
Breakfast Eye-Opener, '87 199
Champagne with Orange Juice, '91 71
Cider, Apple-Orange, '92 20
Cider, Hot Mulled Apple-Orange, '97 301
Cocktail, Citrus Wine, '99 93
Cocktail, Orange-Champagne, '79 39
Cocktail, Tomato-Juice, '83 169
Coffee, Orange, '96 313
Coffee, Viennese Orange, '84 54
Cooler, Apricot-Orange-Carrot, '96 108
Cooler, Citrus, '82 160
Cubes, Florida, '95 201
Flip, Orange-Banana, '82 48
Flips, Orange Blossom, '80 51
Frosty, Orange, '86 101
Frosty Sours, '81 156
Jogger's Sunrise, '93 213
Juicy, Orange, '90 178
Lemonade, Orange-Mint, '88 82
Liqueur, Orange, '81 287
Magnolia Blossoms, '87 72

Magnolias, '82 196
Margaritas, Orange-Lime, '97 140
Mist, Orange-Lemon, '79 288; '80 35
Nog, Orange Spiced, '82 48
Pick-Me-Up, Orange, '80 232
Pineapple Drink, Orange-, '89 35
Pirate's Painkiller, '99 161
Punch, Champagne, '96 277; '98 310
Punch, Champagne Blossom, '99 290
Punch, Citrus Party, '83 141
Punch, Orange Blossom, '83 142
Punch, Orange-Lime, '82 160
Punch, Orange-Mint, '82 121
Punch, Orange Sherbet Party, '83 142
Punch, Orange Soda, '87 214
Punch, Pineapple-Orange, '85 236
Punch, Refreshing Orange, '81 39
Refresher, Grapefruit-Orange, '82 174
Sangría, '81 67
Sangría, Easy Citrus, '80 218
Sangría, Orange, '81 237
Shake, Orange Milk, '84 166
Shake, Peachy Orange, '81 156
Shake, Pineapple-Orange-Banana, '97 172
Shake, Strawberry-Orange Breakfast, '87 186
Shake, Tropical, '87 200
Slush, Banana-Orange, '80 48; '81 155
Slush, Orange, '82 49
Slush, Strawberry-Orange, '83 172
Slush, Vodka-Orange, '89 92
Smoothie, Mango-Orange, '86 216
Smoothie, Orange-Banana, '97 173
Smoothie, Tropical, '81 50
Soda, Cranberry-Orange, '79 148
Sunshine Fizz, '92 44
Syrup, Orange, '96 161
Tea, Marmalade, '98 330
Whiskey Sours, Frozen Orange-, '92 67
Breads
Anise-Orange Bread, '83 295
Apricot-Orange Bread, '92 285
Baba au Orange, '86 138
Biscuits, Orange, '88 85
Blueberry-Orange Bread, '87 140
Breakfast Ring, Orange, '81 229
Coffee Cake, Cranberry-Orange, '82 283
Coffee Cake, Nutty Orange, '95 160
Coffee Cake, Orange, '85 M88
Coffee Cake, Orange Butter, '89 229
Coffee Cake, Orange Marmalade Swirl,
'81 107
Coffee Cake, Orange-Pecan, '86 86
Coffee Ring, Caramel-Orange, '80 45
Cranberry Bread, Orange-, '85 266
Cranberry-Orange Bread, '87 244
Cream Cheese Bread, Orange-, '82 210
French Toast, Orange, '83 292; '84 78; '86 329
French Toast with Orange Sauce, '82 47
Muffins, Banana-Orange, '84 148
Muffins, Orange, '79 236; '81 107; '83 54;
'89 205; '97 271
Muffins, Orange Blossom, '96 54
Muffins, Orange-Date, '92 119; '97 243
Muffins, Orange-Ginger, '89 41
Muffins, Orange-Honey, '88 284
Muffins, Orange-Oatmeal, '85 202
Muffins, Orange-Pecan, '83 96; '99 56
Muffins, Orange-Raisin, '97 153
Muffins, Pecan-Orange, '97 163
Muffins, Streusel-Topped Orange, '84 74
Muffins with Honey Spread, Orange Juice,
'81 229
Nut Bread, Blueberry-Orange, '84 141
Nut Bread, Cranberry-Orange, '80 288

ORANGES, Breads
(continued)

Nut Bread, Orange-, **'82** 75
Nut Loaf, Orange, **'80** 226
Pecan Bread, Glazed Orange-, **'81** 250
Pecan Bread, Orange-, **'79** 148
Pecan Loaves, Orange-, **'79** 215
Puffs, Upside-Down Orange, **'83** 57
Pumpkin Bread, Orange-, **'87** 300
Rolls, Easy Orange, **'89** M131
Rolls, Frosted Hot Orange, **'80** 257
Rolls, Glazed Orange, **'90** 194
Rolls, Kitchen Express Orange, **'98** 252
Rolls, Luscious Orange, **'86** 298
Rolls, Orange, **'80** 22; **'82** 17; **'88** 79; **'96** 321
Rolls, Orange Butter, **'82** 206; **'83** 33
Rolls, Speedy Orange, **'89** 287
Rye Bread, Swedish Orange-, **'85** 111
Scones, Cranberry-Orange, **'97** 45
Scones, Orange-Pecan, **'94** 215
Scones with Orange Butter, Double-Orange, **'97** 44
Tea Bread, Orange, **'79** 234
Toast, Orange Praline, **'79** 36
Toast Topper, Orange, **'79** 36
Whole Wheat Orange Bread, **'85** 5
Broiled Orange Halves, **'85** 288
Broth, Tortellini in Citrus, **'99** 292
Butter, Citrus, **'97** 307
Butter, Honey-Orange, **'79** 36; **'85** 19
Butter, Orange, **'81** 8, 42; **'90** 323; **'92** 319; **'94** 115; **'97** 44
Butter, Orange-Pecan, **'84** 75; **'97** 15
Butter, Prune-Orange, **'92** 49
Butter, Tomato-Curry-Orange, **'93** 159
Candied Orange Peel, **'81** 286
Candied Orange Rind, **'96** 162; **'97** 32
Chutney, Cranberry-Orange, **'79** 292
Chutney, Orange-Cranberry, **'86** 266
Cranberry Oranges, Brandied, **'98** 309
Cream, Beef Fillets with Orange, **'97** 66
Cream Cheese, Orange, **'91** 177
Cream, Orange, **'90** 126
Crêpes, Chocolate-Orange, **'85** 263
Desserts
Alaska, Orange, **'83** 177
Ambrosia, Pineapple-Orange, **'88** 252
Apples, Orange-Pecan Baked, **'85** 45
Apples with Cookie Crumbs, Orange Baked, **'95** 271
Apples with Orange Sauce, Baked, **'84** 314
Baked Orange Elegance, **'80** 13
Balls, Orange, **'94** 331
Bananas Foster, Orange-Glazed, **'91** 91
Bananas with Orange Sauce, Baked, **'79** 115
Bars, Pineapple-Orange, **'82** 129
Baskets, Orange, **'81** 308
Cake, Aztec Pound, **'96** 61
Cake, Chocolate-Orange Pound, **'89** 94
Cake, Fresh Orange, **'83** 300
Cake, Fresh Orange Chiffon, **'88** 179
Cake, General Robert E. Lee Orange-Lemon, **'88** 92
Cake, Mandarin Orange, **'83** 24
Cake, Mandarin-Rum, **'84** 150
Cake, Orange, **'86** 61; **'95** 320
Cake, Orange Angel Food, **'96** 246
Cake, Orange Blossom, **'96** 162
Cake, Orange Butter, **'95** 46
Cake, Orange Chiffon, **'91** 56
Cake, Orange-Coconut Angel Food, **'94** 294
Cake, Orange-Cranberry, **'85** 314

Cake, Orange Cream, **'99** 118
Cake, Orange-Date, **'94** 60
Cake, Orange Liqueur, **'87** 84
Cake, Orange Marmalade, **'85** 53
Cake, Orange Meringue, **'86** 336; **'87** 84
Cake, Orange Nut, **'80** 70
Cake, Orange-Nut Butter, **'80** 254
Cake, Orange-Pecan Crunch, **'83** 10
Cake, Orange-Pecan Pound, **'93** 13
Cake, Orange Pound, **'87** 84, 221; **'92** 69
Cake, Orange Rum, **'79** 2
Cake, Orange-Slice, **'81** 264
Cake, Orange Streusel, **'88** 10
Cake, Rum-Orange Coconut, **'88** 224
Cake, Sour Cream-Orange Pecan Pound, **'89** 207
Cake Squares, Apple-Orange, **'84** 150
Cake Squares, Orange, **'81** 34
Cake Squares, Orange-Pumpkin, **'83** 242
Cake, Williamsburg Orange, **'81** 120; **'82** 23
Candied Orange Zest, **'95** 320
Champagne Oranges, **'93** 83
Cheesecake, Orange, **'81** 84; **'85** 38
Chiffon Dessert, Orange, **'93** 295
Chocolate-Orange Delights, **'93** 52
Chocolate-Orange Roll, **'87** 21
Cookies, Carrot-Orange, **'83** 149
Cookies, Frosted Orange, **'83** 114
Cookies, Orange-Chocolate, **'83** 113
Cookies, Orange-Glazed Oatmeal, **'80** 60
Cookies, Orange-Pecan, **'88** 119
Cookies, Orange Refrigerator, **'86** 230
Cookies, Orange-Slice, **'89** 294
Cookies, Orange Slice, **'98** 324
Cookies, Orange Sugar, **'89** 329
Cookies, White Chocolate-Orange Dream, **'98** 294
Cran-Orange Surprise, **'94** 143
Cream Dessert, Orange, **'80** 254; **'84** 165
Cream, Orange, **'81** 12
Cream, Orange Chantilly, **'84** 156
Cream, Orange-Coconut, **'84** 24
Cream, Orange-Mallow, **'94** 295
Cream, Orange Whipped, **'88** 83
Crème Brûlée, Orange, **'95** 323
Crème, Orange-Tapioca, **'82** M283
Crêpes, Amaretto-and-Orange, **'86** 260
Crêpes, Orange Dream, **'82** 183
Crinkles, Orange, **'95** 272
Crispies, Orange, **'84** 205
Crisp, Orange-Apple, **'80** 295
Cupcakes, Orange, **'97** 32
Dip, Creamy Orange, **'84** 117
Éclairs, Miniature Orange, **'95** 92
Filling, Lemon-Orange, **'81** 71
Filling, Orange, **'79** 229; **'86** 336; **'87** 84; **'88** 224; **'96** 316
Filling, Orange Cream, **'99** 118
Filling, Orange Curd, **'96** 120
Filling, Orange-Pineapple Fried Pie, **'96** 109
Fingers, Orange, **'87** 57
Flambé, Dessert Orange, **'85** 313
Flan, Orange, **'84** 95
Frosted Oranges, **'83** 270
Frosting, Citrus Cream Cheese, **'99** 223
Frosting, Creamy Orange, **'83** 24, 241
Frosting, Orange, **'81** 7; **'86** 61; **'88** 119
Frosting, Orange Butter, **'83** 300
Frosting, Orange Buttercream, **'80** 70; **'99** 117
Frosting, Orange Cream, **'81** 207; **'82** 14
Frosting, Orange-Cream Cheese, **'81** 70; **'82** 16; **'92** 19
Frosting, Orange-Lemon, **'88** 92
Frozen Orange Dessert, **'92** 44

Fruit Dessert Orange, **'84** 314
Fudge, Orange-Walnut, **'92** 288
Glazed Oranges and Pineapple, **'86** 318
Grand Marnier, Oranges, **'92** 82
Grand Marnier, Oranges in, **'95** 142
Granita, Orange, **'88** 118
Ice Cream, Orange, **'97** 160
Ice Cream, Orange-Pineapple, **'86** 117
Ice, Strawberry-Orange, **'86** 196
Ice, Tart Cranberry-Orange, **'86** 317
Juice, Strawberries with Brandied Orange, **'82** 160
Kiwi-and-Orange Dessert, **'93** 295
Meringues, Orange, **'95** 318
Molded Dessert, Orange, **'83** 302
Mousse, Chocolate-Orange, **'81** 16, 205
Mousse, Orange, **'86** 69; **'94** 198
Parfaits, Chilled Orange, **'80** 219
Parfaits, Orange Cream, **'94** 198
Peanut Brittle, Orange, **'80** 302
Pears Flambé, Orange-Poached, **'85** 313
Pears in Orange Sauce, Poached, **'82** 19
Pears, Orange Poached, **'80** 218
Pie, Coconut-Orange Chess, **'89** 169
Pie, Florida Orange, **'91** 43
Pie, Frosty Orange, **'90** 296
Pie, Lemon-Orange, **'85** 172
Pie, Orange Ambrosia, **'80** 237
Pie, Orange Chess, **'88** 204
Pie, Orange Chiffon, **'87** 260
Pie, Orange-Coconut, **'90** 90
Pie, Orange-Coconut Cream, **'94** 208
Pie, Orange Meringue, **'81** 12, 309
Pie, Orange-Pecan, **'79** 282; **'83** 222
Pie, Sweet Potato-Orange, **'88** 207
Poached Oranges, Wine-, **'84** M323
Pops, Hawaiian Orange-Pineapple, **'94** 143
Pops, Orange-Banana, **'82** 129
Pops, Orange Float, **'99** 132
Pralines, Orange, **'92** 313; **'93** 51
Pudding, Mandarin-Almond, **'85** M12
Pudding, Orange, **'81** 85; **'82** 111; **'83** 153
Pudding, Orange Custard, **'88** 174
Pumpkin-Orange Delight, **'86** 321
Rice Cream with Mandarin Oranges, **'85** 317
Roulage, Chocolate-Orange, **'94** 314
Sections with Chocolate and Raspberry Sauce, Orange, **'97** 33
Sherbet Ambrosia Cups, **'82** 159
Sherbet, Banana-Orange, **'83** 162
Sherbet, Orange, **'79** 155
Sherbet with Blackberry Sauce, Orange, **'94** 232
Shortbread Madeleines, Orange, **'88** 242
Shortbread, Orange, **'91** 272
Shortcake, Fresh Orange, **'80** 100
Shortcake, Orange-Strawberry, **'95** 100
Slices, Burgundy-Spiced Orange, **'93** 294
Sorbet, Banana-Orange, **'88** 117
Sorbet, Fresh Orange, **'92** 143
Soufflé, Chilled Orange, **'84** 317; **'86** 189
Soufflé, Frozen Orange, **'79** 211
Soufflé, Grand Marnier, **'79** 281
Soufflé, Orange Dessert, **'83** 206
Special, Orange Blossom, **'79** 48
Squares, Orange-Crunch, **'86** 136
Squash Brûlée, Orange-, **'94** 267
Tapioca Fluff, Orange, **'87** 31
Tarts, Frozen Orange, **'80** 154
Tarts, Orange, **'96** 317
Tarts, Orange Curd, **'92** 193
Topping, Whipped Orange, **'80** 254
Truffles, Orange-Pecan, **'95** 92
Turnovers, Orange-Apple, **'99** 294

Dip, Creamy Orange, '87 247
Dip, Marmalade, '99 324
Dip, Orange Fruit, '96 190
Dip, Orange-Lime, '96 248
Dip, Orange Sour Cream, '79 208
Dip, Spicy Orange, '85 230
Doughnuts, Orange Spiced, '79 136
Dressings
　Blossom Dressing, Orange, '82 266
　Coconut Dressing, Orange-, '80 158
　Coconut-Orange Dressing, '97 93
　Cranberry-Orange Dressing, '91 287
　Curd Dressing, Orange-, '93 22
　Mandarin Dressing, '89 137
　Marmalade-Fruit Dressing, '84 171
　Nutmeg Dressing, Carrot-Raisin Salad with
　　Orange-, '98 19
　Orange Dressing, '81 141; '97 129
　Poppy Seed Dressing, Orange-, '87 187
　Vinaigrette Dressing, Tangy Orange, '93 46
　Vinaigrette, Honey-Orange, '91 255
　Vinaigrette, Orange, '96 65; '97 229; '98 288
　Yogurt Dressing, Orange-, '85 304
Filling, Cheese-and-Orange, '93 159
Filling, Orange, '89 287
Filling, Orange-Cheese, '90 47
French Toast, Orange-Stuffed, '98 54
Fritters, Puffy Orange, '81 169
Glaze. *See* **ORANGES/Sauces and Glazes.**
Granola, Sunny Orange, '84 212
Gravy, Orange, '81 259; '89 323
Grits, Orange, '81 47
Honey Yogurt, Orange Slices with, '91 68
Jelly, Pineapple-Orange Mint, '92 105
Main Dishes
　Catfish Amandine, Mandarin, '84 183
　Chicken à l'Orange, '84 277
　Chicken à l'Orange, Stir-Fry, '83 82
　Chicken Breasts with Orange Sauce, '79 77
　Chicken Breasts with Parslied Rice, Orange,
　　'87 242
　Chicken, Crispy Mandarin, '86 119
　Chicken Drummettes, Orange-Pecan, '93 158
　Chicken, Grilled Ginger-Orange, '91 26
　Chicken in Orange-Almond Sauce, '79 219;
　　'80 13
　Chicken in Orange Sauce, '83 8
　Chicken in Orange Sauce, Skillet, '94 252
　Chicken Livers in Orange Sauce, '82 218
　Chicken, Orange, '83 278; '86 M140
　Chicken, Orange-Avocado, '80 38
　Chicken, Orange Barbecued, '88 123
　Chicken, Skillet-Seared Orange, '96 68
　Chicken Stir-Fry, Kyoto Orange-, '87 96
　Chicken Stir-Fry, Orange-, '84 68
　Chicken with Orange, Lime, and Ginger
　　Sauce, '92 123
　Chuck Roast, Orange Marinated, '85 179
　Cornish Hens, à l'Orange, '95 325
　Cornish Hens, Orange-Glazed, '83 267;
　　'99 293
　Cornish Hens, Orange-Glazed Grilled, '86 250
　Cornish Hens, Orange-Glazed Stuffed, '84 M89
　Cornish Hens with Cranberry-Orange Sauce,
　　'86 119
　Cornish Hens with Orange Glaze, '79 244
　Duck, Chafing Dish Orange, '79 226
　Duck with Orange Sauce, Grilled, '94 305
　Duck with Parsnip Mash, Honey-Orange-
　　Glazed Muscovy, '97 262
　Fish à l'Orange, Fillet of, '89 180
　Halibut with Orange-Curry Sauce, '87 91
　Ham, Cranberry-Orange Glazed, '81 295
　Ham, Orange-Glazed, '89 324

Hens with Cranberry Salsa, Orange-Ginger,
　'98 321
Lamb Chops, Orange, '83 35
Lobster Tails with Spiced Orange Sauce,
　'86 155
Porc à l'Orange, '80 242
Pork Chops, Orange, '84 81
Pork Chops, Orange-Cranberry, '86 335;
　'87 84
Pork Chops, Orange-Glazed, '81 234; '82 25;
　'83 39; '91 84
Pork Loin, Scuppernong-Orange Glazed,
　'98 220
Pork Tenderloin with Orange Marmalade,
　'91 49
Salmon, Orange-Basil, '97 165
Scampi, Orange, '85 303
Snapper à l'Orange, Baked, '85 181
Snapper, Orangy, '88 23
Spareribs, Orange-Glazed, '84 296
Spareribs with Orange Barbecue Sauce,
　'83 11
Swordfish Steaks, Orange-Ginger Marinated,
　'93 271
Turkey Breast with Orange-Raspberry Glaze,
　'91 253
Turkey-Orange Skillet, Oriental, '86 284
Turkey Slices, Orange-, '90 53
Marmalade, Orange, '81 42
Marmalade, Orange-Pineapple, '82 150;
　'89 M156
Marmalade, Peach-Orange, '82 150
Noodles, Orange, '84 177
Nuts, Sherry-Orange, '86 M289
Pancakes, Orange-Yogurt, '87 225
Pancakes with Sunshine Orange Sauce, Orange,
　'97 70
Pears and Oranges, Spicy, '89 305
Pears, Marmalade Breakfast, '83 M203
Pears, Orange-Glazed, '79 247
Pecans, Orange, '84 299; '87 292
Pecans, Orange-Glazed, '97 225
Popcorn, Orange, '86 230
Prunes, Orange-Spiced, '85 224
Relish, Cranberry-Orange, '81 M289; '88 254;
　'99 15
Rice à l'Orange, '90 236
Rice, Miami, '96 86
Rice, Orange, '79 43; '81 175; '82 200
Rice, Orange-Herb, '89 286
Salads
　Almond Salad, Orange-, '99 107
　Ambrosia Supreme, Orange, '79 37
　Aspic, Orange-and-Carrot, '86 199
　Avocado-Orange Salad, '91 44
　Avocado Salad, Orange-, '99 331
　Beet Salad, Orange-and-, '88 43
　Broccoli-Orange Salad, '94 281
　Buttermilk Salad, Orange-, '95 134
　Carrot Salad, Orange-, '80 89; '84 325
　Carrot-Tangerine Salad, '83 316; '84 16
　Cauliflower Salad, Orange-, '82 266
　Cherry-Orange Salad, '79 74; '82 56
　Chicken-and-Orange Salad, Curried, '87 144
　Chicken Salad, '96 67
　Chicken Salad, Persian, '81 12
　Company's Coming Salad, '96 64
　Congealed Salad, Pineapple-Orange, '83 218
　Cottage Cheese Salad, Orange-, '79 44
　Cranberry-Orange Delight, '90 168
　Creamy Orange Salad, '84 124
　Cup, Orange Fruit, '91 277
　Cups, Citrus Salad in Orange, '85 47
　Cups, Orange, '86 92

Cups, Orange Salad, '85 40
Frosted Orange Salad, '81 154; '83 123
Grapefruit-Orange Salad, '91 276
Grapefruit Salad, Orange-, '93 294
Honey-Berry Dressing, Orange Salad with,
　'89 250
Honey Dressing, Orange Salad with, '89 14
Jeweled Orange Salad, '83 210
Jícama-and-Orange Salad, '88 246
Jícama-Orange Salad, '86 83; '90 122
Lobster and Orange Salad, '82 207
Mandarin Chicken, Carousel, '79 88
Mandarin Ham-and-Rice Salad, '87 145
Mandarin Orange and Pineapple Salad,
　'82 266
Mandarin Orange-Lettuce Salad, '92 79
Mandarin Orange Salad, '81 252; '84 161
Mandarin Orange Salad, Congealed, '89 327
Mandarin Orange Tossed Salad, '92 303
Mandarin Pork-and-Spinach Salad, '88 M126
Mandarin Rice Salad, '88 271
Mandarin Salad, Broccoli-, '93 325
Mandarin Salad Molds, '85 54
Mandarin Spinach Salad, '85 163
Mandarin Tossed Salad, '89 12
Marinated Orange-Onion Salad, '91 231;
　'92 68
Mimosa Salad, '98 310
Minted Orange Salad, '92 105
Onion Salad, Orange-, '89 41
Pear Salad, Orange-, '84 164
Poppy Seed Salad, Orange-, '98 87
Quick Orange Salad, '87 80
Red Cabbage Citrus Salad, '94 72
Romaine Salad, Orange-, '84 325; '87 239
Sesame-Citrus Green Salad, '86 33
Sherbet Salad, Orange, '81 154
Shrimp-and-Orange Rice Salad, Zesty, '87 155
Shrimp, Orange, and Olive Salad with Sherry
　Vinaigrette, '93 177
Shrimp Salad, Orange-, '84 197
Slaw, Cabbage-Orange, '79 135
Spinach-and-Orange Salad, '86 15
Spinach, Hot Spiked, '97 195
Spinach Salad, Orange-, '83 316; '84 16
Strawberry Salad with Orange-Curd Dressing,
　Orange-, '93 22
Sunshine Delight, '86 117
Surprise Salad, Orange, '79 12
Tropical Orange Salad, '92 97
Turkey-in-the-Orange Salad, '93 21
Turkish Salad, '96 137
Walnut Salad, Orange, '80 246
Sauces and Glazes
　Butter Glaze, Orange, '90 194
　Caramel Sauce, Pears with Orange-, '95 281
　Chocolate-Orange Sauce, '86 165; '94 314
　Coconut-Orange Sauce, '85 189
　Dessert Sauce, Orange, '86 337; '87 58
　Fresh Orange Glaze, '88 179
　Fresh Orange Sauce, '85 209
　Ginger Sauce, Chicken Breasts with Orange-,
　　'97 47
　Ginger Sauce, Sesame-Crusted Scallops with
　　Orange-, '97 125
　Hard Sauce, Orange, '88 225
　Honey-Orange Sauce, '85 108
　Honey Sauce, Orange-, '97 236
　Liqueur Sauce, Orange, '86 142
　Mandarin Orange Sauce, '89 204
　Mandarin Sauce, '84 60
　Mandarin-Teriyaki Sauce, '96 68
　Maraschino-Orange Sauce, '96 164
　Nutty Orange Glaze, '80 45

ORANGES, Sauces and Glazes
(continued)

Orange Glaze, '79 2; '80 257; '81 34, 107;
  '82 75, 206; '83 33, 114, 140, 267; '84 161;
  '86 298; '92 263; '95 320; '99 293
Orange Sauce, '82 47; '83 10, 277; '84 M286;
  '86 294; '98 83
Pineapple Glaze, Orange-, '81 60
Pineapple-Orange Sauce, '84 14
Raspberry-Orange Sauce, '88 22; '92 154
Salsa, Orange-Black Bean, '98 231
Scuppernong-Orange Glaze, '98 220
Shrimp in Orange Sauce, '99 292
Strawberry-Orange Sauce, '96 95
Sunshine Orange Sauce, '97 70
Sweet Orange Sauce, '93 M325
Syrup, Orange, '80 228; '89 254; '96 164;
  '97 32
Syrup, Orange Marmalade, '96 27
Sauté, Orange-Watercress, '98 83
Slices, Spicy Orange, '81 12
Snack Balls, Orange-Almond, '95 214
Soup, Carrot-Orange, '79 172
Special, Orange Blossom, '88 158
Spread, Orange Cheese, '87 292
Spread, Tropical Cheese, '95 46
Vegetables
Asparagus with Orange Butter Sauce, '85 43
Asparagus with Orange Sauce, '83 46
Beets, Orange, '91 219
Beets, Orange-Ginger, '80 137
Beets, Orange-Glazed, '81 167; '85 289;
  '86 187; '99 24
Beets, Spicy Orange, '94 280
Broccoli, Easy Orange, '85 267
Broccoli with Orange Sauce, '80 243
Brussels Sprouts, Orange, '84 34
Butternut-Orange Bake, '86 295
Cabbage Cooked in Orange Juice, '97 129
Carrots and Turnips, Sunset Orange, '94 213
Carrots in Orange Sauce, '82 107
Carrots, Orange-Fennel, '92 133
Carrots, Orange-Glazed, '79 12; '81 M165;
  '90 M98
Carrots, Orange-Raisin, '80 24
Carrots, Orange-Spiced, '88 18
Carrot Strips, Orangy, '89 312
Celery in Orange Sauce, '79 70
Green Peas in Orange Sauce, '88 97
Leeks in Orange Sauce, '88 86
Potatoes, Orange Mashed, '96 33
Rutabaga, Glazed, '99 284
Squash à l'Orange, '85 230
Sweet Potatoes, Coconut-Orange, '84 252
Sweet Potatoes in Orange Cups, '82 272
Sweet Potatoes, Orange, '86 279
Sweet Potatoes, Orange-Baked, '88 M294
Sweet Potatoes, Orange-Glazed, '81 223;
  '83 280
Sweet Potatoes, Pineapple-Orange, '96 46
Sweet Potato-Orange Bake, '83 226
Sweet Potato-Stuffed Orange Cups, '81 223
Vinaigrette, Grilled Asparagus Salad with
  Orange, '99 102
Vinaigrette, Grilled Fennel and Radicchio with
  Orange, '95 253
Vinaigrette, Orange-Raspberry, '95 144; '96 155
Vinegar, Orange, '95 31
Whip, Orange-Banana, '95 244
ORZO
Grouper with Orzo, Pesto, '97 321
Marinara on Beds of Spinach and Orzo, '93 320

Mozzarella-and-Olive Orzo, '97 249
Primavera, Orzo, '92 192
Sage Orzo, Chicken Breasts with, '98 169
Salad, Artichokes with Orzo, '88 M193
Salad, Confetti Orzo, '92 173
Salad, Peppers Stuffed with Shrimp-and-Orzo,
  '91 203
Salad, Shrimp-and-Orzo, '99 182
Salad with Sesame Dressing, Orzo, '96 137
Shrimp with Orzo, Fire-Roasted, '99 42
Three-Grain Rice, '95 166
OYSTERS
Appetizers
Annapolis, Oysters, '89 195
Artichoke Oysters, '96 154
Bacon, Oysters in, '83 211
Baked Oysters Bienville, '90 27
Barbecued Oysters, '82 247
Bienville, Oysters, '93 257
Casino, Oysters à la, '80 296
Creamed Oysters, '92 254
Dip, Smoked Oyster, '79 233
Dressed Oysters on the Half Shell, '87 M79
Fritters, Oyster, '97 20
Mousse, Oyster, '81 245
Mousse, Smoked Oyster, '84 320; '99 162
Spread, Smoked Oyster, '91 64
Stuffed Oysters, Crabmeat, '94 328
Baked Oysters, Bacon-, '86 132
Baked Oysters Italiano, '89 97
Baked Oysters on the Half Shell, '93 269
Bake, Oyster-and-Corn, '83 34; '84 44
Bisque, Oyster, '83 252; '96 276; '99 320
Brochette, Oysters, '80 56
Casserole, Oyster-and-Spinach, '83 34; '84 44
Casserole, Oyster-and-Wild Rice, '83 34; '84 44
Chesapeake, Oysters, '92 254
Chowder, Oyster, '83 229
Chowder, Oyster-Corn, '83 211
Eggplant-and-Oyster Louisiane, '95 196
Fresh Oysters, Preparing, '82 127
Fried Oysters, '85 104; '99 320
Fried Oysters, Delicious, '83 212
Fried Oysters, Southern, '88 111
Fried Raw Oysters, '81 135; '82 14
Fritters, Oyster, '79 31
Grilled Oysters Mornay, '89 195
Gumbo, Chicken and Oyster, '81 198
Gumbo, Duck, Oyster, and Sausage, '79 226
Gumbo, Seafood, '83 90; '87 210
Johnny Reb, Oysters, '84 213
Loaves, Spinach-Oyster, '84 213
Main Dishes
Baked Oysters over Toast Points, '84 214
Bienville, Oysters, '79 182
Buccaneer, Oysters, '87 40
Casserole, Oyster, '79 228
Casserole, Oyster-and-Chicken, '99 320
Casserole, Wild Rice-Oyster, '86 256
Cornbread, Oysters Casino on, '79 34
Crabmeat, Creamy Oysters and, '83 211
Creamed Oysters in Acorn Squash, '97 20
Creamed Oysters, Pan-Fried Grits with, '93 62
Crêpes, Virginia, '79 264
Dressing, Ma E's Traditional Oyster-
  Cornbread, '96 35
Dressing, Oyster, '79 250
Dressing, Oyster Bread, '82 251
Fried Oyster Bubbles, '80 296
Fry, Hangtown, '80 297
Gino, Oysters à la, '81 126
Ham, Edwards' Oysters and, '86 253
Landmark, Oyster, '84 88
Loaf, Crusty Oyster, '92 254

Mornay, Seafood, '83 67
Omelets, Smoked Oyster, '84 96
Pie, Turkey-and-Oyster, '82 267
Pilaf, Oyster, '97 20
Rockefeller, Oysters, '98 222
Rockefeller, Southern Oysters, '80 212
Sandwich, Oyster Submarine, '80 92
Sautéed Oysters, '86 132
Sautéed Seafood Platter, '83 89
Scalloped Oysters, '79 225; '84 213; '86 132;
  '90 249; '95 318; '99 321
Scalloped Oysters with Macaroni, '80 297
Shrimp Sauce, Oysters in, '87 40
Smoky Oysters Supreme, '87 60
Stewed in Cream, Oysters, '93 50
St. Jacques, Oysters, '80 103
Stuffing, Roast Turkey with Oyster,
  '80 251
Nachos, Texas Oyster, '87 39
Patty Shells, Oysters in, '83 212; '85 257
Pie, Creole Oyster, '84 214
Poor Boys, Oyster-and-Bacon, '87 40
Smoked Oysters, Deviled Eggs with,
  '84 161
Soup, Chicken, Ham, and Oyster, '79 198
Soup, Louisiana Oyster-and-Artichoke, '92 81
Soup, Oyster, '79 228; '83 211
Soup, Oyster-and-Artichoke, '97 21
Soup, Oyster-and-Mushroom, '87 39
Soup, Oyster-Cheese, '84 213
Soup, Oyster-Turnip, '94 328
Spinach Salad with Oysters and Red Wine
  Vinaigrette, '94 327
Stew, Company Oyster, '80 297
Stew, Golden Oyster, '86 132
Stew, Holiday Oyster, '85 264
Stew, Oyster, '80 221
Stew, Oyster-Broccoli, '89 242
Stew, Oyster-Sausage, '89 242
Stew, Potato-Oyster, '89 243
Wild Rice and Oysters, '92 339

Pancakes
Ambrosia Pancakes with Orange Syrup, '89 254
Apple-Filled Pancake, '86 96
Apple Pancakes with Cider Sauce, Spicy, '87 224
Applesauce Pancakes, '79 114
Apple-Topped Pancakes, '93 339
Apricot Delight, '81 42
Baked Pancake, Arkansas German-, '96 53
Banana-Nut Pancakes, '98 160
Best Pancakes, '99 194
Black Bean Pancakes with Gazpacho Butter,
  '92 86
Blueberry Buttermilk Pancakes, '79 114
Blueberry Pancakes, '85 152; '89 138
Blueberry Pancakes, Sour Cream, '81 164
Blue Cornmeal-Blueberry Pancakes, '94 115
Bran Pancakes with Cinnamon Syrup, '91 315
Buttermilk Griddle Cakes, '81 120; '82 22
Buttermilk Pancakes, '83 243; '84 101; '97 256
Buttermilk Pancakes with Fruit Topping, '89 50
Cornmeal Batter Cakes, '87 16
Cornmeal Pancakes, Hearty, '88 129
Corn Pancakes, '93 43
Cottage Cheese Pancakes, '79 115
Cracklin' Cakes, Grannie's, '98 252
Cream Cheese Pancakes, '97 70
Dessert Pancakes, Luau, '88 154
Easy Pancakes, '92 203
Featherweight Pancakes, '99 43
Fluffy Pancakes, '86 137

Fruit Topping, Pancakes with, **'81** 42
Gingerbread Pancakes, **'84** 242; **'95** 282; **'96** 27
Ginger Pancakes, Dessert, **'88** 153
Ham Griddle Cakes, **'89** 255
Honey Pancakes, **'91** 139
Island Pancakes, **'87** 225
Latkes, **'90** 254
Latkes, Potato, **'97** 252
Lemon Pancakes with Strawberry Butter,
    '99 44
Maple-Bacon Oven Pancake, **'89** 255
Mix, Quick Bread, **'81** 90
Noodle Pancake, Szechuan Ginger Stir-Fry with,
    '97 292
Oatmeal-Brown Sugar Pancakes, **'88** 203
Oatmeal Mini-Pancakes with Apple-Pear Sauce,
    '97 M272
Oatmeal Pancakes, **'80** 44; **'89** 107
Oat Pancakes, **'89** 227
Orange Pancakes with Sunshine Orange Sauce,
    '97 70
Orange-Yogurt Pancakes, **'87** 225
Oven-Baked Pancake for Two, **'89** 227
Pancakes, **'81** 90
Peach Pancake, Baked, **'97** 71
Peanut Butter Pancakes, **'97** 271
Pecan Pancakes, Toasted, **'99** 43
Popover Pancake, Brunch, **'96** 28
Potato-Ham Pancakes, **'96** 138
Potato Pancake, **'85** 20
Potato Pancakes, **'79** 115; **'89** 144
Potato Pancakes, German, **'98** 279
Potato Pancakes, Leftover, **'96** 138
Potato Pancakes, Moist, **'80** 36
Potato Pancakes, Old-Fashioned, **'96** 138
Potato Pancakes, Parsley-, **'96** 251; **'97** 103
Potato-Two Potato Pancakes, One, **'96** 138
Pumpkin Pancakes, **'80** 228
Refrigerator Pancakes, Overnight, **'93** 196
Rice Pancakes, **'85** 147
Sauce, Cinnamon-Pecan-Honey Pancake,
    '88 46
Sauce, Peach-Blueberry Pancake, **'82** 177
Sausage Rollups, Pancake-, **'83** 246; **'84** 42
Sausage Wedges, Pancake-, **'93** 196
Sour Cream Pancakes, **'79** 213
Sour Cream Pancakes, Fluffy, **'79** 209
Sour Cream Pancakes with Fruit Topping,
    '90 142
Squash Pancakes, Granola-, **'94** 267
Strawberry Pancakes, **'84** 219
Supper Pancake, **'86** 242
Sweet Potato Pancakes, **'87** 280
Sweet Potato Pancakes with Goat Cheese,
    '96 271
Vegetable Pancakes, **'88** 297; **'98** 236
Vegetable-Rice Pancakes, **'93** 43
Wheat Germ-Banana Pancakes, **'79** 114
Wheat Germ Pancakes, **'86** 242
Wheat Pancakes, Shredded, **'84** 59
Wheat Quick Pancakes, **'85** 278
Whole Grain Pancakes, **'93** 123
Whole Wheat-Oat Pancakes, **'93** 16
Whole Wheat Pancakes, **'83** 18
Zucchini Pancakes, **'93** 43
PARSNIPS
Candied Parsnips, **'86** 224
Fried Parsnips, **'96** 36
Glazed Parsnips, **'91** 220
Mash, Parsnip, **'97** 263
Medley, Parsnip-Carrot, **'96** 36
Scalloped Root Vegetables, **'98** 310
Soufflé, Golden Parsnip, **'83** 266
Sugar-Crusted Parsnips, **'88** 229

PASTAS. *See also* **COUSCOUS; FETTUCCINE;**
    LASAGNA; LINGUINE; MACARONI;
    MANICOTTI; NOODLES; ORZO;
    SALADS/Pasta; SPAGHETTI.
Angel Hair, Goat Cheese-Stuffed Chicken
    Breasts over, **'97** 144
Angel Hair Pasta, Scallops and, **'99** 176
Angel Hair Pasta, Shrimp and Mushrooms with,
    '92 34
Angel Hair Pasta, Szechuan Chicken with,
    '97 91
Angel Hair Pasta with Shrimp and Asparagus,
    '92 100
Angel Hair Pasta with Tomato Cream Sauce,
    '93 292
Antipasto, Pasta, **'85** 286
Asparagus, Tomatoes, and Shrimp, Garlicky
    Pasta with, **'95** 82
Bacon Pasta, **'97** 52
Basil-Cheese Pasta, **'96** 136
Beans and Pasta, **'99** 35
Beans, Pasta with, **'99** 236
Bow Tie Pasta, Spinach and Mushrooms with,
    '95 341
Bow-Tie Pesto, **'94** 231
Bow Ties, Black Beans, and Key Limes, **'96** 291
Bow Ties with Crab and Vegetables, **'98** 233
Bow-Tie with Marinara, **'94** 64
Broccoli Pasta, **'84** 176
Cannelloni, **'85** 60; **'92** 17
Casserole, Crawfish Pasta, **'97** 106
Casserole, Freezer Eggplant-Sausage-Pasta,
    '95 197
Casseroles, Hot Brown Pasta, **'96** 290
Catfish and Artichokes, Pasta with, **'90** 123
Cherry Tomatoes over Pasta, Herbed, **'95** 229
Chicken-and-Broccoli Pasta, **'87** 286
Chicken, Bird's-Nest, **'88** 152
Chicken Caesar Pasta, **'97** 87
Clam Sauce, Pasta with, **'84** 291
Collards and Sausage, Pasta with, **'94** 230
Cucumbers and Pasta, Asian, **'96** 177
Dressing, Pasta Salad, **'86** 121
Fennel, Pasta with, **'98** 46
Frittata, Firecracker Pasta, **'94** 230
Garden-Fresh "Pasta," **'94** M134
Garlic Pasta with Marinara Sauce, **'92** 78
Green Pasta with Shrimp-Mushroom Italienne,
    '79 170
Greens, Pasta with, **'96** 47
Herb-and-Tomato Pasta, **'96** 122
Late-Night Pasta Chez Frank, **'95** 228
Lemon Shrimp and Pasta, **'96** 124
Lentils, Cheesy Pasta and, **'99** 287
Mamma Mia Pasta, **'95** 25
Mediterranean Pasta, **'95** 341; **'96** 122
Minestrone, Dixie, **'94** 230
Mostaccioli Alfredo, **'91** 47
Oregano Pasta, **'84** 176
Pastitsio, **'99** 167
Penne, Garden Sauté with, **'98** 207
Penne Pasta, Chicken, Asparagus, and
    Mushrooms with, **'98** 212
Peppery Pasta, **'94** 164
Pesto and Pasta, **'92** 98
Pesto-Clam Sauce, Pasta with, **'98** 17
Pie, Broccoli-and-Turkey Pasta, **'88** 269
Pimiento Pasta, **'84** 176
Potpourri, Pasta, **'94** 33
Primavera
    Almost Pasta Primavera, **'86** 38
    Chicken-Pasta Primavera, **'91** 72
    Creamy Pasta Primavera, **'95** 167
    Garden Spiral Primavera, **'91** 30

Pasta Primavera, **'85** 86; **'89** 105; **'93** 168;
    '97 228
    Smoked Turkey Pasta Primavera, **'90** 84
    Tomato-Pasta Primavera, **'86** 209
Prosciutto, Party Pasta with, **'94** 176
Provençale, Pasta, **'88** 90
Pumpkin Pasta, **'98** 241
Ravioli, Homemade, **'87** 230
Ravioli, Mediterranean, **'93** 301
Ravioli Pasta, Homemade, **'87** 231
Ravioli, St. Louis Toasted, **'95** 117
Ravioli with Creamy Pesto Sauce, **'92** 79
Rotelle, Chicken and Tomato with, **'87** 108
Rotelle, Shrimp, **'85** 165
Rotini Romano, **'87** 193
Salad Dressing, Herbed Pasta, **'96** 106
Salads
Acini di Pepe Salad, **'83** 163
Artichoke-Pasta Salad, **'94** 180
Bean-Pasta Salad, Marinated, **'94** 167
Bean Salad, Pasta-, **'86** 169
Broccoli-Cauliflower Pasta Salad, **'88** 269
Broccoli-Cheese-Pasta Salad, **'96** 184
Chicken-and-Pasta Salad, Hoisin, **'99** 125
Chicken Pasta Salad, **'88** 89
Chicken-Pasta Salad, Grilled, **'94** 64
Chicken Salad, Tarragon Pasta-, **'87** 155
Confetti-Pasta Salad, Easy, **'92** 220
Crabmeat-Shrimp Pasta Salad, **'86** 208
Crunchy Pasta Salad, **'85** 166
Fruited Pasta Salad, **'92** 108
Garden Pasta Salad, **'86** 188
Ham-and-Pasta Salad, **'90** 128
Ham-Dijon Pasta Salad, **'92** 191
Ham, Pasta Salad with, **'92** 108
Ham-Pecan-Blue Cheese Pasta Salad, **'90** 62
Herbed Pasta-and-Tomato Salad, **'92** 144
Italian Salad, **'87** 145
Luncheon Pasta Salad, **'90** 191
Main-Dish Pasta Salad, **'82** 199
Marinated Bean-Pasta Salad, **'97** 328
Oriental Pasta Salad, **'90** 63
Overnight Pasta Salad, **'82** 276
Pasta Salad, **'84** 139; **'86** 120; **'87** 36; **'89** 217;
    '90 62, 91
Pistachio-Pasta Salad, **'86** 141
Presto Pasta Salad, **'90** 63
Ratatouille Pasta Salad, **'90** 74
Ravioli Salad, Caesar, **'95** 183
Roasted Onion Pasta Salad with Peppered
    Cheese Crisps, **'98** 107
Rotelle Salad, Crunchy, **'86** 209
Rotini Salad, **'88** 42
Salmon-Pasta Salad, **'87** 9
Salmon Salad Shells, **'85** 286
Seafood Pasta Salad, **'90** 62
Seashell Salad, **'86** 209
Shell Salad, Tossed, **'91** 256
Shrimp Salad, Pasta-and-, **'83** 163
Southwestern Pasta Salad, **'94** 278
Tomato-Pasta Salad, **'97** M160
Tortellini-Pesto Salad, **'92** 22
Tortellini Salad, **'89** 237
Tortellini Salad, Chicken, **'87** 288
Tortellini Salad, Garden, **'91** 44
Tortellini Salad, Terrific, **'96** 134
Tuna-Pasta Salad, **'91** 43; **'92** 141
Tuna Pasta Salad, **'92** 108
Turkey 'n' Pasta Salad, Ranch-Style, **'94** 184
Vegetable Pasta Salad, **'89** 256; **'91** 143
Vegetable-Pasta Salad, **'92** 167
Vegetable Salad, Pasta-, **'95** 238
Veggie Salad, Pasta-, **'96** 106
Vermicelli Salad, Shrimp, **'88** 139

PASTAS, Salads
(continued)

Vermicelli Vinaigrette Salad, '82 189
Ziti-Cheddar Salad, '85 165
Sauce, Pecan Pasta, '96 262
Sausage and Pasta, Skillet, '97 267
Scallops and Pasta, Fresh, '83 164
Shells
Bake, Quick Crab, '87 192
Bites, Pesto-Cheese Pasta, '87 251
Casserole, Seashell-Provolone, '80 189
Casserole, Turkey, '96 302
Cavatini, '94 214
Garden Pasta Medley, '89 256
Greens and Bacon, Shelly, '96 290
Jumbo Seashells Florentine, '79 6
Peppers and Broccoli, Pasta with, '91 69
Sausage-Stuffed Shells, '96 102
Seafood and Pasta, '90 234
Spinach Shells, '97 50
Stuffed Shells, Cheesy Beef-, '83 217
Stuffed Shells, Mexican, '91 87
Stuffed Shells, Southwestern, '93 234; '99 238
Stuffed Shells, Spinach-, '85 60; '87 20; '99 64
Stuffed with Five Cheeses, Pasta, '88 197
Tuna Pasta, Stuffed Tomato with, '88 54
Shrimp and Pasta, '91 207
Shrimp and Pasta, Herbed, '92 329; '97 228
Shrimp and Pasta with Cream Sauce, '98 295
Shrimp and Pasta with Two Cheeses, '98 49
Shrimp Élégante, '83 48
Shrimp-Pasta Medley, '88 302
Shrimp Scampi, '95 209
Smoked Salmon-Caper-and-Dill Pasta, '98 169
Snappy Pasta, '83 164
Soup, Bean and Pasta, '94 220
Spinach-Mustard Twist, '86 209
Spinach Pesto-Pasta, '91 314
Steak with Pasta and Sesame-Ginger Butter, '99 142
Straw and Hay Pasta, '80 211
Toasted Rice and Pasta, '95 57
Tomato-Basil Pasta, '94 204
Tomatoes and Basil, Pasta with Fresh, '98 233
Tomato-Garlic Pasta, '94 177
Tomato Pasta, Italian, '93 201
Tomato Pasta, Southwestern, '93 201
Tortellini. *See also* **PASTAS/Salads.**
Carbonara, Creamy Tortellini, '99 171
Carbonara, Tortellini, '91 47
Citrus Broth, Tortellini in, '99 292
Creamy Tortellini, '99 171
Kabobs, Antipasto, '94 144
Parsley-Caper Sauce, Tortellini with, '93 175
Rosemary-Parmesan Sauce, Tortellini with, '92 284
Shrimp and Tortellini, '92 34
Soup, Japanese Tortellini, '96 330
Soup, Sausage-Tortellini, '99 20
Soup, Seafood-Tortellini, '97 324
Soup, Spinach-Tortellini, '99 317
Soup, Tortellini, '98 68
Soup with Tortellini, Italian Sausage, '88 46
Spinach Tortellini with Tomato Sauce, '88 302
Tapas with Spicy Ranch Dip, Tortellini, '98 318
Tomatoes, Quick Pasta and, '92 180
Toss, Pasta-Basil, '87 33
Tricolor Pasta with Clam Sauce, '93 272
Turkey-Basil Pasta, Creamy, '89 216
Vegetable Pasta, Grilled, '97 142
Vegetables and Pasta, Roasted, '93 184

Vegetable Sauce, Pasta with, '83 163
Vegetables, Pasta and, '89 255
Vegetables, Pasta and Garden, '87 192
Vegetable Stir-Fry Pasta, '96 29
Verde, Pasta, '84 201
Vermicelli
Anchovy-Garlic Sauce over Vermicelli, '86 158
Casserole, Chicken-and-Pasta, '97 192
Chicken and Pasta, Quick, '93 14
Clam Sauce, Pasta with, '84 291
Clam Sauce, Vermicelli with, '85 295
Frittata, Pasta, '85 286
Garden Pasta, '82 199
Lemon Vermicelli, '84 329
Mushroom Sauce Supreme on Vermicelli, '86 158
Mushrooms, Vermicelli with, '79 195
Pie, Spinach-Pasta, '85 286
Platter, Cold Pasta, '88 42
Red Clam Sauce, Vermicelli and Sprouts with, '86 143
Salmon-Pesto Vermicelli, '92 200
Scallop-Vegetable Vermicelli, '87 143
Shrimp and Feta Cheese on Vermicelli, '87 108
Soup with Quenelles, Veal-Vermicelli, '94 14
Spinach Sauce, Vermicelli with Fresh, '89 256
Tomato Pasta, Caribbean, '93 201
Tomato Sauce, Vermicelli with, '83 164
Vinaigrette, Italian Pasta, '92 78
Ziti, Baked, '94 65
Ziti with Sausage and Broccoli, '95 340
PÂTÉS
Black-Eyed Pea Pâté, '91 12; '93 97
Braunschweiger Pâté, '83 251
Champignon, Pâté de, '93 171
Cheese Pâté, Four-, '89 284
Cheese Pâté, Layered, '86 105
Cheese Pâté, Sherry, '95 215
Chicken Liver Pâté, '79 153; '81 235; '83 108; '84 205; '88 M132
Chutney-Cheese Pâté, '84 152
Cognac, Pâté with, '86 159
Country Pâté, '86 66
Crab Pâté, '79 233
Cream Cheese Pâté, '80 154
Duck Liver Pâté, '79 227
Duck Pâté, '79 226
en Croûte, Pâté, '86 65
Ham Pâté, '85 279
Lentil Pâté, '92 285
Liver-Cheese Pâté, '85 276
Liver Pâté with Madeira Sauce, '93 323
Maison, Pâté, '84 222
Mock Pâté, '87 251
Mushroom Pâté, '89 157
Pastry, Pâté, '86 65
Pork Pâté with Spinach and Cream, '83 224
Shrimp Pâté on Crostini, '98 316
Shrimp Pâté with Dill Sauce, '85 39
Spread, Quick Pâté, '84 117
Turkey-Mushroom Pâté in Pastry, '92 327
Vegetable-Chicken Pâté, '86 66
Wine Pâté, '90 36
PEACHES
Alaska, Peachy Melba, '88 266
Ambrosia, Peach, '83 53
Baked Peaches, '92 179
Baked Peaches and Sausage, '82 50
Baked Peaches, Spicy, '86 39
Baked Peaches with Ginger, Oven-, '82 170
Bay Laurel Peaches, '90 124

Beverages
Bellinis, '88 77
Bellinis, Frosted, '97 122
Bellini Spritzers, '90 110
Christmas Blossom, '99 321
Cooler, Peach, '85 198; '86 6
Cream, Peaches 'n' Almond, '86 229
Daiquiris, Peach, '90 322
Frost, Peach, '89 155
Frosty, Peach, '81 156; '83 318
Fuzz Buzz, '82 160
Petals, Peach, '90 104
Pick-Me-Up, Peach, '89 183
Refresher, Peach, '86 103
Shake, Peach Melba Sundae, '93 134
Shake, Peachy Orange, '81 156
Shake, Pep, '79 38
Smash, Peach, '88 161
Smoothie, Peachy-Pineapple, '97 173
Smoothie, Strawberry-Peach, '89 182
Bombe with Raspberry Sauce, Creamy, '89 322
Brandied Peaches with Mincemeat, '81 47
Brandy Peaches, '85 275
Bread, Georgia Peach, '79 161
Bread, Peach, '82 170
Butter, Golden Peach, '91 178
Cake, Fresh Peach, '85 178
Cake, Peach-Almond Pound, '89 86
Cake, Peaches and Cream, '80 142
Cake, Peaches-and-Cream, '96 118
Cake, Peach Upside-Down, '87 8
Cake, Peachy Almond-Butter, '90 107
Cake, Peachy Picnic, '79 178
Caramel Peaches, '93 134
Cardinale, Peach, '89 155
Champagne, Peaches, '79 146
Charlotte, Peach, '79 68
Cheesecake, Peaches 'n' Cream, '88 137
Chicken Breasts, Peach-Stuffed, '79 177
Chicken Peach Dinner, '79 77
Chicken, Peachy, '90 212
Chicken with Peaches, Bourbon-Laced Tipsy, '97 136
Chutney, Glazed Ham with Cherry-Peach, '97 315
Cobblers
Apricot Cobbler, Peach-, '99 255
Blueberry Cobbler, Peachy, '80 143
Blueberry-Peach Cobbler, No-Dough, '86 177
Caramel Cobbler, Peach-, '86 300; '87 178
Cranberry-Peach Cobbler, '92 322
Crinkle, Peach, '91 20
Crisp, Peach, '83 113; '92 13; '93 134
Easy Peach Cobbler, '97 137; '99 206
Fresh Peach Cobbler, '82 139; '89 154
Grenadine-Peach Cobbler, '85 178
Lattice-Topped Peach Cobbler, '79 154
Old-Fashioned Peach Cobbler, '82 170
Peach Cobbler, '83 175; '84 178; '90 219; '95 264
(Peach Cobbler), I Fall to Peaches, '96 159
Praline Biscuits, Peach Cobbler with, '92 180
Quick Peach Cobbler, '79 215; '81 142
Spicy Peach Cobbler, '85 178
Supreme, Peach Cobbler, '81 184; '90 313
Compote, Berry-Peach, '82 133
Compote, Peach-Berry, '89 112
Crabapple Peaches, Broiled Pork Chops with, '81 83
Cream, Bavarian Peach, '82 171
Cream Cheese, Peachy, '92 289
Cream, Honeyed Peaches 'n', '93 134
Cream, Peach Almond, '82 108
Cream, Peaches and, '95 196

Cream, Peachy-Apricot, **'86** 163
Crêpes, Fresh Peach, **'84** 186
Crêpes, Peach, **'82** 184
Crisp, Gingered Peach, **'97** 303
Crumble, Easy Peach, **'83** 116
Curried Ham and Peaches, **'82** 60
Custard Dessert, Fresh Peach, **'86** 162
Dessert, Layered Peach, **'95** 196
Dessert, Peach-Blueberry, **'92** 184
Dessert, Peachy Melt-Away, **'87** 298
Dessert, Quick Peach, **'85** 178
Dip, Creole Peach, **'80** 142
Dip, Peachy, **'92** 179
Dressing, Peach, **'90** 180
Dumplings, Peach, **'80** 143; **'85** 177; **'96** 172
Filling, Peach, **'89** 154; **'90** 107; **'96** 119
Flambé, Banana-Peach, **'85** 316
Flambé, Peach Sundaes, **'81** 88
Flip, Peach, **'79** 217
Fluff, Peach, **'95** 176
Foster, Peaches, **'86** 240
Freeze, Creamy Peach, **'82** 144
French Toast, Peach-Filled, **'98** 160
French Toast, Peachy, **'98** 56
Frost, Peach, **'84** 164
Ginger Peaches with Rum, **'84** M323
Gingersnap Peaches, **'85** M329
Ham, Peachy Glazed, **'96** 189
Ham Roast, Peachy, **'86** 118
Honey-Lime Whip, Peaches with, **'85** 108
Ice Cream, Creamy Peach, **'85** 177
Ice Cream, Deluxe Peach, **'80** 176; **'90** 314
Ice Cream, Fresh Peach, **'95** 195
Ice Cream, Peach, **'81** 184; **'82** 171; **'83** 159; **'86** 15; **'93** 135; **'98** 221
Ice Cream, Peach-Almond, **'89** 156
Ice, Peach, **'81** 178
Ice, Peach-Yogurt, **'84** 83
Ketchup, Peach, **'95** 306
Marinated Peaches, **'91** 91
Melba, Peach, **'81** 83; **'83** M114
Meringues, Peach Melba, **'87** 76
Meringues with Buttermilk Custard Sauce, Peach Melba, **'96** 183
Mold, Peachy Berry Cream, **'83** 130
Mousse, Peach, **'85** 54
Mousse, Peach Macaroon, **'80** 153
Muffins, Peachy-Almond, **'86** 301
Muffins, Special Peach, **'84** 74
Nest, Peaches in a Garden, **'87** 154
Pancake, Baked Peach, **'97** 71
Pancake, Brunch Popover, **'96** 28
Parfait, Peach, **'82** 166
Pies
  Blackberry Pie, Peach-and-, **'89** 136
  Blueberry-Peach Pie, **'94** 158
  Chiffon Pie, Peach, **'89** 155
  Cranberry Pie, Peach-, **'83** 249
  Cream Pie, Peaches-and-, **'81** 184
  Filling, Fresh Peach Pie, **'95** 195
  Fresh Peach Pie, **'82** 170; **'95** 195
  Fresh Peach Pie, Elizabeth and Phoebe's, **'96** 119
  Fried Peach Pies, **'81** 272
  Fried Pies, Delicious, **'83** 84
  Fried Pies, Easy Peach, **'85** 178
  Georgia Peach-and-Praline Pie, **'98** 196
  Little Peach Pies, **'86** 303
  Luscious Peach Pie, **'81** 136
  Melba Pie, Peach, **'98** 216
  Mincemeat-Peach Pie, **'80** 295; **'81** 188
  Praline Pie, Peach, **'89** 136
  Quick Peach Pie, **'89** 252
  Rhubarb-Peach Pie, **'86** 140

Pork Chops, Peachy, **'89** 310
Pork Steaks, Peachy, **'79** 166
Preservation
  Butter, Peach, **'82** 308
  Chutney, Peach, **'84** 179; **'96** 207
  Conserve, Peach, **'79** 120
  Honey-Sweet Peaches, **'85** 107
  Jam, Cantaloupe-Peach, **'95** 143
  Jam, Freezer Peach, **'83** 182; **'84** M182
  Jam, Peach, **'93** 135
  Jam, Peach-Plum Freezer, **'85** 130
  Jam, Rosy Peach-Banana, **'80** 142
  Marmalade, Peach-Orange, **'82** 150
  Mincemeat Peaches, **'85** 178
  Pears, Peaches and, **'85** 106
  Pickled Peaches, Perfect, **'85** 178
  Pickles, Peach, **'85** 177; **'99** 170
  Preserves, Cream Cheese and Peach, **'84** 264
  Preserves, Custard, **'98** 126
  Preserves, Honeyed Peach, **'85** 130
  Preserves, Old-Fashioned Peach, **'82** 150
  Preserves, Peach, **'81** 147; **'89** 140
  Relish, Peach, **'85** 136
  Salsa, Peach, **'91** 183
  Spiced Peaches, Brandy, **'80** 142
Pudding, Peachy Bread, **'88** 175
Puffs, Peach Sweet Potato, **'87** 280
Ring, Spicy Peach-Cranberry, **'85** 264
Salads
  Chicken Salad, Peachy, **'97** 193
  Cream Salad, Peaches-and-, **'83** 108
  Easy Peach Salad Supreme, **'79** 177
  Fluff, Peach, **'95** 176
  Frosted Peach Salad, **'82** 145
  Frozen Peach Salad, **'82** 54
  Fruit Salad, Peachy, **'89** 206
  Georgia Peach Salad, **'80** 142
  Indian Chief Salad, **'96** 287
  Kiwi Salad, Peach-and-, **'90** 180
  Party Salad, Peach, **'84** 290
  Pickled Peach Salad, **'80** 104; **'85** 264
  Pinwheel Salad, Peach, **'79** 11
  Slaw, Party Peach, **'86** 250
  Spiced Peach Salad, **'94** 68
  Summer Salad, Georgia, **'92** 179
  Sunny Day Salad, **'96** 90
Sauces
  Berry Sauce, Peach-, **'87** M165
  Blueberry Pancake Sauce, Peach-, **'82** 177
  Blueberry Sauce, Peach-, **'81** 170
  Chicken with Peach Sauce, **'98** 334
  Creamy Peach Sauce, **'85** 189
  Fresh Peach Sauce, **'87** 167
  Fresh Peach Sauce, Creamy, **'79** 177
  Peach Sauce, **'84** 144; **'92** 203
  Pork Loin Dijonnaise with Peach Sauce, **'97** 87
  Praline Sauce, Peach-, **'85** 161
  Salsa, Fresh Peach, **'95** 195
  Salsa, Peach, **'96** 14; **'97** 183
  Salsa, Peachy Green Tomato, **'99** 143
  Strawberry-Peach Sauce, **'92** 154
  Tangy Peach Sauce, **'96** 89
Sherbet Cooler, Peachy, **'91** 187
Sherbet, Peach, **'90** 179
Shortcakes, Spicy Peach, **'89** 154
Sorbet, Peach, **'93** 153; **'97** 110
Soup, Chilled Peach, **'97** 159
Soup, Cream of Peach, **'99** 207
Soup, Peach, **'83** 120, 180
Soup, Peach-Plum, **'87** 157
Spareribs, Peach-Glazed, **'86** 14
Spiced Peach Dessert, **'83** 9
Spiced Peaches, **'91** 72, 148

Spiced Peaches, Ginger, **'86** 15
Spiced Peaches with Nutty Dumplings, **'87** 164
Split, Peach, **'85** 277
Spread, Peachy Cream Cheese, **'90** M215
Spread, Peachy-Raisin, **'86** 326
Strawberry Sauce, Peaches with, **'85** 8
Stuffed Peaches, Macaroon-, **'79** 178
Stuffed Peach Halves, **'86** 196
Sweet Potatoes and Peaches, **'86** 11
Tart, Cream Cheese-Peach, **'99** 169
Tart, Golden Peach Meringue, **'98** 197
Tart, Kiwifruit-Peach, **'88** 20
Tart, Peach Cream, **'90** 173
Tarts, Peachy Keen, **'91** 118
Tart with Brandy Sauce, Peach, **'98** 119
Topping, Peach, **'94** 22
Topping, Raspberry-Peach, **'87** 126
Torte, Frozen Peach, **'93** 135
Trifle, Peach, **'92** 179
Vinaigrette, Roasted Vegetable Salad with Dried Peach, **'97** 265
Vinegar, Peach-Mint, **'95** 190
Wine Sauce, Peaches in, **'79** 184
Yogurt, Frozen Fresh Peach, **'90** 139
PEANUT BUTTER
Apple, Piggy, **'94** 194
Bird's Nests, **'95** 102
Bites, Peanut Butter Elf, **'91** 275
Bread, Peanut Butter, **'86** 171; **'88** 64; **'99** 111
Cake, Chocolate-Peanut Butter, **'84** 240
Cake, Chocolate-Peanut Butter Mousse, **'98** 71
Cake, Fudgy Peanut Butter, **'85** 91
Cake, Peanut Butter, **'79** 51; **'83** M233
Cake, Peanut Butter-and-Jelly, **'85** 34
Cake, Peanut Butter-Banana, **'80** 87
Cake, Peanut Butter-Fudge, **'96** 254
Cake, Peanut Butter Swirl, **'86** 109
Candies
  Balls, Chocolate-Peanut Butter, **'80** 87
  Balls, No-Cook Candy, **'85** 14
  Balls, Peanut Butter-Chocolate, **'80** 269
  Bites, Chocolate-Peanut Butter, **'92** M317
  Chocolate Peanutty Swirls, **'94** M330
  Creams, Peanut Butter, **'79** 273
  Drops, Chocolate-Peanut Butter, **'92** 322
  Eggs, Peanut Butter Easter, **'87** 86
  Fudge Bites, Peanut-, **'91** M231; **'92** M68
  Fudge, Chocolate-Peanut Butter, **'87** 257; **'90** 311
  Fudge, Creamy Peanut Butter, **'92** 240
  Fudge, Diamond, **'92** 193
  Fudge, Double-Good, **'79** M263; **'95** M50
  Fudge, Double Peanut, **'85** 91
  Fudge, Four Chips, **'92** 318
  Fudge, Marbled Peanut Butter, **'88** 65
  Fudge, Peanut Butter, **'80** 302; **'89** 307; **'95** 51
  Fudge-Peanut Butter Chewies, **'98** 215
  Fudge Squares, Chocolate-Peanut Butter, **'97** M54
  Peanut Butter Candy, **'93** 166
  Pralines, Chocolate-Peanut Butter, **'92** 313; **'93** 51
  Pralines, Peanut Butter, **'92** 313; **'93** 51
  Squares, Peanut Butter-Chocolate Candy, **'82** 56
  Tiger Butter, **'86** 48
  Yummies, Peanut Butter, **'83** 223
Cheese Ball, Peanut Butter-, **'86** 136
Cheesecake, Peanut Butter, **'94** 142
Chicken, Peanut Butter-Marmalade, **'81** 282; **'82** 30
Chicken Strips, Nutty, **'99** 111
"Concrete," All Shook Up, **'94** 114
Cones, Chocolate-Peanut Butter, **'85** 14

PEANUT BUTTER
(continued)

Cookies
Bars, Chewy Chocolate Cereal, '97 317
Bars, Peanut Butter, '84 243; '93 166
Bars, Peanut Butter-and-Fudge, '80 M172
Bars, Peanut Butter-Jam, '94 291
Bars, Peanut Butter 'n' Jelly, '83 305
Brownies, Chocolate Chip-Peanut Butter, '84 73
Brownies, Chocolate-Peanut Butter Chip, '91 306
Brownies, Frosted Peanut Butter, '92 272
Brownies, Peanut Butter, '87 199
Chocolate Chip Cookies, Freezer Peanut Butter-, '86 230
Chocolate Chip-Peanut Butter Cookies, '99 68
Chocolate Chunk Cookies, Peanut Butter and, '94 169
Chocolate Kiss Cookies, Peanut Butter-, '86 49
Chocolate-Peanut Butter Cookies, '85 90
Chocolate-Peanut Butter Cups, '97 134
Choco-Peanut Chip Cookies, '92 318
Choco Surprise Cookies, '80 60
Cinnamon Cookies, Peanut Butter-, '84 30
Coconut Cookies, Peanut Butter-, '83 113
Crisp Peanuttiest Cookies, '88 65
Crisps, Peanut Butter, '79 50
Cups, Chocolate-Peanut Butter, '85 14
Double Chip Cookies, '81 301
Double-Chip Peanut Butter Cookies, '89 169
Double Peanut Butter Cookies, '80 209
Easter Basket and Eggs, '95 101
Easy Peanut Butter Cookies, '92 272
Logs, No-Bake Peanut Butter, '84 211
Macaroons, Chewy Peanut Butter, '95 214
Miracle Cookies, '83 149
Monster Cookies, '84 36
No-Bake Peanut Butter Cookies, '94 197
Oatmeal Cookies, Peanut Butter-, '81 218; '84 72
Oatmeal-Peanut Butter Chocolate Chip Cookies, '92 207
Oatmeal-Peanut Butter Cookies, '85 171
Olympic Medal Cookies, '96 180
Peanut Blossom Cookies, '95 245; '96 55; '97 324
Peanut Butter Cookies, '82 56; '87 58
Quick Peanut Butter Cookies, '86 109
Shortbread, Peanut Butter, '95 321
Slice-and-Bakes, Peanut Butter, '82 M185
Snaps, Peanut Butter, '81 237
Spooky Eyes, '95 273
Spooky Ghosts, '98 M256
Squares, Chocolate Chip-Peanut Butter, '84 118
Squares, Peanut Butter, '83 116
Temptations, Peanut Butter, '84 29
Truffle Cookies, Peanut Butter, '93 212
Cooler, Peanut Butter, '84 115
Cupcakes, Chocolate Surprise, '85 91
Delights, Choco-Peanut, '99 197
Dessert, Crunchy Peanut-Buttery, '92 204
Dessert, Peanut Butter, '92 164
Dessert, Rocky Road Pizza, '99 196
Dip, Indonesian, '96 190
Dip, Peanut Butter, '86 135
Dip, Peanut Butter-Honey, '85 19
Dip, Peanut Butter Lovers', '93 162
Filling, Peanut Butter, '96 229
Fingers, Peanut Butter, '79 256

French Toast, Peanut Butter, '93 166
Frosting, Chocolate-Peanut Butter, '84 240; '87 222
Frosting, Creamy Peanut, '80 87
Frosting, Peanut Butter, '83 223; '84 153; '85 34
Frosting, Peanut Butter-Fudge, '87 184
Frosting, Peanut Butter Swirl, '86 109
Frosts, Peanut Butter, '84 153
Frozen Peanut Butter Delight, '88 137
Granola, Peanut Butter, '82 296
Ice Cream, Chocolate Chunk-Peanut Butter, '85 297; '86 120
Ice Cream, Peanut Butter, '81 103; '88 64, 203
Ice Cream Sandwiches, Peanut Butter Cookie, '93 199
Milkshakes, Peanut Butter, '85 198
Monster Mouths, '95 274
Mousse Parfaits, Chocolate-Peanut Butter, '98 71
Muffins, Jelly-Topped Peanut Butter, '96 279
Muffins, Peanut Butter, '80 86; '87 158; '99 111
Muffins, Peanut Butter-Chocolate Chip, '94 167
Muffins, Peanut Butter-Honey, '82 56
Napoleons, Peanut Butter-and-Chocolate, '94 121
Nuggets, Golden North Pole, '99 M309
Pancakes, Peanut Butter, '97 271
Parfait, Bodacious Peanut, '95 167
Parfaits, Crunchy Peanut Butter, '79 176; '80 6
Pie, Chocolate-Peanut Butter, '85 91
Pie, Chocolate-Peanut Butter Ice Cream, '98 244
Pie, Chocolate-Peanut Butter Swirl, '87 262
Pie, Fluffy Peanut Butter, '94 246
Pie, Peanut Butter, '85 275; '86 109; '89 252
Pie, Peanut Butter Cream, '79 50; '88 65
Pie, Peanut Butter Meringue, '84 30
Pie, Tin Roof, '85 91
Pie, "Working for Peanuts," '93 115
Pinecones, Peanut Butter-Suet, '93 286
Pizza, Peanut Butter-Fruit, '94 60
Pudding, Peanut Butter, '85 95; '88 32
Pudding, Peanut Butter-Banana, '93 340
Rollups, Peanut Butter, '99 103
Salad, Thai Green Apple, '99 111
Sandwiches, Peanut Butter-and-Jelly "Fish," '91 177
Sandwiches, Peanut-Cheese-Raisin, '88 140
Sandwiches, Spider, '93 193
Sandwich, Peanut Butter Breakfast, '82 55
Sauce, Chocolate-Peanut Butter, '79 91, M156
Sauce, Hoisin Peanut Dipping, '99 14
Sauce, Pasta with Peanut, '95 252
Sauce, Peanut, '99 134
Sauce, Peanut Butter Barbecue, '81 233
Sauce, Peanut Butter Ice Cream, '84 30
Sauce, Spicy Peanut, '96 93
Shake, PBJ, '93 292
Shake, Peanut Butter, '82 48
Shake, Peanut Butter-Banana, '97 172
Snacks, Chocolate-Peanut Butter, '90 226
Soup, Cream of Peanut, '92 193; '93 288
Soup, Cream of Peanut, '84 29
Soup, Creamy Peanut, '79 50
Soup, Peanut Butter, '89 28
Spread, Peanut Butter, '92 21; '96 90
Tarts, Chocolate-Peanut Butter, '92 277
Tarts, Peanut Butter, '97 329
Vinaigrette, Sesame-Soy, '97 180
Waffles, Honey-Buttered Peanut Butter, '94 M206
Wings and Ribs, Thai, '97 M225
PEANUTS
Apples, Caramel-Peanut, '93 M244
Apples, Peanutty Stuffed, '85 25

Balls, Peanut-Date, '81 92
Bananas, Nutty, '79 251
Bars, Chewy Chocolate Cereal, '97 317
Bars, Chewy Peanut, '80 M172
Bars, Fruit and Nut Granola, '81 49
Bars, Peanut, '89 307
Beef Stir-Fry, Peanutty, '95 157
Bread, Peanut, '87 184
Bread, Peanut Lover's, '93 211
Cake, Chocolate-Caramel-Nut, '83 23
Cake, Chocolate-Peanut Cluster, '87 184
Cakes, Nutty, '89 50
Cake, Super Peanutty Layer, '83 222
Candied Popcorn and Peanuts, '82 295
Candies
Brittle, Golden Peanut, '83 223
Brittle, Never-Fail Peanut, '79 273
Brittle, Orange Peanut, '80 302
Brittle, Peanut, '79 M263; '80 87; '84 298; '92 240
Brittle with Crushed Peanuts, '87 184
Chili Nuts, Hot, '81 254
Chocolate Nut Teasers, '91 35
Chocolate-Peanut Crispies, '93 80
Clusters, Chocolate-Peanut, '81 16
Clusters, Nut, '81 254
Clusters, Peanut, '87 184; '92 288; '98 M282
Clusters, Peanutty, '83 143
Divinity, Peanut, '85 233; '87 M278
Filling, Nut, '91 35
Fudge, Butterscotch-Peanut, '98 M282
Fudge, Double Peanut, '85 91
Squares, Caramel-Peanut, '85 247
Chesapeake Nuts, '93 269
Chicken, Ginger-Nut, '90 M33
Chicken Strips, Nutty, '99 111
Chicken with Peanuts, Oriental, '82 236
Cookies, Chocolate-Peanut, '83 223
Cookies, Crisp Peanuttiest, '88 65
Cookies, Fibber McGee, '95 72
Cookies, Oats-and-Peanut, '89 60
Cookies, Peanutty Oatmeal, '80 106; '83 95
Cookies, Salted Peanut, '87 92
Crunchy Munchies, '94 196
Crust, Peanut-Graham, '99 49
Crust, Peanut-Graham Cracker, '79 50
Crust, Sweet Potatoes with Peanut, '93 212
Dessert, Fudge-Peanut Ice Cream, '88 167
Dessert, Peanut-Chocolate, '80 86
Dressing, Peanut-Ginger, '95 177
Dressing, Roast Turkey with Peanut, '79 283
Filling, Peanut, '93 211
Frosting, Creamy Peanut, '80 87
Fruit Dressing, Nutty, '88 68
Granola, Crunchy Peanut, '90 48
Granola, Superhero, '98 M206
Ice Cream, Chocolate-Covered Peanut, '88 203
Ice Cream, Peanut, '92 132
Mix, Jalapeño Nut, '96 27
Mix, Nutty Snack, '92 22
Muffins, Peanut, '91 223
Pad Thai, '97 202
Pesto and Pasta, Spinach-Peanut, '93 212
Pesto, Thai Peanut, '98 145
Pie, Caramel-Nut Crunch, '94 244
Pie, Caramel-Peanut, '86 259
Pie, Peanut Raisin, '79 85
Pie, Peanutty Ice Cream, '82 56
Pie, "Working for Peanuts," '93 115
Popcorn, Crazy Mixed-Up, '97 245
Popcorn, Oriental, '98 205
Power Munch, '96 180
Puff Nibbles, '84 191
Reindeer Food, Magic, '99 M309

Salad, Broccoli-Peanut, '92 35
Salad, Eight-Layer, '99 107
Salad, Green Bean-Peanut, '86 117
Salad, Nutty Cabbage, '87 42
Salad, Nutty Green, '87 168
Salad, Peanut-Apple, '80 5
Sauce, Hot Indonesian Peanut, '93 211
Sauce, Peanut Dessert, '86 M251
Sauce, Peanut Hot, '86 305
Sauce, Pork Chops with Peanut, '83 29
Sauce, Shrimp with Peanut, '93 303
Sauce, Thai Dipping, '97 236
Sauce, Thai-Style Noodles with Peanut Basil,
   '98 133
Slaw, Banana-Nut, '86 250
Slaw, Chinese Peanut, '93 212
Slaw, Nutty Cabbage, '88 218
Slaw, Peanut, '85 139
Slaw, Peanutty-Pear, '86 250
Snack, Toasted Cereal, '85 215
Soup, Chilled Peanut, '79 130
Soup, Creamy Peanut, '79 50
Soup, Peanut, '87 184
Spiced Nuts, '91 M316
Spicy Nuts, '82 161
Spread, Cheddar-Swiss, '99 106
Sugared Peanuts, '82 249

PEARS
Amaretto Pears with Meringue, '90 M58
Appetizers, Pear-Pecan, '96 262
Apples 'n' Pears, Saucy, '96 72
Baked Apples and Pear, Honey-, '97 303
Baked in Molasses-Port Sauce, Pears, '97 195
Baked Pears à la Mode, '95 129
Baked Pears Elegant, '91 48
Baked Pears, Honey-, '93 47
Belle Helene, Pears, '86 164
Bread, Pear, '80 218
Cake, Ginger-Pear Upside-Down, '97 205
Cake, Pear Preserve, '85 52
Cakes with Praline Sauce, Pear, '96 284
Cake, Upside-Down Sunburst, '87 9
Cake with Caramel Drizzle, Pear, '86 247
Cheesecake, Pear-Berry, '82 141
Cheesecake, Pear-Glazed, '79 67
Chicken and Pears, Glazed, '99 21
Chutney, Pear, '98 243
Cobbler, Best Ever Pear, '82 194
Coconut Pears, Spicy, '83 207
Cookies, Pear Mincemeat, '84 264
Cream, Pears in Orange, '84 245
Crème Chantilly, Holiday Pears with, '91 297
Crème de Menthe Pears, '94 50
Crisp, Cranberry-Pear, '83 207; '97 16
Crisp, Raspberry-Pear, '89 109
Crumble, Pear, '85 221
Dressing, Pear, '83 146
Dumplings, Pear, '97 210
en Croûte, Pears, '93 210
Flaming Pears, '84 313
Fritters, Ol' Timey Pear, '86 51
Gingered Pears, '89 M231
Gratin, Pear-Blue Cheese, '93 328
Honey, Gingered Pear, '97 62
Meringues, Baked Pear, '85 232
Muffins, Pear-Ginger, '91 240
Muscadine Sauce, Pears in, '88 216
Orange-Caramel Sauce, Pears with, '95 281
Pies
   Apple-Pear Pie, '83 249
   Apple-Pear Pull-Up Pie, '98 259
   Apple Pie, Natural Pear-, '88 226
   Backyard Pear Pie, '93 237
   Crumble Pie, Pear, '83 207

Deep-Dish Pear Pie, '80 219
Delicious Pear Pie, '88 226
Double-Crust Pear Pie, '82 194
French Pear Pie, '87 213
Ginger-Pear Pie, '93 48
Macadamia Pie, Pear-, '93 260
Mincemeat Pie, Pear, '84 264; '88 226
Mincemeat Pie, Pear-, '98 258
Mince Pie, Pear-, '81 271
Praline Pie, Pear-, '97 192
Rhubarb-Raspberry Pear Pie, '95 119
Streusel Pie, Pear, '83 234; '84 244; '97 109
Tennessee Pear Pie, '85 230
Poached
   Belle Helene, Pears, '86 164
   Blue, Pears, '99 246
   Caramel Sauce, Poached Pears with White,
      '99 28
   Curried Poached Pears with Coconut-
      Chicken Salad, '97 93
   Custard, Poached Pears in, '88 20
   Dark Chocolate Sauce, Poached Pears with,
      '90 M141
   Honey-Yogurt Sauce, Poached Pears with,
      '92 306
   Lemon Poached Pears, '82 74
   Orange Poached Pears, '80 218
   Orange-Poached Pears Flambé, '85 313
   Orange Sauce, Poached Pears in, '82 19
   Raspberry-Orange Sauce, Poached Pear Fans
      with, '88 22
   Raspberry Sauce, Poached Pears with,
      '84 213; '87 69; '88 223
   Red Wine, Pears in, '82 254
   Red Wine, Pears Poached in, '83 302
   Stewed Pears, '98 280
   Vanilla Poached Pears, '90 57
   Wine-Poached Pears, '98 230
   Wine, Poached Pears in, '82 194
   Wine-Poached Pears with Berry Sauce,
      '86 144
Preservation
   Butter, Pear, '85 130
   Butter, Spiced Pear, '80 218
   Chutney, Pear, '95 251
   Chutney, Pear-Apple, '89 141
   Honey, Pear, '90 159
   Jam, Paradise Pear, '84 300
   Jam, Spiced Pear, '98 214
   Marmalade, Pear, '79 196
   Mincemeat, Pear, '79 196; '84 264; '88 226
   Peaches and Pears, '85 106
   Pickles, Mustard Pear, '79 196
   Preserves, Pear, '82 195
   Relish, Aunt Glennie's Pear, '95 305
   Relish, Pear, '79 196
   Relish, Peppery Pear, '89 141
Pudding, Lemon-Pear, '96 283
Puree, Grapefruit with Pear-Berry, '89 213
Relish, Cranberry-Pear, '85 232
Salads
   Blue Cheese-Pear-Apple Salad, '81 224
   Celery Salad, Pear-and-, '87 56
   Crunchy Pear Salad, '83 234; '84 244
   Festive Fruit Salad, '80 16
   Golden Pear Salad, '91 58
   Harvest Salad with Cider Vinaigrette, '99 322
   Lime Salad, Pear-, '84 152
   Orange-Pear Salad, '84 164
   Pineapple-Pear Delight, '82 54
   Royal Pear Salad, '84 265
   Sautéed Apples, Onions, and Pears over
      Spinach, '94 212
   Slaw, Peanutty-Pear, '86 250

   Slaw, "Think Pink," '94 247
   Spinach Salad, Festive Pear-and-, '85 131
   Spinach Salad with Sautéed Pears, '94 237
   Swiss Cheese Salad, Pear-, '91 237
Sauce, Apple-Pear, '97 M272
Sauce, Pear, '92 164
Shake, Strawberry-Pear, '92 139
Side Dishes
   Baked Pears, Honey-, '93 47
   Bake, Pear-Oatmeal, '89 208
   Blue Cheese Sauce, Brunch Pears with,
      '90 142
   Breakfast Pears, Marmalade, '83 M203
   Breakfast Treat, Pear, '87 72
   Casserole, Pear-Sweet Potato, '86 280
   Crème de Menthe Pears, '94 50
   Filled Pears, Cheese-, '81 268
   Glazed Pears, Orange-, '79 247
   Oranges, Spicy Pears and, '89 305
   Pineapple-Honey Pears, '86 94
   Plate, Pretty Pear, '89 225
   Ruby Pears, '81 288
   Soda Pop Pears, '95 55
   Spiced Fall Pears, '89 M231
   Spiced Pears, '89 305
   Sugared Pears, Maple-, '81 232
   Wine, Pears in Red, '82 254
Sorbet, Pear-Lemon, '88 116
Soup, Pumpkin-Pear, '92 234
Spread, Pear-Cream Cheese, '93 80
Strudel, Pear, '98 253
Stuffed Pears, Almond-, '83 207
Stuffed with Cheese, Pears, '82 290
Sundaes, Quick Pear, '86 71
Tart, Pear, '82 304; '92 72
Tart with White Caramel Sauce, Pear, '92 195
Whip, Pear, '89 94
Wild Rice, Cranberry-Pear, '83 279
PEAS
Baked Peas, Chinese-Style, '86 305
Black-Eyed. *See also* **PEAS/Salads.**
   Best Ever Plain Ole Peas, '88 2
   Black-Eyed Peas, '93 180
   Cajun Black-Eyed Peas, '96 218
   Cajun Peas, '88 3
   Casserole, Reunion Pea, '87 11
   Caviar, Texas, '86 218; '99 84
   Chinese Peas, '88 3
   con Queso, Black-Eyed Pea, '96 274
   Cornbread, Black-Eyed Pea, '98 44
   Creole Black-Eyed Peas, '86 252; '98 22
   Creole Black-Eyes and Rice, '85 6
   Delight, Tomato-Pea, '84 196
   Dinner, Black-Eyed Pea Skillet, '86 6
   Dip, Bill D's Black-Eyed Pea, '97 M89
   Dip, Black-Eyed Pea, '81 8
   Dip, Chili-and-Black-Eyed Pea, '92 155
   Easy Black-Eyed Peas, '99 204
   Farmer's Beans and Rice with Rosemary
      Biscuits, '99 16
   Flips, Pea, '80 7
   Fresh Black-Eyed Peas, '81 M165
   Gravy, Black-Eyed Pea, '87 12
   Ham Hocks, Black-Eyed Peas with, '79 122;
      '89 16
   Hearty Black-Eyed Peas, '85 7
   Hopping Good Peas, '80 7
   Hopping John, '80 7; '90 12; '96 272
   Hopping John, Skillet, '79 10
   Hopping John with Grilled Pork Medaillons,
      '93 229
   Hopping John with Ham, '81 7
   Hot-and-Spicy Black-Eyed Peas, '99 235
   Hummus, Black-Eyed Pea, '94 123

PEAS, Black-Eyed
(continued)

Jalapeño Black-Eyed Peas, **'88** 166
Jambalaya, Black-Eyed Pea, **'92** 70
Jambalaya, Good Luck, **'87** 11
Marinated Black-Eyed Peas, **'82** 156; **'88** 101
Mexican Black-Eyed Peas, **'84** 327
Mexicano, Black-Eyed Peas, **'79** 10
Mexi-Peas, **'88** 3
Passion Peas, **'89** 17
Pâté, Black-Eyed Pea, **'91** 12; **'93** 97
Pickled Black-Eyed Peas, **'79** 10
Pinwheels, Black-Eyed Pea, **'85** 300; **'86** 18
Potatoes, Black-Eyed Pea-Spinach-Stuffed, **'95** 22
Relish, Zesty Black-Eyed Pea, **'95** 56
Rice, Black-Eyed Peas with, **'83** 12; **'90** 208; **'91** 13
Rice with Black-Eyed Peas, **'93** 66
Salsa, Black-Eyed Pea, **'93** 164
Sausage, Black-Eyed Peas with, **'86** 7
Seasoned Black-Eyed Peas, **'85** 138
Soup, Beefy Black-Eyed, **'85** 6
Soup, Black-Eyed Pea, **'97** 213
Southern-Style Black-Eyed Peas, **'82** 107
South-of-the-Border Black-Eyed Peas, **'86** 7
Spaghetti, Black-Eyed Pea, **'81** 7
Special, Black-Eyed Pea, **'86** 7
Spicy Black-Eyed Peas, **'92** 23
Spicy Black-Eyed Peas, Hot-and-, **'84** 9
Spicy Hot Black-Eyed Peas, **'81** 8
Spicy-Hot Black-Eyed Peas, **'90** 135
Spread, Black-Eyed Pea, **'86** 77
Stew, Ham-and-Black-Eyed Pea, **'93** 20
Sweet-and-Sour Black-Eyed Peas, **'85** 290
Sweet-and-Sour Peas, **'88** 3
Tasty Black-Eyed Peas, **'89** 68
Vinaigrette, Black-Eyed Pea, **'86** 7
Casserole, Curry Pea, **'87** 154
English. *See also* **PEAS/Salads.**
Baked Tuna and Peas in Wine Sauce, **'83** 196
Braised Belgian Endive and Peas, **'93** 22
Braised Rice and Peas, **'79** 101
Broil, Tomato-English Pea, **'83** 192
Buttered Peas and Mushrooms, **'82** 204
Buttered Peas with Onions, **'80** 242
Carrots and Peas, Mint-Glazed, **'90** 291
Casserole, Asparagus-and-English Pea, **'86** 324
Casserole, Asparagus and Peas, **'80** 152
Casserole, Asparagus-Pea, **'88** M294
Casserole, Cauliflower-Pea, **'85** 260
Casserole, Cheesy English Pea, **'83** 216
Casserole, English Pea-Pimiento, **'83** 207
Casserole, Quick Fresh English Pea, **'84** 145
Casserole Supreme, Pea, **'82** 281; **'83** 32
Cauliflower and Peas with Curried Almonds, **'79** 221; **'80** 82
Cauliflower, Peas and, **'82** 288
Celery, Deluxe Peas and, **'81** 267
Celery, Peas and, **'93** 289
Company Green Peas, **'91** 31
Continental, Peas, **'84** 254
Country-Style Peas, **'80** 101
Country Style, Peas, **'81** 101
Creamed Peas and New Potatoes, **'79** 102
Creole Peas, Quick, **'84** 123
Curried Peas with Almonds, **'88** M294
Deluxe English Peas, **'84** 68
Deviled Peas in Toast Cups, **'86** 280
Dumplings, Green Peas and, **'80** 102
Glazed English Peas, **'83** 111

Italian Peas, **'81** 83
Lettuce Peas, French, **'86** 62
Medley, English Pea, **'85** 236
Medley, Spring Pea, **'83** 141
Minted Peas, **'83** 141; **'87** 56
Mushrooms, Creamy Peas with, **'84** 196
Mushrooms, English Peas with, **'98** 286
Mushrooms, Green Peas with, **'80** 101
Mushrooms, Peas and, **'83** 141
Onions Stuffed with Peas, **'84** 68
Orange Sauce, Green Peas in, **'88** 97
Party Peas, **'79** 102
Pasta, Peas and, **'99** 68
Perfection, Peas to, **'94** 321
Pignoli, Peas, **'83** 190
Potatoes with Dill, Peas and, **'99** 67
Potato Nest, Peas in a, **'84** M239
Rice, Cashew Fried, **'99** 171
Rice, Holiday Peas and, **'86** 328
Rice, Peas and, **'88** 97
Rice with Green Peas, **'87** 45
Risotto with Shellfish and Peas, **'96** 131
Sauce, Green Pea, **'83** 22
Sautéed Peas and Bacon, **'89** 331
Scallions, Peas and, **'80** 101
Sherry, Peas with, **'80** 102
Soup, Chilled Pea, **'84** 181
Soup, Cold Curried Pea, **'91** 120
Soup Élégante, Pea, **'79** 53
Soup, English Pea, **'96** 56
Soup, Fresh Pea, **'86** 181
Soup, Mardi Gras, **'96** 56
Soup, Pea, **'99** 67
Soup, Peppery Pea, **'82** 271
Soup, Potato-Pea, **'94** 90
Soup, Spring Pea, **'88** M96
Special Peas, **'88** 97; **'95** 133
Field Peas and Spinach, **'99** 169
Ham, Southern Peas and, **'85** 138
Medley, Peas-and-Corn, **'85** 138
Pasta, Peas and, **'93** 139
Pigeon Peas, Rice with, **'92** 157
Salads
Asparagus Salad, Peas-and-, **'83** 141
Black-Eyed Pea Salad, **'80** 112; **'86** 225; **'88** 92, 221; **'90** 173; **'95** 203; **'97** 305; **'98** 52; **'99** 174
Black-Eyed Pea Salad, Fearrington House Goat Cheese and, **'95** 60
Black-Eyed Pea Salad, Marinated, **'93** 190
Black-Eyed Pea Salad, Overnight, **'81** 280
Black-Eyed Pea Salad with Benedictine Dressing, **'98** 83
Black-Eyed Peas, Zesty, **'89** 147
Black-Eyed Salad, Hot Bacon and, **'85** 7
Cauliflower and Pea Salad, Savory, **'81** 280
Cauliflower-Pea Salad, **'87** 231
Cheddar-Pea Salad, **'84** 82
Chicken-and-Black-Eyed Pea Salad, **'97** 305
Chicken-Pea Salad, **'83** 218
Chilled Dilly Peas, **'90** 143
Corn-and-Pea Salad, **'90** 181
Creamy Pea Salad, **'80** 111
Crunchy Pea Salad, **'90** 143
Dilled Pea Salad, **'97** 305; **'98** 18
English Pea-and-Apple Salad, **'87** 24
English Pea Salad, **'81** 280; **'90** 143
English Pea Salad, Cauliflower-, **'95** 66
English Pea Salad, Lettuce-, **'91** 208
English Pea Salad, Marinated, **'82** 54
Green Pea Salad, **'96** 88
Hoppin' John Salad, **'96** 64
Marinated Pea Salad, **'81** 204
Mexi-Pea Salad, **'81** 7

Minted Pea Salad, **'91** 119
Pea Salad, **'98** 274
Plentiful P's Salad, **'87** 12
Rice-Pea Salad, **'85** 163
Special Peas, **'95** 133
Special Pea Salad, **'83** 239
Sugar Snap Pea Salad, **'86** 115
Three Pea Salad, **'84** 290
Snow
Basil Snow Peas and Tomatoes, **'88** M185
Beef and Snow Peas, Oriental, **'79** 105
Beef with Pea Pods, Oriental, **'86** M328
Cashew Pea Pods, **'92** 343
Chicken with Snow Peas, **'83** 137
Chinese Peas, Easy, **'83** 206
Crunchy Snow Peas and Dip, **'86** 62
en Papillote, Fish with Snow Peas, **'86** 144
Medley, Cauliflower-Snow Pea, **'87** 305
Peas and Snow Peas, **'88** 67
Peppers, Minted Peas and, **'90** M99
Pineapple, Snow Peas and, **'91** 120
Piquant, Snow Peas, **'79** 21
Red Pepper, Snow Peas with, **'90** 102
Sesame Snow Peas and Red Pepper, **'84** 175
Shrimp Combo, Snow Pea-, **'79** 57
Shrimp with Snow Peas, **'85** 75
Skillet Snow Peas with Celery, **'84** 123
Slaw, Zesty, **'97** 324
Stir-Fried Peas and Peppers, **'87** 51
Stir-Fry, Beef and Pea, **'82** 98
Stir-Fry Beef and Pea Pods, **'80** 19
Stir-Fry, Beef and Snow Pea, **'82** 98
Stir-Fry Beef and Snow Peas, **'83** 22
Stir-Fry, Chicken and Snow Pea, **'95** 157
Stir-Fry, Potato-Snow Pea, **'86** 173
Stuffed Snow Peas, **'84** 80
Stuffed Snow Peas, Crab-, **'85** 288
Tomatoes, Snow Peas and, **'83** 111
Soup, Country-Style Pea, **'86** 267
Soup, Cream Pea, **'90** 211
Soup, French Market, **'94** 317
Soup Mix, French Market, **'94** 317
Soup, Pea-and-Watercress, **'93** 162
Soup, Split Pea, **'88** 235; **'89** 17; **'90** 198; **'94** 322
Soup, Split Pea and Frankfurter, **'79** 64
Sugar Snap
Appetizers, Sugar Snap Pea, **'86** 115
Basil and Lemon, Sugar Snap Peas with, **'93** 66
Champagne Dressing, Sugar Snap Peas with, **'99** 166
Creamed Sugar Snaps and Carrots, **'93** 139
Dip, Sugar Snap Peas with, **'86** 170
Dip, Sugar Snap, **'88** 91
Pearl Onions, Snap Peas and, **'89** 280
Peppers, Sugar Snaps and, **'93** 139
Potato Salad with Sugar Snap Peas, **'91** 120
Roasted Garlic Dressing, Snap Peas with, **'99** 269
Steamed Sugar Snap Peas, **'99** 71
Vegetable Medley, Spring, **'86** 115
PECANS. *See also* **PRALINE.**
Acorn Squash with Molasses and Pecans, **'85** 205
Appetizers
Ball, Date-Nut, **'92** 326
Ball, Deviled Pecan, **'80** 258
Ball, Party Pecan Cheese, **'81** 235
Ball, Pecan Cheese, **'83** 127
Ball, Pinecone Cheese, **'98** 265
Balls, Date-Nut, **'85** 10
Ball, Tuna-Pecan, **'87** 94
Barbecued Pecans, **'83** 222
Bites, Cheesy Pecan, **'82** 248

Brie, Kahlúa-Pecan, '92 289
Brown Sugar Pecans, '81 266
Candied Nuts, '81 261
Cheese Brick, '99 170
Chesapeake Nuts, '93 269
Chicken Fingers, Buttermilk-Pecan, '93 165
Christmas Eve Pecans, '91 276
Coffee 'n' Spice Pecans, '88 256
Crisps, Blue Cheese, '98 285
Curried Nuts, Spicy, '82 250
Curried Pecans, '91 208
Deviled Nuts, '93 118
Glazed Pecans, '81 254; '82 136
Grapes, Blue Cheese-Pecan, '95 48
Greek Olive Cups, '99 221
Honeycomb Pecans, '84 300
Hot-and-Spicy Pecans, '89 161
Hot Pepper Pecans, '85 4
Hot Smoky Pecans, '98 173
Log, Chicken-Pecan, '81 290
Log, Roquefort Pecan, '89 247
Log, Toasted Pecan Cheese, '86 M288
Mix, Jalapeño Nut, '96 27
Mushrooms, Pecan-Stuffed, '84 261
Nippy Nuts, '93 301
Orange-Glazed Pecans, '97 225
Orange Nuts, Sherry-, '86 M289
Orange Pecans, '84 299; '87 292
Pear-Pecan Appetizers, '96 262
Pepper Pecans, '87 137; '93 79
Pesto-Spiced Nuts, '95 173
Popcorn Balls, Nutty, '88 227
Roasted Bacon Pecans, '96 262
Salted Pecans, Southern, '80 285
Savory Southern Pecans, '95 240
Spiced Nuts, '91 M316
Spiced Pecans, '79 296; '80 31; '81 286
Spicy Pecans, '81 M289; '93 279
Spread, Carrot-Pecan, '96 108
Spread, Nutty Carrot, '94 123
Sugar and Spice Pecans, '82 297
Sugar-and-Spice Pecans, '86 121; '94 272
Sweet-and-Spicy Pecans, '92 321
Tarts, Apricot-Pecan-Brie, '97 236
Tarts, Toasty Southern Pecan, '95 329
Toasted Chili Pecans, '85 154
Toasted Pecans, '84 321; '86 229
Toasted Pecans, Buttery, '88 77
Torte, Showstopping Appetizer, '98 319
Wafers, Pecan-Cheese, '81 119
Wafers, Sage-Pecan Cheese, '93 12
Apples, Orange-Pecan Baked, '85 45
Apples, Taffy Pecan, '99 247
Bars, Creamy No-Bake, '97 166
Biscuits, Elf, '99 309
Blueberry Yum Yum, '98 91
Bourbon-Pecan Alfredo, '96 291
Breads
Apple-Nut Bread, '85 281
Applesauce Nut Bread, '81 305
Applesauce-Pecan Bread, '90 66
Apricot-Nut Loaf, Tasty, '82 10
Apricot-Pecan Bread, '97 266
Banana-Nut Bread, '86 8, 70
Banana-Nut-Raisin Bread, '81 59
Biscuits, Nutty Tea, '89 210
Bourbon-Pecan Bread, '93 308; '96 27
Buns, Nutty, '86 290
Cheddar-Nut Bread, '85 41
Cherry Nut Bread, '81 306; '82 36
Cherry-Nut Bread, Quick, '85 55
Chocolate Date-Nut Bread, '81 284
Coconut-Pecan Coils, '90 196
Cornbread, Pecan, '94 169; '98 252

Crescent Twists, Pecan, '99 47
Date-Nut Loaf, '85 10
Kahlúa Fruit-Nut Bread, '79 235
Lemon-Pecan Bread, '83 54
Maple-Nut Coffee Twist, '86 290
Maraschino Cherry Nut Bread, '79 234
Muffins, Banana-Nut, '93 140
Muffins, Cherry-Nut, '90 87
Muffins, Chunky Pecan, '88 9
Muffins, Cinnamon-Nut, '85 M88
Muffins, Cinnamon-Pecan, '84 219
Muffins, Coffee Cake, '98 160
Muffins, Country Pecan, '83 222
Muffins, Cranberry-Pecan, '84 269
Muffins, Date-Nut, '99 234
Muffins, Nutty Pumpkin, '86 291
Muffins, Orange-Pecan, '83 96; '99 56
Muffins, Pecan, '80 16
Muffins, Pecan-Orange, '97 163
Muffins, Raisin-Nut, '92 46
Muffins, Raisin-Pecan Ginger, '88 9
Muffins, Rum-Nut, '90 87
Orange-Nut Bread, '82 75
Orange Nut Loaf, '80 226
Orange-Pecan Bread, '79 148
Orange-Pecan Bread, Glazed, '81 250
Orange-Pecan Loaves, '79 215
Persimmon Date-Nut Bread, '82 218
Pineapple-Nut Bread, '79 215
Pineapple-Pecan Loaf Bread, '87 256
Popovers, Giant Pecan, '83 208
Prune-Nut Bread, '87 255; '91 55
Pull-Away Bread, Cinnamon, '98 137
Pumpkin-Nut Bread, '83 294
Pumpkin-Pecan Bread, '87 221
Roll, Banana-Nut, '85 112
Rolls, Buttered Rum-Nut, '86 291
Rolls, Caramel-Nut, '86 312
Rolls, Cinnamon-Pecan, '98 251
Rolls, Easy Cinnamon-Pecan, '89 307
Rolls, Oatmeal-Cinnamon-Pecan, '96 50
Rolls, Pecan, '81 62
Scones, Merry Cranberry-Nut Yeast, '99 274
Scones, Mocha-Pecan, '97 45
Scones, Orange-Pecan, '94 215
Strawberry-Nut Bread, '79 24
Wine-Date Nut Bread, '82 253
Brittle, Chocolate, '83 315
Brittle, Microwave Pecan, '97 M245
Brittle, Pecan, '91 272
Broccoli with Lemon Sauce and Pecans, '86 71
Buttered Pecans, Green Beans with, '92 61
Butter, Orange-Pecan, '84 75; '97 15
Butter, Pecan, '97 307
Cakes
Apple-Pecan Cake, '92 167
Banana-Nut Cake, '92 120
Banana Split Cake, '99 48
Bourbon-Pecan Cake, '84 25
Butter Brickle Loaf Cakes, '98 137
Butter Pecan Cake, '80 229
Butter Pecan Cake, Caramel-Filled, '88 278
Candy Bar Cake, '98 90
Carrot Cake, Pecan-, '99 223
Cheesecake, Butter Pecan, '86 61
Cheesecake, Chocolate-Caramel-Pecan, '91 197
Cheesecake, Pecan, '85 38
Cheesecake, Praline, '83 270; '89 93
Chocolate-Nut Cake, Rich, '86 8
Coffee Cake, Apple-Pecan, '84 242
Coffee Cake, Cinnamon-Pecan, '87 69
Coffee Cake, Nutty Orange, '95 160
Coffee Cake, Orange-Pecan, '86 86

Coffee Cake, Pecan-Topped, '81 41
Cupcakes, Apple-Nut, '82 279
Date Nut Cake, '79 176; '80 5
Funnel Cakes, Nutty, '91 233
Kentucky Pecan Cake, '84 263
Maple Nut Cake, '96 17
Orange-Nut Butter Cake, '80 254
Orange Nut Cake, '80 70
Orange-Pecan Crunch Cake, '83 10
Pecan Cake, '97 256
Pie Cake, Pecan, '98 254
Pineapple-Pecan Upside-Down Cake, '84 25
Pound Cake, Bourbon-Pecan, '91 270
Pound Cake, Brown Sugar-Rum, '96 60
Pound Cake, Butterscotch-Pecan, '92 153
Pound Cake, Eggnog-Pecan, '95 313
Pound Cake, Marbled Pecan, '93 313
Pound Cake, Orange-Pecan, '93 13
Pound Cake, Praline, '82 88
Pound Cake, Sour Cream-Orange Pecan, '89 207
Praline Glaze, Pecan Cake with, '82 196
Praline Ice Cream Cake, '80 84
Roulade, Pecan, '87 183
Roulage, Toffee-Pecan, '94 312
Shortcake, Banana-Pecan, '93 43
Candy, Chocolate-Nut Log, '86 335
Caramel Corn, Nutty, '92 317
Caramelized Onion-and-Pecan Brussels Sprouts, '99 254
Caramel O's, '99 M196
Caramel-Pecan Triangles, '99 281
Carrots and Celery with Pecans, '84 254
Casserole, Carrot-Pecan, '93 44; '98 231
Catfish Pecan, '85 53
Catfish, Pecan, '98 329
Chicken, Buttermilk-Pecan, '89 166; '97 252
Chicken Drummettes, Orange-Pecan, '93 158
Chicken, Lemony Pecan, '96 82
Chicken, Nutty Oven-Fried, '85 160
Chicken, Oven-Fried Pecan, '84 288
Chicken, Pecan, '90 54; '99 332
Chocolate Date-Nut Delight, '88 168
Clusters, Pecan, '81 266; '98 305
Clusters, Pecan-Coconut, '86 M251
Clusters, Roasted Pecan, '85 233; '90 310
Coating, Salmon Bake with Pecan-Crunch, '95 209
Cobbler, Apple-Pecan, '84 M198
Coffee, Praline-Flavored, '87 69
Cookies
Bars, Butter Pecan Turtle, '90 70
Bars, Gooey Pecan, '94 133
Bars, Pecan, '82 209
Brownies, Chocolate-Pecan, '81 64
Brownies, Coconut-Pecan-Frosted, '97 99
Brownies, Nutty Blonde, '81 64
Brownies, Nutty Cocoa, '81 64
Brownies, Nutty Fudge, '80 M171
Brownies, Praline, '93 243
Brown Sugar-Pecan Cookies, '91 236
Butter Cookies, Pecan-, '83 113
Butter Pecan Cookies, '82 139
Butter Pecan Shortbread Cookies, '80 282
Butterscotch-Pecan Cookies, '84 36
Cheese Crispies, Pecan-, '87 168
Cherry Nut Nuggets, '81 286
Cherry Pecan Cookies, '82 136
Chocolate Cookies, Chewy, '97 166
Chocolate-Nut Chews, '81 92
Chocolate-Nut Freezer Cookies, '88 217
Crescent Cookies, Pecan, '85 324; '97 274
Crispies, Pecan, '99 337
Easy Pecan Cookies, '80 208

PECANS, Cookies
(continued)

Fruitcake Cookies, **'98** 294
Fudge-Pecan Chewies, Alabama, **'95** 143
Graham Cracker Layered Cookies, **'98** 94
Lemon Pecan Dainties, **'80** 208
Oatmeal-Chocolate Chip Cookies, Nutty, **'82** 185
Oatmeal Cookies, Nutty, **'81** 130
Oatmeal Nut Crispies, **'80** 208
Orange-Pecan Cookies, **'88** 119
Pie Cookies, Pecan, **'92** 289
Praline Cookies, **'91** 271
Praline Shortbread Cookies, **'88** 242
Praline Thumbprint Cookies, **'89** 328
Sandies, Basil-Pecan, **'97** 166
Scotch Bars, Chewy, **'98** M291
Shells, Pecan Lace, **'97** 167
Squares, Congo, **'96** 94
Squares, Lemon-Pecan, **'89** 124
Squares, Pecan, **'79** 205; **'90** 69; **'98** 336
Squares, Twice-Baked Pecan, **'79** 291
Sugar Pecan Crisps, **'86** 230
Sugarplum Sticks, **'95** 321
Cornmeal Rounds, Pecan-, **'95** 99
Crunch, Apple-Nut, **'82** M238
Crunchy Munchies, **'94** 196
Crust, Nutty Oat, **'89** 251
Crust, Pecan, **'86** 317; **'89** 291
Crust, Spiced Nut, **'87** 295
Cupcakes, Apple-Nut, **'82** 279
Dessert, Maple Nut, **'81** 84
Dessert, Nutty Fudgy Frozen, **'94** 28
Dressing, Chicken with Pecan-Rice, **'85** M57
Dressing, Cornbread, Sausage, and Pecan, **'99** 257
Dressing, Fruit-and-Pecan, **'84** 252
Dressing, Mess o' Greens Salad with Warm Pecan, **'98** 250
Dressing, Pecan-Sage, **'80** 262
Dressing, Watermelon Salad with Celery-Nut, **'80** 182
Dumplings, Spiced Peaches with Nutty, **'87** 164
Eggs, Pecan-Stuffed, **'80** 78
Fettuccine, Chicken-Pecan, **'86** 52
Filling, Fruit-Nut, **'80** 289
Filling, Nut, **'91** 35
Filling, Nutty Fruit, **'99** 306
Filling, Pecan Pie, **'98** 254
Fritters, Chocolate-Covered Pecan, **'79** 205
Frosting, Banana-Nut, **'79** 115
Frosting, Butter Pecan, **'80** 229
Frosting, Cherry-Nut Cream Cheese, **'96** 249
Frosting, Chocolate Nut, **'80** 140
Frosting, Coconut-Pecan, **'81** 296; **'83** M233; **'84** 43, 322; **'97** 99
Frosting, Nutty Coconut, **'86** 8
Frosting, Nutty Cream Cheese, **'85** 117; **'96** 263
Frosting, Pecan, **'86** 86
Fruit Compote, Warm Praline, **'85** 260
Fudge, Buttermilk, **'97** 317
Fudge, Cherry Nut, **'83** 315
Fudge, Creamy Nut, **'84** 321
Fudge, Nutty White, **'81** 253
Fudge-Peanut Butter Chewies, **'98** 215
Fudge, Quick Nut, **'83** 316
Garnish, Pastry, **'98** 254
Glazed Nuts, **'88** 222
Glaze, Honey-Nut, **'87** 15
Glaze, Praline, **'82** 196
Goose, Fruit- and Pecan-Stuffed, **'83** 268
Grahams, Praline, **'92** 239

Granola, Nutty, **'90** 95
Green Beans, **'97** 263
Green Beans, Nutty, **'88** M187
Ham, Praline, **'85** 302; **'96** 303
Ice Cream, Butter Pecan, **'80** 176; **'86** 129; **'88** 202
Ice Cream, Butter-Pecan, **'96** 134
Ice Cream, Cherry-Nut, **'86** 129
Ice Cream, Cherry-Pecan, **'88** 203
Ice Cream, Praline, **'89** 318
Ice Cream, Pralines and Cream, **'82** 184; **'83** 159
Ice Cream, Straw-Ba-Nut, **'80** 177
Ice Cream, Strawberry-Banana-Nut, **'88** 203
Millionaires, **'97** M55
Mousse, Butter Pecan, **'95** 286
Onion Flowers with Pecans, Grilled, **'96** 217
Onions with Pecans and Roasted Carrots, Roasted Vidalia, **'92** 340
Orange Pecans, **'84** 299; **'87** 292
Pancakes, Toasted Pecan, **'99** 43
Penuche, Coffee, **'98** 305
Pies and Pastries
Baklava, **'96** 20
Bourbon-Chocolate Pecan Pie, **'98** 258
Bourbon-Pecan Pie, **'85** 90
Bourbon-Pecan Pie, Frozen, **'89** 251
Bourbon-Pecan Pumpkin Pie, **'87** 264
Caramel-Pecan Apple Pie, **'85** 247
Caramel-Pecan Pie, **'88** 282
Cherry-Pecan Pie, **'92** 30
Chocolate-Banana-Pecan Cream Pie, **'94** 210
Chocolate-Pecan Chess Pie, **'93** 251
Chocolate Pecan Pie, **'80** 237; **'83** 12; **'90** 184
Chocolate-Pecan Pie, **'91** 272
Chocolate-Praline Pie, **'86** 259
Choco-Pecan Pie, **'82** 86
Cinnamon-Almond-Pecan Pie, **'98** 89
Coconut-Pecan Chess Pie, **'81** 248
Coconut Pecan Pie, **'81** 161
Coffee Pecan Pie, **'82** 74
Cranberry-Pecan Pie, **'92** 316
Cranberry Pie, Nutty, **'82** 298
Crust, Pecan, **'98** 180
Custard Pecan Pie, **'87** 184
Date-Pecan Pie, **'80** 15
Golden Pecan Pie, **'81** 266
Grandmother's Pecan Pie, **'86** 269
Holiday Pecan Pie, **'81** 296
Honey-Pecan Finger Pies, **'90** 184
Ice Cream Pie, Nutty, **'91** 180
Individual Pecan Pies, **'85** 295
Layered Pecan Pie, **'83** 305
Lemon-Pecan Pie, **'93** 251
Louisiana Pecan Pie, **'92** 83
Maple-Pecan Pie, **'81** 266
Maverick Lunar Pie, **'98** 111
Mincemeat Ice Cream Pie, **'99** 285
Miniature Pecan Pies, **'79** 205; **'86** 13
Mississippi Pecan Pie, **'98** 146
Molasses-Pecan Pie, **'86** 259
Old-Fashioned Pecan Pie, **'81** M269
Orange-Pecan Pie, **'79** 282; **'83** 222
Peach Praline Pie, **'89** 136
Pecan Pie, **'79** 251; **'80** 57; **'85** 255; **'90** 312; **'92** 234; **'98** 275
Praline Pastries, **'89** 318
Pumpkin-Pecan Pie, **'85** 233, 282
Pumpkin Pie, Nutty, **'82** 67
Raisin-Pecan Pie, **'87** 213
Shell, Pecan Pastry, **'97** 275; **'98** 36
Special, Old Pecan Street, **'93** 251
Spicy Pecan Pie, **'84** 240
Strudel, Autumn-Apple, **'98** 253

Sweet Potato-Pecan Pie, **'83** 90
Tart, Apricot-Nut, **'99** 249
Tart, Fudge Truffle-Pecan, **'99** 315
Tart, Honey-Pecan, **'99** 212
Tarts, Apple-Pecan, **'80** 282
Tarts, Bourbon-Chocolate-Pecan, **'96** 264
Tarts, Easy Pecan, **'84** 313
Tarts, Pecan, **'81** 266
Tarts, Special Pecan, **'87** 224
Tart with Caramel Sauce, Chocolate-Pecan, **'93** 296; **'94** 234
Tart with Praline Cream, Pecan, **'90** 256
Tassies, Teatime, **'84** 321
Texas Pecan Pie, **'83** 159
Texas Star Pecan Pie, **'90** 184
Tiny Pecan Pies, **'79** 225
Turtle Pecan Pie, **'93** 250
Popcorn Balls, Nutty, **'88** 227
Popcorn, Crazy Mixed-Up, **'97** 245
Pork Chops with Beer Sauce, Pecan-Breaded, **'95** 266
Pork Loin, Apricot-Pecan Stuffed, **'94** 274
Praline Freeze, **'89** 60; **'90** 48
Praline Pecans, **'97** 285
Pudding, Brown Sugar-Pecan, **'86** M165
Pudding, Pecan-Mocha, **'89** M130
Pudding, with Hot Rum Sauce, Apple-Nut, **'79** 86
Quiche, Chicken-Pecan, **'91** 206
Rice, Island, **'98** 276
Rice, Nutted, **'85** 269
Rice, Pecan, **'85** 53
Rice, Shrimp-and-Scallop Sauté with Pecan, **'90** 317
Roll, Date Nut, **'79** 249
Rolls, Pecan, **'79** 285
Roughy with Brown Butter Sauce, Pecan, **'91** 64
Roulade, Pecan, **'87** 183
Salad, Apple-Nut, **'80** 226
Salad, Beet-Nut, **'79** 74
Salad, Cantaloupe-Pecan, **'86** 178
Salad, Creamy Carrot-Nut, **'86** 331
Salad, Endive, Bacon, and Pecan, **'89** 12
Salad, Ham-Pecan-Blue Cheese Pasta, **'90** 62
Salad, Spinach-Pecan, **'89** 128
Salad, Strawberry-Nut, **'94** 132
Salad, Watercress, **'97** 249
Sauces
Bourbon Praline Sauce, **'81** 170
Butter Pecan Sauce, **'91** 174
Butter Sauce, Pecan-, **'91** 65
Butterscotch-Pecan Sauce, **'82** 212
Chocolate-Praline Sauce, **'85** M295
Cinnamon-Pecan-Honey Pancake Sauce, **'88** 46
Date-Nut Sundae Sauce, **'82** 167
Éclairs with Pecan Sauce, **'83** 219
Pasta Sauce, Pecan, **'96** 262
Peach-Praline Sauce, **'85** 161
Pecan Sauce, **'83** 219
Praline Ice Cream Sauce, **'85** 189
Praline Ice Cream Sauce, Southern, **'86** M227
Praline Sauce, **'83** 25; **'84** 143; **'89** 95; **'92** 282; **'94** 206, 312
Spread, Beet-and-Pecan Sandwich, **'99** 274
Spread, Honey-Nut, **'87** 157
Spread, Nutty Cream Cheese, **'89** 327
Spread, Pimiento Cheese, **'99** 106, 276
Spread, Raisin-Nut, **'95** 79
Squares, Butter Pecan Pie, **'81** 262
Squares, Easy Pecan, **'81** 230
Squash, Apple-and-Pecan-Filled, **'88** 228
Sticky Bun Toast Topper, **'99** M72
Stuffing, Chicken Breasts with Pecan-Sausage, **'94** 212

Stuffing, Cranberry-Pecan, '96 309
Stuffing, Pecan, '79 292; '80 32
Stuffing, Wild Duck with Pecan, '85 269
Sugar-and-Honey Pecans, '86 319
Sugared Pecans, '82 167
Sugarplums, Pecan Shortbread, '83 298
Syrup, Chunky Pecan, '85 278
Syrup, Maple-Nut, '80 228
Toast, Orange Praline, '79 36
Toffee, Microwave, '92 M317
Toffee, Nutty, '79 M263
Topping, Apple-Nut, '93 162
Topping, Butter-Pecan, '95 158
Topping, Cinnamon-Pecan, '85 277
Topping, Crunchy Cereal, '96 216
Topping, Maple-Pecan Ice Cream, '98 317
Topping, Nutty, '85 256
Topping, Pecan, '94 36
Topping, Streusel, '96 216
Torte, Carob-Pecan, '85 218
Torte, Chocolate-Pecan, '89 42
Torte, Graham Cracker-Nut, '97 275; '98 35
Torte, Heavenly Pecan, '81 266
Torte, Mocha-Pecan, '86 26
Trout with Orange Sauce, Pecan-Crusted,
   '98 M82
Turkey Cutlets, Pecan-Crusted, '94 282
Waffles, Pecan, '87 225
Waffles, Pumpkin-Nut, '86 96
Waffles, Southern Chicken-Pecan, '82 231
Wild Rice, Pecan-Lemon, '92 211
Zucchini with Pecans, '87 31

PEPPERMINT
Bavarian, Peppermint, '80 153
Brownies, Chocolate-Peppermint, '88 262
Brownies, Pistachio-Mint, '94 50
Brownies, Southern Chocolate-Mint, '93 216
Cake, Peppermint Candy, '89 254
Cake, Red Velvet Peppermint, '98 308
Cheesecake Bites, Mint, '99 282
Cheesecake, Frozen Peppermint, '94 143
Chocolate Mint Freeze, '88 167
Cookies, Chocolate-Chocolate Chip-
   Peppermint, '97 289
Cookies, Peppermint, '95 322
Cookies, Peppermint Candy, '88 286
Cookies, Peppermint Sandwich, '92 277
Crème Brûlée, Peppermint, '95 323
Dessert, Peppermint Wafer, '79 176; '80 7
Dessert, Triple Mint Ice-Cream Angel, '93 86
Filling, Mint-Cream, '96 229
Filling, Peppermint, '81 119; '89 254
Flip, Hot Peppermint, '86 329
Fondue, Peppermint, '94 332; '95 35
Frosting, Mint Cream, '93 216
Frosting, Peppermint Cream Cheese, '98 308
Frosting, Pink Peppermint Birthday Cake,
   '92 269
Frosting, Quick Peppermint, '98 308
Hot Cocoa Mix, Minted, '91 316
Ice Cream, Peppermint, '80 176; '86 129
Mints, Party, '79 273; '81 119
Mousse, Peppermint, '93 315
Mousse, Peppermint Candy, '82 71; '94 198
Parfait, Peppermint, '93 315
Parfaits, Chocolate-Peppermint, '88 65
Patties, Peppermint, '86 278
Peabody Peppermint Patti, The, '99 321
Pie, Brownie-Mint, '97 303
Pie, Peppermint Candy-Ice Cream, '87 260
Pie, Triple Mint Ice Cream, '98 217
Pralines, Chocolate-Mint, '92 313; '93 51
Rounds, Peppermint, '94 19
Sauce, Chocolate-Peppermint, '94 205

Shortbread, Butter-Mint, '99 28
Snowball Surprises, '93 315
Soufflé, Chocolate Mint, '81 16
Special Mints, '99 323
Squares, Chocolate-Peppermint, '81 119
Twists, Mint, '86 106
Wreaths, Melt-Away Peppermint, '85 324

PEPPERS
Antipasto, Grandpa's, '98 183
Appetizers, Basil-Pepper, '98 133
Burritos, Breakfast, '99 103
Casserole, Southwestern, '99 216
Cherry Pepper Appetizers, Fiery Stuffed, '97 269
Chicken with Angel Hair Pasta, Szechuan, '97 91

Chile
Adobo, Puerco en, '88 116
Ancho Base, '95 205
Ancho-Beer Mashers, '98 248
Ancho Chile Butter, '99 93
Ancho Chile Cream, '87 121
Ancho Chile Sauce, '87 122
Ancho Chile Succotash with Serrano Chile
   Polenta, '98 104
Ancho Cream Sauce, Boneless Pork Chops
   with, '95 205
Casserole, Chile-Cheese, '82 90
Casserole, Chile 'n' Cheese Breakfast, '88 57
Casserole, Chiles Rellenos, '79 84;
   '84 31, 234; '92 18
Casserole, Chili-Corn, '88 266
Casserole, Chili-Rice, '79 54
Casserole, Mexican Rice, '83 31
Casserole, Sausage-Chile Rellenos, '88 52
Caviar, Mexican, '98 135
Cheesecake, Chicken-Chile, '92 42
Cheeses, Mexican Grilled, '97 170
Chicken, Jamaican Jerk, '99 121
Chicken Madrid, '97 326
Chicken with Salsa, Baked Chile, '88 147
Chimichangas (Fried Burritos), '81 196;
   '85 244
con Queso, Chile, '80 194
con Queso Supreme, Chile, '80 265
Dip, Artichoke-Chile, '98 234
Dip, Cheese-and-Chile, '83 31
Dip, Hot Chile, '82 248
Dip, Hot Chile-Beef, '83 218
Dressing, Southwestern Mayonnaise, '99 245
Egg Rolls, Chiles Rellenos, '86 296
Eggs, Chile, '88 80
Enchiladas, Chicken-Chile, '97 313
Enchiladas, New Mexican Flat, '85 245
Green Chile-and-Fish Casserole, '84 32
Green Chile Casserole, Corn-and-, '89 68
Green Chile-Cheese Pie, '84 234
Green Chile-Cornbread Dressing, '93 306
Green Chile Quiche, '83 31
Green Chile Quiche, Squash-and-, '88 143
Green Chile Sauce, '82 220
Green Chiles, Cheese Grits with, '95 208
Green Chile-Sour Cream Enchiladas, '84 234
Green Chiles, Rice and, '83 152
Green Chiles, Stuffed, '93 208
Green Chiles, Stuffed Squash with, '83 148
Grits, Saga Blue-Chile, '98 202
Jelly, Chile Piquín, '94 28
Kabobs, Chile-Beef, '94 251
Oil, Chile Pepper, '96 122
Okra Dills, '97 157
Pico de Gallo, '97 141; '98 87
Poblano Chicken, Creamy, '98 42
Poblanos, Corn-Stuffed, '97 269
Poblanos Stuffed with Pork and Fruit, '97 269
Poblano Vinaigrette, '99 71

Quiche, Chile Pepper, '82 224
Quiche, Shrimp, '83 50
Red Chile Enchilada Sauce, '85 245
Red Chile Powder, '85 245
Red Chile Sauce, '85 245; '94 251; '95 17
Rellenos, Cheese Chiles, '96 24
Rellenos, Chiles (Stuffed Chiles), '82 220;
   '83 150; '88 116; '89 226
Rellenos Potatoes, Papa's, '96 238
Rellenos, Roasted Chiles, '95 64
Rellenos, Southern-Style Chiles, '96 24
Rellenos with Tomatillo Sauce, Roasted
   Chiles, '94 203
Rellenos with Walnut Cream Sauce,
   Havarti-and-Corn-Stuffed Chiles, '93 M275
Rice, Chili-Cheesy, '79 43
Rice, Hot Pepper, '92 310
Rollups, Cream Cheese, '98 134
Salad, Spicy Chile-Tomato, '88 121
Salsa, Double Chile, '91 182
Salsa, Dried Chile, '97 265
Salsa, Pepper, '88 26
Salsa with Homemade Tostados, Hot Chile,
   '88 115
Sauce, Racy Pesto, '97 67
Serrano Chile Blue Cornbread, '94 114
Serrano Chile Polenta, '98 104
Serrano Salsa, Roasted, '95 207
Soufflés, Chile-Cheese, '96 219
Squash, Chile, '84 77
Squash, Mexican, '83 31
Steaks, Mexican Pepper-Cheese, '97 190
Tacos, Shrimp-and-Pepper Soft, '95 339
Tamales, Hot, '83 51
Tamales, Sweet, '83 52
Turnovers, Chile-Ham, '88 64
Verde, Chili, '95 14
Verde, Light Chile, '88 148
Verde, Roasted Salsa, '96 182
Verde Sauce, '93 275
Vinaigrette, Hot Chile, '98 200
Waffles, Corn-Chile, '94 206
Chipotle-Marinated Quail, Pan-Roasted, '98 201
Chipotle Pepper Butter, '97 307
Chipotle Salsa, Chicken-and-Brie Quesadillas
   with, '99 311
Dip, Pepperoncini-Cream Cheese, '91 252
Dressing, Jeweled Hot Bacon, '97 196
Eggs, Tex-Mex Deviled, '97 247
Fajitas with Pico de Gallo, '98 87
Fillet, Acapulco, '98 174
Filling, Crêpe, '96 48
Firecrackers, Texas, '95 96
Frittata, Bell Pepper, '96 204

Green
Beef and Green Peppers, '79 104
Beefed-Up Peppers, '82 186
Black Beans, Traditional Cuban, '98 21
Bread, Pepper, '85 156
Casserole, Peppered Pork Chop, '82 25
Casserole, Peppery Potato, '95 182
Chicken Peppers, Devilish, '80 65
Coleslaw, Memphis-Style, '98 104
Coleslaw, Old-Fashioned, '99 235
Coleslaw, Sour Cream, '99 220
Cups, Potato Salad in Pepper, '79 78
Deluxe, Peppers, '81 159
Dressing, Green Pepper-Onion Salad, '84 12
Fried Pepper Strips, '82 208
Gazpacho, White, '97 181
Hamburger Steak, '99 45
Jelly, Pepper, '79 121
Jelly, Unusual Green Pepper, '82 132
Linguine, Leeks and Peppers with, '98 68

PEPPERS, Green
(continued)

Meatballs with Pineapple and Peppers, **'90** 145
Medley, Pepper-Mushroom, **'90** 98
Mexican Green Peppers, **'80** 65
Muffins, Cheese-and-Pepper, **'84** 139
Onions, Baked Sweet, **'98** 130
Pizza Peppers, **'83** 135
Potato Salad 'n' Peppers, **'83** 135
Ratatouille, **'85** 92
Relish, Pepper, **'83** 183
Relish, Pepper-Onion, **'84** 180
Rice, Charleston, **'97** 310
Rice, Red, **'97** 138
Salad, Ruby-and-Emerald, **'85** 79
Sauce, Green Bell Pepper, **'97** 261
Sauce, Pepper-Onion, **'84** 125
Sauce, Red or Green Pepper, **'91** 85
Sausage and Peppers, Italian, **'84** 9
Sautéed Onions and Peppers, **'83** M148
Sauté, Tomato-Pepper, **'84** 142
Soup, Green Pepper, **'88** 250
Soup, Mexican Cheese, **'97** 268
Spaghetti with Pork and Peppers, **'98** 131
Spread, Roasted Pepper, **'94** 123
Squash Oregano, Summer, **'97** 165
Stacks, Pepper-Cheese, **'87** 80
Steak and Rice, Pepper, **'81** 17
Steak, Pepper, **'81** 273; **'85** 57; **'88** 113
Steak, Pepper-Beef, **'85** 21
Stir-Fried Sweet Peppers with Tomatoes, **'93** 207
Stir-Fry Steak, Pepper, **'81** 240
Stuffed Green Peppers, Beefy, **'81** 86
Stuffed Green Peppers, Ham-, **'80** 65
Stuffed Pepper Medley, **'82** 131
Stuffed Peppers, **'81** 239; **'83** 66; **'84** 202
Stuffed Peppers, Beef-, **'84** 154; **'85** 146; **'91** M127
Stuffed Peppers, Corn-, **'84** 104
Stuffed Peppers, Curried Chicken-, **'87** 19
Stuffed Peppers for Two, **'80** 84
Stuffed Peppers, Ham-and-Corn, **'81** 87
Stuffed Peppers, Hearty, **'88** M214
Stuffed Peppers, Macaroni-and-Cheese-, **'80** 65
Stuffed Peppers, Rice-, **'80** 65; **'99** 241
Stuffed Peppers, Shrimp-, **'80** 162; **'86** 131, 197; **'97** 268
Stuffed Peppers, Spinach-, **'82** 180
Stuffed Peppers with Rice and Ham, **'82** 131
Stuffed with Beef, Peppers, **'84** 72
Taco Peppers, **'81** 86
Turkey with Peppers, **'92** 182
Veal and Peppers, Spaghetti with, **'81** 201; **'82** 14
Guacamole Crisps, **'98** 173
Hush Puppies, Mississippi, **'97** 84
Jalapeño
Biscuits, Cornmeal-Jalapeño, **'94** 214
Black-Eyed Peas, Jalapeño, **'88** 166
Bread, Jalapeño Pepper, **'83** 121
Burgers with Roasted Bell Pepper Ketchup, Jalapeño-Stuffed, **'97** 318
Butter, Jalapeño, **'97** 306
Butter, Jalapeño-Chili, **'98** 156
Casserole, Jalapeño Corn, **'83** 256
Casserole, Jalapeño Rice, **'81** 66
Celery, Jalapeño Stuffed, **'79** 70
Cheese, Jalapeño Pimiento, **'98** 315
Cheese, Shrimp with Herbed Jalapeño, **'87** 112

Cheesy Jalapeño Peppers, **'80** 195
Chicken, Grilled Jalapeño, **'93** 213
Chicken, Grilled Lime-Jalapeño, **'91** 87
Chicken Jalapeño, Easy, **'92** 310
Chicken Legs, Jalapeño Oven-Fried, **'94** 94
Chutney, Jeweled Pepper, **'94** 316
Coleslaw, Jalapeño, **'97** 26
con Queso, Chile, **'97** 25
Cornbread, Beefy Jalapeño, **'82** 142
Cornbread, Cheddar-Jalapeño, **'85** 3
Cornbread, Jalapeño, **'85** 200; **'94** 78; **'98** 178
Cups, Hot Vegetable Pepper, **'88** M188
Dip, Mexican Fiesta, **'98** 234
Eggs, Armadillo, **'97** 270
Fried Jalapeños, **'96** 292
Fritters, Corn-Jalapeño, **'96** 153
Fritters, Squash-Jalapeño, **'98** 249
Grits, Jalapeño Cheese, **'85** 43
Guacamole, Margarita, **'97** 167
Heroes, Open-Faced Jalapeño, **'90** 144
Hominy, Jalapeño, **'82** 51
Jelly, Jalapeño, **'92** 230; **'96** 292
Jelly, Quick Jalapeño Pepper, **'96** 275
Loaf, Jalapeño-Cheese, **'84** 76
Muffins, Jalapeño-Corn, **'93** 164
Mustard, Jalapeño, **'93** 240; **'95** 312
Nachos, Tuna, **'96** 201
Nut Mix, Jalapeño, **'96** 27
Onion Rings, South-of-the-Border, **'96** 217
Pickled Jalapeño Peppers, **'93** 136
Pie, Jalapeño Cheese, **'96** 292
Pork, Jalapeño Grilled, **'99** 160
Pork Tenderloins, Pepper-Honey, **'98** 33
Potatoes, Jalapeño, **'84** 39
Potatoes, Jalapeño-Ham Stuffed, **'81** M61
Puffs, Cajun Hot, **'94** 277
Quesadillas, Bacon-Jalapeño-Tomato, **'95** 240
Quesadillas, Western, **'97** 65
Quiche, Cheesy Jalapeño, **'84** 31
Quiche, Jalapeño-Corn, **'85** 122
Quiche Squares, Cheesy Hot, **'79** 124
Rice, Hot Pepper, **'92** 310
Rice, Jalapeño, **'79** 43
Rice, Jalapeño Hot, **'80** 126
Rollups, Mexican, **'98** 134
Salad, Jalapeño Potato, **'97** 64
Salsa, Cherry, **'99** 156
Salsa, Double Chile, **'91** 182
Salsa, Hot, **'98** 135
Salsa Picante, **'84** 108
Salsa Picante, Homemade, **'81** 67
Salsa Verde, Roasted, **'96** 182
Salsa, Watermelon, **'98** 164
Sauce, Fried Green Tomatillos with Jalapeño Dipping, **'97** 143
Sauce, Hot Chile, **'92** 156
Sauce, Jalapeño, **'80** 193; **'93** 230
Sauce, Jalapeño-Cranberry, **'92** 310
Sauce, Jalapeño Tartar, **'96** 69; **'98** 129
Sauce, San Antonio Hot, **'84** 291
Sausage, Grilled Pork, Cheddar, and Jalapeño, **'98** 311
Sherbet, Jalapeño-Mint, **'98** 202
Spread, Jalapeño-Cheese, **'82** 248
Squares, Jalapeño Cheese, **'80** 195
Stuffed Jalapeño Peppers, **'96** 215
Stuffed Jalapeño Peppers, Fried, **'95** 22
Stuffed Jalapeños, **'98** 234
Stuffed Jalapeños, Fiery Fried, **'90** 118
Stuffed Jalapeños, Hot, **'99** 123
Stuffed Jalapeños, Shrimp-, **'88** 115
Tacos, Shrimp-and-Pepper Soft, **'95** 339
Vinegar, Southwest, **'94** 200

Ketchup, Jalapeño-Stuffed Burgers with Roasted Bell Pepper, **'97** 318
Lamb, Rosemary-Skewered, **'97** 190
Marinated Roasted Peppers, **'97** 123
Pasta with Peppers and Broccoli, **'91** 69
Pizza, Mexican Chicken, **'97** 321
Red
Bread, Roasted Red Bell Pepper, **'95** 241
Brie en Croûte, Stuffed, **'97** 162
Butter, Fillet of Beef with Red Pepper, **'96** 32
Butter, Roasted Red Bell Pepper, **'95** 242
Cheese, Grilled, **'97** 328
Crêpes, Goat Cheese-Filled Cornbread, **'98** 43
Crostini, Roasted Peppers-Feta Cheese, **'96** 87
Cucumber-and-Pepper Combo, **'88** 176
Cups, Hot Vegetable Pepper, **'88** M188
Curried Corn and Sweet Red Peppers, **'95** 47
Dip, Chickpea-and-Red Pepper, **'99** 138
Green Beans with Shallots and Red Bell Pepper, **'97** 251
Jam, Red Bell Pepper, **'95** 242
Jelly, Red Pepper, **'89** M156
Mayonnaise, Roasted Red Pepper, **'98** 144
Okra, Corn, and Peppers, **'87** M151
Peas and Peppers, Minted, **'90** M99
Peas and Peppers, Stir-Fried, **'87** 51
Pizza, Roasted Pepper, **'94** 218
Potatoes with Sweet Red Peppers, **'87** 192
Puree, Red Pepper, **'93** 275
Roasted Red Peppers and Pearl Onions, Green Beans with, **'93** 260
Rollups, Roasted Red Pepper, **'98** 285
Roll with Cilantro Hollandaise Sauce, Southwestern, **'99** 16
Round Steak, Red Pepper, **'88** 214
Salad, Broccoli and Red Pepper, **'83** 224
Salad, Roasted Red Pepper-and-Green Bean, **'99** 322
Salad, Roasted Red Pepper and Watercress, **'90** 55
Salad, Tuna-and-Red Pepper, **'93** 143
Salad with Avocado, Potato, **'98** 332
Sandwiches, Mozzarella-Pepper Bagel, **'98** 145
Sandwiches, Smoked Turkey-Roasted Pepper, **'94** 66
Sauce, Linguine with Red Pepper, **'93** 127
Sauce, Red Bell Pepper, **'99** 267
Sauce, Red or Green Pepper, **'91** 85
Sauce, Red Pepper, **'98** 322
Sauce, Red Pepper-Garlic, **'98** 140
Sauce, Roasted Red Pepper, **'98** 16
Sautéed Peppers and Mushrooms, Herb-Stuffed Chicken with, **'91** 26
Snow Peas and Red Pepper, Sesame, **'84** 175
Snow Peas with Red Pepper, **'90** 102
Soup, Chilled Sweet Red Pepper, **'93** 69
Soup, Cream of Roasted Sweet Red Pepper, **'95** 65
Soup, Red Bell Pepper, **'98** 104
Soup, Roasted Red Pepper, **'96** 245
Soup, Spicy Pepper, **'93** 98
Spread, Roasted Red Bell Pepper, **'97** 217
Squash-and-Pepper Toss, Crisp, **'87** M152
Vinaigrette, Roasted Bell Pepper, **'99** 70
Salad, Grilled Tomato, Bell Pepper, and Portobello, **'98** 211
Salad, Winter Cabbage, **'98** 284
Salsa, Banana, **'96** 85
Salsa, Caribbean, **'96** 70
Salsa, Cha-Cha, **'97** 160
Salsa, Cherry, **'99** 156
Salsa, Fresh Tomatillo, **'97** 143

Salsa, Roasted, '95 130
Sandwich, Giant Ham-and-Pepper, '96 74
Sauce, Creamy Roasted Pepper, '96 183
Scallops and Angel Hair Pasta, '99 176
Shrimp, Charleston Harbor Pickled, '99 275
Shrimp, Marinated, '98 317
Soup, Mardi Gras, '96 56
Soup, Roasted Yellow Bell Pepper, '96 56
Stuffed Peppers, Barbecued Shrimp and
    Cornbread-, '97 261
Stuffed Peppers, Carrot-and-Cabbage, '99 63
Stuffed Peppers, Spicy, '98 243
Sweet
    Chicken Breasts with Curried Peppers,
      '90 227
    Chicken Sauté, Sweet Pepper-, '89 104
    Chicken Scaloppine with Peppers, '85 78
    Chicken, Sicilian, '97 142
    Chowder, Bell Pepper-Cheese, '95 240
    Flank Steak with Sweet Peppers, Grilled,
      '90 138
    Green Beans and Pepper Strips, '86 170
    Kabobs, Pretty Pepper, '90 166
    Kabobs, Summery Squash-and-Pepper,
      '95 193
    Marinated Roasted Peppers, '92 176
    Medley, Cabbage-Onion-Sweet Pepper,
      '96 252; '97 28
    Medley, Rainbow Pepper, '91 126
    Parmesan Pepper Toss, '93 208
    Pasta, Peppery, '94 164
    Pesto, Pepper, '89 103; '90 97
    Relish, Confetti Pepper, '91 195
    Relish, Sweet Pepper, '95 104
    Roasted Bell Peppers in Olive Oil, '95 242
    Roasted Peppers, Marinated, '87 90
    Roasted Peppers with Balsamic Vinaigrette,
      '94 128
    Salad, Chilled Turkey-and-Pepper Stir-Fry,
      '88 140
    Salad, Mixed Pepper, '89 103
    Salad, Mushroom-and-Pepper, '86 68
    Salad, Three-Pepper, '91 162
    Salsa, Mixed Pepper, '91 181
    Salsa, Yellowfin Tuna with Corn, Pepper, and
      Tomato, '94 164
    Sausage and Peppers, '95 165
    Sausage, Sweet Peppery, '95 69
    Sautéed Sweet Peppers, '89 102
    Sauté, Julienne Pepper, '89 104
    Soup, Bell Pepper, '89 103
    Soup, Roasted Pepper-and-Chicken, '90 58
    Soup, Sweet Pepper, '93 277
    Spread, Roasted Pepper, '94 123
    Stuffed with Shrimp-and-Orzo Salad, Peppers,
      '91 203
    Sugar Snaps and Peppers, '93 139
    Tacos, Grilled Pepper, '95 340
    Topping, Rainbow Pepper, '90 117
Terrine with Tomato-Basil Vinaigrette, Blue
    Cheese, '99 288
Turkey and Peppers in Cornbread Crust,
    '95 312
Yellow Pepper Sauce, Poached Salmon with,
    '98 230
PERSIMMONS
Bread, Persimmon, '80 228
Bread, Persimmon Date-Nut, '82 218
Cake, Persimmon, '79 205
Cookies, Persimmon, '96 242
Cookies, Persimmon-Raisin, '85 232
Pie, Persimmon, '79 206
Pudding, Persimmon, '79 206
Salad, Persimmon Fruit, '79 206

PESTOS. *See also* **RELISHES, SALSAS,
    SAUCES, TOPPINGS.**
    Bow-Tie Pesto, '94 231
    Butter, Pesto, '97 307
    Cilantro-Black Walnut Pesto, Littleneck Clams
      with, '97 164
    Cilantro Pesto, '98 145
    Dip, Pesto, '95 93; '97 226
    Fresh Pesto, '86 150
    Garlic Pesto, '84 108
    Nuts, Pesto-Spiced, '95 173
    Pasta, Asian Pesto, '95 189
    Pasta, Pesto and, '92 98
    Peanut Pesto, Thai, '98 145
    Pepper Pesto, '89 103; '90 97
    Pesto, '80 242; '96 207
    Pizza, Nutty Pesto, '97 267
    Primavera, Pesto, '96 170
    Roasted Garlic-Basil Pesto, '98 145
    Roasted Garlic-Rosemary Pesto, '97 46
    Ruth's Pesto, '96 170
    Sage Pesto, '97 22
    Sauce, Pasta with Pesto-Clam, '98 17
    Sauce, Pesto, '89 280; '91 94; '95 267
    Sauce, Racy Pesto, '97 67
    Sauce, Walnut-Parmesan Pesto, '96 251;
      '97 104
    Spinach-Peanut Pesto and Pasta, '93 212
    Spinach Pesto-Pasta, '91 314
    Spinach Pesto Sauce, '93 59
    Thyme Pesto, Sirloin Steaks with, '97 182
    Tomatoes Pesto, '86 150
    Tomato Pesto, Dried, '90 204; '94 249
PETITS FOURS. *See* **CAKES/Petits Fours.**
PHEASANT. *See* **GAME.**
PICANTE SAUCE. *See* **SALSAS, SAUCES.**
PICKLES
    Asparagus, Pickled, '83 46
    Beet Pickles, '81 210
    Beets, Easy Pickled, '80 137
    Beets, Pickled, '81 216; '97 229
    Broccoli, Pickled, '81 308
    Cantaloupe, Sweet Pickled, '89 197
    Carrots, Pickled, '93 12
    Chayote Squash Pickles, '89 197
    Cucumber Chips, '85 176
    Cucumber Pickles, Freezer, '99 87
    Cucumber Pickles, Sour, '85 176
    Cucumber Rounds, Easy Pickled, '90 143
    Cucumber Sandwich Pickles, '81 174
    Dill Pickles, '81 174
    Dill Pickles, Fried, '84 206
    Dills, Lazy Wife, '87 149
    Eggs, Beet Pickled, '84 287
    Eggs, Spiced Pickled, '84 288
    Figs, Pickled, '79 140
    Fire-and-Ice Pickles, '94 316
    Green Tomato Pickles, '87 134
    Icicle Pickles, Sweet, '85 176
    Jalapeño Peppers, Pickled, '93 136
    Lime Pickles, '96 206
    Mixed Pickles, '81 174
    Okra Dills, '97 157
    Okra Pickles, '81 173
    Onion Rings, Pickled Refrigerator, '84 265
    Onions, Pickled Cocktail, '89 197
    Peaches, Perfect Pickled, '85 178
    Peach Pickles, '85 177; '99 170
    Pear Pickles, Mustard, '79 196
    Pineapple, Pickled, '79 24
    Problem Chart, Pickle, '85 176
    Squash Pickles, '81 174; '87 150; '97 119;
      '99 170
    Sweet Pickles, Quick, '87 149

Watermelon Rind Pickles, '81 174; '84 106;
    '98 164
Yellow Squash, Pickled, '93 136
Zucchini, Dilled Fresh, '81 174
PIES, PUFFS, AND PASTRIES
Almond Pie, Toasted, '86 163
Ambrosia Pie, '79 284
Angel Pie, '79 123; '80 238
Apple. *See also* **PIES, PUFFS, AND
    PASTRIES/Cobblers, Crisps, and
    Crumbles; Pastries; Tarts; Turnovers.**
    Amandine Pie, Apple-, '89 215
    American Apple Pie, '91 197
    Applesauce Pie, '98 259; '99 26
    Autumn Apple Pie, '79 205
    Berry-Apple Pie, '88 251
    Blackberry-Apple Pie, '87 130
    Bourbon Pie, Apple-, '95 302
    Brandy-Apple Pie, '86 301
    Brandy Raisin-Apple Pie, '83 192
    Buttermilk Custard Pie, Warm Apple-, '99 98
    Cake, Apple Pie, '82 226
    Chess Pie, Apple-Lemon, '86 220
    Cider Pie, Apple, '84 227
    Cinnamon Crème, Apple Pie with Warm,
      '99 337
    Cinnamon Sauce, Apple Pie with Hot,
      '88 210
    Covered Apple Cake, '89 317
    Cran-Apple Pie, '92 304
    Cranberry-Apple Holiday Pie, '81 M269
    Cranberry-Apple Pie, '79 264
    Cranberry-Apple-Raisin Pie, '98 270
    Cranberry Pie, Apple-, '97 276; '99 M269
    Cream Cheese Pie, Apple-, '81 247
    Custard Pie, Apple, '88 236
    Dutch Apple Pie, '81 105; '82 273
    Easy-Crust Apple Pie, '87 11
    Fresh Apple Pie, '84 178
    Fried Apple Pies, '81 217; '86 302;
      '88 112, 225; '94 61
    Grandmother's Apple Pie, '87 212
    Grated Apple Pie, '83 304
    Holiday Apple Pie, '87 260
    Lemon-Apple Pie, Tart, '80 100
    Maple Pie, Apple-, '97 276
    Mexican Apple Pie, '94 97
    Mincemeat Pie, Apple-, '85 316
    No-Crust Apple Pie, '88 204
    Old-Fashioned Apple Pie, '82 M299; '88 94
    Pear-Apple Pie, Natural, '88 226
    Pear Pie, Apple-, '83 249
    Pear Pull-Up Pie, Apple-, '98 259
    Pineapple Pie, Apple-, '97 276
    Praline-Apple Pie, '99 331
    Raisin Brandy Pie, Apple-, '89 58
    Red Apple Pie, '79 282
    Upside-Down Southern Apple Pie, '88 226
Apricot Fried Pies, '86 269
Apricot Hand Pies, Dried, '98 259
Apricot Pies, Fried, '95 215
Apricot Pies, Special, '94 60
Apricot Pie, Yogurt-, '85 132
Apricot Surprise Pie, '88 99
Banana Cream Pie, '84 48; '87 207
Banana Cream Pie, Hawaiian, '90 105
Banana Pie with Hot Buttered Rum Sauce,
    '88 204
Bavarian Cream Pie, '79 281
Blackberry Cream Pie, '81 132
Blackberry Pie, '84 141; '86 152
Blackberry Pie, Creamy, '88 179
Black Bottom Pie, Weidmann's, '95 118
Black Walnut Pie, '97 275; '98 35

PIES, PUFFS, AND PASTRIES
(continued)

Blueberry. *See also* **PIES, PUFFS, AND PASTRIES/Cobblers, Crisps, and Crumbles.**
Banana Pie, Blueberry-, '93 115
Chilled Blueberry Pie, '89 136
Cream Cheese Pie, Blueberry-, '88 154
Cream Pie, Blueberry, '84 142
Cream Pie, Fresh Blueberry, '80 144
Fresh Blueberry Pie, '83 183; '85 152
Kuchen, Blueberry, '80 143
Old-Fashioned Blueberry Pie, '89 136
Peach Pie, Blueberry-, '94 158
Red, White, and Blueberry Pie, '98 162
Sour Cream Pie, Blueberry-, '83 183
Spicy Blueberry Pie, '96 147
Streusel Pie, Fresh Blueberry, '89 137
Boston Cream Pie, '83 220
Bourbon Pie, Kentucky, '84 87
Boysenberry Pie, '82 133
Brownie Pie, Crustless, '82 33
Bumbleberry Pie, '97 163
Buttermilk Chess Pie, '92 214
Buttermilk-Lemon Cream Pie, '88 99
Buttermilk Lemon Pie, '81 120; '82 23
Buttermilk-Lemon Pie, '88 297
Buttermilk Pie, '82 53; '83 158; '88 93; '92 95; '98 290
Buttermilk Pie, Old-Fashioned, '79 72
Butterscotch Cream Pie, '84 48; '87 207
Butterscotch Meringue Pie, '83 158
Butterscotch Pie, '97 212
Cantaloupe Cream Pie, '79 177
Cantaloupe Meringue Pie, '88 182
Cantaloupe Pie, '86 163
Caramel-Banana Pie, '86 M165
Caramel Banana Pie, Luscious, '79 115
Caramel Meringue Pie, '97 109
Caramel-Nut Crunch Pie, '94 244
Caramel-Peanut Pie, '86 259
Caramel Pie, '96 72
Caramel Pie, Burnt, '82 53
Caviar Pie, '79 154
Cheese. *See also* **PIES, PUFFS, AND PASTRIES/Crusts, Pastries, Tarts, Turnovers, Vegetables.**
Apple-Cream Cheese Pie, '81 247
Blueberry-Cream Cheese Pie, '88 154
Chocolate-Cream Cheese Pie, '80 69
Chocolate Cream Cheese Pie, '92 240
Cottage Cheese Pie, '82 85
Cream Puffs with Chicken Salad, Cheesy, '86 260
Fruited Cheese Pie, '92 228
Hors d'Oeuvre Pie, Cheesy, '88 91
Lemon Cheese Pie, '81 136; '82 146
Lemon-Cottage Cheese Pie, '79 44
Lemon Cottage Cheese Pie, '81 143
Make-Ahead Cheesecake Pie, '81 233
Mincemeat-Cheese Pie, '80 253
Phyllo Cheesecakes, Little, '87 275
Yogurt-Cheese Pie, '82 121
Cherry-Berry Pie, '92 316
Cherry Confetti Pie, No-Bake, '93 114
Cherry Cream Pie with Almond Pastry, '92 30
Cherry Pie, Coconut Crumb, '92 30
Cherry Pie, Easy, '82 299
Cherry Pie, Fresh, '88 178
Cherry Pie, Lemony, '92 30
Cherry Pie, Prize-Winning, '82 57
Cherry Pie, Red, '83 192
Cherry Pie, Scrumptious, '83 250

Chess Pie, Brown Sugar, '86 220
Chess Pie, Old-Fashioned, '86 220
Chocolate. *See also* **PIES, PUFFS, AND PASTRIES/Crusts, Ice Cream, Pastries, Tarts.**
Almond Pie, Creamy Chocolate-, '85 102
Amandine, Chocolate Pie, '83 300
Amaretto Mousse Pie, Chocolate-, '80 180; '81 30
Banana-Pecan Cream Pie, Chocolate-, '94 210
Bavarian Pie, Chocolate, '89 326
Berry Pie, Heavenly Chocolate-, '85 102
Best-Ever Chocolate Pie, '88 M45
Black Bottom Pie, '82 53
Black-Bottom Pie, '98 161
Bourbon Pie, Chocolate, '88 99
Cake, Chocolate Pastry, '91 196
Chess Pie, Chocolate, '81 161; '86 220; '92 13
Chilled Chocolate Pie, '88 99
Chip Pie, Chocolate, '85 114
Coffee Cream Pie, '94 209
Cream Cheese Pie, Chocolate-, '80 69
Cream Cheese Pie, Chocolate, '92 240
Cream Pie, Chocolate, '83 192; '84 49; '87 208; '94 208
Creamy Chocolate Pie, '85 298; '86 119
Double Chocolate Pie, '82 M282
Easy Chocolate Pie, '83 158
Fox Hunter's Pie, '97 109
French Silk Pie, '80 247
Frozen Chocolate Brownie Pie, '96 57
Frozen Chocolate-Macadamia Nut Pie, '96 254
Frozen Chocolate Pie, '80 154
Frozen Chocolate Pie with Pecan Crust, '89 291; '98 180
Fudge Pie, '87 168; '89 252
Fudge Pie, Chocolate, '98 336
Fudge Pie, Sweetheart, '86 316; '90 313
German Chocolate Pie, '93 129
Heaven, Chocolate, '98 323
Heavenly Chocolate Pie, '87 260
Meringue Pie, Chocolate, '80 238; '82 206; '83 158; '92 216
Meringue Pie, Chocolate-Filled, '86 121
Microwave Chocolate Pie, '90 M15
Mint Pie, Brownie-, '97 303
Mocha Crunch Pie, Chocolate-, '81 136
Mocha Pie, '94 168
Mousse Pie, Chocolate, '81 136
Mud Pie, Decadent, '89 252
Mud Pie, Mississippi, '89 26
Mud Pie, Tipsy, '80 255; '97 251
Peanut Butter Pie, Chocolate-, '85 91
Peanut Butter Swirl Pie, Chocolate-, '87 262
Pecan Chess Pie, Chocolate-, '93 251
Pecan Pie, Bourbon-Chocolate, '98 258
Pecan Pie, Choco, '82 86
Pecan Pie, Chocolate, '80 237; '83 12; '90 184
Pecan Pie, Chocolate-, '91 272
Pecan Pie, Turtle, '93 250
Praline Pie, Chocolate-, '86 259
Silk Pie, Chocolate, '88 67
Strawberry-Chocolate Truffle Pie, '89 112
Whipped Cream Pie, Chocolate, '79 124
White Chocolate-Banana Cream Pie, '94 314
Christmas Pie, White, '88 281; '93 289
Cobblers, Crisps, and Crumbles
à la Mode, Apple Cobbler, '97 16
Apple Cobbler, Country, '99 255
Apple Cobbler, Easy, '83 174
Apple Cobbler for Two, '85 261
Apple Cobbler, New-Fashioned, '91 221
Apple Crisp, '84 122; '98 215
Apple Crisp, Tart, '92 226

Apple-Pecan Cobbler, '84 M198
Apple Walnut Cobbler, '79 154
Apple-Walnut Cobbler, '81 248
Apricot Cobbler with Custard Sauce, '97 16
Apricot Cobble Up, '82 138
Berry-Cherry Cobbler, '83 270
Berry Crisp, '83 130
Blackberry-Almond Cobbler, '81 132
Blackberry Cobbler, '82 139; '83 175; '99 131
Blackberry Cobbler, Deep-Dish, '80 186
Blackberry Cobbler, Deluxe, '81 132
Blackberry Cobbler, Juicy, '89 137
Blackberry Cobbler, New-Fashioned, '87 164
Blackberry Cobbler, Southern, '81 132
Blueberry Buckle, '85 30
Blueberry Cobbler, '83 175
Blueberry Cobbler, Easy, '83 183
Blueberry Cobbler, Fresh, '80 144
Blueberry Cobbler, Peachy, '80 143
Blueberry Cobbler, Warm, '98 153
Blueberry Crisp, '84 177
Blueberry Crunch, Fresh, '82 143
Blueberry, Huckle-Buckle, '86 151
Blueberry-Peach Cobbler, No-Dough, '86 177
Blueberry Pinwheel Cobbler, '87 140
Blueberry Slump, Quick, '91 20
Blueberry Upside-Down Cobbler, '96 146
Boysenberry Cobbler, '82 133
Cherry Cobbler, '82 91, 139; '99 156
Cherry Cobbler, Colossal, '89 137
Cherry Cobbler, Fresh, '84 178
Cherry Crisp, '91 20
Cherry Slump, '83 139
Cranberry-and-Apple Cobbler, '84 306; '90 294
Cranberry-Apple Cobbler with Cinnamon Biscuits, '99 256
Cranberry Cobbler, '81 275
Cranberry Cobbler, Easy, '86 260
Cranberry Cobbler Roll, '80 288; '81 248
Cranberry-Peach Cobbler, '92 322
Cranberry-Pear Crisp, '83 207; '97 16
Fig Cobbler, '79 140
Fig Cobbler, Cajun, '94 196
Fig Cobbler, Super, '86 206
Fruit Cobbler, '99 33
Fruit Cobbler, Quick, '91 20
Grenadine-Peach Cobbler, '85 178
Lemon-Blackberry Crisp, '98 171
Muscadine Cobbler, '98 221
Peach-Apricot Cobbler, '99 255
Peach-Caramel Cobbler, '86 300; '87 178
Peach Cobbler, '83 175; '84 178; '90 219; '95 264
Peach Cobbler, Easy, '97 137; '99 206
Peach Cobbler, Fresh, '82 139; '89 154
(Peach Cobbler), I Fall to Peaches, '96 159
Peach Cobbler, Lattice-Topped, '79 154
Peach Cobbler, Old-Fashioned, '82 170
Peach Cobbler, Quick, '79 215; '81 142
Peach Cobbler, Spicy, '85 178
Peach Cobbler Supreme, '81 184; '90 313
Peach Cobbler with Praline Biscuits, '92 180
Peach Crinkle, '91 20
Peach Crisp, '83 113; '92 13; '93 134
Peach Crumble, Easy, '83 116
Pear Cobbler, Best Ever, '82 194
Pear Crumble, '85 221
Pineapple-Apple Betty, '85 46
Plum Brown Betty, Bourbon-, '97 177
Plum Cobbler, '99 254
Plum Cobbler, Crunchy, '88 152
Raspberry-Cherry Cobbler, '93 230
Strawberry Cobbler, Fresh, '96 84
Strawberry-Rhubarb Cobbler, '88 93
Strawberry-Rhubarb Cobbler, Rosy, '79 154

Strawberry-Rhubarb Crisp, '95 119
Sweet Potato Cobbler, '99 M255
Coconut
Blender Coconut Pie, '84 236
Buttermilk-Coconut Pie, '94 246
Caramel Pies, Coconut-, '87 260
Cherry Pie, Coconut Crumb, '92 30
Chess Pie, Coconut, '86 220
Chess Pie, Coconut-Orange, '89 169
Chess Pie, Coconut-Pecan, '81 248
Cloud, Coconut, '80 70
Coconut Pie, '93 115
Cream Pie, Coconut, '80 238; '81 136; '82 85;
'84 49; '87 207; '89 236; '90 312; '98 161
Cream Pie, Fresh Coconut, '80 289
Cream Pie, Surprise Coconut, '92 43
Cream Tarts with Macadamia Nut Crusts,
Coconut, '97 62
Crunch Pie, Coconut, '90 105
Crust, Coconut, '89 160
Custard Pie, Coconut, '82 33
French Coconut Pie, '90 162
Macadamia Nut Pie, Coconut-, '97 110
Macaroon Pie, Coconut, '88 204
Magic Coconut Pie, '79 53
Mock Coconut Pie, '86 200
Orange-Coconut Cream Pie, '94 208
Orange-Coconut Pie, '90 90
Pecan Pie, Coconut, '81 161
Pineapple Pie, Coconut-, '84 256
Puffs, Coconut, '87 277
Quick Coconut Pie, '83 115
Toasted Coconut Pie, '90 105
Coffee Cream Pie, '94 209
Coffee Pie, '96 148
Cracker Pie, '79 113
Cranberry-Cherry Pie, Tart, '87 299
Cranberry Freezer Pie, Festive, '84 306
Cranberry Pie, Frosty, '79 249
Cranberry Pie, Nutty, '82 M298
Cranberry Pie, Walnut-, '87 259
Cranberry-Raisin Pie, '80 283; '85 316
Cranberry Streusel Pie, '98 258
Cran-Raspberry Pie, '87 244
Cream Pie, Texas, '81 181
Crème de Menthe Pie, Quick, '88 127
Crusts. See also **PIES, PUFFS, AND**
PASTRIES/Pastries.
Black Iron Skillet Piecrust, Universal, '99 33
Brown Sugar Crust, '92 118
Butter Crust, '90 173
Cereal Piecrust, Crisp, '82 209; '83 100
Cheese Crust, '80 286; '86 264
Chocolate-Coconut Crust, '87 261
Chocolate-Coconut Pie Shell, '82 210; '83 100
Chocolate Crumb Crust, '87 261
Chocolate Crust, '87 264; '90 M15
Chocolate Cups, '80 207
Chocolate-Macadamia Crumb Crust, '96 254
Chocolate Wafer Crust, '89 42, 93
Cinnamon Meringue Shell, '82 263
Coconut Crust, '89 160
Cookie Crust, Spicy, '88 7
Cracker Crust, '88 97
Crumb Crust, Cheesy, '88 86
Crust, '89 272
Decorating Pie Crusts, '83 248
Deluxe Piecrust, '79 79
Gingersnap Crumb Crust, '96 279
Ginger Snap Crust, '88 138
Gingersnap Crust, '89 93; '90 296; '98 161
Graham Cracker Crust, '79 45; '86 32;
'87 139, 243; '88 M45, 55, 67; '89 93, 326;
'90 296; '91 197, M234, 308; '94 310

Graham Cracker Crust, Microwaved, '82 M141
Graham Cracker Crust, Peanut-, '79 50
Graham Cracker Crusts, '97 162
Graham Crust, Peanut-, '99 49
Italian Sweet Crust, Plum Pie with, '79 162
Lattice Crust, '90 294
Macadamia Nut Crusts, Coconut Cream Tarts
with, '97 62
Nut Crust, Spiced, '87 295
Nutty Oat Crust, '89 251
Oatmeal Piecrust, '79 79
Parmesan Crust, '94 304
Pecan Crust, '86 317; '89 291; '98 180
Perfect Piecrust, Making, '82 234
Pizza Crust, '80 233; '83 226; '86 77
Pizza Crust, Crispy, '87 181
Rice-Cheese Shell, '82 49
Rice Crust, Crispy, '84 43
Spice Crust, '82 298
Sugar Cookie Crust, '93 131
Tart Crust, '84 178; '90 58; '97 86
Vanilla Wafer Crust, '98 216
Whole Wheat Crust, '82 298
Custard Pie, Egg, '99 82
Custard Pie, Old-Fashioned Egg, '82 261
Custard Pie, Perfect, '82 92
Custard Pie, Quick 'n' Easy, '96 28
Daiquiri Pie, '79 68
Daiquiri Pie, Daring, '92 191
Dream Pie, '80 90
Eggnog Chiffon Pie, '86 281
Eggnog Pie, '80 254; '83 205; '86 317; '87 295
Eggnog Pie, Fluffy, '81 M269
Empanadas de Calabaza (Pumpkin Empanadas),
'94 28
Fried Pies, '96 109
Fried Pies, Delicious, '83 84
Fried Pies with Fruit Salsa, Lone Star, '97 124
Fruitcake Pie, '80 237
Fruit Pie, Crispy-Crust, '88 68
Fruit Pie, Dried, '83 249
Fruit Pie, Japanese, '80 238
Fruit Pies, Baked, '84 7
Grapefruit Meringue Pie, '96 56
Grape Juice Pie, '79 123
Grape Pie, '85 212
Grasshopper Freeze, Creamy, '81 180
Grasshopper Pie, '83 145
Ice Cream
Absolutely Divine Ice Cream Pie, '82 181
Caramel Ice Cream Pie, '82 181
Carrot Ice Cream Pie, '86 200
Chocolate-Ice Cream Pie, '87 224
Chocolate Ice Cream Pie, '91 56
Chocolate-Mint Ice Cream Pie, '81 144
Chocolate-Peanut Butter Ice Cream Pie,
'98 244
Coffee Ice Cream Pie, '79 231
Delight, Ice Cream, '80 69
Double-Delight Ice Cream Pie, '89 72
Heavenly Ice Cream Pie, '82 181
Kona Ice Cream Pie, '83 189
Lemon Ice Cream Pie, '80 70
Lemony Ice Cream Pie, '99 207
Meringue-Pecan Crust, Ice Cream Pie with,
'88 127
Mincemeat Ice Cream Pie, '99 285
Mint Ice Cream Pie, Triple, '98 217
Nutty Ice Cream Pie, '91 180
Peanutty Ice Cream Pie, '82 56
Peppermint Candy-Ice Cream Pie, '87 260
Pumpkin Ice Cream Pie, '81 272
Pumpkin-Ice Cream Pie, '87 243
Rum-Fruit Sauce, Ice Cream Pie with, '84 312

Spectacular, Ice-Cream Pie, '90 314
Sundae Pie, Ice Cream, '94 244
Kahlúa Pie, '83 191
Key Lime Pie, '91 42; '96 171
Key Lime Pie, Manny and Isa's, '95 118
Key Lime Pies, '95 86; '97 162
Key Lime Pie with Minted Tropical Salsa, '99 333
Lemon
Aunt Kitty's Lemon Pie, '98 275
Blackberry Crisp, Lemon-, '98 171
Buttermilk-Lemon Cream Pie, '88 99
Buttermilk Lemon Pie, '81 120; '82 23
Buttermilk-Lemon Pie, '88 297
Buttermilk Pie, Lemon-, '91 272
Cheese Pie, Lemon, '81 136; '82 146
Cherry Pie, Lemony, '92 30
Chess Pie, Apple-Lemon, '86 220
Chess Pie, Lemon, '79 32; '82 196
Cottage Cheese Pie, Lemon-, '79 44
Cottage Cheese Pie, Lemon, '81 143
Cream Pie, Frozen Lemon, '82 86
Cream Puffs, Lemon, '93 254
Fluff Pie, Lemon, '92 342; '93 46
Frozen Lemonade Pie, '92 101
Heavenly Pie, '83 158
Ice Cream Pie, Lemon, '80 70
Lemonade Pie, '91 42
Magnolia Pie, '94 210
Meringue Pie, Best-Ever Lemon, '94 208
Meringue Pie, Deluxe Lemon, '81 172; '90 313
Meringue Pie, Lemon, '85 M112; '86 130
Orange Pie, Lemon-, '85 172
Parfait Pie, Lemon, '94 310
Pastry Shell, Lemon in, '84 137
Pecan Pie, Lemon-, '93 251
Slice of Lemon Pie, '84 23
Sour Cream Pie, Lemon-, '82 169
Sponge Pie, Lemon, '83 192
Strawberry Pie, Lemon-, '88 127
Tart Lemon-Apple Pie, '80 100
Tart Lemon Pie, '91 275
Twirl Pie, Lemon, '84 94
Whipped Lemon Pie, '79 124
Lime Chiffon Pie, '86 130
Lime Fluff Pie, '84 43
Lime Party Pies, '92 65
Macadamia Pie, '80 238
Main Dish. See also **PIES, PUFFS, AND**
PASTRIES/Tarts, Turnovers.
Artichoke Pie, '79 25
Beef Pies, Carry-Along, '80 224; '81 56
Beef Pies, Fried, '96 108
Beef Pot Pie, Oriental, '92 253
Beef Pot Pies with Yorkshire Pudding
Topping, '93 45
Beef Roast Pot Pie, '88 296
Bouchées aux Fruits de Mer, '98 267
Breakfast Pie, '86 242
Breakfast Pie, Country, '93 M328
Broccoli-and-Turkey Pasta Pie, '88 269
Broccoli-Beef Pie, '83 196
Burrito Pie, Mexican, '87 287
Calzones, All-Star Pizza, '95 308
Calzones, Easy, '99 133
Cheese-Beef Pie, '85 33
Cheeseburger Pie, '89 121
Cheese Pie, Mexican, '82 9; '83 69
Chicken Breasts in Phyllo Pastry, '91 105
Chicken Breasts Wellington, '84 22
Chicken, Company Creamed, '82 84
Chicken Dumpling Pie, '95 245; '96 55
Chicken in Pastry, '86 122
Chicken in Phyllo, '87 286
Chicken in Puff Pastry, Spinach-Stuffed, '92 125

PIES, PUFFS, AND PASTRIES, Main Dish
(continued)

Chicken Phyllo Pie, Greek, '92 328
Chicken Pie, '81 281; '82 31
Chicken Pie, Biscuit-Topped, '86 157, 264
Chicken Pie, Cheesy Mexican, '82 142
Chicken Pie, Deluxe, '88 298
Chicken Pie, Double-Crust, '87 111
Chicken Pie, Egg-Stra Special, '86 264
Chicken Pie, Nana's, '90 25
Chicken Pie, Savory Southern, '90 24
Chicken Pot Pie, '81 210; '82 114; '84 21;
  '94 21; '95 54, 256; '96 75
Chicken Pot Pie, Double-Crust, '90 220
Chicken Pot Pie, Easy, '83 156; '89 218
Chicken Pot Pie, Old-Fashioned, '92 271
Chicken Pot Pie, Thick 'n' Crusty, '87 267;
  '88 102; '89 67
Chicken Pot Pie with Cheese Crust, '86 264
Chicken Salad in Cream Puff Bowl, '86 232
Chicken-Vegetable Pot Pie, '81 281; '82 30
Chili-Tamale Pie, '82 9; '83 68
Cornbread-Sausage-Apple Pie, '87 171
Cornbread-Tamale Pie, '92 123
Corn Burger Pie, '83 156
Country Pie, '83 155
Enchilada Pie, '83 155
Fish in a Crust, '84 294
Game Pot Pie with Parmesan Crust, '94 304
Green Chile-Cheese Pie, '84 234
Grits-and-Ham Pie, Crustless, '86 103
Grits Fiesta Pie, '92 43
Ham-and-Cheese Pie, '95 256; '96 75
Hamburger Pie, '81 92; '84 13
Ham Pie, Golden, '87 78
Ham Pie with Cheese Crust, '80 286
Ham Pot Pie, '90 25
Ham Towers, Cheesy, '82 77
Hot Dog Deluxe, '97 140
Lamb Pie, '90 26
Meat-and-Potato Pie, '84 23
Meat Loaf in a Wrap, '89 122
Meat Pie, Continental, '95 256; '96 75
Meat Pie, Italian, '89 109
Meat Pie, Mexicali, '81 194
Meat Pie, Old-Fashioned, '82 110
Meat Pie, Reuben, '80 189
Meat Pies, Cornish, '84 23
Meat Pies, Natchitoches, '84 21; '91 241
Oyster Pie, Creole, '84 214
Pancake, Supper, '86 242
Pea Flips, '80 7
Pineapple-Chicken Salad Pie, '80 138
Sausage-and-Cornbread Pie, '90 25
Sausage Log, Phyllo, '84 294
Sausage Pizza Pie, Link-, '85 33
Seafood Pie, Hot, '80 32
Shepherd Pie, '83 116
Shepherd's Pie, '92 168
Shrimp Puffs, Luncheon, '85 72
Sombrero Pie, '81 140
Spaghetti-Ham Pie, '93 19
Spaghetti Pie, '81 32
Spaghetti Pie, Weeknight, '95 312
Spanakopita, '86 58
Spinach-Pasta Pie, '85 286
Taco Pie, '88 256
Taco Pie, Crescent, '80 80
Taco Pie, Double-Crust, '88 272; '89 180
Taco Pies, Individual, '82 M282
Torta Mexican Style, '89 122
Tortilla Pie, '85 M211; '96 135

Tortilla Pie, Montezuma, '83 199
Tumbleweed Pie, '98 205
Tuna Pie with Cheese Roll Crust, '80 286
Tuna-Rice Pie, '84 123
Turkey-and-Dressing Pie, '84 326
Turkey-and-Oyster Pie, '82 267
Turkey-Cheese Pie, '88 264
Turkey Pie, '80 285
Turkey Pie, Crumb-Crust Curried, '86 265
Turkey Pie, Golden, '79 253
Turkey Pie, Lattice-Topped, '81 277; '82 7
Turkey Pie, Potato-Topped, '86 265
Turkey Pot Pie, '86 265; '90 24; '93 45
Turkey Pot Pie with Biscuit Crust, '98 296
Vegetable-Beef Pies, '80 286
Zucchini-Ham-Cheese Pie, '80 272
Mango-Ginger Pie, '88 138
Mango Pie, Green, '79 137
Mincemeat Chiffon Pie, '79 245
Mincemeat-Peach Pie, '80 295; '81 188
Mincemeat Pie, Holiday, '80 282; '83 250; '87 213
Mincemeat Pie, Kentucky, '95 302
Mincemeat Pie, Pear, '84 264; '88 226
Mince Pie, Spirited, '92 316
Mint Pie, Candy-Crust, '92 191
Mocha Meringue Pie, '80 242; '88 163
Molasses Pie, '86 20
Muscadine Pie, '82 202
Nesselrode Pie, Fluffy, '87 261
Orange Ambrosia Pie, '80 237
Orange Blossom Special, '79 48
Orange Chess Pie, '88 204
Orange Chiffon Pie, '87 260
Orange-Coconut Pie, '90 90
Orange Meringue Pie, '81 12, 309
Orange Pie, Florida, '91 43
Orange Pie, Frosty, '90 296
Papaya Pie, '86 53
Pastries. *See also* **PIES, PUFFS, AND**
  PASTRIES/Crusts.
Almond Combs, '84 136
Almond Pastry, '85 177; '89 317; '92 30
Apple Dumplings, Old-Fashioned, '84 226
Apple Flan, '81 309
Apple Foldovers, '84 136
Apple Roll, '82 178
Apple Rolls, Luscious, '88 225
Apple Squares, '92 311
Apple Strudel, '85 259; '89 267; '92 269; '97 238
Apricot Pastries, '83 297
Apricot Pinwheels, '87 276
Baklava, '96 20
Blackberry Roll, '82 178
Blueberry Kuchen, '80 143
Brie en Croûte, Stuffed, '97 162
Briwatts with Fruit, '98 211
Burritos, Hot Phyllo, '98 312
Butter Pastry, Golden, '84 22
Calzones, Spinach-and-Cheese, '95 310
Camembert Bars, '86 58
Cannoli, '80 58
Cheddar Cheese Pastry, '80 219; '82 194
Cheddar Pastry, '86 206
Cheese Danish, '97 31
Cheese Pastries, Date-Filled, '83 259
Cheese Pastry, '88 56
Cheese Puffs, '97 240
Cheese Puffs, Mexican, '87 8
Cheese Rolls, '80 286
Chicken, B'steeya with, '98 210
Chicken Puffs, Appetizer, '85 72
Chipped Beef Spread in Puff Pastry, '98 M335
Chocolate Pastry Shell, '87 262
Chocolate-Raspberry Bags, '95 97

Citrus Pastry, Hint-of-, '93 260
Coconut Puffs, '87 277
Cornmeal Pastry, '81 140
Cornmeal Pastry Cups, '90 69
Cornucopia, Pastry, '95 307
Cream Cheese Danish, '98 325
Cream Cheese Pastries, '80 250
Cream Cheese Pastry, '82 39; '86 24, 78;
  '89 136; '96 228, 264
Cream Cheese Pastry Shells, '86 13
Cream Cheese Pastry Shells, Miniature, '87 190
Cream Cheese Patty Shells, '81 266; '82 249
Cream Cheese Shells, '79 2
Cream Horns, '84 137
Cream Puff Pastry, '85 72; '96 191
Cream Puffs, '98 316
Cream Puffs, Captivating, '81 180
Cream Puff Tree, '96 310
Danish Pastry Puffs, '85 311
Double-Crust Pastry, '81 105; '82 85, M298;
  '83 248; '85 191; '87 299; '88 94, 178
Double-Crust Pastry, Flaky, '82 57
Éclairs, Chocolate, '96 191
Éclairs, Pistachio-Cream, '91 296
Éclairs with Pecan Sauce, '83 219
Empanadas, '92 156
Empanadas, Pumpkin, '82 223
Fig Snacks, Sliced, '86 206
Firecrackers, Texas, '95 96; '99 94
Flaky Pastry, '80 224; '81 56, 210; '83 156
Fruit Basket Strudel, '87 276
Fruit Puff, Giant, '85 72
Garnish, Pastry, '98 254
German Pastries, '86 78
Greek Olive Cups, '99 221
Guava Puffs, '92 247
Heart Tart Pastry, '87 14
Java Cream Puffs, '81 187
Lemon Cream Puffs, '93 254
Light Pastry, '92 95
Make-Ahead Pastry, '82 209; '83 100
Maple Cream Coffee Treat, '90 50
Mexican Fiesta Confection, '82 223
Microwave Pastry, Basic, '82 M142; '85 M113
Mix, Perfect Pastry, '81 142
Mocha Pastry Shell, '81 136
Mushroom-Almond Pastry Cups, '88 210
Napoleon, Giant Apple, '99 282
Napoleons, '84 138
Napoleons, Berry, '94 120
Napoleons, Blueberry, '96 147
Napoleons, Blueberry-Lemon, '94 122
Napoleons, Coffee, '95 276
Napoleons, Peanut Butter-and-Chocolate,
  '94 121
Napoleons, Strawberry, '81 126
Never Fail Pastry, '79 79
Orange Shortcake, Fresh, '80 100
Palmiers, '87 277
Papaya-Pineapple Roll, '94 18
Paste Pastry, Common, '94 17
Pastry, '82 85, 139, 259; '83 84, 91, 175;
  '84 21, 23; '86 24, 25, 242, 259, 303, 326;
  '87 212, 267; '88 103, 198, 225;
  '89 67, 137, 154, 214, 267; '91 23, 241;
  '92 84, 157; '98 272; '99 131
Pastry, Basic, '79 282; '81 M268; '82 114;
  '84 48; '89 215; '91 119; '94 210
Pâté Pastry, '86 65
Pear Dumplings, '97 210
Pears en Croûte, '93 210
Pecan Pastry Shell, '97 275; '98 36
Phyllo Baskets, Walnut-, '93 210
Phyllo Bowls, '95 58

Phyllo Cheesecakes, Little, '87 275
Phyllo-Cheese Triangles, '87 246
Phyllo, Goat Cheese Wrapped in, '99 43
Phyllo Nests, Nutty, '87 277
Phyllo Tartlet Shells, '95 216
Pineapple Phyllo Bundles, '87 277
Piroshki, '92 84
Plum Kuchen, '79 161
Praline Pastries, '89 318
Preserve-Filled Foldovers, '80 7
Processor Pastry, '87 67
Processor Pie Dough, Quick Food, '84 219
Profiteroles, '84 208
Profiteroles with Warm Cranberry Compote,
    Pumpkin-Spiced, '97 264
Puff Pastry, Basic, '84 135
Puff Pastry Baskets, '93 177
Puff Pastry Baskets, Tropical, '93 177
Puff Pastry Bowls, '95 58
Puff Pastry, Quick, '84 207
Puffs, Cocktail, '91 106
Puffs, Sweet, '89 91
Quiche Pastry, '80 M107
Quiche Pastry, Microwaved, '81 M74; '82 M122
Raisin Pastry Bites, '90 86
Raspberry-Nut Strudel, '83 304
Raspberry Party Puffs, '90 170
Roquefort Firecrackers, '97 19
Rugelach, '85 276
Samosas, '89 266
Savory Pastry, '90 24
Seasoned Pastry, '79 253
Sesame Pastry Shell, '82 67
Shell, Pastry, '84 31, 127; '87 262; '89 236;
    '93 289; '94 158
Shell, Perfect Pastry, '81 142
Shells, Cream Cheese Pastry Mini, '99 180
Shells, Pastry, '83 93
Shell, Water-Whipped Baked Pastry, '95 246
Shortcake Pastry, '80 100
Sopaipillas, '89 268
Spanakopita, '96 233
Spinach-and-Cheese Pastries, Greek, '96 76
Spinach-Artichoke-Tomato Puffs, '95 284
Spinach Strudels, '93 249
Strawberry Cream Puffs, '81 95
Strawberry-Lemon Cream Puffs, '87 75
Strudel, Autumn-Apple, '98 253
Strudel, Chicken-Goat Cheese, '98 28
Strudel, Crab-and-Mushroom, '98 28
Strudel, Fig, '98 253
Strudel, Meatless Mexican, '98 29
Strudel, Pear, '98 253
Strudel, Reuben, '98 28
Sugar Cookie Pastry, '91 119
Tart Pastry, '89 232; '90 92; '91 118
Tart Shell, '87 77; '88 20
Tart Shell, Chocolate, '99 315
Tart Shells, '82 304; '83 279; '85 300;
    '86 18, 105; '88 4; '90 84; '91 13
Tart Shells, Cheese, '88 88
Tart Shells, Cheese Pastry, '85 216
Tart Shells, Tea, '85 120
Timbale Shells, '82 108
Triple-Crust Pastry, '80 186
Turkey-Mushroom Pâté in Pastry, '92 327
Tutti-Frutti Cream Puffs, '79 231
Vegetable Oil Pastry, '91 204
Whole Wheat Pastry, '81 229
Peach. See also PIES, PUFFS, AND
    PASTRIES/Cobblers, Crisps, and
    Crumbles; Tarts.
Blackberry Pie, Peach-and-, '89 136
Blueberry-Peach Pie, '94 158

Chiffon Pie, Peach, '89 155
Cranberry Pie, Peach-, '83 249
Cream Pie, Dried Peach, '84 146
Cream Pie, Peaches-and-, '81 184
Filling, Fresh Peach Pie, '95 195
Fresh Peach Pie, '82 170; '95 195
Fresh Peach Pie, Elizabeth and Phoebe's,
    '96 119
Fried Peach Pies, '81 272
Fried Pies, Easy Peach, '85 178
Georgia Peach-and-Praline Pie, '98 196
Little Peach Pie, '86 303
Luscious Peach Pie, '81 136
Melba Pie, Peach, '98 216
Mincemeat-Peach Pie, '80 295; '81 188
Praline Pie, Peach, '89 136
Quick Peach Pie, '89 252
Rhubarb-Peach Pie, '86 140
Peanut Butter Cream Pie, '79 50; '88 65
Peanut Butter Meringue Pie, '84 30
Peanut Butter Pie, '85 275; '86 109; '89 252
Peanut Butter Pie, Fluffy, '94 246
Peanut-Raisin Pie, '79 85
Peanuts" Pie, "Working for, '93 115
Pear
    Backyard Pear Pie, '93 237
    Crumble Pie, Pear, '83 207
    Deep-Dish Pear Pie, '80 219
    Delicious Pear Pie, '88 226
    Double-Crust Pear Pie, '82 194
    Dumplings, Pear, '97 210
    en Croûte, Pears, '93 210
    French Pear Pie, '87 213
    Ginger-Pear Pie, '93 48
    Macadamia Pie, Pear-, '93 260
    Mincemeat Pie, Pear, '84 264; '88 226
    Mincemeat Pie, Pear, '98 258
    Mince Pie, Pear-, '81 271
    Praline Pie, Pear-, '97 192
    Streusel Pie, Pear, '83 234; '84 244; '97 109
    Tart, Pear, '82 304; '92 72
    Tart with White Caramel Sauce, Pear, '92 195
    Tennessee Pear Pie, '85 230
Pecan. See also PIES, PUFFS, AND
    PASTRIES/Crusts, Pastries, Tarts.
Bourbon-Chocolate Pecan Pie, '98 258
Bourbon Pecan Pie, '85 90
Bourbon-Pecan Pie, Frozen, '89 251
Bourbon-Pecan Pumpkin Pie, '87 264
Butter Pecan Pie Squares, '81 262
Caramel-Pecan Apple Pie, '85 247
Caramel-Pecan Pie, '88 282
Cherry-Pecan Pie, '92 30
Chocolate-Banana-Pecan Cream Pie, '94 210
Chocolate-Pecan Chess Pie, '93 251
Chocolate Pecan Pie, '80 237; '83 12; '90 184
Chocolate-Pecan Pie, '91 272
Choco-Pecan Pie, '82 86
Cinnamon-Almond-Pecan Pie, '98 89
Coconut-Pecan Chess Pie, '81 248
Coconut Pecan Pie, '81 161
Coffee Pecan Pie, '82 74
Cranberry-Pecan Pie, '92 316
Custard Pecan Pie, '87 184
Date-Pecan Pie, '80 15
Golden Pecan Pie, '81 266
Grandmother's Pecan Pie, '86 269
Holiday Pecan Pie, '81 296
Honey-Pecan Finger Pies, '90 184
Individual Pecan Pies, '85 295
Layered Pecan Pie, '83 305
Lemon-Pecan Pie, '93 251
Louisiana Pecan Pie, '92 83
Maple-Pecan Pie, '81 266

Miniature Pecan Pies, '79 205; '86 13
Mississippi Pecan Pie, '98 146
Molasses-Pecan Pie, '86 259
Old-Fashioned Pecan Pie, '81 M269
Orange-Pecan Pie, '79 282; '83 222
Pecan Pie, '79 251; '80 57; '85 255; '90 312;
    '92 234; '98 275
Pumpkin-Pecan Pie, '85 233, 282
Pumpkin Pie, Nutty, '82 67
Raisin-Pecan Pie, '87 213
Special, Old Pecan Street, '93 251
Spicy Pecan Pie, '84 240
Sweet Potato-Pecan Pie, '83 90
Texas Pecan Pie, '83 159
Texas Star Pecan Pie, '90 184
Tiny Pecan Pies, '79 225
Turtle Pecan Pie, '93 250
Persimmon Pie, '79 206
Pineapple-Coconut Chess Pie, '92 214
Pineapple-Grits Pie, '96 236
Pineapple Pie, '80 237; '89 252
Pineapple Pie, Double-Crust, '82 85
Pineapple Pie, Fresh, '91 178
Pistachio Pie, '80 56
Plum Cream Pie, Easy, '86 174
Plum Pie, Streusel-Topped, '88 153
Plum Pie with Italian Sweet Crust, '79 162
Pumpkin
    Autumn Pumpkin Pie, '87 213
    Bourbon-Pecan Pumpkin Pie, '87 264
    Chiffon Pie, Pumpkin, '84 312
    Cracked Caramel-Pumpkin Pie, '99 254
    Empanadas, Pumpkin, '82 223
    Festive Pumpkin Pie, '81 M269
    Fluffy Pumpkin Pie, '80 283
    Frosty Pumpkin Pie, '96 279
    Ice Cream Pie, Pumpkin, '81 272
    Ice Cream Pie, Pumpkin-, '87 243
    Mama's Pumpkin Pie, '96 242
    Meringue, Pumpkin Pie with, '92 268
    New-Fashioned Pumpkin Pie, '90 296
    No-Bake Pumpkin Tarts, '86 291
    Nutty Pumpkin Pie, '82 67
    Pecan Pie, Pumpkin-, '85 233, 282
    Praline Pie, Frosty Pumpkin-, '91 M234
    Praline Pie, Pumpkin, '89 136
    Quick Pumpkin Pie, '88 M230
    Rich Pumpkin Pie, '86 292
    Sour Cream-Pumpkin Pie, '84 263
    Spiced Nut Crust, Pumpkin Pie in,
        '87 295
    Spicy Pumpkin Pies, '84 322
    Supreme, Pumpkin Pie, '82 217
    Traditional Pumpkin Pie, '85 256
Raisin Pie, '83 220
Raisin Pie, Spiced, '84 148
Raspberry Baked Alaska Pie, '98 216
Raspberry Cream Pie, '94 209
Rhubarb-Peach Pie, '86 140
Rhubarb-Raisin Pie, '79 112
Rhubarb-Raspberry Pear Pie, '95 119
Rum Bisque Pie, '79 123
Rum Cream Pie, '85 212
Scuppernong Pie, '88 216
Sour Cream Pie, '86 260
Sour Cream Pie, Tropical, '79 176; '80 6
Strawberry Angel Pie, '88 136
Strawberry-Banana Glazed Pie, '81 181
Strawberry-Glaze Pie, '81 141
Strawberry Pie, Chilled, '82 112
Strawberry Pie, Glazed, '82 M142
Strawberry-Rhubarb Pie, '98 99
Strawberry Yogurt Pie, '80 232
Strawberry-Yogurt Pie, '85 122; '86 124

PIES, PUFFS, AND PASTRIES
(continued)

Tarts

Almond Tart, '89 232
Almond Tassies, Lucky, '91 13
Almond Tea Tarts, '85 120
Apple-Cream Cheese Tart, '96 228
Apple Cream Tart, '84 207
Apple-Pecan Tarts, '80 282
Apple Tart, Creamed, '94 17
Apple Tart, Deluxe, '84 227
Apple Tarts, Brandied, '96 284; '99 28
Apple Tart, Upside-Down, '98 35
Apple Tart with Cheese Pastry, '88 225
Apricot-Almond Tart, '97 99
Apricot-Apple Crumb Tart, '94 60
Apricot-Nut Tart, '99 249
Apricot-Pecan-Brie Tarts, '97 236
Apricot Tarts, '79 282; '88 281
Bakewell Tart, '97 110
Berry Tartlets, Fresh, '91 98
Berry Tart, Pick-a-, '91 118
Blackberry Pudding Tarts, '93 200
Blackberry Supremes, '99 179
Black Bottom Mocha-Cream Tart, '92 304
Blue Cheese Appetizer Tarts, '85 300; '86 18
Bouilli, Tarte à la, '83 92
Bourbon-Chocolate-Pecan Tarts, '96 264
Caramel Tarts, '82 43
Caramel Tarts, Tiny, '99 179
Caramel Turtle Truffle Tart, '93 M131
Cheese Tart, Herb-, '87 98
Cheese Tartlets, '88 211
Cherry and Blackberry Tart, '83 225
Cherry Tarts, Cheery, '80 238
Chess Tarts, '90 83
Chicken Salad Tarts, '84 257
Chicken Tarts, Deviled, '94 14
Chocolate-Amaretto Heavenly Tarts, '88 4
Chocolate-Cherry Tart, '97 33
Chocolate Chess Tarts, '92 214
Chocolate Custard Tart, '99 27
Chocolate-Peanut Butter Tarts, '92 277
Chocolate-Pecan Tart with Caramel Sauce,
    '93 296; '94 234
Chocolate Tarts, Bluegrass, '90 84
Coconut Cream Tarts with Macadamia Nut
    Crusts, '97 62
Coffee Tart, '99 67
Country Ham-and-Asparagus Tartlets, '98 82
Cranberry-Apple Tart, '97 M316
Cranberry-Cream Cheese Tarts, '80 154
Cranberry Holiday Tarts, '83 279
Cranberry-Nut Tart, '84 305
Cranberry Tartlets, Fresh, '87 244
Cran-Raspberry Meringue Tarts, '92 286
Cream Cheese-Peach Tart, '99 169
Cream Cheese Tarts, '84 74; '90 312
Derby Tarts, Miniature, '90 92
Dried Tomato-Cheese Tart, '90 203
Eggnog Tarts, Creamy, '79 255
French Silk Tarts, '79 236
Fruit Tart, Fancy, '82 128; '91 119
Fruit Tart, Fresh, '84 178; '90 58
Fruit Tart, King Cake, '96 57
Fruit Tartlets, Fresh, '93 96
Fruit Tart, Open-Face, '84 207
Fruit Tart, Rainbow, '82 304
Fruit Tarts, Bowl-Me-Over Fresh, '93 200
Fudge Truffle-Pecan Tart, '99 315
Grape Tart, Green, '87 77
Grasshopper Tarts, '80 220; '89 275

Ham-and-Cheese Tart, '92 332
Ham Tart, Supreme, '84 22
Heart Tarts, '87 14
Honey-Pecan Tart, '99 212
Kentucky Derby Tarts, '79 102
Key Lime Tart in Coconut Crust, '89 160
Kiwifruit-Peach Tart, '88 20
Kiwifruit Tart, '89 232
Lady Baltimore Tarts, '88 282
Lemon-Cheese Tarts, '79 2
Lemon Ice Cream Tarts, '80 152
Lemon-Sour Cream Tarts, '81 304
Lemon Tart), Caky Flaky Tart (Tart, '96 159
Lemon Tarts, '82 156; '83 79
Lemon Tarts, Berry Good, '91 119
Lemon Tarts, Dainty, '82 304
Lemon Tarts, Golden, '85 191
Lemon Tart Shells, '88 195
Lime-Pineapple Tart, '88 6
Lime Tart, '98 272
Little Bits, '79 196
Midnight Delights, '95 278
Milan, Tart, '87 70
Miniature Tarts, '96 120
Mushroom Tarts, '88 161
Mushroom Tarts, Hot Sherried, '83 78
Onion Tart, Caramelized, '99 96
Orange Curd Tarts, '92 193
Orange Tarts, '96 317
Orange Tarts, Frozen, '80 154
Party Tarts, '95 90
Peach Cream Tart, '90 173
Peach Meringue Tart, Golden, '98 197
Peach Tart with Brandy Sauce, '98 119
Peachy Keen Tarts, '91 118
Peanut Butter Tarts, '97 329
Pear Tart, '82 304; '92 72
Pear Tart with White Caramel Sauce, '92 195
Pecan Tarts, '81 266
Pecan Tarts, Easy, '84 313
Pecan Tarts, Special, '87 224
Pecan Tarts, Toasty Southern, '95 329
Pecan Tart with Praline Cream, '90 256
Picadillo Tarts, '91 279
Pine Nut Tart, '97 86
Pommes, La Tarte aux, '80 125
Portabello Mushroom Tart, Smoked, '94 163
Potato Tarts, Phyllo, '98 69
Prune Tarts, Brandied, '85 223
Puddin' Pies, President Tyler's, '80 43
Pumpkin Tarts, No-Bake, '86 291
Raspberry-Almond Tarts, '99 280
Rutabaga-Spinach Tart, '98 274
Sausage 'n' Cheese Tarts, '88 51
Scuppernong Pudding Tarts, '98 221
Seafood Tartlets, '87 247
Shrimp Tart, '87 70
Spinach Tarts, '82 249
Squash Tart, '96 83
Strawberry Dream Tart, '92 118
Strawberry-Lemon Tart, '89 111
Strawberry Tart, '84 138; '89 272
Strawberry Tarts, '80 70
Sweet Onion Tarts, '95 229
Teatime Tassies, '84 321
Tomato-Basil Tart, '98 132
Tomato Tart, Fresh, '95 170
Tomato Tart, Herbed, '96 94
White Chocolate Chess Tart, '95 303
Tin Roof Pie, '85 91
Transparent Pie, '80 238

Turnovers

Apple Turnovers, Baked, '93 338
Apple Turnovers, Delicious, '86 25

Apple Turnovers, Fried, '81 161
Apple Turnovers, Puffy, '87 276
Apricot Turnovers, Fried, '86 24
Cheesy Sesame Seed Turnovers, '91 252
Chicken Liver Turnovers, '79 141
Cranberry Pockets, '96 320
Fruit Turnovers, '79 150
Ham Turnovers, Party, '82 39
Meat Turnovers, '86 326
Mushroom Turnovers, Hot, '89 285; '97 102
Mushroom Turnovers, Tiny, '86 24
Orange-Apple Turnovers, '99 294
Reuben Turnovers, '94 253
Roast Beef Turnovers, '88 273; '89 180
Salmon-Spinach Turnovers, '83 44
Sausage-Cheese Turnovers, '88 231
Turkey Turnovers, Home-Style, '94 325
Vegetable Turnovers, '86 24
Vanilla Cream Pie, Fruit-Topped, '84 49
Vegetable. *See also* **PIES, PUFFS, AND
    PASTRIES/Tarts, Turnovers.**
Artichoke Flan, '96 22
Broccoli-Cheese Pie, '84 235
Butternut Squash Chiffon Pie, '83 296; '84 285
Butternut Squash Pie, '80 40; '87 212
Butternut Squash Pie, Spicy, '80 296
Carrot Custard Pie, '79 45
Carrot Pie, '83 117
Cauliflower-Carrot Pie, '82 191
Corn Pie, Quick and Cheesy, '82 191
Corn Pie with Fresh Tomato Salsa,
    Buttercrust, '95 181
Florentine Crêpe Pie, '79 34
Green Onion Pie, '98 159
Green Tomato Pie, '79 195
Jalapeño Cheese Pie, '96 292
Mushrooms in Patty Shells, '80 283
Onion-Cheese Pie, '88 86
Onion Pie, '82 191
Pinto Bean Pie, '80 40
Ratatouille Pie, '88 198
Scallopini Pie, '94 133
Spaghetti Squash Pie, '80 186
Spinach Pie, '82 191; '88 56
Spinach Pie, Greek, '85 59
Spinach, Pie Pan, '94 195
Spinach Pie Parma, '96 203
Spinach Pie with Muenster Crust, '95 48
Squash Pie, Spicy, '85 9
Summer Pie, Savory, '99 159
Sweet Potato Cream Pie, Southern, '87 260
Sweet Potato Meringue Pie, '81 126; '83 225
Sweet Potato-Orange Pie, '88 207
Sweet Potato-Pecan Pie, '83 90
Sweet Potato Pie, '79 207; '85 255, 275;
    '86 269; '89 289; '96 131, 326
Sweet Potato Pie, Carolina, '89 295
Sweet Potato Pie, No-Crust, '84 236
Sweet Potato Pie, Old-Fashioned, '79 9
Sweet Potato Pie, Speedy, '90 219
Sweet Potato Pone Pie, '80 288
Tomato Pie, '88 198; '97 249
Wild Mushroom-and-Onion Pot Pies, '98 296
Yam Pie, Louisiana, '81 223
Zucchini Pie, '98 236
Zucchini Pie, Cheesy, '82 191
Zucchini Pie, Italian-Style, '83 43
Watermelon Pie, '95 144
PIMIENTO
Asparagus with Pimientos, '98 286
Ball, Pimiento Cheese, '80 258
Bread, Pimiento-Cheese, '85 223
Casserole, English Pea-Pimiento, '83 207
Eggs, Pimiento-Deviled, '84 143

Hoagies, Bacon, Pimiento, and Cheese, '90 144
Pasta, Pimiento, '84 176
Popovers, Pimiento, '79 138
Salsa, Fiery Steak with Pimiento Cheese, '99 331
Sandwiches, Pimiento Cheese, '82 278
Sandwiches, Pimiento Cheese Finger, '99 86
Sauce, Cauliflower with Pimiento, '87 232
Soup, Cream of Pimiento, '96 45
Soup, Pimiento "Mac and Cheese," '97 M325

Spreads
Cheddar-Swiss Spread, '99 106
Cheese, Fabulous Pimiento, '98 315
Chunky Pimiento Cheese, '86 295
Creamy Pimiento Cheese, '86 296
Creamy Pimiento Cheese Spread, '92 159
Feta-and-Apple Spread, '99 106
Four-Cheese Spread, '99 106
Garlic Pimiento Cheese Spread, '79 58
Ham and Pimiento Spread, '80 285; '81 56
Jalapeño Pimiento Cheese, '98 315
Low-Calorie Pimiento Cheese Spread, '85 215
Pimiento Cheese Spread, '82 35; '83 93;
   '86 127; '99 106, 276
Three Cheeses, Pimiento and, '86 296
West Texas Pimiento Cheese, '84 9
White Cheddar Pimiento Cheese, '99 106
Topping, Pimiento, '83 93

PINEAPPLE
Acorn Squash, Pineapple-Stuffed, '84 255
Appetizer, Shrimp-Pineapple, '85 80
Bacon-Wrapped Pineapple Chunks, '84 25
Baked Pineapple, '83 261; '84 287
Bake, Pineapple, '79 251; '96 84
Bake, Pineapple-Cheese, '79 106
Ball, Pineapple Cheese, '81 160
Ball, Pineapple-Cheese, '84 26
Beans, Hawaiian-Style Baked, '86 210
Beets with Pineapple, '79 249; '82 204
Betty, Pineapple-Apple, '85 46

Beverages
Blue Woo-Woo, '94 226
Bole, '97 245
Coconut-Pineapple Drink, '83 172
Cooler, Pineapple, '90 207
Float, Pineapple Sherbet, '79 148
Hot Buttered Pineapple Drink, '91 260
Lemonade, Pineapple, '93 194
Milk Shake, Banana-Pineapple, '84 59
Milkshake, Pineapple, '87 199
Milk Shake, Pineapple, '94 113
Nectar, Hot Pineapple, '90 21
Nog, Speedy Breakfast, '82 47
Orange-Pineapple Drink, '89 35
Piña Coladas, '95 203; '96 127
Piña Colada Slush, '95 90
Punch, Brew-Ha-Ha, '98 255
Punch, Champagne, '99 30
Punch, False-Kick, '82 121
Punch, Frosty Pineapple, '91 66
Punch, Hot Pineapple, '82 264
Punch, Lime-Pineapple, '83 142
Punch, Pineapple, '79 174; '80 128
Punch, Pineapple-Citrus, '96 134
Punch, Pineapple-Gin, '95 140
Punch, Pineapple-Mint, '88 209
Punch, Pineapple-Orange, '85 236
Punch, Pineapple Sherbet, '95 141
Punch, Spiced Pineapple, '83 33; '92 66
Sangría, Pineapple, '91 176
Shake, Pineapple-Banana, '85 215
Shake, Pineapple-Orange-Banana, '97 172
Shake, Strawberry-Pineapple, '84 166
Slush, Pineapple, '88 82
Slush, Pineapple-Banana, '90 14

Smoothie, Peachy-Pineapple, '97 173
Smoothie, Pineapple, '97 172
Smoothie, Quick Banana-Pineapple, '93 195
Soda, Pineapple, '90 179
Spiced Pineapple Sparkle, '92 322
Strawberry Slush, Pineapple-, '94 227
Tea, Pineapple, '93 165
Wassail, Pineapple-Apricot, '83 275
Yogurt Whirl, Pineapple-, '91 132

Breads
Apricot Bread, Pineapple-, '84 7
Buns, Easy Pineapple, '85 14
Carrot Bread, Pineapple-, '79 106
Carrot-Pineapple Bread, '82 210
Hawaiian Loaf, '80 225
Muffins, Carrot-Pineapple, '81 6
Muffins, Morning Glory, '93 327
Muffins, Pineapple, '81 14, 250
Muffins, Sunshine, '86 9
Nut Bread, Pineapple-, '79 215
Pecan Loaf Bread, Pineapple-, '87 256
Pineapple Bread, '83 139
Puffs, Pineapple Breakfast, '98 326
Rolls, Cranberry-Pineapple, '86 275
Rolls, Pineapple Angel, '89 72
Cabbage with Pineapple, Red, '97 215
Carrots, Pineapple, '83 198
Citrus, Pineapple and Fresh, '89 206
Coffee Cake, Pineapple-Coconut, '94 49
Curried Carrots and Pineapple, '90 228

Desserts
Ambrosia, Pineapple-Orange, '88 252
Baked Pineapple with Natillas Sauce, '83 179
Bars, Pineapple-Orange, '82 129
Basket, Summer Berry, '84 158
Boats with Rum Sauce, Pineapple, '97 192
Cake, Banana Split, '99 48
Cake, Cajun, '87 138
Cake, Carrot, '98 275
Cake, Coconut-Pineapple, '89 56
Cake, Coconut-Pineapple Layer, '80 140
Cake, Fresh Pineapple Upside-Down, '97 204
Cake, Heavenly Pineapple, '83 303
Cake, Lemon-Pineapple, '86 60, 239
Cake, Nanny's Famous Coconut-Pineapple,
   '97 277
Cake, Pineapple-Pecan Upside-Down, '84 25
Cake, Pineapple Pound, '79 148
Cake, Pineapple Right-Side-Up Snack, '99 28
Cake, Pineapple Upside-Down, '80 102; '88 10
Cake Roll, Coconut-Pineapple, '84 304
Cake Roll, Pineapple Upside-Down, '96 162
Cake, Skillet Pineapple Upside-Down, '85 242
Cake, Stacked Pineapple Upside-Down, '86 239
Cake, Zucchini-Pineapple, '95 160
Charlotte, Pineapple, '90 288
Cheesecake, Pineapple, '81 32
Cheesecake, Ultimate Pineapple, '85 38
Chimichangas, Pineapple Dessert, '86 4
Chocolate-Drizzled Pineapple with Raspberry
   Sauce, '90 57
Cookies, Pineapple, '79 216
Cream, Pineapple 'n', '88 202
Crêpes, Mango-Pineapple, '86 216
Delight, Fresh Pineapple, '79 111
Delight, Pineapple-Almond, '85 96
Filling, Orange-Pineapple Fried Pie, '96 109
Filling, Pineapple, '80 140; '83 179; '84 153;
   '89 57; '97 277
Frappé, Hawaiian, '81 178
Fritters, Pineapple, '88 112
Frosting, Pineapple-Cream Cheese, '95 160
Frozen Tropical Paradise, '89 206
Glazed Oranges and Pineapple, '86 318

Glaze, Orange-Pineapple, '81 60
Glaze, Pineapple, '83 143; '85 38; '97 55
Ice Cream, Orange-Pineapple, '86 117
Ice Cream, Pineapple-Mint, '84 186
Meringue-Topped Pineapple, '84 178
Mint Dessert, Pineapple-, '96 127
Mousse, Coconut-Pineapple, '94 198
Mousse, Elegant Pineapple, '79 230
Papaya-Pineapple Roll, '94 18
Parfait, Pineapple, '84 83
Pears, Pineapple-Honey, '86 94
Phyllo Bundles, Pineapple, '87 277
Pie, Apple-Pineapple, '97 276
Pie, Coconut-Pineapple, '84 256
Pie, Double-Crust Pineapple, '82 85
Pie, Fresh Pineapple, '91 178
Pie, Pineapple, '80 237; '89 252
Pie, Pineapple-Chicken Salad, '80 138
Pie, Pineapple-Coconut Chess, '92 214
Pie, Pineapple-Grits, '96 236
Pops, Hawaiian Orange-Pineapple, '94 143
Pops, Pineapple-Yogurt, '91 173
Pudding, Piña Colada Bread, '98 34
Pudding, Pineapple, '80 102
Sauce, Banana-Pineapple, '83 48
Sauce, Pineapple Ice Cream, '81 M289
Sauce, Pineapple-Orange, '84 14
Sauce, Pineapple-Rum, '84 275
Sherbet, Buttermilk, '99 99
Sherbet, Creamy Pineapple, '79 155
Sherbet, Easy Pineapple, '92 199
Sherbet, Lemon-Pineapple, '96 330
Sherbet, Pineapple, '81 177; '84 83; '89 199
Sopaipillas, Pineapple, '83 179
Soufflé, Pineapple Dessert, '80 153
Spritz, Pineapple, '86 94
Sundaes, Mauna Loa, '80 126
Tart, Lime-Pineapple, '88 6
Topping, Cherry-Pineapple, '87 126
Topping, Lemon-Pineapple, '86 60
Topping, Pineapple, '86 239
Trifle, Pineapple Angel Food, '93 86
Tropical Snow, '86 34
Dip, Cheesy Pineapple, '80 249
Dip, Pineapple-Ginger, '86 104
Doughnuts, Pineapple Drop, '83 95
Dressing, Fruit Salad with Pineapple, '85 207
Dressing, Pineapple Cream, '83 81
Dressing, Pineapple-Poppy Seed, '85 55
Fried Pineapple, '81 232
Glaze, Pineapple, '83 143; '84 26; '85 38
Gratin, Pineapple, '93 328
Ham-Pineapple Nibbles, '95 283
Hawaiian Dream Boats, '86 151
Jam, Pineapple, '81 147
Jelly, Pineapple-Orange Mint, '92 105

Main Dishes
Beans and Franks, Hawaiian Baked, '80 136
Beefburgers Hawaiian, '86 137
Beef Kabobs, Pineapple-, '83 212
Burgers, Pineapple, '82 169
Chicken and Pineapple, '81 281; '82 30
Chicken Bake, Pineapple, '82 120
Chicken Breasts, Hawaiian Stuffed, '99 64
Chicken, Hawaiian Sesame, '81 106
Chicken Kabobs, Pineapple-, '86 M328
Chicken, Oriental Pineapple, '84 288
Chicken, Piña Colada, '86 21
Chicken, Pineapple, '83 M194; '85 3
Chicken Stir-Fry, Pineapple-, '89 176
Chicken, Sweet-and-Sour, '97 325
Chicken with Pineapple-Mustard Glaze,
   Roast, '89 83
Chicken with Pineapple, Oriental, '86 42

PINEAPPLE, Main Dishes
(continued)

Chops, Pineapple-Curry Glazed, '82 106
Crab Imperial, Pineapple-, '84 M286
Flank Steak in Mexican Marinade, '98 128
Franks, Hawaiian, '81 202
Ham, Citrus-and-Spice, '88 40
Ham Loaf, Pineapple Upside-Down, '79 253
Ham Patties, Pineapple-, '80 110
Ham, Pineapple-Baked, '86 48
Ham, Pineapple-Flavored, '87 160
Ham-Potato-Pineapple Bake, '93 302
Ham Sandwich Loaf, Pineapple-, '91 167
Kabobs, Pineapple-Pork, '99 144
Loaves, Individual Pineapple, '81 M121
Loaves, Mini Teriyaki, '98 224
Meatballs, Chinese, '87 194
Meatballs with Pineapple and Peppers, '90 145
Meat Loaf, Teriyaki, '98 224
Pork and Pineapple, Polynesian, '83 102
Pork Chops, Hawaiian, '86 212
Pork Chops, Pineapple, '87 M124
Pork, Pineapple, '82 60
Pork, Pineapple Sweet-and-Sour, '82 120
Pork Roast, Pineapple, '79 41
Pot Roast, Hawaiian, '81 298
Pot Roast, Polynesian, '80 59
Marmalade, Orange-Pineapple, '82 150; '89 M156
Marmalade, Strawberry-Pineapple, '85 130
Meatballs, Polynesian, '80 207
Pears, Pineapple-Honey, '86 94
Pickled Pineapple, '79 24
Pizza, Ham-and-Pineapple, '96 169
Preserves, Mango-Pineapple, '79 137
Relish, Cranberry, '98 310
Relish, Pineapple-Coconut, '96 323; '97 27
Rice with Pineapple, Curried, '79 142
Salad Dressing, Pineapple, '81 36
Salads
Boat Aloha, Pineapple, '80 102
Boats Ahoy, Pineapple, '80 148
Buttermilk Salad, Pineapple-, '82 80
Carrot-Pineapple Salad, '91 83
Celery Salad, Pineapple-, '85 95
Chicken Salad, Pineapple-Nut, '83 80
Chicken Salad, South Sea Island, '97 88
Citrus, Pineapple and Fresh, '89 206
Coleslaw, Curried Pineapple, '88 172
Congealed Salad, Pineapple-Cucumber, '83 118
Congealed Salad, Pineapple-Orange, '83 218
Cranberry-Pineapple Salad, Frozen, '91 237
Cucumber-Pineapple Salad, '84 124
Daiquiri Salad, Pineapple, '84 232
Delight, Pineapple-Pear, '82 54
Fresh Pineapple Boats, '83 153
Frosted Salad, Heavenly, '79 286
Frosty Pineapple Salad, '89 278
Fruit Salad, Icy Pineapple-, '87 9
Lime Salad, Pineapple-, '84 320
Macaroni Salad, Pineapple, '79 220
Mandarin Orange and Pineapple Salad, '82 266
Mold, Minted Pineapple, '85 240
Shrimp Salad, Aloha, '95 46
Slaw, Apple-Pineapple, '79 241
Slaw, Cabbage-Pineapple, '92 182
Slaw, Colorful Pineapple, '86 250
Slaw, Pineapple, '94 49; '99 26
Slaw, Pineapple-Almond, '92 171
Slaw Sandwiches, Ham-and-Pineapple, '96 199
Slaw, Zesty, '97 324
Waldorf, Pineapple, '97 86
Waldorf Salad, Pineapple, '92 97

Salsa, Cranberry, '99 316
Salsa, Pineapple, '96 226
Salsa, Spicy Pineapple, '97 165
Sauce, Banana-Pineapple, '83 48
Sauce, Jezebel, '81 29; '82 55
Sauce, Maui, '99 310
Sauce, Pineapple, '84 236; '92 203
Sauce, Pineapple-Curry, '79 252
Sauce, Pineapple-Rhubarb, '88 94
Sauce, Raisin-Pineapple, '82 177
Sauce, Sweet-and-Sour Pineapple, '85 66
Scalloped Pineapple, '79 106; '82 254; '84 M323
Shells, Pineapple, '96 127
Skewered Pineapple and Strawberries, '84 251
Slicing Pineapples, Instructions for, '82 94
Snow Peas and Pineapple, '91 120
Spiced Pineapple, '80 102
Spread, Coconut-Pineapple, '93 309
Spread, Hawaiian Cheese, '87 158
Spread, Pineapple-Cheese, '86 126; '91 167
Spread, Pineapple-Cream Cheese, '82 35
Spread, Pineapple Sandwich, '84 166
Spritz, Pineapple, '86 94
Sweet Potatoes, Pineapple-Orange, '96 46
Vinaigrette, Black Pepper-Pineapple, '97 181
PITA. *See* **APPETIZERS/Pita; BREADS;
  SANDWICHES/Pita.**
PIZZA
Appetizers
Appetizer Pizzas, '89 M118
Cocktail Pizzas, '79 110
Dip, Pizza, '99 65
Horns, Pizza, '89 214
Party Pizzettes, '80 192
Pita Pizzas, '89 19
Shellfish Pizza, '91 224
Shrimp Pizza Wedges, '89 158
Slices, Pizza, '84 269
Snacks, Pizza Party, '86 262
Snacks, Tasty Little Pizza, '79 248
Squares, Pizza, '87 168
Turnovers, Little Pizza, '85 327
Zucchini Pizzas, '88 212
Artichoke and Prosciutto, Pizza with, '87 182
Bagel, Pizza on a, '93 M94
Bake, Upside-Down Pizza, '98 224
Banana Split-Brownie Pizza, '96 M164
Bayou Pizza, The Best of the, '95 268
Beef-and-Sausage Pizza, Double Cheesy, '86 77
Bites, Pizza, '95 244
Blazing Sunset Pizza, '95 267
Blueberry Pizza, '96 147
Bobolis, Easy Cheesy, '92 278
Bread, Pizza Batter, '85 56
Breakfast Pizza, '85 44; '88 288; '90 140, 178;
  '97 172
Burger, Pizza, '87 185
Burgers, All-American Pizza, '92 148
Burgers, Easy Pizza, '82 190
Burger Snacks, Pizza-, '84 30
Burgers, Pizza, '80 M201; '81 73; '89 165
Calzone, '85 94
Calzones, All-Star Pizza, '95 308
Casserole, Microwave Pizza, '89 M248
Casserole, Pizza, '88 273; '89 181
Casserole, Quick Pizza, '83 266
Cheese-and-Mushroom Pizza, '83 226
Cheeseburger Pizza, '97 318
Chicken-and-Purple Onion Pizza, '97 47
Chicken-and-Three-Cheese French Bread
  Pizzas, '96 94
Chicken Pizza, '94 218
Chicken Pizza, Mexican, '97 321
Chocolate Pizza, '91 298

Clam Pizza, Baby, '87 182
Cookie, Pizza, '90 49
Cranberry Dessert Pizzas, '96 320
Crusts
Crispy Pizza Crust, '87 181; '89 64
Parmesan Pizza Crust, '93 58
Pizza Crust, '80 233; '83 226; '85 243; '86 77
Skillet Pizza Crusts, '94 218
Special Pizza Crust, '90 139
Thick Crust, '81 214
Thin Crust, '81 214
Whole Wheat Crust, '94 78
Whole Wheat Pizza Crust, '93 58
Cups, Pizza, '81 215
Deep-Dish Mediterranean Pizza, '80 163
Deep-Dish Pizza Luncheon Pie, '80 286
Deep-Dish Vegetarian Pizza, '85 243
Dessert, Rocky Road Pizza, '99 196
Dogs, Grilled Pizza, '97 139
Easy Pizza, '92 181
Eggplant Pizza, '85 221
Eggplant Pizzas, '98 183
Five-Ring Pizzas, '96 180
French Bread, Pizza on, '82 131
Garden Pizza, '89 108
Grilled Pizza, '97 190
Grilled Pizzas, '93 178; '98 176
Gruyère-Chicken Pizza, '87 182
Ham-and-Eggs Crescent Pizza, '93 47
Ham-and-Pineapple Pizza, '96 169
Hamburger Pizza, Quick, '85 243
Herb Pizza, Easy, '92 99
Homemade Pizza, Best Ever, '80 233
Hot Dog Pizzas, '93 78
Italian-Style Pizza, Original, '87 182
Jazzed-Up Pizza, Jiffy, '83 M314
King Henry Pizza, The, '95 267
Kiwi-Berry Pizza, '86 198; '87 55
Kiwifruit Pizza, '89 306
Lasagna Pizza, '85 285
Maca-Pizza, '99 195
Meatballs, Pizza, '85 86
Meat Loaf, Cheesy Pizza, '81 121
Mexican Pizza, '94 218, 327; '99 119
Pan Pizza, Quick, '86 160
Peanut Butter-Fruit Pizza, '94 60
Pepperoni Pizza, Thick 'n' Crusty, '85 244
Pepper Pizza, Roasted, '94 218
Peppers, Pizza, '83 135
Pesto Pizza, '87 182; '94 218
Pesto Pizza, Nutty, '97 267
Phyllo Pizza, '94 91
Pie, Pizza, '91 23
Pita Pizza Snack, '94 193
Plum-and-Sweet Onion Pizza, '98 193
Pocket Pizzas, Easy, '90 168
Popcorn, Pizza-Flavored, '85 236
Portobello-Pine Nut Pizza, '99 216
Potato Pizzas, Roasted, '99 16
Pumpkins, Pizza, '98 255
Quiche, Pizza, '86 53
Quick Little Pizzas, '88 227
Rollups, Pizza, '99 197
Salad Pizza, '87 182
Sandwiches, Open-Face Pizza, '82 3; '83 85;
  '84 M198; '85 22
Sandwich, Giant Pizza, '80 93
Sauce, Pizza, '84 33; '85 285
Sauce, Traditional Pizza, '95 267
Sausage-Pepperoni Pizza, Spicy, '83 226
Sausage Pie, Link-, '85 33
Shellfish Pizza, '91 224
Shrimp-and-Dried Tomato Pizza, '97 49
Southern Classic Pizza, '95 268

Southwest Deluxe Pizza, '95 268
Speedy Pizza, '81 214
Sticks, Pizza, '98 255
Strawberry Pizza, '79 94
Sunburst, Pizza, '94 245
Supreme, Pizza, '81 214
Taco Pizza, '89 M177; '98 176
Tacos, Pizza-Flavored Chicken, '95 340
Tostada Pizza, '81 16; '82 13
Turkey-Vegetable Pizza, '90 139
Two-Way Pizza, '79 93
Upside-Down Pizza, '91 185
Vegetable Pizza, '89 64; '94 218
Vegetable Pizza, Grilled, '98 176
Vegetable Pizzas, Grilled, '97 323
Vegetarian Pizza, Deep-Dish, '85 243
Vegetarian Processor Pizza, '89 225
Veggie Pizza, '94 78
Veggie Pizzas, '99 97
Veggie Pizza, Southwestern, '95 126
Whole Wheat Pizza, '84 33
Wide-Eyed Pizzas, '90 94
PLANTAINS
Chips, Plantain, '95 M203
Chips), Tostones de Platano (Plantain, '92 158
Fried Plantains, '99 121
PLUMS
Betty, Bourbon-Plum Brown, '97 177
Brandied Plums, '97 176
Bread Pudding, Refrigerator Plum, '97 177
Bread, Sugar Plum, '80 256
Butter, Plum, '88 152
Cake, Plum, '97 177
Chutney, Plum, '84 179
Cobbler, Crunchy Plum, '88 152
Cobbler, Plum, '99 254
Crunch, Layered Plum, '86 174
Fajitas, Plum Good, '94 115
Ham, Plum, '80 110
Jam, Freezer Plum, '89 M156
Jam, Peach-Plum Freezer, '85 130
Jam, Plum Refrigerator, '89 139
Jelly, Plum, '82 150
Kuchen, Plum, '79 161
Muffins, Plum Good, '83 96
Pie, Easy Plum Cream, '86 174
Pie, Streusel-Topped Plum, '88 153
Pie with Italian Sweet Crust, Plum, '79 162
Pizza, Plum-and-Sweet Onion, '98 193
Poached Plums, '90 M141
Port Wine, Plums in, '97 176
Pudding, Flamed Plum, '84 276
Pudding-Gelatin Mold, Plum, '86 300; '87 178
Pudding, Light Plum, '86 318
Pudding, Old-Fashioned Plum, '80 264
Pudding, Plum, '79 281
Salsa, Plum, '97 176
Sauce, Chinese Plum, '82 237
Sauce, Crispy Ribs with Plum, '98 182
Sauce, Fresh Plum, '94 129; '97 176
Sauce, Gingered Plum, '87 175
Sauce, Plum, '80 249; '82 40; '88 152
Sauce, Quail with Red Plum, '80 48
Sauce, Spareribs in Plum, '99 136
Sauce, Spicy Plum, '86 11
Slush, Plum, '84 139
Soup, Chilled Purple Plum, '79 162
Soup, Peach-Plum, '87 157
Soup, Plum, '85 107
POLENTA
Baked Polenta with Cheese and Okra, '99 232
Basic Polenta, '95 164
Grilled Polenta with Black Bean Salsa, '93 155
Sausage, Polenta with, '93 32

Serrano Chile Polenta, '98 104
Triangles, Polenta, '98 181
POMEGRANATE
Salad Dressing, Pomegranate, '96 241
Syrup, Pomegranate, '96 241
Wreath, Tex-Mex, '96 241
POPCORN
Bacon-Cheese Popcorn, '86 74
Balls, Marshmallow Popcorn, '90 226
Balls, Nutty Popcorn, '88 227
Cake, Popcorn-Gumdrop, '87 262
Candied Popcorn and Peanuts, '82 295
Caramel
Baked Caramel Corn, '81 218
Candy, Caramel Corn, '84 243
Caramel Corn, '88 64
Caramel Popcorn, '79 219; '86 M212
Crispy Caramel Popcorn, '85 247
Crunch, Caramel, '95 165
Crunch Popcorn, Caramel, '96 255
Ghoul's Hands, '94 256
Nutty Caramel Corn, '92 317
Oven-Made Caramel Corn, '91 233
Cheese Popcorn, '98 205
Cheesy Barbecue Popcorn, '95 239
Chili Popcorn, '91 17; '95 166
Cinnamon-Popcorn Crunch, '86 136
Crazy Mixed-Up Popcorn, '97 245
Flavored Popcorn, '98 205
Garlic Popcorn, '83 M315
Harvest Popcorn, '84 300
Herb-Seasoned Popcorn, '94 122
Honey-and-Spice Crunch, '94 290
Mexican Popcorn, '98 205
Mix, Curried Popcorn, '86 326
Mix, Party, '96 306; '97 322; '98 234
Munchies, Pop Graham, '96 28
Nutty Popcorn, '85 208
Orange Popcorn, '86 230
Oriental Popcorn, '86 74; '98 205
Pizza-Flavored Popcorn, '85 236
Pizzazz, Popcorn with, '93 245
Pretzel Popcorn, '84 30
Ranch Popcorn, '98 205
Scramble, Popcorn, '87 185
Sesame-Cheese Popcorn, '79 220
Spiced Popcorn Snack, '87 8
PORK. *See also* **BACON, CASSEROLES, HAM, SAUSAGE.**
Apple Cider Pork and Vegetables, '97 210
Backbones, Smoked Country-Style, '82 162
Bake, Pork-and-Noodle, '98 98
Bake, Pork Spaghetti, '81 11
Barbecue
Bannister's Barbecue, '92 166
Barbecued Pork, '80 72
Chops, Barbecued Pork, '81 10
Chops, Barbecued Stuffed, '87 229
Chops, Marinated Barbecued Pork, '79 90
Chops, Oven-Barbecued Pork, '81 234; '82 26; '83 40
Chops with Tangy Barbecue Sauce, Pork, '99 104
Home-Style Barbecue, '88 145
Ribs, Apple Barbecued, '80 111
Ribs, Barbecue, '99 68
Ribs, Barbecued, '80 111; '85 159; '91 205
Ribs, Barbecued Country-Style, '95 237
Ribs, Country-Style Barbecued, '79 42
Ribs, Herbed Barbecued, '86 185
Ribs, Oven-Barbecued Pork, '88 132
Ribs, Smoky Barbecued, '80 111
Ribs, Tangy Barbecued, '83 160
Ribs with Blender Barbecue Sauce, '90 12

Roast, Barbecued Pork, '82 11
Roast, Barbecued Pork Loin, '93 34
Roast, Barbecue Pork, '82 97; '83 104
Roast, Berry Barbecued Pork, '80 288
Roast, Oven-Barbecued Pork, '91 50
Shoulder, Barbecued Pork, '81 111; '82 11
Spareribs, Apple-Barbecue, '90 160
Spareribs, Barbecued, '81 112; '82 12; '86 232; '95 236
Spareribs, Barbecued Country-Style, '80 73
Spareribs, Easy Barbecued, '82 97; '83 104
Spareribs, Saucy Barbecued, '79 14
Spareribs, Southern Barbecued, '79 90
Spareribs, Spicy Barbecued, '84 93
Spareribs, Tangy Barbecued, '82 106
Spareribs with Orange Barbecue Sauce, '83 11
Spicy Barbecued Pork, '84 296
Bean Sauce, Pork-and-Onions with, '85 76
Brunch Eggs, '85 44
Burgers, Hearty Sauced Pork, '84 125
Burgoo, Five-Meat, '87 3
Burgoo, Harry Young's, '87 3
Burgoo, Kentucky, '97 138
Burritos, '80 196
Burritos, Meat-and-Bean, '81 194
Calabaza Guisada con Puerco (Pumpkin Cooked with Pork), '80 193
Casserole, Cheesy Pork, '81 M74
Casserole, Pork, '83 116
Cassoulet, '96 328
Chalupa, Bean, '80 223
Chalupas, Pork, '83 160
Chile Verde, Light, '88 148
Chili, Double-Meat, '79 269; '80 12
Chili Verde, '95 14
Chops. *See also* **PORK/Barbecue.**
Apple-Kraut Pork Chops, '84 50
Apple Pork Chops, '91 198
Apple Pork Chops, Spicy, '87 230
Apricot-Sauced Pork Chops, '85 22
Arlo, Pork, '87 229
Baked Pork Chops and Apples, '81 10
Bake, Fiesta Pork, '79 265
Beans, Pork Chops with Baked, '93 18
Boneless Pork Chops with Ancho Cream Sauce, '95 205
Bourbon-Braised Pork Chops, '85 89
Broiled Pork Chops, '89 191
Broiled Pork Chops with Crabapple Peaches, '81 83
Burritos with Pico de Gallo, Pork, '97 140
Calypso Loin Chops with Mango Salsa, '98 232
Carne Adovada, '91 162
Casserole, Peppered Pork Chop, '81 235; '82 25; '83 39
Casserole, Pork Chop, '94 255
Casserole, Pork Chop-Vegetable, '90 208
Cheesy Pork Chops, '83 102
Chili Chops, '87 10
Chinese Pork Chops, '97 320
Cider-Sauced Pork Chops, '86 213; '87 81
Company Pork Chops, '85 109
Cornbread-Apple Stuffing, Pork Chops with, '99 14
Costillas Rellenos (Stuffed Pork Chops), '82 219
Country Pride Pork Chops, '79 159
Cranberry Pork, '90 293
Cranberry Pork Chops, '80 288; '90 53
Creamy Gravy, Pork Chops and, '81 207
Creole Pork Chops, '83 102
Creole-Style Pork Chops, '91 49
Curried Apricot Pork Chops, '89 191
Dill-Cream Gravy, Pork Chops with, '84 81

PORK, Chops
(continued)

Dinner, Pork Chop, '80 84; '81 180; '88 25
Enchiladas, Pork, '97 M94
Fiesta, Pork Chops, '86 118
Fried Pork Chops with Roasted Vegetables, '98 153
Fruited Pork Chops, '87 194
Fruit-Topped Pork Chops, '94 41
Glazed Apple Pork Chops, '86 300
Glazed Chops, Honey-, '97 200
Glazed Chops, Pineapple-Curry, '82 106
Glazed Chops with Vegetables, '98 132
Glazed Pork Chops, '86 185
Glazed Pork Chops, Apple-, '84 212; '87 35
Glazed Pork Chops, Orange-, '81 234; '82 25; '83 39; '84 234; '91 84
Glazed Pork Chops with Green Mole Sauce, Tamarind-, '95 266
Glazed Pork Chops with Rice, Fruit-, '82 73
Glazed Pork Steaks, '83 178
Gourmet Pork Chops, '79 180
Gravy, Pork Chops and, '96 71
Gravy, Pork Chops in, '91 137
Grilled Pork Chops, '88 113; '98 246
Grilled Pork Chops, Hawaiian, '85 159
Grilled Pork Chops, Marinated, '81 110
Hawaiian Pork Chops, '86 212; '87 82
Herbed Pork Chops, '97 147
Herb-Peppered Pork Chops, '98 60
Honey-Lime Pork Chops, '91 33
Italiano, Pork Chops, '80 72
Italian, Pork Chops, '79 47; '98 334
Jardinière, Pork Chops, '81 112; '82 12
Lemon-Herb Pork Chops, '84 81; '89 M132
Lemony Pork Chops, '88 118
Marinated Pork Chops, '89 249
Meal for Two, Pork Chop, '81 273
Mexican Pork Chops, '99 108
Moo Shu Pork, '99 237
Mustard-Apricot Pork Chops, '89 225
Onion Gravy, Pork Chops in, '99 222
Orange-Cranberry Pork Chops, '86 335; '87 84
Orange Pork Chops, '84 81
Oriental Pork Chops, '84 81; '90 212
Parmesan Pork Chops with Apples, '93 338
Peachy Pork Chops, '89 310
Peanut Sauce, Pork Chops with, '83 29
Pecan-Breaded Pork Chops with Beer Sauce, '95 266
Pineapple Pork Chops, '87 M124
Pleasing Pork Chops, '79 125
Polynesian Pork and Pineapple, '83 102
Potatoes, Pork Chops and Scalloped, '98 16
Potato Scallop, Pork Chops and, '82 114
Rice, Pork Chops and Spanish, '83 103; '85 293
Ripieno, Pork Chops with, '97 245
Risotti, Pork Chops, '81 234; '82 26
Rosemary Pork Chops, '98 329
Salsa, Pork Chops with Black-and-White, '97 200
Saucy Company Pork Chops, '83 102
Saucy Pork Chop, '86 M140
Saucy Pork Dinner, '97 26
Sauerkraut, Pork Chops and, '88 98
Savory Pork Chops, '87 194
Sherry-Apple Pork Chops, '88 40
Sherry, Chops in, '79 125
Skillet Dinner, Pork, '98 131
Skillet Dinner, Pork Chop, '79 125
Skillet Pork Chops, Easy, '79 255
Sour Cream Sauce, Pork Chops with, '83 102

Southwestern Pork Chops, '98 131
Spaghetti with Pork and Peppers, '98 131
Special, Pork Chop, '79 81
Stir-Fry, Mixed Veggie-and-Pork, '99 206
Stuffed Baked Pork Chops, '79 222; '80 64
Stuffed Pork Chops, '84 195; '86 89
Stuffed Pork Chops, Apple-, '79 125
Stuffed Pork Chops, Apple-Crumb, '81 234; '82 26; '83 39
Stuffed Pork Chops, Apricot-, '86 76; '92 219
Stuffed Pork Chops, Apricot-Mushroom, '95 287
Stuffed Pork Chops, Braised, '87 249
Stuffed Pork Chops, Cheese-, '84 81
Stuffed Pork Chops, Easy, '81 10
Stuffed Pork Chops, Fruit-, '82 136
Stuffed Pork Chops, Fruited, '86 197
Stuffed Pork Chops, Rice-, '83 102
Stuffed Pork Chops with Apricot Glaze, '89 M36
Stuffed with Prunes, Pork Chops, '84 7
Sweet-and-Sour Apple Sauce, Pork Chops with, '98 132
Sweet-and-Sour Pork Chops, '83 160
Sweet Potatoes, Pork Chops with, '96 269
Vegetable Pork Chops, Skillet, '85 179
Vegetables, Golden Chops with, '89 218
Vegetables, Pork Chops and Garden, '88 297
Weeknight Pork Chops, '97 200
White Bean Puree, Pork Chops with, '96 226
Chow Mein, Pork, '80 208; '90 101
Combo, Vegetable-Pork, '85 113
Curry, Hurry, '79 103
Cutlets, Apple-Glazed Pork, '92 181
Dinner, Pork-and-Noodles Skillet, '88 199
Dumplings, Steamed Sesame, '97 208
Egg Rolls, '86 81
Egg Rolls, Chinese, '96 101
Eggrolls, Shrimp and Pork, '82 240; '83 18
Egg Rolls, Vietnamese, '96 101
Eggs, Tulsa, '87 95
Hominy, Mexican, '86 255
Hot-and-Spicy Pork, '81 228
Kabobs, Spicy Pork, '82 182
Kung Pao Pork, '96 49
Leg of Pork with Cranberry Glaze, '88 244
Marinated Pork Strips, '92 219
Meatballs in Gravy, '79 136
Meatballs, Sauerkraut, '86 257
Meatballs, Tangy Hawaiian, '79 129
Meat Loaf
Family-Style Meat Loaf, '93 18
Italian Meat Loaf, '79 187
Mozzarella-Layered Meat Loaf, '79 71
Savory Meat Loaf, '87 216
Skillet Liver Loaf, '80 11
Stuffed Meat Loaf, '79 187
Swedish Meat Loaf, '81 M121
Triple Meat Loaf, '79 186
Meat Mixture, Basic, '92 241
Oriental, Pork, '81 212
Paella, Chicken-Pork-Shrimp, '82 245
Pâté, Country, '86 66
Pâté en Croûte, '86 65
Pâté with Spinach and Cream, Pork, '83 224
Picadillo II, '93 72
Pie, Continental Meat, '95 256; '96 75
Pies, Natchitoches Meat, '84 21; '91 241
Pie, Sombrero, '81 140
Pilaf, Fruited Pork, '82 246
Pineapple Pork, '82 60
Poblanos Stuffed with Pork and Fruit, '97 269
Polynesian Pork, '85 78
Posole, '95 226
Rack of Pork, Herb-Crusted, '97 262

Ribs. *See also* **PORK/Barbecue.**
Adams' Ribs, '95 236
Baby Back Ribs, Barbecued, '97 234
Baby Loin Back Ribs, John Wills's, '90 120
Baked and Grilled Spareribs, '97 211
Baked Ribs, Easy, '86 20
Baked Ribs, Lemon, '81 166
Chinese Spareribs, '81 10
Crispy Ribs with Plum Sauce, '98 182
Ginger Pork Ribs, '96 100
Glazed Spareribs, '88 98
Glazed Spareribs, Honey-, '82 163
Glazed Spareribs, Orange-, '84 296
Glazed Spareribs, Peach-, '86 14
Grilled Maple Spareribs, '99 136
Grilled Ribs, Lemon, '81 154
Lemony Sweet Spareribs, '80 73
Maple Spareribs, '99 136
Plantation Ribs, '84 217
Plum Sauce, Spareribs in, '99 136
Puerco en Adobo, '88 116
Saucy Oven Spareribs, '80 207
Saucy-Sweet Ribs, '81 166
Smoked Ribs, '88 169
Smoked Ribs with Honey-Mustard Sauce, '92 168
Smoky Oven Ribs, '81 166
Smoky Ribs, '84 172
Spareribs, Southern, '95 116
Spicy Spareribs, '89 168
Stuffed Spareribs, Fruit-, '79 14
Sweet-and-Sour Ribs, '89 M84
Sweet-and-Sour Spareribs, '83 21
Tangy Ribs and Onions, '99 136
Thai Wings and Ribs, '97 M225
Rice, Pork Fried, '89 99
Risotto, Pork, '82 60
Roasts. *See also* **PORK/Barbecue.**
à l'Orange, Porc, '80 242
Apples and Mushrooms, Roast Pork Loin with, '92 218
Arista of Pork, '81 260
Braised Pork, Brown Sugar, '84 36
Chinese Roast Pork, '91 308
Company Pork Roast, '99 276
Crickhollow Roast Pork, '99 200
Crown Pork Flambé, Stuffed, '83 263
Crown Pork Roast, Stuffed, '89 272
Crown Pork Roast with Cranberry-Pecan Stuffing, '96 309
Crown Roast of Pork, Royal, '80 252
Crown Roast of Pork, Stuffed, '86 323
Crown Roast of Pork with Cranberry-Sausage Stuffing, '88 49
Dijonnaise with Peach Sauce, Pork Loin, '97 87
Glazed Pork Loin, '87 229
Glazed Pork Loin, Scuppernong-Orange, '98 220
Glazed Pork Roast, Cherry-, '91 84
Grilled Pork, Honey-and-Herb, '90 148
Grilled Pork, Jalapeño, '99 160
Grilled Pork Loin, Grandma Ruth's, '96 250
Grilled Pork Loin, Honey-, '92 219
Grilled Pork Roast, '97 323
Honey-Roasted Pork, '96 251
Indonesian Pork Roast, '81 227
Italian Pork Roast, '91 238; '92 27
Loin of Pork, Roast, '84 276
Loin, Roast Pork, '88 221
Loin Roast with Red Currant Sauce, Pork, '89 M84
Mandarin Pork Roast, '83 47
Marinated Pork Loin, Garlic-Honey, '99 334
Marinated Pork Roast, '80 71; '84 260

Minted Pork Loin, '99 96
Peppercorn Pork Roast, '97 248
Pernil (Pork Roast), '92 157
Pineapple Pork Roast, '79 41
Pineapple Sweet-and-Sour Pork, '82 120
Rio Grande Pork Roast, '84 35, 296
Roasted Pork Loin, '96 32
Roasted Pork Loin with Mushrooms and
    Garlic, '92 301
Rolled Pork with Rhubarb Sauce, '96 134
Smoked Pork, '99 81
Smoked Pork Loin Mahogany, '91 148
Smoked Pork Shoulder, '82 225
Spiced Cherry Sauce, Roast Pork with, '89 324
Stew, Baja Pork, '98 283
Stuffed Pork Loin, Apricot-Pecan, '94 274
Stuffed Pork Loin, Fruitcake-, '95 250
Stuffed Pork Loin Roast, Prune-, '80 29
Stuffed Pork Rib Roast, Sausage-, '94 240
Stuffed Pork Roast, '81 111; '82 12; '85 229
Stuffed Pork Shoulder, '81 11
Stuffed Pork, Spinach-and-Herb, '89 193
Stuffed with Wild Rice, Pork Loin, '84 35
Tomato Sauce, Pork Roast with, '87 249
Tropical Pork Loin, '96 86
Zesty Pork Roast, '85 179
Salad, Mandarin Pork-and-Spinach, '88 M126
Salad, Oriental Pork, '92 140
Salad, "Pig in the Garden," '92 255
Salad, Pork-'n'-Bean, '87 83
Salad, Thai Green Apple, '99 111
Sandwiches, Party Pork, '88 M273
Sausage, Pork, '81 55; '97 243
Sauté, Plum Delicious Pork, '89 105
Sesame Pork on Mixed Greens, Hot, '97 19
Sesame Pork Rounds, '89 122
Sloppy Joes, Pork, '86 294
Soup, Guadalajara, '88 30
Soup, Homemade, '79 198
Steaks, Herbed Pork, '80 72
Steaks, Peachy Pork, '79 166
Stew, Bama Brunswick, '87 4
Stew, Breeden Liles's Brunswick, '91 14
Stew, Brunswick, '80 264; '97 315
Stew, Dan Dickerson's Brunswick, '91 16
Stew, Easy Brunswick, '92 280; '99 235
Stew, Georgian Brunswick, '92 35
Stew, Pancho Villa, '94 44
Stew, Sonny Frye's Brunswick, '87 4
Stew, Virginia Ramsey's Favorite Brunswick,
    '91 16
Stir-Fried Pork, '87 51
Stir-Fried Pork in Garlic Sauce, '84 141
St. Tammany, Pork, '82 260
Swedish Porkburgers, '79 42
Sweet-and-Pungent Pork, '86 118
Sweet-and-Sour Pork, '79 42; '80 72, 227;
    '81 26, 104, 111; '82 12; '84 218; '85 34, 194;
    '86 241; '90 317; '92 219
Tamales, '80 195
Tamales, Hot, '83 51
Tasso Fettuccine, Crawfish and, '96 290
Tasso Gravy, '96 270
Tempting Twosome, '81 240
Tenderloin
    Apple Butter Pork Tenderloin, '99 145
    Apple-Ginger Pork Tenderloin, '86 75
    Apple-Mushroom Pork Tenderloin, '95 53
    Apricot Sauce, Pork Tenderloin with, '99 44
    Blue Cheese, Pork Tenderloin with, '86 76
    Cacciatore, Pork, '95 69
    Coriander-Pepper Pork Tenderloin, '99 145
    Curried Pork Tenderloin, '86 76
    Danish Pork Tenderloin, '82 186

Fruit Stuffing and Shiitake Sauce, Pork
    Tenderloin with, '97 218
Glazed Pork Tenderloin, '90 315
Grilled Marinated Pork Tenderloin, '91 199
Grilled Pork Medaillons, '93 229
Grilled Pork Tenderloin, '88 98; '91 163; '94 88
Grilled Pork Tenderloin, Garlic, '90 172
Grilled Pork Tenderloin, Molasses-, '96 265
Grilled Pork Tenderloins, '94 158
Grilled Pork Tenderloin with Apples, Celery,
    and Potatoes, '95 161
Grilled Pork Tenderloin with Brown Sauce,
    '89 32
Grilled Pork Tenderloin with Molasses Sauce,
    '97 193
Grilled Pork with Salsa, '90 128
Grilled Tenderloins, Honey-, '92 199
Herb-Crusted Pork Tenderloin with
    Horseradish-Roasted New Potatoes, '98 168
Herbed Pork Tenderloin with Parmesan-
    Pepper Toasts, '98 242
Honey-Mustard Pork Tenderloin, '95 52
Jamaican Jerk Pork Sandwiches with Apricot
    Mayonnaise, '97 320
Kabobs, Margarita Pork, '98 M223
Kabobs, Pineapple-Pork, '99 144
Lamb Extraordinaire, '99 242
Marinated Pork Tenderloin, '84 175
Marinated Pork Tenderloin with Jezebel
    Sauce, '96 212
Marsala, Pork, '90 35
Medaillons in Mustard Sauce, Pork, '90 96
Medaillons of Pork with Vegetables, '88 223
Medaillons with Chutney Sauce, Pork, '87 35
Medaillons with Fresh Fruit, Pork, '97 104
Medaillons with Port Wine and Dried
    Cranberry Sauce, Pork, '95 330
Mustard Sauce, Pork Tenderloin with,
    '92 302; '99 145
Onion-Balsamic Sauce, Pork Tenderloin with,
    '99 44
Orange Marmalade, Pork Tenderloin with,
    '91 49
Oven-Roasted Vegetables and Pork, '99 259
Parmigiana, Easy Pork, '94 57
Peking Pork Tenderloin, '93 173
Pepper-Honey Pork Tenderloins, '98 33
Piccata, Pork, '94 57; '99 332
Piccata, Pork Tenderloin, '86 76
Pinwheels, Herbed Pork, '92 23
Pinwheels, Spinach-Tenderloin, '89 M118
Platter, Tenderloin, '79 42
Roast Pork Tenderloin, '84 35
Rosemary Pesto, Pork Tenderloin with,
    '98 16
Sandwiches, Beef and Pork Tenderloin,
    '80 175
Scaloppine Marsala, Pork, '94 57
Scaloppine, Olive-Pork, '89 191
Sesame Pork Tenderloin, '95 53
Spiced Pork Tenderloin with Chili-Cranberry
    Glaze, '98 320
Stuffed Pork Tenderloins, Fruit-, '87 270
Stuffed Pork Tenderloin, Southern-Style,
    '99 45
Stuffed Pork Tenderloin, Spinach-and-Bacon,
    '94 81
Stuffed Tenderloin with Praline-Mustard
    Glaze, Apple-, '97 216
Sunrise Pork Tenderloin, '79 103
Towers, Pork Tenderloin, '86 75
Terrine, Jeweled Pork, '84 130
Terrine of Pork and Veal, '93 287
Wontons, Crispy Fried, '83 21

POTATOES. See also SWEET POTATOES.
    Accordion Potatoes, '98 69
    Anna, Potatoes, '97 53
    Appetizers, Fiery Stuffed Cherry Pepper, '97 269
    Appetizers, Potato Shell, '89 M119
    Bacon Dressing, Potatoes with Hot, '88 M294
    Bake, Chive-Potato, '82 229
    Baked. See also POTATOES/Stuffed.
        Avocado-Topped Potatoes, '83 3
        Beef and Chicken-Topped Potatoes, Creamed,
            '83 210
        Broccoli-and-Almond-Topped Potatoes, '83 3
        Broccoli-Topped Baked Potatoes, '86 17
        Buck's Taters, '95 72
        Cheese Potato Skins, '84 M239
        Cheese Sauce, Baked Potatoes with, '83 239
        Cheesy Frank-Topped Potatoes, '83 3
        Cheesy Potato Skins, '82 78
        Chili Potatoes, Roasted, '97 53
        Chili-Topped Potatoes, '83 3; '98 M289
        Crabmeat-Topped Potatoes, '83 3; '95 22
        Croquettes, Baked Potato, '97 30
        Frank-Filled Potatoes, '84 M11
        Fries, Baked Potato, '96 90
        Garden Potato Cups, '83 76
        Garden-Topped Potatoes, '83 4
        Gumbo Potatoes, '95 22
        Mexican-Topped Potatoes, '83 3
        Micro-Baked Potatoes, '81 M61
        Million Dollar Potatoes, '83 210
        Mushroom-Dill-Topped Potatoes, '86 41
        Mushroom Filling in a Peel, '84 214
        New Potatoes, Baked, '90 90
        Oven-Baked Potatoes, Easy, '82 202
        Parmesan-Cream Potatoes, '97 54
        Pleated Potatoes, Baked, '93 54
        Quick Baked Potatoes, '92 M134
        Quick Potatoes, '94 283
        Rosemary-Baked Potatoes, '95 23
        Rosemary-Roasted Potatoes, '95 20
        Salmon-Topped Potatoes, '84 124
        Sausage-Vegetable-Topped Potatoes, '98 29
        Shrimp-Sauced Potatoes, '81 M61
        Skins, Baked Potato, '86 81
        Skins, Cheese Potato, '84 M239
        Skins, Cheesy Potato, '82 78
        Smoked Baked Potatoes, '97 25
        Southwestern Potato Boats, '96 33
        Sweet-and-Sour-Topped Potatoes, '83 4
        Taco-Baked Potatoes, '84 119
        Taco-Topped Potatoes, '93 M18
        Wedges, Potato, '94 M119
    Bake, Ham-Potato-Pineapple, '93 302
    Bake, Herbed Fish and Potato, '79 287
    Bake, Onion-Potato, '83 M195
    Bake, Potato, '83 209
    Barbecued Potatoes, '91 311; '92 26
    Basil-Cheese Potatoes, '90 M316
    Basque-Style Potatoes, '79 46
    Beans and Potatoes, Down-Home, '85 254
    Beans and Potatoes, Snap, '98 177
    Beef Hash, '99 62
    Beets, Potato-Stuffed, '83 234
    Breads
        Biscuits, Potato-Bacon, '94 214
        Bowls, Irish Tater Bread, '96 111
        Dough, Potato Sourdough Bread, '94 324;
            '95 77
        Lightbread, Potato, '80 225
        Loaves, Potato, '86 162
        Old-Fashioned Potato Bread, '86 57
        Potato Bread, '85 56
        Rolls, Easy Potato, '89 287
        Rolls, Feathery Light Potato, '81 305; '82 36

POTATOES, Breads
(continued)

Rolls, Homemade Potato, '82 252
Rolls, Potato, '81 300; '99 290
Rolls, Potato Sourdough, '94 325; '95 77
Rolls, Potato Sourdough Cinnamon, '94 325;
    '95 77
Rolls, Potato Yeast, '87 53; '98 92
Rolls, Refrigerated Potato, '83 254
Rolls, Refrigerator Potato, '87 15
Rolls, Southern Potato, '86 299
Rolls, Super Potato, '85 145
Rolls, Supreme Potato, '82 130
Rolls, Whole Wheat Potato, '89 50
Sourdough Bread, Potato, '94 325; '95 77
Starter Food, '94 324; '95 77
Starter, Potato Sourdough, '94 324; '95 77
Toast, Potato-Crusted Texas, '94 142
Yeast, Potato, '87 53
Breakfast, Farmer's, '81 44
Breakfast Potatoes, '91 68
Breakfast Potatoes, Mexican, '81 209
Broiled Marinated Potatoes, '93 54
Browned Potatoes, Quick, '82 M172
Burgers, Potato-Crusted Crab, '94 139
Burritos, Breakfast, '99 103
Candy, Potato, '79 273
Caraway Potatoes, '85 85
Caraway Potatoes, Cheesy, '86 17
Casseroles
au Gratin, Potatoes, '93 90, 217
au Gratin, Potatoes and Eggs, '79 107
au Gratin, Potatoes-and-Zucchini, '84 5
au Gratin, Shredded Potatoes, '89 69
Breakfast Casserole, Potato, '80 52
Broccoli-Cheese Bake, Potato-, '80 114
Brunch for a Bunch, '88 57
Buffet Potatoes, '98 92
Cheese Casserole, Potato-, '79 101
Cheese Dream, Potato-, '91 307
Cheese Potatoes, Creamy, '88 M146
Cheese Potatoes, Double-, '86 6
Cheese Potatoes, Two-, '80 114
Cheesy Potato Casserole, '80 244; '83 53;
    '92 229
Cheesy Potatoes, '82 211
Chicken Livers and Potatoes, '82 218
Chive Potatoes, Cheesy, '79 46
Christmas Potatoes, '88 252
Cottage Potatoes, '89 69
Creamy Potato Bake, '82 201
Creamy Potato Casserole, '84 M113
Creamy Potatoes with Ham Bits, '87 191
Deviled Potatoes, Hot, '84 296; '85 196
Easy Potato Casserole, '80 114
Egg Casserole, Cheesy Potato-, '84 5
Eggplant Casserole, Potato-, '87 166
Fish and Potato Bake, Herbed, '80 34
Fluffy Potato Casserole, '80 268
Gourmet, Potatoes, '80 114
Gratin, Potato-and-Rutabaga, '96 237
Gratin with Caramelized Onions, Potato-
    Horseradish, '99 314
Gruyère Potatoes, '83 193
Ham-and-Potato Casserole, '83 M87; '96 103
Ham-and-Potato Casserole, Cheesy, '84 326
Hash Brown Cheese Bake, '82 50
Hash Brown-Cheese Bake, '97 323
Hash Brown-Ham-Cheese Bake, '97 323
Hash Brown Potato Casserole, '81 40
Holiday Potato Casserole, '92 302
Irish Potato Casserole, '81 263

Italian Casserole, '80 81
Italian-Style Potatoes, '89 69
Jalapeño Potatoes, '84 39
Lemon and Nutmeg Potatoes, '80 36
Lorraine, Potatoes, '87 190
Mashed Potato Casserole, '85 296; '99 223
Missy Potatoes, '85 259
Moussaka, Potatoes, '93 44
Mushroom-Potato Casserole, '84 5
Olive Potatoes, '80 114
Peppery Potato Casserole, '95 182
Potato Casserole, '87 190; '99 274
Processor Potato Casserole, '86 159
Rosemary's Potatoes, '98 53
Saucy Potato Casserole, '81 276
Saucy Potatoes for Company, '82 202
Sausage-Potato Casserole, '86 217
Scalloped Potatoes, '82 300; '83 211; '92 48
Scalloped Potatoes and Turnips, '85 235
Scalloped Potatoes, Cheesy, '83 82; '96 33
Scalloped Potatoes, Light, '89 311
Scalloped Potatoes, Mushroom, '87 191
Scalloped Potatoes, Party, '87 191
Scalloped Potatoes, Pork Chops and, '98 16
Scalloped Potatoes, Skillet, '79 46
Scalloped Potatoes, Special, '88 162
Scalloped Potatoes, Wayside, '79 283
Scalloped Potatoes, Winter Herb Garden,
    '99 289
Scalloped Potatoes with Pimiento, '81 75
Scalloped Potatoes with Sweet Marjoram and
    Parmesan Cheese, '91 246
Scallop, Pork Chops and Potato, '82 114
Shoestring Potato Tuna Bake, '82 211
Sour Cream Potatoes, '84 39
Thyme-Potato Bake, '96 121
Tomato Bake, Potato-, '86 17
Tomato Casserole, Saucy Potato-, '79 46
Caviar Potatoes, '84 80
Charcoal Potatoes, '88 129
Chicken and Potatoes, Roasted, '98 289
Chicken, Spanish, '98 183
Chili-Cheese Potatoes, '90 M62
Chili, Savory Potato, '83 284
Chowder. *See* **POTATOES/Soups.**
Colcannon, '90 64
Cottage Potatoes, '89 69; '93 M92
Creamed Potatoes, '83 25
Cream-Wine Sauce, Potatoes in, '86 18
Creole Potatoes, '87 138
Crisps, Potato, '96 175
Croquettes, Parmesan Potato, '84 210
Croquettes, Potato, '87 116
Doughnuts, Chocolate-Glazed Potato, '85 6
Doughnuts, Old-Fashioned Potato, '84 56
Dumplings, Chicken and Potato, '99 326
Dumplings, Venison Stew with Potato, '87 304
Egg, Eagle Nest, '99 194
Eggs and Meat, Potatoes with, '91 311; '92 25
Fans, Parmesan Potato, '84 M240
Feta Cheese, Potatoes with, '84 295; '85 196
Fish-and-Potato Platter, '89 M248
Fried
Almond-Fried Potatoes, '82 25
Baskets, Potato, '86 193; '99 166
Chips, Homemade Potato, '82 25
Crinkle-Cut Fries, '99 59
French Fries, '99 59
French Fries, Seasoned, '96 245
Herb French Fries, '82 211
Herb-Fried Potatoes, '82 25
Latkes, '84 318; '90 254
Latkes with Lemon-Date Relish, Potato, '96 271
Nests with Savory Shavings, Potato, '84 209

Okra and Potatoes, Fried, '97 136
Okra-Potato Fry, '81 159
Oven French Fries, '91 122
Oven-Fried Potatoes, '82 25
Oven Fries, Cheesy, '91 187
Oven Fries, Parmesan, '98 235
Patties, Fried Potato, '82 25; '93 54
Patties, Potato-Onion, '95 269
(Plantain Chips), Tostones de Platano, '92 158
Puffs, Potato, '80 36
Shavings, Savory, '84 209
Southern-Fried Potatoes, '82 25; '97 53
Special Potatoes, '83 169
Waffle Chips, '99 59
Wedges, Beer-Batter Potato, '83 211
Frittata, Potato, '89 145
Frittata, Potato-Bacon, '95 269; '98 330
Fritters, Cheese-Stuffed Potato, '96 153
Fritters, Potato-Ham, '98 249
Garlic-Parsley Potatoes, '90 290
Garlic Potatoes, '84 296; '85 196
Gnocchi à la Narciso, '97 246
Golden Potatoes, '96 139
Gratin, Dual Potato, '93 328
Green Beans and Potatoes, '91 221
Grilled Herb Potatoes, '84 172
Grilled Irish Potatoes, '97 53
Grilled Potatoes, Italian, '98 171
Hash, Beef, '95 24
Hash Brown Bake, '95 281
Hash Brown Potatoes, '81 48
Hash Browns, Carrot, '96 107
Hash Browns, Company, '79 268; '80 14
Hash Browns, Convenient, '95 135
Hash Browns, Franks and, '80 166
Hash Brown Skillet Breakfast, '82 5
Hash with Rosemary, Potato, '98 16
Herb Butter, Potatoes with, '81 276
Herbed Potatoes, '91 220
Herb Potatoes, '88 134
Italiano, Potatoes, '89 174
Latkes, Potato, '97 252
Mashed
Ancho-Beer Mashers, '98 248
Bake, Creamy Potato, '88 41
Basic Mashed Potatoes, '92 330
Bites, Mashed Potato, '98 249
Blue Cheese Mashed Potatoes, '92 330
Bowls, Mashed Potato, '97 199
Buttermilk-Basil Mashed Potatoes, '95 330
Casserole, Mashed Potato, '85 296; '99 223
Celery Potatoes, Whipped, '94 305; '99 45
Celery Root Mashed Potatoes, '98 293
Chive-Cream Cheese Mashed Potatoes, '92 330
Chive Mashed Potatoes, '97 308
Crab Marinière, Mashed Potatoes with, '99 165
Cream Cheese Mashed Potatoes, '97 14
Dill-Sour Cream Mashed Potatoes, '92 330
Duchesse, Potatoes, '84 210
Duchess Potatoes, '93 288
Feta Mashed Potatoes, '92 330
Fix-Ahead Mashed Potatoes, '89 70
Fluffy Potatoes, '84 296; '85 196
Garlic-Gruyère Mashed Potatoes, '98 322
Garlic Mashed Potatoes, '92 330; '93 328;
    '97 308
Good Old Mashed Potatoes, '92 215
Harvest Mashed Potatoes, '98 248
Herbed Lemon Mashed Potatoes, '93 208
Horseradish Mashed Potatoes, '98 69, 118
Jazzy Mashed Potatoes, '87 192
Mexican Mashed Potatoes, '92 330
Nest, Peas in a Potato, '84 M239
Nests, Mashed Potato, '94 141

Old-Fashioned Mashed Potatoes, '89 234
Orange Mashed Potatoes, '96 33
Parsnip Mash, '97 263
Pesto Mashed Potatoes, '92 330
Quick-and-Easy Mashed Potatoes, '93 41
Roasted Garlic Mashed Potatoes, '95 288
Roasted Garlic-Parmesan Mashed Potatoes, '97 263
Seasoned Potatoes, '87 253
Snow-Capped Potatoes, '84 255
Stuffed Mashed Potatoes, '98 328
Thunderbolt Potatoes, '94 213
Topping, Mashed Potato, '89 243
Turnips and Potatoes, '79 254
Mexican-Style Potatoes, '91 78
Mustard Greens and Potatoes, '86 224
Mustard Potatoes, '79 32
New Potatoes
Baked New Potatoes, '90 90
Basil Cream Sauce, New Potatoes with, '91 46
Blue Cheese Potatoes, '98 247
Browned New Potatoes, '86 244
Caviar Potatoes, Appetizer, '86 223
Chard and Potatoes, Creamy, '98 250
Cheese Potatoes, Double-, '86 6
Cheesy New Potatoes, '85 156
Creamed Peas and New Potatoes, '79 102
Creamy Potatoes and Broccoli, '92 61
Garden New Potatoes, '91 80
Garlic New Potatoes, '92 54
Green Beans with New Potatoes, '87 164
Ham-Stuffed New Potatoes, '88 211
Herbed New Potatoes, '81 102; '83 9, M148
Lemon-Buttered New Potatoes, '84 149; '90 268; '98 159
Lemon Sauce, New Potatoes with, '86 130
Lemony New Potatoes, '82 158
Medley, New Potato, '90 279
Medley, Potato, '92 61
Parsley-Chive Sauce, New Potatoes with, '84 212
Parsley New Potatoes, '79 122
Roasted Caraway Potatoes, '96 82
Roasted New Potatoes, '90 138
Roasted New Potatoes, Crispy, '98 166
Roasted New Potatoes, Herb-Crusted Pork Tenderloin with Horseradish-, '98 168
Salad, Asparagus-and-New Potato, '86 69
Salad, New Potato, '84 120, 139; '94 162
Seasoned New Potatoes, '87 M151
Skillet, Potato-Vegetable, '92 61
Steamed Potatoes, Lemon-, '86 177
Summertime Potatoes, '86 195
Omelet, Family-Size Potato, '94 31
Omelet, Potato-Sprout, '79 128
Omelets, Country, '91 128
Oven Potatoes, Crispy, '82 96
Pancake, Potato, '85 20
Pancakes, German Potato, '98 279
Pancakes, Leftover Potato, '96 138
Pancakes, Moist Potato, '80 36
Pancakes, Old-Fashioned Potato, '96 138
Pancakes, One Potato-Two Potato, '96 138
Pancakes, Parsley-Potato, '96 251; '97 103
Pancakes, Potato, '79 115; '89 144
Pancakes, Potato-Ham, '96 138
Parmesan-Paprika Potatoes, '99 169
Parmesan Potatoes, '82 270; '90 M62; '92 M341; '93 M46
Parmesan-Potato Fans, '88 M190
Parmesan Potato Wedges, '95 181
Parslied Potatoes, '86 18
Patties, Thunderbolt Potato, '94 213
Peas and Potatoes with Dill, '99 67

Peppers, Potatoes with Sweet Red, '87 192
Pie, Country Breakfast, '93 M328
Pie, Meat-and-Potato, '84 23
Pie, Potato-Topped Turkey, '86 265
Pizzas, Roasted Potato, '99 16
Pork Tenderloin with Apples, Celery, and Potatoes, Grilled, '95 161
Pudding, Carrot-Potato, '94 279
Puff, Potato-Cheese, '95 269
Puffs, Celeried Potato, '89 279
Quiche, Crustless Potato, '83 49
Roasted Potatoes, '99 60
Roasted Potatoes, Carrots, and Leeks, '94 276
Roasted Potatoes, Garlic-, '95 87, 342
Roasted Potatoes, Oven-, '98 103
Rolls. *See* **POTATOES/Breads.**
Rosemary, Potatoes Anna with, '84 209
Roses, Potato, '81 246
Sage Potatoes, '94 320
Salads
Any Day Potato Salad, '81 154
Avocado, Potato Salad with, '98 332
Avocado-Potato Salad with Horseradish Dressing, '96 200
Bacon-Topped Potato Salad, '85 59
Baked Potato Salad, '97 319
Basil Potato Salad, '94 178
Bean Salad, Potato-, '82 301
Blue Cheese-Potato Salad, '91 208
Broccoli-Potato Salad, Hot, '85 23
Charletta's Potato Salad, '98 153
Chunky Potato Salad, '81 M138
Confetti Potato Salad, '80 5; '88 16
Corned Beef-Potato Salad, '85 213
Corned Beef Salad, Potato-, '81 36
Cottage Cheese-Potato Salad, '79 147, 285
Creamy Potato Salad, '80 178; '88 171; '92 241; '98 175
Creole Potato Salad, '99 136
Curried Potato Salad, '99 137
Deluxe Potato Salad, '80 155
Dill-and-Sour Cream Potato Salad, '93 105; '94 100
Dill Potato Salad, '85 213; '94 179; '99 104
Dill Potato Salad, Hot, '79 78
Dutch Potato Salad, Hot, '86 297; '87 176
Festive Potato Salad, '89 315
Fish-Potato Salad, Smoked, '84 233
French-Style Potato Salad, '88 171
Fruity Potato Salad, '85 214
Garden Patch Potato Salad, '84 82
German Potato Salad, '82 134, 239; '84 18; '92 169; '97 195; '98 175
German Potato Salad, Hot, '79 78; '94 254
German-Style Potato Salad, '83 23; '88 M194
Goat Cheese and Potato Salad, Warm, '96 234
Grecian Potato Salad, '82 55
Greek Potato Salad, '98 276
Green Bean-Potato Salad, '83 80
Green Bean-Red Potato Salad, '96 175
Ham-and-Egg Potato Salad, '86 84
Ham and Potato Salad, '80 272
Ham-and-Potato Salad, '95 94
Herbed Potato Salad, '87 171; '94 164
Horseradish Potato Salad, '98 175
Hot-and-Light Potato Salad, '93 90
Hot Potato Greens, '97 20
Hot Potato Salad, '79 78; '81 276; '86 10
Hot Potato Salad Supreme, '79 78
Jalapeño Potato Salad, '97 64
Joy's Potato Salad, '99 83
Layered Creamy Potato Salad, '81 23
Lemon-Basil Potato Salad, '97 63
Marinated Potato Slices, '93 98

Mediterranean Spring Salad, '80 148
Mustard Potato Salad, '86 302
New Potato Salad, '84 120, 139; '94 162
New Potato Salad, Asparagus-and-, '86 69
Olive-Potato Salad, '85 114
Parmesan Potato Salad, Hot, '79 78
Parslied Potato Salad, '85 240
Patio Potato Salad, '90 160
Pepper Cups, Potato Salad in, '79 78
Peppers, Potato Salad 'n', '83 135
Pesto Potato Salad, '90 164
Pickle-Potato Salad, Sweet, '85 213
Pole Bean-Potato Salad, Hot, '79 74
Potato Salad, '90 122; '94 160
Red Potato Salad, '93 119; '96 172
Roasted-Potato Salad, Creamy, '97 161
Salmon-Potato Salad, '87 285
Saucy Potato Salad, '87 123
Savory Potato Salad, '80 30
Shrimp-and-Potato Salad, '96 211
Smoked Salmon Potato Salad, '97 64
Sour Cream Potato Salad, '79 104; '80 79; '99 137
Sour Cream-Potato Salad, '84 149
South-of-the-Border Potato Salad, '94 178
Spicy Potato Salad, '97 305
Steak Salad Niçoise, Grilled, '98 148
Sugar Snap Peas, Potato Salad with, '91 120
Sweet and Sour Potato Salad, '80 152
Sweet-and-Sour Potato Salad, '92 106
Tri Club Potato Salad, '92 166
Tuna-Potato Salad, '84 289
Warm Potato-and-Sausage Salad, '96 25
Warm Potato Salad with Smoked Sausage, '97 267
Scalloped Root Vegetables, '98 310
Skillet Potatoes, Oregano-and-Lemon, '93 54
Skillet Potatoes, Peppy, '86 110
Skins, Baked Potato, '86 81
Skins, Cheesy Potato, '82 78
Skin Snack, Potato, '91 18
Slims, Potato, '81 276
Soufflé, Cheesy Potato, '89 332
Soufflé Potatoes, '84 295; '85 196; '90 14
Soups
Asparagus-Potato Soup, '85 23
Asparagus Soup, '98 290
Bacon Soup, Potato-, '84 M38
Baked Potato Soup, '91 311; '92 26
Beet Soup, Potato-, '88 156
Bisque, Spinach-Potato, '86 66
Bisque, Squash, '98 290
Carrot Soup, Potato-, '88 297
Celery-and-Potato Soup, '84 279
Cheesy Potato-and-Wild Rice Soup, '89 16
Chowder, Mushroom-Potato, '92 331
Chowder, Potato-Corn, '94 66
Chowder, Potato-Vegetable, '98 335
Chowder with Ham, Potato, '99 141
Cream of Potato Soup, '80 M224; '82 21
Cream of Potato Soup, Golden, '86 302
Creamy Potato Soup, '81 19, 98; '84 112
Cucumber-Potato Soup, Chilled, '85 93
Cucumber Soup, Cold Potato-, '88 160
Easy Potato Soup, '92 17
Hearty Potato Soup, '98 292
Holiday Potato Soup, '79 236
Irish Potato Soup, '99 54
Kale Soup, Creamy, '96 203
Leek-and-Potato Soup, '84 112
Leek Soup, Cream of, '99 276
Onion-and-Potato Soup, Creamy, '92 51; '97 304
Pea Soup, Potato-, '94 90

POTATOES, Soups
(continued)

Potato Soup, '82 278; '83 292; '92 263
Sausage-Potato Soup, '80 25
Sausage Soup, Easy Potato-, '98 315
Special Potato Soup, '82 3
Subtle Potato Potage, '80 78
Three-Potato Soup, '86 16
Vichyssoise, '86 181
Vichyssoise with Mint Cream, Cucumber, '98 246
Yogurt Soup, Potato-, '92 217
Steak 'n Potatoes, Skillet, '81 18
Stew, Meatball, '98 30
Stew, Potato-Oyster, '89 243
Stir-Fry, Potato, '93 240
Stir-Fry, Potato-Snow Pea, '86 173
Stuffed
Alfredo, Potatoes, '89 204
Bacon-Stuffed Potatoes, '86 193
Bacon-Stuffed Potatoes, Cheesy, '81 M61
Baked Potatoes, Stuffed, '83 322
Baked Stuffed Potatoes, '84 38
Béchamel Sauce, Stuffed Potatoes with, '84 M239
Black-Eyed Pea-Spinach-Stuffed Potatoes, '95 22
Blue Cheese Potatoes, Bacon-Topped, '79 46
Blue Cheese Stuffed Potatoes, '81 276; '92 M228
Blue Cheese-Stuffed Potatoes, '89 69
Broccoli Bakers, '99 308
Broccoli-Shrimp Stuffed Potatoes, '92 M228
Caviar Potatoes, Appetizer, '86 223
Cheese-and-Chive Potatoes, Creamy, '99 308
Cheese Sauce, Stuffed Potatoes with, '87 192
Chicken-Cheese Stuffed Potatoes, '86 55
Chicken Fajita Spuds, '96 238
Chive-and-Gorgonzola Stuffed Potatoes, Creamy, '99 308
Chives, Potatoes with, '81 M61
Chive-Stuffed Baked Potatoes, '79 52
Chive-Stuffed Potatoes, Cheesy, '91 128
Chive-Stuffed Potatoes, Creamy, '80 268
Crab-Stuffed Potatoes, '91 311; '92 26; '99 307
Crab-Stuffed Potatoes, Cheesy, '86 17
Creamy Stuffed Baked Potatoes, '86 55
Creamy Stuffed Potatoes, '79 211
Fish-Stuffed Potatoes, '92 306
Fluffy Stuffed Potatoes, '86 223
Franks and Potatoes, Stuffed, '81 202
Ham Stuffed Potatoes, '79 210
Hearty Stuffed Potatoes, '89 M282
Herb Stuffed Potatoes, '79 211
Jalapeño-Ham Stuffed Potatoes, '81 M61
Lemon-Herb Stuffed Potatoes, '83 173
Mexican-Stuffed Potatoes, '91 131
Mushroom-Swiss Spuds, '96 M238
Patchwork Potatoes, '86 54
Rellenos Potatoes, Papa's, '96 238
Roquefort, Potatoes, '79 211
Savory Stuffed Potatoes, '81 101
Seafood-Stuffed Potatoes, '95 M192
Shrimp-and-Mushroom Stuffed Potatoes, '99 308
Shrimp Boats, '79 57
Shrimp-Stuffed Potatoes, Creamy, '80 36
South-of-the-Border Stuffed Potatoes, '86 54
Stuffed Potatoes, '89 173
Summertime Potatoes, '86 M195
Tuna Stuffed Potatoes, '79 210
Twice Baked Cottage-Style Potatoes, '91 135
Twice-Baked Potato, '90 M295

Twice-Baked Potatoes, '83 227; '91 185
Vegetable-Topped Stuffed Potatoes, '85 235
Yogurt-Stuffed Potatoes, '88 24
Zesty Stuffed Potatoes, '94 M46
Tacos, Breakfast, '91 316
Tarts, Phyllo Potato, '98 69
Tortilla Campesina, '89 85
Tortilla Española, '92 175
Trout, Sweet Onion-Stuffed, '99 52
Vinaigrette, Potato-Broccoli, '85 84
Wedges, Lemon Potato, '88 21
Wedges, Lemony Potato, '90 M61
POULTRY. *See* **CHICKEN, CORNISH HENS, GAME, TURKEY.**
PRALINE. *See also* **CANDIES/Pralines.**
Almonds, Praline, '97 285
Bananas, Praline, '84 313
Brownies, Praline, '93 243
Buns, Praline, '90 195
Buttercream, Praline, '95 243
Cake, Praline, '81 162
Cake, Praline Ice Cream, '80 84
Cake, Praline Pound, '82 88
Cheesecake, Praline, '83 270; '89 93
Cheesecake, Praline-Crusted, '99 295
Coffee, Praline, '97 17
Coffee, Praline-Flavored, '87 69
Compote, Warm Praline Fruit, '85 260
Cookies, Praline, '91 271
Cookies, Praline Shortbread, '88 242
Cookies, Praline Thumbprint, '89 328
Filling, Praline, '89 328
Freeze, Praline, '89 60; '90 48
French Toast, Praline, '98 55
Glaze, Apple-Stuffed Tenderloin with Praline-Mustard, '97 216
Glaze, Praline, '82 196
Ham, Praline, '85 302; '96 303
Horns, Praline, '96 316
Ice Cream, Praline, '89 318
Ice Cream, Pralines and Cream, '82 184; '83 159
Pastries, Praline, '89 318
Pecans, Praline, '97 285
Pie, Chocolate-Praline, '86 259
Pie, Frosty Pumpkin-Praline, '91 M234
Pie, Georgia Peach-and-Praline, '98 196
Pie, Peach Praline, '89 136
Pie, Pear-Praline, '97 192
Pie, Praline-Apple, '99 331
Pie, Pumpkin Praline, '80 244
Powder, Praline, '95 243
Sauce, Bourbon Praline, '81 170
Sauce, Chocolate-Praline, '85 M295
Sauce, Peach-Praline, '85 161
Sauce, Praline, '83 25; '84 143; '89 95; '92 282; '93 214; '94 206, 312; '96 285
Sauce, Praline Ice Cream, '85 189
Sauce, Southern Praline Ice Cream, '86 M227
Sweet Potatoes, Praline-Topped, '98 96
Toast, Orange Praline, '79 36
Torte, Chocolate Praline, '84 165
Torte, Lucy's Apricot Praline, '95 243
PRESERVES. *See* **JAMS AND JELLIES.**
PRESSURE COOKER
Carrots Polynesian, '79 45
Chicken Marengo, '92 70
Jambalaya, Black-Eyed Pea, '92 70
Roast, Pressure-Cooker, '91 289
Stew, Quick Beef, '92 71
PRETZELS
Brownies, Saucepan Pretzel, '85 171
Chocolate-Covered Pretzels, '82 295
Dressing, Pretzel, '86 280
Flying Brooms, '98 255

Frosted Pretzels, '92 280
Garlands, Pretzel, '93 286
Herb Pretzels with Lower Sodium Horseradish Mustard, '86 325
Homemade Pretzels, '84 159; '91 185
Nuggets, Golden North Pole, '99 M309
Popcorn, Pretzel, '84 30
Reindeer Food, Magic, '99 M309
Soft Pretzels, '83 18
Soft Pretzels, Chewy, '87 159
Whole Wheat Pretzels, '89 20
PRUNES
Bavarian, Prune, '86 223
Bread, Prune-Nut, '87 255; '91 55
Butter, Prune-Orange, '92 49
Cake and Sauce, Prune, '85 118
Cake, Prune, '85 223
Cake, Spicy Prune, '79 136
Chicken with Prunes, Saffron, '97 264
Compote, Baked Prune, '94 50
Merlot, Prunes in, '98 18
Muffins, Miniature Prune, '85 223
Muffins, Spicy Prune, '97 271
Muffins, Wheat Germ-Prune, '81 106
Orange-Spiced Prunes, '85 224
Pork Chops Stuffed with Prunes, '84 7
Pork Loin Roast, Prune-Stuffed, '80 29
Raspberry Prunes, '82 124
Relish, Peppy Prune, '90 227
Stuffed Prunes, '85 47
Tarts, Brandied Prune, '85 223
Tzimmes, '95 102
PUDDINGS. *See also* **CUSTARDS, MOUSSES.**
Apple-Nut Pudding with Hot Rum Sauce, '79 86
Applesauce-Graham Cracker Pudding, '81 34
Banana
Almost Banana Pudding, '88 174
Banana Pudding, '82 53; '84 94; '85 255; '88 16, 32
Basic Banana Pudding, '81 59
Creamy Banana Pudding, '89 M130
Delicious Banana Pudding, '80 9
Fudge-Banana Pudding, '97 331
Mallow Pudding, Banana-, '86 139
No-Bake Banana Pudding, '91 172; '99 197
Old-Fashioned Banana Pudding, '92 94
Peanut Butter-Banana Pudding, '93 340
Pops, Banana Pudding Parfait, '96 180
Sour Cream Banana Pudding, '98 90
Surprise Banana Pudding, '86 7
Trifle, Banana Pudding, '98 273
Beach, The, '95 168
Blackberry Pudding Tarts, '93 200
Blueberry-Raspberry Pudding, Russian, '97 128
Bread
Amish Bread Pudding, '80 8
Apple-Raisin Bread Pudding, '88 175
Apricot Bread Pudding, '85 24
Biscuit Pudding, '79 86; '93 51
Blueberry Bread Pudding, '88 154
Bread Pudding, '89 M130; '90 219
Buttermilk Bread Pudding with Butter-Rum Sauce, '95 134
Cheesy Bread Pudding, '83 68
Chocolate Biscuit Bread Pudding, '94 215
Chocolate Bread Pudding, '80 8
Chocolate Bread Pudding with Whiskey Sauce, '99 277
Cinnamon Toast Pudding with Caramel Sauce, '96 284
Custard Sauce, Bread Pudding with, '97 313
Durfee's Bread Pudding, '96 48
French Bread Pudding, '85 231
Lemon Bread Pudding, Old-Fashioned, '88 95

Mushroom Bread Pudding, '99 58
Old-Fashioned Bread Pudding, '83 213; '88 175
Old-Fashioned Bread Pudding with Bourbon Custard Sauce, '95 271
Old-Fashioned Bread Pudding with Rum Sauce, '88 32
Peachy Bread Pudding, '88 175
Piña Colada Bread Pudding, '98 34
Plum Bread Pudding, Refrigerator, '97 177
Pumpkin Bread Pudding, '98 240
Raisin Bread Pudding, '94 215
Raisin Bread Pudding with Bourbon Sauce, '98 336
Spiced Bread Pudding, '93 52
Sweet Potato Bread Pudding, '94 241
Sweet Roll Pudding, '96 283
Tennessee Bread Pudding with Bourbon Sauce, '93 51
Vanilla Sauce, Bread Pudding with, '97 M15
Whiskey Sauce, Bread Pudding with, '80 58; '90 230; '92 93
Brownie Pudding, '79 265; '80 295
Brown Sugar-Pecan Pudding, '86 M165
Butternut Squash Pudding, '89 M313; '90 M19
Cake, Carrot Pudding, '83 24
Cake, Danish Pudding, '91 269
Cake, Lemon Pudding, '83 106
Cake Pudding, Chocolate, '81 99
Cake Pudding, Hot Fudge Sundae, '88 167
Cake Pudding, Lemon, '92 96; '98 35
Cake Pudding, Wine, '79 230
Cake, Saucy Pudding, '98 196
Cake with Blueberry Sauce, Buttermilk-Lemon Pudding, '95 135
Chocolate-Almond Pudding, '82 M142; '88 24
Chocolate-Almond Silk Pudding, '96 266
Chocolate Pudding, Creamy, '83 106
Chocolate Pudding, Fudgy, '96 285
Chocolate-Rum Dessert, '81 247
Christmas Pudding, '79 230
Christmas Pudding, Flaming, '85 312
Christmas Pudding with Brandy Sauce, Baked, '88 279
Cookies, Pudding-Oatmeal, '98 215
Cranberry Pudding, '84 306
Finger Painting Never Tasted So Good, '95 167
Frozen Ozark Pudding, '88 127
Fruit Pudding Compote, Fresh, '86 151
Hansel Pudding, '80 9
Holland Rusk Pudding, Yia Yia's, '93 124
Hot Fudge Pudding, '81 208
Kugel, Nu Awlins, '94 229
Lemon Fluff Pudding, '85 304
Lemon-Pear Pudding, '96 283
Lemon Pudding, '79 86; '81 99
Lemon Pudding, Layered, '82 128
Mandarin-Almond Pudding, '85 M12
Orange Custard Pudding, '88 174
Orange Pudding, '81 85; '82 111; '83 153
Orange-Tapioca Crème, '82 M283
Peanut Butter-Banana Pudding, '93 340
Peanut Butter Pudding, '85 95; '88 32
Peanut Parfait, Bodacious, '95 167
Pecan-Mocha Pudding, '89 M130
Pineapple Pudding, '80 102
Plum Pudding, '79 281
Plum Pudding, Flamed, '84 276
Plum Pudding-Gelatin Mold, '86 300; '87 178
Plum Pudding, Light, '86 318
Plum Pudding, Old-Fashioned, '80 264
Pumpkin Pudding, '89 M313; '90 M20
Pumpkin Pudding, Baked, '80 244
Raisin-Pumpkin Pudding, '84 315
Raspberry Pudding, '92 92

Rice
Amaretto Rice Pudding, '86 334
Apple Rice Pudding, '91 217
Brown Rice Pudding, '85 77
Creamy Rice Pudding, '81 51, 205
Fruited Rice Pudding, '81 205; '86 95
Fudgy Rice Pudding, '81 205
Old-Fashioned Rice Pudding, '85 147
Raisin-Rice Pudding, '87 46
Velvety Rice Pudding, '81 205
Rum Pudding with Raspberry Sauce, '82 288
Savory
Carrot-Potato Pudding, '94 279
Cheese Pudding, Baked, '86 78
Corn-Cheese Pudding, '80 244
Corn Pudding, '79 276; '81 128; '86 192; '90 219; '98 124; '99 71, 270
Corn Pudding, Baked, '83 314
Corn Pudding, Creamy, '81 267
Corn Pudding, Dashiell, '98 274
Corn Pudding, Easy, '83 280
Corn Pudding, Fresh, '80 157, 165; '89 172
Corn Pudding, Tee's, '95 318
Grits Pudding, '96 28
Onion Pudding, Kathy's, '95 318
Persimmon Pudding, '79 206
Squash Pudding, '82 277; '83 15
Sweet Potato Pudding, '79 244; '86 52
Turnip Pudding, '94 213
Yorkshire Pudding, '80 252; '98 86
Scuppernong Pudding Tarts, '98 221
Snowflake Pudding, '85 30
Snow White Pudding, '85 77
Steamed Date Pudding, '79 86
Steamed Ginger Pudding, '96 283
Steamed Holiday Pudding, '84 275
Steamed Mincemeat Pudding, '80 264
Summer Pudding, '98 217
Tipsy Pudding, Parson's, '80 156
Vanilla Pudding, '88 32
Vanilla Pudding, Creamy, '83 227
Woodford Pudding, '79 86

PUMPKIN
Baked Pumpkin, '82 217
Bars and Cookies
Cake Bars, Pumpkin, '80 245
Chocolate Chip Cookies, Pumpkin-, '93 235
Drop Cookies, Pumpkin, '79 206
Great Pumpkin Cookies, '91 234
Jack-o'-Lantern Cookies, '87 214
Nut Bars, Pumpkin, '82 217
Peppy Pumpkin Cookies, '89 253
Pumpkin Bars, '80 40
Walnut Cookies, Frosted Pumpkin-, '82 217
Bisque, Spicy Pumpkin, '86 67
Breads
Brother Boniface's Pumpkin Bread, '98 26
Coconut Bread, Pumpkin-, '87 255
Cream Cheese and Preserves, Pumpkin Bread with, '84 264
Gingerbread with Caramel Sauce, Pumpkin, '93 235
Harvest Pumpkin Bread, '90 M215
Harvest Pumpkin Loaf, '85 232
Moist Pumpkin Bread, '80 245
Muffins, Monster, '94 256
Muffins, Nutty Pumpkin, '86 291
Muffins, Pumpkin, '79 206, 275; '81 272
Muffins, Pumpkin-Apple, '96 242
Nut Bread, Pumpkin-, '83 294
Oatmeal Loaf, Pumpkin, '81 49
Orange-Pumpkin Bread, '87 300
Pancakes, Pumpkin, '80 228
Pecan Bread, Pumpkin-, '87 221

Pumpkin Bread, '81 8
Rolls, Pumpkin, '87 254
Spiced Pumpkin Bread, '91 233
Cake Bars, Pumpkin, '80 245
Cake, Pumpkin, '81 272; '93 303; '98 241
Cake, Pumpkin Date, '79 251
Cake, Pumpkin Kahlúa, '86 292
Cake, Pumpkin Layer, '80 245
Cake, Pumpkin Pound, '92 235
Cake Squares, Orange-Pumpkin, '83 242
Calabaza Guisada con Puerco (Pumpkin Cooked with Pork), '80 193
Cheesecake, Pumpkin, '80 254; '85 280; '96 268
Chiffon, Pumpkin, '82 216; '86 283; '88 260
Chips, Pumpkin, '98 241
Chocolate Pumpkin, '96 254
Chowder, Pumpkin-Corn, '97 219
Cooked Fresh Pumpkin, '88 M230
Cookies. See PUMPKIN/Bars and Cookies.
Cupcakes, Pumpkin, '85 121
Custard, Pumpkin, '88 279
Delight, Pumpkin-Orange, '86 321
Dessert, Frozen Pumpkin, '88 167
Dessert, Pumpkin Chiffon, '88 128
Doughnut Drops, Pumpkin, '90 323
Empanadas de Calabaza (Pumpkin Empanadas), '94 28
Empanadas, Pumpkin, '82 223
Flan, Pumpkin, '82 217; '97 219
Ice Cream Pumpkin, '96 255
Mold, Pumpkin, '82 311
Mousse, Pumpkin, '91 96; '92 130
Pasta, Pumpkin, '98 241
Pies
Autumn Pumpkin Pie, '87 213
Bourbon-Pecan Pumpkin Pie, '87 264
Chiffon Pie, Pumpkin, '84 312
Cracked Caramel-Pumpkin Pie, '99 254
Festive Pumpkin Pie, '81 M269
Fluffy Pumpkin Pie, '80 283
Frosty Pumpkin Pie, '96 279
Ice Cream Pie, Pumpkin, '81 272
Ice Cream Pie, Pumpkin-, '87 243
Mama's Pumpkin Pie, '96 242
Meringue, Pumpkin Pie with, '92 268
New-Fashioned Pumpkin Pie, '90 296
Nutty Pumpkin Pie, '82 67
Pecan Pie, Pumpkin-, '85 233, 282
Praline Pie, Frosty Pumpkin-, '91 M234
Praline Pie, Pumpkin, '80 244
Quick Pumpkin Pie, '88 M230
Rich Pumpkin Pie, '86 292
Sour Cream-Pumpkin Pie, '84 263
Spiced Nut Crust, Pumpkin Pie in, '87 295
Spicy Pumpkin Pies, '84 322
Supreme, Pumpkin Pie, '82 217
Traditional Pumpkin Pie, '85 256
Pizza Pumpkins, '98 255
Profiteroles with Warm Cranberry Compote, Pumpkin-Spiced, '97 264
Pudding, Baked Pumpkin, '80 244
Pudding, Pumpkin, '89 M313; '90 M20
Pudding, Pumpkin Bread, '98 240
Pudding, Raisin-Pumpkin, '84 315
Risotto with Shrimp, Pumpkin, '98 240
Roll, Pumpkin, '79 206; '91 297
Sauce, Beurre Blanc, '98 240
Sauce, Pumpkin Seed, '88 246
Seeds, Seasoned Pumpkin, '91 234
Seeds, Toasted Pumpkin, '88 M230; '98 241
Soup, Cream of Pumpkin, '93 234
Soup, Curried Pumpkin, '96 242
Soup, Pumpkin, '79 48
Soup, Pumpkin-Pear, '92 234

PUMPKIN
(continued)

Soup, Pumpkin-Tomato, '86 291
Soup with Ginger-Lime Cream, Pumpkin-Corn,
   '95 227
Swirl, Easy Pumpkin, '93 234
Tarts, No-Bake Pumpkin, '86 291
Waffles, Pumpkin, '95 282
Waffles, Pumpkin-Nut, '86 96
Waffles with Mandarin Orange Sauce, Dessert
   Pumpkin, '89 204
PUNCH. *See* **BEVERAGES/Alcoholic, Punch.**

QUAIL. *See* **GAME/Quail.**
QUESADILLAS
Apple Quesadillas, '99 248
Bacon-Jalapeño-Tomato Quesadillas, '95 240
Chicken-and-Black Bean Quesadillas, '96 288
Chicken-and-Brie Quesadillas with Chipotle
   Salsa, '99 311
Chicken Quesadillas, Spicy, '95 42
Easy Quesadillas, '98 M205
Green Chile Quesadillas, '90 121
Quick Quesadillas, '89 87
Salmon Quesadilla with Cucumber Salsa,
   Grilled, '95 131
Sausage Quesadillas, '90 118
Torta, Quesadilla, '97 325
Vegetable Quesadillas, '97 65
Vegetable Quesadilla with Roasted Salsa,
   Northern New Mexican, '95 130
Western Quesadillas, '97 65
QUICHES
Artichoke Quiche, '91 71
Asparagus-Tomato Quiche, '88 198
Broccoli Quiche, Easy, '82 34
Broccoli Quiche, Italian, '85 45
Broccoli-Rice Quiche, '81 228
Casserole, Quiche, '95 33
Cauliflower Quiche, '83 86
Cheese
   Bacon-Cheese Quiches, Miniature, '83 93
   Blue Cheese Quiche, '84 52
   Cheddar-Leek Quiche, '88 198
   Cream Cheese Quiche, '96 203
   Green Onion Quiche, Cheesy, '83 194; '84 42
   Ham-and-Cheese Quiches, Individual, '98 24
   Ham-Cheese Quiche, '79 26
   Ham Quiche, Cheesy, '79 127
   Jalapeño Quiche, Cheesy, '84 31
   Mexican Cheese Pie, '83 69
   Miniature Cheese Quiches, '80 150
   Sausage-Cheddar Quiche, '79 26
   Sealed with a Quiche, '95 135
   Spinach Quiche, Cheesy, '81 228
   Squares, Cheesy Hot Quiche, '79 124
   Squares, Quiche, '84 222
   Swiss Alpine Quiche, '90 18
   Swiss-Zucchini Quiche, '82 49
   Tarragon Cocktail Quiches, '84 127
   Vegetable Quiche, Cheese-, '81 228
   Zucchini Quiche, Cheesy, '83 312
Chicken Divan Quiche, '88 M125
Chicken-Pecan Quiche, '91 206
Chile Pepper Quiche, '82 224
Clam Quiche, '83 215
Crab Quiche, '82 M122, 243
Crab Quiche, Almond-Topped, '79 127
Crab Quiche, Quick, '84 96
Crab Quiche, Sherried, '83 180

Crab Quiche, Simple, '85 207
Eggless Quiche, '87 220
Fiesta Quiche, '92 47
Green Chile Quiche, '83 31
Individual Quiches, '98 101
Jalapeño-Corn Quiche, '85 122
Lorraine, Classic Quiche, '81 131
Lorraine, Mushroom-Quiche, '86 242
Lorraine, Peppery Quiche, '81 228
Lorraine, Perfect Quiche, '79 127
Lorraine, Quiche, '79 40; '80 M108;
   '99 M218
Meat
   Bacon Quiche, '85 60
   Benedict Quiche, '80 M107
   Ham-and-Cheese Quiches, Individual,
      '98 24
   Ham-and-Grits Crustless Quiche, '94 89
   Ham-and-Mushroom Quiche, '81 11
   Ham-and-Vegetable Quiche, '84 326
   Ham-Cheese Quiche, '79 26
   Ham Quiche, '80 110
   Ham Quiche, Cheesy, '79 127
   Ham Quiche, Country, '87 287
   Ham Quiche, Crustless, '84 235
   Sausage-Apple Quiche, Crustless, '87 70
   Sausage-Cheddar Quiche, '79 26
   Sausage Quiche, Easy, '79 261
   Sausage Quiche, Italian, '81 200
   Sausage Quiche, Spicy, '80 M108
   Sausage Quiche, Zucchini-, '83 122
Mexicali Quiche with Avocado Topping, '93 309;
   '94 96
Miniature
   Bacon-Cheese Quiches, Miniature, '83 93
   Cheese Quiches, Miniature, '80 150
   Olive Quiche Appetizers, '86 159
   Shrimp Miniquiches, '87 146
   Spinach Quichelets, '87 67
   Spinach Quiches, Individual, '86 38
   Spinach Quiches, Miniature, '82 38
   Squares, Quiche, '84 222
   Tarragon Cocktail Quiches, '84 127
   Wild Rice-and-Mushroom Quiches, '93 237
Mushroom Quiche, '80 222; '81 244; '89 285
Noël, Quiche, '82 310
Onion Quiche, '83 121
Pastry, Microwaved Quiche, '81 M74;
   '82 M123
Pastry, Quiche, '80 M107
Pizza Quiche, '86 53
Potato Quiche, Crustless, '83 49
Salmon Quiche, '82 87; '87 38
Shrimp Quiche, '83 50
South-of-the-Border Quiche, '93 321
Spinach
   Cheesy Spinach Quiche, '81 228
   Crustless Spinach Quiche, '84 235
   Greek Spinach Quiche, '86 10
   Individual Spinach Quiches, '86 38
   Miniature Spinach Quiches, '82 38
   Mushroom Quiche, Spinach-, '81 M74
   No-Crust Spinach Quiche, '90 142
   Spinach Quiche, '81 44; '85 49; '91 204
   Spinach Quichelets, '87 67
Springtime Quiche, '83 122
Squash-and-Green Chile Quiche, '88 143
Tasty Quiche, '82 264
Vegetable Quiche, '87 M219
Vegetable Quiche, Light, '97 332
Zucchini Frittata, '86 103
Zucchini-Mushroom Quiche, '79 127
Zucchini Pie, Italian-Style, '83 43
Zucchini-Sausage Quiche, '83 122

QUICK & EASY
Appetizers
   Brie, Chutney-Bacon, '90 M292
   Brie in Rye, Raspberry, '93 252
   Caviar, Homemade Cowboy, '94 64
   Cereal Bites, Buttery, '89 97
   Cheese-and-Olive Snack, Open-Faced, '89 97
   Cheese Ball, '91 200
   Cheese Ball, Apple, '98 250
   Cheese Ball, Peppered, '94 118
   Cheese Fondue, Party, '92 20
   Cheese Loaf, Four-Layer, '99 222
   Cheese Snack, '89 98
   Chicken-Cheese Ball, '93 216
   Chicken Strips, Sesame, '98 250
   Cinnamon Sticks, '95 244
   Cocktail Smoky Links, '90 168
   Dip and Vegetable Platter, Curry, '89 327
   Dip, Bean, '89 97
   Dip, Cheese-Crab, '91 200
   Dip, Chili-and-Cheese, '89 M328
   Dip, Fiesta, '92 263
   Dip, Meaty Cheese, '92 160
   Dip, Mexican Artichoke, '90 M292
   Dip, Quick Nacho, '90 168
   Dip, Super Seafood, '90 292
   Dip, Sweet Fruit, '89 328
   Ham Appetillas, '93 63
   Jelly, Garlic Pepper, '99 221
   Kielbasa, Sweet-and-Sour, '89 327
   Mushrooms, Marinated, '91 306
   Nachos, Tex-Mex, '89 97
   Olive Cups, Greek, '99 221
   Olives, Lemon-Garlic, '94 118
   Parmesan Cheese Bites, '99 221
   Pepperoni Pie Hors d'Oeuvres, '98 251
   Pizza Bites, '95 244
   Rollups, Spinach, '98 251
   Spread, Buttery Boursin Cheese, '94 301
   Spread, Cheese, '99 24
   Spread, Chunky Artichoke, '89 98
   Spread, Crabmeat-Horseradish, '90 292
   Spread, Creamy Clam, '91 274
   Spread, Fruited Cream Cheese, '91 306
   Spread, Garlic Boursin Cheese, '94 301
   Spread, Hearts of Palm, '90 M293
   Spread, Nutty Cream Cheese, '89 327
   Spread, Shrimp, '96 104
   Spread, Tuna, '91 305
Apples, Curried, '93 252
Beans, Refried, '96 160
Beans, Skillet Barbecued, '93 217
Beverages
   Cider, Apple-Orange, '92 20
   Orange-Banana Whip, '95 244
   Punch, Percolator, '91 306
   Punch, Pink, '96 190
   Tea, Easy Mint, '91 187
Black Beans and Rice, '89 178
Black Beans and Yellow Rice, '95 126
Breads
   Biscuits, Deluxe Omelet, '98 101
   Biscuits, Easy Herb, '90 283
   Biscuits, Lightnin' Cheese, '90 283
   Biscuits, Quick, '89 30
   Breadsticks, Italian Cheese, '95 126
   Breadsticks, Sesame-Cheese, '97 31
   Cinnamon Loaves, '99 260
   Cinnamon Loaves, Miniature, '99 260
   Croissants, Cream Cheese, '92 159
   Crostini, Feta-Tomato, '92 159
   Danish, Cheese, '97 31
   Focaccia, Herb, '97 31
   French Bread, Chive-Garlic, '89 29

French Bread, Lemony, '97 147
French Bread, Onion-Cheese, '89 29
Garlic Bread, Quick, '90 283
Greek Bread, '89 200
Mayonnaise Bread, '89 29
Muffins, Barbecue, '96 246
Muffins, Orange-Pecan, '99 56
Muffins, Sour Cream, '90 283
Parmesan-Wine Bread, '97 31
Rolls, Almond Crescent, '90 283
Rolls, Cinnamon Tea, '92 263
Rolls, Mayonnaise, '90 283
Rolls, Spoon, '91 275
Sesame Knots, '89 29
Butter, Cilantro, '98 182
Butter, Cinnamon, '92 319
Butter, Green Peppercorn, '90 117
Butter, Orange, '92 319
Butter, Southwestern, '92 320
Coffee Cake, Cowboy, '95 84

Desserts
Apple Dessert, Creamy Dutch, '91 19
Apples and Pear, Honey-Baked, '97 303
Apples 'n' Pears, Saucy, '96 72
Apricot-Almond Squares, '95 272
Bars, Gooey Turtle, '96 M189
Bars, Peanut Butter, '93 166
Blueberry Slump, Quick, '91 20
Brownies, Chocolate-Peanut Butter Chip, '91 306
Brownies, Gooey, '97 133
Brownies, No-Bake, '94 330
Brownies, Rich, '95 84
Cake Dessert Sandwich, Grilled Pound, '94 171
Cake, Éclair, '93 42
Cake, Ice Cream, '89 71
Cake with Strawberry-Banana Topping, Pound, '89 200
Candies, Turtle, '93 M41
Candy, Peanut Butter, '93 166
Cherry Crisp, '91 20
Chocolate Crunchies, '92 50
Chocolate Dip, '92 50
Chocolate-Marshmallow Squares, '92 M50
Chocolate-Peanut Butter Cups, '97 134
Chocolate Peanutty Swirls, '94 M330
Cobbler, Quick Fruit, '91 20
Cookies, Cake Mix, '97 133
Cookies, Cake Mix Oatmeal, '96 247
Cookies, Double-Chocolate, '95 272
Cookies, Keyboard, '94 M330
Cookies, Spider, '93 166
Cranberry-Orange Delight, '90 168
Cream Dessert, Triple, '94 244
Fruit Kabobs, Grilled, '97 147
Fudge, Creamy Peanut Butter, '92 240
Fudge, Microwave Chocolate, '92 M50
Ice Cream Balls, Nutty, '89 72
Ice Cream, Chocolate Cookie, '95 245
Ice Cream, Cinnamon, '95 126
Ice-Cream Dessert, Toffee, '97 134
Ice Cream Sandwiches, Chocolate, '89 72
Ice, Mimosa, '94 24
Lemon Crisps, '95 272
Orange Balls, '94 331
Orange Crinkles, '95 272
Peach Crinkle, '91 20
Peach Crisp, Gingered, '97 303
Pie, Blueberry-Banana, '93 115
Pie, Brownie-Mint, '97 303
Pie, Caramel, '96 72
Pie, Caramel-Nut Crunch, '94 244
Pie, Chocolate Cream Cheese, '92 240

Pie, Coconut, '93 115
Pie, Decadent Mud, '89 252
Pie, Double-Delight Ice Cream, '89 72
Pie, Fudge, '89 252
Pie, Ice Cream Sundae, '94 244
Pie, No-Bake Cherry Confetti, '93 114
Pie, Peanut Butter, '89 252
Pie, Pineapple, '89 252
Pie, Quick Peach, '89 252
Pie, Tart Lemon, '91 275
Pie, "Working for Peanuts," '93 115
Polka Dots, '95 272
Praline Grahams, '92 239
Pudding, No-Bake Banana, '91 172
Sauce, Toffee, '94 72
Sherbet Cooler, Peachy, '91 187
Sherbet, Lemon-Pineapple, '96 330
Strawberries, Christmas, '94 331
Sundae, Hot Apple Spice, '92 239
Topping, Hot Fudge Ice Cream, '98 317
Topping, Maple-Pecan Ice Cream, '98 317
Trifles, Easy Individual, '92 239
Truffles, Bittersweet, '94 330
White Chocolate Salties, '92 50
Dressing, Sweet Cornbread, '97 303
Egg Roll-Ups, Spicy, '90 140
Eggs, Chicken-Stuffed, '98 102
Eggs, Scotch, '98 101
Fettuccine and Vegetables, '97 178
Fettuccine with Poppy Seeds, '91 48
French Toast, Peanut Butter, '93 166
Glaze, Orange, '92 263
Guacamole, '96 160

Main Dishes
Antipasto Kabobs, '94 144
Barbecue, Chuck Roast, '96 71
Beans and Franks, Jiffy, '91 M172
Beef and Broccoli, Quick, '91 123
Beef Burgundy, '95 69
Beef Roll-Ups, Mexican, '90 176
Bow-Tie with Marinara, '94 64
Burgers, Garlic Turkey, '99 135
Burgers, Mushroom, '99 135
Burgers, Spinach-Feta, '99 135
Burritos, Tex-Mex, '95 34
Burritos, Vegetarian, '93 319
Casserole, Chicken, '96 302; '96 103
Casserole, Chicken-and-Pasta, '97 192
Casserole, Chicken-and-Wild Rice, '97 192
Casserole, Chili, '90 176
Casserole, Creamy Chicken-Green Bean, '97 158
Casserole, Ham, '96 302
Casserole, Ham-and-Potato, '96 103
Casserole, Ham Roll, '91 M127
Casserole, Macaroni-Cheese-Beef, '95 125
Casserole, Quiche, '95 33
Casserole, Tuna, '96 103
Casserole, Turkey, '96 302
Casserole, Vegetarian, '96 302
Chicken à la King, '93 14
Chicken and Artichokes, Italian, '95 68
Chicken and Dumplings, Quick, '95 125
Chicken and Pasta, Quick, '93 14
Chicken and Potato Dumplings, '99 326
Chicken and Potatoes, Roasted, '98 289
Chicken and Rice, Creole, '92 262
Chicken and Tortilla Dumplings, '99 327
Chicken, Biscuit Dumplings and, '99 326
Chicken Breasts, Lemon, '89 18
Chicken Breasts, Salsa-Topped, '94 144
Chicken Breast Tarragon, Broiled, '89 310
Chicken Caruso and Rice, '89 177
Chicken, Corn Flake, '91 172

Chicken Delicacy, '99 M23
Chicken, Grilled, '89 200
Chicken, Honey-Lime Grilled, '96 189
Chicken in Mustard Cream Sauce, '92 181
Chicken in Pita, Peppery, '93 62
Chicken-Italian Dressing Bake, '91 199
Chicken, Lemon, '96 49
Chicken, Lemon-Garlic, '90 35
Chicken, Lemon-Pepper, '89 104
Chicken, Mediterranean, '94 72
Chicken Mexicana, '91 M127
Chicken Nuggets, Baked, '89 18
Chicken Nuggets, Sweet-and-Sour, '90 168
Chicken, Oregano, '95 84
Chicken Packets, '96 104
Chicken, Paprika, '95 125
Chicken Pot Pie, Easy, '89 218
Chicken, Quick, '90 117
Chicken, Quick Curried, '89 219
Chicken, Roast, '93 14
Chicken Sauté, Lemon-Dill, '91 186
Chicken Sauté, Sweet Pepper-, '89 104
Chicken Skillet Dinner, Curried, '95 47
Chicken, Szechuan, '98 155
Chicken Tostadas, '93 204
Chicken with Artichokes and Mushrooms, '90 35
Chicken with Creamy Mustard Sauce, Champagne-Poached, '94 24
Chicken with Fennel and Mushrooms, '97 93
Chili, Easy Texas, '90 201
Chili, Quick-and-Easy, '92 20
Chili, Vegetable, '97 179
Chili with Beans, Easy, '92 262
Chimichangas, Oven-Fried Chicken, '90 M175
Chops with Vegetables, Golden, '89 218
Cornish Hens, Jelly-Glazed, '93 251
Crab Bake, Easy, '95 209
Crab Imperial, Easy, '93 128
Crabmeat Brunch Scramble, '95 32
Crab Tostadas, '93 203
Crawfish Delicacy, '99 M23
Eggplant Sauté, '96 135
Eggs, Cheese-Chive Scrambled, '95 34
Enchiladas, Cheese, '95 311
Enchiladas, Pork, '97 M94
Enchiladas, Quicker, '96 103
Enchiladas, Weeknight, '93 63
Filet Mignon with Horseradish Gravy, '92 262
Fish, Caesar's, '90 76
Fish in Caper Sauce, '95 209
Fish, Mexi-Style Oven-Fried, '90 76
Fish, Oven-Fried, '91 172
Flank Steak, Cheese-Stuffed, '98 182
Flounder, Broiled, '89 310
Flounder, Quick Crunchy, '90 76
Frittata, Ham-and-Broccoli, '98 101
Grouper, Guadalajara, '98 17
Grouper with Sautéed Vegetables, '90 M233
Haddock Fillets in White Wine, '90 76
Ham-and-Cheese Bundles, '93 63
Hamburgers Mexicali, '93 217
Hamburgers Teriyaki, '89 309
Ham, Peachy Glazed, '96 189
Ham Slice, Apricot-Glazed, '93 252
Jambalaya, '98 317
Kielbasa-Vegetable Dinner, '91 274
Lasagna, Lots of Noodles, '91 M127
Lasagna, Turkey-Picante, '97 93
Lasagna, Vegetable, '93 320
Linguine, Leeks and Peppers with, '98 68
Linguine, Quick Clam, '90 233
Linguine with Clam Sauce, '89 178
Mahimahi Grape Sauce, '91 218

QUICK & EASY, Main Dishes
(continued)

Manicotti, Make-Ahead, '98 68
Marinara on Beds of Spinach and Orzo, '93 320
Meat Loaf, Easy, '95 125
Mexican Stack-Up, '95 69
Mexicorn Main Dish, '96 189
Omelet, Dill-Cheese-Ham, '95 33
Omelet, Family-Size Potato, '94 31
Omelet Olé, '94 31
Omelet, Shrimp-and-Cheese, '94 31
Pasta, Basil-Cheese, '96 136
Pasta with Pesto-Clam Sauce, '98 17
Pasta with Tomato Cream Sauce, Angel Hair, '93 292
Peppers, Beef-Stuffed, '91 M127
Pizza, Taco, '89 177
Pork Cacciatore, '95 69
Pork Chops and Gravy, '96 71
Pork Chops and Scalloped Potatoes, '98 16
Pork Chops, Herbed, '97 147
Pork Chops, Peachy, '89 310
Pork Cutlets, Apple-Glazed, '92 181
Pork, Kung Pao, '96 49
Pork Marsala, '90 35
Pork Sauté, Plum Delicious, '89 105
Pork Tenderloin, Grilled Marinated, '91 199
Potatoes, Chili-Topped, '98 M289
Quesadillas, Western, '97 65
Rib-Eye Steaks with Roquefort Glaze, '89 310
Rice-and-Black Bean Tostadas, '97 65
Roast, Easy Rump, '93 217
Salmon Bake with Pecan-Crunch Coating, '95 209
Sausage Dinner, Italian, '91 218
Sausage, Sweet Peppery, '95 69
Scallops in Vermouth-Cream Sauce, '96 49
Seafood and Pasta, '90 234
Shrimp-and-Black Bean Tostadas, '93 204
Shrimp and Wine Sauce, '98 50
Shrimp Creole, Easy, '95 68
Shrimp, Fiery Cajun, '91 218
Shrimp Scampi, '95 209
Shrimp Stir-Fry, Cajun, '92 127
Shrimp Versailles, '90 233
Shrimp with Green Peppercorn Tartar Sauce, Boiled, '94 144
Sloppy Joes, '91 172
Snapper, Oven-Fried, '90 75
Snapper with Rosemary, Glazed, '98 51
Sole Royale, '89 104
Spaghetti and Meat Sauce, Quick, '94 64
Spaghetti Pie, Weeknight, '95 312
Spaghetti with Fresh Tomato Sauce, '96 135
Steak and Gravy, Zippy, '90 35
Steak in Pepper Cream, '94 117
Steak Parmesan, '93 41
Stir-Fry Beef and Asparagus, '91 124
Stir-Fry, Chicken and Snow Pea, '95 157
Stir-Fry, Easy Chicken, '91 124
Stir-Fry, Hurry-Up Chicken, '91 124
Stir-Fry, Indian, '92 126
Stir-Fry, Italian, '92 126
Stir-Fry, Mexican, '92 126
Stir-Fry, Orange Roughy, '98 50
Stir-Fry, Peanutty Beef, '95 157
Stir-Fry, Sausage, '98 156
Stroganoff, Beef, '92 20
Swiss Steak Monterey, '99 23
Tacos, Chicken-and-Bean, '93 293
Tacos, Easy, '96 159

Tortilla Pie, '96 135
Tuna, Grilled Florida, '93 128
Turkey and Peppers in Cornbread Crust, '95 312
Turkey-Basil Piccata, '96 49
Turkey Divan, Quick, '89 178
Turkey Sauté, '89 105
Turkey Scaloppine, Easy, '95 M192
Turkey with Peppers, '92 182
Veal Marsala, '91 218
Veal Piccata, '92 181
Vegetarian Sauté, '95 69
Ziti, Baked, '94 65
Mayonnaise, Dill-Garlic, '92 320
Mayonnaise, Italian Herbed, '92 320
Mix, Fish Herb, '98 51
Mix, Jambalaya, '98 317
Mostaccioli Alfredo, '91 47
Pancakes, Easy, '92 203
Pizza, Breakfast, '90 140
Pizza, Southwestern Veggie, '95 126
Quiches, Individual, '98 101
Relish, Quick Corn, '90 M13
Rice, Baked Mushroom, '95 84
Rice, Curried, '98 237
Rice, Jiffy Spanish, '90 M176
Rice, Picadillo, '98 237
Rice Primavera, '98 237
Salads and Salad Dressings
Asparagus and Tomatoes with Herb Vinaigrette, '99 56
Bacon-Lettuce-Mozzarella-and-Tomato Salad, '98 209
Banana Split Salad, '91 58
Bean Salad, Quick, '89 128
Carrot Salad, Harvest, '89 128
Chef's Salad, '98 209
Chicken-Pasta Salad, Grilled, '94 64
Chicken-Rice Salad, '97 93
Chicken Salad Italian, '89 18
Chicken Salad, Peachy, '97 193
Chicken Salad, Roasted, '93 14
Coleslaw, Old-Fashioned Sweet, '93 128
Corn Salad, Festive, '92 263
Fruit Bowl, Colorful, '91 58
Fruit Medley, Yogurt-Granola, '91 58
Fruit Salad, Frozen, '97 158
Fruit Salad, Layered, '91 58
Fruit Salad, Sunny, '91 58
Fruit Salad, Yogurt, '96 247
Greek Salad, '94 202
Green Salad, Garlic-Tarragon, '92 79
Lettuce Salad, Blue Cheese-Stuffed, '94 202
Mandarin Orange-Lettuce Salad, '92 79
Marinara Vinaigrette, '94 64
Marinated Salad, '91 186
Mexican Salad, '94 202
Mushroom Salad, Quick Cheesy-, '89 128
Pasta Salad, '90 62
Pasta Salad, Ham-Pecan-Blue Cheese, '90 62
Pasta Salad, Oriental, '90 63
Pasta Salad, Presto, '90 63
Pasta Salad, Seafood, '90 62
Pear Salad, Golden, '91 58
Red Cabbage Citrus Salad, '94 72
Roquefort Dressing, '93 128
Shrimp Salad, Aloha, '95 46
Slaw, Freezer, '99 260
Spinach-Pecan Salad, '89 128
Summer Italian Salad, Quick, '92 79
Tomato-Asparagus Salad, '92 79
Tomato Flower Salad, '89 128
Tomato-Gruyère-Basil Salad, '99 172
Tuna-and-White Bean Salad, '98 209

Vinaigrette Dressing, '93 41
Wild Rice-Chicken Salad, '99 55
Wild Rice-Shrimp Salad, '99 55
Zucchini Salad, '89 128
Sandwiches
Avocado Deluxe Sandwiches, '99 72
BLT Croissants, '93 158
BLT in Pita Pockets, '93 158
BLT Sandwiches, Curried, '93 158
Breakfast Sandwiches, Cheesy, '90 140
Cheddar Cheese Sandwiches, Hot, '97 179
Chicken 'n' Cheese Sandwiches, Grilled, '99 240
Chicken Parmigiana Sandwich, '94 65
Chicken Toppers, Creamed, '99 240
Cream Cheese Croissants, '92 159
Ham-and-Pineapple Slaw Sandwiches, '96 199
Hamwiches, '96 246
Lettuce Sandwich, Date-Nut, '94 202
Mango-Crab Salad Sandwiches, '99 72
Meatball Sandwiches, Open-Faced, '99 239
Pepperoni Pinwheels, '96 247
Pesto-Sandwich, Grilled Italian, '94 170
Pitas, Fajita, '99 239
Pizzas, Easy Pocket, '90 168
Reuben Sandwiches, Open-Face, '91 199
Spinach Fondue Sandwich, Grilled, '94 171
Tomato-Cheese-Bacon Melts, '99 72
Tuna Melts, Curried, '95 46
Tuna Roll Sandwiches, '96 199
Turkey Sandwich, Waffle-Grilled, '94 170
Vegetable Pita Sandwiches, '96 199
Welsh Rarebit with Tomatoes and Bacon, '92 M159
Sauces
Basil and Cream Sauce, '90 117
Chervil-and-Savory Sauce, '90 117
Chicken Curry Sauce, '90 117
Country Ham Sauce, '90 117
Cranberry-Apple Sauce, '92 203
Dried Tomato Sauce, '96 220; '99 135
Marinara Sauce, '94 64
Peach Sauce, '92 203
Picante-Bean Sauce, '96 220
Pineapple Sauce, '92 203
Salsa, Texas, '96 160
Salsa, Vegetable, '96 220
Salsa Verde, '96 160
Spaghetti Sauce, Slow-Simmered, '96 72
Tomato-Basil Sauce, '96 220
Tomato Sauce, Spicy Gingered, '96 220
Seasoning Blend, Taco, '96 159
Soups and Stews
Asparagus Soup, Creamy, '94 225
Black-Eyed Pea Soup, '97 213
Black, White, and Red All Over Soup, '95 126
Broccoli-and-Chicken Soup, '90 202
Chicken-Corn Soup, Cheesy, '97 158
Chicken Stew, Santa Fe, '97 193
Chili Bean Soup, '96 71
Clam Chowder, '90 202
Clam Chowder, New England, '98 289
Corn Chowder, '90 202
French Soup Maigre, '98 125
Gazpacho, Classic Tomato, '99 172
Mushroom Soup, Sherried, '96 104
Potato Soup, '92 263
Shrimp Chowder, '89 218
Steak Soup, '99 260
Sweet Potato Chowder, Asian, '97 213
Taco Soup, '94 225; '99 36
Tortellini Soup, '98 68
Tortellini Soup, Japanese, '96 330
Tortilla Soup, '90 201

Vegetable-Beef Stew, Shortcut, '89 218
Vegetable Soup, Spicy, '93 293
Veggie Soup, Quick, '91 31
Vidalia Onion Soup, Beefy, '97 212
White Bean Soup, '90 201
White Bean Soup, Spicy, '94 225
Spaghetti with Tomatoes and Garlic, '91 47
Spread, Creamy Pimiento Cheese, '92 159
Spread, Cucumber, '93 158
Spread, Curry, '93 159
Spread, Dijon-Mayo, '96 199
Spread, Garlic-Butter, '96 199
Toast Topper, Sticky Bun, '99 M72
Topping, Rainbow Pepper, '90 117
Tortellini Carbonara, '91 47
Vegetables
Asparagus, Lemon-Sesame, '91 M31
Black-Eyed Peas, Easy, '99 204
Broccoli Casserole, Cheesy, '95 M191
Broccoli Parmesan, '97 302
Brussels Sprouts and Baby Carrots, Glazed, '97 302
Cajun Vegetable Sauté, '92 62
Carrots, Peach-Glazed, '90 M13
Corn-and-Okra Medley, '99 203
Corn and Sweet Red Peppers, Curried, '95 47
Corn on the Cob, Lemony, '89 200
Corn Pudding, '98 124
Cucumbers, Creamy, '92 62
Eggplant, Heavenly, '93 293
Eggplant Parmesan, '95 84
Eggplant Sauté, '96 135
Green Bean-and-Corn Casserole, '99 36
Green Beans, Chinese, '96 330
Green Beans with Buttered Pecans, '92 61
Green Peas, Company, '91 M31
Grilled Vegetables with Cilantro Butter, '98 182
Marinated Vegetables, '99 36
'Maters, Zippy, '99 172
Mexicorn, '96 189
Mexicorn, Black Bean, '96 189
Mexihominy, '96 189
Mushrooms, Sparkling, '94 24
Parmesan Vegetables, '97 147
Potatoes au Gratin, '93 217
Potatoes, Blue Cheese Stuffed, '92 M228
Potatoes, Broccoli-Shrimp Stuffed, '92 M228
Potatoes, Quick-and-Easy Mashed, '93 41
Potatoes, Seafood-Stuffed, '95 M192
Potatoes, Soufflé, '90 M14
Quesadillas, Vegetable, '97 65
Spinach Casserole, '91 M31
Squash Fritters, '99 203
Squash, Skillet, '92 62
Stir-Fry, Convenient Vegetable, '95 157
Stir-Fry, Fresh, '97 179
Stir-Fry, Vegetable, '98 156
Succotash, Quick, '97 302
Sweet Onion Relish, '99 204
Tomatoes, Baked Ranch, '94 72
Tomatoes, Cold Italian, '99 173
Tomatoes, Grilled, '99 173
Zucchini and Carrots, Julienne, '90 M14
Zucchini and Carrots, Sautéed, '92 62
Zucchini Fans, Grilled, '89 200
Waffles, Rice, '98 124
QUINCE
Compote, Baked Quince, '96 241

RABBIT. *See* **GAME.**
RAGOÛTS
Bean Ragoût with Cilantro-Cornmeal Dumplings, '97 209
Chicken Ragoût with Cheddar Dumplings, '94 44
Salmon-and-Vegetable Ragoût, '96 45
Veal-and-Artichoke Ragoût, '94 43
Vegetable Ragoût, '89 172; '98 181
Vegetables, Ragoût of Summer, '98 119
White Bean Ragoût, '96 232
RAISINS
Bars, Raisin, '94 228
Breads
Banana-Nut-Raisin Bread, '81 59
Biscuits, Buttermilk-Raisin, '92 338
Biscuits, Cinnamon-Raisin Breakfast, '93 159
Biscuits, Glazed Raisin, '89 210
Buns, Rum-Raisin, '80 22
Butternut-Raisin Bread, '79 25
Caraway-Raisin Oat Bread, '86 44
Chicken Salad on Raisin Bread, Curried, '85 96
Cinnamon Pull-Aparts, Raisin, '82 205; '83 32
Cinnamon Raisin Bread, '80 22
Cranberry Bread, Raisin-, '81 305; '82 36
Homemade Raisin Bread, '87 300
Muffins, Banana-Raisin, '89 218
Muffins, Breakfast Raisin, '84 59
Muffins, Carrot-and-Raisin, '87 24
Muffins, Cheddar-Raisin, '91 51
Muffins, Orange-Raisin, '97 153
Muffins, Raisin English, '80 75
Muffins, Raisin-Nut, '92 46
Muffins, Raisin-Pecan Ginger, '88 9
Muffins, Whole Wheat Raisin, '85 207
Oatmeal Raisin Bread, '81 14
Oatmeal-Raisin Bread, '83 59
Pastry Bites, Raisin, '90 86
Rolls, Raisin Cinnamon, '81 107
Rolls, Raisin-Cinnamon, '91 240
Rollups, Sweet Raisin, '86 290
Round Raisin Bread, '89 230
Saffron Bread, '96 50
Salt-Free Raisin Batter Bread, '86 33
Scones, Currant, '84 117; '92 332
Scones, Lemon-Raisin, '87 69
Teacakes, Currant, '80 88
Whole Wheat Bread, Raisin-, '93 77
Bugs in a Rug, '95 178
Butter, Raisin, '81 272
Cake, Saucy Pudding, '98 196
Cake, Spicy Raisin Layer, '79 230
Cake, Winter Squash-Spice Bundt, '99 248
Candy, Mixed Raisin, '84 111
Carrots, Orange-Raisin, '80 24
Chocolate-Bran Raisin Jumbos, '91 142
Chutney, Cranberry, '98 318
Chutney, Pear, '98 243
Coffee Cake, Cinnamon-Raisin, '93 180
Coffee Cake, Spicy Raisin, '88 63
Cookies, Alltime Favorite Raisin, '80 24
Cookies, Chocolate-Raisin Oatmeal, '95 136
Cookies, Frosted Oatmeal-Raisin, '79 290
Cookies, Fruitcake, '98 294
Cookies, Nugget, '79 291
Cookies, Oatmeal, '99 280
Cookies, Oatmeal-Raisin, '87 221; '93 127
Cookies, Persimmon-Raisin, '85 232
Cookies, Pudding Oatmeal, '98 215
Filling, Raisin, '90 86
Gingersnaps, Raisin, '85 324
Granola Gorp, '89 59
Granola, Healthful, '97 204

Granola, Superhero, '98 206
Granola Treats, Raisin-, '92 22
Gravy, Currant, '83 276
Ham, Raisin, '80 124
Ice Cream, Rum-Raisin, '97 145
Mix, Raisin-Nut Party, '83 60
Onions, Glazed, '97 306
Pie, Apple-Raisin Brandy, '89 58
Pie, Brandy Raisin-Apple, '83 192
Pie, Cranberry-Apple-Raisin, '98 270
Pie, Cranberry-Raisin, '80 283; '85 316
Pie, Peanut-Raisin, '79 85
Pie, Raisin, '83 220
Pie, Raisin-Pecan, '87 213
Pie, Rhubarb-Raisin, '79 112
Pie, Spiced Raisin, '84 148
Pudding, Apple-Raisin Bread, '88 175
Pudding, Raisin Bread, '94 215
Pudding, Raisin-Pumpkin, '84 315
Pudding, Raisin-Rice, '87 46
Pudding with Bourbon Sauce, Raisin Bread, '98 336
Relish, Raisin, '92 310
Rice, Curried, '98 237
Rice, Island, '98 276
Rice with Curry, Raisin, '85 83
Salad, Carrot-Raisin, '83 117; '84 174; '87 10
Salad, Creamy Broccoli-Raisin, '92 106
Salad, Curried Apple-Raisin, '80 24
Salad with Orange-Nutmeg Dressing, Carrot-Raisin, '97 305; '98 19
Sandwiches, Peanut-Cheese-Raisin, '88 140
Sandwich, Raisin Country, '91 168
Sauce, Baked Ham with Cranberry-Raisin, '88 244
Sauce, Caramel-Raisin, '88 127
Sauce, Ham with Raisin, '82 M76
Sauce, Raisin, '83 59, 215; '84 91, 275; '87 127; '89 58; '99 19
Sauce, Raisin-Pineapple, '82 177
Sauce, Rum-Raisin, '84 7; '94 295
Shake, Amazin' Raisin, '86 195
Shortbread, Rum-Currant, '98 277
Slaw, Sweet Potato-Currant, '93 246
Spread, Creamy Raisin, '90 36
Spread, Peachy-Raisin, '86 326
Spread, Raisin-Nut, '95 79
RASPBERRIES
Appetizer, Orange-Berry, '85 81
Bars, Raspberry, '82 209; '84 212
Bavarian, Raspberry-Strawberry, '89 15
Beverages
"Concrete," Foxtreat, '94 113
Cooler, Raspberry, '89 171
Cranberry-Raspberry Drink, '97 154
Cubes, Berry-Good, '95 201
Fizz, Rosy Raspberry, '90 179
Kir, Raspberry, '86 183
Lemonade, Dazzling, '97 99
Punch, Raspberry-Rosé, '87 242
Punch, Raspberry Sherbet, '95 141
Punch, Raspberry Sparkle, '84 57
Punch, Sunset, '96 278
Shake, Peach Melba Sundae, '93 134
Shake, Raspberry-and-Banana, '89 183
Shakes, Raspberry Milk, '95 238
Shrub, Berry, '95 29
Shrub, Red Raspberry, '97 132
Slush, Watermelon-Berry, '90 137
Smoothie, Four-Berry, '97 173
Spritzers, Raspberry, '99 207
Syrup, Berry, '96 161
Tea, Rasp-Berry Good, '95 200
Tea, Sangría, '94 131

RASPBERRIES
(continued)

Biscuits, Raspberry-Almond, '93 160
Bisque, Banana-Raspberry, '93 161
Bordeaux, Beauberries, '98 18
Brie, Almond-Raspberry, '94 M89
Brie in Rye, Raspberry, '93 252
Brownies, Raspberry, '92 274; '97 M35
Cake, Chocolate-Raspberry, '92 173
Cake, Lemon-Raspberry, '91 247
Cake Loaf, Pretty and Pink Pound, '96 60
Cake, Raspberry-Fudge, '97 34
Cake, White Chocolate-Raspberry, '98 323
Candied Flowers and Raspberries, '98 155
Cheesecake, Chocolate-Raspberry Truffle, '91 270
Chicken, Raspberry, '97 66
Chocolate Cups, Miniature, '87 132
Chocolate-Raspberry Bags, '95 97
Chocolates, Raspberry Cream, '91 36
Cobbler, Berry-Cherry, '83 270
Cobbler, Raspberry-Cherry, '93 230
Coffee Cake, Raspberry, '83 112
Coffee Cake, Raspberry-Cheese, '97 231
Compote, Berry, '81 275
Compote, Berry-Peach, '82 133
Compote, Spicy Grapefruit-Berry, '91 19
Cookies, Raspberry Swirl, '90 111
Crème Brûlée, Berry, '95 323
Crème Brûlée, Double Raspberry, '95 323
Crêpes, Raspberry, '87 126
Crêpes Suzette, Raspberry, '84 84
Crêpes with Yogurt Filling, Fresh Raspberry, '93 123
Crisp, Raspberry-Pear, '89 109
Custard with Raspberries, Almond Crème, '88 174
Custard with Raspberries, Amaretto, '86 152
Dessert, Frozen Raspberry, '84 192
Dessert, Raspberry-Jellyroll, '85 95
Dessert, Raspberry Sauce, '80 147
Dream, Raspberry, '83 108
Dressing, Bibb Salad with Raspberry-Maple, '91 246
Dressing, Mixed Greens with Raspberry, '97 50
Dressing, Peppery Greens with Raspberry, '95 254
Dressing, Raspberry, '87 153; '95 202
Filling, Raspberry, '90 111
Fluff, Raspberry, '89 198
Gazpacho, Berry, '97 181
Glaze, Turkey Breast with Orange-Raspberry, '91 253
Granita, Raspberry Liqueur, '88 117
Granita, Wild Raspberry Tea, '99 89
Ice Cream, Fresh Raspberry, '86 152
Ice Cream, Raspberry, '80 176
Ice, Raspberry, '92 268
Jam, Berry Refrigerator, '89 139
Jam, Mock Raspberry, '96 168
Jam, Raspberry Freezer, '84 M181
Jellyrolls, Raspberry, '93 M255
Lemon Curd with Berries, '90 102
Mayonnaise, Raspberry, '97 107
Mousse in Chocolate Crinkle Cups, Raspberry, '93 270
Mousse, Raspberry, '81 34
Muffins, Lemon-Raspberry, '92 119
Muffins, Raspberry-Streusel, '96 54
Mustard, Raspberry, '95 313
Napoleons, Berry, '94 120

Parfait, White Chocolate-Raspberry Swirl, '93 315
Pie, Bumbleberry, '97 163
Pie, Cherry-Berry, '92 316
Pie, Cran-Raspberry, '87 244
Pie, Raspberry Baked Alaska, '98 216
Pie, Raspberry Cream, '94 209
Pie, Rhubarb-Raspberry Pear, '95 119
Prunes, Raspberry, '82 124
Pudding, Raspberry, '92 92
Pudding, Russian Blueberry-Raspberry, '97 128
Puffs, Raspberry Party, '90 170
Puree, Chocolate Mousse Loaf with Raspberry, '97 34
Puree, Fruit Compote with Raspberry, '88 81
Salad Dressing, Raspberry, '94 158
Salads
Chicken-Raspberry Salad, Marinated, '93 190
Frozen Raspberry Salad, '79 287; '80 35
Fruit Mounds, Raspberry, '79 35
Greens with Raspberries and Walnuts, Mixed, '98 194
Mold, Raspberry Holiday, '84 253
Raspberry Salad, '86 286
Ribbon Salad, Raspberry, '87 236
Walnut Salad, Raspberry-, '94 158
Wine Salad, Raspberry-, '91 256
Sauces
Amaretto Sauce, Raspberry-, '88 130
Berry Sauce, '94 130
Chocolate and Raspberry Sauce, Orange Sections with, '97 33
Crimson Raspberry Sauce, '79 91; '85 30
Custard Sauce, Fresh Berries with Raspberry, '88 163
Duck Breasts with Raspberry Sauce, '87 240
Flambé, Raspberry Sauce, '84 142
Fresh Raspberry Sauce, '93 120
Lemon Sauce, Cheesecake with Raspberry-, '96 30
Melba Sauce, '87 77
Mimosa Sauce, Berry, '90 315
Orange Sauce, Raspberry-, '88 22; '92 154
Peach-Berry Sauce, '87 M165
Poached Pears with Raspberry Sauce, '87 69; '88 223
Raspberry Sauce, '82 289; '83 108;
  '84 73, 213; '87 69, 117, 183; '88 267;
  '89 183, 322; '91 96, 180, 270; '92 130;
  '93 82, 99, 315; '94 295; '95 327;
  '96 183, 310; '98 157, 216; '99 167, 259
Tea-Berry Sauce, '94 130; '99 334
Sherbet, Raspberry, '83 162
Shortbread, Raspberry, '99 29
Shortcake, Chocolate-Raspberry, '95 99
Soufflé, Raspberry, '86 188
Soufflé, Raspberry-Topped, '85 317
Soup, Chilled Raspberry, '81 130
Soup, Sherry-Berry Dessert, '91 180
Spirited Raspberries, '95 142
Strudel, Raspberry-Nut, '83 304
Sweet Potatoes, Raspberry, '87 280
Tart, Bakewell, '97 110
Tartlets, Fresh Berry, '91 98
Tart, Pick-a-Berry, '91 118
Tarts, Berry Good Lemon, '91 119
Tarts, Cran-Raspberry Meringue, '92 286
Tarts, Raspberry-Almond, '99 280
Tea Cake, Raspberry, '91 271
Topping, Raspberry, '85 317
Topping, Raspberry-Peach, '87 126
Trifle, Raspberry, '88 259
Trifles, Individual Raspberry, '99 112
Vinaigrette, Orange-Raspberry, '95 144; '96 155

Vinaigrette, Raspberry, '94 249; '96 275; '97 146; '98 184
Vinegar, Raspberry, '97 146
Vinegar, Raspberry-Lemon, '87 134
Vinegar, Raspberry-Thyme, '95 190
Vinegar, Raspberry Wine, '93 191
RELISHES. *See also* **CHUTNEYS, PESTOS, SALSAS, SAUCES, TOPPINGS.**
Antipasto Relish, '86 327
Apple-Celery Relish, '89 141
Apple Relish, '96 323; '97 27
Apple Relish, Spicy, '84 M323
Avocado Relish, '87 120
Beet Relish, '84 179
Beet Relish, Colorful, '85 136
Black Bean-Tomatillo Relish, '87 121
Black-Eyed Pea Relish, Zesty, '95 56
Cabbage Relish, '83 260
Cabbage Relish, Spanish, '95 270
Cherry-Honey Relish, '97 32
Chow Chow, '82 196
Chowchow, '87 150
Chowchow, Nannie's, '95 250
Confit, Roasted Shallot-Garlic, '94 303
Corn Relish, '81 129, 175; '83 189; '84 107;
  '85 136; '87 120, 245; '92 241
Corn Relish, Easy, '83 260
Corn Relish, Quick, '90 13
Corn Relish, Summer, '89 127
Corn Relish, Sweet, '93 119
Corn Relish, Virginia, '79 283
Crabmeat Relish, '99 198
Cran-Apple Relish, '84 300
Cranberry-Nut Relish, '86 275
Cranberry-Orange Relish, '81 M289; '88 254;
  '99 15
Cranberry-Pear Relish, '85 232
Cranberry Relish, '81 275; '83 144; '85 258, 264;
  '86 283; '87 245; '91 257; '92 341; '95 318;
  '98 310
Cranberry Relish, Frozen, '95 302
Cranberry Relish, Holiday, '88 304
Cranberry Relish, Lemony, '79 243
Cranberry Relish, Old-Fashioned, '82 297
Cranberry Relish, Tipsy, '92 M310
Cucumber Relish, '85 176; '96 23
Eggplant Relish, '95 342
Fruit Relish, Fresh, '95 158
Garden Relish, '83 259
Garden Relish, End-of-the-, '80 179
Green Olive Relish with Coriander, '96 323;
  '97 27
Green Onion Relish, '84 65
Green Tomato Relish, '96 168; '98 124
Green Tomato Sweet Relish, '93 136
India Relish, '84 179
Jerusalem Artichoke Relish, '89 197
Kraut Relish, '91 232
Lemon-Date Relish, '96 271
Mango Relish, '89 198
Onion Relish, '91 79
Onion Relish, Sweet, '93 124; '96 206; '99 204
Orange Slices, Spicy, '81 12
Papaya-Basil Relish, '94 82
Peach Relish, '85 136
Pear Relish, '79 196
Pear Relish, Aunt Glennie's, '95 305
Pear Relish, Peppery, '89 141
Pepper-Onion Relish, '84 180
Pepper Relish, '83 183
Pepper Relish, Confetti, '91 195
Pepper Relish, Sweet, '95 104
Pineapple-Coconut Relish, '96 323; '97 27
Plums, Brandied, '97 176

Prune Relish, Peppy, '90 227
Purple Onion Relish, '95 253
Raisin Relish, '92 310
Salad, Relish, '84 121
Sauerkraut Relish, '85 136
Summer Squash Relish, Pollock with,
    '92 200
Tomato Relish, '85 188
Tomato Relish, Easy, '80 126
Vegetable Relish, '90 147
Vegetable Relish, Eight-, '84 179
White Bean Relish, '93 229
Zucchini Relish, '87 200
Zucchini Relish, Sweet, '95 159

RHUBARB
Ambrosia, Rhubarb, '88 93
Bavarian, Rhubarb-Strawberry, '86 140
Chutney, Rhubarb, '87 245
Cobbler, Rosy Strawberry-Rhubarb, '79 154
Cobbler, Strawberry-Rhubarb, '88 93
Crisp, Rhubarb, '91 146; '92 130
Crisp, Strawberry-Rhubarb, '95 119
Mousse, Rhubarb, '88 93
Pie, Bumbleberry, '97 163
Pie, Rhubarb-Peach, '86 140
Pie, Rhubarb-Raisin, '79 112
Pie, Rhubarb-Raspberry Pear, '95 119
Pie, Strawberry-Rhubarb, '98 99
Salad, Rhubarb, '91 146; '92 129
Salad, Rhubarb Congealed, '86 140
Salad, Tart Rhubarb, '91 146; '92 129
Sauce, Chilled Rhubarb, '88 94
Sauce, Pineapple-Rhubarb, '88 94
Sauce, Rolled Pork with Rhubarb, '96 134
Squares, Rhubarb, '91 146; '92 129
Squares, Rosy Rhubarb, '79 111
Whip, Rhubarb, '79 112

RICE
Almond Rice, '81 195; '85 M112; '89 100; '91 291
à l'Orange, Rice, '90 236
Apple-Cinnamon Rice, '86 249
Arabic Rice, '94 200
Asparagus, Rice and, '93 324
Bacon-Chive Rice, '83 129
Balls, Rice, '81 51
Basic Long-Grain Rice, '83 M285
Basic Molding Rice, '86 221
Basic Quick-Cooking Rice, '83 M285
Basic Rice, '79 64
Beans and Rice. See also **RICE/Salads.**
Black Beans and Rice, '80 222; '89 178;
    '91 82; '95 309
Black Beans and Yellow Rice, '95 126
Black Beans and Yellow Rice, Easy, '92 308
Black Beans with Yellow Rice, '82 2
Cajun Peas, '88 3
Cajun Red Beans and Rice, '83 26
Caribbean Beans and Rice, '99 121
Creole Beans and Rice, '80 223
Farmer's Beans and Rice with Rosemary
    Biscuits, '99 16
New Orleans Red Beans and Rice, '97 235
Red Beans and Rice, '80 58; '83 89; '84 37;
    '87 45; '90 27; '96 218
Red Beans and Rice, Delta, '98 146
Red Beans and Rice, Easy, '90 220;
    '99 M219
Sausage, Beans, and Rice, Texas, '84 296
South Texas Beans and Rice, '85 252
Black-Eyed Peas, Rice with, '93 66
Black-Eyed Peas with Rice, '83 12; '90 208;
    '91 13
Black-Eyes and Rice, Creole, '85 6
Blended Rice, '96 68

Braised Rice, '98 45
Braised Rice and Peas, '79 101
Brown Rice
Brown Rice, '82 275
Calico Brown Rice, '86 33
Casserole, Brown Rice, '87 118
Chicken and Brown Rice, Roast, '83 268
Chicken-Brown Rice Bake, '91 314
Confetti Rice, '89 146
Consommé, Brown Rice, '98 288
Cornish Hens with Brown Rice, '82 275
Garden Rice, '92 12
Mix, Fruited Curry-Rice, '86 326
Mix, Fruited Rice, '97 317
Pancakes, Vegetable-Rice, '93 43
Parmesan, Brown Rice, '84 196
Pecan Rice, '85 53
Pilaf, Brown Rice, '90 136; '91 82
Pudding, Brown Rice, '85 77
Rolls, Crunchy Cabbage-Rice, '85 32
Salad, Brown Rice-and-Vegetable, '84 202
Salad, Brown Rice Confetti, '94 174
Salad, Orange Vinaigrette Rice, '98 288
Spanish Brown Rice, '84 196
Stew, Lentil-Rice, '82 232
Stuffing, Tomatoes with Walnut-Rice, '91 102
Vegetables and Rice, '93 91
Brussels Sprouts and Rice, '79 288; '80 26
Calas, Easy, '92 89
Calas, Quick, '96 64
Calico Rice, '85 83
Casseroles. See also **RICE/Brown Rice,
    Wild Rice.**
Almond Rice, '91 291
au Gratin, Rice, '83 129
au Gratin Supreme, Rice, '86 78
Baked Rice, '94 270
Baked Spicy Rice, '96 125
Beef and Rice, Spiced, '84 285
Black-Eyed Peas with Rice, '83 12
Broccoli-Rice Casserole, '81 101
Broccoli with Rice, Holiday, '87 252
Chantilly, Rice, '86 82
Cheese-Parslied Rice, '89 99
Chicken and Rice, '95 54
Chicken and Rice Casserole, '80 260
Chicken Casserole, '96 302
Chicken Casserole, Rice-and-, '87 154
Chicken-Rice Casserole, '86 52; '99 215
Chicken-Rice Casserole, Creamy, '99 21
Chiles, Rice-and-Cheese con, '89 99
Chiles, Rice and Green, '83 152
Chili-Cheesy Rice, '79 43
Chili-Rice Casserole, '79 54
Colorful Rice Casserole, '82 199
Cornish Hens-and-Rice Casserole, '92 267
Fiesta Rice, '84 76
French Rice, '83 24
Golden Rice, '79 270
Green Rice Casserole, '95 181
Ham-and-Rice Casserole, '84 75
Ham Casserole, '98 314
Ham-Rice-Tomato Bake, '87 78
Jalapeño Rice Casserole, '81 66
Lentils-and-Rice Casserole, '93 301
Mexican Rice Casserole, '83 31
Mushroom Rice, Baked, '95 84
Mushroom Rice, Easy, '89 286
Pepper Rice, Hot, '92 310
Red Rice, Savannah, '95 27
Rice Casserole, '87 45
Sausage-and-Rice Bake, Creole, '88 58
Sausage and Rice Casserole, Oriental,
    '82 M123

Sausage Casserole, Skillet, '99 123
Sausage-Rice Casserole, '82 50; '83 75
Shrimp and Rice Casserole, '79 228
Shrimp-and-Rice Casserole, '94 328
Shrimp Casserole, Spicy, '96 62
Spanish Rice Casserole, '79 192
Spinach Rice, '85 146
Squash Casserole, Creamy Rice and, '95 26
Strata, Cheese-Rice, '81 176
Vegetarian Casserole, '96 302
Zucchini-Rice Casserole Italiano, '89 146
Charleston Rice, '97 310
Chicken-Flavored Rice, '84 M144
Consommé Rice, '80 246
Cream with Mandarin Oranges, Rice, '85 317
Creole Rice, '90 183
Cumin Rice, '85 83
Curried Rice, '90 183; '97 51; '98 237
Curried Rice, Quick, '86 81
Curried Rice with Almonds, '83 M285
Curried Rice with Pineapple, '79 142
Curry-Spiced Rice, '86 M226
Custard, Baked Rice, '92 308
(Date-Nut Rice), Basted Dates and Basted Rice,
    '96 158
Dirty Rice, '86 142
Dressing, Rice, '91 217
Dressing, Southern Rice, '99 256
Empanadas, Easy Turkey, '96 63
Fried Rice
Bacon Fried Rice, '80 115
Calas, Easy, '92 89
Cashew Fried Rice, '99 171
Chicken-Cashew Fried Rice, '99 171
Easy Fried Rice, '84 76
Egg Fried Rice, '79 252; '80 19
Fried Rice, '83 129; '84 197; '88 67
Pork Fried Rice, '89 99
Refried Rice, Shrimp and, '89 176
Sausage, Fried Rice with, '83 12
Special, Fried Rice, '80 56
Turkey Fried Rice, '83 282
Two, Fried Rice for, '81 31
Ginger Rice, Fluffy, '83 102
Glorified Rice, '83 129
Grape Leaves, Stuffed, '94 48
Green Peas, Rice with, '87 45
Green Rice Bake, '79 43
Green Rice, Celebrity, '81 207
Herbed Rice, '83 M285; '93 278
Herb Rice, '91 257
Holiday Rice, '98 289
Honey Rice, '85 83
Hopping John, Skillet, '79 10
Indian Rice, '96 202
Island Rice, '98 276
Lemon Rice, '89 166
Lemony Rice, '99 46
Lentils and Rice, '99 236
Lime-Flavored Rice, '84 175
Lyonnaise, Rice, '83 151
Main Dishes. See also **RICE/Beans and Rice,
    Brown Rice, Pilaf, Risotto, Wild Rice.**
Beef and Cauliflower over Rice, '93 94
Beef and Rice, Curried, '88 164
Beef-and-Rice Dinner, Mexican, '88 199
Beef and Rice, Mango-, '88 138
Beef and Rice, Spicy, '83 231
Beef over Rice Noodles, Shredded, '85 74
Beef Rollups with Rice, Royal, '79 105
Beef Tips on Rice, '85 87
Black-Eyed Peas with Rice, '90 208
Boudin, Old-Fashioned, '85 250
Cabbage Rolls, Stuffed, '88 18

RICE, Main Dishes
(continued)

Chicken-and-Rice Cacciatore, Quick, **'88** 38
Chicken and Rice, Creole, **'92** 262
Chicken and Rice Dressing, **'79** 288
Chicken and Rice, Shortcut, **'90** 220
Chicken-and-Rice Skillet Dinner, **'98** 127
Chicken and Rice, Spicy, **'88** 200
Chicken-and-Rice Valencia, **'85** 113
Chicken Breasts, Celebrity, **'95** 60
Chicken Caruso and Rice, **'89** 177
Chicken Livers and Rice Dish, **'82** 218
Chicken Livers with Rice, **'80** 200; **'81** 58;
  '84 292
Chicken over Confetti Rice Squares,
  Creamed, **'81** 282; **'82** 31
Chicken over Rice, Cajun, **'88** 102; **'89** 67
Chicken-Rice Medaillons in Pepper Pesto,
  '90 97
Chicken, Rice-Stuffed, **'81** 4
Chicken, Rice-Stuffed Roasted, **'88** 38
Chicken, Roasted Stuffed, **'98** 109
Chicken, Sanibel Island, **'97** 66
Chicken with Curried Rice, **'98** 127
Chicken with Pecan-Rice Dressing, **'85** M57
Chicken with Rice, Moorish, **'98** 127
Chicken with Rice, Roast, **'95** 261
Chicken with Rice, Sherry, **'81** 97
Chili with Rice, **'82** 11
Cornish Hens, Rice-Stuffed, **'82** 302
Curried Rice, **'97** 51
Dirty Rice, Hot, **'93** 219
Egg and Rice Bake, **'83** 119
Fruited Rice, Far East, **'81** 175
Ham Rolls, Rice-Stuffed, **'83** 190
Ham with Rice, Curried, **'80** 111
Indian Rice, **'79** 64
Jollof Rice Dinner, **'91** 230; **'92** 325
Lamb Curry with Rice, **'80** 83; **'81** 10
Lentil-and-Rice Supper, **'84** 202
Meatballs Paprikash with Rice, **'85** 31
Mexican Dinner, Quick, **'98** 224
Oriental Rice, **'85** 146
Paella, Chicken-Pork-Shrimp, **'82** 245
Paella, Seafood, **'82** 245
Paella, Spanish, **'85** 26
Paella Valenciana, **'82** 246
Pancakes, Rice, **'85** 147
Peppers, Beef-Stuffed, **'85** 146
Peppers, Rice-Stuffed, **'80** 65; **'99** 241
Pepper Steak and Rice, **'81** 17
Peppers with Rice and Ham, Stuffed, **'82** 131
Pork Chops, Rice-Stuffed, **'83** 102
Red Rice, **'92** 235
Red Rice Jambalaya, **'91** 18
Sausage and Rice, Italian, **'86** 53
Shrimp and Refried Rice, **'89** 176
Shrimp and Rice, Oriental, **'90** 183
Shrimp and Sausage Rice, **'79** 64
Shrimp-and-Scallop Sauté with Pecan Rice,
  '90 317
Shrimp Creole in a Rice Ring, **'86** 222
Shrimp, Curried Rice and, **'83** 231
Strudel, Meatless Mexican, **'98** 29
Tostadas, Rice-and-Black Bean, **'97** 65
Tuna-Rice Pie, **'84** 123
Turkey with Rice Dressing, Roast, **'82** 286
Medley, Rice, **'79** 270
Mélange, Rice, **'87** 240
Mexican Rice
  Dressing, Mexican Rice, **'87** 253
  Jalapeño Hot Rice, **'80** 126

Jalapeño Rice, **'79** 43
Mexican Rice, **'83** 85; **'85** 147; **'91** 217
Mold, Chile-Rice, **'86** 221
Spanish Rice, **'81** 51; **'83** 209; **'90** 183;
  '94 27
Spanish Rice, Jiffy, **'90** 176
Spanish Rice, Pork Chops and, **'83** 103;
  '85 293
Spanish Rice with Tofu, **'88** 26
Spanish-Style Rice, **'83** 152
Spicy Mexican Rice, **'88** 149
Miami Rice, **'96** 86
Mix, Fruited Rice, **'90** 267
Mix, Herb-Rice, **'91** 257
Mold, Curried Rice, **'85** 36
Mold, Saffron Rice, **'86** 221
Mushroom Rice, Baked, **'92** 170
Nutted Rice, **'85** 269
Orange-Herb Rice, **'89** 286
Orange Rice, **'79** 43; **'81** 175; **'82** 200
Oriental Rice, **'85** M12, 146
Oven Rice, **'83** 89
Paella, Garden, **'82** 245
Paella Rice Mix, **'94** 168
Pancakes, Rice, **'85** 147
Parsleyed Rice, **'83** M58
Parsley Rice, **'84** 197; **'85** 95
Parslied Rice, **'87** 167, 243
Parslied Rice, Creamy, **'88** 255
Peas and Rice, **'88** 97
Peas and Rice, Holiday, **'86** 328
Peppered Rice, **'82** 4
Picadillo Rice, **'98** 237
Pigeon Peas, Rice with, **'92** 157
Pilaf
  Apricot Rice Pilaf, **'99** 146
  Browned Rice Pilaf, **'87** 305
  Brown Rice Pilaf, **'90** 136; **'91** 82
  Chicken Pilaf, **'82** 246
  Chicken Pilau, **'99** 184
  Chicken-Vegetable Pilaf, **'97** 51
  Fruit-and-Vegetable Rice Pilaf, **'84** 196
  Fruited Pork Pilaf, **'82** 246
  Fruited Rice Pilaf, Chicken Breasts with,
    '92 307
  Ham Pilaf Mold, **'86** 222
  Lemon-and-Pine Nut Pilaf, **'97** 51
  Lemon Pilaf, **'97** 322
  Lentil Pilaf, Rice-and-, **'88** 17
  Near-Eastern Pilaf, **'82** 246
  Okra Pilaf, **'80** 185; **'82** 126; **'93** 160
  Okra Pilau, **'99** 184
  Oyster Pilaf, **'97** 20
  Rice Pilaf, **'86** 82; **'87** 229; **'88** 42; **'89** 286
  Sausage Pilau, **'99** 184
  Savory Pilaf, **'83** 93
  Shrimp Pilaf, **'82** 246
  Shrimp Pilau, **'99** 184
  Turkey-Asparagus Pilaf, **'88** 200
  Turkey-Rice Pilaf, **'86** 284
  Turkish Pilaf, **'79** 184
  White Rice Pilaf, **'97** 238
  Wild Rice-Fennel Pilaf, **'97** 127
Primavera, Rice, **'98** 237
Pudding, Amaretto Rice, **'86** 334
Pudding, Apple Rice, **'91** 217
Pudding, Creamy Rice, **'81** 51, 205
Pudding, Fruited Rice, **'81** 205; **'86** 95
Pudding, Fudgy Rice, **'81** 205
Pudding, Old-Fashioned Rice, **'85** 147
Pudding, Raisin-Rice, **'87** 46
Pudding, Velvety Rice, **'81** 205
Quiche, Broccoli-Rice, **'81** 228
Raisin Rice with Curry, **'85** 83

Red Rice, **'97** 138
Red Rice, Savannah, **'80** 119; **'89** 286
Ring, Oregano Rice, **'86** 222
Ring, Rice-Carrot, **'79** 246
Ring with Beets, Rice, **'79** 225
Risotto
  alla Milanese, Risotto, **'85** 228
  Baked Risotto, Easy, **'99** 120
  Broccoli Risotto with Parmesan, **'99** 120
  Collards, Risotto with, **'96** 203
  Crawfish Risotto, **'99** 120
  Greens, Risotto with, **'96** 132
  Lemon-Lime Risotto, **'97** 213
  Microwave Risotto, **'97** M213
  Onion Risotto, **'99** 94
  Pinot Noir Risotto with Rosemary Chicken,
    '97 214
  Pistachio Risotto with Saffron, **'98** 272
  Primavera, Risotto, **'95** 163
  Pumpkin Risotto with Shrimp, **'98** 240
  Risotto, **'95** 280
  Seafood Risotto, **'95** 280
  Shellfish and Peas, Risotto with, **'96** 131
  Southwestern Risotto, **'92** 211
  Tomato-Basil Risotto, **'95** 269
  Vegetables, Risotto with, **'98** 193
Rolls, Shrimp-and-Romaine, **'97** 197
Saffron Rice, **'79** 43; **'93** 282; **'97** 51
Saffron Rice Mold, **'86** 221
Salads. *See also* **RICE/Brown Rice, Wild Rice.**
  Artichoke-Chicken-Rice Salad, **'94** 132
  Artichoke-Chicken-Rice Salad,
    Mediterranean, **'97** 321
  Artichoke Hearts, Rice Salad with, **'80** 232
  Artichoke-Rice Salad, **'80** 178; **'81** 41; **'85** 81
  Avocado Salad, Rice-and-, **'89** 146
  Bacon, Rice Salad with, **'79** 52
  Bean-and-Rice Salad, Marinated, **'87** 152
  Bean Salad, Rice-and-, **'85** 22
  Beans-and-Rice Salad, **'91** 44
  Chicken-and-Rice Salad, **'97** 92
  Chicken-and-Rice Salad, Hot, **'83** 22
  Chicken-Rice Salad, **'81** 203; **'97** 93
  Chicken-Rice Salad, Grilled, **'98** 148
  Chicken-Rice Salad, Nutty, **'83** 157
  Chutneyed Rice Salad, **'88** 100
  Colorful Rice Salad, **'81** 253
  Confetti Rice Salad, **'80** 232
  Crunchy Rice Salad, **'82** 302
  Curried Chicken-Rice Salad, **'92** 190
  Curried Rice Salad, **'80** 84; **'85** 147, 220;
    '96 240
  Curry Rice Salad, **'89** 146
  Egg-Rice Salad, **'84** 18; **'86** 169
  Ham-and-Rice Salad, Colorful, **'90** 319
  Ham-and-Rice Salad, Mandarin, **'87** 145
  Ham-Rice Toss, **'82** 40
  Hearty Rice Salad, **'82** 233
  Herbed Rice Salad, **'96** 123
  Hoppin' John Salad, **'96** 64
  Lentils-and-Rice Salad, **'90** 197
  Mandarin Rice Salad, **'88** 271
  Mardi Gras Rice, **'91** 217
  Molded Gazpacho-Rice Salad, **'86** 221
  Mushrooms, Rice Salad with Fresh, **'80** 231
  Paella Salad, **'86** 207
  Pea Salad, Rice-, **'85** 163
  Pebble Salad, **'91** 27
  Pine Nut, Rice, and Feta Salad, **'96** 26; **'98** 331
  Red Rice Salad, Charleston, **'79** 146
  Rice Salad, **'79** 74; **'81** 51
  Salmon-Rice Salad, **'84** 289
  Shrimp-and-Orange Rice Salad, Zesty, **'87** 155
  Shrimp and Rice Salad, **'80** 231; **'82** 207

Shrimp-and-Rice Salad, '92 307
Shrimp-Rice Salad, Baked, '83 22
Shrimp-Rice Salad, Tangy, '84 66
Shrimp Salad, Rice-, '79 270; '92 142
Shrimp Salad, Rice-and-, '83 82
Spinach-Rice Salad, '94 63
Tomatoes and Basil, Rice with, '95 232
Tuna-Rice Salad, '87 202
Vegetable-Rice Salad, '80 148; '83 198; '85 87
Vegetable Salad, Rice-and-, '86 42
Zesty Rice Salad, '81 23
Salsa Rice and Chicken, '99 109
Savory Rice, '89 201
Seasoned Onion Rice, '82 166
Seasoned Rice, '79 244; '83 212
Shell, Rice-Cheese, '82 49
Shrimp Sauté, Confetti, '97 104
Skillet Dinner, Antipasto, '97 327
Soufflé, Rice-Cheese, '79 270
Soup, Chicken-and-Rice, '88 236
Soup, Mushroom-Rice, '90 32
Soup, Tomato-and-Rice, '85 24
Soup, Turkey-Rice, '90 89
Southern Rice, '90 250
Southwestern Rice, '90 121
Spanish Rice. See RICE/Mexican.
Spicy Rice, '83 215; '85 256; '99 214
Steamed Rice, Oven-, '89 226
Strata, Cheese-Rice, '81 176
Stuffing, Rice, '95 290
Stuffing, Rice-and-Onion, '88 246
Succotash, Savory, '96 63
Sweet Jamaican Rice, '96 71
Three-Grain Rice, '95 166
Timbales, Green Rice, '97 62
Timbales, Rice, '94 32
Timbales, Spinach-Rice, '88 271
Toasted Rice and Pasta, '95 57
Tomatoes and Basil, Rice with, '95 232
Tomatoes, Italian-Style, '97 169
Turkey and Rice, Herbed, '97 327
Vegetable-Rice Toss, '91 309
Vegetables, Rice with, '79 64; '85 83
Vegetables, Rice with Spring, '96 132
Waffles, Rice, '98 124
Waldorf Rice, '84 281
Wild Rice. See also RICE/Pilaf.
Almond Wild Rice, '86 50
Belvedere, Wild Rice, '86 82
Bulgur, Wild Rice, '91 83
Casserole, Chicken-and-Wild Rice, '97 192
Casserole, Chicken-Wild Rice, '84 241; '85 65
Casserole, Duck and Wild Rice, '79 224
Casserole, Oyster-and-Wild Rice, '83 34; '84 44
Casserole, Sausage and Wild Rice, '83 196
Casserole, Sausage-Wild Rice, '84 250
Casserole, Veal and Wild Rice, '79 180
Casserole, Wild Rice, '82 199; '95 176
Casserole, Wild Rice-Oyster, '86 256
Chicken and Wild Rice, '79 248
Chicken-Fried Wild Rice, '89 24; '91 132
Chicken Rollups, '88 38
Chicken, Wild Rice-Stuffed, '79 219
Chicken-Wild Rice Supreme, '79 77
Chicken with Wild Rice, Elegant, '80 M76
Cranberry-Pear Wild Rice, '83 279
Creole, Wild Rice-and-Shrimp, '84 292
Dressed-Up Wild Rice, '92 60
Eggs with Wild Rice, Scrambled, '80 42
Gourmet Wild Rice, '89 271
Grapes, Wild Rice with, '95 48
Morels, Wild Rice with, '89 62
Mushrooms, Wild Rice and, '83 278
Oysters, Wild Rice and, '92 339

Pecan-Lemon Wild Rice, '92 211
Popped Wild Rice, '85 65
Pork Loin Stuffed with Wild Rice, '84 35
Quiches, Wild Rice-and-Mushroom, '93 237
Ring, Creamed Mushrooms in Wild Rice, '80 270
Ring, Wild Rice, '83 253
Salad, Crab and Wild Rice, '79 116
Salad, Crab-Wild Rice, '86 207
Salad, Orange Vinaigrette Rice, '98 288
Salad, Oriental Salmon-and-Wild Rice, '94 173
Salad, Springtime Wild Rice, '88 100
Salad, Wild Rice, '85 65; '89 147; '93 191
Salad, Wild Rice-and-Corn, '98 288
Salad, Wild Rice-and-Cranberry, '99 272
Salad, Wild Rice-and-Roasted Vegetable, '99 316
Salad, Wild Rice-Chicken, '83 146; '99 55
Salad, Wild Rice-Green Apple, '92 90
Salad, Wild Rice-Shrimp, '99 55
Salad, Wild Tuna, '95 243
Sausage and Wild Rice, '85 65
Sausage, Wild Rice and, '86 268
Scallops and Wild Rice, '90 129
Soup, Cheesy Potato-and-Wild Rice, '89 16
Soup, Creamy Chicken-and-Wild Rice, '98 M334
Stuffing, Cornish Hens with Wild Rice, '79 222; '80 64; '82 136
Turkey Breast, Wild Rice-Stuffed, '97 281
Yellow Rice, '91 136
Yellow Rice, Black Beans with, '82 2
Yellow Rice, Easy Black Beans and, '92 308
Yellow Rice with Water Chestnuts, '85 24
RISOTTO. See RICE/Risotto.
ROLLS AND BUNS. See also BREADS.
Angel's Wing Rolls, '95 329
Apple Pinwheel, Quick, '85 42
Blueberry Pinwheels, '82 205
Broccoli-Cheddar Rolls, '91 21
Buttered Rum-Nut Rolls, '86 291
Butterscotch Pinwheels, '90 49
Caramel-Chocolate Sticky Buns, Easy, '95 36
Caramel Rolls, Easy, '90 195
Centerpiece Rolls, '94 276
Cheese-Apricot Sweet Rolls, '90 195
Cherry-Almond Rolls, '84 M198
Cinnamon
Chocolate-Cinnamon Buns, '85 5
Cinnamon Buns, '91 68
Cinnamon Rolls, '79 80; '88 290; '92 270; '96 321; '98 325; '99 M284
Crisps, Cinnamon, '81 113
Easy Cinnamon Rolls, '85 290
Glazed Cinnamon Rolls, '86 312
Old-Fashioned Cinnamon Rolls, '86 298; '90 196; '92 226
Pecan Rolls, Cinnamon-, '98 251
Pecan Rolls, Easy Cinnamon-, '89 307
Potato Sourdough Cinnamon Rolls, '94 325; '95 77
Raisin Cinnamon Pull-Aparts, '82 205; '83 32
Raisin Cinnamon Rolls, '81 107
Raisin-Cinnamon Rolls, '91 240
Rollups, Cinnamon Toast, '99 194
Spiral Cinnamon Rolls, '82 205; '83 32
Sticky Buns, Cinnamon, '83 244
Tea Rolls, Cinnamon, '92 263
Tiny Cinnamon Rolls, '97 271; '98 330
Twists, Cinnamon, '83 53
Cornmeal Rolls, '79 60; '89 184
Crescent
Almond Crescent Rolls, '90 283
Apricot-Cheese Crescents, '99 284

Apricot Crescents, '90 181
Butter Crescent Rolls, '95 292
Butter-Rich Crescent Rolls, '81 211
Buttery Crescent Rolls, '83 180
Crescent Rolls, '84 267; '89 235
Deep South Crescent Rolls, '82 309; '83 16
Easy Crescent Rolls, '79 60
Festive Crescents, '80 281
French-Style Crescent Rolls, '82 288
Hurry-Up Crescent Rolls, '97 50
Yogurt Crescent Rolls, '91 123
Croissants, Cream Cheese, '92 159
Crunchy Rolls, '97 160
Dinner
Dinner Rolls, '79 251; '89 312; '93 M326
Fancy Dinner Rolls, '86 299
Freezer Dinner Rolls, '90 251
How to Shape Dinner Rolls, '83 323
Italian Dinner Rolls, '83 254
Italiano Dinner Rolls, '85 32
Refrigerator Dinner Rolls, '81 78
Sour Cream Dinner Rolls, '97 253
Whole Wheat Dinner Rolls, '91 53
Garlic Rolls, Easy, '86 234
Jam Teasers, '81 8
Lemon Knots, Glazed, '86 290
Mayonnaise Rolls, '90 283
Nutty Buns, '86 290
Onion-and-Sesame Rolls, '95 292
Onion-Bacon Rolls, '99 47
Onion-Cheese Buns, '88 218
Onion Rolls, Poppy Seed, '81 63
Orange
Butter Rolls, Orange, '82 206; '83 33
Easy Orange Rolls, '89 M131
Frosted Hot Orange Rolls, '80 257
Glazed Orange Rolls, '90 194
Kitchen Express Orange Rolls, '98 252
Luscious Orange Rolls, '86 298
Orange Rolls, '80 22; '82 17; '88 79; '96 321
Speedy Orange Rolls, '89 287
Parker House Rolls, Italian, '99 47
Parmesan Rolls, '79 181
Parsley-Garlic Rolls, '93 319
Pineapple Buns, Easy, '85 14
Potato
Easy Potato Rolls, '89 287
Feathery Light Potato Rolls, '81 305; '82 36
Homemade Potato Rolls, '82 252
Potato Rolls, '81 300; '99 290
Refrigerated Potato Rolls, '83 254
Refrigerator Potato Rolls, '87 15
Sourdough Cinnamon Rolls, Potato, '94 325; '95 77
Sourdough Rolls, Potato, '94 325; '95 77
Southern Potato Rolls, '86 299
Super Potato Rolls, '85 145
Supreme Potato Rolls, '82 130
Whole Wheat Potato Rolls, '89 50
Yeast Rolls, Potato, '87 53
Pull-Apart Buns, Easy, '83 100
Pumpkin Rolls, '87 254
Quick Rolls, '95 245; '96 54
Raisin Rollups, Sweet, '86 290
Refrigerator
Big-Batch Rolls, '88 289
Bran Rolls, '85 145
Brioche, Morrison House, '96 53
Buttermilk Refrigerator Rolls, '81 120; '82 22
Caramel Breakfast Rolls, '79 193
Caramel-Nut Rolls, '86 312
Cloverleaf Refrigerator Rolls, '80 256
Croissants, '83 54
Herb Rolls, '98 325

ROLLS AND BUNS, Refrigerator
(continued)

Icebox Rolls, '80 242
Lemon Spirals, French, '81 94
Low-Sodium Refrigerator Rolls, '82 67
Overnight Rolls, '86 233
Parker House Refrigerator Rolls, '82 310;
  '83 17
Party Refrigerator Rolls, '79 248
Party Rolls, '98 251
Refrigerator Rolls, '82 287; '91 53
Reuben Buns, '88 298
Sour Cream Rolls, '80 71
Sour Cream Yeast Rolls, '85 259; '90 17; '93 232
Spoon Rolls, '87 15; '91 275
Sweet Rolls, Yummy, '80 281
Three-Day Refrigerator Rolls, '86 306
Twists, Austrian, '80 45
Wixie's Refrigerator Rolls, '99 82
Yeast Rolls, Refrigerator, '81 296, 307;
  '82 309; '83 17, 118; '91 80; '98 109, 325
Romano Sesame Rolls, '87 144
Rum Rolls, Easy, '79 287; '80 35
Sesame Knots, '89 29
Snack Buns, '87 279
Sticky Buns, Christmas Morning, '97 245
Sweet Rolls, Quick Breakfast, '90 195
Toasted Rolls with Herb Butter, '89 70
Wheat
  Dinner Rolls, Whole Wheat, '91 53
  Easy Whole Wheat Rolls, '86 286; '87 74
  Feather Rolls, Shredded Wheat, '82 309;
    '83 16
  Hearty Whole Wheat Bread and Rolls, '79 92
  Honey Wheat Rolls, '83 278
  Honey-Wheat Rolls, Dilled, '83 254
  Light Wheat Rolls, '87 254
  Pan Rolls, Whole Grain, '89 256
  Petite Whole Wheat Rolls, '85 146
  Potato Rolls, Whole Wheat, '89 50
  Wholesome Whole Wheat Rolls, '92 31
  Whole Wheat Buns, '86 236
  Whole Wheat Rolls, '79 275; '90 111; '96 50
Yeast. *See also* **ROLLS AND BUNS/Cinnamon,**
    Crescent, Dinner, Potato, Refrigerator,
    Wheat.
  Anise Rolls, '89 91
  Baguettes and Rolls, '98 168
  Basic Angel Rolls, '89 72
  Best-Ever Yeast Rolls, '90 46
  Blueberry Buns, Deluxe, '81 164
  Bolillos, '88 247
  Bow Ties, '96 321
  Bran Yeast Rolls, '87 116
  Butter-and-Herb Rolls, '86 306
  Butterhorn Rolls, '89 288
  Butterhorns, '84 267
  Buttermilk Rolls, Quick, '83 155
  Buttermilk Yeast Rolls, '79 59
  Caraway Puffs, '82 174
  Cheese Buns, Hurry-Up, '81 300
  Cheese Crescents, '82 18
  Chocolate Sticky Buns, '81 300; '82 124
  Cloverleaf Rolls, '82 18; '96 321
  Cloverleaf Rolls, Light, '83 290
  Coconut-Pecan Coils, '90 196
  Cornmeal Yeast Rolls, '86 177
  Cottage Cheese Rolls, '81 78
  Cranberry-Pineapple Rolls, '86 275
  Cream Cheese Pinches, '87 85
  Crescent Rolls, '97 199
  Dough, Basic Roll, '82 17

Dough, Sweet Roll, '79 80
Easy Yeast Rolls, '81 78; '86 16
Fantan Rolls, French, '80 276
Finger Rolls, '83 254
Hard Rolls, '86 85, 306
Holiday Sparkle Rolls, '83 296
Honey-Oat Buns, '98 27
Honey Oatmeal Buns, '83 154
Honey Rolls, Super, '80 115
Hot Cross Buns, '81 77; '95 100
Hurry-Up Yeast Rolls, '90 90
Jam Kolaches, '85 290
Low-Sodium Yeast Rolls, '84 228
Make-Ahead Yeast Rolls, '95 307
Moravian Feast Buns, '83 295
Oatmeal-Cinnamon-Pecan Rolls, '96 50
Onion Buns, Cheesy, '85 5
Onion Twist Rolls, '89 288
Overnight Yeast Rolls, '96 321
Pan Rolls, '88 76
Pan Rolls, Brown-and-Serve, '91 52
Parkerhouse Rolls, Super, '81 78
Pecan Rolls, '81 62
Pepperoni Rolls, Ground-, '83 244
Pineapple Angel Rolls, '89 72
Pinwheel Rolls, Sweet, '90 46
Potato Yeast Rolls, '98 92
Praline Buns, '90 195
Quick Yeast Rolls, '84 267; '95 45
Refrigerator Yeast Rolls, '81 296, 307; '82 309;
  '83 17, 118; '91 80
Rounds, Individual Bread, '83 159
Rum Buns, '81 299
Rum-Raisin Buns, '80 22
Saffron Rolls, '83 296
Sesame Buns, '82 17
60-Minute Rolls, '96 321
Slow-Rise Yeast Rolls, '97 131
Sourdough Hot Rolls, '82 201
Special Rolls, Extra-, '88 257
Speedy Yeast Rolls, '82 309; '83 17
S Rolls, '96 321
Sticky Buns, '80 23
Sweet Potato Rolls, '93 172; '97 107
Sweet Rolls, Mexican, '81 285
Tasty Rolls, '90 85
Yam Rolls, Golden, '86 299
RUTABAGAS
au Gratin, Rutabaga, '79 254
Bacon, Rutabaga with, '83 243
Boiled Rutabagas, '86 224
Buttered Rutabagas, '81 274
Creamy Rutabaga, '79 254
Fried Rutabaga, '99 285
Glazed Carrots and Rutabaga, Lemon-, '97 46
Glazed Rutabaga, '88 229; '99 284
Gratin, Potato-and-Rutabaga, '96 237
Honey Rutabaga, '91 220
Mashed Rutabagas, '86 295
Roasted Rutabaga, Greek-, '99 285
Simple Rutabaga, '83 243
Skillet, Rutabaga-Cabbage, '99 285
Steamed Rutabagas, '81 274
Tart, Rutabaga-Spinach, '98 274
Whip, Rutabaga, '95 179

SALAD DRESSINGS. *See also*
  MAYONNAISE.
Almond Salad Dressing, '81 37
Apple Dressing, '83 181; '92 216
Apricot Dressing, '99 245
Artichoke Dressing, '84 126

Asian Salad Dressing, '96 327
Avocado Cream, '92 158
Avocado Dressing, '80 15; '92 321; '96 138
Bacon Dressing, Hot, '84 12
Bacon Dressing, Jeweled Hot, '97 196
Balsamic Dressing, '96 137; '99 259
Banana-Poppy Seed Dressing, '98 184
Barbecue Dressing, '99 124
Barbecue Salad Dressing, '80 74
Basil-and-Garlic Dressing, '94 55
Basil Dressing, '88 24
B. B.'s Salad Dressing, '91 65
Benedictine Dressing, '98 83
Blender Dressing, '80 78
Buttermilk Dressing, Down-Home, '84 114
Buttermilk-Honey Dressing, '96 243
Buttermilk Salad Dressing, '79 69
Caesar Salad Dressing, '82 94
Caesar Salad Dressing, Creamy, '96 326
Celery-Honey Dressing, '80 42
Celery Seed Dressing, '82 265
Celery Seed Salad Dressing, '82 94
Cheese
  Barbecue Salad Dressing, Cheesy-, '92 255
  Blue Cheese Dressing, '79 69; '82 166;
    '86 233; '90 286; '97 98; '98 248; '99 244
  Blue Cheese Dressing, Creamy, '81 150;
    '91 307
  Blue Cheese Dressing, Special, '80 30
  Blue Cheese Dressing, Tangy, '87 81
  Blue Cheese Dressing, Zesty, '79 104
  Blue Cheese Salad Dressing, '82 94
  Blue Cheese Salad Dressing, Creamy, '86 123
  Dairy Land Salad Dressing, '86 85
  Fluff Dressing, Cheese, '91 256
  Parmesan Dressing, '86 192
  Romano Dressing, '80 174
  Roquefort Cheese Dressing, Thick, '97 63
  Roquefort Dressing, '79 85; '80 74; '93 128
  Roquefort Dressing, Creamy, '84 12
Citrus-Cilantro Dressing, '93 310; '94 97
Citrus Dressing, '85 92
Coconut Dressing, '87 251
Coconut-Orange Dressing, '97 93
Cooked Dressing, '99 82
Cooked Salad Dressing, '90 231
Cranberry-Orange Dressing, '91 287
Creamy Dressing, '79 159; '83 81; '85 26;
  '92 45, 241; '93 318; '95 66
Creamy Salad Dressing, '83 181
Cucumber-Curry Dressing, '89 179
Cucumber Dressing, '80 74; '90 144
Cucumber-Mint Dressing, '87 153
Cucumber Salad Dressing, Creamy, '82 79
Curried Dressing, '84 115
Curry Dressing, '80 242; '82 78; '97 63
Curry Salad Dressing, '96 326
Date Dressing, '87 57
Delightful Salad Dressing, '83 181
Dijon Dressing, '94 282; '96 176
Dijon-Honey Dressing, '89 45; '99 333
Dill Dressing, '88 182
Dill Dressing, Creamy, '91 213
Dilly Dressing, '80 74
Dressing, '99 316
Egg Dressing, '86 79
French
  Creamy French Dressing, '81 60; '90 286
  French Dressing, '89 46
  Grapefruit French Dressing, '80 101
  Honey French Dressing, '87 81
  Miracle French Dressing, '82 79
  Onion-French Dressing, '84 283
  Piquant French Dressing, '87 202; '88 43

Sassy French Dressing, '99 245
Spicy French Dressing, '81 150; '86 123
Sweet French Dressing, '82 94
Tangy French Dressing, '84 12
Tomato-Honey French Dressing, '81 105
Fruit
Avocado Fruit Salad Dressing, '82 93
Coconut-Fruit Dressing, Tangy, '84 171
Creamy Fruit Salad Dressing, '82 94
Dressing for Fruit Salad, '87 81
Fluffy Fruit Dressing, '79 69
Fresh Fruit Dressing, '87 134
Fruit Salad Dressing, '79 69; '93 184
Lime-Honey Fruit Salad Dressing, '87 81
Marmalade-Fruit Dressing, '84 171
Red Fruit Salad Dressing, '83 231
Salad Dressing for Fruit, '86 40
Sweet-and-Sour Fruit Dressing, '84 125
Whipped Cream Fruit Dressing, '79 270
Garden Dew Dressing, '86 50
Garlic-Herb Salad Dressing, Creamy, '84 66
Garlic Salad Dressing, '86 123
Ginger Dressing, '82 194; '88 61; '90 160;
    '93 290; '96 127
Grapefruit Salad Dressing, '84 262
Greek Goddess Dressing, '81 150
Greek Salad Dressing, '90 286
Green Pepper-Onion Salad Dressing, '84 12
Guacamole Dressing, '92 64
Herb Dressing, '80 122
Herbed Salad Dressing, '99 245
Herb-Mayonnaise Sauce, '85 73
Herb Salad Dressing, '86 40
Honey-Applesauce Salad Dressing, '99 210
Honey-Dijon Salad Dressing, Creamy, '99 245
Honey Dressing, '79 242; '83 146; '87 129
Honey-Lemon Dressing, '95 133
Honey-Lime Dressing, '83 139; '93 71
Honey-Mustard Dressing, '90 55, 111, 146
Honey-Walnut Dressing, '93 107
Horseradish Dressing, '96 200
Italian
Cream Dressing, Italian, '89 83
Creamy Italian-American Salad Dressing, '79 69
Grapefruit Salad Dressing, '84 262
Italian Dressing, '79 52; '85 261; '89 166
Italian Salad Dressing, '80 82; '84 12
Sour Cream Italian Dressing, '89 45
Special Italian Dressing, '79 190
Lemon-and-Herb Dressing, '92 108
Lemon-Caper Dressing, '96 69
Lemon Cream Dressing, '82 170
Lemon Dressing, Creamy, '88 M193
Lemon-Herb Dressing, '97 92
Lemon-Herb Dressing, '82 67
Lemon-Molasses Dressing, '97 195
Lemon-Pepper Dressing, '87 55
Lemon Salad Dressing, '79 8
Lime Dressing, '79 2; '83 120
Lime-Honey Dressing, '92 213
Lime-Parsley Dressing, '85 131
Lime Sherbet Dressing, '80 221
Magnificent Seven Salad Dressing, '89 45
Margarita Dressing, '94 107
Mayonnaise Dressing, '86 11
Mayonnaise Dressing, Herbed-, '86 119
Mayonnaise Dressing, Southwestern, '99 245
Mint Dressing, '80 183
Mint Dressing, Fresh, '84 126
Mix, Salad Dressing, '99 245
Mustard Dressing, '80 112
Mustard Dressing, Tangy, '93 323
Olive Oil Dressing, '84 266
Olive Oil, Flavored, '89 193

Orange Blossom Dressing, '82 266
Orange-Coconut Dressing, '80 158
Orange Cream, '90 126
Orange-Curd Dressing, '93 22
Orange Dressing, '81 141
Orange-Poppy Seed Dressing, '87 187
Oregano Dressing, '86 141
Oriental Dressing, '91 277
Oriental Salad Dressing, '96 93
Papaya Seed Dressing, '95 204
Paprika Dressing, '86 191
Parmesan Dressing, '97 326
Pasta Salad Dressing, '86 121
Pasta Salad Dressing, Herbed, '96 106
Peach Dressing, '90 180
Peanut-Ginger Dressing, '95 177
Pear Dressing, '83 146
Pepper Dressing, '80 174
Peppery Salad Dressing, '79 69
Pesto Salad Dressing, '86 150
Pineapple Cream Dressing, '83 81
Pineapple-Poppy Seed Dressing, '85 55
Pineapple Salad Dressing, '81 36
Pomegranate Salad Dressing, '96 241
Poppy Seed Dressing, '80 152; '81 63, 252;
    '83 153, 316; '84 16; '86 123, 305; '88 78;
    '91 169; '92 191; '93 65, 168; '96 240
Poppy Seed Dressing, Blender, '79 176
Raspberry Dressing, '87 153; '95 202
Raspberry Salad Dressing, '94 158
Red Wine Dressing, '98 246
Rémoulade Dressing, '86 123
Rémoulade Sauce, '99 164
Rosemary Dressing, '81 131
Rum Dressing, '80 139
Russian Dressing, '80 4
Russian Sour Cream Dressing, '79 55
Russian-Style Dressing, '83 181
Russian-Style Salad Dressing, '86 305
Salad Dressing, '90 161
Sesame Dressing, '96 137
Sesame Seed Dressing, '87 81
Sesame-Soy Dressing, '93 106
Slaw Dressing, Sweet, '98 184
Sour Cream Dressing, '82 165; '86 331
Sour Cream Sauce, '87 233
Southwestern Dressing, Spicy, '94 136
Southwestern Salad Dressing, Creamy, '94 278
Soy Dressing, '86 191
Soy-Ginger Salad Dressing, '96 123
Soy-Sesame Dressing, '87 153
Spinach Salad Dressing, '83 181; '93 250
Stay Trim Dressing, '86 40
Strawberry Dressing, Creamy, '84 161
Sweet-and-Sour Dressing, '80 247; '84 70, 161;
    '85 163; '87 305; '89 62; '91 126; '94 281
Sweet-Sour Dressing, '80 246
Tangy Dressing, '83 9
Tangy Red Dressing, '86 191
Tangy Salad Dressing, '80 146; '84 115
Tarragon Dressing, '90 55
Thousand Island Dressing, '80 74; '81 104;
    '83 135; '86 123
Thousand Island Dressing, Special, '82 79
Tomato Salad Dressing, Fresh, '83 193
Tossed Salad Dressing, '84 115
Touchdown Salad Dressing, '81 197
Vanilla Oil, '94 243
Vinaigrette
Apple Cider Vinaigrette, '98 284
Asian Vinaigrette, '97 146; '98 142
Balsamic Dressing, '95 281
Balsamic Vinaigrette, '99 230
Basic Vinaigrette, '94 249

Basil-Honey Dressing, '97 30
Basil-Red Wine Vinaigrette, '96 65
Basil Vinaigrette, '93 106; '97 146
Beet Vinaigrette, '97 229
Black Pepper-Pineapple Vinaigrette, '97 181
Black Pepper Vinaigrette, '98 284
Blue Cheese Vinaigrette, '89 45; '90 55, 280
Caper Vinaigrette, '91 310
Cider Vinaigrette, '99 322
Cilantro-Lime Vinaigrette, '94 77
Cilantro Vinaigrette, '97 126
Cranberry Vinaigrette, '98 321
Creamy Vinaigrette, '98 130
Croutons, Vinaigrette Dressing and, '86 M288
Curry Vinaigrette, Warm, '93 107
Dijon Vinaigrette, '95 301
Dried Peach Vinaigrette, Roasted Vegetable
    Salad with, '97 265
Dried Tomato Vinaigrette, '93 272
Garlic-Blue Cheese Vinaigrette, '92 57
Garlic-Chive Vinaigrette, '91 44
Garlic Dressing, '79 269; '80 14
Garlic-Ginger Vinaigrette Dressing, '92 195
Garlic Vinaigrette, '95 65
Ginger-Curry Vinaigrette, '97 146
Greens and Vinaigrette, '98 168
Greens, Vinaigrette with, '98 184
Herbed Salad Dressing, '88 29
Herbed Vinaigrette, '93 120
Herb Vinaigrette, Fresh, '99 183
Honey-Mustard Vinaigrette, '94 249
Honey-Orange Vinaigrette, '91 255
Hot Chile Vinaigrette, '98 200
Italian Vinaigrette, Red, '97 46
Lemon-Basil Vinaigrette, '94 205
Lemon-Dill Vinaigrette, '99 27
Lemon-Honey Vinaigrette, '96 65
Lemon Vinaigrette, '95 31
Marinara Vinaigrette, '94 64
Mustard Vinaigrette, '96 184
Orange-Raspberry Vinaigrette, '95 144;
    '96 155
Orange Vinaigrette, '96 65; '97 229;
    '98 288
Orange Vinaigrette Dressing, Tangy, '92 341;
    '93 46
Oregano-Vinaigrette Dressing, '79 113
Papaya Vinaigrette Dressing, '95 206
Pistachio-Lime Vinaigrette, '97 148
Poppy Seed Vinaigrette, '94 249
Raspberry Vinaigrette, '94 249; '96 275;
    '97 146; '98 184
Red Wine Vinaigrette, '94 327
Roasted Bell Pepper Vinaigrette, '99 70
Roasted Garlic Vinaigrette, '97 47
Sesame-Soy Vinaigrette, '97 180
Soy Vinaigrette, '97 18
Spicy Dressing, '80 55
Sweet-and-Sour Balsamic Vinaigrette,
    '97 146
Tarragon Vinaigrette, '94 201
Tomato-Basil Vinaigrette, '99 288
Vanilla Vinaigrette, '94 242
Versatile Vinaigrette, '93 140
Vidalia Onion Vinaigrette, '99 168
Vinaigrette, '94 179; '95 61; '99 107
Vinaigrette Dressing, '79 171; '87 138;
    '89 12, 220, 256; '90 173; '92 303; '93 41;
    '95 231; '97 250
White Wine Vinaigrette, '89 46
Wine Vinegar Dressing, '92 91; '93 126
Walnut Dressing, '99 125
Whipped Cream Salad Dressing, '82 145
Wine Dressing, Creamy, '85 20

SALAD DRESSINGS
(continued)

Yogurt
Coconut Dressing, **'87** 251
Creamy Dressing, **'93** 318
Cucumber-Mint Dressing, **'87** 153
Dill Dressing, **'88** 182
Garden Dressing, Spring, **'85** 157
Ginger-Yogurt Dressing, **'81** 302
Herb Dressing, Yogurt-, **'92** 96
Honey-Lime Dressing, **'93** 71
Honey-Mustard Dressing, **'90** 111
Honey Poppy Seed Dressing, Yogurt-, **'83** 177
Honey-Yogurt Dressing, **'93** 172
Horseradish Dressing, **'87** 152; **'91** 32
Lemon-Yogurt Dressing, **'93** 17
Lemon-Yogurt Slaw or Salad Dressing, **'88** 54
Orange-Yogurt Dressing, **'85** 304
Strawberry Dressing, Creamy, **'84** 161
Sweet-Hot Yogurt Dressing, **'86** 40
Yogurt Dressing, **'85** 59, 215; **'88** 27
Yogurt Salad Dressing, **'79** 69
Zesty Salad Dressing, **'92** 60
SALADS. *See also* **AMBROSIA, ASPIC, SLAWS.**
Acini di Pepe Salad, **'83** 163
Alfalfa-Celery Salad, Overnight, **'82** 97
Antipasto, Easy, **'85** 114
Antipasto, Pasta, **'85** 286
Antipasto Salad, **'84** 66; **'89** 145
Antipasto, Salad, **'96** 161
Antipasto Salad, Layered, **'92** 220
Apple. *See also* **SALADS/Congealed, Rice, Waldorf.**
Apple Salad, **'87** 233
Beet Salad, Apple-, **'91** 237
Blue Cheese Dressing, Apple Salad with, **'87** 103
Blue Cheese-Pear-Apple Salad, **'81** 224
Bran Salad, Lemony Apple-, **'86** 223
Carrot Salad, Apple-, **'85** 22
Cheesy Apple Salad, **'86** 301
Chicken-Apple Salad, **'90** 216
Crunchy Apple Salad, **'80** 138
Double Apple Salad, **'84** 227
English Pea-and-Apple Salad, **'87** 24
Fresh Apple Salad, **'81** 207
Frozen Apple-Cream Salad, **'82** 80
Grapefruit-Apple Salad, **'89** 41
Nut Salad, Apple-, **'80** 226
Peanut-Apple Salad, **'80** 5
Raisin Salad, Curried Apple-, **'80** 24
Sesame-Apple Toss, **'88** 21
Snow Salad, Apple, **'81** 224
Spicy Apple Salad, **'85** 215
Spinach Salad, Apple-, **'99** 222
Stuffed Apple Ring Salad, **'91** 198
Stuffed Apple Salad, **'92** 266
Summer Apple Salad, **'80** 149
Swiss-Apple Salad, **'84** 81
Thai Green Apple Salad, **'99** 111
Turkey-Apple Salad, **'88** 123; **'90** 181
Wedges with Poppyseed Dressing, Apple, **'86** 131
Zucchini Salad, Apple-and-, **'97** 216
Apricot Salad, Frosted, **'80** 248
Artichoke-Goat Cheese Salad, **'98** 118
Artichoke-Pasta Salad, **'94** 180
Artichoke-Rice Salad, **'80** 178; **'81** 41; **'85** 81
Artichoke Salad, **'86** 333
Artichoke Salad, Marinated, **'83** 241; **'95** 66
Artichokes Vinaigrette, **'88** 101
Artichokes with Orzo Salad, **'88** M193

Artichoke-Tomato Salad, **'82** 239
Asian Salad Gift, **'96** 327
Asparagus
Artichoke Salad, Asparagus-, **'85** 162
Asparagus Salad, **'94** 67
Chicken Salad, Asparagus-, **'89** 83
Chicken Salad with Asparagus, Curried, **'81** 36
Crab-and-Asparagus Salad, **'92** 141
Cups, Asparagus Salad, **'83** 47
Easy Asparagus Salad, **'88** 131
Egg Salad, Asparagus-and-, **'86** 305
Horseradish Salad, Asparagus-, **'87** 80
Marinated Asparagus, **'83** 46; **'86** 92
Marinated Asparagus Medley, **'91** 105
Marinated Asparagus Salad, **'79** 20
Papaya Salsa, Asparagus Salad with, **'97** 144
Peas-and-Asparagus Salad, **'83** 141
Tarragon Marinade, Asparagus with, **'83** 47
Tomatoes with Herb Vinaigrette, Asparagus and, **'99** 56
Vinaigrette, Asparagus, **'80** 77; **'90** 138
Vinaigrette, Asparagus Salad, **'88** 56
Vinaigrette, Light Asparagus, **'82** 50
Yogurt Dressing, Asparagus with, **'79** 66
Australian Outback Salad, **'92** 45
Avocado Acapulco, **'83** 2
Avocado and Zucchini Salad, Creamy, **'79** 208
Avocado Garbanzo Salad, **'81** 33
Avocado-Grapefruit Salad, **'85** 26; **'93** 282
Avocado-Melon Salad, **'82** 164
Avocado-Orange Salad, **'91** 44
Avocado Salad, **'81** 195; **'82** 9; **'83** 69; **'92** 246; **'97** 250
Avocado Salad, Citrus-, **'82** 265
Avocado Salad, Spanish, **'87** 41
Avocados, Salmon-Stuffed, **'86** 74
Avocados, Shrimp-Filled, **'83** 2
Avocado with Crabmeat, **'86** 119
Bacon-Lettuce-Mozzarella-and-Tomato Salad, **'98** 209
Banana Salad, **'87** 80
Banana Salad, Frozen, **'82** 80, 132
Bananas, Nutty, **'79** 251
Barley-Broccoli Salad, **'90** 135
Barley Salad, **'92** 212
Bean
Black Bean-and-Barley Salad, **'94** 174
Black Bean-and-Cheese Salad, **'92** 217
Black Bean Salad, **'89** 217; **'97** 196; **'98** 208
Chicken-Black Bean Salad, **'99** 124
Chilled Bean Salad, **'80** 178
Cucumber-Bean Salad, **'83** 81
Five-Bean Salad, Hot, **'81** 149
Four-Bean Salad, **'79** 20; **'84** 82
Full o' Beans Salad, **'81** 38
Garbanzo Salad, **'82** 2
Garbanzo Salad, Avocado-, **'81** 33
Green Bean-and-Tomato Salad, **'86** 180
Green Bean-Peanut Salad, **'86** 117
Green Bean-Potato Salad, **'83** 80
Green Bean-Red Potato Salad, **'96** 175
Green Bean Salad, **'87** 90
Green Bean Salad, Cold, **'84** 106
Green Bean Salad, Crispy, **'82** 239
Green Bean Salad, German, **'92** 169
Green Bean Salad, Hot, **'86** 298; **'87** 176
Green Bean Salad, Lettuce and, **'80** 79
Green Bean Salad, Molded, **'85** 252
Green Bean Salad, Paprika-, **'86** 191
Green Bean Salad, Pickled, **'82** 239
Green Bean Salad, Roasted Red Pepper-and-, **'99** 322
Green Bean Salad, Speedy, **'84** 283

Green Bean Salad, Tomato-and-, **'97** 162
Green Beans-and-Cheese Salad, **'91** 159
Green Beans, Dill-Icious, **'98** 53
Green Beans, Marinated, **'83** 145
Green Beans Vinaigrette, **'83** 25
Green Beans Vinaigrette, Kentucky Wonder, **'94** 158
Green Bean, Walnut, and Feta Salad, **'96** 273
Hacienda Salad, **'81** 67
Hominy-Bean Salad, **'88** 266
Hot German-Style Bean Salad, **'91** 314
Kidney Bean-Salami Pasta Toss, **'85** 165
Lima Beans, Chilly, **'81** 206
Lima Bean-Tomato Salad, **'85** 137
Lima Salad), You Lima My Life (Paprika, **'96** 159
Marinated Bean-and-Rice Salad, **'87** 152
Marinated Bean-Pasta Salad, **'94** 167; **'97** 328
Marinated Bean Salad, **'85** 137, 296; **'89** 314; **'93** 312; **'94** 167; **'98** 331
Marinated Bean Salad, Crunchy, **'84** 197
Marinated Corn-Bean Salad, **'87** 9
Mexican Salad, **'81** 113; **'94** 202
Mexican-Style Salad, **'83** 240
Mexican Tossed Salad, **'81** 280
Mixed Bean Salad, **'83** 217
Niçoise, Salad, **'86** 35
Overnight Fiesta Salad, **'83** 80
Pasta-Bean Salad, **'86** 169
Pinto Salad, **'86** 169
Pole Bean-Potato Salad, Hot, **'79** 74
Pork-'n'-Bean Salad, **'87** 83
Potato-Bean Salad, **'82** 301
Quick Bean Salad, **'89** 128
Rice-and-Bean Salad, **'85** 22
Rice Salad, Beans-and-, **'91** 44
Sandwiches, Bean Salad, **'81** 243
Saucy Bean Salad, **'84** 18
Sausage Salad, Bean-and-, **'91** 313
Six-Bean Salad, Colorful, **'87** 82
Southwest Salad, **'81** 113
Spicy Bean Salad, **'96** 46
Sprout Salad, Bean, **'82** 113
Supreme Bean Salad, **'91** 202
Sweet-and-Sour Bean Salad, **'85** 198; **'86** 147
White Bean Salad, Tuna-and-, **'98** 209
White Beans, Caesar Salad with, **'93** 30
White Bean-Tuna Salad, **'98** 208
Beet-and-Sugared Walnut Salad with Orange Vinaigrette, Roasted, **'97** 229
Beet, Apple, and Walnut Salad, **'98** 269
Beet Salad, Marinated, **'83** 216
Beets and Cauliflower, Chilled, **'80** 137
Berry Grapefruit Cup, **'79** 242
Black Cherry Salad, Frozen, **'89** 163
Blue Cheese-Pear-Apple Salad, **'81** 224
Blue Cheese Salad, **'88** 48
Boats, Salad, **'80** 93
Broccoli. *See also* **SALADS/Cauliflower.**
Broccoli Salad, **'82** 24; **'85** 249; **'90** 292; **'95** 95; **'99** 84
Carrot-Broccoli Salad, **'99** 26
Cauliflower Pasta Salad, Broccoli-, **'88** 269
Cauliflower Salad, Broccoli-, **'92** 97
Cauliflower Salad, Broccoli and, **'81** 280
Cauliflower Salad, Broccoli 'n', **'90** 32
Cauliflower Salad, Creamy Broccoli and, **'81** 23
Cauliflower Toss, Crunchy Broccoli and, **'83** 25
Cheese-Pasta Salad, Broccoli-, **'96** 184
Chilled Broccoli with Lemon Dressing, **'88** 270
Corn Salad, Broccoli-, **'87** 24
Creamy Broccoli Salad, **'79** 143

Crunchy Broccoli Salad, '83 39
Curried Broccoli Salad, '86 225
Fresh Broccoli Salad, '82 34; '87 103
Mandarin Salad, Broccoli-, '93 325
Marinated Broccoli, '81 40
Marinated Broccoli Salad, '83 240
Medley, Broccoli, '81 206
Orange Salad, Broccoli-, '94 281
Peanut Salad, Broccoli-, '92 35
Raisin Salad, Creamy Broccoli-, '92 106
Red Pepper Salad, Broccoli and, '83 224
Supreme, Broccoli Salad, '83 260
Warm Broccoli Salad, '92 35
Brussels Sprouts Salad, '87 233
Cabbage and Fruit Salad, '79 286
Cabbage Salad, '87 120, 233
Cabbage Salad, Austrian Hash with, '95 262
Cabbage Salad, Chinese, '81 271
Cabbage Salad, Garden, '81 210
Cabbage Salad, Nutty, '87 42
Cabbage Salad, Overnight, '79 83
Cabbage Salad, Tangy, '82 55
Cabbage Salad, Wilted, '94 281
Cabbage Salad, Winter, '98 284
Cabbage, Sweet-Sour Red, '79 5
Caesar
  Caesar Salad, '80 112; '86 80; '92 71; '99 265
  Chicken Caesar Salad, '96 26
  Easy Caesar Salad, '87 116
  Flippo Caesar Salad, '87 61
  Gift, Caesar Salad, '96 326
  Greek Caesar Salad, '96 64
  Margarita Salad, Caesar, '94 107
  Maui Caesar Salad, '94 107
  Mock Caesar Salad, '92 283
  Oriental Caesar Salad, '94 107
  Romaine Caesar Salad, Baby, '97 128
  Southern Caesar Salad, '94 106
  Turkey Caesar Salad, '93 320
  White Beans, Caesar Salad with, '93 30
Cantaloupe-Cheese Salad, '88 184
Cantaloupe Colada Salad, '97 148
Cantaloupe Cooler Salad, '79 176
Cantaloupe-Pecan Salad, '86 178
Cantaloupe Salad, '86 182
Cantaloupe-Spinach Salad with Pistachio-Lime
  Vinaigrette, '97 148
Carrot
  Apple-Carrot Salad, '85 22
  Broccoli Salad, Carrot-, '99 26
  Caraway Salad, Carrot-, '89 105
  Favorite Carrot Salad, '80 33
  Fruit Toss, Carrot-, '82 235
  Harvest Carrot Salad, '89 128
  Honey-Sweet Carrot Salad, '89 161
  Marinated Carrots, Creamy, '87 200
  Orange-Carrot Salad, '80 89; '84 325
  Raisin Salad, Carrot-, '83 117; '84 174; '87 10
  Raisin Salad with Orange-Nutmeg Dressing,
    Carrot-, '97 305; '98 19
  Ring, Festive Carrot, '82 16
  Seed Salad, Fruity Carrot-and-, '86 223
  Shredded Carrot Salad, '80 178
  Simple Carrot Salad, '82 101; '84 152
  Sunshine Carrot Salad, '82 132
  Sweet-and-Sour Carrot Salad, '98 211
  Tangerine Salad, Carrot-, '83 316; '84 16
  Turkey-Carrot Salad, '86 283
  Turnip-and-Carrot Salad, '91 212
  Zucchini Salad, Carrot-and-, '83 240
Cauliflower. See also **SALADS/Broccoli.**
  Beets and Cauliflower, Chilled, '80 137
  Broccoli Crunch, Cauliflower-, '88 216
  Broccoli Salad, Cauliflower-, '79 20

Broccoli Toss, Cauliflower-, '82 54
Broccoli Toss, Italian Cauliflower-, '88 269
Brussels Sprouts Salad, Cauliflower-, '83 240
Cauliflower Salad, '79 221; '80 83; '81 225;
  '84 291; '85 240, 279; '92 36
Celery-and-Cauliflower Salad, '83 39
Corned Beef-Cauliflower Salad, '83 16
Creamy Cauliflower Salad, '82 102
Crunchy Cauliflower Salad, '80 4; '82 75
English Pea Salad, Cauliflower-, '95 66
Layered Cauliflower Salad, '83 240
Marinated Cauliflower Salad, '82 303; '84 232
Olive Toss, Cauliflower-, '85 198; '86 147
Orange-Cauliflower Salad, '82 266
Parmesan and Bacon, Cauliflower with,
  '96 137
Pea Salad, Cauliflower-, '87 231
Pea Salad, Savory Cauliflower and, '81 280
Sweet-and-Sour Cauliflower Salad, '81 2
Vegetable Salad, Cauliflower-, '85 158
Celery Salad, '79 70
Cheese Salad, Warm, '97 246
Cheesy Italian Salad, '84 33
Chef's
  Bowl, Chef's Salad, '84 66
  Chef's Salad, '86 186; '98 209
  Combination Chef's Salad, '86 47
  Fruited Chef Salad, '85 222
  Fruit Salad, Chef's, '86 35
  Garden Salad, Chef's, '83 146
  Mexican Chef Salad, '85 84; '92 64
  Microwave Chef Salad, '90 M146
  Vinaigrette Chef's Salad, '81 9
  Zucchini Chef's Salad, '83 143
Cherry-Orange Salad, '79 74; '82 56
Cherry Salad, Delicious Frozen, '81 252
Cherry Salad, Fresh, '83 120
Cherry Salad, Frozen, '79 126
Cherry Salad with Honey-Lime Dressing, '83 139
Cherry Salad with Sherry Dressing, '79 165
Chicken
  Almond-Chicken Salad Shanghai, '90 160
  Almond Salad, Chicken-, '81 133
  Aloha Chicken Salad, '80 297
  Amandine, Chicken Salad, '81 37
  Ambrosia, Chicken Salad, '85 216
  Apple Salad, Chicken-, '90 216
  Apricot-Chicken Salad, '99 163
  Apricot Salsa, Chicken with, '98 126
  Artichoke-Chicken-Rice Salad, '94 132
  Artichoke-Chicken-Rice Salad,
    Mediterranean, '97 321
  Artichokes, Chicken Salad with, '86 186
  Asian Chicken Salad, '99 124
  Asparagus-Chicken Salad, '89 83
  Aspic-Topped Chicken Salad, '88 88
  Avocado-Chicken Salad, '87 107
  Avocado Salad, Chicken-, '80 139
  Avocado Salad, Fruited Chicken, '82 101
  Avocado Salad Platter, Chicken-, '83 2
  Avocado Salad, Tossed Chicken-, '80 4
  Avocados, Chicken Salad in, '85 216
  Baked Chicken Salad, '86 297; '87 176
  Barbecue Chicken Salad, Warm, '99 124
  Basil-Chicken-Vegetable Salad, '92 162
  Black Bean Salad, Chicken-, '99 124
  Black-Eyed Pea Salad, Chicken-and-, '97 305
  BLT Chicken Salad, '87 144
  Blue Cheese Chicken Salad, '94 81
  Blue Cheese, Chicken Salad with, '97 97
  Broccoli-Chicken Salad, '90 129
  Caesar Salad, Chicken, '96 26
  Celery Salad, Chicken-, '81 187
  Chicken Salad, '86 232, 261; '96 67

Chop Suey Salad, '81 37
Chutney-Chicken Salad, '87 74
Chutney Salad, Chicken, '82 108
Coconut-Chicken Salad, Curried Poached
  Pears with, '97 93
Coleslaw, Chicken, '84 2
Cream Puff Bowl, Chicken Salad in, '86 232
Crisp Salad, Crunchy, '95 28
Crunchy Chicken Salad, '86 157, 207
Curried Chicken-and-Orange Salad, '87 144
Curried Chicken-Rice Salad, '92 190
Curried Chicken Salad, '79 219; '84 66; '85 96;
  '86 131; '89 176
Curried Chicken Salad on Raisin Bread,
  '85 96
Curried Chicken Salad, Royal, '96 200
Curried Chicken Salad with Asparagus, '81 36
Dilled Chicken Salad, '91 212
Fancy Chicken Salad, '79 55
Filling, Chicken Salad, '87 106
Fried Chicken Ginger Salad, '93 290
Fruit, Chicken Salad with, '82 171
Fruited Chicken Salad, '84 25, 290; '88 88;
  '90 318
Fruited Chicken Salad in Avocados, '87 41
Fruit Salad, Chicken-, '82 79; '90 234
Fruity Chicken Salad, '83 157
Grapes, Chicken Salad with, '86 117
Greek Chicken Salad, '97 92; '98 329
Green Salad with Chicken, Mixed, '80 54
Grilled Asian Chicken Salad, '96 158
Grilled Chicken-and-Fruit Salad, '96 155
Grilled Chicken on Greens, '99 201
Grilled Chicken-Rice Salad, '98 148
Grilled Chicken Salad, Moroccan, '95 231
Grilled Chicken Salad with Mango Chutney,
  '96 182
Hoisin Chicken-and-Pasta Salad, '99 125
Hot Chicken Salad, '81 201; '83 196; '98 290
Hot Chicken Salad, Country Club-Style, '86 10
Hot Chicken Salad, Crunchy, '80 138
Hot Chicken Salad Pinwheel, '80 139
Italian, Chicken Salad, '89 18
Layered Chicken Salad, '89 162
Macadamia Chicken Salad, '80 138
Macaroni-Chicken Salad, '85 296; '86 302
Macaroni-Chicken Salad, Dilled, '92 142
Mama Hudson's Chicken Salad, '93 238
Mandarin Chicken, Carousel, '79 88
Mango, Chicken Salad with, '86 215
Marinated Chicken-Grape Salad, '85 74
Marinated Chicken-Raspberry Salad, '93 190
Mexican Chicken Salad, '85 84; '88 272
Minted Chicken Salad, '92 104
Nectarine Chicken Salad, '79 175
Noodle Salad, Chicken, '95 25
Old-Fashioned Chicken Salad, '83 79
Oriental Chicken Salad, '85 216; '88 271;
  '91 43; '96 92
Oriental, Chicken Salad, '90 146
Overnight Salad, '97 305; '98 18
Parmesan-Chicken Salad, '98 234
Pasta-Chicken Salad, Tarragon, '87 155
Pasta Salad, Chicken, '88 89
Pasta Salad, Grilled Chicken-, '94 64
Peachy Chicken Salad, '97 193
Pea Salad, Chicken-, '83 218
Persian Chicken Salad, '81 12
Pineapple-Chicken Salad Pie, '80 138
Pineapple-Nut Chicken Salad, '83 80
Pocket, Chicken Salad in a, '88 139
Polynesian Chicken Salad, '88 272
Poulet Rémoulade, '87 144
Rice Salad, Chicken-, '81 203; '97 93

SALADS, Chicken
(continued)

Rice Salad, Chicken-and-, **'97** 92
Rice Salad, Hot Chicken-and-, **'83** 22
Rice Salad, Nutty Chicken-, **'83** 157
Roasted Chicken Salad, **'93** 14
Sandwiches, Asian Chicken Salad, **'98** 223
Sandwiches, Chicken-Salad Finger, **'85** 119
Sandwiches, Hot Chicken Salad, **'96** 74
South Sea Island Chicken Salad, **'97** 88
Southwestern Chicken Salad, **'88** 88
Spaghetti Salad, Chicken-, **'90** 146
Special Chicken Salad, **'85** 82; **'87** 183;
    '88 M193
Spinach-Strawberry Salad, Chicken-, **'97** 92
Spinach Tossed Salad, Chicken-and-, **'83** 157
Spread, Chicken Salad Party, **'88** M8
Stack-Up Salad, Chicken, **'83** 80
Summer Chicken Salad, **'83** 145
Summery Chicken Salad, **'95** 138
Super Chicken Salad, **'82** 174
Supreme, Chicken Salad, **'79** 107, 152; **'89** 176
Taco Chicken Salad, Ranch, **'97** 315
Taco Salad, Chicken, **'94** M136
Tahitian Chicken Salad, **'84** 120
Tarragon Chicken Salad, **'90** 199
Tarts, Chicken Salad, **'84** 257
Thai Chicken Salad, **'95** 177
Thai Lettuce Folds, **'94** 47
Tortellini Salad, Chicken, **'87** 288
Tortilla Salads, Mexican Chicken, **'95** 129
Tropical Chicken Boats for Two, **'82** 186
Tropical Chicken Salad, **'85** 216; **'96** 127
Twist, Chicken Salad with a, **'84** 221
Vegetable-Chicken Salad, **'91** 287
Walnut-Chicken Salad, **'89** 14; **'96** 243
Walnut Salad, Sunburst Chicken-and-, **'93** 91
Wild Rice-Chicken Salad, **'83** 146; **'99** 55
Citrus-Blue Cheese Salad, **'92** 220
Citrus Salad, **'87** 103
Citrus Salad Bowl, **'86** 335; **'87** 83
Citrus Salad in Orange Cups, **'85** 47
Citrus Salad, Southern-Style, **'84** 262
Citrus Salad, Tangy, **'89** 34
Citrus Vinaigrette Salad, **'86** 192
Congealed
Apple-Apricot Salad, **'88** 121
Apple Cider Salad, **'83** 123
Apple Cider Salad Mold, **'85** 54
Apple Crunch Salad, **'84** 232; **'86** 331
Apple Salad, Congealed, **'85** 252
Apple Salad, Triple, **'88** 122
Apricot Fruit Salad, **'82** 132
Apricot Nectar Salad, **'83** 218; **'87** 236
Apricot Salad, **'81** 251; **'83** 123
Apricot Salad, Creamy, **'85** 263
Asheville Salad, **'86** 199
Asparagus-Cucumber Mold, **'85** 252
Asparagus Mold, **'80** 104
Asparagus Mousse Salad, **'86** 252
Asparagus Salad, **'88** 121
Asparagus Salad, Congealed, **'83** 260
Asparagus Salad, Creamy Lemon-, **'93** 116
Asparagus Salad, Tart, **'81** 203
Avocado Crunch Salad, Congealed, **'85** 26
Avocado Salad, Congealed, **'84** 266
Avocado Salads, Congealed, **'87** 42
Beet-Nut Salad, **'79** 74
Beet Salad Mold, **'82** 267
Beet Salad, Pickled, **'83** 234
Beet Salad, Tangy, **'86** 199
Berry Salad, Layered, **'79** 173

Broccoli Salad, Congealed, **'84** 124
Cantaloupe, Southern Plantation, **'82** 179
Carrot-Nut Salad, Creamy, **'86** 331
Carrot-Pineapple Salad, **'91** 83
Carrot Salad, **'82** 137
Cauliflower-Lemon Salad, **'81** 23
Cheese Molds, Snowcap, **'79** 242
Cherry-Apple Salad, **'86** 31
Cherry Cola Salad, **'80** 104
Cherry-Cola Salad, **'91** 224; **'95** 94
Cherry-Salad, Best, **'82** 302
Cherry Salad, Congealed, **'89** 278
Cherry Salad, Festive, **'84** 265
Cherry Salad, Port Wine-, **'86** 11
Cherry Salad, Sweet, **'89** 326
Cherry-Wine Salad, Elegant, **'82** 56
Chicken-Cucumber Mold, **'80** 175
Chicken Jewel Ring Salad, **'83** 282
Chicken-Pea Salad, **'83** 218
Chicken Salad Mold, **'83** 80; **'84** 163
Chicken Salad Ring, **'90** 175
Chile-Tomato Salad, Spicy, **'88** 121
Christmas Salad, **'88** 249
Christmas Snow Salad, **'82** 266
Citrus Mold, Sparkling, **'86** 331
Citrus Salad Mold, Golden, **'85** 303
Corned Beef Salad, **'80** 104
Corned Beef Salad, Molded, **'82** 86
Crabmeat-and-Asparagus, Congealed Salad
    with, **'84** 86
Cranberry-Apple Mold, **'89** 277
Cranberry Congealed Salad, **'91** 296
Cranberry Gelatin Mold, **'92** 271
Cranberry Mold, **'79** 250
Cranberry-Orange Delight, **'90** 168
Cranberry Ring, **'90** 291
Cranberry Salad, **'99** 290
Cranberry Salad, Congealed, **'90** 124
Cranberry Salad, Festive, **'81** 264, 296
Cranberry Salad, Frosted, **'90** 288
Cranberry Salad, Holiday, **'82** 266, 288;
    '95 301
Cranberry Salad, Jellied, **'83** 279; **'85** 281
Cranberry Salad, Layered, **'84** 322; **'86** 325
Cranberry Salad Ring, **'80** 247
Crème de Menthe Salad, **'82** 122
Creole Salad, **'79** 147
Cucumber Mold, Creamy, **'84** 164
Cucumber Mousse, **'88** 121
Cucumber-Pineapple Salad, **'84** 124
Cucumber Salad, Creamy, **'86** 147; **'92** 97
Cucumber Salad Mold, **'82** 111; **'83** 81, 253
Eggnog Christmas Salad, **'86** 281
Egg Salad, Deviled, **'83** 124
Emerald Salad, **'81** 143
Emerald Salad, Snowy, **'87** 311
Fall Salad with Ginger Dressing, **'82** 194
Frosted Salad, Heavenly, **'79** 286
Fruit, Jeweled Congealed Fresh, **'95** 89
Fruit Mold, Sherried, **'90** 124
Fruit Salad, Cherry, **'87** 236
Fruit Salad, Sparkling, **'82** 266
Fruit Salad, Spiced Autumn, **'87** 228
Garden-Patch Salad Molds, **'86** 283
Garden Salad, Molded, **'86** 199
Gazpacho Molded Salad, **'92** 323
Gazpacho Salad Mold, **'87** 311
Gazpacho Salad, Molded, **'79** 159
Gazpacho Salad with Avocado Cream,
    Congealed, **'92** 158
Grape-Cantaloupe Mold, Double, **'79** 173
Grapefruit Congealed Salad, **'83** 190
Grapefruit-Orange Salad, **'91** 276
Grapefruit Salad, **'83** 124; **'84** 325; **'88** 122

Grapefruit Salad, Congealed, **'84** 325; **'85** 279
Grape Salad Mold, **'83** 120
Green Bean Salad, Molded, **'85** 252
Green Spring Salad, **'83** 124
Ham Salad, Congealed, **'81** 36
Holiday Jewel Salad, **'81** 252
Horseradish Salad, **'85** 66
Layered Congealed Salad, **'81** 143
Layered Holiday Salad, **'81** 252
Layered Salad, Make Ahead, **'81** 296
Layer Mold, Three-, **'82** 54
Lemon-Cheese Salad, **'85** 240
Lemon-Cranberry Congealed Salad, **'87** 311
Lemon-Cream Salad, **'88** 250
Lemon-Cucumber Mold, **'87** 90
Lemon Mold, Cheesy, **'79** 241
Lemon-Onion Salad, **'85** 252
Lemon-Tomato Salad, Congealed, **'89** 178
Lemon-Vegetable Congealed Salad, **'85** 22
Lime-Carrot Salad, **'92** 65
Lime-Cheese Salad, Frosted, **'79** 286
Lime Sherbet Salad, **'80** 154
Mandarin Orange Salad, Congealed, **'89** 327
Mandarin Salad Molds, **'85** 54
Melon Ball Salad, Congealed, **'84** 125
Mimosa Salad, **'98** 310
Mincemeat Salad, **'94** 282
Mincemeat Salad, Holiday, **'85** 263
Molds, Perfection, **'81** 153
Mosaic Salad, **'89** 313
Orange-Buttermilk Salad, **'95** 134
Orange-Pear Salad, **'84** 164
Orange Salad, Creamy, **'84** 124
Orange Salad, Frosted, **'81** 154; **'83** 123
Orange Salad, Jeweled, **'83** 210
Orange Sherbet Salad, **'81** 154
Orange Surprise Salad, **'79** 12
Peach-Cranberry Ring, Spicy, **'85** 264
Peaches-and-Cream Salad, **'83** 108
Peach Fluff, **'95** 176
Peach Frost, **'84** 164
Peach Party Salad, **'84** 290
Peach Pinwheel Salad, **'79** 11
Peach Salad, Pickled, **'80** 104; **'85** 264
Peach Salad, Spiced, **'94** 68
Peachy Berry Cream Mold, **'83** 130
Pear-Lime Salad, **'84** 152
Pear Salad, Royal, **'84** 265
Pimiento Salad, Sunshine, **'84** 124
Pineapple-Buttermilk Salad, **'82** 80
Pineapple-Cucumber Congealed Salad,
    '83 118
Pineapple Daiquiri Salad, **'84** 232
Pineapple-Lime Salad, **'84** 320
Pineapple Mold, Minted, **'85** 240
Pineapple-Orange Congealed Salad, **'83** 218
Pineapple-Pear Delight, **'82** 54
Raspberry Fruit Mounds, **'79** 35
Raspberry Holiday Mold, **'84** 253
Raspberry Ribbon Salad, **'87** 236
Raspberry Salad, **'86** 286
Raspberry-Wine Salad, **'91** 256
Rhubarb Congealed Salad, **'86** 140
Rhubarb Salad, **'91** 146; **'92** 129
Rhubarb Salad, Tart, **'91** 146; **'92** 129
Roquefort Salad, Creamy, **'79** 73
Ruby-and-Emerald Salad, **'85** 79
Salmon Salad, Chilly, **'80** 104
Sangría Salad, **'86** 331
Shrimp Salad, **'84** 221
Strawberry-Nut Salad, **'94** 132
Strawberry Salad, Hidden Treasure, **'79** 11
Strawberry-Wine Salad Mold, **'83** 261
Sunshine Delight, **'86** 117

Tomato Mold, Tangy, '79 74
Tomato Ring, Tangy, '84 164
Tomato Salad, Frozen, '84 52
Tomato-Vegetable Ring, '81 302
Tuna-Cheese Mold, Creamy, '81 135
Tuna Ring, Creamy, '80 275
Tuna Salad, Congealed, '84 163
Tuna Salad, Creamy, '82 87, 208
Tuna Salad, Luncheon, '81 135
Vegetable Congealed Salad, Cheesy-, '86 199
Vegetable Congealed Salad, Fresh, '91 229
Vegetable Relish Salad, '82 267
Vegetable Salad, Congealed, '79 276
Vegetable Salad, Congealed Fresh, '82 240
Waldorf Salad, Congealed, '82 80
Waldorf Salad, Molded, '84 326
Corn-and-Pea Salad, '90 181
Cornbread Salad, '87 172
Cornbread Salad, Mexican, '95 210
Corn-in-the-Shuck Salad, '93 236
Corn Salad, '80 247; '81 139; '85 236; '91 27;
   '95 214
Corn Salad, Chilled, '79 20
Corn Salad, Confetti, '96 168
Corn Salad, Festive, '92 263
Corn Salad, Fresh, '91 126; '94 162
Corn Salad, Marinated, '89 126
Corn Salad, Roasted, '97 196
Corn Salad, Shoepeg, '81 23
Corn Salad, Tangy, '88 176
Corn Salad, Tasty, '84 289
Cottage Cheese-Banana Splits, '87 56
Cottage Cheese Salad, Different, '85 328; '86 22
Cottage Cheese Salad in Tomatoes, '86 208
Cottage Cheese Salad, Out-of-This-World, '79 44
Cottage-Tomato Salad, '85 163
Couscous Salad, Curried, '91 44
Couscous Salad with Dried Tomato Vinaigrette,
   '96 244
Cranberry. See also **SALADS/Congealed.**
   Cheese Ribbon Salad, Cranberry-, '79 241
   Christmas Salad, Cranberry, '79 243
   Cloud, Cranberry, '90 287
   Cranberry Salad, '88 250
   Frozen Cranberry-Pineapple Salad, '91 237
   Holiday Salad, Cranberry, '89 277
   Oriental, Cranberry, '79 126
   Tart Cranberry Salad, '79 286
   Whipped Cream Salad, Cranberry-, '83 261
   Wild Rice-and-Cranberry Salad, '99 272
Crunchy-Creamy Salad, '88 100
Cucumber-Almond Salad, '86 147
Cucumber and Tomato Salad, Dilled, '81 153
Cucumber Cooler, Simple, '86 147
Cucumber Mousse, '79 11
Cucumber Mousse with Dill Sauce, '95 216
Cucumber Salad, Dilled, '82 229; '92 72; '93 65
Cucumber Salad, Marinated, '82 111
Cucumbers and Artichokes, Marinated, '82 111
Cucumbers, Cool, '84 152
Cucumbers in Sour Cream, '79 52; '80 178
Cucumber-Tomato Salad, '90 144
Cucumber-Vinaigrette Oriental, '85 198; '86 147
Cucumber-Yogurt Salad, '87 33
Cukes and Scallions, '91 168
Curried Salad Gift, '96 326
Curry Salad, Hot Indian, '83 23
Eggplant Salad, '90 99
Egg-Rice Salad, '84 18; '86 169
Egg Salad, Bacon-Horseradish, '94 181
Egg Salad, Green Vegetable and, '79 191
Egg Salad Spread, Cottage-, '82 146
Egg Salad Tacos, Mexican, '94 181
Egg Salad, Yolkless, '94 181

Endive, Bacon, and Pecan Salad, '89 12
Endive-Tomato Starburst Salad, '93 323
Endive with Arugula Tabbouleh, '98 67
Escarole-and-Bacon Salad, '84 85
Fennel and Radicchio with Orange Vinaigrette,
   Grilled, '95 253
Fennel Salad, Marinated, '93 56
Fish. See also **SALADS/Seafood.**
   Confetti Salad, '80 4
   Crawfish Salad, Dilled, '83 126
   Meal-in-One Salad, '82 232
   Salmon-and-Macaroni Salad, '81 114
   Salmon on Mixed Greens with Creamy Dill
      Dressing, '93 143
   Salmon-Pasta Salad, '87 9
   Salmon-Rice Salad, '84 289
   Salmon Salad, '89 99
   Salmon Salad, Broiled, '92 108
   Salmon Salad, Chilled Poached, '96 68
   Salmon Salad, Crunchy, '81 148
   Salmon Salad, Scandinavian, '98 208
   Salmon Salad Shells, '85 286
   Salmon Salad, Simple, '91 23
   Salmon Salad, Summertime, '82 207
   Salmon-Spinach Salad, '87 145
   Salmon-Stuffed Avocados, '86 74
   Trout-and-Tomato Salad with Black Pepper
      Vinaigrette, '98 284
   Tuna-and-Cannellini Bean Salad, '86 143
   Tuna-and-Red Pepper Salad, '93 143
   Tuna-and-White Bean Salad, '98 209
   Tuna Chef Salad, '82 78
   Tuna-Egg Salad, '81 135
   Tuna Macaroni Salad, '83 44
   Tuna-Macaroni Salad, '83 145; '84 66
   Tuna-Mac in Tomatoes, '87 188
   Tuna-Pasta Salad, '91 43; '92 141
   Tuna Pasta Salad, '92 108
   Tuna-Potato Salad, '84 289
   Tuna-Rice Salad, '87 202
   Tuna Salad, Cheese-Sauced, '87 M124
   Tuna Salad, Company, '87 201
   Tuna Salad, Crunchy, '87 201
   Tuna Salad, Curried, '86 208
   Tuna Salad, Favorite, '82 208
   Tuna Salad, Flavorful, '81 37
   Tuna Salad, Fresh Greens and, '80 55
   Tuna Salad, Layered, '84 221
   Tuna Salad Rolls, Hot, '84 281
   Tuna Salad, Swiss, '86 186
   Tuna Salad, White Bean-, '98 208
   Tuna Salad, Whole Wheat Macaroni-, '84 193
   Tuna Salad, Wild, '95 243
   Tuna Salad with Grapes, Curried, '87 201
   Tuna-Taco Salad, '87 145
Freezer Salad, '94 118
Fruit. See also **SALADS/Congealed.**
   Almond-Citrus Salad, '96 274
   Ambrosia, Mixed Fruit, '83 10
   Avocado Fruit Salad, '87 41
   Avocado-Fruit Salad with Honey-Yogurt
      Dressing, '93 172
   Banana Split Salad, '91 58
   Berry-Citrus Twist, '95 100
   Cabbage and Fruit Salad, '79 286
   Chef Salad, Fruited, '85 222
   Chef's Fruit Salad, '86 35
   Chicken-and-Fruit Salad, Grilled, '96 155
   Chicken-Fruit Salad, '82 79; '90 234
   Chicken Salad, Fruited, '84 25, 290; '88 88;
      '90 318
   Chicken Salad, Fruity, '83 157
   Chicken Salad in Avocados, Fruited, '87 41
   Chicken Salad with Fruit, '82 171

Chilled Fruit with Dressing, '85 222
Citrus-and-Avocado Salad, '99 26
Citrus and Greens with Orange-Ginger
   Dressing, '96 240
Citrus-Cilantro Dressing, Fruit Salad with,
   '93 310; '94 97
Citrus Dressing, Fruit Salad with, '88 6
Coconut Fruit Bowl, '83 111
Coconut Salad, Chunky Fruit-and-, '84 24
Colorful Fruit Salad, '82 113
Cottage Cheese-and-Fruit Salad, '86 16
Cottage-Fruit Split, '86 169
Cracked Wheat-Fruit Salad, '96 240
Cream Dressing, Fruit Salad with, '89 277
Creamy Fruit Salad, '84 265
Creamy Holiday Fruit Salad, '90 251
Cups, Royal Fruit, '81 146
Cups, Sangría Fruit, '89 34
Cups with Pineapple Cream Dressing, Fruit,
   '83 81
Curried Fruit Salad, '85 107
Date Dressing, Fruit Salad with, '87 57
Delight, Fruit, '86 131
Dressed-Up Fruit, '82 5
Easy Fruit Salad, '80 221
Easy Patio Fruit Salad, '88 184
Favorite Fruit Salad, '99 220
Festive Fruit Salad, '80 16
Fresh Fruit Bowl, Sparkling, '80 146
Fresh Fruit Cup with Mint Dressing, '80 183
Fresh Fruit Salad, '82 165; '97 122
Fresh Fruit Salad with Celery-Honey
   Dressing, '80 42
Fresh Fruit Salad with Poppy-Seed Dressing,
   '80 137
Fresh Fruit Salad with Poppy Seed Dressing,
   '91 168
Fresh Fruit with Lemon Sauce, '82 290
Frisky Fruit Salad, '85 46
Frozen Fruit Salad, '83 110; '97 158
Frozen Fruit Salad, Dreamy, '79 126
Frozen Fruit Salad, Luscious, '81 204
Frozen Fruit Salad, Summertime, '89 111
Frozen Salad, Christmas Wreath, '79 241
Fruit Salad, '83 209; '89 277
Gingered Fruit Salad, '95 95
Glazed Fruit Salad, '83 48; '84 290
Green Fruit Salad with Honey-Lime Dressing,
   '93 71
Hawaiian Fruit Dish, '82 112
Heavenly Salad, '81 252
Holiday Fruit Salad, '87 236
Honeydew Fruit Boats, '81 147
Honeydew Fruit Bowl, '84 186
Honey Dressing, Fruit Salad with, '87 129
Honey Fruit Salad, '80 276
Honey-Lemon Dressing, Fruit Salad with,
   '93 21
Hurry-Up Fruit Salad, '87 236
Jícama-Fruit Salad, '86 83
Layered Fruit Salad, '84 290; '89 277; '91 58
Lemonade Fruit Salad, '84 24
Lemon Freeze, Fruity, '82 145
Lettuce and Fruit Salad with Poppy Seed
   Dressing, '80 152
Main Dish Fruit Salad, '83 119
Marinated Fruit Bowl, '80 297
Marinated Fruit Deluxe, '81 146
Medley, Chilled Fruit, '84 60
Medley, Fruit Cup, '85 47
Mélange Delight, Fruit, '81 302
Melon Balls in Watermelon Sauce, '79 177
Melon-Citrus Mingle, '79 177
Melon Cocktail, Minted, '81 146

SALADS, Fruit
(continued)

Melon Cooler, '81 146
Melon Mélange, '84 139
Melon Salad, Summertime, '82 101
Melon Salad with Orange-Raspberry
  Vinaigrette, Grilled, '95 144
Minted Fruit Medley, '80 182
Minted Fruit Toss, '99 160
Mint-Gin Fruit Salad, '92 92
Mint Sauce, Fruit Salad with, '88 M96
Mixed Fruit Cup, '87 233
Mixed Fruit Salad, Banana-, '79 270
Multi-Fruit Salad, '93 184
Nut Salad, Cheesy Fruit-'n'-, '87 56
Old-Fashioned Fruit Salad, '82 80
Orange Cream, Fresh Fruit Salad with,
  '90 126
Orange Fruit Cup, '91 277
Oriental Dressing, Fruit Salad with, '91 277
Party Freeze Salad, '82 145
Pasta Salad, Fruited, '92 108
Peachy Fruit Salad, '89 206
Persimmon Fruit Salad, '79 206
Picks, Fruit on, '80 159
Pineapple Dressing, Fruit Salad with, '85 207
Pineapple-Fruit Salad, Icy, '87 9
Platter, Fresh Fruit Salad, '92 213
Platter, Fruit Salad, '83 261
Poppy Seed Dressing, Fruit Salad with, '88 78
Quick-and-Easy Fruit Salad, '81 99
Refreshing Fruit Salad, '85 92
Rhapsody, Fruit, '80 158
Rum, Fruit Cup with, '83 55
Sherried Fruit Mélange, '80 158
Shrimp Salad, Fruited, '86 156
Sour Cream Fruit Salad, '80 138
Spiced Fruit Salad, '98 54
Springtime Fruit Salad, '81 96
Summer Fruit Salad, '82 164; '92 171
Summer Salad, '93 179
Summer Salad, Favorite, '80 158
Summer Salad, Georgia, '92 179
Sunny Day Salad, '96 90
Sunny Fruit Salad, '91 58
Sunny Salad, '80 138
Sweet-and-Sour Fruit Salad, '80 13; '84 125
Tossed Fruit Salad, '92 106
Tropical Fruit Salad, '89 306
Tropical Fruit Salad with Fresh Mint
  Dressing, '84 126
Turkey Salad, Fruit-and-, '89 176
Turkey Salad, Fruit-and-Spice, '94 325
Twenty-Four-Hour Fruit Salad, '96 279
Vanilla Fruit Cup, '80 183
Watermelon Fruit Basket, '84 161
White Wine, Fruit in, '81 48
Winter Fruit Delight, '80 243
Winter Fruit Salad, '80 248; '82 23
Winter Fruit with Poppy Seed Dressing,
  '95 317
Wreath, Della Robbia Fruit, '87 294
Wreath, Tex-Mex, '96 241
Yogurt Fruit Salad, '81 114; '96 247
Yogurt-Granola Fruit Medley, '91 58
Gazpacho Salad, '91 313
Gorgonzola-Walnut Salad, '96 170
Grapefruit-Apple Salad, '89 41
Grapefruit-Avocado Salad, '83 316; '84 16;
  '89 41
Grapefruit-Banana Salad with Celery Seed
  Dressing, '91 237

Grapefruit Combo Salad, '80 50
Grapefruit-Cucumber Salad, '80 100
Grapefruit Winter Salad, '84 24
Greek Salad, '87 103; '93 208; '94 160, 202
Greek Salad, Dawn's World-Famous, '98 276
Greek-Style Salad, '91 27
Green. *See also* **SALADS/Caesar, Spinach.**
  Apple and Brie, Salad Greens with, '93 241
  Baby Lettuces with Vidalia Onion Vinaigrette,
    Salad of, '99 168
  Baked Goat Cheese Salad, '96 26
  Balsamico, Insalata, '94 46
  Balsamic-Pesto Salad, '96 274
  B.B.'s Salad Dressing, Green Salad with,
    '91 65
  Bibb Salad, Tossed, '87 128
  Bibb Salad with Raspberry-Maple Dressing,
    '91 246
  Boston Lettuce and Watercress Salad, '93 65
  Bouquet, A Salad, '91 44
  California Green Salad, '81 84
  Cantaloupe Green Salad, '91 126
  Chinese Green Salad, '88 48
  Citrus Green Salad, '85 304
  Citrus Salad, Southern-Style, '84 262
  Collard Greens Salad, '96 325
  Combination Salad Bowl, '85 132
  Combo Salad Bowl, '81 9
  Company's Coming Salad, '79 113; '96 64
  Cranberry-Topped Green Salad, '87 311
  Crimson Greens, '87 153
  Crunchy Green Salad, '89 321
  Cucumber Asian Greens, '98 66
  Dijon Vinaigrette, Greens with, '98 332
  Endive Salad, Avocado-, '94 88
  Endive-Watercress Salad, '93 22
  Fast-and-Easy Salad, '85 M328
  Fenron Salad, '79 85
  Garden Salad, '85 92; '92 60
  Garden Salad Centerpiece, '83 171
  Garden Salad, Herbed, '85 328; '86 22
  Garden Salad, Summer, '87 153
  Garden Salad Toss, '81 9
  Garden Salad with Buttermilk Dressing,
    '96 94
  Garden Salad with Rosemary Dressing, Fresh,
    '81 131
  Garlic-Tarragon Green Salad, '92 79
  Goat Cheese and Greens, '90 54
  Grapefruit Salad, Greens and, '95 301
  Grecian Green Salad, '84 266
  Grecian Tossed Salad, '79 174
  Herbed Earl Grey Vinaigrette, Salad Greens
    with, '99 89
  Hill Country Salad, '81 9
  Hot Chile Vinaigrette, Greens with,
    '98 200
  Lemon-Dill Vinaigrette, Green Salad with,
    '99 27
  Lemony French Dressing, Green Salad with,
    '85 67
  Lettuce, Cheesy Stuffed, '79 175
  Lettuce, Confetti-Stuffed, '87 24
  Lettuce, Delicate Garden, '87 62
  Lettuce-English Pea Salad, '91 208
  Lettuce, Garden-Stuffed, '83 135
  Lettuce Salad, Blue Cheese Stuffed, '94 202
  Lettuce Salad, French, '84 187
  Lettuce Salad, Tennessee-Killed, '88 86
  Lettuce Salad, Wilted, '82 302
  Lettuce Salad, Wilted Bacon-and-, '85 69
  Lettuces with Mustard Vinaigrette, Baby, '93 67
  Lettuce Wedges with Pimiento Dressing,
    '84 212

Lettuce, Wilted, '86 269
Lettuce with Sour Cream Dressing Deluxe,
  '88 48
Marinated Cheese Dressing, Green Salad
  with, '93 206
Mediterranean Salad, '90 99
Mesclun with Tarragon Dressing, '90 55
Mess o' Greens Salad with Warm Pecan
  Dressing, '98 250
Mint-Fresh Green Salad, '92 105
Mixed Green Salad, '90 230
Mixed Green Salad, Wilted, '85 69
Mixed Green Salad with Chicken, '80 54
Mixed Greens, Hot Sesame Pork on, '97 19
Mixed Greens Salad, '87 62
Mixed Greens with Blue Cheese Vinaigrette,
  '89 274; '90 280
Mixed Greens with Parmesan Walnuts,
  '95 301
Mixed Greens with Raspberries and Walnuts,
  '98 194
Mixed Greens with Raspberry Dressing,
  '97 50
Mixed Greens with Roquefort Firecrackers,
  '97 19
Mixed Greens with Tarragon Vinaigrette,
  '95 326
Mixed Greens with Walnuts, '99 107
Nutty Green Salad, '87 168
Orange-Poppy Seed Salad, '98 87
Oriental, Green Salad, '85 92
Peppery Greens with Raspberry Dressing,
  '95 254
Red-and-Green Salad, '90 55
Rich Green Salad, '99 203
Robust Salad, '90 181
Romaine Salad, Tangy, '80 155
Romaine-Spinach Salad, '89 123
Romaine with Caper Vinaigrette, Hearts of,
  '91 310
Salmagundi Salad, '83 146
Savory Green Salad, '82 74
Sensational Salad, '84 320
Sesame-Citrus Green Salad, '86 33
Shrimp, Green Salad with, '88 49
Simply Good Salad, '85 131
Soy Dressing, Green Salad with, '86 191
Spring Salad, '87 62
Spring Salad, Mediterranean, '80 148
Spring Salad Wedges, '87 62
Summer Salad, Crisp, '85 92
Summertime Salad, '79 143; '84 195
Sweet-and-Sour Green Salad, '94 281
Tangy Wilted Salad, '85 69
Tarragon Salad, '97 165
Tossed Mixed Green Salad, '84 126
Tossed Salad, Blue Cheese, '84 195
Tossed Salad, Boston, '84 85
Tossed Salad, Colorful, '90 55
Tossed Salad, Radish-Dressed, '79 104
Veggies with Fried Okra Croutons, Salad
  Greens and, '96 178
Vinaigrette, Greens and, '98 168
Vinaigrette with Greens, '98 184
Watercress-and-Mushroom Salad, '88 104
Watercress Salad, '97 249
Watercress Salad, Roasted Red Pepper and,
  '90 55
Winter Green Holiday Salad with Cranberry
  Vinaigrette, '98 321
Winter Salad, '95 280
Guacamole Salad, '80 14; '87 181
Guacamole-Tomato Salad, '81 302
Harvest Salad with Cider Vinaigrette, '99 322

Hearts of Palm Salad, **'81** 252; **'89** 276; **'96** 86
Hearts-of-Palm Salad, **'87** 138
Hearts of Palm Salad with Basil-and-Garlic
    Dressing, **'94** 55
Herb Salad, **'87** 90
Honeydew Salad with Apricot Cream Dressing,
    '84 191
Hoppin' John Salad, **'96** 64
Ice Cream Salad, **'79** 126
Indian Chief Salad, **'96** 287
Italian Bread Salad, **'99** 259
Italian Salad, **'87** 145
Jícama-and-Orange Salad, **'88** 246
Jícama-Orange Salad, **'86** 83; **'90** 122
Jícama Salad, **'87** 123
Layered Overnight Salad, **'90** 319
Layered Salad, **'86** 35, 79
Layered Salad, Cheesy, **'81** 37
Layered Salad Deluxe, **'81** 153
Layered Salad, Hearty, **'86** 79
Layered Salad, Majestic, **'86** 79
Layered Salad, Make-Ahead, **'81** 296
Layered Salad, Overnight, **'81** 188
Layer Salad, Eight-, **'99** 107
Legumes, Marinated, **'90** 197
Lentil Salad, Mediterranean, **'96** 239
Lentils-and-Rice Salad, **'90** 197
Macaroni. *See* **SALADS/Pasta.**
Magnolia Blossom Salad, **'89** 123
Main-Dish Salad, **'86** 191
Mandarin, Salad, **'84** 231
Mandarin Spinach Salad, **'85** 163
Mandarin Tossed Salad, **'89** 12
Mango Salad, **'79** 137
Mango Salad, Fresh, **'84** 126
Meal in a Bowl, **'96** 138
Meal-in-One Salad, **'86** 43
Meat
    Beef-and-Broccoli Salad, **'87** 187
    Beef Fajita Salad, **'91** 70
    Beef Salad, Gingered, **'88** 61
    Beef Salad Niçoise, **'99** 159
    Beef Salad, Peking, **'88** 60
    Beef Salad, Stir-Fry, **'96** 129
    Beef Salad, Tangy, **'87** M218
    Beef Salad, Western-Style, **'93** 321
    Beef Salad with Cilantro, **'97** 202
    Beef Salad, Zesty, **'79** 56
    Beef Vinaigrette Salad, **'95** 177
    Chili Salad, Spicy, **'86** 71
    Committee, Salad by, **'87** 288
    Corned Beef-Cauliflower Salad, **'83** 16
    Corned Beef-Potato Salad, **'85** 213
    Corned Beef Salad, **'80** 104
    Corned Beef Salad, Molded, **'82** 86
    Corned Beef Salad, Potato-, **'81** 36
    Corned Beef Salad, Vegetable-, **'80** 148
    Dude Ranch Salad, **'80** 15
    Ham-and-Apple Salad, **'88** 139
    Ham-and-Cheese Salad, **'88** 138
    Ham and Cheese Toss, **'79** 55
    Ham and Macaroni Salad, **'79** 220
    Ham-and-Pasta Salad, **'90** 128
    Ham-and-Rice Salad, Colorful, **'90** 319
    Ham-and-Rice Salad, Mandarin, **'87** 145
    Ham-Dijon Pasta Salad, **'92** 191
    Ham 'n Egg Salad, **'81** 36
    Ham-Noodle Salad, **'85** 249
    Ham-Rice Toss, **'82** 40
    Ham Salad, Congealed, **'81** 36
    Ham Salad, Crunchy Baked, **'83** 23
    Ham Salad, Fruited, **'81** 36, 146
    Ham Salad, Hearty, **'82** 40
    Ham Salad Sandwich, Tangy, **'80** 272

Ham Salad, Spicy Italian, **'85** 74
Ham Salad Spread, **'87** 92
Ham Salad, Tropical, **'89** 175
Ham-Sweet Potato Salad, Hawaiian, **'82** 232
Mexican Dinner Salad, **'98** 330
Mexican Salad in a Shell, **'86** 4
Mexican Salad Supper, **'82** 9; **'83** 68
Paella Salad, **'86** 207
"Pig in the Garden" Salad, **'92** 255
Pork-and-Spinach Salad, Mandarin, **'88** M126
Pork Salad, Oriental, **'92** 140
Roast Beef Salad, **'80** 223; **'81** 56; **'90** 318
Roast Beef Salad, Cucumber-, **'89** 162
Rolls, Hearty Salad, **'81** 206
Sirloin Salad, Grilled, **'94** 129
Steak Salad Cups, Pepper, **'86** 206
Steak Salad, Greek, **'92** 107
Steak Salad with Peach Salsa, **'97** 183
Taco Salad, **'79** 56; **'83** 145; **'84** 221; **'85** 84;
    '89 332; **'90** 20
Taco Salad Cups, **'85** M29
Taco Salad, Party, **'97** 19
Taco Salad, Spicy, **'87** 287
Melon-and-Prosciutto Salad, **'92** 191
Melon Balls, Minted, **'87** 162
Melon-Berry Salad, **'90** 180
Melon Salad with Dill Dressing, **'88** 182
Mexican Salad with Avocado Dressing, **'92** 321
Mexicorn-Bean Salad, **'96** 184
Middle Eastern Salad, **'87** 107
Minestrone Salad, **'79** 220
Mix, Muffy Salad, **'94** 34
Mozzarella-Tomato-Basil Salad, Fresh, **'93** 131
Mushroom-and-Pepper Salad, **'86** 68
Mushroom Salad, Fabulous, **'81** 190
Mushroom Salad, Fresh, **'93** 65
Mushroom Salad, Marinated, **'88** 215; **'90** 181
Mushroom Salad, Quick Cheesy-, **'89** 128
Mushrooms in Rosemary-Red Wine Vinaigrette,
    Marinated, **'97** 63
Mushroom-Zucchini Salad, **'85** 8
Okra-Corn-and-Tomato Vinaigrette, **'90** 173
Okra Salad, **'90** 155
Okra Salad, Fried, **'97** M157
Olive Clubhouse Salad, **'81** 114
Olive Salad, **'98** 184
Olive Salad, Doodles, **'94** 35
Olive Salad, Italian, **'94** 35
Olive Salad, Mexican, **'85** 84
Onion Salad, Grilled, **'99** 96
Onion Salad, Roasted, **'95** 65
Orange
    Almond Salad, Orange-, **'99** 107
    Avocado Salad, Orange-, **'99** 331
    Beet Salad, Orange-and-, **'88** 43
    Carrot Salad, Orange-, **'80** 89; **'84** 325
    Cauliflower Salad, Orange-, **'82** 266
    Cottage Cheese Salad, Orange-, **'79** 44
    Cups, Orange, **'86** 92
    Cups, Orange Salad, **'85** 40
    Grapefruit Salad, Orange-, **'93** 294
    Honey-Berry Dressing, Orange Salad with,
        '89 250
    Honey Dressing, Orange Salad with, **'89** 14
    Mandarin Orange and Pineapple Salad,
        '82 266
    Mandarin Orange-Lettuce Salad, **'92** 79
    Mandarin Orange Salad, **'81** 252; **'84** 161
    Mandarin Orange Tossed Salad, **'92** 303
    Marinated, Orange-Onion Salad, **'91** 231;
        '92 68
    Onion Salad, Orange-, **'89** 41
    Quick Orange Salad, **'87** 80
    Romaine Salad, Orange-, **'84** 325; **'87** 239

Shrimp Salad, Orange-, **'84** 197
Spinach Salad, Orange-, **'83** 316; **'84** 16
Strawberry Salad with Orange-Curd Dressing,
    Orange-, **'93** 22
Tropical Orange Salad, **'92** 97
Walnut Salad, Orange, **'80** 246
Oriental Salad Bowl, **'87** 153
Orzo Salad, Confetti, **'92** 173
Orzo Salad with Sesame Dressing, **'96** 137
Paella Salad, **'86** 207
Pasta
    Artichoke-Pasta Salad, **'94** 180
    Bean-Pasta Salad, Marinated, **'94** 167
    Bean Salad, Pasta-, **'86** 169
    Broccoli-Cauliflower Pasta Salad, **'88** 269
    Caesar Salad Pasta, **'95** 230
    Chicken Pasta Salad, **'88** 89
    Chicken-Pasta Salad, Grilled, **'94** 64
    Chicken Salad, Tarragon Pasta-, **'87** 155
    Cold Pasta Platter, **'88** 42
    Crabmeat-Shrimp Pasta Salad, **'86** 208
    Crunchy Pasta Salad, **'85** 166
    Easy Confetti-Pasta Salad, **'92** 220
    Fruited Pasta Salad, **'92** 108
    Garden Pasta Salad, **'86** 188
    Ham, Pasta Salad with, **'92** 108
    Ham-Pecan-Blue Cheese Pasta Salad, **'90** 62
    Herbed Pasta-and-Tomato Salad, **'92** 144
    Hoisin Chicken-and-Pasta Salad, **'99** 125
    Luncheon Pasta Salad, **'90** 191
    Macaroni and Cheese Salad, **'97** 203
    Macaroni-Cheese Salad, Dilled, **'86** 208
    Macaroni-Chicken Salad, **'85** 296; **'86** 302
    Macaroni-Chicken Salad, Dilled, **'92** 142
    Macaroni-Crabmeat Salad, **'81** 153
    Macaroni-Ham Salad, **'85** 218
    Macaroni Salad, **'87** 92
    Macaroni Salad, Barbecue, **'82** 276
    Macaroni Salad, Confetti, **'82** 132; **'85** 297
    Macaroni Salad, Crunchy, **'82** 24
    Macaroni Salad, Dilled, **'89** 161
    Macaroni Salad for Two, **'81** 31
    Macaroni Salad, Garden, **'84** 290; **'92** 64
    Macaroni Salad, Gourmet, **'81** 253
    Macaroni Salad, Hearty, **'84** 90
    Macaroni Salad, Pineapple, **'79** 220
    Macaroni Salad, Refreshing, **'80** 177
    Macaroni Salad, Shell, **'92** 163
    Macaroni Salad, Spiral, **'82** 276
    Macaroni Salad, Sweet-and-Sour, **'85** 166
    Macaroni Salad, Taco, **'85** 165
    Macaroni Salad Véronique, **'85** 164
    Macaroni-Salmon Salad, **'82** 232
    Macaroni Shell Salad, **'87** 38
    Macaroni-Shrimp Salad, **'85** 121
    Macaroni-Shrimp Salad, Festive, **'85** 165
    Macaroni Toss, Corkscrew, **'83** 163
    Macaroni-Tuna Salad, Whole Wheat, **'84** 193
    Macaroni-Vegetable Salad, **'86** 209
    Main-Dish Pasta Salad, **'82** 199
    Marinated Bean-Pasta Salad, **'97** 328
    Mediterranean Salad, **'95** 132
    Medley, Garden Pasta, **'89** 256
    Oriental Pasta Salad, **'90** 63
    Overnight Pasta Salad, **'82** 276
    Pasta Salad, **'84** 139; **'86** 120; **'87** 36; **'90** 62, 91
    Pistachio-Pasta Salad, **'86** 141
    Plentiful P's Salad, **'87** 12
    Presto Pasta Salad, **'90** 63
    Ramen Noodle Salad, **'88** 41
    Ratatouille Pasta Salad, **'90** 74
    Ravioli Salad, Caesar, **'95** 183
    Roasted Onion Pasta Salad with Peppered
        Cheese Crisps, **'98** 107

SALADS, Pasta
(continued)

Rotelle Salad, Crunchy, **'86** 209
Rotini Salad, **'88** 42
Seafood Pasta Salad, **'90** 62
Seashell Salad, **'86** 209
Shell Salad, Tossed, **'86** 209
Shrimp Salad, Pasta-and-, **'83** 163
Snappy Pasta, **'83** 164
Southwestern Pasta Salad, **'94** 278
Spaghetti Salad, **'82** 277; **'84** 205
Spaghetti Salad, Chicken-, **'90** 146
Spinach-Mustard Twist, **'86** 209
Tomato-Pasta Salad, **'97** M160
Tortellini-Pesto Salad, **'92** 22
Tortellini Salad, **'89** 237
Tortellini Salad, Chicken, **'87** 288
Tortellini Salad, Garden, **'91** 44
Tortellini Salad, Terrific, **'96** 134
Turkey 'n' Pasta Salad, Ranch-Style, **'94** 184
Vegetable Salad, Pasta-, **'95** 238
Veggie Salad, Pasta-, **'96** 106
Vermicelli Vinaigrette Salad, **'82** 189
Vinaigrette, Italian Pasta, **'92** 78
Ziti-Cheddar Salad, **'85** 165
Pea
Asparagus Salad, Peas-and-, **'83** 141
Black-Eyed Pea Salad, **'80** 112; **'86** 225;
'88 92, 221; **'90** 173; **'95** 203; **'97** 305;
'98 52; **'99** 174
Black-Eyed Pea Salad, Chicken-and-, **'97** 305
Black-Eyed Pea Salad, Fearrington House
Goat Cheese and, **'95** 60
Black-Eyed Pea Salad, Marinated, **'93** 190
Black-Eyed Pea Salad, Overnight, **'81** 280
Black-Eyed Pea Salad with Benedictine
Dressing, **'98** 83
Black-Eyed Peas, Marinated, **'82** 156
Black-Eyed Peas, Zesty, **'89** 147
Black-Eyed Pea Vinaigrette, **'86** 7
Black-Eyed Salad, Hot Bacon and, **'85** 7
Cauliflower and Pea Salad, Savory, **'81** 280
Cauliflower-Pea Salad, **'87** 231
Cheddar-Pea Salad, **'84** 82
Chicken-Pea Salad, **'83** 218
Corn-and-Pea Salad, **'90** 181
Creamy Pea Salad, **'80** 111
Crunchy Pea Salad, **'90** 143
Dilled Pea Salad, **'97** 305; **'98** 18
English Pea-and-Apple Salad, **'87** 24
English Pea Salad, **'81** 280; **'90** 143
English Pea Salad, Cauliflower-, **'95** 66
English Pea Salad, Marinated, **'82** 54
Green Pea Salad, **'96** 88
Marinated Pea Salad, **'81** 204
Mexi-Pea Salad, **'81** 7
Minted Pea Salad, **'91** 119
Pea Salad, **'98** 274
Plentiful P's Salad, **'87** 12
Special Peas, **'95** 133
Special Pea Salad, **'83** 239
Sugar Snap Pea Salad, **'86** 115
Three Pea Salad, **'84** 290
Peach-and-Kiwi Salad, **'90** 180
Peaches in a Garden Nest, **'87** 154
Peach Salad, Frosted, **'82** 145
Peach Salad, Frozen, **'82** 54
Peach Salad, Georgia, **'80** 142
Peach Salad Supreme, Easy, **'79** 177
Peanut-Apple Salad, **'80** 5
Pear-and-Celery Salad, **'87** 56
Pear-and-Spinach Salad, Festive, **'85** 131

Pear Plate, Pretty, **'89** 225
Pear Salad, Crunchy, **'83** 234; **'84** 244
Pear Salad, Golden, **'91** 58
Pear-Swiss Cheese Salad, **'91** 237
Pepper-Cheese Stacks, **'87** 80
Pepperoni-and-Broccoli Salad, **'83** 216
Pepper Salad, Mixed, **'89** 103
Pepper Salad, Three-, **'91** 162
Pineapple Boat Aloha, **'80** 102
Pineapple Boats Ahoy, **'80** 148
Pineapple Boats, Fresh, **'83** 153
Pineapple-Celery Salad, **'85** 95
Pineapple Salad, Frosty, **'89** 278
Pineapple Waldorf, **'97** 86
Pineapple Waldorf Salad, **'92** 97
Pita Salad Sandwiches, **'83** 134
Pizza, Salad, **'87** 182
Portobello Salad, Grilled, **'99** 216
Potato Salads, Cold
Any Day Potato Salad, **'81** 154
Asparagus-and-New Potato Salad, **'86** 69
Avocado, Potato Salad with, **'98** 332
Avocado-Potato Salad with Horseradish
Dressing, **'96** 200
Bacon-Topped Potato Salad, **'85** 59
Baked Potato Salad, **'97** 319
Basil Potato Salad, **'94** 178
Bean Salad, Potato-, **'82** 301
Blue Cheese-Potato Salad, **'91** 208
Charletta's Potato Salad, **'98** 153
Chunky Potato Salad, **'81** M138
Confetti Potato Salad, **'80** 5; **'88** 16
Corned Beef-Potato Salad, **'85** 213
Corned Beef Salad, Potato-, **'81** 36
Cottage Cheese-Potato Salad, **'79** 147, 285
Creamy Potato Salad, **'80** 178; **'88** 171;
'92 241; **'98** 175
Creole Potato Salad, **'99** 136
Curried Potato Salad, **'99** 137
Deluxe Potato Salad, **'80** 155
Dill-and-Sour Cream Potato Salad, **'93** 105;
'94 100
Dill Potato Salad, **'85** 213; **'94** 179; **'99** 104
Festive Potato Salad, **'89** 315
Fish-Potato Salad, Smoked, **'84** 233
French-Style Potato Salad, **'88** 171
Fruity Potato Salad, **'85** 214
Garden Patch Potato Salad, **'84** 82
German Potato Salad, **'84** 18
Grecian Potato Salad, **'82** 55
Greek Potato Salad, **'98** 276
Green Bean-Potato Salad, **'83** 80
Green Bean-Red Potato Salad, **'96** 175
Ham-and-Egg Potato Salad, **'86** 84
Ham and Potato Salad, **'80** 272
Ham-and-Potato Salad, **'95** 94
Herbed Potato Salad, **'87** 171; **'94** 164
Horseradish Potato Salad, **'98** 175
Jalapeño Potato Salad, **'97** 64
Joy's Potato Salad, **'99** 83
Layered Creamy Potato Salad, **'81** 23
Marinated Potato Slices, **'93** 98
Mustard Potato Salad, **'86** 302
New Potato Salad, **'84** 120, 139; **'94** 162
Olive-Potato Salad, **'85** 114
Parslied Potato Salad, **'85** 240
Patio Potato Salad, **'90** 160
Peppers, Potato Salad 'n', **'83** 135
Pickle-Potato Salad, Sweet, **'85** 213
Potato Salad, **'90** 122; **'94** 160
Red Potato Salad, **'93** 119; **'96** 172
Roasted-Potato Salad, Creamy, **'97** 161
Salmon-Potato Salad, **'87** 285
Salmon Potato Salad, Smoked, **'97** 64

Saucy Potato Salad, **'87** 123
Savory Potato Salad, **'80** 30
Shrimp-and-Potato Salad, **'96** 211
Sour Cream Potato Salad, **'79** 104; **'80** 79;
'99 137
Sour Cream-Potato Salad, **'84** 149
South-of-the-Border Potato Salad, **'94** 178
Spicy Potato Salad, **'97** 305
Spring Salad, Mediterranean, **'80** 148
Sweet and Sour Potato Salad, **'80** 152
Sweet Potato-Apple Salad, **'96** 240
Sweet Potato Salad, Fresh, **'86** 226
Tri Club Potato Salad, **'92** 166
Tuna-Potato Salad, **'84** 289
Potato Salads, Hot or Warm
Baked Potato Salad, **'97** 319
Broccoli-Potato Salad, Hot, **'85** 23
Dill Potato Salad, Hot, **'79** 78
Dutch Potato Salad, Hot, **'86** 297; **'87** 176
German Potato Salad, **'82** 134, 239; **'92** 169;
'97 195; **'98** 175
German Potato Salad, Hot, **'79** 78; **'94** 254
German-Style Potato Salad, **'83** 23; **'88** M194
Goat Cheese and Potato Salad, Warm, **'96** 234
Greens, Hot Potato, **'97** 20
Lemon-Basil Potato Salad, **'97** 63
Light Potato Salad, Hot-and-, **'93** 90
Parmesan Potato Salad, Hot, **'79** 78
Pepper Cups, Potato Salad in, **'79** 78
Pesto Potato Salad, **'90** 164
Pole Bean-Potato Salad, Hot, **'79** 74
Potato Salad, Hot, **'79** 78; **'81** 276; **'86** 10
Sausage Salad, Warm Potato-and-, **'96** 25
Savory Potato Salad, **'80** 30
Smoked Sausage, Warm Potato Salad with,
'97 267
Sugar Snap Peas, Potato Salad with, **'91** 120
Supreme, Hot Potato Salad, **'79** 78
Sweet-and-Sour Potato Salad, **'92** 106
Sweet Potato Salad with Rosemary-Honey
Vinaigrette, **'98** 243
Ramen Noodle Salad, **'97** 18
Raspberry Salad, Frozen, **'79** 287; **'80** 35
Raspberry-Walnut Salad, **'94** 158
Red Cabbage Citrus Salad, **'94** 72
Relish Salad, **'84** 121
Rice. *See also* **SALADS/Vegetable.**
Artichoke-Chicken-Rice Salad,
Mediterranean, **'97** 321
Artichoke Hearts, Rice Salad with, **'80** 232
Artichoke-Rice Salad, **'80** 178; **'81** 41; **'85** 81
Avocado Salad, Rice-and-, **'89** 146
Bacon, Rice Salad with, **'79** 52
Bean-and-Rice Salad, Marinated, **'87** 152
Bean Salad, Rice-and-, **'85** 22
Beans-and-Rice Salad, **'91** 44
Brown Rice-and-Vegetable Salad, **'84** 202
Brown Rice Confetti Salad, **'94** 174
Chicken-and-Rice Salad, **'97** 92
Chicken-and-Rice Salad, Hot, **'83** 22
Chicken-Rice Salad, **'81** 203; **'97** 93
Chicken-Rice Salad, Curried, **'92** 190
Chicken-Rice Salad, Nutty, **'83** 157
Chutneyed Rice Salad, **'88** 100
Colorful Rice Salad, **'81** 253
Confetti Rice Salad, **'80** 232
Crunchy Rice Salad, **'82** 302
Curried Rice Salad, **'80** 84; **'85** 147, 220; **'96** 240
Curry Rice Salad, **'89** 146
Egg-Rice Salad, **'84** 18; **'86** 169
Hearty Rice Salad, **'82** 233
Herbed Rice Salad, **'96** 123
Madras Salad, **'86** 82
Mandarin Rice Salad, **'88** 271

Mardi Gras Rice, '91 217
Meal-in-One Salad, '86 43
Molded Gazpacho-Rice Salad, '86 221
Mushrooms, Rice Salad with Fresh, '80 231
Orange Vinaigrette Rice Salad, '98 288
Paella Salad, '86 207
Pea Salad, Rice-, '85 163
Pebble Salad, '91 27
Pine Nut, Rice, and Feta Salad, '96 26; '98 331
Red Rice Salad, Charleston, '79 146
Rice Salad, '79 74; '81 51
Ring, Rice-Carrot, '79 246
Shrimp Salad, Rice-, '79 270; '92 142
Shrimp Salad, Rice-and-, '83 82
Spinach-Rice Salad, '94 63
Tomatoes and Basil, Rice with, '95 232
Tuna Salad, Wild, '95 243
Vegetable-Rice Salad, '80 148; '83 198; '85 87
Wild Rice-and-Corn Salad, '98 288
Wild Rice-and-Cranberry Salad, '99 272
Wild Rice-and-Roasted Vegetable Salad, '99 316
Wild Rice-Chicken Salad, '83 146; '99 55
Wild Rice-Green Apple Salad, '92 90
Wild Rice Salad, '85 65; '89 147; '93 191
Wild Rice Salad, Crab-, '86 207
Wild Rice Salad, Crab and, '79 116
Wild Rice Salad, Oriental Salmon-and-, '94 173
Wild Rice Salad, Springtime, '88 100
Wild Rice-Shrimp Salad, '99 55
Zesty Rice Salad, '81 23
Roasted Red Pepper-and-Green Bean Salad, '99 322
Sandwich, Tuscan Feta Salad, '99 289
Sauerkraut Salad, '80 178; '97 195
Sauerkraut Salad, Crunchy, '87 9
Seafood. *See also* **SALADS/Fish, Shrimp.**
Baked Seafood Salad, '86 10
Blue Crab Salad with Asian Vinaigrette, '98 142
Crab-and-Asparagus Salad, '92 141
Crab-and-Endive Salad, Marinated, '93 22
Crab and Wild Rice Salad, '79 116
Crab-Avocado Salad, '81 114
Crab Cakes with Greens and Dijon Dressing, '96 176
Crab Louis, '95 94
Crabmeat, Avocado with, '86 119
Crabmeat Luncheon Salad, '82 207
Crabmeat Salad, '91 169
Crabmeat Salad with Creamy Gingered Dressing, Caribbean, '97 263
Crabmeat-Shrimp Pasta Salad, '86 208
Crab Mousse, '79 117
Crab Salad, Chesapeake, '89 195
Crab Salad, Cucumber-and-, '98 208
Crab Salad, Delightful, '87 145
Crab Salad Sandwiches, Mango-, '99 72
Crab-Wild Rice Salad, '86 207
Fleur-de-lis Salad, '99 164
Hot Seafood Salad, '79 117; '80 164
Lobster and Orange Salad, '82 207
Lobster Salad, '89 249; '90 69
Lobster Salad with Tarragon Vinaigrette, '97 163
Paella Salad, '86 207
Polynesian Seafood Salad, '79 57
Seafood Salad, '90 88
Smoky Seafood Salad, '84 46
Sussex Shores, Seafood Salad, '93 98
Tropical Salad, '85 91
Sesame-Almond Salad, '89 123
Shallot Salad, Caramelized, '96 308

Shrimp
Aloha Shrimp Salad, '95 46
Avocado Salad, Shrimp and, '80 266
Avocados, Shrimp-Filled, '83 2
Avocado Stuffed with Shrimp Salad, '82 207
Baked Shrimp-Rice Salad, '83 22
Bowl, Mediterranean Shrimp, '80 174
Caribbean Shrimp-and-Black Bean Salad, '93 143
Couscous Salad, Shrimp-and-, '96 157
Creamy Shrimp Salad, '79 56
Croissants, Shrimp Salad on, '96 175
Curry Salad, Melon and Shrimp, '97 129
Egg Salad, Tossed Shrimp-, '80 4
Endive Salad, Shrimp-, '85 73
Filling, Shrimp Salad, '87 106
Grapefruit-and-Shrimp Salad, '88 5
Green Salad with Shrimp, '88 49
Half Shell, Shrimp Salad on the, '86 73
Individual Shrimp Salads, '83 146
Layered Shrimp Salad, '88 100
Macaroni Salad, Shrimp, '79 220
Macaroni Salad, Shrimp-, '85 219
Marinated Shrimp Salad, '85 82; '93 321; '99 169
Mousse, Shrimp, '79 57
Orange, and Olive Salad with Sherry Vinaigrette, Shrimp, '93 177
Orange-Shrimp Salad, '84 197
Oriental Shrimp Salad, '91 313
Orzo Salad, Peppers Stuffed with Shrimp-and-, '91 203
Orzo Salad, Shrimp-and-, '99 182
Pastry, Shrimp Salad in, '86 105
Picnic Shrimp Salad, '95 182
Potato Salad, Shrimp-and-, '96 211
Rémoulade, Shrimp, '90 255
Rice Salad, Shrimp and, '80 231; '82 207
Rice Salad, Shrimp-and-, '92 307
Rotelle, Shrimp, '85 165
Shrimp Salad, '81 94; '86 186; '93 238; '98 333
Sandwiches, Shrimp-and-Egg Salad, '94 182
Sandwiches, Shrimp Salad, '90 178
Super Shrimp Salad, '81 37
Tangy Shrimp-Rice Salad, '84 66
Vegetable-Shrimp Salad, '79 190
Vermicelli Salad, Shrimp, '88 139
Wild Rice-Shrimp Salad, '99 55
Zesty Shrimp-and-Orange Rice Salad, '87 155
Southwestern Spiral Salad, '98 66
Spaghetti Squash Salad, '99 M322
Spaghetti Squash Salad, Marinated, '94 134
Spinach
Apple-Onion Vinaigrette, Spinach Salad with, '94 276
Apple Salad, Spinach-, '90 89; '92 13; '97 308
Apple-Spinach Salad, '97 14; '99 222
Apricot Salad, Spinach-, '94 63
Arranged Spinach Salad, '91 210; '92 160
Bacon Salad, Spinach and, '81 143
Beet Salad, Spinach-, '83 227
Blue Cheese Salad, Spinach-, '82 166
Blues, Spinach Salad with the, '95 66
Chili-Lime Dressing, Spinach Salad with, '94 63
Citrus Dressing, Spinach Salad with, '88 133
Citrus Spinach Salad, '90 59
Combination Spinach Salad, '85 327; '86 22
Creamy Dressing, Crisp Spinach Salad with, '83 81
Creamy Spinach Salad, '83 60
Crunchy Spinach Salad, '80 147; '81 225
Curry Spinach Salad, '80 242
Dijon Spinach Salad, '89 282

Dried Tomato Vinaigrette, Spinach Salad with, '93 272
Easy Spinach Salad, '91 249
Enoki Salad, Spinach-, '89 62
Festive Spinach Salad, '80 247
French Spinach Salad, '79 8
Fresh Spinach Salad, '82 73; '83 240; '84 15, 77; '86 130
Fresh Spinach Salad Delight, '80 146
Garlic-Ginger Vinaigrette Dressing, Spinach Salad with, '92 195
Green Spinach Salad, '79 142
Grits-Spinach Salad, Stacked, '98 66
Honey Dressing, Spinach Salad with, '90 16
Hot Bacon Dressing, Spinach Salad with, '82 211
Hot Spiked Spinach, '97 195
Kiwifruit Salad, Spinach-, '87 305
Lamb Salad, Spinach-, '85 58
Layered Spinach Salad, '80 5; '89 163
Lettuce Salad, Layered Spinach-, '84 266
Mandarin Spinach Salad, '85 163
Minted Spinach Salad, '94 63
Mushroom Salad, Spinach and, '80 112
Mustard Twist, Spinach-, '86 209
Onion Salad Bowl, Spinach-and-, '81 157
Orange Dressing, Spinach Salad with, '87 187
Orange Salad, Spinach-and-, '86 15
Orange-Spinach Salad, '83 316; '84 16
Oriental Spinach Salad, '82 23
Oysters and Red Wine Vinaigrette, Spinach Salad with, '94 327
Pear-and-Spinach Salad, Festive, '85 131
Pecan Salad, Spinach-, '89 128
Pickled Spinach, '81 69
Poppy Seed Dressing, Spinach Salad with, '91 210; '92 160
Pork-and-Spinach Salad, Mandarin, '88 M126
Raspberry Cream Dressing, Spinach Salad with, '94 321
Rice Salad, Spinach-, '94 63
Russian Dressing, Spinach Salad with, '79 144
Sesame Salad, Spinach-, '91 211; '92 160
Sesame Spinach Salad, '90 292
Southern Spinach Salad, '80 55
Special Spinach Salad, '80 78
Spicy Dressing, Fresh Spinach with, '80 55
Spinach Salad, '82 102; '86 302; '87 62; '88 299; '92 281, 341; '93 46, 65
Springtime Spinach Salad, '81 114
Sprout Salad, Fresh Spinach-, '82 281; '83 42
Strawberry-Spinach Salad, '91 169; '93 168
Sun-Dried Tomato Salad, Spinach and, '93 250
Supreme, Spinach Salad, '79 243
Sweet-Sour Spinach Salad, '85 M112
Tropical Spinach Salad, '90 231
Wilted, Spinach Salad, '81 M4; '89 123; '91 210; '92 160; '93 125
Zesty Spinach Salad, '79 88
Sprout Salad, '90 137
Sprout Salad, Crunchy, '98 52
Sprout Salad, Spanish, '85 327; '86 22
Steak Salad Niçoise, Grilled, '98 148
Strawberry Salad, Frozen, '94 119
Strawberry Yogurt Salad, '80 232
Suzie or Steven Salad, '98 204
Tabbouleh, '85 148; '93 70; '99 175
Tabbouleh Salad, '91 70; '92 212; '94 174
(Tabbouleh Salad), Boot Scoot Tabbouli, '96 159
Taco Salad, '79 56; '83 145; '84 221; '85 84; '89 332; '90 20
Taco Salad Cups, '85 M29
Taco Salad, Meatless, '81 204

SALADS
(continued)

Taco Salad, Party, '97 19
Taco Salad, Spicy, '87 287
Tofu Salad, '88 27
Tomato. *See also* **SALADS/Congealed.**
  Artichoke-Tomato Salad, '82 239
  Asparagus and Tomatoes with Herb
    Vinaigrette, '99 56
  Asparagus Salad, Tomato-, '92 79
  Avocado Salad, Tomato-, '86 74
  Basil-and-Tomato Couscous Salad, '94 175
  Basil-Mozzarella Salad, Tomato-, '95 171
  Cherry Tomato Salad, '87 156
  Cottage Cheese Salad in Tomatoes, '86 208
  Cottage-Tomato Salad, '85 163
  Cucumber and Tomato Salad, Dilled, '81 153
  Cucumber-Onion Salad, Tomato-, '81 239
  Cucumber Salad, Tomato-, '86 218; '92 199
  Cucumber Salad with Yogurt-Herb Dressing,
    Tomato-, '92 96
  Cucumber Summer Salad, Tomato-and-, '93 141
  Cucumber-Tomato Salad, '90 144
  Endive-Tomato Starburst Salad, '93 323
  Feta Salad, Tomato-, '81 246; '91 168
  Flower Salad, Tomato, '89 128
  Green Bean Salad, Tomato-and-, '97 162
  Gruyère-Basil Salad, Tomato-, '99 172
  Guacamole-Tomato Salad, '81 302
  Herbed Tomatoes, '83 173
  Herb Salad, Tomato-, '89 220
  Lima Bean-Tomato Salad, '85 137
  Marinated Salsa Tomatoes, '82 164
  Marinated Tomato and Brie Salad, '95 95
  Marinated Tomato-and-Cucumber Salad,
    '92 216
  Marinated Tomatoes, '85 156, 163; '89 174, 202
  Marinated Tomato Slices, '83 193
  Mozzarella Salad, Tomato-, '89 220
  Mozzarella-Tomato-Basil Salad, Fresh, '93 131
  Okra-Corn-and-Tomato Vinaigrette, '90 173
  Onion, and Cucumber in Italian Dressing,
    Tomato, '81 83
  Oregano, Tomatoes, '83 145
  Pasta Salad, Tomato-, '97 M160
  Petal Salad, Tomato, '79 88
  Refresher, Tomato, '81 94
  Relish Salad, Tomato, '83 111
  Slices with Lemon Dressing, Tomato, '87 167
  Stuffed Tomatoes, Avocado-, '82 101
  Stuffed Tomatoes, Cold, '80 100
  Stuffed Tomato Salad, Artichoke-, '82 101
  Stuffed Tomato Salad, Crab-, '80 148
  Stuffed Tomato Salad, Oriental-, '82 101
  Stuffed with Sea Slaw, Tomatoes, '89 96
  Summer Tomato Salad, '94 201
  Summer Tomato Treat, '79 143
  Trout-and-Tomato Salad with Black Pepper
    Vinaigrette, '98 284
  Tuna with Warm Tomato Salad, '97 179
  Vidalia-Tomato Salad, '84 65
  Vinaigrette, Tomato-Basil, '87 89
  Vinaigrette, Tomatoes, '84 106
  Watercress-Tomato Salad, '85 132
Tossed Salad with Parmesan Dressing, '86 192
Turkey
  Bacon Dressing, Turkey Salad with Hot,
    '87 285
  Bake, Turkey Salad, '79 253
  Carrot Salad, Turkey-, '86 283
  Curried, Turkey Salad, '88 140
  Curried Turkey Salad, Chutney, '98 314

Fruit-and-Spice Turkey Salad, '94 325
Fruitful Turkey Salad, '84 197
Fruit Salad, Turkey-, '79 56
Fruit Salad, Turkey, '83 233; '84 244
Holiday Turkey Salad, '84 320
Honey-Mustard Turkey Salad, '92 309
Hot Turkey Salad, '86 10, 297; '87 176
Layered Turkey Salad, '86 332; '92 220
Macaroni Salad, Turkey, '83 282
Orange Salad, Turkey-in-the-, '93 21
Polynesian Turkey Salad, '87 285
Ranch-Style Turkey 'n' Pasta Salad, '94 184
Sandwiches, Turkey Salad Pita, '87 202; '88 43
Smoked Turkey Salad, '96 184
Southwestern Turkey Salad, '91 313
Stir-Fry Salad, Chilled Turkey-and-Pepper,
  '88 140
Straw Salad, Turkey-in-the-, '96 286
Taco Salad, Turkey, '95 25
Turkey Salad, '90 318
Waldorf Salad with Yogurt Dressing, Turkey,
  '88 53
Walnuts, Turkey Salad with Sautéed, '86 117
Zucchini Salad, Turkey-, '85 74
Turkish Salad, '96 137
Turnip-and-Carrot Salad, '91 212
Turnip Salad, '85 235
Turnip Salad, Irish, '94 178
Vegetable. *See also* **SALADS/Congealed,**
  Pasta.
  Antipasto, Vegetable, '85 263
  Basil-Chicken-Vegetable Salad, '92 162
  Boats, Salad, '80 93
  Calico Salad, '82 35
  Cauliflower-Vegetable Salad, '85 158
  Chicken Salad, Vegetable-, '91 287
  Chinese Salad, '80 4
  Composée, Salad, '79 171
  Composé, Salad, '93 126
  Corned Beef Salad, Vegetable-, '80 148
  Creamy Vegetable Salad, '79 47
  Creole Salad, '79 147
  Crunchy Vegetable Salad, '79 11; '80 217;
    '83 216
  Different Vegetable Salad, '82 143
  Easy Vegetable Salad, '83 316; '84 16
  Extravaganza, Salad, '87 233
  Garden Marinade, '81 23
  Garden Medley Salad, '80 122
  Garden Salad, '87 62; '89 166
  Garden Salad Bowl, '82 239
  Garden Salad with Tomato-Cream Cheese
    Dressing, '79 173
  Greek Salad, Garden, '86 173
  Greek Vegetable Salad, '99 202
  Green-and-White Vegetable Salad, '79 286
  Green Vegetable and Egg Salad, '79 191
  Green Vegetable Salad, Overnight, '80 5
  Grilled Vegetable Salad, '94 203
  Healthy Salad, '95 133
  Horseradish Dressing, Vegetable Salad with,
    '92 85
  Italian Garden Salad, '99 203
  Italian Vegetable Salad, '81 253; '82 19
  Luncheon Salad, '84 232
  Marinade, Fresh Vegetable, '83 209
  Marinade, Garden, '81 23
  Marinade, Medley, '79 20
  Marinade, Tossed Vegetable, '84 266
  Marinated Combo Salad, '82 267
  Marinated Garden Vegetables, '87 252
  Marinated Mixed Vegetables, '89 276; '92 106
  Marinated Salad, '83 170; '91 186
  Marinated Salad, Eight-Vegetable, '80 218

Marinated Salad, Zesty, '90 90
Marinated Summer Salad, '81 153
Marinated Tex-Mex Salad, '93 106
Marinated Vegetable-Bacon Bowl, '79 191
Marinated Vegetable Patch Salad, '84 232
Marinated Vegetables, '79 146; '81 239;
  '85 67; '88 4, 170
Marinated Vegetable Salad, '79 106, 143;
  '81 280; '82 163; '83 260; '84 13; '87 243;
  '92 64, 91; '97 219
Marinated Vegetable Salad, Crispy, '84 193
Marinated Vegetable Salad, Fresh, '86 173
Marinated Vegetables, Sweet-and-Sour,
  '83 266
Marinated Vegetables, Zesty, '82 272
Marinate, Fresh Vegetable, '80 33; '81 230
Meal-in-One Salad, '82 232
Medley Salad, Vegetable, '88 86
Mexican Salad, '81 36, 113
Minted Vegetable Medley, '88 23; '98 158
Mixed Vegetable Salad, '80 115; '81 302;
  '82 239; '83 317; '84 16; '86 136
Next-Day Vegetable Salad, '83 81
Oriental Salad, Make-Ahead, '82 163
Oriental Vegetable Salad, '84 290
Overnight Vegetable Salad, '90 33
Party Vegetable Salad, '86 79
Pasta and Vegetables, '89 255
Pasta Salad, Vegetable, '89 256; '91 143
Pasta Salad, Vegetable-, '92 167
Pebble Salad, '91 27
Pita Bread Salad, '95 86
Primavera Salad, '93 140
Quick Summer Italian Salad, '92 79
Rainbow Vegetable Salad, '83 111
Red, White, and Green Salad, '90 18
Refrigerated Vegetable Salad, '84 120
Rice-and-Vegetable Salad, '86 42
Riviera, Salade, '89 12
Roasted Vegetable Salad, Wild Rice-and-,
  '99 316
Rolls, Picnic Salad, '79 127
Rolls, Vegetable Salad, '82 278
Salad, Vegetable, '98 92
Senator's Salad, '79 191
Seven-Layer Vegetable Salad, '79 88
Spaghetti-Vegetable Salad, '97 196
Spring Vegetable Salad, '88 48
Sprout Salad, Crunchy, '96 45
Summer Salad with Citrus Marinade, '92 133
Swedish Vegetable Salad, '82 23
Sweet-and-Sour Vegetable Salad, '81 25
Tangy Vegetable Toss, '79 144
Tarragon-Vegetable Salad, '85 288
Tomato, Bell Pepper, and Portobello Salad,
  Grilled, '98 211
Variety Salad, '79 113
Vinaigrette Salad, Vegetable-Chicken, '86 135
Vinaigrette, Vegetables, '82 225, 290
Walnuts, Vegetable Salad with, '86 118
Warm Vegetable Salad, '95 174
Winter Salad, '97 304
Winter Vegetable Salad, '86 42
Zucchini-Corn Marinated Salad, '98 236
Waldorf. *See also* **SALADS/Congealed.**
  Creamy Waldorf Salad, '87 311
  Deluxe Waldorf Salad, '83 81
  Frozen Waldorf Salad, '79 126; '82 145
  Jiffy Waldorf Salad, '88 100
  New Wave Waldorf Salad, '92 36
  Old-Fashioned Waldorf Salad, '81 295
  Overnight Waldorf Salad, '81 309
  Pineapple Waldorf, '97 86
  Pineapple Waldorf Salad, '92 97

Southern Classic Waldorf Salad, '92 36
Tropical Waldorf Salad, '89 12
Turkey Waldorf Salad with Yogurt Dressing,
   '88 53
Waldorf Salad, '89 278; '97 204
Watercress Salad, '79 144
Watercress-Tomato Salad, '85 132
Watermelon Salad with Celery-Nut Dressing,
   '80 182
Watermelon Sparkle, '84 191
Wheat Berry-and-Roasted Corn Salad,
   '94 175
Wheat Salad with Citrus and Mint, '99 163
Winter Salad, '98 19
Yogurt-Cucumber Salad, '82 122
Yogurt Salad, Frozen, '92 303
Zucchini-Artichoke Salad, '91 229
Zucchini Chef's Salad, '83 143
Zucchini, Marinated, '80 33
Zucchini Salad, '82 104; '87 103; '89 128
Zucchini Salad, Marinated, '82 164; '90 32
Zucchini Salad, Summer, '95 229

SALMON
Bake with Pecan-Crunch Coating, Salmon,
   '95 209
Ball, Salmon, '80 149; '86 262
Ball, Smoky Salmon Cheese, '82 247
Barbecued Salmon, '81 181
Broiled Salmon with Dijon-Caper Cream Sauce,
   '98 329
Burgers, Salmon, '89 98; '95 24; '98 144
Canapés, Smoked Salmon, '99 140
Carbonara, Salmon, '83 43
Casserole, Salmon, '81 22
Cheesecake, Smoked Salmon, '99 92
Chili-Rubbed Salmon, '97 124
Chilled Salmon with Dill Sauce, '84 285
Chowder, Salmon, '97 125
Croquettes, Baked Salmon, '81 22
Fettuccine, Salmon, '90 123
Fillets with Red Wine Garlic Sauce, Salmon,
   '94 250
Fillets with Sweet Corn Relish, Salmon, '93 119
Florentine, Salmon, '83 43
Kabobs, Salmon, '81 182
Loaf, Easy Salmon, '80 4
Loaf, Savory Salmon, '92 33
Loaf with Cucumber-Dill Sauce, Salmon, '86 5
Log, Salmon, '81 22
Log, Salmon Party, '98 154
Mousse, Irresistible Salmon, '79 284
Mousse, Salmon, '83 79
Mousse, Salmon Dill, '81 21
Mushrooms and Green Onions, Fresh Salmon
   with, '93 180
Orange-Basil Salmon, '97 165
Parchment, Salmon in, '95 311
Pasta, Smoked Salmon-Caper-and-Dill, '98 169
Patties, Cheesy Salmon, '89 99
Patties, Open-Faced Salmon, '87 M218
Patties, Salmon, '92 215
Patties with Lemon-Cheese Sauce, Salmon,
   '91 24
Patties with Sauce, Salmon, '88 164
Poached Salmon, '83 35
Poached Salmon with Emerald Sauce, '90 63
Poached Salmon with Horseradish Sauce,
   '91 183
Poached Salmon with Yellow Pepper Sauce,
   '98 230
Potatoes, Salmon-Topped, '84 124
Quesadilla with Cucumber Salsa, Grilled
   Salmon, '95 131
Quiche, Salmon, '82 87; '87 38

Ragoût, Salmon-and-Vegetable, '96 45
Roll, Salmon Party, '83 127
Salads
Avocados, Salmon-Stuffed, '86 74
Broiled Salmon Salad, '92 108
Chilly Salmon Salad, '80 104
Crunchy Salmon Salad, '81 148
Greens with Creamy Dill Dressing, Salmon on
   Mixed, '93 143
Macaroni Salad, Salmon-and-, '81 114
Macaroni-Salmon Salad, '82 232
Pasta Salad, Salmon-, '87 9
Poached Salmon Salad, Chilled, '96 68
Potato Salad, Salmon-, '87 285
Potato Salad, Smoked Salmon, '97 64
Rice Salad, Salmon-, '84 289
Salmon Salad, '89 99
Scandinavian Salmon Salad, '98 208
Shells, Salmon Salad, '85 286
Simple Salmon Salad, '91 23
Spinach Salad, Salmon-, '87 145
Summertime Salmon Salad, '82 207
Wild Rice Salad, Oriental Salmon-and-,
   '94 173
Salsa, Smoked Salmon, '96 272
Scalloped Salmon, '81 273
Scalloped Salmon for Two, '89 98
Scaloppine with Vegetable Confetti and Pernod
   Sauce, Salmon, '94 172
Sesame-Crusted Salmon with Ginger
   Vinaigrette, '95 162
Smoked Salmon, '95 114
Smoked Salmon and Cucumber Tartlets, '95 216
Smoked Salmon, Drizzled, '88 91
Smoked Salmon or Mackerel, '84 46
Soufflé, Fresh Salmon, '81 182
Spread, Salmon, '81 149
Spread, Salmon-and-Horseradish, '87 146
Spread, Smoked Salmon, '84 324; '98 285
Spread with Capers, Smoked Salmon, '98 49
Steaks, Baked Salmon, '85 54
Steaks, Glazed Salmon, '86 256
Steaks, Grilled Herbed Salmon, '93 176
Steaks, Grilled Salmon, '94 278
Steaks, Marinated Salmon, '87 6
Steaks, Mint-Marinated Salmon, '96 175
Steaks, Oven-Fried Salmon, '81 181
Steaks with Dill Sauce, Salmon, '85 164
Steaks with Lemon-Mustard Sauce, Salmon,
   '97 124
Steaks with Tarragon Butter, Salmon, '87 155
Steaks with Tarragon Sauce, Grilled Salmon,
   '97 42
Teriyaki Salmon, Glazed, '97 124
Terrine, Layered Salmon-and-Spinach, '84 132
Turnovers, Salmon-Spinach, '83 44
Vermicelli, Salmon-Pesto, '92 200
SALSAS. *See also* **CHUTNEYS, PESTOS,
   RELISHES, SAUCES, TOPPINGS.**
Apricot Salsa, '98 126
Artichoke-Tomato Salsa, '96 182
Avocado-Corn Salsa, '94 201; '99 335
Avocado-Feta Salsa, '96 15
Avocado Salsa, '91 182
Banana Salsa, '96 85
Black-and-White Salsa, Pork Chops with,
   '97 200
Black Bean-and-Corn Salsa, '94 80
Black Bean-Corn Salsa, '96 126
Black Bean Salsa, '93 155; '94 161; '97 226
Black-Eyed Pea Salsa, '93 164
Broiled Salsa Parmesan, '98 33
Caribbean Salsa, '96 70
Cha-Cha Salsa, '97 160; '98 333

Cheesecake, Salsa, '98 33
Cherry Salsa, '99 156
Chile Salsa, Double, '91 182
Chile Salsa with Homemade Tostados, Hot,
   '88 115
Chipotle Salsa, Chicken-and-Brie Quesadillas
   with, '99 311
Chunky Salsa, '86 130; '90 206
Citrus Salsa, Grilled Shrimp with, '97 141
Colorful Salsa, '99 119
Corn-Black Bean Salsa, '96 15
Corn, Pepper, and Tomato Salsa, Yellowfin Tuna
   with, '94 164
Corn Salsa, Grilled, '99 162
Corn Salsa, Spicy, '93 322
Corn Salsa, Sweet, '95 156
Cranberry-Citrus Salsa, '97 290
Cranberry Salsa, '98 321; '99 316
Cruda, Salsa, '87 180; '88 148
Cucumber-Dill Salsa, '95 107
Cucumber Salsa, '95 131
Dried Chile Salsa, '97 265
Fresh Salsa, '95 42
Fresh Summer Salsa, '87 89
Fruit Salsa, '97 124
Garden Salsa, '91 182
Green Salsa, Creamy, '91 162
Green Tomato Salsa, Peachy, '99 143
Hill Country Salsa, '97 123
Hot Mexican Salsa, '85 136
Hot Salsa, '98 135
Kale with Salsa, Southwest, '94 246
Kiwifruit Salsa, Hot, '94 82
Mango Salsa, '91 182; '95 104; '98 232
Mango Salsa, Minted, '96 206
Melon Salsa, Hot, '95 144
Mexi-Corn Salsa, '91 182
One-Minute Salsa, '95 93
Onion Salsa, Fiesta, '94 82
Orange-Black Bean Salsa, '98 231
Papaya Salsa, '94 173
Papaya Salsa, Asparagus Salad with, '97 144
Peach Salsa, '91 183; '96 14; '97 183
Peach Salsa, Fresh, '95 195
Pepper Salsa, '88 26
Pepper Salsa, Mixed, '91 181
Picante, Homemade Salsa, '81 67
Picante with Shrimp, Salsa, '92 210
Pimiento Cheese Salsa, Fiery Steak with, '99 331
Pineapple Salsa, '96 226
Pineapple Salsa, Spicy, '97 165
Plum Salsa, '97 176
Poblano Salsa, '91 135
Red Bean Salsa, '97 227
Red Salsa, '90 172
Roasted Salsa, '95 130
Roasted Salsa Verde, '96 182
Salmon Salsa, Smoked, '96 272
Salsa, '80 196; '87 217; '88 147; '97 171
Serrano Salsa, Roasted, '95 207
Southwestern Salsa with Black Beans and Corn,
   '96 275
Summer Salsa, '98 172
Sweet Salsa, '98 174
Texas Salsa, '99 160
Tomatillo Salsa, '92 245
Tomatillo Salsa, Fresh, '97 143
Tomatillo Salsa, Roasted, '95 64
Tomato-Avocado Salsa, '94 83
Tomato-Basil Salsa, Pan-Fried Roughy with,
   '99 123
Tomato-Mango Salsa, Seared Scallops with,
   '95 122
Tomato Salsa, '87 120; '96 15

SALSAS
(continued)

Tomato Salsa, Fresh, '91 182; '95 181
Tomato Salsa, Roasted, '95 64
Tomato Salsa, Three, '93 138
Tropical Rainbow Salsa, '94 161
Tropical Salsa, '96 14
Tropical Salsa, Key Lime Pie with Minted, '99 333
Vegetable Salsa, '96 208, 220
Vegetable Salsa, Fresh, '98 194
Vegetable Salsa, Greek, '98 32
Vegetable Salsa, Shrimp Skewers with, '98 32, 223
Verde, Salsa, '91 182; '96 160
Warm-and-Spicy Salsa, '99 279
Watermelon Salsa, '98 164
Yellow Tomato Salsa, '87 122

SANDWICHES
Apple Breakfast Sandwiches, '92 332
Apple-Cinnamon Breakfast Sandwiches, '85 298
Apple Party Sandwiches, '92 234
Apple Sandwiches, '79 164; '80 130
Asparagus Grill Sandwiches, '79 164; '80 130
Asparagus Sandwich, Warm, '99 102
Asparagus Spear Sandwiches, '84 165
Avocado, Bacon, and Cheese Sandwiches, '87 279
Avocado Deluxe Sandwiches, '99 72
Bacon, Cheese, and Tomato Sandwiches, '84 14
Bacon-Cheese Sandwiches, Grilled, '83 242
Bacon, Pimiento, and Cheese Hoagies, '90 144
Bacon Sandwiches, Open-Faced Cheesy, '80 78
Bagel, Breakfast on a, '94 66
Bagels, Meal-in-One, '88 159
Bar, Super Summer Sandwich, '91 143
Basket of Sandwiches, Bread, '86 126
Beef. *See also* **SANDWICHES/Pita.**
Bacon, and Blue Cheese Sandwiches, Beef, '96 23
Barbecue Beef Sandwiches, '99 327
Barbecued Beef Sandwiches, '81 25; '82 31; '83 34
Barbecue Sandwiches, Debate, '97 234
Beef-Eater Sandwiches, '86 72
Calzones, Ground Beef, '97 95
Cheeseburger Biscuits, '79 194
Corned Beef and Cheese Sandwich, '79 214
Corned Beef Sandwiches, '83 291; '85 242; '92 23
Corned Beef Sandwiches, Barbecued, '83 130
Corned Beef Sandwiches, Grilled, '87 54
Dilly Beef Sandwiches, '98 288
Flank Steak Sandwiches with Apple Barbecue Sauce, '99 173
French Beef Slice, '79 125
French Dip Sandwiches, '97 211
Gumbo Joes, '88 158
Jalapeño Heroes, Open-Faced, '90 144
Kraut Sandwich, Beef-and-, '91 167
Loaf, Big Wheel, '84 281
Meatball Sandwich, Giant, '92 196
Open-Faced Italian Sandwich, Beef-and-Artichoke, '98 22
Pizza Sandwiches, Open-Face, '82 3; '83 85; '84 M198; '85 22
Pork Tenderloin Sandwiches, Beef and, '80 175
Reuben Puffs, '98 231
Reuben Sandwiches, '80 M201
Reuben Sandwiches, Broiled, '81 240; '83 69
Reuben Sandwiches, Crispy, '85 299

Reuben Sandwiches, Grilled, '81 206
Reuben Sandwiches, Open-Face, '91 199
Reuben Sandwich, Rolled, '99 219
Reubens, Oven-Grilled, '97 304
Reubens, Party, '90 61
Roast Beef Hero Sandwich, '91 167
Roll-Ups, Savory Beef and Cheese, '96 235
Sloppy Joes, '91 172
Steak Bagel Sandwiches, '96 249
Steak Sandwiches, '96 136
Steak Stroganoff Sandwiches, '85 110
Taco Joes, '91 167
Tenderloin Picnic Sandwiches, Beef, '90 91
Wake-Up Sandwiches, '84 58
BLT Croissants, '93 158
BLT Sandwiches, Curried, '93 158
BLT's, Cheesy, '85 92
Breakfast Sandwiches, '80 52; '82 M123; '89 M230
Breakfast Sandwiches, Cheesy, '90 140
Breakfast Sandwiches, Open-Faced, '92 140
Brown Bread-Cream Cheese Sandwiches, '87 M6
Bunwiches, '80 92
Calla Lily Sandwiches, '91 106
Calzone, '85 94
Cheddar Cheese Sandwiches, Hot, '97 179
Cheese Sandwiches, Hot French, '82 3
Cheese Sandwiches, Leafy, '90 56
Cheese Sandwiches with Artichoke-Tomato Salsa, Herbed, '96 182
Cheese Tea Sandwiches, '92 276
Chicken. *See also* **SANDWICHES/Pita.**
Artichokes, Chicken Salad with, '86 186
Bagel Sandwiches, Chicken-Benedict, '96 250
Baked Chicken Sandwiches, '79 164; '80 130; '84 165
Cheese Chicken Sandwich, Ham 'n', '95 153
Cheese Sandwiches, Toasted Chicken-and-, '85 242
Cheesy Chicken Sandwiches, '82 190
Chutney-Chicken Croissants, '92 22
Club Sandwiches, Chicken, '86 160
Creamed Chicken Toppers, '99 240
Crispy Chicken Sandwich, '81 114
Curried Chicken Salad on Raisin Bread, '85 96
Curried Chicken Tea Sandwiches, '97 23
Dagwoods, Chicken-Avocado, '96 200; '99 337
English Muffin Delight, '82 45
Finger Sandwiches, Chicken-Salad, '85 119
Gouda Lover's Chicken Sandwiches, '99 195
Grilled Chicken 'n' Cheese Sandwiches, '99 240
Hot Chicken Sandwiches, '83 291
Jamaican Chicken Sandwich, '95 153
Jerk Chicken Sandwich, '98 333
Marinated Chicken in a Sandwich, '86 185
Marinated Chicken Sandwiches, '86 M45
Mozzarella Melt, Italian Chicken-, '95 153
Open-Faced Mexican Sandwiches, '98 230
Open-Faced Sandwiches, Summer, '99 201
Parmigiana Sandwich, Chicken, '94 65
Puffed Chicken Sandwiches, '82 35
Salad Sandwiches, Asian Chicken, '98 223
Salad Sandwiches, Hot Chicken, '96 74
Saucy Chick-Wiches, '81 25; '82 31; '83 34
Southwestern Chicken Sandwiches, '96 23
Spread, Tasty Chicken, '84 193
Sprout Sandwiches, Polynesian, '85 51
Sub, Chicken, '98 287
Chili con Queso Sandwiches, Grilled, '96 139
Christmas Tree Sandwiches, '92 279

Club Sandwich Bar, Easy, '91 279
Club Sandwiches, Double-Decker, '91 231; '92 68
Club Sandwiches, Tangy, '80 93
Confetti Sandwiches, '79 236
Crab Burgers, Potato-Crusted, '94 139
Crostini, Feta-Tomato, '92 159
Cucumber Pinwheel Sandwiches, '85 120
Cucumber Sandwiches, '88 159; '90 81; '94 14; '97 99
Cucumber Sandwiches, Dainty, '81 119
Curried Tea Sandwiches, '91 314
Date-Nut Lettuce Sandwich, '94 202
Deli Stuffed Sandwich, '98 287
Dried Tomato-and-Basil Sandwiches, '99 274
Eggplant Sandwiches, '99 240
Eggplant Sandwiches, Baked, '82 230
Eggplant Sandwiches, Open-Face, '95 124
Eggplant, Tomato, and Feta Sandwiches, '98 106
Egg Sandwiches, Open-Face, '83 292; '84 78; '86 160
Egg Sandwiches, Open-Faced Cheesy, '86 67
Egg Sandwiches, Saucy, '91 160
Eggsclusive Sandwiches, '79 164; '80 130
Eggs-Tra Special Sandwiches, '81 240; '83 69
Eggwiches, Croissant, '91 160
Feta Salad Sandwich, Tuscan, '99 289
Fish. *See also* **SANDWICHES/Pita.**
Amberjack Sandwiches, Grilled, '91 195
Grouper Sandwiches, Batter-Fried, '96 197
Heroes, Neptune, '84 281
Tuna Burgers, Zippy, '81 135
Tuna Cheesies, '82 191
Tuna Club Sandwiches, '83 134
Tuna Melts, Curried, '95 46
Tuna Melts, Hot, '95 126; '96 201
Tuna Melt, Southwestern, '96 201
Tuna Melts, Southwestern, '95 127
Tuna Melts, Tempting, '88 158
Tuna Salad Rolls, Hot, '84 281
Tuna Salad, Swiss, '86 186
Tuna Sandwich Boats, '91 166
Tuna Sandwiches, French Toasted, '80 275
Tuna Sandwiches, Hot, '85 299; '86 M194
Tuna Waffle-Wich, Hot, '88 272; '89 181
Focaccia Sandwiches, '98 53
Frankfurter Sandwiches, '84 M11
French Toast Sandwiches, Strawberry-, '91 160
Fruit-and-Cheese Breakfast Sandwiches, '89 M21
Fruit Sandwiches, Glazed Breakfast, '93 178
Garden Sandwiches, Grilled, '98 315
Garden Sandwiches, Open-Faced, '87 105
Garden, The, '83 134
Good-Start Sandwiches, '99 134
Grilled Bacon, Cheese, and Tomato Sandwiches, '97 170
Grilled Cheese, '97 328
Grilled Cheese Sandwiches, '82 M172; '94 167
Grilled Cheese Sandwich, Mexican, '92 63
Grilled Cheeses, Mexican, '97 170
Grilled Sandwiches, Tasty, '84 30
Grills, Double Cheese, '97 170
Grills, Triple Cheese, '97 170
Guacamole Sandwiches, '82 9; '83 68
Guacamole Subs, '84 293
Ham. *See also* **SANDWICHES/Pita.**
Asparagus-and-Ham Melt Sandwiches, '88 M96
Baked Ham Sandwiches, '81 29
Basket of Sandwiches, Bread, '86 126
Blue Cheese-Ham Sandwiches, Creamy, '87 279
Cheese-and-Ham Striped Tea Sandwiches, Cheshire Claret, '94 16
Cheese Chicken Sandwich, Ham 'n', '95 153

Cheese Rolls, Ham-and-, '82 3
Cheese Sandwiches, Hot Ham-and-, '85 299
Cheese Sandwiches, Tiny Ham-and-, '99 87
Cheese Sandwich Round, Ham-and-, '94 326
Cheese Sandwich, Tex-Mex Ham-and-, '86 4
Country Ham Loaves, '86 255
Croissant Sandwiches, '89 161
Deviled Delight, '83 130
French Market Sandwiches, '98 230
Giant Ham-and-Pepper Sandwich, '96 74
Grinder Sandwich, '85 299
Hamwiches, '96 246
Hideaways, Ham, '81 29
Hot Ham Sandwiches, '79 214
Hot Rods, Ham, '86 136
Loaf, Big Wheel, '84 281
Omelet Sandwich, '86 95
Open-Face Ham Sandwiches, '82 40; '85 8
Open-Face Sandwiches, '84 13
Party Ham Sandwiches, '97 240
Pineapple-Ham Sandwich Loaf, '91 167
Pineapple Slaw Sandwiches, Ham-and-, '96 199
Po-Boy, Pain-Perdu, '93 291
Salad Boats, '80 93
Salad Sandwich, Tangy Ham, '80 272
Sebastian, The, '94 184
Swiss, Ham and Eggs à la, '88 158
Swiss Sandwiches, Ham-and-, '98 287
Swiss Sandwiches, Tangy Ham-and-, '85 164
Turkey Specials, Cheesy Ham-and-, '84 14
Virginia Ham Sandwiches, '80 155
Yummy Sandwiches, '81 229
Hamburgers, Meatless Walnut, '96 243
Hearts of Palm Sandwich, '92 191
Heroes, Healthy, '90 177
Hero, E-Z, '92 63
Hot Browns, '98 287
Hot Brown Sandwiches, '80 M202
Italian Pesto Sandwich, Grilled, '94 170
Lamb Sandwiches, '97 107
Loaf, Mediterranean Picnic, '96 156
Mayflower Sandwiches, '96 287
Meal-in-One Sandwiches, '80 218
Meatball Sandwiches, Open-Faced, '99 239
Monte Cristo Sandwiches, '83 134; '97 319
Mozzarella-Pepper Bagel Sandwiches, '98 145
Muffaletta-Style Po-Boys, '83 230
Muffin Stacks, Mushroom-Topped, '80 271
Muffuletta, Doodles, '94 35
Muffuletta Loaf, '97 86
Muffuletta, Napoleon House, '94 35
Muffulettas, '98 184
"Muffy" Sandwich, Fertitta's, '94 34
Mushroom Bagel Sandwiches with Curry-
    Mustard Sauce, '96 249
Mushroom Sandwiches, Toasted, '87 281
Open-Faced Sandwiches, '79 214
Open-Faced Sandwiches, Super, '97 52
Orange Blossom Special, '88 158
Party Sandwiches, Double-Filled, '93 159
Peanut Butter-and-Jelly "Fish" Sandwiches,
    '91 177
Peanut Butter-and-Jelly Sandwiches, Christmas
    Tree, '85 319
Peanut Butter Breakfast Sandwich, '82 55
Peanut-Cheese-Raisin Sandwiches, '88 140
Pimiento Cheese Finger Sandwiches, '99 86
Pimiento Cheese Sandwiches, '82 278
Pita
    Alfalfa Pocket Bread Sandwiches, '82 282;
    '83 41
    Bavarian Pita Sandwiches, '83 31
    Bean Salad Sandwiches, '81 243
    Beef Pitas, Curried, '85 220

Beef Pocket Sandwich, Saucy, '80 92
Beef Salad Pocket Sandwiches, '83 267
BLT in Pita Pockets, '93 158
Breakfast Pita Pockets, '89 M21
Chef's Salad, '86 186
Chicken-Almond Pocket Sandwiches, '81 240;
    '83 69
Chicken Pita, Oriental, '89 216
Chicken Salad in a Pocket, '88 139
Denver Pita Sandwiches, '86 M12
Dried Beef Pita Sandwiches, '86 160
Fajita Pitas, '99 239
Falafel Sandwiches, '96 23
Ham-and-Cheese Pita Pockets, '90 271
Ham-and-Cheese Pita Sandwiches, '87 202;
    '88 44
Ham and Swiss in the Pocket, '83 31
Hearty Pocket Sandwiches, '80 93
Hot Pita Sandwiches, '83 217; '87 M6
Lamb Pockets with Dilled Cucumber Topping,
    '87 104
Oriental Stuffed Pockets, '79 14
Pita Sandwiches, '84 139
Salad Sandwiches, Pita, '83 134
Sloppy Joe Pocket Sandwiches, '81 200
Spinach-Walnut Pitas, '87 202; '88 43
Steaks, Greek Pocket, '81 262
Stuffed Pita, '89 87
Stuffed Pitas, Acadian, '90 177
Tabbouleh Pitas, '98 105
Taco Pitas, '83 31
Tuna-in-a-Pita Pocket, '87 202
Tuna Pockets, '88 139
Tuna Roll Sandwiches, '96 199
Turkey-Mozzarella Rounds, '82 3
Turkey Salad Pita Sandwiches, '87 202; '88 43
Vegetable Pita Sandwiches, '96 199
Vegetable Pockets, '85 215
Vegetarian Pita Sandwiches, '84 193
Pizza Sandwiches, Open-Face, '82 3; '83 85;
    '84 M198; '85 22
Pizza Sandwich, Giant, '80 93
Pork Sandwiches, Party, '88 M273
Pork Sandwiches with Apricot Mayonnaise,
    Jamaican Jerk, '97 320
Pound Cake Dessert Sandwich, Grilled, '94 171
Raisin Country Sandwich, '91 168
Rarebit, Tangy Welsh, '88 159
Rarebit, Uptown Welsh, '87 279
Rarebit with Tomatoes and Bacon, Welsh,
    '92 M159
Salad Rolls, Hearty, '81 206
Salami Sandwiches, Open-Faced, '87 279
Sausage and Pepper Loaves, Italian, '83 11
Sausage Burgers, '96 102
Sausage-Cheese Loaves, '88 235
Sausage-Cheese Muffin Sandwiches, '92 M212
Sausage in a Sleeping Bag, '98 206
Sausage Sandwiches with Mustard Sauce,
    '84 250
Sausage Sandwich, Italian, '80 92
Sausage Sloppy Joes, Italian, '86 160
Sausage-Stuffed French Loaf, '90 19
Seafood. See also SANDWICHES/Pita.
    Caribbean Seafood Sandwiches, '98 105
    Club Sandwich, South Seas, '84 282
    Crab-and-Cheese Sandwiches, Hot, '87 279
    Crab Cake Sandwiches, Miniature, '96 306
    Crabmeat Sandwiches, '84 285
    Crabmeat Sandwiches, Avocado-, '83 2
    Crabmeat Sandwiches, Deluxe, '81 M74
    Crab Salad Sandwiches, Mango-, '99 72
    Crab Sandwiches, Open-Faced, '87 106
    Crab Sandwiches, Puffy, '83 291

Crab Tomato Sandwiches, Open-Face, '81 29
English Muffin Delight, '82 45
Hot Brown, Seafood, '88 158
Oyster-and-Bacon Poor Boys, '87 40
Oyster Loaves, Spinach-, '84 213
Oyster Submarine Sandwich, '80 92
Po'Boy, Grilled Seafood, '96 244
Shrimp-and-Egg Salad Sandwiches, '94 182
Shrimp-Cheese Sandwiches, '85 242
Shrimp Destin, '82 29
Shrimp Po' Boys, '97 312
Shrimp Salad, '86 186
Shrimp Salad on Croissants, '96 175
Shrimp Salad Sandwiches, '90 178
Sloppy Toms, '91 51
Snack Buns, '87 279
Snackwiches, '88 172
Spider Sandwiches, '93 193
Spinach Fondue Sandwiches, Grilled, '99 337
Spinach Fondue Sandwich, Grilled, '94 171
Spinach Sandwiches, Fresh, '85 59
Squash Sandwiches, Skillet, '98 144
Stacking Sandwiches, '86 127
Stromboli, '88 272
Stuffed Sandwich, Italian, '99 15
Stuffin' Muffin, '99 193
Submarine Sandwiches, Superb, '84 250
Sweet Smoky Sandwiches, '97 219
Tea Sandwiches, Gingered, '84 116
Tempting Twosome, '81 240; '83 69
Tofu-Veggie Sandwiches, Open-Face, '86 5
Tomatillo Sandwiches, Open-Faced, '92 246
Tomato-Cheese-Bacon Melts, '99 72
Tomatoes with Cheese Sauce over Toast, '88 159
Tomato Sandwich, Floyd's Favorite, '95 172
Torta, Mediterranean, '98 23
Tortilla Stack-Ups, '92 196
Tuna. See SANDWICHES/Fish.
Turkey-Asparagus Sandwiches, '96 74
Turkey-Cheese Dogs, '97 203
Turkey-Cheese Puffs, '87 301
Turkey-Cranberry Croissant, '96 320
Turkey Hero Sandwiches, '92 196
Turkey Hero with Garlic Sauce, '90 145
Turkey-in-the-Slaw Sandwich, '90 177
Turkey, Mozzarella, and Blackberry Sandwiches,
    Smoked, '99 220
Turkey Open-Facers, '82 190
Turkey-Roasted Pepper Sandwiches, Smoked,
    '94 66
Turkey Sandwich, Hot, '93 306
Turkey Sandwich, Waffle-Grilled, '94 170
Turkey Tea Sandwiches, '99 86
Vegetable Garden Heroes, '84 14
Vegetable Puff Sandwich, '85 51
Vegetable Salad Rolls, '82 278
Vegetable Sandwiches, Creamy, '97 122
Vegetarian Melt, Open-Faced, '87 106
Vegewiches, '99 86
Veggie Sandwich, Big, '92 196
Victoria Sandwiches, '94 16
Vidalia Sandwiches on Salt-Rising Bread, '79 145
Watercress-Cucumber Sandwiches, '97 108
Watercress Sandwiches, '90 82
Wreath, Festive Sandwich, '86 333
Zucchini Sandwiches, Open-Faced, '88 159
SAUCES. See also CHOCOLATE/ Sauces;
    CHUTNEYS; DESSERTS/Sauces;
    GRAVIES; MARINADES; MUSTARD/
    Sauces; PESTOS; RELISHES; SALSAS;
    SYRUPS; TOPPINGS.
Aioli, Picante, '99 53
Alfredo Sauce, '94 84
Almond Sauce, Asparagus with, '91 117

SAUCES
(continued)

Ancho Chile Cream, **'87** 121
Ancho Chile Sauce, **'87** 122
Anchovy-Garlic Sauce over Vermicelli, **'86** 158
Avgolemono Sauce, **'94** 48
Balsamic Sauce, **'98** 319
Barbecue
    Apple Barbecue Sauce, **'99** 173
    Bannister's Barbecue Sauce, **'92** 166
    Barbecue Sauce, **'84** 172; **'86** 153; **'88** 218;
      '91 16, 205; **'93** 129; **'94** 27
    Basting Sauce, **'90** 120
    Beer Barbecue Sauce, **'84** 173
    Bourbon Barbecue Sauce, **'85** 90
    Crickhollow Barbecue Sauce, **'99** 200
    Dressed-Up Barbecue Sauce, **'84** 173
    Eastern-Style Barbecue Sauce, **'88** 145
    Easy Barbecue Sauce, **'79** 90; **'82** 178
    Handcrafted Barbecue Sauce, **'98** 45
    John Wills's Barbecue Sauce, **'92** 255
    Lemon Barbecue Sauce, Herbed, **'94** 154;
      '98 334
    Lemony Barbecue Sauce, **'95** 31
    Maple Syrup Barbecue Sauce, **'94** 154
    Mustard Barbecue Sauce, **'84** 173
    Oven Barbecue Sauce, **'82** 233
    Paprika Barbecue Sauce, **'79** 90
    Peanut Butter Barbecue Sauce, **'81** 233
    Piquant Barbecue Sauce, **'79** 159
    Savory Barbecue Sauce, **'86** 153
    Southwest Barbecue Sauce, Spicy, **'94** 154
    Special Barbecue Sauce, **'82** 177
    Sweet Sauce, **'90** 120
    Tangy Barbecue Sauce, **'97** 323; **'99** 104
    Texas Barbecue Sauce, **'99** 210
    Thick and Robust Barbecue Sauce, **'94** 95
    Thick and Sweet Barbecue Sauce, **'94** 95
    Thin and Tasty Barbecue Sauce, **'94** 95
    Tomato Barbecue Sauce, Fresh, **'84** 172
    Western-Style Barbecue Sauce, **'88** 145
    White Barbecue Sauce, **'94** 95
    White Barbecue Sauce, Chicken with,
      '89 M84; **'97** 322
    Zippy Barbecue Sauce, **'92** 166
Basil and Cream Sauce, **'90** 118
Basil-Brown Butter Sauce, **'93** 92
Basil Cream, **'89** 159
Basil Cream Sauce, New Potatoes with, **'91** 46
Basil Sauce, **'90** 85
Basil Sauce, Asparagus with, **'86** 33
Bean Sauce, Pork-and-Onions with, **'85** 76
Béarnaise Sauce, **'83** 138; **'85** 37; **'86** 193;
  '89 201; **'96** 133, 174
Béarnaise Sauce, Blender, **'81** 90
Béarnaise Sauce, Classic, **'86** 244
Béarnaise Sauce, Quick, **'82** 84
Béchamel Sauce, **'80** 190; **'83** 277; **'84** M239;
  '87 286; **'91** 94; **'96** 239
Beef Sauce, Szechuan Noodles with Spicy,
  '97 95
Beer Sauce, **'95** 266
Beurre Blanc Sauce, **'98** 240
Black Bean Sauce, **'93** 59; **'98** 46
Black Bean Sauce, Spicy Beef Fillets with,
  '97 184
Bordelaise Sauce, **'83** 138, 262
Bouillon Sauce, **'80** 8
Brandy-Butter Sauce, **'79** 230
Brandy Sauce, Carrots in, **'83** 86
Brandy Sauce, Lemony-Butter Steak with, **'85** 78
Broccoli Sauce, **'91** 85

Brown Butter Sauce, **'91** 65
Brown Sauce, **'89** 32; **'94** 15, 240
Buttermilk Sauce, **'84** 6
Butter Sauce, **'86** 268
Butter Sauce, Vegetable, **'86** 174
Catsup Sauce, **'81** 228
Catsup Topping, **'81** 170
Champagne-Saffron Sauce, Scallops with,
  '93 177
Champagne Sauce, **'90** 29
Champagne Sauce, Chicken Breasts with, **'86** 49
Chanterelle Brown Sauce, **'89** 62
Cheese
    Blue Cheese Sauce, **'90** 142; **'94** 320
    Blue Cheese Sauce, Fettuccine with, **'98** 247
    Brussels Sprouts with Cheese Sauce, **'79** 246
    Cheddar Cheese Sauce, **'91** 286
    Cheddar-Cider Sauce, **'98** 242
    Cheese Sauce, **'79** M156; **'81** 43, 44, 225;
      '82 M123; **'83** 49, 138, 188; **'84** 57; **'85** 92;
      '86 241; **'88** 78, 272; **'89** 181, 229; **'90** 235;
      '93 48
    Cottage Cheese Sauce, **'87** 232
    Cream Sauce, Cheesy, **'82** 79
    Easy Cheese Sauce, **'79** 22
    Garlic-Cheese Sauce, **'84** M70
    Guilt-Free Cheese Sauce, **'93** M95
    Heather Sauce, **'84** 182
    Lemon-Cheese Sauce, **'91** 24
    Lemony Cheese Sauce, **'84** 183
    Monterey Jack Sauce, **'84** 293
    Mornay Sauce, **'80** 120; **'81** 90; **'83** 138;
      '84 295; **'89** 195
    Mushroom-Cheese Sauce, **'83** 190; **'86** 48
    Parmesan Cheese Sauce, **'79** 165; **'80** 162;
      '85 143
    Parmesan Sauce, **'92** 17
    Rich Cheese Sauce, **'81** 89
    Roquefort Sauce, **'89** 321
    Seafood Cheese Sauce, **'89** 240
    Swiss Cheese Sauce, **'79** 35; **'87** 289; **'88** 135
    Swiss Sauce, **'83** M195
    Swiss Sauce, Creamy, **'80** M53
    Topper, Vegetable-Cheese Potato, **'86** 6
    Turnips in Cheese Sauce, **'84** 229
    Vegetable-Cheese Sauce, **'85** M152
    Vegetable Sauce, Cheesy, **'92** M134
    Walnut-Parmesan Pesto Sauce, **'97** 104
Chervil-and-Savory Sauce, **'90** 117
Chervil Sauce, **'83** 128
Chicken Curry Sauce, **'90** 117
Chicken Sauce, Creamy, **'81** 91
Chile Sauce, Hot, **'92** 156
Chili Meat Sauce, **'83** 4
Chili Sauce, **'81** 175; **'94** 287
Chili Sauce, Chunky, **'85** 188
Chili Sauce, Spicy, **'87** 127
Chive Sauce, Steamed Broccoli with Tangy,
  '83 101
Cider-Port Wine Reduction Sauce, **'96** 245
Cider Sauce, **'87** 224
Cilantro Cream, **'87** 121
Cilantro Vinaigrette, **'97** 126
Clam Sauce, Tricolor Pasta with, **'93** 272
Cocktail Sauce, **'87** 128; **'90** 242
Cocktail Sauce, Boiled Shrimp with, **'79** 151
Cocktail Sauce, Coastal, **'92** 254
Cocktail Sauce, Delta, **'91** 147
Cocktail Sauce, French Fried Zucchini with,
  '86 146
Cocktail Sauce, Southwestern, **'98** 46
Cocktail Sauce, Spicy, **'83** 258
Corn Sauce, Fresh, **'98** 43
Country Ham Sauce, **'90** 117; **'96** 24

Cream Sauce, **'85** 291; **'93** 157
Cream Sauce, Brandied, **'82** 70
Cream Sauce, Peppery, **'88** 206
Cream Sauce, Sherried, **'84** 210; **'85** M152
Cream Sauce, Shrimp in, **'84** M286
Cream Sauce, Spicy, **'82** 45
Cream-Wine Sauce, Potatoes in, **'86** 18
Creamy Sauce, **'79** 41
Creolaise Sauce, **'83** 91, 262
Creole Sauce, **'89** 228; **'90** 28; **'92** 87; **'98** 98, 142
Cress Sauce, **'96** 176
Cucumber Cream Sauce, **'92** 33
Cucumber-Dill Sauce, **'86** 5; **'91** 62; **'92** 51
Cucumber Dipping Sauce, **'94** 47
Cucumber Sauce, **'82** 111; **'84** M286; **'92** 41
Cucumber Sauce, Lamb Burgers with, **'98** 102
Cucumber Sauce, Lemony, **'89** 245
Cucumber Sauce, Tuna Steaks with, **'97** 180
Cumberland Sauce, **'92** 309
Currant Jelly Sauce, Quail with, **'86** 94
Currant Sauce, **'87** 240
Curried Cream Sauce, Turkey Slices with, **'91** 60
Curried Rum Sauce, **'91** 164
Curried Sour Cream Sauce, **'90** 174
Curry-Mustard Sauce, **'96** 249
Curry Sauce, **'79** M156; **'83** 138; **'84** M71; **'94** 54;
  '95 18; **'97** 170; **'99** 92
Curry Sauce, Asparagus with, **'90** 17
Curry Sauce, Chicken, **'90** 117
Custard Sauce, **'89** 291
Custard Sauce, Bourbon, **'95** 271
Dijon-Caper Cream Sauce, Broiled Salmon with,
  '98 329
Dill Sauce, **'84** M70, 107; **'85** 39; **'88** 162; **'95** 216;
  '98 157
Dill Sauce, Chilled Salmon with, **'84** 285
Dill Sauce, Creamy, **'79** M156; **'94** 42
Dill Sauce, Salmon Steaks with, **'85** 164
Dipper's Delight, **'98** 93
Dipping Sauce, Citrus, **'97** 208
Dipping Sauce, "Come Back," **'96** 213
Dipping Sauce, Hoisin Peanut, **'99** 14
Dipping Sauce, Thai, **'97** 236
Dunk Sauce, John's, **'97** 129
Egg Foo Yong Sauce, **'86** 232
Emerald Sauce, **'90** 63
Enchilada Sauce, **'81** 194
Enchilada Sauce, Red Chile, **'85** 245
Florentine Sauce, **'93** 48
Foo Yong Sauce, **'80** 223
French Sauce, Broccoli with, **'81** 295
Fruit
    Apple-Bourbon Sauce, **'99** 142
    Apple-Horseradish Sauce, **'82** 229
    Apple-Pear Sauce, **'97** M272
    Apple Sauce, Pork Chops with Sweet-and-
      Sour, **'98** 132
    Apricot Sauce, **'87** 172
    Apricot-Sauced Pork Chops, **'85** 22
    Apricot Sauce, Pork Tenderloin with, **'99** 44
    Avocado-Lime Sauce, Grilled Swordfish with,
      '97 127
    Avocado Sauce, **'80** 198; **'83** 200
    Avocado-Tomatillo Sauce, **'95** 206
    Blueberry Sauce, **'80** 144; **'86** 248
    Cherry Sauce, **'83** 276; **'84** 91; **'91** 67
    Cherry Sauce, Elegant, **'79** M156
    Cherry Sauce, Roast Ducklings with,
      '86 312
    Cherry Sauce, Roast Pork with Spiced,
      '89 324
    Cherry Sauce, Royal, **'85** 224; **'86** 83
    Cherry Sauce, Spicy, **'83** 244
    Cherry-Wine Sauce, **'95** 285

Citrus Sauce, Stuffed Flounder Rolls with, '85 180
Cranberry-Apple Sauce, '92 203
Cranberry-Apricot Sauce, Fresh, '87 243
Cranberry Juice Sauce, '85 224; '86 83
Cranberry-Raisin Sauce, Baked Ham with, '88 244
Cranberry Sauce, '92 269
Cranberry Sauce, Baked, '88 257
Cranberry Sauce, Cornish Hens with, '79 180
Cranberry Sauce, Fresh, '79 283; '84 275
Cranberry Sauce, Spiced, '96 267
Cranberry Sauce, Tart, '83 261
Cranberry Wine Sauce, '83 276
Devonshire Cream, Mock, '81 288
Devonshire Sauce, Processor, '86 337; '87 58
Fruit Sauce, '81 177
Grand Marnier Fruit Sauce, '90 93
Grape Sauce, Mahimahi in, '91 218
Lemon Basting Sauce, '95 32
Lemon-Butter Sauce, '84 252; '92 337
Lemon-Celery Sauce, Baked Fillets in, '84 91
Lemon-Cheese Sauce, '91 24
Lemon Cream Sauce, '99 53
Lemon Cream Sauce, Braised Chicken Breast in, '94 184
Lemon Garlic Sauce, Shrimp in, '83 67
Lemon-Herb Sauce, Hot, '91 286
Lemon Meunière Sauce, '88 222
Lemon-Mustard Sauce, Salmon Steaks with, '97 124
Lemon Parsley Sauce, '81 106
Lemon-Parsley Sauce, '93 48
Lemon Sauce, '82 290
Lemon Sauce, Asparagus with, '86 62
Lemon Sauce, Chicken Scallopini with, '86 156
Lemon Sauce, Zesty, '97 318
Lime-Saffron Sauce, '94 71
Lime Sauce, Honey-, '82 85
Lime Sauce, Sour Cream-, '91 286
Mandarin-Almond Cream Sauce, '84 183
Mandarin Sauce, '84 60
Mandarin-Teriyaki Sauce, '96 68
Maraschino-Orange Sauce, '96 164
Mimosa, Sauce, '88 288
Orange-Almond Sauce, Chicken in, '79 219; '80 13
Orange Butter Sauce, Asparagus with, '85 43
Orange-Ginger Sauce, Chicken Breasts with, '97 47
Orange-Ginger Sauce, Sesame-Crusted Scallops with, '97 125
Orange-Honey Sauce, '97 236
Orange, Lime, and Ginger Sauce, Chicken with, '92 123
Orange Liqueur Sauce, '86 142
Orange Sauce, '82 47; '83 10, 277; '84 M286; '98 83
Orange Sauce, Asparagus with, '83 46
Orange Sauce, Brussels Sprouts in, '86 55
Orange Sauce, Celery in, '79 70
Orange Sauce, Chicken Breasts with, '79 77
Orange Sauce, Grilled Duck with, '94 305
Orange Sauce, Lobster Tails with Spiced, '86 155
Orange Sauce, Sweet, '93 M325
Orange Sauce, Shrimp in, '99 292
Orange Sauce, Sunshine, '97 70
Peach-Blueberry Pancake Sauce, '82 177
Peach-Blueberry Sauce, '81 170
Peach Sauce, '92 203
Peach Sauce, Creamy Fresh, '79 177

Peach Sauce, Pork Loin Dijonnaise with, '97 87
Peach Sauce, Tangy, '96 89
Pineapple-Curry Sauce, '79 252
Pineapple-Rhubarb Sauce, '88 94
Pineapple Sauce, '84 236; '92 203
Pineapple Sauce, Raisin-, '82 177
Plum Sauce, '80 249; '82 40; '88 152
Plum Sauce, Chinese, '82 237
Plum Sauce, Crispy Ribs with, '98 182
Plum Sauce, Fresh, '97 176
Plum Sauce, Gingered, '87 175
Plum Sauce, Red, '80 49
Plum Sauce, Spareribs in, '99 136
Plum Sauce, Spicy, '86 11
Strawberry-Banana Sauce, '81 41
Tangy Sauce for Fruit, '90 161
White Grape Sauce, '80 38
Garlic Buerre Blanc Sauce, '88 222
Garlic-Butter Sauce, '95 327
Garlic-Chive Butter Sauce, '90 96
Garlic-Ginger Butter Sauce, '94 89
Garlic Sauce, '92 56
Garlic Sauce, Roasted, '95 268; '98 176
Garlic Sauce, Stir-Fried Pork in, '84 141
Garlic Sauce, Turkey Hero with, '90 145
Ginger-Soy Sauce, '91 33
Ginger Vinaigrette, '95 162
Goat Cheese Sauce, Asparagus with, '93 116
Greek Sauce, '91 183
Green Bell Pepper Sauce, '97 261
Green Chile Sauce, '82 220
Green Mole Sauce, '95 267
Green Pea Sauce, '83 22
Green Sauce, Herbed, '86 244
Grill Basting Sauce, '95 236
Guacamole, '89 226
Ham-and-Mushroom Sauce, Steak with, '83 109
Herb Butter Sauce, Corn with, '79 150
Herb-Mayonnaise Sauce, '85 73
Herb Sauce, '91 29
Herb Sauce, Green, '83 36
Hollandaise Sauce, '80 M107, M268; '81 90; '83 137; '85 295; '86 94; '87 195; '88 58, M177, 222; '89 24; '92 93; '95 86; '98 55
Hollandaise Sauce, Blender, '79 39; '82 84, 234
Hollandaise Sauce, Broccoli with, '79 244, 276
Hollandaise Sauce, Broccoli with Mock, '82 272
Hollandaise Sauce, Classic, '88 53
Hollandaise Sauce, Easy Dilled, '92 107
Hollandaise Sauce, Lime, '93 121
Hollandaise Sauce, Mock, '85 49; '93 68
Hollandaise-Shrimp Sauce, Flounder with, '86 234
Hollandaise, Tangy, '85 148
Hollandaise, Three-Pepper, '96 52
Honey-Butter Sauce, '85 18; '98 45
Honey-Lemon Mustard Sauce, '84 275
Honey-Mustard Sauce, '85 13
Honey-Mustard Sauce, Smoked Ribs with, '92 168
Honey-Poppy Seed Sauce, '93 13
Honey Sauce, '99 210
Honey Sauce, Chicken in, '89 82
Horseradish-Mustard Sauce, Creamy, '88 M177
Horseradish Sauce, '84 190; '85 224; '86 83; '87 127; '88 207, M273; '91 183; '93 215
Horseradish Sauce and Curried Bananas, Fillets with, '85 230
Horseradish Sauce, Broccoli with, '81 2; '83 206; '84 33
Horseradish Sauce, Carrots and Broccoli with, '91 246

Horseradish Sour Cream, '86 244
Hot Diggity Dog Sauce, '93 198
Hot Sauce, '79 185; '83 74
Hot Sauce, San Antonio, '84 291
Hunter Sauce, '95 317
Italian Sauce, '80 63; '90 67
Italian Sauce, Quick, '82 230
Italian-Style Sauce, '83 250
Jalapeño-Cranberry Sauce, '92 310
Jalapeño Dipping Sauce, Fried Green Tomatillos with, '97 143
Jalapeño Sauce, '80 193
Jalapeño Tartar Sauce, '96 69; '98 129
Jezebel Sauce, '81 29; '82 55; '93 331; '96 212
Juniper Sauce, '93 278
Lingonberry Sauce, Turkey Tenderloins with, '97 289
Mahogany Sauce, '91 148
Maple Brown Sauce, '96 232
Maple-Cider Sauce, '95 288
Marinara Sauce, '82 178; '89 239; '92 18
Maui Sauce, '99 310
Mediterranean Sauce, '94 83
Meunière Sauce, '80 57
Mexican Sauce, '80 198
Microwaving Sauces, '84 M70
Mint Sauce, '84 107; '88 M96
Mint Sauce over Vegetables, '92 104
Molasses Sauce, Grilled Pork Tenderloin with, '97 193
Mole Sauce, Burgundy, '98 174
Mushroom-Dill Sauce, '80 271
Mushroom Sauce, '81 90, 200; '82 46; '83 71, 205, 212; '84 M70; '85 40; '86 198; '87 36, 186, 284; '91 221
Mushroom Sauce, Chicken with, '99 22
Mushroom Sauce, Eggs Baked in, '93 47
Mushroom Sauce, Filet Mignon with, '94 250
Mushroom Sauce, Savory, '96 236
Mushroom Sauce, Spicy Sherried, '89 239
Mushroom Sauce Supreme on Vermicelli, '86 158
Mushroom-Wine Sauce, '84 84; '86 24
Natillas Sauce, '83 179
Niçoise, Sauce, '96 190
Olive-Butter Sauce, Broccoli with, '83 118
Onion-Balsamic Sauce, '99 44
Onion Cream Sauce, '87 232
Onion-Mushroom Sauce, '85 224; '86 84
Onion-Parsley Sauce, '85 148
Onion Sauce, '82 72; '87 248
Onion Sauce, Brussels Sprouts in, '81 308
Pancake Sauce, Cinnamon-Pecan-Honey, '88 46
Parsley-Caper Sauce, Tortellini with, '93 175
Parsley-Chive Sauce, '84 212
Parsley-Garlic Sauce, '83 138; '84 M70
Parsley Sauce, '82 248; '86 108
Peanut Basil Sauce, Thai-Style Noodles with, '98 133
Peanut Dipping Sauce, Hoisin, '99 14
Peanut Hot Sauce, '86 305
Peanut Sauce, '99 134
Peanut Sauce, Hot Indonesian, '93 211
Peanut Sauce, Shrimp with, '93 303
Peanut Sauce, Spicy, '96 93
Pecan-Butter Sauce, '91 65
Pecan Pasta Sauce, '96 262
Pepper-Onion Sauce, '84 125
Pesto-Clam Sauce, Pasta with, '98 17
Pesto Sauce, '89 280; '91 94; '95 267
Pesto Sauce, Racy, '97 67
Picante-Bean Sauce, '96 220
Pico de Gallo, '98 174
Pig Sauce, '98 203

SAUCES
(continued)

Pintos, Texas Souper, '98 51
Pizza Sauce, Traditional, '95 267
Port Wine Sauce, '84 252
Pumpkin Seed Sauce, '88 246
Raisin Sauce, '83 59, 215; '84 91, 275; '87 127;
     '89 58; '99 19
Raisin Sauce, Ham with, '82 M76
Red Bell Pepper Sauce, '99 267
Red Chile Sauce, '94 251; '95 17
Red Chili Sauce, '85 245
Red Hot Sauce, '93 158
Red or Green Pepper Sauce, '91 85
Red Pepper-Garlic Sauce, '98 140
Red Pepper Sauce, '98 322
Red Sauce, Zippy, '91 147
Red Wine-Butter Sauce, '96 173
Red Wine Garlic Sauce, '94 250
Rémoulade, Braised Shrimp with Garlic, '98 133
Rémoulade, Criolla, '97 227
Rémoulade Sauce, '80 58; '81 89; '82 178;
     '91 147; '93 280; '94 139; '99 164
Rémoulade Sauce, Shrimp with, '91 29
Rhubarb Sauce, Chilled, '88 94
Roasted Pepper Sauce, Creamy, '96 183
Roasted Red Pepper Sauce, '98 16
Rosemary-Parmesan Sauce, Tortellini with,
     '92 284
Rosemary Sauce, '97 127
Rum Sauce, Mango-Spiced, '86 215
Sauerbraten Sauce, '93 16
Savory Sauce, '84 196
Seafood
Clam Sauce, Linguine with, '84 124; '88 90;
     '89 178
Clam Sauce, Pasta with, '84 291
Clam Sauce, Vermicelli and Sprouts with Red,
     '86 143
Clam Sauce, Vermicelli with, '85 295
Clam Sauce with Linguine, '84 9
Crab and Shrimp Sauce Piquante, '83 92
Crab Marinara Sauce, Quick, '85 M151
Delight, Seafood Sauce, '82 91
Linguine with Seafood Sauce, '83 232
Red Seafood Sauce, '95 107
Seafood Sauce, '79 3; '82 84; '83 36; '86 304;
     '89 239
Shrimp-and-Almond Sauce, '87 282
Shrimp Sauce, '87 138, 232
Shrimp Sauce, Broccoli and Cauliflower with,
     '84 248
Shrimp Sauce, Flounder Fillets in, '83 227
Stone Crab Mustard Sauce, '80 3
Stone Crab Sauce, Tangy, '80 3
Sesame Sauce, Vegetables with, '83 112
Shallot-Thyme Sauce, '96 121
Sherry Sauce, '87 96
Shiitake Madeira Sauce, Filet Mignons with,
     '95 265
Shiitake Sauce, Pork Tenderloin with Fruit
     Stuffing and, '97 218
Sofrito, '92 158
Sour Cream-Dill Sauce, Mushrooms in, '84 215
Sour Cream-Horseradish Sauce, '88 4
Sour Cream, Mock, '83 71, 205
Sour Cream Sauce, '82 68; '84 132; '87 233;
     '93 162
Sour Cream Sauce, Broccoli with, '87 127
Soy Sauce, Grilled Trout with Ginger and,
     '85 228
Spaghetti Sauce, Grisanti, '94 194

Spicy Sauce, '99 291
Spinach Pasta Sauce, '93 71
Spinach Sauce, Fettuccine with, '84 329
Spinach Sauce, Vermicelli with Fresh, '89 256
Sunshine Sauce, '87 96
Sweet-and-Sour Sauce, '80 20; '85 12, 34;
     '86 240
Taco Sauce, '82 M283; '93 69
Tahini Sauce, '96 23
Tarragon-Mustard Sauce, Turkey Cutlets with,
     '93 239
Tarragon Sauce, '83 56; '84 190; '87 229; '97 42
Tartar Sauce, '79 184; '81 134; '82 135; '86 233;
     '91 147; '95 107, 155; '99 174
Tartar Sauce, Boiled Shrimp with Green
     Peppercorn, '94 144
Tartar Sauce, Bold-and-Spicy, '86 180
Tartar Sauce, Creamy, '80 164
Tartar Sauce, Lemony, '95 32
Tartar Sauce, Quick, '87 128
Tempura Sauce, Basic, '81 68
Teriyaki Sauce, '93 258
The Sauce, '95 237
Tomatillo Sauce, '94 231; '95 206; '97 25
Tomatillo Sauce, Roasted Chiles Rellenos with,
     '94 203
Tomato
Basil Cream, Tomato-, '99 240
Basil Sauce, Tomato, '91 85
Basil Sauce, Tomato-, '92 180; '96 220;
     '97 144
Basil-Tomato Sauce, '92 198; '93 25, 48, 65
Caper Sauce, Turkey Cutlets with Tomato-,
     '91 61
Chunky Tomato Sauce, '95 264
Cream Sauce, Angel Hair Pasta with Tomato,
     '93 292
Cream Sauce, Linguine with Tomato-, '86 158
Cream, Tomato, '94 70
Creamy Tomato Sauce, '93 71
Cucumber Sauce, Tomato-, '98 45
Dried Tomato Sauce, '96 220; '99 135
Fish in Tomato Sauce, '85 75
Fresh Tomato Sauce, '83 224; '87 171
Fresh Tomato Sauce over Basil Pasta, '93 176
Gingered Tomato Sauce, Spicy, '96 220
Green Chiles, Tomato Sauce with, '81 196
Herbed Fresh Tomato Sauce, '85 M151
Herbed Tomato Sauce, '86 277
Hot Sauce, Kleberg, '94 28
Italian-Style Tomato Sauce, '87 182
Italian Tomato Sauce, '82 M68; '92 57
Italian Tomato Sauce for Spaghetti, '81 134
Light Tomato Sauce, '97 246
Marinara Sauce, '89 239; '92 18; '94 64;
     '99 266
Meat Sauce, Italian, '83 193
Picante Sauce, '94 116
Picante Sauce, Homemade, '90 205
Picante Sauce, Processed, '91 257
Pico de Gallo, '79 185; '86 19; '97 141
Pizza Sauce, '80 163; '84 33; '85 285
Ranchero Sauce, '96 168
Rancheros Sauce, '88 148
Red Pepper-Tomato Sauce, '93 59
Refrigerator Tomato Sauce, '85 188
Roasted Garlic-Tomato Sauce, '97 46
Seasoned Tomato Sauce, '83 150
Spaghetti Meat Sauce for 4, Easy, '92 244
Spaghetti Meat Sauce for 25, Easy, '92 245
Spaghetti Sauce, Beer, '85 13
Spaghetti Sauce, Dried Tomato, '90 202
Spaghetti Sauce, Herbed, '85 13
Spaghetti Sauce, Lentil, '90 198

Spaghetti Sauce, Slow-Simmered, '96 72
Spaghetti Sauce, Thick, '84 118
Spaghetti Sauce, Turkey, '85 13
Spicy Sauce, '84 77
Spicy Tomato Sauce, '84 294; '88 19
Taco Sauce, '94 30
Tarragon-Tomato Sauce, '84 131
Tomato Sauce, '85 193, 244; '87 249; '88 116;
     '97 96, 269; '99 270
Vermicelli with Tomato Sauce, '83 164
Zesty Tomato Sauce, '98 176
Vanilla Wine Sauce, Pan-Fried Grouper with,
     '94 241
Vegetable Sauce, '89 98
Vegetable Sauce, Greek Fish with, '82 72
Vegetable Sauce, Pasta with, '83 163
Vegetable Sauce, Tangy, '89 280
Velouté Sauce, '84 22
Venison Reduction Sauce, '94 303
Verde Sauce, '93 275
Vermouth-Cream Sauce, Scallops in, '96 49
Vidalia Onion Sauce, '99 52
Vinaigrette, Versatile, '93 141
Vinegar Basting Sauce, '91 205
Walnut Cream Sauce, '93 275
Walnut-Parmesan Pesto Sauce, '96 251
Walnut Sauce, Spaghetti with Parsley and, '80 30
Watercress Sauce, '91 85
Whiskey Sauce, '80 58
White Butter Sauce, '92 107
White Sauce, '82 269; '83 138, 245; '87 166
White Sauce, Asparagus, '80 147
White Sauce, Basic, '79 M156; '81 89
White Sauce, Low-Calorie, Medium, '87 26
White Sauce, Medium, '93 48
White Sauce, Thick, '82 42
Wine Reduction Sauce, '94 270
Wine Sauce, Beef Cubes in, '79 264
Wine Sauce, Broccoli with, '84 187
Wine Sauce, Chicken in, '80 8
Wine Sauce, Marsala, '81 77
Wine Sauce, Mushrooms with, '85 292
Wine Sauce, Red Snapper in, '85 138
Wine Sauce, Shrimp and, '98 50
Wine Sauce, Skillet Steak in Red, '85 21
Wine Sauce, Veal and Carrots in, '86 M139
Wine Sauce, White, '84 132; '89 24; '92 41;
     '93 49
Yellow Pepper Sauce, Poached Salmon with,
     '98 230
Yogurt-Horseradish Sauce, '85 66
Yogurt Sauce, '89 283
Yogurt Sauce, Creamy, '91 238; '92 28
Yogurt Sauce, Lamb Meatballs with, '85 132
Zesty Sauce, '94 82; '97 312
Zippy Sauce, '86 44
Zucchini-Mushroom Sauce, '93 71
Zucchini Sauce, Spaghetti with, '81 38
SAUERKRAUT
Bratwurst and Sauerkraut, '84 250
Bratwurst Dinner, Krause's Café, '87 238
Cake, Sauerkraut, '94 254
Franks, Beany Kraut and, '79 64
Homemade Sauerkraut, '81 216
Meatballs, Sauerkraut, '86 257
Pork Chops and Sauerkraut, '88 98
Relish, Kraut, '91 232
Relish, Sauerkraut, '85 136
Reuben Puffs, '98 231
Reuben Sandwiches, '80 M201
Reuben Sandwiches, Broiled, '81 240; '83 69
Reuben Sandwiches, Crispy, '85 299
Reuben Sandwiches, Grilled, '81 206
Reuben Sandwiches, Open-Face, '91 199

Reuben Sandwich, Rolled, '99 219
Reubens, Oven-Grilled, '97 304
Reubens, Party, '90 61
Reuben Turnovers, '94 253
Salad, Crunchy Sauerkraut, '87 9
Salad, Sauerkraut, '80 178; '97 195
Sandwich, Beef-and-Kraut, '91 167
Sausage and Kraut, '83 11
SAUSAGE
Acorn Squash, Sausage-Stuffed, '81 231; '83 296;
    '84 285
Acorn Squash with Sausage, '85 9
Andouille, '92 242
Andouille Gumbo, Chicken-, '98 14
Appetizers
Balls in Cheese Pastry, Sausage, '80 248
Balls, Sausage, '98 93
Balls, Sausage-Apple, '90 85
Balls, Venison Sausage, '80 42
Basil-Pepper Appetizers, '98 133
Cheese Queso, Chunky, '99 279
Chile con Queso Supreme, '80 265
Cocktail Sausages, Saucy, '87 173
Cocktail Smoky Links, '90 168
Dip, Braunschweiger-and-Beer, '85 69
Dip, Chili con Queso, '86 81
Italian Sausage-Stuffed Mushrooms, '83 127
Kielbasa, Sweet-and-Sour, '89 327
Meatballs, Chestnut, '79 110
Meatballs, Crisp German, '92 326
Meatballs, Sweet-and-Sour, '82 247
Mushrooms, Sausage-Stuffed, '80 248;
    '91 164
Pepperoni Pie Hors d'Oeuvres, '98 251
Phyllo Bites, Sausage-Mushroom-, '89 284
Pizza Snacks, Tasty Little, '79 248
Puffs, Cajun Hot, '94 277
Quesadillas, Sausage, '90 118
Rolls with Sweet-and-Sour Sauce, Sausage,
    '83 74
Rye Appetizers, Party, '86 262
Ryes, Sausage Party, '89 315
Salami Rollups, '90 226
Smoked Sausages with Mustard Sauce, '81 56
Squares, Chile-Sausage, '86 297
Sticks, Beef, '93 331
Sweet-and-Sour Sausage, '88 296
Turkey Sausage Turnovers, '95 239
Baked Peaches and Sausage, '82 50
Baked Sausage Patties, '90 82
Bake, Sausage Egg, '81 225
Barbecued Sausage, '86 153
Basic Sausage, '88 104
Beans, and Rice, Texas Sausage, '84 296
Beans, Spicy-Hot, '89 17
Black-Eyed Peas, Creole, '98 22
Black-Eyed Peas, Easy, '99 204
Black-Eyed Peas Mexicano, '79 10
Black-Eyed Peas with Sausage, '86 7
Boudin, Old-Fashioned, '85 250
Bratwurst and Sauerkraut, '84 250
Bratwurst Dinner, Krause's Café, '87 238
Bratwurst, Grilled, '94 253
Breads
Biscuit Bites, Sausage, '84 95
Biscuits, Cheesy Sausage, '80 78
Biscuits, Ham, '99 233
Biscuits, Pepperoni, '84 95
Biscuits, Southern Sausage and, '82 43
Biscuits with Sausage, Angel Heart, '87 156
Biscuits with Sausage, Best, '99 103
Muffins, Cheesy Sausage, '92 252; '93 144
Muffins, Sausage, '88 52; '95 49
Muffins, Sausage-Cheese, '86 213

Pig-in-a-Blanket Bread, '99 134
Rolls, Ground-Pepperoni, '83 244
Waffles, Sausage, '83 50
Breakfast Delight, '93 195
Breakfast Dish, Sausage-Apricot, '82 10
Burritos, Breakfast, '84 57; '90 192
Cabbage, Italian Stuffed, '84 294
Cabbage Rolls, Hot-and-Spicy, '84 249
Cabbage, Sausage-Sauced, '81 271
Cabbage, Stuffed, '84 282
Casseroles
Beefy Sausage Dinner, '80 M9
Breakfast Casserole, '91 285; '99 273
Breakfast Casserole, Sausage, '81 270
Breakfast Casserole, Sausage-Mushroom,
    '86 95
Broccoli Casserole, Sausage and, '80 33
Brunch Casserole, '82 124
Brunch for a Bunch, '88 57
Cheese Bake, Sausage-, '88 58
Cheesy Sausage Casserole, '82 124
Chile Rellenos Casserole, Sausage-, '88 52
Chiles Rellenos Casserole, '98 48
Country Sausage Casserole, '79 192
Creole Sausage-and-Rice Bake, '88 58
Crunchy Sausage Casserole, '81 288
Easy Sausage Casserole, '87 M189
Egg Casserole, Sausage-, '86 M12
Egg Casserole, Sausage-and-, '94 284
Eggplant Parmesan, '86 53
Eggplant-Sausage Bake, '85 221
Eggplant-Sausage Casserole, '84 215
Eggplant-Sausage-Pasta Casserole, Freezer,
    '95 197
Grits-Sausage Casserole, '84 75; '86 241
Ground Beef and Sausage Casserole, '80 260
Hawaiian Sausage Casserole, '85 42
Hominy-Sausage Bake, '88 51
Italian Casserole, '90 238
Italian Sausage Brunch, '88 57
Jambalaya Casserole, Sausage, '82 M203
Lasagna Florentine, Creamy, '91 94
Lasagna, Gourmet White, '96 225
Lasagna, Italian Sausage, '96 225
Lasagna Maria, '90 191
Lasagna Rollups, Sausage-, '80 236
Lasagna, Sausage, '83 288
Lasagna Sausage Pinwheels, '79 6
Manicotti, Saucy Stuffed, '83 288
Noodle Bake, Sausage-, '81 52
Noodle Casserole, Sausage and, '82 123
Noodle Casserole, Sausage-and-, '95 255
Paella Casserole, '95 254
Potato Casserole, Sausage-, '86 217
Rice Casserole, Oriental Sausage and,
    '82 M123
Rice Casserole, Sausage-, '82 50; '83 75
Salami-Corn Casserole, '80 209
Sausage Casserole, '81 112; '82 12
Shells, Sausage-Stuffed, '96 102
Skillet Sausage Casserole, '99 123
Smoked Sausage-Egg Bake, '85 248
Spanish Rice Casserole, '79 192
Strata, Christmas Morning, '95 282
Swiss Sausage Casserole, '80 209
Venison-Vegetable Bake, '87 304
Wild Rice and Sausage, '86 268
Wild Rice Casserole, Sausage-, '84 250
Wild Rice Casserole, Sausage and, '83 196
Zucchini and Sausages, Baked, '80 300
Cassoulet, '96 328
Chicken Rolls Élégante, '80 210
Chicken Sausage with Fennel, '98 312
Chicken with Tomatoes and Sausage, '97 266

Chili, Beefy Sausage, '82 11
Chili, Company, '82 311
Chili con Carne, Beef and Sausage, '83 284
Chili Goes Southwest, Basic, '93 326
Chili, Hearty Kielbasa, '91 28
Chili, Hotto Lotto, '89 316
Chili-I-Cious, '89 315
Chili, Lolly's Pop, '89 316
Chili, Now, Thatsa, '95 16
Chili, Sausage-Beef, '86 232
Chili, Texas-Style, '82 311; '83 30
Chorizo, '92 241
Chorizo and Egg Tortillas, '81 193
Chorizo, Breakfast, '91 77
Chorizo Carbonara, '94 230
Chorizo Grits with Red Bean Salsa,
    Shrimp-Manchego-, '97 227
Chorizo (Spicy Spanish Sausage), '81 193
Chorizo Substitute, '87 238
Chowder, Clam-and-Sausage, '94 104
Chowder, Sausage-Bean, '83 20
Corn Boil, Monroe County, '96 167
Country Sausage, '88 104; '92 242
Country Sausage, Spiced, '88 104
Crêpes, Apple Breakfast, '97 331
Crêpes, Cheesy Sausage, '82 240; '83 71
Crêpes, Sausage, '88 295
Crêpes, Sausage-Filled, '79 39; '98 266; '99 25
Dinner, Sausage-and-Bean, '95 108
Dinner, Sausage-Vegetable, '84 250
Dressing, Cajun, '82 307
Dressing, Cornbread-and-Sausage, '83 213
Dressing, Cornbread-Sausage, '82 307; '85 280
Dressing, Cornbread, Sausage, and Pecan,
    '99 257
Dressing, Fruited Turkey, '99 257
Dressing, Harvest Sausage, '88 254
Dressing, Sausage, '86 280
Dressing, Sausage-Apple, '93 305; '94 296
Dressing, Sausage-Cornbread, '95 289
Dressing, Southern Rice, '99 256
Dressing, Turkey with Sausage-Cornbread,
    '83 287
Eggplant, Sausage Stuffed, '81 204
Eggplant, Sausage-Stuffed, '91 211
Eggs, Armadillo, '97 270
Eggs Creole, '92 86
Eggs, Scotch, '79 261; '83 289; '98 101
Filling, Omelet with Sausage, '81 43
Garlic Sausage, '88 104
Gravy, Sausage, '92 271; '94 20; '97 243
Grilled Pork, Cheddar, and Jalapeño Sausage,
    '98 311
Grits and Sausage, Country, '83 54
Grits Italiano, '92 43
Grits, Nassau, '99 214
Grits, Sausage, '86 92
Grits, Sausage-Cheese, '90 238
Grits with Sausage, '99 233
Gumbo, Chicken-and-Sausage, '89 275; '90 256;
    '94 20
Gumbo, Dove and Sausage, '81 199
Gumbo, Duck, Oyster, and Sausage, '79 226
Gumbo, The Gullah House, '92 237
Gumbo Ya Ya, '87 210
Gumbo z'Herbes, '94 239
Homemade Sausage, Spicy, '84 320
Hominy-Sausage Skillet, '81 29
Italian Meat Sauce, '83 193
Italian Sauce with Noodles, '84 250
Italian Sausage, '88 104; '92 242
Italian Sausage and Peppers, '84 9
Italian Sausage and Rice, '86 53
Italian Sausage Dinner, '91 218

SAUSAGE

(continued)

Italian Sausage Quiche, '81 200
Italian Sausage Soup, '84 235
Italian Sausage Soup with Tortellini, '88 46
Italian Sausage Supper, '88 164
Italian Sausage-Zucchini Soup, '84 4
Italian Turkey Sausage, Marinara Sauce with, '89 239
Jalapeños, Hot Stuffed, '99 123
Jambalaya, Chicken-and-Sausage, '88 200; '91 216
Jambalaya, Creole, '81 51
Jambalaya de Covington, '87 211
Jambalaya, Northshore, '87 45
Jambalaya, 1-2-3, '97 301
Jambalaya, Oven, '84 44
Jambalaya, Sausage, '80 210; '84 249
Jambalaya, Smoked Sausage, '79 42
Jambalaya, Smoky Cajun, '96 62
Jambalaya, Trail, '93 179
Kielbasa, '92 242
Kielbasa and Cabbage, '85 67; '89 M196
Kielbasa, Cabbage, '87 42
Kielbasa-Vegetable Dinner, '91 274
Kraut, Sausage and, '83 11
Loaf, Hawaiian Ham, '79 71
Loaf, Skillet Liver, '80 11
Log, Phyllo Sausage, '84 294
Log, Stuffed Beef, '79 71
Main Dish, Sausage-Eggplant, '80 211
Meatballs and Sausage, Spicy, '79 163
Meat Loaf, Mozzarella-Layered, '79 71
Mexican Luncheon, '87 192
Minestrone, Cheesy, '99 17
Omelet, Puffy Sausage, '80 M268
Onions, Baked Stuffed, '83 135
Paella, '97 328
Pancake-Sausage Wedges, '93 196
Pasta with Broccoli and Sausage, '87 109; '97 266
Pasta with Collards and Sausage, '94 230
Pasta with Sausage and Mixed Vegetables, '84 249
Patties, Apples on Sausage, '82 120
Pepperoni-and-Broccoli Salad, '83 216
Pepperoni Pasta, '83 105
Pepperoni Pinwheels, '96 247
Pepperoni-Squash Toss, '84 127
Peppers, Sausage and, '95 165
Pie, Breakfast, '86 242
Pie, Cornbread-Sausage-Apple, '87 171
Pie, Sausage-and-Cornbread, '90 25
Pie, Tumbleweed, '98 205
Pilau, Sausage, '99 184
Pintos and Sausage, Hearty, '88 296
Pinwheels, Sausage, '80 209; '93 238
Pizza, Breakfast, '85 44; '88 288
Pizza, Double Cheesy Beef-and-Sausage, '86 77
Pizza Luncheon Pie, Deep-Dish, '80 286
Pizza Peppers, '83 135
Pizza Pie, Link-Sausage, '85 33
Pizza, Speedy, '81 214
Pizza, Spicy Sausage-Pepperoni, '83 226
Pizza, The King Henry, '95 267
Pizza, Thick 'n' Crusty Pepperoni, '85 244
Polenta with Sausage, '93 32
Polish Sausage, Cabbage with, '83 104
Pork Rib Roast, Sausage Stuffed, '94 240
Pork Sausage, '81 55; '97 243
Pork Sausage Ring, '80 49
Potatoes, Mexican-Topped, '83 3

Potatoes, Sausage-Vegetable-Topped, '98 29
Potatoes with Eggs and Meat, '91 311; '92 25
Potato Salad with Smoked Sausage, Warm, '97 267
Quiche, Crustless Sausage-Apple, '87 70
Quiche, Easy Sausage, '79 261
Quiche, Pizza, '86 53
Quiche, Sausage-Cheddar, '79 26
Quiche, South-of-the-Border, '93 321
Quiche, Spicy Sausage, '80 M108
Quiche with Avocado Topping, Mexicali, '93 309; '94 96
Quiche, Zucchini-Sausage, '83 122
Ratatouille, Sausage, '89 248
Red Beans and Rice, Delta, '98 146
Red Beans and Rice, New Orleans, '97 235
Rice, Shrimp and Sausage, '79 64
Rice with Sausage, Fried, '83 12
Risotto, Redneck, '98 107
Rollups, Pancake-Sausage, '83 246; '84 42
Rollups, Sausage-Bacon, '88 51
Roll-Ups, Spicy Egg, '90 140
Salad, Bean-and-Sausage, '91 313
Salad, Warm Potato-and-Sausage, '96 25
Sandwiches
Breakfast Pita Pockets, '89 M21
Breakfast Sandwiches, '80 52
Bun, Sausage in a, '89 M22
Burgers, All-American Pizza, '92 148
Burgers, Sausage, '83 212; '96 102
Calzone, '85 94
Cheese Muffin Sandwiches, Sausage-, '92 M212
Italian Sausage and Pepper Loaves, '83 11
Italian Sausage Sandwich, '80 92
Italian Sausage Sloppy Joes, '86 160
Loaf, Sausage-Stuffed French, '90 19
Loaves, Sausage-Cheese, '88 235
Muffuletta Loaf, '97 86
Mustard Sauce, Sausage Sandwiches with, '84 250
Pepperoni and Cheese Loaf, '82 32
Pizza Sandwich, Giant, '80 93
Salami Sandwiches, Open-Faced, '87 279
Sleeping Bag, Sausage in a, '98 206
Shrimp and Sausage over Creamy Grits with Tasso Gravy, Spicy, '92 236
Shrimp Sausage, '97 164
Skillet Dinner, Sausage, '83 29
Skillet Express, Sausage, '83 117
Skillet, Mexican-Style, '83 12
Skillet Sausage and Pasta, '97 267
Skillet Supper, Sausage, '85 293
Smoked Sausage, '86 154
Smoked Sausage, Chicken Gumbo with, '81 199
Smoked Sausage Jambalaya, '79 42
Smoked Sausage Stew, '82 231
Soup, Easy Potato-Sausage, '98 315
Soup, Polish Sausage, '99 317
Soup, Sausage and Okra, '80 209
Soup, Sausage-Bean, '85 88
Soup, Sausage-Potato, '80 25
Soup, Sausage, Spinach, and Bean, '99 311
Soup, Sausage-Tortellini, '99 20
Soup, Spicy Sausage-Bean, '83 229
Soup, Sweet Potato-and-Sausage, '95 23
Spaghetti Dinner, Sausage, '79 194
Spaghetti, Italian, '81 38
Spaghetti, Italian Zucchini, '85 2
Spaghetti, Real Italian, '81 233
Spaghetti, Sausage, '83 160
Spicy Sausage, Dieters', '85 49
Squares, Chile-Sausage, '86 297
Squares, Sausage-Onion, '83 112

Squash, Harvest, '80 214
Squash, Sausage-Stuffed, '81 183
Stew, Frogmore, '92 236
Stew, Oyster-Sausage, '89 242
Stew, Venison Sausage, '87 238
Stir-Fry, Sausage, '82 236; '98 156
Stir-Fry Sausage and Vegetables, '86 213; '87 82
Strata, Sausage, '83 243; '84 101
Stuffing, Chicken Breasts with Pecan-Sausage, '94 212
Stuffing, Crown Roast of Pork with Cranberry-Sausage, '88 49
Stuffing, Sausage, '99 293
Stuffing, Sausage-and-Wild Mushroom, '96 267
Summer Sausage, '99 85
Supper, Cabbage, '89 314
Supper, Sausage-Bean, '86 52
Surprise, Sausage, '83 245; '84 42
Sweet Peppery Sausage, '95 69
Tacos, Breakfast, '80 43; '95 340
Taquitos, Breakfast, '87 237
Tarts, Sausage 'n' Cheese, '88 51
Tomatoes, Italian-Style, '97 169
Tomatoes, Sausage-Stuffed, '80 47
Tortilla Campesina, '89 85
Tortillas, Egg-and-Sausage, '83 246; '84 42
Turban Squash, Sausage-Stuffed, '80 214
Turnovers, Sausage-Cheese, '88 231; '89 22
Vegetables and Sausage, Spicy, '80 82
Vegetable Skillet, Sausage-, '96 102
Wild Rice, Sausage and, '85 65
Ziti with Sausage and Broccoli, '95 340
Zucchini and Sausage, Sautéed, '83 289

SCALLOPS

Angel Hair Pasta, Scallops and, '99 176
Appetizer, Scallop, '86 155
Appetizers, Flaky Scallop, '86 327
Artichokes Stuffed with Shrimp and Scallops, '84 174
Bacon-Wrapped Scallops, '87 94
Bacon-Wrapped Scallops with Orange-Honey Sauce, '97 236
Baked Gruyère Scallops, '92 57
Bay Scallops, Linguine with, '97 201
Broiled Scallops, '91 170
Broiled Scallops with Tartar Sauce, '80 164
Broth with Black Beans and Cilantro, Southwestern Scallop, '87 123
Casserole, Scallop, '79 228
Ceviche (Marinated Raw Fish), '82 220
Champagne-Saffron Sauce, Scallops with, '93 177
Cheese Scallops, Chip and, '80 301
Coquilles Saint Cyrano, '86 90
Coquilles St. Jacques, '97 201
Creamy Scallops and Mushrooms, '83 144
Crêpes, Coquilles St. Jacques, '83 13
en Brochette with Vegetables, Scallops, '80 163
Fettuccine, Scallop-Mushroom, '96 198
Ginger Scallops, '99 177
Grilled Orange Scallops with Cilantro-Lime Vinaigrette, '94 77
Grilled Scallops, Marinated, '84 171
Kabobs, Grilled Scallop, '83 101
Kabobs, Grilled Shrimp-and-Scallop, '92 210
Kabobs, Scallop-Bacon, '81 111
Kabobs, Sea Scallop, '82 162
Maple Scallops, '99 176
Mornay, Scallops, '80 164
Mornay, Shrimp and Scallops, '97 238
Mustard Sauce, Scallops with, '84 163
Pasta, Fresh Scallops and, '83 164

Provençal, Scallops, '85 66
Rumaki, Scallop, '98 M173
Sautéed Scallops with Cranberry Relish, '83 144
Sauté, Scallop, '88 28
Sauté, Shrimp-and-Scallop, '85 103
Sauté with Pecan Rice, Shrimp-and-Scallop,
    '90 317
Savannah, Scallops, '79 145
Seared Scallops with Tomato-Mango Salsa,
    '95 122
Seared Sea Scallops with Tomato Puree, '97 201
Sesame-Crusted Scallops with Orange-Ginger
    Sauce, '97 125
Sherried Scallops, '83 281
Stir-Fry, Scallop, '94 32
Supreme, Seafood, '82 284
Tostada, Grilled Scallops, '87 120
Vegetable Nests, Scallops in, '91 70
Vegetables, Bay Scallops with, '84 233
Vermicelli, Scallop-Vegetable, '87 143
Vermouth-Cream Sauce, Scallops in, '96 49
Véronique, Scallops, '83 144
Wild Rice, Scallops and, '90 129
Wine, Scallops in, '91 48
SCONES. See BREADS/Scones.
SEAFOOD. See also CASSEROLES, CLAMS,
    CRAB, CRAWFISH, FISH, LOBSTER,
    OYSTERS, SALMON, SCALLOPS,
    SHRIMP, TUNA.
Appetizer, Layered Seafood, '88 2
Bisque, Seafood, '86 66
Boil, Low Country Seafood, '80 119
Boil, Southern Shellfish, '93 258
Bouchées aux Fruits de Mer, '98 267
Bouillabaisse, Florida, '79 158
Brochette, Seafood, '87 96
Broiled Shellfish, Quick, '79 228
Butter, Seafood, '97 306
Cakes with Jalapeño Tartar Sauce, Seafood,
    '98 129
Casserole, Seafood, '87 109; '89 63
Chowder, Curried Seafood, '94 103
Chowder, Seafood, '85 9; '92 122
Chowder, Southern Seafood, '83 20
Cioppino, Gulf Coast, '94 102
Delight, Seafood, '86 208
Dip, Hot Artichoke-Seafood, '80 241
Dip, Hot Artichoke Seafood, '85 M212
Dip, Hot Cheesy Seafood, '84 221
Dip, Seafood, '79 3
Dip, Super Seafood, '90 292
Eggplant, Seafood Stuffed, '79 187
Gumbos
    Cajun Seafood Gumbo, '94 238
    Champion Seafood Gumbo, '86 293
    Chicken-Ham-Seafood Gumbo, '81 6
    Creole Gumbo, '86 228
    Creole Gumbo, Quick, '82 87
    Creole Seafood Gumbo, '82 278
    Ham and Seafood Gumbo, '81 199
    Okra Gumbo, Light Seafood-, '86 155
    Seafood Gumbo, '79 198, 286; '80 34; '81 5;
        '83 90; '84 87, 92; '87 210; '90 154; '96 98
    Spicy Seafood Gumbo, '91 207
    Whole Crabs, Seafood Gumbo with, '85 2
Hot Brown, Seafood, '88 158
Imperials, Individual Seafood, '84 162
Jambalaya, Three-Seafood, '82 126
Linguine, Seafood, '79 227
Manicotti, Seafood, '94 195
Mayonnaise, Seafood with Dill, '86 234
Mold, Chilled Seafood, '86 70
Mornay, Seafood, '83 67
Mussels Linguine, '90 M112

Mussel Soup, '93 259
Oriental Marinade, Seafood in, '98 128
Paella, Chicken-Seafood, '88 68
Paella, Party, '88 M189
Paella, Seafood, '82 245
Papillote, Ocean, '84 M287
Parmesan, Savannah Seafood, '99 312
Pasta, Seafood and, '90 234
Pie, Hot Seafood, '80 32
Po' Boy, Grilled Seafood, '96 244
Potatoes, Seafood-Stuffed, '95 M192
Prawns with Winter Cabbage Salad, '98 284
Risotto, Seafood, '95 280
Risotto with Shellfish and Peas, '96 131
Robert, Seafood, '97 106
Salads
    Baked Seafood Salad, '86 10
    Hot Seafood Salad, '79 117; '80 164
    Paella Salad, '86 207
    Pasta Salad, Seafood, '90 62
    Polynesian Seafood Salad, '79 57
    Seafood Salad, '90 88
    Seaside Salad, '86 183
    Slaw, Seafood, '79 56
    Smoky Seafood Salad, '84 46
    Sussex Shores, Seafood Salad, '93 98
Sandwiches, Caribbean Seafood, '98 105
Sauce Delight, Seafood, '82 91
Sauce, Linguine with Seafood, '83 232
Sauce, Red Seafood, '95 107
Sauce, Seafood, '79 3; '82 48; '86 304; '89 239
Sauce, Seafood Cheese, '89 240
Sautéed Seafood Platter, '83 89
Seasoning Blend, Bay Seafood, '92 121
Seasoning Blend, Fish-and-Seafood, '88 28
Seasoning Rub, Seafood, '93 101
Soup, Seafood-Tortellini, '97 324
Spread, Grandma Reed's Seafood, '98 268
Spread, Seafood, '86 M58; '87 146
Spread, Seafood Sandwich, '82 87
Stew, Seafood, '84 280
Stir-Fry with Noodle Pancake, Szechuan Ginger,
    '97 292
Stock, Seafood, '94 238
Supreme, Seafood, '82 284
Tartlets, Seafood, '87 247
Tempura, Basic, '81 68
Tempura, Cornmeal, '81 68
Terrine with Dill Sauce, Asparagus-Seafood,
    '98 157
SEASONINGS. See also MARINADES, OILS,
    SPICE.
Adobo, '92 158
Bay Seafood Seasoning Blend, '92 121
Better-Than-Potpourri Brew, '95 271
Blend, Seasoning, '82 296
Court-Bouillon, '98 229
Creole Rub, '93 101
Creole Seasoning Blend, '92 121
Dry Rub, Biltmore, '99 231
Essence, Emeril's, '99 198
Fish-and-Seafood Seasoning Blend, '88 28
Five-Spice Powder Blend, '92 121
Garlic, Herbed Roasted, '94 177
Garlic Puree, Roasted, '92 55
Garlic, Roasted, '94 177; '96 304
Greek Seasoning Blend, '92 121
Gremolata, '95 280
Ground Seasoning Blend, '92 121
Herb Rub, '93 102
Herb Seasoning, '99 63
Herbs Seasoning Blend, '92 121
Hoisin Mixture, '99 125
Italian Breadcrumb Mix, '99 265

Jerk Rub, '93 101
Lemon-Mint Sugar, '95 32
Lemon Squeezers, '95 32
Meat Seasoning, '98 62
Meat Seasoning Blend, '88 29
Mexican Rub, '93 102
Mix, Fish Herb, '98 51
Mix, GOPPS Seasoning, '92 305
Mix, Seasoning, '91 64
Mix, Weaver D's Seasoning, '96 248
Moroccan Spice Rub, '95 231
Olive Oil, Basil-Infused, '95 231
Olive Oil, Lemon-Infused, '95 231
Poultry Seasoning Blend, '88 28
Rub, Master Class Barbecue, '98 244
Salt, Gourmet Seasoning, '82 297; '97 254
Sazon, '92 157
Seafood Seasoning Rub, '93 101
Southwest Seasoning, '95 266
Taco Seasoning Blend, '96 159
Vanilla Extract, '94 243; '97 288
Vanilla Sugar, '94 243
Vegetable Seasoning Blend, '88 29
SHERBETS. See also ICE CREAMS.
Ambrosia Cups, Sherbet, '82 159
Apricot Sherbet, '81 177; '92 164
Avocado Sherbet, '83 162
Banana-Orange Sherbet, '83 162
Beverages
    Float, Pineapple Sherbet, '79 148
    Orange-Banana Smoothie, '97 173
    Pineapple Smoothie, '97 172
    Punch, Double Sherbet, '79 232
    Punch, Orange Sherbet Party, '83 142
    Punch, Pineapple Sherbet, '95 141
    Punch, Raspberry Sherbet, '95 141
    Smoothie, Citrus, '99 196
Blackberry Sherbet, 1-2-3, '99 130
Buttermilk Sherbet, '84 184; '99 99
Cantaloupe Sherbet, '88 183
Cantaloupe Sherbet, Frosty, '82 144
Cranberry Sherbet, '88 280
Dessert, Layered Sherbet, '87 109
Fruit Punch Sherbet, '86 129
Fruit Sherbet, Freezer, '86 334
Fruit Sherbet, Frozen, '79 155
Fruit Sherbet, Instant, '85 158
Jalapeño-Mint Sherbet, '98 202
Lemon Cream Sherbet, '79 114
Lemon-Pineapple Sherbet, '96 330
Lemon Sherbet, '91 309
Lime Sherbet, '82 159; '89 202
Lime Sherbet, Creamy, '84 165
Macaroon-Sherbet Frozen Dessert, '79 212
Mexican Sherbet, '79 155
Mint Sherbet, Fresh, '88 23
Nectarine Sherbet, '89 199
Orange Sherbet, '79 155
Orange Sherbet Salad, '81 154
Orange Sherbet with Blackberry Sauce, '94 232
Peach Sherbet, '90 179
Pineapple Sherbet, '81 177; '84 83; '89 199
Pineapple Sherbet, Creamy, '79 155
Pineapple Sherbet, Easy, '92 199
Raspberry Sherbet, '83 162
Strawberry Sherbet, '82 112, 160
Watermelon Sherbet, '79 155; '92 124
Watermelon Sherbet, Light, '81 147
SHRIMP
Appetizers
    Artichoke-and-Shrimp Appetizer, '93 271
    Bacon, Shrimp 'n', '98 222
    Ball, Curried Shrimp Cheese, '86 135
    Balls, Curried Shrimp, '94 180

SHRIMP, Appetizers
(continued)

Ball, Shrimp-Cheese, '85 208
Barbecue Shrimp, '96 210; '97 58
Bayou, Shrimp, '88 261
Bites, Bacon-Shrimp, '98 234; '99 213
Boiled Shrimp, Spicy, '83 320; '84 289
Boiled Shrimp with Cocktail Sauce, '79 151
Boil, Southern Shellfish, '93 258
Braised Shrimp with Garlic Rémoulade, '98 133
Cajun Shrimp, '89 283
Canapés, Shrimp, '84 116
Canapés, Shrimp-and-Cucumber, '93 164
Cheese, Shrimp with Herbed Jalapeño,
    '87 112
Cocktail, Shrimp, '87 173; '96 174
Coconut-Beer Shrimp, '85 230; '89 23
Croustades, Shrimp, '97 23
Dilled Shrimp, '88 150
Dip, Chunky Shrimp, '96 214
Dip, Hot Shrimp, '87 190
Dip, Monterey Shrimp, '99 M65
Dippers, Shrimp, '84 324
Dip, Quick Shrimp, '79 153
Dip, Shrimp, '86 84; '88 M261; '98 67
Dip, Zesty Shrimp, '80 150
Double-Dip Shrimp, '99 112
Egg Rolls, '86 81
Eggrolls, Shrimp and Pork, '82 240; '83 18
Filling, Shrimp, '89 320
Fried Marinated Shrimp with Mango Slaw,
    '93 31
Grilled Zucchini-Wrapped Shrimp, '98 200
Jalapeños, Shrimp-Stuffed, '88 115
Kabobs, Appetizer Shrimp, '91 251
Kabobs, Shrimp, '80 150
Key West Shrimp, '94 278
Lemon Shrimp, Luscious, '88 150
Manale, Shrimp, '86 268
Marinated Shrimp and Artichokes, '97 89;
    '98 335
Marinated Shrimp and Cucumber, '91 166
Marinated Shrimp, Icy, '84 215
Miniquiches, Shrimp, '87 146
Mold, Shrimp, '87 94
Mold with Asparagus, Shrimp, '93 214
Mousse, Shrimp, '79 57; '87 196, 251
Mushrooms, Shrimp-Stuffed, '80 M135; '99 324
Oven-Fried Shrimp with Marmalade Dip,
    '99 324
Pâté on Crostini, Shrimp, '98 316
Pâté with Dill Sauce, Shrimp, '85 39
Pickled Shrimp, '94 182
Pickled Shrimp, Charleston Harbor, '99 275
Pickled Shrimp, New Orleans, '79 145
Pickle, Shrimp-in-a-, '86 326
Pineapple Appetizer, Shrimp-, '85 80
Pizza Wedges, Shrimp, '89 158
Puffs, Gouda-Shrimp, '79 234
Puffs, Shrimp, '96 211; '98 316
Rémoulade, Shrimp, '83 173; '90 255
Rock Shrimp Conga, '80 2
Rounds, Shrimp, '98 167
Salsa Picante with Shrimp, '92 210
Sesame Shrimp, '95 92
Sherried Garlic Shrimp, '92 175
Skewers with Vegetable Salsa, Shrimp, '98 32
Soufflé Roll, Shrimp, '89 320
Spread, Chunky Shrimp, '85 300; '86 18
Spread, Curried Shrimp, '87 158
Spread, Shrimp, '81 306; '85 135; '87 111;
    '93 205; '96 104

Spread, Shrimp-Cucumber, '79 81
Spread, Tempting Shrimp, '79 57
Spread, Zippy Shrimp, '90 36
Toast, Shrimp, '86 91
Tree, Shrimp, '83 320; '84 288; '85 318
Vegetable Appetizer, Shrimp-and-, '97 161
Zucchini-Shrimp Appetizers, '89 311
Ariosto, Shrimp and Chicken, '79 31
Artichokes, Shrimp-Stuffed, '84 67; '87 55
Artichokes, Shrimp Stuffed, '94 62
Artichokes Stuffed with Shrimp and Scallops,
    '84 174
au Gratin, Crab, Shrimp, and Artichoke, '90 240
au Gratin, Shrimp, '85 79
Avocados, Shrimp-Filled, '83 2
Baked Shrimp, '87 35
Baked Shrimp, Spicy, '97 324
Barbecued Shrimp, '82 74; '84 93; '90 28
Barbecued Shrimp and Cornbread-Stuffed
    Peppers, '97 261
Barbecued Shrimp, Cajun, '87 95
Boats, Shrimp, '79 57
Boiled Shrimp, '79 3
Boiled Shrimp, Ray Kidd's, '84 87
Boiled Shrimp, Special, '83 36
Boiled Shrimp Supper, '94 200
Boiled Shrimp with Green Peppercorn Tartar
    Sauce, '94 144
Breakfast Shrimp, Classic Charleston, '93 60
Broiled Shrimp, Beer-, '87 142
Broiled Shrimp, Garlic-, '83 193
Broiled Shrimp, Lemon-Garlic, '82 29; '86 182
Broiled Shrimp Supreme, '79 3
Butter, Shrimp, '92 91
Cajun Shrimp, Fiery, '91 218
Cashew Shrimp Supreme, '83 29
Casserole, Chayotes and Shrimp, '80 230
Casserole, Crab-and-Shrimp, '84 71
Casserole, Miss Hannah's, '92 236
Casserole, Shrimp, '85 240
Casserole, Shrimp-and-Chicken, '91 102
Casserole, Shrimp-and-Noodle, '90 240
Casserole, Shrimp and Rice, '79 228
Casserole, Shrimp-and-Rice, '94 328
Casserole, Spicy Shrimp, '96 62
Casserole, Turkey-and-Shrimp Florentine, '92 122
Catfish, Crown Room's Shrimp-Stuffed, '84 182
C'est Bon, Shrimp, '94 195
Cheesecake, Shrimp-and-Gruyère, '92 57
Chicken Breasts, Stuffed, '88 50
Chow Mein, Shrimp, '82 30
Creamed Shrimp on Pecan-Cornmeal Rounds,
    '95 99
Cream Sauce, Shrimp in, '84 M286
Creole, Easy Shrimp, '95 68
Creole in a Rice Ring, Shrimp, '86 222
Creole, Shrimp, '86 256; '87 18; '90 M220;
    '93 282; '96 210
Creole, Special Shrimp, '87 172
Creole, Spicy Shrimp, '79 181
Creole, Wild Rice-and-Shrimp, '84 292
Croquettes, Nannie's Shrimp, '98 316
Curry
Charleston-Style Shrimp Curry, '84 109
Creamy Shrimp Curry, '90 145
Curried Shrimp, '84 110
Eggs, Saucy Shrimp-Curried, '84 143
Polynesian Shrimp Curry, '89 23
Quick Curried Shrimp, '84 M198
Rice and Shrimp, Curried, '83 231
Sauce, Hawaiian Shrimp with Curry, '94 54
Shrimp Curry, '99 91
Shrimp Malai Curry, '84 110
Sour Cream and Shrimp Curry, '81 10

Sour Cream Shrimp Curry, '80 83
West Indian Curried Shrimp, '79 227
Dee-Lish, Shrimp, '90 216
de Jonghe, Shrimp, '79 228
Delight, English Muffin, '82 45
Delight, Shrimp, '79 192
Destin, Shrimp, '82 29
Dijonnaise, Shrimp, '87 91
Dilled Sauced Shrimp, '86 88
Dinner, Jollof Rice, '91 230; '92 325
di Santo, Shrimp, '99 265
Egg Foo Yong, '80 19; '86 232
Egg Foo Yong, Shrimp, '83 22
Eggplant à la Creole, '96 177
Eggplant, Shrimp-Stuffed, '92 99
Eggrolls, Shrimp and Pork, '82 240; '83 18
Egg Rolls, Vietnamese, '96 101
Eggs, Shrimp and Crab Scrambled, '79 261
Élégante, Shrimp, '83 48
Enchiladas in Tomatillo Sauce, Shrimp, '95 310
en Papillote, Shrimp Cancun, '91 136
en Papillote, Shrimp with Asparagus, '86 145
Étouffée, Crab-and-Shrimp, '89 96
Étouffée, Shrimp, '79 4; '90 229
Filling, Shrimp and Dill, '97 171
Fire-Roasted Shrimp with Orzo, '99 42
Fish with Shrimp, Veracruz, '86 130
Flambé, Prawns, '89 24
Florentine, Chicken-and-Shrimp, '89 64
Flounder Stuffed with Shrimp, '88 51
Fondue, Shrimp, '86 244
French-Fried Shrimp, '79 4
French Shrimp, '80 85
Fresh Shrimp, Preparing, '82 127
Fried Marinated Shrimp with Mango Slaw, '93 31
Fried Shrimp, Coconut, '96 248
Fried Shrimp, Golden, '82 29
Fried Shrimp, Gulf Coast, '91 29
Fried Shrimp, Puffy, '79 4
Fried Shrimp with Apricot Sauce, '87 172
Garlic-Buttered Shrimp, '86 M226
Garlic Shrimp, '79 268; '80 14
Gin and Ginger, Shrimp with, '95 205
Grilled Garlic Shrimp, '99 178
Grilled Margarita-Marinated Shrimp, '97 167
Grilled Shrimp, '85 103
Grilled Shrimp with Citrus Salsa, '97 141
Grilled Sweet-and-Sour Shrimp, '97 100
Grits with Red Bean Salsa, Shrimp-Manchego-
    Chorizo, '97 227
Gumbo, Old-Style Shrimp, '98 97
Gumbo, Shrimp-Crab, '98 15
Hoisin Shrimp, '99 237
Honeyed Shrimp, Tangy, '94 32
Kabobs, Grilled Shrimp-and-Scallop, '92 210
Kabobs, Marinated Shrimp, '84 276; '85 158
Kabobs, Shrimp, '80 150, 184
Kabobs, Steak-and-Shrimp, '80 184
Lamb Chops with Shrimp, '88 58
Lemon Butter, Shrimp in, '84 163
Lemon Garlic Sauce, Shrimp in, '83 67
Lemon Shrimp, Luscious, '88 150
Marinara, Shrimp, '84 233
Marinated and Grilled Shrimp, '87 141
Marinated Shrimp, '98 317
Marinated Shrimp, Grilled, '87 173
Marinated Shrimp, Zesty, '87 173
Mediterranean Shrimp Bowl, '80 174
Medley, Eggplant-Shrimp, '79 188
Melba, Shrimp, '84 86
Mirlitons, Stuffed, '97 263
Mornay, Shrimp and Scallops, '97 238
Mustard-Vinegar Sauce, Shrimp with, '93 240
Omelet, Shrimp-and-Cheddar, '84 57

Omelet, Shrimp-and-Cheese, '94 31
Omelet, Shrimp-and-Vegetable Oven, '99 286
Orange Sauce, Shrimp in, '99 292
Oven Shrimp, Vic's, '95 215
Pad Thai, '97 202
Paella, '97 328
Paella Casserole, '95 254
Paella, Chicken-Pork-Shrimp, '82 245
Paella, Party, '88 M189
Paella, Shrimp-and-Chicken, '94 168
Paella, Spanish, '85 26
Paella Valenciana, '82 246
Pasta. *See also* **SHRIMP/Salads.**
  Angel Hair Pasta, Shrimp and Mushrooms
    with, '92 34
  Angel Hair Pasta with Shrimp and Asparagus,
    '92 100
  Asparagus, Tomatoes, and Shrimp, Garlicky
    Pasta with, '95 82
  Cheeses, Shrimp and Pasta with Two, '98 49
  Cream Sauce, Shrimp and Pasta with, '98 295
  Fettuccine and Shrimp with Dried Tomato
    Pesto, '94 249
  Fettuccine, Dilled Shrimp with, '99 141
  Fettuccine, Shrimp, '94 84; '96 210
  Fettuccine with Shrimp and Tomatoes, '96 198
  Green Pasta with Shrimp-Mushroom
    Italienne, '79 170
  Herbed Shrimp and Pasta, '92 329; '97 228
  Lemon Shrimp and Pasta, '96 124
  Linguine, Artichoke and Shrimp, '95 210
  Linguine, Spicy Shrimp and, '92 34
  Manicotti, Shrimp, '97 96
  Mediterranean Shrimp and Pasta, '95 286
  Medley, Shrimp-Pasta, '88 302
  Noodles, Creamy Shrimp and, '92 100
  Noodles with Shrimp, Hoisin, '98 233
  Primavera, Shrimp with Pasta, '93 168
  Rotelle, Shrimp, '85 165
  Salad, Pasta-and-Shrimp, '83 163
  Sautéed Shrimp and Pasta, '96 288
  Scampi, Shrimp, '95 209
  Shrimp and Pasta, '91 207
  Spaghetti, Shrimp-and-Vegetable, '91 170
  Spaghetti with Black Olives, Shrimp, '85 13
  Spicy Pasta and Shrimp, '97 67
  Tomato Pasta, Shrimp-, '98 172
  Tortellini, Shrimp and, '92 34
  Vermicelli Salad, Shrimp, '88 139
  Vermicelli, Shrimp and Feta Cheese on,
    '87 108
Patties, Shrimp, '92 128
Peanut Sauce, Shrimp with, '93 303
Peppers, Shrimp-Stuffed, '80 162; '86 131, 197;
  '97 268
Peppers, Spicy Stuffed, '98 243
Pickled Shrimp, '79 3
Pilaf, Shrimp, '82 246
Pilau, Shrimp, '99 184
Pizza, Shrimp-and-Dried Tomato, '97 49
Pizza, The Best of the Bayou, '95 268
Platter with Béarnaise Sauce, Artichoke and
  Shrimp, '96 132
Po' Boys, Shrimp, '97 312
Polynesian Shrimp, '79 3
Potatoes, Broccoli-Shrimp Stuffed, '92 M228
Potatoes, Creamy Shrimp-Stuffed, '80 36
Potatoes, Shrimp-and-Mushroom Stuffed,
  '99 308
Potatoes, Shrimp-Sauced, '81 M61
Puff, Shrimp-Crab, '79 57
Puffs, Luncheon Shrimp, '85 72
Puppies, Hot-to-Trot Shrimp, '97 84
Quesadillas with Shrimp and Brie, '94 173

Quiche, Shrimp, '83 50
Rémoulade Sauce, Shrimp with, '91 29
Rice, Oriental Shrimp and, '90 183
Rice, Shrimp and Refried, '89 176
Rice, Shrimp and Sausage, '79 64
Risotto with Shrimp, Pumpkin, '98 240
Rock Shrimp Tails, Batter-Fried, '80 2
Rock Shrimp Tails, Broiled, '80 3
Rock Shrimp Tails, Sweet-and-Sour, '80 3
Rolls, Shrimp-and-Romaine, '97 197
Rollups, Shrimp-Stuffed, '82 234
Sailor Shrimp for Two, '82 276
Salads
  Aloha Shrimp Salad, '95 46
  Aspic, Shrimp-Coleslaw, '79 88
  Aspic, Shrimp-Cucumber, '83 108
  Aspic with Shrimp, Tomato, '79 241
  Avocado Salad, Shrimp and, '80 266
  Avocado Stuffed with Shrimp Salad,
    '82 207
  Black Bean Salad, Caribbean Shrimp-and-,
    '93 143
  Boiled Shrimp, '79 3
  Couscous Salad, Shrimp-and-, '96 157
  Crabmeat-Shrimp Pasta Salad, '86 208
  Creamy Shrimp Salad, '79 56
  Croissants, Shrimp Salad on, '96 175
  Egg Salad Sandwiches, Shrimp-and-,
    '94 182
  Endive Salad, Shrimp-, '85 73
  Filling, Shrimp Salad, '87 106
  Fleur-de-lis Salad, '99 164
  Fruited Shrimp Salad, '86 156
  Grapefruit-and-Shrimp Salad, '88 5
  Greek Salad, Dawn's World-Famous, '98 276
  Green Salad with Shrimp, '88 49
  Half Shell, Shrimp Salad on the, '86 73
  Individual Shrimp Salads, '83 146
  Layered Shrimp Salad, '88 100
  Macaroni Salad, Shrimp, '79 220
  Macaroni Salad, Shrimp-, '85 219
  Macaroni-Shrimp Salad, '85 121
  Macaroni-Shrimp Salad, Festive, '85 165
  Marinated Shrimp Salad, '85 82; '93 321;
    '99 169
  Melon and Shrimp Curry Salad, '97 129
  Orange, and Olive Salad with Sherry
    Vinaigrette, Shrimp, '93 177
  Orange Rice Salad, Zesty Shrimp-and-, '87 155
  Orange-Shrimp Salad, '84 197
  Oriental Shrimp Salad, '91 313
  Orzo Salad, Shrimp-and-, '99 182
  Pasta-and-Shrimp Salad, '83 163
  Pastry, Shrimp Salad in, '86 105
  Peppers Stuffed with Shrimp-and-Orzo Salad,
    '91 203
  Picnic Shrimp Salad, '95 182
  Potato Salad, Shrimp-and-, '96 211
  Rice-and-Shrimp Salad, '83 82
  Rice Salad, Baked Shrimp-, '83 22
  Rice Salad, Shrimp and, '80 231; '82 207
  Rice Salad, Shrimp and, '92 307
  Rice Salad, Tangy Shrimp-, '84 66
  Rice-Shrimp Salad, '79 270; '92 142
  Sandwiches, Shrimp Salad, '90 178
  Sea Slaw, Tomatoes Stuffed with, '89 96
  Shrimp Salad, '81 94; '84 221; '86 186;
    '93 238; '98 333
  Super Shrimp Salad, '81 37
  Tossed Shrimp-Egg Salad, '80 4
  Vegetable-Shrimp Salad, '79 190
  Vermicelli Salad, Shrimp, '88 139
  Walnut Salad, Shrimp-, '86 182
  Wild Rice-Shrimp Salad, '99 55

Sandwiches, Shrimp-Cheese, '85 242
Sauce, Broccoli and Cauliflower with Shrimp,
  '84 248
Sauce, Flounder Fillets in Shrimp, '83 227
Sauce, Flounder with Hollandaise-Shrimp,
  '86 234
Sauce, Oysters in Shrimp, '87 40
Sauce Piquante, Crab and Shrimp, '83 92
Sauce, Shrimp, '87 138, 232
Sauce, Shrimp-and-Almond, '87 282
Sausage over Creamy Grits with Tasso Gravy,
  Spicy Shrimp and, '92 236
Sausage, Shrimp, '97 164
Sauté, Confetti Shrimp, '97 104
Sautéed Shrimp, '79 3
Sautéed Shrimp and Thai Coconut Broth with
  Noodles, '98 295
Sautéed Shrimp with Cranberry-Citrus Salsa,
  '97 290
Sauté, Shrimp-and-Grouper, '87 91
Sauté, Shrimp-and-Scallop, '85 103
Sauté with Pecan Rice, Shrimp-and-Scallop,
  '90 317
Scampi, Easy, '84 291
Scampi, Orange, '85 303
Scampi, Quick, '88 301
Scampi, Shrimp, '84 230; '92 117; '93 70
Sesame Shrimp, '95 92
Shells, Creamy Shrimp, '79 4
Sirloin Supreme, Shrimp and, '81 131
Skewers with Vegetable Salsa, Shrimp,
  '98 32, 223
Skillet, Quick Shrimp, '87 50
Smoked Shrimp, Citrus-Marinated, '95 114
Snow Pea-Shrimp Combo, '79 57
Snow Peas, Shrimp with, '85 75
Soups
  Bisque, Okra-and-Shrimp, '97 156
  Bisque, Seafarer's, '98 67
  Bisque, Shrimp, '95 19
  Bisque, Shrimp-Chile, '94 272
  Bisque, Shrimp-Cucumber, '79 172
  Bisque, Shrimp-Vegetable, '82 313; '83 66
  Bisque, Tomato-Shrimp, '86 66
  Bouillabaisse, Marcelle's, '99 200
  Chowder, Shrimp, '89 218
  Chowder, Shrimp and Corn, '79 199
  Corn Soup, Shrimp-and-, '84 88
  Corn Soup with Shiitakes and Shrimp, Sweet,
    '99 168
  Enchilada Soup, Shrimp, '94 103
  Gazpacho, Shrimp-Cream Cheese, '94 137
  Gumbo, Crab and Shrimp, '81 200
  Gumbo, Quick Shrimp, '86 71
  Gumbo, Shrimp, '81 199
  Jambalaya, Creole Shrimp, '92 99
  Mushroom Soup, Shrimp-, '85 87
  Okra-and-Shrimp Soup, '94 323
  Stock, Shrimp, '93 60
Spread, Shrimp, '81 306; '85 135; '87 111;
  '93 205; '96 104
Spread, Shrimp-Cucumber, '79 81
Steak and Shrimp, '88 123
Stew and Grits, Shrimp, '80 118
Stewed Shrimp with Dumplings, '79 31
Stew, Frogmore, '92 236
Stew over Grits, Shrimp, '88 126; '89 47
Stew, Shrimp, '83 4
Stir-Fry, Beef-and-Shrimp, '93 32
Stir-Fry, Cajun Shrimp, '92 127
Stir-Fry Shrimp, '96 129
Stir-Fry, Shrimp-and-Vegetable Medley, '99 205
Stir-Fry Shrimp and Vegetables, '87 91
Stroganoff, Oven-Baked Shrimp, '81 297

SHRIMP
(continued)

Stroganoff, Shrimp, '79 81
Stuffed Shrimp Bundles, Crab-, '81 176
Stuffed Shrimp, Crab-, '84 259
Stuffed Shrimp, Parmesan-, '85 103
Stuffed Shrimp with Hollandaise Sauce, '95 86
Sweet-and-Sour Shrimp, '83 278; '90 M112
Sweet-and-Sour Shrimp and Chicken, '87 267;
   '88 103; '89 66
Szechuan Shrimp, '86 173
Tacos, Shrimp-and-Pepper Soft, '95 339
Tart, Shrimp, '87 70
Tempura "Shrimps," French-Fried, '97 128
Topping, Shrimp, '93 291
Tostadas, Shrimp-and-Black Bean, '93 204
Vegetables, Shrimp and, '82 6
Versailles, Shrimp, '90 233
Wine Sauce, Shrimp and, '98 50
Yellow Squash, Shrimp-Stuffed, '84 194

SLAWS
Apple-Carrot Slaw, '92 243
Apple Coleslaw, '89 315
Apple-Pineapple Slaw, '79 241
Apple Slaw, Fresh, '81 63
Apple Slaw, Nutty, '88 216
Asian Slaw, '99 108
Asian Slaw, Crispy, '97 180
Aspic, Shrimp-Coleslaw, '79 88
Bacon Coleslaw, '83 58
Banana-Nut Slaw, '86 250
Barbecue Coleslaw, '97 139
Barbecue Coleslaw, Best, '97 214
Blue Cheese Coleslaw, '89 13; '95 270
Broccoli Slaw, Sweet, '96 20; '98 332
Broccoli Slaw, Zesty, '93 246
Cabbage-Orange Slaw, '79 135
Cabbage-Pineapple Slaw, '92 182
Cabbage Slaw, Fresh, '85 139
Cabbage Slaw, Nutty, '88 218
Cabbage Slaw, Sweet, '79 76
Cauliflower Slaw, '92 167
Celery Root-and-Carrot Slaw, Shredded, '98 293
Chicken Coleslaw, '84 2
Chili Coleslaw, '80 178
Chinese Cabbage Slaw, '89 312
Coleslaw, '79 152; '82 135
Colorful Coleslaw, '88 166
Confetti Slaw, '89 48
Cooked Dressing, Aunt Beulah's Coleslaw with,
   '99 82
Corn and Cabbage Slaw, '79 135
Cottage Coleslaw, '80 64
Country-Style Coleslaw, '83 59
Creamy Coleslaw, '83 170; '98 244
Crunchy Coleslaw, '86 295
Cucumber Slaw, Creamy, '89 49
Curried Coleslaw, '85 139
Dressing, Sweet Slaw, '98 184
Freezer Coleslaw, '89 49
Freezer Slaw, '81 279; '82 24; '83 154; '99 260
Frozen Coleslaw, '82 102
Fruit Coleslaw, Three-, '86 250
Fruited Coleslaw, '83 209; '85 139
Grape-Poppy Seed Slaw, '86 225
Grapes and Almonds, Coleslaw with, '83 59
Green Bean Slaw, '95 108
Guacamole Mexican Coleslaw, '82 302
Ham Coleslaw, '84 195
Healthy Slaw, '92 183
Hot-and-Creamy Dutch Slaw, '87 127
Hot-and-Sour Chinese Slaw, '85 139

Hot Slaw, '89 49
Jalapeño Coleslaw, '97 26
Kentucky Coleslaw, '81 216
Layered Coleslaw, '86 180
Layered Slaw, '93 214
Lemon-Yogurt Coleslaw, Grilled Chicken
   Breasts with, '98 148
Light and Creamy Coleslaw, '93 318
Make-Ahead Coleslaw, '81 155
Mango Slaw, '93 31; '94 71
Marinated Coleslaw, '79 135
Marinated Slaw, '91 229
Memphis Slaw, '91 28
Memphis-Style Coleslaw, '98 104
Mexicali Coleslaw, '84 18
Mexican Coleslaw, '89 48
Mustard Slaw, Texas, '88 172
Old-Fashioned Coleslaw, '80 120; '82 225;
   '99 235
Old-Fashioned Slaw, '84 149
Old-Fashioned Sweet Coleslaw, '93 128
Overnight Cabbage Slaw, '81 88; '82 7
Overnight Coleslaw, '79 135
Overnight Slaw, '79 5; '92 280
Peach Slaw, Party, '86 250
Peanut Slaw, '85 139
Peanut Slaw, Chinese, '93 212
Pear Slaw, Peanutty-, '86 250
Peppery Hot Coleslaw, '98 159
Pineapple-Almond Slaw, '92 171
Pineapple Coleslaw, Curried, '88 172
Pineapple Slaw, '94 49; '99 26
Pineapple Slaw, Colorful, '86 250
Polka Dot Slaw, '83 59
Red Bean Slaw, '79 247
Red Cabbage-and-Apple Slaw, '87 31; '91 309
Red Cabbage Slaw, '95 153
Seafood Slaw, '79 56
Sea Slaw, Tomatoes Stuffed with, '89 96
Silks, Slaw, '93 236
Sour Cream Coleslaw, '99 220
Sour Cream Slaw, '87 10
Swedish Slaw, '79 135
Sweet and Crunchy Slaw, '79 104
Sweet-and-Sour Hot Slaw, '92 63
Sweet-and-Sour Slaw, '81 237
Sweet-and-Sour Slaw, Confetti, '98 89
Sweet Onion Slaw, '98 171
Sweet Potato-Currant Slaw, '93 246
Tangy Coleslaw, '83 59
"Think Pink" Slaw, '94 247
Tomatoes, Coleslaw with, '80 34
Turnip Slaw, '89 245
Vegetable Slaw, '81 280
Zesty Slaw, '82 127; '97 324
Zucchini Coleslaw, Fiesta, '91 168

SLOW COOKER
Bean Bake, Slow Cooker, '99 88
Black-Eyed Peas, Hot-and-Spicy, '99 235
Butter, Slow Cooker Apple, '97 235
Cheese Queso, Chunky, '99 279
Desserts
   Apples 'n' Pears, Saucy, '96 72
   Pie, Caramel, '96 72
Main Dishes
   Barbecue, Chuck Roast, '96 71
   Eye of Round, Slow Cooker Spicy Marinated,
      '99 291
   Ham, Pinto Beans with, '97 210
   Pork and Vegetables, Apple Cider, '97 210
   Pork Chops and Gravy, '96 71
   Ribs, Barbecued Baby Back, '97 234
   Roast, Pumpernickel, '97 234
   Roast, Slow Cooker Chuck, '98 32

Oatmeal in a Slow Cooker with Ice Cream,
   '99 193
Red Beans and Rice, New Orleans, '97 235
Sandwiches, Debate Barbecue, '97 234
Sandwiches, French Dip, '97 211
Sauce, Slow-Simmered Spaghetti, '96 72
Soups and Stews
   Black Bean Soup, '98 291
   Brunswick Stew, Easy, '99 235
   Chicken Brunswick Stew, '97 234
   Chili Bean Soup, '96 71
   Potato Soup, Hearty, '98 292
   Steak Soup, '99 260
   Texas Stew, '97 211
   Tortilla Soup, '98 291
   Vegetable Soup, '98 32, 291

SOUFFLÉS
Blue Cheese Soufflé, '91 244
Cheddar Cheese Soufflé, '98 24
Cheese Soufflé, '79 72, 261; '94 116
Cheese Soufflé for Two, '81 226
Cheese Soufflé, Rolled, '89 13
Cheese Soufflés, Three-, '96 219
Cheese Soufflé, Three-Egg, '87 234
Chicken-Chestnut Soufflé, '79 107
Chile-Cheese Soufflés, '96 219
Cornbread, Soufflé, '96 34
Crab Soufflé Spread, '85 4
Cups, Hot Soufflé, '85 284
Dessert
   Apricot Soufflé, Baked, '88 267
   au Chocolat Cointreau, Soufflé, '94 56
   Banana Daiquiri Soufflé, '84 317
   Blintz Soufflé, '88 155
   Brandy Alexander Soufflé, '82 173; '83 M114
   Bread Pudding Soufflé, Creole, '92 87
   Chocolate Mint Soufflé, '81 16
   Chocolate Soufflé, '84 317; '94 46
   Chocolate Soufflé, Light, '83 278
   Chocolate Soufflé with White Chocolate
      Mousse, '98 57
   Coconut Soufflé, '79 73; '85 212
   Cranberry-Topped Holiday Soufflé, '84 306
   Cream Cheese Soufflé, '88 11
   Daiquiri Soufflé, Elegant, '80 69
   Devonshire Soufflé, Chilled, '88 279
   Grand Marnier Soufflé, '79 281
   Grand Marnier Soufflés, '89 290
   Grasshopper Soufflé, '81 248; '86 188
   Kahlúa Soufflé, '82 173
   Lemon-Lime Soufflé, Cold, '84 24
   Lemon Sauce Soufflés, Quick, '88 43
   Lemon Soufflé, '82 170, 252; '94 199
   Lemon Soufflé, Tart, '85 82
   Lemon Soufflé with Raspberry-Amaretto
      Sauce, Frozen, '88 130
   Orange Dessert Soufflé, '83 206
   Orange Soufflé, Chilled, '84 317; '86 189
   Orange Soufflé, Frozen, '79 211
   Pineapple Dessert Soufflé, '80 153
   Raspberry Soufflé, '86 188
   Raspberry-Topped Soufflé, '85 317
   Vanilla Soufflé, Frozen, '79 230; '82 173
   Vanilla Soufflés with Vanilla Crème Sauce,
      '94 242; '96 155
Egg Soufflé Casserole, '83 55
Egg Soufflés, Little, '83 57
Frozen Soufflés, Individual, '80 52
Grits Soufflé, '80 30
Grits Soufflé, Garlic-Cheese, '99 18
Grits Soufflé, Mexican, '79 55
Ham Breakfast Soufflé, Virginia, '93 121
Ham Soufflé with Cucumber Sauce, '92 41
Individual Soufflés, '80 190

Parmesan Soufflés, '97 280
Pizzaola Soufflé, Italian, '98 232
Pizzaola Soufflé, Mexican, '98 232
Rice-Cheese Soufflé, '79 270
Roll, Southwestern Soufflé, '97 171
Salmon Soufflé, Fresh, '81 182
Shrimp Soufflé Roll, '89 320
Sour Cream Soufflé, '80 43
Turkey Soufflé, '80 271
Vegetable
Asparagus Soufflé, '79 66; '83 265; '89 89
Broccoli Soufflé, '81 24
Broccoli Soufflé, Golden, '84 283
Broccoli Soufflés, '96 218
Butternut Soufflé, '83 266
Butternut Squash Soufflé, '97 270
Carrot Puff, '89 89
Carrot Soufflé, '79 73; '83 265; '98 231; '99 25
Carrot Soufflés, '96 309
Cauliflower Soufflé, '82 76; '89 279; '90 17
Corn-and-Cheese Soufflé, '88 122
Mushroom Soufflés, '87 282
Onion Soufflé, '79 247
Parsnip Soufflé, Golden, '83 266
Potatoes, Soufflé, '84 295; '85 196; '90 14
Potato Soufflé, Cheesy, '89 332
Spinach Soufflé, '79 73; '81 304; '84 78; '85 248; '86 108
Spinach Soufflé, Cheese-and-, '98 235
Spinach Soufflé, Cheesy, '81 53
Spinach Soufflé Deluxe, '79 8
Spinach Soufflé Roll, '80 215
Squash Soufflé, '95 215
Squash Soufflé, Cheesy, '82 146
Sweet Potato Soufflé, '82 286; '86 121; '93 325; '96 247
Turnip Soufflé, '79 254
Yellow Squash Soufflé, '89 89
Zucchini-and-Corn Soufflé, '83 265
Zucchini-Corn Soufflés, '97 203
Zucchini Soufflé, '79 157
SOUPS. See also CHILI, CHOWDERS, GUMBOS, JAMBALAYAS, STEWS.
Acorn-Butternut Soup, Creamy, '96 216
Acorn Squash Soup, '91 294
Acorn Squash Soup, Cream of, '94 268
Acorn Squash-Thyme Soup, '99 252
Almond Soup, '79 48
Artichoke Cream Soup, '94 62
Artichoke Soup, '89 269
Artichoke Soup, Cream of, '82 232
Asparagus Soup, '84 67; '98 290
Asparagus Soup, Cream of, '84 111
Asparagus Soup, Creamy, '94 225
Avocado-Banana-Yogurt Soup, '80 78
Avocado-Mushroom Soup, Creamy, '85 25
Avocado Soup, '88 160
Avocado Soup, Chilled, '81 34; '87 37; '93 108
Avocado Soup, Creamy, '79 107
Avocado Soup, Sherried, '84 181
Bacon, Lettuce, and Tomato Soup, '91 207
Bean
Bacon Soup, Bean and, '83 26
Barley Soup, Hearty Bean-and-, '86 304
"Bean Counter" Soup, '92 80
Beanolla Soup, '94 248
Bean Soup, '80 25
Black Beans and Cilantro, Southwestern Scallop Broth with, '87 123
Black Bean Soup, '88 30, 266; '89 28; '93 231; '98 291
Black Bean Soup, Carolina, '92 139
Black Bean Soup, Marge Clyde's, '96 29
Cabbage-Bean Soup, '97 301

Capitol Hill Bean Soup, '80 222
Chicken Soup, Bean-, '99 283
Chili Bean Soup, '96 71
Chill-Chaser Soup, '87 282
Drunken Bean Soup, '87 283
French Market Soup, '85 277; '92 49; '94 317
Green Bean Soup, Cream of, '84 111
Ham-and-Bean Soup, '84 4
Hominy Soup, Bean-and-, '95 23
Leafy Bean Soup, '86 223
Minestra, '97 246
Mix, Bean Soup, '99 283
Mix, French Market Soup, '85 277; '94 317
Navy Bean Soup, '84 280; '96 19
Navy Bean Soup, Chunky, '83 291
Navy Bean Soup, Savory, '87 282
Pasta Soup, Bean and, '94 220
Quick Bean Soup, '99 97
Red Bean Soup with Walnuts, '96 243
Refried Bean Soup, '96 136
Sausage-Bean Soup, '85 88
Sausage-Bean Soup, Spicy, '83 229
Three-Bean Soup, '89 17
Three-Bean Soup, Spicy, '91 28
Turkey Soup, Bean-and-, '93 319
White Bean Pot, '86 194
White Bean Soup, '83 229; '90 201
White Bean Soup, Spicy, '94 225
Bell Pepper Soup, '89 103
Bisques
Banana-Raspberry Bisque, '93 161
Clam Bisque, '86 228
Crab-and-Corn Bisque, '87 137
Crab-and-Leek Bisque, '94 104
Crab-and-Spinach Bisque, '97 241
Crab Bisque, '88 251
Mushroom Bisque, Brisk, '81 190
Okra-and-Shrimp Bisque, '97 156
Oyster Bisque, '83 252; '96 276; '99 320
Pumpkin Bisque, Spicy, '86 67
Seafarer's Bisque, '97 67
Seafood Bisque, '86 66
Shrimp Bisque, '95 19
Shrimp-Chile Bisque, '94 272
Shrimp-Cucumber Bisque, '79 172
Shrimp-Vegetable Bisque, '82 313; '83 66
Spinach-Potato Bisque, '86 66
Squash Bisque, '84 280; '98 290
Stone Crab Bisque, '96 86
Tomato-Basil Bisque, Make-Ahead, '93 322
Tomato-Shrimp Bisque, '86 66
Tuna Bisque, '79 76
Black-Eyed Pea Soup, '97 213
Black-Eyed Soup, Beefy, '85 6
Black, White, and Red All Over Soup, '95 126
Borscht, Crawfish, '92 84
Borscht, Ruby Red, '83 176
Bouillabaisse, Florida, '79 158
Bouillon, Court-, '98 229
Bouillon, Redfish Court, '83 290; '84 93
Bouillon, Tomato, '83 8
Bourbon with Molasses Sauce, Burned, '95 17
Bread Bowls, Italian, '98 292
Broccoli
Broccoli Soup, '86 161, M194; '87 288
Cheesy-Broccoli Soup, '86 258
Chicken Soup, Broccoli-and-, '90 202
Creamed Broccoli Soup, '85 24
Cream of Broccoli Soup, '79 130; '80 188, M225; '82 314; '83 66; '86 259
Cream-of-Broccoli Soup, '88 56
Cream of Broccoli Soup, Light, '93 17
Cream of Broccoli Soup, Mock, '85 288

Creamy Broccoli Soup, '81 75; '82 13; '83 99; '91 307
Easy Broccoli Soup, '81 307
Fresh Broccoli Soup, '91 86
Hot Broccoli Soup, '81 235; '83 44
Swiss Soup, Broccoli-, '86 6
Butternut-and-Apple Soup, Creamed, '88 228
Butternut Soup, Creamy, '96 216
Butternut Squash Soup, '95 62
Cabbage Soup, '83 291; '85 88
Cabbage Soup, Sweet-and-Sour, '89 314
Carrot
Butternut Squash Soup with Parslied Croutons, Carrot-and-, '97 217
Carrot Soup, '80 88; '89 146; '98 123
Cheesy Carrot Soup, '81 262
Chilled Carrot-Mint Soup, '90 M168
Cream of Carrot Soup, '81 307; '88 46; '91 69
Cream Soup, Carrot, '90 210
Creamy Carrot Soup, '92 218
Curried Carrot Soup, '82 157
Leek Soup, Carrot-, '86 34
Orange Soup, Carrot-, '79 172
Savory Carrot Soup, '84 107
Tomato Soup, Cream of Carrot-and-, '94 176
Cauliflower and Caraway Soup, '82 264
Cauliflower and Watercress Soup, Cream of, '83 126
Cauliflower Soup, '90 211; '99 318
Cauliflower Soup, Cream of, '87 M7; '88 12; '96 277
Cauliflower Soup, Creamy, '82 76
Cauliflower Soup, Fresh, '84 279
Celery Soup, Burnet-, '84 107
Celery Soup, Cream of, '79 71; '90 210
Celery Soup, Light Cream-of-, '82 279
Cheese. See also SOUPS/Onion, Vegetable.
Anytime Soup, Cheesy, '81 307; '82 314; '83 66
Bacon-Beer Cheese Soup, '87 M7
Bacon-Topped Cheese Soup, '80 M224
Beer-Cheese Soup, '84 246
Blue Satin Soup, '98 248
Broccoli Soup, Cheese-and-, '89 276
Chunky Cheese Soup, '98 31
Cream Cheese Soup, Austrian, '98 M85
Cream of Cheese Soup, '83 99
Favorite Cheese Soup, Uncle Ed's, '94 228
Gazebo Cheese Soup, '90 158
Hearty Cheese Soup, '84 4
Herbed Cheese Soup, '96 219
Macaroni and Cheese Soup, '95 264
Mexican Cheese Soup, '97 268
Minestrone, Cheesy, '99 17
Monterey Jack Cheese Soup, '81 112; '85 M211
Pimiento "Mac and Cheese" Soup, '97 M325
Velvet Soup, Cheese, '80 74; '92 193
Vichyssoise, Velvety Roquefort, '83 223
Chicken. See SOUPS/Poultry.
Chocolate Soup, Mexican, '96 277
Cilantro Soup with Black Bean Salsa, Cream of, '97 226
Consommé aux Champignons, '79 48
Consommé, Brown Rice, '98 288
Corn-and-Bourbon Soup, '92 194
Corned Beef Soup, '83 16
Corn Soup, '80 56; '85 243; '87 156
Corn Soup, Cream of, '90 210
Corn Soup, Favorite, '85 155
Corn Soup, Grilled, '87 121
Corn Soup, Pimiento-, '89 126
Corn Soup with Shiitakes and Shrimp, Sweet, '99 168
Cucumber-Buttermilk Soup, Chilled, '95 134

SOUPS
(continued)

Cucumber Soup, Chilled, '79 144
Cucumber Soup, Cold, '79 130; '81 130
Cucumber Soup, Cold Minted, '86 34
Cucumber Soup, Cream of, '81 98
Cucumber Soup, Creamy, '80 171
Cucumber Soup, Dilled, '90 M167
Cucumber-Yogurt Soup, '82 157; '83 205
Curried Soup, '81 130
Dill Soup, Cold, '84 107
Egg Drop Soup, '83 21; '86 16
Egg-Drop Soup, '85 M12
Egg Drop Soup, Lemon-, '93 81
Egg Flower Soup, '81 307; '82 313; '83 65
Egg-Lemon Soup, '96 88
Eggplant Soup, Herbed, '90 173
Eggplant Supper Soup, '85 221
English Pea Soup, '96 56
Fish Soup with Garlic Mayonnaise, Rich, '92 56
French Soup Maigre, '98 125
Fruit. *See also* SOUPS/Gazpacho.
    Apple Soup, Creamed Butternut-and-, '88 228
    Avocado-Banana-Yogurt Soup, '80 78
    Cantaloupe Soup, '83 120; '88 160
    Cantaloupe Soup, Chilled, '81 156; '97 148
    Cantaloupe Soup, Fresh, '84 190
    Chilled Fresh Fruit Soup, '88 160
    Cold Fresh Fruit Soup, '87 157
    Dessert, Fruit Soup, '79 172
    Dried Fruit Soup, '79 23
    Egg-Lemon Soup, '96 88
    Fruit Soup, '87 98
    Fruit Soup, Fresh, '98 196
    Lemon-Egg Drop Soup, '93 81
    Lemon Soup, '85 94
    Lime Soup, '88 31
    Mango-Cantaloupe Soup, Chilled, '96 205
    Melon Soup, '80 182
    Melon Soup, Swirled, '87 162
    Orange Soup, Carrot-, '79 172
    Peach-Plum Soup, '87 157
    Peach Soup, '83 120, 180
    Peach Soup, Chilled, '97 159
    Peach Soup, Cream of, '99 207
    Pear Soup, Pumpkin-, '92 234
    Plum Soup, '85 107
    Plum Soup, Chilled Purple, '79 162
    Raspberry Soup, Chilled, '81 130
    Sherry-Berry Dessert Soup, '91 180
    Strawberry-Banana Soup, '86 181
    Strawberry Soup, '88 160
    Strawberry Soup, Cold, '82 157
    Strawberry Soup Supreme, '81 M144
    Swedish Fruit Soup, '82 313; '83 65
    Yogurt Fruit Soup, '86 176
Gazpacho
    Berry Gazpacho, '97 181
    Blender Gazpacho, '85 93
    Chilled Gazpacho, '84 138
    Citrus Gazpacho, '96 70
    Classy Gazpacho, '89 220
    Cool Gazpacho, '83 140
    Crab Gazpacho, '97 181
    Gazpacho, '79 172; '80 266; '81 98; '82 73;
        '84 112; '85 164; '91 94; '92 64; '93 215
    Herbed Gazpacho, '95 175
    Saucy Gazpacho, '82 157
    Secret Gazpacho, '93 161
    Shrimp-Cream Cheese Gazpacho, '94 137
    Spring Gazpacho, '81 112
    Summer Gazpacho, '84 181

Tomato-Avocado-Corn Gazpacho, '97 182
Tomato Gazpacho, Classic, '99 172
Tropical Gazpacho, '95 204
Vegetable Gazpacho, Grilled, '97 181
Vegetable Gazpacho, Smoked, '93 156
White Gazpacho, '97 181
Green Pepper Soup, '88 250
Green Soup, '98 23
Greens Soup, Cream with, '94 277
Guadalajara Soup, '88 30
Ham-and-Bean Soup, Spicy, '94 322
Hamburger Soup, '80 263
Ham Soup, Hearty, '82 4
Harvest Soup, '79 101
Homemade Soup, '79 198
Hot-and-Sour Soup, '83 68; '91 50
Italian Soup, Chunky, '99 20
Kale Soup, Creamy, '96 203
Leek Soup, Cream of, '99 276
Lentil Soup, '83 292; '86 304; '91 28; '97 304;
    '98 19
Lentil Soup, Beefy, '87 282
Lentil Soup, Spanish-Style, '96 239
Mardi Gras Soup, '96 56
Meatball Soup, Mexican, '98 315
Minestrone, '82 4
Minestrone, Dixie, '94 230
Minestrone Soup, '84 202; '86 144; '91 258
Minestrone Soup Mix, '91 258
Mushroom-Onion Soup, '80 25
Mushroom-Rice Soup, '90 32
Mushroom Soup, '82 286; '86 M73; '94 54
Mushroom Soup, Chunky, '88 12
Mushroom Soup, Cream of, '84 5; '85 93, 261
Mushroom Soup, Creamy, '79 243; '81 307
Mushroom Soup, Curried, '84 M89
Mushroom Soup, Elegant, '83 99
Mushroom Soup, Fresh, '81 109; '90 190
Mushroom Soup, Sherried, '96 104
Mushroom Soup, Shrimp-, '85 87
Mushroom Soup, Wild, '98 281
Mustard Green Soup, Cream of, '93 280
Nuts, Soup, '96 106
Okra Soup, Charleston, '87 156
Okra Soup with Fou-Fou, '96 325
Onion
    Beefy Vidalia Onion Soup, '97 212
    Cheese Soup, Onion-, '87 81
    Classic Onion Soup, '84 65
    Creamy Onion Soup, '90 211
    Double-Cheese Onion Soup, '85 227
    Double Cheese-Topped Onion Soup, '79 49
    Easy Onion Soup, '85 226
    French Onion-Beef Soup, '87 54
    French Onion Soup, '79 49; '80 188; '83 126;
        '85 226; '86 M212; '90 31; '93 246
    French Onion Soup, Shortcut, '85 M328
    French Onion Soup, Toasty, '81 306
    Green Onion Soup, '84 112
    Green Onion Soup, Creamed, '83 82
    Mushroom-Onion Soup, '80 25
    Onion Soup, '99 96
    Oven-Browned Onion Soup, '79 49
    Potato Soup, Creamy Onion-and-, '92 51;
        '97 304
    Rich Onion Soup, '85 226
    Superb Onion Soup, '81 86
    Three-Onion Soup, '96 217
Pea-and-Watercress Soup, '93 162
Peanut Butter Soup, '89 28
Peanut Butter Soup, Cream of, '84 29
Peanut Soup, '87 184
Peanut Soup, Chilled, '79 130
Peanut Soup, Cream of, '92 193; '93 288

Peanut Soup, Creamy, '79 50
Pea Soup, '99 67
Pea Soup, Chilled, '84 181
Pea Soup, Cold Curried, '91 120
Pea Soup, Country-Style, '86 267
Pea Soup, Cream, '90 211
Pea Soup Élégante, '79 53
Pea Soup, Fresh, '86 181
Pea Soup, Peppery, '82 271
Pea Soup, Potato-, '94 90
Pea Soup, Spring, '88 M96
Pepper Soup, Spicy, '93 98
Pepper Soup, Sweet, '93 277
Pimiento Soup, Cream of, '96 45
Potato
    Asparagus-Potato Soup, '85 23
    Bacon Soup, Potato-, '84 M38
    Baked Potato Soup, '91 311; '92 26
    Beet Soup, Potato-, '88 156
    Carrot Soup, Potato-, '88 297
    Celery-and-Potato Soup, '84 279
    Chilled Cucumber-Potato Soup, '85 93
    Cold Potato-Cucumber Soup, '88 160
    Cream of Potato Soup, '80 M224; '82 21
    Cream of Potato Soup, Golden, '86 302
    Creamy Potato Soup, '81 19, 98; '84 112
    Easy Potato Soup, '92 17
    Hearty Potato Soup, '98 292
    Holiday Potato Soup, '79 236
    Irish Potato Soup, '99 54
    Leek-and-Potato Soup, '84 112
    Onion-and-Potato Soup, Creamy, '97 304
    Pea Soup, Potato-, '94 90
    Potato Soup, '82 278; '83 292; '92 263
    Sausage-Potato Soup, '80 25
    Sausage Soup, Easy Potato-, '98 315
    Special Potato Soup, '82 3
    Subtle Potato Potage, '80 78
    Sweet Potato-and-Sausage Soup, '95 23
    Sweet Potato Soup, '88 250
    Sweet Potato Soup with Rum Cream, '98 271
    Sweet Potato Velouté, '94 238
    Three-Potato Soup, '86 16
    Wild Rice Soup, Cheesy Potato-and-, '89 16
    Yogurt Soup, Potato-, '92 217
Pot-of-Gold Soup, '86 259
Poultry
    Chicken-Almond Cream Soup, '92 21
    Chicken-and-Rice Soup, '88 236
    Chicken-and-Wild Rice Soup, Creamy,
        '98 M334
    Chicken, Artichoke, and Mushroom Soup,
        '92 324
    Chicken Broth, Easy Microwave, '90 M167
    Chicken-Corn Soup, Cheesy, '97 158
    Chicken Enchilada Soup, '86 22
    Chicken, Ham, and Oyster Soup, '79 198
    Chicken Noodle Soup, '80 264; '95 45; '98 30
    Chicken-Noodle Soup, Chunky, '88 12
    Chicken Noodle Soup, Creamy, '99 20
    Chicken Soup, '81 98
    Chicken Soup, Bean-, '99 283
    Chicken Soup, Cream of, '85 243
    Chicken Soup, Creamy Asparagus-and-,
        '95 82
    Chicken Soup, Curried, '86 34
    Chicken Soup, Homemade, '82 34
    Chicken Soup, Mexican, '84 234
    Chicken Soup, Quick, '86 M72
    Chicken Soup, Roasted Pepper-and-, '90 58
    Chicken Soup, Spicy, '97 268
    Chicken Stock, '95 18
    Chicken-Vegetable Soup, '88 18; '99 60
    Stock, Light Poultry, '90 31

Turkey-Barley Soup, '91 312
Turkey Carcass Soup, '86 284
Turkey-Noodle Soup, '91 312
Turkey-Noodle Soup Mix, '89 330
Turkey-Rice Soup, '90 89
Turkey Soup, Curried, '86 332
Turkey Soup, Tempting, '98 314
Turkey Soup, Williamsburg, '90 287
Turkey-Vegetable Soup, '84 4; '88 264; '91 312
Pumpkin-Corn Soup with Ginger-Lime Cream, '95 227
Pumpkin-Pear Soup, '92 234
Pumpkin Soup, '79 48
Pumpkin Soup, Cream of, '93 234
Pumpkin Soup, Curried, '96 242
Red Bell Pepper Soup, '98 104
Red Pepper Soup, Chilled Sweet, '93 69
Reuben Soup, Cream of, '97 26
Roasted Red Pepper Soup, '96 245
Roasted Yellow Bell Pepper Soup, '96 56
Sausage and Okra Soup, '80 209
Sausage Soup, Italian, '84 235
Sausage Soup, Polish, '99 317
Sausage Soup with Tortellini, Italian, '88 46
Sausage, Spinach, and Bean Soup, '99 311
Sausage-Tortellini Soup, '99 20
Sausage-Zucchini Soup, Italian, '84 4
Seafood
Bouillabaisse, Marcelle's, '99 200
Cioppino, Gulf Coast, '94 102
Clam Florentine Soup, '85 23
Crabmeat Soup, '84 123
Crab Soup, Beaufort, '92 238
Crab Soup, Cream of, '88 302
Crab Soup, Creamy, '80 M224
Crab Soup, Elegant, '80 188
Crab Soup, Fresh Corn-and-, '92 183
Crab Soup, Old-Fashioned, '90 71
Crab Soup, Plantation, '92 237
Crab Soup, Quick, '84 279
Crab Soup, Steamboat's Cream of, '81 127
Lobster Soup, Spicy Thai, '94 102
Mussel Soup, '93 259
Oyster-and-Artichoke Soup, '97 21
Oyster-and-Artichoke Soup, Louisiana, '92 81
Oyster-and-Mushroom Soup, '87 39
Oyster-Cheese Soup, '84 213
Oyster Soup, '79 228; '83 211
Oyster-Turnip Soup, '94 328
Scallop Broth with Black Beans and Cilantro, Southwestern, '87 123
She-Crab Soup with Marigold, '79 32
Shrimp-and-Corn Soup, '84 88
Shrimp Enchilada Soup, '94 103
Shrimp Soup, Okra-and-, '94 323
Stock, Seafood, '94 238
Tortellini Soup, Seafood-, '97 324
Shiitake Soup, Cream of, '95 265
Sopa de Lima, '79 211
Southwest Soup, '86 255
Spinach Soup, Cream of, '82 38; '90 211
Spinach Soup, Hot Cream of, '84 29
Spinach Soup, Oriental, '83 151
Spinach Soup with Meatballs, Italian, '92 331
Spinach-Tortellini Soup, '99 317
Split Pea and Frankfurter Soup, '79 64
Split Pea Soup, '88 235; '89 17; '94 322
Squash Soup, '94 134
Squash Soup, Chilled, '92 173
Squash Soup, Cold Cream of, '81 130
Squash Soup, Cream of, '81 246
Squash Soup, Perky, '85 20
Steak Soup, '99 260
Stock, Beef, '95 17

Stock, Brown Meat, '90 31
Stock, Chicken, '95 18
Stock, Fish, '95 19
Stock, Homemade Fish, '92 237
Stock, Light Poultry, '95 31
Stock, Quick Full-Bodied, '95 17
Stock, Seafood, '94 238
Stock, Vegetable, '90 31
Stock, Venison, '94 302
Summer Soup, Dilled, '99 182
Summer Squash Soup, '83 99; '84 193; '85 136
Sweet Red Pepper Soup, Cream of Roasted, '95 65
Taco Soup, '94 225; '99 36
Tamale Soup, '95 213
Tomatillo Soup with Crunchy Jicama, '92 245; '97 143
Tomato
Appetizer Tomato Soup, '86 258
Celery Soup, Tomato-, '83 M58
Chilled Tomato Soup, '82 155
Cioppino, Gulf Coast, '94 102
Cold Tomato Soup, '88 160
Consommé, Tomato, '88 250
Cream of Tomato Soup with Lemon Basil, '96 124
Cream of Tomato Soup with Parmesan Cheese, '86 161
Cream Soup, Refreshing Tomato, '79 172
Cream Soup, Tomato-Basil, '97 198
Creamy Tomato Soup, '83 267; '86 258
Dried Tomato-Cream Soup, '90 203
Easy Tomato Soup, '84 14
Fire Water, '80 188
Fresh Tomato Soup, '83 140
Herbed Yogurt and Parmesan Toasts, Tomato Soup with, '96 66
Hot Tomato Juice Soup, '86 302
Iced Tomato Soup, '79 170
Mexican Tomato Soup, Icy-Spicy, '90 155
Plus, Tomato Soup, '88 170
Pumpkin-Tomato Soup, '86 291
Rice Soup, Tomato-and-, '85 24
Savory Tomato Soup, '94 91
Sour Cream-Topped Tomato Soup, '80 246
Summer Tomato Soup, '79 130
Tomato Potage, '79 250
Tomato Soup, '81 236; '83 44; '89 217
Vegetable Soup, Tomato-, '81 M177; '86 9
Tortellini Soup, '98 68
Tortellini Soup, Japanese, '96 330
Tortilla Soup, '88 31, 245; '90 201; '93 197, 274; '94 136; '98 291; '99 310
Tortilla Soup, Spicy, '90 32; '93 108
Turkey. *See* **SOUPS/Poultry.**
Turnip Soup, '92 217
Turnip Soup, Creamy, '84 279
Turtle Soup, '92 92
Turtle Soup au Sherry, '80 56
Veal-Vermicelli Soup with Quenelles, '94 14
Vegetable
Bean Soup, Vegetable-, '83 317
Beef-and-Barley Vegetable Soup, '89 31
Beef and Vegetable Soup, Quick Italian, '96 235
Beef Soup, Hearty Vegetable-, '84 102
Beef Soup, Spicy Vegetable-, '88 11
Beef Soup, Vegetable-, '88 296; '99 219
Beefy Vegetable Soup, '79 113; '84 M38
Beefy Vegetable Soup, Quick, '80 25
Broth, Savory Vegetable, '81 230
Burger Soup, Vegetable-, '82 6
Cheese Soup, Creamy Vegetable-, '81 244
Cheese Soup, Creamy Vegetable, '83 230

Cheese Soup, Vegetable-, '89 15
Cheesy Vegetable Soup, '80 73; '97 241
Chicken-Vegetable Soup, '99 60
Chili Vegetable Soup, '94 120
Chunky Vegetable Soup, '89 M283
Clear Vegetable Soup, '79 130
Cold Garden Vegetable Soup, '84 197
Down-Home Vegetable Soup, '90 32
Garden Harvest Soup, Italian, '90 M167
Garden Soup, '85 241
Garden Vegetable Soup, '83 140; '86 160
Hearty Vegetable Soup, '80 26
Leek-Vegetable Soup, '86 304
Light Vegetable Soup, '84 280
Marvelous Vegetable Soup, '82 3
Mix, Vegetable Soup, '84 148
Old-Fashioned Vegetable Soup, '86 304
Pot Liquor Soup, '98 273
Quick Vegetable Soup, '79 190; '85 24, 32
Quick Veggie Soup, '91 31
Southwestern Vegetable Soup, '97 268
Spicy Vegetable Soup, '79 198; '93 293; '99 337
Stock, Vegetable, '90 31
Vegetable Soup, '80 128; '84 148; '85 106; '86 187; '87 83, 123; '88 266; '93 157; '98 32, 291
Venison Soup, '82 216
Vichyssoise, '86 181
Vichyssoise, Cucumber, '94 90
Vichyssoise, Velvety Roquefort, '83 223
Vichyssoise with Mint Cream, Cucumber, '98 246
Watercress-and-Leek Soup, '86 161
Watercress Soup, '79 82; '88 104
Watercress Soup, Cream of, '96 66
Zucchini Soup, '82 104; '84 181; '86 181; '89 14
Zucchini Soup, Chilled, '87 90
Zucchini Soup, Cold, '85 265; '92 64; '99 164
Zucchini Soup, Cream of, '83 99
Zucchini Soup, Creamy, '83 140
Zucchini Soup, Dilled, '90 88
Zucchini Soup, Watercress-, '91 72
Zucchini Soup with Cilantro, '93 130
Zucchini Soup with Fresh Vegetable Salsa, Chilled, '98 194
SPAETZLE
Spaetzle, '99 242
SPAGHETTI
All-in-One Spaghetti, '98 295
Bacon Spaghetti, '86 213; '87 82
Black Bean Spaghetti, '92 217
Black-Eyed Pea Spaghetti, '81 7
Carbonara, Chorizo, '94 230
Carbonara, Salmon, '83 43
Carbonara, Spaghetti, '85 34; '87 167
Carbonara, Spaghetti alla, '81 38
Casseroles
Asparagus-Spaghetti Casserole, '80 77
Beef Casserole, Spaghetti and, '79 129
Casserole Spaghetti, '95 132
Chicken-Spaghetti Casserole, '84 15
Florentine Bake, Cheesy, '95 131
Ham-and-Turkey Spaghetti, '95 19
Italian Casserole, '90 238
Low-Fat Spaghetti Casserole, '99 215
Pork Spaghetti Bake, '81 11
Spaghetti Casserole, '84 241
Tetrazzini, Chicken, '79 268; '80 75; '83 288; '99 61
Tetrazzini, Ham, '82 77; '84 241
Tetrazzini, Herbed Turkey, '86 47
Cheese Spaghetti, Three-, '83 105
Chicken Spaghetti, '83 105; '87 221; '98 329

SPAGHETTI

(continued)

Chicken-Vegetable Spaghetti, '92 281; '98 296
Chili, Cincinnati, '96 18
Chili-Spaghetti, Herbed, '84 222
Clam Sauce, Pasta with, '84 291
Crawfish Spaghetti, '85 104
Easy Spaghetti, '83 M317; '84 72; '92 66
Etcetera, Spaghetti, '83 105
Ham Spaghetti Skillet, '83 283
Herbal Dressing, Spaghetti with, '86 158
Hot Dog and Spaghetti Skillet, '83 144
Italian Spaghetti, '81 38
Italian Spaghetti, Real, '81 233
Lemon-Garlic Pasta, '95 181
Marzetti's Spaghetti, '99 85
Meatballs, Spaghetti-and-Herb, '84 75
Meatballs, Spaghetti with, '81 38
Meaty Spaghetti, '82 19
Mushroom Pasta 1-2-3, '97 102
Mushrooms, Spicy Spaghetti with, '85 2
Onions, Spaghetti with Smothered, '97 229
Parmesan Noodles, Cheesy, '83 M7
Parsley and Walnut Sauce, Spaghetti with, '80 30
Parsley, Spaghetti with, '80 236
Peanut Sauce, Pasta with, '95 252
Pepperoni Pasta, '83 105
Pepperoni Spaghetti, Quick, '88 40
Pie, Spaghetti, '81 M32
Pie, Spaghetti-Ham, '93 19
Pie, Weeknight Spaghetti, '95 312
Pizzazz, Spaghetti with, '80 85
Pork and Peppers, Spaghetti with, '98 131
Pot Roast with Spaghetti, '80 59
Salad, Chicken-Spaghetti, '90 146
Salad, Mediterranean, '95 132
Salad, Spaghetti, '82 277; '84 205
Salad, Spaghetti-Vegetable, '97 196
Sauces
Beer Spaghetti Sauce, '85 13
Grisanti Spaghetti Sauce, '94 194
Herbed Spaghetti Sauce, '85 13
Italian Tomato Sauce for Spaghetti, '81 134
Meat Sauce, Quick Spaghetti and, '94 64
Slow-Simmered Spaghetti Sauce, '96 72
Thick Spaghetti Sauce, '84 118
Turkey Spaghetti Sauce, '85 13
Vegetable Sauce, Pasta with, '83 163
Zucchini Sauce, Spaghetti with, '81 38
Sausage Spaghetti, '83 160
Sausage Spaghetti Dinner, '79 194
Shrimp and Pasta, '91 207
Shrimp-and-Vegetable Spaghetti, '91 170
Shrimp Spaghetti with Black Olives, '85 13
Soup, Creamy Chicken Noodle, '99 20
Szechuan Noodle Toss, '91 30
Thick-and-Spicy Spaghetti, '83 287
Tomatoes and Garlic, Spaghetti with, '91 47
Tomato Pasta, Italian, '93 201
Tomato Sauce, Spaghetti with Fresh, '96 135
Veal and Peppers, Spaghetti with, '81 201; '82 14
Veal Spaghetti, '84 276
Vegetable Sauce, Pasta with, '83 163
Vegetables, Spaghetti with, '85 67
Vegetables with Spaghetti, Fresh, '86 257
Vegetables with Spaghetti, Sautéed, '81 89
Zucchini Spaghetti, '83 160
Zucchini Spaghetti, Italian, '85 2
SPICE. *See also* **SEASONINGS.**
Balls, Decorative Ribbon-Spice, '84 325
Blend, Five-Spice Powder, '92 121
Dry Spices, '90 120

Mix, Mulled Wine Spice, '85 266
Mix, Tex-Mex Spice, '94 135
Rub, Moroccan Spice, '95 231
SPINACH
Appetizers
Bread, Spinach, '83 121
Cheese Bites, Spinach-, '94 23
Cheesecake, Spinach-Herb, '99 139
Cheesecake, Spinach-Mushroom, '92 326
con Queso, Easy Spinach, '88 101
Cups, Cottage Cheese-Spinach, '87 190
Dip, Beef-and-Spinach, '99 65
Dip, Cheesy Spinach, '82 59
Dip, Creamy Spinach, '88 132
Dip, Florentine Artichoke, '96 274
Dip, Hot Spinach, '80 249
Dip, Hot Spinach-Cheese, '89 48
Dip in Cabbage, Spinach, '82 155
Dip in Sourdough Round, Spinach, '98 173
Dip, Pine Nut-Spinach, '99 138
Dip, Spinach, '80 86; '86 159; '87 25, 214;
   '93 324
Filling, Spinach, '95 316
Loaf, Four-Layer Cheese, '99 222
Madeleine in Chafing Dish, Spinach, '85 319
Mushrooms, Spinach-Stuffed, '86 81;
   '88 131, M261; '89 M133
Pastries, Greek Spinach-and-Cheese, '96 76
Pâté with Spinach and Cream, Pork, '83 224
Phyllo-Spinach Triangles, '87 53
Phyllo Triangles, Spinach-Filled, '84 52
Phyllo Triangles, Spinach-Ricotta, '88 212
Pinwheels, Spinach-Tenderloin, '89 M118
Puffs, Cheese-and-Spinach, '87 246
Puffs, Spinach, '95 316
Puffs, Spinach-Artichoke-Tomato, '95 284
Quichelets, Spinach, '87 67
Quiche, No-Crust Spinach, '90 142
Quiches, Miniature Spinach, '82 38
Rollups, Spinach, '98 251
Sauce, Herbed Green, '86 244
Spanakopita, '96 233
Spread, Parmesan-Spinach, '93 55
Spread, Savory Spinach, '82 180
Spread, Spinach, '88 132
Spread, Spinach-Bacon, '92 M310
Squares, Spinach, '88 131
Strudels, Spinach, '93 249
Supreme, Layered Spinach, '82 38
Tarts, Spinach, '82 249
Terrine, Layered Salmon-and-Spinach, '84 132
Wontons, Spinach, '83 74
Apples, Onions, and Pears over Spinach,
   Sautéed, '94 212
Baked Spinach, Gourmet, '82 180
Bisque, Crab-and-Spinach, '97 241
Bisque, Spinach-Potato, '86 66
Bread, Spinach, '83 121; '87 144
Burgers, Spinach-Feta, '99 135
Calzones, Spinach-and-Cheese, '95 310
Casseroles
Artichoke Bake, Spinach-, '95 48
Artichoke Casserole, Spinach-, '88 252; '93 44
Artichoke Casserole, Spinach and, '81 103
Beef Casserole, Spinach and, '79 192
Beef-Macaroni Casserole, Spinach-, '83 313
Cannelloni, '85 60; '92 17
Celery Casserole, Spinach-and-, '84 294
Cheese Bake, Spinach-, '88 10
Cheese Casserole, Spinach-, '83 216; '89 64
Cheesy Florentine Bake, '95 131
Cheesy Spinach Casserole, '81 263
Company Spinach, '89 280
Cottage Cheese-and-Spinach Casserole, '84 77

Crab and Spinach Casserole, Creamy, '80 3
Creamy Spinach Bake, '89 68
Creamy Spinach Casserole, '86 111
Delight, Spinach, '84 M144
Egg Casserole, Spinach and, '82 270
Eggplant-Spinach Casserole, '99 217
Enchiladas, Chicken-and-Spinach, '91 222
Enchiladas, Spinach, '83 60; '84 14
Florentine Casserole, Turkey-and-Shrimp,
   '92 122
Florentine, Chicken-and-Shrimp, '89 64
Florentine, Creamy Lasagna, '91 94
Florentine, Jumbo Seashells, '79 6
Florentine, Lasagna, '88 196
Florentine, Salmon, '83 43
Florentine, Turkey, '88 264
Lasagna, Cheesy Spinach, '80 32; '83 204
Lasagna Florentine, Chicken, '95 158
Lasagna, Spinach, '79 25; '81 243
Lasagna, Spinach-Bean, '92 96
Manicotti, Spinach, '82 199
Manicotti, Spinach-Stuffed, '88 255
Oyster-and-Spinach Casserole, '83 34; '84 44
Parmesan Casserole, Spinach-, '82 281; '83 32
Parmesan, Spinach, '93 72
Puff, Spinach-Cheese, '84 96
Rice Bake, Green, '79 43
Rice, Spinach, '85 146
Ricotta Bake, Spinach-, '88 97
Roll-Ups, Ham and Spinach, '81 143
Scalloped Spinach with Cheese, '79 8
Shells, Spinach-Stuffed, '85 60
Spinach Casserole, '79 265; '91 31; '99 271
Supreme, Spinach, '84 77
Surprise, Spinach, '82 42
Turkey-Spinach Casserole, '84 71
Cheesecake, Spinach Pesto, '90 175
Cheesy Topped Spinach, '84 85
Chicken Breasts, Fried Spinach-Stuffed, '88 206
Chicken, Garlic-Spinach, '92 56
Chicken in Puff Pastry, Spinach-Stuffed, '92 125
Chicken, Lemon-Spinach, '97 104
Chicken Rolls, Spinach-Stuffed, '86 248
Chinese Spinach, '79 179; '82 39
Chinese Spinach Sauté, '83 208
Cornbread, Spinach, '95 49
Couscous, Spinach-and-Onion, '98 23
Creamed Spinach, '81 54; '86 110; '96 252;
   '97 28
Creamed Spinach in Pastry Shells, '89 280
Creamed Spinach with Noodles, '84 29
Creamy Spinach, '85 289
Crêpes, Spinach-Ricotta, '81 52
Custards, Savory Spinach-Gorgonzola, '99 313
Eggs Oso Grande, '98 279
Eggs Sardou, '92 93
Enchiladas, Spinach, '83 60; '84 14
Fettuccine, Creamy Basil Chicken with Spinach,
   '97 328
Field Peas and Spinach, '99 169
Filling, Spinach, '79 34
Filling, Spinach and Feta, '97 171
Filling, Spinach-Mushroom, '80 215
Filling, Spinach-Ricotta, '81 53
Fish in a Wrap, '97 64
Florentine, Baked Eggs, '86 M12
Florentine, Cheesy Trout, '85 53
Florentine, Chicken, '93 107
Florentine Crêpe Cups, '89 44
Florentine Crêpe Pie, '79 34
Florentine, Crêpes, '80 190
Florentine, Eggs, '79 39; '83 56
Florentine, Fish, '86 35
Florentine in Parchment, Fish, '87 22

Florentine Sauce, '93 48
Florentine, Stuffed Mushrooms, '82 270
Florentine-Style Eggs, '82 38
Florentine with Mushroom Sauce, Chicken,
　'87 250
Frittata, Spinach, '81 53
Garden, The, '83 134
Greek Sunburst, '94 245
Grits, Garlicky Ham-and-Spinach, '94 177
Lemon and Pepper, Spinach with, '97 105
Lemon Spinach, Creamy, '82 302
Lemon Spinach with Feta, '85 190
Loaves, Spinach-Oyster, '84 213
Macaroni with Spinach, Baked, '99 244
Marinara on Beds of Spinach and Orzo, '93 320
Meat Loaf, Spinach, '96 131
Meat Loaf, Spinach-Stuffed Turkey, '97 24
Mushrooms, Spinach with, '80 19
Nests, Baked Eggs in Spinach, '82 70
Noodles, Chicken and Spinach, '82 19
Omelet, Spinach-Cheese, '83 119
Oysters Rockefeller, '98 222
Parmesan Spinach, Savory, '85 68
Pastas
　Bow Tie Pasta, Spinach and Mushrooms with,
　　'95 341
　Fantastic, Spinach, '93 173
　Fettuccine and Spinach, '88 90
　Fettuccine, Easy Chicken with Spinach,
　　'88 89
　Fettuccine, Fresh Spinach, '83 60
　Fettuccine, Spinach, '82 179
　Fettuccine with Mustard Greens, Spinach,
　　'94 247
　Fettuccine with Spinach Sauce, '84 329
　Green Pasta with Shrimp-Mushroom
　　Italienne, '79 170
　Linguine with Spinach, '91 30
　Pesto and Pasta, Spinach-Peanut, '93 212
　Pesto-Pasta, Spinach, '91 314
　Pie, Spinach-Pasta, '85 286
　Sauce, Spinach Pasta, '93 71
　Shells, Spinach, '97 50
　Shells, Spinach-Stuffed, '87 20; '99 64
　Tortellini with Tomato Sauce, Spinach,
　　'88 302
　Verde, Pasta, '84 201
　Vermicelli with Fresh Spinach Sauce, '89 256
Peppers, Spinach-Stuffed, '82 180
Pesto, Orange Roughy with Spinach, '88 M192
Pesto, Squash Stuffed with Spinach, '89 M133
Pie, Greek Spinach, '85 59
Pie Pan Spinach, '94 195
Pie Parma, Spinach, '96 203
Pie, Spinach, '82 191; '88 56
Pie, Spinach-Pasta, '85 286
Pie with Muenster Crust, Spinach, '95 48
Pinwheels, Flank Steak-and-Spinach, '95 56
Pitas, Spinach-Walnut, '87 202; '88 43
Pork, Spinach-and-Herb Stuffed, '89 193
Pork Tenderloin, Spinach-and-Bacon Stuffed,
　'94 81
Potatoes, Black-Eyed Pea-Spinach-Stuffed,
　'95 22
Quiche, Cheesy Spinach, '81 228
Quiche, Crustless Spinach, '84 235
Quiche, Greek Spinach, '86 10
Quiche, No-Crust Spinach, '90 142
Quiches, Individual Spinach, '86 38
Quiche, Spinach, '81 44; '85 49; '91 204
Quiche, Spinach-Mushroom, '81 M74
Ring au Fromage, Spinach, '79 8
Roll, Feta Cheese-Spinach, '91 22
Rolls, Spinach-Ham, '88 78

Rollups, Chicken and Spinach, '80 90; '82 M68
Roll-Ups, Ham and Spinach, '81 143
Rollups, Spinach-and-Ham, '86 84
Salad Dressing, Spinach, '83 181; '93 250
Salads
　Apple-Onion Vinaigrette, Spinach Salad with,
　　'94 276
　Apple Salad, Spinach-, '90 89; '92 13; '97 308
　Apple-Spinach Salad, '97 14; '99 222
　Apricot Salad, Spinach-, '94 63
　Arranged Spinach Salad, '91 210; '92 160
　Bacon Dressing, Spinach Salad with Hot,
　　'82 211
　Bacon Salad, Spinach and, '81 143
　Beet Salad, Spinach-, '83 227
　Blue Cheese Salad, Spinach-, '82 166
　Blues, Spinach Salad with the, '95 66
　Cantaloupe-Spinach Salad with Pistachio-
　　Lime Vinaigrette, '97 148
　Chicken-and-Spinach Tossed Salad, '83 157
　Chicken-Spinach-Strawberry Salad, '97 92
　Chili-Lime Dressing, Spinach Salad with,
　　'94 63
　Citrus Dressing, Spinach Salad with, '88 133
　Citrus Spinach Salad, '90 59
　Combination Spinach Salad, '85 327; '86 22
　Creamy Spinach Salad, '83 60
　Crisp Spinach Salad with Creamy Dressing,
　　'83 81
　Crunchy Spinach Salad, '80 147; '81 225
　Curry Spinach Salad, '80 242
　Dijon Spinach Salad, '89 282
　Dried Tomato Vinaigrette, Spinach Salad with,
　　'93 272
　Easy Spinach Salad, '91 249
　Enoki Salad, Spinach-, '89 62
　Festive Spinach Salad, '80 247
　French Spinach Salad, '79 8
　Fresh Spinach Salad, '82 73; '83 240;
　　'84 15, 77; '86 130
　Fresh Spinach Salad Delight, '80 146
　Fresh Spinach with Spicy Dressing, '80 55
　Garlic-Ginger Vinaigrette Dressing, Spinach
　　Salad with, '92 195
　Green Spinach Salad, '79 142
　Grits-Spinach Salad, Stacked, '98 66
　Honey Dressing, Spinach Salad with, '90 16
　Hot Spiked Spinach, '97 195
　Kiwifruit Salad, Spinach-, '87 305
　Lamb Salad, Spinach-, '85 58
　Layered Salad, Make-Ahead, '81 296
　Layered Spinach-Lettuce Salad, '84 266
　Layered Spinach Salad, '80 5; '89 163
　Mandarin Spinach Salad, '85 163
　Minted Spinach Salad, '94 63
　Mushroom Salad, Spinach and, '80 112
　Onion Salad Bowl, Spinach-and-, '81 157
　Orange Dressing, Spinach Salad with, '87 187
　Orange Salad, Spinach-and-, '86 15
　Orange-Spinach Salad, '83 316; '84 16
　Oriental Spinach Salad, '82 23
　Oysters and Red Wine Vinaigrette, Spinach
　　Salad with, '94 327
　Pears, Spinach Salad with Sautéed, '94 237
　Pecan Salad, Spinach-, '89 128
　Pickled Spinach, '81 69
　Poppy Seed Dressing, Spinach Salad with, '91
　　210; '92 160
　Pork-and-Spinach Salad, Mandarin, '88 M126
　Raspberry Cream Dressing, Spinach Salad
　　with, '94 321
　Rice Salad, Spinach-, '94 63
　Romaine-Spinach Salad, '89 123
　Russian Dressing, Spinach Salad with, '79 144

Salmon-Spinach Salad, '87 145
Sesame Salad, Spinach-, '91 211; '92 160
Sesame Spinach Salad, '90 292
Southern Spinach Salad, '80 55
Special Spinach Salad, '80 78
Spinach Salad, '82 102; '86 302; '87 62;
　'88 299; '92 281, 341; '93 46, 65
Springtime Spinach Salad, '81 114
Sprout Salad, Fresh Spinach-, '82 281; '83 42
Strawberry-Spinach Salad, '91 169; '93 168
Sun-Dried Tomato Salad, Spinach and,
　'93 250
Supreme, Spinach Salad, '79 243
Sweet-Sour Spinach Salad, '85 M112
Tropical Spinach Salad, '90 231
Turkish Salad, '96 137
Twist, Spinach-Mustard, '86 209
Vinaigrette Spinach, '79 8
Wilted Spinach Salad, '81 M4; '89 123;
　'91 210; '92 160; '93 125
Zesty Spinach Salad, '79 88
Sandwiches, Fresh Spinach, '85 59
Sandwiches, Grilled Spinach Fondue, '99 337
Sandwich, Grilled Spinach Fondue, '94 171
Sauce, Emerald, '90 63
Sauce, Fettuccine with Spinach, '84 329
Sauce, Herbed Green, '86 244
Sauce, Spinach Pesto, '93 59
Sautéed Spinach, '93 250
Sauté, Fresh Spinach, '93 55
Sesame Spinach, '98 24
Skillet Spinach, '96 19
Soufflé, Cheese-and-Spinach, '98 235
Soufflé, Cheesy Spinach, '81 53
Soufflé Deluxe, Spinach, '79 8
Soufflé Roll, Spinach, '80 215
Soufflé, Spinach, '79 73; '81 304; '84 78; '85 248;
　'86 108
Soup, Cream of Spinach, '82 38; '90 211
Soup, Cream with Greens, '94 277
Soup, Green, '98 23
Soup, Hot Cream of Spinach, '84 29
Soup, Oriental Spinach, '83 151
Soup, Sausage, Spinach, and Bean, '99 311
Soup, Spinach-Tortellini, '99 317
Soup with Meatballs, Italian Spinach, '92 331
Spanakopita, '86 58; '96 233
Squares, Spinach, '95 49
Squash, Spinach-Stuffed, '82 4; '91 14; '97 119
Stir-Fry Spinach, '81 182
Strudels, Spinach, '93 249
Supreme, Layered Spinach, '82 38
Tart Milan, '87 70
Tart, Rutabaga-Spinach, '98 274
Tenderloin, Spinach-Stuffed, '89 311
Tenderloin, Stuffed Tuscany, '99 269
Terrine, Layered Salmon-and-Spinach, '84 132
Timbales, Green Rice, '97 62
Timbales, Spinach, '84 29
Timbales, Spinach-Rice, '88 271
Tomatoes, Baked Spinach, '90 92
Tomatoes, Spinach-Stuffed, '89 203; '93 281
Tomatoes, Spinach-Stuffed Baked, '86 14
Tomatoes, Spinach-Topped, '88 265; '94 321
Tomatoes, Veracruz, '97 169
Turnovers, Salmon-Spinach, '83 44
Zucchini Boats with Spinach, '82 252
SPREADS. See also **APPETIZERS/Spreads.**
Aioli, Shortcut, '93 157
Ambrosia Spread, '92 50
Apple-Date Spread, '91 231; '92 67
Beef Spread, Hot, '83 50
Beet-and-Pecan Sandwich Spread, '99 274
Braunschweiger-Onion Spread, '79 82

SPREADS

(continued)

Bread Spread, Party, '82 161
Caraway Spread, '85 276
Caviar Spread, Creamy, '92 58
Cheese
  Almond Cheese Spread, '87 292
  Aloha Spread, '83 93
  Avocado-Cheese Spread, Herbed, '98 335
  Bacon-Cheese Spread, '83 241
  Basil-Cheese Spread, Fresh, '97 108
  Beer Cheese Spread, '81 69; '94 123
  Beer-Cheese Spread, '85 69
  Beer Spread, Cheesy, '87 196
  Blue Cheese Spread, '95 79; '97 240
  Boursin Cheese Spread, Buttery, '94 301
  Boursin Cheese Spread, Garlic, '94 301
  Brie Spread, Apricot, '86 275
  Cheddar-Swiss Spread, '99 106
  Cheese Spread, '86 135; '96 122; '99 24
  Chile-Cheese Spread, '86 297; '99 336
  Chili Cheese Spread, '93 242
  Chocolate Cheese Spread, '87 292
  Chocolate Chip Cheese Loaves, '91 299;
    '92 264
  Coconut-Cranberry Cheese Spread, '92 328
  Confetti Cheese Spread, '84 256
  Cottage Cheese Spread, '87 107
  Cream Cheese-Olive Spread, '82 35
  Cream Cheese Spread, Apricot-, '82 161;
    '87 158
  Cream Cheese Spread, Caviar-, '84 256
  Cream Cheese Spread, Cucumber and,
    '82 140
  Cream Cheese Spread, Deviled, '81 235
  Cream Cheese Spread, Herb-, '83 24
  Cream Cheese Spread, Nutty, '89 327
  Cream Cheese Spread, Peachy, '90 M215
  Cream Cheese Spread, Pear-, '93 80
  Cream Cheese Spread, Pineapple-, '82 35
  Cream Cheese Spread, Tri-Flavored, '98 134
  Dried Tomato-Cheese Spread, '90 204
  Edam-Sherry Spread, '84 257
  Feta-and-Apple Spread, '99 106
  Four-Cheese Spread, '99 106
  Fruit and Cheese Spread, '81 245
  Fruit-and-Cheese Spread, Nutty, '87 246
  German Cheese Spread, '79 82
  Gouda Cheese Spread, '90 36
  Green Onion-Cheese Spread, '92 24
  Gruyère-Apple Spread, '81 160
  Hawaiian Cheese Spread, '87 158
  Herb-Cheese Spread, '91 124
  Herbed Cheese, '88 152
  Herbed Cheese Spread, '87 247
  Horseradish Spread, Cheese-, '84 222
  Italian Spread, '85 135
  Jalapeño-Cheese Spread, '82 248
  Make-Ahead Cheese Spread, '93 324
  Mexican Cheese Spread, '90 119
  Olive Spread, Cheese-, '79 82
  Orange Cheese Spread, '87 292
  Pimiento Cheese Spread, '82 35; '83 93;
    '86 127; '99 106, 276
  Pimiento Cheese Spread, Creamy, '92 159
  Pimiento Cheese Spread, Garlic, '79 58
  Pimiento Cheese Spread, Low-Calorie,
    '85 215
  Pineapple-Cheese Spread, '86 126; '91 167
  Raisin-Nut Spread, '95 79
  Sandwich Spread, Benedictine, '80 299
  Sandwich Spread, Chunky, '82 140

Sombrero Spread, '87 111
Strawberry Spread, '95 79
Sweet Cheese Spread, Creamy, '79 264
Sweet 'n' Sour Spread, '86 184
Swiss Cheese Spread, '90 60
Tipsy Cheese Spread, '80 150
Tomato-Cheese Spread, '81 157
Tomato-Cheese Spread, Fiery, '87 196
White Cheddar Pimiento Cheese, '99 106
Zesty Cheese Spread, '82 140
Zippy Cheese Spread, '85 4
Cherry Spread, '93 309
Chicken Salad Party Spread, '88 M8
Chicken Spread, Festive, '87 158
Chicken Spread, Low-Fat, '82 290
Chicken Spread, Tasty, '84 193
Chive-Mustard Spread, '91 12
Chutney Spread, Curried, '89 283
Coconut-Pineapple Spread, '93 309
Corn-and-Walnut Spread, '96 26
Corned Beef Spread, '87 196
Cranberry-Butter Spread, '99 86
Cranberry Salsa with Sweet Potato Chips, '93 332
Curry Spread, '93 159
Date Spread, Breakfast, '84 7
Date-Walnut Spread, '87 292
Deviled Delight, '83 130
Dijon-Mayo Spread, '96 199
Egg Salad Spread, '86 127
Egg Salad Spread, Cottage-, '82 146
Egg, Sour Cream, and Caviar Spread, '85 279
Fish Spread, Smoked, '92 305
Fruit Spread, '85 135
Fruit Spread, Sugarless, '84 60
Garbanzo Bean Spread, Herbed, '99 160
Garlic-Butter Spread, '96 199
Garlic Puree, Roasted, '92 55
Garlic Spread, '85 111
Ham-and-Egg Spread, '79 59
Ham and Pimiento Spread, '80 285; '81 56
Ham Spread, '86 126
Ham Spread, Buttery, '95 93; '97 98
Ham Spread, Cold, '82 248
Ham Spread, Country, '87 8
Ham Spread, Deviled, '79 81
Ham Spread, Hawaiian, '87 106
Honey Mustard-Butter Spread, '99 86
Honey-Nut Spread, '87 157
Honey Spread, '81 229
Horseradish-Ham Spread, '91 167
Horseradish, Homemade, '92 25
Horseradish Spread, '90 243
Hummus, '96 158
Lentil Spread, '99 288
Liver Spread, '89 161
Liver Spread, Sherried, '80 86
Mustard Spread, '86 105
Olive Spread, Creamy, '81 290
Olive Spread, Tomatoes with, '85 114
Orange Toast Topper, '79 36
Party Spread, Spicy, '97 240
Peanut Butter Spread, '92 21; '96 90
Pineapple Sandwich Spread, '84 166
Raisin Spread, Creamy, '90 36
Raisin Spread, Peachy-, '86 326
Relish Spread, Creamy, '93 217
Roasted Garlic Canapés, '96 95
Salad Dressing Spread, '82 140
Seafood. *See also* **SPREADS/Trout, Tuna,
  Whitefish.**
  Clam Spread, Creamy, '91 274
  Crabmeat-Horseradish Spread, '90 292
  Crabmeat Spread, '79 81
  Crabmeat Spread, Layered, '83 127

Crab Soufflé Spread, '85 4
Crab Spread, '93 167
Crab Spread, Baked, '80 86
Crab Spread, Superb, '81 255
Oyster Spread, Smoked, '91 64
Salmon-and-Horseradish Spread, '87 146
Salmon Spread, '81 149
Salmon Spread, Smoked, '84 324
Salmon Spread with Capers, Smoked, '98 49
Sandwich Spread, Seafood, '82 87
Seafood Spread, '86 M58; '87 146
Shrimp-Cucumber Spread, '79 81
Shrimp Spread, '81 306; '85 135; '87 111;
  '93 205; '96 104
Shrimp Spread, Chunky, '85 300
Shrimp Spread, Curried, '87 158
Shrimp Spread, Tempting, '79 57
Shrimp Spread, Zippy, '90 36
Tuna Tapenade, '95 127
Spinach-Bacon Spread, '92 M310
Spinach Spread, '88 132
Spinach Spread, Savory, '82 180
Strawberry Spread, Light, '85 55
Sweet 'n' Sour Spread, '86 184
Trout Spread, Smoked, '84 47
Tuna Spread, '83 174; '91 305
Tuna Spread, Chunky, '89 147
Turkey Party Spread, '83 282
Turkey Spread, Curried, '92 16
Vegetable
  Antipasto Spread, '81 25
  Artichoke-Crab Spread, Hot, '85 81
  Artichoke Hearts with Caviar, '79 142
  Artichoke Spread, Hot, '79 110
  Broccamoli Curry Spread, '88 55
  Carrot Spread, Nutty, '94 123
  Cucumber Spread, '79 295; '80 31; '93 158
  Eggplant Spread, '86 278
  Egg Spread, Vegetable-, '87 106
  Garden Spread, '86 135
  Green Onion-Cheese Spread, '92 24
  Green Tomato Sandwich Spread, '95 172
  Guacamole Spread, '90 119
  Hearts of Palm Spread, '90 293
  Mushroom Spread, Hot, '81 190
  Party Spread, Vegetable, '84 166
  Pepper Spread, Roasted, '94 123
  Radish Spread, Fresh, '84 166
  Roasted Red Bell Pepper Spread, '97 217
  Sandwich Spread, Benedictine, '80 299
  Sandwich Spread, Home-Style, '80 179
  Sandwich Spread, Vegetable, '83 174; '85 135
  Tomato Spread, '94 123
  Vegetable Spread, '90 144
  Watercress Spread, '88 103
White Bean Spread, '93 30; '95 279; '96 122
Whitefish Spread, Smoked, '92 58
SPROUTS
Asparagus and Bean Sprouts, '96 95
Beans with Sprouts, Sweet-and-Sour, '86 32
Beef and Bean Sprouts, '82 281; '83 42
Meat Loaf, Sprout, '85 51
Omelet, Potato-Sprout, '79 128
Omelet, Rising Sun, '82 281
Patties, Ham-Sprout, '85 51
Rolls with Thai Dipping Sauce, Summer, '97 236
Salad, Bean Sprout, '82 113
Salad, Crunchy Sprout, '96 45
Salad, Fresh Spinach-Sprout, '82 281; '83 42
Salad, Spanish Sprout, '85 327; '86 22
Salad, Sprout, '90 137
Sandwiches, Alfalfa Pocket Bread, '82 282;
  '83 41
Sandwiches, Polynesian Sprout, '85 51

SQUASH. *See also* CHAYOTES, ZUCCHINI.

Acorn. *See also* SQUASH/Stuffed.
Bake, Acorn Squash, '83 280
Baked Sweet Dumpling Squash, '94 266
Bake, Squash, '82 107
Bowls, Acorn Squash, '96 216
Bread, Squash, '79 210
Butter, Acorn Squash-and-Bourbon, '94 266
Cake, Acorn Squash, '96 216
Cake, Winter Squash-Spice Bundt, '99 248
Delight, Acorn Squash, '81 267
Grilled Acorn Squash with Rosemary, '96 266
Orange Squash Brûlée, '94 267
Oysters in Acorn Squash, Creamed, '97 20
Pancakes, Granola-Squash, '94 267
Puppies, Acorn Squash, '94 268
Puree, Basic Acorn Squash, '94 267
Rings, Easy Glazed Acorn, '81 M231
Rings, Glazed Acorn, '80 214
Sherried Acorn Squash, '85 9
Soup, Acorn Squash, '91 294
Soup, Acorn Squash-Thyme, '99 252
Soup, Cream of Acorn Squash, '94 268
Soup, Creamy Acorn-Butternut, '96 216
Baby Squash, '93 118
Basil Butter, Squash and Cherry Tomatoes in, '98 328

Butternut. *See also* SQUASH/Stuffed.
Bake, Butternut-Orange, '86 295
Baked Butternut Squash, '85 205
Bake, Squash and Apple, '79 210
Bisque, Squash, '84 280
Bread, Butternut-Raisin, '79 25
Bread, Squash, '79 210
Casserole, Butternut, '83 280
Casserole, Butternut Squash, '79 210; '96 216
Casserole, Squash and Apple, '79 209
Casserole, Sweet Butternut, '83 256
Pie, Butternut Squash, '80 40; '87 212
Pie, Butternut Squash Chiffon, '83 296; '84 285
Pie, Spicy Butternut Squash, '80 296
Pie, Spicy Squash, '85 9
Pudding, Butternut Squash, '89 M313; '90 M19
Pudding, Squash, '82 277; '83 15
Puff, Butternut Squash, '85 205
Ring, Butternut Squash, '81 M232
Sauté, Savory Butternut, '85 205
Skillet Butternut and Bacon, '85 9
Soufflé, Butternut, '83 266
Soufflé, Butternut Squash, '97 270
Soup, Butternut Squash, '95 62
Soup, Creamed Butternut-and-Apple, '88 228
Soup, Creamy Acorn-Butternut, '96 216
Soup, Creamy Butternut, '96 216
Soup with Parslied Croutons, Carrot-and-Butternut Squash, '97 217
Stir-Fry, Honey-Butternut, '93 184
Sunshine Squash, '85 205
Whipped Butternut Squash, '94 302
Whipped Squash, Tasty, '82 277; '83 15
Cajun Squash, '88 142
Calabacitas, '95 130
Casserole, Calico Squash, '90 290
Casserole, Squash, '87 163; '89 159; '90 161; '92 342
Casserole, Two-Squash, '79 101
Chile Squash, '84 77
con Crema, Squash, '89 148
Delight, Squash, '90 236
Dilled Summer Squash, '96 148
Dressing, Squash, '95 290
Dressing, Turkey with Squash, '87 248

Greek-Style Squash, '92 26
Greek-Style Squashes, '96 88
Hubbard Squash, Tart, '80 214
Kabobs, Summery Squash-and-Pepper, '95 193
Marinated Squash Medley, '94 126
Medley, Carrot-Lima-Squash, '80 123
Medley, Fresh Squash, '81 M165
Medley, Sautéed Vegetable, '83 101
Medley, Squash, '81 139; '84 128
Mirliton Balls, '90 217
Muffins, Squash, '91 69
Oregano, Summer Squash, '97 165
"Pasta," Garden-Fresh, '94 M134
Pattypan-Zucchini Skillet, '82 103
Pickles, Squash, '87 150; '99 170
Pie, Mock Coconut, '86 200
Pie, Scallopini, '94 133
Puff, Golden Squash, '82 288
Relish, Pollock with Summer Squash, '92 200
Rosemary, Summer Squash with, '88 143
Sandwiches, Skillet Squash, '98 144
Sauté, Squash, '82 67
Scallop, Green-and-Gold, '81 159
Skillet Squash, '82 195
Soup, Dilled Summer, '99 182
Spaghetti Squash, '92 340
Spaghetti Squash and Chicken Skillet Casserole, '94 134
Spaghetti Squash, Asian, '94 268
Spaghetti Squash Lasagna, '84 127
Spaghetti Squash Pie, '80 186
Spaghetti Squash Salad, '99 M322
Spaghetti Squash Salad, Marinated, '94 134
Spaghetti Squash Sauté, '98 212
Spaghetti Squash, Sautéed Vegetables with, '84 128
Spaghetti Squash with Meat Sauce, '88 M180
Spaghetti Squash with Sesame Eggplant, '92 252
Stir-Fried Squash Medley, '80 123
Stir-Fry, Squash, '80 184
Stir-Fry, Two-Squash, '86 174

Stuffed
Acorn Squash, Apple-Stuffed, '83 296; '84 285
Acorn Squash, Baked, '81 24
Acorn Squash, Cranberry-Filled, '81 M231
Acorn Squash, Custard-Filled, '86 334
Acorn Squash, Deluxe, '80 215
Acorn Squash, Fruited, '85 235; '90 228
Acorn Squash, Fruit-Stuffed, '81 295
Acorn Squash, Ham-Stuffed, '81 239; '83 66
Acorn Squash-Mushroom Puree, '93 305
Acorn Squash, Pineapple-Stuffed, '84 255
Acorn Squash, Sausage-Stuffed, '81 M231; '83 296; '84 285
Acorn Squash, Stuffed, '82 277; '83 15
Acorn Squash with Molasses and Pecans, '85 205
Acorn Squash with Nutmeg, '85 267
Acorn Squash with Sausage, '85 9
Acorn Squash with Spiced Cranberry Sauce, Gingered, '96 267
Apple-and-Pecan-Filled Squash, '88 228
Apple-Stuffed Squash, '85 206
Baked Squash, Stuffed, '85 206
Beef-Stuffed Squash, '83 134
Butternut Squash, Apple-Stuffed, '81 232
Chayote, Stuffed, '92 247
Cheesy Stuffed Squash, '82 134
Crumb-Stuffed Squash, '89 148
Green Chiles, Stuffed Squash with, '83 148
Harvest Squash, '80 214
Maple-Flavored Stuffed Squash, '85 205
Mexican, Stuffed Squash, '90 200
Mirlitons, Stuffed, '90 217; '93 278

Parmesan-Stuffed Squash Boats, '79 156
Pattypan Squash, Stuffed, '82 103; '85 136; '88 142
Plantation Squash, '79 225
Sausage-Stuffed Squash, '81 183
Spinach Pesto, Squash Stuffed with, '89 M133
Spinach-Stuffed Squash, '82 4; '91 14; '97 119
Stuffed Squash, '98 177
Turban Chicken Curry, '94 266
Turban Squash, Sausage-Stuffed, '80 214
Turban Squash, Stuffed Turks, '88 228
Vegetable-Stuffed Squash, '84 104
White Squash, Stuffed, '90 M201
Yellow Squash, Garden-Stuffed, '84 106
Yellow Squash, Italian Stuffed, '86 111
Yellow Squash, Mushroom-Stuffed, '84 154
Yellow Squash, Shrimp-Stuffed, '84 194
Yellow Squash with Cheese Sauce, Stuffed, '80 162
Summer Squash, Southern, '98 207
Tart, Squash, '96 83
Tomatoes, Squash-Stuffed, '82 102
Tomato Squash, '86 111
Toss, Pepperoni-Squash, '84 127
Turban Squash, Glazed, '81 24

Yellow. *See also* SQUASH/Stuffed.
à l'Orange, Squash, '85 230
Amarillo Squash, '99 M218
Bacon-Flavored Squash, '82 158
Bake, Cheddar-Squash, '84 M113, 128
Bake, Cheesy Squash, '80 183
Bake, Squash and Tomato, '95 180
Beans, and Tomatoes, Squash, '83 148
Bisque, Squash, '98 290
Bread, Spicy Squash, '83 121
Bread, Yellow Squash, '84 140
Buttered Summer Squash, '81 84
Cake, Squash, '86 200
Casserole, Baked Squash, '83 149
Casserole, Blender Squash, '81 212
Casserole, Cheesy Squash, '79 123; '82 M21
Casserole, Chicken-Squash, '95 121
Casserole, Company Squash, '81 183
Casserole, Creamy Rice and Squash, '95 26
Casserole, Crunchy Squash, '84 293
Casserole, Fresh Squash, '82 204
Casserole, Hearty Tex-Mex Squash-Chicken, '99 312
Casserole, Jiffy Squash, '81 M144
Casserole, Squash, '96 244, 252; '97 29
Casserole, Squash and Egg, '80 146
Casserole, Squash-Carrot, '81 157
Casserole, Summer Squash, '81 102, 184
Casserole, Yellow Squash, '79 179; '85 135; '88 166
Casserole, Zippy Squash, '80 183
Country Club Squash, '79 158; '88 M16
Croquettes, Squash, '79 157; '83 148; '88 142; '97 118
Dip, Yellow Squash-Zucchini, '89 48
Dressing, Squash, '83 315; '86 280
Fiesta Squash, '82 102
Fried Yellow Squash, '86 211
Fritters, Squash, '89 68; '99 203
Fritters, Squash-Jalapeño, '98 249
Greek-Style Squash, '91 285
Grilled Squash and Onion, '79 150
Grilled Squash Fans, '97 118
Grilled Summer Squash and Tomatoes, '99 144
Grilled Vegetables, '84 172
Marinated Cucumbers and Squash, '86 146
Medley, Summer Garden, '84 158
Mexican Squash, '82 103

SQUASH, Yellow
(continued)

Muffins, Yellow Squash, '81 163
Nicholas, Squash, '94 236
Nosh, Squash, '90 147
Pats, Squash, '80 298; '81 25
Patties, Squash, '79 158
Patties, Summer Squash, '81 184
Pickled Yellow Squash, '93 136
Pickles, Squash, '81 174; '97 119
Posh Squash, '81 159
Puffs, Yellow Squash, '82 103
Puppies, Squash, '83 170
Quiche, Squash-and-Green Chile, '88 143
Rings, Asparagus in Squash, '87 68
Savory Squash, '99 111
Skillet Squash, '92 62
Skillet Summer Squash, '82 96
Soufflé, Cheesy Squash, '82 146
Soufflé, Squash, '95 215
Soufflé, Yellow Squash, '89 89
Soup, Chilled Squash, '92 173
Soup, Cold Cream of Squash, '81 130
Soup, Cream of Squash, '81 246
Soup, Perky Squash, '85 20
Soup, Squash, '94 134
Soup, Summer Squash, '83 99; '85 136
South-of-the-Border Squash, '89 148; '96 178
Stir-Fried Squash, '97 118
Stir-Fried Squash Medley, '80 123
Summer Squash, '80 127; '85 105
Toss, Asparagus-Carrot-Squash, '91 45
Toss, Crisp Squash-and-Pepper, '87 M152
Toss, Simple Squash, '85 M142
Vegetable-Herb Trio, '83 172

STEWS. *See also* **CHILI, CHOWDERS, GUMBOS, JAMBALAYAS, RAGOÛTS, SOUPS.**
Bean Pot, White, '86 194
Beef-and-Celery Root Stew, '98 292
Beef-and-Onion Stew, '87 18
Beef and Vegetable Stew, Sweet-and-Sour, '85 87
Beef Stew, '86 51; '90 230; '96 16
Beef Stew, Burgundy, '88 234
Beef Stew, Company, '83 85; '97 198
Beef Stew, Oven, '79 222; '80 64
Beef Stew, Quick, '86 302; '92 71
Beef Stew, Spicy, '86 228
Beef Stew with Dumplings, '84 3
Beef Stew with Parsley Dumplings, '81 76; '82 13; '85 M246
Brown Stew, '85 239
Brunswick
Aunt Willette's Brunswick Stew, '85 320
Bama Brunswick Stew, '87 4
Blakely Brunswick Stew, '87 4
Breeden Liles's Brunswick Stew, '91 14
Brunswick Stew, '80 264; '97 138, 315
Chicken Brunswick Stew, '97 234
Chicken Stew, Brunswick, '87 4
Dan Dickerson's Brunswick Stew, '91 16
Easy Brunswick Stew, '92 280; '99 235
Family-Size Brunswick Stew, Van Doyle's, '91 14
Favorite Brunswick Stew, Virginia Ramsey's, '91 16
Gay Neale's Brunswick Stew, '91 17
Georgian Brunswick Stew, '92 35
Jeff Daniel's Brunswick Stew, '91 16
Sonny Frye's Brunswick Stew, '87 4
Virginian Brunswick Stew, '92 34

Burgoo, Five-Meat, '87 3
Burgoo, Harry Young's, '87 3
Burgoo, Kentucky, '88 235; '97 138
Burgoo, Old-Fashioned, '87 3
Burgundy Stew with Drop Dumplings, '83 125
Caldo de Rez (Mexican Beef Stew), '89 276
Catfish Stew, Cajun-Style, '88 12
Chicken, Kale, and Chickpea Stew, '98 47
Chicken Stew, '97 26
Chicken Stew and Dumplings, '84 4
Chicken Stew, Chili-, '90 319
Chicken Stew, Santa Fe, '97 193
Chili Stew, Red, '95 226
Emerald Isle Stew, '95 71
Étouffée, Okra, '98 207
Étouffée, Roasted Quail, '96 34
Fish-and-Vegetable Stew, '87 220
Fisherman's Stew, '81 98
Fricassee, White Chicken, '98 122
Frogmore Stew, '92 236
Game Pot Pie with Parmesan Crust, '94 304
Ham-and-Black-Eyed Pea Stew, '93 20
Hamburger Oven Stew, '84 4
Hungarian Stew with Noodles, '80 263
Hunter's Stew, '85 270
Irish Stew, '90 64
Lamb-and-Okra Stew, '97 156
Lamb Stew, '79 293; '88 58
Lamb Stew-in-a-Loaf, '85 37
Lamb Stew with Popovers, '94 43
Lentil-Rice Stew, '82 232
Meatball Stew, '79 198; '98 30
Mexican Stew, '82 231
Mexican Stew Olé, '86 296
Minestrone Stew, '93 184
Okra Stew, Old-Fashioned, '84 158
Okra Stew, Quick, '97 88
Oyster-Broccoli Stew, '89 242
Oyster-Sausage Stew, '89 242
Oyster Stew, '80 221
Oyster Stew, Company, '80 297
Oyster Stew, Golden, '86 132
Oyster Stew, Holiday, '85 264
Pancho Villa Stew, '94 44
Pollo en Pipián, Mexican, '88 31
Pork Stew, Baja, '98 283
Potato-Oyster Stew, '89 243
Reggae Rundown, '96 71
Rib-Tickling Stew, Campeche Bay, '89 317
Sausage Stew, Smoked, '82 231
Seafood Stew, '84 280
Shrimp Creole, '93 282; '96 210
Shrimp Creole, Spicy, '79 181
Shrimp Creole, Wild Rice-and-, '84 292
Shrimp Stew, '83 4
Shrimp Stew and Grits, '80 118
Shrimp Stew over Grits, '88 126; '89 47
Strader Stew, '89 28
Succotash with Serrano Chile Polenta, Ancho Chile, '98 104
Texas Stew, '97 211
Turkey Stew, Hearty, '79 252
Turkey-Tomato Stew, '90 279
Tzimmes with Brisket, Mixed Fruit, '93 114
Vegetable-Beef Stew, '94 323
Vegetable-Beef Stew, Shortcut, '89 218
Vegetable Stew, Mixed, '84 13
Vegetable Tagine, '96 289
Venison Sausage Stew, '87 238
Venison Stew, '86 294
Venison Stew with Potato Dumplings, '87 304
White Wine Stew, '82 228

STIR-FRY. *See* **WOK COOKING.**
STRAWBERRIES
Almond Cream Dip with Strawberries, '92 164
Arnaud, Strawberries, '93 50
Banana-Berry Flip, '88 215; '89 20
Bars, Strawberry, '81 301
Bavarian, Raspberry-Strawberry, '89 15
Bavarian, Rhubarb-Strawberry, '86 140
Beets, Strawberry-Glazed, '83 234
Best-Dressed Berries, '96 317
Beverages
Brandied Orange Juice, Strawberries with, '82 160
Calypso, Coco-Berry, '89 171
Coolers, Strawberry, '92 67
Cooler, Strawberry, '83 56; '84 51
Cooler, Strawberry-Mint, '84 57
Cooler, Watermelon-Strawberry, '98 178
Cubes, Berry-Good, '95 201
Daiquiris, Creamy Strawberry, '91 66
Daiquiris, Strawberry, '90 125; '98 99
Daiquiri, Strawberry, '81 156
Float, Strawberry-Banana, '87 160
Frost, Banana-Strawberry, '87 199
Frozen Strawberry Refresher, '93 213
Ice Mold, Strawberry, '91 278
Ice Ring, Strawberry, '94 176
Lemonade, Berry Delicious, '93 205
Lemonade, Strawberry, '80 160
Milkshake, Fresh Strawberry, '82 113
Milk Shake, Strawberry, '94 113
Mimosa, Sparkling Strawberry, '88 169
Pineapple-Strawberry Slush, '94 227
Punch, Berry, '92 67
Punch, Berry-Colada, '96 277
Punch, Champagne, '98 310
Punch, Creamy Strawberry, '86 195
Punch, Strawberry, '90 273
Punch, Strawberry Champagne, '90 315
Punch, Strawberry-Lemonade, '85 116; '91 175
Sangría, Teaberry, '87 147
Shake, Strawberry, '97 172
Shake, Strawberry-Banana, '89 35; '97 172
Shake, Strawberry-Cheesecake, '92 44
Shake, Strawberry-Orange Breakfast, '87 186
Shake, Strawberry-Pear, '92 139
Shake, Strawberry-Pineapple, '84 166
Shake, Strawberry-Yogurt, '87 199
Shrub, Berry, '95 29
Slurp, Strawberry, '81 96
Slush, Strawberry, '98 178
Slush, Strawberry-Orange, '83 172
Smoothie, Four-Berry, '97 173
Smoothie, Strawberry, '86 183; '97 173
Smoothie, Strawberry-Banana, '81 59
Smoothie, Strawberry-Peach, '89 182
Smoothie, Tropical, '81 50
Soda, Old-Fashioned Strawberry, '79 149
Soda, Strawberry, '84 115
Sparkler, Strawberry, '99 49
Spritzer, Strawberry, '90 14; '97 272
Syrup, Berry, '96 161
Tea, Berry-Mint Iced, '98 332
Tea, Sparkling Strawberry, '94 131
Tea, Strawberry, '88 248
Bordeaux, Beauberries, '98 18
Bread, Strawberry, '81 250; '83 140; '84 49
Bread, Strawberry Jam, '79 216
Bread, Strawberry-Nut, '79 24
Butter, Strawberry, '79 36; '81 286; '91 71; '99 44, 234
Cake, Chocolate-Strawberry Basket, '98 100
Cake Roll, Strawberries 'n Cream Sponge, '81 95

Cake Roll, Strawberry, '79 49; '83 129; '84 305; '85 172
Cake, Strawberry Cream, '86 61
Cake, Strawberry Crunch, '79 288; '80 35
Cake, Strawberry Delight, '85 30
Cake, Strawberry Meringue, '86 240
Cake, Strawberry-Studded White Chocolate Mousse, '99 154
Cake, Strawberry Yogurt Layer, '94 85
Cake with Strawberries and Chocolate Glaze, White, '87 76
Carousel, Strawberry, '91 247
Cheesecake, Almost Strawberry, '86 32
Cheesecake, Pear-Berry, '82 M141
Cherry-Berry on a Cloud, '79 94
Chocolate Combo, Strawberry-, '85 96
Chocolate-Dipped Strawberries, '98 M100
Christmas Strawberries, '87 293; '94 331
Citrus Twist, Berry-, '95 100
Cobbler, Fresh Strawberry, '96 84
Cobbler, Rosy Strawberry-Rhubarb, '79 154
Cobbler, Strawberry-Rhubarb, '88 93
Coffee Cake, Strawberry, '85 46
Compote, Peach-Berry, '89 112
Cookie Tarts, Strawberry, '89 112
Cream, Chocolate Baskets with Berry, '92 118
Cream Dip, Fresh Strawberries with, '90 86
Cream in Vanilla Lace Cups, Strawberry, '98 93
Cream Puffs, Strawberry, '81 95
Cream Puffs, Strawberry-Lemon, '87 75
Cream, Strawberries and, '82 100; '92 132
Cream, Strawberries in, '89 88
Cream, Strawberries 'n', '90 30
Cream, Strawberries 'n Lemon, '85 120
Cream, Strawberries with Chocolate, '85 81
Cream, Strawberries with French, '83 191
Cream, Strawberries with Strawberry, '84 108
Cream, Strawberry, '88 153
Cream with Fresh Strawberries, Almond, '87 93
Crêpes, Nutritious Brunch, '80 44
Crêpes, Strawberry Dessert, '83 122
Crisp, Strawberry-Rhubarb, '95 119
Croissants, Strawberry or Apricot, '96 303
Deep-Fried Strawberries, '84 109
Delight, Frozen Strawberry, '82 112, 174
Delight, Strawberry, '81 85
Delight, Strawberry Cheese, '79 50
Delight, Strawberry Yogurt, '85 77
Dessert, Chilled Strawberry, '84 164
Dessert, Glazed Strawberry, '84 33
Dessert, Honeydew-Berry, '83 120
Dessert, Strawberry, '83 123
Dessert, Strawberry-Cream Cheese, '83 123
Dessert, Strawberry-Lemon, '86 162
Dessert, Strawberry-Yogurt, '90 295
Dessert, Summer Strawberry, '92 143
Dessert, Sweet-and-Sour Strawberry, '92 54
Dipped Strawberries, '94 17
Divinity, Strawberry, '91 272
Dressing, Creamy Strawberry, '84 161
French Toast Sandwiches, Strawberry-, '91 160
Frosting, Strawberry, '89 184
Frost, Strawberry, '81 279; '82 24; '83 154
Frozen Strawberry Cups, '91 173
Fudge Balls, Strawberry, '93 80
Gazpacho, Berry, '97 181
Glaze, Strawberry, '80 35; '83 142
Ham, Strawberry-Glazed, '91 84
Ice Cream Crêpes, Strawberry, '87 290; '88 135
Ice Cream, Fresh Strawberry, '89 111
Ice Cream, Homemade Strawberry, '84 184
Ice Cream, Old-Fashioned Strawberry, '79 94
Ice Cream Roll, Strawberry, '84 105
Ice Cream, Straw-Ba-Nut, '80 177

Ice Cream, Strawberry, '80 177; '98 221
Ice Cream, Strawberry-Banana-Nut, '88 203
Ice Cream Torte, Chocolate-Strawberry, '79 7
Ice Cream, Very Strawberry, '81 155
Ice Milk, Fresh Strawberry, '92 94
Ice, Strawberry, '84 175; '85 108
Ice, Strawberry-Orange, '86 196
Jamaica, Strawberries, '85 161; '93 239
Jam, Christmas, '88 288
Jam, Strawberry, '89 138
Jam, Strawberry Freezer, '84 M182
Jellyroll, Easy, '82 176
Jelly, Strawberry, '81 147
Juliet, Strawberries, '84 82
Lemon Cream, Strawberries with, '90 170
Marmalade, Strawberry-Pineapple, '85 130
Marsala, Strawberries, '88 171
Melon, Berry-Filled, '86 93
Meringues, Strawberry, '84 188
Mousse, Fresh Strawberry, '82 72
Mousse, Strawberry, '81 95
Mousse, Strawberry-Lemon, '82 128
Muffins, Strawberry, '99 234
Napoleons, Strawberry, '81 126
Nests, Strawberry Coconut, '88 136
Omelet, Strawberry-Sour Cream, '89 229
Pancakes, Strawberry, '84 219
Parfait, Crunchy Strawberry-Yogurt, '79 124
Parfaits, Frosty Strawberry, '85 213
Parfaits, Strawberry-Lemon, '84 198
Parfait, Strawberry, '79 99
Parfait, Surprise Strawberry, '86 151
Pie, Bumbleberry, '97 163
Pie, Chilled Strawberry, '82 112
Pie, Glazed Strawberry, '82 M142
Pie, Heavenly Chocolate-Berry, '85 102
Pie, Lemon-Strawberry, '88 127
Pie, Red, White, and Blueberry, '98 162
Pie, Strawberry Angel, '88 136
Pie, Strawberry-Banana Glazed, '81 181
Pie, Strawberry-Chocolate Truffle, '89 112
Pie, Strawberry-Glaze, '81 141
Pie, Strawberry-Rhubarb, '98 99
Pie, Strawberry Yogurt, '80 232
Pie, Strawberry-Yogurt, '85 122; '86 124
Pizza, Kiwi-Berry, '86 198; '87 55
Pizza, Strawberry, '79 94
Popsicles, Smoothie Strawberry, '82 112
Pops, Strawberry-Cinnamon, '99 132
Pound Cake with Mint Berries and Cream, Lemon, '99 183
Preserves Deluxe, Strawberry, '82 150
Preserves, Freezer Strawberry, '82 112
Preserves, Quick Strawberry-Fig, '96 194
Preserves, Strawberry, '79 120; '81 96
Pudding, Summer, '98 217
Puff, Strawberry, '82 5
Raspberry Custard Sauce, Fresh Berries with, '88 163
Ring, Strawberry-Cheese, '86 14
Rock Cream with Strawberries, Old-Fashioned, '90 125
Roll, Heavenly Strawberry, '82 176
Roll, Strawberry, '82 120
Romanoff, Strawberries, '84 108; '88 95; '91 126; '94 68
Romanoff, Strawberry-Almond, '98 99
Ruby Strawberries, '82 100
Sabayon, Strawberries, '79 94
Salad, Chicken-Spinach-Strawberry, '97 92
Salad, Frozen Strawberry, '94 119
Salad, Hidden Treasure Strawberry, '79 11
Salad, Mimosa, '98 310
Salad Mold, Strawberry-Wine, '83 261

Salad, Strawberry-Nut, '94 132
Salad, Strawberry-Spinach, '91 169; '93 168
Salad, Strawberry Yogurt, '80 232
Salad with Orange-Curd Dressing, Orange-Strawberry, '93 22
Sauces
    Amaretto-Strawberry Sauce, '87 M165
    Arnaud Sauce, Strawberries, '93 50
    Banana Sauce, Strawberry-, '81 41
    Berry Sauce, '87 290; '88 135; '95 103
    Brandied Strawberry Sauce, '88 196
    Butter Sauce, Strawberry-, '96 87
    Crunchy Topping, Strawberry Sauce with, '81 170
    Dumplings, Strawberry Sauce with, '84 314
    Fresh Strawberry Sauce, '82 177
    Melon Wedges with Berry Sauce, '86 178
    Mimosa Sauce, Berry, '90 315
    Old-Fashioned Strawberry Sauce, '94 130
    Orange Sauce, Strawberry-, '96 95
    Peaches with Strawberry Sauce, '85 8
    Peach Sauce, Strawberry-, '92 154
    Strawberry Sauce, '84 144; '87 93, 198; '92 85; '94 121
Sherbet, Strawberry, '82 112, 160
Shortcake, A Favorite Strawberry, '88 136
Shortcake, Chocolate-Strawberry, '89 216
Shortcake, Elegant Strawberry, '88 37
Shortcake Jubilee, Strawberry, '88 209
Shortcake, Orange-Strawberry, '95 100
Shortcake Shells, Strawberry, '88 196
Shortcake Squares, Strawberry, '86 124
Shortcakes, Strawberry Crispy, '93 42
Shortcake, Strawberry, '81 96; '83 122; '92 184; '94 162
Shortcake, Strawberry Pinwheel, '89 112
Shortcakes with Mint Cream, Strawberry, '97 144
Skewered Pineapple and Strawberries, '84 251
Sorbet, Strawberry, '88 117; '93 153
Sorbet, Strawberry-Champagne, '83 162; '95 20
Sorbet, Strawberry Margarita, '89 111
Sorbet, Strawberry-Passion Fruit, '98 180
Sorbet, Very Berry, '90 85
Soup, Cold Strawberry, '82 157
Soup, Sherry-Berry Dessert, '91 180
Soup, Strawberry, '88 160
Soup, Strawberry-Banana, '86 181
Soup Supreme, Strawberry, '81 M144
Spiked Strawberries, '97 58
Spread, Light Strawberry, '85 55
Spread, Strawberry, '95 79
Spumoni and Berries, '91 204
Squares, Strawberry Shortcake, '85 122
Stuffed Strawberries, '98 155
Stuffed Strawberries with Walnuts, '85 122; '86 124
Sundaes, Hot Strawberry, '81 M5
Supreme, Banana-Berry, '81 205
Swirl, Strawberry, '84 108
Tartlets, Fresh Berry, '91 98
Tarts, Berry Good Lemon, '91 119
Tarts, Strawberry, '80 70
Tart, Strawberry, '84 138; '89 272
Tart, Strawberry Dream, '92 118
Tart, Strawberry-Lemon, '89 111
Tea Cakes and Fresh Strawberries, Telia's, '98 110
Topping, Pound Cake with Strawberry-Banana, '89 200
Topping, Strawberry, '86 32; '90 142
Topping, Strawberry-Banana, '87 125
Torte, Spring, '91 57
Torte, Strawberry Meringue, '88 136

STRAWBERRIES
(continued)

Treasure, Berried, '89 124
Trifle, Easy Strawberry, '88 201
Whip, Strawberry, '89 198
White Chocolate, Strawberries Dipped in, '90 83
Zabaglione, Strawberries, '81 95

STROGANOFF
Beef Burgundy Stroganoff, '85 31
Beef Stroganoff, '79 163; '81 179; '91 134; '93 18
Beef Stroganoff, Light, '86 36
Beef Stroganoff, Quick, '92 20; '99 327
Casserole, Stroganoff, '98 48
Chicken Livers Stroganoff, '80 200; '81 57
Chicken Livers Supreme, '81 298
Chicken Stroganoff, '99 41
Crab Stroganoff, '79 116
Crawfish Stroganoff, '91 89
Ground Beef Stroganoff, '84 71
Hamburger Stroganoff, '82 108, 110
Hamburger Stroganoff, Easy, '79 208
Ham Stroganoff, '82 40
Ham Stroganoff on Cheesy Onion Biscuits, '95 98
Liver Stroganoff, '79 54
Meatballs, European Veal, '85 30
Meatballs Paprikash with Rice, '85 31
Meatball Stroganoff, '81 297
Mushroom-Meatball Stroganoff, '85 85
Mushroom Stroganoff, '81 298
Quail Stroganoff, '99 41
Quickie Stroganoff, '81 200
Shrimp Stroganoff, '79 81
Shrimp Stroganoff, Oven-Baked, '81 297
Sirloin Stroganoff, '81 297
Steak Stroganoff Sandwiches, '85 110
Steak Stroganoff with Parslied Noodles, '85 31
Tofu, Stroganoff, '84 202
Turkey Stroganoff, '91 61
Veal Stroganoff, '79 108

STUFFINGS. *See also* DRESSINGS.
Apple-Crumb Stuffing, '81 234; '82 26; '83 39
Apple-Walnut Stuffing, '95 289
Barley-Mushroom Stuffing, Cornish Hens with, '97 242
Cornbread-Apple Stuffing, Pork Chops with, '99 14
Cornbread Stuffing, '94 305
Crabmeat Stuffing, '94 68
Crabmeat Stuffing, Chicken Breasts with, '85 302
Crab Stuffing, Tropical Orange Roughy with, '99 122
Cranberry-Pecan Stuffing, '96 309
Cranberry-Sausage Stuffing, Crown Roast of Pork with, '88 49
Fruited Stuffing, Cornish Hens with, '90 191
Fruited Stuffing Mix, '89 331
Fruit Stuffing and Shiitake Sauce, Pork Tenderloin with, '97 218
Grits Stuffing, '96 270
Low-Sodium Stuffing, '82 66
Mushroom Stuffing, Grilled Rainbow Trout with, '97 162
Oyster Stuffing, Roast Turkey with, '80 251
Pecan-Sausage Stuffing, Chicken Breasts with, '94 212
Pecan Stuffing, '79 292; '80 32
Pecan Stuffing, Wild Duck with, '85 269
Rice-and-Onion Stuffing, '88 246
Rice Stuffing, '95 290
Sausage-and-Wild Mushroom Stuffing, '96 267

Sausage Stuffing, '99 293
Tangerine Stuffing, '90 16
Walnut-Rice Stuffing, Tomatoes with, '91 102
Wild Rice Stuffing, Cornish Hens with, '79 222; '80 64; '82 136

SWEET-AND-SOUR
Beets, Sweet-and-Sour, '81 167; '82 22; '89 314
Black-Eyed Peas, Sweet-and-Sour, '85 290
Burgers, Sweet-and-Sour, '90 128
Cabbage, Sweet-and-Sour, '86 295; '87 189
Cabbage, Sweet-Sour Red, '79 5
Carrots, Sweet-and-Sour, '82 137
Chicken Nuggets, Sweet-and-Sour, '90 168
Chicken Stir-Fry, Sweet-and-Sour, '98 204
Chicken, Sweet-and-Sour, '79 106; '86 217, 240; '90 161; '91 202; '97 325
Chicken, Sweet-and-Sour Lemon, '84 93
Chicken Wings, Sweet-and-Sour, '90 206; '96 110
Dessert, Sweet-and-Sour Strawberry, '92 54
Dressing, Sweet-and-Sour, '80 247; '84 70, 161; '85 163; '87 305; '89 62; '91 126; '94 281
Dressing, Sweet-and-Sour Fruit, '84 125
Dressing, Sweet-Sour, '80 246
Fish, Sweet-and-Sour, '80 M54
Green Beans and Carrots, Sweet-and-Sour, '83 6
Green Beans, Sweet-and-Sour, '79 184; '81 158; '82 90; '91 250
Ham, Sweet-and-Sour Glazed, '88 M15
Ham, Sweet-Sour Glazed, '83 311
Kale, Sweet-and-Sour, '80 298
Kielbasa, Sweet-and-Sour, '89 327
Liver, Sweet-and-Sour, '81 277
Marinade, Sweet-and-Sour, '86 113; '87 115
Meatballs, Sweet-and-Sour, '82 233, 247; '86 240; '99 325
Meatballs, Sweet-and-Sour Party, '79 233
Onions, Sweet-and-Sour Baked, '90 34
Pearl Onions, Sweet-and-Sour, '96 216
Peas, Sweet-and-Sour, '88 3
Pork Chops, Sweet-and-Sour, '83 160
Pork, Pineapple Sweet-and-Sour, '82 120
Pork, Sweet-and-Sour, '79 42; '80 72, 227; '81 26, 104, 111; '82 12; '84 218; '85 34, 194; '86 241; '90 317; '92 219
Potatoes, Sweet-and-Sour-Topped, '83 4
Pot Roast, Sweet-and-Sour, '83 8; '99 291
Riblets, Sweet-and-Sour, '85 276
Ribs, Sweet-and-Sour, '89 M84
Ribs, Sweet-and-Sour Grilled, '98 331

Salads
Asparagus, Sweet-and-Sour, '89 159
Bean Salad, Sweet-and-Sour, '85 198; '86 147
Beans, Sweet-and-Sour, '87 197
Beans with Sprouts, Sweet-and-Sour, '86 32
Carrot Salad, Sweet-and-Sour, '98 211
Cauliflower Salad, Sweet-and-Sour, '81 2
Fruit Salad, Sweet-and-Sour, '80 13; '84 125
Green Salad, Sweet-and-Sour, '94 281
Macaroni Salad, Sweet-and-Sour, '85 166
Potato Salad, Sweet and Sour, '80 152
Potato Salad, Sweet-and-Sour, '92 106
Slaw, Confetti Sweet-and-Sour, '98 89
Slaw, Sweet-and-Sour, '81 237
Slaw, Sweet-and-Sour Hot, '92 63
Spinach Salad, Sweet-and-Sour, '85 M112
Vegetable Salad, Sweet-and-Sour, '81 25
Sauce, Pork Chops with Sweet-and-Sour Apple, '98 132
Sauce, Sausage Rolls with Sweet-and-Sour, '83 74
Sauce, Sweet-and-Sour, '80 20; '85 12, 34; '86 240
Sauce, Sweet-and-Sour Pineapple, '85 66
Sausage, Sweet-and-Sour, '88 296

Shrimp and Chicken, Sweet-and-Sour, '87 267; '88 103; '89 66
Shrimp, Grilled Sweet-and-Sour, '97 100
Shrimp, Sweet-and-Sour, '83 278; '90 M112
Shrimp Tails, Sweet-and-Sour Rock, '80 3
Snap Beans, Sweet-and-Sour, '89 173
Soup, Sweet-and-Sour Cabbage, '89 314
Spareribs, Sweet-and-Sour, '83 21
Spread, Sweet 'n' Sour, '86 184
Steaks, Sweet-and-Sour Marinated, '83 110
Stew, Sweet-and-Sour Beef and Vegetable, '85 87
Turkey, Sweet-and-Sour, '79 252
Turnips, Sweet-and-Sour, '81 274
Vegetables, Sweet-and-Sour Marinated, '83 266
Vinaigrette, Sweet-and-Sour Balsamic, '97 146

SWEET POTATOES
Apple Shells, Sweet Potatoes in, '85 206
Apples, Sweet Potato-Stuffed, '97 216
Apple-Stuffed Sweet Potatoes, '88 207
Apricot Glaze, Sweet Potatoes with, '89 331
Bake, Southern Sweet Potato, '85 229
Bake, Sweet Potato-Apricot, '85 206
Balls, Sweet Potato, '86 312
Boats, Sweet Potato, '80 287
Brandied Sweet Potatoes, '97 248
Breads
Biscuits, Sweet Potato, '80 287; '84 140; '89 210; '98 222
Biscuits, Sweet Potato Angel, '93 312
Muffins, Sweet Potato, '81 224; '85 6; '87 280; '92 31
Muffins, Yam, '79 7
Rolls, Golden Yams, '86 299
Rolls, Sweet Potato, '93 172; '97 107
Broiled Sweet Potatoes, Coconut-, '84 231
Butter, Sweet Potato, '95 M290
Candied Sweet Potatoes, '79 9, 251; '86 111; '88 207; '97 312
Candied Sweet Potatoes, Nannie's, '95 306
Casseroles
Apple Bake, Sweet Potato-, '83 25; '86 282
Apple Casserole, Sweet Potato-and-, '94 280
Apple Casserole, Sweet Potatoes-and-, '90 228
Applesauce Sweet Potatoes, '91 292; '92 256
Apples, Sweet Potatoes and, '97 249
Apricot Sweet Potatoes, '82 228
Bake, Sweet Potato, '80 287
Banana Casserole, Sweet Potato-, '86 276
Berries Casserole, Sweet Potatoes-and-, '84 231
Bourbon Sweet Potatoes, '86 324; '87 280
Candied Sweet Potatoes, '88 207
Coconut-Orange Sweet Potatoes, '84 252
Delight, Sweet Potato, '86 335; '87 83
Eggnog Casserole, Sweet Potato-, '95 291
Festive Sweet Potatoes, '80 244
Glazed Sweet Potato Casserole, '90 250
Glazed Sweet Potatoes, Tropical, '83 226
Holiday Sweet Potato Bake, '90 291
Mashed Sweet Potatoes, '98 269
Orange Bake, Sweet Potato-, '83 226
Peaches, Sweet Potatoes and, '86 11
Pear-Sweet Potato Casserole, '86 280
Pineapple-Orange Sweet Potatoes, '96 46
Pones, Sweet Potato, '96 270
Praline-Topped Sweet Potatoes, '98 96
Puree, Carrot-and-Sweet Potato, '94 56
Royale, Sweet Potatoes, '91 250
Rum Casserole, Sweet Potato-, '84 231
Scallop, Yam-and-Apple, '91 199
Sherry and Walnuts, Sweet Potatoes with, '86 286

Surprise, Holiday Sweet Potato, '84 254
Surprise, Sweet Potato, '81 267; '97 139
Sweet Potato Casserole, '79 289; '80 26;
  '85 256; '89 279
Yams, Cornwallis, '79 276
Chips, Boniato, '92 247
Chips, Sweet Potato, '91 138; '93 332; '95 M203;
  '97 63
Chips with Blue Cheese, Sweet Potato, '93 290
Chowder, Asian Sweet Potato, '97 213
Chutney, Sweet Potato, '99 45
Cinnamon-Apple Sweet Potatoes, '95 M23
Croquettes, Sweet Potato, '81 223; '96 238
Cups, Sunshine Sweet Potato, '82 195
Desserts
  Cake, Sweet Potato, '79 207; '89 295
  Cake, Sweet Potato Loaf, '81 224
  Cake, Sweet Potato Pound, '83 85
  Cake, Sweet Potato Surprise, '80 287
  Cheesecake, Sweet Potato, '80 287; '96 312
  Cheesecake, Yam, '81 224
  Cobbler, Sweet Potato, '99 M255
  Flan, Sweet Potato, '95 291
  Pie, Carolina Sweet Potato, '89 295
  Pie, Louisiana Yam, '81 223
  Pie, No-Crust Sweet Potato, '84 236
  Pie, Old-Fashioned Sweet Potato, '79 9
  Pie, Southern Sweet Potato Cream, '87 260
  Pie, Speedy Sweet Potato, '90 219
  Pie, Sweet Potato, '79 207; '85 255, 275;
    '86 269; '89 289; '96 131, 326
  Pie, Sweet Potato Meringue, '81 126; '83 225
  Pie, Sweet Potato-Orange, '88 207
  Pie, Sweet Potato-Pecan, '83 90
  Pie, Sweet Potato Pone, '80 288
  Pudding, Sweet Potato, '80 228; '86 52
  Pudding, Sweet Potato Bread, '94 241
  Roll, Sweet Potato Log, '82 227
  Torte, Caramel-Sweet Potato, '96 312
French-Fried Sweet Potatoes, '81 223
Fried Sweet Potatoes, '83 226
Fried Sweet Potato Strips, '94 238
Fritters, Golden Sweet Potato, '79 9
Fritters, Sweet Potato, '88 44
Glazed Sweet Potatoes, '85 206; '89 274
Glazed Sweet Potatoes, Apple-, '82 303
Glazed Sweet Potatoes, Apricot-, '81 295
Glazed Sweet Potatoes, Orange-, '81 223;
  '83 280
Gravy, Roast Duck with Sweet Potato-Eggplant,
  '83 90
Grilled Sweet Potatoes, '93 213
Hash, Sweet Potato, '92 337
Maple-Ginger Cream, Sweet Potatoes with,
  '97 27
Mashed Sweet Potatoes, '85 25
Mashed Sweet Potatoes with Cumin, '99 244
Orange-Baked Sweet Potatoes, '88 M294
Orange Cups, Sweet Potatoes in, '82 272
Orange Cups, Sweet Potato-Stuffed, '81 223
Orange Sweet Potatoes, '86 279
Oven-Fried Sweet Potatoes with Chutney,
  '93 241
Pancakes, Sweet Potato, '87 280
Pancakes with Goat Cheese, Sweet Potato,
  '96 271
Peaks, Sweet Potato, '95 291
Peanut Crust, Sweet Potatoes with, '93 212
Pones, Sweet Potato, '96 270
Pork Chops with Sweet Potatoes, '96 269
Pork Dinner, Saucy, '97 26
Pudding, Sweet Potato, '79 244; '80 228; '86 52
Puffs, Peach Sweet Potato, '87 280
Puffs, Sweet Potato, '87 253

Puff, Sweet Potato, '85 235
Puree, Carrot-Sweet Potato, '92 90
Puree, Sweet Potato, '92 306
Raspberry Sweet Potatoes, '87 280
Sage Vinaigrette, Sweet Potatoes with, '97 270
Salad, Fresh Sweet Potato, '86 226
Salad, Hawaiian Ham-Sweet Potato, '82 232
Salad, Sweet Potato-Apple, '96 240
Salad with Rosemary-Honey Vinaigrette, Sweet
  Potato, '98 243
Scalloped Root Vegetables, '98 310
Slaw, Sweet Potato-Currant, '93 246
Soufflé, Sweet Potato, '82 286; '86 121; '93 325;
  '96 247
Soup, Sweet Potato, '88 250
Soup, Sweet Potato-and-Sausage, '95 23
Soup with Rum Cream, Sweet Potato, '98 271
Stacked Sweet Potato Blues, '95 290
Stuffed Baked Sweet Potatoes, '79 207; '84 231
Stuffed Sweet Potatoes, '86 224
Stuffed Sweet Potatoes, Bacon-, '86 224
Stuffed Sweet Potatoes, Coconut-, '82 204
Stuffed Sweet Potatoes, Fluffy, '79 9
Stuffed with Apples, Sweet Potatoes, '82 228
Supreme, Sweet Potato, '94 196
Tzimmes, '95 102
Tzimmes, Sweet Potato-Beef, '92 234
Velouté, Sweet Potato, '94 238
Waffles, Sweet Potato, '88 208
Waffles with Orange Butter, Sweet Potato,
  '90 323
Yams, Bourbon, '90 232
Yams, Brandied, '94 273
Yams Cointreau, '92 192
Yams, Rosemary-Garlic, '93 174
SWISS CHARD
  Bundles, Swiss Chard, '94 48
  Buttered Chard, '83 36
  Creamy Chard and Potatoes, '98 250
  Sautéed Chard with Onion and Apple, '98 48
  Tomatoes, Swiss Chard with, '83 36
SYRUPS
  Almond Syrup, '82 47
  Anise Sugar Syrup, '86 248
  Apple Syrup, Spiced, '79 114
  Apricot Fruit Syrup, '82 10
  Barbecue Sauce, Maple Syrup, '94 154
  Berry Syrup, '96 161
  Blackberry Syrup, '99 131
  Bourbon Syrup, '98 277
  Caramel Syrup, '82 43
  Caramel Syrup, Citrus Compote with,
    '98 313
  Cherry-Lemonade Syrup, '86 214
  Cinnamon Syrup, '91 315
  Citrus Syrup, Sweet, '86 270
  Fruit Syrup, '86 176
  Ginger Syrup, '96 161
  Honey Syrup, '96 21
  Kirsch Syrup, '80 280
  Madeira Syrup, '98 247
  Maple-Honey-Cinnamon Syrup, '85 19
  Maple-Nut Syrup, '80 228
  Maple Syrup, '81 120; '82 23; '93 16
  Maple Syrup, Homemade, '79 114
  Mint Syrup, '90 89; '96 161; '97 120
  Orange Marmalade Syrup, '96 27
  Orange Syrup, '80 228; '89 254; '96 161, 164;
    '97 32
  Pecan Syrup, Chunky, '85 278
  Pomegranate Syrup, '96 241
  Rum Syrup, '95 313
  Simple Syrup, '99 161
  Sugar Syrup, '93 29; '96 161

TABBOULEH
  Appetizers, Endive with Arugula Tabbouleh,
    '98 67
  Couscous, Tabbouleh, '96 251
  Endive with Arugula Tabbouleh, '98 67
  Pitas, Tabbouleh, '98 105
  Salad), Boot Scoot Tabbouli (Tabbouleh, '96 159
  Salad, Tabbouleh, '92 212; '94 174
  Tabbouleh, '93 70; '99 175
TACOS
  al Carbón, Tacos, '86 19
  al Carbón, Tailgate Tacos, '79 185
  Appetizer, Layered Taco, '84 206
  Bake, Taco, '97 326
  Bake, Taco Beef-Noodle, '81 141
  Basic Tacos, '83 199
  Beef Tacos, Soft, '91 88
  Biscuit Bites, Taco, '91 89
  Breakfast Tacos, '80 43; '91 316; '95 340
  Burgers, Taco, '98 224
  Casserole, Taco, '80 33
  Chicken-and-Bean Tacos, '93 293
  Chicken Skewers, Taco-, '99 119
  Chicken Tacos, Pizza-Flavored, '95 340
  Corn Chip Tacos, '81 67
  Deep-Dish Taco Squares, '91 88
  Dessert Tacos, '97 141
  Dip, Hot Taco, '93 238
  Easy Tacos, '96 159
  Egg Salad Tacos, Mexican, '94 181
  Fish Tacos, Barbecued, '95 339
  Jiffy Tacos, '83 M318
  Joes, Taco, '91 167
  Lentil Tacos, '88 197
  Lobster Taco with Yellow Tomato Salsa and
    Jícama Salad, Warm, '87 122
  Margarita Tacos, '97 167
  Microwave Tacos, '88 M213
  Navajo Tacos, '84 246
  Peppers, Taco, '81 86
  Pepper Tacos, Grilled, '95 340
  Pie, Crescent Taco, '80 80
  Pie, Double-Crust Taco, '88 272; '89 180
  Pies, Individual Taco, '82 M282
  Pie, Taco, '88 256
  Pitas, Taco, '83 31
  Pizza, Taco, '89 M177; '98 176
  Potatoes, Taco-Topped, '93 M18
  Rolls, Chinese Taco, '95 339
  Salad, Chicken Taco, '94 M136
  Salad Cups, Taco, '85 M29
  Salad, Meatless Taco, '81 204
  Salad, Party Taco, '97 19
  Salad, Spicy Taco, '87 287
  Salad, Taco, '79 56; '83 145; '85 84; '89 332;
    '90 20
  Salad, Taco Macaroni, '85 165
  Salad, Tuna-Taco, '87 145
  Sauce, Taco, '82 M283; '93 69; '94 30
  Seasoning Blend, Taco, '96 159
  Shrimp-and-Pepper Soft Tacos, '95 339
  Soup, Taco, '94 225; '99 36
  Tacos, '80 196
  Tassies, Taco, '95 339
TAMALES
  Bake, Cornbread Tamale, '79 163
  Casserole, Quick Tamale, '94 255
  Chicken Tamales, '88 151
  Dessert Tamales, Mango, '94 190
  Dressing, Corny Cornbread, '99 258
  Hot Tamales, '83 51
  Meatballs, Tamale, '80 194
  Miniature Tamales, '85 154
  Mozzarella Tamale, '95 70

TAMALES
(continued)

Pie, Chili-Tamale, '82 9; '83 68
Pie, Cornbread-Tamale, '92 123
Soup, Tamale, '95 213
Sweet Tamales, '83 52
Tamales, '80 195

TEA
Cake, Tea Pound, '99 90
Granita, Ginger Tea, '98 334
Granita, Mint Tea, '88 117
Granita, Wild Raspberry Tea, '99 89
Hot
Almond Tea, '85 43; '86 329
Apple-Cinnamon Tea, Hot, '87 57
Apricot Tea, Hot Spiced, '88 248
Brew, Quilter's, '85 43
Cider Tea, '98 241; '99 335
Citrus Tea, Hot, '83 275
Fruit Tea, Christmas, '83 275
Fruit Tea, Hot Spiced, '87 242
Grape Tea, Spiced, '79 174
Hawaiian Tea, '87 57
Honey Tea, '81 105
Johnny Appleseed Tea, '85 23
Marmalade Tea, '98 330
Minted Tea, '86 101
Mint Tea, Moroccan, '98 211
Mix, Deluxe Spiced Tea, '88 257
Mix, Friendship Tea, '83 283
Mix, Spiced Tea, '86 32
Mix, Sugar-Free Spiced Tea, '91 258
Punch, Cran-Grape-Tea, '92 209
Punch, Spiked Tea, '86 101
Russian Tea, Hot, '97 274
Spiced Tea, Hot, '83 244
Strawberry Tea, '88 248
Yaupon Tea, '79 31
Ice Cream, Orange Pekoe-Chocolate, '99 90
Iced
Almond-Lemonade Tea, '86 229; '99 207
Almond Tea, '89 212; '97 226
Apple Tea, Iced, '98 84
Berry-Mint Iced Tea, '98 332
Bubbly Iced Tea, '81 168
Cider Tea, '98 241
Citrus-Mint Tea Cooler, '92 105
Citrus Tea, Iced, '85 162
Cranberry-Apple Tea, '88 169
Cranberry Tea, '94 131; '97 121, 160
Cubes, Frozen Tea, '85 161
Fruit-and-Mint Iced Tea, '98 84
Fruited Tea Cooler, '94 131
Fruit Tea, Refreshing, '97 122
Ginger-Almond Tea, '94 131
Ginger Tea, '81 100; '96 100
Grapefruit Tea, '92 67
Grape Tea, Spiced, '79 174
Hawaiian Tea, '87 57
Juleps, Tea, '99 90
Lemon-Mint Tea, '85 162
Lemon Tea, '82 156
Lemon Tea Tingler, '95 200
Lime-Mint Tea, '97 122
Lime Tea, '98 198
Long Island Iced Tea, Southern, '90 207
Minted Tea, '88 163; '92 54
Mint Tea, '87 107; '90 89
Mint Tea, Easy, '91 187
Mint Tea, Fresh, '95 88
Mint Tea, Frosted, '84 161

Mint Tea, Fruited, '88 79; '91 81
Mint Tea, Iced, '83 170
Mint Tea, Moroccan, '98 211
Pineapple Tea, '93 165
Punch, Apple-Tea, '85 82
Punch, Bourbon-Tea, '87 57
Punch, Citrus-Tea, '85 116
Punch, Cran-Grape-Tea, '92 209
Punch, Southern Fresh Fruit, '99 70
Punch, Tea, '90 143, 207
Rasp-Berry Good Tea, '95 200
Sangría, Mock Tea, '99 336
Sangría Tea, '94 131
Sangría, Teaberry, '87 147
Sangría Tea, Pink, '95 200
Sparkling Summer Tea, '96 172
Spiced Iced Tea, '91 209; '97 121
Spiced Tea Cooler, '83 55
Strawberry Tea, Sparkling, '94 131
Summer Tea, '85 162
Summertime Tea, '81 167
Sun Tea, Southern, '81 168
Sweet Tea, '98 84
Tropical Tea-Ser, '95 200
White Grape Iced Tea, '98 84
White Grape Juice Tea, '87 57
Yaupon Tea, '79 31
Jelly, Red Zinger, '99 89
Sauce, Tea-Berry, '94 130; '99 334
Vinaigrette, Salad Greens with Herbed Earl Grey, '99 89

TEMPURA
Basic Tempura, '81 68
Chicken Tempura Delight, '85 66
Cornmeal Tempura, '81 68
Green Onions, Tempura-Battered, '96 93
Sauce, Basic Tempura, '81 68
Sauce, Mustard-Sour Cream, '81 68
"Shrimps," French-Fried Tempura, '97 128
Vegetable Tempura, '79 112

TERRINES
Asparagus-Seafood Terrine with Dill Sauce, '98 157
Banana Split Terrine, '96 164
Black Bean Terrine with Fresh Tomato Coulis and Jalapeño Sauce, '93 230
Black Bean Terrine with Goat Cheese, '87 120
Blue Cheese Terrine with Tomato-Basil Vinaigrette, '99 288
Cheese Terrine, Basil-, '96 322
Cheese Terrine, Italian, '93 64
Chicken-Leek Terrine, Cold, '92 145
Chicken Terrine Ring, '84 132
Chicken-Vegetable Terrine, '84 131
Fruit Terrine with Raspberry Sauce, '98 157
Pork and Veal, Terrine of, '93 287
Pork Terrine, Jeweled, '84 130
Salmon-and-Spinach Terrine, Layered, '84 132
Veal Terrine with Mustard Sauce, '93 118
Vegetable-Chicken Terrine, '83 224

TIMBALES
Cheesy Mexicali Appetizer, '82 108
Chicken Chutney Salad, '82 108
Corn-and-Zucchini Timbales, '92 100
Green Rice Timbales, '97 62
Grits Timbales, '88 223
Grits Timbales, Chives-, '90 172
Hamburger Stroganoff, '82 108
Peach Almond Cream, '82 108
Rice Timbales, '94 32
Shells, Timbale, '82 108
Shrimp Sauté, Confetti, '97 104
Spinach-Rice Timbales, '88 271
Spinach Timbales, '84 29

TOFU
Dip, Tofu, '86 109
Drink, Tofruitti Breakfast, '88 26
Lasagna, Tofu, '83 312
Rice with Tofu, Spanish, '88 26
Salad, Tofu, '88 27
Sandwiches, Open-Face Tofu-Veggie, '86 5
Stroganoff Tofu, '84 202

TOMATILLOS
Beef Saltillo (Beef with Tomatillos), '82 219
Fillets Tomatillo, '94 135
Green Tomatillos with Jalapeño Dipping Sauce, Fried, '97 143
Relish, Black Bean-Tomatillo, '87 121
Salsa, Fresh Tomatillo, '97 143
Salsa, Roasted Tomatillo, '95 64
Salsa, Tomatillo, '92 245
Salsa Verde, '96 160
Sandwiches, Open-Faced Tomatillo, '92 246
Sauce, Avocado-Tomatillo, '95 206
Sauce, Roasted Chiles Rellenos with Tomatillo, '94 203
Sauce, Shrimp Enchiladas in Tomatillo, '95 310
Sauce, Tomatillo, '94 231; '95 206; '97 25
Soup with Crunchy Jícama, Tomatillo, '92 245; '97 143
Vinaigrette, Poblano, '99 71

TOMATOES
Appetizers, Oven-Baked Tomato, '95 172
au Gratin, Zucchini and Tomato, '82 208
Bake, Chicken-Tomato, '83 35
Baked Cheddar Tomatoes, '85 43
Baked Ranch Tomatoes, '94 72
Baked Tomatoes, '83 53; '87 197
Baked Tomato Halves, Zippy, '81 182
Bake, Ham-Rice-Tomato, '87 78
Bake, Okra-and-Tomato, '89 173
Bake, Okra-Tomato, '80 298; '81 26
Bake, Potato-Tomato, '86 17
Bake, Tomato-and-Artichoke Heart, '85 81
Bake, Zucchini and Tomato, '82 158
Basil, and Cheese, Tomato, '95 165
Basil, Zucchini and Tomatoes, '89 147
Bean-and-Tomato Skillet, '90 316
Beans and Tomatoes, Basil, '83 172
Beans, Texas, '97 139
Beef with Tomatoes and Artichokes, '92 282
Biscuit Cakes, Tomato-Eggplant, '95 170
Biscuits, Tomato, '86 72
Biscuits, Tomato-Herb, '94 215
Bowl, Tomato, '81 69
Breaded Tomatoes, '95 180
Bread, Herbed Tomato-Cheese, '88 143
Bread, Tomato-Cheese, '98 172; '99 M157
Broiled Tomatoes, '80 152
Broiled Tomatoes, Quick, '79 153
Broiled Tomatoes, Romano, '80 42
Broiled Tomatoes with Dill Sauce, '80 161
Broiled Tomatoes with Mushroom Sauce, '81 103
Broil, Tomato-English Pea, '83 192
Burgers, Stuffed Southwestern-Style, '99 201
Butterbeans, Bacon, and Tomatoes, '96 36
Butter, Tomato, '86 128
Butter, Tomato-Curry-Orange, '93 159
Cabbage and Tomatoes, '83 104
Cabbage and Tomatoes, Tasty, '86 72
Cacciatore, Chicken, '86 42
Canned Flavored Tomatoes, '95 217
Canning Tomatoes, '80 128; '85 106
Caponata, '98 50
Casserole, Corn and Tomato, '81 127
Casserole, Corn-and-Tomato, '84 145
Casserole, Eggplant-and-Tomato, '83 187

Casserole, Saucy Potato-Tomato, '79 46
Casserole, Scalloped Tomato, '88 144
Casserole, Zucchini-and-Tomato, '88 265
Catsup, Spicy Tomato, '83 182
Cauliflower au Gratin, '99 59
Cheese Herbed-Topped Tomatoes, '86 108
Cheese Sauce over Toast, Tomatoes with, '88 159
Cheese-Topped Tomatoes, '81 160
Cheesy Puff-Top Tomatoes, '86 187
Cherry. *See also* **TOMATOES/Dried.**
  Basil Butter, Squash and Cherry Tomatoes in, '98 328
  Bites, Tomato, '84 80
  Brown Butter Sauce, Cherry Tomatoes in, '81 168
  Caviar Tomatoes, '91 12
  Cheesy Cherry Tomatoes, '83 135
  Green Beans with Cherry Tomatoes, '86 177
  Herbed Cherry Tomatoes, '82 128
  Pasta, Herbed Cherry Tomatoes over, '95 229
  Rockefeller, Tomatoes, '97 169
  Rum, Cherry Tomatoes with, '83 192
  Salad, Cherry Tomato, '87 156
  Sautéed Roma Tomatoes, '92 338
  Stuffed Cherry Tomatoes, '84 160; '88 95, 212; '92 25
  Stuffed Cherry Tomatoes, Crab-, '82 289; '88 78
  Stuffed Cherry Tomatoes, Cucumber-, '88 262
  Stuffed Cherry Tomatoes, Tuna-, '89 214
Chicken, Tomato-Baked, '81 281; '82 30
Chicken with Tomatoes and Sausage, '97 266
Chili, Chilly Night, '99 317
Chili in a Biscuit Bowl, '98 224
Chutney, Tomato, '99 143
Chutney, Tomato-Apple, '84 180
Cocktail, Tomato, '83 M203
Cocktail, Tomato-Clam, '87 252
Cocktail, Tomato Juice, '79 212; '83 230; '90 12
Cocktail, Tomato-Orange Juice, '83 169
Cocktail, Zesty Tomato Juice, '83 289
Couscous, Tabbouleh, '97 103
Cream, Tomato, '94 70
Creole-Style Tomatoes-and-Corn, '84 142
Crêpes, Southwestern Cornbread, '98 42
Croissants, BLT, '93 158
Crostini, Festive, '99 M325
Crostini, Feta-Tomato, '92 159
Crostini, Tomato, '99 230
Delight, Tomato-Pea, '84 196
Dip, Bacon-and-Tomato, '90 147
Dip, Fiesta, '96 212
Dressing, Fresh Tomato Salad, '83 193
Dressing, Garden Salad with Tomato-Cream Cheese, '79 173
Dressing, Tomato-Honey French, '81 105
Dried
  Cheese Balls with Sun-Dried Tomatoes, '94 317
  Cherry Tomatoes, Marinated Dried, '93 23
  Chicken, Undercover, '97 64
  Dip, Cottage Cheese Sun-Dried Tomato, '93 13
  Fettuccine, Chicken and Dried Tomatoes over, '98 233
  Focaccia, Dried Tomato, '94 65
  Focaccia, Fast Rosemary-Dried Tomato, '98 53
  Goat Cheese, Dried Tomato Mock, '97 105
  Goat Cheese with Sun-Dried Tomatoes and Rosemary, '93 175
  Hummus, Creamy Dried Tomato, '95 284
  Mayonnaise, Dried Tomato, '98 144

Meat Loaf with Sun-Dried Tomatoes and Herbs, '92 192
  Pesto, Dried Tomato, '90 204; '94 249
  Pizza, Shrimp-and-Dried Tomato, '97 49
  Salad, Spinach and Sun-Dried Tomato, '93 250
  Sandwiches, Dried Tomato-and-Basil, '99 274
  Sauce, Dried Tomato, '99 135
  Sauce, Dried Tomato Spaghetti, '90 202
  Soup, Dried Tomato-Cream, '90 203
  Spread, Dried Tomato-Cheese, '90 204
  Spread, Tri-Flavored Cream Cheese, '98 134
  Tart, Dried Tomato-Cheese, '90 203
  Torte, Tomato-Cheese, '97 49
  Vinaigrette, Couscous Salad with Dried Tomato, '96 244
  Vinaigrette, Dried Tomato, '93 272
Dumplings, Tomato, '88 144; '97 209
Eggs Benedict, Bacon-and-Tomato, '87 195
Eggs, Layered, '96 97
Eggs Oso Grande, '98 279
Enchiladas, Enticing, '99 57
Fettuccine with Shrimp and Tomatoes, '96 198
Fire-and-Ice Tomatoes, '87 92
Flank Steak, Tomato-Stuffed, '97 49
Fried Herb Tomatoes, '88 144
Fried Red Tomatoes, '81 102
Fried Ripe Tomatoes, '81 168
Fried Ripe Tomatoes with Gravy, '82 180
Fried Tomatoes with Bacon, Saucy, '81 210
Fried Tomatoes with Gravy, '86 211
Gazpacho-Stuffed Endive, '95 287
Gratin, Tomato-Zucchini, '95 171
Gravy, Southwestern, '99 34
Gravy, Spicy Tomato, '95 172
Gravy, Tomato, '93 18; '99 35
Greek Tomatoes, '98 173
Green
  Baked Green Tomatoes, Herb-, '85 214
  Curried Green Tomatoes, '93 138
  Fried Green Tomato Cheeseburgers, '94 138
  Fried Green Tomatoes, '79 123; '80 178; '81 210; '85 214; '95 171; '98 172
  "Fried" Green Tomatoes, '89 174
  Fried Green Tomatoes, Blue Willow, '99 143
  Fried Green Tomato Napoleons, '99 230
  Fried Okra and Green Tomatoes, '93 160
  Grilled Summer Squash and Tomatoes, '99 144
  Hot Tomatoes, '93 138
  Italian-Sauced Green Tomatoes, '85 214
  Jam, Green Tomato, '79 121
  Okra and Green Tomatoes, '79 160
  Oven-Fried Green Tomatoes, '82 107; '91 122
  Pickled Green Tomatoes, '99 143
  Pickles, Green Tomato, '87 134
  Pie, Green Tomato, '79 195
  Relish, Green Tomato, '96 168; '98 124
  Relish, Green Tomato Sweet, '93 136
  Salsa, Peachy Green Tomato, '99 143
  Spread, Green Tomato Sandwich, '95 172
Green Beans, Tomato-Feta, '99 59
Green Beans with Tomatoes, '85 137
Grilled Okra and Tomatoes, '98 124
Grilled Tomatoes, '85 158; '99 173
Grilled Tomatoes, Cheesy, '79 150
Grilled Tomatoes with Basil Vinaigrette, '97 168
Grits, Hot Tomato, '95 171
Grouper, Guadalajara, '98 17
Guacamole, Margarita, '97 167
Herbed Tomatoes, '81 102; '82 49; '83 173
Herbed Tomato Slices, '89 173
Hush Puppies, Creole, '98 43
Hush Puppies, Green Onion-Tomato, '97 84

Hush Puppies, Tomato-Onion, '91 201
Italian Tomatoes, Cold, '99 173
Juice, Homemade Tomato, '81 50
Juice, Spicy Tomato, '85 189
Kale with Tomato and Onion, '92 244
Kale with Tomatoes, Spicy, '99 243
Lentils, Tex-Mex, '99 288
Lima and Tomato Combo, Hot, '83 219
Mahimahi, Middle Eastern, '96 92
Marinade, Bright Tomato, '88 176
Marinara Vinaigrette, '94 64
Marinated Sliced Tomatoes, '92 173
Medley, Okra-Corn-Tomato, '81 159
Medley, Tomato, '81 159
Melts, Tomato-Cheese-Bacon, '99 72
Mexicorn, '96 189
Muffins, Tomato Corn, '81 137
Mustard, Green Beans and Tomatoes with, '87 83
Mustard Tomatoes, Zippy, '86 M226
Okra and Tomatoes, '80 185; '81 139; '92 215; '98 286
Okra and Tomatoes, Fresh, '81 M165; '87 89
Okra Caponata, '97 157
Okra, Corn, and Tomatoes, '95 203
Okra-Tomato Combo, '83 157
Okra, Tomatoes and, '86 170; '87 164
Okra, Tomatoes with, '85 106
Onions, Baked Sweet, '98 130
Parmesan Tomatoes, '80 161
Pastas. *See also* **TOMATOES/Sauces.**
  Asparagus, Tomatoes, and Shrimp, Garlicky Pasta with, '95 82
  Basil Pasta, Tomato-, '94 204
  Caribbean Tomato Pasta, '93 201
  Fettuccine, Chicken-and-Tomatoes over, '90 204
  Fresh Tomatoes and Basil, Pasta with, '98 233
  Garlic Pasta, Tomato-, '94 177
  Herb-and-Tomato Pasta, '96 122
  Italian Tomato Pasta, '93 201
  Late-Night Pasta Chez Frank, '95 228
  Macaroni, Cheese, and Tomatoes, '95 213
  Primavera, Tomato-Pasta, '86 209
  Quick Pasta and Tomatoes, '92 180
  Rotelle, Chicken and Tomato with, '87 108
  Shrimp-Tomato Pasta, '98 172
  Southwestern Tomato Pasta, '93 201
  Spaghetti, All-in-One, '98 295
  Spaghetti with Tomatoes and Garlic, '91 47
  Toss, Tomato-Olive Pasta, '86 209
Pesto, Bow-Tie, '94 231
Pesto, Tomatoes, '86 150
Pie, Tomato, '88 198; '97 249
Pita Pockets, BLT in, '93 158
Pizza, Nutty Pesto, '97 267
Pizzas, Roasted Potato, '99 16
Potato Boats, Southwestern, '96 33
Preserves, Tomato, '98 214
Provençal, Tomatoes, '82 181
Puffs, Spinach-Artichoke-Tomato, '95 284
Puree, Seared Sea Scallops with Tomato, '97 201
Puree, Seasoned Tomato, '83 182
Quesadillas, Bacon-Jalapeño-Tomato, '95 240
Quesadillas with Chipotle Salsa, Chicken-and-Brie, '99 311
Quiche, Asparagus-Tomato, '88 198
Red Beans and Couscous, '99 22
Refresher, Tomato, '81 94; '83 318
Refried Beans, Easy, '99 57
Relish, Easy Tomato, '80 126
Relish, End-of-the-Garden, '80 179
Relish, Tomato, '85 188
Rice, Blended, '96 68

TOMATOES

(continued)

Rice, Charleston, '97 310
Rice, Red, '92 235; '97 138
Rice with Tomatoes and Basil, '95 232
Risotto, Tomato-Basil, '95 269
Roma Tomatoes, Sautéed, '92 338
Ropa Vieja, '98 20
Rose, Tomato, '82 51; '85 338
Salads
　Artichoke-Stuffed Tomato Salad, '82 101
　Artichoke-Tomato Salad, '82 239
　Asparagus and Tomatoes, Fresh, '94 162
　Asparagus and Tomatoes with Herb
　　Vinaigrette, '99 56
　Asparagus Salad, Tomato-, '92 79
　Aspic, Bloody Mary-Tomato, '81 77
　Aspic, Chicken in Tomato, '84 190
　Aspic, Chili Sauce Tomato, '85 252
　Aspic, Classic Tomato, '91 229
　Aspic, Gazpacho, '96 65
　Aspic, Herbed Tomato, '81 73
　Aspic, Layered Tomato, '90 99
　Aspic, Light Tomato, '85 83
　Aspic, Ranch Tomato, '83 218
　Aspic, Spicy Tomato, '81 40; '89 288
　Aspic, Tangy Tomato, '83 124
　Aspic, Tomato-Artichoke, '84 320; '86 92
　Aspic, Tomato-Crab, '85 287
　Aspic with Shrimp, Tomato, '79 241
　Avocado Salad, Tomato-, '86 74
　Bacon-Lettuce-Mozzarella-and-Tomato Salad,
　　'98 209
　Basil-and-Tomato Couscous Salad, '94 175
　Basil-Mozzarella Salad, Tomato-, '95 171
　Chile-Tomato Salad, Spicy, '88 121
　Citrus Marinade, Summer Salad with, '92 133
　Coleslaw with Tomatoes, '80 34
　Congealed Lemon-Tomato Salad, '89 178
　Cottage Cheese Salad in Tomatoes, '86 208
　Cottage-Tomato Salad, '85 163
　Crab-Stuffed Tomato Salad, '80 148
　Cucumber and Tomato Salad, Dilled, '81 153
　Cucumber-Onion Salad, Tomato-, '81 239
　Cucumber on Tomatoes, Dilled, '84 142
　Cucumber Salad, Tomato-, '86 218; '92 199
　Cucumber Salad with Yogurt-Herb Dressing,
　　Tomato-, '92 96
　Cucumber Summer Salad, Tomato-and-,
　　'93 141
　Cucumber-Tomato Salad, '90 144
　Endive-Tomato Starburst Salad, '93 323
　Feta Salad, Tomato-, '81 246; '91 168
　Flower Salad, Tomato, '89 128
　Frozen Tomato Salad, '84 52
　Green Bean Salad, Tomato-and-, '97 162
　Grilled Tomato, Bell Pepper, and Portobello
　　Salad, '98 211
　Gruyère-Basil Salad, Tomato-, '99 172
　Guacamole-Tomato Salad, '81 302
　Herbed Pasta-and-Tomato Salad, '92 144
　Herbed Tomatoes, '83 173
　Herb Salad, Tomato-, '89 220
　Italian Dressing, Tomato, Onion, and
　　Cucumber in, '81 83
　Italiano, Tomatoes, '88 29
　Lemon Dressing, Tomato Slices with,
　　'87 167
　Lima Bean-Tomato Salad, '85 137
　Marinated Salad, '83 170
　Marinated Salsa Tomatoes, '82 164
　Marinated Tomato and Brie Salad, '95 95

Marinated Tomato-and-Cucumber Salad,
　'92 216
Marinated Tomatoes, '85 156, 163;
　'89 174, 202
Marinated Tomato Slices, '82 134; '83 193
Mexican Dinner Salad, '98 330
Mold, Tangy Tomato, '79 74
Mozzarella Salad, Tomato-, '89 220
Mozzarella-Tomato-Basil Salad, Fresh, '93 131
Olive Spread, Tomatoes with, '85 114
Oregano Tomatoes, '83 145
Pasta Salad, Tomato-, '97 M160
Petal Salad, Tomato, '79 88
Red, White, and Green Salad, '90 18
Relish Salad, Tomato, '83 111
Ring, Tangy Tomato, '84 164
Ring, Tomato-Vegetable, '81 302
Ruby-and-Emerald Salad, '85 79
Stuffed Tomato Salad, Oriental-, '82 101
Summer Tomato Salad, '94 201
Summer Tomato Treat, '79 143
Trout-and-Tomato Salad with Black Pepper
　Vinaigrette, '98 284
Tuna with Warm Tomato Salad, '97 179
Vidalia-Tomato Salad, '84 65
Vinaigrette, Marinara, '94 64
Vinaigrette, Okra-Corn-and-Tomato, '90 173
Vinaigrette, Tomato-Basil, '87 89
Vinaigrette, Tomatoes, '84 106
Watercress-Tomato Salad, '85 132
Sandwiches, Bacon, Cheese, and Tomato, '84 14
Sandwiches, Curried BLT, '93 158
Sandwiches, Eggplant, Tomato, and Feta, '98 106
Sandwiches, Grilled Bacon, Cheese, and
　Tomato, '97 170
Sandwiches, Open-Face Crab Tomato, '81 29
Sandwiches, Super Open-Faced, '97 52
Sandwich, Floyd's Favorite Tomato, '95 172
Sauces
　Asparagus with Tomato Sauce, '83 46
　Basil Cream, Tomato-, '99 240
　Basil Sauce, Tomato, '91 85
　Basil Sauce, Tomato-, '92 180; '96 220; '97 144
　Basil-Tomato Sauce, '92 198; '93 25, 48, 65
　Caper Sauce, Turkey Cutlets with Tomato-,
　　'91 61
　Chili Sauce, '94 287
　Chunky Tomato Sauce, '95 264
　Cocktail Sauce, Southwestern, '98 46
　Coulis, Fresh Tomato, '93 230
　Cream Sauce, Angel Hair Pasta with Tomato,
　　'93 292
　Cream Sauce, Linguine with Tomato-, '86 158
　Cream, Tomato, '94 70
　Creamy Tomato Sauce, '93 71
　Creole Sauce, '98 98
　Cucumber Sauce, Tomato-, '98 45
　Dried Tomato Sauce, '96 220
　Fish in Tomato Sauce, '85 75
　Fresh Tomato Sauce, '83 224; '87 171
　Fresh Tomato Sauce over Basil Pasta, '93 176
　Fresh Tomato Sauce, Spaghetti with, '96 135
　Gingered Tomato Sauce, Spicy, '96 220
　Green Chiles, Tomato Sauce with, '81 196
　Hamburgers with Tomato Sauce, '81 73
　Herbed Fresh Tomato Sauce, '85 M151
　Hot Sauce, Kleberg, '94 28
　Italian-Style Tomato Sauce, '87 182
　Italian Tomato Sauce, '82 M68; '92 57
　Italian Tomato Sauce for Spaghetti, '81 134
　Light Tomato Sauce, '97 246
　Marinara Sauce, '94 64; '99 266
　Pesto, Bow-Tie, '94 231
　Pesto, Tomatoes, '86 150

Pico de Gallo, '96 227; '97 141; '98 87
Pintos, Texas Souper, '98 51
Pizza Sauce, Traditional, '95 267
Ranchero Sauce, '96 168
Red Pepper-Tomato Sauce, '93 59
Refrigerator Tomato Sauce, '85 188
Roasted Garlic-Tomato Sauce, '97 46
Salsa, '88 147; '97 171
Salsa, Artichoke-Tomato, '96 182
Salsa, Chunky, '86 130; '90 206
Salsa, Fresh, '95 42
Salsa, Fresh Tomato, '91 182; '95 181
Salsa, Hot, '98 135
Salsa, Mango, '98 232
Salsa, One-Minute, '95 93
Salsa, Pan-Fried Roughy with Tomato-Basil,
　'99 123
Salsa, Red, '90 172
Salsa, Roasted Tomato, '95 64
Salsa, Seared Scallops with Tomato-Mango,
　'95 122
Salsa, Summer, '98 172
Salsa, Texas, '96 160
Salsa, Three Tomato, '93 138
Salsa, Tomato, '87 120; '96 15
Salsa, Tomato-Avocado, '94 83
Salsa, Warm-and-Spicy, '99 279
Salsa, Yellowfin Tuna with Corn, Pepper, and
　Tomato, '94 164
Salsa, Yellow Tomato, '87 122
Seasoned Tomato Sauce, '83 150
Spicy Tomato Sauce, '84 294; '88 19
Spinach Tortellini with Tomato Sauce, '88 302
Tarragon-Tomato Sauce, '84 131
Tomato Sauce, '85 193, 244; '87 249; '88 116;
　'97 96, 269; '99 270
Vegetable-Tomato Sauce, Turkey Patties in,
　'87 18
Vermicelli with Tomato Sauce, '83 164
Zesty Tomato Sauce, '98 176
Sauté, Tomato-Pepper, '84 142
Scalloped Tomatoes, '84 142
Scalloped Tomato Slices, '81 168
Scallops, Ginger, '99 177
Sesame Tomatoes, '84 142
Sipper, Peppy Tomato, '94 227
Sipper, Spicy Tomato, '86 229
Skillet, Cabbage-and-Tomato, '86 110
Skillet Tomatoes, '81 108
Skillet, Zucchini-Tomato, '93 206
Sloppy Joe Cups, '98 204
Snow Peas and Tomatoes, '83 111
Snow Peas and Tomatoes, Basil, '88 M185
Soufflé, Italian Pizzola, '98 232
Soups
　Appetizer Tomato Soup, '86 258
　Bacon, Lettuce, and Tomato Soup, '91 207
　Bisque, Make-Ahead Tomato-Basil, '93 322
　Bisque, Tomato-Shrimp, '86 66
　Black, White, and Red All Over Soup, '95 126
　Bouillon, New Year's Tomato, '94 24
　Bouillon, Tomato, '83 8
　Carrot-and-Tomato Soup, Cream of, '94 176
　Celery Soup, Tomato-, '83 M58
　Chilled Tomato Soup, '82 155
　Chowder, Tomato-Clam, '84 251
　Cioppino, Gulf Coast, '94 102
　Cold Tomato Soup, '88 160
　Consommé, Tomato, '88 250
　Cream of Tomato Soup with Lemon Basil,
　　'96 124
　Cream of Tomato Soup with Parmesan
　　Cheese, '86 161
　Cream Soup, Refreshing Tomato, '79 172

Cream Soup, Tomato-Basil, '97 198
Creamy Tomato Soup, '83 267; '86 258
Easy Tomato Soup, '84 14
French Market Soup, '94 317
Fresh Tomato Soup, '83 140
Gazpacho, Classic Tomato, '99 172
Gazpacho, Tomato-Avocado-Corn, '97 182
Herbed Yogurt and Parmesan Toasts, Tomato
    Soup with, '96 66
Hot Tomato Juice Soup, '86 302
Iced Tomato Soup, '79 170
Italian Soup, Chunky, '99 20
Mexican Tomato Soup, Icy-Spicy, '90 155
Plus, Tomato Soup, '88 170
Potage, Tomato, '79 250
Pumpkin-Tomato Soup, '86 291
Rice Soup, Tomato-and-, '85 24
Savory Tomato Soup, '94 91
Sour Cream-Topped Tomato Soup, '80 246
Summer Tomato Soup, '79 130
Tomato Soup, '81 236; '83 44; '89 217
Tortellini Soup, '98 68
Tortilla Soup, '98 291
Vegetable Soup, Tomato-, '81 M177; '86 9
Spicy Tomato Warm-Up, '95 328
Spinach-Topped Tomatoes, '88 265; '94 321
Spread, Fiery Tomato-Cheese, '87 196
Spread, Home-Style Sandwich, '80 179
Spread, Tomato, '94 123
Spread, Tomato-Cheese, '81 157
Squash and Tomato Bake, '95 180
Squash, Beans, and Tomatoes, '83 148
Squash, Tomato, '86 111
Stack-Ups, Jiffy Tomato, '80 161
Stewed Tomatoes, '83 182
Stewed Tomatoes and Greens, '95 234
Stew, Turkey-Tomato, '90 279
Stir-Fried Sweet Peppers with Tomatoes, '93 207
Stir-Fry, Italian, '92 126
Stir-Fry, Tomato-Zucchini, '80 158
Stir-Fry, Zucchini-and-Tomato, '85 108
Strata, Tomato-Cheese, '81 209

Stuffed
Avocado-Stuffed Tomatoes, '82 101
Bacon-and-Egg-Stuffed Tomatoes, '80 162
Baked Spinach Tomatoes, '90 92
Baked Stuffed Tomatoes, '88 162
Baked Tangy Tomatoes, '81 168
Baked Tomatoes with Corn, '80 161
Bean-Stuffed Tomatoes, '84 34
Broccoli-Stuffed Tomatoes, '83 136; '93 216
Buffet Tomatoes, '82 180
Cheese-Stuffed Tomatoes, '91 69
Cheesy Stuffed Tomatoes, '80 161
Chile-Cheese Stuffed Tomatoes, '94 141
Cold Stuffed Tomatoes, '80 100
Cornbread-Stuffed Tomatoes, '97 169
Corn-Stuffed Tomatoes, '82 270
Crab-and-Avocado Stuffed Tomatoes,
    '94 141
Cups, Turkey-Tomato, '84 119
Curry Sauce, Stuffed Tomatoes with, '97 170
Delights, Tomato, '81 140
Easy Stuffed Tomatoes, '82 264
Eggs-and-Tomato Slices, Stuffed, '84 152
Herbed Tomatoes, '82 49
Homestead Tomatoes, Stuffed, '96 87
Hot Tomatoes, '93 138
Italian-Style Tomatoes, '97 169
Maque Chou Stuffed Tomatoes, '87 89
Mushroom-Stuffed Tomatoes, '86 218; '96 106
Parmesan-Stuffed Tomatoes, '92 182
Provençal Tomatoes, '98 267

Puffs, Tomato Cheese, '81 48
Sausage-Stuffed Tomatoes, '80 47
Scalloped Tomatoes, Stuffed, '90 29
Sea Slaw, Tomatoes Stuffed with, '89 96
Spinach-Stuffed Baked Tomatoes, '86 14
Spinach-Stuffed Tomatoes, '89 203; '93 281
Squash-Stuffed Tomatoes, '82 102
Stuffed Tomatoes, '83 252; '96 82
Tuna-Mac in Tomatoes, '87 188
Tuna Pasta, Stuffed Tomato with, '88 54
Turkey Stuffed Tomatoes, '94 140
Vegetable Stuffed Tomatoes, '94 141
Veracruz Tomatoes, '97 169
Walnut-Rice Stuffing, Tomatoes with, '91 102
Swiss Chard with Tomatoes, '83 36
Swiss Steak Monterey, '99 23
Tabbouleh, '99 175
Tart, Fresh Tomato, '95 170
Tart, Herbed Tomato, '96 94
Tart, Tomato-Basil, '98 132
Tenderloin, Stuffed Tuscany, '99 269
Venison and Tomatoes, '85 270
Vinaigrette, Tomato-Basil, '99 288
Vinegar, Tomato-Herb, '94 200
Welsh Rarebit with Tomatoes and Bacon,
    '92 M159
Zippy 'Maters, '99 172
Zucchini and Tomato with Herbs, '92 182
TOPPINGS. *See also* **FROSTINGS, GLAZES,
    PESTOS, RELISHES, SALSAS,
    SAUCES, SYRUPS.**
Savory
Almond-Garlic Streusel, '95 159
Almonds, Sweet-and-Spicy, '96 274
Apple Topping, '89 107
Avocado Topping, '93 309; '94 96
Biscuit Topping, '86 157, 265
Black Pepper-Pineapple Vinaigrette, '97 181
Blue Cheese Burger Topping, '93 218
Butter-Pecan Topping, '95 158
Catsup Topping, '81 170
Cereal Topping, Crunchy, '96 216
Cheese Topping, '86 233
Chili Topping, '94 22
Cilantro-Lime Cream, '98 129
Crabmeat Topping, '91 64
Cream, Mock Devonshire, '81 288
Crumble Mix, Asian, '96 327
Devonshire Cream, Mock, '99 275
Eggs and Cheese, '95 165
Fruit Dressing, Nutty, '85 68
Fruit Fluff, Tropical, '88 68
Fruit Topping, '81 42; '87 225; '89 50
Ginger-Lime Cream, '95 227
Grecian Skillet Rib Eyes, '96 234
Guacamole, '96 170
Guac, Baine's, '98 88
Hazelnut Whipped Cream, '94 16
Honey Topping, '83 154
Horseradish Cream, '90 96
Ketchup, Christmas, '97 254
Ketchup, Hoisin, '94 138
Lemon Curd, '87 139
Mushrooms, Garlic and, '95 165
Nutty Topping, '86 16
Oat Crunch Topping, '89 108
Oatmeal Cookie Topping, '95 291
Olive Salad, Doodles, '94 35
Olive Salad, Italian, '94 35
Orange Dressing, '97 129
Peach Ketchup, '95 306
Peach Topping, '94 22
Pecan Topping, '94 36
Pepper Topping, Rainbow, '90 117

Pico de Gallo, '96 227; '97 141; '98 87
Pimiento Topping, '83 93
Potato Topping, Mashed, '89 243
Red Pepper Puree, '93 275
Roasted Red Bell Pepper Spread, '97 217
Roquefort Firecrackers, '97 19
Rum Cream, '98 271
Salad Mix, Muffy, '94 34
Salad Topping, Curry, '96 326
Sausage and Peppers, '95 165
Shrimp Topping, '93 291
Sour Cream Topping, Spicy, '95 15
Southwestern Dressing, '91 195
Strawberry Topping, '90 142
Streusel, '85 326
Streusel Topping, '94 280
Sweet Potato Chips, '97 63
Tomato, Basil, and Cheese, '95 165
Turkey-Vegetable Topping, '94 22
Vegetable Topping, '79 79
Yogurt-Cheese Topping, '88 55
Sweet
Almond Topping, '85 152; '86 200
Apple-Nut Topping, '93 162
Apples 'n' Pears, Saucy, '96 72
Apricot Flambé Topping, '98 127
Bananas Hawaiian, '89 94
Blackberries Chantilly, '99 130
Blackberry Syrup, '99 131
Brown Sugar Topping, '81 162
Caramel Drizzle, '86 247
Chantilly Cream, '83 91
Chocolate Cream, '94 57
Chocolate Ganache, '97 282
Chocolate-Peanut Topping, '79 222
Cinnamon Crème, Apple Pie with Warm,
    '99 337
Cinnamon-Pecan Topping, '85 277
Cream Topping, Spicy, '85 177
Crème Chantilly, '91 297
Crème Chantilly, Gingered, '96 163
Crème Pâtissière, '83 225
Crumb Topping, '83 183; '88 216
Fruit Fluff, Tropical, '88 68
Fruity Dessert Topping, '82 167
Ginger Cream Topping, '84 312
Hot Fudge Ice Cream Topping, '98 317
Kahlúa Cream, '91 197
Key Lime Curd, '96 126
Lemon-Blueberry Cream, '92 153
Lemon Cream, '82 237
Lemon Curd, '94 315
Lemon-Pineapple Topping, '86 60
Lime-Rum Cream, '93 169
Maple-Pecan Ice Cream Topping, '98 317
Mocha Cream, '94 47
Nutty Topping, '85 256
Orange-Mallow Cream, '94 295
Oranges in Grand Marnier, '95 142
Orange Topping, Whipped, '80 254
Paint, Egg Yolk, '86 322
Papaya Topping, '86 181
Pear Whip, '89 94
Pineapple Topping, '86 239
Powdered Sugar Paints, '97 286
Raspberries, Spirited, '95 142
Raspberry Topping, '85 317
Rum Cream, '88 154
Rum Cream Topping, '80 255
Rumtopf, '95 142
Sour Cream Topping, '85 298; '86 120
Sticky Bun Toast Topper, '99 M72
Strawberry Cream, '88 153
Strawberry Topping, '86 32

TOPPINGS, Sweet
(continued)

    Streusel Topping, **'88** 154, M275; **'96** 216
    Sugar, Colored, **'99** 179
    Sugars, Colored, **'90** 21
    Vanilla Cream, **'81** 248
    Whipped Cream Topping, **'87** 264; **'89** 154
    Whipped Topping, Reduced-Calorie, **'85** 55

TORTES. *See* **CAKES/Tortes.**

TORTILLAS. *See also* **BURRITOS,
    ENCHILADAS, FAJITAS,
    QUESADILLAS, TAMALES.**

Appetizers, Tex-Mex Tortilla, **'86** 297
Bake, Chicken Tortilla, **'82** 89
Bake, Texas Tortilla, **'94** 285
Baskets, Tortilla, **'94** 97
Bites, Tortilla, **'95** 42
Buñuelos, **'80** 199
Buñuelos, King-Size, **'86** 5
Burgers, Tortilla, **'94** 138
Campesina, Tortilla, **'89** 85
Casserole, Cabin Mexican, **'97** 95
Casserole, Chicken Tortilla, **'81** 166
Casserole, El Dorado, **'81** 140
Casserole, Mexican Chicken, **'82** 143
Chalupas, Bean, **'83** 313
Chalupas, Chicken, **'79** 185
Chalupas, Chicken-Olive, **'81** 227
Chalupas, Texas Turkey, **'80** 196
Cheese Tortilla Snack, Two-, **'90** 119
Cheesy Tortillas, **'81** 62
Chicken Acapulco, **'84** 32
Chicken, King Ranch, **'99** 330
Chicken-Tortilla Stack, Cheesy, **'86** 3
Chicken Tostadas, **'93** 204
Chilaquiles, **'82** 220
Chilaquiles con Pollo, **'81** 66
Chimichangas, **'86** 114
Chimichangas, Apple, **'95** 43
Chimichangas, Baked Spicy Beef, **'97** 319
Chimichangas, Chicken, **'98** 95
Chimichangas, Oven-Fried Beef, **'92** 124
Chimichangas, Pineapple Dessert, **'86** 4
Chimichangas, Traditional Spicy Beef, **'97** 319
Chips, Corn Tortilla, **'91** 17
Chips, Light Tortilla, **'90** 278; **'91** 257
Chips, Tortilla, **'91** 137
Chorizo and Egg Tortillas, **'81** 193
Crackers, Tortilla-Lime, **'99** 17
Dinner, Quick Mexican, **'98** 224
Dippers, Rolled Tortilla, **'86** 4
Dumplings, Chicken and Tortilla, **'99** 327
Egg-and-Sausage Tortillas, **'83** 246; **'84** 42
Eggs Sonora, **'80** 196
Española, Tortilla, **'92** 175
Fillet, Acapulco, **'98** 174
Flautas, **'83** 199
Flautas, Rancho Ramillete, **'96** M125
Flautas with Guacamole, Chicken, **'89** 226
Flour Tortillas, **'81** 303; **'95** 44
Flour Tortillas, Never-Fail, **'80** 198
Franks, Mexican, **'93** 78
Garlic Crisps, **'99** 60
Ham Appetillas, **'93** 63
Huevos Rancheros, **'82** 197; **'91** 77
Lasagna, Mexican, **'98** 283
Lasagna, Texas, **'98** 52
Migas, **'94** 26; **'98** 312
Picadillo, **'84** 118
Pie, Mexican Cheese, **'82** 9; **'83** 69
Pie, Montezuma Tortilla, **'83** 199
Pie, Tortilla, **'85** M211; **'96** 135

Pizza, Mexican, **'99** 119
Rollups, Cream Cheese, **'98** 134
Rollups, Mexican, **'98** 134
Roll-Ups, Mexican Beef, **'90** 176
Rollups, Pizza, **'99** 197
Rollups, Roasted Red Pepper, **'98** 285
Rollups, Spinach, **'95** 251
Rollups, Tortilla, **'89** 87
Rollups, Vegetable, **'98** 134
Salad in a Shell, Mexican, **'86** 4
Salads, Mexican Chicken Tortilla, **'95** 129
Salad, Southwestern Spiral, **'98** 66
Sandwiches, Caribbean Seafood, **'98** 105
Sandwiches, Guacamole, **'82** 9; **'83** 68
Sandwiches, Tuna Roll, **'96** 199
Sandwich, Tex-Mex Ham-and-Cheese, **'86** 4
Snacks, Pesto Tortilla, **'89** 19
Soup, Spicy Tortilla, **'90** 32; **'93** 108
Soup, Tortilla, **'88** 31, 245; **'90** 201; **'93** 197, 274;
    '94 136; **'98** 291; **'99** 310
Stack-Ups, Tortilla, **'92** 196
Steak, Matt's Chicken-Fried, **'97** 25
Stew, Baja Pork, **'98** 283
Tacoritos, **'90** 133
Tostada Compuestas, **'81** 194
Tostadas, Chicken, **'95** 122
Tostadas, Crab, **'93** 203
Tostadas, Crispy, **'83** 2
Tostadas, Party, **'98** M33
Tostadas, Quick Chicken, **'99** 159
Tostadas, Rice-and-Black Bean, **'97** 65
Tostadas, Shrimp-and-Black Bean, **'93** 204
Tostadas, Super, **'83** 199
Triangles, Tortilla, **'94** 107
Wraps, Western, **'99** 194

TUNA

Appetizers

    Ball, Tuna-Pecan, **'87** 94
    Cherry Tomatoes, Tuna-Stuffed, **'89** 214
    Dip, Low-Cal Tuna, **'87** 25
    Dip, Tasty Tuna, **'96** 190
    Dip, Tuna-Curry, **'84** 31
    Mold, Creamy Tuna-Cheese, **'81** 135
    Mound, Tuna, **'80** 276
    Mousse, Tuna, **'80** 275
    Nachos, Tuna, **'96** 201
    Spread, Chunky Tuna, **'89** 147
    Spread, Tuna, **'83** 174; **'91** 305
Baked Tuna and Peas in Wine Sauce, **'83** 196
Bake, Shoestring Potato Tuna, **'82** 211
Barbecued Tuna, **'80** 275
Bisque, Tuna, **'79** 76
Broiled Tuna with Rosemary, **'93** 127
Burgers, Tuna, **'95** 128; **'96** 139
Burgers, Zippy Tuna, **'81** 135
Casserole, Biscuit-Topped Tuna, **'79** 113
Casserole, Easy Tuna, **'82** M203
Casserole, Nippy Tuna, **'84** 241
Casserole, Tangy Tuna-Broccoli, **'83** 75
Casserole, Tuna, **'82** 119; **'96** 103
Casserole, Tuna Vegetable, **'81** 135
Casserole with Cheese Swirls, Tuna, **'88** 256
Cheesies, Tuna, **'82** 191
Chopsticks, Tuna, **'94** 255
Creamed Chipped Tuna, **'95** 127
Croquettes, Tuna-Egg, **'80** 275
Croquettes with Parsley Sauce, Tuna, **'86** 108
Grilled Florida Tuna, **'93** 128
Grilled Tuna, Inland, **'96** 197
Grilled Tuna with Poblano Salsa, **'91** 135
Jambalaya, Tuna, **'83** 44
Lasagna, Tuna, **'83** 44; **'84** 123
Lemon and Capers, Tuna with, **'97** 180
Loaf, Mediterranean Picnic, **'96** 156

Macaroni Treat, Tuna-, **'82** 131
Melts, Curried Tuna, **'95** 46
Melts, Hot Tuna, **'95** 126; **'96** 201
Melt, Southwestern Tuna, **'96** 201
Melts, Tempting Tuna, **'88** 158
Mustard Sauce, Tuna with Tangy, **'92** 201
Nachos, Tuna, **'95** 127
Pie, Tuna-Rice, **'84** 123
Pie with Cheese Roll Crust, Tuna, **'80** 286
Pita Pocket, Tuna-in-a-, **'87** 202
Pockets, Tuna, **'88** 139
Potatoes, Tuna-Stuffed, **'79** 210

Salads

    Cannellini Bean Salad, Tuna-and-, **'86** 143
    Cheese-Sauced Tuna Salad, **'87** M124
    Chef Salad, Tuna, **'82** 78
    Company Tuna Salad, **'87** 201
    Confetti Salad, **'80** 4
    Congealed Tuna Salad, **'84** 163
    Creamy Tuna Salad, **'82** 87, 208
    Crunchy Tuna Salad, **'87** 201
    Cucumber Tuna Boats, **'83** 136
    Curried Tuna Salad, **'86** 208
    Curried Tuna Salad with Grapes, **'87** 201
    Egg Salad, Tuna-, **'81** 135
    Eggs, Tuna-Stuffed, **'83** 83
    Favorite Tuna Salad, **'82** 208
    Flavorful Tuna Salad, **'81** 37
    Greens and Tuna Salad, Fresh, **'80** 55
    Hot Tuna Salad Rolls, **'84** 281
    Layered Tuna Salad, **'84** 221
    Luncheon Tuna Salad, **'81** 135
    Macaroni Salad, Tuna, **'83** 44, 145
    Macaroni Salad, Tuna-, **'84** 66
    Macaroni-Tuna Salad, Whole Wheat, **'84** 193
    Meal-in-One Salad, **'82** 232
    Pasta Salad, Tuna-, **'91** 43; **'92** 141
    Pasta Salad, Tuna, **'92** 108
    Pasta, Stuffed Tomato with Tuna, **'88** 54
    Potato Salad, Tuna-, **'84** 289
    Red Pepper Salad, Tuna-and-, **'93** 143
    Rice Salad, Tuna-, **'87** 202
    Ring, Creamy Tuna, **'80** 275
    Swiss Tuna Salad, **'86** 186
    Taco Salad, Tuna-, **'87** 145
    Tomatoes, Tuna-Mac in, **'87** 188
    Tomato Salad, Tuna with Warm, **'97** 179
    White Bean Salad, Tuna-and-, **'98** 209
    White Bean-Tuna Salad, **'98** 208
    Wild Tuna Salad, **'95** 243
Sandwich Boats, Tuna, **'91** 166
Sandwiches, French Toasted Tuna, **'80** 275
Sandwiches, Hot Tuna, **'85** 299; **'86** M194
Sandwiches, Tuna Club, **'83** 134
Sandwiches, Tuna Roll, **'96** 199
Southwestern Tuna Melts, **'95** 127
Steaks, Grilled Tuna, **'90** 129
Steaks on Mixed Greens with Lemon-Basil
    Vinaigrette, Seared Tuna, **'94** 205
Steaks with Cucumber Sauce, Tuna, **'97** 180
Steaks with Tarragon Butter, Tuna,
    '92 328
Tapenade, Tuna, **'95** 127; **'96** 201
Vegetables, Tuna with Sautéed, **'98** 222
Waffle-Wich, Hot Tuna, **'88** 272; **'89** 181
Yellowfin Tuna with Corn, Pepper, and Tomato
    Salsa, **'94** 164

TURKEY

Appetizers, Turkey, **'91** 314
Baked Turkey, Cider, **'83** 263
Bake, Layered Ham and Turkey, **'79** 252
Barbecue, Turkey, **'90** 158
Black-Eyed Peas, Creole, **'98** 22
Braised Turkey Breast, **'84** 260

Breast and Gravy, Savory Seasoned Turkey, '89 M309
Breast, Apple-Rosemary Turkey, '99 253
Breast, Citrus-Marinated Turkey, '94 272
Breast, Herb Butter-Basted Turkey, '86 285
Breast, Herbed Turkey, '92 266
Breast, Smoky Turkey, '89 323
Breast with Orange-Raspberry Glaze, Turkey, '91 253
Buffet Turkey, '80 29
Burgers, Garlic Turkey, '99 135
Burgers, Turkey, '98 22
Cabbage Rolls, Stuffed, '88 18
Casserole, Crunchy Turkey, '89 M282
Casserole, Day-After-the-Holiday, '96 276
Casserole, Golden Turkey, '80 271
Casserole, Stuffed Turkey, '88 246
Casserole, Turkey, '84 327; '96 302
Casserole, Turkey-and-Broccoli, '86 332
Casserole, Turkey-and-Shrimp Florentine, '92 122
Casserole, Turkey-Asparagus, '86 284
Casserole, Turkey-Olive, '87 268
Casserole, Turkey-Spinach, '84 71
Casserole, Turkey-Swiss, '86 283
Chalupas, Texas Turkey, '80 196
Chili, Southwestern, '91 284
Chili Topping, '84 246
Chili, Turkey-Bean, '88 M213
Chowder, Turkey, '85 10; '91 312
Chowder, Turkey-Corn, '81 98; '96 279
Cornbread Crust, Turkey and Peppers in, '95 312
Creamed Turkey, Southern, '80 272
Crêpes, Elegant Turkey, '83 282
Crêpes, Turkey, '92 41
Cups, Turkey-Tomato, '84 119
Curried Cream Sauce, Turkey Slices with, '91 60
Cutlets, Oven-Fried Turkey, '91 121
Cutlets, Pecan-Crusted Turkey, '94 282
Cutlets with Pepper Salsa, Spicy Turkey, '88 26
Cutlets with Sage Gravy, Turkey, '96 268
Cutlets with Tarragon-Mustard Sauce, Turkey, '93 239
Cutlets with Tomato-Caper Sauce, Turkey, '91 61
Deep-Fried Turkey, '92 339
Divan, Creamy Turkey, '90 M34
Divan, Quick Turkey, '89 178
Divan, Turkey, '82 268
Dressing, Easy Turkey and, '79 296
Dressing, Fruited Turkey, '99 257
Dressing, Turkey, '85 298
Drumsticks, Grilled Turkey, '89 168
Empanadas, Easy Turkey, '96 63
Fast-and-Savory Turkey, '87 306
Florentine, Turkey, '88 264
Galantine of Turkey, '85 150
Giblet Dressing and Turkey Gravy, Turkey with, '91 254
Gravy, Savory Turkey and, '94 326
Gravy, Turkey, '91 255; '94 306
Grilled Turkey Breast with Cranberry Salsa, '95 252
Gumbo, Turkey, '82 268; '85 258
Hash, Turkey, '95 262
Herbed Turkey-in-a-Bag, '91 253
Indian Turkey, '85 302
Italiano, Turkey, '91 62
Jambalaya de Covington, '87 211
Kabobs, Turkey-and-Fruit, '88 140
Lazy Day Turkey, '93 93
Loaf, Cranberry-Glazed Turkey, '86 171
Loaf, Ground Turkey, '86 171

Loaf, Turkey, '92 33
Marinated Turkey, Benny Sauce, '98 306
Marinated Turkey with Peppery Milk Gravy, Buttermilk-, '98 311
Meatballs, Turkey, '89 237
Meat Loaf, Spinach-Stuffed Turkey, '97 24
Meat Mixture, Basic, '92 241
Mix, Ground Meat, '89 143
Nachos, Turkey, '90 118
New Year's Turkey, '97 255
Oriental Turkey, '82 268
Parmesan, Turkey, '82 268
Parmigiana, Turkey, '87 193
Pasta
    Basil Pasta, Creamy Turkey-, '89 216
    Lasagna, Easy, '92 M197; '93 24
    Lasagna, Lean, '86 37
    Lasagna, Turkey, '83 239; '91 130
    Lasagna, Turkey-Picante, '97 93
    Noodle Bake, Turkey, '93 243
    Noodle-Poppyseed Casserole, Turkey-, '90 239
    Noodle Soup Mix, Turkey-, '89 330
    Noodle Soup, Turkey-, '91 312
    Pie, Broccoli-and-Turkey Pasta, '88 269
    Primavera, Smoked Turkey Pasta, '90 84
    Salad, Ranch-Style Turkey 'n' Pasta, '94 184
    Spaghetti, Ham-and-Turkey, '95 19
    Spaghetti Sauce, Turkey, '85 13
    Stroganoff, Turkey, '91 61
    Tetrazzini, Herbed Turkey, '86 47
Pâté in Pastry, Turkey-Mushroom, '92 327
Patties in Vegetable-Tomato Sauce, Turkey, '87 18
Patties, Stuffed Ground Turkey, '86 171
Peppers, Turkey with, '92 182
Piccata, Turkey, '91 137
Piccata, Turkey-Basil, '96 49
Piccata with Caper Sauce, Turkey, '98 49
Pie, Crumb-Crust Curried Turkey, '86 265
Pie, Golden Turkey, '79 253
Pie, Italian Meat, '89 109
Pie, Lattice-Topped Turkey, '81 277; '82 7
Pie, Potato-Topped Turkey, '86 265
Pie, Turkey, '80 285
Pie, Turkey-and-Dressing, '84 326
Pie, Turkey-and-Oyster, '82 267
Pie, Turkey-Cheese, '88 264
Pie, Turkey Pot, '86 265; '90 24; '93 45
Pie with Biscuit Crust, Turkey Pot, '98 296
Pilaf, Turkey-Asparagus, '88 200
Pilaf, Turkey-Rice, '86 284
Pizza, Turkey-Vegetable, '90 139
Puffs, Turkey-Cheese, '87 301
Rice, Herbed Turkey and, '97 327
Rice, Turkey Fried, '83 282
Roasted Turkey, Apple-Rosemary, '99 252
Roasted Turkey Breasts, Jackie's, '98 269
Roasted Turkey, Rosemary, '99 312
Roasted Turkey with Sausage-and-Wild Mushroom Stuffing, '96 266
Roast Turkey, '79 250; '80 262; '86 47; '88 253; '90 321
Roast Turkey and Cornbread Dressing, '89 324
Roast Turkey and Giblet Gravy, '94 308
Roast Turkey Breast and Gravy, '88 303
Roast Turkey Breast with Special Gravy, '86 282
Roast Turkey, How to, '83 286
Roast Turkey with Grandmother's Dressing, Madeira, '91 254
Roast Turkey with Herbs, '95 305
Roast Turkey with Oyster Stuffing, '80 251
Roast Turkey with Peanut Dressing, '79 283

Roast Turkey with Rice Dressing, '82 286
Rollups, Turkey, '86 198
Salads
    Apple Salad, Turkey-, '88 123; '90 181
    Bake, Turkey Salad, '79 253
    Caesar Salad, Turkey, '93 320
    Carrot Salad, Turkey-, '86 283
    Curried Turkey Salad, '88 140
    Curried Turkey Salad, Chutney, '98 314
    Fruit-and-Spice Turkey Salad, '94 325
    Fruit-and-Turkey Salad, '89 176
    Fruitful Turkey Salad, '84 197
    Fruit Salad, Turkey-, '79 56
    Fruit Salad, Turkey, '83 233; '84 244
    Holiday Turkey Salad, '84 320
    Honey-Mustard Turkey Salad, '92 309
    Hot Bacon Dressing, Turkey Salad with, '87 285
    Hot Turkey Salad, '86 10, 297; '87 176
    Layered Turkey Salad, '86 332; '92 220
    Macaroni Salad, Turkey, '83 282
    Meal-in-One Salad, '86 43
    Orange Salad, Turkey-in-the-, '93 21
    Pasta Salad, Ranch-Style Turkey 'n', '94 184
    Polynesian Turkey Salad, '87 285
    Sandwiches, Turkey Salad Pita, '87 202; '88 43
    Sautéed Walnuts, Turkey Salad with, '86 117
    Smoked Turkey Salad, '96 184
    Southwestern Turkey Salad, '91 313
    Stir-Fry Salad, Chilled Turkey-and-Pepper, '88 140
    Straw Salad, Turkey-in-the-, '96 286
    Taco Salad, Turkey, '95 25
    Turkey Salad, '90 318
    Waldorf Salad with Yogurt Dressing, Turkey, '88 53
    Zucchini Salad, Turkey-, '85 74
Sandwiches
    Asparagus Sandwiches, Turkey-, '96 74
    Burgers, All-American Pizza, '92 148
    Burgers, Grilled Turkey, '91 61
    Burgers, Pizza, '89 165
    Cheese Dogs, Turkey-, '97 203
    Club Sandwiches, Double-Decker, '91 231; '92 68
    Croissant, Turkey-Cranberry, '96 320
    Ham-and-Turkey Specials, Cheesy, '84 14
    Hero Sandwiches, Turkey, '92 196
    Hero with Garlic Sauce, Turkey, '90 145
    Hot Browns, '98 287
    Hot Brown Sandwiches, '80 M202
    Hot Turkey Sandwich, '93 306
    Mayflower Sandwiches, '96 287
    Meal-in-One Sandwiches, '80 218
    Monte Cristo Sandwiches, '83 134; '97 319
    Mozzarella Rounds, Turkey-, '82 3
    Open-Faced Sandwiches, '79 214
    Open-Facers, Turkey, '82 190
    Roast Turkey, '90 321
    Slaw Sandwich, Turkey-in-the-, '90 177
    Sloppy Toms, '91 51
    Smoked Turkey, Mozzarella, and Blackberry Sandwiches, '99 220
    Smoked Turkey-Roasted Pepper Sandwiches, '94 66
    Stuffed Sandwich, Deli, '98 287
    Sweet Smoky Sandwiches, '97 219
    Tea Sandwiches, Turkey, '99 86
    Waffle-Grilled Turkey Sandwich, '94 170
Sausage-Cornbread Dressing, Turkey with, '83 287
Sausage, Marinara Sauce with Italian Turkey, '89 239

TURKEY

(continued)

Sauté, Creamy Turkey, '93 19
Sauté, Turkey, '89 105
Scaloppine, Easy Turkey, '95 M192
Schnitzel, Turkey, '84 230
Skillet, Oriental Turkey-Orange, '86 284
Skillet Turkey Dinner, '91 61
Slices, Orange-Turkey, '90 53
Smoked Turkey, '79 293; '84 160; '85 258;
   '90 249
Smoked Turkey Breast, '88 169
Smoked Turkey Medley, '90 128
Smoked Turkey, Seasoned, '97 85
Soufflé, Turkey, '80 271
Soup, Bean-and-Turkey, '93 319
Soup, Curried Turkey, '86 332
Soup Mix, Turkey-Noodle, '89 330
Soup, Tempting Turkey, '98 314
Soup, Turkey-Barley, '91 312
Soup, Turkey Carcass, '86 284
Soup, Turkey-Noodle, '91 312
Soup, Turkey-Rice, '90 89
Soup, Turkey-Vegetable, '84 4; '88 264; '91 312
Soup, Williamsburg Turkey, '90 287
Spread, Curried Turkey, '92 16
Spread, Turkey Party, '83 282
Squash Dressing, Turkey with, '87 248
Steaks, Grilled Marinated Turkey, '93 170
Stew, Hearty Turkey, '79 252
Stew, Turkey-Tomato, '90 279
Stir-Fry, Italian, '92 126
Stir-Fry, Turkey-Broccoli, '91 62
Stock, Light Poultry, '90 31
Stuffed Turkey Breast, '87 270; '89 322
Stuffed Turkey Breast, Wild Rice-, '97 281
Stuffed Turkey Breast with Seasoned Dressing,
   '83 320; '84 128
Sweet-and-Sour Turkey, '79 252
Tarragon Cream, Turkey with, '91 60
Tenderloins, Lime-Buttered Turkey, '92 127
Tenderloins with Lingonberry Sauce, Turkey,
   '97 289
Tomatoes, Turkey Stuffed, '94 140
Topping, Turkey-Vegetable, '94 22
Treats, Turkey, '93 256
Turnovers, Home-Style Turkey, '94 325
Turnovers, Turkey Sausage, '95 239
Wild Turkey, Country-Fried, '94 306
TURNIP GREENS. *See* **GREENS.**
TURNIPS
au Gratin, Turnip, '79 289
au Gratin, Turnips, '84 229; '88 229; '89 244
Boiled Turnips, '83 242
Braised Turnips, '91 219
Casserole, Baked Turnip, '82 274
Casserole, Turnip, '83 242; '84 229
Cheese Sauce, Turnips in, '84 229
Creamy Cooked Turnips, '86 224
Dip, Turnip Green, '91 13
Fried Turnips, Shoestring, '81 274
Gingered Turnips, '82 274
Glazed Turnips, '81 274
Greens and Ham Hock, Southern Turnip, '80 119
Greens, Fresh Turnip, '92 339
Greens, Old-Fashioned Turnip, '85 255
Greens, Turnip, '90 13, 232; '95 306
Greens, Turnip-and-Collard, '92 215
Greens with Turnips, Turnip, '84 230
Hash Brown Turnips, '79 254
Julienne, Turnips and Carrots, '86 295
Onions, Turnips and, '83 242

Orange Carrots and Turnips, Sunset, '94 213
Parsleyed Turnips and Carrots, '79 253
Party Turnips, '84 230
Potatoes, Turnips and, '79 254
Pudding, Turnip, '94 213
Salad, Irish Turnip, '94 178
Salad, Turnip, '85 235
Salad, Turnip-and-Carrot, '91 212
Saucy Turnips, '85 289
Sauté, Carrot-Turnip, '93 241
Scalloped Potatoes and Turnips, '85 235
Scalloped Turnips, '79 254
Slaw, Turnip, '89 245
Soufflé, Turnip, '79 254
Soup, Creamy Turnip, '84 279
Soup, Oyster-Turnip, '94 328
Soup, Turnip, '92 271
Southern Turnips, '87 190
Stir-Fry, Turnip-and-Carrot, '96 36
Supreme, Turnip, '79 254
Sweet-and-Sour Turnips, '81 274
TURTLE
Fried Cooter (Soft-Shell Turtle), '80 99
Soup au Sherry, Turtle, '80 56
Soup, Turtle, '92 92
TZIMMES
Fruit Tzimmes with Brisket, Mixed, '93 114
Sweet Potato-Beef Tzimmes, '92 234
Tzimmes, '95 102

Vanilla

Almond Crunch, Vanilla, '93 243
Beach, The, '95 168
Cake, Vanilla Chiffon, '79 266
Cheesecake, Creamy Vanilla, '89 93
Cookies 'n' Cream Dessert, Gold-Dusted, '94 271
Cookies, Vanilla Slice-and-Bake, '85 171
Cream, Vanilla, '81 248; '83 M115; '97 272
Crescents, Vanilla, '82 307
Cupcakes, Golden Vanilla, '85 121
Cupcakes, Vanilla, '92 14
Cups, Vanilla Lace, '98 M93
Custard, Baked Vanilla, '82 129
Custard, Vanilla, '99 27
Dessert, Glorified Vanilla Sherry, '81 85
Extract, Home-Brewed Vanilla, '83 228
Extract, Homemade Vanilla, '83 228
Extract, Vanilla, '94 243; '97 288
Finger Painting Never Tasted So Good, '95 167
Fondant, Faux, '98 M154
Frosting, Vanilla, '84 36; '85 236; '92 14, 274
Frosting, Vanilla Buttercream, '92 239; '94 99;
   '96 229; '97 111; '99 117
Frosting, Vanilla-Rum, '85 324
Frosty, French Vanilla, '79 148
Fruit Cup, Vanilla, '80 183
Glaze, Vanilla, '85 M89; '89 211
Ice Cream, Basic Vanilla, '88 202
Ice Cream, Country Vanilla, '82 143
Ice Cream) Helado, Caramel-Vanilla (Caramel-
   Vanilla, '81 67
Ice Cream, Honey-Vanilla, '95 178
Ice Cream, Old-Fashioned Vanilla, '97 166
Ice Cream Pumpkin, '96 255
Ice Cream Spectacular, Vanilla, '82 166
Ice Cream, Vanilla, '80 176; '86 129; '91 174
Ice Cream, Vanilla Custard, '92 148; '96 145;
   '98 221
Oil, Vanilla, '94 243
Parfait, Bodacious Peanut, '95 167
Parfaits, Hooray, '96 229
Pears, Vanilla Poached, '90 57

Pie, Fruit-Topped Vanilla Cream, '84 49
Pralines, Vanilla, '92 313; '93 51
Pudding, Creamy Vanilla, '83 227
Pudding, Vanilla, '88 32
Sauce, Almond-Vanilla Custard, '88 M177
Sauce, Pan-Fried Grouper with Vanilla Wine,
   '94 241
Sauce, Vanilla, '97 M15
Sauce, Vanilla Crème, '94 243; '96 155
Sauce, Vanilla Custard, '99 27
Shortbread, Scottish, '94 242
Soufflé, Frozen Vanilla, '79 230; '82 173
Soufflés with Vanilla Crème Sauce, Vanilla,
   '94 242; '96 155
Spooky Ghosts, '98 M256
Sugar, Vanilla, '94 243
Vinaigrette, Vanilla, '94 242
VEAL
Amaretto-Lime Veal, '93 54
Amelio, Veal, '86 142
au Madeira, Veal, '81 131
Birds, Veal, '84 260
Burgoo, Five-Meat, '87 3
Casserole, Veal and Wild Rice, '79 180
Casserole, Veal Cutlet, '79 109
Chops, Apple Veal, '87 220
Chops, Herb-Peppered Veal, '98 60
Chops Mediterranean, Veal, '79 108
Company Veal and Carrots, '85 22
Cordon Bleu, Veal, '87 219
Cutlets, Stuffed Veal, '92 329
Cutlets with Leeks and Zinfandel Cream, Veal,
   '96 237
Delight, Veal, '79 109
Grilled Pork Chops, '98 246
Herbed Veal and Onions, '79 108
Herbed Veal with Wine, '86 193
Italian Style, Veal, '82 M68
Lemon Veal, '93 35
Lemon Veal Piccata, '86 118
Lemon Veal with Artichoke Hearts, '87 219
Marsala, Veal, '91 218, 310
Marsala, Veal-and-Mushrooms, '89 44
Meatballs, European Veal, '85 30
Meat Loaf, Italian, '79 187
Meat Loaf, Savory, '87 216
Meat Loaf, Triple, '79 186
Meat Loaf, Veal, '93 292
New Orleans Veal with Crabmeat, '86 94
Osso Buco, '98 260
Paprika, Veal, '88 113
Parmigiana, Veal, '81 227
Peppercorns, Veal with Green, '87 220
Picante, Veal, '87 31
Piccata, Veal, '92 181
Piccata with Capers, Veal, '87 142
Ragoût, Veal-and-Artichoke, '94 43
Roast, Best Baked Veal, '87 219
Roast with Vegetables, Veal, '89 71
Sauce, Noodles with Veal, '80 236
Sauté, Veal-Cepe, '89 62
Savory Veal, '83 281
Scallopini à la Marsala, Veal, '79 109
Scallopini Marsala, Veal, '85 295
Scallopini of Veal al Sorriso, '79 85
Scallopini, Veal, '83 8, 125
Scallopini with Shiitakes, Veal, '99 232
Schnitzel, Swiss, '80 189
Skillet Veal, '83 200
Soup with Quenelles, Veal-Vermicelli, '94 14
Spaghetti, Veal, '84 276
Spaghetti with Veal and Peppers, '81 201; '82 14
Steak, Veal, '82 276
Stock, Brown Meat, '90 31

Stroganoff, Veal, '79 108
Supreme, Veal, '85 109
Sweetbreads, Creamed, '90 82
Swirls, Veal-and-Smithfield Ham, '86 253
Terrine of Pork and Veal, '93 287
Terrine with Mustard Sauce, Veal, '93 118
Turkey, New Year's, '97 255
Wine Sauce, Veal and Carrots in, '81 31;
  '86 M139
VEGETABLES. *See also* **specific types and
  CASSEROLES.**
à la Grill, Vegetables, '88 130
Antipasto Skillet Dinner, '97 327
Appetizers
  Antipasto, Easy, '92 24
  Antipasto, Grandpa's, '98 183
  Antipasto, Vegetable, '85 263
  Bites, Veggie, '91 171
  Canapés, Vegetable, '91 252
  Caviar, Texas, '99 84
  Cheesecake, Roasted Vegetable, '99 140
  Cheesecake, Vegetable, '96 110
  Cocktail, Fresh Vegetable, '82 165
  Dip and Vegetable Platter, Curry, '89 327
  Dip, Creamy Vegetable, '83 180
  Dip, Cucumber-Cheese Vegetable, '83 128
  Dip, Fresh Vegetable, '80 249
  Dip, Herb Vegetable, '89 269
  Dip, Starburst Vegetable, '82 248
  Dip, Tangy Vegetable, '87 196
  Dip, Vegetable, '79 52; '82 161
  Dip, Vegetable Garden, '85 215
  Dip, Zippy Vegetable, '84 256
  Egg Rolls, Vegetarian, '86 148
  Fresh Vegetable Party Tray, '82 122
  Fresh Vegetables, Parsley-Dill Dip with, '85 79
  Fried Veggies, '96 19
  Hot Vegetable Juice Appetizer, '93 324
  Marinated Vegetable Medley, '85 319; '95 91
  Marinated Vegetables, '94 183; '96 213
  Marinated Vegetables Italian, '90 242
  Mushroom Caps, Vegetable, '81 246
  Nachos, Vegetable, '91 17
  Pâté, Vegetable-Chicken, '86 66
  Platter with Creamy Honey-Herb Dip,
    Vegetable, '98 135
  Relish Tree, Christmas, '84 257
  Rice with Spring Vegetables, '96 132
  Rollups, Vegetable, '98 134
  Salsa, Greek Vegetable, '98 32
  Salsa, Shrimp Skewers with Vegetable, '98 32
  Shrimp-and-Vegetable Appetizer, '97 161
  Spread, Garden, '86 135
  Spread, Garden Vegetable, '93 184
  Spread, Vegetable, '90 144
  Spread, Vegetable Party, '84 166
  Tarragon Vegetable Appetizer, '83 277
  Terrine, Chicken-Vegetable, '84 131
  Terrine, Vegetable-Chicken, '83 224
Apple Cider Pork and Vegetables, '97 210
Bake, Winter, '99 273
Bake with Sweet Bacon Dressing,
  Vegetable-Chicken, '93 108
Barbecue Hobo Supper, '99 108
Barley and Vegetables, '91 81
Beef and Vegetables, Company, '88 234
Beef and Vegetables, Savory, '79 163
Blanching Chart, Microwave, '80 M181
Bread, Breakaway Vegetable, '82 74
Bread, Herb-Vegetable-Cheese, '88 172
Bundles, Vegetable, '93 181
Buñuelos, '93 29
Burgers, Beef-and-Vegetable, '84 125
Burgers, Beefy Vegetable, '98 143

Burgers, Vegetable, '89 164
Burgoo, Kentucky, '97 138
Burritos, Tony's Veggie, '96 289
Burritos, Vegetable, '80 197; '90 134; '92 138
Burritos, Vegetarian, '93 319
Burritos with Avocado Sauce, Vegetable, '83 200
Buttermilk Sauce, Vegetables with, '84 6
Cabbage Rolls, Vegetarian, '91 86
Calabacitas, '95 130
Casseroles
  Beef and Vegetable Chow Mein Casserole,
    '83 313
  Beefy Vegetable Casserole, '79 248
  Cashew Casserole, '95 166
  Cheesy Vegetable Casserole, '81 103
  Creamy Vegetable Casserole, '98 96
  Curry Casserole, Vegetable-, '91 286; '92 27
  Enchiladas, Meatless, '93 106
  Fresh Vegetable Casserole, '82 225
  Garden Casserole, '82 168; '88 122
  Garden Medley, '98 236
  Ham Casserole, Vegetable-and-, '84 91
  Lasagna Casserole, Vegetable, '92 198; '93 25
  Lasagna, Cheesy Vegetable, '79 84
  Lasagna, Colorful Vegetable, '87 19
  Lasagna, Garden, '83 119
  Lasagna, Roasted Vegetable-Meat, '99 M332
  Lasagna, Vegetable, '84 201; '93 320; '95 211;
    '96 47; '99 97
  Layered Vegetable Casserole, '91 286; '92 27
  Macaroni Primavera, '96 73
  Medley Bake, Vegetable, '81 268
  Medley, Green Vegetable, '79 287; '80 34
  Medley, Vegetable-Cheese, '99 M287
  Mexican Vegetarian Casserole, '96 276
  Mixed Vegetable Casserole, '83 208, 256;
    '86 327
  Mixed-Vegetable Casserole, '87 154
  Noodle Casserole, Vegetable, '91 30
  Pork Combo, Vegetable-, '85 113
  Scalloped Mixed Vegetables, '83 5
  Squares, Checkerboard Vegetable, '96 178
  Strata, Vegetable-Cheese, '98 98
  Swiss Vegetable Medley, '95 26
  Tuna Vegetable Casserole, '81 135
  Vegetarian Casserole, '96 302
  Veggies Casserole, '88 123
  Wine Sauce Casserole, Vegetables in, '95 133
  Winter Root Vegetable Casserole, '98 265
Cassoulet, Vegetarian, '96 329
Cheesecake, Layered Vegetable, '91 62; '92 51
Chicken and Dumplings with Vegetables,
  '85 M56
Chicken-and-Vegetable Platter, '88 M52
Chicken and Vegetables, '88 165
Chicken and Vegetables, Creamed, '91 90
Chicken and Vegetables, Ginger-Poached,
  '98 229
Chicken and Vegetables, Grilled, '99 200
Chicken and Vegetables, Jim's, '99 237
Chicken and Vegetables, Roast, '81 3
Chicken and Vegetables Vermouth, '87 M37
Chicken and Vegetables with Ginger-Soy Sauce,
  '91 32
Chicken Breast with Turned Vegetables and
  Chive Sauce, Poached, '94 309
Chicken Cacciatore, '99 213
Chicken Chow Mein, '98 283
Chicken, Foil-Wrapped, '99 108
Chicken, Roasted Stuffed, '98 109
Chicken Sausage with Fennel, '98 312
Chicken Skillet, Confetti, '97 327
Chicken Strips and Vegetables, Marinated,
  '90 110

Chicken, Vegetable-Stuffed, '89 M65
Chicken, Whole Poached, '98 229
Chicken with Vegetables, Roasted, '98 108
Chicken with Vegetables Vinaigrette, Grilled,
  '91 26
Chicken with Wine-Soaked Vegetables, Baked,
  '84 277
Chili, Bodacious, '95 14
Chili, Mom's, '93 292
Chili, Vegetable, '91 28; '97 179
Chili, Vegetarian, '84 280, 327; '91 284
Chops with Vegetables, Glazed, '98 132
Chops with Vegetables, Golden, '89 218
Chowchow, Nannie's, '95 250
con Queso, Chile, '97 25
Cornbread-Vegetable Supper, '97 319
Cornish Hens with Vegetables, Tarragon
  Roasted, '94 79
Couscous, Vegetables and, '96 136
Crabs, Fried Stuffed Soft-Shell, '98 140
Crackers, Vegetable, '96 105
Crawfish Delicacy, '99 M23
Creamed Spring Vegetables, '87 127
Crêpes, Chicken-Vegetable, '83 70
Crêpes, Vegetable-Filled Bran, '86 44
Croutons, Vegetable-Flavored, '84 148
Crunchy Vegetables, '99 43
Curry, Vegetable, '99 91
Dilled Vegetable Sticks, '88 179
Dinner, Jollof Rice, '91 230; '92 325
Egg Rolls, Vegetarian, '86 148
Enchiladas, Meatless, '93 106
Enchiladas, Vegetable-Cheese, '94 42
en Papillote, Chicken and Vegetables, '86 145
Étouffée, Roasted Quail, '96 34
Fennel, Braised, '88 46
Fennel, Italian-Style Braised, '93 56
Fennel with Garlic Butter, Steamed, '93 56
Fettuccine and Vegetables, '97 178
Fish-and-Vegetable Dinner, '91 196
Fish and Vegetables, Cheesy, '94 254
Fish and Vegetables, Grilled, '89 179
Fish Rolls, Vegetable-Filled, '86 M251
Fish with Vegetables, Poached, '89 332; '90 18
Flounder Rolls, Vegetable-Stuffed, '87 6
Flounder-Vegetable Medley, '85 217
Freezing Chart, Vegetable, '85 185
Fresh Vegetable Potpourri, '79 208
Fries, Mixed Vegetable, '96 140
Frittata, Fresh Vegetable, '93 140
Frittata, Vegetable, '92 48; '93 183
Garbanzo-Black Bean Medley, '99 236
Garden Combo, '86 172
Garden Harvest, '85 M142
Garden Surprise, '83 112
Garnishes, '82 280; '85 338, 339
Glazed Vegetables, '97 105
Grilled Vegetable Medley, '98 158
Grilled Vegetables, '84 172; '92 124, 231;
  '96 123, 173
Grilled Vegetables, Italian-Style, '92 143
Grilled Vegetable Skewers, '94 160
Grilled Vegetables, Marinated, '95 162
Grilled Vegetables with Cilantro Butter, '98 182
Grouper with Confetti Vegetables, '88 M189
Ham-and-Vegetables, Skillet, '84 90
Hash, Vegetable, '95 262
Herbed-Smoked Vegetables, '85 145
Heroes, Vegetable Garden, '84 14
Honey-Dijon Vegetables, '98 311
Juice Delight, Vegetable, '84 58
Julienne Vegetables, '93 31
Julienne Vegetables with Walnuts, '86 M251
Kabobs, Beef-and-Vegetable, '91 148

VEGETABLES
(continued)

Kabobs, Fresh Vegetable, '81 158; '92 101
Kabobs, Grilled Vegetable, '93 170
Kabobs, Marinated Vegetable, '83 M195
Kabobs, Tangy Marinated Vegetable, '88 142
Kabobs, Vegetable, '87 116
Kabobs with Vegetables, Beef, '90 148
Kabobs with Vegetables, Marinated Beef,
   '99 292
Kielbasa-Vegetable Dinner, '91 274
Kugel, Vegetable-Noodle, '96 228
Lamb with Vegetables, Fillets of, '85 36
Lamb with Vegetables, Roasted, '98 266
Lemon Vegetables, '93 83
Lentils and Vegetables, Savory, '98 29
Limping Susan, '90 155
Liver with Vegetables, Calf's, '85 219
Loaf, Beef-Vegetable, '79 164
Loaf, Pureed Vegetable-Cheese, '85 297
Loaf, Vegetable Meat, '85 M29
Marinade, Fresh Vegetable, '83 209
Marinade, Vegetable, '92 231
Marinated Vegetable Medley, '85 319; '89 14
Marinated Vegetables, '79 146; '81 239; '85 67;
   '86 286; '96 176; '98 178; '99 36, 105
Marinated Vegetables, Honey-Mustard, '93 236
Marinated Vegetables, Sweet-and-Sour, '83 266
Meatballs and Vegetables with Horseradish
   Dressing, '91 32
Medley, Baked Vegetable, '81 75
Medley, Crunchy Vegetable, '84 254
Medley, Fresh Vegetable, '85 155
Medley, Garden Vegetable, '91 45
Medley, Herbed Vegetable, '99 46
Medley, Italian Vegetable, '88 143
Medley, Masala Vegetable, '94 56
Medley, Mixed Vegetable, '82 126
Medley, Sautéed Vegetable, '83 101
Medley, Skillet Vegetable, '81 134
Medley, Spring Vegetable, '86 115
Medley, Summer Garden, '84 158
Medley, Summer Vegetable, '83 208
Medley, Vegetable, '79 102; '83 112; '86 327;
   '89 M129
Microwaving Fresh Vegetables, '82 M138
Migas, '98 312
Minestrone, Cheesy, '99 17
Mint Sauce over Vegetables, '92 104
Mirlitons, Stuffed, '97 263
Mixed Vegetables, '83 M195
Mixed Vegetables, Tangy, '96 273
Mosaic of Vegetables, '98 280
Mushroom Caps, Vegetable, '81 246
Nests, Scallops in Vegetable, '91 70
Olive Butter, Vegetables Tossed in, '91 295
Omelet, Beefy Vegetable, '83 188
Omelet, Cheddar-Vegetable, '83 205
Omelet, Cheesy Vegetable, '85 49
Omelet, Fresh Vegetable, '84 211
Omelet, Garden, '99 174
Omelet, Golden Vegetable, '82 123
Omelet Primavera, '87 71
Omelet, Puffy Vegetable, '83 188
Omelet, Shrimp-and-Vegetable Oven, '99 286
Omelet, Vegetable-Pasta Oven, '99 286
Omelet, Vegetarian, '84 114
Open-Faced Vegetarian Melt, '87 106
Orange Roughy, Vegetable-Topped, '93 67
Orange Roughy with Vegetables, Basil-, '92 98
Osso Buco, '98 260
Packets, Vegetable, '97 64

Paella, '97 328
Paella, Garden, '82 245
Paella, Spanish, '85 26
Pancakes, Vegetable, '88 297; '98 236
Pancakes, Vegetable-Rice, '93 43
Parmesan Vegetables, '97 147
Pasta
   Beans and Pasta, '99 35
   Bow Ties with Crab and Vegetables, '98 233
   Fennel, Pasta with, '98 46
   Fettuccine Primavera, '89 238; '94 85
   Fettuccine, Vegetable, '83 312
   Garden Pasta, '82 199
   Garden Vegetables, Pasta and, '87 192
   Grilled Vegetable Pasta, '97 142
   Linguine with Roasted Vegetables, Traveling,
      '93 178
   Mediterranean Pasta, '95 341
   Mixed Vegetables, Pasta with Sausage and,
      '84 249
   Noodle Ring, Beef and Vegetables in a, '85 285
   Orzo Primavera, '92 192
   Penne, Garden Sauté with, '98 207
   Potpourri, Pasta, '94 33
   Primavera, Almost Pasta, '86 38
   Primavera, Chicken-Pasta, '91 72
   Primavera, Creamy Pasta, '95 167
   Primavera, Garden Spiral, '91 30
   Primavera, Pasta, '85 86; '89 105; '93 168;
      '97 228
   Primavera, Smoked Turkey Pasta, '90 84
   Roasted Vegetables and Pasta, '93 184
   Sauce, Pasta with Vegetable, '83 163
   Spaghetti, Chicken-Vegetable, '92 281
   Spaghetti, Fresh Vegetables with, '86 257
   Spaghetti, Sautéed Vegetables with, '81 89
   Spaghetti, Shrimp-and-Vegetable, '91 170
   Spaghetti with Vegetables, '85 67
   Stir-Fry Pasta, Vegetable, '96 29
   Vermicelli, Scallop-Vegetable, '87 143
Peperonata, '97 291
Pepper Cups, Hot Vegetable, '88 M188
Peppers, Spicy Stuffed, '98 243
Pesto Primavera, '96 170
Pie, Chicken-Vegetable Pot, '81 281; '82 30
Pie, Savory Summer, '99 159
Pies, Vegetable-Beef, '80 286
Pilaf, Barley-Vegetable, '91 33
Pilaf, Chicken-Vegetable, '97 51
Pilaf, Fruit-and-Vegetable Rice, '84 196
Pilau, Chicken, '99 184
Pilau, Shrimp, '99 184
Pizza, Blazing Sunset, '95 267
Pizza, Deep-Dish Vegetarian, '85 243
Pizza, Garden, '89 108
Pizza, Grilled Vegetable, '98 176
Pizzas, Grilled Vegetable, '97 323
Pizza, Southwestern Veggie, '95 126
Pizzas, Veggie, '99 97
Pizza, Turkey-Vegetable, '90 139
Pizza, Vegetable, '89 64; '94 218
Pizza, Vegetarian Processor, '89 225
Pizza, Veggie, '94 78
Platter, Fresh Vegetable, '92 60
Platter, Vegetable, '88 M187
Pockets, Vegetable, '85 215
Pork Chops and Garden Vegetables, '88 297
Pork Chops, Skillet Vegetable, '85 179
Pork Skillet Dinner, '98 131
Pork with Vegetables, Medallions of, '88 223
Potatoes, Sausage-Vegetable-Topped, '98 29
Potatoes, Vegetable-Topped Stuffed, '85 235
Pot Pie with Biscuit Crust, Turkey, '98 296
Pot Roast Medley, Vegetable-, '83 319

Pot Roast of Beef with Vegetables, '98 65
Pot Roast with Vegetables, '80 59; '81 M208
Pot Roast with Vegetables, Marinated, '88 M52
Primavera, Rice, '98 237
Punch, Hot Vegetable, '93 12
Puree, Smoked Vegetable, '93 156
Quesadillas, Vegetable, '97 65
Quesadilla with Roasted Salsa, Northern New
   Mexican Vegetable, '95 130
Quiche, Cheese-Vegetable, '81 228
Quiche, Ham-and-Vegetable, '84 326
Quiche, Light Vegetable, '97 332
Quiche, Vegetable, '87 M219
Ragoût of Summer Vegetables, '98 119
Ragoût, Salmon-and-Vegetable, '96 45
Ragoût, Vegetable, '89 172; '98 181
Ratatouille, '84 105, 243; '85 92; '89 174
Ratatouille-Bran Stuffed Eggplant, '86 44
Ratatouille, Eggplant-Zucchini, '81 205
Ratatouille, Microwave, '95 M232
Ratatouille Niçoise, '81 22
Ratatouille Pie, '88 198
Ratatouille, Quick-and-Easy, '80 212
Ratatouille, Sausage, '89 248
Ratatouille-Stuffed Eggplant, '83 187
Ratatouille-Stuffed Onions, '96 91
Ratatouille Supreme, '86 172
Reggae Rundown, '96 71
Relish, Eight-Vegetable, '84 179
Relish, Garden, '83 259
Relish, Vegetable, '90 147
Rib-Eyes, Italian, '98 215
Ribs, Braised Short, '98 44
Rice, Garden, '92 12
Rice, Picadillo, '98 237
Rice Pilaf, White, '97 238
Rice, Spicy, '99 214
Rice Toss, Vegetable-, '91 309
Rice, Vegetables and, '93 91
Rice with Spring Vegetables, '96 132
Rice with Vegetables, '79 64; '85 83
Risotto, Microwave, '97 M213
Risotto Primavera, '95 163
Risotto with Vegetables, '98 193
Roast, Easy Banquet, '99 291
Roasted Baby Vegetables, '98 61
Roasted Fall Vegetables, Honey-Glazed, '99 244
Roasted Summer Vegetables, '98 213
Roasted Vegetables, '95 64; '99 143
Roasted Vegetables and Pork, Oven-, '99 259
Roasted Vegetables, Fried Pork Chops with,
   '98 153
Roasted Vegetables, Honey-, '97 29
Roasted Winter Vegetables, '97 281
Rolls with Thai Dipping Sauce, Summer, '97 236
Salads
   Antipasto, Salad, '96 161
   Aspic, Cheesy Vegetable, '81 73
   Aspic with Horseradish Dressing, Crisp
      Vegetable, '87 152
   Boats, Salad, '80 93
   Brown Rice-and-Vegetable Salad, '84 202
   Calico Salad, '82 35
   Cauliflower-Vegetable Salad, '85 158
   Chef's Salad, '98 209
   Chicken Salad, Vegetable-, '91 287
   Chicken-Vegetable Salad, Basil-, '92 162
   Chicken Vinaigrette Salad, Vegetable-, '86 135
   Chinese Salad, '80 4
   Composée, Salad, '79 171
   Composé, Salad, '93 126
   Congealed Fresh Vegetable Salad, '82 240
   Congealed Salad, Cheesy-Vegetable, '86 199
   Congealed Salad, Fresh Vegetable, '91 229

Congealed Salad, Lemon-Vegetable, '85 22
Congealed Vegetable Salad, '79 276
Corned Beef Salad, Vegetable-, '80 148
Creamy Vegetable Salad, '79 47
Creole Salad, '79 147
Crunchy Vegetable Salad, '79 11; '80 217; '83 216
Different Vegetable Salad, '82 143
Easy Vegetable Salad, '83 316; '84 16
Eight-Layer Salad, '99 107
Fennel Salad, Marinated, '93 56
Freezer Salad, '94 118
Garden Medley Salad, '80 122
Garden Salad, '87 62
Garden Salad Bowl, '82 239
Greek Salad, '93 208
Greek Salad, Dawn's World-Famous, '98 276
Greek Salad, Garden, '86 173
Greek Vegetable Salad, '99 202
Green-and-White Vegetable Salad, '79 286
Green Salad, Rich, '99 203
Greens and Veggies with Fried Okra Croutons, Salad, '96 178
Green Vegetable and Egg Salad, '79 191
Green Vegetable Salad, Overnight, '80 5
Grilled Vegetable Salad, '94 203
Healthy Salad, '95 133
Horseradish Dressing, Vegetable Salad with, '92 85
Italian Garden Salad, '99 203
Italian Vegetable Salad, '81 253; '82 19
Luncheon Salad, '84 232
Macaroni-Vegetable Salad, '86 209
Marinade, Garden, '81 23
Marinade, Medley, '79 20
Marinade, Tossed Vegetable, '84 266
Marinated Combo Salad, '82 267
Marinated Garden Vegetables, '87 252
Marinated Mixed Vegetables, '89 276; '92 106
Marinated Salad, '91 186
Marinated Salad, Eight-Vegetable, '80 218
Marinated Summer Salad, '81 153
Marinated Vegetable-Bacon Bowl, '79 191
Marinated Vegetable Medley, '95 91
Marinated Vegetable Patch Salad, '84 232
Marinated Vegetables, '85 67; '86 286; '88 4, 170
Marinated Vegetable Salad, '79 106, 143; '81 280; '82 163; '83 260; '84 13; '87 243; '92 64, 91; '97 219
Marinated Vegetable Salad, Crispy, '84 193
Marinated Vegetable Salad, Fresh, '86 173
Marinated Vegetables, Honey-Mustard, '93 236
Marinated Vegetables, Zesty, '82 272
Marinated Vegetable Toss, '82 113
Marinated Veggies, '91 46
Marinate, Fresh Vegetable, '80 33; '81 230
Meal in a Bowl, '96 138
Meal-in-One Salad, '82 232
Mediterranean Salad, '95 132
Medley Salad, Vegetable, '88 86
Mexican Salad, '81 113
Minted Vegetable Salad, '88 23; '98 158
Mixed Vegetable Salad, '80 115; '81 302; '82 239; '83 317; '84 16; '86 136
Next-Day Vegetable Salad, '83 81
Niçoise, Beef Salad, '99 159
Olive Salad, '98 184
Oriental Salad, Make-Ahead, '82 163
Oriental Vegetable Salad, '84 290
Overnight Salad, '98 18
Overnight Vegetable Salad, '90 33
Pasta and Vegetables, '89 255

Pasta Salad, Ratatouille, '90 74
Pasta Salad, Vegetable, '89 256; '91 143
Pasta Salad, Vegetable-, '92 167
Pasta Salad with Peppered Cheese Crisps, Roasted Onion, '98 107
Pasta-Vegetable Salad, '95 238
Pasta-Veggie Salad, '96 106
Pebble Salad, '91 27
Pita Bread Salad, '95 86
Primavera Salad, '93 140
Quick Summer Italian Salad, '92 79
Rainbow Vegetable Salad, '83 111
Refrigerated Vegetable Salad, '84 120
Relish Salad, Vegetable, '82 267
Rice-and-Vegetable Salad, '86 42
Rice Salad, Vegetable-, '80 148; '83 198; '85 87
Ring, Tomato-Vegetable, '81 302
Riviera, Salade, '89 12
Roasted Vegetable Salad with Dried Peach Vinaigrette, '97 265
Rolls, Vegetable Salad, '82 278
Senator's Salad, '79 191
Seven-Layer Vegetable Salad, '79 88
Shrimp Salad, Vegetable-, '79 190
Slaw, Confetti Sweet-and-Sour, '98 89
Slaw, Layered, '93 214
Slaw, Vegetable, '81 280
Spaghetti-Vegetable Salad, '97 196
Spring Vegetable Salad, '88 48
Sprout Salad, Crunchy, '98 52
Summertime Salad, '79 143
Suzie or Steven Salad, '98 204
Swedish Vegetable Salad, '82 23
Sweet-and-Sour Vegetable Salad, '81 25
Tangy Vegetable Toss, '79 144
Tarragon-Vegetable Salad, '85 288
Tortellini Salad, Garden, '91 44
Tortellini Salad, Terrific, '96 134
Variety Salad, '79 113
Vegetable Salad, '98 92
Vinaigrette, Vegetables, '82 225, 290
Walnuts, Vegetable Salad with, '86 118
Warm Vegetable Salad, '95 174
Wild Rice-and-Roasted Vegetable Salad, '99 316
Winter Salad, '97 304
Winter Vegetable Salad, '86 42
Salmon Scaloppine with Vegetable Confetti and Pernod Sauce, '94 172
Salsa, Cha-Cha, '97 160; '98 333
Salsa, Colorful, '99 119
Salsa, Fresh Vegetable, '98 194
Salsa, Garden, '91 182
Salsa, Hill Country, '97 123
Salsa, Shrimp Skewers with Vegetable, '98 32, 223
Salsa, Tropical, '96 14
Salsa, Vegetable, '96 208, 220
Sandwich, Big Veggie, '92 196
Sandwiches, Creamy Vegetable, '97 122
Sandwiches, Focaccia, '98 53
Sandwiches, Grilled Garden, '98 315
Sandwiches, Open-Face Tofu-Veggie, '86 5
Sandwiches, Summer Open-Faced, '99 201
Sandwiches, Vegetable Pita, '96 199
Sandwiches, Vegetarian Pita, '84 193
Sandwich, Vegetable Puff, '85 51
Sauce, Cheesy Vegetable, '92 M134
Sauce, Creole, '98 98
Sauce, Greek Fish with Vegetable, '82 72
Sauce, Tangy Vegetable, '89 280
Sauce, Turkey Patties in Vegetable-Tomato, '87 18
Sauce, Vegetable, '89 98

Sauce, Vegetable Butter, '86 174
Sauce, Vegetable-Cheese, '85 M152
Sausage, Spicy Vegetables and, '80 82
Sausage Vegetable Dinner, '84 250
Sausage-Vegetable Skillet, '96 102
Sauté, Cajun Vegetable, '92 62
Sautéed Vegetables, Grouper with, '90 M233
Sautéed Vegetables, Tuna with, '98 222
Sautéed Vegetables with Spaghetti Squash, '84 128
Sauté, Garden, '87 90
Sautéing Fresh Vegetables, '82 138
Sauté, Tossed Vegetable, '92 138
Sauté, Vegetable-Egg, '96 204
Sauté, Vegetarian, '95 69
Scalloped Root Vegetables, '98 310
Scallops en Brochette with Vegetables, '80 163
Scallops with Vegetables, Bay, '84 233
Seafood Robert, '97 106
Seasoning Blend, Vegetable, '88 29
Sesame Sauce, Vegetables with, '83 112
Shrimp and Vegetables, '82 6
Skillet Dinner, Fresh Vegetable, '95 229
Skillet, Potato-Vegetable, '92 61
Skillet, Vegetable-Beef, '86 172
Skillet Zucchini Combo, '96 178
Soufflé Roll, Southwestern, '97 171
Soups
  Bean Soup, Vegetable-, '83 317
  Beef-and-Barley Vegetable Soup, '89 31
  Beef and Vegetable Soup, Quick Italian, '96 235
  Beef Soup, Hearty Vegetable-, '84 102
  Beef Soup, Spicy Vegetable-, '88 11
  Beef Soup, Vegetable-, '88 296; '99 219
  Beefy Vegetable Soup, '79 113; '84 M38
  Beefy Vegetable Soup, Quick, '80 25
  Bisque, Shrimp-Vegetable, '82 313; '83 66
  Bouillabaisse, Marcelle's, '99 200
  Broth, Savory Vegetable, '81 230
  Burger Soup, Vegetable-, '82 6
  Cheese Soup, Creamy Vegetable-, '81 244
  Cheese Soup, Creamy Vegetable, '83 230
  Cheese Soup, Vegetable-, '89 15
  Cheesy Vegetable Soup, '80 73; '97 241
  Chicken-Vegetable Soup, '88 18; '99 60
  Chili Vegetable Soup, '94 120
  Chocolate Soup, Mexican, '96 277
  Chowder, Cheesy Vegetable, '80 25; '83 20
  Chowder, Chicken-and-Roasted Vegetable, '97 21
  Chowder, Creamy Chicken-Vegetable, '92 20
  Chowder, Easy Vegetable, '97 304
  Chowder, Harvest, '83 317
  Chowder, Hearty Vegetable, '88 56
  Chowder, Mixed Greens, '97 262
  Chowder, Oven-Roasted Vegetable, '95 229
  Chowder, Potato-Vegetable, '98 335
  Chunky Vegetable Soup, '89 M283
  Clear Vegetable Soup, '79 130
  Down-Home Vegetable Soup, '90 32
  French Soup Maigre, '98 125
  Garden Soup, '85 241
  Garden Vegetable Soup, '83 140; '86 160
  Garden Vegetable Soup, Cold, '84 197
  Gazpacho, '84 112; '85 164
  Gazpacho, Chilled, '84 138
  Gazpacho, Cool, '83 140
  Gazpacho, Grilled Vegetable, '97 181
  Gazpacho, Smoked Vegetable, '93 156
  Gazpacho, Spring, '81 112
  Gazpacho, Summer, '84 181
  Harvest Soup, '79 101
  Hearty Vegetable Soup, '80 26

VEGETABLES, Soups
(continued)

Homemade Soup, **'79** 198
Leek-Vegetable Soup, **'86** 304
Light Vegetable Soup, **'84** 280
Marvelous Vegetable Soup, **'82** 3
Meatball Soup, Mexican, **'98** 315
Mix, Vegetable Soup, **'84** 148
Old-Fashioned Vegetable Soup, **'86** 304
Pot Liquor Soup, **'98** 273
Quick Vegetable Soup, **'79** 190; **'85** 24, 32
Quick Veggie Soup, **'91** 31
Southwestern Vegetable Soup, **'97** 268
Spicy Vegetable Soup, **'79** 198; **'93** 293;
   '99 337
Stock, Vegetable, **'90** 31
Tomato-Vegetable Soup, **'81** 177; **'86** 9
Turkey Soup, Tempting, **'98** 314
Turkey-Vegetable Soup, **'84** 4; **'88** 264; **'91** 312
Vegetable Soup, **'80** 128; **'84** 148; **'85** 106;
   '86 187; **'87** 83, 123; **'88** 266; **'93** 157;
   '98 32, 291
Spaghetti, Chicken-Vegetable, **'98** 296
Spread, Vegetable-Egg, **'87** 106
Spread, Vegetable Sandwich, **'83** 174; **'85** 135
Spring Rolls, **'99** 238
Squash, Stuffed, **'98** 177
Squash, Vegetable-Stuffed, **'84** 104
Steak with Pasta and Sesame-Ginger Butter,
   '99 142
Steak with Vegetables, Skewered, **'81** 124
Steak with Vegetables, Swiss, **'81** 273
Steamed and Minted Garden Toss, **'83** 173
Steamed Dinner, Easy, **'83** M314
Steamed Fish and Vegetables, **'91** 32
Steamed Garden Vegetables, **'93** 155
Steamed Herbed Vegetables, **'93** M303
Steamed Vegetable Medley, **'86** 50; **'90** 29
Steamed Vegetables with Garlic-Ginger Butter
   Sauce, **'94** 89
Steamed Vegetables with Mustard Sauce,
   '83 208
Steaming Fresh Vegetables, **'82** 138, 183
Stew, Easy Brunswick, **'99** 235
Stew, Fish-and-Vegetable, **'87** 220
Stew, Minestrone, **'93** 184
Stew, Mixed Vegetable, **'84** 13
Stew, Shortcut Vegetable-Beef, **'89** 218
Stew, Sweet-and-Sour Beef and Vegetable,
   '85 87
Stew, Texas, **'97** 211
Stew, Vegetable-Beef, **'94** 323
Stir-Fry. *See also* **WOK COOKING.**
Almond-Vegetable Stir-Fry, **'86** 222
Beef and Vegetables, Stir-Fried, **'88** 301
Beef-and-Vegetables, Stir-Fry, **'84** 141
Beef-and-Vegetable Stir-Fry, **'81** 211; **'87** 22;
   '99 204
Beef with Chinese Vegetables, **'81** 211
Beef with Oriental Vegetables, **'84** 140
Chicken and Vegetables, Almond, **'86** 21
Chicken and Vegetables, Chinese, **'81** 212
Chicken and Vegetables, Lemon, **'88** 118
Chicken and Vegetables, Stir-Fry, **'86** 249
Chicken-and-Vegetables, Stir-Fry, **'86** 68
Chicken and Vegetable Stir-Fry, **'82** 237
Chicken-and-Vegetable Stir-Fry, **'96** 19
Chicken and Vegetables, Walnut, **'85** 194
Chicken Stir-Fry, Sweet-and-Sour, **'98** 204
Chicken, Stir-Fry Vegetables with, **'84** 195
Chicken-Vegetable Stir-Fry, **'83** 151;
   '84 13, 141

Chicken with Vegetables, Stir-Fry, **'96** 128
Chinese Vegetable Pouches, **'94** 34
Convenient Vegetable Stir-Fry, **'95** 157
Curried Vegetables, **'89** 219
Curry, Stir-Fried Vegetables with, **'87** 51
Fresh Stir-Fry, **'97** 179
Glazed Stir-Fry Vegetables, **'99** 205
Glazed Stir-Fry Vegetables and Chicken,
   '99 205
Lo Mein, Vegetable, **'97** 321
Medley, Chinese Vegetable, **'84** 33
Medley, Stir-Fry, **'88** 156
Medley Stir-Fry, Vegetable, **'85** 109; **'99** 205
Mixed Vegetable Stir-Fry, **'79** 268; **'80** 14
Mixed Veggie-and-Pork Stir-Fry, **'99** 206
Mixed Veggie Stir-Fry, **'99** 206
Orange Roughy-and-Vegetable Stir-Fry, **'91** 50
Orange Roughy Stir-Fry, **'98** 50
Oriental Vegetables, **'84** 26; **'85** 108
Sausage and Vegetables, Stir-Fry, **'86** 213;
   '87 82
Sausage Stir-Fry, **'98** 156
Shrimp-and-Vegetable Medley Stir-Fry,
   '99 205
Shrimp and Vegetables, Stir-Fry, **'87** 91
Skillet-Fried Vegetables, **'88** 156
Steak-and-Vegetable Stir-Fry, **'84** 8
Stir-Fried Vegetables, **'79** 217; **'83** 193; **'90** 136
Stir-Frying Fresh Vegetables, **'82** 138
Three-Vegetable Stir-Fry, **'86** 174
Vegetable Stir-Fry, **'79** 214; **'82** M172, 208;
   '84 104; **'98** 156; **'99** 204
Succotash, **'85** 106; **'98** 177
Succotash, Easy, **'80** 165
Succotash, Quick, **'97** 302
Succotash, Summer, **'86** 170
Succotash with Serrano Chile Polenta, Ancho
   Chile, **'98** 104
Summer Vegetables, **'91** 136
Supper, Vegetarian, **'86** 222
Tagine, Vegetable, **'96** 289
Tangy Vegetable Toss, **'97** 306
Tempura, Basic, **'81** 68
Tempura, Cornmeal, **'81** 68
Tempura, Vegetable, **'79** 112
Terrine, Chicken-Vegetable, **'84** 131
Terrine, Vegetable-Chicken, **'83** 224
Tomatoes, Vegetable Stuffed, **'94** 141
Topper, Vegetable-Cheese Potato, **'86** 6
Topping, Turkey-Vegetable, **'94** 22
Topping, Vegetable, **'79** 79
Torta, Mediterranean, **'98** 23
Torte, Layered Vegetable, **'84** 52
Trio, Vegetable-Herb, **'83** 172
Trout, Cornmeal-Crusted, **'99** 52
Turkey Breasts, Jackie's Roasted, **'98** 269
Turnovers, Vegetable, **'86** 24
Tzimmes, **'95** 102
Veal Roast with Vegetables, **'89** 71
Vegewiches, **'99** 86
Venison-Vegetable Bake, **'87** 304
Yataklete Kilkil, **'95** 71
Yuca Con Mojo, **'93** 29
VENISON. *See* **GAME.**
VINEGARS
Basil Vinegar, **'93** 218
Cranberry Vinegar, **'91** 288
Dill-and-Chive Vinegar, **'84** 300
Garlic-Basil Vinegar, **'85** 124
Herb Vinegar, Five-, **'85** 124
Herb Vinegar, Homemade, **'79** 100
Herb Vinegar, Mixed, **'84** 107
Lemon-Mint Vinegar, **'85** 124
Lemon Vinegar, **'95** 31; **'96** 124

Mango-Cilantro Vinegar, **'95** 190
Mint Vinegar, **'92** 104
Orange Vinegar, **'95** 31
Oregano-Lemon Vinegar, Spicy, **'85** 124
Peach-Mint Vinegar, **'95** 190
Raspberry-Lemon Vinegar, **'87** 134
Raspberry-Thyme Vinegar, **'95** 190
Raspberry Vinegar, **'97** 146
Rosemary-Red Wine Vinegar, **'97** 62
Shallot-Tarragon-Garlic Vinegar, **'93** 191
Southwest Vinegar, **'94** 200
Tarragon-Dill Vinegar, **'85** 124
Tarragon Vinegar, **'84** 107; **'89** 194; **'94** 201;
   '97 165
Tomato-Herb Vinegar, **'94** 200

W AFFLES

Banana-Ginger Waffles, **'86** 96
Banana-Oatmeal Waffles, **'94** 206
Banana Split Waffles, **'89** 205
Belgian Waffles, **'94** 206
Brunch Waffles, Crunchy, **'81** 41
Chicken-Pecan Waffles, Southern, **'82** 231
Chocolate Waffles with Strawberry Cream,
   '88 153
Club Soda Waffles, **'94** 206
Cornbread Waffles, **'79** 265; **'91** 90; **'98** 42
Corn-Chile Waffles, **'94** 206
Cornmeal Waffles, **'85** 201; **'94** 22
French Toast, Waffled, **'82** 47
French Waffles, **'86** 138
Fudge Waffles, **'94** 205
Gingerbread Waffles, **'91** 68
Gingerbread Waffles with Apples and Caramel,
   '98 M237
Ham Waffles, **'80** 44
Light Waffles, **'91** 139
Oat Bran Waffles, **'92** 139
Oatmeal-Nut Waffles, **'83** 96
Oatmeal Waffles, **'89** 107
Peanut Butter Waffles, Honey-Buttered,
   '94 M206
Pecan Waffles, **'87** 225
Pumpkin-Nut Waffles, **'86** 96
Pumpkin Waffles, **'95** 282
Pumpkin Waffles with Mandarin Orange Sauce,
   Dessert, **'89** 204
Quick Bread Mix, **'81** 90
Quick Mix Waffles, **'86** 9
Refrigerator Waffles, Best Ever, **'87** 225
Rice Waffles, **'98** 124
Sausage Waffles, **'83** 50
Sorghum-Ginger Waffles, **'85** 239
Southern Waffles, **'87** 225
Sundae, Breakfast, **'98** 206
Sweet Potato Waffles, **'88** 208
Sweet Potato Waffles with Orange Butter,
   '90 323
Tuna Waffle-Wich, Hot, **'88** 272; **'89** 181
Wacky Waffles, **'93** 195
Waffles, **'81** 90
Walnut Waffles, Crunchy, **'85** 48
Whole Wheat Dessert Waffle, **'79** 92
Whole Wheat Waffles, **'84** 228
WALNUTS
Apple-Date-Nut Ring, **'90** 212
Bonbons, Coconut-Black Walnut, **'82** 307
Breads
   Apple-Nut Bread, **'79** 12
   Apple-Nut Bread, Fresh, **'87** 256
   Applesauce-Honey Nut Bread, **'87** 300
   Apricot-Nut Bread, **'79** 24

Carrot-Walnut Bread, '88 284
Cherry Nut Bread, '81 306; '82 36
Chocolate Date-Nut Bread, '81 284
Cinnamon-Nut Bubble Bread, '80 22
Cranberry-Orange Nut Bread, '80 288
Date-Nut Bread, '85 306
Honey-Walnut Swirl, '80 21
Loaf, Apricot-Nut, '81 8
Loaf, Blue Ribbon Date-Walnut, '80 15
Loaf, Nutty Wheat, '90 65
Muffins, Carrot-Date-Nut, '86 262
Muffins, Nutty Pumpkin, '86 291
Scones, Merry Cranberry-Nut Yeast, '99 274
Twists, Fruit-Nut, '82 253
Walnut Bread, '93 77
Wine-Date Nut Bread, '82 253
Brie, Walnut-Baked, '93 241
Brie, Walnut-Fried, '86 244
Broccoli, English Walnut, '89 68
Brownies, Amaretto-Walnut, '99 311
Brownies, Chocolate-Walnut, '89 325
Brownies for Passover, '99 56
Brownies, Walnut-Cream Cheese, '84 240
Burgers, Nutty, '87 185
Burgers, Walnut, '89 163
Cake, Apple-Nut, '87 76; '96 268
Cake, Apple-Walnut, '94 242
Cake, Black Walnut, '80 253; '84 316; '90 308
Cake, Black Walnut Pound, '92 16
Cake, Orange Nut, '80 70
Cake, Orange-Nut Butter, '80 254
Cake Roll, Date-Nut, '89 94
Cake, Saucy Pudding, '98 196
Cakes, Mini-Mincemeat Nut, '88 257
Cake, Yogurt-Lemon-Nut, '89 169
Candied Nuts, '81 261
Carrots with Walnuts, Julienne, '84 188
Cheese, Nutty Date Dessert, '87 299
Chicken and Vegetables, Walnut, '85 194
Chicken Breasts, Walnut-Stuffed, '85 293
Chicken, Crispy Walnut, '90 89
Chicken, Deep-Fried Walnut, '87 175
Chicken, Walnut, '85 126
Chocolate-Nut Chews, '81 92
Cobbler, Apple-Walnut, '79 154; '81 248
Coffee Cake, Cranberry-Nut, '81 250
Coffee Cake, Sour Cream-Walnut, '79 209
Coffee Cake, Walnut, '93 124
Cookies, Apple-Nut, '80 228
Cookies, Frosted Pumpkin-Walnut, '82 217
Cookies, Nutty Oatmeal, '81 130
Cookies, Rich Date-Nut Chocolate Chip, '92 207
Cookies, Simply Walnut, '91 236
Cookies, Walnut, '81 301; '97 275; '98 35
Cupcakes, Apple-Nut, '82 279
Cups, Chocolate-Walnut, '85 213
Date Drops, Stuffed, '97 247
Dressing, Green Beans with Walnut, '94 279
Dressing, Honey-Walnut, '93 107
Dressing, Walnut, '99 125
Figs with Prosciutto, Walnuts, and Cream, '96 194
Fillets, Blue Cheese-Walnut Stuffed, '95 327
Filling, Honey-Walnut, '80 21
Finikia, '96 21
Fried Walnuts, Chinese, '81 254
Frosting, Chocolate, '99 271
Frosting, Nutty Coconut, '86 8
Fruit, Cheese, and Nuts, '93 324
Fudge, Buttermilk, '97 317
Fudge, Nutty White, '81 253
Fudge, Orange-Walnut, '92 288
Green Beans, Lemon-Walnut, '93 304

Greens with Raspberries and Walnuts, Mixed, '98 194
Greens with Walnuts, Mixed, '99 107
Hamburgers, Meatless Walnut, '96 243
Ice Cream Balls, Nutty, '89 72
Mandel Bread, '99 57
Meatballs, Mock, '81 243
Mousse, Coffee-Nut, '86 319
Parmesan Walnuts, Mixed Greens with, '95 301
Pears Blue, '99 246
Pesto, Littleneck Clams with Cilantro-Black Walnut, '97 164
Phyllo Baskets, Walnut-, '93 210
Pie, Black-and-White Fudge, '99 249
Pie, Black Walnut, '97 275; '98 35
Pie, Walnut-Cranberry, '87 259
Pitas, Spinach-Walnut, '87 202; '88 43
Salad, Asian Chicken, '99 124
Salad, Beet, Apple, and Walnut, '98 269
Salad, Gorgonzola-Walnut, '96 170
Salad, Green Bean, Walnut, and Feta, '96 273
Salad, Orange Walnut, '80 246
Salad, Raspberry-Walnut, '94 158
Salad, Shrimp-Walnut, '86 182
Salad, Sunburst Chicken-and-Walnut, '93 91
Salad, Walnut-Chicken, '89 14; '96 243
Salad with Orange Vinaigrette, Roasted Beet-and-Sugared Walnut, '97 229
Salad with Walnuts, Vegetable, '86 118
Sandwich, Date-Nut Lettuce, '94 202
Sauce, Apricot-Walnut Hard, '88 153
Sauce, Spaghetti with Parsley and Walnut, '80 30
Sauce, Walnut Cream, '93 275
Sauce, Walnut-Parmesan Pesto, '96 251; '97 104
Sauté, Broccoli and Walnut, '95 52
Sautéed Walnuts, Turkey Salad with, '86 117
Sherry-Orange Nuts, '86 M289
Slaw, Nutty Apple, '88 216
Soup with Walnuts, Red Bean, '96 243
Spice Kisses, '89 295
Spread, Corn-and-Walnut, '96 26
Spread, Date-Walnut, '87 292
Spread, Date-Walnut-Cheese, '96 322
Spread, Nutty Fruit-and-Cheese, '87 246
Strawberries with Walnuts, Stuffed, '85 122; '86 124
Stuffing, Apple-Walnut, '95 289
Stuffing, Tomatoes with Walnut-Rice, '91 102
Sweet Potatoes with Sherry and Walnuts, '86 286
Syrup, Maple-Nut, '80 228
Tart, Apricot-Nut, '99 249
Topping, Nutty, '86 16
Vegetables with Walnuts, Julienne, '86 M251
Waffles, Crunchy Walnut, '85 48
Zucchini with Walnuts, '84 213
WATERMELON. See MELONS.
WHAT'S FOR SUPPER?
Appetizers, Fiery Stuffed Cherry Pepper, '97 269
Black-Eyed Peas, Hot-and-Spicy, '99 235
Breads
    Breadsticks, Parmesan-Garlic, '99 46
    Cornbread, Buttermilk, '99 235
    Rolls, Hurry-Up Crescent, '97 50
Cheese Crisps, Peppered, '98 107
Cobbler, Warm Blueberry, '98 153
Fried Rice, Cashew, '99 171
Macaroni-Mushroom Bake, '97 96
Main Dishes
    Barbecue Hobo Supper, '99 108
    Beef à la Beer, '98 64
    Beef à la Mode, '98 122
    Beef Stroganoff, Quick, '99 327
    Burgers, Taco, '98 224

Casserole, Beef, Cheese, and Noodle, '99 58
Casserole, Chiles Rellenos, '98 48
Casserole, Creamy Chicken-Rice, '99 21
Casserole, Fajita, '97 96
Casserole, Ham, '98 314
Casserole, Stroganoff, '98 48
Catfish Parmesan, '99 91
Chicken and Pears, Glazed, '99 21
Chicken and Vegetables, Grilled, '99 200
Chicken-Cashew Fried Rice, '99 171
Chicken Curry, Indian-Style, '97 119
Chicken, Dijon, '99 21
Chicken, Foil-Wrapped, '99 108
Chicken, Marmalade Baked, '99 286
Chicken, Pinot Noir Risotto with Rosemary, '97 214
Chicken, Undercover, '97 64
Chili in a Biscuit Bowl, '98 224
Corn Puppies, '97 140
Dinner, Quick Mexican, '98 224
Drumsticks, Tangy, '97 120
Eggs, Armadillo, '97 270
Enchiladas, Enticing, '99 57
Fillets, Crispy Baked, '99 90
Fish, Baked, '98 122
Fish, Caribbean, '99 109
Fish in a Wrap, '97 64
Fricassee, White Chicken, '98 122
Hamburger-Corn Bake, '99 58
Hot Dog Deluxe, '97 140
Kabobs, Pineapple-Pork, '99 144
Loaves, Mini Teriyaki, '98 224
Meat Loaf, Easy, '97 24
Meat Loaf, Spinach-Stuffed Turkey, '97 24
Meat Loaf, Teriyaki, '98 224
Meat Loaf with Feta Cheese, Lamb, '97 24
Omelet, Shrimp-and-Vegetable Oven, '99 286
Omelet, Vegetable-Pasta Oven, '99 286
Peppers, Shrimp-Stuffed, '97 268
Pizza Bake, Upside-Down, '98 224
Pizza Dogs, Grilled, '97 139
Poblanos, Corn-Stuffed, '97 269
Poblanos Stuffed with Pork and Fruit, '97 269
Pork Chops in Onion Gravy, '99 222
Pork Chops, Mexican, '99 108
Pork Chops with Roasted Vegetables, Fried, '98 153
Pork Tenderloin, Apple Butter, '99 145
Pork Tenderloin, Coriander-Pepper, '99 145
Pork Tenderloin with Mustard Sauce, '99 145
Pot Roast, Mexican, '98 64
Pot Roast of Beef with Vegetables, '98 65
Pot Roast, Old-Fashioned, '98 64
Pot Roast with Dumplings, '98 245
Risotto, Redneck, '98 107
Roast, Barbecue, '98 245
Roast Beef, Sunday, '99 327
Shrimp and Pasta with Cream Sauce, '98 295
Shrimp Manicotti, '97 96
Spaghetti, All-in-One, '98 295
Spaghetti, Chicken-Vegetable, '98 296
Spinach Shells, '97 50
Steak, Hamburger, '99 45
Thighs, Grilled Tarragon-Dijon, '97 120
Tuna Steaks with Cucumber Sauce, '97 180
Tuna with Lemon and Capers, '97 180
Tuna with Warm Tomato Salad, '97 179
Penne, Garden Sauté with, '98 207
Refried Beans, Easy, '99 57
Risotto, Lemon-Lime, '97 213
Risotto, Microwave, '97 M213

WHAT'S FOR SUPPER?
(continued)

Salads and Salad Dressings
Apple-Spinach Salad, '99 222
Bacon Dressing, Jeweled Hot, '97 196
Black Bean Salad, '97 196; '98 208
Chicken on Greens, Grilled, '99 201
Coleslaw, Old-Fashioned, '99 235
Corn Salad, Roasted, '97 196
Greens with Raspberry Dressing, Mixed,
   '97 50
Pasta Salad with Peppered Cheese Crisps,
   Roasted Onion, '98 107
Potato Salad, Charletta's, '98 153
Potato Salad, German, '97 195
Spaghetti-Vegetable Salad, '97 196
Turkey Salad, Chutney Curried, '98 314

Sandwiches
Barbecue Beef Sandwiches, '99 327
Beef-and-Artichoke Open-Faced Italian
   Sandwich, '98 22
Open-Faced Sandwiches, Summer, '99 201
Torta, Mediterranean, '98 23
Sauce, Tomato, '97 96, 269

Soup and Stews
Brunswick Stew, Easy, '99 235
Étouffée, Okra, '98 207
Turkey Soup, Tempting, '98 314
Tortellini, Creamy, '99 171

Vegetables
Broccoli, Garlic, '99 46
Carrots and Green Beans, Dilled, '99 223
Corn Fritters, '98 207
Medley, Vegetable-Cheese, '99 M287
Packets, Vegetable, '97 64
Potato Casserole, Mashed, '99 223
Potatoes, Whipped Celery, '99 45
Spinach, Hot Spiked, '97 195
Squash, Southern Summer, '98 207

WHEAT GERM
Biscuits, Wheat Germ, '86 261
Bread, Banana Wheat, '81 14
Cookies, Breakfast, '97 52
Crackers, Oatmeal-Wheat Germ, '84 236
Crisps, Sesame Wheat, '81 106
Muffins, Carrot-Wheat, '88 9
Muffins, Wheat Germ-Prune, '81 106
Pancakes, Wheat Germ, '86 242
Pancakes, Wheat Germ-Banana, '79 114
Squares, Spicy Wheat Germ, '80 44

WILD RICE. *See* **RICE/Wild Rice.**

WOK COOKING
Beef
Asparagus, Stir-Fry Beef and, '91 124
Broccoli and Beef, Stir-Fry, '83 110
Broccoli, Quick Beef and, '91 123
Broccoli, Stir-Fry Beef and, '79 47
Broccoli Stir-Fry, Beef-and-, '91 46
Carrot Stir-Fry, Beef-and-, '98 335
Chinese Beef Stir-Fry, '83 151
Chinese-Style Beef, '87 50
Chinese Vegetables, Beef with, '81 211
Coconut-Beef Stir-Fry, '97 18
Hungarian Stir-Fry, '93 64
Indian Stir-Fry, '92 126
Italian Beef Stir-Fry, '99 35
Lime-Ginger Beef Stir-Fry, '92 65
Meatballs, Sweet-and-Sour, '86 240
Mongolian Beef, '85 2, 75
Mongolian Beef Stir-Fry, '89 25
Oriental Beef, '85 20
Oriental Vegetables, Beef with, '84 140

Peanutty Beef Stir-Fry, '95 157
Pea Pods, Stir-Fry Beef and, '80 19
Shredded Beef over Rice Noodles, '85 74
Shrimp Stir-Fry, Beef-and-, '93 32
Snow Peas, Oriental Beef and, '79 105
Snow Peas, Stir-Fry Beef and, '83 22
Snow Pea Stir-Fry, Beef and, '82 98
Steak, Chinese Pepper, '82 236
Steak, Fast-and-Easy Stir-Fried, '87 50
Steak, Pepper Stir-Fry, '81 240
Steak Sukiyaki, Flank, '88 233
Stew, Beef, '86 51
Stir-Fried Beef, '84 26
Teriyaki Stir-Fry, '83 110
Thai Lemon Beef, '97 292
Vegetables, Stir-Fried Beef and, '88 301
Vegetables, Stir-Fry Beef-and-, '84 141
Vegetable Stir-Fry, Beef-and-, '81 211; '87 22;
   '99 204
Wontons, Tex-Mex, '87 196
Catfish Stir, '84 184
Cheese Wontons with Hot Sauce, '83 74
Chicken
Almond Chicken and Vegetables, '86 21
à l'Orange, Stir-Fry Chicken, '83 82
Braised Bourbon Chicken, '86 51
Broccoli Stir-Fry, Chicken-, '82 33
Cashew Chicken, '79 255; '83 21
Cashews, Chicken with, '79 207
Cashews, Szechwan Chicken with, '81 212
Chinese, Chicken, '94 33
Chinese Chicken and Vegetables, '81 212
Chinese Chicken Stir-Fry, '90 100
Chinese-Style Dinner, '84 26
Curry, Stir-Fried Chicken, '87 51
Easy Chicken Stir-Fry, '91 124
Garden, Chicken-in-a-, '80 18
Herb-Chicken Stir-Fry, '89 177
Hurry-Up Chicken Stir-Fry, '91 124
Lemon Chicken, '86 173
Mexican Stir-Fry, '92 126
Orange-Chicken Stir-Fry, '84 68
Orange-Chicken Stir-Fry, Kyoto, '87 96
Oriental Chicken with Peanuts, '82 236
Oriental Chicken with Pineapple, '86 42
Pineapple-Chicken Stir-Fry, '89 176
Plum Sauce, Chicken with, '82 236
Princess Chicken, '86 122
Shiitake-Chicken Stir-Fry, '89 61
Snow Pea Stir-Fry, Chicken and, '95 157
Soy and Wine, Chicken in, '84 26
Sweet-and-Sour Chicken, '86 240
Szechuan Chicken, '98 155
Szechwan Chicken, '83 85
Tempura Delight, Chicken, '85 66
Vegetables and Chicken, Glazed Stir-Fry,
   '99 205
Vegetables, Jim's Chicken and, '99 237
Vegetables, Stir-Fry Chicken with, '96 128
Vegetable Stir-Fry, Chicken-, '83 151;
   '84 13, 141
Vegetable Stir-Fry, Chicken-and-, '82 237;
   '86 68; '96 19
Vegetables with Chicken, Stir-Fry, '84 195
Walnut Chicken, '85 126
Walnut Chicken and Vegetables, '85 194
Zesty Stir-Fried Chicken, '83 82
Zucchini Stir-Fry, Chicken-, '84 50
Egg Rolls, '86 81
Egg Rolls, Scrumptious, '96 101
Eggrolls, Shrimp and Pork, '82 240; '83 18
Ham and Zucchini Stir-Fry, '79 47
Ham Stir-Fry, Easy, '86 332
Indian Stir-Fry, '92 126

Orange Roughy-and-Vegetable Stir-Fry, '91 50
Orange Roughy Stir-Fry, '98 50
Pasta Potpourri, '94 33
Pear Fritters, Ol' Timey, '86 51
Pork-and-Onions with Bean Sauce, '85 76
Pork, Hot-and-Spicy, '81 228
Pork in Garlic Sauce, Stir-Fried, '84 141
Pork, Kung Pao, '96 49
Pork, Moo Shu, '99 237
Pork Oriental, '81 212
Pork, Stir-Fried, '87 51
Pork, Sweet-and-Sour, '79 42; '80 227; '81 26;
   '85 34, 194
Pork Tenderloin, Curried, '86 76
Rice, Easy Fried, '84 76
Rice, Egg Fried, '80 19
Rice Special, Fried, '80 56
Rice with Sausage, Fried, '83 12
Sausage Rolls with Sweet-and-Sour Sauce,
   '83 74
Sausage Stir-Fry, '82 236; '98 156
Scallop Stir-Fry, '94 32
Shrimp and Refried Rice, '89 176
Shrimp and Sirloin Supreme, '81 131
Shrimp-and-Vegetable Medley Stir-Fry, '99 205
Shrimp and Vegetables, Stir-Fry, '87 91
Shrimp, Hoisin, '99 237
Shrimp Skillet, Quick, '87 50
Shrimp, Stir-Fry, '96 129
Shrimp Stir-Fry, Cajun, '92 127
Shrimp, Szechuan, '86 173
Shrimp, Tangy Honeyed, '94 32
Shrimp with Snow Peas, '85 75
Sugar Flips, '83 74
Swordfish Stir-Fry, '96 128
Szechuan Ginger Stir-Fry with Noodle Pancake,
   '97 292
Turkey
Broccoli Stir-Fry, Turkey-, '91 62
Italian Stir-Fry, '92 126
Spring Rolls, '99 238
Vegetables
Asparagus and Mushrooms, '85 108
Asparagus, Stir-Fried, '87 52
Bok Choy-Broccoli Stir-Fry, '84 2
Bok Choy, Stir-Fried, '97 105
Broccoli, Jade-Green, '80 12
Broccoli, Stir-Fried, '83 227
Broccoli, Stir-Fry, '80 19
Broccoli with Sesame, '80 13
Broccoli with Sesame Seeds, '82 34
Brussels Sprouts Stir-Fry, '81 308
Cabbage, Lemon-Butter, '88 156
Cabbage, Stir-Fried, '81 75, 271; '85 109
Chinese Vegetable Medley, '84 33
Chinese Vegetable Pouches, '94 34
Convenient Vegetable Stir-Fry, '95 157
Curry, Stir-Fried Vegetables with, '87 51
Egg Rolls, Vegetarian, '86 148
Fresh Stir-Fry, '97 179
Glazed Stir-Fry Vegetables, '99 205
Green Bean Medley, '85 108
Green Beans, Stir-Fried, '85 148
Greens, Stir-Fried, '94 33; '97 270
Medley, Stir-Fry, '88 156
Medley Stir-Fry, Vegetable, '85 109; '99 205
Mixed Vegetable Stir-Fry, '79 268; '80 14
Mixed Veggie Stir-Fry, '99 206
Mushrooms with Bacon, Stir-Fried, '80 123
Onion-Asparagus Stir-Fry, Sweet, '98 135
Oriental Vegetables, '84 26; '85 108
Pasta Potpourri, '94 33
Pasta, Vegetable Stir-Fry, '96 29
Peas and Peppers, Stir-Fried, '87 51

Potato-Snow Pea Stir-Fry, '86 173
Skillet-Fried Vegetables, '88 156
Spinach, Chinese, '79 179
Spinach, Stir-Fry, '81 182
Spinach with Mushrooms, '80 19
Spinach Wontons, '83 74
Squash Medley, '84 128
Squash Medley, Stir-Fried, '80 123
Squash, Stir-Fried, '97 118
Squash Stir-Fry, '80 184
Squash Stir-Fry, Two-, '86 174
Sweet Potato Pudding, '86 52
Three-Vegetable Stir-Fry, '86 174
Tomato-Zucchini Stir-Fry, '80 158
Turnip-and-Carrot Stir-Fry, '96 36
Vegetables, Stir-Fried, '79 217; '83 193;
    '90 136
Vegetable Stir-Fry, '82 208; '84 104; '99 204
Zucchini-and-Tomato Stir-Fry, '85 108
Zucchini, Italian-Style, '80 123
Zucchini Pesto, '84 194
Zucchini Toss, Stir-Fry, '88 156
Veggie-and-Pork Stir-Fry, Mixed, '99 206
WONTONS
Bowls, Wonton Wrapper, '95 58
Cheese Wontons with Hot Sauce, '83 74
Chicken Wontons, '92 284
Chicken Wontons with Hoisin Peanut Dipping
    Sauce, '99 14
Chips, Baked Wonton, '91 138
Chips, Cinnamon-and-Sugar Wonton, '91 138
Chips, Garlic Wonton, '91 138
Chips, Lemon-and-Herb Wonton, '91 138
Chips, Parmesan Cheese Wonton, '91 138
Fried Wonton Envelopes, '95 96
Fried Wontons, Crispy, '83 21
Fruit-Filled Wontons, '85 287
Nibbles, Wonton, '85 287
Pork on Mixed Greens, Hot Sesame, '97 19
Preparation Techniques, '83 74
Sausage Rolls with Sweet-and-Sour Sauce,
    '83 74
Sesame Dumplings, Steamed, '97 208
Spinach Wontons, '83 74
Sugar Flips, '83 74
Tex-Mex Wontons, '87 196

YOGURT
Apples, Honey-Yogurt, '92 46
Bread, Yogurt, '97 130
Breakfast-in-a-Bowl, '89 87
Carambola-Yogurt Calypso, '90 169
Chicken, Grilled Yogurt-Lemon, '81 111
Chicken, Savory Yogurt, '91 238; '92 28
Chicken, Yogurt-Sesame, '90 216
Coffee Freeze, Amaretto-, '99 161
Coleslaw, Grilled Chicken Breasts with
    Lemon-Yogurt, '98 148
Desserts
Bars, Lemon Yogurt Wheat, '79 93
Cake, Strawberry Yogurt Layer, '94 85
Cake, Yogurt-Lemon-Nut, '89 169
Cake, Yogurt Pound, '84 10
Chocolate Yogurt, Mocha Sauce with, '92 243
Ice, Apricot Yogurt, '81 177
Ice Milk, Banana Yogurt, '89 199
Ice, Peach-Yogurt, '84 83
Lemon-Chiffon Frozen Yogurt, '85 54
Nectarines Royale, '85 132
Parfait, Crunchy Strawberry-Yogurt, '79 124
Peach Yogurt, Frozen Fresh, '90 139
Pie, Strawberry Yogurt, '80 232

Pie, Strawberry-Yogurt, '85 122; '86 124
Pie, Yogurt-Apricot, '85 132
Pie, Yogurt-Cheese, '82 121
Pops, Pineapple-Yogurt, '91 173
Sauce, Honey-Yogurt, '92 307
Strawberry Smoothie, '97 173
Strawberry Yogurt Delight, '85 77
Strawberry-Yogurt Dessert, '90 295
Tortoni, Apricot-Yogurt, '95 124
Vanilla Frozen Yogurt, '87 125
Dip, Cucumber-Yogurt, '99 93
Dip, Curry, '85 132
Dip, Fruited Yogurt, '84 171
Dip, Yogurt, '94 21
Dip, Yogurt Herring, '80 232
Dressing, Asparagus with Yogurt, '79 66
Dressing, Ginger-Yogurt, '81 302
Dressing, Honey-Yogurt, '93 172
Dressing, Lemon-Yogurt, '93 17
Dressing, Orange-Yogurt, '85 304
Dressing, Sweet-Hot Yogurt, '86 40
Dressing, Turkey Waldorf Salad with Yogurt,
    '88 53
Dressing, Yogurt, '85 59, 215; '88 27
Dressing, Yogurt-Herb, '92 96
Dressing, Yogurt-Honey Poppy Seed, '83 177
Dressing, Yogurt Salad, '79 69
Filling, Fresh Raspberry Crêpes with Yogurt,
    '93 123
Fruit Medley, Yogurt-Granola, '91 58
Herbed Yogurt, '96 66
Honey Yogurt, Orange Slices with, '91 68
Lima Beans, Minted, '98 86
Muffins, Yogurt, '88 55
Muffins, Yogurt-Muesli, '90 215
Omelet, Yogurt-Avocado, '81 33
Pancakes, Orange-Yogurt, '87 225
Pineapple-Yogurt Whirl, '91 132
Potatoes, Yogurt-Stuffed, '88 24
Rolls, Yogurt Crescent, '91 123
Salad, Crème de Menthe, '82 122
Salad, Cucumber-Yogurt, '87 33
Salad, Frozen Yogurt, '92 303
Salad, Strawberry Yogurt, '80 232
Salad, Yogurt-Cucumber, '82 122
Salad, Yogurt Fruit, '81 114; '96 247
Sauce, Creamy Yogurt, '91 238; '92 28
Sauce, Lamb Meatballs with Yogurt, '85 132
Sauce, Yogurt, '89 283
Sauce, Yogurt-Horseradish, '85 66
Shake, Strawberry-Yogurt, '87 199
Slaw or Salad Dressing, Lemon-Yogurt, '88 54
Smoothie, Fruited Honey-Yogurt, '88 231; '89 23
Smoothie, Honey-Yogurt, '97 326
Snack, Yogurt, '88 55
Soup, Avocado-Banana-Yogurt, '80 78
Soup, Cucumber-Yogurt, '82 157; '83 205
Soup, Potato-Yogurt, '92 217
Soup, Yogurt Fruit, '86 176
Sundae, Breakfast, '98 206
Topping, Yogurt-Cheese, '88 55

ZUCCHINI
Appetizers
Caviar, Zucchini, '88 212
Crab-Zucchini Bites, '84 M216
Dip, Yellow Squash-Zucchini, '89 48
French Fried Zucchini with Cocktail Sauce,
    '86 146
French Fries, Zucchini, '82 78
Fries, Zucchini, '90 147
Hors d'Oeuvres, Zucchini, '80 151

Pizzas, Zucchini, '88 212
Scalloped Zucchini Bites, '91 165
Shrimp Appetizers, Zucchini-, '89 311
Baked Zucchini, '83 209
Baked Zucchini Fans, '87 243
Bars, Zucchini, '85 77
Basil, Zucchini and Tomatoes, '89 147
Boats with Spinach, Zucchini, '82 252
Boats, Zucchini, '85 M143
Breads
Apple Bread, Zucchini-, '87 255
Banana-Zucchini Bread, '85 326
Carrot Bread, Zucchini-, '83 190
Chocolate-Zucchini Bread, '93 308
Fritters, Cheesy Zucchini, '88 44
Fritters, Zucchini, '81 163
Honey Bread, Zucchini-, '89 143
Loaves, Zucchini, '96 130
Muffins, Zucchini, '83 121; '86 146
Spiced Zucchini Bread, '79 161; '86 162
Spicy Zucchini Bread, '81 305; '82 36
Squares, Zucchini, '82 103
Zucchini Bread, '85 111; '86 93
Broiled Zucchini, Quick-and-Easy, '86 169
Buttered Zucchini and Carrots, '83 252
Cajun Squash, '88 142
Cake, Chocolate-Zucchini, '85 156
Cake, Zucchini, '79 24
Cake, Zucchini-Carrot, '93 20
Cake, Zucchini-Pineapple, '95 160
Calabaza Guisada con Puerco (Pumpkin Cooked
    with Pork), '80 193
Carrots and Zucchini, '84 262
Carrots, Zucchini with Baby, '88 24
Casseroles
au Gratin, Potatoes-and-Zucchini, '84 5
au Gratin, Zucchini and Tomato, '82 208
Bacon, Zucchini, and Cornbread Bake,
    '99 123
Beef Bake, Zucchini-, '86 146
Calabaza Mexicana (Mexican Squash),
    '81 196
Carrot and Zucchini Casserole, '83 256
Carrot Casserole, Zucchini-, '99 61
Cheese-Egg-Zucchini Casserole, '84 114
Cheesy Zucchini Casserole, '82 168; '84 145
Corn-Zucchini Bake, '79 178
Egg Casserole, Zucchini-, '84 M113
Eggplant and Zucchini, Italian-Style, '79 289;
    '80 26
Italian Squash, '79 158
Italian Zucchini Casserole, '85 59
Jack Casserole, Zucchini-, '85 296
Lasagna, Garden, '83 119
Lasagna, Zucchini, '85 194
Manicotti, Zucchini, '84 194
Mexican Squash, '83 31
Parmesan, Zucchini, '81 108
Parmesan Zucchini, '81 234
Rice Casserole Italiano, Zucchini-, '89 146
Sausages Baked Zucchini and, '80 300
Scallop, Green-and-Gold, '81 159
Squash Bake, '82 107
Squash Casserole, '96 252
Stuffed Zucchini with Pasta, '97 101
Tomato Bake, Zucchini and, '82 158
Tomato Casserole, Zucchini-and-, '88 265
Zucchini Casserole, '79 157; '87 154
Chicken, Moroccan Garlic, '99 15
Coleslaw, Fiesta Zucchini, '91 168
Cookies, Spicy Zucchini, '97 273
Corn and Zucchini, '83 190
Corn Combo, Zucchini-, '86 218
Corn, Zucchini and, '86 177

Zucchini   229

ZUCCHINI
(continued)

Crab Cakes, Mock, '95 159
Crêpes, Zucchini, '79 157
Crispies, Zucchini, '95 179
Delight, Zucchini-Basil, '85 267
Dilled Fresh Zucchini, '81 174
Dilled Summer Squash, '96 148
Dilled Zucchini and Corn, '83 173
Dressing, Zucchini, '86 282
Easy Zucchini, '87 167
Eggplant and Squash, '83 187
Eggplant and Zucchini, Sautéed, '82 96
Fans, Baked Zucchini, '88 246
Fans, Herb Butter Zucchini, '90 201
Fans, Zucchini, '91 33
Fried Zucchini Strips, '81 184
Fries, Parmesan-Zucchini, '95 129
Frittata, Corn-and-Squash, '89 144
Frittata, Zucchini, '86 103
Fritters, Cheesy Zucchini, '88 44
Fritters, Zucchini, '81 163
Fruitcake, Zucchini, '88 284
Fry, Zucchini, '81 102
Gratin, Tomato-Zucchini, '95 171
Green Beans with Zucchini, '84 128
Grilled Zucchini Fans, '89 200
Grilled Zucchini with Feta, Greek, '95 190
Herbed Zucchini, '84 104
Italiano, Zucchini, '81 183
Italian Squash, '79 158
Italian-Style Zucchini, '80 123
Italian Zucchini, '83 M147
Julienne Zucchini and Carrots, '90 M14
Lemon-Garlic Zucchini, '89 226
Marinated Squash Medley, '94 126
Marinated Zucchini, '80 33; '89 102
Medley, Zucchini-and-Corn, '80 298; '81 25
Mexican Style, Zucchini, '80 184
Omelet, Zucchini, '81 99
Oven-Fried Zucchini, '86 211
Oven-Fried Zucchini Spears, '91 121
Pancakes, Zucchini, '93 43

Parmesan, Zucchini, '81 108; '82 103
Pecans, Zucchini with, '87 31
Pesto, Zucchini, '84 194
Pie, Cheesy Zucchini, '82 103
Pie, Italian-Style Zucchini, '83 43
Pie, Zucchini, '98 236
Pie, Zucchini-Ham-Cheese, '80 272
Pollo con Calabacita (Mexican Chicken with Zucchini), '82 219
Provençal, Zucchini, '86 146
Quiche, Cheesy Zucchini, '83 312
Quiche, Swiss-Zucchini, '82 49
Quiche, Zucchini-Mushroom, '79 127
Quiche, Zucchini-Sausage, '83 122
Ratatouille, Eggplant-Zucchini, '81 205
Relish, Pollock with Summer Squash, '92 200
Relish, Sweet Zucchini, '95 159
Relish, Zucchini, '87 200
Rosemary, Summer Squash with, '88 143
Salad, Apple-and-Zucchini, '97 216
Salad, Carrot-and-Zucchini, '83 240
Salad, Creamy Avocado and Zucchini, '79 208
Salad, Marinated Zucchini, '82 164; '90 32
Salad, Mushroom-Zucchini, '85 8
Salad, Summer Zucchini, '95 229
Salad, Turkey-Zucchini, '85 74
Salad, Zucchini, '82 104; '87 103; '89 128
Salad, Zucchini-Artichoke, '91 229
Salad, Zucchini Chef's, '83 143
Salad, Zucchini-Corn Marinated, '98 236
Sandwiches, Open-Faced Zucchini, '88 159
Sandwiches, Skillet Squash, '98 144
Sauce, Spaghetti with Zucchini, '81 38
Sauce, Zucchini-Mushroom, '93 71
Sautéed Zucchini, '83 86; '92 60
Sautéed Zucchini and Carrots, '92 62, 99
Sautéed Zucchini and Sausage, '83 289
Sautéed Zucchini with Mushrooms, '94 135
Sauté, Zucchini, '81 183; '84 35
Scramble, Zucchini-Basil, '87 34
Shrimp, Grilled Zucchini-Wrapped, '98 200
Skillet, Pattypan-Zucchini, '82 103
Skillet, Squash, '82 195
Skillet, Zippy Zucchini, '82 158

Skillet Zucchini Combo, '96 178
Skillet, Zucchini-Tomato, '93 206
Soufflés, Zucchini-Corn, '97 203
Soufflé, Zucchini, '79 157
Soufflé, Zucchini-and-Corn, '83 265
Soups
Chilled Zucchini Soup, '87 90
Chilled Zucchini Soup with Fresh Vegetable Salsa, '98 194
Cilantro, Zucchini Soup with, '93 130
Cold Zucchini Soup, '85 265; '92 64; '99 164
Cream of Zucchini Soup, '83 99
Creamy Zucchini Soup, '83 140
Dilled Summer Soup, '99 182
Dilled Zucchini Soup, '90 88
Green Soup, '98 23
Italian Sausage-Zucchini Soup, '84 4
Summer Squash Soup, '84 193
Watercress-Zucchini Soup, '91 72
Zucchini Soup, '82 104; '84 181; '86 181; '89 14
South-of-the-Border Zucchini, '85 135
Spaghetti, Italian Zucchini, '85 2
Spaghetti, Zucchini, '83 160
Stir-Fried Squash Medley, '80 123
Stir-Fry, Chicken-Zucchini, '84 50
Stir-Fry, Ham and Zucchini, '79 47
Stir-Fry, Squash, '80 184
Stir-Fry, Tomato-Zucchini, '80 158
Stir-Fry, Two-Squash, '86 174
Stir-Fry, Zucchini-and-Tomato, '85 108
Stir-Fry Zucchini Toss, '88 156
Stuffed Zucchini, '86 54, 187; '89 M133
Stuffed Zucchini, Beef-, '86 M139
Stuffed Zucchini, Ham and Cheese, '79 157
Stuffed Zucchini, Italian, '84 119
Stuffed Zucchini Main Dish, '79 215
Stuffed Zucchini, Savory, '80 161
Stuffed Zucchini Supreme, '83 136
Stuffing, Haddock Fillets with Zucchini, '88 M191
Timbales, Corn-and-Zucchini, '92 100
Tomatoes with Herbs, Zucchini and, '92 182
Toss, Zucchini, '91 292

FAVORITE RECIPES JOURNAL

*Jot down your family's and your favorite recipes for quick and
handy reference. And don't forget to include the dishes that drew
rave reviews when company came for dinner.*

RECIPE	SOURCE/PAGE	REMARKS
Appetizers & Beverages		
Breads		
Desserts		

FAVORITE RECIPES JOURNAL *(continued)*

RECIPE	SOURCE/PAGE	REMARKS

Main Dishes

Side Dishes

Soups & Salads